ADJUNCT

RETURN @ END OF
Semester or employment

Thanks

FIFTH EDITION

ON COOKING

A TEXTBOOK OF CULINARY FUNDAMENTALS

Approach and Philosophy of ON COOKING

On Cooking, Fifith Edition, follows the model established in our previous editions, which have prepared thousands of students for successful careers in the culinary arts by building a strong foundation based in sound fundamental techniques. Students and instructors alike have praised *On Cooking* for its comprehensive yet accessible coverage of culinary skills and cooking procedures.

On Cooking focuses on teaching the hows and whys of cooking. *On Cooking* starts with general procedures, highlighting fundamental principles and skills, and then presents specific applications and sample recipes. Core cooking principles are explained as the background for learning proper cooking techniques. Once mastered, these techniques can be used to cook a wide array of foods. The culinary arts are shown in cultural and historical context as well so that students understand how different techniques form the basis for various cuisines.

Chapters focus on six areas essential to a well-rounded culinary professional:

1 Professionalism Background chapters introduce students to the field with material on food history, food safety and menu planning. Food safety information has been updated to reflect the most recent regulations.

2 Preparation *On Cooking* covers those core subjects with which all culinary students should be familiar before stepping into the kitchen. Equipment, basic knife skills and mise en place concepts and techniques are presented. Staple ingredients such as dairy products, herbs, spices and flavor profiles are covered.

3 Cooking Fundamental cooking techniques are explained and then demonstrated with a wide range of recipes. Individual chapters focus on different categories of key ingredients: meats, poultry, fish, eggs, vegetables and so forth. A new chapter devoted to healthy cooking completes this emphasis.

4 Garde Manger Cold kitchen preparations from salad and sandwich making to more complex charcuterie preparations are covered. We present this material in sufficient depth to support a unit on garde manger skills, including charcuterie and hors d'oeuvre.

5 Baking Several chapters cover the aspects of bread and pastry making that every student should know. The material is sufficient to support a stand-alone unit on bread baking and dessert preparation.

6 Presentation Chapters on plate and buffet presentation demonstrate traditional and contemporary techniques for enhancing the visual presentation of food, along with the basics of buffet setup and management.

NEW TO THIS EDITION

▶ **Fresh new design,** including more than **250 new photographs, line drawings and illustrations** provide clear representation of core techniques that are the foundation of any good culinary textbook.

▶ Content updates reflect **current trends in the culinary arts,** such as sustainable/seasonal cooking, small plate dishes, global techniques, Asian knife skills, molecular trends, sous-vide cooking and international cuisine.

▶ **New Healthy Cooking chapter combines** material on basic nutrition, healthy cooking techniques and cooking for special diets such as vegetarian or allergic diets.

▶ **Increased emphasis on sanitation** through more safety alerts reflects current restaurant industry concerns.

▶ **Expanded coverage of flavors** offered in new sidebars; expanded coverage of small plates and additional plate presentation techniques.

▶ **Greatly enhanced support package,** including MyCulinaryLab™ 2.0, instructor's manual featuring performance-based learning activities, improved test bank and lecture-based PowerPoint™ slides.

► **Expanded Recipe Testing Program** Hundreds of recipes featured in *On Cooking*, 5e, were tested by chef-instructors at leading culinary schools across the country. This unparalleled program ensures accuracy, clarity and instructional value. (We invite qualified chef-instructors to test recipes for upcoming projects. If you would like more information regarding the program, or would like to sign up to be part of the Pearson Test Kitchen, please visit **www.pearsontestkitchen.com**.)

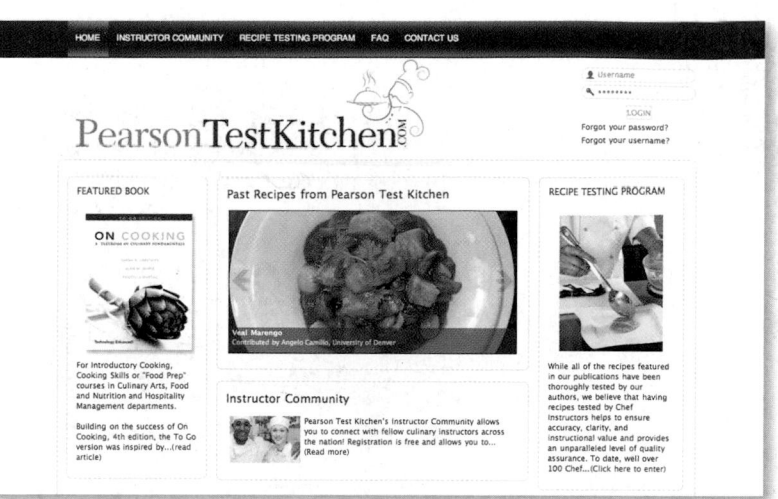

GUIDED TOUR **FOR THE READER**

Easy to navigate, *On Cooking* is broken down into bite-size subsections as reflected in the table of contents. We invite you to take the Guided Tour to capture the flavor of *On Cooking*.

HALLMARK FEATURES

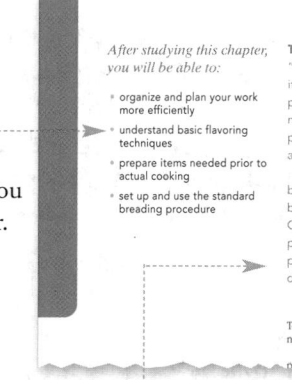

After studying this chapter, you will be able to:

- organize and plan your work more efficiently
- understand basic flavoring techniques
- prepare items needed prior to actual cooking
- set up and use the standard breading procedure

THE FRENCH TERM *MISE EN PLACE* (meez ahn plahs) literally means "to put in place" or "everything in its place." But in the culinary context, it means much more. Escoffier defined the phrase as "those elementary preparations that are constantly resorted to during the various steps of most culinary preparations." He meant, essentially, gathering and prepping the ingredients to be cooked as well as assembling the tools and equipment necessary to cook them.

In this chapter, we discuss many of the basics that must be in place before cooking begins: for example, creating bouquets garnis, clarifying butter, making bread crumbs, toasting nuts and battering foods. Chopping, dicing, cutting and slicing—important techniques used to prepare foods as well—are discussed in Chapter 5, Knife Skills; specific preparations, such as roasting peppers and trimming pineapples, are discussed elsewhere.

The concept of mise en place is simple: A chef should have at hand everything he or she needs to prepare and serve food in an organized and efficient manner.

Proper mise en place can consist of just a few items—for example, those needed to prepare a small quantity of chicken soup. Or it can be quite extensive—for example,

Learning Objectives

Each chapter begins with clearly stated objectives that enable you to focus on what you should achieve by the end of the chapter.

Chapter Introduction

Chapter introductions summarize the main themes in each chapter and help reinforce topics.

palate (1) the complex of smell, taste and touch receptors that contribute to a person's ability to recognize and appreciate flavors; (2) the range of an individual's recognition and appreciation of flavors

unami the taste sensation caused by the naturally occurring amino acid glutamate; gives food a savory richness or meatiness; found primarily in fermented foods and those to which monosodium glutamate has been added

cuisson (kwee-sohn) the liquid used for shallow poaching

Margin Definitions

Important terms appear in the margins to help you master new terminology. There is a helpful phonetic pronunciation guide for non-English terms.

Safety Alerts

Brief notes remind you of safety concerns and encourage you to incorporate food safety and sanitation into your regular kitchen activities.

SAFETY ALERT

Never leave an egg dish at room temperature for more than 1 hour, including preparation and service time. Never reuse a container after it has held raw eggs without thoroughly cleaning and sanitizing it.

PROCEDURE FOR **WHIPPING EGG WHITES**

1. Use fresh egg whites that are completely free of egg yolk and other impurities. Warm the egg whites to room temperature before whipping; this helps a better foam to form.
2. Use a clean bowl and whisk. Even a tiny amount of fat can prevent the egg whites from foaming properly.
3. Whip the whites until very foamy, then add salt or cream of tartar as directed.
4. Continue whipping until soft peaks form, then gradually add granulated sugar as directed.
5. Whip until stiff peaks form. Properly whipped egg whites should be moist and shiny; overwhipping will make the egg whites appear dry and spongy or curdled.
6. Use the whipped egg whites immediately. If liquid begins to separate from the whipped egg whites, discard them; they cannot be rewhipped successfully.

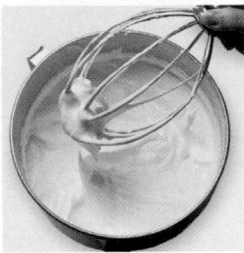

1. Egg whites whipped to soft peaks.　2. Egg whites whipped to stiff peaks.　3. Spongy, overw...

◀ Procedures

Step-by-step color photographs of various stages in the preparation of ingredients and dishes help you visualize unfamiliar techniques and encourage you to review classroom or kitchen activities whenever necessary.

▼ Product Identification

Hundreds of original color photographs help you recognize and identify ingredients. You can explore a huge variety of items such as fruits, berries, chocolates, fresh herbs, fish, dried spices, game, meats and fine cheeses.

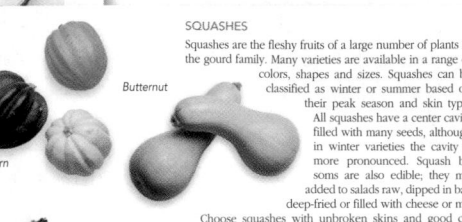

SQUASHES

Squashes are the fleshy fruits of a large number of plants in the gourd family. Many varieties are available in a range of colors, shapes and sizes. Squashes can be classified as winter or summer based on their peak season and skin type. All squashes have a center cavity filled with many seeds, although in winter varieties the cavity is more pronounced. Squash blossoms are also edible; they may be added to salads raw, dipped in batter and deep-fried or filled with cheese or meat and baked.

Choose squashes with unbroken skins and good color for the variety. Avoid any squash with soft, moist spots.

Winter Squashes

Winter squashes include the acorn, butternut, Hubbard, pumpkin and spaghetti varieties. They have hard skins (shells) and seeds, neither of which is generally eaten. The flesh, which may be removed from the shell before or after cooking, tends to be sweeter and more strongly flavored than that of summer squash. Winter squashes are rarely used raw; they can be baked, steamed or sautéed. Most winter squashes can also be puréed for soups or pie fillings. Their peak season is October through March.

Summer Squashes

Summer squashes include the pattypan, yellow crookneck and zucchini varieties. They have soft edible skins and seeds that are generally not re-

THE VERSATILE EGG

For versatility, the egg has few rivals. Poached eggs work in breakfast and brunch dishes but also complement tender green salads. When stuffed, hard-boiled eggs become simple hors d'oeuvre. Finely chopped and bound with mayonnaise, hard-boiled eggs fill sandwiches and canapés. Omelets, quiches and scrambled eggs benefit from countless additions, including finely diced bell peppers, onions, mushrooms, zucchini or tomatoes; cottage cheese, creamy goat cheese or any variety of shredded firm cheese; crumbled bacon or pancetta; diced ham, turkey or beef; bits of smoked salmon, cooked shrimp or cooked sausage; and fresh herbs.

◀ **New!** Flavor sidebars show how flavoring ingredients may be used to change the character of a dish.

MISE EN PLACE

▶ Heat water.
▶ Peel and Mince onions.
▶ Grate cheese.

◀ Mise en Place

French for "put in place," this feature accompanying in-chapter recipes provides a list of what you must do before starting a recipe, such as preheating the oven, chopping nuts or melting butter.

Line Drawings ▶

Detailed line drawings illustrate tools and equipment without brand identification. Other drawings depict the skeletal structure of meat animals, fish and poultry.

◀ Icons

Icons identify additional recipes that are accessible through electronic resources, as well as recipes that are vegetarian or healthy options.

Healthy

Vegetarian

Additional Online Resources

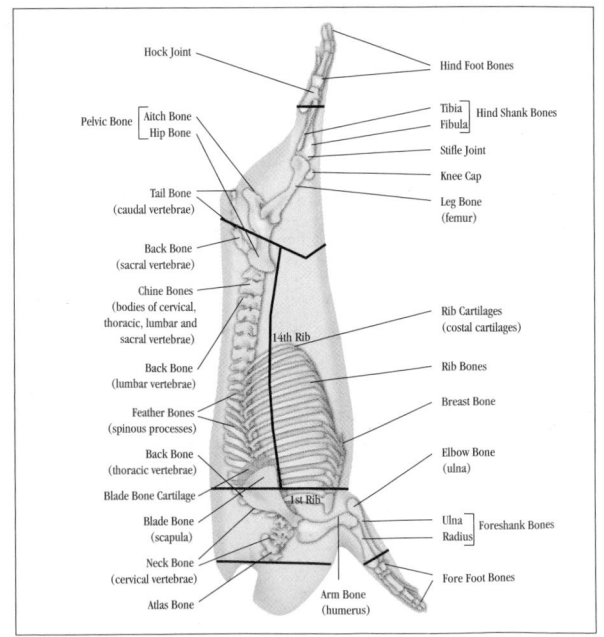

FIGURE 16.1 ▶ The skeletal structure of a hog.

Recipes

Measurements

All recipes include both U.S. and metric measurements. To aid in teaching scaling and consistent baking practices, we also provide metric equivalents for all temperatures, pan sizes and length measurements throughout the text.

Illustrations

Recipes are illustrated with both sequential photos showing fabrication and assembly of dishes and many finished-dish photos that show you the author's finished work created while testing the recipes.

Variations

Recipe variations show you how to modify recipes to create new dishes.

Nutritional Analysis

All recipes include a nutritional analysis prepared by a registered dietician.

Grilled vegetables served with grilled chicken breast

PROCEDURE FOR **BROILING OR GRILLING VEGETABLES**

1. Heat the grill or broiler.
2. Use a wire brush to remove any charred or burnt particles that may be stuck to the broiler or grill grate. The grate may be wiped with a lightly oiled towel to remove any remaining particles and help season it.
3. Prepare the vegetables to be broiled or grilled by cutting them into appropriate shapes and sizes, then seasoning, marinating or otherwise preparing them as desired or directed in the recipe.
4. Place the vegetables on the broiler grate, broiler platter or grill grate and cook to the desired doneness while developing the proper surface color.

GRILLED VEGETABLE SKEWERS

Yield: 12 Skewers   **Method:** Grilling

Marinade:		
Rice wine vinegar	4 fl. oz.	120 ml
Vegetable oil	8 fl. oz.	240 ml
Garlic, chopped	1 oz.	30 g
Dried thyme	2 tsp.	10 ml
Salt	1 Tbsp.	15 ml
Black pepper	½ tsp.	2 ml
Zucchini	6 oz.	180 g
Yellow squash	6 oz.	180 g
Broccoli florets, large	12	12
Cauliflower florets, large	12	12
Onion, large dice	24 pieces	24 pieces
Red bell pepper, large dice	12 pieces	12 pieces
Mushroom caps, medium	12	12

1. Combine all the marinade ingredients and set aside.
2. Cut the zucchini and yellow squash into ½-inch- (1.2-centimeter-) thick semicircles.
3. Blanch and refresh the zucchini, yellow squash, broccoli florets, cauliflower florets, onion and bell pepper as discussed later under Moist-Heat Cooking Methods.
4. Drain the vegetables well and combine them with the marinade. Add the mushroom caps to the marinade. Marinate the vegetables for 30 to 45 minutes, remove and drain well.
5. Skewer the vegetables by alternating them on 6-inch (10-centimeter) bamboo skewers.
6. Place the vegetable skewers on a hot grill and cook until done, turning as needed. The vegetables should brown and char lightly during cooking. Serve hot.

VARIATION:

Grilled Sliced Vegetables—Slice the zucchini, yellow squash, onion and bell pepper into large pieces. Marinate and then grill these vegetables along with the broccoli, cauliflower and mushroom caps without skewering.

Approximate values per serving: **Calories** 60, **Total fat** 2.5 g, **Saturated fat** 0 g, **Cholesterol** 0 mg, **Sodium** 610 mg, **Total carbohydrates** 8 g, **Protein** 2 g, **Vitamin C** 90%, **Claims**—low fat; no cholesterol; good source of fiber

ROASTING AND BAKING

The terms *roasting* and *baking* are used interchangeably when referring to vegetables. Roasting or baking is used to bring out the natural sweetness of many vegetables while preserving their nutritional values. The procedures are basically the same as those for roasting meats.

MISE EN PLACE
◄ Peel and chop garlic.
◄ Wash broccoli and cauliflower and cut into large florets.
◄ Peel and dice onion.
◄ Wash and seed bell pepper and cut into large dice.
◄ Wash mushroom caps.

Grilling skewers of marinated vegetables.

Grilled sliced vegetables as an accompaniment to an entrée plate.

Sidebars

Sidebars present information on food history, food in culture and the background of professional foodservice. These sidebars help you understand the culinary arts in a wider social context.

Questions for Discussion and Terms to Know

Questions for Discussion, which appear at the end of each chapter, encourage you to integrate theory and technique into a broader understanding of the material. Web-based activities, indicated by the this icon, encourage you to conduct original research and seek answers from outside your primary classroom material.

Comprehensive Learning

FOR THE STUDENT

MyCulinaryLab™, a dynamic online tool, supports the many ways students learn. *MyCulinaryLab™* enables the student to study and master the content online on their own time and at their own pace. Media-rich personalized study plans are based on the student's performance using the site's interactive testing and games.

NEW! Simulations provide students with an interactive learning experience on topics such as:
FABRICATION: beef, lamb, pork, veal, flatfish and round fish

COOKING METHODS: broiling, grilling, roasting and baking, sautéing, pan frying, deep frying, poaching, simmering, boiling, steaming, braising and stewing

NEW! Culinary Math Primer. Success in the culinary arts requires a strong grasp of mathematics.

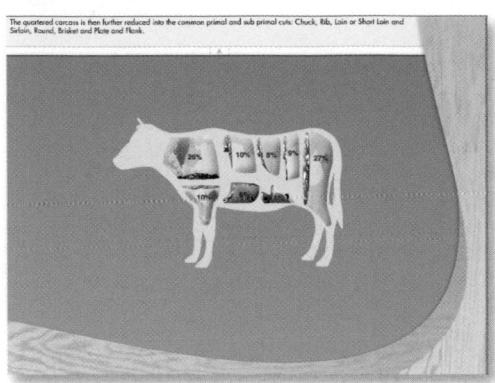

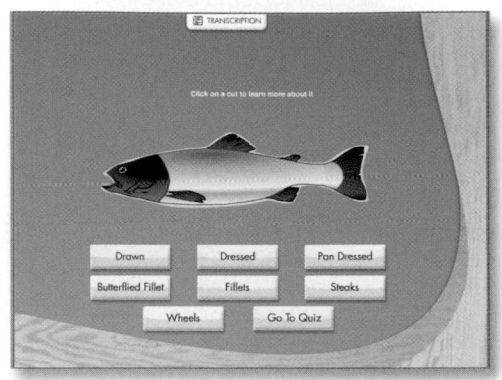

A chef needs to be able to accurately cost recipes; set menu prices; calculate food and beverage cost percentages and labor costs; as well as forecast, budget, read and understand profit and loss statements. The Culinary Math Primer provides students with a pretest to assess a student's competence in critical culinary math skills. It builds a personalized study plan to provide remediation and practice to help students gain confidence and proficiency in critical topics such as fractions and decimals, kitchen measurements, yield percentages, ratios, recipe costing and conversions.

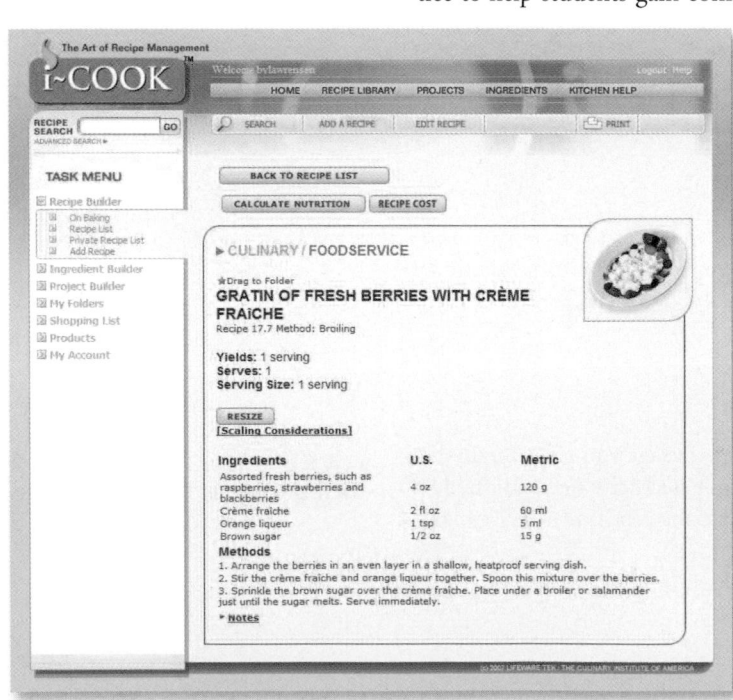

i-COOK™ is a Web-based recipe management tool designed to enhance and simplify the culinary education experience. Created by a team of culinary foodservice management and interactive technology experts in collaboration with The Culinary Institute of America, i-COOK™ facilitates the process of creating, editing, sharing, publishing and archiving recipe content.

Student Study Guide

Authored by Christine Stamm-Griffin, the Student Study Guide (ISBN-10: 0-13-510889-6) allows students to test their knowledge of key concepts and vocabulary by chapter. The study guide provides an excellent way for students to review for tests using a variety of practice techniques.

and Teaching Package

FOR THE INSTRUCTOR

Manage your Course with MyCulinaryLab™

MyCulinaryLab is an easy-to-use online resource designed to supplement a traditional lecture course. It provides instructors with basic course management capabilities in the areas of course organization, grades, communication and personalization of content. Instructors benefit from course management tools such as a robust grade book, integrated course email and reporting tools.
Reporting features include: Data tracking and reporting for students, grades and question usage Provides detailed results of students' performance and use of the program.

Qualified adopters can download the following instructor supplements by registering at our Instructors' Resource Center at **www.pearsoned.com**. (For Qualified Adopters)

Online Instructor's Manual

Includes chapter outlines, examination questions and answers, performance-based learning activities, answers to end-of-chapter questions for discussion and maps to ACF skill standards and competencies. (**ISBN-10:** 0-13-510890-X)

PowerPoint Lecture Presentations

This comprehensive set of slides can be used by instructors for class presentations or by students for lecture preview or review. There is a presentation for each chapter, including a selection of full-color photographs from the book. (**ISBN-10:** 0-13-510898-5)

TestGen (Computerized Test Bank)

TestGen contains text-based questions in a format that enables instructors to choose questions in order to create their own examinations. (**ISBN-10:** 0-13-510929-9)

For additional information on media resources or instructor materials,
please contact Prentice Hall faculty services at 1-800-526-0485

FIFTH EDITION

ON COOKING
A TEXTBOOK OF CULINARY FUNDAMENTALS

SARAH R. LABENSKY, CCP

ALAN M. HAUSE

PRISCILLA A. MARTEL

Photographs by Richard Embery
Drawings by William E. Ingram

Pearson
Boston   Columbus   Indianapolis   New York   San Francisco   Upper Saddle River
Amsterdam   Cape Town   Dubai   London   Madrid   Milan   Munich   Paris   Montreal
Toronto   Delhi   Mexico City   Sao Paulo   Sydney   Hong Kong   Seoul   Singapore   Taipei   Tokyo

Editor in Chief: Vernon R. Anthony
Senior Acquisitions Editor: William R. Lawrensen
Editorial Assistant: Lara Dimmick
Director of Marketing: David Gesell
Senior Marketing Manager: Leigh Ann Sims
Assistant Marketing Manager: Alicia Wozniak
Marketing Assistant: Les Roberts
Senior Managing Editor: JoEllen Gohr
Associate Managing Editor: Alexandrina Benedicto Wolf
AV Project Manager: Janet Portisch
Senior Operations Supervisor: Pat Tonneman
Operations Specialist: Deidra Skahill
Senior Art Director: John Christiana
Manager, Rights and Permissions: Beth Brenzel
Image Permission Coordinator: Frances Toepfer
Image Specialists: Joseph Conti, Ron Walko
Interior Design: Maureen Eide and John Christiana
Cover Design: John Christiana
Cover Art: © Yuri Arcurs/iStockphoto.com
Media Director: Ally Graesser
Lead Media Project Manager: Karen Bretz
Supplements Editor: Sonya Kottcamp
Full-Service Project Management: Linda Zuk, WordCraft LLC
Composition: S4Carlisle Publishing Services
Printer/Binder: Courier/Kendallville
Cover Printer: Lehigh-Phoenix Color
Text Font: Garamond

Credits and acknowledgments for illustrations, photos, and text borrowed from other sources and reproduced, with permission, in this textbook appear on page 1183.

Library of Congress Cataloging-in-Publication Data
Labensky, Sarah R.
  On cooking : a textbook of culinary fundamentals / Sarah R. Labensky, Alan
M. Hause, Priscilla A. Martel; photographs by Richard Embery; drawings by
William E. Ingram.—5th ed.
    p. cm.
  Includes bibliographical references and index.
  ISBN 0-13-715576-X (978-0-13-715576-7) 1. Cookery. I. Hause, Alan M. II.
Martel, Priscilla. II. Title.
  TX651.L333 2011
  641.5—dc22   2009043941

10 9 8 7 6 5 4

Prentice Hall,
an imprint of

ISBN 10:   0-13-715576-X
ISBN 13: 978-0-13-715576-7

www.pearsonhighered.com

CONTENTS

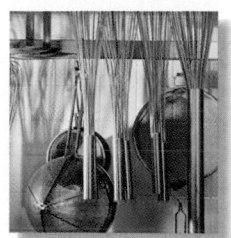

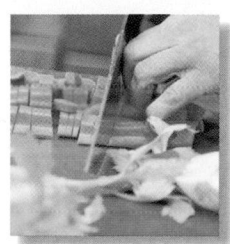

CONTENTS

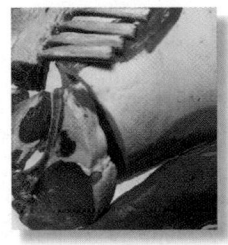

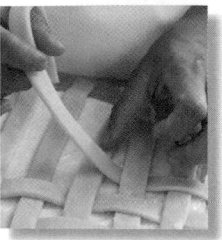
CONTENTS

CHAPTER **THIRTY-THREE**

CAKES AND FROSTINGS
1006

CHAPTER **THIRTY-FOUR**

CUSTARDS, CREAMS, FROZEN DESSERTS
AND DESSERT SAUCES
1046

CHAPTER **THIRTY-FIVE**

PLATE PRESENTATION
1078

CHAPTER **THIRTY-SIX**

BUFFET PRESENTATION
1092

CONTENTS

PREFACE

Learning to cook is much more than simply learning to follow a recipe. Consequently, *On Cooking*, Fifth Edition, is not a cookbook or a collection of recipes. It is a carefully designed text intended to teach you the fundamentals of the culinary arts and to prepare you for a rewarding career in the food service industry.

This book is extensively illustrated with photographs and line illustrations to help you identify foods and equipment. The goal of *On Cooking* is to focus on general procedures, highlighting fundamental principles and skills, whether it be for preparing a yeast bread or grilling a piece of fish. We discuss both the how and why of cooking. Only then are specific applications and sample recipes given. Most recipes include photographs of the finished dish, ready for service. Many procedures are illustrated with step-by-step photographs as well.

Numerous hotel and restaurant chefs throughout the country contributed recipes to this book, usually accompanied by photographs of the dishes as prepared in their kitchens. These recipes and illustrations enable you to explore different techniques and presentation styles. Teaching professionals from culinary schools across the country also share some of their most successful recipes in this new edition.

In order to provide you with a sense of the rich traditions of cookery, informative sidebars on food history, chef biographies and other topics are scattered throughout the book. Also included are several short essays written by prominent culinarians on topics ranging from tempering chocolate to tasting spicy foods. Sidebars that relate to flavors and flavorings have been added throughout the book to enhance your understanding of key cooking ingredients.

We wish you much success in your culinary career and hope that this text will continue to inform and inspire you long after graduation.

A NOTE ON RECIPES

Recipes are important and useful as a means of standardizing food preparation and recording information. We include recipes that are designed primarily to reinforce and explain techniques and procedures presented in the text. Many recipe yields are intentionally low in order to be less intimidating to beginning cooks and more useful in small schools and kitchens.

All ingredients are listed in both U.S. and metric measurements. The metric equivalents are rounded off to even, easily measured amounts. You should consider these ingredient lists as separate recipes or formulas; do not measure some ingredients according to the metric amounts and other ingredients according to the U.S. amounts or the proportions will not be accurate and the intended result will not be achieved. Throughout this book, unless otherwise noted:

▶ *mirepoix* refers to a preparation of 2 parts onion, 1 part celery and 1 part carrot by weight
▶ *pepper* refers to ground black pepper, preferably freshly ground
▶ *butter* refers to whole, unsalted butter
▶ *milk* refers to whole or reduced fat (not nonfat) milk, and
▶ *TT* means "to taste"

Detailed procedures for standard techniques are presented in the text and generally are not repeated in each recipe (for example, "deglaze the pan" or "monté au beurre"). Variations appear at the end of selected recipes. These variations give you the opportunity to see how one set of techniques or procedures can be used to prepare different dishes with only minor modifications.

A mise en place feature is included with recipes that appear in the front section of recipe chapters. Ingredients that require preparation before beginning to prepare the recipe are listed in the margin. You should consult this brief checklist after you read the recipe but before you begin to cook. Headnotes that describe the cultural or historical background of a dish or the unique techniques used in its preparation appear with many recipes. This short text should help enhance your understanding of a cuisine or cooking technique.

No matter how detailed the written recipe, however, we must assume that you have certain knowledge, skills and judgment. It becomes a judgment call to know, for example, when a loaf of bread or a casserole is finished cooking. Ovens may vary in efficiency. For these reasons, we give alternate tests for doneness, as well as timing each recipe. Use your developing skills to determine when a dish is fully cooked. You should also rely upon the knowledge and skills of your instructor for guidance. Although some skills and an understanding of theory can be acquired through reading and study, no book can substitute for repeated hands-on preparation and observation.

A registered dietician analyzed all the recipes in this book using nutritional analysis software that incorporates data from the U.S. Department of Agriculture, research laboratories and food manufacturers. The nutrient information provided here should be used only as a reference, however. A margin of error of approximately 20 percent can be expected because of natural variations in ingredients.

Preparation techniques and serving sizes may also significantly alter the values of many nutrients. For the nutritional analysis, if a recipe offers a choice of ingredients, the first-mentioned ingredient is the one used. Ingredients listed as "to taste" (TT) and "as needed" are omitted from the analysis. Corn oil and whole milk are used throughout for "vegetable oil" and "milk," respectively. In cases of a range of ingredient quantities or numbers of servings, the average is used.

 Throughout this book various recipes are marked with the apple symbol. This symbol identifies dishes that are particularly low in calories, fat, saturated fat or sodium; they may also be a good source of vitamins, protein, fiber or calcium.

 Vegetarian dishes are indicated with a green vegetable symbol. These recipes do not contain meat, fish, shellfish or poultry, but may contain dairy products and/or eggs. (We do not use this symbol for the baked goods recipes in Chapters 30 through 34, however, because none of them contains meat, fish, shellfish or poultry.) Vegetarian dishes are not necessarily low in calories, fat or sodium; nor are they automatically good sources of vitamins, protein, fiber or calcium.

 The World Wide Web symbol appears next to end-of-chapter discussion questions whose answers may be researched on the Internet.

ACKNOWLEDGMENTS

This book would not have been possible without the assistance and support of many people. Special thanks to our photographer, Richard Embery, for his talent, professionalism and commitment to quality; and to Sharon Salomon, MS, RD, for assistance with the preparation of the Healthy Cooking chapter. The nutritional analysis for this edition was prepared by Mindy Hermann, MS, RD, whose thoroughness and prompt replies were greatly appreciated. Thanks also to Bill Ingram for his artistry. We are also grateful to the many chefs, restaurateurs, writers and culinary professionals who provided recipes and essays for this book.

Alan thanks his wife Chantal for her support and understanding while his attention is diverted from family to endless hours of production on each edition of the text. He also thanks his new son Logan Micheal Hause for his patience and understanding, however limited it has been, while Daddy sat in front of the computer. He also thanks his many coworkers and friends who contributed to the success of the text, including: Charles Blonkenfeld, Gregory Reynolds, Reynalda Montes, Rosalino Morales, Estella Morales, Juan Soto, Jim Curry, Christopher Torres, Martin van de Brug, Kathleen Doeller, Gayleen Cooley, April Kilgore, Katelin Lindblom, Vanessa Arce, Chaz Frankenfield, Marisol Statton, Raul Cisneros, Kenny Penberton, Kirk Guerrero and Maria Moreno. Finally, he thanks Priscilla Martel for her patience, consistency, expertise and professionalism. It has been a pleasure to get to know her and work with her on this project.

Sarah offers her sincere thanks and appreciation to Priscilla Martel for adding her expertise and insight to this edition of the text. She would also like to thank the many students she has worked with over the years. They are the real reason that books such as this are written.

Priscilla would like to acknowledge the contributions of Carole Pierce and J. Patrick Truhn, two fine writers and editors, and the support of Todd Bates, Doerte McManus, Robin Schremp and Eddy Van Damme.

The authors wish to thank the following companies for their generous donations of equipment and supplies: J.A. Henckels Zwillingswerk, Inc., All-Clad Metalcrafters, Inc. and Parrish's Cake Decorating Supplies, Inc. We are most appreciative of the support of the Hotel Adlon Kempinski Berlin and Sabina C. Held for the use of photographs. We also wish to thank Joan and Tim O'Connor of Honeymoon Sweets Bakery, Demarle USA, Shamrock Foods Company, KitchenAid Home Appliances, Taylor Environmental Instruments, Hobart Corporation, Jeff and Sue Reising of Arizona Ostrich Fillet, Randy Dougherty of ISF International, Kristine Cueto, Manager Hotel Operations, Rosenthal USA, Ltd., Maureen Ryan, National Restaurant Association, Marci Wilson, American Cheese Society and TechneUSA.

Finally, we wish to thank everyone involved in this project at Prentice Hall, including Vernon Anthony, Editor-in-Chief; William Lawrensen, Senior Acquisitions Editor; John Christiana, Manager of Design Development; Alexandrina Wolf, Associate Managing Editor; Sonya Kottcamp, Development Editor; Leigh Ann Sims, Executive Marketing Manager; and Linda Zuk, Project Editor at WordCraft LLC. We also remain indebted to Robin Baliszewski, Acquisitions Editor of the first edition and current Pearson Director for People, for her support and friendship.

ADDITIONAL CREDITS

The reviewers of *On Cooking* provided many excellent suggestions and ideas for improving the text: Scott Brunson, Mission College; Leonard G. Bailey II, National Institute for Culinary Arts at Mountain State University; and Leslie G. Jett, University of Missouri–Columbia. The quality of the reviews was outstanding and played a major role in the preparation of this revision. Their assistance and expertise is greatly appreciated.

The authors wish to thank the instructors who participated in our focus group and helped us refine the contents of this revision.

Brandon Harpster,
Southeast Community College

Mary G. Trometter,
Pennsylvania College of Technology

Fiona McKenzie,
Sandhills Community College

Louis R. Woods, Jr.,
Anne Arundel Community College

We extend our thanks to the many chefs and instructors who took the time to complete our general survey regarding introductory cooking textbooks. Their feedback has contributed greatly to the production of our text.

Karin Allen, Utah State University
Chris Argento, Nassau Community College
Mike Artlip, Kendall College
Victor Bagan, Hibbing Community College
Jeff Bane, The Chef's Academy, Harrison College
Todd Barrios, CEC, Northwestern State University
Erica Beirman, Iowa State University
Paul John Bernhardt, Diablo Valley College
LeRoy Blanchard, Los Angeles Trade Technical College
Patricia Bowman, Johnson & Wales University
Eric Breckoff, J. Sargeant Reynolds Community College
Scott Bright, The Chef's Academy
Tracey Brigman, University of Georgia
Stephen Burgeson, Buffalo State College
Angelo Camillo, Daniels College of Business–University of Denver
Kristina Campbell, Columbus Technical College
Mary Ann Campbell, Trenholm State Technical College
Michael Carmel, Culinary Institute of Charleston at Trident Technical College
Mark Carpenter, MBA, CEC, Del Mar College
Paul Carrier, Madison Area Technical College
Melinda Casady, Oregon Culinary Institute
Amy Chaffin, West Central Technical College
Dorothy Chen-Maynard, California State University–Santa Barbara
Jerry Comar, Johnson & Wales University
Matt Cooper, Mott Community College
Sharron Coplin, Ohio State University
Anne Corr, Penn State University
Philip Cragg, Atlantic Cape Community College
William Crawford, Moatt Community College
Sylvia Crixell, Texas State University–San Marcos
Chris Crosthwaite, Lane Community College
Chris Currier, Sandhills Community College
Scott Dahlberg, WOR-WIC Community College
Jacqueline deChabert-Rios, East Carolina University
Michael Downey, St. Louis Community College at Forest Park
Charles Drabkin, Edmonds Community College
Jerome Drosos, Triton College
Jodi Lee Duryea, University of North Texas
Kimberly Emery, SUNY–Plattsburgh
Richard Exley, Scottsdale Culinary Institute
Doug Flick, Johnson County Community College
Debbie Foster, Ball State University
Thomas Gaddis, Pellissippi State Community College

Wendy Gordon, Rockland Community College
Debra Gourley, Ivy Tech Community College
Clarke Griffin, Kaskaskia College
Lauri Griffin, Ivy Tech Community College
Jeff Hamblin, Brigham Young University–Idaho
Brandon Harpster, Southeast Community College
Joe Harrold, Florida Community College at Jacksonville
Ed Hennessy, Delaware Technical and Community College
Vern Hickman, Boise State University
Martina Hilldorfer, Kauai Community College
Carol Himes, Pueblo Community College
David Hoffman, Mohawk Valley Community College
Thomas Hosley, Carteret Community College
Julie Hosman Kulm, Boise State University, College of Applied Tech
John Hudoc, Robert Morris College
Sharon Hunt, Fort Valley State University
Dorothy Johnston, Erie Community College
Wendy Jordan, Le Cordon Bleu College of Culinary Arts–Las Vegas
Thomas Kaltenecker, Elgin Community College
Debbie Kern, Delgado Community College
Linda Kinney, University of Massachusetts
Kathy Knight, University of Mississippi
Chris Koch, Drexel University
Claude Lambertz, University of Nevada–Las Vegas
Steve Lammers, Olympic College
Barbara Lang, Cornell University–School of Hotel Administration
Joe LaVilla, Art Institute of Phoenix
Julie Lee, Western Kentucky University
Peter Lehmuller, Johnson & Wales University
Dean Louic, Maui Community College
Beth Lulinski, Northern Illinois University
George Macht, College of DuPage
Mark Mattern, Art Institute of Jacksonville
Donnie McBride, North Arkansas College
Paula McKeehan, Tarleton State University
Fiona McKenzie, Sandhills Community College
Ken Mertes, Robert Morris College
David Miller, Idaho State University–College of Technology
Maria Montemagni, College of the Sequoias
Sylvia H. Marple, University of New Hampshire
Judy Myhand, Louisiana State University
Karla Nardi, National Park Community College
Ethel Nettles, Michigan State University
Darla O'Dwyer, Stephen F. Austin State University
Erich Ogle, Mississippi University for Women
Lisa O'Neill, East Central Community College
Joel Papcun, Great Lakes Culinary Institute
Ellen Piazza, Saint Louis Community College
Christine Piccin, Santa Rosa Junior College
Tony Pisacano, Ogeechee Technical College
Leonard Pringle, San Jacinto College–Central
Joan E. Quinn, Northern Illinois University
Charles Robertson, Illinois Central College
Colin Roche, Johnson & Wales University
Gary Rodrick, University of Florida
Linda Rosner, Lexington College
Charles Rossi, St. Louis Community College

Warren Sackler, Rochester Institute of Technology
Carl Sandberg, Gwinnett Technical College
Janet Saros, Montgomery College
Craig Schmantowsky, Lynn University
Jules Schmitz, Cascade Culinary Institute
Bridget Schwartz, Bainbridge College
Janet Shaffer, Lake Washington Technical College
Gregg Shiosaki, Seattle Central Community College
Cory Shute, Kansas City Kansas Community College, Technical Education Center
Curtis Smith, Spokane Community College
Wayne Smith, Western Colorado Community College
Beth Sonnier, El Centro College
Stephen Sparks, South Seattle Community College
Rupert Spies, Cornell University, School of Hotel Administration
Nancy St. John, Bridgewater College
Brian Stahlsmith, Mercyhurst College
Trent Starks, The Keeter Center–College of the Ozarks
Wendy Stocks, Purdue University–Calumet
Linda Sullivan, Indiana University of Pennsylvania
Janis Taylor, Freed-Hardeman University
Klaus Tenbergen, California State University–Fresno
Clorice Thomas-Haysbert, University of Delaware
Peter Tobin, Inland Northwest Culinary Academy at Spokane Community College
Arthur Tolve, Bergen Community College
Mary Trometter, Pennsylvania College of Technology
Armando Trujillo, Pima Community College
Katrina Warner, Tarrant County College, Southeast Campus
Diana Watson-Maile, East Central University
Boo Wells, Jefferson Community College
Seunghee Wie, California State University–Sacramento
Brenda Wilkening, Estrella Mountain Community College
Gay Winterringer, PhD, RD, Mission College
Chris Woodruff, Lake Michigan College
Louis Woods, Anne Arundel Community College
Mark Wright, Erie Community College (State University of New York)
Charles Ziccardi, Drexel University–Goodwin College of Professional Studies

Grateful acknowledgment is extended to the following schools for testing various recipes from this text for accuracy, level of difficulty and appropriateness. Their feedback helped the authors refine recipes so that the concerns of the classroom appear on the printed page.

G. Allen Akmon,
Sullivan University

Leslie Bartosh,
Alvin Community College

Bea Beasley,
Santa Rosa Junior College

Carol Bennett,
Central Arizona College

Frank Benowitz,
Mercer County Community College

Ben Black,
Culinary Institue of Charleston at
Trident Techincal College

Larry Bressler,
California School of Culinary Arts,
Le Cordon Bleu Program

Scott Bright,
The Chefs Academy, Harrison College

Tracey Brigman,
University of Georgia

Angelo Camillo,
Daniels College of Business,
University of Denver

Paul Carrier,
Milwaukee Area Technical College

Melinda Casady,
Oregon Culinary Institute

Susan Ciriello,
Art Institute of Washington

Jerry Comar,
Johnson & Wales University

Chris Crosthwaite,
Lane Community College

Cathy Cunningham,
Tennessee Technological University

Jacqueline deChabert-Rios,
East Carolina University

Richard Donnelly,
East Stroudsburg University

Jodi Lee Duryea,
University of North Texas

Tuesday Eastlack,
Northwest Arkansas
Community College

Sari Edelstein,
Simmons College

Thom England,
Ivy Tech Community College of
Central Indiana

Naomi Everett,
University of Alaska

Melanie Ewalt,
Kirkwood Community College

Richard Exley,
Scottsdale Culinary Institute

Francois Faloppa,
Macomb Community College

Stephen Fernald,
Lake Tahoe Community College

Edward Fernandez,
Kapiolani Community College

Deborah Foster,
Ball State University

Wendy Gordon,
SUNY Rockland Community College

Kristen Grissom,
Daytona State College

Marian Grubor,
West Virginia Northern Community
College

Jeff Hamblin,
Brigham Young University-Idaho

Lois Hand,
Bob Jones University

Brandon Harpster,
Southeast Community College

Kathleen Hassett,
Horry-Georgetown Technical College

Michael Herbert,
Northern Virginia Community College

David Horsfield,
Kirkwood Community College

Julie Hosman Kulm,
Boise State University

Robert Hudson,
Pikes Peak Community College

Robert "Miles" Huff,
Culinary Institute of Charleston at
Trident Technical College

Barry Infuso,
Pima Community College

Bruce Johnson,
Salt Lake City Community College

Dorothy Johnston,
Erie Community College

Melodie Jordan,
Keystone College

Deborah Karasek,
Bob Jones University

Debbie Kern,
Delgado Community College

Mary Ann Kiernan,
Syracuse University

Christopher Koch,
Drexel University

Cindy Komarinski,
Westmoreland County
Community College

Heinz Lauer,
Le Cordon Bleu College of Culinary
Arts Las Vegas

Julie Lee,
Western Kentucky University

Larry Lewis,
San Diego Culinary Institute

Dean Louie,
Maui Culinary Academy

Beth Lulinski,
Northern Illinois University

Nicole Martinelli,
Keiser University

Dean Massey,
Clover Park Technical College

Fiona McKenzie,
Sandhills Community College

Brenden Mesch,
The Art Institute of Dallas

Maria Montemagni,
College of the Sequoias

Andrea Nickels,
Robert Morris College

Adrienne O'Brien,
Luna Community College

Charlie Olawsky,
Grand Rapids Community College

Shelly Owens,
Metropolitan State College of Denver

Clarence Pan,
Daytona State College

Jayne Pearson,
Manchester Community College

Donna Pease,
Technical College of the Lowcountry

Sean M. Perrodin,
San Jacinto College–North Campus

Toussaint Potter,
Art Institute of California–Sacramento

Joan E. Quinn,
Northern Illinois University

Scott Rudolph,
California State Polytechnic
University–Pomona

Craig Schmantowsky,
Lynn University

Jules Schmitz,
Central Oregon Community College

Dave Schneider,
Macomb Community College

Janet Shaffer,
Lake Washington Technical College

Cherie Simpson,
The University of Alabama

Wayne Smith,
Western Colorado Community College

James Swenson,
MilitaryChefs.com

Jim Switzenberg,
Harrisburg Area Community College

Katie Thomas,
Blackhawk Technical College

George Thompson,
Oregon Culinary Institute

Mary Trometter,
Pennsylvania College of Technology

Anna Turner,
Bob Jones University

Katrina Warner,
Tarrant County College

Diana Watson-Maile,
East Central University

Lorna Williams,
Bob Jones University

Josef Wollinger,
Blackhawk Technical College

Louis Woods,
Anne Arundel Community College

Kimberly Youkstetter,
Salter College

Michael Zema,
Elgin Community College

RECIPES

Recipes printed in color are available on electronic media.

CHAPTER ELEVEN

SOUPS

CHAPTER TWELVE

PRINCIPLES OF MEAT COOKERY

CHAPTER THIRTEEN

BEEF

CHAPTER FOURTEEN

VEAL

CHAPTER FIFTEEN

LAMB

CHAPTER SIXTEEN

PORK

CHAPTER SEVENTEEN

POULTRY

CHAPTER EIGHTEEN

GAME

CHAPTER NINETEEN

FISH AND SHELLFISH

CHAPTER TWENTY

EGGS AND BREAKFAST

CHAPTER TWENTY-ONE

VEGETABLES

CHAPTER TWENTY-TWO

POTATOES, GRAINS AND PASTA

CHAPTER **TWENTY-THREE**

HEALTHY COOKING

CHAPTER **TWENTY-FOUR**

SALADS AND SALAD DRESSINGS

CHAPTER TWENTY-EIGHT

HORS D'OEUVRE AND CANAPÉS

CHAPTER THIRTY

QUICK BREADS

CHAPTER THIRTY-ONE

YEAST BREADS

CHAPTER THIRTY-TWO

PIES, PASTRIES AND COOKIES

ON COOKING

CHAPTER ONE

PROFESSIONALISM

cooking (1) the transfer of energy from a heat source to a food; this energy alters the food's molecular structure, changing its texture, flavor, aroma and appearance; (2) the preparation of food for consumption

cookery the art, practice or work of cooking

professional cooking a system of cooking based on a knowledge of and appreciation for ingredients and procedures

LIKE ANY FINE ART, great cookery requires taste and creativity, an appreciation of beauty and a mastery of technique. Like the sciences, successful cookery demands knowledge and an understanding of basic principles. And like any successful leader, today's professional chefs must exercise sound judgment and be committed to achieving excellence in their endeavors.

This book describes foods and cooking equipment, explains culinary principles and cooking techniques and provides recipes using these principles and techniques. No book, however, can provide taste, creativity, commitment and judgment. For these, chefs must rely on themselves.

CHEFS AND RESTAURANTS

Cooks have produced food in quantity for as long as people have eaten together. For millennia, chefs have catered to the often elaborate dining needs of the wealthy and powerful, whether they be Asian, Native American, European or African. And for centuries, vendors in China, Europe and elsewhere have sold to the public foods that they prepared themselves or bought from others.

But the history of the professional chef is of relatively recent origin. Its cast is mostly French, and it is intertwined with the history of restaurants—for only with the development of restaurants during the late 18th and early 19th centuries were chefs expected to produce, efficiently and economically, different dishes at different times for different diners.

The 18th Century—Boulanger's Restaurant

The word *restaurant* is derived from the French word *restaurer* ("to restore"). Since the 16th century, the word *restorative* had been used to describe rich and highly flavored soups or stews capable of restoring lost strength. Restoratives, like all other cooked foods offered and purchased outside the home, were made by guild members. Each guild had a monopoly on preparing certain food items. For example, during the reign of Henri IV of France (1553–1610), there were separate guilds for *rôtisseurs* (who cooked *la grosse viande*, the main cuts of meat), *pâtissiers* (who cooked poultry, pies and tarts), *tamisiers* (who baked breads), *vinaigriers* (who made sauces and some stews, including some restoratives), *traiteurs* (who made ragoûts) and *porte-chapes* (caterers who organized feasts and celebrations).

The French claim that the first modern restaurant opened one day in 1765 when a Parisian tavern keeper, a Monsieur Boulanger, hung a sign advertising the sale of his special restorative, a dish of sheep feet in white sauce. His establishment closed shortly thereafter as the result of a lawsuit brought by a guild whose members claimed that Boulanger was infringing on their exclusive right to sell prepared dishes. Boulanger triumphed in court and later reopened.

Boulanger's establishment differed from the inns and taverns that had existed throughout Europe for centuries. These inns and taverns served foods prepared (usually off premises) by the appropriate guild. The food—of which there was little choice—was offered by the keeper as incidental to the establishment's primary function: providing sleeping accommodations or drink. Customers were served family style and ate at communal tables. Boulanger's contribution to the food service industry was to serve a variety of foods prepared on premises to customers whose primary interest was dining.

Several other restaurants opened in Paris during the succeeding decades, including the Grande Taverne de Londres in 1782. Its owner, Antoine Beauvilliers (1754–1817), was the former steward to the Comte de Provence, later King Louis XVIII of France. He advanced the development of the modern restaurant by offering his wealthy patrons a menu listing

to nontraditional ingredients, and ingredients have been combined in new and previously unorthodox fashions. For chefs with knowledge, skill, taste and judgment, this works.

The Late 20th and Early 21st Century— An American Culinary Revolution

During the last 30 to 40 years, broad changes first launched in the United States have affected the global culinary landscape. Two such trends are "bold, ethnic flavors" and "fresh food, simply prepared."

The first trend is due, in large part, to an unlikely source: the Immigration Act of 1965. Under its provisions, a large number of Asians immigrated to the United States.. They brought with them their rich culinary traditions and ignited America's love affair with fiery hot cuisines. By the late 1970s, many Americans were no longer content with overly salty pseudo-Chinese dishes. They demanded authenticity and developed cravings for spicy dishes from Szechuan and Hunan provinces, Vietnam and Thailand. At the same time, Mexican food left the barrio and became mainstream. Even authentic regional Mexican dishes are now commonplace throughout America.

During this same time period, restaurateurs and chefs began Americanizing the principles of French *nouvelle cuisine*. When Alice Waters opened Chez Panisse in Berkeley, California, in 1971, her goal was to serve fresh food, simply prepared. Rejecting the growing popularity of processed and packaged foods, Waters wanted to use fresh, seasonal and locally grown produce in simple preparations that preserved and emphasized the foods' natural flavors. Chez Panisse and the many chefs who passed through its kitchen launched a new style of cuisine that became known as **New American cuisine**. As Waters's culinary philosophy spread across the United States, farmers and chefs began working together to make fresh, locally grown foods available, and producers and suppliers began developing domestic sources for some of the high-quality ingredients that were once available only from overseas.

This ushered in a period of bold experimentation. American chefs began to combine ingredients and preparation methods from a variety of cuisines. Their work resulted in **fusion cuisine**. With fusion cuisine, ingredients or preparation methods associated with one ethnic or regional cuisine are combined with those of another. A fillet of Norwegian salmon might be grilled over hickory wood, and then served on a bed of Japanese soba noodles, for example, whereas a traditional French duck confit may now be seasoned with lemongrass, ginger and chiles. The fluidity of international borders, the accessibility of global travel and the popularity of the Internet have made the larders of the world available to chefs everywhere. With a few clicks chefs can access recipes, menus and ingredients from virtually anywhere.

At the same time that chefs are sourcing ingredients globally, they are also working in tandem with farmers to supply their diners with fresh flavors while preserving local agriculture and heirloom varieties. The concern for locally raised ingredients, referred to as the **farm-to-table movement**, has influenced chefs to serve fresh seasonal foods, such as wild greens or pastured pork, that is produced within a few miles of their restaurants.

Along with this new interest in and appreciation for American ingredients and American tastes has come a new respect for American chefs. Many European and American food writers and pundits now consider American chefs to be among the best in the world, a fact they often triumph, while at the same time expressing their concern about the general decline of French cuisine and the exodus of European chefs to America. In addition, the American public has taken food to heart.

Many chefs have been elevated to celebrity status; an entire cable television network is devoted to cooking. Bookstore and library shelves are jammed with cookbooks, and newspapers and magazines regularly review restaurants and report on culinary trends. With gourmet shops and cookware stores in most malls, cooking has become both a hobby and a spectator sport. All this has helped inspire a generation of American teenagers to pursue careers behind the stove—and in front of the camera.

FERNAND POINT (1897–1955)

A massive man with a monumental personality, Point refined and modernized the classic cuisine of Escoffier. By doing so, he laid the foundations for *nouvelle cuisine*.

Point received his early training in some of the finest hotel-restaurant kitchens in Paris. In 1922, he and his family moved to Vienne, a city in southwest France near Lyon, and opened a restaurant. Two years later his father left the restaurant to Fernand, who renamed it La Pyramide. During the succeeding years, it became one of the culinary wonders of the world.

Point disdained dominating sauces and distracting accompaniments and garnishes. He believed that each dish should have a single dominant ingredient, flavor or theme; garnishes must be simple and match "like a tie to a suit." Procedure was of great importance. He devoted equal efforts to frying an egg and creating the marjolaine (a light almond and hazelnut spongecake filled with chocolate and praline buttercreams). His goal was to use the finest raw ingredients to produce perfect food that looked elegant and simple. But simplicity was not easy to achieve. As he once said, "a béarnaise sauce is simply an egg yolk, a shallot, a little tarragon vinegar, and butter, but it takes years of practice for the result to be perfect."

ethnic cuisine the cuisine of a group of people having a common cultural heritage, as opposed to the cuisine of a group of people bound together by geography or political factors

fusion cuisine the blending or use of ingredients and/or preparation methods from various ethnic, regional or national cuisines in the same dish; also known as transnational cuisine

farm-to-table movement an awareness of the source of ingredients with an emphasis on serving locally grown and minimally processed foods in season

global cuisine foods (often commercially produced items) or preparation methods that have become ubiquitous throughout the world; for example, curries and French-fried potatoes

national cuisine the characteristic cuisine of a nation

regional cuisine a set of recipes based on local ingredients, traditions and practices; within a larger geographical, political, cultural or social unit, regional cuisines are often variations of one another that blend together to create a national cuisine

INFLUENCES ON MODERN FOOD SERVICE OPERATIONS

From Monsieur Boulanger's humble establishment, a great industry has grown. Today, more than 945,000 public dining facilities operate in the United States alone. The dramatic growth and diversification of the food service industry is due in part to the Industrial Revolution and the social and economic changes it wrought, including the introduction of new technologies, foods, concerns and consumers.

New Technologies

Technology has always had a profound effect on cooking. For example, the development of clay and, later, metal vessels that could contain liquids and withstand as well as conduct heat offered prehistoric cooks the opportunity to stew, make soups and porridge, pickle and brine foods and control fermentation. But it was not until the rapid technological advances fostered by the Industrial Revolution that anything approaching the modern kitchen was possible.

One of the most important advancements was the introduction of the cast-iron stove. Prior to the 19th century, most cooking was done on spits or grills or in cauldrons or pots set on or in a wood- or coal-burning hearth. Hearthside cooking did not lend itself well to the simultaneous preparation of many items or to items requiring constant and delicate attention. With the introduction of cast-iron stoves during the 1800s (first wood- and coal-burning; by midcentury, gas; and by the early 20th century, electric), cooks could more comfortably and safely approach the heat source and control its temperatures. They could also efficiently prepare and hold for later use or service a multitude of smaller amounts of items requiring different cooking methods or ingredients, a necessity at a restaurant simultaneously catering to different diners' demands.

GASTON LENÔTRE (1920–2008)

Gaston Lenôtre started baking in the heart of Normandy in the 1930s. By age 15, he had passed his professional exams. In 1947, he bought the boulangerie/ pâtisserie of his boss in Pont Audemer. His bakery became a destination for sophisticated Parisians on their way to their country estates. In 1957 he was enticed to open a shop in Paris in the stylish 16th arrondissement. It was the first of more than a baker's dozen of locations, plus a vast catering business that literally catered to *"le tout Paris."*

His third location in Plaisir outside Paris, a vast production kitchen, became the heart of his expanding empire. In 1971, he began an in-house school, L'École Lenôtre, to train workers he would need for his expansion. But here is where Gaston Lenôtre showed himself to be much more than a talented baker and inspired businessman. There was a crisis in the trade at the time due to a lack of qualified bakers, so Lenôtre opened the school, a few years later, to the entire professional community. For a fee, even his competitors could come learn from his

Meilleurs Ouvriers de France—chefs recognized by the French government as the best artisans in the trade.

As befitting a native of Normandy, the heart of France's dairy industry, Lenôtre's innovations came in the area of Bavarians,

charlottes and fruit mousses. Many of his cakes and tortes became modern classics. La Feuille d'Automne, Le Concorde, L'Opéra and the Charlotte Cécile seemed to be in all the Parisian bakeries in the early 1980s. Lenôtre mastered the technique of freezing, using it with respect to protect the quality of his products without adulterating them. He used the latest technology and had a staff of laboratory experts to maintain the integrity of his products. Proper freezing preserves the product, extending its shelf life without the chemicals and preservatives common in industrial food production. Many professionals believe that Lenôtre single-handedly saved the pastry profession when it was threatened by mass production.

Many consider Lenôtre the father of modern French pastry, and his impact is felt worldwide. Today, whether you go to Rio de Janeiro, Disney World in Florida, Lebanon or Las Vegas, you will find Lenôtre's name on the marquee.

—ALEX MILES is a Pastry Chef and Culinary Educator in Dijon, France

Also of great importance were developments in food preservation and storage techniques. For thousands of years, food had been preserved by sun-drying, salting, smoking, pickling, sugar-curing or fermenting. Although useful, these procedures destroy or distort the appearance and flavor of most foods. By the early 19th century, preserving techniques that had minimal effect on appearance and flavor began to emerge. For example, by 1800, the Frenchman François Appert successfully "canned" foods by subjecting foods stored in sterilized glass jars to very high heat. An early mechanical refrigerator was developed by the mid-1800s; soon reliable iceboxes, refrigerators and, later, freezers were available. During the 20th century, freeze-drying, vacuum-packing and irradiation became common preservation techniques.

While advancements were being made in preservation and storage techniques, developments in transportation technology were also underway. During the 19th century, steam-powered ships and railroads brought foods quickly to market from distant suppliers. Indeed, by the 1870s, Chicago meat packers were routinely supplying Europe with beef from the western Great Plains. During the 20th century, temperature-controlled cargo ships, trains, trucks and airplanes all were used as part of an integrated worldwide food transportation network. Combined with dependable food preservation and storage techniques, improved transportation networks have freed chefs from seasonal and geographic limitations in their choice of foods and have expanded consumers' culinary horizons.

FERRAN ADRIÀ (1962–)

Cooking is a language through which all the following properties may be expressed: harmony, creativity, happiness, beauty, poetry, complexity, magic, humor, provocation and culture.
—Ferran Adrià

Ferran Adrià is an experimental Spanish chef called the Salvador Dalí of the kitchen. Adrià's restaurant, elBulli (slang for "the bulldog"), has been voted World's Best Restaurant four times by Britain's *Restaurant* magazine. ElBulli also has three Michelin stars, the highest rating, an award it has maintained since 1997.

Born near Barcelona, this food futurist planned a business career before a temporary dishwashing job redirected his path. Inspired by classic cuisine and an encouraging chef, Adrià began his self-education, reading from cover to cover *El Práctico*, a cooking manual edited by a Spanish chef heavily influenced by Escoffier. A month working at elBulli, a prestigious resort restaurant in the tiny town of Roses on the Costa Brava, was an experience so stimulating that he returned there upon completion of his military service in 1984.

At the time, the cuisine at elBulli was heavily influenced by *nouvelle cuisine*, then at its height. Working alongside the restaurant's chef, Adrià created new versions of acclaimed French dishes, earning the restaurant its first star in the influential Michelin Guide. He enhanced his skills and knowledge of classic technique through brief apprenticeships in top kitchens in France. But in 1987, Adrià heard an expression that was to change his direction as a chef. "Creativity means not copying," said Jacques Maximin, then chef of Le Chanticleer in Nice, France. At that moment Adrià and his team committed themselves to reinventing cuisine as we know it.

Today the food served at elBulli engages all of one's senses. Dinner is a tasting menu of up to 35 bite-sized dishes.

What appears to be cooked may actually be flash frozen. An herb clipped to a spoon allows guests to smell the aroma before tasting the herb in the dish. Warm foam that tastes of carrots or mushrooms, hot gelatin, encapsulated mango purée that resembles egg yolks and ravioli filled with liquid are some of the show-stopping techniques for which Adrià has become known. At the vanguard of experimental cooking, Adrià and staff spend 6 months each year working with food technologists, industrial designers and artists experimenting with new techniques. The chef and his staff have documented their style of cooking in a 23-point synthesis. Using the freshest ingredients and mastery of technique are given, they write. But all foods are of equal gastronomic value, with a preference for vegetables and seafood to create a "light, harmonic cuisine" based on classic and modern technologies.

Among those who have worked at elBulli, Chef Grant Achatz of Alinea in Chicago and Chef Wylie Dufresne of wd-50 in New York City have become leaders in this emerging modern style of cooking. Indicative of the appeal of this challenging cuisine, millions of prospective customers vie for one of only 8000 seats at the restaurant each year.

Engineering advancements also have facilitated or even eliminated much routine kitchen work. Since the start of the Industrial Revolution, chefs have come to rely increasingly on mechanical and motorized food processors, mixers and cutters as well as a wealth of sophisticated kitchen equipment such as high-carbon stainless steel knife blades, infrared thermometers and induction cooktops.

During the 1990s, scientists, particularly in the United States, France and Spain, began to see food preparation as a distinct and worthy field of exploration. Chefs and home cooks wanted to understand why food behaved as it did, why traditional cooking techniques sometimes failed and how to improve their culinary skills. These scientists began working under the umbrella of **molecular gastronomy**, a term coined by the French scientist Hervé This in 1988. Inspired by the experiments of molecular gastronomy, some contemporary chefs are reinventing the notion of cooking by employing ingredients and machinery more common in industrial food manufacturing than in classic kitchens. This offshoot of the molecular gastronomy or culinary science movement includes a group of daring, innovative chefs practicing a form of *haute cuisine* that integrates classic French cuisine with the highest-quality ingredients and previously unthinkable presentations.

The founding chef of this as yet unnamed movement is Ferran Adrià of the elBulli restaurant in Spain. Practitioners in the United States include Wylie Dufresne at wd-50 in New York, Homaro Cantu at Moto in Chicago and Grant Achatz at Alinea, also in Chicago. The hallmarks of this high-tech cuisine are dehydrators, edible menus, savory-sweet combinations, smoke infused with intense flavors and −30°F antigriddles that "cook" liquefied food. These chefs produce foods that look like one thing, taste like something totally different and smell like childhood memories. Although few restaurants are going to the extreme of replacing their cooktops with water baths and chemical freezers, many of the tools and techniques that these avant-garde chefs perfected are now being widely used and appreciated.

New Foods

Modern food preservation, storage and transportation techniques have made both fresh and exotic foods regularly available to chefs and consumers.

Advancements in agriculture such as the switch from organic to chemical fertilizers and the introduction of pesticides and drought- or pest-resistant strains have resulted in increased yields of healthy crops. Traditional hybridization techniques and, more recently, genetic engineering have produced new or improved grains and, for better or for worse, fruits and vegetables that have a longer shelf life and are more amenable to mass-production handling, storage and transportation methods.

Likewise, advancements in animal husbandry and aquaculture have led to a more reliable supply of leaner meat, poultry and fish. Moreover, foods found traditionally only in the wild (for example, game, wild rice and many mushrooms) are now being raised commercially and are routinely available.

Food preservation and processing techniques have also led to the development of packaged, prepared convenience foods, some of which are actually quite good. After careful thought and testing, today's chef can rely on some of these products. Doing so allows greater flexibility and more time to devote to other preparations.

New Concerns

Consumer concerns about nutrition and diet have fueled changes in the food service industry. Obviously, what we eat affects our health. Adequate amounts of certain nutrients promote good health by preventing deficiencies; good nutrition also helps prevent chronic diseases and increases longevity. Chefs should provide their customers with nutritious foods.

The public has long been concerned about food safety. Federal, state and local governments have helped promote food safety by inspecting and grading meats and poultry, regulating label contents for packaged foods and setting sanitation standards. All of these

molecular gastronomy a contemporary scientific movement that investigates the chemistry and physics behind the preparation of foods and dishes

standards, especially sanitation standards, affect the way foods are prepared, stored and served.

Concerns about nutrition and food safety have also resulted in renewed interest in organically grown fruits and vegetables and free-range-raised animals.

New Consumers

Demographic and social changes have contributed to the diversification of the food service industry by creating or identifying new consumer groups with their own desires or needs. By tailoring their menu, prices and décor accordingly, food service operations can cater to consumers defined by age (baby boomers and seniors, in particular), type of household (singles, couples and families), income, education and geography.

Since World War II, there has also been a rapid increase in the number and types of institutions providing food services. These include hospitals, schools, retirement centers, sports facilities, private clubs, hotels and resorts (which may in turn have fine dining, coffee shop, quick service, banquet and room service facilities), factories and office complexes. Each of these institutions presents the professional chef with unique challenges, whether they be culinary, dietary or budgetary.

Through travel or exposure to the many books and magazines about food, consumers are becoming better educated and more sophisticated. Educated consumers provide a market for new foods and cuisines as well as an appreciation for a job well done.

Although some consumers may frequent a particular restaurant because its chef or owner is a celebrity or the restaurant is riding high on a crest of fad or fashion, most consumers choose a restaurant—whether it be a fast-food burger place or an elegant French restaurant—because it provides quality food at a cost they are willing to pay. To remain successful, then, the restaurant must carefully balance its commitment to quality with marketplace realities.

THE FOOD SERVICE OPERATION

To function efficiently, a food service operation must be well organized and staffed with appropriate personnel. This staff is traditionally called a **brigade**. Escoffier is credited with developing the kitchen brigade system used in large restaurant kitchens; modern kitchens use a simplified version of this brigade in order to reduce labor costs and streamline operations. Although a chef will be most familiar with the back-of-the-house or kitchen brigade, he or she should also understand how the dining room or front of the house is organized.

The Modern Kitchen Brigade

Today's food service operations are generally led by an **executive chef**, who coordinates kitchen activities and directs the kitchen staff's training and work efforts. The executive chef plans menus and creates recipes. He or she sets and enforces nutrition, safety and sanitation standards and participates in (or at least observes) the preparation and presentation of menu items to ensure that quality standards are rigorously and consistently maintained. He or she is also responsible for purchasing food items and, often, equipment. In some food service operations, the executive chef may assist in designing the menu, dining room and kitchen. He or she trains the dining room staff so that they can correctly answer questions about the menu. He or she may also work with food purveyors, catering directors, equipment vendors, financial consultants, the media, sanitation inspectors and dietitians. In some operations, chefs with some or all of these responsibilities may be referred to as a chef de cuisine.

The executive chef is assisted by a **sous-chef** or **executive sous-chef**, whose primary responsibility is to make sure that the food is prepared, portioned, garnished and

brigade a system of staffing a kitchen so that each worker is assigned a set of specific tasks; these tasks are often related by cooking method, equipment or the types of foods being produced

presented according to the executive chef's standards. The sous-chef may be the cook principally responsible for producing menu items and supervising the kitchen.

Large hotels and conference centers with multiple dining facilities may have one or more **area chefs**, each responsible for a specific facility or function. There could be, for instance, an area chef responsible for each of the hotel's restaurants as well as a banquet chef. Area chefs usually report to the executive chef. Each area chef, in turn, has a brigade working under him or her.

Line cooks (or section cooks) are responsible for preparing menu items according to recipe specifications. They may be assigned to a specific area, such as the broiler cook, fry cook or pantry station. A *roundsman* or *swing cook* is capable of working several stations and is assigned wherever needed during each shift.

The **pastry chef** is responsible for developing recipes for and preparing desserts, pastries, frozen desserts and breads. He or she is usually responsible for purchasing the food items used in the bakeshop.

Prep cooks, **assistants** and **apprentices** are employed as entry-level workers throughout modern kitchens.

New styles of dining have created new positions since Escoffier's days. The most notable is the **short-order cook**, who is responsible for quickly preparing foods to order in smaller operations. He or she will work the broiler, deep-fat fryer and griddle as well

THE CLASSIC KITCHEN BRIGADE

From the chaos and redundancy found in the private kitchens of the 19th century's aristocracy, Escoffier created a distinct hierarchy of responsibilities and functions for food service operations.

At the top is the *chef de cuisine* or *chef*, who is responsible for all operations, developing menu items and setting the kitchen's tone and tempo.

His or her principal assistant is the *sous-chef* (the under chef or second chef), who is responsible for scheduling personnel and replacing the chef and station chefs as necessary. The *sous-chef* also often functions as the *aboyeur* (expediter or announcer), who accepts the orders from the dining room, relays them to the various station chefs and then reviews the dishes before service.

The *chefs de partie* (station chefs) produce the menu items under the direct supervision of the chef or *sous-chef*. Previously, whenever a cook needed an item, he or his assistants produced it; thus several cooks could be making the same sauce or basic preparation. Under Escoffier's system, each station chef is assigned a specific task based on either the cooking method and equipment or the category of items to be produced. They include the following:

- The *saucier* (sauté station chef), who holds one of the most demanding

jobs in the classical kitchen, is responsible for all sautéed items and most sauces.
- The *poissonier* (fish station chef) is responsible for fish and shellfish items and their sauces.
- The *grillardin* (grill station chef) is responsible for all grilled items.
- The *friturier* (fry station chef) is responsible for all fried items.
- The *rôtisseur* (roast station chef) is responsible for all roasted items and jus or other related sauces.
- The *potager* (soup station chef) is responsible for soups and stocks.
- The *légumier* (vegetable station chef) is responsible for all vegetable and starch items.
- The *potager* and *légumier* functions are often combined into a single vegetable station whose chef is known as the *entremetier*. *Entremets* were the courses served after the roast; they usually comprised vegetables, fruits, fritters or sweet items (the sorbet served before the main course in some contemporary restaurants is a vestigial *entremet*).
- The *garde-manger* (pantry chef) is responsible for cold food preparations, including salads and salad dressings, cold appetizers,

charcuterie items, pâtés, terrines and similar dishes. The *garde-manger* supervises the *boucher* (butcher), who is responsible for butchering meats and poultry, as well as the chefs responsible for hors d'oeuvre and breakfast items.
- The *tournant*, also known as the roundsman or swing cook, works where needed.
- The *pâtissier* (pastry chef) is responsible for all baked items, including breads, pastries and desserts. Unlike the several station chefs, the *pâtissier* is not necessarily under the *sous-chef's* supervision. The *pâtissier* supervises the *boulanger* (bread baker), who makes the breads, rolls and baked dough containers used for other menu items (for example, bouchées and feuilletés); the *confiseur*, who makes candies and petit fours; the *glacier*, who makes all chilled and frozen desserts; and the *décorateur*, who makes showpieces and special cakes.
- Depending on the size and needs of any station or area, there may be one or more *demi-chefs* (assistants) and *commis* (apprentices) who work with the station chef or pastry chef to learn the area.

THE DINING ROOM

Like the back-of-the-house (that is, kitchen) staff, the front-of-the-house (that is, dining room) staff is also organized into a brigade. A traditional dining room brigade is led by the **dining room manager** (French *maître d'hotel* or *maître d'*), who generally trains all service personnel, oversees wine selections and works with the chef to develop the menu. He or she organizes the seating chart and may also seat the guests. Working subordinate to him or her are the following:

- The **wine steward** (Fr. *sommelier*), who is responsible for the wine service, including purchasing wines, assisting guests in selecting wines and serving the wines.
- The **headwaiter** (Fr. *chef de salle*), who is responsible for service throughout the dining room or a section of it. In smaller operations, his or her role may be assumed by the *maître d'* or a captain.
- The **captains** (Fr. *chefs d'étage*), who are responsible for explaining the menu to guests and taking their orders. They are also responsible for any tableside preparations.
- The **front waiters** (Fr. *chefs de rang*), who are responsible for assuring that the tables are set properly for each course, foods are delivered properly to the proper tables and the needs of the guests are met.
- The **back waiters** (Fr. *demi-chefs de rang* or *commis de rang*, also known as dining room attendants or buspersons), who are responsible for clearing plates, refilling water glasses and other general tasks appropriate for new dining room workers.

Whether a restaurant uses this entire array of staff depends on the nature and size of the restaurant and the type of service provided.

---

as make sandwiches and even some sautéed items. Another is the **institutional cook**, who generally works with large quantities of packaged or prepared foods for a captive market such as a school, hospital or prison.

A restaurant may employ a **master chef** (Fr. *maître cuisinier*), **master pastry chef** (Fr. *maître pâtissier*) or a **master baker** (Fr. *maître boulanger*, Gr. *bäckermeister*). These titles recognize the highest level of achievement; only highly skilled and experienced professionals who have demonstrated their expertise and knowledge in written and practical exams are entitled to use them. These titles recall the European guild tradition still alive in many countries today. In France and Germany, for example, a chef, pastry chef or baker must pursue many years of classroom and job training, work as an apprentice and pass numerous examinations before acquiring the right to call himself or herself a "master." In the United States, several professional organizations administer programs that certify the professional experience of chefs, pastry chefs and bakers among others in the culinary field. (See Appendix I.)

THE PROFESSIONAL CHEF

Although there is no one recipe for producing a good professional chef, we believe that with knowledge, skill, taste, judgment, dedication and pride a student chef will mature into a professional chef.

Knowledge

Chefs must be able to identify, purchase, utilize and prepare a wide variety of foods. They should be able to train and supervise a safe, skilled and efficient staff. To do all this successfully, chefs must possess a body of knowledge and understand and apply certain scientific and business principles. Schooling helps. A professional culinary program should, at a minimum, provide the student chef with a basic knowledge of foods, food styles and the methods used to prepare foods. Student chefs should also understand sanitation, nutrition and business procedures such as food costing.

This book is designed to help students learn these basics. Many chapters have extensive sections identifying foods and equipment. Throughout this book, we emphasize culinary principles, not recipes. Whenever possible, whether it be preparing puff pastry or grilling a steak, we focus on the general procedure, highlighting fundamental principles

ON EXPERIENCE

Sight, feel, hearing, and smell taught me about food. By touching a piece of meat, I learned to determine its degree of doneness. Raw meat was spongy, well-done meat hard. I learned precisely how to determine all the stages in between by pushing a finger against the surface of the meat. Hearing was significant, too. The snap of an asparagus spear, the crunch of an apple, the pop of a grape are all indicators of freshness and quality. I learned to listen to the sizzling sound of a chicken roasting in the oven. When *le poulet chant* (the chicken sings), I knew that the layers of fat had clarified, signifying that the chicken was nearly done. Smell was of importance in recognizing quality. A fresh fish smells of the sea, seaweed, and salt. Fresh meat has a sweet smell, fresh poultry practically no smell at all. Melon, pears, tomatoes, raspberries, oranges and the like each have their own distinctive fragrance when perfectly ripe.

LA TOQUE BLANCHE

Although the toque traces its origin to the monasteries of the 6th century, the style worn today was introduced at the end of the 19th century. Most chefs now wear a standard 6- or 9-inch-high toque, but historically, a cook's rank in the kitchen dictated the type of hat worn. Beginners wore flat-topped calottes; cooks with more advanced skills wore low toques and the master chefs wore high toques called *dodin-bouffants*. Culinary lore holds that the toque's pleats—101 in all—represent the 101 ways its wearer can successfully prepare eggs.

gastronomy the art and science of eating well

gourmet a connoisseur of fine food and drink

gourmand a connoisseur of fine food and drink, often to excess

gourmet foods foods of the highest quality, perfectly prepared and beautifully presented

and skills; we discuss both the how and why of cooking. Only then are specific applications and sample recipes given. We also want students to have a sense of the rich tradition of cookery, so informative sidebars on food history, chef biographies and other topics are scattered throughout the book. The electronic media that accompanies this book are designed to enhance the learning experience while exposing students to the usefulness of computer technology in the contemporary kitchen.

In this way, we follow the trail blazed by Escoffier, who wrote in the introduction to *Le Guide culinaire* that his book is not intended to be a compendium of recipes slavishly followed, but rather a tool that leaves his colleagues "free to develop their own methods and follow their own inspiration; . . . the art of cooking . . . will evolve as a society evolves . . . only basic rules remain unalterable."

As with any profession, an education does not stop at graduation. The acquisition of knowledge continues after the student chef joins the ranks of the employed. He or she should take additional classes on unique or ethnic cuisines, nutrition, business management or specialized skills. He or she should regularly review some of the many periodicals and books devoted to cooking, should travel and should try new dishes to broaden his or her culinary horizons. The professional chef should also become involved in professional organizations (see Appendix I) in order to meet his or her peers and exchange ideas.

Skill

Culinary schooling alone does not make a student a chef. Nothing but practical, hands-on experience will provide even the most academically gifted student with the skills needed to produce, consistently and efficiently, quality foods or to organize, train, motivate and supervise a staff.

Many food service operations recognize that new workers, even those who have graduated from culinary programs, need time and experience to develop and hone their skills. Therefore, many graduates start in entry-level positions. Do not be discouraged; advancement will come, and the training pays off in the long run. Today, culinary styles and fashions change frequently. What does not go out of fashion are well-trained, skilled and knowledgeable chefs. They can adapt.

Taste

No matter how knowledgeable or skilled the chef, he or she must be able to produce foods that taste great, or the consumer will not return. A chef can do so only if he or she is confident about his or her own sense of taste.

Our total perception of taste is a complex combination of smell, taste, sight, sound and texture. All senses are involved in the enjoyment of eating; all must be considered in creating or preparing a dish. The chef should develop a taste memory by sampling foods, both familiar and unfamiliar. The chef should also think about what he or she tastes, making notes and experimenting with flavor combinations and cooking methods. But a chef should not be inventive simply for the sake of invention. Rather, he or she must consider how the flavors, appearances, textures and aromas of various foods will interact to create a total taste experience.

Judgment

Selecting menu items, determining how much of what item to order, deciding whether and how to combine ingredients and approving finished items for service are all matters of judgment. Although knowledge and skill play a role in developing judgment, sound judgment comes only with experience. And real experience is often accompanied by failure. Do not be upset or surprised when a dish does not turn out as you expected. Learn from your mistakes as well as from your successes; only then will you develop sound judgment.

Dedication

Becoming a chef is hard work; so is being one. The work is often physically taxing, the hours are usually long and the pace is frequently hectic. Despite these pressures, the chef is expected to efficiently produce consistently fine foods that are properly prepared, seasoned, garnished and presented. To do so, the chef must be dedicated to the job.

The dedicated chef should never falter. The food service industry is competitive and depends on the continuing goodwill of an often fickle public. One bad dish or one off night can result in a disgruntled diner and lost business. The chef should always be mindful of the food prepared and the customer served.

The chef must also be dedicated to his or her staff. Virtually all food service operations rely on teamwork to get the job done well. Good teamwork requires a positive attitude and dedication to a shared goal, which is as impressive to a prospective employer as well-honed technical skills.

Pride

Not only is it important that the job be well done, but the professional chef should have a sense of pride in doing it well. Pride should also extend to personal appearance and behavior in and around the kitchen. The professional chef should be well-groomed and in a clean, well-maintained uniform when working.

The professional chef's uniform consists of comfortable shoes, trousers (either solid white, solid black, black-and-white checked or black-and-white striped), a white double-breasted jacket, an apron and a neckerchief usually knotted or tied cravat style. The uniform has certain utilitarian aspects: Checked trousers disguise stains; the double-breasted white jacket can be rebuttoned to hide dirt, and the double layer of fabric protects from scalds and burns; the neckerchief absorbs facial perspiration; and the apron protects the uniform and insulates the body. This uniform should be worn with pride. Shoes should be polished; trousers and jacket should be pressed. The crowning element of the uniform is the toque, the tall white hat worn by chefs almost everywhere.

---

1. Describe the kitchen brigade system. What is its significance in today's professional kitchens?

2. What are the roles of a chef, sous-chef and line cook in a modern kitchen?

3. Describe the differences in a meal prepared by Carême and one prepared by Point.

4. List and explain three technological advances affecting food preparation.

5. Discuss the societal changes that have contributed to diversification in the modern food service industry.

6. The newspapers in most large cities as well as national food magazines publish restaurant reviews. Use the Internet to find restaurant reviews from a city other than the one in which you live. Select one or two restaurants where you would like to dine the next time you visit that city. Why did you select these particular establishments? **www**

7. The James Beard Foundation recognizes and honors outstanding American chefs each year. Who was James Beard? Which chefs are currently considered some of the most outstanding in the United States? Why? **www**

QUESTIONS FOR DISCUSSION

Terms to Know

chef	back of the
guild	house
cuisine	front of the
restaurateur	house
brigade	food service
executive chef	skill
chef de cuisine	taste
sous-chef	judgment
line cook	toque
expediter	

> " Our lives are not in the lap of the gods,
> but in the lap of our cooks. "
>
> —Lin Yutang, Chinese-American writer,
> in *The Importance of Living*, 1937

CHAPTER TWO

FOOD SAFETY AND SANITATION

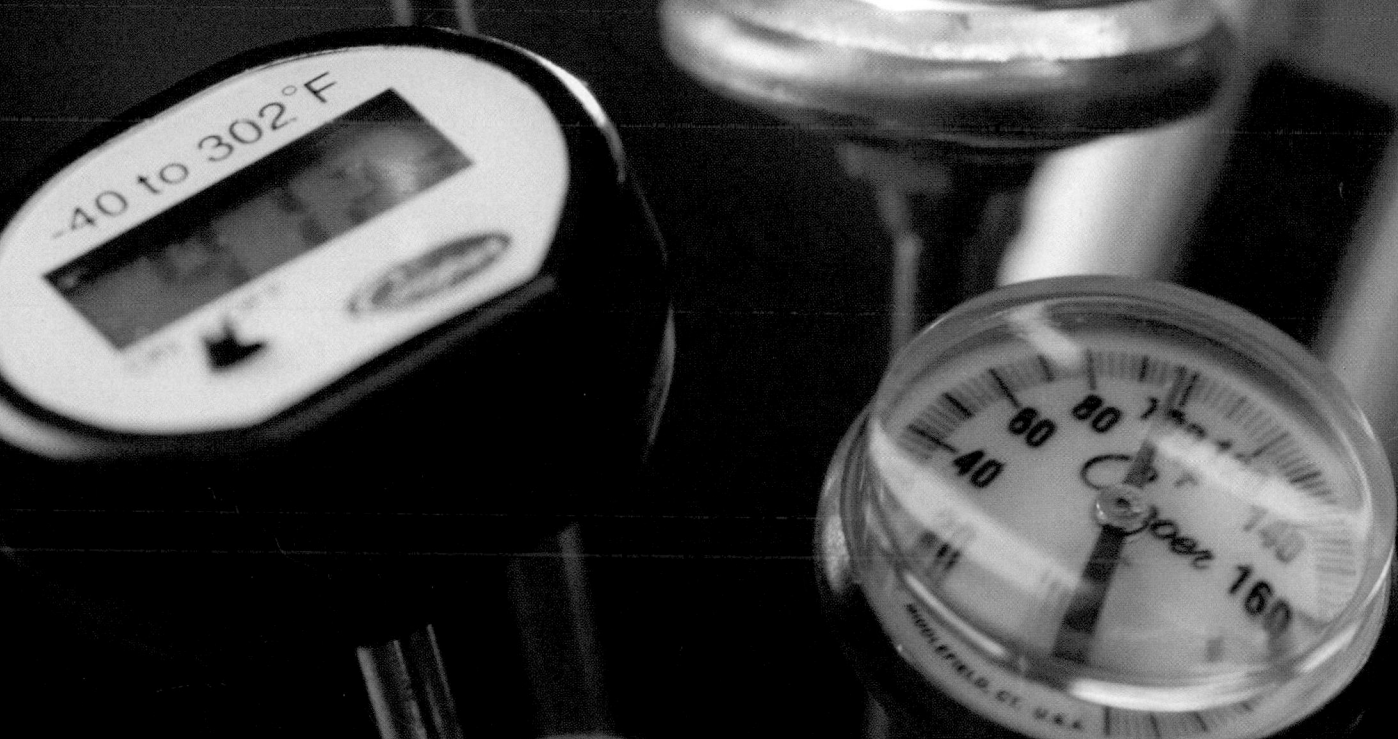

THE U.S. PUBLIC HEALTH SERVICE identifies more than 40 diseases that can be transmitted through food. Many can cause serious illness; some are even deadly. Therefore, providing consumers with safe food is the food handler's most important responsibility. Unfortunately, food handlers are also the primary cause of food-related illnesses.

Understanding what causes food-borne illnesses and what can be done to prevent them will help students be better able to protect their customers. This chapter, however, is not meant to be a complete discussion of sanitation in food service operations. But it should alert students to practices that can result in food-borne illnesses.

Federal, state, county and municipal health, building and other codes are designed in part to ensure that food is handled in a safe and proper manner. Chefs should always consult the local health department for information and guidance, and always be conscious of what they can do to create and maintain a safe product as well as a safe environment for their customers, their fellow employees and themselves.

Sanitation refers to the creation and maintenance of conditions that will prevent food contamination or food-borne illness. **Contamination** refers to the presence, generally unintended, of harmful organisms or substances. Contaminants can be (1) biological, (2) chemical or (3) physical. When consumed in sufficient quantities, food-borne contaminants can cause illness or injury, long-lasting disease or even death.

Contamination occurs in two ways: direct contamination and cross-contamination. **Direct contamination** is the contamination of raw foods or the plants or animals from which they come, in their natural settings or habitats. Chemical and biological contaminants such as bacteria and fungi are present in the air, soil and water. So, foods can be easily contaminated by their general exposure to the environment: Grains can become contaminated by soil fumigants in the field, and shellfish can become contaminated by ingesting toxic marine algae.

Chemicals and microorganisms generally cannot move on their own, however. They need to be transported, an event known as **cross-contamination**. The major cause of cross-contamination is people. Food handlers can transfer biological, chemical and physical contaminants to food while processing, preparing, cooking or serving it. It is therefore necessary to view sanitation as the correction of problems caused by direct contamination and the prevention of problems caused by cross-contamination during processing and service.

DIRECT CONTAMINATION

Biological Contaminants

Several **microorganisms**, primarily bacteria, parasites, viruses and fungi, can cause biologically based food-borne illnesses. By understanding how these organisms live and reproduce, students can better understand how to protect food from them.

BACTERIA

Bacteria, which are single-celled microorganisms, are the leading cause of food-borne illnesses. See Figure 2.1. Some bacteria are beneficial, such as those that aid in digesting food or decomposing garbage. Certain beneficial bacteria are used to make cheese, yogurt and sauerkraut. Other bacteria spoil food, but without rendering it unfit for

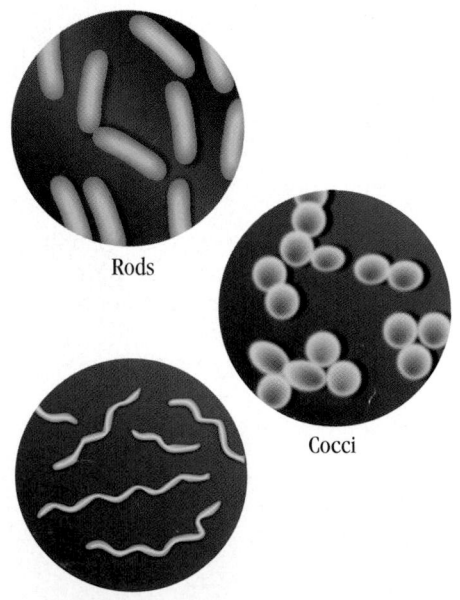

Rods

Cocci

Spirilla

FIGURE 2.1 ▶ Bacteria can be classified by shape: Rods are short, tubular structures; cocci are discs, some of which form clusters; and spirilla are corkscrews.

54

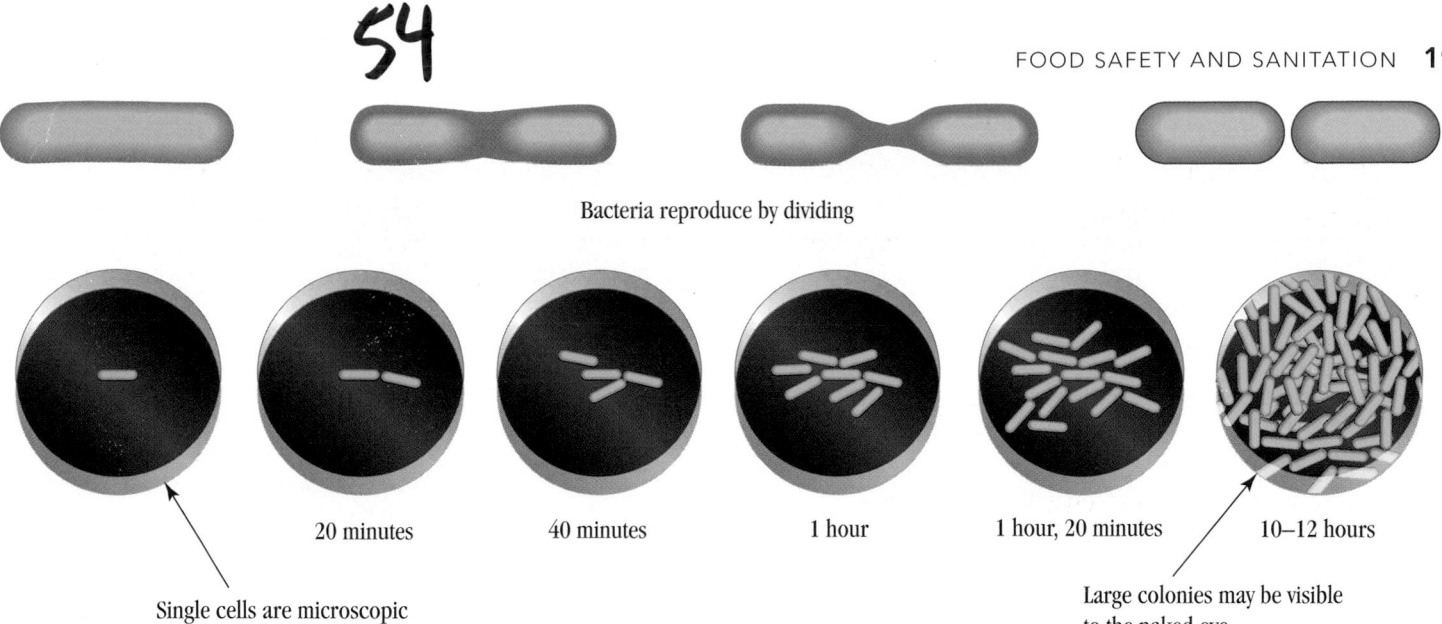

Bacteria reproduce by dividing

20 minutes   40 minutes   1 hour   1 hour, 20 minutes   10–12 hours

Single cells are microscopic

Large colonies may be visible
to the naked eye

FIGURE 2.2 ▶ One bacterium divides into two; the two bacteria each divide, creating four; the four become 16 and so on. It takes only a very short time for one bacterium to produce millions more.

human consumption. These bacteria, called **putrefactives**, are not a sanitation concern. (Indeed, in some cultures, they are not even a culinary concern. Cultures differ on what constitutes "bad" meat, for example, and game is sometimes hung for a time to allow bacteria to grow.) The bacteria that are dangerous when consumed by humans are called **pathogenic**. These bacteria must be destroyed or controlled in a food service operation.

Most bacteria reproduce by binary fission: Their genetic material is first duplicated and the nucleus then splits, each new nucleus taking some of the cellular material with it. See Figure 2.2. Under favorable conditions each bacterium can divide every 15–30 minutes. Within 12 hours, one bacterium can become a colony of 72 billion bacteria, more than enough to cause serious illness.

Some rod-shaped bacteria are capable of forming spores. Spores are thick-walled structures used as protection against a hostile environment. The bacteria essentially hibernate within their spores, where they can survive extreme conditions that would otherwise destroy them. When conditions become favorable, the bacteria return to a viable state. This is important in food sanitation because heating or sanitizing techniques may not destroy bacterial spores.

Intoxications and Infections

Depending on the particular microorganism, pathogenic bacteria can cause illnesses in humans in one of three ways: by intoxication, infection or toxin-mediated infection. See Table 2.1.

Botulism is a well-known example of an **intoxication**. Certain bacteria produce **toxins**, by-products of their life processes. You cannot smell, see or taste toxins. Ingesting these toxin-producing bacteria by themselves does not cause illness. But toxins that are ingested can poison the consumer. Proper food-handling techniques are critical in preventing an intoxication because even if a food is cooked to a sufficiently high temperature to kill all bacteria present, the toxins they leave behind are usually not destroyed.

The second type of bacterial illness is an **infection**. Salmonella is an especially well known example. An infection occurs when live pathogenic bacteria (infectants) are ingested. The bacteria then live in the consumer's intestinal tract. It is the living bacteria, not their waste products, that cause an illness. Infectants must be alive when eaten for them to do any harm. Fortunately, these bacteria can be destroyed by cooking foods to sufficiently high temperatures, usually 165°F (74°C) or higher.

The third type of bacterial illness has characteristics of both an intoxication and an infection, and is referred to as a **toxin-mediated infection**. Examples are *Clostridium perfringens* and *Escherichia coli* 0157:H7. When these living organisms are ingested, they establish colonies in human or animal intestinal tracts, where they then produce toxins.

physical hazard a danger to the safety of food caused by particles such as glass chips, metal shavings, bits of wood or other foreign matter

chemical hazard a danger to the safety of food caused by chemical substances, especially cleaning agents, pesticides and toxic metals

biological hazard a danger to the safety of food caused by disease-causing microorganisms such as bacteria, molds, yeasts, viruses or fungi

microorganisms single-celled organisms as well as tiny plants and animals that can be seen only through a microscope

pathogen any organism that causes disease; usually refers to bacteria; undetectable by smell, sight or taste, pathogens are responsible for as many as 95 percent of all food-borne illnesses

TABLE 2.1 CHARACTERISTICS OF BACTERIAL ILLNESSES

COMMON NAME	ORGANISM	FORM	COMMON SOURCES	PREVENTION
Staph	*Staphylococcus aureus*	Toxin Intoxication	Starchy foods, cold meats, bakery items, custards, milk products, humans with infected wounds or sores	Wash hands and utensils before use; exclude unhealthy food handlers; avoid having foods at room temperature
Perfringens or CP	*Clostridium perfringens*	Cells and toxin Toxin-mediated	Reheated meats, sauces, stews, casseroles, beans	Keep cooked foods at an internal temperature of 135°F (57°C) or higher; reheat leftovers to an internal temperature of 165°F (74°C) or higher
Botulism	*Clostridium botulinum*	Toxin, cells, spores Intoxication	Cooked foods held for an extended time at warm temperatures with limited oxygen: rice, potatoes, smoked fish, canned vegetables, soil	Keep cooked foods at an internal temperature of 135°F (57°C) or higher or 41°F (5°C) or lower; reheat leftovers thoroughly; discard swollen cans; do not use home-canned products
Salmonella	*Salmonella*	Cells Infection	Poultry, eggs, milk, meats, produce, fecal contamination	Thoroughly cook all meat, poultry, fish and eggs; avoid cross-contamination with raw foods; maintain good personal hygiene
Strep	*Streptococcus*	Cells Infection	Infected food handlers	Do not allow employees to work if ill; protect foods from customers' coughs and sneezes
E. coli or 0157	*Escherichia coli 0157:H7* (enteropathogenic strains)	Cells and toxins Toxin-mediated	Any food, especially raw milk, raw vegetables, raw or rare beef, humans	Thoroughly cook or reheat items; use only pasteurized dairy products
Listeria	*Listeria monocytogenes*	Cells Infection	Milk products, ice cream, frozen yogurt, raw vegetables, poultry, meat, seafood, humans, deli meats	Avoid raw milk and cheese made from unpasteurized milk; keep storage areas clean

These bacteria are particularly dangerous for young children, the elderly and people with weakened immune systems.

Preventing Bacterial Intoxications and Infections

All bacteria, like other living things, need certain conditions in order to complete their life cycles. Like humans, they need food, a comfortable temperature, moisture, the proper pH, the proper atmosphere and time. The best way to prevent bacterial intoxications and infections is to attack the factors bacteria need to survive and multiply.

Certain conditions enhance the growth of bacteria:

▶ Food
▶ Temperature
▶ Time
▶ Moisture
▶ Acid/alkali balance
▶ Atmosphere

FOOD　Bacteria need food for energy and growth. The foods on which bacteria thrive are referred to as **potentially hazardous foods (PHF)** or **time/temperature controlled for safety (TCS) foods.** They are generally high in protein and include animal-based products, cooked grains and some raw and cooked vegetables. These foods and items containing these foods must be handled with great care.

THE FOOD-BORNE ILLNESS CRISIS IN AMERICA

America is confronted with a food-related health crisis of unprecedented proportions. The latest official estimate from the Centers for Disease Control and Prevention (CDC) is that there are some 76 million incidents of food-related illness in the United States annually. Of these, an estimated 325,000 Americans are hospitalized and 5,000 die each year. Some recent evidence indicates that these incidents have slightly decreased, and a new study is currently underway. Yet this remains a major crisis, and many Americans who suffer from food poisoning are not even aware of the cause. Symptoms may take a week or longer to appear, and victims frequently incorrectly attribute the distress and discomfort to stomach flu. It is not until the victims' afflictions become acute that tests are taken to determine the real cause. For those at risk—children, the elderly and anyone with a compromised immune system—this is frequently too late and the consequences can be deadly.

In his best-selling book *Fast Food Nation*, Eric Schlosser points out that one cause for this increase in food-borne illnesses is the vast expansion of the meat-packing industry due to increased demand from the fast-food industry. Indeed, recent *E. coli* outbreaks have been traced to meat processors' operations, just as *Salmonella* has increasingly been traced to poultry operations.

While the health problems that Schlosser raises are important and should not be glossed over, they should not be exaggerated either. The Food Safety and Inspection Service (FSIS), a branch of the U.S. Department of Agriculture (USDA), has tested thousands of samples of ground beef since 1996. Of these, few have tested positive for *E. coli* and none of these samples were associated with any outbreak of illness. Recently FSIS inspections of meat-processing plants have increased, but incidences of *E. coli* have decreased. Even if health problems in the meat-packing industry were somehow solved tomorrow, food-borne illnesses would likely still be on the rise. The Government Accounting Office has estimated that 85 percent of food-borne illnesses comes from fruits, vegetables, seafood and cheeses—not meat or poultry. Fortunately, poisoning from *E. coli* is among the more uncommon food-borne diseases, with an estimated 73,000 cases each year from all sources.

Schlosser also raises legitimate concerns about the fat and nutritional content of the food served in fast-food establishments. Obesity and high cholesterol can cause health problems, and consuming vast quantities of fast food can contribute to potential illness. However, for most Americans an occasional trip to McDonald's is not hazardous to their health. It just depends on the rest of their diet. And popular images to the contrary, fast-food establishments have a good record of cleanliness when compared with other restaurants—and particularly when compared with home kitchens.

In fact, food safety experts have concluded that the home is the number one place where food-borne illnesses originate. Indeed, most home kitchens would not pass food inspections that public facilities regularly pass with flying colors. And most cases of illnesses caused by *E. coli* and *Salmonella*, even those originating at meat and poultry packers, could have been averted if home cooks had followed basic health procedures: properly storing meat and poultry, frequently washing their hands, promptly disinfecting all areas touched by raw meat or poultry and correctly cooking foods at the appropriate high temperatures for the appropriate period of time.

Of course, food inspections need to be increased and conditions improved at some meat- and poultry-packing plants. However, while blaming particular elements in the food system may bring visibility to serious problems, contamination can occur at many points along the way in the food system. If this food-related health crisis is to be controlled, it must be approached systemically from the farm to the fork.

—ANDREW F. SMITH teaches culinary history at the New School University and is the author of 13 books on culinary topics. He is editor in chief of the *Oxford Encyclopedia of Food and Drink in America*

TEMPERATURE   **Temperature** is the most important factor in the pathogenic bacteria's environment because it is the factor most easily controlled by food service workers. Most microorganisms are destroyed at high temperatures. Freezing slows but does not stop growth, nor does it destroy bacteria.

Most bacteria that cause food-borne illnesses multiply rapidly at temperatures between 70°F and 125°F (21°C and 52°C). Therefore, the broad range of temperatures between 41°F and 135°F (5°C and 57°C) is referred to as the **temperature danger zone**. See Figure 2.3. Keeping foods out of the temperature danger zone reduces the bacteria's ability to thrive and reproduce.

To control the growth of any bacteria that may be present, it is important to maintain the internal temperature of food at 135°F (57°C) or above or 41°F (5°C) or below. Simply stated: Keep hot foods hot and cold foods cold. Potentially hazardous foods or time/temperature controlled for safety foods should be heated or cooled quickly so that they are within the temperature danger zone as briefly as possible. This is known as the **time-and-temperature principle**.

Keep hot foods hot. The high internal temperatures reached during proper cooking kill most of the bacteria that can cause food-borne illnesses. (See Table 2.2.) When foods are reheated, the internal temperature should quickly reach or exceed 165°F (74°C) in order

THE TEMPERATURE DANGER ZONE

The temperature danger zone is a broad range of temperatures in which most of the bacteria that cause food-borne illnesses multiply rapidly. The 2005 Model Food Code of the Food and Drug Administration (FDA), October 2007 revision, indicates that the temperature danger zone begins at 41°F (5°C) and ends at 135°F (57°C). Regulations in some localities and with some organizations may vary, however. This text uses the range recommended by the FDA.

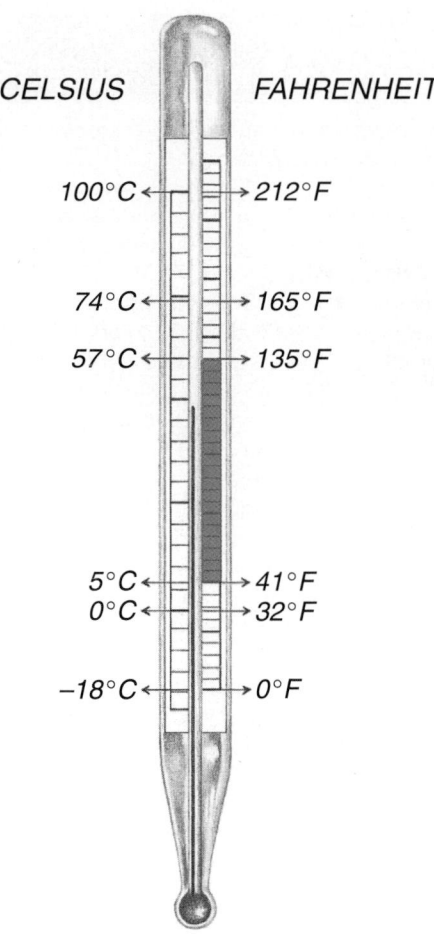

CELSIUS   FAHRENHEIT

100°C ←→ 212°F

74°C ←→ 165°F

57°C ←→ 135°F

5°C ←→ 41°F
0°C ←→ 32°F

−18°C ←→ 0°F

FIGURE 2.3 ▶ The temperature danger zone.

to kill any bacteria that may have grown during storage. Once properly heated, hot foods must be held at temperatures of 135°F (57°C) or higher. (Holding food at 140°F/60°C offers an additional safeguard.) Foods that are to be displayed or served hot must be heated rapidly to reduce the time within the temperature danger zone. When heating or reheating foods:

▶ Heat small quantities at a time.

▶ Stir frequently.

▶ Heat foods as close to service time as possible.

▶ Use preheated ingredients whenever possible to prepare hot foods.

▶ Never use a steam table for heating or reheating foods. Bring reheated food to an appropriate internal temperature (at least 165°F/74°C) before placing it in the steam table for holding.

Keep cold foods cold. Foods that are to be displayed, stored or served cold must be cooled rapidly. When cooling foods:

▶ Refrigerate semisolid foods at 41°F (5°C) or below in containers that are less than 2 inches deep. (Increased surface area decreases cooling time.)

▶ Avoid crowding the refrigerator; allow air to circulate around foods.

▶ Vent hot foods in an ice-water bath, as illustrated in Chapter 10, Stocks and Sauces.

▶ Prechill ingredients such as mayonnaise before preparing cold foods.

▶ Store cooked foods above raw foods to prevent cross-contamination.

Keep frozen foods frozen. Freezing at 0°F (−18°C) or below essentially stops bacterial growth but will not kill the bacteria. Do not place hot foods in a standard freezer. This will not cool the food any faster, and the release of heat can raise the temperature of other foods in the freezer. Only a special blast freezer can be used for chilling hot items. If one is not available, cool hot foods as mentioned earlier before freezing them. When frozen foods are thawed, bacteria that are present will begin to grow. Therefore:

▶ Never thaw foods at room temperature.

▶ Thaw foods gradually under refrigeration to maintain the food's temperature at 41°F (5°C) or less. Place thawing foods in a container to prevent cross-contamination from dripping or leaking liquids.

▶ Thaw foods under running water at a temperature of 70°F (21°C) or cooler.

▶ Thaw foods in a microwave only if the food will be prepared and served immediately.

POTENTIALLY HAZARDOUS FOODS OR TIME/TEMPERATURE CONTROLLED FOR SAFETY FOODS

A potentially hazardous food (PHF), which may require time/temperature control for safety (TCS), is any food or food ingredient that will support the rapid growth of infectious or toxigenic microorganisms, or the slower growth of *Clostridium botulinum*. PHF/TCS foods include the following:

■ Food from an animal source (for example, meat, fish, shellfish, poultry, milk and eggs)

■ Food from a plant that has been heat-treated (for example, cooked rice, beans, potatoes, soy products and pasta)

■ Raw seed sprouts

■ Cut melons

■ Cut tomatoes or mixtures of cut tomatoes that are not acidified or

otherwise appropriately modified at a processing plant

■ Garlic-in-oil mixtures that are not acidified or otherwise appropriately modified at a processing plant

■ Foods containing any of the preceding items (for example, custards, sauces and casseroles)

TABLE 2.2 RECOMMENDED INTERNAL COOKING TEMPERATURES

PRODUCT	TEMPERATURE
Beef, pork, veal or lamb steaks or chops	Cook to 145°F/63°C for 15 seconds
Beef, pork, veal or lamb, roasts	Cook to 145°F/63°C for 4 minutes
Egg dishes	Cook to 155°F/68°C; if the dish is uncooked, use only pasteurized eggs
Eggs	Cook until the yolk and white are firm OR cook to 145°F/63°C for 15 seconds if prepared for a customer's immediate order
Fish and shellfish	Cook to 145°F/63°C for 15 seconds; shells should open
Game, commercial	Cook to 145°F/63°C for 15 seconds
Ground beef, veal, pork or lamb	Cook to 155°F/68°C for 15 seconds
Ham and bacon	Cook to 155°F/68°C for 15 seconds
Poultry or wild game, whole or ground	Cook to 165°F/74°C for 15 seconds
Ratites and injected meats (commercially flavored with marinade or brine)	Cook to 155°F/68°C for 15 seconds
Stuffing, stuffed meat, stuffed fish, stuffed pasta and casseroles	Cook to 165°F/74°C for 15 seconds
Any PHF/TCS foods cooked in a microwave	Cook to 165°F/74°C, then let stand for 2 minutes

(SOURCES: USDA Food Safety and Inspection Service; FDA 2005 Model Food Code, October 5, 2007, Supplement.)

TIME When bacteria are moved from one place to another, they require time to adjust to new conditions. This resting period, during which very little growth occurs, is known as the **lag phase** and may last from 1 to 4 hours. It is followed by the **log phase**, a period of accelerated growth, and then by the **stationary phase**, which lasts until the bacteria begin to crowd others within their colony, creating competition for food, space and moisture. This begins the **decline** or **negative-growth phase**, during which bacteria die at an accelerated rate. See Figure 2.4.

Because of the lag phase, foods can be in the temperature danger zone for very short periods during preparation without an unacceptable increase in bacterial growth. Exposure to the temperature danger zone is cumulative, however, and should not exceed 4 hours total. The less time food is in the temperature danger zone, the less opportunity bacteria have to multiply.

MOISTURE Bacteria need a certain amount of moisture, which is expressed as water activity or A_w. Water itself has an A_w of 1.0. Any food with an A_w of 0.85 or greater is considered PHF/TCS food. Bacteria cannot flourish where the A_w is too low, usually below 0.85. This explains why dry foods such as flour, sugar and crackers are rarely subject to bacterial infestations. A low A_w only halts bacterial growth, however; it does not kill the microorganisms. When dried foods such as beans or rice are rehydrated, any bacteria present can flourish and the food may become potentially hazardous, requiring time/temperature control for safety.

ACID/ALKALI BALANCE Bacteria are affected by the **pH** of their environment. Although they can survive in a wider range, they prefer a neutral environment with a pH of 6.6 to 7.5. Growth is usually halted if the pH is 4.6 or less. So acidic foods such as lemon juice, tomatoes and vinegar create an unfavorable environment for bacteria. Simply adding an acidic ingredient to foods should not, however, be relied on to destroy bacteria or preserve foods. The amount of acidity appropriate for flavoring is not sufficient to ensure the destruction of bacteria.

pH a measurement of the acid or alkali content of a solution, expressed on a scale of 0 to 14.0. A pH of 7.0 is considered neutral or balanced. The lower the pH value, the more acidic the substance. The higher the pH value, the more alkaline the substance.

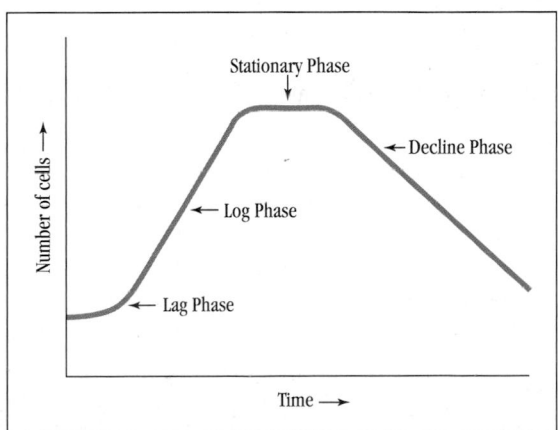

FIGURE 2.4 ▶ Bacterial growth curve.

MAD COW DISEASE

During the past several years, medical authorities have found links between a disease in cattle called bovine spongiform encephalopathy (BSE, popularly known as "mad cow disease") and an extremely rare disease in humans called new variant Creutzfeldt-Jakob disease (nvCJD). Both BSE and nvCJD are slowly degenerative and invariably fatal diseases affecting the central nervous system. Researchers know that these diseases have unusually long incubation periods, but do not know exactly what causes them. They believe that BSE is spread in cattle through feed that has been made, in part, with processed ingredients from slaughtered animals that carried the unknown infectious agent. They also believe that nvCJD is probably contracted by eating meat or other products processed from infected animals. So far, the worst of the known BSE outbreaks has been confined to Europe, principally Great Britain, and even there only a few people have been diagnosed with nvCJD.

Very few cases of BSE or nvCJD have been reported in the United States. For more than a decade, federal authorities have restricted the importation of certain species of live animals and products derived from them originating in countries suffering or suspected of suffering from outbreaks of BSE. They also actively monitor American meat-packing facilities for any signs of BSE in cattle waiting to be slaughtered, and long ago banned the sale of the type of feed associated with BSE in Europe.

Responsible government and nongovernmental authorities continue to assure the American public that it is safe to eat American beef.

ATMOSPHERE Bacteria need an appropriate atmosphere. Some bacteria, known as **aerobic**, thrive on oxygen, whereas others, known as **anaerobic**, cannot survive in its presence. Still others, known as **facultative**, can adapt and will survive with or without oxygen. Unfortunately, most pathogenic bacteria are facultative.

Canning, which creates an anaerobic atmosphere, destroys bacteria that need oxygen. But it also creates a favorable atmosphere for anaerobic and facultative bacteria. A complete vacuum need not be formed for anaerobic bacteria to thrive, however. A tight foil covering, a complete layer of fat or even a well-fitting lid can create an atmosphere sufficiently devoid of oxygen to permit the growth of anaerobic bacteria.

PARASITES

Parasites are tiny organisms that depend on nutrients from a living host to complete their life cycle. Animals, poultry, fish, shellfish and humans can all play host to parasites. Several types of very small parasitic worms can enter an animal through contaminated feed, then settle in the host's intestinal tract or muscles, where they grow and reproduce.

Trichinosis is caused by eating undercooked meat (usually game or pork) infected with trichina larvae. Although trichinosis has been virtually eradicated by grain-feeding hogs and testing them before slaughter, some cases still occur each year. Traditionally, it was thought that pork must be cooked to internal temperatures of 170°F (77°C) or higher to eradicate the larvae. This generally resulted in a dry, tough product. Scientists have now determined that trichina larvae are killed if held at 137°F (58°C) for 10 seconds. The FDA currently recommends cooking pork products to an internal temperature of 145°F (63°C) or above for 15 seconds. The National Livestock and Meat Board and the USDA recommend cooking all pork products to 160°F (71°C), however.

Anisakiasis is another illness caused by parasitic roundworms. *Anisakis* worms reside in the organs of fish, especially bottom feeders or those taken from contaminated waters. Raw or undercooked fish are most often implicated in anisakiasis. Fish should be thoroughly cleaned immediately after being caught so that the parasites do not have an opportunity to spread. Thorough cooking to a minimum internal temperature of 135°F (57°C) is the only way to destroy the larvae, as they can survive even highly acidic marinades.

Cyclospora infections are caused by a single-celled parasite found in water or food contaminated by infected feces. Produce from undeveloped countries is a common source of cyclospora parasites, as is untreated water. Avoiding such products is the best prevention method.

VIRUSES

Viruses cause other biologically based food-borne illnesses such as hepatitis A and Norovirus (formerly called the Norwalk virus). Viruses are among the smallest known forms of life. They invade the living cells of a host, take over those cells' genetic material and cause the cells to produce more viruses.

Viruses do not require a host to survive, however. They can survive—but not multiply—while lying on any food or food contact surface. Unlike bacteria, viruses can be present on any food, not just a PHF/TCS food. The food or food contact surface simply becomes a means of transportation between hosts.

Unlike bacteria, viruses are not affected by the water activity, pH or oxygen content of their environment. Some, however, can be destroyed by temperatures higher than 176°F (80°C). Basically, the only way to prevent food-borne viral illnesses is to prevent contamination in the first place.

Hepatitis A often enters the food supply through shellfish harvested from polluted waters. The virus is carried by humans, some of whom may never know they are infected, and is transmitted by poor personal hygiene and cross-contamination. The actual source of contamination may be hard to establish, though, because it sometimes takes months for symptoms to appear.

Norovirus is spread almost entirely by poor personal hygiene among infected food handlers. The virus is found in human feces, contaminated water or vegetables fertilized by manure. The virus can be destroyed by high cooking temperatures but not by sanitizing solutions or freezing. In fact, Norovirus has even been found in ice cubes.

Foods most likely to transmit viral diseases are those that are not heated after handling. These include salads, sandwiches, milk, baked products, uncooked fish and shellfish and sliced meats. The best techniques for avoiding viral food-borne illnesses are to observe good personal hygiene habits, avoid cross-contamination and use only foods obtained from reputable sources.

FUNGI

Fungi are a large group of plants ranging from single-celled organisms to giant mushrooms. Fungi are everywhere: in the soil, air and water. Poisonous mushrooms, a type of fungus, can cause illness or death if consumed. The most common fungi, however, are molds and yeasts.

Molds

Molds are algae like fungi that form long filaments or strands. These filaments often extend into the air, appearing as cottony or velvety masses on food. Large colonies of mold are easily visible to the naked eye. Although many food molds are not dangerous, and some are even very beneficial, rare types known as mycotoxicoses form toxins that have been linked to food-borne illnesses. For the most part, however, molds affect only the appearance and flavor of foods. They cause discoloration, odors and off-flavors.

Unlike bacteria, molds can grow on almost any food at almost any temperature, moist or dry, acidic or alkaline. Mold cells can be destroyed by heating to 135°F (57°C) for 10 minutes. Their toxins are heat resistant, however, and are not destroyed by normal cooking methods. Therefore, foods that develop mold should be discarded, and any container or storage area cleaned and sanitized.

Yeasts

Yeasts require water and carbohydrates (sugar or starch) for survival. As the organisms consume carbohydrates, they expel alcohol and carbon dioxide gas through a process known as **fermentation**. Fermentation is of great benefit in making breads and alcoholic beverages.

Although naturally occurring yeasts have not been proven to be harmful to humans, they can cause foods to spoil and develop off-flavors, odors and discoloration. Yeasts are killed at temperatures of 136°F (58°C) or above.

Chemical Contaminants

Contamination of foods by a wide variety of chemicals is a very real and serious danger in which the public has shown a strong interest. Chemical contamination is usually inadvertent and invisible, making it extremely difficult to detect. The only way to avoid such hazards is for everyone working in a food service operation to follow proper procedures when handling foods or chemicals.

Chemical hazards include contamination with (1) residual chemicals used in growing the food supply, (2) food service chemicals and (3) toxic metals.

RESIDUAL CHEMICALS

Chemicals such as antibiotics, fertilizers, insecticides and herbicides have brought about great progress in controlling plant, animal and human diseases, permitting greater food yields and stimulating animal growth. The benefits derived from these chemicals, however, must be contrasted with the adverse effects on humans when they are used indiscriminately or improperly.

The danger of these chemicals lies in the possible contamination of human foods, which occurs when chemical residues remain after the intended goal is achieved. Fruits and vegetables must be washed and peeled properly to reduce the risk of consuming residual chemicals.

FOOD SERVICE CHEMICALS

A more common contamination problem involves the common chemicals found in almost every food service operation. Cleaners, polishes, pesticides and abrasives are often poisonous to humans. Illness and even death can result from foods contaminated by such common items as bug spray, drain cleaner, oven cleaner or silver polish. These

FOOT-AND-MOUTH DISEASE

Although humans are not susceptible to foot-and-mouth disease (FMD; also known as hoof-and-mouth disease), it could have a severe impact on our food supply. Foot-and-mouth disease affects animals with cloven hooves such as cattle, swine, sheep, goats and deer. Nearly 100 percent of the animals exposed to the virus ultimately become infected. The disease is rarely fatal, but those that survive are often debilitated and experience severe loss in milk or meat production.

Fortunately, there has not been a reported case of FMD in the United States for more than 80 years. But a 2001 outbreak of FMD in Europe resulted in the destruction of hundreds of thousands of cattle and pigs. Milk and meat production declined and farmers and meat packers suffered tremendous economic losses.

The U.S. government continues to take steps to ensure that a similar outbreak does not take place here. When FMD is detected, the importation of certain animals and animal products from countries with infected animal populations is prohibited. In addition, as the FMD virus can be transported by humans and on their clothes and possessions, travelers from countries with infected animal populations are prohibited from bringing with them most agricultural products, and they and their possessions can be subjected to varying degrees of decontamination procedures.

chemicals pose a hazard if used or stored near food supplies. Even improperly washing or rinsing dishes and utensils leaves a soap residue, which is then transmitted via food to anyone using the item.

To avoid food service chemical contamination, make sure all cleaning chemicals are clearly labeled and stored well away from food preparation and storage areas. Always use these products as directed by the manufacturer; never reuse a chemical container or package.

TOXIC METALS

Another type of chemical contamination occurs when metals such as lead, mercury, copper, zinc and antimony are dispersed in food or water. For example:

▶ Metals can accumulate in fish and shellfish living in polluted waters or in plants grown in soil contaminated by the metals.

▶ Using an acidic food such as tomatoes or wine in a zinc (galvanized) or unlined copper container causes metal ions to be released into the food.

▶ Antimony is used in bonding enamelware; it can be released into food when the enamel is chipped or cracked, so the use of enamelware is prohibited in food service facilities.

▶ Lead enters the water supply from lead pipes and solder, and is found in the glaze on some imported ceramic items.

Consuming any of these metals can cause poisoning.

To prevent metal contamination, use only approved food service equipment and utensils and re-tin copper cookware as needed. Never serve fish or shellfish that was illegally harvested or obtained from uninspected sources.

Physical Contaminants

Physical contaminants include foreign objects that find their way into foods by mistake. Examples include metal shavings created by a worn can opener, pieces of glass from a broken container, hair and dirt. Physical contaminants may be created by intentional tampering, but they are most likely the result of poor safety and sanitation practices or a lack of training.

CROSS-CONTAMINATION

Generally, microorganisms and other contaminants cannot move by themselves. Rather, they are carried to foods and food contact surfaces by humans, rodents or insects. This transfer is referred to as cross-contamination.

Cross-contamination is the process by which one item, such as your finger or a cutting board, becomes contaminated and then contaminates another food or tool. For example, suppose a chef's knife and cutting board are used in butchering a PHF/TCS food such as a chicken, and the chicken was directly contaminated with salmonella at the hatchery. If the knife and board are not cleaned and sanitized properly, anything that touches them can also become contaminated. So even though cooking the chicken to an appropriate internal temperature may destroy the salmonella in the chicken, the uncooked salad greens cut on the same cutting board or with the same knife can contain live bacteria.

Cross-contamination can occur with bacteria or other microorganisms, chemicals, dirt and debris. Side towels are an especially common source of cross-contamination. If a cook uses a side towel to wipe a spill off the floor, then uses that same towel to dry his hands after visiting the restroom, he has recontaminated his hands with whatever bacteria or dirt was on the floor. Cross-contamination also occurs when raw foods come in contact with cooked foods. Never store cooked food below raw food in a refrigerator, and never return cooked food to the container that held the raw food. Cross-contamination

---

STEPS TO PREVENT CROSS-CONTAMINATION

▪ Wash hands frequently—before and after touching raw food; after touching anything that may contaminate the hands (after removing the garbage, using the restroom, coughing, eating, smoking or touching dirty clothes or side towels); before putting on single-use gloves and when changing to a new pair.

▪ Properly sanitize all knives, cutting boards and equipment after each task.

▪ Use color-coded cutting boards for poultry, meats and produce.

▪ Discard soiled side towels. (Don't use side towels to wipe the floor, then your hands.)

▪ Use single-use gloves and change them frequently.

▪ Use clean tongs and bakery tissue paper when handling foods for immediate service.

▪ Use the two-spoon method when tasting foods.

can also occur easily from smoking, drinking or eating, unless hands are properly washed after each of these activities.

Even with proper hand washing, food service workers should strive to minimize direct contact with prepared food by using single-use gloves, clean tongs, tasting spoons, bakery tissue paper and other appropriate tools. Be aware that disposable gloves can prevent cross-contamination only when used properly. Wash hands before putting on disposable gloves because microorganisms on the hands could contaminate the gloves. Gloves, along with proper bandaging, must always be worn if there is a cut or infection on the hand. Wear single-use gloves for only one task; for example, change gloves immediately after handling raw poultry, and when switching from making sandwiches to making salads. Change gloves as often as necessary, when they are torn or after 4 hours of continual use. Do not wash or try to reuse disposable gloves. To remove a glove, grab the cuff, peel the glove off inside out over the fingers and then throw it away. Check your local regulations; some health departments require the use of disposable gloves when handling any ready-to-eat foods.

Reducing Cross-Contamination

Cross-contamination can be reduced or even prevented by (1) personal cleanliness, (2) dish and equipment cleanliness and (3) pest management.

PERSONAL CLEANLINESS

To produce clean, sanitary food, all food handlers must maintain high standards of personal cleanliness and hygiene. This begins with good grooming.

Humans provide the ideal environment for the growth of microorganisms. Everyone harbors bacteria in the nose and mouth. These bacteria are easily spread by sneezing or coughing, by not disposing of tissues properly and by not washing hands frequently and properly. Touching your body and then touching food or utensils transfers bacteria. Hands should be washed before and after handling raw food; after smoking, drinking or eating; after coughing or sneezing; after removing the garbage; and after touching dirty clothes, side towels or anything that may contaminate the hands. Human waste carries many dangerous microorganisms, so it is especially important to wash your hands thoroughly after visiting the restroom. An employee who is ill should not be allowed in the kitchen. If during work, an employee develops symptoms such as fever, diarrhea, vomiting, sore throat with fever or jaundice, he or she must report to a manager and request to be dismissed until recovered.

Current research shows that the human immunodeficiency virus (HIV), the causative agent of AIDS, is not spread by food. According to the Centers for Disease Control and Prevention (CDC), food service workers infected with HIV should not be restricted from work unless there is another infection or illness.

You can do several things to decrease the risk of an illness being spread by poor personal hygiene:

▶ Wash your hands frequently and thoroughly. Gloves are not a substitute for proper hand washing.

▶ Keep your fingernails short, clean and neat. Do not bite your nails or wear nail polish or artificial nails.

▶ Keep any cut or wound antiseptically bandaged. An injured hand should also be covered with a disposable glove.

▶ Bathe daily, or more often if required.

▶ Keep your hair clean and restrained.

▶ Wear work clothes that are clean and neat. Avoid wearing jewelry or watches.

▶ Do not eat, drink, smoke or chew gum in food preparation areas.

DISH AND EQUIPMENT CLEANLINESS

One of the requirements for any food service facility is cleanability. But there is an important difference between *clean* and *sanitary*. **Clean** means that the item has no visible

---

SAFETY ALERT
Tasting Food

To avoid cross-contamination, a two-spoon tasting method should be used when sampling in the professional kitchen. To safely taste food, use a clean spoon to remove some of the food from the pan in which it was made or stored. Pour that food into a second clean spoon before tasting it. This prevents the soiled spoon from going back into the food being prepared. Keep a supply of clean spoons for this purpose near all cooking and preparation stations.

clean to remove visible dirt and soil

PROCEDURE FOR **PROPER HAND WASHING**

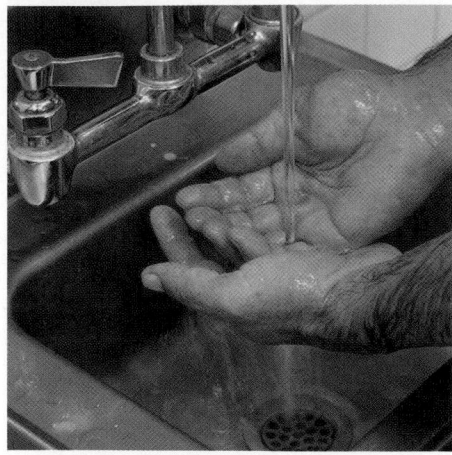

❶ Using hot water (100°F/38°C), wet hands and forearms.

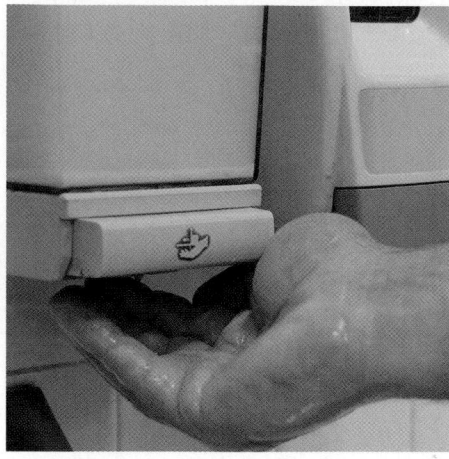

❷ Apply an antibacterial soap.

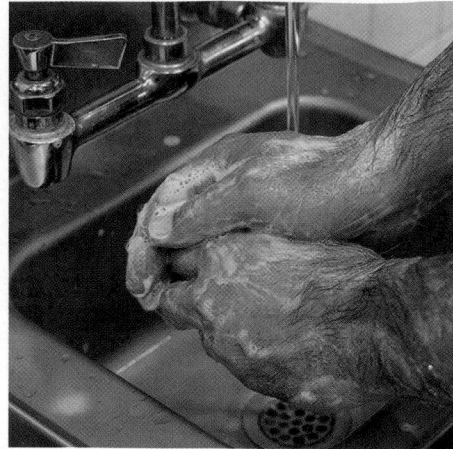

❸ Rub hands and arms briskly with soapy lather for at least 20 seconds.

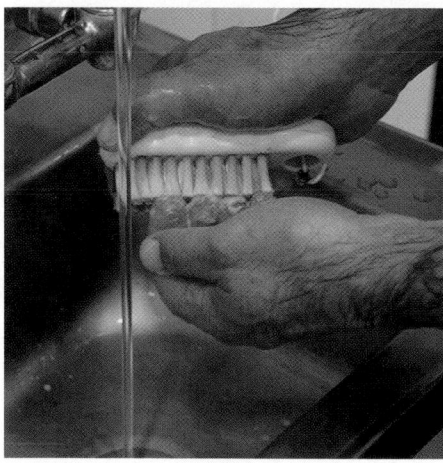

❹ Scrub between fingers and clean nails with a clean nail brush.

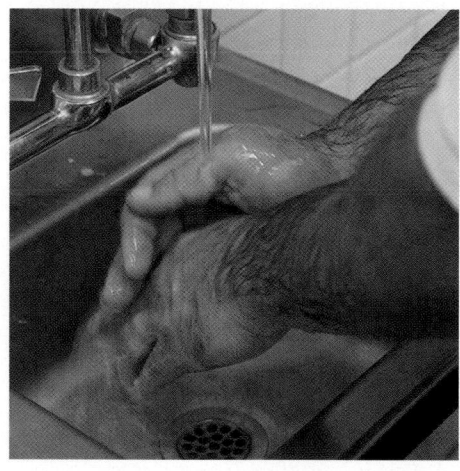

❺ Rinse thoroughly under hot running water. Reapply soap and scrub hands and forearms for another 5–10 seconds. Rinse again.

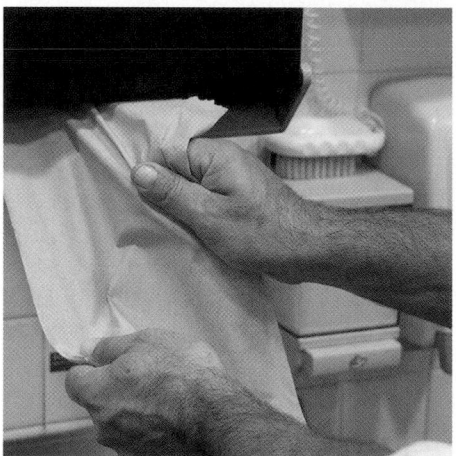

❻ Dry hands and arms with a single-use towel, using the towel to turn off the water. Discard the towel in a trash receptacle.

sanitize to reduce pathogenic organisms to safe levels

soil on it. **Sanitary** means that harmful substances are reduced to safe levels. Thus, something may be clean without being sanitary; the visible dirt can be removed, but disease-causing microorganisms can remain.

The cleaning of dishes, pots, pans and utensils in a food service operation involves both removing soil and sanitizing. Soil can be removed manually or by machine. Sanitizing can be accomplished with heat or chemical disinfectants.

Procedures for manually washing, rinsing and sanitizing dishes and equipment generally follow the three-compartment sink setup shown in Figure 2.5. The dishwasher must do the following:

❶ Scrape and spray the item to remove soil.

❷ Wash the item in the first sink compartment using 110°F (43°C) water and an approved detergent. A brush or cloth may be used to remove any remaining soil.

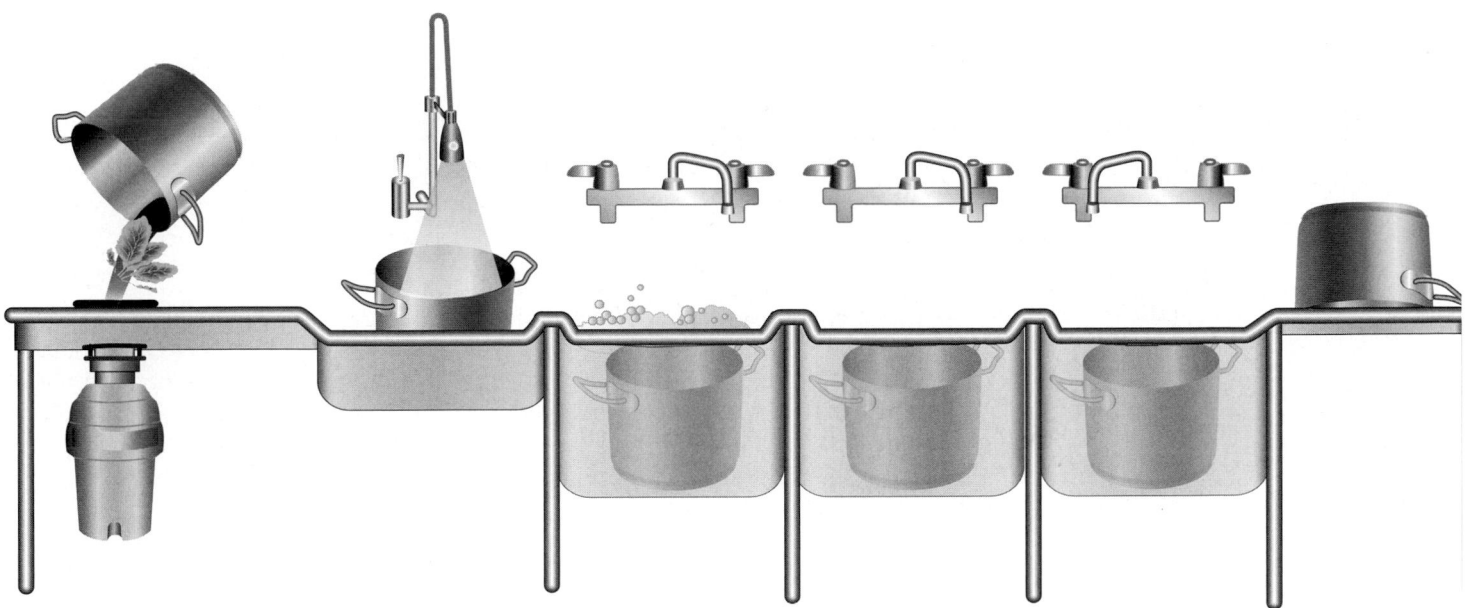

FIGURE 2.5 ▶ The three-compartment sink procedure—scrape, spray, wash, rinse, sanitize and air-dry each item.

❸ Rinse the item in the second sink compartment using clear, 110°F (43°C) water.

❹ Sanitize the item in the third sink compartment by either:
   a. immersing it in 171°F (77°C) water for at least 30 seconds, or
   b. immersing it in an approved chemical sanitizing solution used according to the manufacturer's directions.

❺ Empty, clean and refill each sink compartment as necessary, and check the water temperature regularly.

Food service items, dishes, silverware and utensils should always be allowed to air-dry, as towel drying may recontaminate them. Any cracked or chipped china should be discarded, as it can harbor bacteria that pose a food safety hazard.

Machine-washing dishes or utensils follows a similar procedure. The dishwasher should first scrape and rinse items as needed, then load the items into dishwasher racks so that the spray of water will reach all surfaces. The machine cleans the items with a detergent, then sanitizes them with either a hot-water rinse (at least 180°F/82°C) or a chemical disinfectant. When the machine cycle is complete, items should be inspected for residual soil, allowed to air-dry and stored in a clean area.

Work tables and stationary equipment must also be cleaned and sanitized properly. Equipment and surfaces, including floors, walls and worktables, should be easily exposed for inspection and cleaning and should be constructed so that soil can be removed effectively and efficiently with normal cleaning procedures. A thorough cleaning schedule should be implemented and closely monitored to prevent problems from developing.

The following points are important to the safety and cleanliness of any food service facility:

▶ Equipment should be disassembled for cleaning; any immersible pieces should be cleaned and sanitized like other items.

▶ All worktables or other food contact surfaces should be cleaned with detergent, then sanitized with a clean cloth dipped in a sanitizing solution. Combining 1 gallon (4 liters) lukewarm water with 1 tablespoon (15 milliliters) chlorine bleach makes an acceptable sanitizing solution. This solution must be replaced every 2 hours. Other chemical sanitizers should be prepared and used according to health department and manufacturer's directions.

sterilize to destroy all living microorganisms

SAFETY ALERT

Use a clean cloth dipped in sanitizing solution when wiping off your knives, utensils or cutting board during work. An acceptable solution can be made by combining 1 gallon lukewarm water with 1 tablespoon (15 milliliters) chlorine bleach. Replace this solution every 2 hours. Store this solution below work areas to prevent accidentally spilling it onto food or food preparation areas.

► Surfaces, especially work surfaces with which food may come in contact, should be smooth and free of cracks, crevices or seams in which soil and microorganisms can hide.

► Floors should be nonabsorbent and should not become slippery when wet.

► Walls and ceilings should be smooth and light-colored so that soil is easier to see.

► Light should be ample and well located throughout food preparation and storage areas. All lightbulbs should be covered with a sleeve or globe to protect surroundings from shattered glass.

A kitchen's design can also affect food safety and sanitation. Food preparation equipment should be arranged in such a way as to decrease the chances of cross-contamination. The workflow should eliminate crisscrossing and backtracking. Employees should be able to reach storage, refrigeration and cleanup areas easily. Dish- and pot-washing areas and garbage facilities should be kept as far from food preparation and storage areas as possible. Cleaning supplies and other chemicals should be stored away from foods.

PEST MANAGEMENT

Food can be contaminated by insects (for example, roaches and flies) and rodents (for example, mice and rats). These pests carry many harmful bacteria on their bodies, thus contaminating any surface with which they come in contact. An insect or rodent infestation is usually considered a serious health risk and should be dealt with immediately and thoroughly. Pests must be controlled by (1) building them out of the facility, (2) creating an environment in which they cannot find food, water or shelter, and (3) relying on professional extermination.

The best defense against pests is to prevent infestations in the first place by building them out. Any crack—no matter how small—in door frames, walls or windowsills should be repaired immediately, and all drains, pipes and vents should be well sealed. Inspect all deliveries thoroughly, and reject any packages or containers found to contain evidence of pests.

Flies are a perfect method of transportation for bacteria because they feed and breed on human waste and garbage. Use screens or "fly fans" (also known as air curtains) to keep them out in the first place. Controlling garbage is also essential because moist, warm, decaying organic material attracts flies and provides favorable conditions for eggs to hatch and larvae to grow.

Pest management also requires creating an inhospitable environment for pests. Store all food and supplies at least 6 inches off the floor and 6 inches away from walls. **Rotate stock** often to disrupt nesting places and breeding habits. Provide good ventilation in storerooms to remove humidity, airborne contaminants, grease and fumes. Do not allow water to stand in drains, sinks or buckets, as cockroaches are attracted to moisture. Clean up spills and crumbs immediately and completely to reduce their food supply.

Despite the best efforts to build pests out and maintain proper housekeeping standards, it is still important to watch for the presence of pests. For example, cockroaches leave a strong, oily odor and feces that look like large grains of pepper. Cockroaches prefer to search for food and water in the dark, so seeing any cockroach on the move in the daylight is an indication of a large infestation.

Rodents (mice and rats) tend to hide during the day, so an infestation may be rather serious before any creature is actually seen. Rodent droppings, which are shiny black to brownish gray, may be evident, however. Rodent nests made from scraps of paper, hair or other soft materials may be spotted.

Should an infestation occur, consult a licensed pest control operator immediately. With early detection and proper treatment, infestations can be eliminated. Employees should be very careful in attempting to use pesticides or insecticides themselves. These chemicals are toxic to humans as well as to pests. Great care must be used to prevent contaminating food or exposing workers or customers to the chemicals.

rotate stock to use products in the order in which they were received; all perishable and semiperishable goods, whether fresh, frozen, canned or dry, should be used according to the first in, first out (FIFO) principle

HACCP SYSTEMS

Now that you understand what contaminants are and how they can be destroyed or controlled, it is necessary to put this information into practice during day-to-day operations. Although local health departments regularly inspect all food service facilities, continual self-inspection and control are essential for maintaining sanitary conditions.

Hazard Analysis Critical Control Points (HACCP) is proving to be an effective and efficient system for managing and maintaining sanitary conditions in all types of food service operations. Developed in 1971 for NASA to ensure food safety for astronauts, HACCP (pronounced HASS-ip) is a rigorous system of self-inspection. It focuses on the flow of food through the food service facility, from the decision to include an item on the menu through service to the consumer. A **critical control point** in that flow is any step during the processing of a food when a mistake can result in the transmission, growth or survival of pathogenic bacteria.

The HACCP process begins by identifying the steps and evaluating the type and severity of hazard that can occur. It then identifies what actions can be taken to reduce or prevent each risk of hazard. See Table 2.3. The activities that present the highest risk of hazard should be monitored most closely. For example, a cook's failure to wash his or her hands before handling cooked food presents a greater risk of hazard than a dirty floor. In other words, hazards must be prioritized, and the correction of critical concerns should take priority.

Note that the standards (or what some might call boundaries) applied in a formal HACCP system are no different from those that should be rigorously followed in any food service operation. HACCP does not impose new or different food safety standards; it is merely a system for ensuring that those standards are actually followed.

One way to ensure compliance is to frequently check and record the temperature of PHF/TCS foods during cooking, cooling and holding. Maintaining written time-and-temperature logs enables management to evaluate and adjust procedures as necessary. Whatever system is followed, all personnel must be constantly aware of and responsive to risks and problems associated with the safety of the food they serve.

One way that a food service operation can make workers aware of potential hazards and the critical actions that are necessary to avoid those hazards is by including detailed safety information in every recipe. Figure 2.6 shows the recipe for Beef Stroganoff, as it would appear with all critical control points (CCP) noted. Writing this much detail into every one of an operation's standardized recipes serves as a constant reminder to employees of both the specific actions necessary and the importance of food safety to the operation.

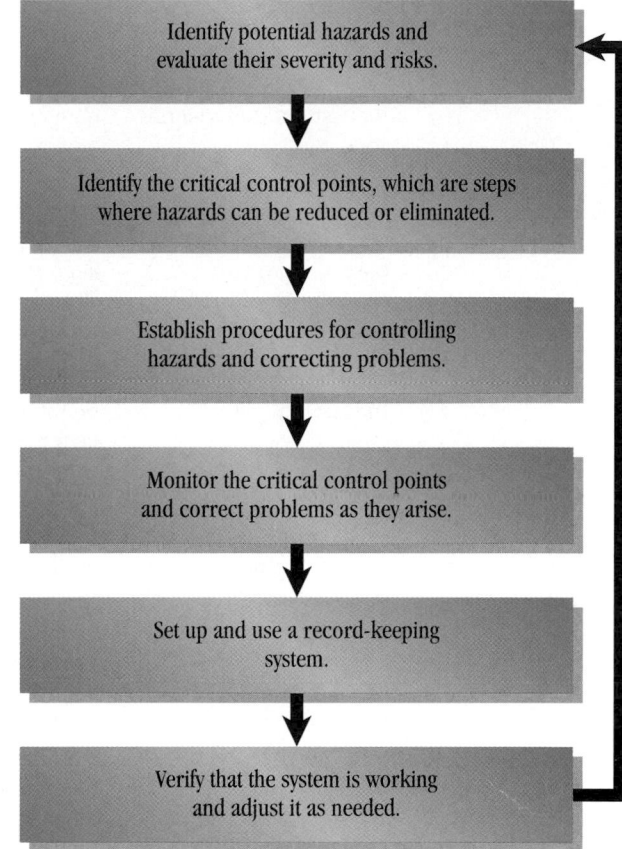

A HACCP SYSTEM FLOWCHART

Identify potential hazards and evaluate their severity and risks.

↓

Identify the critical control points, which are steps where hazards can be reduced or eliminated.

↓

Establish procedures for controlling hazards and correcting problems.

↓

Monitor the critical control points and correct problems as they arise.

↓

Set up and use a record-keeping system.

↓

Verify that the system is working and adjust it as needed.

critical control point a step during the processing of food when a mistake can result in the transmission, growth or survival of pathogenic bacteria

TABLE 2.3 HACCP ANALYSIS—THE FLOW OF FOOD

CONTROL POINT	HAZARDS	STANDARDS	CRITICAL ACTIONS
Selecting the menu and recipes	PHF/TCS foods; human hands involved in food preparation	Analyze menus and recipes for control points; wash hands frequently; use single-use gloves as appropriate	Plan physical work flow; train employees
Receiving	Contaminated or spoiled goods; PHF/TCS foods in the temperature danger zone	Do not accept torn bags, dented cans, broken glass containers or leaking or damaged packages; frozen food should be received at 0°F (–18°C) or below and refrigerated food at 41°F (5°C) or below	Inspect all deliveries and reject as necessary
Storing	Cross-contamination to and from other foods; bacterial growth; spoilage; improper holding temperatures	Avoid crowding and allow air to circulate in freezers and refrigerators; rotate stock and keep storage areas clean, dry and well lit; store frozen food at 0°F (–18°C) or below and refrigerated food at 41°F (5°C) or below	Maintain proper temperatures and other storage conditions; discard if necessary
Preparing	Cross-contamination; bacterial growth	Keep PHF/TCS foods at 41°F (5°C) or below or 135°F (57°C) or above; thaw frozen foods under refrigeration or under cold running water (70°F/21°C) for no more than 2 hours	Avoid the temperature danger zone; maintain good personal hygiene and use sanitary utensils
Cooking	Bacterial survival; physical or chemical contamination	Heat foods to the appropriate internal temperature; reheat leftover foods to at least 165°F (74°C)	Cook foods to their proper temperatures
Holding and service	Bacterial growth; contamination	Maintain hot holding temperatures at 135°F (57°C) or above and cold holding temperatures at 41°F (5°C) or below; do not mix new product with old and discard food after 2 hours of being held at room temperature	Maintain proper temperatures and use sanitary equipment
Cooling leftovers	Bacterial growth	Spread food into clean, shallow, metal containers; use an ice bath; stir periodically during cooling; cool to 70°F (21°C) within 2 hours, then cool to 41°F (5°C) or below within 4 hours; cover and refrigerate; store cooked food above raw	Cool foods quickly; label and store them properly
Reheating	Bacterial survival and growth	Use leftovers within 4 days; heat leftovers to 165°F (74°C) for 15 seconds within 2 hours; do not mix old product with new and discard secondary leftovers	Reheat food quickly (do not use a steam table) and as close to serving time as possible; reheat smaller quantities as needed; discard if necessary

BEEF STROGANOFF

Yield: 8 Servings, 8 oz. (240 g) each   **Method:** Sautéing

Tenderloin tips, émincé	2 lb.	960 g
Clarified butter	3 Tbsp.	45 ml
Onion, medium dice	4 oz.	120 g
Mushrooms, halved	1 lb.	480 g
Demi-glace	10 fl. oz.	300 ml
Heavy cream	10 fl. oz.	300 ml
Sour cream	8 oz.	240 g
Dijon mustard	1 Tbsp.	15 ml
Fresh dill, chopped	1 Tbsp.	15 ml
Fresh parsley, chopped	1 Tbsp.	15 ml
Salt and pepper	TT	TT
Egg noodles, cooked	24 oz.	720 g

PRE-PREPARATION

A. Wash hands before handling food, after handling raw foods and after any interruptions in work.
B. Cut the beef tenderloin using a clean, sanitized knife and cutting board. Place the émincé into a clean container, cover and refrigerate until ready to use. If work is interrupted, return the beef to refrigerated storage during the interruption.
C. Measure the demi-glace, cream and sour cream, cover and keep refrigerated until ready to use.
D. Chop the onions and herbs using a clean, sanitized knife and cutting board.

PREPARATION

CCP 1. Sauté the tenderloin tips in the butter, searing on all sides. Remove the meat **to a clean container and hold at 135° F (57°C) or higher for no more than 2 hours.**
2. Add the onion to the pan and sauté lightly. Add the mushrooms and sauté until dry.
3. Add the demi-glace. Bring to a boil, reduce to a simmer and cook for 10 minutes.
CCP 4. Add the cream, sour cream, mustard and any meat juices that accumulated while holding the meat. **Cook until an internal temperature of 145°F (63°C) is maintained for at least 15 seconds.**
CCP 5. Return the meat to the sauce. **Cook until the meat reaches an internal temperature of 145°F (63°C).** Stir in the dill and parsley. Adjust the seasonings and serve over hot egg noodles.

HOLDING

CCP Transfer the sauce to a clean steam table pan and cover. Hold for service in a preheated steam table at **135°F (57°C) or higher. Use within 4 hours.**

LEFTOVERS

CCP Place in shallow metal pans with a product depth of no more than 2 inches. **Cool from 135°F (57°C) to 70°F (21°C) within 2 hours and from 70°F (21°C) to 41°F (5°C) or lower within 4 additional hours,** for a total cooling time of not more than 6 hours. Cover and store in a refrigerator so that the internal product temperature is 41°F (5°C) or less. Use leftovers within 4 days.

REHEATING

CCP Reheat Stroganoff to an internal temperature of **165°F (74°C) or higher for 15 seconds within 2 hours;** discard any product that is not consumed within 4 hours.

NOTES:
Measure all internal temperatures with a clean, sanitized thermocouple or thermometer.
Once cooked, egg noodles are a potentially hazardous food and should be held and stored accordingly.

FIGURE 2.6 ▶ A recipe showing critical control points (CCPs).

STORAGE AND FOOD LABELING

Proper food labeling and good record keeping are as important as safe food-handling practices to prevent cross-contamination and food spoilage. Food labels should be used to date all foods that are made for kitchen use as well as leftovers. Systems for labeling foods vary in every operation. Once placed in clean sanitized storage containers, food prepared for later use should be labeled with the product name and the date and time it was made. Some health department regulations require that food be labeled with the day or date by which the food must be consumed on premises, sold or discarded. Once labeled and then refrigerated or frozen, products will be easily identifiable by the entire kitchen staff.

FRI
Viernes

Item: _____
Shelf
Life: _____ Qty: _____ Emp: _____
☐ AM
Date: _____ ☐ PM
☐ AM
Use By: _____ ☐ PM

Temp: _____ _____ _____

Sample of a label used to identify and date foods after preparation

THE SAFE WORKER

Kitchens are filled with objects that can cut, burn, break, crush or sprain the human body. The best ways to prevent work-related injuries are proper training, good work habits and careful supervision.

The federal government enacted legislation designed to reduce hazards in the work area, thereby reducing accidents. The Occupational Safety and Health Act (OSHA) covers a broad range of safety matters. Employers who fail to follow its rules can be severely fined. Unfortunately, human error is the leading cause of accidents, and no amount of legislation can protect someone who doesn't work in a safe manner.

Personal Safety

Safe behavior on the job reflects pride, professionalism and consideration for fellow workers. The following list should alert you to conditions and activities aimed at preventing accidents and injuries:

▶ Clean up spills as soon as they occur.
▶ Learn to operate equipment properly; always use guards and safety devices.
▶ Wear clothing that fits properly; avoid wearing jewelry, which may get caught in equipment.
▶ Use knives and other equipment for their intended purposes only. When walking in the kitchen, carry knives close to your side with the point down.
▶ Keep exits, aisles and stairs clear and unobstructed.
▶ Always assume pots and pans are hot; handle them with dry towels.
▶ Position pot and pan handles out of the aisles so that they do not get bumped.
▶ Get help or use a cart when lifting or moving heavy objects.
▶ Avoid back injury by lifting with your leg muscles; stoop, don't bend, when lifting.
▶ Use an appropriately placed ladder or stool for climbing; do not use a chair, box, drawer or shelf.
▶ Keep breakable items away from food storage or production areas.
▶ Never leave a pan of oil unattended; hot fat can ignite when overheated.
▶ Warn people when you must walk behind them, especially when carrying a hot pan.

Fire Safety

From grease flare-ups on cooktops to major fires caused by dirty ventilation hoods, fires can develop into serious threats in busy professional kitchens. Understanding the danger posed by fires and having a proper fire safety program in place is of utmost importance in a professional kitchen. Fire extinguishers contain different types of chemicals effective on various types of fires. (See Chapter 4, page 72.) Learn which types of fire extinguishers to use for specific combustible materials. Regulations require that commercial kitchens be outfitted with ventilation hoods and professional sprinkler systems. Grease fires in ventilation hoods are the primary cause of restaurant fires; thorough and regular cleaning prevents hazardous grease buildup. All fire suppression systems should be inspected regularly. When faced with a serious fire, do not waste time. Immediately call for help. Shut off all exhaust fans and turn off kitchen equipment if time permits. Close the kitchen doors and evacuate the premises.

Deep-fat fryers pose a serious fire threat, and employee training should include instruction on the proper operation and cleaning of such equipment. In addition, large quantities of hot fat can cause severe burns if not properly handled. When liquids come into contact with the heated fat, hot steam is released. Take care when adding foods to all deep-fat fryers to prevent getting burned. The threat is more extreme when a large quantity of liquid hits the hot grease. Keep containers of liquids away from deep-fat fryers to avoid accidentally spilling liquid into the hot fat and causing a hazardous steam explosion.

Chef uniforms were designed with comfort and safety in mind; the double front panels and long sleeves help prevent burns. Clothing and towels can catch on fire, however. If an employee's garments catch on fire, use a safety blanket to wrap the person and smother the flames. Although it is generally best to use an appropriate fire extinguisher to douse kitchen fires, some simple measures can be useful for extinguishing a small flame in a pan. Immediately cover a pan in which a small oil flare-up occurs; lack of oxygen will extinguish the flame. To extinguish a small grease flare-up in a pan or on a cooktop, douse it quickly with a generous amount of baking soda or salt.

First Aid

Some accidents will inevitably occur, and it is important to act appropriately in the event of an injury or emergency. This may mean calling for help or providing first aid. Every food service operation should be equipped with a complete first-aid kit. Municipal regulations may specify the exact contents of the kit. Be sure that the kit is conveniently located and well stocked at all times.

The American Red Cross and local public health departments offer training in first aid, cardiopulmonary resuscitation (CPR) and the Heimlich maneuver used for choking victims. All employees should be trained in basic emergency procedures. A list of emergency telephone numbers should be posted by each telephone.

QUESTIONS FOR DISCUSSION

1. Foods can be contaminated in several ways. Explain the differences between biological, chemical and physical contamination. Give an example of each.

2. Under what conditions will bacteria thrive? Explain what you can do to alter these conditions.

3. What is the temperature danger zone? What is its significance in food preparation?

4. Explain how improper or inadequate pest management can lead to food-borne illnesses.

5. Define HACCP. How is this system used in a typical food service facility?

6. Visit the Web sites of the U.S. Department of Agriculture and the Food and Drug Administration. What is the Model Food Code? What types of programs do these agencies offer for training consumers about food safety? wWWw

Terms to Know

sanitation	temperature
contamination	danger zone
direct	time-and-
contamination	temperature
cross-	principle
contamination	water activity
bacteria	aerobic bacteria
putrefactives	anaerobic
spores	bacteria
intoxication	facultative
toxins	bacteria
infection	trichinosis
toxin-mediated	hepatitis A
infection	Norovirus
potentially	molds
hazardous	chemical
foods (PHF)	contaminants
time/temperature	tasting spoons
controlled for	HACCP
safety (TCS)	OSHA
foods	

CHAPTER THREE

MENUS AND RECIPES

...TANA
A PLANCHA
PLANCHA
ANCHA
PLANCHA
NCHA
AUNA
PLANCHA
Y MARISCO

BOGAVANTE

...DINES GREEN
CUTTLEFISH GRILLE
BATTER FRIED SQU
SMALL SQUID GRI
DUBLIN BAY PRAWN
PRAWNS
LARGE GRILLED
SCAMPI PRAWNS GRILL
CODFISH GRILLED
LOBSTER "LLAUNA" CAT
BIG CASSEROLE of SEAFO
BIG PLATTER GRILLED
BIG PLATTER SEAFOOD
PLATTER SEAFOOD GR
SEAFOOD WITH

O
ETA
GRE
RICO
N
AGRETA

GREEK SALAD
RUSSIAN SALAD
SEAFOOD SALAD
OCTOPUS COCKTAIL
WHITE ANCHOVIES VINAIGRETTE
ANCHOVIES FROM THE CANTAB
FRIED "PADRON" PEPPERS
ARTICHOKES WITH VIN
SPANISH OMELETTE
POTATOES "VIN
SPICY
L AJILLO FRIED POTATOES
INERA

After studying this chapter, you will be able to:

- appreciate the different types and styles of menus
- understand the purpose of standardized recipes
- convert recipe yield amounts
- appreciate the need for cost controls in any food service operation

entrée the main dish of an American meal, usually meat, poultry, fish or shellfish accompanied by a vegetable and starch; in France, the first course, served before the fish and meat courses

TODAY'S PROFESSIONAL CHEFS must master more than the basics of béchamel, butchering and bread baking. They must be equally skilled in the business of food services. This means knowing what products cost and how to control and maintain food costs. It also means understanding how accurate measurements, portion control and proper food handling directly affect the food service operation's bottom line.

This chapter introduces various types and styles of menus. It then explains a standardized recipe format and presents information on measurements and techniques for changing or converting recipe yields. It describes methods for determining unit and recipe costs and concludes with a discussion of methods for controlling food costs.

THE MENU

Whether it lists Spanish dishes, hamburgers, just desserts or classic cuisine and whether the prices are inexpensive or exorbitant, the menu is the soul of every food service operation. Its purposes are to identify for the consumer the foods and beverages the operation offers, to create consumer enthusiasm and to increase sales. When combined with good food and good service, a good menu helps ensure success.

Most menus offer consumers sufficient selections to build an entire meal. A typical North American meal consists of three courses. The first course may be a hot or cold appetizer, soup or salad. The second course is the **entrée** or main dish, usually meat, poultry, fish or shellfish accompanied by a vegetable and starch. The third course is dessert, either a sweet preparation or fruit and cheese. For a more formal meal, there may be a progression of first courses, including a hot or cold appetizer and soup, as well as a fish course served before the main dish (which, in this case, would not be fish). For a meal served in the European tradition, the salad would be presented as a palate cleanser after the main dish and before the dessert.

Types of Menus

Menus are classified according to the regularity with which the foods are offered:

1. **Static or fixed menu**—All patrons are offered the same foods every day. Once a static menu is developed and established, it rarely changes. Static menus are typically found in fast-food operations, ethnic restaurants, steakhouses and the like. Static menus can also be used in institutional settings. For example, a static menu at an elementary school could offer students, along with a vegetable and dessert, the same luncheon choices every school day: a cheeseburger, fish sticks, chicken tacos, pizza wedges or a sandwich.

2. **Cycle menu**—A cycle menu is developed for a set period; at the end of that period it repeats itself (that is, on a seven-day cycle, the same menu is used every Monday). Some cycle menus are written on a seasonal basis, with a new menu for each season to take advantage of product availability. Cycle menus are used commonly in schools, hospitals and other institutions. Although cycle menus may be repetitious, the repetition is not necessarily noticeable to diners because of the length of the cycles.

3. **Market menu**—A market menu is based on product availability during a specific period; it is written to use foods when they are in peak season or readily available. Market menus are becoming increasingly popular with chefs (and consumers) because they challenge the chef's ingenuity in using fresh, seasonal products. Market menus are short-lived, however, because of limited product availability and perishability. In fact, they often change daily.

④ **Hybrid menu**—A hybrid menu combines a static menu with a cycle menu or a market menu of specials.

Food service operations may have separate menus for breakfast, lunch and dinner, often referred to as day parts. If all three meals are available all day and are listed on the same menu, the menu is known as a **California menu;** California menus are typically found in 24-hour restaurants. Depending on the food service operation's objectives, separate specialty menus for drinks, hors d'oeuvre, desserts, brunch or afternoon tea, for example, are used.

Regardless of whether the menu is static, cycle, market or hybrid, it can offer consumers the opportunity to purchase their selections à la carte, semi à la carte, table d'hôte or some combination of the three.

① **À la carte**—Every food and beverage item is priced and ordered separately.
② **Semi à la carte**—With this popular menu style, some food items (particularly appetizers and desserts) are priced and ordered separately, while the entrée is accompanied by and priced to include other items, such as a salad, starch or vegetable.
③ **Table d'hôte or *prix fixe***—This menu offers a complete meal at a set price. (The term *table d'hôte* is French for "host's table" and is derived from the innkeeper's practice of seating all guests at a large communal table and serving them all the same meal.) A table d'hôte meal can range from very elegant to a diner's blue-plate special. A *prix fixe* menu may offer choices at a fixed price, whereas a table d'hôte menu usually offers no choice.

Many menus combine à la carte, semi à la carte and table d'hôte choices. For example, appetizers, salads and desserts may be available à la carte; entrées may be offered semi à la carte (served with a salad, starch and vegetable), while the daily special is a complete (table d'hôte or *prix fixe*) meal.

Menu Language

The menu is the principal way in which the food service operation, including the chef, communicates with the consumer. A well-designed menu often reflects the input of design, marketing, art and other consultants as well as the chef and management. The type of folds, cover, artwork, layout, typefaces, colors and paper are all important considerations. But the most important consideration is the language.

The menu should list the foods offered. It may include descriptions such as the preparation method, essential ingredients and service method as well as the quality, cut and quantity of product. For example, the menu can list "Porterhouse Steak" or "Mesquite-Grilled 16-oz. Angus Beef Porterhouse Steak."

TRUTH IN ADVERTISING

Salmon

Federal as well as some state and local laws require that certain menu language be accurate. Areas of particular concern include statements about quantity, quality, grade and freshness. Accurate references to an item's source are also important. If brand names are used, those brands must be served. If the restaurant claims to be serving "Fresh Dover Sole," it must be just that, not frozen sole from New England. (On the other hand, like French or Russian dressing, "English mint sauce" is a generic name for a style of food, so using that geographical adjective is appropriate even if the mint sauce is made in Arizona.) A reference to "our own fresh-baked" desserts means that the restaurant regularly bakes the desserts on premises, serves them soon after baking and does not substitute commercially prepared or frozen goods.

NUTRITIONAL STATEMENTS

As discussed in Chapter 23, Healthy Cooking, the FDA carefully regulates the language used on packaged food labels. In 1997, the FDA extended its nutrition labeling regulations to restaurant menus. These regulations are intended to prevent restaurants from making misleading health or nutrition claims. For example, terms such as *light, healthy* and *heart-healthy* must be accurate and documented. The standards for calculating and presenting that information are far less stringent than the regulations for packaged foods, however.

THE TASTING MENU

In addition to their à la carte menus, restaurants are increasingly offering tasting menus (Fr. *menu dégustation*, It. *degustazione*), small portions served in four, five or more courses for a fixed price. A tasting menu allows consumers the opportunity to sample a wider range of dishes than would normally be eaten in one meal. The best examples of such menus are carefully crafted by the chef so that each dish complements the next and courses are not merely a hodgepodge of everything in the kitchen. Chefs frequently design tasting menus with a theme such as "spring asparagus" in which each course highlights the ingredient in a new guise. A selection of wines can accompany a tasting menu. For ease of service, restaurants usually require that the tasting menu be ordered by the entire table.

recipe a set of written instructions for producing a specific food or beverage; also known as a formula

standardized recipe a recipe producing a known quality and quantity of food for a specific operation

Restaurants may support their claims with data from any "reasonable" source and may present that information in any format, including verbally. Nutritional data is not required for menu items that do not carry a nutritional content or health claim, although numerous states and municipalities have introduced legislation requiring that nutritional information be posted on menu boards and printed menus.

STANDARDIZED RECIPES

Menu writing and **recipe** development are mutually dependent activities. Once the menu is created, **standardized recipes** should be prepared for each item. A standardized recipe is one that will produce a known quality and quantity of food for a specific operation. It specifies (1) the type and amount of each ingredient, (2) the preparation and cooking procedures and (3) the yield and portion size.

Standardized recipes are not found in books or provided by manufacturers; they are recipes customized to a specific operation—cooking time, temperature and utensils should be based on the equipment actually available. Yield should be adjusted to an amount appropriate for that operation. A recipe must be tested repeatedly and adjusted to fit the facility and the chef's needs before it can be considered standardized.

Standardized recipes are a tool for the chef and management. The written forms assist with training cooks, educating service staff and controlling financial matters. They help ensure that customers receive a consistent quality and quantity of product. And they are essential for accurate recipe costing and menu pricing. Each recipe should be complete, consistent and simple to read and follow. These recipe forms should be stored in a readily accessible place. Index cards, notebook binders or a computerized database may be used, depending on the size and complexity of the operation.

MEASUREMENTS AND CONVERSIONS

Measurement Formats

Accurate measurements are among the most important aspects of food production. Ingredients and portions must be measured correctly to ensure consistent product quality. In other words, the chef must be able to prepare a recipe the same way each time, and portion sizes must be the same from one order to the next. In a kitchen, measurements may be made in three ways: weight, volume and count.

Weight refers to the mass or heaviness of a substance. It is expressed in terms such as grams, ounces, pounds and tons. Weight may be used to measure liquid or dry ingredients (for example, 2 pounds of eggs for a bread recipe) and portions (for example, 4 ounces of sliced turkey for a sandwich). Because weight is generally the most accurate form of measurement, portion scales or balance scales are commonly used in kitchens.

Volume refers to the space occupied by a substance. This is mathematically expressed as *height* × *width* × *length*. It is expressed in terms such as cups, quarts, gallons, teaspoons, fluid ounces, bushels and liters. Volume is most commonly used to measure liquids. It may also be used for dry ingredients when the amount is too small to be weighed accurately (for example, ¼ teaspoon of salt). Although measuring by volume is somewhat less accurate than measuring by weight, volume measurements are generally quicker to do.

Frequently mistakes are made in food preparation by chefs who assume wrongly that weight and volume are equal. Do not be fooled! One cup does not always equal 8 ounces. Although it is true that 1 standard cup contains 8 fluid ounces, it is not true that the contents of that standard cup will weigh 8 ounces. For example, the weight of 1 cup of diced apples will vary depending on the size of the apple pieces. Errors are commonly made in the bakeshop by cooks who assume that 8 ounces of flour is the same as 1 cup of flour. In fact, 1 cup of flour weighs only about 4½ ounces.

It is not unusual to see both weight and volume measurements used in a single recipe. When a recipe ingredient is expressed in weight, weigh it. When it is expressed as a volume, measure it. Like most rules, however, this one has exceptions. The weight and volume of water, butter, eggs and milk are, in each case, the same. For these ingredients you

FANNIE MERRITT FARMER (1857–1915)

Fannie Farmer is more than the name on a cookbook. She was an early, vigorous and influential proponent of scientific cooking, nutrition and academic training for culinary professionals.

At age 30, Farmer enrolled in the Boston Cooking School. The school's curriculum was not designed to graduate chefs, but rather to produce cooking teachers. After graduating from the two-year course, Farmer stayed on, first as assistant principal and then as principal.

During her years there (and, indeed, for the rest of her career) she was obsessed with accurate measurements. She waged a campaign to eliminate measurements such as a "wineglass" of liquid, a "handful" of flour, a chunk of butter the "size of an egg" or a "heaping spoonful" of salt. For, as she once wrote, "correct measurements are absolutely necessary to insure the best results." Farmer also sought to replace the European system of measuring ingredients by weight with, for her, a more scientific measurement system based on volume and level measures (for example, a level tablespoon). To a great degree, she succeeded.

Her writings reflect her concern for accurate measurements. Her first book, *The Boston Cooking School Cookbook* (1896), includes clearly written recipes with precise measurements. Later editions add recipe yields, oven temperatures and baking times.

Farmer wrote other cookbooks, including *A New Book of Cookery* (first published in 1912 and republished in several revised versions). Her writings never address the joys of cooking and eating; rather, they reflect a scientific approach to cooking and rely on clearly written, accurately measured recipes for good, solid food.

---

may use whichever measurement is most convenient. Some common abbreviations for weight and volume measurements appear in Table 3.1.

Count refers to the number of individual items. Count is used in recipes (for example, 4 eggs) and in portion control (for example, 2 fish fillets or 1 ear of corn). Count is also commonly used in purchasing to indicate the size of the individual items. For example, a "96 count" case of lemons means that a 40-pound case contains 96 individual lemons; a "115-count" case means that the same 40-pound case contains 115 individual lemons. So each lemon in the 96-count case is larger than those in the 115-count case. Shrimp is another item commonly sold by count. One pound of shrimp may contain from eight to several hundred shrimp, depending on the size of the individual pieces. When placing an order, the chef must specify the desired count. For example, when ordering one pound of 21–25-count shrimp, the chef expects to receive not fewer than 21 nor more than 25 pieces.

Measurement Systems

The measurement formats of weight, volume and count are used in both the U.S. and metric measurement systems. Both of these systems are used in modern food service operations, so chefs should be able to prepare recipes written in either one.

The U.S. system, with which most students probably are familiar, is actually the more difficult system to understand. It uses pounds for weight and cups for volume.

The metric system is the most commonly used system in the world. Developed in France during the late 18th century, it was intended to fill the need for a mathematically rational and uniform system of measurement. The metric system is a decimal system in which the gram, liter and meter are the basic units of weight, volume and length, respectively. Larger and smaller units of weight, volume and length are formed by adding a prefix to the words *gram*, *liter* and *meter*. Some of the more commonly used prefixes in food service operations are *deca-* (10), *kilo-* (1000), *deci-* (1/10) and *milli-* (1/1000). Thus a kilogram is 1000 grams; a decameter is 10 meters; a milliliter is 1/1000 of a liter. Because the metric system is based on multiples of 10, it is extremely easy to increase or decrease amounts.

The most important thing for a chef to know about the metric system is that one does not need to convert between the metric system and the U.S. system in recipe preparation. If a recipe is written in metric units, use metric measuring equipment; if it is written in

TABLE 3.1 COMMON ABBREVIATIONS	
teaspoon	= tsp.
tablespoon	= Tbsp.
cup	= c.
pint	= pt.
quart	= qt.
gram	= g
milliliter	= ml
liter	= lt
ounce	= oz.
fluid ounce	= fl. oz.
pound	= lb.
kilogram	= kg

NOTE ON MEASUREMENTS

All ingredients in this book are listed in both U.S. and metric measurements. The metric equivalents are rounded off to even, easily measured amounts. Consider these ingredient lists as separate recipes or formulas; do not measure some ingredients according to the metric amounts and other ingredients according to the U.S. amount or the proportions will not be accurate and the intended result will not be achieved.

U.S. units, use U.S. measuring equipment. Luckily, most modern measuring equipment is calibrated in both U.S. and metric increments. The need to convert amounts will arise only if the proper equipment is unavailable.

Converting Grams and Ounces

As you can see from Table 3.2, 1 ounce equals 28.35 grams and 1 fluid ounce equals 29.57 milliliters. So to convert ounces/fluid ounces to grams/milliliters, multiply the number of ounces by 28 or 29, using a number that is rounded for convenience.

$$8 \text{ oz.} \times 28 = 224 \text{ g}$$
$$8 \text{ fl. oz.} \times 29 = 232 \text{ ml}$$

Likewise to convert grams/milliliters to ounces/fluid ounces, divide the number of grams/milliliters by 28 or 29 (rounded for convenience).

$$224 \text{ g} \div 28 = 8 \text{ oz.}$$
$$224 \text{ ml} \div 29 = 7.72 \text{ fl. oz.}$$

To help you develop a framework for judging conversions, remember that:

▶ A kilogram is about 2.2 pounds.
▶ A gram is about 1/30 ounce.
▶ A pound is about 450 grams.
▶ A liter is slightly more than a quart.
▶ A centimeter is slightly less than ½ inch.
▶ 0°C (32°F) is the freezing point of water.
▶ 100°C (212°F) is the boiling point of water.

These approximations are not a substitute for accurate conversions, however. Appendix II contains additional information on equivalents and metric conversions. There is no substitute for knowing this information. In fact, it should become second nature to you.

TABLE 3.2 COMMON EQUIVALENTS

dash	=	⅛ teaspoon
3 teaspoons	=	1 tablespoon
2 tablespoons	=	1 fl. oz.
4 tablespoons	=	¼ cup (2 fl. oz.)
5⅓ tablespoons	=	⅓ cup (2⅔ fl. oz.)
16 tablespoons	=	1 cup (8 fl. oz.)
2 cups	=	1 pint (16 fl. oz.)
2 pints	=	1 quart (32 fl. oz.)
4 quarts	=	1 gallon (128 fl. oz.)
2 gallons	=	1 peck
4 pecks	=	1 bushel
1 gram	=	0.035 ounce (1/30 oz.)
1 ounce	=	28.35 grams (often rounded to 30 for convenience)
454 grams	=	1 pound
2.2 pounds	=	1 kilogram (1000 grams)
1 teaspoon	=	5 milliliters
1 tablespoon	=	15 milliliters
1 fluid ounce	=	29.57 milliliters (often rounded to 30 for convenience)
1 cup	=	0.24 liter
1 gallon	=	3.80 liters

RECIPE CONVERSIONS

Whether it produces 6 servings or 60, every recipe is designed to produce or **yield** a specific amount of product. A recipe's yield may be expressed in volume, weight or servings (for example, 1 quart of sauce; 8 pounds of bread dough; 8 half-cup servings). If the expected yield does not meet the chef's needs, he or she must convert (that is, increase or decrease) the ingredient amounts. Recipe conversion is sometimes complicated by portion size conversion. For example, it may be necessary to convert a recipe that initially produces twenty-four 8-ounce servings of soup into a recipe that produces sixty-two 6-ounce servings.

It is just as easy to change yields by uneven amounts as it is to double or halve recipes. The mathematical principle is the same: Each ingredient is multiplied by a **conversion factor (C.F.)**. Do not take shortcuts by estimating recipe amounts or conversion factors. Inaccurate conversions lead to inedible foods, embarrassing shortages or wasteful excesses. Take the time to learn and apply proper conversion techniques.

yield the total amount of a product made from a specific recipe; also, the amount of a food item remaining after cleaning or processing

conversion factor (C.F.) the number used to increase or decrease ingredient quantities and recipe yields

Converting Total Yield

When portion size is unimportant or remains the same, recipe yield is converted by a simple two-step process:

Step 1 Divide the desired (new) yield by the recipe (old) yield to obtain the conversion factor (C.F.).

$$\text{New yield} \div \text{Old yield} = \text{Conversion factor}$$

Step 2 Multiply each ingredient quantity by the conversion factor to obtain the new quantity.

$$\text{Old quantity} \times \text{Conversion factor} = \text{New quantity}$$

$$\frac{\text{New Yield}}{\text{Old Yield}} = \text{C.F.}$$

$$\text{Old Quantity} \times \text{C.F.} = \text{New Quantity}$$

EXAMPLE 3.1

You need to convert a recipe for cauliflower soup. The present recipe yields 1½ gallons. You need to make only ¾ gallon.

Step 1 Determine the conversion factor:

$$0.75 \text{ gallon} \div 1.5 \text{ gallons} = 0.5$$

Note that any unit can be used, as long as the same unit is used with both the new and the old recipes. For example, the same conversion factor would be obtained if the recipe amounts were converted to fluid ounces:

$$96 \text{ fluid ounces} \div 192 \text{ fluid ounces} = 0.5$$

Step 2 Apply the conversion factor to each ingredient in the soup recipe:

CAULIFLOWER SOUP	old quantity	×	C.F.	=	new quantity
Cauliflower, chopped	5 lb.	×	0.5	=	2½ lb.
Celery stalks	4	×	0.5	=	2
Onion	1	×	0.5	=	½
Chicken stock	2 qt.	×	0.5	=	1 qt.
Heavy cream	3 pt.	×	0.5	=	1½ pt.

Converting Portion Size

Sometimes the amount of food served as a portion must be changed. For example, new soup cups may hold less than cups now being used, or a banquet menu may require a smaller entrée portion than is normally served à la carte. A few additional steps are necessary to convert recipes when portion sizes must also be changed. This is easy to understand if you think in terms of the total amount of a food item that is needed in relation to the total amount of that item (yield) produced by the current recipe. The key is to find a common denominator for the new and old recipes: ounces, grams, cups, servings and so on. Any unit can be used, as long as the same unit is used with both the new and the old recipes.

No. of Portions × Portion Size = Yield

Step 1   Determine the total yield of the existing recipe by multiplying the number of portions by the portion size.

Original portions × Original portion size = Total (old) yield

Step 2   Determine the total yield desired by multiplying the new number of portions by the new portion size.

Desired portions × Desired portion size = Total (new) yield

$$\frac{\text{New Yield}}{\text{Old Yield}} = \text{C.F.}$$

Step 3   Obtain the conversion factor as described earlier.

Total new yield ÷ Total old yield = Conversion factor

Old Quantity × C.F. = New Quantity

Step 4   Multiply each ingredient quantity by the conversion factor.

Old quantity × Conversion factor = New quantity

EXAMPLE 3.2

Returning to the cauliflower soup: The original recipe produced 1½ gallons or 48 4-ounce servings. Now you need 72 6-ounce servings.

Step 1   Total original yield is 48 × 4 = 192 ounces.

Step 2   Total desired yield is 72 × 6 = 432 ounces.

Step 3   The conversion factor is calculated by dividing total new yield by total old yield:

432 ÷ 192 = 2.25

Step 4   Old ingredient quantities are multiplied by the conversion factor to determine the new quantities:

CAULIFLOWER SOUP

	old quantity	×	C.F.	=	new quantity
Cauliflower, chopped	5 lb.	×	2.25	=	11.25 lb.
Celery stalks	4	×	2.25	=	9
Onion	1	×	2.25	=	2.25
Chicken stock	2 qt.	×	2.25	=	4.5 qt.
Heavy cream	3 pt.	×	2.25	=	6.75 pt.

Additional Conversion Problems

When making large recipe changes—for example, from 5 to 25 portions or 600 to 300 portions—you may encounter additional problems. The mathematical conversions described here do not take into account changes in equipment, evaporation rates, unforeseen recipe errors or cooking times. Chefs learn to use their judgment, knowledge of cooking principles and skills to compensate for these factors.

EQUIPMENT

When the size of a recipe changes, the equipment necessary to produce it must change as well. Problems arise, however, when the production techniques previously used no longer work with the new quantity of ingredients. For example, if a small muffin recipe can be mixed by hand, an increased batch size may require the use of a mixer. But if mixing time remains the same, the batter may become overmixed, resulting in poor-quality muffins. Trying to prepare a small amount of product in equipment that is too large for the task can also affect its quality.

EVAPORATION

Equipment changes can also affect product quality because of changes in evaporation rates. Increasing a soup recipe may require substituting a tilt skillet for a saucepan. But because a tilt skillet provides more surface area for evaporation than does a saucepan, reduction time must be decreased to prevent overthickening the soup. The increased evaporation caused by increased surface area may also alter the strength of the seasonings.

RECIPE ERRORS

A recipe may contain errors in ingredients or techniques that are not obvious when it is prepared in small quantities. When increased, however, small mistakes often become big (and obvious) ones, and the final product suffers. The only solution is to test recipes carefully and rely on your knowledge of cooking principles to compensate for unexpected problems.

TIME

Do not multiply time specifications given in a recipe by the conversion factor used with the recipe's ingredients. All things being equal, cooking time will not change when recipe size changes. For example, a muffin requires the same amount of baking time whether you prepare 1 dozen or 14 dozen. Cooking time will be affected, however, by changes in evaporation rate or heat conduction caused by equipment changes. And an oven filled to capacity may lose more heat, thus slowing the baking time. Mixing time may change when recipe size is changed. Different equipment may perform mixing tasks more or less efficiently than previously used equipment. Again, rely on experience and good judgment.

CALCULATING UNIT COSTS AND RECIPE COSTS

Unit Costs

Food service operations purchase most foods from suppliers in bulk or wholesale packages. For example, canned goods are purchased by the case; produce by the flat, case or lug; and flour and sugar in 25- or 50-pound bags. Even fish and meats are often purchased in large cuts, not individual serving-sized portions. The purchased amount is rarely used for a single recipe, however. It must be broken down into smaller units such as pounds, cups, quarts or ounces.

In order to allocate the proper ingredient costs to the recipe being prepared, it is necessary to convert **as-purchased (A.P.) costs or prices** to **unit costs or prices.** To find the unit cost (that is, the cost of a particular unit, say, a single egg) in a package containing multiple units (for example, a 30-dozen case), divide the A.P. cost of the package by the number of units in the package.

A.P. cost ÷ Number of units = Cost per unit

EXAMPLE 3.3

A case of #10 cans contains six individual cans. If a case of tomato paste costs $23.50, then each can costs $3.92.

$23.50 A.P. case cost ÷ 6 cans per case = $3.92 cost per can

If your recipe uses less than the total can, you must continue dividing the cost of the can until you arrive at the appropriate unit amount. Continuing with the tomato paste example, if you need only 1 cup of tomato paste, divide the can price ($3.92) by the total number of cups contained in the can to arrive at the cost per cup (unit). The list of canned-good sizes in Appendix II shows that a #10 can contains approximately 13 cups. Using the formula, each cup costs $0.30.

$3.92 cost per can ÷ 13 cups per can = $0.30 cost per cup

The cost of 1 cup can be reduced even further if necessary. If the recipe uses only 1 tablespoon of tomato paste, divide the cost per cup by the number of tablespoons in a cup. As you can see, the cost for 1 tablespoon of this tomato paste is $0.018.

$0.30 cost per cup ÷ 16 tablespoons per cup = $.018 cost per tablespoon

as purchased (A.P.) the condition or cost of an item as it is purchased or received from the supplier

unit cost the price paid to acquire one of the specified units

$$\frac{A.P.\ \$}{\#\ of\ Units} = \$\ per\ Unit$$

edible portion (E.P.) the amount of a food item available for consumption or use after trimming or fabrication; a smaller, more convenient portion of a larger or bulk unit

yield test measuring and weighing an ingredient before and after trimming to determine the usable portion; used to determine the quantity of an ingredient to purchase as well as actual ingredient cost

yield percentage the ratio of the usable weight of an ingredient after cleaning and trimming to the quantity purchased, calculated by dividing the trimmed weight by the as-purchased weight of the ingredient

E.P. weight ÷ A.P. weight
= Yield percentage

E.P. quantity ÷ Yield percentage
= A.P. quantity

A.P. cost per pound ÷ Yield percentage
= E.P. cost per pound

So when you are calculating the total cost of a recipe containing a tablespoon of tomato paste, the unit cost will be $.018 or 1.8¢.

Cost information is usually provided to the chef or manager from purchase invoices. It may also be necessary to examine a product's label or package to determine some information such as actual weight of the contents or size of ingredients contained within a package.

Yield Percentage

Many ingredients such as fruit and vegetables require cleaning and trimming before they are ready for use in a recipe. Once a potato is peeled, for example, the peels are discarded and the remaining **edible portion (E.P.)** is what is left. (In the case of baked potatoes, the whole potato is used and the E.P. is the same as the A.P.) To determine the actual cost of the edible portion of an ingredient, chefs conduct a **yield test** to determine the **yield percentage,** which can be used to determine the as-purchased (A.P.) quantity for the recipe as well as the actual cost per pound of the ingredient. The edible portion (E.P.) or the weight of the ingredient after it is prepared for cooking divided by the weight of the ingredient as purchased (A.P.) gives the yield percentage for that food item.

E.P. weight ÷ A.P. weight = Yield percentage

Step 1   Weigh the ingredient as purchased before cleaning, trimming and peeling.
Step 2   Peel, trim and clean the ingredient as required in the standardized recipe.
Step 3   Weigh the trimmed product to obtain the E.P.
Step 4   Divide the E.P. weight by the A.P. weight to obtain the yield percentage.

EXAMPLE 3.4

The weight of 5 pounds of potatoes (A.P.) after peeling is 4 pounds (E.P.). Dividing 4 pounds peeled potatoes (E.P.) by 5 pounds unpeeled potatoes (A.P.) gives an 80% yield percentage.

4 pounds peeled potatoes (E.P.) ÷ 5 pounds unpeeled potatoes (A.P.)
= 80% yield percentage

USING YIELD PERCENTAGE TO CALCULATE A.P. QUANTITY

Often recipes are written listing the edible portion of an ingredient. The chef must then calculate the A.P. quantity required. To find the A.P. quantity needed for a recipe, divide the E.P. quantity in the recipe by the yield percentage.

E.P. quantity ÷ Yield percentage = A.P. quantity

EXAMPLE 3.5

A recipe calls for 12 pounds of peeled potatoes with an 80% yield percentage; therefore 15 pounds of potatoes will be required.

12 pounds (E.P.) ÷ 0.80 (yield percentage) = 15 pounds (A.P.)

Because trimming decreases the usable quantity of an ingredient, the cost of the ingredient must be increased by the amount that is discarded. Chefs can use the yield percentage to accurately calculate the cost of an ingredient after trimming.

A.P. cost per pound ÷ Yield percentage = E.P. cost per pound

EXAMPLE 3.6

Potatoes cost $0.41 per pound and have a yield percentage of 80%; therefore the true cost of the edible portion of peeled potatoes is $0.51 per pound.

$0.41 per pound (A.P.) ÷ 0.80 (yield percentage) = $0.51 per pound (E.P.)

Chefs periodically conduct yield tests on items requiring fabrication and trimming to ensure that they are properly costing ingredients. Tables listing average yields of common ingredients are also available in books and from meat, poultry and fish purveyors. The butchering of meats, poultry and fish as well as other foods is complicated by the fact that these ingredients can yield trim and bones usable in other preparations. The calculation of E.P. cost must take this into consideration.

Recipe Costs

A standardized recipe, listing the ingredients and their amounts, as well as the number and size of the portions, must be established in order to determine the cost of a completed menu item. Once an accurate recipe is written, the **total recipe cost** is calculated with the following two-step procedure:

Step 1   Determine the cost for the given quantity of each recipe ingredient with the unit costing procedures described earlier.

Step 2   Add all the ingredient costs together to obtain the total recipe cost.

The total recipe cost can then be broken down into the **cost per portion,** which is the most useful figure for food cost controls. To arrive at cost per portion, divide the total recipe cost by the total number of servings or portions produced by that recipe.

Total recipe cost ÷ Number of portions = Cost per portion

The Recipe Costing Form shown in Figure 3.1 is useful for organizing recipe costing information. It provides space for listing each ingredient, the quantity of each ingredient needed, the cost of each unit (E.P.), and the total cost for the ingredient. Total yield, portion size and cost per portion are listed at the bottom of the form. Note that there is no space for recipe procedures, because these are generally irrelevant in recipe costing.

Selling Prices

The cost of a portion of food is just one factor used to determine the selling price of a dish on the menu. The portion cost of several recipes may need to be calculated in order to determine what it costs to serve a finished dish. Each item served on the plate, such as the

total recipe cost the total cost of ingredients for a particular recipe; it does not reflect overhead, labor, fixed expenses or profit

cost per portion the amount of the total recipe cost divided by the number of portions produced from that recipe; the cost of one serving

$$\frac{\text{Recipe \$}}{\text{\# of portions}} = \text{\$ per portion}$$

RECIPE COSTING FORM

Menu Item __Beef Stew_____   Date _____

Total Yield ____200 fl. oz._____   Portion Size ____12 1/2 fl. oz.____

| INGREDIENT | QUANTITY | COST | | | RECIPE COST |
		A.P. ($)	Yield %	E.P. ($)	
Beef, cubes	6 lb.			$3.60/lb.	$21.60
Corn oil	3 Tbsp.	6.78/gal.		0.42/c.	0.08
Flour	1½ oz.	13.50/50 lb.		0.27/lb.	0.03
Beef stock	2 qt.	2.50/gal.		0.62/qt.	1.24
Carrots, diced	1 lb.	.56/lb.	82%	0.68/lb.	0.68
Potatoes, diced	2 lb.	.41/lb.	80%	0.51/lb.	1.02
Onions	2	.15 each		0.15 each	0.30
Salt	TT				-0-

TOTAL RECIPE COST $ ____24.95____

Number of Portions _____16_____

Cost per Portion $ _____1.559_____

FIGURE 3.1 ▶ Recipe costing form.

MENU COSTING FORM

Menu Item _Beef Stew with Parsley Buttered Noodles and Green Beans_

INGREDIENT	RECIPE COST
Beef Stew	$1.559
Parsley Buttered Noodles	0.24
Green Beans	0.44
Roll and butter	0.32
Total plate cost	$2.559
Desired food cost percentage	35%
Proposed menu selling price	$7.311

FIGURE 3.2 ▶ Menu costing form.

overhead costs expenses related to operating a business, including but not limited to costs for advertising, equipment leasing, insurance, property rent, supplies and utilities

food cost percentage the ratio of the cost of foods used to the total food sales during a set period, calculated by dividing the cost of food used by the total sales in a restaurant

$$\frac{\text{Plate cost}}{\text{Desired cost \%}} = \text{Selling price}$$

buttered noodles and green beans that may accompany the Beef Stew in Figure 3.1, contributes to the total **plate cost** for that item, as shown in Figure 3.2. In addition, as in any business, a food service operation incurs numerous **overhead costs** in the preparation and service of a menu. Typically these include the cost of kitchen and dining room labor and employment taxes, utilities, rent, supplies, linens, advertising and promotional expenses along with myriad other expenses necessary for the business to operate successfully. Working closely with its chef, restaurant management determines the **food cost percentage** it needs to achieve to be profitable. This percentage represents the cost of all food used divided by the total sales in a restaurant. Kitchen waste, inefficient trimming of meats and inconsistent portion sizes all contribute to increases in food cost and decreased profitability.

The food cost percentage is one of many methods that can be used to determine selling prices of each individual menu item in the following manner:

Step 1   Determine the total cost of all components in a finished plate.

Step 2   Divide the total plate cost by the desired food cost percentage.

Plate cost ÷ Food cost % = Selling price

EXAMPLE 3.7

To determine the selling price for the Beef Stew in Figure 3.2, if management wants to achieve a 35% food cost, divide the total plate cost of $2.559 by 35%.

$2.559 ÷ 35% = $7.311 (proposed selling price)

Selling prices may be adjusted by management to fit a particular pricing format, rounding cents to the nearest dollar or adding a flat sum to cover additional costs. Chefs work closely with food service managers to keep the food cost percentage within established guidelines. Taking periodic physical **inventory** helps management verify that the proper quantities of food are being used.

inventory the listing and counting of all foods in the kitchen, storerooms and refrigerators

✳CONTROLLING FOOD COSTS

Many things affect food costs in any given operation; most can be controlled by the chef or manager. These controls do not require mathematical calculations or formulas, just basic management skills and a good dose of common sense. The following factors all have an impact on the operation's bottom line:

▶ Menu

▶ Purchasing/ordering

▶ Receiving

- ▶ Storing
- ▶ Issuing
- ▶ Kitchen procedures
- ▶ Establishing standard portions
- ▶ Waste
- ▶ Sales and service

Chefs tend to focus their control efforts in the area of kitchen preparation. Although this may seem logical, it is not adequate. A good chef is involved in all aspects of the operation to help prevent problems from arising or to correct those that may occur.

MENU

A profitable menu is based on many variables, including customer desires, physical space and equipment, ingredient availability, cost of goods sold, employee skills and competition. All management personnel, including the chef, should be consulted when planning the menu. Menu changes, though possibly desirable, must be executed with as much care as the original design.

PURCHASING/ORDERING

Purchasing techniques have a direct impact on cost controls. On the one hand, **parstock (par)** must be adequate for efficient operations; on the other hand, too much inventory wastes space and resources and may spoil. Before any items are ordered, purchasing specifications should be established and communicated to potential purveyors. Specifications should precisely describe the item, including grade, quality, packaging and unit size. Each operation should design its own form to best meet its specific needs. A sample specification form is shown in Figure 3.3. This information can be used to obtain price quotes from several purveyors. Update these quotes periodically to ensure that you are getting the best value for your money.

parstock (par) the amount of stock necessary to cover operating needs between deliveries

RECEIVING

Whether goods are received by a full-time clerk, as they are in a large hotel, or by the chef or kitchen manager, certain standards should be observed. The person signing for merchandise should first confirm that the items were actually ordered. Second, determine whether the items listed on the invoice are the ones being delivered and that the price and quantity listed are accurate. Third, the items, especially meats and produce, should be checked for quality, freshness and weight. The temperature of all perishable items should be carefully checked at the time of delivery to ensure compliance with food safety standards. Established purchase specifications should be readily available for anyone responsible for receiving goods. If an item does not meet any of these purchase specifications or is not within acceptable temperature ranges on arrival, the product should be refused.

FIFO (first in, first out) a system of rotating inventory, particularly perishable and semiperishable goods, in which items are used in the order in which they are received

STORING

Proper storage of foodstuffs is crucial in order to prevent spoilage, pilferage and waste. Stock must be rotated so that the older items are used first. Such a system for rotating stock is referred to as **FIFO (first in, first out)**. Dry storage areas should be well ventilated and lit to prevent pest infestation and mold. Freezers and refrigerators should be easily accessible, operating properly and kept clean and organized.

ISSUING

It may be necessary, particularly in larger operations, to limit storeroom access to specific personnel. Maintaining ongoing inventory records or parstock sheets helps the ordering process. Controlling issuances eliminates waste caused by multiple opened containers and ensures proper stock rotation.

KITCHEN PROCEDURES: ESTABLISHING STANDARD PORTIONS

Standardizing portions is essential to controlling food costs. Unless portion quantity is uniform, it will be impossible to compute portion costs accurately. Portion discrepancies can also confuse or mislead customers. Chefs can check plates that

MEAT PURCHASING SPECIFICATIONS	
Product:	
Menu Item:	
Grade/Quality:	NAMP/IMPS#:
Packaging:	
Pricing Unit:	
Delivery Conditions:	
Comments:	

FIGURE 3.3 ▶ Specification form.

have been cleared from the table; large quantities of waste could suggest a serious and costly problem.

Actual portion sizes depend on the food service operation itself, the menu, the prices and the customers' desires. Some items are generally purchased preportioned for convenience (for example, steaks are sold in uniform cuts, baking potatoes are available in uniform sizes, butter comes in preportioned pats and bread comes sliced for service). Other items must be portioned by the establishment before service. Special equipment makes consistent portioning easy. There are machines to slice meats, cutting guides for cakes and pies and portion scales for weighing quantities. Standardized portion scoops and ladles are indispensable for serving vegetables, soups, stews, salads and similar foods. Many of these items are discussed and illustrated in Chapter 4, Tools and Equipment.

Once acceptable portion sizes are established, employees must be properly trained to present them. If each employee of a sandwich shop prepared sandwiches the way he or she would like to eat them, customers would probably never receive the same sandwich twice. Customers may become confused and decide not to risk a repeat visit. Obviously, carelessness in portioning can also drastically affect food cost.

KITCHEN PROCEDURES: WASTE

The chef must also control waste from overproduction or failure to use leftovers. With an adequate sales history, the chef can accurately estimate the quantity of food to prepare for each week, day or meal. An organized kitchen staff works from lists prepared by the head chef or station chefs outlining the type and quantities of products to be made. A well-planned "prep list" keeps work flow organized and waste to a minimum. The less waste generated in food preparation, the lower the overall food cost will be.

If the menu is designed properly, the chef can also use leftovers and trim from product fabrication. When planning the menu, the chef should identify all trim and create uses for it before putting the menu into service. The chain muscle trimmed from beef tenderloin, for example, can be used for kebabs. Whole chickens should not be purchased if the menu only calls for boneless breast. Other dishes using the legs and carcass should be on the menu; otherwise, boned chicken breasts should be purchased. Anticipating uses for leftovers helps reduce waste. Leftover roast turkey from a holiday menu can be used on a turkey club sandwich at the next service. Chefs should avoid using highly perishable items that have limited use on a menu, such as an expensive garnish.

SALES AND SERVICE

An improperly trained sales staff can undo even the most rigorous food cost controls. Front-of-the-house personnel are, after all, ultimately responsible for the sales portion of the food cost equation. Prices charged must be accurate and complete. Poor service can lead to the need to "comp" (serve for free) an excessive amount of food. Dropped or spilled foods do not generate revenues. Proper training is once again critical. The dining room manager and the chef should work together to educate servers about menu items and sales techniques.

QUESTIONS FOR DISCUSSION

1. Describe the four types of menus. Can each type of menu offer foods à la carte, semi à la carte and/or table d'hôte? Explain your answer.

2. Discuss three factors in food preparation that affect successful recipe size changes.

3. Why is it important to calculate the portion cost of a recipe in professional food service operations? Why is the full recipe cost inadequate?

4. List several factors, other than kitchen procedures, that a chef should examine when looking for ways to control food costs.

5. Several recipe costing software programs are available online. Research two of these programs. What are their advantages and disadvantages? Why is it important for cooks to learn to calculate recipe costs without the aid of a computer? **WWW**

Terms to Know

course	food production
day part	portion size
tasting menu	selling price
menu language	recipe costing
nutritional	menu planning
statements	trim
measurements	

> "And, indeed, is there not something holy about a great kitchen? The scoured gleam of row upon row of metal vessels dangling from hooks or reposing on their shelves till needed with the air of so many chalices waiting for the celebration of the sacrament of food."
>
> —ANGELA CARTER, BRITISH NOVELIST (1940–1992)

CHAPTER FOUR

TOOLS AND EQUIPMENT

After studying this chapter, you will be able to:

- recognize a variety of professional kitchen tools and equipment
- select and care for knives
- understand how a professional kitchen is organized

HAVING THE PROPER TOOLS AND EQUIPMENT for a particular task may mean the difference between a job well done and one done carelessly, incorrectly or even dangerously. This chapter introduces most of the tools and equipment typically used in a professional kitchen. Items are divided into categories according to their function: hand tools, knives, measuring and portioning devices, cookware, strainers and sieves, processing equipment, storage containers, heavy equipment, buffet equipment and safety equipment.

A wide variety of specialized tools and equipment is available to today's chef. Breading machines, croissant shapers and doughnut glazers are designed to speed production by reducing handwork. Other devices—for instance, a duck press or a couscousière— are used only for unique tasks in preparing a few menu items. Much of this specialized equipment is quite expensive and found only in food manufacturing operations or specialized kitchens; a discussion of it is beyond the scope of this chapter. Brief descriptions of some of these specialized devices are, however, found in the Glossary. Baking pans and tools are discussed in Chapter 29, Principles of the Bakeshop.

Before using any equipment, personnel should study the operator's manual or have someone experienced with the particular item instruct them on proper procedures for its use and cleaning. And remember, always think safety first.

STANDARDS FOR TOOLS AND EQUIPMENT

NSF International (NSF), previously known as the National Sanitation Foundation, promulgates consensus standards for the design, construction and installation of kitchen tools, cookware and equipment. Many states and municipalities require that food service operations use only NSF-certified equipment. Although NSF certification is voluntary, most manufacturers submit their designs to NSF for certification to show that they are suitable for use in professional food service operations. Certified equipment bears the NSF mark shown in Figure 4.1.

NSF standards reflect the following requirements:

1. Equipment must be easily cleaned.
2. All food contact surfaces must be nontoxic (under intended end-use conditions), nonabsorbent, corrosion resistant and nonreactive.
3. All food contact surfaces must be smooth—that is, free of pits, cracks, crevices, ledges, rivet heads and bolts.
4. Internal corners and edges must be rounded and smooth; external corners and angles must be smooth and sealed.
5. Coating materials must be nontoxic and easily cleaned; coatings must resist chipping and cracking.
6. Waste and waste liquids must be easily removed.

FIGURE 4.1 ▶ The NSF mark.

SELECTING TOOLS AND EQUIPMENT

In general, only commercial food service tools and equipment should be used in a professional kitchen. Look for tools that are well constructed. For example, joints should be welded, not bonded with solder; handles should be comfortable, with rounded borders; plastic and rubber parts should be seamless.

Before purchasing or leasing any equipment, you should evaluate several factors:

❶ Is this equipment necessary for producing menu items?
❷ Will this equipment perform the job required in the space available?
❸ Is this equipment the most economical for the operation's specific needs?
❹ Is this equipment easy to clean, maintain and repair?

HAND TOOLS

Hand tools are designed to aid in cutting, shaping, moving or combining foods. They have few, if any, moving parts. Knives, discussed separately later, are the most important hand tools. Sturdiness, durability and safety are the watchwords when selecting hand tools. Choose tools that can withstand the heavy use of a professional kitchen and those that are easily cleaned.

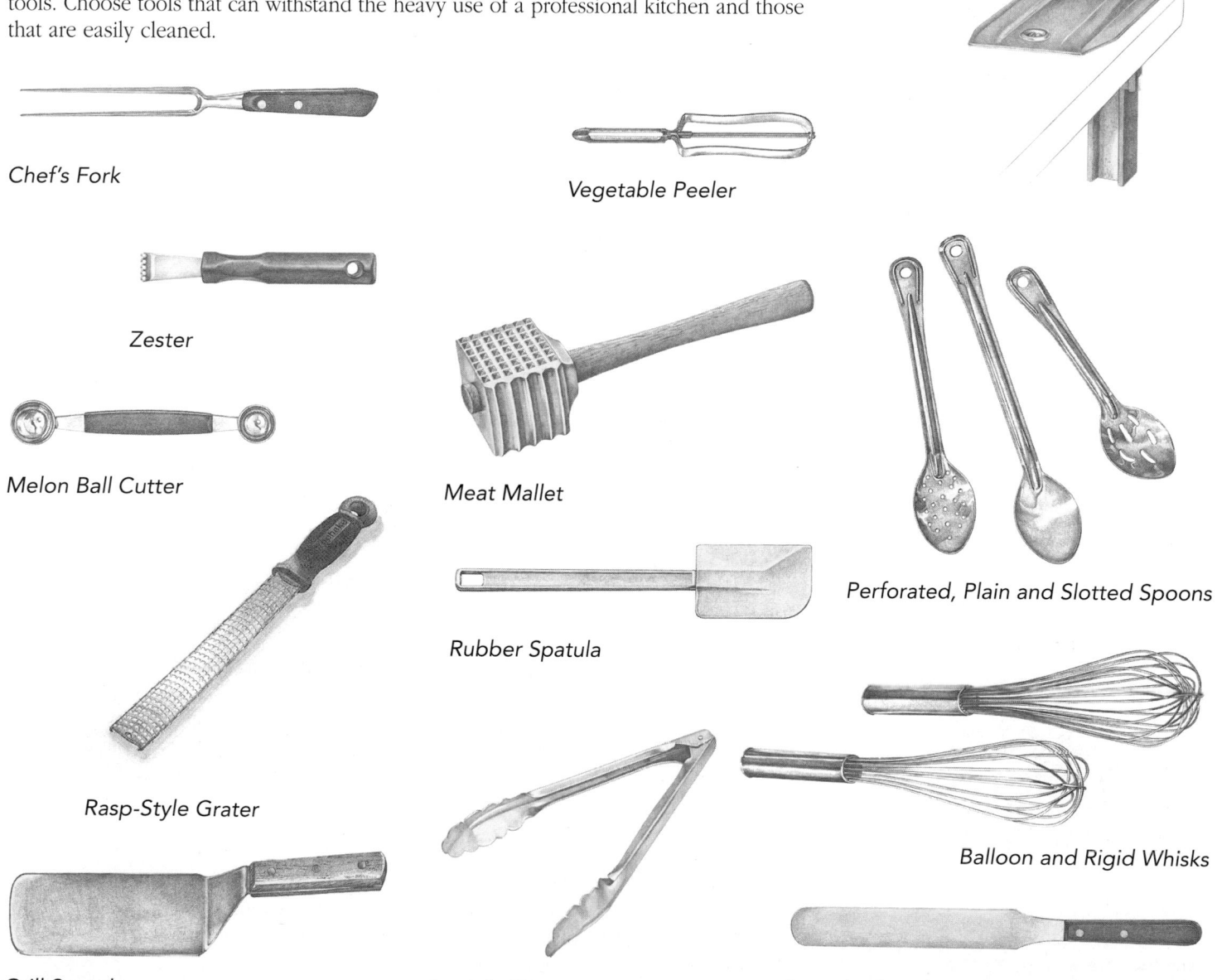

Table-Mounted Can Opener

Chef's Fork

Vegetable Peeler

Zester

Melon Ball Cutter

Meat Mallet

Perforated, Plain and Slotted Spoons

Rasp-Style Grater

Rubber Spatula

Balloon and Rigid Whisks

Grill Spatula

Straight Tongs

Straight Spatula (Cake Spatula)

KNIVES

Knives are the most important items in the chef's tool kit. With a sharp knife, the skilled chef can accomplish a number of tasks more quickly and efficiently than any machine. Good-quality knives are expensive but will last for many years with proper care. Select easily sharpened, well-constructed knives that are comfortable and balanced in your hand. Knife construction and commonly used knives are discussed here; knife safety and care as well as cutting techniques are discussed in Chapter 5, Knife Skills.

Knife Construction

A good knife begins with a single piece of metal, stamped, cut or—best of all—forged and tempered into a blade of the desired shape. The following metals are generally used for knife blades:

❶ **Carbon steel**—An alloy of carbon and iron, carbon steel is traditionally used for blades because it is soft enough to be sharpened easily. It corrodes and discolors easily, however, especially when used with acidic foods.

❷ **Stainless steel**—Stainless steel will not rust, corrode or discolor and is extremely durable. A stainless steel blade is much more difficult to sharpen than a carbon steel one, although once an edge is established, it lasts longer than the edge on a carbon steel blade.

❸ **High-carbon stainless steel**—An alloy combining the best features of carbon steel and stainless steel, high-carbon stainless steel neither corrodes nor discolors and can be sharpened almost as easily as carbon steel. It is now the most frequently used metal for blades.

❹ **Ceramic**—A ceramic called zirconium oxide is now used to make knife blades that are extremely sharp, very easy to clean, rustproof and nonreactive. With proper care, ceramic blades will remain sharp for years, but when sharpening is needed, it must be done professionally on special diamond wheels. Material costs and tariffs make ceramic-bladed knives very expensive. Although this ceramic is highly durable, it does not have the flexibility of metal, so never use a ceramic knife to pry anything, to strike a hard surface (for example, when crushing garlic or chopping through bones) or to cut against a china or ceramic surface.

A portion of the blade, known as the tang, fits inside the handle, as shown in Figure 4.2. The best knives are constructed with a full tang running the length of the handle; they also have a bolster where the blade meets the handle (the bolster is part of the blade, not a separate collar). Less expensive knives may have a ¾-length tang or a thin "rattail" tang. Neither provides as much support, durability or balance as a full tang.

Knife handles are often made of hard woods infused with plastic and riveted to the tang. Molded polypropylene handles are permanently bonded to a tang without seams or rivets. Stainless steel handles welded directly to the blade are durable but very lightweight. Any handle should be shaped for comfort and ground smooth to eliminate crevices where bacteria can grow.

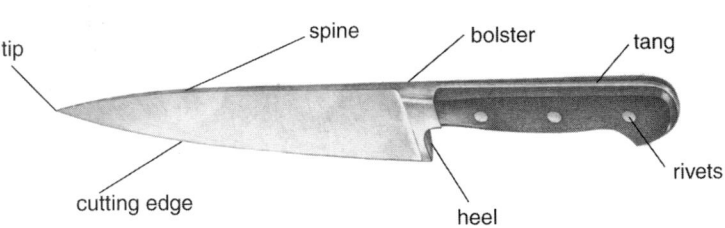

FIGURE 4.2 ▶ The parts of a chef's knife.

Knife Shapes and Sharpening Equipment

A chef will collect many knives during his or her career, many with specialized functions not described here. This list includes only the most basic knives and sharpening equipment.

FRENCH OR CHEF'S KNIFE

An all-purpose knife used for chopping, slicing and mincing. Its rigid 8- to 14-inch-long blade is wide at the heel and tapers to a point at the tip.

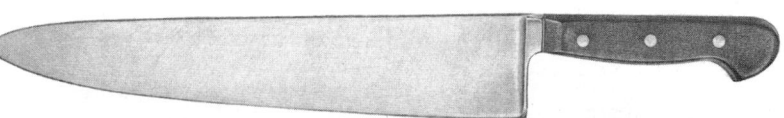

French or Chef's Knife

UTILITY KNIFE

An all-purpose knife used for cutting fruits and vegetables and carving poultry. Its rigid 6- to 8-inch-long blade is shaped like a chef's knife but narrower.

Utility Knife

BONING KNIFE

A smaller knife with a thin blade used to separate meat from bone. The blade is usually 5 to 7 inches long and may be flexible or rigid.

Rigid Boning Knife

PARING KNIFE

A short knife used for detail work or cutting fruits and vegetables. The rigid blade is from 2 to 4 inches long. A tournée or **bird's-beak knife** is similar to a paring knife but with a curved blade; it is used to cut curved surfaces or tournée vegetables.

Paring Knife

CLEAVER

A knife with a large, heavy rectangular blade used for chopping or cutting through bones.

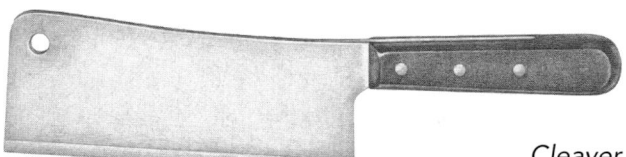

Cleaver

SLICER

A knife with a long, thin blade used primarily for slicing cooked meat. The tip may be round or pointed, and the blade may be flexible or rigid. A similar knife with a serrated edge is used for slicing bread or pastry items.

Flexible Slicer

Serrated Slicer

BUTCHER KNIFE

Sometimes known as a **scimitar** because the rigid blade curves up in a 25-degree angle at the tip, it is used for fabricating raw meat and is available with 6- to 14-inch blades.

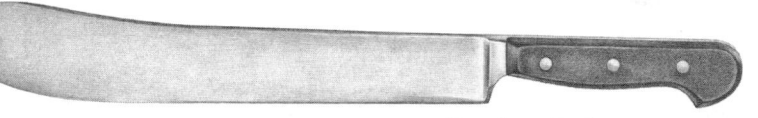

Butcher Knife or Scimitar

OYSTER AND CLAM KNIVES

The short, rigid blades of these knives are used to open oyster and clam shells. The tips are blunt; only the clam knife has a sharp edge.

Oyster Knife

STEEL

A scored, slightly abrasive steel rod used to hone or straighten a blade immediately after and between sharpenings.

Clam Knife

Steel

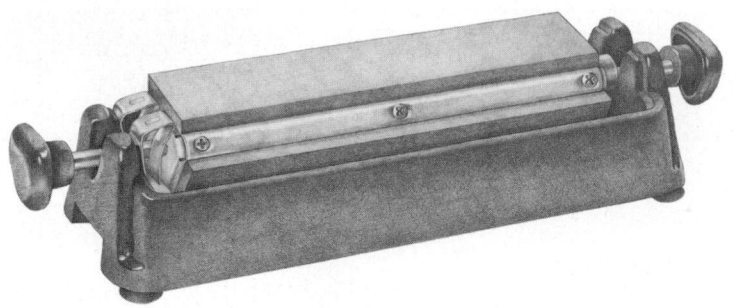

Three-Sided Sharpening Stone

SHARPENING STONE

Also known as a **whetstone**, a flat brick of synthetic abrasives that is used to put an edge on a dull blade. Various grit sizes are available. The most practical sets include both coarse- and fine-grit stones.

MEASURING AND PORTIONING DEVICES

Recipe ingredients must be measured precisely, especially in the bakeshop, and foods should be measured when served to control portion size and cost. The devices used to measure and portion foods are, for the most part, hand tools designed to make food preparation and service easier and more precise. The accuracy they afford prevents the cost of mistakes made when accurate measurements are ignored.

Measurements may be based on weight (for example, grams, ounces, pounds) or volume (for example, teaspoons, cups, gallons). Therefore, it is necessary to have available several measuring devices, including liquid and dry measuring cups and a variety of scales. Thermometers and timers are also measuring devices and are discussed here. When purchasing measuring devices, look for quality construction and accurate markings.

SCALES

Scales are necessary to determine the weight of an ingredient or a portion of food (for example, the sliced meat for a sandwich). Portion scales use a spring mechanism, round dial and single flat tray. They are available calibrated in grams, ounces or pounds. Electronic scales also use a spring mechanism but provide digital readouts. They are often required where foods are priced for sale by weight. An automatic tare feature allows the user to ignore the weight of the container used to hold loose ingredients on the scale, a feature that makes measuring accurately more convenient. Balance scales (also known as baker's scales) use a two-tray, free-weight counterbalance system. A balance scale allows more weight to be measured at one time because it is not limited by spring capacity.

Any scale must be properly used and maintained to provide an accurate reading. Never pick up a scale by its platform, as this can damage the balancing mechanism.

JAPANESE KNIVES

Numerous specialized knives used in Japanese cooking are popular additions to a chef's toolkit. Traditional Japanese knives have an asymmetrical blade, basically flat on one side and beveled to a sharp edge on the other side, which facilitates precise cutting. The **usuba** has a rectangular blade and is used to cut thin vegetable garnishes. The **yanagiba** has a thin 8-to-14-inch-long straight blade traditionally used to cut translucent slices of raw fish fillets called sashimi and sushi rolls. The **deba** has a wide, sturdy 5-to-7-inch-long wedge-shaped blade used for butchering and boning fish.

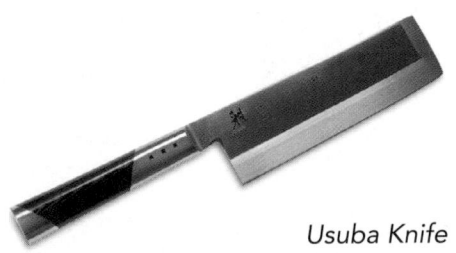

Usuba Knife

Yanagiba Sashimi Knife

Deba Knife

Balance or Baker's Scale

Portion Scale

VOLUME MEASURES

Ingredients may be measured by volume using measuring spoons and measuring cups. Measuring spoons sold as a set usually include ¼-teaspoon, ½-teaspoon, 1-teaspoon and 1-tablespoon units (or the metric equivalent). Liquid measuring cups are available in capacities from 1 cup to 1 gallon. They have a lip or pour spout above the top line of measurement to prevent spills. Measuring cups for dry ingredients are usually sold in sets of ¼-, ⅓- ½- and 1-cup units. They do not have pour spouts, so the top of the cup is level with the top measurement specified. Glass measuring cups are not recommended because they can break. Avoid using bent or dented measuring cups, as the damage may distort the measurement capacity.

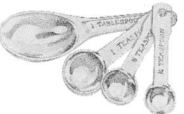

Measuring Spoons

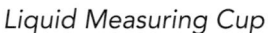

Liquid Measuring Cup

Dry Measuring Cups

LADLES

Long-handled ladles are useful for portioning liquids such as stocks, sauces and soups. The capacity, in ounces or milliliters, is stamped on the handle.

PORTION SCOOPS

Portion scoops (also known as dishers) resemble ice cream scoops. They come in a range of standardized sizes and have a lever-operated blade for releasing their contents. Scoops are useful for portioning salads, vegetables, muffin batters or other soft foods. A number, stamped on either the handle or the release mechanism, indicates the number of level scoopfuls per quart. The higher the scoop number, the smaller the scoop's capacity. See Table 4.1.

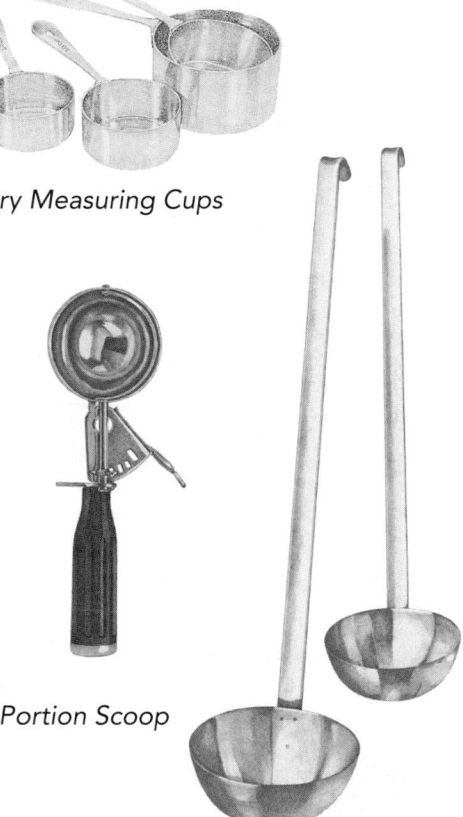

Portion Scoop

Ladles

TABLE 4.1 PORTION SCOOP CAPACITIES

SCOOP NUMBER	APPROXIMATE VOLUME		APPROXIMATE WEIGHT*	
	U.S.	METRIC	U.S.	METRIC
6	⅔ c.	160 ml	5 oz.	160 g
8	½ c.	120 ml	4 oz.	120 g
10	3 fl. oz.	90 ml	3–3½ oz.	85–100 g
12	⅓ c.	80 ml	2½–3 oz.	75–85 g
16	¼ c.	60 ml	2 oz.	60 g
20	1½ fl. oz.	45 ml	1½ oz.	45 g
24	1⅓ fl. oz.	40 ml	1⅓ oz.	40 g
30	1 fl. oz.	30 ml	1 oz.	30 g
40	0.8 fl. oz.	24 ml	0.8 oz.	24 g
60	½ fl. oz.	15 ml	½ oz.	15 g

*Weights are approximate because they vary by food.

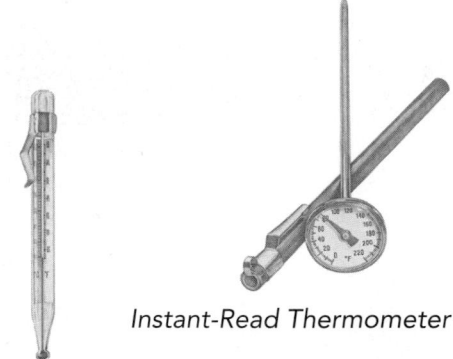

Instant-Read Thermometer

Candy Thermometer

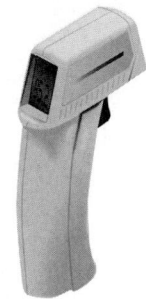

Digital Infrared Thermometer

HOW TO CALIBRATE A STEM-TYPE THERMOMETER

All stem-type thermometers should be calibrated at least weekly as well as whenever they are dropped. To calibrate a stem-type thermometer, fill a glass with shaved ice, then add water. Place the thermometer in the ice slush and wait until the temperature reading stabilizes. Following the manufacturer's directions, adjust the thermometer's calibration nut until the temperature reads 32°F (0°C). Check the calibration by returning the thermometer to the slush. Then repeat the procedure, substituting boiling water for the ice slush, and calibrate the thermometer at 212°F (100°C).

THERMOMETERS

Various types of thermometers are used in the kitchen.

Stem-type thermometers, including instant-read models, are inserted into foods to obtain temperature readings. Temperatures are shown on either a dial noted by an arrow or a digital readout. An instant-read thermometer is a small stem-type model, designed to be carried in a pocket and used to provide quick temperature readings. An instant-read thermometer should not be left in foods that are cooking because doing so damages the thermometer. Sanitize the stem of any thermometer before use in order to avoid cross-contamination.

Candy and fat thermometers measure temperatures up to 400°F (204°C) using mercury in a column of glass. A back clip attaches the thermometer to the pan, keeping the chef's hands free. Be careful not to subject glass thermometers to quick temperature changes, as the glass may shatter.

Electronic probe thermometers are now reasonably priced and commonly used in food service facilities. These thermometers provide immediate, clear, digital readouts from a handheld unit attached to a metal probe (some are conveniently designed so that the probe is embedded in the tines of a long-handled fork or the bowl of a ladle). A detachable probe is especially useful inside an oven and for deep-frying and grilling.

The latest advancement in thermometers relies on infrared sensors with laser sightings. Infrared thermometers can instantly monitor the surface temperature of foods during cooking or holding and the temperature of goods at receiving and in storage. Units can respond to a wide range of temperatures in less than a second without actually touching the food, thus avoiding any risk of cross-contamination.

Because proper temperatures must be maintained for holding and storing foods, oven and refrigerator thermometers are also useful. Select thermometers with easy-to-read dials or column divisions.

TIMERS

Portable kitchen timers are useful for any busy chef. Small digital timers can be carried in a pocket; some even time three functions at once. Select a timer with a loud alarm signal and long timing capability.

COOKWARE

Cookware includes the sauté pans and stockpots used on the stove top as well as the roasting pans, hotel pans and specialty molds used inside the oven. Cookware should be selected for its size, shape, ability to conduct heat evenly and overall quality of construction.

Metals and Heat Conduction

Cookware that fails to distribute heat evenly may cause hot spots that burn foods. Because different metals conduct heat at different rates, and thicker layers of metal conduct heat more evenly than thinner ones, the most important considerations when choosing cookware are the type and thickness (known as the gauge) of the material used. No one cookware or material suits every process or need, however; always select the most appropriate material for the task at hand.

COPPER

Copper is an excellent conductor: It heats rapidly and evenly and cools quickly. Indeed, unlined copper pots are unsurpassed for cooking sugar and fruit mixtures. But copper cookware is extremely expensive. It also requires a great deal of care and is often quite heavy. Moreover, because copper may react with some foods, copper cookware usually has a tin lining, which is soft and easily scratched. Because of these problems, copper is now often sandwiched between layers of stainless steel or aluminum in the bottom of pots and pans.

ALUMINUM

Aluminum is the metal used most commonly in commercial utensils. It is lightweight and, after copper, conducts heat best. Aluminum is a soft metal, though, so it should be treated with care to avoid dents. Do not use aluminum containers for storage or for cooking acidic foods because the metal reacts chemically with many foods. Light-colored foods, such as soups or sauces, may be discolored when cooked in aluminum, especially if stirred with a metal whisk or spoon.

Anodized aluminum has a hard, dark, corrosion-resistant surface that helps prevent sticking and discoloration.

STAINLESS STEEL

Although stainless steel conducts and retains heat poorly, it is a hard, durable metal particularly useful for holding foods and for low-temperature cooking in which hot spots and scorching are not problems. Stainless steel pots and pans are available with aluminum or copper bonded to the bottom or with an aluminum-layered core. Although expensive, such cookware combines the rapid, uniform heat conductivity of copper and aluminum with the strength, durability and nonreactivity of stainless steel. Stainless steel is also ideal for storage containers because it does not react with foods.

CAST IRON

Cast-iron cookware distributes heat evenly and holds high temperatures well. It is often used in griddles and large skillets. Although relatively inexpensive, cast iron is extremely heavy and brittle. It must be kept properly conditioned and dry to prevent rust and pitting.

Other Materials

GLASS

Glass retains heat well but conducts it poorly. It does not react with foods. Tempered glass is suitable for microwave cooking provided it does not have any metal band or decoration. Commercial operations rarely use glass cookware because of the danger of breakage.

CERAMICS

Ceramics, including earthenware, porcelain and stoneware, are used primarily for baking dishes, casseroles and baking stones because they conduct heat uniformly and retain temperatures well. Ceramics are nonreactive, inexpensive and generally suitable for use in a microwave oven (provided there is no metal in the glaze). Ceramics are easily chipped or cracked, however, and should not be used over a direct flame. Also, quick temperature changes may cause the cookware to crack or shatter.

PLASTIC

Plastic containers are frequently used in commercial kitchens for food storage or service, but they cannot be used for heating or cooking except in a microwave oven. Plastic microwave cookware is made of phenolic resin. It is easy to clean, relatively inexpensive and rigidly shaped, but its glasslike structure is brittle, and it can crack or shatter.

ENAMELWARE

Pans lined with enamel should not be used for cooking; in many areas, their use in commercial kitchens is prohibited by law. The enamel can chip or crack easily, providing good places for bacteria to grow. Also, the chemicals used to bond the enamel to the cookware can cause food poisoning if ingested.

Nonstick Coatings

Without affecting a metal's ability to conduct heat, a polymer (plastic) known as polytetrafluoroethylene (PTFE) and marketed under the trade names Teflon and Silverstone may be applied to many types of cookware. It provides a slippery, nonreactive finish

SILICONE BAKEWARE

In the 1980s, flexible silicone baking materials became available for use in the professional kitchen. Made from pure silicone or fiberglass impregnated with food-grade silicone, this light material resists sticking and can withstand temperatures from freezing to 485°F (251°C). Baking pan liners made from silicone materials rarely require greasing and are useful for baking as well as candy and chocolate work. Heat-resistant spatulas and pot holders made from silicone are effective and popular. Sheets of baking molds made from these materials are used to form individual cakes, petit fours and desserts, as well as ice cream and frozen desserts. Often these pans are called by the brand names used by their manufacturers, among them Silpats, Flexipan, Gastroflex, Silform and Elastomolds.

Small Cakes Baked in Silicone Molds

that prevents food from sticking and allows the use of less fat in cooking. Cookware with nonstick coatings requires a great deal of care, however, because the coatings can scratch, chip and blister. Do not use metal spoons or spatulas in cookware with nonstick coatings.

Common Cookware

POTS

Pots are large round vessels with straight sides and two loop handles. Available in a range of sizes based on volume, they are used on the stove top for making stocks or soups, or for boiling or simmering foods, particularly where rapid evaporation is not desired. Flat or fitted lids are available.

PANS

Pans are round vessels with one long handle and straight or sloped sides. They are usually smaller and shallower than pots. Pans are available in a range of diameters and are used for general stove top cooking, especially sautéing, frying or reducing liquids rapidly.

Stock Pot with Spigot

Sauce Pot

Saucepan

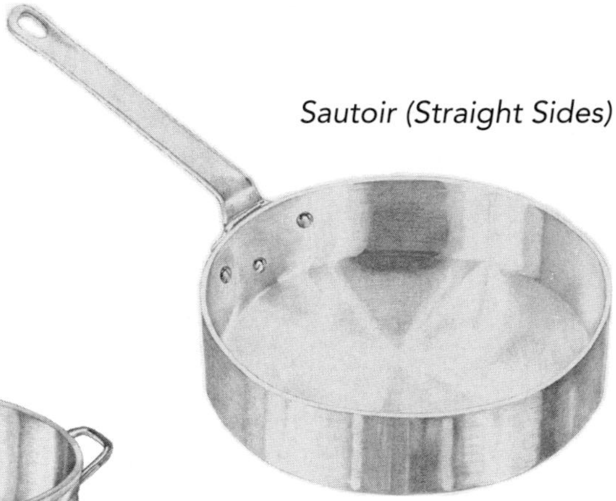

Sautoir (Straight Sides)

Rondeau/Brazier

Cast-Iron Skillet (Griswold)

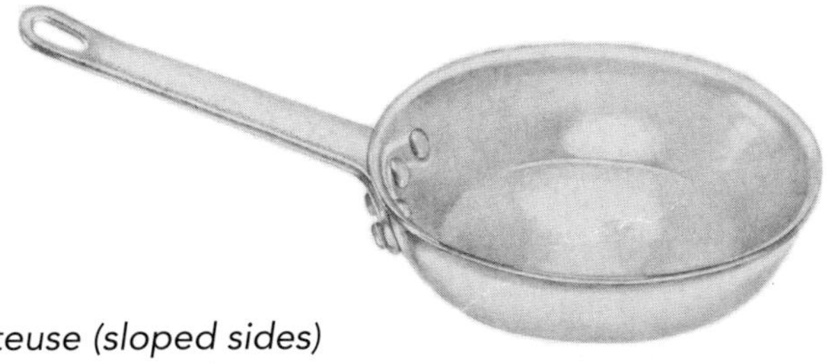

Sauteuse (sloped sides)

WOKS

Originally used to prepare Asian foods, woks are now found in many professional kitchens. Their round bottoms and curved sides diffuse heat and make it easy to toss or stir contents. Their large domed lids retain heat for steaming vegetables. Woks are useful for quickly sautéing strips of meat, simmering a whole fish or deep-frying appetizers. Stove top woks range in diameter from 12 to 30 inches; larger built-in gas or electric models are also available.

Wok

HOTEL PANS

Hotel pans (also known as steam table pans) are rectangular stainless steel pans designed to hold food for service in steam tables. Hotel pans are also used for baking, roasting or poaching inside an oven. Perforated pans useful for draining, steaming or icing down foods are also available. The standard full-size pan is 12 × 20 inches, with pans one-half, one-third, one-sixth and other fractions of this size available. Hotel pan depth is standardized at 2 inches (referred to as a "200 pan"), 4, 6 and 8 inches.

Hotel Pans

MOLDS

Pâté molds are available in several shapes and sizes and are usually made from tinned steel. Those with hinged sides, whether smooth or patterned, are more properly referred to as pâté en croûte molds. The hinged sides make it easier to remove the baked pâté. Terrine molds are traditionally lidded earthenware or enameled cast-iron containers used for baking ground meat mixtures. They may be round, oval or rectangular. **Timbale molds** are small (about 4 ounces) metal or ceramic containers used for molding aspic or baking individual portions of mousse, custard or vegetables. Their slightly flared sides allow the contents to release cleanly when inverted.

Pâté en Croûte Mold

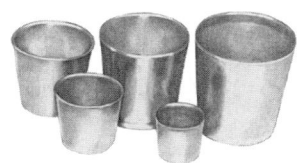

Timbales

STRAINERS AND SIEVES

Strainers and sieves are used primarily to aerate and remove impurities from dry ingredients and drain or purée cooked foods. Strainers, colanders, drum sieves, china caps and chinois are nonmechanical devices with a stainless steel mesh or screen through which food passes. The size of the mesh or screen varies from extremely fine to several millimeters wide; select the fineness best suited for the task at hand.

Colander

Round Mesh Strainer

ROMAN POTS, SOUTHERN STILLS AND CRAFT FAIRS

Lead is poisonous. Ingesting it can cause severe gastrointestinal pains, anemia and central nervous system disorders, including intelligence and memory deficits and behavioral changes.

The unwitting and dangerous consumption of lead is not limited to children eating peeling paint chips. Some historians suggest that the use of lead cookware and lead-lined storage vessels and water pipes may have caused pervasive lead poisoning among the elite of the Roman empire and thus contributed to the empire's decline. There is also ample evidence that from ancient times until just a few hundred years ago, wine was heated in lead vessels to sweeten it. This had a disastrous effect on the drinker and, for several centuries in countries throughout Europe, on the wine purveyor as well. The former could be poisoned, and the latter could be punished by death for selling adulterated wine. More recently, it was found that much of the moonshine whiskey produced in the American South contained lead in potentially toxic ranges. The source was determined to be the lead solder used in homemade stills, some of which even included old lead-containing car radiators as condensers.

Although commercially available cookware does not contain lead, be careful of imported pottery and those lovely hand-thrown pots found at craft fairs—there could be lead in the glaze.

Drum Sieve (Tamis)

Reinforced Mesh Strainer (Chinois)

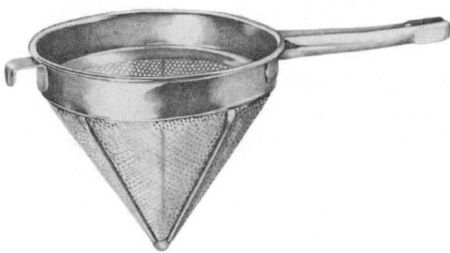

Perforated Metal Strainer (China Cap)

CHINOIS AND CHINA CAP

Both the chinois and china cap are cone-shaped metal strainers. The conical shape allows liquids to filter through small openings. The body of a chinois is made from a very fine mesh screen, while a china cap has a perforated metal body. Both are used for straining stocks and sauces, with the chinois being particularly useful for consommé. A china cap can also be used with a pestle to purée soft foods.

SKIMMER AND SPIDER

Skimmer

Both the skimmer and spider are long-handled tools used to remove foods or impurities from liquids. The flat, perforated disk of a skimmer is used for skimming stocks or removing foods from soups or stocks. The spider has a finer mesh disk, which makes it better for retrieving items from hot fat. Wooden-handled spiders are available but are less sturdy and harder to clean than all-metal designs.

CHEESECLOTH

Spider

Cheesecloth is a loosely woven cotton gauze used for straining stocks and sauces and wrapping poultry or fish for poaching. Cheesecloth is also indispensable for making sachets. Always rinse cheesecloth thoroughly before use; this removes lint and prevents the cheesecloth from absorbing other liquids.

FOOD MILL

A food mill purées and strains food at the same time. Food is placed in the hopper and a hand-crank mechanism turns a blade in the hopper against a perforated disk, forcing the food through the disk. Most models have interchangeable disks with various-sized holes. Choose a mill that can be taken apart easily for cleaning.

FLOUR SIFTER

A sifter is used for aerating, blending and removing impurities from dry ingredients such as flour, cocoa and leavening agents. The 8-cup hand-crank sifter shown here uses four curved rods to brush the contents through a curved mesh screen. The sifter should have a medium-fine screen and a comfortable handle. The French **tamis** is a drum-shaped sieve useful for sifting ingredients as well as for straining thick purées to remove lumps and seeds.

Food Mill

Flour Sifter

PROCESSING EQUIPMENT

Processing equipment includes both electrical and nonelectrical mechanical devices used to chop, purée, slice, grind or mix foods. Before using any such equipment, be sure to review its operating procedures and ask for assistance if necessary. Always turn the equipment off and disconnect the power before disassembling, cleaning or moving the appliance. Report any problems or malfunctions immediately. *Never place your hand into any machinery when the power is on. Processing equipment is powerful and can cause serious injury.*

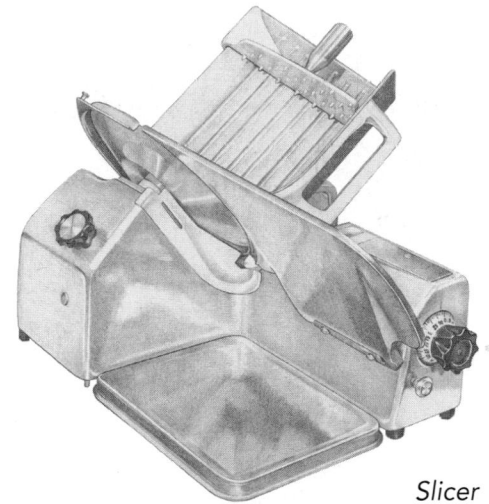

Slicer

SLICER

An electric slicer is used to cut meat, bread, cheese or raw vegetables into uniform slices. It has a circular blade that rotates at high speed. Food is placed in a carrier, then passed (manually or by an electric motor) against the blade. Slice thickness is determined by the distance between the blade and the carrier. Because of the speed with which the blade rotates, foods can be cut into extremely thin slices very quickly. An electric slicer is convenient for preparing moderate to large quantities of food, but the time required to disassemble and clean the equipment makes it impractical when slicing only a few items.

MANDOLINE

A mandoline is a manually operated slicer made of stainless steel with adjustable slicing blades. It is also used to make julienne and waffle-cut slices. Its narrow, rectangular body sits on the work counter at a 45-degree angle. Foods are passed against a blade to obtain uniform slices. It is useful for slicing small quantities of fruits or vegetables when using a large electric slicer would be unwarranted. To avoid injury, always use a hand guard or steel glove when using a mandoline.

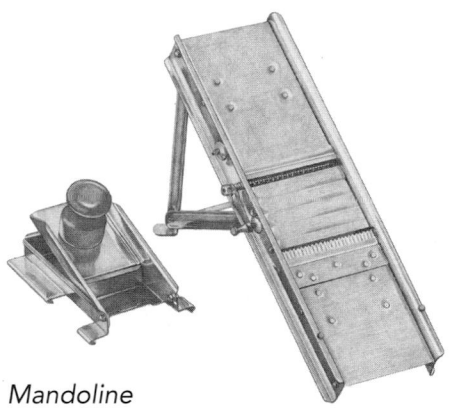

Mandoline

FOOD CHOPPER OR BUFFALO CHOPPER

This chopper is used to process moderate to large quantities of food to a uniform size, such as chopping onions or grinding bread for crumbs. The food is placed in a large bowl rotating beneath a hood, where curved blades chop it. The size of the cut depends on how long the food is left in the machine. Buffalo choppers are available in floor or tabletop models. The motor can usually be fitted with a variety of other tools such as a meat grinder or a slicer/shredder, making it even more useful.

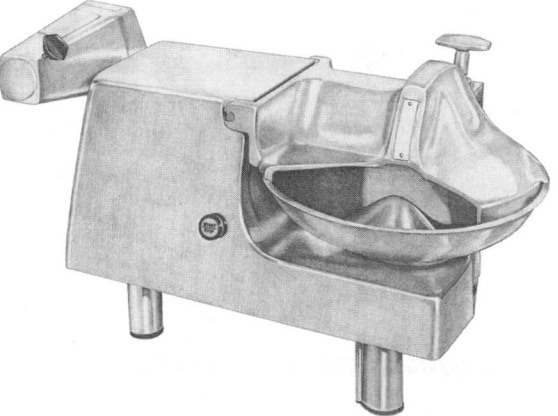

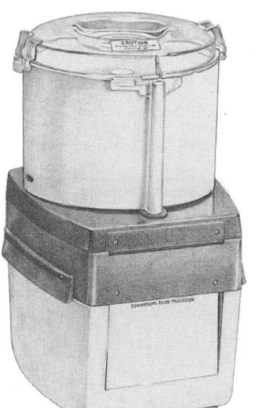

FOOD PROCESSOR

A food processor has a motor housing with a removable bowl and S-shaped blade. It is used, for example, to purée cooked foods, chop nuts, prepare compound butters and emulsify sauces. Special disks can be added that slice, shred or julienne foods. Bowl capacity and motor power vary; select a model large enough for your most common tasks.

BLENDER

Though similar in principle to a food processor, a blender has a tall, narrow food container and a four-pronged blade. Its design and whirlpool action are better for processing liquids or liquefying foods quickly. A blender is used to prepare smooth drinks, purée soups and sauces, blend batters and chop ice. A **vertical cutter/mixer** (VCM) operates like a very large, powerful blender. A VCM is usually floor-mounted and has a capacity of 15 to 80 quarts.

Food Processor

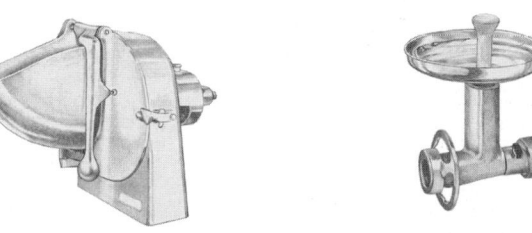

Buffalo Chopper with Slicer and Meat Grinder Attachments

Heavy-Duty Blender

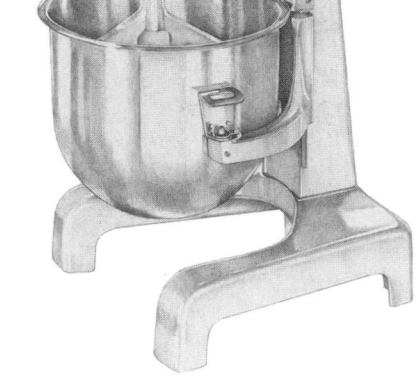

20-Quart Mixer and Attachments

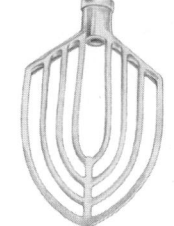

Immersion Blender

Flat Paddle

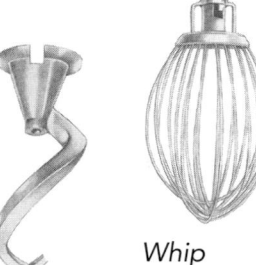

Dough Hook

Whip

IMMERSION BLENDER

An immersion blender—as well as its household counterpart called a hand blender or wand—is a long shaft fitted with a rotating four-pronged blade at the bottom. Operated by pressing a button in the handle, an immersion blender is used to purée a soft food, soup or sauce directly in the container in which it was prepared, eliminating the need to transfer the food from one container to another. This is especially useful when working with hot foods. Small cordless, rechargeable models are convenient for puréeing or mixing small quantities or beverages, but larger heavy-duty electric models are more practical in commercial kitchens.

MIXER

A vertical mixer is indispensable in the bakeshop and most kitchens. The U-shaped arms hold a metal mixing bowl in place; the selected mixing attachment fits onto the rotating head. The three common mixing attachments are the whip (used for whipping eggs or cream), the paddle (used for general mixing) and the dough hook (used for kneading bread). Most mixers have several operating speeds. Bench models range in capacity from 4.5 to 20 quarts, whereas floor mixers can hold as much as 140 quarts. Some mixers can be fitted with shredder/slicers, meat grinders, juicers or power strainers, making the equipment more versatile.

JUICER

Two types of juicers are available: reamers and extractors. **Reamers**, also known as citrus juicers, remove juice from citrus fruits. They can be manual or electric. Manual models use a lever arm to squeeze the fruit with increased pressure. They are most often used to prepare small to moderate amounts of juice for cooking or beverages. Juice extractors are electrical devices that create juice by liquefying raw fruits, vegetables and herbs. They use centrifugal force to filter out fiber and pulp.

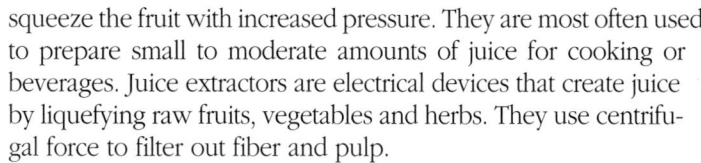

Citrus Juicer

CREAM WHIPPER

A cream whipper is designed to aerate and dispense whipped cream. It is composed of a stainless steel canister to hold the cream and a tight-fitting lid with a single-use cartridge or charger of nitrous oxide gas. Once discharged into the canister, the gas dissolves in the fat of the cream, pressurizing its contents. When dispensed, the gas turns into air bubbles and the cream expands and lightens. This tool can also be used to create and dispense cold or hot foams made from smooth and light soups, stocks or purées.

STORAGE CONTAINERS

Proper storage containers are necessary for keeping leftovers and opened packages of food safe for consumption. Proper storage can also reduce the costs incurred by waste or spoilage.

Although stainless steel pans such as hotel pans are suitable and useful for some items, the expense of stainless steel and the lack of airtight lids makes these pans impractical for general storage purposes. Aluminum containers are not recommended because the metal can react with even mildly acidic items. Glass containers are generally not allowed in commercial kitchens because of the hazards of broken glass. The most useful storage containers are those made of high-density plastic such as polyethylene and polypropylene.

Storage containers must have well-fitting lids and should be available in a variety of sizes, including some that are small enough to hold even minimal quantities of food without allowing too much exposure to oxygen. Round and square plastic containers are widely available. Flat, snap-on lids allow containers to be stacked for more efficient storage. Containers may be clear or opaque white, which helps protect light-sensitive foods. Larger containers may be fitted with handles and spigots, making them especially suited for storing stock. Some storage containers are marked with graduated measurements so that content quantity can be determined at a glance.

Large quantities of dry ingredients, such as flour, sugar and rice, can be stored in rolling bins. The bins should be seamless with rounded corners for easy cleaning. They should have well-fitting but easy-to-open lids and should move easily on well-balanced casters.

Storage Containers

HEAVY EQUIPMENT

Heavy equipment includes the gas-, electric- or steam-operated appliances used for cooking, reheating or holding foods. It also includes dishwashers and refrigeration units. These items are usually installed in a fixed location determined by the kitchen's traffic flow and space limitations.

Heavy equipment may be purchased or leased new or used. Used equipment is most often purchased in an effort to save money. Although the initial cost is generally less for used equipment, the buyer should also consider the lack of a manufacturer's warranty or dealership guarantee and how the equipment was maintained by the prior owner. Functional used equipment is satisfactory for back-of-the-house areas, but it is usually better to purchase new equipment if it will be visible to the customer. Leasing equipment may be appropriate for some operations. The cost of leasing is less than purchasing, and if something goes wrong with the equipment, the operator is generally not responsible for repairs or service charges.

STOVE TOPS

Stove tops or ranges are often the most important cooking equipment in the kitchen. They have one or more burners powered by gas or electricity. The burners may be open or covered with a cast-iron or steel plate. Open burners supply quick, direct heat that is easy to regulate. A steel plate, known as a **flat top**, supplies even but less intense heat. Although it takes longer to heat than a burner, the flat top supports heavier

Flat-Top Range

Griddle

weights and makes a larger area available for cooking. Many stoves include both flat tops and open burner arrangements.

Griddles are similar to flat tops except they are made of a thinner metal plate. Foods are usually cooked directly on the griddle's surface, not in pots or pans, which can nick or scratch the surface. The surface should be properly cleaned and conditioned after each use. Griddles are popular for short-order and fast-food-type operations.

OVENS

An oven is an enclosed space where food is cooked by being surrounded with hot, dry air. Conventional ovens are often located beneath the stove top. They have a heating element located at the unit's bottom or floor, and pans are placed on adjustable wire racks inside the oven's cavity. See Figure 4.3. Conventional ovens may also be separate, freestanding units or decks stacked one on top of the other. In stack ovens, pans are placed directly on the deck or floor and not on wire racks.

Convection ovens use internal fans to circulate the hot air. This tends to cook foods more quickly and evenly. Convection ovens are almost always freestanding units, powered by either gas or electricity. Because convection ovens cook foods more quickly, temperatures may need to be reduced by 25°F to 50°F (10°C to 20°C) from those recommended for conventional ovens.

Stack Oven

INDUCTION— A NEW HEAT WAVE

Induction cooking uses special conductive coils called inductors placed below the stove top's surface in combination with flat-bottomed cookware made of cast iron or magnetic stainless steel. The coil generates a magnetic current so that the cookware is heated rapidly with magnetic friction. Heat energy is then transferred from the cookware to the food by conduction. The cooking surface, which is made of a solid ceramic material, remains cool. Only the cookware and its contents get hot. This means that induction systems are extremely efficient with instant response time because power is directed into the cooking utensil, not the surrounding air.

Induction cooking is gaining acceptance in professional kitchens because of the speed with which foods can be heated and the ease of cleanup. Induction burners are useful in the bakeshop, where there may be only a limited need for direct-heat cooking; they are portable and maintain a safer, cooler cooking environment.

Induction Cooktop

Convection Oven

FIGURE 4.3 ▶ Gas burner and griddle with dual ovens and an overhead broiler (salamander).

WOOD-BURNING OVENS

The ancient practice of baking in a retained-heat masonry oven has been revived in recent years, with many upscale restaurants and artisan bakeries installing brick or adobe ovens for baking pizzas and breads as well as for roasting fish, poultry and vegetables. These ovens have a curved interior chamber that is usually recessed into a wall. Although gas-fired models are available, wood-firing is more traditional and provides the aromas and flavors associated with brick ovens. A wood fire is built inside the oven to heat the brick chamber. The ashes are then swept out and the food is placed on the flat oven floor. Breads and pizzas baked in direct contact with the hot masonry rise better than in a conventional oven and develop a unique crisp crust. The combination of high heat and wood smoke adds distinctive flavors to foods.

Wood-Burning Oven

MICROWAVE OVENS

Microwave ovens are electrically powered ovens used to cook or reheat foods. They are available in a range of sizes and power settings. Microwave ovens will not brown foods unless fitted with special browning elements. Microwave cooking is discussed in more detail in Chapter 9, Principles of Cooking.

BROILERS AND GRILLS

Broilers and grills are generally used to prepare meats, fish and poultry. For a grill, the heat source is beneath the rack on which the food is placed. For a broiler, the heat source is above the food. Most broilers are gas powered; grills may be gas or electric or may burn wood or charcoal. A **salamander** is a small overhead broiler primarily used to

Gas Grill

Rotisserie

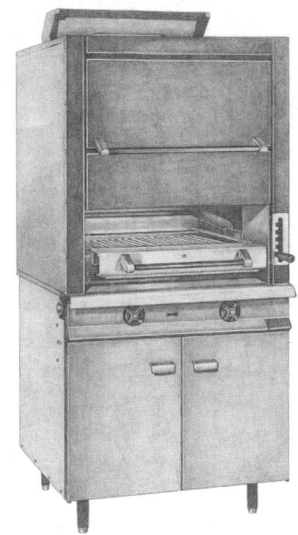

Overhead Broiler

finish or top-brown foods. See Figure 4.3. A **rotisserie** is similar to a broiler except that the food is placed on a revolving spit in front of the heat source. The unit may be open or enclosed like an oven; it is most often used for cooking poultry or meats.

TILTING SKILLETS

Tilting skillets are large, freestanding, flat-bottomed pans about 6 inches deep with an internal heating element below the pan's bottom. They are usually made of stainless steel with a cover and have a hand-crank mechanism that turns or tilts the pan to pour out the contents. Tilting skillets can be used as stockpots, braziers, fry pans, griddles or steam tables, making them one of the most versatile of commercial appliances.

STEAM KETTLES

Steam kettles (also known as steam-jacketed kettles) are similar to stockpots except they are heated from the bottom and sides by steam circulating between layers of stainless steel. The steam may be generated internally or from an outside source. Because steam heats the kettle's sides, foods cook more quickly and evenly than they would in a pot sitting on the stove top. Steam kettles are most often used for making sauces, soups, custards and stocks. Steam kettles are available in a range of sizes, from a 2-gallon tabletop model to a 100-gallon floor model. Some models have a tilting mechanism that allows the contents to be poured out; others have a spigot near the bottom through which liquids can be drained.

Steam Kettle

Tilting Skillet

STEAMERS

Pressure and convection steamers are used to cook foods rapidly and evenly, using direct contact with steam. Pressure steamers heat water above the boiling point in sealed compartments; the high temperature and sealed compartment increase the internal pressure in a range of 4 to 15 pounds per square inch. The increased pressure and temperature cook the foods rapidly. Convection steamers generate steam in an internal boiler, then release it over the foods in a cooking chamber. Both types of steamers are ideal for cooking vegetables with minimal loss of flavor or nutrients.

DEEP-FAT FRYERS

Deep-fat fryers are used to cook foods in a large amount of hot fat. Fryers are sized by the amount of fat they hold. Most commercial fryers range between 15 and 82 pounds. Fryers can be either gas or electric and are thermostatically controlled for temperatures between 200°F and 400°F (90°C and 200°C).

Deep-Fat Fryer

Convection Steamer

SPECIALIZED EQUIPMENT FOR NEW AND EMERGING CULINARY TECHNIQUES

Chefs are adopting new tools and cooking equipment to facilitate many modern and experimental cooking techniques. One of the more widely discussed new techniques is *sous vide* (French for "under vacuum"), a type of low-temperature cooking in which foods are vacuum-sealed in pouches, then cooked for an extended period in a water bath. Chefs such as Thomas Keller have discovered that this method, also known as *cook-chill*, which has been used since the 1960s for preparing cured and frozen meats, also produces tender, flavorful fresh meat, fish and seafood. The reduced oxygen environment of foods packaged under vacuum concentrates flavors and extends the shelf life of dishes prepared using this method. In addition, the temperatures for *sous vide* cooking, ranging from 125°F (51°C) to 195°F (90°C), rarely exceed the desired temperature of the finished dish, resulting in foods that are precisely cooked but not overcooked. (Food safety is ensured by cooking the foods the proper length of time at a constant temperature.)

Two essential pieces of equipment are required for sous vide cooking: a chamber vacuum machine and a thermal circulator or immersion circulator. The chamber vacuum machine allows solids and liquids to be packaged in food-grade polyethylene bags in order to seal in flavor and prevent water from touching the food to be cooked. A thermal circulator is attached to a vessel of water, where the pouched foods are then cooked in the warm flowing bath. The heating element and temperature controls on the circulator maintain the precise and constant temperatures required for *sous vide* cooking. Because foods cooked *sous vide* resemble poached or braised foods, they are often finished for service by browning conventionally in a pan or using a handheld propane torch.

Accurate temperature control and proper cooking time is essential when cooking foods *sous vide* at the low temperatures in which bacteria can thrive. The Model Food Code requires that a detailed HAACP program including time and temperature monitoring be in place in any food service operation using *sous vide* cooking methods. Before employing *sous vide* techniques in any food service operation, consult local health authorities to learn what technical training, licensing and record keeping is required.

Among the tools migrating from the chemistry laboratory to the kitchen are microscopically fine heat-resistant filters. With perforations a mere 100 microns (0.004 inch) thick, these filters can be used for clarifying stock and making clear colorless consommé. The vacuum rotary evap-

Immersion Heat Circulator and Thermal Bath

orator, a costly lab instrument used to distill mixtures, has been adapted for kitchen use to reduce liquids without applying heat and to impregnate foods with flavors. One device inspired by the science lab is the anti-griddle, which resembles a flat top on which food is frozen, not cooked. The surface of the anti-griddle, chilled to –30°F (–34°C), "sears" food with cold. Hot purées and liquids can be sealed on the outside with cold and still be warm or liquid inside.

When choosing a fryer, look for a fry tank with curved, easy-to-clean sloping sides. Some fryers have a cold zone (an area of reduced temperature) at the bottom of the fry tank to trap particles. This prevents them from burning, creating off-flavors and shortening the life of the fryer fat.

Deep-fryers usually come with steel wire baskets to hold the food during cooking. Fryer baskets are usually lowered into the fat and raised manually, although some models have automatic basket mechanisms. The most important factor when choosing a deep-fryer is **recovery time**. Recovery time is the length of time it takes the fat to return to the desired cooking temperature after food is submerged in it. When food is submerged, heat is immediately transferred to the food from the fat. This heat transfer lowers the fat's temperature. The more food added at one time, the greater the drop in the fat's temperature. If the temperature drops too much or does not return quickly to the proper cooking temperature, the food may absorb excess fat and become greasy.

REFRIGERATORS

Proper refrigeration space is an essential component of any kitchen. Many foods must be stored at low temperatures to maintain quality and safety. Most commercial refrigeration is of two types: walk-in units and reach-in or upright units.

A walk-in is a large, room-sized box capable of holding hundreds of pounds of food on adjustable shelves. A separate freezer walk-in may be positioned nearby or even inside a refrigerated walk-in.

Reach-ins may be individual units or parts of a bank of units, each with shelves approximately the size of a full sheet pan. Reach-in refrigerators and freezers are usually located throughout the kitchen to provide quick access to foods. Small units may also be placed beneath the work counters. Freezers and refrigerators are available in a wide range of sizes and door designs to suit any operation.

Other forms of commercial refrigeration include chilled drawers located beneath a work area that are just large enough to accommodate a hotel pan, and display cases used to show foods to the customer.

DISHWASHERS

Mechanical dishwashers are available to wash, rinse and sanitize dishware, glassware, cookware and utensils. Small models clean one rack of items at a time, whereas larger models can handle several racks simultaneously on a conveyor belt system. Sanitation is accomplished either with extremely hot water (180°F/82°C) or with chemicals automatically dispensed during the final rinse cycle. Any dishwashing area should be carefully organized for efficient use of equipment and employees and to prevent recontamination of clean items.

RACKS

Rolling racks are metal frames designed to hold a number of sheet trays in a space-saving manner. They are useful for storing trays of items waiting to be placed in the oven or for receiving hot pans directly from an oven.

Insulated Carrier

BUFFET EQUIPMENT

Food service operations that prepare buffets or cater off-premise events need a variety of specialized equipment to ensure that food is handled safely and efficiently and displayed appropriately. Proper temperatures must be maintained during transportation, display and service.

Insulated carriers hold food at its current temperature for a time. They are designed to hold hotel pans or sheet pans and are available with wheels for easy movement. Some are available with a spigot for serving hot or cold beverages. Any carrier should be easy to clean and of a convenient size for the space available and the type of operation.

Temperature remains a concern when arranging food on a buffet table. **Chafing dishes** are commonly used for keeping hot foods hot during service. Chafing dishes are designed so that cans of solid fuel can be placed under a deep hotel pan of hot water. Like a double boiler or bain marie, the hot water then helps maintain the temperature of food placed in a second hotel pan suspended over the first. Chafing dishes, however, should never be used to heat food. Chafing dishes are available in several sizes and shapes, but the most convenient are those based on the size of a standard hotel pan. Round, deep chafing dishes are useful for serving soups or sauces. Exteriors can be plain or ornate and made of silver, copper or stainless steel.

Chafing Dish

Roast beef, turkey, ham and other large cuts of meat are sometimes carved on a buffet in front of guests. **Heat lamps** can be used to keep these foods warm. Heat lamps are also useful for maintaining the temperature of pizza or fried foods, which may become soggy if held in a chafing dish.

Pastries, breads and cold foods can be arranged on a variety of platters, trays, baskets and serving pieces, depending on the size and style of the buffet. Some of the most elegant

Heat Lamp

and traditional serving pieces are flat display mirrors. These may be plastic or glass and are available in a wide variety of shapes and sizes. The edges should be sealed in easy-to-clean plastic to prevent chipping.

Although many of these items can be rented, operations that regularly serve buffets may prefer to invest in their own transportation and serving equipment.

SAFETY EQUIPMENT

Safety devices, many of which are required by federal, state or local law, are critical to the well-being of a food service operation although they are not used in food preparation. Failing to include safety equipment in a kitchen or failing to maintain it properly endangers workers and customers.

FIRE EXTINGUISHERS

Fire extinguishers are canisters of foam, dry chemicals (such as sodium bicarbonate or potassium bicarbonate) or pressurized water used to extinguish small fires. They must be placed within sight of and easily reached from the work areas in which fires are likely to occur. Different classes of extinguishers use different chemicals to fight different types of fires. The appropriate class must be used for the specific fire. See Table 4.2. Fire extinguishers must be recharged and checked from time to time. Be sure they have not been discharged, tampered with or otherwise damaged.

Remember the acronym **P.A.S.S.** for the four steps to follow when using any fire extinguisher:

▶ **Pull**—Pull the safety pin on the extinguisher.
▶ **Aim**—Aim the extinguisher hose at the base of the fire.
▶ **Squeeze**—Squeeze the handle to discharge the material.
▶ **Sweep**—Sweep the hose from side to side across the base of the fire.

TABLE 4.2   FIRE EXTINGUISHERS

CLASS	SYMBOL	USE
Class A		Fires involving ordinary combustibles such as wood, paper, cloth or plastic
Class B		Fires involving grease or flammable liquids such as gasoline, paint or alcohol
Class C		Fires involving electrical equipment or wiring
Class K		Fires involving cooking oils or fat and fats in commercial cooking equipment

Combination extinguishers—AB, BC and ABC—are also available.

VENTILATION SYSTEMS

Ventilation systems (also called ventilation hoods) are commonly installed over cooking equipment to remove vapors, heat and smoke. Some systems include fire extinguishing agents or sprinklers. A properly operating hood makes the kitchen more comfortable for the staff and reduces the danger of fire. The system should be designed, installed and inspected by professionals, then cleaned and maintained regularly.

FIRST-AID KITS

First-aid supplies should be stored in a clearly marked box, conspicuously located near food preparation areas. State and local laws may specify the kit's exact contents. Generally, they should include a first-aid manual, bandages, gauze dressings, adhesive tape, antiseptics, scissors, cold packs and other supplies. The kit should be checked regularly and items replaced as needed. In addition, cards with emergency telephone numbers should be placed inside the first-aid kit and near a telephone.

PROTECTIVE GEAR

All kitchens should be equipped with high quality heat-resistant gloves or pot holders to be used when handling hot pans and other equipment. In kitchens where a large quantity of shellfish is opened or a meat slicer is used, steel-mesh safety gloves may be required. Made from stainless steel woven into a fine fiber, these gloves recall medieval armor and are effective at preventing puncture or slicing wounds.

THE PROFESSIONAL KITCHEN

The kitchen is the heart of the food service operation. There, food and other items are received, stored, prepared and plated for service; dining room staff places orders, retrieves foods that are ready for service and returns dirty service items; dishes and other wares are cleaned and stored; and the chef conducts business. But commercial space is expensive, and most food service operators recognize that the greater number of customers served, the greater the revenues. Often this translates into a large dining area and small kitchen and storage facilities. Therefore, when designing a kitchen, it is important to use the space wisely so that each of its functions can be accomplished efficiently.

Kitchen design begins with a consideration of the tasks to be performed. Analyzing the menu identifies these tasks. A restaurant featuring steaks and chops, for example, will need areas to fabricate and grill meats. If it relies on commercially prepared desserts and breads, it will not need a bakeshop but will still need space to store and plate baked goods.

Once all food preparation tasks are identified, a work area for each particular task is designated. These work areas are called **work stations**. At a steak restaurant, an important work station is the broiler. If the restaurant serves fried foods, it will also need a fry station. The size and design of each work station is determined by the volume of food the operation intends to produce.

Usually work stations using the same or similar equipment for related tasks are grouped into **work sections**. See Table 4.3. (Note that work stations correspond to the kitchen brigade system discussed in Chapter 1, Professionalism.) For example, a typical full-service restaurant will have a hot-foods section that includes broiler, fry, griddle, sauté and sauce stations. The principal cooking equipment (a range, broiler, deep-fat fryer, oven, griddle and so on) will be arranged in a line under a ventilation hood. During service each work station within the hot-foods section may be staffed by a different line cook, but the proximity of the stations allows one line cook to cover more than one station if the kitchen is shorthanded or when business is slow.

When designing the work area, one must also consider what equipment and storage facilities can be placed beneath or on top of other equipment. For example, in a bakeshop, rolling storage bins for flour and sugar may be located beneath the work surface, while mixing bowls and dry ingredients are stored on shelves above. Ideally, each station should be designed so that the cook takes no more than three steps in any direction to perform all of his or her assigned station tasks.

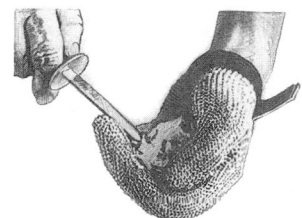

Mesh Safety Gloves

TABLE 4.3	WORK SECTIONS AND THEIR STATIONS
SECTIONS	**STATIONS**
Hot-foods section	Broiler station Fry station Griddle station Sauté/sauce station Holding
Garde-manger section	Salad greens cleaning Salad preparation Cold foods preparation Sandwich station Showpiece preparation
Bakery section	Mixing station Dough holding and proofing Dough rolling and forming Baking and cooling Dessert preparation* Frozen dessert preparation* Plating desserts*
Banquet section	Steam cooking Dry-heat cooking (roasting, broiling)
Short-order section	Holding and plating Griddle station Fry station Broiler station
Beverage section	Hot beverage station Cold beverage station Alcoholic beverage station

*These stations are sometimes found in the garde-manger section.

In addition to the work sections where the menu items are produced, a typical restaurant kitchen includes areas dedicated to the following functions:

❶ **Receiving and storing foods and other items.** Most kitchens will need freezer, refrigerator and dry-goods storage facilities. Each should have proper temperature, humidity and light controls in order to properly and safely maintain the stored items. Typically there is a combination of central and section storage. For example, up to 100 pounds of flour and sugar can be stored in rolling bins under a worktable in the bakeshop, while several hundreds of pounds more remain in a central dry-goods area. Similarly, one box of salt can be stored near the hot line for immediate use, while the remainder of the case is stored in a central dry-goods area. Additional storage space will be needed for cleaning and paper supplies, dishes and other service ware.

❷ **Washing dishes and other equipment.** These dish- and equipment-washing facilities should have their own sinks. Food preparation and hand-washing sinks must be separate.

❸ **Employee use.** Restrooms, locker facilities and an office are also found in most food service facilities.

The guiding principle behind a good kitchen design is to maximize the flow of goods and staff from one area to the next and within each area itself. Maximizing flow creates an efficient work environment and helps reduce preparation and service time.

ALEXIS SOYER (1809–1858)

The father of the contemporary celebrity chef was Alexis Soyer, a Frenchman whose tragically short working life was spent mostly in London. He was a flamboyant, talented and egocentric showman. He was also a renowned chef, restaurateur, social activist, author, purveyor of prepared foods and inventor.

In 1831, Soyer left his thriving catering business and restaurant in Paris for London. (A scandal was rumored to be behind his sudden departure.) There he quickly established a reputation as a talented chef in the latest French fashion. By 1838, he was employed at a gentlemen's club called the Reform. Able to assist in planning the club's new kitchen facility, Soyer installed the most modern equipment: gas ovens with temperature controls, a steam-driven mechanical spit and a storage locker cooled by running water. From this modern kitchen he produced his signature dish: lamb chops Reform.

The Reform was founded by members of the Liberal party, a political party interested in social reform. Their chef soon joined the party ranks. He developed recipes for inexpensive, nutritious soups for the working class and in 1847 went to Ireland and opened soup kitchens to feed those who were starving as a result of the potato famine.

His most important writings reflect his interests in good food for the masses. The intended audience for *The Modern Housewife* (1849) was the middle class; the growing urban working class was the intended audience for his second book, *A Schilling Cookery for the People* (1855).

Courtesy of Barbara Wheaton

In 1851, Soyer opened his own lavishly decorated and expensively equipped restaurant called the Gastronomic Symposium of All Nations. It closed shortly thereafter, in part because of Soyer's debts, in part because he lost his operating license as a result of the rowdiness in the restaurant's American-style bar, at which customers were publicly served cocktails for the first time in London.

In addition to cooking and writing, Soyer created and marketed several prepared food items: Soyer's Sauce, Soyer's Nectar and Soyer's Relish. He was also fascinated with kitchen gadgets and invented several, including a sink stopper, jelly mold, egg cooker and coffeepot. The most notable, however, was a portable "Magic Stove" weighing less than 4 pounds, similar to a modern chafing dish. Soyer's final triumph was in the Crimean War (1854–1857). He developed army rations, reorganized field and hospital kitchens and introduced one of his last inventions, the campaign stove. Portable, efficient and requiring little fuel, it was used by the British army for the next 90 years.

---

1. What is NSF International? What is its significance with regard to commercial kitchen equipment?

2. List the parts of a chef's knife and describe the knife's construction.

3. List six materials used to make commercial cookware and describe the advantages and disadvantages of each.

4. Describe six pieces of equipment that can be used to slice or chop foods.

5. List four classes of fire extinguishers. For each one, describe its designating symbol and identify the type or types of fire it should be used to extinguish.

6. Explain the relationship between work sections and work stations and the kitchen brigade system discussed in Chapter 1, Professionalism.

7. Use the Internet to locate vendors, obtain specifications and compare warranties and prices for a piece of commercial kitchen equipment. **WWW**

8. Research information on selecting and installing a wood-burning oven in a commercial kitchen.

QUESTIONS FOR DISCUSSION

Terms to Know

NSF	conduction
knife	gauge
construction	calibrate
tang	convection oven
bolster	recovery time
whetstone	P.A.S.S.
tare	work stations
portioning	work sections

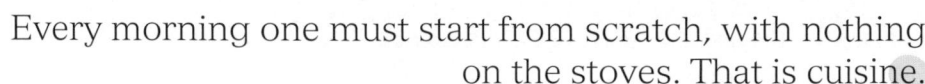

> "Every morning one must start from scratch, with nothing on the stoves. That is cuisine."
>
> —FERNAND POINT, FRENCH RESTAURATEUR (1897–1955)

CHAPTER FIVE

KNIFE SKILLS

After studying this chapter, you will be able to:

- care for knives properly
- use knives properly
- cut foods into a variety of classic shapes

EVERY PROFESSIONAL MUST BECOME SKILLED in the use of certain tools. The professional chef is no exception. One of the most important tools the student chef must master is the knife. Good knife skills are critical to a chef's success because the knife is the most commonly used tool in the kitchen. Every chef spends countless hours slicing, dicing, mincing and chopping. Learning to perform these tasks safely and efficiently is an essential part of a student's training.

At first, professional knives may feel large and awkward and the techniques discussed in this chapter may not seem all that efficient. But as students become familiar with knives and practice their knife skills, using knives correctly will become second nature.

Knives are identified in Chapter 4, Tools and Equipment. Here we show how they are used to cut vegetables. The techniques presented, however, can be used for almost any food that holds its shape when cut. Knife skills for butchering and fabricating meat, poultry, fish and shellfish are discussed in Chapter 12, Principles of Meat Cookery, through Chapter 19, Fish and Shellfish.

A note about language: Many of the classic cuts are known by their French names: *julienne*, for example. Although these words are nouns and entered the English language as nouns (for example, a julienne of carrot), they are also used as verbs (to julienne a carrot) and adjectives (julienned carrots).

USING YOUR KNIFE SAFELY

The first rule of knife safety is to think about what you are doing. Other basic rules of knife safety are as follows:

1. Use the correct knife for the task at hand.
2. Always cut away from yourself.
3. Always cut on a cutting board. Do not cut on glass, marble or metal.
4. Place a damp towel underneath the cutting board to keep it from sliding as you cut.
5. Keep knives sharp; a dull knife is more dangerous than a sharp one.
6. When carrying a knife, hold it point down, parallel and close to your leg as you walk.
7. A falling knife has no handle. Do not attempt to catch a falling knife; step back and allow it to fall.
8. Never leave a knife in a sink of water; anyone reaching into the sink could be injured or the knife could be dented by pots or other utensils.

CARING FOR YOUR KNIFE

Knife Sharpening

A sharpening stone called a **whetstone** is used to put an edge on a dull knife blade. To use a whetstone, place the heel of the blade against the whetstone at a 20-degree angle.

Keeping that angle, press down on the blade while pushing it away from you in one long arc, as if to slice off a thin piece of the stone. The entire length of the blade should come in contact with the stone during each sweep. Repeat the procedure on both sides of the blade until it is sufficiently sharp. With a triple-faced stone, such as that shown here, you progress from the coarsest to the finest surface. Any whetstone can be moistened with either water or mineral oil, but not both. Do not use vegetable oil on a whetstone because it will soon become rancid and gummy.

A **steel** does not sharpen a knife. Rather, it is used to hone or straighten the blade immediately after and between sharpenings. To use a steel, place the blade against the steel at a 20-degree angle. Then draw the blade along the entire length of the steel. Repeat the technique several times on each side of the blade.

Washing and Storing Knives

Proper sanitation of knives is essential to prevent cross-contamination. Always sanitize, rinse and dry knives by hand immediately after each use. Do not wash knives in commercial dishwashers. The heat and harsh chemicals can damage the edge and the handle. In addition, the knife could injure an unsuspecting worker if left in a sink full of water.

To prevent dulling their blades, store knives so that their blades never touch other knives or tools. Slotted knife holders or magnetized strips can be wall-mounted near work stations. The portable knife kit, made from flexible washable material, is designed to hold each knife in an individual protective sleeve.

GRIPPING YOUR KNIFE

There are several different ways to grip a knife. Use the grip that is most comfortable for you or the one dictated by the job at hand. Whichever grip you use should be firm but not so tight that your hand becomes tired. Gripping styles are shown here.

When sharpening a knife against a three-sided whetstone, go from the coarsest to the finest surface.

Honing a knife against a steel straightens the blade between sharpenings.

The most common grip: Hold the handle with three fingers while gripping the blade between the thumb and index finger.

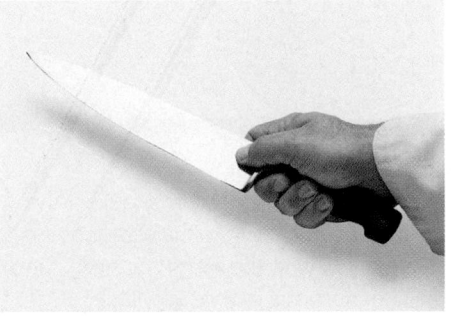

A variation on the most common grip: Grip the handle with four fingers and place the thumb on the front of the handle.

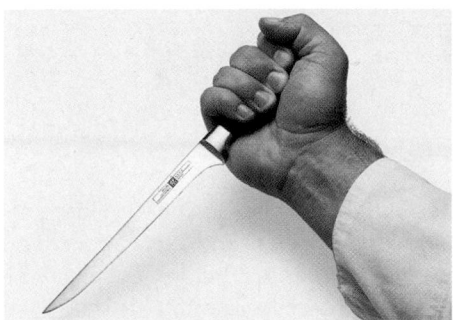

The underhand grip for a rigid boning knife: Grip the handle in a fist with four fingers and thumb. This grip allows you to use the knife tip to cut around joints and separate flesh from bone when boning meat and poultry.

CONTROLLING YOUR KNIFE

To safely produce even cuts, you must control (or guide) your knife with one hand and hold the item being cut with the other. Always allow the blade's sharp edge to do the cutting. Never force the blade through the item being cut. Use smooth, even strokes. Using a dull knife or excessive force with any knife produces, at best, poor results and, at worst, a significant safety risk. Cutting without using your hand as a guide may also be dangerous. Two safe cutting methods that produce good results are shown here.

Gripping Knives: Method A

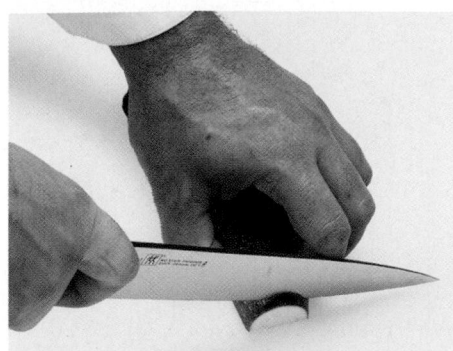

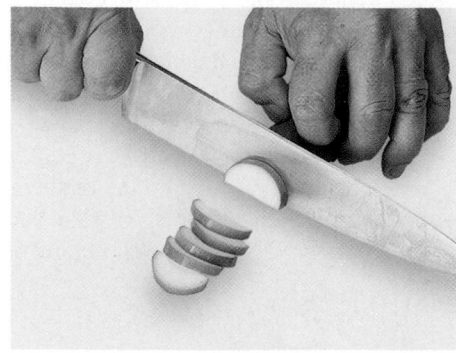

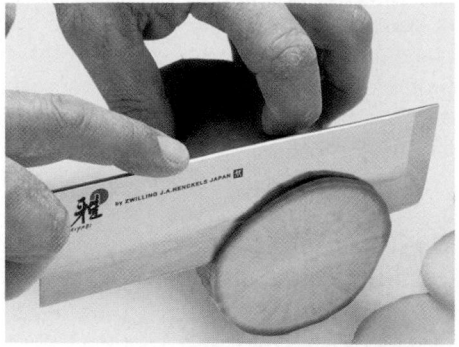

❶ Keeping your fingertips curled back, grip the item being cut with three fingertips and your thumb. Hold the knife in the other hand. While keeping the knife's tip on the cutting board, lift the heel of the knife.

❷ Using the second joint of your index finger as a guide, cut a slice using a smooth, even, downward stroke. Adjust the position of the guiding finger after each slice to produce slices of equal size. After a few cuts, slide your fingertips and thumb down the length of the item and continue slicing. For this slicing technique, the knife's tip acts as the fulcrum.

❸ An index finger placed on top of the blade steadies a traditional Japanese knife when slicing using Method A.

Gripping Knives: Method B

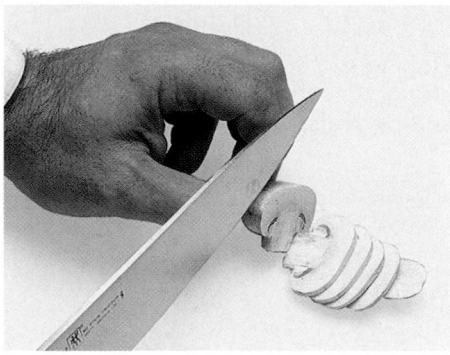

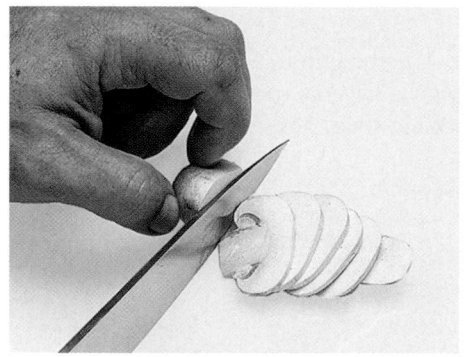

❶ Grip the item as described in Method A. Using the second joint of your index finger as a guide, lift the knife's tip and slice by drawing the knife slightly back toward you and down through the item, cutting the item to the desired thickness.

❷ The motion of the knife should come almost entirely from the wrist, not the elbow. Allow the weight of the knife to do most of the work; very little downward pressure needs to be applied to the knife. For this slicing technique, your wrist should act as the fulcrum.

CUTTING WITH YOUR KNIFE

A knife is used to shape an item and reduce its size. Uniformity of size and shape ensures even cooking and enhances the appearance of the finished product. Items are shaped by slicing, chopping, dicing, mincing and other special cutting techniques.

Slicing

To slice is to cut an item into relatively broad, thin pieces. Slices may be either the finished cut or the first step in producing other cuts. Slicing is typically used to create three specialty cuts: chiffonade, rondelle and diagonal. Slicing skills are also used to produce oblique or roll cuts and lozenges.

A **chiffonade** is a preparation of finely sliced or shredded leafy vegetables used as a garnish or a base under cold presentations. As shown here, slicing spinach en chiffonade is a relatively simple process.

chiffonade (chef-fon-nahd) to finely slice or shred leafy vegetables or herbs

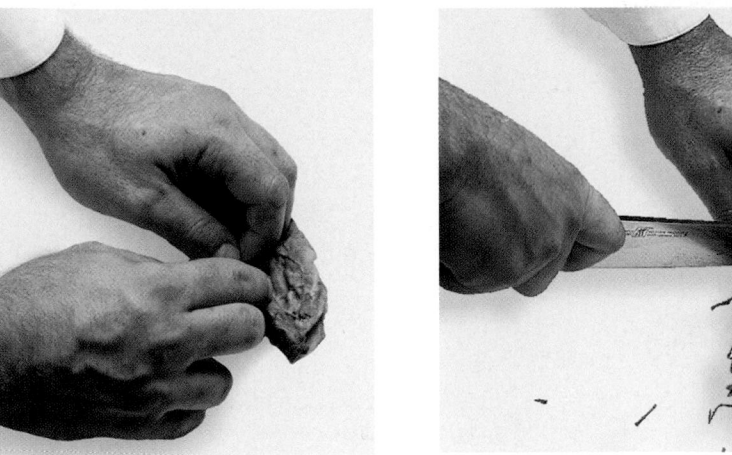

❶ Wash and destem the leaves as necessary. Stack several leaves on top of each other and roll them tightly like a cigar.

❷ Make fine slices across the leaves while holding the leaf roll tightly.

As seen here, **rondelles** or **rounds** are easily made disk-shaped slices of cylindrical vegetables or fruits.

rondelles (ron-dellz) disk-shaped slices

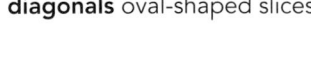

Peel the item (if desired) and place it on a cutting board. Make even slices perpendicular to the item being cut.

Diagonals or bias cuts are elongated or oval-shaped slices of cylindrical vegetables or fruits. They are produced with a cut similar to that used to cut rondelles except that the knife is held at an angle to the item being cut.

diagonals oval-shaped slices

Peel the item (if desired) and place it on a cutting board. Position the knife at the desired angle to the item being cut and slice it evenly.

oblique cuts (oh-bleek) small pieces with two angle-cut sides

Oblique-cut or **roll-cut** items are small pieces with two angle-cut sides. It is a relatively simple cut most often used on carrots and parsnips.

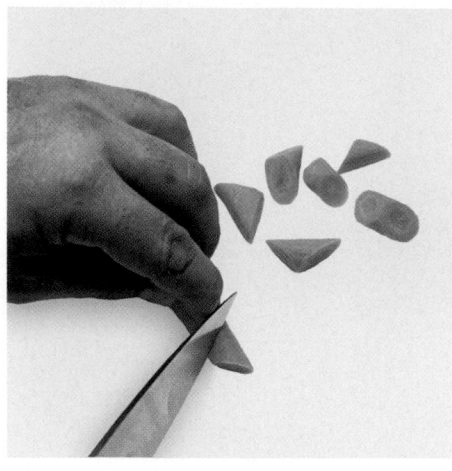

Place the peeled item on a cutting board. Holding the knife at a 45-degree angle, make the first cut. Roll the item a half turn, keeping the knife at the same angle, and make another cut. The result is a wedge-shaped piece with two angled sides.

lozenges diamond-shaped pieces, usually of firm vegetables

Lozenges are diamond-shaped cuts prepared from firm vegetables such as carrots, turnips, rutabagas and potatoes.

❶ Slice the item into long slices of the desired thickness. Then cut the slices into strips of the desired width.

❷ Cut the strips at an angle to produce diamond shapes.

HORIZONTAL SLICING

To horizontal slice is to **butterfly** or cut a pocket into meats, poultry or fish. It is also a method of cutting used to thinly slice soft vegetables.

butterfly to slice boneless meat, poultry or fish nearly in half lengthwise so that it spreads open like a book

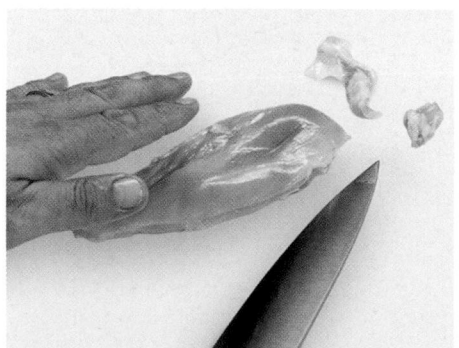

❶ With your hand opened and your fingers arched upward, hold the item to be cut firmly in the center of your palm.

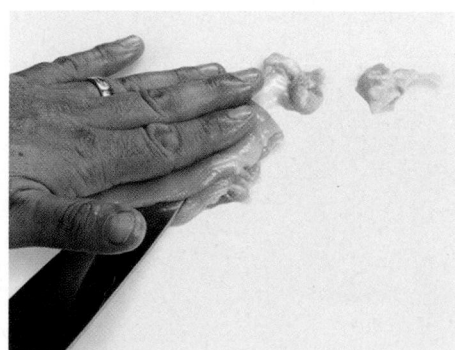

❷ Holding the knife parallel to the table, slice a pocket to the desired depth, or cut through the item completely.

Chopping

To **chop** is to cut an item into small pieces when uniformity of size and shape is neither necessary (for example, coarsely chopped onions for a mirepoix that will be removed from the stock before service) nor feasible (for example, parsley).

COARSE CHOPPING

Coarse chopping does not mean carelessly hacking up food. Rather, the procedure is identical to that used for slicing but without the emphasis on uniformity. Coarsely chopped pieces should measure approximately ¾ inch × ¾ inch × ¾ inch (2 cm × 2 cm × 2 cm).

chop to cut into pieces when uniformity of size and shape is not important

Grip the knife as for slicing. Hold the item being chopped with your other hand. It may not be necessary to use your finger as a guide because uniformity is not crucial.

CHOPPING PARSLEY AND SIMILAR FOODS

Parsley can be cut very coarsely or very finely. As shown here, it is easy to chop parsley and similar foods properly regardless of the desired fineness.

❶ Wash the parsley in cold water; drain well. Remove the parsley sprigs from the stems.

❷ Grip the knife in one hand. With the other hand spread flat, hold the knife's tip on the cutting board. Keeping the knife's tip on the board, chop the parsley sprigs by rocking the curved blade of the knife up and down while moving the knife back and forth over the parsley.

❸ Place the chopped parsley in a clean kitchen towel or a double layer of cheesecloth. Rinse it under cold water and squeeze out as much water as possible. The chopped parsley should be dry and fluffy.

CHOPPING GARLIC

A daily chore in many food service facilities, peeling and chopping garlic is a simple job made easy with the procedure shown here.

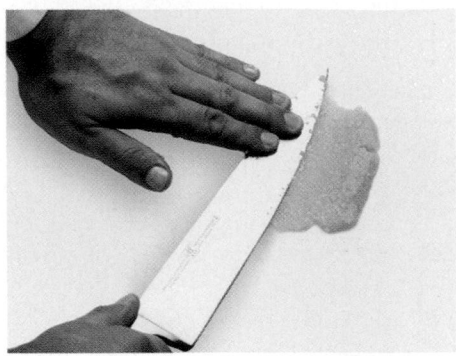

❶ Break the head of garlic into individual cloves with your hands. Lightly crush the cloves using the flat edge of a chef's knife or a mallet. They will break open and the peel can be separated easily from the garlic flesh.

❷ With a flat hand, hold the knife's tip on the cutting board. Using a rocking motion, chop the garlic cloves to the desired size. Garlic is usually chopped very finely.

❸ Garlic paste can be made by first finely chopping the garlic and then turning the knife on an angle and repeatedly dragging the edge of the knife along the cutting board, mashing the garlic.

dice to cut into cubes with six equal-sized sides

Cutting Sticks and Dicing

To **dice** is to cut an item into cubes. The techniques described here are most often used when uniformity of size and shape is important (for example, julienned carrots for a salad or brunoised vegetables for a garnish).

Before an item can be diced, it must be cut into sticks such as juliennes and bâtonnets. These sticks are then reduced through dicing into the classic cuts known as brunoise, small dice, medium dice, large dice and paysanne. Although most cooks have some notion of what size and shape "small diced" potatoes or julienne carrots may be, there are specific sizes and shapes for these cuts. They are as follows:

Julienne—(ju-lee-en) a stick-shaped item with dimensions of ⅛ inch × ⅛ inch × 2 inches (3 mm × 3 mm × 5 cm). When used with potatoes, this cut is sometimes referred to as an allumette (al-yoo-meht). A fine julienne has dimensions of ⅟₁₆ inch × ⅟₁₆ inch × 2 inches (1.5 mm × 1.5 mm × 5 cm).

Bâtonnet—(bah-toh-nay) a stick-shaped item with dimensions of ¼ inch × ¼ inch × 2 inches (6 mm × 6 mm × 5 cm).

Brunoise—(broo-nwaz) a cube-shaped item with dimensions of ⅛ inch × ⅛ inch × ⅛ inch (3 mm × 3 mm × 3 mm). A ⅟₁₆-inch (1.5-mm) cube is referred to as a fine brunoise.

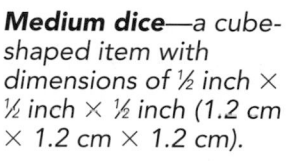

Medium dice—a cube-shaped item with dimensions of ½ inch × ½ inch × ½ inch (1.2 cm × 1.2 cm × 1.2 cm).

Small dice—a cube-shaped item with dimensions of ¼ inch × ¼ inch × ¼ inch (6 mm × 6 mm × 6 mm).

Large dice—a cube-shaped item with dimensions of ¾ inch × ¾ inch × ¾ inch (2 cm × 2 cm × 2 cm).

Paysanne—(pahy-sahn) a flat, square, round or triangular item with dimensions of ½ inch × ½ inch × ⅛ inch (1.2 cm × 1.2 cm × 3 mm).

CUTTING JULIENNE AND BÂTONNET

Julienne and bâtonnet are matchstick-shaped cuts prepared using the same procedure as cutting sticks for dicing.

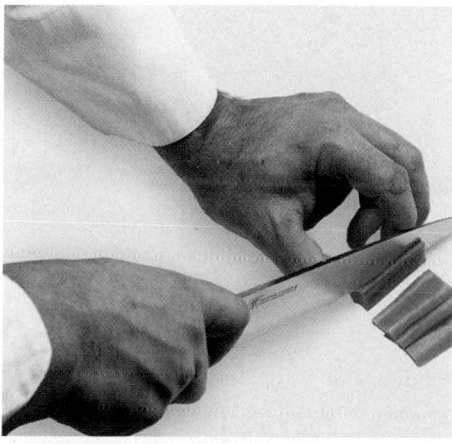

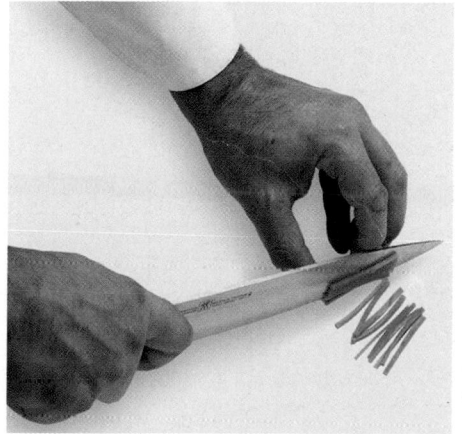

❶ Peel the item (if desired) and square off the sides. Trim the item so that the slices cut from it will be the proper length. Cut even slices of the desired thickness, ⅛ inch (3 mm) for julienne or ¼ inch (6 mm) for bâtonnet.

❷ Stack the slices and cut them evenly into sticks that are the same thickness as the slices.

Cutting paysanne from a ½-inch × ½-inch (6-mm × 6-mm) stick.

CUTTING BRUNOISE AND SMALL, MEDIUM AND LARGE DICE

Brunoise as well as small, medium and large dice are made by first cutting the item into sticks following the procedure for cutting julienne or bâtonnet, then making cuts perpendicular to the length of the sticks to produce small cubes. Making a ⅛-inch (3-mm) cut perpendicular to the length of a julienne produces a brunoise. Similarly, a fine julienne (¹⁄₁₆ inch × ¹⁄₁₆ inch × 2 inches) is used to produce a fine brunoise. Making a ¼-inch (6-mm) cut perpendicular to the length of a bâtonnet produces a small dice. A ½-inch (1.2-cm) cut from a ½-inch (1.2-cm) stick produces a medium dice, and a ¾-inch (1.8-cm) cut from a ¾-inch (1.8-cm) stick produces a large dice.

CUTTING PAYSANNE

Paysanne is a classic vegetable cut for garnishing soups and other dishes. It could be described as a very thin ½-inch cube. It is produced by following the procedures for dicing, but in the final step the ½-inch × ½-inch (1.2-cm × 1.2-cm) sticks are cut into slices ⅛-inch (3 mm) thick. The term *paysanne* is also used to refer to similarly sized round or triangular pieces.

DICING AN ONION

Onions are easily peeled and diced to any size desired using the procedure shown here.

❶ Using a paring knife, remove the stem end. Trim the root end but leave it nearly intact (this helps prevent the onion from falling apart while dicing). Peel away the outer skin; be careful not to remove and waste too much onion.

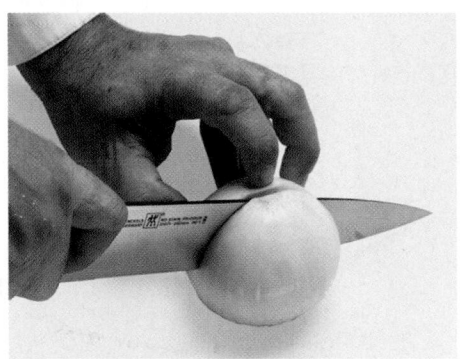

❷ Cut the onion in half through the stem and root. Place the cut side down on the cutting board.

❸ Cut parallel slices of the desired thickness vertically through the onion from the root toward the stem end without cutting completely through the root end.

❹ Make a single horizontal cut on a small onion or two horizontal cuts on a large onion through the width of the onion, again without cutting through the root end.

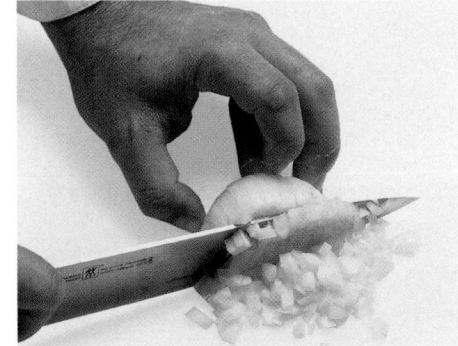

❺ Turn the onion and cut slices perpendicular to the other slices to produce diced onion.

Mincing

To **mince** is to cut an item into very small pieces. The terms *finely chopped* and *minced* are often used interchangeably and are most often used when referring to garlic, shallots, herbs and other foods that do not have to be uniform in shape.

mince to cut into very small pieces when uniformity of shape is not important

MINCING SHALLOTS

The procedure for mincing shallots is shown here.

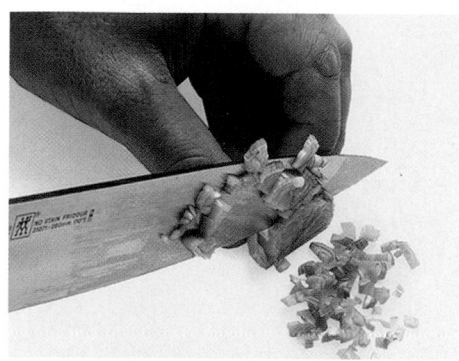

❶ Peel and dice the shallots, following the procedure for peeling and dicing an onion.

❷ With a flat hand, hold the knife's tip on the cutting board. Using a rocking motion, mince the shallots with the heel of the knife.

Tourner

Tourner (toor-nay; "to turn" in French) is a cutting technique that results in a football-shaped finished product with seven equal sides and flat ends. The size of the finished product may vary, the most common being 2 inches (5 cm) long and 1 to 1½ inches (2.5 to 3.5 cm) in diameter. This is a more complicated procedure than other cuts, and it takes considerable practice to produce good, consistent results.

tourner (toor-nay) to cut into football-shaped pieces with seven equal sides and blunt ends

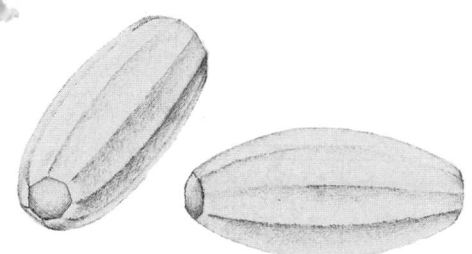

❶ Cut the item being "turned" into pieces 2 inches (5 cm) × ¾ to 1 inch (2 to 2.5 cm). Each piece should have flat ends. (Potatoes, turnips and beets may be cut into as many as six or eight pieces; carrots can simply be cut into 2-inch lengths.) Peeling is optional because in most cases the item's entire surface area is trimmed away.

❷ Holding the item between the thumb and forefinger, use a tourné knife or a paring knife to cut seven curved sides on the item, creating a flat-ended, football-shaped product.

parisienne (pah-ree-zee-en) spheres of fruits or vegetables cut with a small melon ball cutter

Parisiennes

A melon ball cutter or Parisienne scoop can be used to cut fruits and vegetables into uniform spheres, or **Parisiennes**. Small balls or spheres of fresh melon can be used in fruit salad, while tiny spheres of carrot, turnip, squash and so on can be used as a side dish or to garnish soup or an entrée. Melon ball cutters are available in a range of sizes, the smallest of which has an approximately ⅜-inch (9-mm) diameter and is known as a Parisienne (or Parisian) scoop.

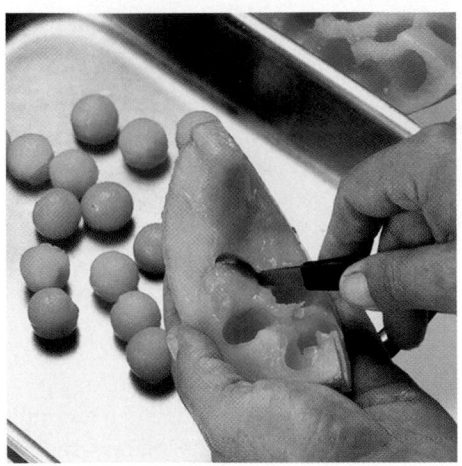

❶ Cut each scoop with a pressing and twisting motion.

❷ Make the cuts as close together as possible in order to minimize trim loss.

Using a Mandoline

gaufrette (goh-freht) a thin lattice or waffle-textured slice of vegetable cut on a mandoline

The mandoline is a nonmechanical cutting tool. It does jobs that can be done with a chef's knife, such as very thinly sliced apples or large quantities of julienned vegetables, quickly, easily, and very accurately. It can also produce cuts such as a ridged slice or **gaufrette** that cannot be done with a conventional chef's knife.

When using the mandoline, always use the guard or a steel-mesh glove to protect your hand.

❶ To use a mandoline, position the legs and set the blade to the desired shape and thickness.

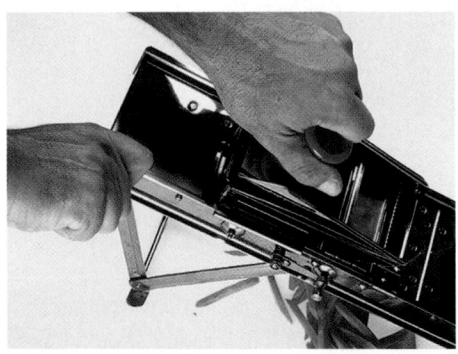

❷ Slide the guard into place.

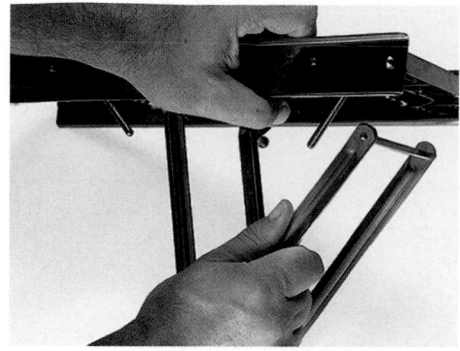

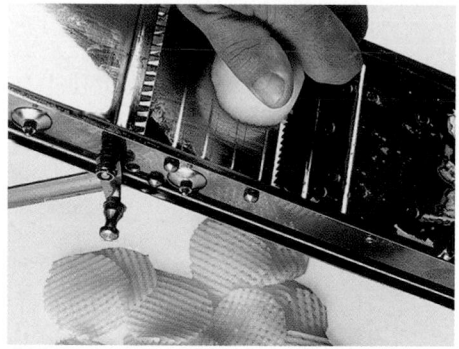

③ To slice, slide the item against the blade with a single, smooth stroke.

④ To cut gaufrette, select the ridged blade and set it to the desired thickness. Make the first slice, turn the item 60 to 90 degrees and make a second slice. Turn the item back to the original position and make another slice, and so on.

QUESTIONS FOR DISCUSSION

① Explain the step-by-step procedures for sharpening a knife using a three-sided whetstone.

② What is the purpose of a steel? How is it used?

③ Why is it necessary to cut vegetables into uniform shapes and sizes?

④ Describe the following cutting procedures: slicing, chopping and dicing.

⑤ Identify the dimensions of the following cuts: julienne, bâtonnet, brunoise, small dice, medium dice, large dice and paysanne.

⑥ Describe the procedure for making tournéed vegetables.

⑦ Describe three preparations for which a mandoline would be useful.

⑧ A large number of vendors sell professional-quality knives through their Web sites. What are the advantages and disadvantages of buying knives from an online source? ᴡᴡᴡ

Terms to Know

sharpening	chop
whetstone	dice
steel	julienne
grip	bâtonnet
uniformity	brunoise
oblique cut	payasanne
roll cut	mince
chiffonade	tourner
rondelle	parisienne
diagonal	gaufrette
butterfly	

CHAPTER SIX

FLAVORS AND FLAVORINGS

IT IS THE CHEF'S ROLE TO consistently present well-flavored foods—to excite the consumer's brain and palate. This can be accomplished by an act as simple as sprinkling a bit of salt over a ripe watermelon to enhance the melon's natural sweetness or as complicated as using a long-simmered stock made from wild mushrooms to enrich a sauce flavored with herbs and wine. In either case, the chef must understand how to flavor foods and be able to recognize flavoring ingredients and know how to use them. This chapter looks at the sense of taste and smell and the flavoring ingredients used in the professional kitchen to enhance foods. Flavorings—the herbs, spices, salt, oils, vinegars, condiments, wines and other alcoholic beverages typically used to create, enhance or alter the natural flavors of a dish—are featured. Flavorings used primarily for baked goods and desserts are discussed in Chapter 29, Principles of the Bakeshop.

FLAVORS

From the simplest grunt of pleasure upon biting into a chunk of grilled steak to the most sophisticated discourse on the fruity top notes of a full-bodied Cabernet Sauvignon, people have long attempted to describe the flavors of food. This is done by describing physical perceptions ("it tastes sugary" or "it feels greasy") or the recognition of a flavor ("I can sense the rosemary" or "there is a hint of strawberries"). In either case, the terms *flavor* and *taste* are often confused. Although often used interchangeably, they are not synonymous.

flavor an identifiable or distinctive quality of a food, drink or other substance perceived with the combined senses of taste, touch and smell

taste the sensations, as interpreted by the brain, of what we detect when food, drink or other substances come in contact with our taste buds

mouthfeel the sensation created in the mouth by a combination of a food's taste, smell, texture and temperature

aroma the sensations, as interpreted by the brain, of what we detect when a substance comes in contact with sense receptors in the nose

palate (1) the complex of smell, taste and touch receptors that contribute to a person's ability to recognize and appreciate flavors; (2) the range of an individual's recognition and appreciation of flavors

Flavor is a combination of the tastes, aromas and other sensations caused by the presence of a foreign substance in the mouth. **Tastes** are the sensations we detect when a substance comes in contact with the taste buds on the tongue (sweet, sour, salt, bitter and umami). Some substances irritate other nerves on the tongue or embedded in the fleshy areas of the mouth. These nerves respond to sensations of pain, heat or cold, or sensations our brain interprets as spiciness, pungency or astringency. **Mouthfeel** refers to the sensation created in the mouth by a combination of a food's taste, smell, texture and temperature. **Aromas** are the odors that enter the nose or float up through the back of the mouth to activate smell receptors in the nose. Whenever a particular taste, sensation and/or aroma is detected, a set of neurons in the brain is excited and, with experience, we learn to recognize these patterns as the flavor of bananas, chocolate, grilled lamb or sour milk. Each person has a unique ability to recognize and appreciate thousands of these patterns. This compendium of flavors and the ability to recognize them is sometimes referred to as the **palate**.

Tastes: Sweet, Sour, Salty, Bitter and Now Umami

Over the centuries, various cultures have developed complex philosophies based, in part, on the basic tastes they found in the foods they ate. For example, as early as 1000 B.C.E., the Chinese were describing the five-taste scheme that they still adhere to today. For them, each of the basic tastes—sweet, sour, salty, bitter and pungent/hot/spicy—is associated with a vital organ of the body, a certain season, a specific element of nature, or an astrological sign. Maintaining the proper balance of tastes in a dish or during a meal assists in the maintenance of good health and good fortune.

About the same time, in what is now India, the practice of ayurvedic medicine was developing. Indians recognized six tastes (and still do): sweet, sour, salty, spicy/

pungent, bitter and astringent. Based on the tastes of various herbs and spices, practitioners of ayurvedic medicine associate them with specific vital organs or bodily systems. Indian cooks attempt to create dishes with a balance of all six tastes, in part to encourage good health.

As the understanding of the human body evolved, the definition of taste came to be based more on science than on a balancing of elements. Today, taste is defined as the sensations detected when substances come in contact with the taste buds on the tongue, a process described more fully in the sidebar on page 94. For many years, western cultures have identified four tastes:

Sweet—For most people, sweetness is the most pleasurable and often sought-after taste, although, ironically, the fewer sweet-tasting foods we consume, the more enhanced our ability to recognize sweetness becomes. A food's sweetness comes from the naturally occurring sugars it contains (for example, sucrose and fructose) or sweeteners added to it. This sweetness can sometimes be enhanced by adding a small amount of a sour, bitter or salty taste. Adding too much sourness, bitterness or saltiness, however, will lessen our perception of the food's sweetness.

Sour—Considered the opposite of sweet, a sour taste is found in acidic foods and, like sweetness, can vary greatly in intensity. Many foods with a dominant sour taste, such as red currants or sour cream, also contain a slight sweetness. Often a sour taste can be improved by adding a little sweetness or negated by adding a large amount of a sweet ingredient.

Salty—With the notable exception of oysters and other shellfish and seaweed, the presence of a salty taste in a food is the result of the cook's decision to add the mineral sodium chloride, known as salt, or to use a previously salted ingredient such as salt-cured fish or soy sauce. Salt helps finish a dish, heightening or enhancing its other flavors. Dishes that lack salt often taste flat. Like the taste of sweetness, the less salt consumed on a regular basis, the more saltiness we can detect in foods.

Bitter—Although the bitter taste caused by alkaloids and other organic substances may occasionally be appreciated, such as when tasting beer, dark chocolate, fermented cheese or coffee, a bitter-flavored ingredient that is not balanced by sour or salty flavors is generally disliked. Bitter is an acquired taste in all cultures. The natural human aversion to bitterness is believed to function as a survival mechanism, warning us of inedible or toxic foods. Many foods that are good for us, such as herbs and vegetables, especially those in the cabbage family, are bitter. But, when used as a side note in a dish, or when the bitterness is offset by salt or sugar, these foods go from mouth-puckering to delicious.

In the past several years, many western researchers have begun to recognize a fifth taste, akin to the **savory** taste long recognized as the fifth taste in Japanese cuisine. Called **umami** (from the Japanese word *umai*, meaning "delicious"), this fifth taste does not have a simple English translation. Rather, for some people it refers to a food's savory characteristic; for others to the richness or fullness of a dish's overall taste, and still others, the meatiness or meat taste of a dish.

Taste buds sense umami in the presence of several substances, including the naturally occurring amino acid glutamate and its commercially produced counterpart known as monosodium glutamate (MSG). Cheeses, meats, rich stocks, soy sauce, shellfish, fatty fish, mushrooms, tomatoes and wine are all high in glutamate and produce the taste sensation of umami. Aged or fermented foods also provide umami.

Often food professionals and others refer to tastes in addition to sweet, sour, salty, bitter and umami. Typically, they describe something as pungent, hot, spicy or piquant or something that is astringent, sharp or dry. None of these terms, however, fit the definition of a taste, as none are detected solely by taste buds. Rather, these sensations are detected by nerve endings embedded in the fleshy part of the mouth. When irritated by the presence of compounds such as piperine (the active ingredient in black peppercorns) or capsaicin (the active ingredient in chiles), these nerves register a burning sensation that the brain translates as the hot and spicy "taste" of a dish.

savory a food that is not sweet

umami the taste sensation caused by the naturally occurring amino acid glutamate; gives food a savory richness or meatiness; found primarily in fermented foods and those to which monosodium glutamate has been added

HOW WE EXPERIENCE TASTE AND SMELL

The smallest functional unit of taste is the taste bud. These specialized sensory organs can be found on the tongue within three different kinds of **papillae** (Figure 1), as well as the back of the throat and the roof of the mouth. Each taste bud contains several **taste receptor cells**, and **taste compounds** interact with the tops of these specialized cells, which then transmit taste information through a nerve to the brain. The process of tasting begins when a substance is placed in the mouth and taste compounds begin to dissolve in saliva. Mastication, or chewing, further breaks down the substance and increases the concentration of taste compounds dissolved in the saliva. Once dissolved in saliva, the taste compounds have the potential to stimulate taste receptors and ultimately elicit taste sensations. Because compounds must dissolve in the saliva in order to reach the taste receptors, taste compounds must be water-soluble.

The process of smelling begins when odor compounds reach the olfactory neurons, the specialized sensing organs of smell. Olfactory neurons are located at the top of the nasal cavity and are clustered together in the **olfactory bulb** (Figure 2). A separate olfactory bulb rests at the bottom of each hemisphere of the brain and at the top of each nasal cavity. Odor compounds can reach these receptors through two different pathways: orthonasally via the external nares (or **nostrils**) or retronasally via the internal nares. When we sniff or experience odors that are external to our bodies, we are smelling orthonasally. Once we place a substance in our mouth, the aromas we are experiencing are being delivered through the **retronasal path**. Regardless of route, in order for odor compounds to reach the olfactory receptors they must be able to volatilize, or dissolve in air. Since air is hydrophobic, this means most odor compounds do not dissolve well in water, dissolving better in oils.

A pervasive myth (based upon misinterpretation of an article written in German in the 1800s) is that you experience certain taste qualities on only certain areas of the tongue (sweet on the tip, bitter in the back, salt on the front sides and sour on the back sides). In fact, you can taste all taste compounds everywhere on your tongue, and it is easy to prove this to yourself by placing various items representative of sweet, sour, salty, bitter, and even umami on the tip of your tongue. You will be able to immediately perceive any taste at the tongue tip (or anywhere else you have taste buds) and will not need to wait for bitter compounds to diffuse to the back, sour to the back sides, or salt to the sides.

—JEANNINE DELWICHE, PH.D., an expert in sensory science and chemosensory psychophysics, is a senior scientist at Firmenich, Inc., as well as an adjunct faculty member of both The Ohio State University and Brock University

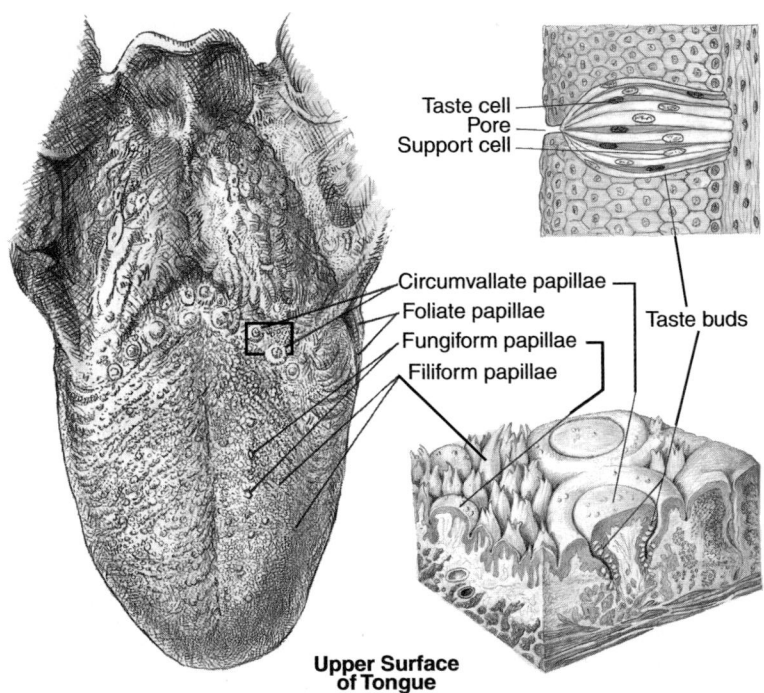

Taste cell
Pore
Support cell

Circumvallate papillae
Foliate papillae
Fungiform papillae
Filiform papillae

Taste buds

Upper Surface of Tongue

FIGURE 1 ▶ The human tongue and taste buds.

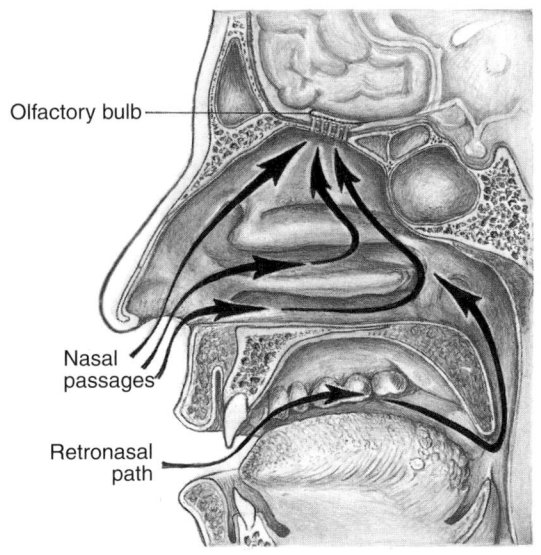

Olfactory bulb

Nasal passages

Retronasal path

FIGURE 2 ▶ The human olfactory system.

Factors Affecting Perception of Flavors

Obviously, the most important factors affecting the flavor of a dish are the quantity, quality and concentration of the flavoring ingredients. (With practice, a chef gains a feel for the proper proportions.) Other factors that affect one's perception of flavors include the following:

Temperature—Foods at warm temperatures offer the strongest tastes. Heating foods releases volatile flavor compounds, which intensifies one's perceptions of odors. This is why fine cheese is served at room temperature to improve its eating quality and flavor. Foods tend to lose their sour or sweet tastes both the colder and the hotter they become. Saltiness, however, is perceived differently at extreme cold temperatures; the same quantity of salt in a solution is perceived more strongly when very cold than when merely cool or warm. Therefore, it is best to adjust a dish's final flavors at its serving temperature. That is, *season hot foods when they are hot and cold foods when they are cold.*

Consistency—A food's consistency affects its flavor. Two items with the same amount of taste and smell compounds that differ in texture will differ in their perceived intensity; the thicker item will take longer to reach its peak intensity and will have a less intense flavor. For example, two batches of sweetened heavy cream made from the same ingredients in the same proportions can taste different if one is whipped and the other is unwhipped; the whipped cream has more volume and therefore a milder flavor.

Presence of contrasting tastes—Sweet and sour are considered opposites, and often the addition of one to a food dominated by the other will enhance the food's overall flavor. For example, adding a little sugar to vinaigrette reduces the dressing's sourness; adding a squeeze of lemon to a broiled lobster reduces the shellfish's sweetness. But add too much, and the dominant taste will be negated. Likewise, adding something sweet, sour or salty to a dish with a predominantly bitter flavor will cut the bitterness.

Presence of fats—Many of the chemical compounds that create tastes and aromas are dissolved in the fats naturally occurring in foods or added to foods during cooking. As these compounds are slowly released by evaporation or saliva, they provide a sustained taste sensation. If, however, there is too little fat, the flavor compounds may not be released efficiently, resulting in a dish with little sustained flavor. Too much fat poses another problem; it can coat the tongue and interfere with the ability of taste receptors to perceive flavor compounds.

Color—A food's color affects how the consumer will perceive the food's flavor before it is even tasted. When foods or beverages lack their customary color, they are less readily identified correctly than when appropriately colored. As color level changes to match normal expectations, our perception of taste and flavor intensity increases. A miscue created by the perceived flavor (the flavor associated with the color) can have an adverse impact on the consumer's appreciation of the actual flavor. For example, if the predominant flavor of a dessert is lemon, the dessert or some component of the dessert should be yellow; a green color will trigger an expectation of lime and the possible disappointment of the consumer. Similarly, the dark ruby-red flesh of a blood orange looks different from the bright orange flesh of a Valencia orange. This tonal difference can create the expectation of a different, non-orangey flavor, even though the blood orange's flavor is similar to that of other sweet orange varieties. Likewise, a sliced apple that has turned brown may suggest an off-flavor, although there is none.

Of special note is the perception and appreciation of saltiness, which varies from one person to another. What one person perceives as highly salted, another may find ideal. And, over time, one's taste adapts to the level of saltiness in food. Continual exposure to highly salted foods will increase one's tolerance of salt. Similarly, one can develop an appreciation over time for less salty food by decreasing the amount consumed.

SUPERTASTERS, MEDIUM TASTERS AND NONTASTERS

Recent research into the physiology of taste has shown that some people detect a greater degree of a taste in foods than others. Called **supertasters** by Professor Linda Bartoshuk of the University of Florida's Center for Smell and Taste, these people may have more taste buds than average, possibly twice as many as **nontasters** or **medium tasters**. In addition to detecting strongly bitter flavors where many people do not (for example, in coffee, broccoli, Brussels sprouts, grapefruit juice and green tea), supertasters also tend to perceive artificial sweeteners as sweeter than do the rest of the population and with a bitter aftertaste that most people miss. Similarly, supertasters find the spicy heat generated by capsaicin to be more pronounced, sometimes unbearably so, than does the average person.

A person's responsiveness to tastes appears to influence food choices. Supertasters tend to avoid strong-tasting foods such as coffee, rich or very sweet desserts, greasy or spicy meats, and green leafy vegetables. They also tend not to crave fats or sugars. Cooks who are nontasters may not realize when a food would be too sweet or too bitter to medium tasters or supertasters. And supertaster cooks may unconsciously avoid using foods that would be perfectly delicious to everyone else. It is easy to determine one's taste level with special chemically treated test papers.

COMPROMISES TO THE PERCEPTION OF TASTE

The sense of taste can be challenged by factors both within and beyond one's control. Age and general health can diminish one's perception of flavor, as can fatigue and stress. Chefs need to be aware of the age and health of their clientele, adjusting the seasoning of foods served according to their needs. Here are some factors, described by Jeannine Delwiche, Ph.D., that can affect one's taste perceptions.

Age—"The bad news is that taste and smell sensitivity does decline as we age. The good news is that it declines at a slower rate than our vision and hearing. The sense of smell tends to decline earlier than the sense of taste. There is a great deal of variance across individuals, with some showing declines earlier than others."

Health—"An acute condition, such as a cold, can result in a temporary loss of smell. The presence of mucus can prevent airflow, preventing the odor compounds from reaching the olfactory receptors. In contrast, the sense of taste would remain largely unaffected. Medications can also alter the perception of taste and smell. Some medications suppress the perceptions of saltiness, while others result in chronic perception of bitterness. Still other medications alter salivary flow, making it difficult to swallow dry foods. A further complication is the underlying conditions for taking medication. If an individual is taking high blood pressure medications, not only may the medication have a direct impact on perceived taste, but the same individual is likely to be on a sodium-restricted diet."

Smoking—"Anecdotal reports from those who quit smoking strongly indicate that smoking diminishes odor sensitivity. This is further supported by evidence indicating that people who smoke generally are less sensitive to odors than those who do not. In contrast, evidence indicates that if one waits two hours after smoking, the sense of taste is unaltered. Immediately after smoking, however, taste sensitivity is lowered."

FLAVORING FOOD

The judicious use of **flavorings** and **seasonings** transforms raw ingredients such as beef chuck into the aromatic stew Boeuf Bourguignonne or plain noodles into a fragrant bowl of pasta with Pesto Sauce. Mastery of flavoring and seasoning foods is the hallmark of a true culinary professional. Culinary tradition provides chefs with myriad flavor combinations to use when preparing dishes. What would apple pie be without cinnamon? Or a hot dog without mustard? The recipes in this book use classic and traditional flavor combinations as well as such modern flavor pairings as coffee in a sauce for beef. Familiarity with the science of taste and smell as well as the ingredients described in this chapter will enhance your ability to season foods. The sections on international flavor principles at the end of this chapter provide more specific information on flavor combinations common in various regions of the world, as do the sidebars in this and other chapters in this book.

Flavor Profiles

A food's **flavor profile** describes its flavor from the moment the consumer gets the first whiff of its aroma until he or she swallows that last morsel. It is a convenient way to articulate and evaluate a dish's sensory characteristics as well as identify contrasting or complementing items that could be served with it.

A food's flavor profile consists of one or more of the following elements:

Top notes or high notes—the sharp, first flavors or aromas that come from citrus, herbs, spices and many condiments. These top notes provide instant impact and dissipate quickly.

Middle notes—the second wave of flavors and aromas. More subtle and more lingering than top notes, middle notes come from dairy products, poultry, some vegetables, fish and some meats.

ABOUT FLAVORS

Flavor is to food what hue is to color. It is what timbre is to music. (*Flavor* is adjective; *food* is noun.) Each ingredient has its own particular character, which is altered by every other ingredient it encounters. A secret ingredient is one that mysteriously improves the flavor of a dish without calling attention to itself. It is either undetectable or extremely subtle, but its presence is crucial because the dish would not be nearly as good without it.

Primary flavors are those that are obvious, such as the flavors of chicken and tarragon in a chicken tarragon, shrimp and garlic in a shrimp scampi, or beef and red wine in a beef à la Bourguignonne. Secret ingredients belong to the realm of secondary flavors. However obvious it is that you need tarragon to prepare a chicken tarragon, you would not achieve the most interesting result using only tarragon. Tarragon, in this case, needs secondary ingredients—a hint of celery seed and anise—to make it taste more like quintessential tarragon and at the same time more than tarragon. In this way, primary flavors often depend on secret ingredients to make them more interesting and complex. Using only one herb or spice to achieve a certain taste usually results in a lackluster dish—each mouthful tastes the same. Whether they function in a primary or secondary way, flavors combine in only three different ways: They marry, oppose, or juxtapose.

When flavors marry, they combine to form one taste. Some secondary flavors marry with primary ones to create a new flavor greater than the sum of its parts, and often two flavors can do the job better than one. It may sound like an eccentric combination, but vanilla marries with the flavor of lobster, making it taste more like the essence of lobster than lobster does on its own. And when ginger and molasses marry, they create a flavor superior to either alone.

Opposite flavors can highlight or cancel each other; they can cut or balance each other. Sweet/sour, sweet/salty, sweet/hot, salty/sour, and salty/tart are all opposites. Salt and sugar are so opposed, in fact, that when used in equal amounts they cancel each other entirely. Sweet relish helps cancel the salty flavor of hot dogs. Chinese sauces usually contain some sugar to help balance the saltiness of soy sauce.

Knowing how to combine many flavors and aromas to achieve a simple and pure result (and knowing when not to combine flavors) will make you a better, more confident cook. Good cooks over the centuries have known these things intuitively—but they've had neither the huge variety of ingredients nor the knowledge of world cuisines that we have today.

—CHEF MICHAEL ROBERTS
is the author of *Secret Ingredients*

Low notes or bass notes—the most dominant, lingering flavors. These flavors consist of the basic tastes (especially sweetness, sourness, saltiness and umami) and come from foods such as anchovies, beans, chocolate, dried mushrooms, fish sauce, tomatoes, most meats (especially beef and game) and garlic. Or they can be created by smoking or caramelizing the food's sugars during grilling, broiling and other dry-heat cooking processes.

Aftertaste or finish—the final flavor that remains in the mouth after swallowing; for example, the lingering bitterness of coffee or chocolate or the pungency of black pepper or strong mustard.

Roundness—the unity of the dish's various flavors achieved through the judicious use of butter, cream, coconut milk, reduced stocks, salt, sugar and the like; these ingredients cause the other flavorings to linger without necessarily adding their own dominant taste or flavor.

Depth of flavor—whether the dish has a broad range of flavor notes.

These expressions can be applied to any dish to describe its sensory characteristics. For example, Roman-Style Free-Range Chicken (page 427) has a flavor profile with a top note of rosemary. Its middle notes are contributed by the chicken, and the low notes from the anchovies and garlic. There is an aftertaste of garlic and vinegar. The sauce adds roundness to the chicken, thus creating a dish with a fine depth of flavor.

An experienced chef is able to taste and evaluate a dish, adjusting flavorings, ingredients and cooking technique as needed to create an appealing balance of flavors.

Describing Aromas and Flavors in Food

Food scientists and professional tasters make their living describing the smell and taste of foods. Many have attempted to standardize the language used to describe both positive and negative aromas and flavors. Frequently they employ flavor wheels or other charts

TABLE 6.1   COMMON FLAVOR DESCRIPTIONS

TYPE OF AROMA OR FLAVOR	FOODS WITH SUCH CHARACTERISTICS
Green, grassy	Green bell peppers, raw apple skins
Fruity, esterlike	Bananas, apples
Citrus, terpenic	Lemons, limes
Minty, camphoraceous	Fresh mint, rosemary
Floral, sweet	Roses, violets, honey
Spicy, herbaceous	Allspice, cinnamon, nutmeg
Woody, smoky	Smoked foods
Roasty, burnt	Coffee, toasted bread
Caramel, nutty	Burnt sugar, molasses
Bouillon, high vegetable protein	Meat stock
Meaty, animalic	Roasted meat
Fatty, rancid	Fishy smell
Sulfurous, alliaceous	Onions, garlic, rotten egg
Mushroom, earthy	Cooked mushrooms, damp soil, yeasty bread
Celery, soupy	Celery, parsnip
Dairy, buttery	Cheese

seasoning an item added to enhance the natural flavors of a food without dramatically changing its taste; salt is the most common seasoning

flavoring an item that adds a new taste to a food and alters its natural flavors; flavorings include herbs, spices, vinegars and condiments; the terms seasoning and flavoring are often used interchangeably

herb any of a large group of aromatic plants whose leaves, stems or flowers are used as a flavoring; used either dried or fresh

aromatic a food added to enhance the natural aromas of another food; aromatics include most flavorings, such as herbs and spices, as well as some vegetables

spice any of a large group of aromatic plants whose bark, roots, seeds, buds or berries are used as a flavoring; usually used in dried form, either whole or ground

condiment traditionally, any item added to a dish for flavor, including herbs, spices and vinegars; now also refers to cooked or prepared flavorings such as prepared mustards, relishes, bottled sauces and pickles

to identify and organize the flavors and tastes found in specific food items. For example, there are flavor wheels devoted to chocolate, wine, catfish, Italian cheese, coffee, citrus fruits and just about every other category of food and beverage on the market. These charts help food scientists, product developers and quality-control tasters to speak a common language when describing the flavors they encounter.

Table 6.1 shows one list used by chemists to describe 16 broad categories of tastes and smells that correspond to the major chemicals found in aromas and tastes. Such a list is helpful when trying to analyze and describe the flavors in a dish.

FLAVORINGS: HERBS AND SPICES

Herbs and spices are used as **flavorings**. **Herbs** refer to the large group of **aromatic** plants whose leaves, stems or flowers are used to add flavors to other foods. Most herbs are available fresh or dried. Because drying alters their flavors and aromas, fresh herbs are generally preferred and should be used if possible. **Spices** are strongly flavored or aromatic portions of plants used as flavorings, **condiments** or aromatics. Spices are the bark, roots, seeds, buds or berries of plants, most of which grow naturally only in tropical climates. Spices are almost always used in their dried form, rarely fresh, and can usually be purchased whole or ground. Some plants—dill, for example—can be used as both an herb (its leaves) and a spice (its seeds).

Herbs

Basil (Fr. *basilic*) is considered one of the great culinary herbs. It is available in a variety of "flavors"— cinnamon, garlic, lemon, even chocolate—but the most

Basil

common is sweet basil. Sweet basil has light green, tender leaves and small white flowers. Its flavor is strong, warm and slightly peppery, with a hint of cloves. Basil is used in Mediterranean and some Southeast Asian cuisines and has a special affinity for garlic and tomatoes. When purchasing fresh basil, look for bright green leaves; avoid flower buds and wilted or rust-colored leaves. Dried sweet basil is readily available but has a decidedly weaker flavor.

Opal basil is named for its vivid purple color. It has a tougher, crinkled leaf and a medium-strong flavor. Opal basil may be substituted for sweet basil in cooking, and its appearance makes it a distinctive garnish.

Bay (Fr. *laurier*), also known as sweet laurel, is a small tree from Asia that produces tough, glossy leaves with a sweet balsamic aroma and peppery flavor. Bay symbolized wisdom and glory in ancient Rome; the leaves were used to form crowns or "laurels" worn by emperors and victorious athletes. In cooking, dried bay leaves are often preferred over the more bitter fresh leaves. Essential in French cuisine, bay leaves are part of the traditional bouquet garni and court bouillon. Whole dried leaves are usually added to a dish at the start of cooking, then removed when sufficient flavor has been extracted.

Bay Leaves

Opal Basil

Chervil (Fr. *cerfeuil*), also known as sweet cicely, is native to Russia and the Middle East. Its lacy, fernlike leaves are similar to parsley and can be used as a garnish. Chervil's flavor is delicate, similar to parsley but with the distinctive aroma of anise. It should not be heated for long periods. Chervil is commonly used in French cuisine and is one of the traditional *fines herbes*.

Chervil

Chives (Fr. *ciboulettes*) are perhaps the most delicate and sophisticated members of the onion family. Their hollow, thin grass-green stems grow in clumps and produce round, pale purple flowers, which are used as a garnish. Chives may be purchased dried, quick-frozen or fresh. They have a mild onion flavor and bright green color. Chives complement eggs, poultry, potatoes, fish and shellfish. They should not be cooked for long periods or at high temperatures. Chives make an excellent garnish when snipped with scissors or carefully chopped and sprinkled over finished soups or sauces.

Garlic chives, also known as Chinese chives, actually belong to another plant species. They have flat, solid (not hollow) stems and a mild garlic flavor. They may be used in place of regular chives if their garlic flavor is desired.

Garlic Chives

Chives

Cilantro (Fr. *coriandre*; Sp. *culantro*) is the green leafy portion of the plant that yields seeds known as coriander. The flavors of the two portions of this plant are very different and cannot be substituted for each other. Cilantro, also known as Chinese parsley, is sharp and tangy with a strong aroma and an almost citrus flavor. It is widely used in Asian, Mexican and South American cuisines, especially in salads and sauces. It should not be subjected to heat, and cilantro's flavor is completely destroyed by drying. Do not use yellow or discolored leaves or the tough stems. When used in excess, cilantro can impart a soapy taste to foods.

Curry leaves (Hindi *karipatta*; *kitha neem*) are the distinctively flavored leaves of a small tree that grows wild in the Himalayan foothills, southern India and Sri Lanka. They look like small shiny bay leaves and have a strong currylike fragrance and a citrus-curry flavor. Often added to a preparation whole, then removed before

Cilantro

Curry Leaves

Dill

Epazote

Lemongrass

Marjoram

serving, they can also be minced or finely chopped for marinades and sauces. Choose fresh bright green leaves, if possible, or frozen leaves; dried leaves have virtually no flavor. Although used in making southern Indian and Thai dishes, curry leaves (also known as neem leaves) must not be confused with curry powder, which is discussed later.

Dill (Fr. *aneth*), a member of the parsley family, has tiny, aromatic, yellow flowers and feathery, delicate blue-green leaves. The leaves taste like parsley, but sharper, with a touch of anise. Dill seeds are flat, oval and brown, with a bitter flavor similar to caraway. Both the seeds and the leaves of the dill plant are used in cooking. Dill is commonly used in Scandinavian and central European cuisines, particularly with fish and potatoes. Both leaves and seeds are used in pickling and sour dishes. Dill leaves are available fresh or dried but lose their aroma and flavor during cooking, so add them only after the dish is removed from the heat. Dill seeds are available whole or ground and are used in fish dishes, pickles and breads.

Epazote, also known as wormseed or stinkweed, grows wild throughout the Americas. It has a strong aroma similar to kerosene and a wild flavor. Fresh epazote is used in salads and as a flavoring in Mexican and Southwestern cuisines. It is often cooked with beans to reduce their gaseousness. Dried epazote is brewed to make a beverage.

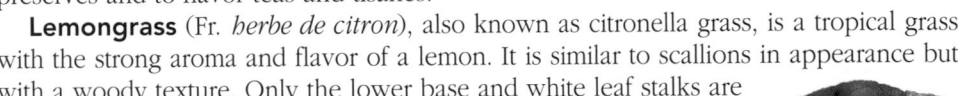

Lavender is an evergreen with thin leaves and tall stems bearing spikes of tiny purple flowers. Although lavender is known primarily for its aroma, which is widely used in perfumes, soaps and cosmetics, the flowers are also used as a flavoring, particularly in Middle Eastern and Provençal cuisines. These flowers have a sweet, lemony flavor and can be crystallized and used as a garnish. Lavender is also used in jams and preserves and to flavor teas and tisanes.

Lavender

Lemongrass (Fr. *herbe de citron*), also known as citronella grass, is a tropical grass with the strong aroma and flavor of a lemon. It is similar to scallions in appearance but with a woody texture. Only the lower base and white leaf stalks are used. Available fresh or quick-frozen, lemongrass is widely used in Southeast Asian cuisines.

Lime leaves from a species of thorny lime trees (*Citrus hystrix*) are used much like bay leaves to flavor soups and stews in Thai and other Asian cuisines. These small, dark green leaves have a bright citrus floral aroma. Fragrant lime leaves are available fresh in the United States now that these trees are cultivated domestically.

Fragrant Lime Leaves

Lovage (Fr. *céleri bâtard*, "false celery") has tall stalks and large dark green celery-like leaves. The leaves, stalks and seeds (which are commonly known as **celery seeds**) have a strong celery flavor. This plant is also known as sea parsley and smallage; the leaves and stalks are used in salads and stews and the seeds are used for flavoring.

Marjoram (Fr. *marjolaine*), also known as sweet marjoram, is a flowering herb native to the Mediterranean and used since ancient times. Its flavor is similar to thyme but sweeter; it also has a stronger aroma. Marjoram is now used in many European cuisines. Although it is available fresh, marjoram is one of the few herbs whose flavor increases when dried. Wild marjoram is more commonly known as oregano.

Mint (Fr. *menthe*), a large family of herbs, includes many species and flavors (even chocolate). Spearmint is the most common garden and commercial variety. It has soft, bright green leaves and a tart aroma and flavor. Mint does not blend well with other herbs, so its use is confined to specific dishes, usually fruits or fatty meats such as lamb. Mint has an affinity for chocolate. It can also be brewed into a beverage or used as a garnish.

Spearmint

Peppermint has thin, stiff, pointed leaves and a sharper menthol flavor and aroma. Fresh peppermint is used less often in cooking or as a garnish than spearmint, but peppermint oil is a common flavoring in sweets and candies.

Peppermint

Oregano

Oregano (Fr. *origan*), also known as wild marjoram, is a pungent, peppery herb used in Mediterranean cuisines, particularly Greek and Italian, as well as in Mexican cuisine. It is a classic complement to tomatoes. Oregano's thin, woody stalks bear clumps of tiny, dark green leaves, which are available dried and crushed.

Parsley (Fr. *persil*) is probably the best known and most widely used herb in the world. It grows in almost all climates and is available in many varieties, all of which are rich in vitamins and minerals. The most common type in the United States and Northern Europe is **curly parsley**. It has small curly leaves and a bright green color. Its flavor is tangy and clean. Other cuisines use a variety sometimes known as **Italian parsley**, which has flat leaves, a darker color and coarser flavor. Curly parsley is a ubiquitous garnish; both types can be used in virtually any food except sweets. Parsley stalks have a stronger flavor than the leaves and are part of the standard bouquet garni. Chopped parsley forms the basis of any fine herb blend.

Parsley

Rosemary (Fr. *romarin*) is an evergreen bush that grows wild in warm, dry climates worldwide. It has stiff, needlelike leaves; some varieties bear pale blue flowers. It is highly aromatic, with a slight odor of camphor or pine. Rosemary is best used fresh. When dried, it loses flavor, and its leaves become very hard and unpleasant to chew. Whole rosemary stems may be added to a dish such as a stew and then removed when enough flavor has been imparted. They may also be added to a bouquet garni. Rosemary has a great affinity for roasted and grilled meats, especially lamb.

Rosemary

Italian Parsley

Sage (Fr. *sauge*) was used as a medicine for centuries before it entered the kitchen as a culinary herb. Culinary sage has narrow, fuzzy, gray-green leaves and blue flowers. Its flavor is strong and balsamic, with notes of camphor. Sage is used in poultry dishes, with fatty meats or brewed as a beverage. Sage's strong flavor does not blend well with other herbs. It dries well and is available in whole or chopped leaves or rubbed (coarsely ground).

Savory (Fr. *sariette*) has been used since ancient times. Its leaves are small and narrow, and it has a sharp, bitter flavor, vaguely like thyme. It dries well and is used in bean dishes, sausages and fine herb blends. Although the variety called *summer savory* is most common and popular, a variety called *winter savory* is also available.

Sage

Savory

Tarragon (Fr. *estragon*), another of the great culinary herbs, is native to Siberia. It is a bushy plant with long, narrow, dark green leaves and tiny gray flowers. Tarragon goes well with fish and tomatoes and is essential in many French dishes such as béarnaise sauce and fine herb blends. Its flavor is strong and diffuses quickly through foods. It is available dried, but drying may cause haylike flavors to develop.

Tarragon

Thyme

Aleppo Pepper

Allspice

Thyme (Fr. *thym*) has been popular since 3500 B.C.E., when Egyptians used it as a medicine and for embalming. Thyme is a small, bushy plant with woody stems, tiny green-gray leaves and purple flowers. Its flavor is strong but refined, with notes of sage. Thyme dries well and complements virtually all types of meat, poultry, fish, shellfish and vegetables. It is often included in a bouquet garni or added to stocks.

Spices

Aleppo pepper (ah-LEHP-oh) is made from bright red chiles grown in Turkey and northern Syria. The sun-dried Aleppo chiles are seeded and crushed, then used as a condiment. It has a sharp, but sweet, fruity flavor, with only mild heat (15,000 Scoville units, discussed in Chapter 21, Vegetables). Although it is a member of the *capsicum* family, Aleppo pepper is used more like ground peppercorns (*piper nigrum*) than a chile. Also known as Halaby pepper, it adds an authentic Mediterranean flavor and fragrance to foods.

Allspice (Fr. *quatre-épices*), also known as Jamaican pepper, is the dried berry of a tree that flourishes in Jamaica, and one of the few spices still grown exclusively in the New World. Allspice is available whole; in berries that look like large, rough, brown peppercorns; or ground. Ground allspice is not a mixture of spices, although it does taste like a blend of cinnamon, cloves and nutmeg. Allspice is now used throughout the world, in everything from cakes to curries, and is often included in peppercorn blends.

Anise (Fr. *anis*) is native to the eastern Mediterranean, where it was widely used by ancient civilizations. Today it is grown commercially in warm climates throughout India, North Africa and southern Europe. The tiny, gray-green egg-shaped seeds have a distinctively strong, sweet flavor, similar to licorice and fennel. When anise seeds turn brown, they are stale and should

Anise Seeds

FROM THE LABORATORY TO THE DINING TABLE: HOW FLAVORINGS ARE MADE

Flavor creation, like the culinary art, is a blend of science and creativity. The role of science is to identify the minute trace components of food that define its characteristic odor. This is done using a combination of techniques—gas chromatography, liquid chromatography, mass spectrometry and nuclear magnetic resonance to produce an analysis of the volatile organic compounds in the food. The analysis of sautéed chicken, for example, would contain hundreds of ingredients at levels ranging from parts per million down to fractions of a part per billion.

A purely scientific approach to formulation would involve such complex interactions that it would take a lifetime to make one flavor. At this stage creativity has to take over. The creative process is similar to that used by a chef. The flavorist attempts to form a mental picture of the possible combinations of the key parts of the composition that trigger the recognition of "chicken." Depending on the flavor type, this may be anywhere from two or three components to as many as fifteen. Typically fruits, herbs, and spices are relatively simple; heated or processed foods such as cooked chicken, beer or roasted coffee are more complex.

Once the basic chicken profile has been established, the secondary notes can be built up. In this case we would reproduce the sautéed character. We would also push the character of the flavor in the best direction for the target audience. Whether a skin note should be included would be a typical question.

So far we have considered only odor. It is very easy to confuse flavor, taste and odor, but in reality odor is the key differentiating characteristic that separates great food from simply good food. Although odor is far more important than taste, a flavor lacking any taste components will not taste very authentic. The next step is to build in subtle taste characteristics; perhaps a hint of bitterness would add realism to this flavor?

At this stage our flavor might contain as many as 60 ingredients, which could be chemicals derived from nature or natural extracts, so it is a fairly complex mixture. It will have omitted many of the components found in the analysis and concentrated on the attractive elements of the flavor. The object is not to duplicate nature, but rather to learn from nature and beat her at her own game.

Finally the flavor is tailored to the end use. Many factors in finished food can alter the consumer's perception of flavor; processing temperature, fat content and storage conditions are the most important. High processing temperature will cause a differential loss of the more volatile components, the top notes, and this must be rectified by either modifying the formulation or protecting the flavor from the heat process.

—JOHN WRIGHT, author and independent flavorist, was vice president of Global Technical Business Development for International Flavors & Fragrances Inc.

A PINCH OF HISTORY

Spices have been used for many purposes for thousands of years. Egyptian papyri dating back to 2800 B.C.E. identify several spices native to the Middle and Far East that were used by the ruling and priestly classes for therapeutic, cosmetic, medicinal, ritualistic and culinary purposes. By 300 C.E., the Romans were regularly importing spices for use as perfumes, medicines, preservatives and ingredients from China and India via long, difficult caravan journeys over sea and land. Spices were extremely expensive and unavailable to all but the wealthiest citizens.

After Rome fell in the second half of the fifth century C.E., much of the overland route through southern Europe became prey to bandits; after Constantinople fell in 1453, the Ottoman Turks controlled the spice routes through the Middle East. Spice costs soared and economies based on the spice trade, such as that of Venice, were at risk.

By then highly spiced food had become common, especially in wealthier households. So, in part to maintain their culinary norm, the Europeans set out to break the Ottoman Turk monopoly. These efforts led to Columbus's exploration of the Americas and Vasco da Gama's discovery of a sea route to India. Although the New World contained none of the spices for which Columbus was searching, it provided many previously unknown foods and flavorings that subsequently changed European tables forever, including chiles, vanilla, tomatoes, potatoes and chocolate.

Formation of the Dutch East India Company in 1602 marked the start of the Dutch colonial empire and made spices from what is now Indonesia, whose Molucca Islands were once referred to as the "Spice Islands," widely available to the growing European middle classes. The transplantation and cultivation of spice plants eventually weakened the once-powerful trading empires until, by the 19th century, no European country could monopolize trade. Prices fell dramatically.

---

be discarded. Anise is used in pastries as well as fish, shellfish and vegetable dishes, and is commonly used in alcoholic beverages (for example, Pernod and ouzo). The green leaves of the anise plant are occasionally used fresh as an herb or in salads.

Star anise, also known as Chinese anise, is the dried, star-shaped fruit of a Chinese magnolia tree. Although it is botanically unrelated, its flavor is similar to anise seeds but more bitter and pungent. It is an essential flavor in many Chinese dishes and one of the components of five-spice powder.

Star Anise

Annatto Seeds

Annatto seeds (Fr. *roucou*) are the small, brick-red triangular seeds of a shrub from South America and the Caribbean. Annatto seeds add a mild, peppery flavor to rice, fish and shellfish dishes and are crushed to make Mexican achiote paste. Because they impart a bright yellow-orange color to foods, annatto seeds are commonly used as a natural food coloring, especially in cheeses and margarine.

Asafetida (ah-sah-FEH-teh-dah; also spelled asafoetida) is a pale brown resin made from the sap of a giant fennel-like plant native to India and Iran. Also known as devil's dung, it has a garlicky flavor and a strong unpleasant fetid aroma (the aroma is not transferred to food being flavored). Available powdered or in lump form, it is used—very sparingly—as a flavoring in Indian and Middle Eastern cuisines.

Capers (Fr. *capres*) come from a small bush that grows wild throughout the Mediterranean basin. Its unopened flower buds have been pickled and used as a condiment for thousands of years. Fresh capers are not used, as the sharp, salty-sour flavor develops only after curing in strongly salted white vinegar. The finest capers are the smallest, known as nonpareils, which are produced in France's Provence region. Capers are used in a variety of sauces (tartare, rémoulade) and are excellent with fish and game. Capers will keep for long periods if moistened by their original liquid. Do not add or substitute vinegar, however, as this causes the capers to spoil.

Capers

Caraway (Fr. *carvi*) is perhaps the world's oldest spice. Its use has been traced to the Stone Age, and seeds have been found in ancient Egyptian tombs. The caraway plant grows wild in Europe and temperate regions of Asia. It produces a small, crescent-shaped brown seed with the peppery flavor of rye. Seeds may be purchased whole or ground. (The leaves have a mild, bland flavor and are rarely used in cooking.) Caraway is a very European flavor, used extensively in German and Austrian dishes, particularly breads, meats and cabbage. It is also used in alcoholic beverages and cheeses.

Caraway Seeds

Cardamom Seeds

Chile refers to the plant, **chili** refers to the stewlike dish containing chiles and **chilli** refers to the commercial spice powder

Cayenne Pepper

Paprika

Crushed Chiles

Cloves

Cardamom (Fr. *cardamome*) is one of the most expensive spices, second only to saffron in cost. Its seeds are encased in 1/4-inch- (6-millimeter-) long light green or brown pods. Cardamom is highly aromatic. Its flavor, lemony with notes of camphor, is quite strong and is used in both sweet and savory dishes. Cardamom is widely used in Indian and Middle Eastern cuisines, where it is also used to flavor coffee. Scandinavians use cardamom to flavor breads and pastries. Ground cardamom loses its flavor rapidly and is easily adulterated, so it is best to purchase whole seeds and grind your own as needed.

Chiles, including paprika, chile peppers, bell peppers and cayenne, are members of the capsicum plant family. Although cultivated for thousands of years in the West Indies and Americas, capsicum peppers were unknown in the Old World prior to Spanish explorations during the 15th century. Capsicum peppers come in all shapes and sizes, with a wide range of flavors, from sweet to extremely hot. Some capsicums are used as a vegetable; others are dried, ground and used as a spice. Fresh chiles and bell peppers are discussed in Chapter 21, Vegetables. Capsicums are botanically unrelated to *Piper nigrum*, the black peppercorns discussed later.

Cayenne, sometimes simply labeled "red pepper," is ground from a blend of several particularly hot types of dried red chile peppers. Its flavor is extremely hot and pungent; it has a bright orange-red color and fine texture.

Paprika, also known as Hungarian pepper, is a bright red powder ground from specific varieties of red-ripened and dried chiles. Paprika's flavor ranges from sweet to pungent; its aroma is distinctive and strong. It is essential to many Spanish and eastern European dishes. Mild paprika is meant to be used in generous quantities and may be sprinkled on prepared foods as a garnish.

Chile powders are made from a wide variety of dried chile peppers, ranging from sweet and mild to extremely hot and pungent. The finest pure chile powders come from dried chiles that are simply roasted, ground and sieved. Commercial chilli powder, an American invention, is actually a combination of spices—oregano, cumin, garlic and other flavorings—intended for use in Mexican dishes. Each brand is different and should be sampled before using.

Chilli Powder

Crushed chiles, also known as chile flakes, are blended from dried, coarsely crushed chiles. They are quite hot and are used in sauces and meat dishes.

Cinnamon (Fr. *cannelle*) and its cousin cassia are among the oldest known spices: Cinnamon's use is recorded in China as early as 2500 B.C.E., and the Far East still produces most of these products. Both cinnamon and cassia come from the bark of small evergreen trees, peeled from branches in thin layers and dried in the sun. High-quality cinnamon should be pale brown and thin, rolled up like paper into sticks known as quills. Cassia is coarser and has a stronger, less subtle flavor than cinnamon. Consequently, it is cheaper than true cinnamon. Cinnamon is usually purchased ground because it is difficult to grind. Cinnamon sticks are used when long cooking times allow for sufficient flavor to be extracted (for example, in stews or curries). Cinnamon's flavor is

Ground Cinnamon and Cinnamon Sticks

most often associated with pastries and sweets, but it has a great affinity for lamb and spicy dishes. Labeling laws do not require that packages distinguish between cassia and cinnamon, so most of what is sold as cinnamon in the United States is actually cassia, blended for consistent flavor and aroma.

Cloves (Fr. *clous de girofle*) are the unopened buds of evergreen trees that flourish in muggy tropical regions. When dried, whole cloves have hard, sharp prongs that can be used to push them into other foods, such as onions or fruit, in order to provide flavor. Cloves are extremely pungent, with a sweet, astringent aroma. A small amount provides a great deal of flavor. Cloves are used in desserts and meat dishes, preserves and liquors. They may be purchased whole or ground.

Coriander Seeds

Coriander (Fr. *coriandre*) seeds come from the cilantro plant. They are round and beige, with a distinctive sweet, spicy flavor and strong aroma. Unlike other plants in which the seeds and the leaves carry the same flavor and aroma, coriander and cilantro are very different. Coriander seeds are available whole or ground and are frequently used in Indian cuisine and pickling mixtures.

Cumin is the seed of a small delicate plant of the parsley family that grows in North Africa and the Middle East. The small seeds are available whole or ground and look (but do not taste) like caraway seeds. Cumin has a strong earthy flavor and tends to dominate any dish in which it is included. It is used in Indian, Middle Eastern and Mexican cuisines, in sausages and in a few cheeses.

Fennel (Fr. *fenouil*) is a perennial plant with feathery leaves and tiny flowers long cultivated in India and China as a medicine and cure for witchcraft. Its seeds are greenish brown with prominent ridges and short, hairlike fibers. Their taste and aroma are similar to anise, though not as sweet. Whole seeds are widely used in Italian stews and sausages; central European cuisines use fennel with fish, pork, pickles and vegetables. Ground seeds can also be used in breads, cakes and cookies. The same plant produces a bulbous stalk used as a vegetable.

Fenugreek (Fr. *fenugrec*), grown in Mediterranean countries since ancient times, is a small, beanlike plant with a tiny flower. The seeds, available whole or ground, are pebble shaped and transfer their pale orange color to the foods with which they are cooked. Their flavor is bittersweet, like burnt sugar with a bitter aftertaste. Fenugreek is a staple in Indian cuisines, especially curries and chutneys.

Filé powder (fee-LAY) is the dried, ground leaf of the sassafras plant. Long used by Choctaw Indians, it is now most commonly used as a thickener and flavoring in Cajun and Creole cuisines. Filé is also used as a table condiment to add a spicy note to stews, gumbo and the like. The powder forms strings if allowed to boil, so it should be added during the last minutes of cooking.

Galangal (guh-LANG-guhl) is the rhizome of a plant native to India and Southeast Asia. The rhizome has a reddish skin, an orange or whitish flesh and a peppery, gingerlike flavor and piny aroma. Also known as galanga root, Thai ginger and Laos ginger, it is peeled and crushed for use in Thai and Indonesian cuisines. Fresh ginger is an appropriate substitute.

Ginger (Fr. *gingembre*) is a well-known spice obtained from the rhizome of a tall, flowering tropical plant. Fresh ginger is known as a "hand" because it looks vaguely like a group of knobby fingers. It has grayish-tan skin and a pale yellow, fibrous interior. Fresh ginger should be plump and firm with smooth skin. It should keep for about a month under refrigeration. Its flavor is fiery but sweet, with notes of lemon and rosemary. Fresh ginger is widely available and is used in Indian and Asian cuisines. It has a special affinity for chicken, beef and curries. Ginger is also available peeled and pickled in vinegar, candied in sugar or preserved in alcohol or syrup. Dried, ground ginger is a fine yellow powder widely used in pastries. Its flavor is spicier and not as sweet as fresh ginger.

Grains of paradise are the seeds of a perennial reedlike plant indigenous to the West African coast. Related to cardamom, grains of paradise have a spicy, warm and slightly bitter flavor, similar to peppercorns. In fact, grains of paradise were traditionally used in place of black pepper and are also known as Guinea pepper or Melegueta pepper. Now enjoying a resurgence in popularity and increased availability, they are ground and used primarily in West African and Magreb dishes, and in the spice blend known as ras el hanout.

Horseradish (Fr. *raifort*) is the large off-white taproot of a hardy perennial (unrelated to radishes) that flourishes in cool climates. Fresh roots should be firm and plump; they will not have the distinctive horseradish aroma unless cut or bruised. The outer skin and inner core of a fresh horseradish root can have an unpleasant flavor and should be discarded. Typically used in Russian and central European cuisines, especially as an accompaniment to roasted meats and fish and shellfish dishes, horseradish is usually served grated, creamed into a sauce or as part of a compound butter or mustard preparation. If

Cumin

Fennel

Fenugreek

Filé Powder

Ginger Root

Grains of Paradise

Horseradish Root

Juniper Berries

Mustard Seeds   Ground Mustard

Whole Nutmegs with
Ground Mace (left) and
Ground Nutmeg (right)

Mace

Green Peppercorns

Pink Peppercorns

Szechuan Pepper

horseradish is cooked, heat can destroy its flavor and pungency, so any horseradish should be added near the end of cooking.

Juniper (Fr. *genièvre*) is an evergreen bush grown throughout the Northern Hemisphere. It produces round purple berries with a sweet flavor similar to pine. Juniper berries are used for flavoring gin and other alcoholic beverages, and are crushed and incorporated in game dishes, particularly venison and wild boar.

Mustard seeds (Fr. *moutarde*), available in black, brown and yellow, come from three different plants in the cabbage family. Mustard seeds are small, hard spheres with a bitter flavor. The seeds have no aroma, but their flavor is sharp and fiery hot. Yellow seeds have the mildest and black seeds the strongest flavor. All are sold whole and can be crushed for cooking. Mustard seeds are a standard component of pickling spices and are processed and blended for prepared mustards, which we discuss later. Ground or dry mustard is a bright yellow powder made from a blend of ground seeds, wheat flour and turmeric.

Nutmeg (Fr. *muscade*) and **mace** come from the yellow plumlike fruit of a large tropical evergreen. These fruits are dried and opened to reveal the seed known as nutmeg. A bright red lacy coating or *aril* surrounds the seed; the aril is the spice mace. Whole nutmegs are oval and look rather like a piece of smooth wood. The flavor and aroma of nutmeg are strong and sweet, and a small quantity provides a great deal of flavor. Nutmeg should be grated directly into a dish as needed; once grated, flavor loss is rapid. Nutmeg is used in many European cuisines, mainly in pastries and sweets, but is also important in meat and savory dishes.

Mace is an expensive spice, with a flavor similar to nutmeg but more refined. It is almost always purchased ground and retains its flavor longer than other ground spices. Mace is used primarily in pastry items.

Peppercorns (Fr. *poivre*) are the berries of a vine plant (*Piper nigrum*) native to tropical Asia. Peppercorns should not be confused with the chile (*capsicum*) peppers discussed earlier. Peppercorns vary in size, color, pungency and flavor. Many of these differences are the result of variations in climate and growing conditions. Good-quality pepper is expensive and should be purchased whole and ground fresh in a peppermill as needed. Whole peppercorns will last indefinitely if kept dry. They should be stored well covered in a cool, dark place.

Black and **white peppercorns** are produced from the same plant, but are picked and processed differently. For black peppercorns, the berries are picked when green and simply dried whole in the sun. Black pepper has a warm, pungent flavor and aroma. Tellicherry peppercorns from the southwest coast of India are generally considered the finest black peppercorns in the world and are priced accordingly. For white peppercorns, the berries are allowed to ripen until they turn red. The ripened berries are allowed to ferment, then the outer layer of skin is washed off. Nowadays, white pepper may be produced by mechanically removing the outer skin from black peppercorns. This is not true white pepper, and the resulting product should be labeled "decorticated." White pepper has fewer aromas than black pepper but is useful in white sauces or when the appearance of black speckles is undesirable.

Black Pepper (left)
and White Pepper
(right)

Green peppercorns are unripened berries that are either freeze-dried or pickled in brine or vinegar. Pickled green peppercorns are soft, with a fresh, sour flavor similar to capers. They are excellent in spiced butters and sauces or with fish.

Pink peppercorns (Fr. *baies roses*) are actually the berries of a South American tree, not a vine pepper plant. Pink peppercorns are available dried or pickled in vinegar. Although they are attractive, their flavor is bitter and pinelike, with less spiciness than true pepper.

Szechuan pepper (also spelled *Szechwan* and *Sichuan*) is the dried red berries of the prickly ash tree native to China. Also known as anise pepper and Chinese pepper, the berries have an extremely hot, peppery, spicy flavor with citrus overtones and are used in Chinese cuisines and as part of Chinese five-spice powder. In Japanese cuisine, a green variety called sancho is used to season grilled fish and meats.

Poppy seeds (Fr. *pavot*) are the ripened seeds of the opium poppy, which flourishes in the Middle East and India. (When ripe, the seeds do not contain any of the medicinal alkaloids found elsewhere in the plant.) The tiny blue-gray seeds are round and hard with a sweet, nutty flavor. Poppy seeds are used in pastries and breads.

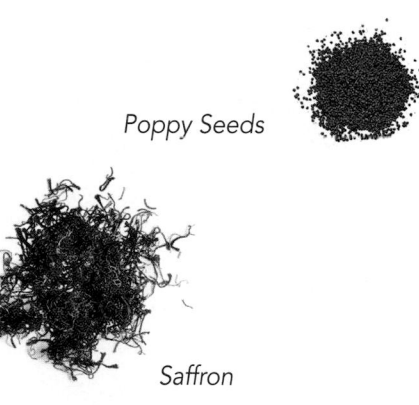

Poppy Seeds

Saffron (Fr. *safran*) comes from the dried stigmas of the saffron crocus. Each flower bears only three threadlike stigmas, and each must be picked by hand. It takes about 250,000 flowers to produce one pound of saffron, making it the most expensive spice in the world. Beware of bargains; there is no such thing as cheap saffron. Luckily, a tiny pinch is enough to color and flavor a large quantity of food. Good saffron should be a brilliant orange color, not yellow, with a strong aroma and a bitter, honeylike taste. Saffron produces a yellow dye that diffuses through any warm liquid. Valencia or Spanish saffron is considered the finest. It is commonly used with fish and shellfish (a necessity for bouillabaisse) and rice dishes such as paella and risotto. When using saffron threads, first crush them gently, then soak them in some hot liquid from the recipe. Powdered saffron is less expensive but more easily adulterated. It may be added directly to the other ingredients when cooking.

Saffron

Sesame seeds, also known as benne seeds, are native to India. They are small, flat ovals, with a creamy white color. Their taste is nutty and earthy, with a pronounced aroma when roasted or ground into a paste (known as tahini). Sesame seeds are the source of sesame oil, which has a mild, nutty flavor and does not go rancid easily. Sesame seeds are roasted and used in or as a garnish for breads and meat dishes. They are popular in Indian and Asian cuisines, with a black variety of seeds most popular as a Japanese condiment.

Sesame Seeds

Sumac is a red powder made from the dried petals and berries of a shrub native to Turkey. It has a sour, citric flavor and is used throughout the Middle East. Early colonists made a beverage similar to lemonade from a variety of sumac they found in North America.

Sumac

Tamarind (Fr. *tamarin*; Sp. and It. *tamarindo*), also known as an Indian date, is the brown, bean-shaped pod of the tamarind tree, which is native to Africa. Although naturally sweet, tamarind also contains 12% tartaric acid, which makes it extremely tart. It is commonly used in Indian curries and Mediterranean cooking as a souring agent and in the West Indies in fruit drinks. Tamarind is sold as a concentrate or in sticky blocks of crushed pods, pulp and seeds, which should be soaked in warm water for about 5 minutes, then squeezed through a sieve. Tamarind's high pectin content is useful in chutneys and jams, and it is often included in barbecue sauces and marinades. It is a key ingredient in Worcestershire sauce.

Tamarind Pods

Tamarind Paste

Turmeric (Fr. *curcuma*), also known as Indian saffron, is produced from the rhizome of a flowering tropical plant related to ginger. It has a mild, woodsy aroma. It is most often available dried and usually ground although fresh turmeric appears in ethnic markets. Turmeric is renowned for its vibrant yellow color and is used as a food coloring and dye. Turmeric's flavor is distinctive and strong; it should not be substituted for saffron. Turmeric is a traditional ingredient in Indian curries, to which it imparts color as well as flavor.

Turmeric

Wasabi is a pale green root similar, but unrelated, to horseradish. It has a strong aroma and a sharp, cleansing flavor with herbal overtones that is a bit hotter than that of horseradish. Fresh wasabi is rarely found outside Japan, but tins of powder and tubes of paste are readily available. It is commonly served with sushi and sashimi and can be used to add a spicy Asian note to other dishes, such as mashed potatoes or a compound butter.

Wasabi

Herb and Spice Blends

Many cuisines have created recognizable combinations of flavors that are found in a variety of dishes. Although many of these blends are available ready-prepared for convenience, most can be mixed by the chef as needed. (And commercial blends can contain large amounts of salt.) A few of the more common herb and spice blends are described here. In addition, a recipe for Blackened Steak Seasoning appears on page 978.

Five-Spice Powder

Curry Powder

Herbes de Provence

Pickling Spice

Za'atar

Chinese five-spice powder is a combination of equal parts finely ground Szechuan pepper, star anise, cloves, cinnamon and fennel seeds. This blend is widely used in Chinese and some Vietnamese foods and is excellent with pork and in pâtés.

Curry powder is a European invention that probably took its name from the Tamil word *kari*, meaning "sauce." Created by 19th-century Britons returning from colonial India, it was meant to be the complete spicing for a "curry" dish. There are as many different formulas for curry powder as there are manufacturers, some mild and sweet (Bombay or Chinese style), others hot and pungent (Madras style). Typical ingredients in curry powder are black pepper, cinnamon, cloves, coriander, cumin, ginger, mace and turmeric.

Fine herbs (Fr. *fines herbes*) are a combination of parsley, tarragon, chervil and chives widely used in French cuisine. The mixture is available dried, or it can be created from fresh ingredients.

Jamaican jerk seasoning is a powdered or wet mixture used on the Caribbean island of the same name made from a combination of spices that typically includes thyme, ground spices such as allspice, cinnamon, cloves, and ginger as well as onions and garlic. Chicken and pork are typically rubbed or marinated in the blend, then grilled.

Herbes de Provence (airb duh pro-VAWNS) is a blend of dried herbs commonly grown and used in southern France. Commercial blends usually include thyme, rosemary, bay leaf, basil, fennel seeds, savory and lavender. The herb blend is used with grilled or roasted meat, fish or chicken; in vegetable dishes; on pizza; and even in steamed rice and yeast breads.

Italian seasoning blend is a commercially prepared mixture of dried basil, oregano, sage, marjoram, rosemary, thyme, savory and other herbs associated with Italian cuisine.

Masala (mah-SAH-lah) is a flavorful, aromatic blend of roasted and ground spices used in Indian cuisines. A **garam masala** (gah-RAHM) is a masala made with hot spices (*garam* means warm or hot). A dry garam masala usually contains peppercorns, cardamom, cinnamon, cloves, coriander, nutmeg, turmeric, bay leaves and fennel seeds and is added toward the end of cooking or sprinkled on the food just before service. Adding coconut milk, oil or sometimes tamarind water to a dry garam masala makes a wet garam masala. A wet garam masala is typically added at the start of cooking.

Pickling spice, as with other blends, varies by manufacturer. Most pickling spice blends are based on black peppercorns and red chiles, with some or all of the following added: allspice, cloves, ginger, mustard seeds, coriander seeds, bay leaves and dill. These blends are useful in making cucumber or vegetable pickles as well as in stews and soups.

Quatre-épices (kah-tray-PEES), literally "four spices" in French and also the French word for allspice, is a peppery mixture of black peppercorns with lesser amounts of nutmeg, cloves and dried ginger. Sometimes cinnamon or allspice is included. Quatre-épices is used in charcuterie and long-simmered stews.

Ras el hanout (rass al ha-noot) is a common Moroccan spice blend varying greatly from supplier to supplier. It typically contains 20 or more spices, such as turmeric, cinnamon, cloves, grains of paradise, coriander, cumin, cardamom, peppercorns, dried chiles, dried flower petals and, allegedly, an aphrodisiac or two. It is sold whole and ground by the cook as necessary to flavor stews, rice, couscous and game dishes.

Seasoned salts are commercially blended products containing salt and one or more natural flavoring ingredients such as garlic, spices or celery seeds and, often, monosodium glutamate.

Za'atar (ZAH-tar) is a blend of dried thyme, wild oregano, sumac and sesame seeds used through the Middle East on flatbreads or mixed with olive oil as a condiment.

Storing Herbs and Spices

Fresh herbs should be kept refrigerated at 34°F–40°F (2°C–4°C). Large bouquets can be stored upright, their leaves loosely covered with plastic wrap and their stems submerged in water. Smaller bunches should be stored loosely covered with a damp towel. Excess fresh herbs can be dried for later use in an electric dehydrator or spread out on baking sheets in a 100°F (38°C) oven.

Dried herbs and spices should be stored in airtight, opaque containers in a cool, dry place. Avoid light and heat, both of which destroy delicate flavors. If stored properly, dried herbs should last for 2 to 3 months.

Using Herbs and Spices

Herbs and spices are a simple, inexpensive way to bring individuality and variety to foods. They add neither fat nor sodium and virtually no calories to foods; most contain only 3 to 10 calories per teaspoon. Table 6.2 lists just a few uses for some of the more common herbs and spices.

Although the flavors and aromas of fresh herbs are generally preferred, dried herbs are widely used because they are readily available and convenient. Use less dried herb than you would fresh herb. The loss of moisture strengthens and concentrates the flavor in dried herbs. In general, use only one-half to one-third as much dried herb as fresh in any given recipe. For example, if a recipe calls for 1 tablespoon of fresh basil, substitute only 1 teaspoon of dried basil. More can usually be added later if necessary. The delicate aroma and flavors of fresh herbs is volatile. Most fresh herbs such as chives, parsley, cilantro, basil and tarragon are best when added at the end of cooking.

Spices are often available whole or ground. Once ground, they lose their flavors rapidly, however. Whole spices should keep their flavors for at least 6 to 9 months if stored properly. Stale spices lose their spicy aroma and develop a bitter or musty aftertaste. Discard them.

Most dried spices need to be added early in order for their flavor to develop during the cooking. Whole spices take the longest; ground spices release their flavor more quickly. In some preparations, Indian curries for example, ground spices are first cooked

TABLE 6.2 USES FOR SOME COMMON HERBS AND SPICES

FLAVORING	FORM	SUGGESTED USES
Allspice	Whole or ground	Fruits, relishes, braised meats, quickbreads and spice cookies
Anise	Whole or ground	Asian cuisines, pastries, breads, cheeses
Basil	Fresh or dried	Tomatoes, salads, eggs, fish, chicken, lamb, cheeses, savory breads, pizza
Caraway	Whole or ground	Rye bread, cabbage, beans, pork, beef, veal
Cardamom	Ground	Sweet dough, cookies
Chervil	Fresh	Chicken, fish, eggs, salads, soups, vegetables
Chives	Fresh or dried	Eggs, fish, chicken, soups, potatoes, cheeses
Cilantro	Fresh leaves	Salsa, salads, Mexican cuisine, fish, shellfish, chicken
Cinnamon	Whole or ground	Infused in syrups for compotes, fruit, pies, pastries, breads, ice cream
Cloves	Whole or ground	Marinades, baked goods, braised meats, pickles, fruits, beverages, stocks
Cumin	Whole or ground	Chili, sausages, stews, eggs
Dill	Fresh or dried leaves; whole seeds	Leaves or seeds in soups, salads, fish, shellfish, vegetables, breads; seeds in pickles, potatoes, vegetables
Fennel	Whole seeds	Sausages, stews, sauces, pickling, lamb, eggs
Ginger	Fresh or powder	Asian, Caribbean and Indian cuisines; pastries, curries, stews, meats
Mace	Ground	Pâtés, sausage, spice breads, cookies
Marjoram	Fresh or dried	Sausages, pâtés, meats, poultry, stews, green vegetables, tomatoes, game
Mint	Fresh or dried	Infused in sauces, soups
Nutmeg	Ground	Curries, relishes, rice, eggs, custards, beverages
Rosemary	Fresh or dried	Lamb, veal, beef, poultry, game, marinades, stews
Saffron	Threads or ground	Rice, breads, potatoes, soups, stews, chicken, fish, shellfish
Sage	Fresh or dried	Poultry, charcuterie, pork, stuffings, pasta, beans, tomatoes
Tarragon	Fresh or dried	Chicken, fish, eggs, salad dressings, sauces, tomatoes
Thyme	Fresh or dried	Fish, chicken, meats, stews, charcuterie, soups, tomatoes
Turmeric	Fresh or powder	Curries, relishes, rice, eggs, breads

in oil to release their aromas before being added to a dish. Some dried spices such as black pepper may become bitter when cooked for an extended period of time, however. In uncooked dishes that call for ground spices (for example, salad dressings), the mixture should be allowed to stand for several hours to develop good flavor.

Creating dishes with appealing and complex flavors comes with practice and a solid understanding and appreciation of flavoring ingredients. Although some flavoring combinations are timeless—rosemary with lamb, dill with salmon, nutmeg with spinach, caraway with rye bread—less common pairings can be equally delicious and far more exciting. Chefs must be willing and able to experiment with new flavors. But first they must become familiar with the distinctive flavors and aromas of an herb, spice, condiment, vinegar or the like. Then chefs can experiment, always bearing in mind the following guidelines:

▶ Flavorings should not hide the taste or aroma of the primary ingredient.

▶ Flavorings should be combined in balance, so as not to overwhelm the palate.

▶ Flavorings should not be used to disguise poor quality or poorly prepared products.

▶ Flavorings should be added sparingly when foods are to be cooked over an extended period of time. When reduced during cooking, flavorings can intensify and overpower the dish.

▶ Taste and season foods frequently during cooking.

Even in a well-tested recipe, the quantity of flavorings may need to be adjusted because of a change in brands or the condition of the ingredients. A chef should strive to develop his or her palate to recognize and correct subtle variances as necessary.

SALT

Salt (Fr. *sel*) is the most basic seasoning, and its use is universal. It preserves foods, heightens their flavors and provides the distinctive taste of saltiness. The presence of salt can be tasted easily but not smelled. Salt suppresses bitter flavors, making the sweet and sour ones more prominent. The flavor of salt will not evaporate or dissipate during cooking, so it should be added to foods carefully, according to taste. Remember, more salt can always be added to a dish, but too much salt cannot be removed nor can its flavor be masked if too much salt has been added.

Culinary or **table salt** is sodium chloride (NaCl), one of the minerals essential to human life. Salt contains no calories, proteins, fats or carbohydrates. It is available from several sources, each with its own flavor and degree of saltiness.

Rock salt, mined from underground deposits, is available in both edible and nonedible forms. It is used in ice cream churns, for thawing frozen sidewalks and, in edible form, in salt mills.

Common **kitchen** or table salt is produced by pumping water through underground salt deposits, then bringing the brine to the surface to evaporate, leaving behind crystals. Chemicals are usually added to prevent table salt from absorbing moisture and thus keep it free-flowing. Iodized salt is commonly used in the United States. The iodine has no effect on the salt's flavor or use; it is simply added to provide an easily available source of iodine, an important nutrient, to a large number of people.

Kosher salt has large, irregular crystals and is used in the "koshering" or curing of meats. It is purified rock salt that contains no iodine or additives. It can be substituted for common kitchen salt. Some chefs prefer it to table salt because they prefer its flavor and it dissolves more easily than other salts.

Sea salt is obtained, not surprisingly, by evaporating seawater. The evaporation can be done naturally by drying the salt in the sun (unrefined sea salt) or by boiling the salty liquid (refined sea salt). Unlike other table salts, unrefined sea salt contains additional mineral salts such as magnesium, calcium and potassium, which give it a stronger, more complex flavor and a grayish-brown color. The region where it is produced can also affect its flavor and color. For example, salt from the Mediterranean Sea will taste different from salt

Rock Salt

Kosher Salt

obtained from the Indian Ocean or the English Channel. Sea salt is considerably more expensive than other table salts and is often reserved for finishing a dish or used as a condiment.

Sel gris is a sea salt harvested off the coast of Normandy, France. It is slightly wet and takes its gray color from minerals in the clay from which it is collected. **Fleur de sel**, which means "flower of salt," is salt that collects on rocks in the sel gris marshes. It forms delicate crystals and has little color because it has not come into contact with the clay.

Some **specialty salts** are actually mined from the earth, such as that from the foothills of the Himalayan Mountains. The presence of iron and copper along with other minerals gives Himalayan salt a pink hue and distinct flavor. Black salt, common in traditional Indian recipes, is mined rock salt; minerals and other components in the salt give it a dark color and sulfurous taste. **Smoked salt** is a type of flavored salt made by smoking the salt over a smoldering fire. It can also be made by adding liquid smoke to a salt solution before it is evaporated.

Because it is nonorganic, salt keeps indefinitely. It will, however, absorb moisture from the atmosphere, which prevents it from flowing properly. Salt is a powerful preservative; its presence stops or greatly slows down the growth of many undesirable microorganisms. Salt is used to preserve meats, vegetables and fish. It is also used to develop desirable flavors in bacon, ham, cheeses and fish products as well as pickled vegetables.

Fleur de Sel

OILS

Oils (Fr. *huiles*) are a type of fat that remains liquid at room temperature. Cooking oils are refined from various seeds, plants and vegetables. (Other fats, such as butter and margarine, are discussed in Chapter 7, Dairy Products; fats for deep-frying are discussed in Chapter 9, Principles of Cooking.) They are included here as flavorings because each oil, along with its cooking properties, has specific flavor and aroma characteristics that should be considered when choosing an oil as a cooking medium or as an ingredient.

When purchasing oils, consider their use, **smoke point**, flavor and cost. Fats, including oils and **shortenings**, are manufactured for specific purposes such as deep-frying, cake baking, salad dressings and sautéing. Most food service operations purchase different ones for each of these needs. Fats break down at different temperatures. When fats break down, their chemical structure is altered; the triglyceride molecules that make up fat are converted into individual fatty acids. These acids add undesirable flavors to the fat and can ruin the flavor of the food being cooked. The temperature at which a given fat begins to break down and smoke is known as its smoke point. Choose fats with higher smoke points for high-temperature cooking such as deep-frying and sautéing.

The flavor and cost of each oil must also be considered. For example, both corn oil and walnut oil can be used in a salad dressing. Their selection may depend on balancing cost (corn oil is less expensive) against flavor (walnut oil has a stronger, more distinctive flavor).

When fats spoil, they are said to go **rancid**. Rancidity is a chemical change caused by exposure to air, light or heat. It results in objectionable flavors and odors. Different fats turn rancid at different rates, but all fats benefit from refrigerated storage away from moisture, light and air. (Some oils are packaged in colored glass containers because certain tints of green and yellow block the damaging light rays that can cause an oil to go rancid.) Although oils may become thick and cloudy under refrigeration, this is not a cause for concern. The oils will return to their clear, liquid states at room temperature. Stored fats should also be covered to prevent them from absorbing odors.

Vegetable oils are extracted from a variety of plants, including corn, cottonseed, peanuts, grape seeds and soybeans, by pressure or chemical solvents. The oil is then refined and cleaned to remove unwanted colors, odors or flavors. Vegetable oils are virtually odorless and have a neutral flavor. Because they contain no animal products, they are cholesterol-free. If a commercial product contains only one type of oil, it is labeled "pure" (as in "pure corn oil"). Products labeled "vegetable oil" are blended from several sources. Products labeled "salad oil" are highly refined blends of vegetable oil.

smoke point the temperature at which a fat begins to break down and smoke

flash point the temperature at which a fat ignites and small flames appear on the surface of the fat

shortening (1) a white, flavorless, solid fat formulated for baking or deep-frying; (2) any fat used in baking to tenderize the product by shortening gluten strands

Canola Oil

Extra Virgin Olive Oil

Canola oil is processed from rapeseeds. Its popularity is growing rapidly because it contains no cholesterol and has a high percentage of monounsaturated fat. Canola oil is useful for frying and general cooking because it has no flavor and a high smoke point.

Nut oils are extracted from a variety of nuts and are almost always packaged as a "pure" product, never blended. A nut oil should have the strong flavor and aroma of the nut from which it was processed. Popular examples are walnut and hazelnut oils. These oils are used to give flavor to salad dressings, marinades and other dishes. But heat diminishes their flavor, so nut oils are not recommended for frying or baking. Nut oils tend to go rancid quickly and therefore are usually packaged in small containers.

Olive oil (Fr. *huile d'olive*) is the only oil that is extracted from a fruit rather than a seed, nut or grain. Olive oil is produced primarily in Spain, Italy, France, Greece and North Africa; California produces a relatively minor amount of olive oil. Like wine, olive oils vary in color and flavor according to the variety of tree, the ripeness of the olives, the type of soil, the climate and the producer's preferences. Colors range from dark green to almost clear, depending on the ripeness of the olives at the time of pressing and the amount of subsequent refining. Color is not a good indication of flavor, however. Flavor is ultimately a matter of personal preference. Stronger-flavored oil may be desired for some foods, whereas milder oil is better for others. Good olive oil should be thicker than refined vegetable oils, but not so thick that it has a fatty texture.

The label designations—extra virgin, virgin and pure—refer to the acidity of the oil (a low acid content is preferable) and the extent of processing used to extract the oil. The first cold-pressing of the olives results in virgin oil. (The designation "virgin" is used only when the oil is 100% unadulterated olive oil, unheated and without any chemical processing.) Virgin oil may still vary in quality depending on the level of free acidity, expressed as oleic acid. Extra virgin oil is virgin oil with not more than 1% free acidity (oleic acid); virgin oil may have up to 3%. Pure olive oil is processed from the pulp left after the first pressing using heat and chemicals. Pure oil is lighter in flavor and less expensive than virgin oil.

Sesame oil is produced from the seeds of a large annual herb native to India. The tiny seeds range from white to tan to black, depending on the variety. The oil has a nutty, slightly bitter flavor, which becomes even more pronounced when the seeds are toasted prior to pressing for oil. Toasted sesame oil is used as a condiment or flavoring oil in China, Japan and Korea, whereas the milder oil pressed from raw seeds is used for baking and cooking in Mediterranean, Jewish and Indian cuisine.

Flavored oils, also known as **infused oils**, are an interesting and increasingly popular condiment. These oils may be used as a dip for breads, a cooking medium or a flavoring accent in marinades, dressings, sauces or other dishes. Flavors include basil and other herbs, garlic, citrus and spice. Flavored oils are generally prepared with olive oil for additional flavor or canola oil, both considered more healthful than other fats.

Top-quality commercially flavored oils are prepared by extracting aromatic oils from the flavoring ingredients and then emulsifying them with a high-grade oil; any impurities are then removed by placing the oil in a centrifuge. Using the aromatic oils of the flavoring ingredients yields a more intense flavor than merely steeping the same ingredients in the oil. Flavored oils should be stored as you would any other high-quality oil.

Hazelnut Oil

VINEGARS

Vinegar (Fr. *vinaigre*) is a thin, sour liquid used for thousands of years as a preservative, cooking ingredient, condiment and cleaning solution. Vinegar is obtained through the fermentation of wine or other alcoholic liquid. Bacteria attack the alcohol in the solution, turning it into acetic acid. No alcohol remains when the transformation is complete. The quality of vinegar depends on the quality of the wine or other liquid on which it is based. Vinegar flavors are as varied as the liquids from which they are made.

Vinegars should be clear and clean-looking, never cloudy or muddy. Commercial vinegars are pasteurized, so an unopened bottle should last indefinitely in a cool, dark place. Once opened, vinegars should last about 3 months if tightly capped. Any sediment that develops can be strained out; if mold develops, discard the vinegar.

Wine vinegars are as old as wine itself. They may be made from white or red wine, sherry or even Champagne, and should bear the color and flavor hallmarks of the wine used. Wine vinegars are preferred in French and Mediterranean cuisines.

Malt vinegar is produced from malted barley. Its slightly sweet, mild flavor is used as a condiment, especially with fried foods.

Distilled vinegar, made from grain alcohol, is completely clear with a stronger vinegary flavor and higher acid content than other vinegars. It is preferred for pickling and preserving.

Cider vinegar is produced from unpasteurized apple juice or cider. It is pale brown in color with a mild acidity and fruity aroma. Cider vinegar is particularly popular in the United States.

Rice vinegar is a clear, slightly sweet product brewed from rice wine. Its flavor is clean and elegant, making it useful in a variety of dishes, especially those of Japanese or Asian origin.

Flavored vinegars are simply traditional vinegars in which herbs, spices, fruits or other foods are steeped to infuse their flavors. They are easily produced from commercial wine or distilled vinegars, using any herb, spice or fruit desired. Inferior flavored vinegars are made by adding the desired flavoring to low-grade vinegar. The use of flavored vinegars is extremely popular but definitely not new. Clove, raspberry and fennel vinegars were sold on the streets of Paris during the 13th century. Making fruit-flavored vinegars was also one of the responsibilities of American housewives during the 18th and 19th centuries.

Balsamic vinegar (It. *aceto balsamico*) is newly popular in the United States, though it has been produced in Italy for more than 800 years. To produce traditional balsamic vinegar, red or white wine made from specially cultivated grapes (white Trebbiano and red Lambrusco grapes among others) is reduced, then aged in a succession of wooden barrels made from a variety of woods—oak, cherry, locust, ash, mulberry and juniper—for at least 4, but sometimes up to 50, years. The resulting liquid is dark reddish-brown and sweet. Balsamic vinegar has a high acid level, but the sweetness covers the tart flavor, making it very mellow. True balsamic is extremely expensive because of the long aging process and the small quantities available. Most of the commercial products imported from Italy are now made by a quick caramelization and flavoring process. Balsamic is excellent as a condiment or seasoning and has a remarkable affinity for tomatoes and strawberries.

Balsamic Vinegar, Raspberry Vinegar and Cider Vinegar

relish a cooked or pickled sauce usually made with vegetables or fruits and often used as a condiment; can be smooth or chunky, sweet or savory, and hot or mild

pickle (1) to preserve food in a brine or vinegar solution; (2) food that has been preserved in a seasoned brine or vinegar, especially cucumbers; pickled cucumbers are available whole, sliced, in wedges, or chopped as a relish, and may be sweet, sour, dill-flavored or hot and spicy

CONDIMENTS

Strictly speaking, a condiment is any food added to a dish for flavor, including herbs, spices and vinegars. Today, however, condiments more often refer to cooked or prepared flavorings, such as prepared mustards, **relishes**, bottled sauces and **pickles** served to accompany foods. We discuss several frequently used condiments here. These staples may be used to alter or enhance the flavor of a dish during cooking or added to a completed dish at the table by the consumer.

Chipotle in adobo is a Latin American seasoning made from smoked jalapeño chiles cooked in a tomato, onion and spice purée and is used as a rub or as an ingredient in sauces.

Chutney (from the Hindi word for *catnip*) is a pungent relish made from fruits, spices and herbs and is frequently used in Indian cooking.

Fermented black bean sauce is a Chinese condiment and flavoring ingredient made from black soybeans that have been heavily salted, then fermented and either slightly mashed (whole bean sauce) or puréed (paste). Both versions are usually mixed

Fermented Black Bean Sauce

FROM YOUR GROCER'S SHELF

Even the most sophisticated food service operation occasionally uses prepared condiments or flavorings. The products described here are widely used and available from grocery stores or wholesale purveyors. Some are brand-name items that have become almost synonymous with the product itself; others are available from several manufacturers.

Barbecue sauce—Commercial barbecue sauce is a mixture of tomatoes, vinegar and spices used primarily for marinating or basting meat, poultry or fish. A tremendous variety of barbecue sauces are available, with various flavors, textures and aromas. Sample several before selecting the most appropriate for your specific needs.

Chile sauce—Asian chile sauce, also known as *sambol* or *oelek* or hot sauce, varies somewhat depending on the country of origin or style, but all are thick, reddish-orange and extremely pungent and spicy. They usually contain pieces of chiles and/or garlic and less vinegar than Louisiana-style hot sauce. Asian cuisines incorporate these bottled sauces in curries and other dishes and use them as table condiments. One of the most popular and readily available brands is the Vietnamese-style chili garlic sauce with a rooster logo, made in California. Imported Sauce Sriracha, named after a port town in southern Thailand, is also widely available.

Hoisin sauce—Hoisin sauce is a dark, thick, salty-sweet sauce made from fermented soybeans, vinegar, garlic and caramel. It is used in Chinese dishes or served as a dipping sauce.

Old Bay brand seasoning—Old Bay is a dry spice blend containing celery salt, dry mustard, paprika and other flavorings. It is widely used in shellfish preparations, especially boiled shrimp and crab.

Oyster sauce—Oyster sauce is a thick, dark sauce made from oyster extract. It has a salty-sweet flavor and a rich aroma. Oyster sauce is often used with stir-fried meats and poultry.

Pickapeppa brand sauce—Pickapeppa sauce is a dark, thick, sweet-hot blend of tomatoes, onions, sugar, vinegar, mango, raisins, tamarinds and spices. Produced in Jamaica, it is used as a condiment for meat, game or fish and as a seasoning in sauces, soups and dressings.

Tabasco brand sauce—Tabasco sauce is a thin, bright-red liquid blended from vinegar, chiles and salt. Its fiery flavor is widely used in sauces, soups and prepared dishes; it is a popular condiment for Mexican, southern and southwestern cuisines. Tabasco sauce has been produced in Louisiana since 1868. Other "Louisiana-style" hot sauces (those containing only peppers, vinegar and salt) may be substituted.

Worcestershire sauce—Worcestershire sauce is a thin, dark brown liquid made from malt vinegar, tamarind, molasses and spices. It is used as a condiment for beef and as a seasoning in sauces, soups, stews and prepared dishes. Its flavor should be rich and full, but not salty.

Fish Sauce

Yellow Mustard

Dijon Mustard

with hoisin, chile sauce or minced garlic to produce a sauce that has an intense, pungent, salty flavor. Yellow bean sauces are similar, but milder and sweeter.

Fish sauce (Viet. *nuoc mam*; Thai *nam pla*) is the liquid drained from fermenting salted anchovy-like fish. It is a thin, golden to light brown liquid with a very pungent odor and salty flavor. There is no substitute for the savory richness that it adds to food and it is considered an essential flavoring and condiment throughout Southeast Asia, where it is used in and served with most every sort of dish.

Ketchup (also known as catsup or catchup) originally referred to any salty extract from fish, fruits or vegetables. Prepared tomato ketchup is really a sauce, created in America and used worldwide as a flavoring ingredient or condiment. It is bright red and thick, with a tangy, sweet-sour flavor. Ketchup can be stored either in the refrigerator or at room temperature; it should keep well for up to 4 months after opening. Ketchup does not turn rancid or develop mold, but it will darken and lose flavor as it ages.

Prepared mustard is a mixture of crushed mustard seeds, vinegar or wine, and salt or spices. It can be flavored in many ways—with herbs, onions, peppers and even citrus zest. It can be a smooth paste or coarse and chunky, depending on how finely the seeds are ground and whether the skins are strained out. Prepared mustard gets its tangy flavor from an essential oil that forms only when the seeds are crushed and mixed with water. Prepared mustard can be used as a condiment, particularly with meat and charcuterie items, or as a flavoring ingredient in sauces, stews and marinades.

Dijon mustard takes its name from a town and the surrounding region in France that produces about half of the world's mustard. French mustard labeled "Dijon" must, by law,

Whole-Grain Mustard

Brown Mustard

be produced only in that region. Dijon and Dijon-style mustards are smooth with a rich, complex flavor.

English and Chinese mustards are made from mustard flour and cool water. They are extremely hot and powerful. American or "ball-park" mustard is mild and vinegary with a bright yellow color. Unless it contains a high percentage of oil, mustard never really spoils; its flavor just fades away. Because of its high acid content, mustard is not prone to rancidity, but it will oxidize and develop a dark surface crust. Once opened, mustard should be kept well-covered and refrigerated.

Soy sauce is a thin, dark brown liquid fermented from cooked soybeans, wheat and salt. Available in several flavors and strengths, it is ubiquitous in most Asian cuisines. Light soy sauce is thin, with a light brown color and a very salty flavor. Dark soy sauce is thicker and dark brown, with a sweet, less salty flavor. **Tamari** is a Japanese-style soy sauce made without wheat, although its name may be applied to a variety of Japanese-style soy sauces. Necessary for preparing many Asian dishes, soy sauce is also used in marinades and sauces and as an all-purpose condiment. Other common soy-based sauces and condiments include teriyaki sauce and fermented bean paste (miso), made by fermenting soybeans with a grain such as rice or barley.

Soy Sauce

Tahini is a thick, oily paste made of ground toasted sesame seeds. It is thick and slightly grainy, with an ivory to grayish-tan color. Tahini can be bland or salty, depending on the manufacturer. Its toasted, nutty flavor is widely used in Middle Eastern and Mediterranean cuisine, especially in sauces and spreads such as hummus. Tahini is also useful in vegetarian dishes and is relatively high in protein and vitamins.

WINES, BEERS, BRANDIES, LIQUORS AND LIQUEURS

Wines, **beers**, **brandies**, **liquors** and **liqueurs** are frequently used in the kitchen, most often as flavorings, but also as primary ingredients in marinades and sauces or even as a cooking medium (pears poached in red wine, for instance). Wines are used to flavor and frequently to tenderize foods in marinades, to add flavor during or at the end of cooking, and to deglaze a pan to add flavor to a sauce. Brandy, especially the classic orange-flavored Grand Marnier, is a common bakeshop flavoring. Brandy complements fruits and rounds off the flavors of custards and creams. Liqueurs are selected for their specific flavors: amaretto for almond, Kahlúa for coffee, crème de cassis for black currant. They are used either to add flavors or to enhance other flavors in a dish. Liquors such as rum, bourbon and whiskey can be used for their own distinctive flavors or to blend with other flavors such as chocolate and coffee.

Because alcoholic beverages are used as flavorings, basic information about them is included here to familiarize the student chef with the basics of wine, beer and spirits. Brief guidelines for choosing appropriate wines or other alcoholic beverages as flavorings as well as guidelines on how to use them as flavorings are also included. As with other flavoring ingredients, patience, research, experimentation and practice will help develop a chef's feel for what alcoholic beverage—and how much—will best enhance a specific dish.

Wine

THE WINE-MAKING PROCESS

The process of transforming grapes into a still wine is called **vinification**. Freshly harvested grapes are gently crushed in order to release their juices. While in the crusher, stems and other undesirable matter are separated from the juice and grape skins.

wine an alcoholic beverage made from the fermented juice of grapes; may be sparkling (effervescent) or still (non-effervescent) or fortified with additional alcohol

beer an alcoholic beverage made from water, hops and malted barley, fermented by yeast

brandy an alcoholic beverage made by distilling wine or the fermented mash of grapes or other fruits

liquor an alcoholic beverage made by distilling grains, fruits, vegetables or other foods; includes rum, whiskey and vodka

liqueur a strong, sweet, syrupy alcoholic beverage made by mixing or redistilling neutral spirits with fruits, flowers, herbs, spices or other flavorings; also known as a cordial

vintner a winemaker

viniculture the art and science of making wine from grapes

viticulture the art and science of growing grapes used to make wines; factors considered include soil, topography (particularly, sunlight and drainage) and microclimate (temperature and rainfall)

fermentation the process by which yeast converts sugar into alcohol and carbon dioxide

Wooden Cork Pull

Waiter's Corkscrew

Lever-Type Corkscrew

If the **vintner** is making a **red wine**, both the crushed grapes (typically black-skinned grapes) and the juice are then transferred to a fermentation tank and allowed to ferment. As the red wine ferments, the grape skins release **tannins**, which give many red wines their distinctive astringent characteristic and slightly bitter taste.

If the vintner is making a **white wine**, the grape skins (typically from green- or white-skinned grapes, although occasionally black-skinned grapes are used) and juice pass through a wine press, where the juice is separated from the skins. For white wines, only the juice is allowed to ferment. If the vintner is making a **rosé wine** (ro-zay) or a blush wine, black grape skins are left in contact with the juice just long enough to add the desired amount of color.

After the juice is transferred to a fermentation tank, the vintner adds yeast to start the **fermentation** process. During fermentation, the yeast converts the sugar from the grape juice to alcohol and carbon dioxide. Fermentation generally lasts for 2 to 4 weeks and creates many of the wine's flavors and aromas.

Once fermentation is complete, red wines are pressed to remove the skins from the wine and then filtered to remove the yeast. White wines are allowed to settle and the yeast is filtered out. The wines are then stored in either stainless steel tanks or oak barrels for aging. Aging wines in oak barrels adds mellow vanilla, butter and oak flavors. White wines are normally aged for less time than red wines, usually no more than a year. When the vintner has determined that the wine has aged sufficiently, the wine is removed from the tank or barrel and bottled, corked and labeled.

Grape Varietals

Most wines sold in the United States are labeled according to the grape variety from which they are made. (The U.S. government requires that 75 percent of the wine come from a particular grape before that varietal can be named on the label.)

Most of the world's wine is made from one or more of the many varieties of the *Vitis vinifera* family of grapes. The most popular red wine grape varietals are Cabernet Sauvignon, Merlot, Nebbiolo, Pinot Noir, Syrah and Sangiovese. Popular white wine varietals include Chardonnay, Riesling, Pinot Grigio and Sauvignon Blanc.

Wines may also be labeled by their place of origin, and the names given to many European wines, particularly from France and Italy, actually refer to specific locations where the wine is produced. For example, Chablis, a popular white wine from the district of Chablis in France's northern Burgundy region, is made from Chardonnay grapes. Likewise, Chianti is a place in Italy's Tuscany region and refers to wine produced in that region from the Sangiovese grape. A number of countries, led by France and Italy, have implemented systems to ensure that wines bottled and sold under such district names are exclusively from grapes produced in that geographic area. French labels will state "AOC" (for "*appellation d'origine contrôlée*") and Italian labels "DOC" (for "*denominazione di origine controllata*") to designate such wines.

Sparkling Wines

Sparkling wines are still wines that undergo a complete second fermentation. The carbon dioxide generated during this second fermentation gives a sparkling wine its effervescence. After the initial fermentation, a sparkling wine is allowed to age for approximately 5 months. The vintner then adds extra yeast and sugar to the wine and allows it to undergo a second fermentation that lasts for a year or so.

For Champagne (shahm-PAHN-ya) and sparkling wines made like champagne (only a sparkling wine from the Champagne region of France can be called champagne), the second fermentation takes place in the bottle. Called **méthode champenoise**, the process requires that the wine be aged for one to two years after its second fermentation. Alternatively, the vintner can use the **charmat process**. With this less expensive process, the second fermentation takes place in a tank, and then the carbonated wine is bottled.

Champagne and other sparkling wines are classified by their degree of sweetness. From driest to sweetest, they are Natural or Au Sauvage, Brut, Extra Dry, Dry or Sec, Demi-Sec and Doux.

Fortified Wines

Wines usually have an alcohol content of 10–15%. Fortified wines are wines whose alcohol content has been increased to 18–22% by the addition of neutral grape spirits or grape brandy. If the brandy is added before fermentation is complete, the fortified wine will be quite sweet, as the extra alcohol stops the fermentation process before the yeast can digest all the sugars. If the brandy is added after fermentation is complete, the fortified wine will be drier. The best-known fortified wines—and the ones most often used in cooking—are listed next.

Port is traditionally produced in the Duoro valley of Portugal from a blend of five red wine grape varieties. Ports are generally divided into three categories. **Tawny ports** are pale brown and mellow, with a less fruity flavor than other ports. They are aged in wooden casks, sometimes for 20 or 30 years, before bottling. **Vintage ports** have a deep, dark brick or burgundy color and a rich, sweet flavor. Vintage ports are aged in their bottles, sometimes as long as several decades, before being consumed. They are considered the finest of ports and are too rare and expensive to use in cooking. **Ruby ports** are blends of younger ports of lesser quality than those designated as vintage ports. They tend to have a bright, almost crimson color and a sweet, fruity flavor. Several domestic ports, both ruby and tawny styles, are available and are reasonably priced and suitable for kitchen use.

Sherry is a fortified white wine from the Jerez region of southern Spain. Sherries can range from pale golden yellow and very dry to amber colored, thick and sweet with a pronounced nutty or dried fruit flavor and aroma. True aged Spanish sherries can be extremely expensive, but several domestic producers make both dry and sweet (cream) versions that are suitable for cooking use. Products labeled "cooking sherry" should be avoided at all cost, however, as these are inferior-quality, highly salted products.

Madeira, a fortified wine from the island of Madeira, is made from white wine grapes. Its characteristic light brown color and toffee-caramel flavor are produced when the developing wine is placed in wooden barrels and heated for a period of time, a process called *estufagem*. Madeira is sometimes used in desserts and in meat dishes.

Marsala, a fortified wine from western Sicily, is made from grapes that are dried prior to fermentation. This increases the resulting wine's sugar content. After fermentation and fortification, Marsala is aged in wooden barrels, which mellows its flavors. Marsalas are brown-colored and available in two styles, dry and sweet; both styles can be used in baked goods, pastries and veal and chicken dishes.

Evaluating Wines

Each grape varietal used to make a wine displays certain hallmark aroma and flavor characteristics in the finished product. This does not mean, however, that all wines made from the same grape varietal will have exactly the same aromas and flavors. Take, for example, a Merlot from Australia and one from California. They may share a certain smooth, juicy, mellow flavor with strong plum, black currant, black cherry and herbal or minty notes. But they will not be identical beverages. Rather, differences in the conditions under which the grapes were grown or the techniques the vintners used to make the wines will create noticeable differences between them. That said, the hallmark flavor and aroma characteristics of several of the world's most popular wine grapes are set forth in Tables 6.3 and 6.4. Often vintners blend two or more grape varietals in order to create a wine with the best attributes of a number of grapes. The infinite combinations account for the wide number of wines available and the vast differences between them.

As with any other flavoring, a chef should evaluate wines before using them. Wines that are not suitable for drinking are also not suitable for cooking purposes. When tasting wine, three basic attributes should be considered: aroma, flavor and body.

▶ **Aroma**—Most wines present a collection of different aromas. Called a bouquet or nose, individual aromas can often be distinguished (especially with practice) from a complex bouquet. The wine's aroma reminds the taster of some other scent, usually that of a fruit, flower, herb, spice or other easily distinguished item. For example, when evaluating the bouquet of a Cabernet Sauvignon, many people recognize the aromas of black currants, green bell peppers, chocolate, mint and/or leather as well as fruit jams if the wine is young and cedar and tobacco when it is aged. Likewise,

TABLE 6.3 PRINCIPAL RED WINE GRAPES

GRAPE VARIETALS	HALLMARK FLAVOR AND AROMA CHARACTERISTICS	ACIDITY	TANNINS	BODY	COMMON FOOD PAIRINGS
Cabernet Sauvignon (KA-bair-nay so-veen-yawn)	Assertive, rich, full flavor with fruity, black currant, chocolate, green bell pepper, mint or spice notes; jams when young, cedar and tobacco when older	Moderate	Moderate to prominent	Medium to full	Lamb and beef, especially if grilled; game, especially venison; strong cheeses
Merlot (mare-low)	Soft, smooth, juicy, mellow flavor with strong plum, black currant, black cherry and herbal or minty notes	Low	Low to moderate	Medium	Highly spiced dishes; savory foods with a hint of sweetness; grilled meats; fish and shellfish; strong cheeses; chocolate
Pinot Noir (pee-noe nwahr)	Rich, complex, flavor with cherry, raspberry and smoky or earthy notes and a velvety, silky texture	Moderate to high	Low to moderate	Light to medium	Game birds; rich, fatty fish or shellfish; roast beef; strong cheeses
Zinfandel (zin-fahn-DELL)	Robust, ripe, fruity, spicy flavors with blackberry or raspberry jam and black pepper notes	Low to moderate	Moderate to substantial	Medium to full	Roasted lamb; dishes flavored with garlic, black pepper and other strong flavorings; chili con carne and other hearty, spicy dishes; vegetable dishes; strong cheeses
Sangiovese (sahn-joe-VAY-zeh)	Earthy, hearty flavor with black cherry, raisin or floral (especially violet) notes	Moderate to high	Moderate	Light to medium	Veal; beef; lamb; hearty chicken dishes; tomato-based dishes
Syrah (see-rah) or Shiraz (shih-rhaz)	Rich flavor with sweet fruity, spice, floral or black pepper notes	Low to moderate	Moderate to prominent	Medium	Peppery, tangy, spicy foods; grilled meats; game

the hallmark aromas of a Sauvignon Blanc are cut grass, fresh green herbs, asparagus and other vegetables.

► **Flavor**—The alcohol in wine contributes very little to its flavor. Rather, vintners try to create flavors by adjusting the balances between the sugars and acids in the wine. These sugars and acids interact, exciting the taste buds to recognize the wine as sweet, dry or somewhere in between. The resulting flavor attributes are usually described with words based on a sweet/sour continuum (syrupy, sweet, crisp, tart or dry, for example), a general theme (for instance, fruity, herbaceous or spicy) or a reference to an attribute more akin to mouthfeel than flavor: smooth, velvety, silky and so on. **Initial taste** is the first impression of a wine's flavors; when constructing a wine's flavor profile, these would be the top notes. **Finish** is how long the flavor lasts after the wine is swallowed.

Tannins are complex organic compounds concentrated in the grape's skin, pits and stems. Tannins give red wines their characteristic astringent sensation and slightly bitter taste. Because grape parts are separated from the juice early in the white-wine-making process, for the most part, tannins present in a white wine are usually the result of the wine being aged in oak casks.

Because the skins are present during fermentation in red wines, red wines tend to have more dominant and complex fruity flavors than white wines. These fruity flavors tend to mask the acidity more commonly associated with white wines. White wines are generally served chilled because acidic flavors (the tart or sour taste) are less pronounced at colder temperatures.

► **Body**—The body is the weight of the wine in the mouth and is generally related to the amount of alcohol and/or glycerin it contains. A wine's body is usually described as light, medium or full.

TABLE 6.4 PRINCIPAL WHITE WINE GRAPES

GRAPE VARIETALS	HALLMARK FLAVOR AND AROMA CHARACTERISTICS	ACIDITY	BODY	COMMON FOOD PAIRINGS
Chardonnay (shar-doe-nay)	Full, rich flavor with a buttery texture and apple, green apple or tropical fruit notes; if aged in oak, may have vanilla or spicy notes	Moderate to high	Light to medium	Fish; shellfish, especially lobster; veal; chicken; foods flavored with herbs; foods served with rich or creamy sauces
Chenin Blanc (sheh-nan blahn)	Somewhat muted, tart acidic flavor with pine, melon or citrus notes; also used for a slightly sweet wine with similar notes	Very high	Light to medium	Light, summer foods; sweet or delicately flavored shellfish or fish; chicken; most cheeses; Asian foods
Pinot Grigio (pee-noe gree-joe) or Pinot Gris (pee-noe gree)	Crisp, dry, somewhat muted flavor with pine, orange rind and earthy or metallic notes	Moderate	Medium	Vegetables; fish; shellfish; pasta dishes; chicken
Riesling (REESE-ling)	Usually sweet but balanced by a strong steely acidity; apricot, citrus, peach or floral notes	Moderate to high	Light; medium to heavy as a dessert wine	Spicy foods; Asian foods; highly seasoned chicken dishes; shellfish; most cheeses
Sauvignon Blanc (so-veen-yawn blahn)	Bright, crisp, green, tangy flavor with grassy, herb or citrus notes	High	Medium	Spicy foods; tomato-based dishes; rich or fatty fish, especially salmon; most cheeses

MATCHING WINE AND FOOD

The only rule about matching wine and food is that there are no rules. The best food and wine pairings are simply those that the diner enjoys. With this in mind, consider the following guidelines.

Match Colors

Traditionally, red wines were served only with beef, veal, pork and lamb; white wines with only fish, shellfish and poultry. Although this rule may still be true for many pairings, do not be afraid to ignore it once in a while. Try, for example, a strong, oaky Chardonnay with grilled beef or a highly acidic, low-tannin red such as Sangiovese (Chianti), Pinot Noir or Beaujolais with fish or shellfish.

Match Tastes

▶ **Sweet**—Dishes with an element of sweetness often pair well with sweet or slightly sweet wines—the sweetness of one complements the sweetness of the other. If the same dish were served with a dry wine, the sweetness in the dish could make the wine taste a bit sour. Because **dessert wines** are so sweet, they are often difficult to pair with any food. A sweet dessert wine such as Sauternes does, however, complement the fatty richness in foie gras or lobster with a rich cream sauce.

▶ **Sour**—If a dish has a citrus, especially lemony, top note, usually an acidic wine goes well with it. Wines with a high acid content frequently taste less acidic when paired with salty or sweet foods.

▶ **Salty**—Salty foods will mute the sweetness and enhance the fruitiness of a wine.

▶ **Bitter**—Be careful of pairing a wine high in tannins such as a Syrah or Cabernet Sauvignon with a food equally rich in tannins, such as walnuts. The combination will render the wine almost unbearably bitter, dry and astringent.

▶ **Umami**—The richer the food, often the more robust the wine needed to complement it.

dessert wines sweet wines made from grapes left on the vine until they are overly ripe, such as Sauternes or wines labeled "Late Harvest"; during fermentation, some of the sugar is not converted to alcohol, but remains in the wine, giving it its characteristic intense sweet taste

Match Strengths

A delicate dish often goes best with a light, gentle wine, usually a white wine. A richly sauced or meaty dish might be best served with a strong, assertive wine, generally a red wine.

Match Opposites

Sometimes the perfect wine for pungent, spicy foods is a sweet or slightly sweet wine. Similarly, an acidic wine sometimes goes well with rich creamy or buttery sauces. Along the same vein, pair complex wines with simple dishes and simple wines with complex dishes.

Match Origins

Wines often developed alongside regional cuisines and thus they often have an affinity for each other. For example, cheeses or other foods from the Loire Valley of France pair exceptionally well with wines from that region, such as Sancerre (Sauvignon Blanc) or Chenin Blanc.

SELECTING WINES TO USE AS FLAVORINGS

The concepts just described for matching wines with foods have some bearing on what wines a chef should choose as flavoring ingredients. If a chef is wedded to a particular food-and-wine pairing and the dish calls for wine as an ingredient, it is often best to use the same or a similar wine (that is, a less expensive wine made from the same grape varietal) as the flavoring.

A chef should choose good-quality wines at cost-effective prices. Finding such wines may take time, but they are available. Often recipes will specify only a general type of wine. Here are some suggestions on what to use if a recipe calls for specific wines:

White wine or dry white wine—Consider a simple, fruity Chardonnay or a dry, herby Sauvignon Blanc. Avoid wines with a sharp, acidic flavor and those with an excessive oaky or woody flavor. When a dessert calls for white wine, such as for poached pears, a sweet wine might be appropriate.

Sweet or slightly sweet white wine—Consider a Riesling or Chenin Blanc or even a white Zinfandel.

Red wine or dry red wine—Consider a simple, fruity red wine with a low to moderately low tannin content. A Pinot Noir or a medium-bodied Merlot or red Zinfandel is usually a good choice.

Sweet red wine—Consider the rich flavor of a ruby port or possibly a red Zinfandel.

Sparkling wine—Consider using a sweet, fruity one (sparkling wines lose their effervescence once exposed to air and heat).

Dessert wine—Consider one labeled "Late Harvest."

Beer

THE BEER-MAKING PROCESS

Beer is an alcoholic beverage containing from 3% to 12% alcohol by volume. It is made from water, hops and malted barley, fermented by yeast (like wine) to produce alcohol and carbon dioxide. In Germany, by law only these four ingredients may be used, but in the United States and elsewhere another unmalted, less expensive grain such as rice or corn is often added to lighten the product.

Barley is converted into malt by steeping the dry grain in cool water for several days, allowing it to germinate and produce the sugar-producing enzymes required for the fermentation process. Once the barley has reached the desired sugar and enzyme levels, the grain is dried with warm air to establish color and flavor. The longer the drying period, the darker the resulting malt. A slow, gentle drying produces pale malts and a corresponding light-colored and -bodied brew, whereas more intense heat develops dark malts that may be characterized as "caramelized," "chocolate" or "toasted." To brew beer, the ground barley malt is "mashed" or soaked in hot water, producing a brown liquid called the wort. **Hops,** the cone-shaped flowers of the vine *Humulus lupulus*, provide bitterness and

Hops Flowers

aroma. They are added to the wort, which is then boiled for 1 to 2 hours, allowing the hops to flavor the brew.

Fermentation yeasts, selected according to the type of beer produced, are then added to the cooled wort. The fermentation process, which produces alcohol and carbon dioxide, can last from a few days in the case of ales to several weeks for lagers. Once fermentation is complete, the beer is transferred to storage vats for conditioning, a process that removes unwanted flavors and develops natural carbonation. This stage can also vary widely, from a few days to a few months before the beer is filtered and bottled.

Unlike wine, beer does not improve with age and is best consumed as soon as possible after production. Light and heat both adversely alter beer's flavor. Brown bottles are generally used to filter damaging rays. Beer is best stored between 50°F and 55°F (10°C and 13°C). Although Americans tend to serve beer ice-cold, this practice limits the appreciation of its full flavor. Lagers are ideally served at approximately 50°F (10°C), whereas ales should be served at about 60°F (15°C).

EVALUATING BEERS

Many characteristics influence the final outcome of the brewing process: the quality of the water, the type of malt, the hops used, the species of yeast selected for fermentation and the length of the fermentation and conditioning stages, as well as any additives. The combined effects of these elements determine the color, body, astringency, taste, alcohol content and aroma of the finished product. Beers may be divided into two broad groups: **ales** and **lagers**. Ales are made with yeast that rise to the top during the fermentation process, producing an aromatic, cloudy brew; porter and stout are the darkest and most potent ales. Lagers are made with yeast that falls to the bottom during fermentation and are characteristically light, clear, and crisp. Pilsner is a popular style of pale, light lager associated with the ancient brewing center in Plzen in the western Czech Republic. Most of the mass-market beer produced today is lager, but regional and microbreweries often specialize in ales.

Although all ales and lagers share certain general characteristics, within each group there are immense variations, as demonstrated in Table 6.5.

MATCHING BEER AND FOOD

Beer can be served with far more than pizza or barbecue; simply consider the following guidelines.

Match Tastes

Fruit beers, such as Belgian *kriek*, are often paired with meat or dessert dishes based on fruits.

TABLE 6.5 CHARACTERISTICS OF BEER

TYPE OF BEER	COLOR	ALCOHOL CONTENT	BODY	FLAVOR	COMMON FOOD PAIRINGS
American pilsner	Light	Very low	Light	Little aroma or bitterness	Spicy foods
Belgian lambic	Light	Moderate	Light	Sour	Sharp cheese; fruit desserts; dark chocolate
Brown ale	Red to brown	Low	Full-bodied	Sweet, nutty	Sausages; smoked fish; game; salad
European lager	Light	Moderate	Moderate	Bitter, floral finish	Most meat and fish dishes; German sausage; pretzels
Pale ale	Light	Low	Moderate	Bitter, fruity, floral	Spicy foods; smoked or fried seafood; beef; lamb; game
Porter	Dark	Moderate	Full-bodied	Bitter	Barbecue; hearty meat dishes; oysters; shellfish; smoked salmon; strong cheeses
Stout; bock	Very dark	High	Full-bodied	Sweet; malty	Chocolate, nut or fruit desserts; heavy meat dishes; goulash; spicy desserts

Match Strengths

Strong beers, such as porter and stout ales or bock lager, are frequently paired with strong tastes, such as sharp cheeses, game and spicy desserts.

Match Opposites

Beer, particularly lighter brew, is often preferable as a pairing with particularly spicy foods of East and Southeast Asia, Africa, the southwestern United States or Latin America, which may overpower wine. In Italy, beer is often drunk with pizza, which frequently contains such acidic ingredients as anchovies or artichokes, or multiple ingredients, which would challenge a single wine.

Match Origins

Beers of a given country are often paired with foods of that country—for example, German bratwurst or pretzels with German lager, or fiery Thai food with Thai pilsners.

SELECTING BEERS TO USE AS FLAVORINGS

Beer is frequently used as a flavoring in the cuisines of northern France and Belgium, where it appears in such dishes as carbonnade, a stew flavored with beer. Because of beer's slight bitterness, sugar or brown sugar is often added to balance the flavor. Beer can also be used in marinades and to deglaze and prepare sauces in the same manner as wine. In the United States, beer is frequently used in batters for foods being deep-fat fried, such as fish, and vegetables, such as Beer-Battered Onion Rings (page 598).

Brandy

Brandy is an alcoholic beverage made by distilling fermented fruit juice (wine) or fruit pulp and skin. Brandies typically fall into one of three categories:

▶ **Grape brandy** is a brandy distilled from white wine or fermented grape pulp and skins. It is aged in wooden casks (usually oak), which contributes to its rich, amber-brown colors and imparts additional mellowing flavors and aromas.

Cognac, one of the best-known brandies, is made in France's Cognac region (and only brandy made there can be called Cognac). Cognac is twice distilled from blends of various wines that tend to be thin, tart and low in alcohol—bad for drinking but great for brandy making. After distillation, the brandy is aged in oak casks. Virtually all Cognacs sold are blends of brandies from different vintners and different years. Traditionally Cognacs are labeled according to their age. Some common grades are V.S. (Very Special, at least 2½ years old), V.S.O.P. (Very Superior Old Pale, at least 4½ years old) and XO, Napoleon or Extra, at least 6 years old.

Armagnac is another well-known French brandy from the Armagnac region of southwestern France; it is slightly drier and heavier than Cognac.

▶ **Fruit brandy** is any brandy made from fermenting fruits other than grapes. This term should not be confused with **fruit-flavored brandy**, which is a grape brandy that has been flavored with the extract of another fruit. Well-known fruit brandies include **Calvados**, an apple brandy from Normandy, France; **Kirschwasser**, a cherry brandy from Bavaria, Germany; **Framboise**, a raspberry brandy from Alsace, France; **Poire**, a pear brandy from Alsace, France; and **Slivovitz**, a plum brandy from eastern Europe and the Balkans.

As with wines, when choosing a brandy as a flavoring, it does not necessarily pay to skimp on costs. The brandy does not have to be the most expensive brand, but it should have a rich, full, mellow flavor. Try, for example, an inexpensive but genuine Cognac (one that is graded V.S.). If the recipe calls for a fruit brandy, make sure to use one. Do not use a fruit brandy with added artificial flavors, a fruit-flavored brandy or a fruit-flavored liqueur. These products have different flavors, bodies, degrees of sweetness and alcohol contents than fruit brandies.

Liquors

Liquors are alcoholic beverages distilled from fermented grains, vegetables or the like. In **distillation**, the water component of a fermented liquid is cooked off and the alcohol is

distillation the separation of alcohol from a liquid (or, during the production of alcoholic beverages, from a fermented mash); it is accomplished by heating the liquid or mash to a gas that contains alcohol vapors; this steam is then condensed into the desired alcoholic liquid (beverage) concentrated. The resulting clear liquid can be colored or flavored during aging. The alcohol content of liquors ranges from 20% to 75% by volume, which is also expressed as "proof." Proof is double the amount of alcohol by volume; for example, a vodka that is 80 proof is 40% alcohol by volume.

Gin is a clear spirit distilled from grains and flavored with juniper berries, citrus peels and spices.

Rum is distilled from fermented sugar cane juice or molasses. Its character varies according to its color: **White rums**, which are clear and colorless, are relatively dry and light; **amber** or **gold rums** are similar to white rums but with a slightly stronger flavor and a pale golden color; **dark rums** have a strong molasses flavor, a dark brown color and a heavy body. Rums are a popular flavoring for desserts and baked goods.

Tequila is a clear to amber-colored spirit made in the Tequila region of Mexico from the fermented sap of the agave.

Vodka is, traditionally, a flavorless and colorless liquor distilled from potatoes, fruits, grains and/or other plant products. Most of the world's vodka is actually made from wheat. Many newer types of vodka are flavored, either by including the flavorings in the mash during distillation or by adding flavors afterward.

Whiskey (the English, Scots and Canadians spell it without the *e*) is distilled from various grains. After distillation, whiskey is aged in oak barrels until the flavors are mellow and smooth. There are many types of whiskies. **Bourbon** is produced in Kentucky and is distilled from a mash containing at least 51% corn, then aged in charred new oak barrels. It is slightly sweet and pairs well with desserts as well as rich meats such as duck, pork and game. **Irish whiskey** resembles Scotch, but without the smoky flavor. **Rye whiskey** is an American whiskey made from rye. **Scotch whisky** is distilled from malted barley and has a distinctive smoky or peaty flavor.

Liqueurs

Liqueurs are traditionally made from herbs, fruits, nuts, spices, flowers or other flavorings infused into an alcohol base. The base can be **neutral spirits**, brandy, rum or whiskey. All liqueurs have varying degrees of added sugar. Many newer liqueurs, especially less expensive products, are made with flavoring extracts, essential oils and even artificial flavors. **Cream liqueurs** are liqueurs blended with cream. They are thick, with mild, comforting flavors. They do not keep long once opened, so they need to be stored in the refrigerator. **Crème liqueurs**, such as crème de cacao, crème de menthe and crème de cassis, contain no cream. Rather, additional sugar gives them a thick, syrupy, creamy texture and a very sweet flavor.

When using a liqueur as a flavoring, look for products with rich, true, natural flavors. Also bear in mind that a liqueur and a crème liqueur flavored with the same ingredients are not the same products and should not be used interchangeably. So if a recipe calls for the coffee-flavored liqueur Kahlúa, use it and not a crème de café product; the latter will have a more syrupy texture and a sweeter flavor. Similarly, if a recipe calls for a proprietary blend such as Drambuie or Chambord, do not skimp on some lesser-quality generic product; customers may know the difference. Many of the liqueurs commonly used as flavorings are listed in Table 6.6.

Guidelines for Cooking with Wines, Beers, Brandies, Liquors and Liqueurs

▶ **Use quality products**—Heating a mediocre wine, brandy, liqueur or liquor tends to bring out the worst characteristics of the product, especially its acidic properties.

▶ **Pay attention to cooking time once wine or other alcoholic beverages have been added**—The longer a dish cooks, the more alcohol evaporates, thus concentrating its flavors, especially acidic flavors. Because alcohol evaporates at a lower temperature than water (172°F/86°C), the flavorings suspended in the alcohol are reduced and concentrated faster than flavorings suspended in water.

▶ **Brown foods before adding wine or other alcoholic beverages to a dish such as a sauce or stew**—This allows the surface of the foods to caramelize before liquid is added. As the wine is reduced, all of the flavors will blend together.

neutral spirits or **grain spirits** pure alcohol (ethanol or ethyl alcohol); they are odorless, tasteless and a very potent 190 proof (95% alcohol)

FLAMBÉING: COOKING WITH ALCOHOL

Often a dish will require flaming or flambéing, which means igniting brandy, rum or other liquor so that the alcohol burns off and the flavor of the liquor is retained. When alcohol comes into contact with a flame, it can ignite. So, in order to avoid singed eyebrows and kitchen fires, be careful when adding wine, brandy, liqueurs or liquor to a dish on or near the stove.

When a dish calls for flambéing, stand away from the pan being flamed. Never pour alcohol directly from a bottle into a hot pan because the flames can travel up into the bottle, causing it to explode. Heat the liquor until warm. This can be done in the pan in which the food is cooking, such as for Pepper Steaks (page 318), or in a separate pan, such as for Strawberry Crêpes Fitzgerald (page 561). Tilt the pan away from you before igniting the liquor to avoid having the flames leap from the pan. The flame from a gas burner or match will ignite the alcohol. Allow the flame to subside before finishing the preparation.

TABLE 6.6   LIQUEURS COMMONLY USED AS FLAVORINGS

LIQUEUR	ALCOHOL BASE	FLAVORINGS
Amaretto	Grape brandy	Almonds and apricots
B&B	Grape brandy	Bénédictine and brandy
Bénédictine	Grape brandy	Herbs, spices and citrus peels
Campari	Neutral spirits	130 different herbs, plants, peels and aromatics
Cassis	Neutral spirits	Black currants, herbs, roots, plants and peels
Chambord	Grape brandy	Black raspberries
Chartreuse	Grape brandy	More than 125 herbs and other flavorings
Cointreau	Grape brandy	Bitter orange peel
Crème de cacao	Neutral spirits	Chocolate
Crème de café	Neutral spirits	Coffee
Crème de cassis	Neutral spirits	Black currants
Crème de menthe	Neutral spirits	Peppermint
Curaçao	Neutral spirits	Bitter orange
Drambuie	Scotch whisky	Honey
Frangelico	Neutral spirits	Hazelnuts
Galliano	Neutral spirits	Anise, licorice and vanilla
Grand Marnier	Grape brandy	Bitter oranges
Irish Crème	Irish whiskey	Cream and sugar
Kahlúa	Neutral spirits	Coffee
Kirsch	Neutral spirits	Cherries
Limoncello	Neutral spirits, vodka	Lemons
Malibu	White rum	Coconut
Midori	Neutral spirits	Melons
Ouzo	Neutral spirits	Anise seed and herbs
Pernod	Neutral spirits	Anise seed and licorice
Pimm's No. 1 Cup	Gin	Herbs, botanicals and fruit extracts
Sambuca	Neutral spirits	Anise seed and elderberries
Sloe gin	Gin, neutral spirits	Sloe berries
Southern Comfort	American whiskey	Peaches and oranges
Tia Maria	Cask-aged rum	Coffee beans and spices
Triple Sec	Grape brandy	Bitter orange peel

▶ **Alcohol and acids in wine may interact with aluminum or cast-iron cookware**—Some chefs therefore prefer to use nonreactive cookware when cooking with wine or other alcoholic beverages.

For many, the consumption of alcohol is a concern. The amount of alcohol left after a wine or other alcoholic beverage has been added as a flavoring depends on how and for how long the dish is cooked. A dish flambéed tableside with Cognac that is allowed to burn out before being served, for example, may retain very little of its original alcohol content. But a chicken breast that has been marinated in white wine and then quickly sautéed could retain as much as 75 percent of the alcohol from the marinade. If, however, the same chicken breast is cooked over medium heat for 15 minutes, as much as 60 percent of the alcohol will evaporate out. Simmering the same chicken breast over low heat for approximately 2 hours or more will reduce the alcohol content to 10 percent or even less.

INTERNATIONAL FLAVOR PRINCIPLES

The proper study of world cuisines would occupy many books and many years of reading, traveling and tasting. Luckily for both culinary students and working chefs, the essence of the world's many cuisines can be distilled into an evaluation of six general components: primary ingredients (protein and starches); religious influences; typical cooking methods; cooking liquids; fats; and flavorings. Many of the ingredients used in a cuisine are the result of climate and geography. For example, the climate and landscape of northern Italy is good for grazing cattle, so beef, veal, butter and dairy products are more common there than in southern Italy, where seafood and olive oil prevail. Religious proscriptions against consuming certain meats, such as beef or pork, or drinking alcoholic beverages obviously impacts the cuisine of any region or culture that abides by such dictates. But the key point is the herbs and spices used to flavor the primary ingredients. Whether a cuisine utilizes tomatoes, chilies, lemon, basil or fennel may be the result of indigenous foodstuffs or may linger from long-ago trade practices.

For example, the primary ingredients of a Thai dish might be seafood and rice plus vegetables. These items would generally be cooked quickly by sautéing or stir-frying with water or fish sauce as a liquid component. Thai cuisine relies on palm or coconut oil, rather than butter or olive oil, which affects that cuisine's distinctive taste as well. Flavoring ingredients such as chilies (from the New World), fresh herbs, fish sauce or curry (from Thailand's neighbor India) complete the picture, and result in a dish that is recognizably Thai.

Although this six-part framework offers an almost stereotypically broad description of a cuisine, it presents a profile that most diners would recognize on their plate. This approach can also be useful for chefs in deconstructing dishes or imparting ethnic flavors to their own preparations.

In *Ethnic Cuisine: The Flavor Principle Cookbook*, Elisabeth Rozin writes: "Every culture tends to combine a small number of flavoring ingredients so frequently and so consistently that they become definitive of that particular cuisine" (p. xiv). She calls these defining flavors "flavor principles" and notes that they are "designed to abstract what is absolutely fundamental about a cuisine and, thus, to serve as a guide in cooking and developing new recipes" (p. xvii). She identifies the following flavor principles:

► Central Asia: cinnamon, fruit, nuts

► China: generally—soy sauce, rice wine, fresh ginger
      Northern China (Mandarin/Peking)—miso and/or garlic and/or sesame
      Western China (Szechuan)—sweet, sour and hot
      Southern (Canton)—black beans, garlic

► Eastern Europe (Jewish): onion and chicken fat

► Eastern and northern Europe: sour cream and dill or paprika or allspice or caraway

► France: generally—olive oil, garlic and basil or wine and herb or butter and/or sour cream and/or cheese plus wine and/or stock
      Provence—olive oil, thyme, rosemary, marjoram, sage plus tomato as a variation
      Normandy—apple, cider, Calvados

► Greece: tomato, cinnamon or olive oil, lemon, oregano

► India: Northern—cumin, ginger, garlic
      Southern—mustard seed, coconut, tamarind, chile

► Italy: generally—olive oil, garlic, basil
      Northern Italy—wine vinegar, garlic
      Southern Italy—olive oil, garlic, parsley, anchovy, tomato

► Japan: soy sauce, sake, sugar

► Mexico: tomato and chile or lime and chile

► North Africa: cumin, coriander, cinnamon, ginger, onion and/or tomato and/or fruit

► Spain: olive oil, garlic, nut or olive oil, onion, pepper, tomato

► Thailand: fish sauce, curry, chile

► West Africa: tomato, peanut, chile

Some of the flavor principles of selected international cuisines are discussed in the following essays.

SIGNATURE FLAVORS OF THE MEDITERRANEAN

"The Mediterranean is not even a single sea, it is a complex of seas . . . it is the sea of vineyards and olive trees as much as the sea of the long-oared galleys and the round ships of merchants . . .," wrote French historian Fernand Braudel in *The Mediterranean*. The ancients called the Mediterranean Sea *mare nostrum*, "our sea." Before national borders were defined, the fertile land and waters of the Mediterranean basin defined a regional culture and its rich cuisine.

The flavors of the Mediterranean (Greece, Turkey, Syria, Lebanon, Egypt, Jordan, Israel, North Africa, Spain, southern France, southern Italy, Sicily and Sardinia) are those from a quilt of local ingredients, many of which are native to the region—foods perfumed with heady olive oil and pungent green herbs such as wild thyme, fennel and rosemary—and from foods easily transported across its waters. Since Greek and Roman times, cultivation of key ingredients, which today define Mediterranean cooking, has flourished. Almond and citrus groves still thrive where they were planted to please Caesar. Romans established Sicily as its granary; durum wheat grown there fed armies from Rome to Tunis.

Wild mushrooms and chestnuts in Avignon, France

Whether in the port of Nice, in the foothills of the Parnassos Mountains in Greece or in a busy port town of Egypt, the flavors and primary ingredients in the foods served will be the same. Bold flavors using seasonally available ingredients are prepared using simple cooking techniques such as grilling, braising and simmering. Because all of the regions that border the Mediterranean have their roots in a rugged agrarian and fishing lifestyle, fresh, seasonal ingredients are prized. The labor involved in raising animals for food is respected; every part of the chicken, lamb or pig will be used.

Chef and food writer Joyce Goldstein has studied the signature food and flavor components of Mediterranean cooking. She has charted the cooking in the following list, useful to the chef looking to understand the cuisines of the region.

- **Olives and olive oil**
- **Primary vegetables**—garlic, eggplant, peppers and tomatoes
- **Secondary vegetables**—artichokes, beans, asparagus, spinach, squashes, pumpkin

- **Greens**—escarole, chard, chicory, dandelion, cabbage, broccoli rabe, spinach, cress, purslane, mesclun
- **Nuts**—walnuts, almonds, hazelnuts, pine nuts, pistachios
- **Dried fruits**—apricots, raisins, prunes, currants, figs
- **Citrus**—lemons, oranges, clementines
- **Fruit**—apricots, figs, dates, quince, pomegranate, pears, peaches, cherries
- **Grains**—rice, corn (polenta) and wheat in the form of farro, couscous, cracked wheat and bulgur, pasta, breads, flatbreads, phyllo, ouarka
- **Dried beans**—lentils, chickpeas, favas, cannellini
- **Yogurt, cheeses**—feta, haloumi, Parmesan, ricotta, pecorino, Fontina, mascarpone, taleggio, goat cheese, Manchego, Gruyère
- **Grapes and wine**
- **Spices, herbs and aromatics**—allspice, anise seed, cardamom, cayenne, cinnamon, coriander, cumin, ginger, peppercorns, saffron, turmeric; basil, cilantro, dill, lavender, marjoram, mint, oregano, parsley, rosemary, tarragon, thyme; orange and rose flower waters, honey

Fruit display in a market in Italy

Artichokes in Sicily

THE FLAVORS OF ASIA

Asian flavors are as diverse as the people who inhabit the more than 30 countries of Asia. Each country, region, city, town or village touts a rich culinary heritage that in many cases has evolved over thousands of years. Each region has developed unique combinations of tastes to create distinctive Asian flavors.

Sweetness can be as subtle as a raw shrimp served atop a pillow of seasoned rice at a Japanese sushi bar. The Chinese use rock sugar in simmered dishes. (It gives an evident sheen to the finished sauce.) In the tropics, one finds palm sugar in aromatic Thai coconut curries, in spicy Indonesia peanut satay sauce or drizzled over shaved ice in Malaysia. Indonesian sweet soy sauce coats skewers of meat before they are grilled over smoky coals. And ripe fruits are highly regarded at the end of a meal.

To balance the sweet ingredients, Asian cooks pull from a library of souring agents. Limes are preferred over lemons, as is a slightly sweet vinegar made from rice wine. Tamarind, widely known as *asam*, is sour without being overly acidic. Unripe mangoes' sourness plays center stage in green mango salad in Vietnam. The Japanese use *yuzu*, a tangerine-sized citron, combined with soy sauce and dashi, Japanese stock, for a dipping sauce.

Subtle bitter notes are prized in Asian cuisine. Ginseng is used not only for its medicinal properties but also for its bitter taste in Chinese broths, for example. In the Philippines, slices of bitter gourd are simmered with garlic and fatty pork. The Vietnamese prepare a syrup of bitter caramelized sugar that is combined with black pepper, fish sauce and shallots for simmering a type of local catfish. Astringency of tea is appreciated across the globe. In Asian cuisine, the flavor goes from the cup onto the plate. Tea, brown sugar and rice are combined and used to smoke duck, giving it a mahogany finish and a slightly bitter taste.

The use of monosodium glutamate (MSG) is heavily relied on in most Asian homes and restaurants. They use it judiciously, yet they use it often. Many con-

Produce market in India

temporary chefs prefer to use ingredients that are naturally high in glutamic acid because the savory mouthfeel lasts longer than any of our other primary tastes. The amount of free glutamic acid increases as fruit ripens and meat ages and, through fermentation, it enhances flavor during these processes. The Japanese are on the forefront of harnessing this taste naturally when they make miso—the fermented soybean paste that is used for soups, sauces and marinades.

Other contributors to the Asian flavor palate include the top notes of fragrant lime or orange rind and a generous use of herbs and spices. In Vietnam, copious amounts of herbs are used throughout the meal, especially in *pho*, noodle soup. A paste of aromatic lemongrass, galangal, turmeric, garlic, shrimp paste, coriander root, and fragrant lime zest creates the base of curries across the southeast regions. In India, dry spice mixtures are ground after toasting to enhance their inherent character.

Using contrasting temperatures throughout a meal and on one plate is a hallmark of Asian cuisine. This is where the Chinese concept of yin and yang, which promotes a harmony of contrasting elements, comes into play. For example, cool rice noodles may be topped with hot

grilled fish perfumed with Asian basil and dill. A topping of crunchy peanuts and a salty-sour blast of *nuoc cham*, Vietnam's fish sauce, further accentuates the contrast of temperatures and textures. In a Singaporean chicken satay, cool cubes of cucumber are skewered and dipped into the spicy peanut sauce right along with the hot skewers of poultry.

Chemesthesis, or the stimulation of the trigeminal nerve, is an often-overlooked part of flavor. But anyone would agree that the spice of capsaicin from chile peppers is an important element of flavor in Asian cuisine. Most experienced sashimi aficionados have pushed beyond their tolerance at least once by consuming too much wasabi on a piece of yellowtail. This burning sensation is an important part of Asian cuisine, as is mustard in Indian cuisine, in which mustard seeds, powder and oil are all used in many applications. Also associated with this sensation is what I refer to as *coolth*, the cool sensation experienced with herbs such as mint.

The crunch of a prawn chip, the crispness of a pickled cucumber or the slipperiness of sea cucumber are all examples of how textures and sound form an important part of Asian foods. Even the sizzle of a wok excites the palate. *Nori*, a type of seaweed, is toasted slightly before wrapping sushi rice, creating a crispy and chewy mouthfeel. Traditionally only the crispy skin of Peking duck is served wrapped in the hoisin-coated pancake.

The Asian flavor profile is a culmination of all the senses. Taste, smell, sight, sound and touch interplay to create one of the most exciting cuisines around. With the large influx of immigrants from Asia, one can now find authentic Asian cooking in many cities across the United States. An educated and experienced chef can elevate the dining experience with the deliberate manipulation of raw ingredients, mastering of cooking techniques and dramatic presentations. Now more than ever, Asian flavors are appearing in restaurants across the globe.

—ROBERT DANHI is an educator, cookbook author and Asian cuisine specialist

CHILES: THE FIERY HEART OF MEXICAN COOKING

Many Americans first taste Mexican cooking in one of the many fast-food chains that punctuate strip malls. Unfortunately, for some, this caricature of the foods of Mexico is the only thing they ever will know. Others, especially if they live in communities with a sizable Mexican population, have access to places owned and run by Mexican-American families who specialize in versions of the specific regional foods from where they have familial ties. These vary from the traditional border foods of Texas, Arizona, New Mexico and California—all once part of Mexico—to those of more recent generations of migrants from throughout Mexico.

Diverse regional differences exist throughout Mexico, but the one common strand that ties together the flavor profile of Mexican cuisine is chiles. Fresh, dried or pickled, their distinctive picante flavor is always present at the table in some form. The most common use are the vibrant tongue-tingling salsas and condiments that are found in or on almost any dish: soups, rice, beans, egg dishes and, of course, the myriad of different tacos and other *antojitos* (Spanish for "little whim," used to describe any appetizer).

In Yucatán, salsas will be made with the hottest of hot and herbaceous-flavored *habanero* chile, usually just ground into a paste and thinned with lime juice. In Guadalajara, the incendiary dried *chile de árbol* would flavor the salsa of choice, either puréed with tomatillos or blended with crushed sesame and pumpkin seeds, garlic and spices. These other ingredients go a long way toward rounding off the burning sensation of the chile.

The large dried chiles—the *ancho*, *mulattos*, *guajillo* and *pasilla*, to name the most common—are used more for their flavors than for heat and play an important

Chiles in a market in Mexico

role as an ingredient in hearty soups, stews, *moles* and *pipianes*, and in red-sauced *enchiladas*, *chilaquiles* and *tamales*. Each chile adds its own characteristic flavor. The *ancho* provides a fruity, slightly bittersweet element; the *mulatto*, although it looks like a black version of the *ancho*, has a less sweet, but still well-rounded flavor, which is only medium-hot. The *guajillo*, on the other hand, has a strong, straight, medium-hot chile flavor. There is nothing subtle about this chile. The deliciously picante hot *chile pasilla* has the most complex, rather astringent flavor of all. For some dishes, such as *moles*, two or three different varieties of these chiles would be blended to get the expected flavor for that particular dish. Each region has its own specialties.

The unique, smoky-flavored *chile chipotle* (a smoke-dried *jalapeño*) is used as a condiment, appears in salsas and in such classic dishes as the *tinga* from Puebla, and is now becoming trendy in the United States, even being used to flavor fine chocolates. And then there are *chiles rellenos*, in which the chile is the primary focus. Most commonly they are made from both fresh *chiles poblanos* and *jalapeños* or their dried versions, *chiles anchos* and the smoky *chipotles* and

stuffed with cheese or *picadillo*—a medley of meat, fish or chicken and nuts, raisins and spices.

There are now other ethnic cuisines in which chiles play a major role, such as India, Thailand and several provinces of China, but for the Mexican palate it is not just the use of chiles that is an important element; equally essential are the techniques utilized. The first is roasting or toasting to deepen and mellow the flavor. Large green chiles are blistered over a flame and the charred surface rubbed off. To enhance the flavor of dried chiles they often are briefly toasted on a *comal* until the color changes and their pungent aroma invades the air. The same roasting or toasting process is used as well with garlic, onion and even tomatoes, and when preparing moles, all of the seeds, nuts and spices are toasted or fried separately before becoming a part of this complex sauce. Another technique used to concentrate the flavors of cooked sauces is to fry the blended ingredients in very hot fat, sizzling, sputtering and spewing, until it becomes thick and dark.

For all the regional differences, there remains the commonality of the basic indigenous ingredients—corn, beans, squash and tomatoes, with chiles to enliven the cuisine. These staple ingredients and the cooking techniques are the very foundation of Mexican food. The native seafood, avocados, papayas, pineapple and other tropical fruits and herbs, along with the rice, wheat, spices, citrus fruit and meat from the livestock and poultry, first introduced by the Spanish, only enrich this wondrous cuisine.

—MARILYN TAUSEND is the author of several Mexican cookbooks and leads culinary tours to Mexico

CREOLE FLAVORS

For many, the words *Creole cooking* conjure up images of crawfish, jambalaya and the foods associated with New Orleans. But food historian and cookbook author Dr. Jessica Harris sees Creole cooking in a broader light. She feels that Creole food is the food of the southern Atlantic rim, "resulting from the confluence of the Columbian exchange, the Atlantic slave trade, and the European age of exploration, and extending over subsequent migrations of Indian, Chinese, Levantines, and more Europeans."

By her definition, Creole food is that found in Brazil, the Caribbean, Cuba, the West Indies, coastal Mexico, the southern United States and places in between. It is a cuisine composed of rice dishes such as jambalaya and red beans and rice, known as *moros y cristianos* in Cuba. Spices and hot sauces such as Tabasco or the searing Scotch Bonnet sauces served in the Caribbean are used frequently. And pork, fresh, salted or smoked, is of utmost importance.

Her discussion of the role of dried, smoked and pickled foods is of particular interest, for it suggests broad roots for many tastes prevalent in contemporary American cooking. Here she maps how the preference for these flavors migrated from one part of the world to another.

Market in Guadaloupe

"It is undeniable that there is a cultural curve that extends from Africa to the New World, then upward from coastal South America into the Caribbean and beyond. This curve is fascinating, as Africa's hold on culture mutates as the curve moves northward. Tribal influences change and vary, the intensity of Africanisms heightens or decreases all along the arc, but the African culture is always present. This also applies to the use of seasoning ingredients.

"On the African continent, there is a tradition of using dried or smoked ingredients to season soupy stews. Senegal's *guedge* and *yète* and the superfunky dried, smoked shrimp of the République du Benin are examples. In the New World, dried ingredients are used as well, and dried, smoked shrimp are still a major seasoning ingredient in the Afro-Brazilian cooking of the state of Bahia. As the arc moves northward, the dried ingredients give way to the pickled pork and smoked and salted fish that are used to season the pots of the Caribbean. Salt cod, a legacy of the slave trade, pickled and smoked herring from the seafarers, and the pickled pork that was also aboard ship take over seasoning duty from smoked shrimp, and the result is a change in flavor. Further North, in the southern United States, smoked ingredients return with seasoning pieces of fatback or even leftover ham or ham hocks, when available. Codfish turns up rarely, if ever, unless the cook comes from the Cape Verde Islands or is a transplanted Caribbean native. The constant throughout is the cardinal importance of the flavoring piece of meat, and the need for getting as much flavor as possible from as little animal protein as possible."

—From *Beyond Gumbo: Creole Fusion Food from the Atlantic Rim*, by JESSICA B. HARRIS (New York, Simon & Schuster, 2003)

1. What are some factors that can affect flavors? Discuss how this relates to cooking certain foods.

2. What is a flavoring? Does every kitchen keep the same flavorings on hand? Explain your answer.

3. What are the differences between an herb and a spice? Give an example of a plant that is used as both an herb and a spice.

4. If a recipe calls for a fresh herb and you only have the herb dried, what do you do? Explain your answer.

5. How are condiments used by chefs and by customers?

6. Describe ways in which wines and other alcoholic beverages are used to flavor foods.

7. Use the Internet to learn about the type of research being conducted by flavor and sensory research institutions such as the Monell Chemical Senses Center. WWW

8. Research the typical foods of the region of the world which your grandparents were born. Discuss how the climate and geography has played a part in the evolution of the most popular dishes from those areas.

Terms to Know

umami	flavor profile
taste receptor cells	flavor notes
olfactory bulb	garum masala
nostrils	table salt
retronasal path	rancid
pungent	oleic acid
astringent	condiments
capsaicin	vinification
consistency of food	initial taste
supertaster	finish
	flambéing

CHAPTER SEVEN

DAIRY PRODUCTS

ewe's milk milk produced by a female sheep; it has approximately 7.9% milkfat, 11.4% milk solids and 80.7% water

goat's milk milk produced by a female goat; it has approximately 4.1% milkfat, 8.9% milk solids and 87% water

water buffalo's milk milk produced by a female water buffalo; it has approximately 7.5% milkfat, 10.3% milk solids and 82.2% water

DAIRY PRODUCTS INCLUDE COW'S MILK AND foods produced from cow's milk such as butter, yogurt, sour cream and cheese. The milk of other mammals, namely, goats, sheep (ewe) and buffalo, is also made into cheeses that are used in commercial food service operations. Dairy products are extremely versatile and are used throughout the kitchen, served either as is or as ingredients in foods as varied as soups, salads, breads and desserts.

MILK

Milk is not only a popular beverage, it is also an ingredient in many dishes. It provides texture, flavor, color and nutritional value for cooked or baked items. Indeed, milk is one of the most nutritious foods available, providing proteins, vitamins and minerals (particularly calcium). But milk is also highly perishable and an excellent bacterial breeding ground. Care must be exercised when handling and storing milk and other dairy products.

Whole milk—that is, milk as it comes from the cow—consists of water primarily (about 88%). It contains approximately 3.5% milkfat and 8.5% other milk solids (proteins, milk sugar [lactose] and minerals).

Whole milk is graded A, B or C according to standards recommended by the U.S. Public Health Service. Grades are assigned based on bacterial count, with Grade A products having the lowest count. Grades B and C, though still safe and wholesome, are rarely available for retail or commercial use. Fresh whole milk is not available raw, but must be processed as we describe shortly.

Processing Techniques

PASTEURIZATION

By law, all Grade A milk must be pasteurized prior to retail sale. Pasteurization is the process of heating milk to a sufficiently high temperature for a sufficient length of time to destroy pathogenic bacteria. This typically requires holding milk at a temperature of 161°F (72°C) for 15 seconds. Pasteurization also destroys enzymes that cause spoilage, thus increasing shelf life. Milk's nutritional value is not significantly affected by pasteurization.

ULTRA-PASTEURIZATION

Ultra-pasteurization is a process in which milk is heated to a very high temperature (275°F/135°C) for a very short time (2 to 4 seconds) in order to destroy virtually all bacteria. Ultra-pasteurization is most often used with whipping cream and individual creamers. Although the process may reduce cream's whipping properties, it extends its shelf life dramatically.

ULTRA-HIGH-TEMPERATURE PROCESSING

Ultra-high-temperature (UHT) processing is a form of ultra-pasteurization in which milk is held at a temperature of 280°F–300°F (138°C–150°C) for 2 to 6 seconds. It is then packed in sterile containers under sterile conditions and aseptically sealed to prevent bacteria from entering the container. Unopened UHT milk can be stored without refrigeration for at least 3 months. Although UHT milk can be stored unrefrigerated, it should be chilled before serving and stored like fresh milk once opened. UHT processing may give milk a slightly cooked taste, but it has no significant effect on milk's nutritional value. Long available in Europe, it is now gaining popularity in the United States.

HOMOGENIZATION

Homogenization is a process in which the fat globules in whole milk are reduced in size and permanently dispersed throughout the liquid. This prevents the fat from clumping together and rising to the surface as a layer of cream. Although homogenization is not required, milk sold commercially is generally homogenized because it ensures a uniform consistency, a whiter color and a richer taste.

MILKFAT REMOVAL

Whole milk can also be processed in a centrifuge to remove all or a portion of the milkfat, resulting in reduced-fat, low-fat and nonfat milks. All reduced-fat milks must still be nutritionally equivalent to full-fat milk and must provide at least the same amounts of the fat-soluble vitamins A and D as full-fat milk.

Reduced-fat or less-fat milk is whole milk from which sufficient milkfat has been removed to produce a liquid with 2% milkfat. **Low-fat** or little-fat milk contains 1% milkfat. **Nonfat** milk, also referred to as fat-free, no-fat or skim milk, has had as much milkfat removed as possible. The fat content must be less than 0.5%.

STORAGE

Fluid milk is a potentially hazardous food and should be kept refrigerated at or below 41°F (5°C). Its shelf life is reduced by half for every 5-degree rise in temperature above 41°F (5°C). Keep milk containers closed to prevent absorption of odors and flavors. Freezing is not recommended.

Concentrated Milks

Concentrated or condensed milk products are produced by using a vacuum to remove all or part of the water from whole milk. The resulting products have a high concentration of milkfat and milk solids and an extended shelf life.

Evaporated milk is produced by removing approximately 60% of the water from whole, homogenized milk. The concentrated liquid is canned and heat-sterilized. This results in a cooked flavor and darker color. Evaporated skim milk, with a milkfat content of 0.5%, is also available. A can of evaporated milk requires no refrigeration until opened, although the can should be stored in a cool place. Evaporated milk can be reconstituted with an equal amount of water and used like whole milk for cooking or drinking.

Sweetened condensed milk is similar to evaporated milk in that 60% of the water has been removed. But unlike evaporated milk, sweetened condensed milk contains large amounts of sugar (40 to 45%). Sweetened condensed milk is also canned; the canning process darkens the color and adds a caramel flavor. Sweetened condensed milk cannot be substituted for whole milk or evaporated milk because of its sugar content. Its distinctive flavor is most often found in desserts and confections.

Dry milk powder is made by removing virtually all the moisture from pasteurized milk. Dry whole milk, nonfat milk and buttermilk are available. The lack of moisture prevents the growth of microorganisms and allows dry milk powders to be stored for extended periods without refrigeration. Powdered milks can be reconstituted with water and used like fresh milk. Milk powder may also be added to foods directly, with additional liquid included in the recipe. This procedure is typical in bread making and does not alter the function of the milk or the flavor in the finished product.

Cream

Cream is a rich, liquid milk product containing at least 18% fat. It must be pasteurized or ultra-pasteurized and may be homogenized. Cream has a slight yellow or ivory color and is more viscous than milk. It is used throughout the kitchen to give flavor and body to sauces, soups and desserts. Whipping cream, containing not less than 30% milkfat, can be whipped into a stiff foam and used in pastries and desserts. Cream is marketed in several forms with different fat contents, as described here.

Half-and-half is a mixture of whole milk and cream containing between 10% and 18% milkfat. It is often served with cereal or coffee, but does not contain enough fat to whip into a foam.

Light cream, **coffee cream** and **table cream** are all products with more than 18% but less than 30% milkfat. These products are often used in baked goods or soups as well as with coffee, fruit and cereal.

Light whipping cream or, simply, **whipping cream**, contains between 30% and 36% milkfat. It is generally used for thickening and enriching sauces and making ice cream. It can be whipped into a foam and used as a dessert topping or folded into custards or mousses to add flavor and lightness.

Heavy whipping cream or, simply, **heavy cream**, contains not less than 36% milkfat. It whips easily and holds its whipped texture longer than other creams. It must be pasteurized, but is rarely homogenized. Heavy cream is used throughout the kitchen in the same ways as light whipping cream.

STORAGE

Ultra-pasteurized cream will keep for 6 to 8 weeks if refrigerated at or below 41°F (5°C). Unwhipped cream should not be frozen. Keep cream away from strong odors and bright lights, as they can adversely affect its flavor.

Cultured Dairy Products

Cultured dairy products such as yogurt, buttermilk and sour cream are produced by adding specific bacterial cultures to fluid dairy products. The bacteria convert the milk sugar **lactose** into lactic acid, giving these products their body and tangy, unique flavors. The acid content also retards the growth of undesirable microorganisms; thus cultured products have been used for centuries to preserve milk.

Buttermilk originally referred to the liquid remaining after cream was churned into butter. Today, buttermilk is produced by adding a culture (*Streptococcus lactis*) to fresh, pasteurized skim or low-fat milk. This results in tart milk with a thick texture. Buttermilk is most often used as a beverage or in baked goods.

Sour cream is produced by adding the same culture to pasteurized, homogenized light cream. The resulting product is a white, tangy gel used as a condiment or to give baked goods a distinctive flavor. Sour cream must have a milkfat content of not less than 18%.

Crème fraîche is a cultured cream popular in French cuisine. Although thinner and richer than sour cream, it has a similar tart, tangy flavor. It is used extensively in soups and sauces, especially with poultry, rabbit and lamb dishes. It is easily prepared from the following recipe.

Yogurt is a thick, tart, custardlike product made from milk (either whole, low-fat or nonfat) cultured with *Lactobacillus bulgaricus* and *Streptococcus thermophilus*. Though touted as a health or diet food, yogurt contains the same amount of milkfat as the milk from which it is made. Yogurt may also contain a variety of sweeteners, flavorings and fruits. Greek yogurt is a more creamy and dense style of yogurt, made by straining more of the whey from the product or by adding additional milk protein solids. (Authentic Greek yogurt is often made with sheep's milk.) Yogurt is generally eaten as is, but may be used in baked products, salad dressings and frozen desserts. It is used in many Middle Eastern cuisines.

lactose a disaccharide that occurs naturally in mammalian milk; milk sugar

---

BUTTERMILK IN A PINCH

To make a buttermilk substitute when none is available, combine 8 fluid ounces (240 milliliters) whole milk with 1/2 fluid ounce (15 milliliters) white vinegar or lemon juice. The mixture should begin to curdle in 15 minutes. Stir well before using. Combining 2 fluid ounces (60 milliliters) whole milk with 6 fluid ounces (180 milliliters) plain yogurt will also work as a buttermilk substitute.

CRÈME FRAÎCHE

Yield: 16 fl. oz. (480 ml)

Heavy cream, not ultra-pasteurized	16 fl. oz.	480 ml
Buttermilk, with active cultures	1 fl. oz.	30 ml

1. Heat the cream to approximately 100°F (43°C).
2. Remove the cream from the heat and stir in the buttermilk.
3. Allow the mixture to stand in a warm place, loosely covered, until it thickens, approximately 12 to 36 hours.
4. Chill thoroughly before using. Crème fraîche will keep for up to 10 days in the refrigerator.

Approximate values per 1-fl.-oz. (30-ml) serving: **Calories** 90, **Total fat** 10 g, **Saturated fat** 6 g, **Cholesterol** 35 mg, **Sodium** 10 mg, **Total carbohydrates** 1 g, **Protein** 1 g, **Vitamin A** 10%, Claims—very low sodium

STORAGE

Cultured products are potentially hazardous foods and should be kept refrigerated at or below 41°F (5°C). Under proper conditions, sour cream will last up to 4 weeks, yogurt up to 3 weeks and buttermilk up to 2 weeks. Freezing is not recommended for these products, but dishes prepared with cultured products generally can be frozen.

Butter

Butter is a fatty substance produced by agitating or churning cream. Its flavor is unequaled in sauces, breads and pastries. Butter contains at least 80% milkfat, not more than 16% water and 2–4% milk solids. It may or may not contain added salt. Butter is firm when chilled and soft at room temperature. It melts into a liquid at approximately 93°F (33°C) and reaches the smoke point at 260°F (127°C).

Sweet butter is simply another name for unsalted butter. **Salted butter**, as the name implies, is butter with salt added. Typically 1.7% salt is used, although exact amounts vary from producer to producer. Salt not only changes the butter's flavor, it also extends its keeping qualities. When using salted butter in cooking or baking, the salt content must be considered in the total recipe.

European-style butter contains more milkfat than regular butter, usually 82–86%, and very little or no added salt. It is often churned from cultured cream, giving it a more intense, buttery flavor. It may be used in lieu of any regular butter in cooking or baking.

Whipped butter is made by incorporating air into the butter. This increases its volume and spreadability, but also increases the speed with which the butter will become rancid. Because of the change in density, whipped butter should not be substituted in recipes calling for regular butter.

Clarified butter is butter that has had its water and milk solids removed by a process called clarification. Although **whole butter** can be used for cooking or sauce making, sometimes a more stable and consistent product will be achieved by using clarified butter. The clarification process is described in Chapter 8, Mise en Place.

STORAGE

With its high fat content, butter is extremely prone to **rancidity**. Butter that is rancid will develop a harsh bitter taste and deep yellow to brown color. To preserve its freshness, butter should be well wrapped and stored at temperatures between 32°F and 35°F (0°C and 2°C). Unsalted butter is best kept frozen until needed. If well wrapped, frozen butter will keep for up to 9 months at a temperature of 0°F (–18°C).

Margarine

Margarine is not a dairy product but is included in this section because it is so frequently substituted for butter in cooking, baking and table service. Margarine is manufactured from animal or vegetable fats or a combination of such fats. Flavorings, colorings, emulsifiers, preservatives and vitamins are added, and the mixture is firmed or solidified by exposure to hydrogen gas at very high temperatures, a process known as hydrogenation. Generally, the firmer the margarine, the greater the degree of hydrogenation and the longer its shelf life. Like butter, margarine is approximately 80% fat and 16% water. But even the finest margarine cannot match the flavor of butter.

Margarine packaged in tubs is softer and more spreadable than solid products and generally contains more water and air. Indeed, diet margarine is approximately 50% water. Because of their decreased density, these soft products should not be substituted for regular butter or margarine in cooking or baking.

Specially formulated and blended margarine is available for commercial use in making puff pastry, croissant doughs, frostings and the like.

GRADING BUTTER

Government grading is not mandatory, but most processors submit their butters for testing. The USDA label on the package assures the buyer that the butter meets federal standards for the grade indicated:

- USDA Grade AA—butter of superior quality, with a fresh, sweet flavor and aroma, a smooth, creamy texture and good spreadability.
- USDA Grade A—butter of very good quality, with a pleasing flavor and fairly smooth texture.
- USDA Grade B—butter of standard quality, made from sour cream; has an acceptable flavor but lacks the flavor, texture and body of Grades AA and A. Grade B is most often used in the manufacture of foods.

whole butter butter that is not clarified, whipped or reduced-fat

rancidity the decomposition of fats by exposure to oxygen, resulting in off-flavors and destruction of nutritive components

NUTRITION

Dairy products are naturally high in vitamins, minerals and protein. Often liquid products such as milk are fortified with additional vitamins and minerals, especially vitamins A and D. Because milk and butter are animal products, they do contain cholesterol. Their overall fat content varies depending on the amount of milkfat left after processing.

NATURAL CHEESES

Cheese (Fr. *fromage*; It. *formaggio*) is one of the oldest and most widely used foods known to humankind. It is served alone or as a principal ingredient in or an accompaniment to countless dishes. Cheese is commonly used in commercial kitchens, appearing in everything from breakfast to snacks to desserts.

Hundreds of natural cheeses are produced worldwide. Although their shapes, ages and flavors vary according to local preferences and traditions, all natural cheeses are produced in the same basic fashion as has been used for centuries. Each starts with a mammal's milk; cows, goats and sheep are the most commonly used. The milk proteins (known as *casein*) are coagulated with the addition of an enzyme, usually rennet, which is found in calves' stomachs. As the milk coagulates, it separates into solid curds and liquid whey. After draining off the whey, either the curds are made into fresh cheese, such as ricotta or cottage cheese, or the curds are further processed by cutting, kneading and cooking. The resulting substance, known as "green cheese," is packed into molds to drain. Salt or special bacteria may be added to the molded cheeses, which are then allowed to age or ripen under controlled conditions to develop the desired texture, color and flavor.

Cheeses are a product of their environment, which is why most fine cheeses cannot be reproduced outside their native locale. The breed and feed of the milk animal, the wild spores and molds in the air and even the wind currents in a storage area can affect the manner in which a cheese develops. (Roquefort, for example, develops its distinctive flavor from aging in particular caves filled with crosscurrents of cool, moist air.)

Some cheeses develop a natural rind or surface because of the application of bacteria (bloomy rind) or by repeated washing with brine (washed rind). Most natural rinds may be eaten if desired. Other cheeses are coated with an inedible wax rind to prevent moisture loss. (Cheeses that are smoked are frequently coated with a brown wax rind.) Fresh cheeses have no rind whatsoever.

Moisture and fat contents are good indicators of a cheese's texture and shelf life. The higher the moisture content, the softer the product and the more perishable it will be. Low-moisture cheeses may be used for grating and will keep for several weeks if properly stored. (Reduced water activity levels prohibit bacterial growth.) Fat content ranges from low fat (less than 20% fat) to double cream (at least 60% fat) and triple cream (at least 72% fat). Cheeses with a high fat content will be creamier and have a richer flavor and texture than low-fat products.

Most cheeses contain high percentages of fat and protein. Cheese is also rich in calcium, phosphorus and vitamin A. As animal products, natural cheeses contain cholesterol. Today, many low-fat and even nonfat processed cheeses are available. Sodium has also been reduced or eliminated from some modern products.

The FDA allows the manufacture and distribution of raw-milk cheeses provided that they are aged more than 60 days at a temperature not less than 35°F (2°C).

Cheese Varieties

Cheeses can be classified by country of origin, ripening method, fat content or texture. Here we classify fine cheeses by texture and have adopted five categories: fresh or unripened, soft, semisoft, firm and hard. A separate section on goat's-milk cheeses is also included.

FRESH OR UNRIPENED CHEESES

Fresh cheeses are uncooked and unripened. Referred to as *fromage blanc* or *fromage frais* in French, they are generally mild and creamy with a tart tanginess. They should not taste acidic or bitter. Fresh cheeses have a moisture content of 40–80% and are highly perishable.

MAKING MOZZARELLA

In Italy, mozzarella is made every day; it is meant to be consumed just as often. Before there was refrigeration, the balls of mozzarella were stored in well water to keep them cool, which is where the tradition originated of storing fresh mozzarella in liquid.

Once the milk is coagulated and the curds are cut, the mass is slowly stirred to enhance the whey's expulsion. A few hours later, when the curds are mature, they are removed from the whey, chopped or shredded and then mixed with hot water.

To test the exact amount of maturity, a handful of curds is dipped into a bucket of hot water for 10 seconds. When the curds are removed, they should be kneaded briefly and then, holding the mass with two hands, it should be pulled and stretched out to determine its maturity. When it can be stretched as thin and opaque as tissue paper, it is exactly ready to be strung. At this point, small amounts of curd are dumped into a small vat and stirred with hot water using a paddle. This is known as "stringing" the cheese because as the curds are mixed with the water they begin to melt somewhat and become stringy. The more the cheese is stirred, the longer the strings are stretched. Eventually, all the strings come together to make a large mass of satiny-smooth cheese. In Italian, the word *filare* means "to string"; therefore, all cheeses that are strung are members of the *pasta filata* family.

When stringing is complete, the cheese is ready to be shaped and hand-formed into balls. The balls are tossed immediately into vats of cool water so they will maintain the desired shapes. When cool, the balls are immersed in brine solution and then wrapped in parchment paper.

—PAULA LAMBERT owns the Mozzarella Company in Dallas, Texas

Cream cheese is a soft cow's milk cheese from the United States containing approximately 35% fat. It is available in various-sized solid white blocks or whipped and flavored. It is used throughout the kitchen in baking, dips, dressings and confections and is popular as a spread for bagels and toast. **Feta** is a semisoft Greek or Italian product made from sheep's and/or goat's milk. It is a white, flaky cheese that is pickled (but not ripened) and stored in brine water, giving it a shelf life of 4 to 6 weeks. Its flavor becomes sharper and saltier with age. Feta is good for snacks and salads and melts easily for sauces and fillings.

Feta

Mascarpone (mas-cahr-POHN-ay) is a soft cow's-milk cheese originally from Italy's Lombard region. It contains 70–75% fat and is extremely smooth and creamy. Mascarpone is highly perishable and is available in bulk or in 8- or 16-ounce tubs. With its pale ivory color and rich, sweet flavor, it is useful in both sweet and savory sauces as well as desserts. It is also eaten plain, with fresh fruit or spread on bread and sprinkled with cocoa or sugar.

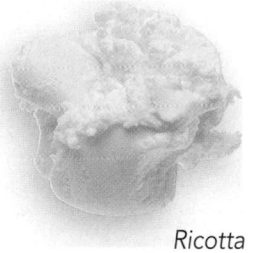

Mascarpone

Mozzarella (maht-suh-REHL-lah) is a firm Italian cheese traditionally made with water buffalo's milk (today, cow's milk is more common) and containing 40–45% fat. Mozzarella becomes elastic when melted and is well known as "pizza cheese." Fresh mozzarella is excellent in salads or topped simply with olive oil and herbs. It is a very mild white cheese best eaten within hours of production. Commercial mozzarella is rather bland and rubbery and is best reserved for cooking, for which it may be purchased already shredded.

Mozzarella

Queso Oaxaca (KEH-soh wah-HA-kaa), also known as Quesillo or Asadero, is one of the most popular cheeses of Mexico. It is a cow's-milk *pasta filata* or stretched-curd cheese that is kneaded and wound into balls, then soaked in brine for several minutes. It is pulled apart into thin strings before being used to fill tortillas or melted over cooked dishes. Queso Oaxaca is a good melting cheese with a smooth semisoft texture, white color and 45% fat content. It is invaluable in preparing Mexican and Mexican-American dishes such as quesadillas, nachos and tacos, and is also available blended with herbs, spices or chiles.

Queso Oaxaca

Ricotta (rih-COH-tah) is a soft Italian cheese, similar to American cottage cheese, made from the whey left when other cow's-milk cheeses are produced. It contains only 4–10% fat. It is white or ivory in color and fluffy, with a small grain and sweet flavor. Ricotta is an important ingredient in many pasta dishes and desserts. It can be made easily with the following recipe.

Ricotta

RICOTTA CHEESE

THE ART INSTITUTE OF WASHINGTON, ARLINGTON, VA

Former Chef Instructor John Harrison

Yield: 8 oz. (240 g)

Milk	1 qt.	960 ml
Fresh lime juice	3 fl. oz.	90 ml

1. Allow the milk to reach room temperature in a covered container.
2. In a stainless steel saucepan slowly heat the milk to 180°F (82°C), stirring often. Hold the heated milk at 180°F (82°C) for 5 minutes.
3. Remove the milk from the heat and gently stir it while adding the lime juice. Continue to stir until curds form.
4. Gently pour the curds into a strainer or china cap lined with new, rinsed cheesecloth. Allow the whey (liquid) to separate and drain away from the curds (solids). Discard the whey.
5. Allow the cheese to rest undisturbed for 1 hour. For a firm, dry ricotta, lift the corners of the cheese-cloth and tie them together with twine. Suspend the bag in a tall, covered container, place it in the refrigerator and allow the cheese to drain for 4 hours or overnight.
6. Unwrap the cheese. Season it with salt if desired. Use the cheese as you would use commercially produced ricotta.

Approximate values per 1-oz. (30-g) serving: **Calories** 80, **Total fat** 4 g, **Saturated fat** 2.5 g, **Cholesterol** 15 mg, **Sodium** 60 mg, **Total carbohydrates** 7 g, **Protein** 4 g, **Calcium** 15%

1. Heat the milk to 180°F (82°C).

2. Gently stir in the lime juice.

3. Strain the mixture through cheesecloth.

4. The finished ricotta.

SOFT CHEESES

Soft cheeses are characterized by their thin skins and creamy centers. They are among the most delicious and popular of cheeses. They ripen quickly and are at their peak for only a few days, sometimes less. Moisture content ranges from 50–75%.

Brie (bree) is a rind-ripened French cheese made with cow's milk and containing about 60% fat. Brie is made in round, flat disks weighing 2 or 4 pounds (1 or 2 kilograms); it is coated with a bloomy white rind. At the peak of ripeness, it is creamy and rich, with a texture that oozes. Selecting a properly ripened Brie is a matter of judgment and experience. Select a cheese that is bulging a bit inside its rind; there should be just the beginning of a brown coloring on the rind. If underripe, Brie will be bland with a hard, chalky core. Once the cheese is cut, it will not ripen any further. If overripe, Brie will have a brownish rind that may be gummy or sagging and will smell strongly of ammonia. The rind is edible, but trim it off if preferred. The classic after-dinner cheese, Brie is also used in soups, sauces and hors d'oeuvres.

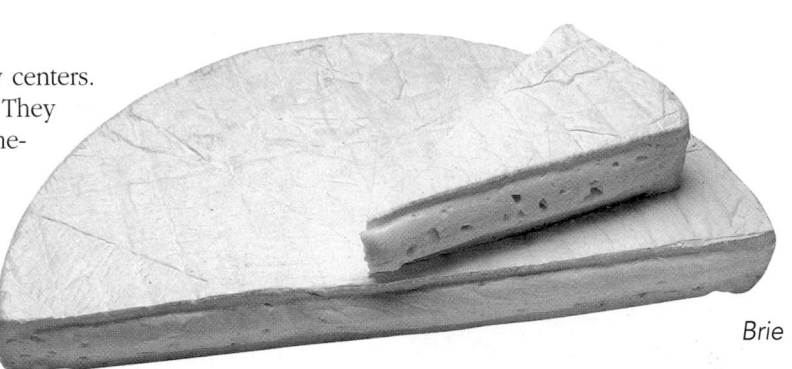

Brie

Boursin (boor-SAHN) is a triple-cream cow's-milk cheese from France containing approximately 75% fat. Boursin is usually flavored with peppers, herbs or garlic. It is rindless, with a smooth, creamy texture, and is packed in small, foil-wrapped cylinders. Boursin is a good breakfast cheese and a welcome addition to any cheese board. It is also a popular filling for baked chicken. A substitute can be prepared using the following recipe.

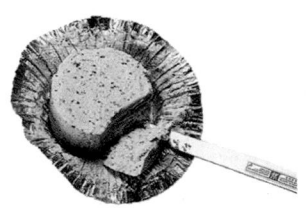

Boursin

HERB CHEESE SPREAD

Yield: 1 lb. 4 oz. (600 g); 5 Ramekins, 4 oz. (120 g) each

Unsalted butter, softened	4 oz.	120 g
Cream cheese, softened	1 lb.	480 g
Fine sea salt	½ tsp.	2 ml
Heavy cream	0.5 fl. oz.	15 ml
Fresh garlic, minced	½ oz.	15 g
Fresh chives, minced	2 Tbsp.	30 ml
Parsley, minced	1 Tbsp.	15 ml
White pepper, ground	¼ tsp.	1 ml

1. Blend the butter and cream cheese in the bowl of a mixer fitted with the paddle attachment on medium speed until smooth.
2. Dissolve the salt in the cream. Add the cream and remaining ingredients to the cheese. Scrape down the bowl and blend thoroughly.
3. Pack the cheese mixture into five 4-ounce molds lined with plastic wrap.
4. Chill thoroughly before using. This herb cheese will keep for up to 4 days in the refrigerator.

Approximate values per 1-oz. (30-g) serving: **Calories** 90, **Total fat** 10 g, **Saturated fat** 6 g, **Cholesterol** 35 mg, **Sodium** 10 mg, **Total carbohydrates** 1 g, **Protein** 1 g, **Vitamin A** 10%

Camembert (kam-uhm-BAIR) is a rind-ripened cheese from France containing approximately 45% fat. Camembert is creamy, like Brie, but milder. It is shaped in small round or oval disks and is coated with a white bloomy rind. Selecting a properly ripened Camembert is similar to selecting a Brie, but Camembert will become overripe and ammoniated even more quickly than Brie. Camembert is an excellent dessert or after-dinner cheese and goes particularly well with fruit.

Taleggio (tahl-EH-gee-oh) is a semisoft cheese that has been produced since the 10th century in a small town near Bergamo in the Lombardy region of Italy. Made with pasteurized or unpasteurized cow's milk, it contains 48% fat and is aged for 1 to 2 months.

Taleggio

Cabrales

Taleggio has an orange-colored washed rind that is edible but pungent. It is molded in a distinctive 8-inch square, approximately 2 inches thick. Its nutty, salty flavor and strong aroma become softer, creamier and more piquant with age. Serve as a dessert cheese with a strong red wine, crusty bread and fruit, or with a salad at the end of a meal.

SEMISOFT CHEESES

Semisoft cheeses include many mild, buttery cheeses with smooth, sliceable textures. Some semisoft cheeses are also known as monastery or Trappist cheeses because their development is traced to monasteries, some recipes having originated during the Middle Ages. The moisture content of semisoft cheeses ranges from 40–50%.

Cabrales (kah-BRAH-layss) is a blue-veined Spanish cheese made primarily from a blend of raw goat's, ewe's and cow's milks and containing 45–48% fat. Its wrapper made from large maple, oak or sycamore leaves is easily recognized. The outer foil wrapper is marked with the *Denominación de Origen* (D.O.) logo, and each 5- to 9-pound (2.5- to 4.5-kilogram) wheel is stamped with a unique number. It is aged for 3 to 6 months under the cold, humid and breezy conditions in natural caves found in the Asturias region. Cabrales has a moist, crumbly interior with purple-blue veins and a rough, salt-cured rind. It has a thick, creamy texture, a strong aroma and a complex sour, piquant flavor. Cabrales is especially good with salami and a full-bodied red wine or for dessert with a sweet sherry such as Pedro Ximenex.

Fontina (fon-TEE-nah) is a cow's-milk cheese from Italy's Piedmont region containing approximately 45% fat. The original, known as **Fontina Val D'Aosta**, has a dark gold, crusty rind; the pale gold, dense interior has a few small holes. It is nutty and rich. The original must have a purple trademark stamped on the rind. Imitation Fontinas (properly known as **Fontal** or **Fontinella**) are produced in Denmark, France, Sweden, the United States and other regions of Italy. They tend to be softer, with less depth of flavor, and may have a rubbery texture. Real Fontina is a good after-dinner cheese; the imitations are used in sauces, soups or sandwiches.

Gorgonzola (gohr-guhn-ZOH-lah) is a blue-veined cow's-milk cheese from Italy containing 48% fat. Gorgonzola has a white or ivory interior with bluish-green veins. It is creamier than other blues such as Stilton or Roquefort, with a somewhat more pungent, spicy, earthy flavor. White Gorgonzola has no veins but a similar flavor, while aged Gorgonzola is drier and crumbly with a very strong, sharp flavor. The milder Gorgonzolas are excellent with fresh peaches or pears or crumbled in a salad. Gorgonzola is also used in sauces and pasta dishes.

Gorgonzola

Havarti

Gouda (GOO-dah) is a Dutch cheese containing approximately 48% fat. Gouda is sold in various-sized wheels covered with red or yellow wax. The cheese is yellow with a few small holes and a mild, buttery flavor. Gouda may be sold soon after production, or it may be aged for several months, resulting in a firmer, more flavorful cheese. Gouda is widely popular for snacking and sandwiches.

Havarti (hah-VAHR-tee) is a cow's-milk monastery-style cheese from Denmark containing 45–60% fat. Havarti is also known as **Danish Tilsit** or by the brand name **Dofino**. Pale yellow with many small, irregular holes, it is sold in small rounds, rectangular blocks or loaves. Havarti has a mild flavor and creamy texture. It is often flavored with dill, caraway seeds or peppers. Havarti is very popular for snacking and in sandwiches.

Roquefort

Port du Salut (por doo suh-LOO) is a monastery cow's-milk product from France containing approximately 50% fat. Port du Salut (also known as Port Salut) is smooth, rich and savory. It is shaped in thick wheels with a dense, pale yellow interior and an edible, bright orange rind. The Danish version is known as Esrom. One of the best and most authentic Port du Saluts has the initials S.A.F.R. stamped on the rind. Lesser-quality brands may be bland and rubbery. It is popular for breakfast and snacking, especially with fruit.

Roquefort (ROHK-fohr) is a blue-veined sheep's-milk cheese from France containing approximately 45% fat. It was first mentioned in a text dated to 79 C.E., and Roquefort producers have held a legal monopoly over making this cheese since 1411. Roquefort is intensely pungent with a rich, salty flavor and strong aroma. It is a white paste with veins of blue mold and a thin natural rind shaped into thick, foil-wrapped cylinders. Roquefort is always aged for at least 3 months in the limestone caves of Mount Combalou. Since 1926, no producer outside this region can legally use the name Roquefort or even "Roquefort-style." Roquefort is an excellent choice for serving before or after dinner and is, of course, essential for Roquefort dressing.

Stilton is a blue-veined cow's-milk cheese from Great Britain containing 45% fat. Stilton is one of the oldest and grandest cheeses in the world. It has a white or pale yellow interior with evenly spaced blue veins. Stilton's distinctive flavor is pungent, rich and tangy, combining the best of blues and cheddars. It is aged in cool ripening rooms for 4 to 6 months to develop the blue veining; it is then sold in tall cylinders with a crusty, edible rind. Stilton should be wrapped in a cloth dampened with salt water and stored at cool temperatures, but not refrigerated. It is best served alone or with plain crackers, dried fruit or vintage port.

blue cheese (1) a generic term for any cheese containing visible blue-green molds that contribute a characteristic tart, sharp flavor and aroma; also known as a blue-veined cheese or bleu; (2) a group of Roquefort-style cheeses made in the United States and Canada from cow's or goat's milk rather than ewe's milk and injected with molds that form blue-green veins; also known as blue mold cheese or blue-veined cheese

Stilton

FIRM CHEESES

Firm cheeses are not hard or brittle. Some are close-textured and flaky, like Cheddar; others are dense, holey cheeses like Emmenthaler. Most firm cheeses are actually imitators of these two classics. Their moisture content ranges from 30–40%.

Cheddars are widely produced in North America, Australia and Great Britain. **American Cheddar** is a cow's-milk cheese made primarily in New York, Wisconsin, Vermont and Oregon, containing from 45–50% fat. The best cheddars are made from raw milk and aged for several months. (Raw milk may be used in the United States provided the cheese is then aged at least 60 days.) They have a dense, crumbly texture. Cheddars may be white or colored orange with vegetable dyes, depending on local preference. Flavors range from mild to very sharp, depending on the age of the cheese. **Colby** and **Longhorn** are two well-known mild, soft-textured Wisconsin Cheddars. Cheddars are sold in a variety of shapes and sizes, often coated with wax. Good-quality Cheddars are welcome additions to any cheese board, whereas those of lesser quality are better reserved for cooking and sandwiches. Canadian and **English Cheddars** are also cow's-milk cheeses containing approximately 45–48% fat. They tend to be dryer and more sharply flavored than American cheddars because of additional aging and are popular for snacking and in soups.

Emmenthaler (EM-en-tah-ler) is a cow's-milk cheese from Switzerland containing approximately 45% fat. Emmenthaler is the original Swiss cheese; it accounts for more than half of Switzerland's cheese production. It is mellow, rich and nutty with a natural

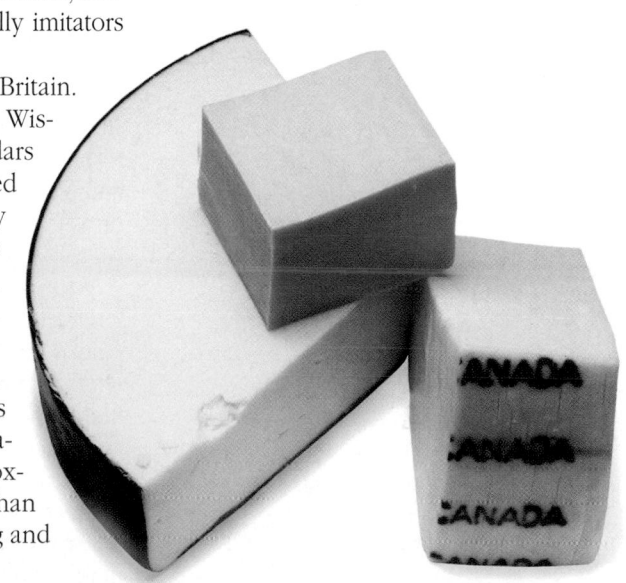

American Cheddar—Wisconsin Sharp, Vermont Cabot, Canadian Black Diamond

fondue a Swiss specialty made with melted cheese, wine and flavorings; eaten by dipping pieces of bread into the hot mixture with long forks

Gruyère

Manchego

Monterey Jack

rind and a light yellow interior full of large holes. It is ripened in three stages with the aid of fermenting bacteria. The holes or "eyes" are caused by gases expanding inside the cheese during fermentation. Authentic Emmenthaler is sold in 200-pound (90-kilogram) wheels with the word *Switzerland* stamped on the rind like the spokes of a wheel. Emmenthaler, one of the basic **fondue** cheeses, is also popular for sandwiches, snacks and after dinner with fruit and nuts.

Gruyère (groo-YAIR) is a cow's-milk cheese made near Fribourg in the Swiss Alps and containing approximately 45–50% fat. Gruyère is often imitated, as the name is not legally protected. True Gruyère is moist and highly flavorful, with a sweet nuttiness similar to Emmenthaler. Gruyère is aged for up to 12 months and then sold in huge wheels. It should have small, well-spaced holes and a brown, wrinkled rind. Gruyère melts easily and is often used with meats and in sauces, but it is also appropriate before or after dinner. A similar cheese is **Comté** (CON-tay), also called Gruyère de Comté. It is cow's-milk cheese from the Jura Mountain region of France made from raw milk of the red and white Montbeliard breed. A moist firm cheese, Comté is one of the most popular cheeses in France, with distinctive flavors of dried fruit and nuts.

Jarlsberg (YAHRLZ-behrg) is a Swiss-type cow's-milk cheese from Norway containing approximately 45% fat. Jarlsberg closely resembles Emmenthaler in both flavor and appearance. It is mild with a delicate, sweet flavor and large holes. Jarlsberg has a pale yellow interior; it is coated with yellow wax and sold in huge wheels. It has a long shelf life and is popular for sandwiches and snacks and in cooking.

Manchego (mahn-CHAY-goh) is the best-known and most widely available Spanish sheep's-milk cheese. Its ivory to pale yellow interior is firm and compact with a few small air pockets. It has a buttery and slightly piquant flavor with an aftertaste of sheep's milk. The inedible rind is black, gray or beige with a very distinctive zigzag pattern imprinted by the traditional esparto grass molds.

There are two types of Manchego: farmhouse style, made with unpasteurized sheep's milk, and industrial, made with pasteurized milk. For both, only milk from Manchega sheep raised in the La Mancha region is used. Manchego is aged from 2 months (*fresco*) to 1 year (*curado*) to 2 years (*añejo* or *viejo*) and contains 45–57% fat. Its intense flavor and crumbly texture make it excellent for eating as is, with bread or fruit or as the focal point of antipasto with a robust red wine or a dry sherry.

Monterey Jack is a cheddarlike cow's-milk cheese from California containing 50% fat. It is very mild and rich, with a pale ivory interior. It is sold in wheels or loaves coated with dark wax. "Jack" is often flavored with peppers or herbs and is good for snacking and sandwiches. Dry-aged Jack develops a tough, wrinkled brown rind and a rich, firm yellow interior. It has a nutty, sharp flavor and is dry enough for grating.

Provolone (pro-voh-LOH-neh) is a cow's-milk cheese from southern Italy containing approximately 45% fat. Provolone *dolce*, aged only 2 months, is mild, with a smooth texture. Provolone

Emmenthaler (Swiss)

Provolone

piccante, aged up to 6 months, is stronger and somewhat flaky or stringy. Smoked provolone is also popular, especially for snacking. Provolone is shaped in various ways, from huge salamis to plump spheres to tiny piglets shaped by hand. It is excellent in sandwiches and for cooking and is often used for melting and in pizza and pasta dishes.

HARD CHEESES

Hard cheeses are not simply cheeses that have been allowed to dry out. Rather, they are carefully aged for extended periods and have a moisture content of about 30%. Hard cheeses are most often used for grating; the best flavor will come from cheeses grated as needed. Even the finest hard cheeses begin to lose their flavor within hours of grating. The most famous and popular of the hard cheeses are those from Italy, where they are known as *grana*. Hard cheeses can also be served as a table cheese or with a salad.

Asiago

Asiago (ah-zee-AH-go) is a cow's-milk cheese from Italy containing approximately 30% fat. After only one year of aging, Asiago is sharp and nutty with a cheddarlike texture. If aged for 2 years or more, Asiago becomes dry, brittle and suitable for grating. Either version should be an even white to pale yellow in color with no dark spots, cracks or strong aromas. Asiago melts easily and is often used in cooking.

Grana Padano (gran-ah pa-DAN-o) is produced throughout Northern Italy from partly skim raw cow's milk. It is formed into large cylinders, salted and aged for at least 270 days, resulting in a hard, dark beige crust and a firm white to straw-yellow interior with a granular texture and the aroma of almonds. It is excellent for grating, and its sweet yet salty flavor is also enjoyed with fruit and wine.

Parmigiano-Reggiano (Parmesan) (pahr-me-ZHAN-no reg-gee-AH-no) is a cow's-milk cheese made exclusively in the region near Parma, Italy, containing from 32–35% fat. Parmigiano-Reggiano is one of the world's oldest and most widely copied cheeses. Used primarily for grating and cooking, it is rich, spicy and sharp with a golden interior and a hard oily rind. It should not be overly salty or bitter. Reggiano, as it is known, is produced only from mid-April to mid-November. It is shaped into huge wheels of about 80 pounds (36 kilograms) each, with the name stenciled repeatedly around the rind. Imitation Parmesan is produced in the United States, Argentina and elsewhere, but none can match the distinctive flavor of freshly grated Reggiano.

Parmigiano-Reggiano (Parmesan)

Pecorino Romano (peh-coh-REE-no roh-MAH-no) is a sheep's-milk cheese from central and southern Italy containing approximately 35% fat. Romano is very brittle and sharper than other grating cheeses, with a "sheepy" tang. Its light, grainy interior is whiter than Parmesan or Asiago. It is packed in large cylinders with a yellow rind. Romano is often substituted for, or combined with, Parmesan in cooking, but it is also good eaten with olives, sausages and red wine.

GOAT'S-MILK CHEESES

Because of their increasing popularity, cheeses made from goat's milk deserve a few words of their own. Although goats give less milk than cows, their milk is higher in fat and protein and richer and more concentrated in flavor. Cheeses made with goat's milk have a sharp, tangy flavor. They may range in texture from very soft and fresh to very hard, depending on age.

Chèvre (shehv; French for "goat") refers to small, soft, creamy cheeses produced in a variety of shapes: cones, disks, pyramids or logs. Chèvres are often coated with ash, herbs or seasonings. They are excellent for cooking and complement a wide variety of flavors. Unfortunately, they have a short shelf life, perhaps only 2 weeks. Cheese labeled *pur chèvre* must be made with 100% goat's milk; others may be a mixture of cow's and goat's milk.

Assorted Soft and Goat's-Milk Cheeses (clockwise starting from the top right): log of herb-coated French goat's cheese, French Banon wrapped in leaves, cinder-coated French Sainte Maure, French Chabichon goat's cheese, French Cabichou marinated in olive oil, herbs and peppercorns and, in the center, French Camembert

The finest goat's-milk cheeses usually come from France. Preferred brands include Bûcheron, exported from France in 5-pound (2-kilogram) logs; Chevrotin, one of the mildest; and Montrachet, a tangy soft cheese from the Burgundy wine region. Numerous North American producers have developed excellent goat's-milk cheeses in a wide variety of shapes and styles.

CHEESE TERMINOLOGY

The following terms often appear on cheese labels and may help identify or appreciate new or unfamiliar cheeses:

Affiné—French term for a cured or properly ripened cheese

Bleu—French for "blue"

Brique or *briquette*—refers to a group of French brick-shaped cheeses

Brosse—French term for cheeses that are brushed with liquid or oil during ripening

Capra—Italian for goat's-milk cheese

Carré—French term for square, flat cheeses

Cendré—French term for cheeses ripened in ashes

Coulant—French for "flowing," used to describe ripe Brie, Camembert and other cheeses when their interiors ooze or flow

Ferme or *fermier*—French adjective used to indicate farm-produced cheeses

Kaas—Dutch for "cheese"

Käse—German for "cheese"

Lait cru—French term for raw milk

Laiterie or *laitier*—French for "dairy"; appears on factory-made cheeses

Matières grasses—French term for dry matter

Mi chèvre—a French product so labeled must contain at least 25% goat's milk

Ost—Scandinavian for "cheese"

Pecorino—Italian term for all sheep's-milk cheeses

Queso—Spanish for "cheese"

Râpé—French term applied to cheeses that are suitable for grating

Tome or *tomme*—term used by the French, Italians and Swiss to refer to mountain cheeses, particularly from the Pyrénées or Savoie regions

Tyrophile—one who loves cheese

Vaccino—Italian term for cow's-milk cheese

Vache—French term for cow's-milk cheese

PROCESSED CHEESES

Pasteurized processed cheese is made from a combination of aged and green cheeses mixed with emulsifiers and flavorings, pasteurized and poured into molds to solidify. Manufacturers can thus produce cheeses with consistent textures and flavors. Processed cheeses are commonly used in food service operations because they are less expensive than natural cheeses. And, because they will not age or ripen, their shelf life is greatly extended. Nutritionally, processed cheeses generally contain less protein, calcium and vitamin A and more sodium than natural cheeses.

Processed cheese food contains less natural cheese (but at least 51% by weight) and more moisture than regular processed cheese. Often vegetable oils and milk solids are added, making cheese food soft and spreadable.

Imitation cheese is usually manufactured with dairy by-products and soy products mixed with emulsifiers, colorings and flavoring agents and enzymes. Although considerably less expensive than natural cheese, imitation cheese tends to be dense and rubbery, with little flavor other than that of salt.

SERVING CHEESES

Cheeses may be served at any time of day. In Northern Europe, they are common for breakfast; in Great Britain, they are a staple at lunch. Cheeses are widely used for sandwiches, snacks and cooking in America, and they are often served following the entrée or instead of dessert at formal dinners.

The flavor and texture of natural cheeses are best at room temperature. So, except for fresh cheeses, all cheeses should be removed from the refrigerator 30 minutes to an hour before service to allow them to come to room temperature. Fresh cheeses, such as cottage and cream, should be eaten chilled.

Any selection of fine cheeses should include a variety of flavors and textures: from mild to sharp, from soft to creamy to firm. Use a variety of shapes and colors for visual appeal. Do not precut the cheeses, as this only causes them to become dry. Provide an adequate supply of serving knives so that stronger-flavored cheeses will not combine with and overpower milder ones. Fine cheeses are best appreciated with plain bread and crackers, as salted or seasoned crackers can mask the cheese's flavor. Noncitrus fruits are also a nice accompaniment.

STORAGE

Most cheeses are best kept refrigerated, well wrapped to keep odors out and moisture in. Firm and hard cheeses can be kept for several weeks; fresh cheeses will spoil in 7 to 10 days because of their high moisture content. Some cheeses that have become hard or dry may still be grated for cooking or baking. Freezing is possible but not recommended because it changes the cheese's texture, making it mealy or tough.

COOKING WITH CHEESE

When heated, cheese can melt into a tough, stringy mass because of its high protein content. Long exposure to heat can also cause cheese mixtures to curdle and separate. Lower-fat cheeses, such as cottage, feta and commercially prepared low-fat products, are especially difficult to heat. Therefore, it is important to use low temperatures and short cooking times. Cheeses can be incorporated into sauces and soups by first grating the cheese while cold. The small pieces will then melt quickly and evenly. Add cheese toward the end of cooking, and do not allow cheese mixtures to boil. Hold cheese mixtures warm over a bain marie or indirect heat.

AMERICAN CHEESE PRODUCTION

The first cheese factory in the United States was built in 1851 in Oneida County, New York. Herkimer County, which adjoins Oneida County, soon became the center of the American cheese industry and remained so for the next 50 years. During this time, the largest cheese market in the world was at Little Falls, New York, where farm-produced cheeses and cheeses from more than 200 factories were sold. At the turn of the century, as New York's population increased, there was a corresponding increase in demand for fluid milk. Because dairies could receive more money for fluid milk than for cheese, cheese production declined.

Although New York still produces some outstanding cheddars, the bulk of the American cheese industry gradually moved westward, eventually settling in Wisconsin's rich farmlands. The United States is now the world's largest manufacturer of cheeses, producing nearly twice as many pounds per year as its nearest competitor, France.

Over the last fifteen years there has been a resurgence of interest in traditional cheesemaking in the United States. According to the American Cheese Society there are now at least 380 artisan producers scattered throughout the United States. These artisan cheeses are mostly handmade in small batches using all types of milk. They include farmstead cheeses, which by definition must be made on the producer's property with milk from the producer's own herd or flock. Artisan cheeses are often sold at local farmer's markets.

Cheeseboard Ready for Service (starting from the top right): Shropshire Blue from Great Britain, Layered Huntsman Cheese from Great Britain, Italian Pecorino Pepato and in the center a wedge of ripe Brie cheese

When melting a cheese topping, place the dish 4 to 6 inches from the heating element or broiler and broil only until the cheese melts. Cheese can taste scorched and the fats can separate if overheated. Dry, high-fat cheeses such as Parmesan and pecorino can tolerate heat better and are good choices for toppings.

WINE AND CHEESE: CLASSIC COMBINATIONS

Some cheeses are delicious with beers or ales. Others are best with strong coffee or apple cider, and nothing accompanies a Cheddar cheese sandwich as well as ice-cold milk. For most cheeses, however, the ultimate partner is wine. Wine and cheese bring out the best in each other. The proteins and fats in cheeses take the edge off harsh or acidic wines, whereas the tannins and acids in wines bring out the creamy richness of cheeses.

Because of their natural affinity, certain pairings are universal favorites: Stilton with port, Camembert with Bordeaux, Roquefort with Sauternes and English Cheddar with Burgundy. Although taste preferences are an individual matter, cheese-wine marriages follow two schools of thought: either pair likes or pair opposites.

Pairing like with like is simple: Cheeses are often best served with wines produced in the same region. For example, a white Burgundy such as Montrachet would be an excellent choice for cheeses from Burgundy; goat cheeses from the Rhone Valley go well with wines of that region. Hearty Italian wines such as Chianti, Barolo and Valpolicella are delicious with Italian cheese—Gorgonzola, Provolone, Taleggio. And a dry, aged Monterey Jack is perhaps the perfect mate for California Zinfandel.

Opposites do attract, however. Sweet wines such as Sauternes and Gewürztraminer go well with sharp, tangy blues, especially Roquefort. And light, sparkling wines such as Champagne or Spanish Cava are a nice complement to rich, creamy cheeses such as Brie and Camembert.

QUESTIONS FOR DISCUSSION

1. What is milkfat, and how is it used in classifying milk-based products?
2. If a recipe calls for whole milk and you have only dried milk, what do you do? Explain your answer.
3. The texture and shelf life of cheese depends on what two factors?
4. Cheeses are categorized as fresh, soft, semisoft, firm and hard. Give two examples of each, and explain how they are generally used.
5. The FDA and many states currently ban the sale of raw milk or products, such as cheese, made from raw milk. Several groups, including the American Cheese Society, the Campaign for Real Milk, the Raw Milk Cheese Association and some organic dairy farmers are fighting to legalize the sale of these products. What arguments are used in support of and in opposition to the sale of raw milk products?
6. Use the Internet to locate a U.S. producer of European-style goat cheeses. What varieties of goat cheeses do they market? WWW

Terms to Know

pasteurization
homogenization
skim milk
evaporated milk
cream
buttermilk
crème fraîche
clarified butter
margarine
natural cheese
rind
bloomy rind
washed rind
chèvre

> *"When you become a good cook, you become a good craftsman, first. You repeat and repeat and repeat until your hands know how to move without thinking about it.*

—JACQUES PÉPIN, FRENCH CHEF AND TEACHER (1935–)

CHAPTER EIGHT

MISE EN PLACE

- organize and plan your work more efficiently
- understand basic flavoring techniques
- prepare items needed prior to actual cooking
- set up and use the standard breading procedure

THE FRENCH TERM *MISE EN PLACE* (meez ahn plahs) literally means "to put in place" or "everything in its place." But in the culinary context, it means much more. Escoffier defined the phrase as "those elementary preparations that are constantly resorted to during the various steps of most culinary preparations." He meant, essentially, gathering and prepping the ingredients to be cooked as well as assembling the tools and equipment necessary to cook them.

In this chapter, we discuss many of the basics that must be in place before cooking begins: for example, creating bouquets garnis, clarifying butter, making bread crumbs, toasting nuts and battering foods. Chopping, dicing, cutting and slicing—important techniques used to prepare foods as well—are discussed in Chapter 5, Knife Skills; specific preparations, such as roasting peppers and trimming pineapples, are discussed elsewhere.

The concept of mise en place is simple: A chef should have at hand everything he or she needs to prepare and serve food in an organized and efficient manner.

Proper mise en place can consist of just a few items—for example, those needed to prepare a small quantity of chicken soup. Or it can be quite extensive—for example, when setting up the hot line for a busy restaurant with a large menu. A proper mise en place requires the chef to consider work patterns, ingredient lists and tool and equipment needs.

Mise en place will differ from one restaurant to another. A banquet chef's mise en place could include organizing large quantities of meats, vegetables, salad ingredients, breads, condiments and pastries for several dinners, all with different menus. Regardless of the specific menu, banquet mise en place may also include gathering hot boxes, plates, chafing dishes, tongs, spoons and ladles, and setting up the dish-up line. The mise en place for the broiler station at a steakhouse could include properly storing raw steaks and chops that will be cooked to order, as well as gathering the salt, pepper, prepared sauces and accompaniments that are used during cooking or served with the finished items. The broiler cook could also be responsible for gathering plates, building a charcoal fire for the grill, and stocking his or her work area with hand tools, towels and sanitizing solution. In the restaurant situation, unlike in banquet work, the cook's mise en place is probably identical night after night. A waiter's mise en place could include brewing tea, cutting lemon wedges and refilling salt and pepper shakers—preparations that will make work go more smoothly during actual service. Regardless of the number of items used or the complexity of the recipes being prepared, completing a proper mise en place requires careful planning, efficient organization and attention to detail.

Coordination of multiple tasks is also important. An organized cook will think about everything that needs to be done and the most efficient way to complete those tasks before beginning the actual work. Taking the time to first plan the day's activities can eliminate unnecessary steps and conserve resources.

Proper mise en place also requires a good sense of timing. Knowing how long before service to begin a task, or how far in advance of service some preparations can be made, allows a cook to better plan for the efficient execution of his or her duties. In this type of planning, it is also important to consider food safety issues, such as those relating to time and temperature controls. See Chapter 2, Food Safety and Sanitation, for detailed information.

SELECTING TOOLS AND EQUIPMENT

An important step in creating the proper mise en place is to identify and gather all of the tools and equipment that will be needed to prepare a recipe properly or to work a station efficiently. The tools and equipment used to prepare, cook and store foods are discussed in Chapter 4, Tools and Equipment. A few general rules to bear in mind:

▶ All tools, equipment and work surfaces must be clean and sanitized.

▶ Knives should be honed and sharpened.

▶ Measuring devices should be checked periodically for accuracy.

▶ Ovens and cooking surfaces should be preheated, as necessary.

▶ Mixing bowls, saucepans and storage containers should be the correct size for the task at hand.

▶ Serving plates, cookware, utensils, hand tools and other necessary smallwares should be gathered and stored nearby.

▶ Foods should be gathered and stored conveniently at the proper temperatures.

▶ Expiration dates on foods should be checked periodically for validity.

▶ Sanitizing solution, hand towels, disposable gloves and trash receptacles should be conveniently located.

MEASURING INGREDIENTS

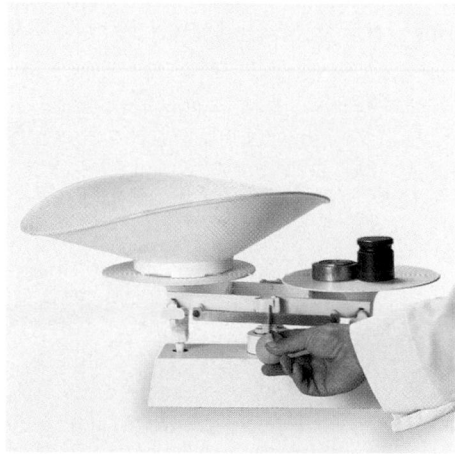

❶ To use a balance scale to weigh an ingredient, place an empty container on the left, then set a counterbalance to that container on the right. Use weights and the sliding beam weight to add an amount equal to the amount of the ingredient needed.

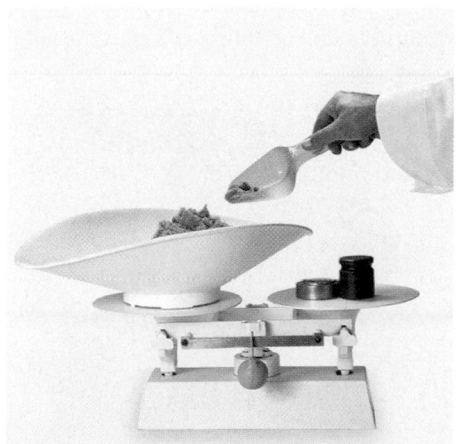

❷ Place the ingredient on the left side of the scale until the two platforms are balanced.

In order to reproduce foods consistently and for the same cost day after day, it is important that the ingredients be measured accurately each time. As explained in more detail in Chapter 3, Menus and Recipes, ingredients may be measured by weight, volume or count. Weight refers to the mass or heaviness of an item and is measured using a scale. Volume refers to the space occupied by a substance and is measured with graduated measuring cups and spoons. Count refers to the number of individual items. It is

THE PREP LIST

Imagine trying to cross a stream by stepping on many different rocks. If you look at only one rock at a time, you will never have a clear picture of where you need to step next to safely get to the other side. You may completely miss the next step and find that now you have to backtrack and waste time or not get across at all. A prep list is the blueprint for how food production is going to be achieved during the work day. It gives the cook an overview of what needs to be done, how long it may take, the order in which assignments should be completed, and how each cook may interact with others in the kitchen. A prep list is not just rewriting recipes. It is reading through recipes and composing a written map of how to accomplish the tasks necessary to prepare the recipe.

The first step in organizing your work is to read and understand the recipes you will be using. Reading the recipe alerts you to other components such as sauces or stocks that must be prepared in advance. You may find that you need to change the proportions of the recipe to meet production needs. Next, it is important to break down each dish by the steps necessary to complete the mise en place and prep. This will assist you in gathering ingredients for all of your prep at one time instead of getting an item multiple times on each occasion that it is called for in the recipe.

Once each item is identified and quantified, the next step is to schedule your tasks through prioritization. Decide what needs to be done first and at what time or on what day the task should be started and completed. Follow the detailed task list you started with and this will assist you in determining the priority of your work. Do not leave anything to chance by trying to keep track of things in your head. The prep list is not only for your benefit. It can be used if another cook is assigned to help you or is needed to take over your work assignments. A clearly written prep list will allow the prep work to be completed efficiently and effectively.

—CHEF DAVID ROSENTHAL is former Department Chair of the Contra Costa College Culinary Program

important to remember that foods do not weigh their volume. In other words, although 1 cup contains 8 fluid ounces, 1 cup of flour, honey, cinnamon, and so on do not *weigh* 8 ounces.

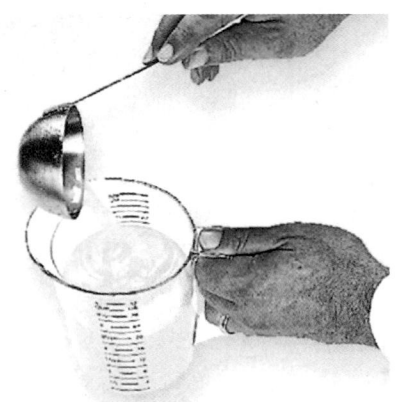

Liquids should be measured in liquid measuring cups, which may be marked in U.S. and/or metric units.

Small amounts of dry ingredients are measured by overfilling the appropriate measuring spoon, then leveling the ingredient.

PREPARING INGREDIENTS

Some ingredients that are used frequently throughout the kitchen are often prepared in large quantities so that they are ready when needed for a specific recipe. For example, dry bread crumbs can be made and stored whenever a supply of bread is available. Large quantities of butter can be clarified on a back burner while other operations proceed on the line. These chores may be simple, but they are time-consuming. An entry-level cook may be assigned responsibility for this type of mise en place. Never feel that such chores are menial; consider, instead, how frustrating it would be for the chef to run out of a simple item just when it is needed during service.

Clarifying Butter

Unsalted whole butter is approximately 80% fat, 16% water and 4% milk solids. Although whole butter can be used for cooking or sauce making, sometimes a more stable and consistent product will be achieved by using butter that has had the water and milk solids removed by a process called **clarification**.

ghee a form of clarified butter in which the milk solids remain with the fat and are allowed to brown; originating in India and now used worldwide as an ingredient and cooking medium, it has a long shelf life, a high smoke point and a nutty, caramel-like flavor

PROCEDURE FOR **CLARIFYING BUTTER**

1. Slowly warm the butter in a saucepan over low heat without boiling or agitation. As the butter melts, the milk solids rise to the top as a foam and the water sinks to the bottom.
2. When the butter is completely melted, skim the milk solids from the top.
3. When all the milk solids have been removed, ladle the butterfat into a clean saucepan, being careful to leave the water in the bottom of the pan.
4. The clarified butter is now ready to use. One pound (454 grams) of whole butter will yield approximately 12 ounces (340 grams) of clarified butter—a yield of 75%.

Clarified butter will keep for extended periods in either the freezer or refrigerator.

Skimming milk solids from the surface of melted butter.

Ladling the butterfat into a clean pan.

Toasting Nuts and Spices

Nuts are often toasted lightly before being used in baked goods, breadings, salads and sauces. Whole spices are sometimes toasted before being ground for a sauce or used as a garnish. Toasting not only browns the food, it brings out its flavor and makes it crispier and crunchier. To toast nuts or spices in the oven or on the stove top, spread them out in one layer so they cook evenly. Watch them closely, as they can develop bitter scorched flavors and burn easily. A light color and fragrant aroma indicates nuts and spices that are toasted not burnt.

Making Bread Crumbs

Almost any bread can be used to make crumbs; the choice depends on how the crumbs will be used. **Fresh bread crumbs** are made from fresh bread that is slightly dried out, approximately two to four days old. If the bread is too fresh, the crumbs will be gummy and stick together; if the bread is too stale, the crumbs will taste stale as well. **Dry bread crumbs** are made from bread that has been lightly toasted in a warm oven. Do not make crumbs from stale or molding bread, as these undesirable flavors will be apparent when the crumbs are used.

To make crumbs, the bread is cubed or torn into pieces and ground in a food processor. Dried bread can be processed to a finer consistency than fresh bread. After processing, the crumbs should be passed through a tamis and stored in a tightly closed plastic container in a cool, dry place. For additional flavors, dried herbs and spices may be mixed into the crumbs.

Toasting sesame seeds in a dry sauté pan on the stove top.

PROCEDURE FOR **MAKING BREADCRUMBS**

❶ Grind chunks of bread in a food processor.

❷ Pass the crumbs through a tamis or sieve so that they will be the same size.

FLAVORING FOODS

Foods are often flavored with herbs or spices, marinades or rubs before they are actually cooked. This may require the chef to prepare various flavoring or seasoning mixtures and wait for a period of time between steps in a recipe.

Bouquet Garni and Sachet

A bouquet garni and sachet are used to introduce flavorings, seasonings and aromatics into stocks, sauces, soups and stews.

A **bouquet garni** is a selection of herbs (usually fresh) and vegetables tied into a bundle with twine. A standard bouquet garni consists of parsley stems, celery, thyme, leeks and carrots.

A **sachet** (also known as a *sachet d'épices*) is made by tying seasonings together in cheesecloth. A standard sachet consists of peppercorns, bay leaves, parsley stems, thyme, cloves and, optionally, garlic. The exact quantity of these ingredients is determined by the amount of liquid the sachet is meant to flavor.

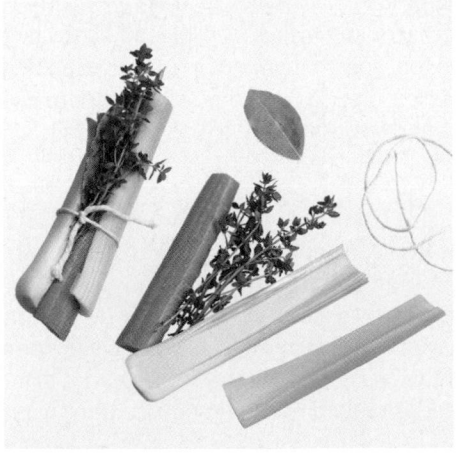

Bouquet Garni

Sachet

Bouquets garni and sachets are used to add flavors in such a way that they can be easily removed from a dish when their flavors have been extracted. A similar technique,

Oignon Piqué

although less commonly used, is an **oignon piqué** (also known as an *onion piquet*). To prepare an oignon piqué, peel the onion and trim off the root end. Attach one or two dried bay leaves to the onion using whole cloves as pins. The oignon piqué is then simmered in milk or stock to extract flavors.

An **oignon brûlé** (also known as *onion brûlé*), French for "burnt onion," is used to flavor and color stocks, sauces and soups such as consommé. To prepare an onion brûlé, peel the onion, trim off the root end and cut it in half. Place the onion halves cut sides down in a dry skillet over medium-high heat. Cook until the onion halves char and darken. The oignon brûlé is then simmered in stocks or soups to give them a clear caramel color.

Oignon Brûlé

Marinades

Marinating is the process of soaking meat or poultry in a seasoned liquid to flavor and tenderize it. Marinades can be a simple blend (herbs, seasonings and oil) or a complicated cooked recipe (red wine, fruit and other ingredients). Mild marinades should be used on more delicate meats, such as veal. Game and beef require strongly flavored marinades. In wine-based marinades, white wine is usually used for white meats and poultry, and red wine is used for red meats. Not only does the wine add a distinctive flavor, but the acids in it break down connective tissues and help tenderize the meat.

Poultry, veal and pork generally require less time to marinate than game, beef and lamb. Smaller pieces of meat take less time than larger pieces. When marinating, be sure to cover the meat or poultry completely, then keep it refrigerated. The quantity of marinade needed will vary depending on the size and form of the product; 2 pounds of boneless chicken breasts will require less marinade to cover than 2 pounds of whole Cornish game hens. Stir or turn foods frequently so that the marinade can penetrate evenly.

Some chefs prefer to marinate food in heavy-duty plastic food storage bags. These are useful for smaller quantities and allow for easy disposal of leftover marinades with less risk of cross-contamination. Label the bags properly and be sure to seal them tightly to prevent leaks.

Marinating chicken breasts.

Rubs and Pastes

Additional flavors can be added to meat, fish and poultry by rubbing them with a mixture of fresh or dried herbs and spices ground together with a mortar and pestle or in a spice grinder. The flavoring blend, called a **rub**, can be used dried, or it can be mixed with a little oil, lemon juice, prepared mustard or ground fresh garlic or ginger to make a **paste** (also known as a **wet rub**). Rubs and pastes add flavor and, often, a bit of crispy crust. They do not, however, generally act as a tenderizer. They are most often used on foods that will be cooked with dry heat, especially by grilling, broiling, baking or roasting.

To apply a rub or paste, slather the mixture over the entire surface of the food to be flavored. Use enough pressure to make sure that the rub or paste adheres. (Pastes tend to adhere better than rubs.) The thicker the covering or the longer it remains on the food before cooking, the more pronounced the flavor. If the rubbed food is to be left for some time so that the flavors can be absorbed, it should be covered, refrigerated and turned from time to time.

It is best to wear disposable gloves when applying a rub or paste. Some spices can irritate or stain the skin, and cross-contamination can occur from handling raw meats.

Applying a dry rub to beef.

Steeping

Steeping is the process of soaking dry ingredients in a liquid (usually hot) in order to either soften a food or **infuse** its flavor into the liquid. Spices, coffee beans and nuts are often steeped in hot milk to extract their flavors. The milk is then used to flavor other foods during cooking. For example, coffee beans can be steeped in hot milk and then strained out, with the coffee-flavored milk being used to make a custard sauce.

infuse to flavor a liquid by steeping it with ingredients such as tea, coffee, herbs or spices

Steeping is also used for rehydrating dried fruits and vegetables such as raisins and mushrooms. Typically, the softened fruits or vegetables will be used in a recipe and the liquid discarded. Additional flavors can be achieved by using wine, spirits, stock or other flavored liquids as the rehydrating medium.

Note that in both situations, the steeping mixture is generally covered and removed from the heat to avoid evaporation or reduction of the liquid.

Steeping a vanilla bean and cinnamon sticks in warm milk to extract their flavors.

Steeping raisins in hot water to rehydrate.

PREPARING TO COOK

Some techniques are done very close to or almost as a part of the final preparation of a dish.

Breading and Battering Foods

BREADING

meal (1) the coarsely ground seeds of any edible grain such as corn or oats; (2) any dried, ground substance (such as bonemeal)

A breaded item is any food that is coated with bread crumbs, cracker meal, cornmeal or other dry **meal** to protect it during cooking. Breaded foods can be seasoned before the breading is applied, or seasonings may be added to the flour, bread crumbs or meal before the main item is coated. Breaded foods are generally cooked by deep-frying or pan-frying. The breading makes a solid coating that seals during cooking and prevents the fat from coming in direct contact with the food, which would make it greasy.

STANDARD BREADING PROCEDURE

For breading meats, poultry, fish, shellfish or vegetables, a three-step process is typically used. Called the **standard breading procedure**, it gives foods a relatively thick, crisp coating.

1. Pat the food dry and dredge it in seasoned flour. The flour adds seasoning to the food, helps seal it, and allows the egg wash to adhere.
2. Dip the floured food in an egg wash. The egg wash should contain whole eggs whisked together with approximately 1 tablespoon (15 milliliters) milk or water per egg. The egg wash will cause the crumbs or meal to completely coat the item and form a tight seal when the food is cooked.
3. Coat the food with bread crumbs, cracker crumbs or other dry meal. Shake off excess crumbs and place the breaded item in a pan. As additional breaded items are added to the pan, align them in a single layer; do not stack them or the breadings will get soggy and the foods will stick together.
4. To ensure that breading adheres after cooking, refrigerate breaded foods for at least 30 minutes before frying.

| Product to be breaded | Flour | Egg wash | Bread crumbs | Pan to hold breaded product |

FIGURE 8.1 ▶ Setup for the standard breading procedure.

Figure 8.1 shows the proper setup for breading foods using the standard breading procedure. The following procedure helps bread foods more efficiently:

1 Assemble the mise en place as shown in Figure 8.1.

2 With your left hand, place the food to be breaded in the flour and coat it evenly. With the same hand, remove the floured item, shake off the excess flour and place it in the egg wash.

3 With your right hand, remove the item from the egg wash and place it in the bread crumbs or meal.

4 With your left hand, cover the item with crumbs or meal and press lightly to make sure the item is completely and evenly coated. Shake off the excess crumbs or meal and place the breaded food in the empty pan for finished product.

The key is to use one hand for the liquid ingredients and the other hand for the dry ingredients. This prevents your fingers from becoming coated with layer after layer of breading.

BATTERING

Batters, like breading, coat the food being cooked, keeping it moist and preventing it from becoming excessively greasy. Batters consist of a liquid such as water, milk or beer, combined with a starch such as flour or cornstarch. Many batters also contain a leavening agent such as baking powder or whipped egg whites. Two common batters are beer batter, which uses the beer for leavening as well as for flavor and is illustrated in the recipe for Beer Battered Onion Rings (page 598), and tempura batter, which is used in Tempura Vegetables with Dipping Sauce (page 618). Items coated with a batter are cooked immediately, usually by deep-frying or pan-frying. Figure 8.2 shows the proper setup for battering foods using the standard battering procedure.

PROCEDURE FOR **BATTERING FOODS**

1 Prepare the batter.

2 Pat the food dry and dredge in flour if desired.

3 Dip the item in the batter and place it directly in the hot fat.

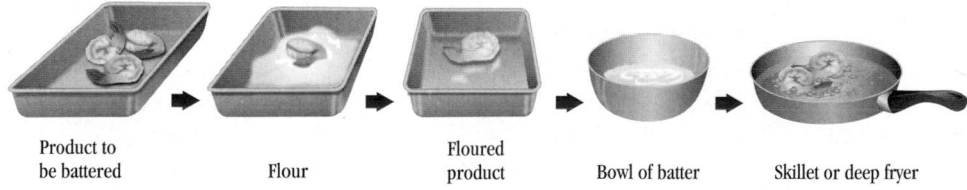

| Product to be battered | Flour | Floured product | Bowl of batter | Skillet or deep fryer |

FIGURE 8.2 ▶ Setup for the standard battering procedure.

blanching very briefly and partially cooking a food in boiling water or hot fat; used to assist preparation (for example, to loosen peels from vegetables), as part of a combination cooking method or to remove undesirable flavors

parboiling partially cooking a food in boiling or simmering liquid; similar to blanching but the cooking time is longer

parcooking partially cooking a food by any cooking method

shocking also called refreshing; the technique of quickly chilling blanched or parcooked foods in ice water; prevents further cooking and sets colors

Blanching and Parboiling

Some foods, especially vegetables, are **blanched** or **parboiled** before being used in a recipe. To do so, they are immersed in a large quantity of a boiling or simmering liquid—oil or water—and partially cooked. This **parcooking** assists preparation (for example, it loosens peels from vegetables), removes undesirable flavors, softens firm foods, sets colors and shortens final cooking times. The only difference between blanching and parboiling is cooking time. Blanching is done quickly, usually only a few seconds. Parboiling lasts longer, usually several minutes. Foods that are blanched or parboiled in water (rather than fat) are often **shocked** or **refreshed** in ice water to halt the cooking process.

❶ Blanch or parboil the food as desired in boiling water.

❷ Remove the food from the cooking liquid and submerge it in ice water to refresh.

Making an Ice Bath

Because of the risk of food-borne illness, it is important to cool hot foods quickly to a temperature below 41°F (5°C) before storing them in the refrigerator. An ice bath is an easy, efficient way to do so. An ice bath is also necessary for shocking or refreshing blanched or parcooked vegetables and for stopping the cooking of delicate mixtures such as custards.

An ice bath is simply a container of ice cubes and cold water. The combination of ice and water will chill foods more rapidly than a container of only ice. The food being chilled will also cool faster if it is in a metal container, rather than one made of plastic or glass. The container should be submerged into the ice bath so that the level of ingredients contained is at or below the level of liquid in the ice bath. Constant stirring speeds the cooling process.

Chilling Vanilla Custard Sauce in an ice bath.

1. Discuss how to create a prep list at the start of each day. Describe how the prep list can make work flow more smoothly.

2. Explain the differences between breading and battering foods.

3. Describe the correct mise en place for the standard breading procedure.

4. Choose a dessert recipe from the baking chapters of this book and describe the proper mise en place for preparing that dish.

5. How can the concepts of mise en place be applied to activities outside the kitchen?

6. Food service distributors supply many ingredients, products and equipment to assist chefs and restaurants with mise en place. Use the Internet to research three or four products or supplies that are designed to simplify the preparation process in a restaurant or other foodservice operation. Discuss the advantages and disadvantages to using these products. wWw

QUESTIONS FOR DISCUSSION

Terms to Know

mise en place
expiration dates
mass
volume
clarification
bouquet garni
sachet
marinate
dry rub

wet rub
rehydrating
standard breading procedure
battering
ice bath
refreshing

> "The qualities of an exceptional cook are akin to those of a successful tightrope walker: an abiding passion for the task, courage to go out on a limb and an impeccable sense of balance."
>
> —BRYAN MILLER, AMERICAN FOOD WRITER

PRINCIPLES OF COOKING

COOKING CAN BE DEFINED AS THE transfer of energy from a heat source to a food. This energy alters the food's molecular structure, changing its texture, flavor, aroma and appearance. But why is food cooked at all? The obvious answer is that cooking makes food taste better. Cooking also destroys undesirable microorganisms and makes foods easier to ingest and digest.

To cook foods successfully, you must first understand the ways in which heat is transferred: conduction, convection and radiation. You should also understand what the application of heat does to the proteins, sugars, starches, water and fats in foods.

Perhaps most important, you must understand the cooking methods used to transfer heat: broiling, grilling, roasting and baking, sautéing, pan-frying, deep-frying, poaching, simmering, boiling, steaming, braising and stewing. Each method is used for many types of food, so you will be applying one or more of them every time you cook. The cooking method you select gives the finished product a specific texture, appearance, aroma and flavor. A thorough understanding of the basic procedures involved in each cooking method helps you produce consistent, high-quality products.

This chapter describes each of the cooking methods and uses photographs to outline their general procedures. Detailed procedures and recipes applying these methods to specific foods are found in subsequent chapters.

HEAT TRANSFER

Heat is a type of energy. When a substance gets hot, its molecules have absorbed energy, which causes the molecules to vibrate rapidly, expand and bounce off one another. As the molecules move, they collide with nearby molecules, causing a transfer of heat energy. The faster the molecules within a substance move, the higher its temperature. This is true whether the substance is air, water, an aluminum pot or a sirloin steak.

Heat energy may be transferred *to* foods via conduction, convection or radiation as shown in Figure 9.1. Heat then travels *through* foods by conduction. Only heat is transferred—cold is simply the absence of heat, so cold cannot be transferred from one substance to another.

Conduction

Conduction is the most straightforward means of heat transfer. It is simply the movement of heat from one item to another through direct contact. For example, when the flame of a gas burner touches the bottom of a sauté pan, heat is conducted to the pan. The metal of the pan then conducts heat to the surface of the food lying in that pan.

Some materials conduct heat better than others. Water is a better conductor of heat than air. This explains why a potato cooks much faster in boiling water than in an oven, and why you cannot place your hand in boiling water at a temperature of 212°F (100°C), but can place your hand, at least very briefly, into a 400°F (200°C) oven. Generally, metals are good conductors (as discussed in Chapter 4, Tools and Equipment, copper and aluminum are the best conductors), and liquids and gases are poor conductors.

FIGURE 9.1 ▶ Arrows indicate heat patterns during conduction, convection and radiation.

Conduction is a relatively slow method of heat transfer because there must be physical contact to transfer energy from one molecule to adjacent molecules. Consider what happens when a metal spoon is placed in a pot of simmering soup. At first the spoon handle remains cool. Gradually, however, heat travels up the handle, making it warmer and warmer, until it becomes too hot to touch.

Conduction is important in all cooking methods because it is responsible for the movement of heat from the surface of a food to its interior. As the molecules near the food's exterior gather energy, they move more and more rapidly. As they move, they conduct heat to the molecules nearby, thus transferring heat through the food (from the exterior of the item to the interior).

In conventional heating methods (nonmicrowave), the heat source causes food molecules to react largely from the surface inward so that layers of molecules heat in succession. This produces a range of temperatures within the food, which means that the outside can brown and form a crust long before the interior is noticeably warmer. That is why a steak can be fully cooked on the outside but still rare on the inside.

Convection

Convection refers to the transfer of heat through a fluid, which may be liquid or gas. Convection is actually a combination of conduction and a mixing in which molecules in a fluid (whether air, water or fat) move from a warmer area to a cooler one. There are two types of convection: natural and mechanical.

Natural convection occurs because of the tendency of warm liquids and gases to rise while cooler ones fall. This causes a constant natural circulation of heat. For example, when a pot of stock is placed over a gas burner, the molecules at the bottom of the pot are warmed. These molecules rise while cooler, heavier molecules sink. Upon reaching the pot's bottom, the cooler molecules are warmed and begin to rise. This ongoing cycle creates currents within the stock, and these currents distribute the heat throughout the stock.

Mechanical convection relies on fans or stirring to circulate heat more quickly and evenly. This explains why foods heat faster and more evenly when stirred. Convection ovens are equipped with fans to increase the circulation of air currents, thus speeding up the cooking process. But even conventional ovens (that is, not convection ovens) rely on the natural circulation patterns of heated air to transfer heat energy to items being baked or roasted.

Radiation

Unlike conduction and convection, **radiation** does not require physical contact between the heat source and the food being cooked. Instead, energy is transferred by waves of heat or light striking the food. Two kinds of radiant heat are used in the kitchen: infrared and microwave.

Infrared cooking uses an electric or ceramic element heated to such a high temperature that it gives off waves of radiant heat that cook the food. Radiant heat waves travel at the speed of light in any direction (unlike convection heat, which only rises) until they are absorbed by a food. Infrared cooking is commonly used with toasters and broilers. The glowing coals of a fire are another example of radiant heat.

Microwave cooking relies on radiation generated by a special oven to penetrate the food, where it agitates water molecules, creating friction and heat. This energy then spreads throughout the food by conduction (and by convection in liquids). Microwave cooking is much faster than other methods because energy penetrates the food up to a depth of several centimeters, setting all water molecules in motion at the same time. Heat is generated quickly and uniformly throughout the food. Microwave cooking does not brown foods, however, and often gives meats a dry, mushy texture, making microwave ovens an unacceptable replacement for traditional ovens.

Because microwave radiation affects only water molecules, a completely waterless material (such as a plate) will not get hot. Any warmth felt in a plate used when microwaving food usually results from heat being conducted from the food to the plate.

Microwave cooking requires the use of certain types of utensils, usually heat-resistant glass or microwavable plastic. But even heat-resistant glass can shatter and is not recommended for professional use. The aluminum and stainless steel utensils most common in professional kitchens cannot be used because metal deflects microwaves, and this can damage the oven.

THE EFFECTS OF HEAT

Foods are composed of proteins, carbohydrates (starches and sugars), water and fats, plus small amounts of minerals and vitamins. Changes in the shape, texture, color and flavor of foods may occur when heat is applied to each of these nutrients. By understanding these changes and learning to control them, you will be able to prepare foods with the characteristics desired. Although volumes are written on these subjects, it is sufficient for you to know the following processes as you begin your study of cooking.

Proteins Coagulate

The heating of protein during cooking changes its structure, causing it to coagulate. Proteins are large, complex molecules found in every living cell, plant as well as animal. They are formed from amino acids that are chemically bonded into long, loosely folded chains. In the presence of heat, the protein chains unfold (denature), which allows them to rebond and solidify into a solid mass. In other words, as proteins cook, they lose moisture, shrink and become firm. (See Figure 9.2.) **Coagulation** refers to the irreversible transformation of proteins from a liquid or semiliquid state to a solid state. Common examples of protein coagulation are the firming of meat fibers during cooking, egg whites changing from a clear liquid to a white solid when heated and the

coagulation the irreversible transformation of proteins from a liquid or semiliquid state to a solid state

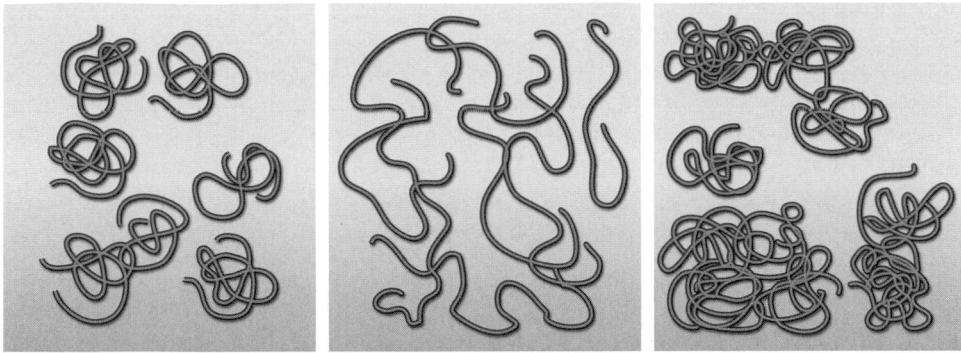

FIGURE 9.2 ▶ Protein coagulation, from left: loosely folded protein chain; denatured protein; coagulated protein.

setting of the structure of wheat proteins (known as gluten) in bread during baking. The process of coagulation begins as proteins are heated to 140°F (60°C). Most proteins complete coagulation at 160°F to 185°F (71°C to 85°C).

Starches Gelatinize

Gelatinization is the proper term for the cooking of starches. Starches are complex carbohydrates present in plants and grains such as potatoes, wheat, rice and corn. When a mixture of starch and liquid is heated, remarkable changes occur. The starch granules absorb water, causing them to swell, soften and clarify slightly. The liquid visibly thickens because of the water being absorbed into the starch granules and the granules themselves swelling to occupy more space.

Gelatinization occurs gradually over a range of temperatures—150°F to 212°F (66°C to 100°C)—depending on the type of starch used. Starch gelatinization affects not only sauces or liquids to which starches are added for the express purpose of thickening, but also any mixture of starch and liquid that is heated. For example, the flour (a starch) in cake batter gelatinizes by absorbing the water from eggs, milk or other ingredients as the batter bakes. This causes part of the firming and drying associated with baked goods. (See Figure 9.3.)

gelatinization the process by which starch granules are cooked; they absorb moisture when placed in a liquid and heated; as the moisture is absorbed, the product swells, softens and clarifies slightly

Sugars Caramelize

The process of cooking sugars is properly known as **caramelization**. Sugars are simple carbohydrates used by all plants and animals to store energy. As sugars cook, they gradually

caramelization the process of cooking sugars; the browning of sugar enhances the flavor and appearance of foods

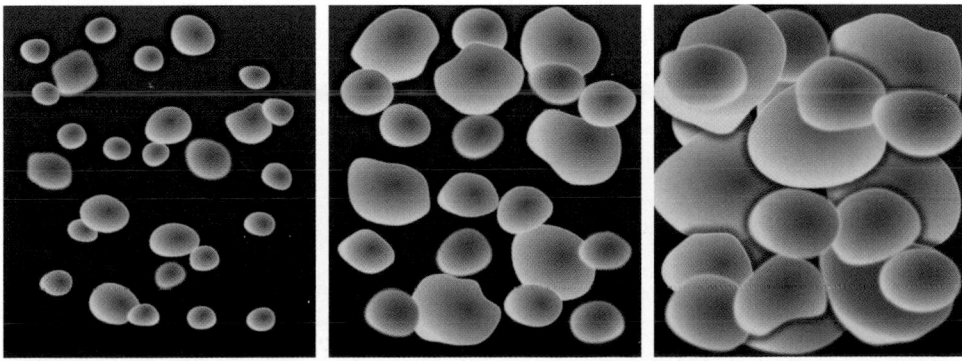

FIGURE 9.3 ▶ Gelatinization of starch, from left: uncooked starch granules floating in a liquid; starch beginning to swell when heated; fully gelatinized starches binding into a solid mass.

Maillard reaction the process whereby sugar breaks down in the presence of protein

darken from golden to deep brown and change flavor. Caramelized sugar is used in many sauces, candies and desserts. But caramelized sugar is also partly responsible for the flavor and color of bread crusts and the browning of meats and vegetables. In fact, the process of caramelization is responsible for most flavors we associate with cooking. The **Maillard reaction**, named for the French scientist who discovered this principle, describes the process of sugar breaking down in the presence of protein. Maillard browning results in darkening as well as the development of complex, meaty and baked flavors. (Some of the aromas and flavors of roasted nuts, chocolate and coffee derive from Maillard browning.)

Sucrose (common table sugar) begins to brown at about 338°F (170°C). The naturally occurring sugars in other foods, such as maltose, lactose and fructose, also caramelize, but at varying temperatures. Because high temperatures are required for browning (that is, caramelizing), most foods will brown only on the outside and only through the application of dry heat. Because water cannot be heated above 212°F (100°C), foods cooked with moist-heat methods do not get hot enough to caramelize. Foods cooked with dry-heat methods, including those using fats, will reach the high temperatures at which browning occurs.

Water Evaporates

All foods contain some water. Some foods, especially eggs, milk and leafy vegetables, are almost entirely water. Even as much as 75 percent of raw meat is water. As the internal temperature of a food increases, water molecules move faster and faster until the water turns to a gas (steam) and vaporizes. This **evaporation** of water is responsible for the drying of foods during cooking.

Fats Melt

Fat is an energy source for the plant or animal in which it is stored. Fats are smooth, greasy substances that do not dissolve in water. Their texture varies from very firm to liquid. Oils are simply fats that remain liquid at room temperature. Fats **melt** when heated; that is, they gradually soften, then liquefy. Fats will not evaporate. Most fats can be heated to very high temperatures without burning, so they can be used as a cooking medium to brown foods.

COOKING METHODS

Foods can be cooked in air, fat, water or steam. These are collectively known as **cooking media**. There are two general types of cooking methods: dry heat and moist heat. (See Table 9.1.)

Dry-heat cooking methods are those using air or fat. They are broiling, grilling, roasting and baking, sautéing, pan-frying and deep-frying. Foods cooked using dry-heat cooking methods have a rich flavor caused by browning because moisture on the surface of food evaporates.

Moist-heat cooking methods are those using water or steam. They are poaching, simmering, boiling and steaming. Moist-heat cooking methods are used to tenderize and emphasize the natural flavors of food.

TABLE 9.1 COOKING METHODS

METHOD	MEDIUM	EQUIPMENT
Dry-Heat Cooking Methods		
Broiling	Air	Overhead broiler, salamander, rotisserie
Grilling	Air	Grill
Roasting	Air	Oven
Baking	Air	Oven
Sautéing	Fat	Stove top
Pan-frying	Fat	Stove top, tilt skillet
Deep-frying	Fat	Deep-fat fryer
Moist-Heat Cooking Methods		
Poaching	Water or other liquid	Stove top, oven, steam-jacketed kettle, tilt skillet
Simmering	Water or other liquid	Stove top, steam-jacketed kettle, tilt skillet
Boiling	Water or other liquid	Stove top, steam-jacketed kettle, tilt skillet
Steaming	Steam	Stove top, convection steamer
Combination Cooking Methods		
Braising	Fat, then liquid	Stove top, oven, tilt skillet
Stewing	Fat, then liquid	Stove top, oven, tilt skillet

Other cooking methods employ a combination of dry- and moist-heat cooking methods. The two most significant of these **combination cooking methods** are braising and stewing.

Each of these cooking methods can be applied to a wide variety of foods—meats, fish, vegetables and even pastries. Here we describe each of the cooking methods and use photographs to outline their general procedures. Detailed procedures and recipes applying these methods to specific foods are found in subsequent chapters.

Dry-Heat Cooking Methods

Cooking by dry heat is the process of applying heat either directly, by subjecting the food to the heat of a flame, or indirectly, by surrounding the food with heated air or heated fat.

BROILING

Broiling uses radiant heat from an overhead source to cook foods. The temperature at the heat source can be as high as 2000°F (1093°C). The food to be broiled is placed on a preheated metal grate. Radiant heat from overhead cooks the food, while the hot grate below marks it with attractive crosshatch marks.

Delicate foods that may be damaged by being placed directly on a metal grate or foods on which crosshatch marks are not desirable may be placed on a preheated heatproof platter and then placed under the broiler. Cooking will take place through indirect heat from the preheated platter as well as by direct heat from the broiler's overhead heat source.

PROCEDURE FOR **BROILING FOODS**

❶ Heat the broiler or salamander to its highest setting.

❷ If necessary, use a wire brush to remove any charred or burnt particles that may be stuck to the broiler grate. The grate can be wiped with a lightly oiled towel to remove any remaining particles and to help season it.

❸ Cut, trim or otherwise prepare the food to be broiled. (Thicker pieces of food will take longer to cook.) Marinate, rub or season it, as desired. Many foods can be brushed lightly with oil to keep them from sticking to the grate.

❹ Place the food in the broiler, presentation side down. If necessary, use a fork or tongs to turn or flip the item without piercing its surface.

❺ Cook the food to the desired degree of doneness while developing the proper surface color. To do so, adjust the position of the item on the broiler, or adjust the distance between the grate and heat source. Doneness is often determined by touch, internal temperature or specific visual cues (for example, clear juices running from poultry).

❶ Preheat the grate under the broiler, then pull it out and place the food on the hot grate, presentation side down. If the item is oblong, place it at a 45-degree angle to the bars on the cooking grate. Slide the grate back under the broiler and cook long enough for the food to develop lines where it touches the grate. Pull the sliding grate out again and turn the food over at a 90-degree angle, working from left to right.

❷ Pull the sliding grate out of the broiler to turn the food as necessary in order to cook it evenly. Note the handle visible on the right, which can be used to adjust the distance between the grate and the heat source. Smaller pieces of food can often be cooked closer to the source of heat.

❸ Remove the cooked item from the broiler grate.

GRILLING

Although similar to broiling, grilling uses a heat source located beneath the cooking surface. Grills may be electric or gas, or they can burn wood or charcoal, which will add a smoky flavor to the food. Specific woods such as mesquite, hickory or vine clippings can be used to create special flavors. Grilled foods are often identified by cross-hatch markings.

PROCEDURE FOR **GRILLING FOODS**

❶ Heat the grill.

❷ If necessary, use a wire brush to remove any charred or burnt particles that may be stuck to the grill grate. The grate can be wiped with a lightly oiled towel to remove any remaining particles and to help season it.

❸ Cut, trim or otherwise prepare the food to be grilled. Marinate, rub or season it, as desired. Many foods can be brushed lightly with oil to keep them from sticking to the grate.

❹ Place the food on the grill, presentation side down. If practical, rotate the food 90 degrees to produce the attractive crosshatch marks associated with grilling. Then use a fork or tongs to turn or flip the item without piercing its surface.

❺ Cook the food to the desired degree of doneness while developing the proper surface color. To do so, adjust the position of the item on the grill, or adjust the distance between the grate and heat source. Doneness is often determined by touch, internal temperature or specific visual cues (for example, clear juices running from poultry).

❶ Decide which side of the grilled food will be presented face up to the customer. Place the food on the hot grill with this side facing down. If the item is oblong, place it at a 45-degree angle to the bars on the cooking grate. Cook long enough for the food to develop dark charred lines where it touches the grate.

❷ Rotate the food 90 degrees and allow it to cook long enough for the grates to char it to the same extent as in Step 1.

❸ Turn the food over and finish cooking it. It is usually unnecessary to create the crosshatch markings on the reverse side because the customer will not see this side.

ROASTING AND BAKING

Roasting and baking are the processes of surrounding a food with dry, heated air in a closed environment. The term *roasting* is usually applied to meats and poultry, whereas *baking* is used when referring to fish, fruits, vegetables, starches, breads and pastry items. Heat is transferred by convection to the food's surface and then penetrates the food by conduction. The surface dehydrates and the food browns from caramelization, completing the cooking process.

Poêléing (poe-el-lay-ing) is a cooking method similar to both roasting and braising. The food is cooked in an oven, but in a covered pot with aromatic vegetables and bacon fat or butter, so that it steams in its own juices. Also known as butter roasting, the French poêlé technique is perhaps most similar to pot-roasting. Like a typical roasted dish (and unlike a typical braised dish), this method is used for tender cuts of meats and poultry that do not require long, slow cooking, and no additional liquid is added during cooking. The meat or poultry can first be browned in hot fat, or it can be browned toward the end of cooking by removing the lid of the cooking vessel. Doneness is determined using the same techniques as those used for roasting. The meat or poultry is usually served with a sauce made from the pan juices mixed with a liquid and finished in the same way as a sauce for a braised dish. A recipe for Poêlé of Chicken with Pearl Onions and Mushrooms is given on page 414.

PROCEDURE FOR **ROASTING OR BAKING FOODS**

❶ Preheat the oven.

❷ Cut, trim or otherwise prepare the food to be roasted or baked. Marinate or season as desired. Brush with oil or butter, as appropriate.

❸ Place the food on a rack or directly in a roasting pan or baking dish.

❹ Roast the food, generally uncovered, at the desired temperature. **Baste** as necessary.

❺ Cook to the desired internal temperature or doneness, remembering that many foods will undergo **carryover cooking** after they are removed from the oven.

baste to moisten foods during cooking (usually grilling, broiling or roasting) with melted fat, pan drippings, a sauce or other liquids to prevent drying and to add flavor

carryover cooking the cooking that occurs after a food is removed from a heat source; it is accomplished by the residual heat remaining in the food

❶ Season the item to be roasted, arrange it in an uncovered pan and place it in a preheated oven.

❷ Use a thermometer to check the internal temperature of the item being roasted.

SAFETY ALERT
Cooking with Hot Oil

When hot oil comes into contact with liquid, it can spatter, causing severe burns. Use caution when placing foods into hot fat. When pan-frying, slide food into the heated pan, letting it fall away from you so that splatters do not cause burns. Pat moist foods dry with paper towels before adding them to a deep fryer.

Oil heated to its flash point can ignite, causing burns or a serious kitchen fire. When oil is heated to its smoke point, it begins to break down, creating acrolein, a harsh-smelling chemical compound. This offensive smell is a good warning that hot oil may be close to its flash point. Turn off the heat and carefully remove the pan of oil from its heat source. Cover with a tight-fitting lid to smother any flames. Allow the oil to cool completely before discarding.

SAUTÉING

Sautéing is a dry-heat cooking method that uses conduction to transfer heat from a hot sauté pan to food with the aid of a small amount of fat. Heat then penetrates the food through conduction. High temperatures are used to sauté, and the foods are usually cut thinly or into small pieces to promote even cooking.

To sauté foods properly, begin by heating a sauté pan on the stove top, then add a small amount of fat. The fat should just cover the bottom of the pan. Heat the fat to the point where it just begins to smoke. The food to be cooked should be as dry as possible when it is added to the pan to promote browning and to prevent excessive spattering. Place the food in the pan in a single layer. (The pan should be just large enough to hold the food in a single layer; a pan that is too large may cause the fat to burn.) The heat should be adjusted so that the food cooks thoroughly; it should not be so hot that the outside of the food burns before the inside is cooked. The pan should be hot enough so that any surface moisture on the food evaporates quickly. The food should be turned or tossed periodically to develop the proper color. Larger items should be turned using a fork or tongs without piercing the surface. Smaller items are often turned by using the sauteuse's sloped sides to flip them back on top of themselves. When tossing sautéed foods, keep the pan in contact with the heat source as much as possible to prevent it from cooling. Sautéing sometimes includes the preparation of a sauce directly in the pan after the main item has been removed.

Stir-frying is a variation of sautéing. A wok is used instead of a sauté pan; the curved sides and rounded bottom of the wok diffuse heat efficiently and facilitate tossing and stirring. When stir-frying, the heat is kept at a constant high temperature. Otherwise, stir-frying procedures are the same as those outlined for sautéing and will not be discussed separately here.

PROCEDURE FOR **SAUTÉING FOODS**

1. Cut, pound or otherwise prepare the food to be sautéed. Season it and dredge it in flour, if desired.
2. Heat a sauté pan and add enough fat (typically, oil or clarified butter) to just cover the pan's bottom.
3. Add the food to the sauté pan in a single layer, presentation side down. Do not crowd the pan.
4. Adjust the temperature so that the food's exterior browns properly without burning and the interior cooks. The heat should be high enough to complete the cooking process before the food begins to stew in its own juices.
5. Turn or toss the food as needed. Avoid burns by not splashing hot fat.
6. Cook until done. Doneness is usually determined by timing or touch.

1. Heat a small amount of oil in the sauté pan before adding the food.

2. The sloped edge of the pan can be used to toss the food.

3. The item being sautéed should be cooked quickly.

PAN-FRYING

Pan-frying shares similarities with both sautéing and deep-frying. It is a dry-heat cooking method in which heat is transferred by conduction from the pan to the food, using a moderate amount of fat. Heat is also transferred to the food from the hot fat by convection. Foods to be pan-fried are usually coated in breading. This forms a seal that keeps the food moist and prevents the hot fat from penetrating the food and causing it to become greasy. (Breading procedures are explained in Chapter 8, Mise en Place.)

To pan-fry foods properly, first heat the fat in a sauté pan. Use enough fat so that when the food to be cooked is added, the fat comes one-third to halfway up the item being cooked. The fat should be at a temperature somewhat lower than that used for sautéing; it should not smoke but should be hot enough so that when the food is added it crackles and spatters from the rapid vaporization of moisture. If the temperature is too low, the food will absorb excessive amounts of fat; if it is too high, the food will burn on the outside before the interior is fully cooked. When the food is properly browned on one side, use a fork or tongs to turn it without piercing. Always turn the food away from you to prevent being burned by any fat that may splash. When the food is fully cooked, remove it from the pan, drain it on absorbent paper and serve it immediately.

PROCEDURE FOR **PAN-FRYING FOODS**

❶ Cut, pound or otherwise prepare the food to be pan-fried; then bread, batter or flour it as desired.

❷ Heat a moderate amount of fat or oil in a heavy pan—usually enough to cover the item one-third to halfway up its sides.

❸ Add the food to the pan, being careful not to splash the hot fat.

❹ Fry the food on one side until brown. Using tongs, turn and brown the other side. Generally, pan-fried foods are fully cooked when they are well browned on both sides.

❺ Remove the food from the pan and drain it on absorbent paper before serving.

❶ Use tongs to carefully place the item being pan-fried into a moderate amount of hot oil.

❷ Turn the item to brown the other side.

❸ Drain the cooked item on absorbent paper.

DEEP-FRYING

Deep-frying is a dry-heat cooking method that uses conduction and convection to transfer heat to food submerged in hot fat. Although conceptually similar to boiling, deep-frying is not a moist-heat cooking method because the liquid fat contains no water. A key difference between boiling and deep-frying is the temperature of the cooking medium. The boiling point, 212°F (100°C), is the hottest temperature at which food can be cooked in water. At this temperature, most foods require a long cooking period and surface sugars cannot caramelize. With deep-frying, temperatures up to 400°F (200°C) are used. These high temperatures cook food more quickly and allow the food's surface to brown.

Foods to be deep-fried are usually first coated in batter or breading. This preserves moisture and prevents the food from absorbing excessive quantities of fat. Foods to be deep-fried should be of a size and shape that allows them to float freely in the fat. Foods that are to be deep-fried together should be of uniform size and shape. Delicately flavored foods should not be deep-fried in the same fat used for more strongly flavored ones, as the former could develop an odd taste from residual flavors left in the fat. Deep-fried foods should cook thoroughly while developing an attractive deep golden-brown color.

Today, most deep-frying is done in specially designed commercial fryers. These deep-fat fryers have built-in thermostats, making temperature control more precise. Deep-frying foods in a saucepan on the stove top is discouraged because it is both difficult and dangerous.

Recovery time is usually very slow, and temperatures are difficult to control. Also, the fat can spill easily, leading to injuries or creating a fire hazard.

To deep-fry food, first heat the fat or oil to a temperature between 325°F and 375°F (160°C and 190°C). The cooking medium's temperature can be adjusted within this range

recovery time the length of time it takes a cooking medium such as fat or water to return to the desired cooking temperature after food is submerged in it to allow the interior of thicker foods or frozen foods to cook before their surfaces become too dark. The fat must be hot enough to quickly seal the surface of the food so that it does not become excessively greasy, yet it should not be so hot that the food's surface burns before the interior is cooked.

There are two methods of deep-frying: the basket method and the swimming method. The **basket method** uses a basket to hold foods that are breaded, are individually quick-frozen or otherwise will not tend to stick together during cooking. The basket is removed from the fryer and filled as much as two-thirds full of product. (Do not fill the basket while it is hanging over the fat, as this allows unnecessary salt and food particles to fall into the fat, shortening its life.) The filled basket is then submerged in the hot fat. When cooking is completed, the basket is used to remove the foods from the fat and hold them while excess fat drains off.

A variation on this procedure is the **double-basket method**. It is used because many foods float as they deep-fry. This may produce undesirable results because the portion of the food not submerged may not cook. To prevent this and to promote even cooking, a second basket is placed over the food held in the first basket, keeping the food submerged in the fat.

Most battered foods initially sink to the bottom when placed in hot fat, then rise to the top as they cook. Because they would stick to a basket, the **swimming method** is used for these foods. With the swimming method, battered foods are carefully dropped directly into the hot fat. (Baskets are not used.) They will rise to the top as they cook. When the surface that is in contact with the fat is properly browned, the food is turned over with a spider or a pair of tongs so that it can cook evenly on both sides. When done, the product is removed and drained, again using a spider or tongs.

PROCEDURE FOR **DEEP-FRYING FOODS**

1. Cut, trim or otherwise prepare the food to be deep-fried. Bread or batter it, as desired.
2. Heat the oil or fat to the desired temperature.
3. Using either the basket method or the swimming method, carefully place the food in the hot fat.
4. Deep-fry the food until done. Doneness is usually determined by timing, surface color or sampling.
5. Remove the deep-fried food from the fryer and hold it over the cooking fat, allowing the excess fat to drain off.
6. Transfer the food to a hotel pan either lined with absorbent paper or fitted with a rack.
7. If the deep-fried items are to be held for later service, place them under a heat lamp; steam tables will not keep fried foods properly hot.

The basket method of deep-frying.

The double-basket method of deep-frying.

The swimming method of deep-frying.

TABLE 9.2 REACTION TEMPERATURES OF FATS

FAT	MELT POINT	SMOKE POINT	FLASH POINT
Butter	92–98°F/33–36°C	260°F/127°C	Possible at any temperature above 300°F/150°C
Butter, clarified	92–98°F/33–36°C	335–380°F/168–193°C	Possible at any temperature above 300°F/150°C
Lard	89–98°F/32–36°C	370°F/188°C	n/a
Deep-fryer shortening, heavy-duty, premium	102°F/39°C	440°F/227°C	690°F/365°C
Canola oil	n/a	430–448°F/221–230°C	553–560°F/289–293°C
Corn oil	40–50°F/4–7°C	450°F/232°C	610°F/321°C
Cocoa butter	88–93°F/31–34°C	n/a	n/a
Cottonseed oil	55°F/13°C	450°F/232°C	650°F/343°C
Margarine	94–98°F/34–36°C	410–430°F/210–221°C	Possible at any temperature above 300°F/150°C
Olive oil, extra virgin	32°F/0°C	350–410°F/177–210°C	n/a
Olive oil, pure or pomace	32°F/0°C	410–440°F/210°C–227°C	437°F/225°C
Peanut oil	28°F/–2°C	450°F/232°C	540°F/282°C
Shortening, vegetable, all-purpose	120°F/49°C	410°F/210°C	625°F/329°C
Soybean oil	–5°F/–20°C	495°F/257°C	540°F/282°C
Walnut oil	n/a	350–400°F/177–204°C	620°F/326°C

n/a = not available

This data was compiled from a variety of sources and is meant as a guideline only. Because reaction temperatures depend on the exact type and ratio of fatty acids present, the actual temperatures will vary depending on the brand or manufacturer of the fat in question. Temperatures are for clean, previously unused fats. Heating a fat, even one time, can lower the smoke and flash points dramatically.

Fats for Deep-Frying

Many types of fats can be used for deep-frying. Although animal fats, such as rendered beef fat, are sometimes used to impart their specific flavors to deep-fried foods, their low smoke points generally make them unsuitable for deep-frying unless blended with vegetable fats. By far the most common fats used for deep-frying are vegetable oils such as soybean, peanut and canola oil, all of which have high smoke points and are relatively inexpensive. See Table 9.2.

Specially formulated deep-frying compounds are also available. These are usually composed of a vegetable oil or oils to which antifoaming agents, antioxidants and preservatives have been added. These additives increase the oil's usable life and raise its smoke point.

Deep-fryer fats may also be hydrogenated. **Hydrogenation** is a chemical process that adds hydrogen to oil, turning the liquid oil into a solid (margarine is hydrogenated vegetable oil). Hydrogenated fats are more resistant to oxidation and chemical breakdown.

To choose the right fat, consider flavor, smoke point and resistance to chemical breakdown. High-quality frying fat should have a clean or natural flavor and a high smoke point and, when properly maintained, should be resistant to chemical breakdown.

Properly maintaining deep-fryer fat will greatly extend its useful life. (See Figure 9.4 and Table 9.3.) To do so:

❶ Store the fat in tightly sealed containers away from strong light; cover the deep fryer when not in use. Prolonged exposure to air and light turns fat rancid.

❷ Skim and remove food particles from the fat's surface during frying. Food particles cause fat to break down; if they are not removed, they will accumulate in the fryer and burn.

FIGURE 9.4 ▶ Clean fat for frying (left) is clear, free from off-odors and light in color. Fat that has darkened (right) should be discarded.

❸ Do not salt food over the fat. Salt causes fat to break down chemically.

❹ Prevent excessive water from coming into contact with the fat; pat-dry moist foods as much as possible before cooking and dry the fryer, baskets and utensils well after cleaning. Water, like salt, causes fat to break down.

❺ Do not overheat the fat (turn the fryer down or off if not in use). High temperatures break down the fat.

❻ Filter the fat each day or after each shift if the fryer is heavily used. Best results are obtained by using a filtering machine designed specifically for this purpose. Many large commercial fryers even have built-in filter systems. Less well-equipped operations can simply pour the hot fat through a paper filter.

Moist-Heat Cooking Methods

Cooking with moist heat is the process of applying heat to food by submerging it directly into a hot liquid or by exposing it to steam. Each of the following moist-heat cooking methods can be applied to a variety of foods. (See Table 9.4)

POACHING

Poaching is a moist-heat cooking method that uses convection to transfer heat from a liquid to a food. It is most often associated with delicately flavored foods that do not require lengthy cooking times to tenderize them, such as eggs, fruit or fish.

For poaching, the food is placed in a liquid held at temperatures between 160°F and 180°F (71°C and 82°C). The surface of the liquid should show only slight movement, but no bubbles. It is important to maintain the desired temperature throughout the cooking process. Do not allow the liquid to reach a boil, because the agitation will cause meats to become tough and stringy and will destroy tender foods such as fresh fruit or fish.

The flavor of the poaching liquid strongly affects the ultimate flavor of the finished product, so stock, **court bouillon** or broth is generally used. The liquid used to poach a food is sometimes used to make an accompanying sauce.

TABLE 9.3

FRYER FAT CAN BE DAMAGED BY

Salt

Water

Overheating

Food particles

Oxygen

CHANGE FRYER FAT WHEN IT

Becomes dark

Smokes

Foams

Develops off-flavors

---

court bouillon a liquid in which fish or vegetable are poached; made by simmering vegetables and seasonings in water and an acidic liquid such as vinegar or wine

---

TABLE 9.4 MOIST-HEAT COOKING METHODS

METHOD	LIQUID'S TEMPERATURE	LIQUID'S CONDITION	USES
Poaching	160–180°F/71–82°C	Liquid moves slightly but no bubbles	Eggs, fish, fruits
Simmering	185–205°F/85–96°C	Small bubbles break through the liquid's surface	Meats, stews, chicken
Boiling	212°F/100°C	Large bubbles and rapid movement	Vegetables, pasta
Steaming	212°F or higher/100°C or higher	Food is in contact only with the steam generated by a boiling liquid	Vegetables, fish, shellfish

Poaching (160°F–180°F/71°C–82°C).

Simmering (185°F–205°F/85°C–96°C).

Boiling (212°F/100°C).

There are two methods of poaching: submersion poaching and shallow poaching. For **submersion poaching**, the food is completely covered with the cooking liquid. There should not be too much excess liquid, however, as this could leach away much of the food's flavor. Nor should there be too little, as that could leave a portion of the food exposed, preventing it from cooking.

For **shallow poaching**, the food is placed in just enough liquid to come approximately halfway up its sides. The liquid, called a **cuisson**, is brought to a simmer on the stove top. The pan is then covered with a piece of buttered parchment paper or a lid, and cooking is completed either on the stove top or in the oven. Shallow poaching combines aspects of poaching and steaming.

cuisson (kwee-sohn) the liquid used for shallow poaching

PROCEDURE FOR **POACHING FOODS**

1. Cut, trim or otherwise prepare the food to be poached.
2. Bring an adequate amount of cooking liquid to the desired starting temperature. (For some items, the cooking liquid is first brought to a boil and then reduced to the poaching temperature.) Place the food in the liquid.
3. For submersion poaching, the liquid should completely cover the food.
4. For shallow poaching, the liquid should come approximately halfway up the side of the food. If shallow poaching, cover the pan with a piece of buttered parchment paper or a lid.
5. Maintaining the proper temperature, poach the food to the desired doneness in the oven or on the stove top. Doneness is generally determined by timing, internal temperature or tenderness.
6. Remove the food and hold it for service in a portion of the cooking liquid or, using an ice bath, cool it in the cooking liquid.
7. The cooking liquid can sometimes be used to prepare an accompanying sauce or reserved for use in other dishes.

1. Season the poaching liquid as desired and bring it to the correct temperature.

2. Carefully place the food item into the poaching liquid.

3. Remove the cooked food from the poaching liquid.

SIMMERING

Simmering is another moist-heat cooking method that uses convection to transfer heat from a liquid to a food. It is often associated with foods that need to be tenderized through long, slow, moist cooking, such as less tender cuts of meat. Properly simmered foods should be moist and very tender. For simmering, the food is submerged in a liquid held at temperatures between 185°F and 205°F (85°C and 96°C). Because simmering temperatures are slightly higher than those used for poaching, there should be more action on the liquid's surface, with a few air bubbles breaking through.

As with poaching, the liquid used for simmering has a great effect on the food's flavor. Be sure to use a well-flavored stock or broth and to add mirepoix, herbs and seasonings as needed.

PROCEDURE FOR **SIMMERING FOODS**

❶ Cut, trim or otherwise prepare the food to be simmered.

❷ Bring an adequate amount of the cooking liquid to the appropriate temperature (some foods, especially smoked or cured items, are started in a cold liquid). There should be enough liquid to cover the food completely.

❸ Add the food to the simmering liquid.

❹ Maintaining the proper cooking temperature throughout the process, simmer the food to the desired doneness. Doneness is generally determined by timing or tenderness.

❺ Remove the item and hold it for service in a portion of the cooking liquid or, using an ice bath, cool the food in its cooking liquid.

❶ The item being simmered should be fully submerged in the seasoned liquid.

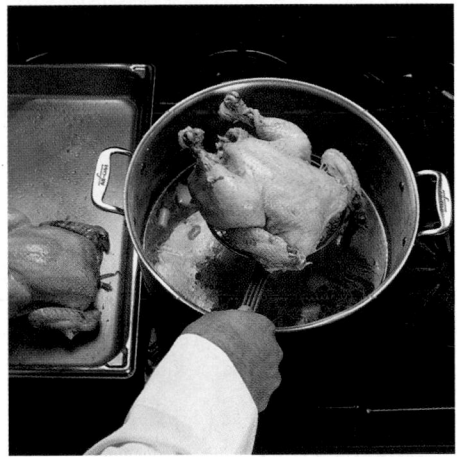

❷ Remove the cooked item from the liquid.

BOILING

Boiling is another moist-heat cooking method that uses the process of convection to transfer heat from a liquid to a food. Boiling uses large amounts of rapidly bubbling liquid to cook foods. The turbulent waters and the relatively high temperatures cook foods more quickly than do poaching or simmering. Few foods, however, are cooked by true boiling. Most "boiled" meats are actually simmered. Even "hard-boiled" eggs are really only simmered. Starches such as pasta and potatoes are among the only types of food that are truly boiled.

Under normal atmospheric pressure at sea level, water boils at 212°F (100°C). The addition of other ingredients or a change in atmospheric pressure can change the boiling point, however. As altitude increases, the boiling point decreases because of the drop in atmospheric pressure. For every 1000 feet above sea level, the boiling point of water drops 2°F (1°C). In the mile-high city of Denver, for example, water boils at 203°F (95°C). Because the boiling temperature is lower, it will take longer to cook foods in Denver than in, for example, Miami.

The addition of alcohol also lowers the boiling point of water because alcohol boils at about 175°F (80°C). In contrast, the addition of salt, sugar or other substances raises the boiling point slightly. This means that foods cooked in salted water cook faster because the boiling point is one or two degrees higher than normal.

Use as much water as practical when boiling food. Whenever food is added to boiling water, it lowers the water's temperature. The greater the amount of water, however, the faster it will return to a boil.

PROCEDURE FOR **BOILING FOODS**

❶ Bring an appropriate amount of a liquid to a boil over high heat. Add oil or seasonings, if desired.

❷ Add the food to be boiled to the rapidly boiling water. Bring the liquid back to a boil and adjust the temperature to maintain the boil.

❸ Cook until done. Doneness is usually determined by timing or texture.

❹ Remove the boiled food from the cooking liquid, draining any excess liquid.

❺ Serve the boiled food immediately. Some boiled foods can be refreshed in cold water and held for later service.

❶ Bring the cooking liquid to a full boil. When the item being cooked is added to the liquid, its temperature will fall.

❷ After a boiled item such as pasta is cooked, it may be drained through a colander.

STEAMING

Steaming is a moist-heat cooking method that uses the process of convection to transfer heat from the steam to the food being cooked. It is most often associated with tender, delicately flavored foods, such as fish and vegetables, which do not require long cooking times. Steaming tends to enhance a food's natural flavor and helps retain its nutrients. Properly steamed foods should be moist and tender. Additional flavor can be introduced by adding wine, stock, aromatics, spices or herbs to the liquid used as the steaming medium. The steaming liquid can also often be used to make a sauce to be served with the steamed food.

The food to be steamed is usually placed in a basket or rack above a boiling liquid. The food should not touch the liquid; it should be positioned so that the steam can circulate around it. (Some foods, such as shellfish and ears of corn, however, can be placed directly in a shallow pool of boiling water.) A lid should be placed on the steaming pot to trap the steam and also create a slight pressure within the pot, which speeds the cooking process.

Another type of steaming uses a convection steamer. Convection steamers use pressurized steam to cook food very quickly in an enclosed chamber. Convection steamer cooking does not result in a flavored liquid that can be used to make a sauce.

Steamed foods should be served immediately. If held for later service, they should be refreshed and refrigerated until used.

PROCEDURE FOR **STEAMING FOODS**

1. Cut, trim or otherwise prepare the food to be steamed.
2. If a convection steamer is not being used, prepare a steaming liquid and bring it to a boil in a covered pan or double boiler.
3. Place the food to be steamed on a rack, in a basket or on a perforated pan in a single layer. Do not crowd the items. Place the rack, basket or pan over the boiling liquid.
4. Alternatively, place the food in a shallow pool of the cooking liquid.
5. Cover the cooking assemblage and cook to the desired doneness. Doneness is usually determined by timing, color or tenderness.

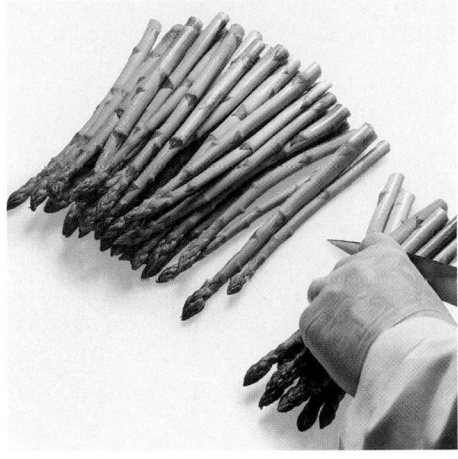

1. Trim items before steaming them so that they cook evenly.

2. A perforated hotel pan can be set over a deeper pan of water, covered and used as a steamer.

Combination Cooking Methods

Some cooking methods employ both dry-heat and moist-heat cooking techniques. The two principal combination methods are braising and stewing. In both methods, the first step is usually to brown the main item using dry heat. The second step is to complete cooking by simmering the food in a liquid. Combination methods are often used for less tender but flavorful cuts of meat as well as for poultry and some vegetables.

1. First brown the item being braised in fat.

2. Add liquid to the pan.

3. The item can be basted with the liquid during cooking.

BRAISING

Braised foods benefit from the best qualities of both dry- and moist-heat cooking methods. Foods to be braised are usually large pieces that are first browned in a small amount of fat at high temperatures. As with sautéing, heat is transferred from the pan to the food mainly by the process of conduction. Vegetables and seasonings are added, and enough sauce or liquid is added to come one-third to halfway up the item being cooked. The pan is covered, and the heat is reduced. The food is then cooked at low heat, using a combination of simmering and steaming to transfer heat from the liquid (conduction) and the air (convection) to the food. This can be done on the stove top or in the oven. A long, slow cooking period helps tenderize the main item. Braised foods are usually served with a sauce made from the cooking liquid.

PROCEDURE FOR **BRAISING FOODS**

1. Cut, trim or otherwise prepare the food to be braised. Dredge it in flour, if desired.
2. Heat a small amount of fat in a heavy pan.
3. Sear the food on all sides. Some foods—notably, meats—should be removed from the pan after they are seared.
4. Add any other ingredients and sauté.
5. Add flour or roux, if used.
6. Add the cooking liquid; it should partially cover the food being braised.
7. Add aromatics and seasonings.
8. If the principal item was removed, return it to the pan.
9. Cover the pan and bring the cooking liquid to a simmer. Cook slowly, either on the stove top or in an oven at 250°F–300°F (120°C–150°C). Baste and turn the food as needed.
10. When the principal item is cooked, remove it from the pan and hold it in a warm place.
11. Prepare a sauce from the braising liquid if desired. This may be done by reducing the liquid on the stove top to intensify its flavors. If the food was braised in an unthickened stock, the stock may now be thickened using a roux, arrowroot or cornstarch. Strain the sauce or, if desired, purée the mirepoix and other ingredients and return them to the sauce. Adjust the sauce's consistency as desired.

STEWING

Stewing also uses a combination of dry- and moist-heat cooking methods. Stewing is most often associated with smaller pieces of food that are first cooked either by browning them in a small amount of fat or oil or by blanching them in a liquid. Cooking is then finished in a liquid or sauce. Stewed foods have enough liquid added to cover them completely and are simmered at a constant temperature until tender. Cooking time is generally shorter for stewing than for braising because the main items are smaller.

PROCEDURE FOR **STEWING FOODS**

1. Trim and cut the food to be stewed into small, uniform-sized pieces. Dredge the pieces in flour, if desired.
2. Heat a small amount of fat in a heavy pan. Then sear the food on all sides, developing color as desired.
3. Add any other ingredients and sauté.
4. Add flour or roux.
5. Gradually add the cooking liquid, stirring to prevent lumps. The liquid should completely cover the principal items.
6. Bring the stew to the appropriate temperature. Cover and place in the oven at 250°F–300°F (120°C–150°C) or continue to simmer on the stove top until the principal items are tender.
7. Remove the principal items and hold them in a warm place.

8. Thicken the sauce as desired.

9. Return the principal items to the stew. If not added during the cooking process, vegetables and other garnishes may be cooked separately and added to the finished stew.

1. First brown the item being stewed in a small amount of fat.

2. Add flour to make a roux.

3. Add liquid to the pan.

4. Degrease the finished stew as necessary.

1. Describe the differences between conduction and convection. Identify four cooking methods that rely on both conduction and convection to heat foods. Explain your choices.

2. Identify two cooking methods that rely on infrared heat. What is the principal difference between these methods?

3. At the same temperature, will a food cook faster in a convection oven or a conventional oven? Explain your answer.

4. Describe the process of caramelization and its significance in food preparation. Will a braised food have a caramelized surface? Explain your answer.

5. Describe the process of coagulation and its significance in food preparation. Will a pure fat coagulate if heated? Explain your answer.

6. Describe the process of gelatinization and its significance in food preparation. Will a pure fat gelatinize? Explain your answer.

7. Name and describe two styles of deep-frying.

8. Use the Internet to research some of the cooking methods used in the food processing industry to prepare meats and poultry for the deli case. Discuss the cooking methods used and compare them with the techniques illustrated in this chapter. **www**

QUESTIONS FOR DISCUSSION

Terms to Know

energy	poêléing
conduction	stir-frying
convection	basket method
natural convection	double-basket method
mechanical convection	swimming method
radiation	hydrogenation
infrared cooking	submersion poaching
microwave cooking	shallow poaching
evaporation	
melting	

CHAPTER TEN

STOCKS AND SAUCES

fond (1) French for "stock" or "base"; (2) the concentrated juices, drippings and bits of food left in pans after foods are roasted or sautéed; it is used to flavor sauces made directly in the pans in which foods were cooked

A STOCK IS A FLAVORED LIQUID. A good stock is the key to a great soup, sauce or braised dish. The French appropriately call a stock *fond* ("base"), as stocks are the basis for many classic and modern dishes.

A **sauce** is a thickened liquid used to flavor and enhance other foods. A good sauce adds flavor, moisture, richness and visual appeal. A sauce should complement food; it should never disguise it. A sauce can be hot or cold, sweet or savory, smooth or chunky.

Although the thought of preparing stocks and sauces may be intimidating, the procedures are really quite simple. Carefully follow the basic procedures outlined in this chapter, use high-quality ingredients and, with practice and experience, you will soon be producing fine stocks and sauces.

This chapter addresses classical hot sauces as well as coulis, contemporary broths, flavored oils, salsas and relishes. Cold sauces, generally based on mayonnaise and vinaigrettes, are discussed in Chapter 24, Salads and Salad Dressings; dessert sauces are discussed in Chapter 34, Custards, Creams, Frozen Desserts and Dessert Sauces.

STOCKS

There are several types of stocks. Although they are all made from a combination of bones, vegetables, seasonings and liquids, each type uses specific procedures to give it distinctive characteristics.

A **white stock** is made by simmering chicken, veal or beef bones in water with vegetables and seasonings. The stock remains relatively colorless during the cooking process.

A **brown stock** is made from chicken, veal, beef or game bones and vegetables, all of which are caramelized before being simmered in water with seasonings. The stock has a rich, dark color.

Both a **fish stock** and a **fumet** are made by slowly cooking fish bones or crustacean shells and vegetables without coloring them, then simmering them in water with seasonings for a short time. For a fumet, wine and lemon juice are also added. The resulting stock or fumet is a strongly flavored, relatively colorless liquid.

A **court bouillon** is made by simmering vegetables and seasonings in water and an acidic liquid such as vinegar or wine. It is used to poach fish or vegetables.

The quality of a stock is judged by four characteristics: body, flavor, clarity and color. Body develops when collagen proteins dissolve in protein-based stock. Vegetable stocks have less body than meat stocks because they lack animal protein. Flavoring vegetables such as mirepoix, herb sachets and the proper ratios of ingredients to liquid give stocks their flavor. Clarity is achieved by removing impurities during stock making. Many ingredients contribute to a stock's color. Vegetables such as leeks and carrots give white stock a light color. Browned bones and tomato paste give color to dark stocks. Improper uses of coloring ingredients can overwhelm the color and flavor of a stock.

Ingredients

The basic ingredients of any stock are bones, a vegetable mixture known as a mirepoix, seasonings and water.

BONES

Bones are the most important ingredient; they add flavor, richness and color to the stock. Traditionally, the kitchen or butcher shop saved the day's bones to make stock. But because many meats and poultry items are now purchased precut or portioned, food service operations often purchase bones specifically for stock making.

Different bones release their flavor at different rates. Even though the bones are cut into 3- to 4-inch (8- to 10-centimeter) pieces, a stock made entirely of beef and/or veal bones requires 6 to 8 hours of cooking time, whereas a stock made entirely from chicken bones requires only 5 to 6 hours.

Beef and Veal Bones

The best bones for beef and veal stock are from younger animals. They contain a higher percentage of **cartilage** and other **connective tissue** than do bones from more mature animals. Connective tissue has a high **collagen** content. Through the cooking process, the collagen is converted into **gelatin** and water. The gelatin adds richness and body to the finished stock.

The best beef and veal bones are back, neck and shank bones, as they have high collagen contents. Beef and veal bones should be cut with a meat saw into small pieces, approximately 3 to 4 inches (8 to 10 centimeters) long, so that they can release as much flavor as possible while the stock cooks.

Chicken Bones

The best bones for chicken stock are from the neck and back. If a whole chicken carcass is used, it can be cut up for easier handling.

Fish Bones

The best bones for fish stock are from lean fish such as sole, flounder, whiting or turbot. Bones from fatty fish (for example, salmon, tuna and swordfish) do not produce good stock because of their high fat content and distinctive flavors. The entire fish carcass can be used, but it should be cut up with a cleaver or heavy knife for easy handling and even extraction of flavors. After cutting, the pieces should be rinsed in cold water to remove blood, loose scales and other impurities.

Other Bones

Lamb, turkey, game and ham bones can also be used for white or brown stocks. Although mixing bones is generally acceptable, be careful of blending strongly flavored bones, such as those from lamb or game, with beef, veal or chicken bones. The former's strong flavors may not be appropriate or desirable in the finished product.

MIREPOIX

A mirepoix is a mixture of onions, carrots and celery added to a stock to enhance its flavor and aroma. Although chefs differ on the ratio of vegetables, generally a mixture of 50 percent onions, 25 percent carrots and 25 percent celery, by weight, is used. (Unless otherwise noted, any reference to mirepoix in this book refers to this ratio.) For a brown stock, onion skins may be used to add color. It is not necessary to peel the carrots or celery because flavor, not aesthetics, is important.

The size into which the mirepoix is chopped is determined by the stock's cooking time: The shorter the cooking time, the smaller the vegetables must be chopped to ensure that all possible flavor is extracted. For white or brown stocks made from beef or veal bones, the vegetables should be coarsely chopped into large, 1- to 2-inch (2.5- to 5-centimeter) pieces. For chicken and fish stocks, the vegetables should be more finely chopped into ½-inch (1.2-centimeter) pieces.

A white mirepoix is made by replacing the carrots in a standard mirepoix with parsnips and adding mushrooms and leeks. Some chefs prefer to use a white mirepoix when making a white stock, as it produces a lighter product. Sometimes parsnips, mushrooms and leeks are added to a standard mirepoix for additional flavors.

cartilage also known as gristle; a tough, elastic, whitish connective tissue that helps give structure to an animal's body

connective tissue tissue found throughout an animal's body that binds together and supports other tissues such as muscles

collagen a protein found in nearly all connective tissue; it dissolves when cooked with moisture

gelatin a tasteless and odorless mixture of proteins (especially collagen) extracted from boiling bones, connective tissue and other animal parts; when dissolved in a hot liquid and then cooled, it forms a jellylike substance used as a thickener and stabilizer

matignon a standard mirepoix plus diced smoked bacon or smoked ham and, depending on the dish, mushrooms and herbs; sometimes called an edible mirepoix, it is usually cut more uniformly than a standard mirepoix and left in the finished dish as a garnish

 Formula for standard mirepoix = 50% onions + 25% carrots + 25% celery by weight

Mirepoix ingredients

SEASONINGS

Principal stock seasonings are peppercorns, bay leaves, thyme, parsley stems and, optionally, garlic. These seasonings generally can be left whole. A stock is cooked long enough for all of their flavors to be extracted, so there is no reason to chop or grind them. Seasonings generally are added to the stock at the start of cooking. Some chefs do not add seasonings to beef or veal stock until midway through the cooking process, however, because of the extended cooking times. Seasonings can be added as a sachet d'épices or a bouquet garni.

Salt, an otherwise important seasoning, is not added to stock. Because a stock has a variety of uses, it is impossible for the chef to know how much salt to add when preparing it. If, for example, the stock was seasoned to taste with salt, the chef could not reduce it later; salt is not lost through reduction, and the concentrated product would taste too salty. Similarly, seasoning the stock to taste with salt could prevent the chef from adding other ingredients that are high in salt when finishing a recipe. Unlike many seasonings whose flavors must be incorporated into a product through lengthy cooking periods, salt can be added at any time during the cooking process with the same effect.

Principles of Stock Making

The following principles, outlined in Figure 10.1, apply to all stocks. You should follow them in order to achieve the highest-quality stocks possible. Consult Table 10.1 when problems arise.

A. START THE STOCK IN COLD WATER

The ingredients should always be covered with cold water. When bones are covered with cold water, blood and other impurities dissolve. As the water heats, the impurities coagulate and rise to the surface, where they can be removed easily by skimming. If the bones were covered with hot water, the impurities would coagulate more quickly and remain dispersed in the stock without rising to the top, making the stock cloudy.

If the water level falls below the bones during cooking, add water to cover them. Flavor cannot be extracted from bones not under water, and bones exposed to the air will darken and discolor a white stock.

B. SIMMER THE STOCK GENTLY

The stock should be brought to a boil and then reduced to a simmer, a temperature of approximately 185°F (85°C). While simmering, the ingredients release their flavors into the liquid. If kept at a simmer, the liquid will remain clear as it reduces and the stock develops.

Never boil a stock for any length of time. Rapid boiling of a stock, even for a few minutes, causes impurities and fats to blend with the liquid, making it cloudy.

C. SKIM THE STOCK FREQUENTLY

A stock should be skimmed often to remove the fat and impurities that rise to the surface during cooking. If they are not removed, they may make the stock cloudy.

D. STRAIN THE STOCK CAREFULLY

Once a stock finishes cooking, the liquid must be separated from the bones, vegetables and other solid ingredients. In order to keep the liquid clear, it is important not to disturb the solid ingredients when removing the liquid. This is easily accomplished if the stock is cooked in a steam kettle or stockpot with a spigot at the bottom.

If the stock is cooked in a standard stockpot, to strain it:

1. Skim as much fat and as many impurities from the surface as possible before removing the stockpot from the heat.
2. After removing the pot from the heat, carefully ladle the stock from the pot without stirring it.
3. Strain the stock through a china cap lined with several layers of cheesecloth.

Start the stock in cold water.
Simmer the stock gently.
Skim the stock frequently.
Strain the stock carefully.
Cool the stock quickly.
Store the stock properly.
Degrease the stock.

FIGURE 10.1 ▶ Principles of stock making.

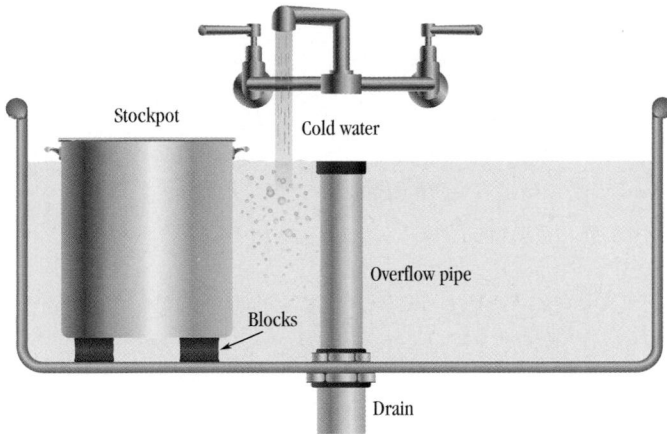

FIGURE 10.2 ▶ Venting a stockpot.

E. COOL THE STOCK QUICKLY

Most stocks are prepared in large quantities, cooled and held for later use. Great care must be taken when cooling a stock to prevent food-borne illnesses or souring. To cool a stock below the temperature danger zone quickly and safely:

1. Keep the stock in a metal container. A plastic container insulates the stock and delays cooling.
2. Vent the stockpot in an empty sink by placing it on blocks or a rack. This allows water to circulate on all sides and below the pot when the sink is filled with water. See Figure 10.2.
3. Install an overflow pipe in the drain and fill the sink with cold water or a combination of cold water and ice. Make sure that the weight of the stockpot is adequate to keep it from tipping over.
4. Let cold water run into the sink and drain out the overflow pipe. Stir the stock frequently to facilitate even, quick cooling.

In addition to this venting procedure, cooling wands can be used to speed the cooling of stocks, soups, sauces and other liquids. These wands (also known as ice paddles) are hollow plastic containers that can be filled with water or ice, sealed, frozen and then used to stir and cool liquids. Clean and sanitize the wand after each use to prevent cross-contamination.

F. STORE THE STOCK PROPERLY

Once the stock is cooled, transfer it to a sanitized covered container (either plastic or metal) and store it in the refrigerator. As the stock chills, fat rises to its surface and solidifies. If left intact, this layer of fat helps preserve the stock. Stocks can be stored for up to 1 week under refrigeration or frozen for several months.

G. DEGREASE THE STOCK

Degreasing a stock is simple: When a stock is refrigerated, fat rises to its surface, hardens and is easily lifted or scraped away before the stock is reheated.

White Stock

A white or neutral stock may be made from beef, veal or chicken bones. The finished stock should have a good flavor, good clarity, high gelatin content and little or no color. Veal bones are most often used, but any combination of beef, veal or chicken bones may be used.

BLANCHING BONES

Chefs disagree on whether the bones for a white stock should be blanched to remove impurities. Some chefs argue that blanching keeps the stock as clear and colorless as possible; others argue that blanching removes nutrients and flavor.

Lifting fat from the surface of a cold stock.

degrease to remove fat from the surface of a liquid such as a stock or sauce by skimming, scraping or lifting congealed fat

PROCEDURE FOR **BLANCHING BONES**

If you choose to blanch the bones:

1. Wash the cut-up bones, place them in a stockpot and cover them with cold water.
2. Bring the water to a boil over high heat.
3. As soon as the water boils, skim the rising impurities. Drain the water from the bones and discard it.
4. Refill the pot with cold water and proceed with the stock recipe.

WHITE STOCK

MISE EN PLACE

▶ Cut up and wash bones.
▶ Peel and chop onions, carrots and celery for mirepoix.
▶ Prepare herb sachet.

Yield: 2 gal. (7.6 lt)

Bones, veal, chicken or beef	15 lb.	7.2 kg
Cold water	3 gal.	11.5 lt
Mirepoix	2 lb.	960 g
Sachet:		
Bay leaves	2	2
Dried thyme	½ tsp.	2 ml
Peppercorns, crushed	½ tsp.	2 ml
Parsley stems	8	8

1. Cut the washed bones into pieces approximately 3–4 inches (8–10 centimeters) long.
2. Place the bones in a stockpot and cover them with cold water. If blanching, bring the water to a boil, skimming off the scum that rises to the surface. Drain off the water and the impurities. Then add the 3 gallons (11.5 liters) cold water and bring to a boil. Reduce to a simmer.
3. If not blanching the bones, bring the cold water to a boil. Reduce to a simmer and skim the scum that forms.
4. Add the mirepoix and sachet to the simmering stock.
5. Continue simmering and skimming the stock for 6 to 8 hours. (If only chicken bones are used, simmer for 3 to 4 hours.)
6. Strain, cool and refrigerate.

Approximate values per 1-fl.-oz. (30-ml) serving: **Calories** 4, **Total fat** 0.1 g, **Saturated fat** 0.1 g, **Cholesterol** 0 mg, **Sodium** 5 mg, **Total carbohydrates** 0 g, **Protein** 0.2 g, **Claims**—fat free; very low sodium

1. Adding water to bones for white stock.

2. Skimming the white stock.

3. Adding mirepoix to the white stock and seasonings.

Brown Stock

A brown stock is made from chicken, veal, beef or game bones. The finished stock should have a good flavor, rich dark brown color, good body and high gelatin content.

The primary differences between a brown stock and a white stock are that for a brown stock, the bones and mirepoix are caramelized before being simmered and a tomato product is added. These extra steps provide the finished stock with a rich dark color and a more intense flavor.

CARAMELIZING

Caramelization is the process of browning the sugars found on the surface of most foods. This gives the stock its characteristic flavor and color.

PROCEDURE FOR **CARAMELIZING BONES**

For caramelizing, do not wash or blanch the bones as this retards browning. To caramelize:

1. Place the cut-up bones in a roasting pan one layer deep. It is better to roast several pans of bones than to overfill one pan.
2. Roast the bones for approximately 1 hour in a hot oven (375°F/190°C). Stirring occasionally, brown the bones thoroughly, but do not allow them to burn.
3. Transfer the roasted bones from the pan to the stockpot.

DEGLAZING THE PAN

After the bones are caramelized, the excess fat should be removed and reserved for future use. The caramelized and coagulated proteins remaining in the roasting pan are very flavorful. To utilize them, **deglaze** the pan.

remouillage (rhur-moo-yahj) French for "rewetting"; a stock produced by reusing the bones left from making another stock. After draining the original stock from the stockpot, add fresh mirepoix, a new sachet and enough water to cover the bones and mirepoix, and a second stock can be made. A remouillage is treated like the original stock; allow it to simmer for 4 to 5 hours before straining. A remouillage will not be as clear or as flavorful as the original stock, however. It is often used to make glazes or in place of water when making stocks.

PROCEDURE FOR **DEGLAZING THE PAN**

1. Place the pan on the stove top over medium heat and add enough water to cover the bottom of the pan approximately ½ inch (1.2 centimeters) deep.
2. Stir and scrape the pan bottom to dissolve and remove all the caramelized materials while the water heats.
3. Pour the deglazing liquid (also known as the deglazing liquor) over the bones in the stockpot.

deglaze to swirl or stir a liquid (usually wine or stock) in a sauté pan or other pan to dissolve cooked food particles remaining on the bottom; the resulting mixture often becomes the base for a sauce

PROCEDURE FOR **CARAMELIZING MIREPOIX**

1. Add a little of the reserved fat from the roasted bones to the roasting pan after it has been deglazed. (Or use a sautoir large enough to contain all the mirepoix comfortably.)
2. Sauté the mirepoix, browning all the vegetables well and evenly without burning them.
3. Add the caramelized mirepoix to the stockpot.

Almost any tomato product can be used in a brown stock: fresh tomatoes, canned whole tomatoes, crushed tomatoes, tomato purée or paste. If using a concentrated tomato product such as paste or purée, use approximately half the amount by weight of fresh or canned tomatoes. The tomato product should be added to the stockpot when the mirepoix is added.

MISE EN PLACE

▶ Cut up and wash bones.
▶ Peel and chop onions, carrots and celery for mirepoix.
▶ Prepare herb sachet.

BROWN STOCK

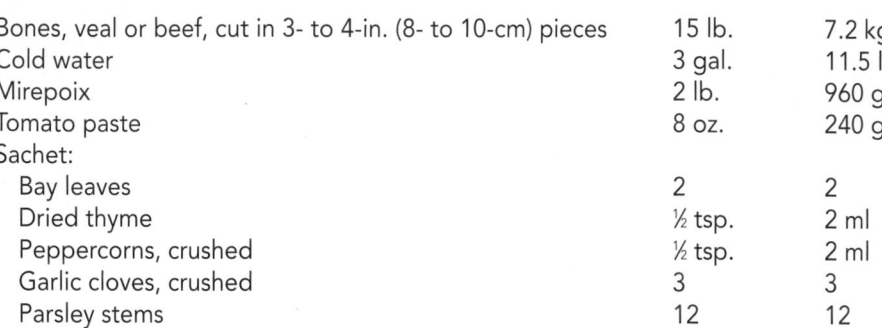

Yield: 2 gal. (7.6 lt)

Bones, veal or beef, cut in 3- to 4-in. (8- to 10-cm) pieces	15 lb.	7.2 kg
Cold water	3 gal.	11.5 lt
Mirepoix	2 lb.	960 g
Tomato paste	8 oz.	240 g
Sachet:		
Bay leaves	2	2
Dried thyme	½ tsp.	2 ml
Peppercorns, crushed	½ tsp.	2 ml
Garlic cloves, crushed	3	3
Parsley stems	12	12

① Place the bones in a roasting pan, one layer deep, and brown in a 375°F (190°C) oven. Turn the bones occasionally to brown them evenly.

② Remove the bones and place them in a stockpot. Pour off the fat from the roasting pan and reserve it.

③ Deglaze the roasting pan with part of the cold water.

④ Add the deglazing liquor and the rest of the cold water to the bones, covering them completely. Bring to a boil and reduce to a simmer.

⑤ Add a portion of the reserved fat to the roasting pan and sauté the mirepoix until evenly browned. Then add it to the simmering stock.

⑥ Add the tomato paste and sachet to the stock and continue to simmer for 6 to 8 hours, skimming as necessary.

⑦ Strain, cool and refrigerate.

Approximate values per 1-fl.-oz. (30-ml) serving: **Calories** 3, **Total fat** 0 g, **Saturated fat** 0 g, **Cholesterol** 0.3 mg, **Sodium** 105 mg, **Total carbohydrates** 0 g, **Protein** 0 g, **Claims**—fat free; low sodium

① Caramelizing the bones.

② Deglazing the pan with water.

③ Caramelizing the mirepoix.

④ Adding the proper amount of water.

Fish Stock and Fish Fumet

A fish stock and a fish fumet (foo-may) are similar and can be used interchangeably in most recipes. Both are clear with a pronounced fish flavor and very light body. A fumet, however, is more strongly flavored and aromatic and contains an acidic ingredient such as white wine and/or lemon juice.

Only the bones and heads of lean fish and crustacean shells are used to make fish stock. Oily fish such as mackerel, salmon or tuna are not used because their pronounced flavor would overwhelm the stock. The fish bones and shells used to make a fish stock

COMMERCIAL BASES

Commercially produced flavor (or convenience) bases are widely used in food service operations. They are powdered or paste flavorings added to water to create stocks or, when used in smaller amounts, to enhance the flavor of sauces and soups. These products are also sold as bouillon cubes or granules. Although inferior to well-made stocks, flavor bases do reduce the labor involved in the production of stocks, sauces and soups. Used properly, they also ensure a consistent product. Because most bases do not contain gelatin, stocks and sauces made from them do not benefit from reduction. (Frozen glace de viande and demi-glace are increasingly available from meat and other food service suppliers.)

Bases vary greatly in quality and price. Sodium (salt) is the main ingredient in many bases. Better bases are made primarily of meat, poultry or fish extracts. To judge the quality of a flavor base, prepare it according to package directions and compare the flavor to that of a well-made stock. The flavor base can be improved by adding a mirepoix, standard sachet and a few appropriate bones to the mixture, then simmering for 1 or 2 hours. It can then be strained, stored and used like a regular stock. Although convenience bases are widely used in the industry, it is important to remember that even the best base is a poor substitute for a well-made stock.

or fumet should be washed but never blanched because blanching removes too much flavor. They may be **sweated** without browning if desired, however. Because of the size and structure of fish bones and crustacean shells, stocks and fumets made from them require much less cooking time than even a chicken stock; 30 to 45 minutes is usually sufficient to extract full flavor. Mirepoix or other vegetables should be cut small so that all of their flavors can be extracted during the short cooking time.

The procedure for making a fish stock is very similar to that for making a white stock.

sweat to cook a food in a pan (usually covered), without browning, over low heat until the item softens and releases moisture; sweating allows the food to release its flavor more quickly when cooked with other foods

FISH STOCK

Yield: 1 gal. (3.8 lt)

Mirepoix, small dice	1 lb.	480 g
Mushroom trimmings	8 oz.	240 g
Clarified butter	2 fl. oz.	60 ml
Fish bones or crustacean shells	10 lb.	4.8 kg
Water	5 qt.	4.8 lt
Sachet:		
Bay leaves	2	2
Dried thyme	½ tsp.	2 ml
Peppercorns, crushed	¼ tsp.	1 ml
Parsley stems	8	8

1. Sweat mirepoix and mushroom trimmings in butter until tender for 1 to 2 minutes.
2. Combine all ingredients except the sachet in a stockpot.
3. Bring to a simmer and skim impurities as necessary.
4. Add the sachet and simmer uncovered for 30 to 45 minutes.
5. Strain, cool and refrigerate.

Approximate values per 1-fl.-oz. (30-ml) serving: **Calories** 5, **Total fat** 0 g, **Saturated fat** 0 g, **Cholesterol** 0 mg, **Sodium** 100 mg, **Total carbohydrates** 0 g, **Protein** 1 g, **Claims**—fat free; low sodium

MISE EN PLACE

◄ Peel and chop onions, carrots and celery for mirepoix.
◄ Wash fish bones or shells.
◄ Prepare herb sachet.

Adding cold water to fish bones.

A fish stock is sometimes used to make a fish fumet; if so, the resulting product is very strongly flavored. A fish fumet is also flavored with white wine and lemon juice. When making a fumet, sweat the bones and vegetables before adding the cooking liquid and seasonings.

FISH FUMET

Yield: 2 gal. (7.6 lt)

MISE EN PLACE
▶ Peel onions and chop into small dice.
▶ Cut up and wash bones.

Whole butter	2 oz.	60 g
Onions, small dice	1 lb.	480 g
Parsley stems	12	12
Fish bones	10 lb.	4.8 kg
Dry white wine	24 fl. oz.	720 ml
Lemon juice	2 fl. oz.	60 ml
Cold water or fish stock	7 qt.	6.7 lt
Mushroom trimmings	2 oz.	60 g
Fresh thyme	1 sprig	1 sprig
Lemon slices	10	10

① Sweating the onions, parsley stems and fish bones.

① Melt the butter in a stockpot.

② Add the onions, parsley stems and fish bones. Cover the pot and sweat the bones over low heat.

③ Sprinkle the bones with the wine and lemon juice.

④ Add the cold water or stock, mushroom trimmings, thyme and lemon slices. Bring to a boil, reduce to a simmer and cook approximately 30 minutes, skimming frequently.

⑤ Strain, cool and refrigerate.

Approximate values per 1-fl.-oz. (30-ml) serving: **Calories** 5, **Total fat** 0.7 g, **Saturated fat** 0.2 g, **Cholesterol** 0.5 mg, **Sodium** 90 g, **Total carbohydrates** 0 g, **Protein** 1 g, **Claims**—fat free; low sodium

② Adding cold water and seasonings.

Vegetable Stock

A good vegetable stock should be clear and light-colored. Because no animal products are used, it has no gelatin content and little body. A vegetable stock can be used instead of a meat-based stock in most recipes. This substitution is useful when preparing vegetarian dishes or as a lighter, more healthful alternative when preparing sauces and soups. Although almost any combination of vegetables can be used for stock making, more variety is not always better. Sometimes a vegetable stock made with one or two vegetables that complement the finished dish particularly well will produce better results than a stock made with many vegetables. Strongly flavored vegetables such as asparagus, broccoli and other cruciferous vegetables, spinach and bitter greens, for example, should be avoided when making an all-purpose vegetable stock. Potatoes and other starchy vegetables will cloud the stock and should not be used unless clarity is not a concern.

VEGETABLE STOCK

Yield: 1 gal. (3.8 lt)

MISE EN PLACE
▶ Peel and chop onions, carrots and celery for mirepoix.
▶ Clean, peel and chop leek, garlic cloves, fennel and turnip.
▶ Wash and dice tomato.
▶ Prepare herb sachet.

Vegetable oil	2 fl. oz.	60 ml
Mirepoix, small dice	2 lb.	960 g
Leek, white and green parts, chopped	8 oz.	240 g
Garlic cloves, chopped	4	4
Fennel, small dice	4 oz.	120 g
Turnip, diced	2 oz.	60 g
Tomato, diced	2 oz.	60 g
White wine	8 fl. oz.	240 ml
Water	1 gal.	3.8 lt
Sachet:		
Bay leaf	1	1
Dried thyme	½ tsp.	2 ml
Peppercorns, crushed	¼ tsp.	1 ml
Parsley stems	8	8

1. Heat the oil. Add the mirepoix, leek, garlic, fennel, turnip and tomato and sweat for 10 minutes.
2. Add the wine, water and sachet.
3. Bring the mixture to a boil, reduce to a simmer and cook for 45 minutes.
4. Strain, cool and refrigerate.

Approximate values per 1-fl.-oz. (30-ml) serving: **Calories** 5, **Total fat** 0 g, **Saturated fat** 0 g, **Cholesterol** 0 mg, **Sodium** 0 mg, **Total carbohydrates** 0 g, **Protein** 0 g, **Claims**—fat free; low calorie

Court Bouillon

A court bouillon (bool-yawn), though not actually a stock, is prepared in much the same manner as stocks, so it is included here. A court bouillon (French for "short broth") is a flavored liquid, usually water and wine or vinegar, in which vegetables and seasonings have been simmered to impart their flavors and aromas.

Court bouillon is most commonly used to poach foods such as fish and shellfish. Recipes vary depending on the foods to be poached. Although a court bouillon can be made in advance and refrigerated for later use, its simplicity lends itself to fresh preparation whenever needed.

Adding cold water to sweated vegetables.

COURT BOUILLON

Yield: 1 gal. (3.8 lt)

Water	1 gal.	3.8 lt
Vinegar	6 fl. oz.	180 ml
Lemon juice	2 fl. oz.	60 ml
Mirepoix	1 lb. 8 oz.	720 g
Bay leaves	4	4
Peppercorns, crushed	1 tsp.	5 ml
Dried thyme	1 pinch	1 pinch
Parsley stems	1 bunch	1 bunch

1. Combine all ingredients and bring to a boil.
2. Reduce to a simmer and cook for 45 minutes.
3. Strain and use immediately or cool and refrigerate.

Note: This recipe can be used for poaching almost any fish, but it is particularly well suited to salmon, trout and shellfish. When poaching freshwater fish, replace the water and vinegar with equal parts white wine and water.

Approximate values per 1-fl.-oz. (30-ml) serving: **Calories** 3, **Total fat** 0 g, **Saturated fat** 0 g, **Cholesterol** 0 mg, **Sodium** 0 mg, **Total carbohydrates** 0 g, **Protein** 0 g, **Claims**—fat free; low sodium

Nage

An aromatic court bouillon is sometimes served as a light sauce or broth with fish or shellfish. This is known as a nage (nahj), and dishes served in this manner are described as *à la nage* (French for "swimming"). After the fish or shellfish is cooked, additional herbs and aromatic vegetables are added to the cooking liquid, which is then reduced slightly and strained.

Alternatively, the used court bouillon can be strained, chilled, and clarified with egg whites and aromatic vegetables in the same manner as a consommé, discussed in Chapter 11, Soups. Finally, whole butter or cream may be added to a nage for richness.

LIME LEAVES, LEMON GRASS

Court Bouillon lends itself to a variety of flavorings customized to the dish in which it is being used. Adding fragrant lime leaves, lemon grass or fresh ginger gives court bouillon an exotic flavor profile suitable for Asian fish dishes. Likewise, adding a mixture of mild dried chilies and cilantro to the preparation brings a Latin flair to the broth.

MISE EN PLACE

▶ Peel and chop onions, carrots and celery for mirepoix.
▶ Crush peppercorns.

Glaze

A glaze is the dramatic reduction and concentration of a stock. One gallon (4 liters) of stock produces only 8 to 16 fluid ounces (240 to 480 milliliters) of glaze. *Glace de viande* is made from brown stock, reduced until it becomes dark and syrupy. *Glace de volaille* is made from chicken stock, and *glace de poisson* from fish stock.

Glazes are added to soups or sauces to increase and intensify flavors. They are also used as a source of intense flavoring for several of the small sauces discussed next.

PROCEDURE FOR **REDUCING A STOCK TO A GLAZE**

❶ Simmer the stock over very low heat. Be careful not to let it burn, and skim it often.

❷ As it reduces and the volume decreases, transfer the liquid into progressively smaller saucepans. Strain the liquid each time it is transferred into a smaller saucepan.

❸ Strain it a final time, cool and refrigerate. A properly made glaze will keep for several months under refrigeration.

❶ A properly thickened glaze made from brown stock.

❷ Chilled glace de viande.

TABLE 10.1	TROUBLESHOOTING CHART FOR STOCKS	
PROBLEM	**REASON**	**SOLUTION**
Cloudy	Impurities	Start stock in cold water
	Stock boiled during cooking	Strain through layers of cheesecloth
Lack of flavor	Not cooked long enough	Increase cooking time
	Inadequate seasoning	Add more flavoring ingredients
	Improper ratio of bones to water	Add more bones
Lack of color	Improperly caramelized bones and mirepoix	Caramelize bones and mirepoix until darker
	Not cooked long enough	Cook longer
Lack of body	Wrong bones used	Use bones with a higher content of connective tissue
	Insufficient reduction	Cook longer
	Improper ratio of bones to water	Add more bones
Too salty	Commercial base used	Change base or make own stock; do not salt stock
	Salt added during cooking	

SAUCES

With a few exceptions, a sauce is a liquid plus thickening agent plus seasonings. Any chef can produce fine sauces by learning to do the following:

① Make good stocks.
② Use thickening agents properly to achieve the desired texture, flavor and appearance.
③ Use seasonings properly to achieve the desired flavors.

Classic hot sauces are divided into two groups: **mother** or **leading sauces** (Fr. *sauce mère*) and **small** or **compound sauces**. The five classic mother sauces are béchamel, velouté, espagnole (brown), tomato and hollandaise. Except for hollandaise, leading sauces are rarely served as is; more often they are used to create the many small sauces.

Not all sauces fall into the traditional classifications, however. Some sauces use purées of fruits or vegetables as their base; they are known as **coulis**. Others, such as **beurre blanc** (French for "white butter") and **beurre rouge** ("red butter"), are based on an acidic reduction in which whole butter is incorporated. **Flavored butters**, **flavored oils**, **salsas**, **relishes** and **pan gravy** are also used as sauces in modern food service operations.

Thickening Agents

One of the most traditional and commonly used methods for thickening sauces is through the gelatinization of starches. As discussed in Chapter 9, Principles of Cooking, gelatinization is the process by which starch granules absorb moisture when placed in a liquid and heated. As the moisture is absorbed, the product thickens. Starches generally used to thicken sauces are flour, cornstarch and arrowroot. Gelatinization may sound easy, but it takes practice to produce a good sauce that:

▶ Is lump-free
▶ Has a good clean flavor that is not pasty or floury
▶ Has a consistency that will coat the back of a spoon (the French call this **nappé**)
▶ Will not separate or break when the sauce is held or reduced

nappé (nap-ay) the consistency of a liquid, usually a sauce, that will coat the back of a spoon; from the verb *naper* in French or *nap* in English, meaning to coat a food with sauce

ROUX

Roux (roo) is the principal means used to thicken sauces. It is a combination of equal parts, by weight, of flour and fat, cooked together to form a paste. Cooking the flour in fat coats the starch granules with the fat and prevents them from lumping together or forming lumps when introduced into a liquid. In large production kitchens, large amounts of roux are prepared and held for use as needed. Smaller operations may make roux as required for each recipe.

There are three types of roux:

① **White roux** is cooked only briefly and should be removed from the heat as soon as it develops a frothy, bubbly appearance. It is used in white sauces, such as béchamel, or in dishes where little or no color is desired.
② **Blond roux** is cooked slightly longer than white roux and should begin to take on a little color as the flour caramelizes. It is used in ivory-colored sauces, such as velouté, or where a richer flavor is desired.
③ **Brown roux** is cooked until it develops a darker color and a nutty aroma and flavor. Brown roux is used in brown sauces and dishes where a dark color is desired. It is important to remember that cooking a starch before adding a liquid breaks down the starch granules and prevents gelatinization from occurring. Therefore, because brown roux is cooked longer than white roux, more brown roux is required to thicken a given quantity of liquid.

White, Blond and Brown Roux

A SAUCY HISTORY

The word *sauce* is derived from the Latin word *salus*, meaning "salted." This derivation is entirely logical. For millennia, salt has been the basic condiment for enhancing or disguising the flavor of many foods.

Cooks of ancient Rome flavored dishes with *garum*, a golden-colored sauce made from fermented fish entrails combined with brine, condiments, water and wine or vinegar. They also used a sauce referred to as a "single" made from oil, wine and brine. When boiled with herbs and saffron, it became a "double" sauce. To this the Byzantines later added pepper, cloves, cinnamon, cardamom and coriander or spikenard (a fragrant ointment made from grains).

Medieval chefs were fond of either very spicy or sweet-and-sour sauces. A typical sauce for roasted meat consisted of powdered cinnamon, mustard, red wine and a sweetener such as honey. Bits of stale or grilled bread were used as a thickener. Other sauces were based on verjuice, an acidic stock prepared from the juice of unripe grapes. To it were added other fruit juices, honey, flower petals and herbs or spices. Perhaps this was done to hide the taste of salt-cured or less-than-fresh meats, or, more likely, to showcase the host's wealth.

Guillaume Tirel (ca. 1312–1395), who called himself **Taillevent,** was the master chef for Charles V of France. Around 1375, Taillevent wrote *Le Viandier*, the oldest known French cookbook. It includes 17 sauces. Among them is a recipe for a *cameline* sauce, made from grilled bread soaked in wine. The wine-soaked bread is then drained, squeeze-dried and ground with cinnamon, ginger, pepper, cloves and nutmeg; this mixture is diluted with vinegar. There is also a recipe for a sauce called *taillemaslée*, made of fried onions, verjuice, vinegar and mustard.

Sauces enjoyed in Renaissance Italy and France were prepared much like those of the Middle Ages, but in an important development for modern cuisine, many were based on broths thickened with cream, butter and egg yolks and flavored with herbs and spices. Recipes for some sauces of the Renaissance, such as poivrade and Robert, are recognizable today. Many con-

Taillevent dressed as a sergeant-at-arms with three cooking pots on his shield from his grave marker.

sider **François Pierre de La Varenne** (1618–1678) to be one of the founding fathers of French cuisine. His treatises, especially *Le Cuisinier français* (1651), detail the early development, methods and manners of French cuisine. His analysis and recipes mark a departure from medieval cookery and a French cuisine heavily influenced by Italian traditions. His uniquely modern writings include recipes for new foods (especially fruits and vegetables native to the Americas or the Far East) and for indigenous foods (such as saltwater fish) that were becoming more popular. La Varenne is credited with introducing roux as a thickening agent for sauces, especially velouté sauces. He emphasized the importance of fonds and the reduction of cooking juices to concentrate flavors. He also popularized the use of bouquets garni to flavor stocks and sauces.

During the early 18th century, the chef to the French Duc de Levis-Mirepoix pioneered the use of onions, celery and carrots to enhance the flavor and aroma of stocks. The mixture, named for the chef's employer, soon became the standard. An enriched stock greatly improves the quality of the sauces derived from it. Antonin Carême developed the modern system for classifying hundreds of sauces in the early 19th century. Although it is unknown how many sauces Carême actually invented, he wrote treatises containing the theories and recipes for many of the sauces still used today. Carême's extravagant lists were simplified by chefs later in the 19th century, most notably by Auguste Escoffier.

PROCEDURE FOR **PREPARING ROUX**

Cooking the roux.

Whether it will be white, blond or brown, the procedure for making a roux is the same:

1. Using a heavy saucepan to prevent scorching, heat the clarified butter or other fat.
2. Add all the flour and stir to form a paste. Although all-purpose flour can be used, it is better to use cake or pastry flour because they contain a higher percentage of starch. Do not use high-gluten flour because of its greatly reduced starch content. (Flours are discussed in Chapter 29, Principles of the Bakeshop.)
3. Cook the paste over medium heat until the desired color is achieved. Stir the roux often to avoid burning. Burnt roux will not thicken a liquid; it will simply add dark specks and an undesirable flavor.

The temperature and amount of roux being prepared determine the exact length of cooking time. Generally, however, a white roux needs to cook for only a few minutes, long enough to minimize the raw flour taste. Blond roux is cooked longer, until the paste begins to change to a slightly darker color. Brown roux requires a much longer cooking time to develop its characteristic color and aroma. A good roux will be stiff, not runny or pourable.

INCORPORATING ROUX INTO A LIQUID

There are two ways to incorporate roux into a liquid without causing lumps:

❶ Cold stock can be added to the hot roux while stirring vigorously with a whisk.

❷ Room-temperature roux can be added to a hot stock while stirring vigorously with a whisk.

When the roux and the liquid are completely incorporated and the sauce begins to boil, it is necessary to cook the sauce for a time to remove any raw flour taste that may remain. Most chefs feel a minimum of 20 minutes is necessary.

GUIDELINES FOR USING ROUX

❶ Avoid using aluminum pots. The scraping action of the whisk will turn light sauces gray and will impart a metallic flavor.

❷ Use sufficiently heavy pots to prevent sauces from scorching or burning during extended cooking times.

❸ Avoid extreme temperatures. Roux should be no colder than room temperature so that the fat is not fully solidified. Extremely hot roux is dangerous and can spatter when combined with a liquid. Stocks should not be ice cold when combined with roux; the roux will become very cold, and the solidified pieces may be very difficult to work out with a whisk.

❹ Avoid overthickening. See Table 10.2. Roux does not begin to thicken a sauce until the sauce is almost at the boiling point; the thickening action continues for several minutes while the sauce simmers. If a sauce is to cook for a long time, it will also be thickened by reduction.

CORNSTARCH

Cornstarch, a very fine white powder, is a pure starch derived from corn. It is used widely as a thickening agent for hot and cold sauces and is especially popular in Asian cuisines for thickening sauces and soups. Liquids thickened with cornstarch have a glossy sheen that may or may not be desirable.

One unit of cornstarch thickens about twice as much liquid as an equal unit of flour. Sauces thickened with cornstarch are less stable than those thickened with roux because cornstarch can break down and lose its thickening power after prolonged heating. Products thickened with cornstarch should not be reheated.

(a)
Cold stock
Hot roux

(b)
Hot stock
Cold roux

When thickening stock with roux, either (a) add cold stock to hot roux or (b) add cold roux to hot stock.

TABLE 10.2		PROPORTIONS OF ROUX TO LIQUID					
FLOUR	+	**BUTTER**	=	**ROUX**	+	**LIQUID**	=	**SAUCE**
6 oz./180 g	+	6 oz./180 g	=	12 oz./360 g	+	1 gal./4 lt	=	light
8 oz./240 g	+	8 oz./240 g	=	1 lb./480 g	+	1 gal./4 lt	=	medium
12 oz./360 g	+	12 oz./360 g	=	24 oz./720 g	+	1 gal./4 lt	=	heavy

Variables: The starch content of a flour determines its thickening power. Cake flour, being lowest in protein and highest in starch, has more thickening power than bread flour, which is high in protein and low in starch. In addition, a dark roux has less thickening power than a lighter one, so more will be needed to thicken an equal amount of liquid.

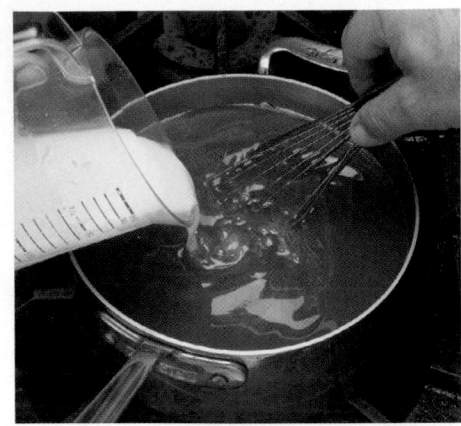

Whisking cornstarch slurry into simmering liquid.

slurry a mixture of raw starch and cold liquid used for thickening

Incorporating Cornstarch

Cornstarch must be mixed with a cool liquid before it is introduced into a hot one. The cool liquid separates the grains of starch and allows them to begin absorbing liquid without lumping. A solution of a starch and a cool liquid is called a **slurry**.

The starch slurry may be added to either a hot or cold liquid. If added to a hot liquid, it must be stirred continuously during incorporation. Unlike roux, cornstarch begins to thicken almost immediately if the liquid is hot. Sauces thickened with cornstarch must be cooked gently until the raw starch flavor disappears, usually about 5 minutes.

ARROWROOT

Arrowroot, derived from the roots of several tropical plants, is similar in texture, appearance and thickening power to cornstarch and is used in exactly the same manner. Arrowroot does not break down as quickly as cornstarch, and it produces a slightly clearer finished product although it is much more expensive.

BEURRE MANIÉ

Beurre manié (burr mahn-yay) is a combination of equal amounts, by weight, of flour and soft whole butter. Beurre manié is used for quick thickening at the end of the cooking process. The butter also adds shine and flavor to the sauce as it melts.

PROCEDURE FOR **USING BEURRE MANIÉ**

❶ Knead flour and butter together until smooth.

❷ Form the mixture into pea-sized balls, then whisk the beurre manié gradually into a simmering sauce.

LIAISON

Unlike the thickeners already described, a liaison (lee-yeh-zon) does not thicken a sauce through gelatinization. A liaison is a mixture of egg yolks and heavy cream; it adds richness and smoothness with minimal thickening. Special care must be taken to prevent the yolks from coagulating when they are added to a hot liquid because this could curdle the sauce.

PROCEDURE FOR **USING A LIAISON**

tempering gradually raising the temperature of a cold liquid such as eggs by slowly stirring in a hot liquid

❶ Whisk together one part egg yolk and three parts whipping cream. Combining the yolk with cream raises the temperature at which the yolk's proteins coagulate, making it easier to incorporate them into a sauce without lumping or curdling.

❷ **Temper** the egg yolk and cream mixture by slowly adding a small amount of the hot liquid while stirring continuously.

❸ When enough of the hot liquid has been added to the liaison to warm it thoroughly, begin adding the warmed liaison to the remaining hot liquid. Be sure to stir the mixture carefully to prevent the yolk from overcooking or lumping. Plain egg yolks coagulate at temperatures between 149°F and 158°F (65°C and 70°C). Mixing them with cream raises the temperatures at which they coagulate to approximately 180°F–185°F (82°C–85°C). Temperatures over 185°F (85°C) will cause the yolks to curdle. Great care must be taken to hold the sauce above 135°F (57°C) for food safety and sanitation reasons, yet below 185°F (85°C) to prevent curdling.

① Adding hot liquid to the egg yolk and cream mixture.

② Adding the tempered egg yolk and cream liaison to the hot liquid.

EMULSIFICATION

Sauces can also be thickened by the process of **emulsification**, whereby unmixable liquids such as oil and water are forced into a uniform, creamy state. Usually an emulsifying agent such as the lecithin found in egg yolks must be present to aid in the process. The action of stirring or whisking a sauce to incorporate the ingredients will produce an emulsion that is **permanent**, **semipermanent** or **temporary**. A permanent emulsion, such as that formed when making mayonnaise, will last for several days. A semipermanent emulsion will last for a few hours. Hollandaise sauce, discussed on page 208, is one example of a

emulsification the process by which generally unmixable liquids, such as oil and water, are forced into a uniform distribution

---

EMULSIONS

An emulsion is formed when unblendable ingredients such as fat and water are forced into a creamy state through the action of beating, blending, shaking, stirring or whisking. The agitation breaks the fat into microscopic droplets that are dispersed in the water.

In scientific terms, this is called a fat-in-water emulsion, where the fat (the dispersed phase) is dispersed into water (the continuous phase). Cream and milk are examples of fat-in-water emulsions created during the process of homogenization. Butter whisked into vinegar and egg yolks for hollandaise sauce is another example of a fat-in-water emulsion. The microscopic droplets of fat suspended in the liquid give the emulsion its creamy, cloudy appearance.

Visualizing an emulsion. Left: Oil floats on the surface of water before blending. Right: Vigorous stirring disperses the oil throughout the water.

semipermanent emulsion. A temporary emulsion will last very briefly and usually does not contain an emulsifying agent. Rather, vigorous whisking aerates the mixture, causing the temporary suspension of liquids. Such is the case when oil and vinegar are whisked together to make a simple salad dressing. Emulsified sauces are discussed in detail in Chapter 24, Salads and Salad Dressings.

Finishing Techniques

REDUCTION

reduction cooking a liquid such as a sauce until its quantity decreases through evaporation. To reduce by one-half means that one-half of the original amount remains. To reduce by three-fourths means that only one-fourth of the original amount remains. To reduce *au sec* means that the liquid is cooked until nearly dry.

As sauces cook, moisture is released in the form of steam. As steam escapes, the remaining ingredients concentrate, thickening the sauce and strengthening the flavors. This process, known as **reduction**, is commonly used to thicken sauces because no starches or other flavor-altering ingredients are needed. Sauces are often finished by allowing them to reduce until the desired consistency is reached.

STRAINING

Smoothness is important to the success of most sauces. They can be strained through either a china cap lined with several layers of cheesecloth or a fine-mesh chinois. As discussed later, often vegetables, herbs, spices and other seasonings are added to a sauce for flavor. Straining removes these ingredients as well as any lumps of roux or thickener remaining in the sauce after the desired flavor and consistency have been reached.

MONTER AU BEURRE

Monter au beurre (mohn-tay ah burr) is the process of swirling or whisking whole butter into a sauce to give it shine, flavor and richness. Compound or flavored butters, discussed later, can be used in place of whole butter to add specific flavors. Monter au beurre is widely used to enrich and finish small sauces.

Using a wire whisk to finish a sauce with whole butter.

Using a hand blender to finish a sauce with whole butter.

Sauce Families

Leading, **grand** or **mother sauces** are the foundation for the entire classic repertoire of hot sauces. The five leading sauces—béchamel, velouté, espagnole (also known as brown), tomato and hollandaise—can be seasoned and garnished to create a wide variety of small or compound sauces. These five leading sauces are distinguished principally by the liquids and thickeners used to create them. See Table 10.3.

Small or **compound sauces** are grouped into families based on their leading sauce. Some small sauces have a variety of uses; others are traditional accompaniments for specific foods. A small sauce may be named for its ingredients, place of origin or creator. Although there are numerous classic small sauces, we have included only a few of the more popular ones following each of the leading sauce recipes.

TABLE 10.3	SAUCE FAMILIES	
MOTHER SAUCE	**LIQUID**	**THICKENER**
Béchamel	Milk	Roux
Velouté	White stock	Roux
Veal velouté	Veal stock	
Chicken velouté	Chicken stock	
Fish velouté	Fish stock	
Espagnole (brown sauce)	Brown stock	Roux
Tomato sauce	Tomato	Roux (optional)
Hollandaise	Butter	Egg yolks

THE BÉCHAMEL FAMILY

Named for its creator, Louis de Béchameil (1630–1703), steward to Louis XIV of France, béchamel (bay-shah-mell) sauce is the easiest mother sauce to prepare. Traditionally, it is made by adding heavy cream to a thick veal velouté. Although some chefs still believe a béchamel should contain veal stock, today the sauce is almost always made by thickening scalded milk with a white roux and adding seasonings. Often used for vegetable, egg and gratin dishes, béchamel has fallen into relative disfavor recently because of its rich, heavy nature. It is nevertheless important to understand its production and its place in traditional sauce making.

A properly made béchamel is rich, creamy and absolutely smooth with no hint of graininess. The flavors of the onion and clove used to season it should be apparent but not overwhelm the sauce's clean, milky taste. The sauce should be the color of heavy cream and have a deep luster. It should be thick enough to coat foods lightly but should not taste like the roux used to thicken it.

BÉCHAMEL

Yield: 1 gal. (3.8 lt)

Onion piquet	1	1
Milk	1 gal.	3.8 lt
Flour	8 oz.	240 g
Clarified butter	8 fl. oz.	240 ml
Salt and white pepper	TT	TT
Nutmeg	TT	TT

White Baylca–

1. Add the onion piquet to the milk in a heavy saucepan and simmer for 20 minutes.
2. In a separate pot, make a white roux with the flour and butter.
3. Remove the onion piquet from the milk. Gradually add the hot milk to the roux while stirring constantly with a whisk to prevent lumps. Bring to a boil.
4. Reduce the sauce to a simmer, add the seasonings and continue cooking for 30 minutes.
5. Strain the sauce through a china cap lined with cheesecloth. Melted butter can be carefully ladled over the surface of the sauce to prevent a skin from forming. Hold for service or cool in a water bath.

Approximate values per 6-fl.-oz. (180-ml) serving: **Calories** 240, **Total fat** 15 g, **Saturated fat** 9 g, **Cholesterol** 50 mg, **Sodium** 180 mg, **Total carbohydrates** 18 g, **Protein** 7 g, **Vitamin A** 15%, **Calcium** 25%

Small Béchamel Sauces

With a good béchamel, producing the small sauces in its family is quite simple. The quantities given are for 1 quart (approximately 1 liter) of béchamel. The final step for each recipe is to season to taste with salt and pepper.

MISE EN PLACE

◀ Tack a bay leaf onto a small peeled onion using a clove to make onion piquet.

TABLE 10.4   VELOUTÉ SAUCES

Fish stock	+	Roux	=	Velouté				
Chicken stock	+	Roux	=	Velouté	+	Cream	=	Suprême
Chicken stock	+	Roux	=	Velouté	+	Liaison and lemon	=	Allemande
Veal stock	+	Roux	=	Velouté	+	Liaison and lemon	=	Allemande

CHEESE Add to béchamel 8 ounces (240 grams) grated Cheddar or American cheese, a dash of Worcestershire sauce and 1 tablespoon (15 milliliters) dry mustard.

CREAM SAUCE Add to béchamel 8–12 fluid ounces (240–360 milliliters) scalded cream and a few drops of lemon juice.

MORNAY Add to béchamel 4 ounces (120 grams) grated Gruyère and 1 ounce (30 grams) grated Parmesan. Thin as desired with scalded cream. Remove the sauce from the heat and swirl in 2 ounces (60 grams) whole butter.

NANTUA Add to béchamel 4 fluid ounces (120 milliliters) heavy cream and 6 ounces (180 grams) crayfish butter (page 212). Add paprika to achieve the desired color. Garnish the finished sauce with diced crayfish meat.

SOUBISE (MODERN) Sweat 1 pound (480 grams) diced onions in 1 ounce (30 grams) whole butter without browning. Add béchamel and simmer until the onions are fully cooked. Strain through a fine chinois.

THE VELOUTÉ FAMILY

Velouté (veh-loo-TAY) sauces are made by thickening a white stock or fish stock with roux. The white stock can be made from veal or chicken bones. A velouté sauce made from veal or chicken stock is usually used to make one of two intermediary sauces—allemande and suprême—from which many small sauces are derived. **Allemande** sauce is made by adding lemon juice and a liaison to either a veal or chicken velouté. (The stock used depends on the dish with which the sauce will be served.) **Suprême** sauce is made by adding cream to a chicken velouté. See Table 10.4.

A properly made velouté should be rich, smooth and lump-free. If made from chicken or fish stock, it should taste of chicken or fish. A velouté made from veal stock should have a more neutral flavor. The sauce should be ivory-colored, with a deep luster. It should be thick enough to cling to foods without tasting like the roux used to thicken it.

allemande (ah-leh-MAHND) an intermediary sauce made by adding lemon juice and a liaison to chicken or veal velouté

suprême (soo-prem) an intermediary sauce made by adding cream to chicken velouté

VELOUTÉ

Yield: 1 gal. (3.8 lt)

Clarified butter	8 fl. oz.	240 ml
Flour	8 oz.	240 g
Chicken, veal or fish stock	5 qt.	4.8 lt
Salt and white pepper	TT	TT

1. Heat the butter in a heavy saucepan. Add the flour and cook to make a blond roux.
2. Gradually add the stock to the roux, stirring constantly with a whisk to prevent lumps. Bring to a boil and reduce to a simmer. (Seasonings are optional; their use depends on the seasonings in the stock and the sauce's intended use.)
3. Simmer and reduce to 1 gallon (3.8 liters), approximately 30 minutes.
4. Strain through a china cap lined with cheesecloth.
5. Melted butter may be carefully ladled over the surface of the sauce to prevent a skin from forming. Hold for service or cool in a water bath.

Approximate values per 1-fl.-oz. (30-ml) serving: **Calories** 25, **Total fat** 1.5 g, **Saturated fat** 1 g, **Cholesterol** 5 mg, **Sodium** 140 mg, **Total carbohydrates** 2 g, **Protein** 1 g

Small Fish Velouté Sauces

A few small sauces can be made from fish velouté. The quantities given are for 1 quart (approximately 1 liter) fish velouté sauce. The final step for each recipe is to season to taste with salt and pepper.

BERCY Sauté 2 ounces (60 grams) finely diced shallots in butter. Then add 8 fluid ounces (240 milliliters) dry white wine and 8 fluid ounces (240 milliliters) fish stock. Reduce this mixture by one-third and add the fish velouté. Finish with butter and garnish with chopped parsley.

CARDINAL Add 8 fluid ounces (240 milliliters) fish stock to 1 quart (1 liter) fish velouté. Reduce this mixture by half and add 16 fluid ounces (480 milliliters) heavy cream and a dash of cayenne pepper. Bring to a boil and swirl in 1½ ounces (45 grams) lobster butter (page 212). Garnish with chopped lobster coral at service time.

NORMANDY Add 4 ounces (120 grams) mushroom trimmings and 4 fluid ounces (120 milliliters) fish stock to 1 quart (960 milliliters) fish velouté. Reduce by one-third and finish with an egg yolk and cream liaison. Strain through a fine chinois.

ALLEMANDE SAUCE

Yield: 1 gal. (3.8 lt)

Veal or chicken velouté sauce	1 gal.	3.8 lt
Egg yolks	8	8
Heavy cream	24 fl. oz.	720 ml
Lemon juice	1 fl. oz.	30 ml
Salt and white pepper	TT	TT

1. Bring the velouté to a simmer.
2. In a stainless steel bowl, whip the egg yolks with the cream to create a liaison. Ladle approximately one-third of the hot velouté sauce into this mixture, while whisking, to temper the yolk-and-cream mixture.
3. When one-third of the velouté has been incorporated into the now-warmed yolk-and-cream mixture, gradually add the liaison to the remaining velouté sauce while whisking continuously.
4. Reheat the sauce. Do not let it boil.
5. Add the lemon juice; season with salt and white pepper to taste.
6. Strain through a china cap lined with cheesecloth.

Approximate values per 1-fl.-oz. (30-ml) serving: **Calories** 40, **Total fat** 3.5 g, **Saturated fat** 2 g, **Cholesterol** 25 mg, **Sodium** 95 mg, **Total carbohydrates** 1 g, **Protein** 1 g, **Vitamin A** 4%

Small Allemande Sauces

Several small sauces are easily produced from an allemande sauce made with either a chicken or veal velouté. The quantities given are for 1 quart (approximately 1 liter) allemande. The final step for each recipe is to season to taste with salt and pepper.

AURORA Add to allemande 2 ounces (60 grams) tomato paste and finish with 1 ounce (30 grams) butter.

HORSERADISH Add to allemande 4 fluid ounces (120 milliliters) heavy cream and 1 teaspoon (5 milliliters) dry mustard. Just before service add 2 ounces (60 grams) freshly grated horseradish. The horseradish should not be cooked with the sauce.

MUSHROOM Sauté 4 ounces (120 grams) sliced mushrooms in ½ ounce (15 grams) whole butter; add 2 teaspoons (10 milliliters) lemon juice. Then add the allemande to the mushrooms. Do not strain.

POULETTE Sauté 8 ounces (240 grams) sliced mushrooms and ½ ounce (15 grams) diced shallot in 1 ounce (30 grams) whole butter. Add to the allemande; then add 2 fluid ounces (60 milliliters) heavy cream. Finish with lemon juice to taste and 1 tablespoon (15 milliliters) chopped parsley.

SUPRÊME SAUCE

Yield: 1 gal. (3.8 lt)

Chicken velouté sauce	1 gal.	3.8 lt
Mushroom trimmings	8 oz.	240 g
Heavy cream	1 qt.	960 ml
Salt and white pepper	TT	TT

1. Simmer the velouté sauce with the mushroom trimmings until reduced by one-fourth.
2. Gradually whisk in the cream and return to a simmer.
3. Adjust the seasonings.
4. Strain through a china cap lined with cheesecloth.

Approximate values per 1-fl.-oz. (30-ml) serving: **Calories** 45, **Total fat** 4 g, **Saturated fat** 2.5 g, **Cholesterol** 15 mg, **Sodium** 95 mg, **Total carbohydrates** 1 g, **Protein** 1 g, **Vitamin A** 4%

Small Suprême Sauces

The following small sauces are easily made from a suprême sauce. The quantities given are for 1 quart (approximately 1 liter) suprême sauce. The final step for each recipe is to season to taste with salt and pepper.

ALBUFERA Add to suprême sauce 3 fluid ounces (90 milliliters) glace de volaille and 2 ounces (60 grams) red pepper butter (page 212).

HUNGARIAN Sweat 2 ounces (60 grams) diced onion in 1 tablespoon (15 milliliters) whole butter. Add 1 tablespoon (15 milliliters) paprika. Stir in suprême sauce. Cook for 2 to 3 minutes, strain and finish with whole butter.

IVORY Add to suprême sauce 3 fluid ounces (90 milliliters) glace de volaille.

THE ESPAGNOLE FAMILY

The mother sauce of the espagnole (ess-spah-nyol) or brown sauce family is full-bodied and rich. It is made from a brown stock to which brown roux, mirepoix and tomato purée have been added. Most often this sauce is used to produce demi-glace. Brown stock is also used to make jus lié. Demi-glace and jus lié are intermediary sauces used to create the small sauces of the espagnole family.

MISE EN PLACE

▶ Peel and chop onions, carrots and celery for mirepoix.
▶ Prepare herb sachet.

ESPAGNOLE (BROWN SAUCE)

Yield: 1 gal. (3.8 lt)

Mirepoix, medium dice	2 lb.	960 g
Clarified butter	8 fl. oz.	240 ml
Flour	8 oz.	240 g
Brown stock	5 qt.	4.8 lt
Tomato purée	8 oz.	240 g
Sachet:		
Bay leaf	1	1
Dried thyme	½ tsp.	2 ml
Peppercorns, crushed	¼ tsp.	1 ml
Parsley stems	8	8
Salt and pepper	TT	TT

1. Sauté the mirepoix in the butter until well caramelized.
2. Add the flour and cook to make a brown roux.
3. Add the stock and tomato purée. Stir to break up any lumps of roux. Bring to a boil; reduce to a simmer.

4 Add the sachet.

5 Simmer for approximately 1½ hours, allowing the sauce to reduce. Skim the surface as needed to remove impurities.

6 Strain the sauce through a china cap lined with several layers of cheesecloth. Adjust seasonings and cool in a water bath or hold for service.

Approximate values per 1-fl.-oz. (30-ml) serving: **Calories** 35, **Total fat** 2 g, **Saturated fat** 1 g, **Cholesterol** 5 mg, **Sodium** 150 mg, **Total carbohydrates** 4 g, **Protein** 1 g, **Vitamin A** 6%, **Claims**—low fat; low calorie

Demi-Glace

Brown stock is used to make the espagnole or brown sauce described earlier. Espagnole sauce can then be made into demi-glace, which in turn is used to make the small sauces of the espagnole family. Demi-glace is half brown sauce, half brown stock, reduced by half. It is usually finished with a small amount of Madeira or sherry wine. Because demi-glace creates a richer, more flavorful base, it produces finer small sauces than those made directly from a brown sauce.

A properly made demi-glace is rich, smooth and lump-free. Its prominent roasted flavor comes from the bones used for the brown stock. There should be no taste of roux. The caramelized bones and mirepoix as well as the tomato product contribute to its glossy dark brown, almost chocolate, color. It should be thick enough to cling to food without being pasty or heavy.

DEMI-GLACE

Yield: 1 qt. (960 ml)

Brown stock	1 qt.	960 ml
Brown sauce	1 qt.	960 ml

1 Combine the stock and sauce in a saucepan over medium heat.

2 Simmer until the mixture is reduced by half (a yield of 1 quart or 960 milliliters).

3 Strain and cool in a water bath.

Approximate values per 1-fl.-oz. (30-ml) serving: **Calories** 30, **Total fat** 1.5 g, **Saturated fat** 0.5 g, **Cholesterol** 5 mg, **Sodium** 200 mg, **Total carbohydrates** 4 g, **Protein** 1 g, **Vitamin A** 6%, **Claims**—low fat; low calorie

Jus Lié

Jus lié (zhoo lee-ay), also known as fond lié, is used like a demi-glace, especially to produce small sauces. Jus lié is lighter and easier to make than a demi-glace, however. It is made in one of two ways:

1 A rich brown stock is thickened with cornstarch or arrowroot and seasoned.

2 A rich brown stock is simmered and reduced so that it thickens naturally because of the concentrated amounts of gelatin and other proteins.

The starch-thickened method is a quick alternative to the long-simmering demi-glace. But because it is simply a brown stock thickened with cornstarch or arrowroot, it will be only as good as the stock with which it was begun. Sauces made from reduced stock usually have a better flavor but can be expensive to produce because of high food costs and lengthy reduction time.

A properly made jus lié is very rich and smooth. It shares many flavor characteristics with demi-glace. Its color should be dark brown and glossy from the concentrated gelatin content. Its consistency is somewhat lighter than demi-glace, but it should still cling lightly to foods.

Small Brown Sauces

Demi-glace and jus lié are used to produce many small sauces. The quantities given are for 1 quart (approximately 1 liter) demi-glace or jus lié. The final step for each recipe is to season to taste with salt and pepper.

BORDELAISE Combine 16 fluid ounces (480 milliliters) dry red wine, 2 ounces (60 grams) chopped shallots, 1 bay leaf, 1 sprig thyme and 1 pinch black pepper in a saucepan. Reduce by three-fourths, then add demi-glace and simmer for 15 minutes. Strain through a fine chinois. Finish with 2 ounces (60 grams) whole butter and garnish with sliced, poached beef marrow.

CHASSEUR (HUNTER'S SAUCE) Sauté 4 ounces (120 grams) sliced mushrooms and ½ ounce (15 grams) diced shallots in whole butter. Add 8 fluid ounces (240 milliliters) white wine and reduce by three-fourths. Then add demi-glace and 6 ounces (180 grams) diced tomatoes; simmer for 5 minutes. Do not strain. Garnish with chopped parsley.

CHÂTEAUBRIAND Combine 16 fluid ounces (480 milliliters) dry white wine and 2 ounces (60 grams) diced shallots. Reduce the mixture by two-thirds. Add demi-glace and reduce by half. Season to taste with lemon juice and cayenne pepper. Do not strain. Swirl in 4 ounces (120 grams) whole butter to finish and garnish with chopped fresh tarragon.

CHEVREUIL Prepare a poivrade sauce but add 6 ounces (180 grams) bacon or game trimmings to the mirepoix. Finish with 4 fluid ounces (120 milliliters) red wine and a dash of cayenne pepper.

MADEIRA OR PORT Bring demi-glace to a boil and reduce slightly. Then add 4 fluid ounces (120 milliliters) Madeira wine or ruby port.

MARCHAND DE VIN Reduce 8 fluid ounces (240 milliliters) dry red wine and 2 ounces (60 grams) diced shallots by two-thirds. Then add demi-glace, simmer and strain.

MUSHROOM Blanch 8 ounces (240 grams) mushroom caps in 8 fluid ounces (240 milliliters) boiling water seasoned with salt and lemon juice. Drain the mushrooms, saving the liquid. Reduce this liquid to 2 tablespoons (30 milliliters) and add it to the demi-glace. Just before service stir in 2 ounces (60 grams) whole butter and the mushroom caps.

PÉRIGUEUX Add finely diced truffles to Madeira sauce. **Périgourdine** sauce is the same as périgueux, except that the truffles are cut into relatively thick slices.

PIQUANT Combine 1 ounce (30 grams) shallots, 4 fluid ounces (120 milliliters) white wine and 4 fluid ounces (120 milliliters) white wine vinegar. Reduce the mixture by two-thirds. Then add demi-glace and simmer for 10 minutes. Add 2 ounces (60 grams) diced cornichons, 1 tablespoon (15 milliliters) fresh tarragon, 1 tablespoon (15 milliliters) fresh parsley and 1 tablespoon (15 milliliters) fresh chervil. Do not strain.

POIVRADE Sweat 12 ounces (360 grams) mirepoix in 2 tablespoons (30 milliliters) oil. Add 1 bay leaf, 1 sprig thyme and 4 parsley stems. Then add 16 fluid ounces (480 milliliters) vinegar and 4 fluid ounces (120 milliliters) white wine. Reduce by half, add demi-glace and simmer for 40 minutes. Then add 20 crushed peppercorns and simmer for 5 more minutes. Strain through a fine chinois and finish with up to 2 ounces (60 grams) whole butter.

ROBERT Sauté 8 ounces (240 grams) chopped onion in 1 ounce (30 grams) whole butter. Add 8 fluid ounces (240 milliliters) dry white wine and reduce by two-thirds. Add demi-glace and simmer for 10 minutes. Strain and then add 2 teaspoons (10 milliliters) prepared Dijon mustard and 1 tablespoon (15 milliliters) granulated sugar. If the finished Robert sauce is garnished with sliced sour pickles, preferably cornichons, it is known as **Charcutière**.

THE TOMATO SAUCE FAMILY

Classic tomato sauce is made from tomatoes, vegetables, seasonings and white stock and thickened with a blond or brown roux. In today's kitchens, however, most tomato sauces

---

POIVRADE POUR GIBIER

Poivrade is also the name given to a flavorful sauce traditionally made with game stock and seasoned with peppercorns. It is used for the wonderful Sauce Grand Veneur, one of the most complex small sauces in the classic repertoire. For Grand Veneur, game stock is flavored with demi-glace and finished with cream and currant jelly. The sweetness balances the strong flavor of the game meats.

are not thickened with roux. Rather, they are created from tomatoes, herbs, spices, vegetables and other flavoring ingredients simmered together and puréed.

A **gastrique** is sometimes added to reduce the acidity of a tomato sauce. To prepare a gastrique, caramelize a small amount of sugar, then thin or deglaze with vinegar. This mixture is then used to finish the tomato sauce.

A properly made tomato sauce is thick, rich and full-flavored. Its texture should be grainier than most other classic sauces, but it should still be smooth. The vegetables and other seasonings should add flavor, but none should be pronounced. Tomato sauce should not be bitter, acidic or overly sweet. It should be deep red and thick enough to cling to foods.

gastrique (gas-streek) caramelized sugar deglazed with vinegar; used to flavor tomato or savory fruit sauces

---

TOMATO SAUCE

Yield: 1 gal. (3.8 lt)

Salt pork, small dice	4 oz.	120 g
Mirepoix	1 lb. 8 oz.	720 g
Tomatoes, fresh or canned	3 qt.	2.8 lt
Tomato purée	2 qt.	1.9 lt
Sachet:		
Dried thyme	1 tsp.	5 ml
Bay leaves	3	3
Garlic cloves	3	3
Parsley stems	10	10
Peppercorns, crushed	½ tsp.	2 ml
Salt	1½ oz.	45 g
Granulated sugar	¾ oz.	20 g
White stock	3 qt.	2.8 lt
Pork bones	2 lb.	960 g

1. **Render** the salt pork over medium heat.
2. Add the mirepoix and sauté, but do not brown.
3. Add the tomatoes, tomato purée, sachet, salt and sugar.
4. Add the stock and bones.
5. Simmer slowly for 1 to 2 hours or until the desired consistency has been reached.
6. Remove the bones and sachet and pass the sauce through a food mill. Cool in a water bath and refrigerate.

Approximate values per 1-fl.-oz. (30-ml) serving: **Calories** 30, **Total fat** 0.5 g, **Saturated fat** 0.2 g, **Cholesterol** 0.7 mg, **Sodium** 240 mg, **Total carbohydrates** 4 g, **Protein** 2 g, **Vitamin A** 6%, **Claims**—low fat; low calorie

Small Tomato Sauces

The following small sauces are made by adding the listed ingredients to 1 quart (1 liter) tomato sauce. The final step for each recipe is to season to taste with salt and pepper.

CREOLE Sauté 6 ounces (180 grams) finely diced onion, 4 ounces (120 grams) thinly sliced celery and 1 teaspoon (5 milliliters) garlic in 1 fluid ounce (30 milliliters) oil. Add tomato sauce, a bay leaf and 1 pinch thyme; simmer for 15 minutes. Then add 4 ounces (120 grams) finely diced green pepper and a dash of hot pepper sauce; simmer for 15 minutes longer. Remove the bay leaf.

SPANISH Prepare creole sauce as directed, adding 4 ounces (120 grams) sliced mushrooms to the sautéed onions. Garnish with sliced black or green olives.

MILANAISE Sauté 5 ounces (150 grams) sliced mushrooms in ½ ounce (15 grams) whole butter. Add tomato sauce and then stir in 5 ounces (150 grams) cooked ham (julienne) and 5 ounces (150 grams) cooked tongue (julienne). Bring to a simmer.

MISE EN PLACE
◄ Rinse and dry salt pork and chop into fine dice.
◄ Peel and chop onions, carrots and celery for mirepoix.
◄ Prepare herb sachet.
◄ Wash pork bones.

render (1) to melt and clarify fat; (2) to cook meat in order to remove the fat

1. Passing the sauce through a food mill.

2. The finished sauce.

Broken hollandaise separates, appearing thin and curdled.

THE HOLLANDAISE FAMILY

Hollandaise and the small sauces derived from it are emulsified sauces. Egg yolks, which contain large amounts of lecithin, a natural emulsifier, are used to emulsify warm butter and a small amount of water, lemon juice or vinegar. When the egg yolks are vigorously whipped with the liquid while the warm butter is slowly added, the lecithin coats the individual fat droplets and holds them in suspension in the liquid.

A properly made hollandaise is smooth, buttery, pale lemon-yellow-colored and very rich. It is lump-free and should not exhibit any signs of separation. The buttery flavor should dominate but not mask the flavors of the egg, lemon and vinegar. The sauce should be frothy and light, not heavy like a mayonnaise.

Temperatures and Sanitation Concerns

Temperatures play an important role in the proper production of a hollandaise sauce. As the egg yolks and liquid are whisked together, they are cooked over a bain marie until they thicken to the consistency of slightly whipped cream. Do not overheat this mixture, because even slightly cooked eggs lose their ability to emulsify. The clarified butter used to make the sauce should be warm but not so hot as to further cook the egg yolks. Although hollandaise sauce can be made from whole butter, a more stable and consistent product will be achieved by using clarified butter. (Clarification is described in Chapter 8, Mise en Place.)

Rescuing a Broken Hollandaise

Occasionally, a hollandaise will break or separate and appear thin, grainy or even lumpy. A sauce breaks when the emulsion has not formed or the emulsified butter, eggs and liquid have separated. This may happen for several reasons: The temperature of the eggs or butter may have been too high or too low; the butter may have been added too quickly; the egg yolks may have been overcooked; too much butter may have been added or the sauce may not have been whipped vigorously enough.

To rescue and re-emulsify broken hollandaise you must first determine whether it is too hot or too cold. If it is too hot, allow the sauce to cool. If it is too cold, reheat the sauce over a double boiler before attempting to rescue it.

For 1 quart (approximately 1 liter) of broken sauce, place 1 tablespoon (15 milliliters) water in a clean stainless steel bowl and slowly beat in the broken sauce. If the problem seems to be that the eggs were overcooked or too much butter was added, add a yolk to the water before incorporating the broken sauce.

HOLLANDAISE

MISE EN PLACE

▶ Crush white peppercorns.
▶ Warm clarified butter.

Yield: 24 fl. oz. (720 ml)

White peppercorns, crushed	½ tsp.	2 ml
White wine vinegar	3 fl. oz.	90 ml
Water	2 fl. oz.	60 ml
Egg yolks, pasteurized	6	6
Lemon juice	1½ fl. oz.	45 ml
Clarified butter, warm	1 pt.	480 ml
Salt and white pepper	TT	TT
Cayenne pepper	TT	TT

1. Combine the peppercorns, vinegar and water in a small saucepan and reduce by one-half.
2. Place the egg yolks in a stainless steel bowl. Strain the vinegar-and-pepper reduction through a chinois into the yolks. There should be ½ fluid ounce (15 milliliters) acidic reduction for each egg yolk used.
3. Place the bowl over a double boiler, whipping the mixture continuously with a wire whip. As the yolks cook, the mixture will thicken. When the mixture is thick enough to leave a trail across the surface when the whip is drawn away, remove the bowl from the double boiler. Do not overcook the egg yolks.
4. Whip in 1 fluid ounce (30 milliliters) lemon juice to stop the yolks from cooking.
5. Begin to add the warm clarified butter to the egg yolk mixture a few drops at a time, while constantly whipping the mixture to form an emulsion. Once the emulsion is started, the butter may be added more quickly. Continue until all the butter is incorporated.
6. Whip in the remaining lemon juice. Adjust the seasonings.
7. Strain the sauce through cheesecloth if necessary and hold for service in a warm (not simmering) bain marie. This sauce may be held for approximately 1 to 1½ hours.

Approximate values per 1-fl.-oz. (30-ml) serving: **Calories** 170, **Total fat** 18 g, **Saturated fat** 11 g, **Cholesterol** 90 mg, **Sodium** 180 mg, **Total carbohydrates** 0 g, **Protein** 1 g, **Vitamin A** 20%

1. Combining the egg yolks with the vinegar and pepper reduction in a stainless steel bowl.

2. Whipping the mixture over a double boiler until it is thick enough to leave a trail when the whip is removed.

3. Using a kitchen towel and saucepot to firmly hold the bowl containing the yolks, add the butter slowly while whipping continuously.

4. Hollandaise at the proper consistency.

Small Hollandaise Sauces

The following small sauces are easily made by adding the listed ingredients to 1 quart (approximately 1 liter) hollandaise. The final step for each recipe is to season to taste with salt and pepper. Béarnaise is presented here as a small sauce although some chefs consider it a leading sauce.

BÉARNAISE (bair-NAYZ) Combine 2 ounces (60 grams) chopped shallots, 5 tablespoons (75 milliliters) chopped fresh tarragon, 3 tablespoons (45 milliliters) chopped fresh chervil and 1 teaspoon (5 milliliters) crushed peppercorns with 8 fluid ounces (240 milliliters) white wine vinegar. Reduce to 2 fluid ounces (60 milliliters). Add this reduction to the egg yolks and proceed with the hollandaise recipe. Strain the finished sauce and season to taste with salt and cayenne pepper. Garnish with additional chopped fresh tarragon.

CHORON Combine 2 ounces (60 grams) tomato paste and 2 fluid ounces (60 milliliters) heavy cream; add the mixture to a béarnaise.

FOYOT Add to béarnaise 3 fluid ounces (90 milliliters) melted glace de viande.

GRIMROD Infuse a hollandaise sauce with saffron.

glaçage (glah-sahge) browning or glazing a food, usually under a salamander or broiler

beurre fondu (burr fon-DOO) French for "melted butter"; it is often served over steamed vegetables such as asparagus or poached white fish

beurre noir (burr NWAR) French for "black butter"; used to describe whole butter cooked until dark brown (not black); sometimes flavored with vinegar or lemon juice, capers and parsley and served over fish, eggs and vegetables

beurre noisette (burr nwah-ZEHT) French for "brown butter"; used to describe butter cooked until it is a light brown color; it is flavored and used in much the same manner as beurre noir

MALTAISE Add to hollandaise 2 fluid ounces (60 milliliters) orange juice and 2 teaspoons (10 milliliters) finely grated orange zest. Blood oranges are traditionally used for this sauce.

MOUSSELINE (CHANTILLY SAUCE) Whip 8 fluid ounces (240 milliliters) heavy cream until stiff. Fold it into the hollandaise just before service. Mousseline sauce is also used as a **glaçage** coating.

Beurre Blanc and Beurre Rouge

Beurre blanc (burr blahnk) and beurre rouge (burr rooge) are emulsified butter sauces made without egg yolks. The small amounts of lecithin and other emulsifiers naturally found in butter are used to form an oil-in-water emulsion. Although similar to hollandaise in concept, they are not considered either classic leading or compound sauces. Beurre blancs are thinner and lighter than hollandaise and béarnaise. They should be smooth and slightly thicker than heavy cream.

Beurre blanc and beurre rouge are made from three main ingredients: shallots, white (Fr. *blanc*) wine or red (Fr. *rouge*) wine and whole butter (not clarified). The shallots and wine provide flavor, while the butter becomes the sauce. A good beurre blanc or beurre rouge is rich and buttery, with a neutral flavor that responds well to other seasonings and flavorings, thereby lending itself to the addition of herbs, spices and vegetable purées to complement the dish with which it is served. Its pale color changes depending on the flavorings added. It should be light and airy yet still liquid, while thick enough to cling to food.

PROCEDURE FOR **PREPARING BEURRE BLANC OR BEURRE ROUGE**

au sec (oh sek) cooked until nearly dry

1. Use a nonaluminum pan to prevent discoloring the sauce. Do not use a thin-walled or nonstick pan, as heat is not evenly distributed in a thin-walled pan and a nonstick pan makes it difficult for an emulsion to set.
2. Over medium heat, reduce the wine, shallots and herbs or other seasonings, if used, until **au sec** (that is, nearly dry). Some chefs add a small amount of heavy cream at this point and reduce the mixture. Although not necessary, the added cream helps stabilize the finished sauce.
3. Whisk in cold butter a small amount at a time. The butter should be well chilled, as this allows the butterfat, water and milk solids to be gradually incorporated into the sauce as the butter melts and the mixture is whisked.
4. When all the butter is incorporated, strain the sauce and hold in a bain marie.

TEMPERATURE

Do not let the sauce become too hot. At 136°F (58°C) some of the emulsifying proteins begin to break down and release the butterfat they hold in emulsion. Extended periods at temperatures over 136°F (58°C) will cause the sauce to separate. If the sauce separates, it can be corrected by cooling to approximately 110°F–120°F (43°C–49°C) and whisking to reincorporate the butterfat.

If the sauce is allowed to cool below 85°F (30°C), the butterfat will solidify. If the sauce is reheated it will separate into butterfat and water; whisking will not re-emulsify it. Cold beurre blanc can be used as a soft, flavored butter, however, simply by whisking it at room temperature until it smooths out to the consistency of mayonnaise.

BEURRE BLANC

Yield: 1 qt. (960 ml)

White wine vinegar	1 fl. oz.	30 ml
White wine	4 fl. oz.	120 ml
Salt	1½ tsp.	7 ml
White pepper	½ tsp.	2 ml
Shallot, minced	1 oz.	30 g
Whole butter, chilled	2 lb.	960 g

1 Combine the white wine, white wine vinegar, salt, white pepper and shallot in a small saucepan. Reduce the mixture until approximately 2 tablespoons (30 milliliters) of liquid remain. If more than 2 tablespoons of liquid are allowed to remain, the resulting sauce will be too thin. For a thicker sauce, reduce the mixture au sec.

2 Cut the butter into pieces approximately 1 ounce (30 grams) in weight. Over low heat, whisk in the butter a few pieces at a time, using the chilled butter to keep the sauce between 100°F and 120°F (38°C and 49°C).

3 Once all the butter has been incorporated, remove the saucepan from the heat. Strain through a chinois and hold the sauce at a temperature between 100°F and 130°F (38°C and 54°C) for service.

VARIATIONS:

Beurre Rouge—Substitute a dry red wine for the white wine and red wine vinegar for the white wine vinegar.

Lemon-Dill—Heat 2 tablespoons (30 milliliters) lemon juice and whisk it into the beurre blanc. Stir in 4 tablespoons (60 milliliters) chopped fresh dill.

Pink Peppercorn—Add 2 tablespoons (30 milliliters) coarsely crushed pink peppercorns to the shallot-wine reduction when making beurre rouge. Garnish the finished sauce with whole pink peppercorns.

Approximate values per 1-fl.-oz. (30-ml) serving: **Calories** 210, **Total fat** 23 g, **Saturated fat** 14 g, **Cholesterol** 60 mg, **Sodium** 340 mg, **Total carbohydrates** 0 g, **Protein** 0 g, **Vitamin A** 20%

Compound Butters

A compound butter is made by incorporating various seasonings into softened whole butter. These butters, also known as *beurres composés*, give flavor and color to small sauces or may be served as sauces in their own right. For example, a slice of maître d'hôtel butter (parsley butter) is often placed on a grilled steak or piece of fish at the time of service. The butter quickly melts, creating a sauce for the beef or fish.

Butter and flavoring ingredients can be combined with a blender, food processor or mixer. Using parchment paper or plastic wrap, the butter is then rolled into a cylinder, chilled and sliced as needed. Or it can be piped into rosettes and refrigerated until firm. Most compound butters will keep for 2 to 3 days in the refrigerator, or they can be frozen for longer storage.

RECIPES FOR COMPOUND BUTTERS

For each of the following butters, add the listed ingredients to 1 pound (480 grams) of softened, unsalted butter. The compound butter should then be seasoned with salt and pepper to taste.

BASIL BUTTER Mince 2 ounces (60 grams) fresh basil and 2 ounces (60 grams) shallots; add to the butter with 2 teaspoons (10 milliliters) lemon juice.

HERB BUTTER Add to the butter up to 1 cup (240 milliliters) mixed chopped fresh herbs such as parsley, dill, chives, tarragon or chervil.

MISE EN PLACE

◀ Peel and mince shallot.

1 Reducing the shallots and wine au sec.

2 Whisking in the cold butter a little at a time.

3 Straining the sauce.

PROCEDURE FOR **PREPARING COMPOUND BUTTER**

1 Placing the butter on the plastic wrap.

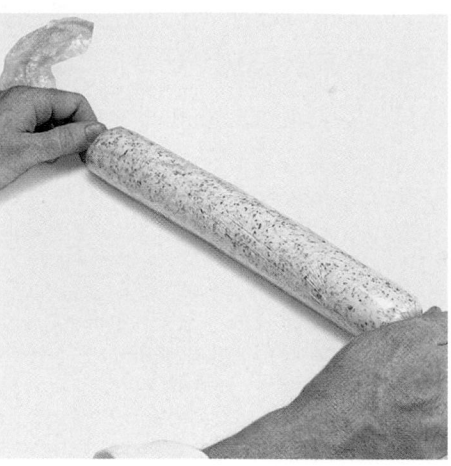

2 Rolling the butter in the plastic wrap to form a cylinder.

LOBSTER OR CRAYFISH BUTTER Grind 8 ounces (240 grams) cooked lobster or crayfish meat, shells and/or coral with 1 pound (480 grams) butter. Place in a saucepan and clarify. Strain the butter through a fine chinois lined with cheesecloth. Refrigerate, then remove the butterfat when firm.

MAÎTRE D'HÔTEL BUTTER Mix into the butter 4 tablespoons (60 milliliters) finely chopped fresh parsley, 3 tablespoons (45 milliliters) lemon juice and a dash of white pepper.

MONTPELIER BUTTER Blanch 1 ounce (30 grams) fresh parsley, 1 ounce (30 grams) fresh chervil, 1 ounce (30 grams) watercress and 1 ounce (30 grams) fresh tarragon in boiling water. Drain thoroughly. Mince 2 hard-boiled egg yolks, 2 garlic cloves and 2 sour gherkin pickles. Blend everything into the butter.

RED PEPPER BUTTER Purée 8 ounces (240 grams) roasted, peeled red bell peppers until liquid, then add to the butter.

SHALLOT BUTTER Blanch 8 ounces (240 grams) peeled shallots in boiling water. Dry and finely dice them and mix with the butter.

Pan Gravy

Pan gravy is aptly named: It is made directly in the pan used to roast the poultry, beef, lamb or pork that the gravy will accompany. Pan gravy is actually a sauce; it is a liquid thickened with a roux. Pan gravy gains additional flavors from the drippings left in the roasting pan and by using a portion of the fat rendered during the roasting process to make the roux. This technique is used in the recipe for Roast Turkey with Chestnut Dressing and Giblet Gravy (page 410).

A properly made pan gravy should have all the characteristics of any brown sauce except that it has a meatier flavor as a result of the pan drippings.

gravy a sauce made from meat or poultry juices combined with a liquid and thickening agent; usually made in the pan in which the meat or poultry was cooked

PROCEDURE FOR **PREPARING PAN GRAVY**

1 Remove the cooked meat or poultry from the roasting pan.

2 If mirepoix was not added during the roasting process, add it to the pan containing the drippings and fat.

3 Place the roasting pan on the stove top and clarify the fat by cooking off any remaining moisture.

4 Pour off the fat, reserving it to make the roux.

5. Deglaze the pan using an appropriate stock. The deglazing liquid may be transferred to a saucepan for easier handling, or the gravy may be finished directly in the roasting pan.

6. Add enough stock or water to the deglazing liquid to yield the proper amount of finished gravy.

7. Determine the amount of roux needed to thicken the liquid and prepare it in a separate pan, using a portion of the reserved fat.

8. Add the roux to the liquid and bring the mixture to a simmer. Simmer until the mirepoix is well cooked, the flavor is extracted and the flour taste is cooked out.

9. Strain the gravy and adjust the seasonings.

1. Deglazing the roasting pan.

2. Thickening the gravy with a roux.

3. Straining the gravy.

Pan Sauces

Sauces served with sautéed meats, poultry or fish are often made directly in the sauté pan in which the dish was cooked. Once the food is sautéed, it is removed from the pan and kept warm while the sauce is prepared. Stock, jus lié or other liquid is added to deglaze the pan. Like pan gravy, these pan sauces gain flavor from the drippings left in the pan. Unlike pan gravy, pan sauces are usually thickened by reduction, not with a starch. Pan sauces are discussed in Chapter 12, Principles of Meat Cookery.

Coulis

The term *coulis* most often refers to a sauce made from a purée of vegetables and/or fruit that is strained before serving. A vegetable coulis can be served as either a hot or a cold accompaniment to other vegetables, starches, meat, poultry, fish or shellfish. It is often made from a single vegetable base (popular examples include broccoli, tomatoes and sweet red peppers) cooked with flavoring ingredients such as onions, garlic, shallots, herbs and spices and then puréed. An appropriate liquid (stock, water or cream) may be added to thin the purée if necessary. Vegetable coulis are often prepared with very little fat and served as a healthy alternative to a heavier, classic sauce.

A fruit coulis, often made from fresh or frozen berries, is generally used as a dessert sauce. It is usually as simple as puréed fruit thinned to the desired consistency with sugar syrup.

Typically, both vegetable and fruit coulis have a texture similar to that of a thin tomato sauce. But their textures can range from slightly grainy to almost lumpy, depending on their intended use. The flavor and color of a coulis should be that of the main ingredient. The flavors of herbs, spices and other flavoring ingredients should only complement and not dominate the coulis.

coulis (koo-lee) a sauce made from a purée of vegetables and/or fruit; may be served hot or cold

PROCEDURE FOR **PREPARING A COULIS**

Here we include a procedure for making a vegetable coulis. Procedures for making fruit coulis are included as recipes in Chapter 34, Custards, Creams, Frozen Desserts and Dessert Sauces.

❶ Cook the main ingredient and any additional flavoring ingredients with an appropriate liquid.

❷ Purée the main ingredient and flavoring ingredients in a food mill, blender or food processor.

❸ Combine the purée with the appropriate liquid and simmer to blend the flavors.

❹ Strain, then thin and season the coulis as desired.

RED PEPPER COULIS

MISE EN PLACE

▶ Peel and chop garlic.
▶ Peel the onion and chop into small dice.
▶ Wash red peppers and chop into medium dice.

Yield: 1 qt. (960 ml)

Vegetable oil	1 fl. oz.	30 ml
Garlic, chopped	2 tsp.	10 ml
Onion, small dice	3 oz.	90 g
Red bell peppers, medium dice	3 lb.	1.4 kg
White wine	8 fl. oz.	240 ml
Chicken stock	1 pt.	480 ml
Salt and pepper	TT	TT

❶ Heat the oil and sweat the garlic and onion until translucent, without browning.

❷ Add the bell peppers and sweat until tender.

❸ Deglaze the pan with the wine.

❹ Add the stock, bring to a simmer and cook for 15 minutes. Season with salt and pepper.

❺ Purée in a blender or food processor and strain through a china cap.

❻ Adjust the consistency and seasonings and hold for service.

Approximate values per 1-fl.-oz. (30-ml) serving: **Calories** 20, **Total fat** 1 g, **Saturated fat** 0 g, **Cholesterol** 0 mg, **Sodium** 45 mg, **Total carbohydrates** 2 g, **Protein** 1 g, **Vitamin C** 50%, **Claims**—low fat; low sodium; low calorie

❶ Sweating the red peppers.

❷ Puréeing the cooked peppers.

❸ Straining the coulis.

Contemporary Sauces

Modern chefs and menu writers are relying less on traditional sauces and more on salsas, relishes, juices, broths, essences and infused oils in their work. Unlike classic sauces, these modern accompaniments do not rely on meat-based stocks and starch thickeners, but rather on fresh vegetables, vegetable juices, aromatic broths and intensely flavored oils. The names for these sauces are not codified, as are those in the classic sauce repertoire. Chefs apply various terms freely, using whatever name best fits the dish and the overall menu. Most of these contemporary sauces can be prepared more quickly than their classic counterparts, and the use of fresh fruits and vegetables enhances the healthfulness of the dish. These so-called contemporary or modern sauces may have a lighter body and less fat than classic sauces, but they are still derived from classical culinary techniques and principles. The sauces should be appropriate in flavor, texture and appearance and should complement, not overwhelm, the food they accompany.

SALSA AND RELISH

Many people think of salsa (Spanish for "sauce") as a chunky mixture of raw vegetables and chiles eaten with chips or ladled over Mexican food; they think of relish as a sweet green condiment spooned onto a hot dog. But salsas and relishes—generally, cold chunky mixtures of herbs, spices, fruits and/or vegetables—can be used as sauces for many meat, poultry, fish and shellfish items. They can include ingredients such as oranges, pineapple, papaya, black beans, jicama, tomatillos and an array of other vegetables.

Although not members of any classic sauce family, salsas, **chutnies,** and relishes are currently enjoying great popularity because of their intense fresh flavors, ease of preparation and low fat and calorie content. Salsas and relishes are often a riot of colors, textures and flavors, simultaneously cool and hot, spicy and sweet.

chutney a sweet-and-sour condiment made of fruits and/or vegetables cooked in vinegar with sugar and spices; some chutneys are reduced to a purée, whereas others retain recognizable pieces of their ingredients

PROCEDURE FOR **PREPARING A SALSA OR RELISH**

1. Cut or chop the ingredients.
2. Precook and chill items as directed in the recipe.
3. Toss all ingredients together and refrigerate, allowing the flavors to combine for at least 30 minutes before service.

PICO DE GALLO (TOMATO SALSA)

Yield: 1 qt. (960 ml)

Tomatoes, seeded, small dice	5	5
Green onions, sliced	1 bunch	1 bunch
Garlic cloves, minced	3	3
Fresh cilantro, chopped	½ bunch	½ bunch
Jalapeños, chopped fine	3	3
Lemon juice	2 fl. oz.	60 ml
Cumin, ground	½ tsp.	2 ml
Salt and pepper	TT	TT

1. Combine all ingredients and gently toss. Adjust seasonings and refrigerate.

Approximate values per 1-fl.-oz. (30-ml) serving: **Calories** 5, **Total fat** 0 g, **Saturated fat** 0 g, **Cholesterol** 0 mg, **Sodium** 30 mg, **Total carbohydrates** 1 g, **Protein** 0 g, **Claims**—fat free; very low sodium; low calorie

MISE EN PLACE

◄ Wash and peel vegetables, if necessary.
◄ Chop tomatoes into small dice.
◄ Slice green onions.
◄ Mince garlic cloves.
◄ Chop cilantro leaves.
◄ Remove seeds from jalapeños and finely chop.

VEGETABLE JUICE SAUCES

Juice extractors make it possible to prepare juice from fresh, uncooked vegetables such as carrots, beets and spinach. Thinner and smoother than a purée, vegetable juice can be heated, reduced, flavored and enriched with butter to create colorful, intensely flavored

essence a sauce made from a concentrated vegetable juice

sauces. Cream or stock can be added to finish the sauce. Sauces made from vegetable juices are sometimes referred to as an **essence** or **tea** on menus.

Juice from a single type of vegetable provides the purest, most pronounced flavor, but two or more vegetables sometimes can be combined successfully. Be careful of mixing too many flavors and colors in the juice, however. Juiced vegetable sauces are particularly appropriate with pasta, fish, shellfish and poultry, and they can be useful in vegetarian cuisine or as a healthier alternative to classic sauces.

PROCEDURE FOR **PREPARING A VEGETABLE JUICE SAUCE**

1. Wash and peel vegetables as needed.
2. Process the vegetables through a juice extractor.
3. Place the juice in a saucepan and add stock, lemon juice, herbs or other flavorings as desired.
4. Bring the sauce to a simmer and reduce as necessary.
5. Strain the sauce through a fine chinois.
6. Adjust the seasonings and whisk in whole butter to finish.

MISE EN PLACE

▶ Wash celery and put through juice extractor.
▶ Wash tomatoes and put through juice extractor.
▶ Chop fresh thyme.

Juicing the celery.

THYME-SCENTED CELERY ESSENCE

STOUFFER STANFORD COURT HOTEL, SAN FRANCISCO, CA
Former Executive Chef Ercolino Crugnale

Yield: 1 qt. (960 ml)

Celery juice	1 qt.	960 ml
Tomato juice	1 pt.	480 ml
Fresh thyme, chopped	½ oz.	15 g
Whole butter	6 oz.	180 g
Salt	TT	TT
Tabasco sauce	TT	TT

1. Combine the celery juice, tomato juice and thyme. Bring to a simmer and reduce to 24 fluid ounces (720 milliliters).
2. Whisk in the butter and adjust the seasonings with salt and Tabasco sauce.
3. Strain through a chinois.

Approximate values per 1-fl.-oz. (30-ml) serving: **Calories** 50, **Total fat** 4.5 g, **Saturated fat** 2.4 g, **Cholesterol** 10 mg, **Sodium** 200 mg, **Total carbohydrates** 2 g, **Protein** 0 g

BROTH

Broth, which also appears on menus as a **tea**, **au jus**, **essence** or **nage**, is a thin, flavorful liquid served in a pool beneath the main food. The broth should not be so abundant as to turn an entrée into a soup, but it should provide moisture and flavor. The essence, broth or nage is often made by simply reducing and straining the liquid in which the main food was cooked. Alternatively, a specifically flavored stock—tomato, for example—can be prepared, then clarified like consommé to create a broth or essence to accompany an appetizer or entrée.

FLAVORED OIL

Small amounts of intensely flavored oils can be used to dress or garnish a variety of dishes. Salads, soups, vegetable and starch dishes and entrées can be enhanced with a drizzle of colorful, appropriately flavored oil. Because such small quantities are used, these oils provide flavor and moisture without adding too many calories or fat.

Unless the flavoring ingredient goes especially well with olive oil (for example, basil), select a high-quality but neutral oil such as peanut, safflower or canola. Although flavoring ingredients can be simply steeped in oil for a time, a better way to flavor oil

SAFETY ALERT
Handling Flavored Oils

Flavored oils must be stored under refrigeration. Raw garlic, fresh herbs or other fresh ingredients can become potentially hazardous foods or time/temperature controlled for safety foods (PHF/TCS foods) when added to oil. Serve them within 2 days of preparation.

is to crush, purée or cook the flavoring ingredients first. Warming the oil before infusing it with dry herbs or spices is recommended, as is **decanting** the oil to remove solids before using.

Modern chefs are also using vinaigrettes, a combination of oil and vinegar, citrus or other acidic liquid, as quick light sauces. Vinaigrettes give the illusion of lightness that many health-conscious customers are demanding, although the oil in such sauces can raise the fat and calorie content substantially. Vinaigrettes are discussed in Chapter 24, Salads and Salad Dressings.

decant to separate liquid from solids without disturbing the sediment by pouring off the liquid; vintage wines are often decanted to remove sediment

vinaigrette a temporary emulsion of oil and vinegar seasoned with salt and pepper

PROCEDURE FOR **PREPARING A FLAVORED OIL**

1. Purée or chop fresh herbs, fruits or vegetables. Sweat dry spices or seeds in a small amount of oil to form a paste.
2. Place the selected oil and the flavoring ingredients in a jar or other tightly lidded container.
3. Allow the mixture to stand at room temperature until sufficient flavor is extracted. This may take from 1 to 24 hours. Shake the jar periodically. Do not allow the flavoring ingredients to remain in the oil indefinitely, as the flavor may become harsh or bitter.
4. Strain the oil through a chinois lined with a coffee filter.
5. Store the flavored oil in a covered container in the refrigerator.

SHALLOT CURRY OIL

Yield: 8 fl. oz. (240 ml)

Canola oil	8 fl. oz.	240 ml
Shallot, minced	1	1
Curry powder	4 Tbsp.	60 ml
Water	2 fl. oz.	60 ml

1. In a small saucepan, heat 1 tablespoon (15 milliliters) oil over medium heat. Add the shallot and sauté until softened and translucent. Do not allow the shallot to brown.
2. Add the curry powder and sauté for 1 to 2 minutes.
3. Stir in the water and bring the mixture to a boil. Reduce the heat and simmer until most of the water evaporates, leaving a paste of curry and shallots.
4. Remove from the heat and stir in the remaining oil.
5. Place the mixture in a lidded jar and set aside at room temperature for 6 to 8 hours. Shake the jar occasionally.
6. Strain the oil through a chinois lined with a coffee filter. Place the flavored oil in a covered container and refrigerate until ready to use.

Approximate values per 1-fl.-oz. (30-ml) serving: **Calories** 208, **Total fat** 23 g, **Saturated fat** 2 g, **Cholesterol** 0 mg, **Sodium** 1 mg, **Total carbohydrates** 1 g, **Protein** 0 g, **Claims**—no cholesterol; no sodium

MISE EN PLACE
◀ Peel and mince shallot.

Sauces are used in many recipes in this book and in the professional kitchen. Table 10.5 lists some of the sauces discussed in this chapter and describes common ways to use them. Table 10.6 is a troubleshooting chart to be used when problems arise.

TABLE 10.5 USING SAUCES

SAUCE	QUALITIES	SMALL SAUCE OR FLAVORINGS	USE
Béchamel	Smooth, rich and creamy; no graininess; cream-colored with rich sheen	Cream Cheese Mornay Nantua Soubise	Vegetables, pasta, eggs, fish, shellfish Vegetables, pasta Fish, shellfish, poultry, vegetables Fish, shellfish Veal, pork, eggs

Velouté	Smooth and rich; ivory-colored; good flavor of the stock used; not pasty or heavy	Fish Velouté
		  Bercy
		  Cardinal
		  Normandy
		Allemande (veal or chicken)
		  Aurora
		  Horseradish
		  Mushroom
		  Poulette
		Suprême (chicken)
		  Albufera
		  Hungarian
		  Ivory
			
			Poached fish
			Lobster, white fish, crab, eggs
			Delicate white fish, oysters
			
			Eggs, chicken, sweetbreads
			Roast beef, corned beef, baked ham
			Sautéed poultry, white meats
			Vegetables, sweetbreads
			
			Braised poultry, sweetbreads
			Eggs, chicken, chops, sweetbreads
			Eggs, braised poultry

Espagnole	Smooth and rich; dark brown color; good meat flavor	Bordelaise Chasseur Châteaubriand Chevreuil Madeira/Port Marchand de vin Mushroom Périgueux/Périgourdine Piquant Poivrade Robert	Sautéed or grilled meats Sautéed or grilled meats and poultry Broiled meats Roasted meats and game Grilled or roasted meats and game, ham Grilled or roasted meats Sautéed or grilled meats and poultry Sautéed poultry, grilled meats and game, sweetbreads Pork Grilled or roasted meats, game Pork
Tomato	Thick and rich; slightly grainy; full-flavored	Tomato Creole Spanish Milanaise	Meats, poultry, vegetables, pasta and for making small sauces Fish, eggs, chicken Eggs, fish Pasta, grilled or sautéed poultry and white meats

Hollandaise	Smooth and rich; buttery flavor; light and slightly frothy; pale yellow color; no signs of separating	Béarnaise
		  Choron
		  Foyot
		Grimrod
		Maltaise
		Mousseline
			Grilled or sautéed meats and fish
			Grilled meats and fish
			Grilled meats and fish
			Eggs, poached fish
			Poached fish
			Poached fish, eggs, vegetables

Beurre blanc and beurre rouge	Rich and buttery; thinner than hollandaise; light and airy; pale-colored	Wide variety of seasonings and flavorings may be used	Steamed, grilled or poached fish, chicken or vegetables
Compound butter	Flavor ingredients should be evenly distributed	Wide variety of seasonings and flavorings may be used	Grilled meats, poultry and fish; finishing sauces
Pan gravy (jus lié)	Smooth; deep rich color; meaty flavor	Made from pan drippings	Roasted meats and poultry
Coulis	Rich color; moderately thin, grainy texture; strongly flavored	Made with a wide variety of vegetables or fruits	Vegetables, grilled or poached meats, poultry and fish
Salsa and relish	Chunky; bright colors; not watery	Made with a wide variety of vegetables, fruits and seasonings	Meats, fish, vegetables and poultry; used as a sauce or condiment
Flavored oil	Smooth; bright colors; intense flavors	Made with a variety of herbs, spices and seasonings	Used as a garnish

TABLE 10.6   TROUBLESHOOTING CHART FOR SAUCES

PROBLEM	REASON	SOLUTION
Lumpy	Roux undercooked	Increase cooking time of roux
	Stock cold when roux added	Heat stock before adding roux; strain through chinois to remove lumps
	Cornstarch not properly dissolved	Strain, make cornstarch slurry and cook until thickened, stirring constantly
Pasty or floury taste	Sauce undercooked after starch was added	Increase cooking time
Grainy texture	Starch or flour not properly gelatinized	Increase cooking time
	Eggs overheated in liaison	Discard sauce
Thick consistency	Too much thickener	Decrease thickener; add additional liquid
	Sauce reduced too much	Decrease cooking time; add additional liquid
Thin consistency	Not enough thickener	Add more roux or cornstarch slurry
	Starch-thickened sauce overheated	Do not reheat sauces thickened with cornstarch
	Insufficiently reduced	Continue cooking until sauce thickens
Separates, breaks	Temporary emulsion failed	Whisk sauce again (vinaigrette); cool to 110°F–120°F (43°C–49°C), then whisk again to reincorporate fat (beurre blanc); reheat sauce over double boiler, then beat into water (hollandaise)
	Eggs overcooked	Beat an egg yolk and water together, then beat into sauce (hollandaise); discard sauce if liaison was used and overheated
Gray color or metallic taste	Aluminum pan used	Discard (cream sauce); use nonreactive pan to make cream sauce

❶ Why are the bones of younger animals preferred for making stocks?

❷ Why should a stock made from beef or veal bones cook longer than a stock made from fish bones? What is the result if a stock does not cook long enough?

❸ What can cause a stock to become cloudy? How can you prevent this from happening?

❹ List three differences in the production of a white stock and a brown stock.

❺ List the five classic mother sauces and explain how they are used to prepare small sauces.

❻ Why is demi-glace preferred when making brown sauces? Is jus lié different from classic demi-glace? Can they be used interchangeably?

❼ Why are temperatures important when making hollandaise sauce? What precautions must be taken when holding hollandaise for service?

❽ Compare a beurre blanc and a hollandaise sauce. How are they similar? How are they different?

❾ How are compound butters used in making sauces? What are the ingredients for a traditional maître d'hôtel butter?

❿ What are the differences between a salsa, a chutney and a relish? Can these items be used in place of classic sauces? Explain your answer.

⓫ What are the differences between a vegetable juice sauce and a broth?

⓬ Chefs and restaurateurs are constantly experimenting with new ingredients and new techniques. Use the Internet to research the variety of stocks and sauces chefs are using in various regions of the country. Discuss and compare the preparation techniques required for these variations. **WWW**

QUESTIONS FOR DISCUSSION

Terms to Know

fumet
court bouillon
standard
    mirepoix
white mirepoix
skim
blanching bones
à la nage
glace de viande
leading, grand or
    mother sauces
emulsifying agent

permanent,
    semipermanent
    or temporary
    emulsion
dispersed phase
continuous phase
monter au beurre
small or
    compound
    sauces
pan gravy

MARCHAND DE VIN (RED WINE SAUCE)

BRENNAN'S RESTAURANT, NEW ORLEANS, LA

Chef Michael Roussel (1938–2005)

Yield: 24 fl. oz. (720 ml)   **Method:** Roux-thickened

Unsalted butter	3 oz.	90 g
Onion, chopped fine	2 oz.	60 g
Garlic, chopped fine	1½ tsp.	7 ml
Green onion, chopped fine	2 oz.	60 g
Boiled ham, chopped fine	2 oz.	60 g
Mushroom, chopped fine	2 oz.	60 g
All-purpose flour	1½ oz.	45 g
Worcestershire sauce	2 Tbsp.	30 ml
Beef stock	1 pt.	480 ml
Red wine	4 fl. oz.	120 ml
Dried thyme	1½ tsp.	7 ml
Bay leaf	1	1
Fresh parsley, chopped fine	1½ oz.	45 g
Salt and pepper	TT	TT

1. Melt the butter in a large saucepan and sauté the onion, garlic, green onion and ham for 5 minutes.
2. Add the mushroom, reduce the heat to medium and cook for 2 minutes.
3. Blend in the flour and cook, stirring, for 4 minutes. Then add the Worcestershire sauce, stock, wine, thyme and bay leaf. Simmer until the sauce thickens, approximately 1 hour.
4. At service, remove the bay leaf and add the parsley. Season to taste with salt and pepper.
5. For a smoother texture, pass the sauce through a fine-mesh strainer before adding the parsley.

Approximate values per 1½-oz. (45-ml) serving: **Calories** 45, **Total fat** 3 g, **Saturated fat** 2 g, **Cholesterol** 10 mg, **Sodium** 100 mg, **Total carbohydrates** 3 g, **Protein** 1 g, **Vitamin A** 15%

ROASTED GARLIC SAUCE

SIMPLICITY CATERING, FALLS CHURCH, VA

Chef Leland Atkinson

Yield: 12 fl. oz. (360 ml)

Shallot, minced	4 Tbsp.	60 ml
Clarified butter	1 Tbsp.	15 ml
Madeira wine	4 fl. oz.	120 ml
Fresh thyme	1 sprig	1 sprig
Bay leaf	1	1
Garlic head, trimmed and roasted	1	1
Demi-glace	1 pt.	480 ml
Roux	as needed	as needed
Salt and pepper	TT	TT

1. Sauté the shallot lightly in the clarified butter until slightly caramelized.
2. Add the wine, thyme and bay leaf and reduce by one-third.
3. Squeeze in the garlic, discarding the skins and root.
4. Add the demi-glace and reduce by one-third.
5. Thicken slightly with roux if desired, adjust the seasonings and force through a fine strainer.

Approximate values per 1-fl.-oz. (30-ml) serving: **Calories** 15, **Total fat** 1 g, **Saturated fat** 0.5 g, **Cholesterol** 5 mg, **Sodium** 240 mg, **Total carbohydrates** 0 g, **Protein** 0 g

HORSERADISH CREAM SAUCE

BRENNAN'S RESTAURANT, NEW ORLEANS, LA
Chef Michael Roussel (1938–2005)

Yield: 24 fl. oz. (720 ml)

Heavy cream	1 qt.	960 ml
Salt	½ tsp.	2 ml
White pepper	½ tsp.	2 ml
Whole butter	½ tsp.	2 ml
All-purpose flour	4 Tbsp.	60 ml
Horseradish, grated	4 Tbsp.	60 ml

1. Combine the cream, salt and white pepper in a saucepan. Heat over medium heat. Do not allow the cream to boil.
2. Rub the butter and flour together to form small balls (beurre manié).
3. Add the beurre manié to the simmering cream. Cook until the sauce is smooth, then add the horseradish. Serve warm.

Approximate values per 1-fl.-oz. (30-ml) serving: **Calories** 140, **Total fat** 15 g, **Saturated fat** 9 g, **Cholesterol** 55 mg, **Sodium** 65 mg, **Total carbohydrates** 2 g, **Protein** 1 g, **Vitamin A** 10%

DUXELLES SAUCE

Yield: 1½ pt. (720 ml)

Mushrooms, chopped fine	8 oz.	240 g
Shallot, chopped fine	3 oz.	90 g
Clarified butter	1 fl. oz.	30 ml
Olive oil	1 fl. oz.	30 ml
Dry white wine	12 fl. oz.	360 ml
Demi-glace	1 pt.	480 ml
Heavy cream	2 fl. oz.	60 ml
Salt and pepper	TT	TT
Fresh parsley, chopped fine	1 Tbsp.	15 ml

1. Sauté the mushrooms and shallot in the butter and oil. The mushrooms will release their liquid and darken. Cook until completely dry.
2. Deglaze with the wine and reduce by two-thirds.
3. Add the demi-glace. Bring to a boil, then simmer for 5 minutes.
4. Stir in the cream. Adjust the seasonings. Garnish with parsley.

Approximate values per 1-fl.-oz. (30-ml) serving: **Calories** 100, **Total fat** 10 g, **Saturated fat** 6 g, **Cholesterol** 30 mg, **Sodium** 40 g, **Total carbohydrates** 2 g, **Protein** 1 g, **Vitamin A** 15%

duxelles a coarse paste made of finely chopped mushrooms sautéed with shallots in butter; used in sauces and stuffing

FRESH TOMATO SAUCE FOR PASTA

Yield: 2½ qt. (2.4 lt)

Onion, small dice	8 oz.	240 g
Carrot, small dice	4 oz.	120 g
Garlic, minced	1 Tbsp.	15 ml
Olive oil	2 fl. oz.	60 ml
Tomato concassée	7 lb.	3.3 kg
Fresh oregano	1 Tbsp.	15 ml
Fresh thyme	2 tsp.	10 ml
Salt	1 tsp.	5 ml
Pepper	½ tsp.	2 ml
Fresh basil, chopped	½ oz.	15 g

1. Sweat the onion, carrot and garlic in the oil until tender.
2. Add the tomato concassée, oregano and thyme. Simmer for approximately 1 hour or until the desired consistency is reached.
3. Pass the sauce through a food mill if a smooth consistency is desired. Do not purée if a chunkier sauce is desired.
4. Adjust the seasonings and add the basil.

Approximate values per 1-fl.-oz. (30-ml) serving: **Calories** 20, **Total fat** 1 g, **Saturated fat** 0 g, **Cholesterol** 0 mg, **Sodium** 35 mg, **Total carbohydrates** 2 g, **Protein** 0 g, **Vitamin C** 15%, **Claims**—low fat; low sodium; low calorie

BOLOGNESE SAUCE

Bolognese sauce is named for the city of Bologna in Italy's culinary heartland. The mirepoix that gives this sauce its characteristic flavor is called soffrito *in Italian. The length of cooking time and the degree to which the mirepoix is cooked alters the taste and texture of the finished sauce. Serve this sauce over spaghetti or any wide noodle.*

Yield: 1 qt. (960 ml)

Mirepoix, fine dice	8 oz.	240 g
Olive oil	2 fl. oz.	60 ml
Whole butter	1 oz.	30 g
Ground beef	1 lb.	480 g
White wine	8 fl. oz.	240 ml
Milk	6 fl. oz.	180 ml
Nutmeg	TT	TT
Tomato concassée	2 lb.	1 kg
White stock	approx. 8 fl. oz.	approx. 240 ml
Salt and pepper	TT	TT

1. Sauté the mirepoix in the oil and butter until tender. Add the beef and cook until no pink remains. Drain fat if necessary.
2. Add the wine. Cook and reduce the wine until nearly dry.
3. Add the milk and season with nutmeg. Cook and reduce the milk until nearly dry.
4. Add the tomato concassée and 8 fluid ounces (240 milliliters) stock; season with salt and pepper. Simmer for 1½ to 2 hours, adding stock only if needed to prevent scorching. Adjust the seasonings.

Approximate values per 2-fl.-oz. (60-ml) serving: **Calories** 100, **Total fat** 8 g, **Saturated fat** 3 g, **Cholesterol** 20 mg, **Sodium** 230 mg, **Total carbohydrates** 4 g, **Protein** 4 g, **Vitamin C** 20%

MOLE

Mole or "mixture" in Spanish is a harmonious blend of fresh and dried chiles, spices, seeds, nuts and chocolate that is used to simmer poultry, especially turkey and other meats. Variations of this savory sauce are found throughout Mexico, where mole recipes are revered to be served at festive occasions.

Yield: 1 qt. (960 ml)

Cinnamon stick	1	1
Allspice	1/2 tsp.	2 ml
Guajillo chiles	2	2
Pasilla chiles	2	2
Sesame seeds	4 oz.	120 g
Pumpkin seeds	6 oz.	180 g
Cumin seeds	1 tsp.	5 ml
Onion, small	1	1
Olive oil	as needed	as needed
Plum tomatoes	4	4
Garlic cloves	4	4
Fresh thyme	1 sprig	1 sprig
Dried oregano	1 tsp.	5 ml
Chicken stock	1 qt.	960 ml
Salt	TT	TT
Semisweet chocolate, chopped	2 oz.	60 g

❶ Roasting the tomatoes.

1. Grind the cinnamon and allspice in a spice grinder.
2. Stem and seed the guajillo and pasilla chiles. Break them into small pieces and simmer them in water for 15 minutes. Drain well.
3. Combine the sesame seeds, pumpkin seeds and cumin seeds and fry them in a dry sauté pan until well toasted.
4. Slice the onion approximately 1/2 inch (1.2 centimeters) thick. Brush the slices with oil and grill until well colored.

❷ Combining ingredients in a sauce pan.

5. Roast the tomatoes over the open flame of a gas burner until they are evenly charred and blistered. Remove the cores, peel the tomatoes and chop them coarsely.
6. Combine the cinnamon and allspice with the chiles, toasted seeds, onion, tomatoes, garlic, thyme, oregano and stock in a saucepan. Season with salt and bring to a boil. Reduce to a simmer and cook for 15 minutes. Remove from the heat, cool and remove the sprig of thyme.
7. Blend the mixture in a blender until smooth. Strain through a china cap and stir in the chocolate until melted. Adjust the seasonings.
8. Serve the mole over grilled chicken, turkey, duck, quail or a meat such as pork or rabbit. Or, reheat cooked turkey or chicken pieces in the sauce until hot and serve with a portion of the sauce.

Approximate values per 1-fl.-oz. (30-ml) serving: **Calories** 70, **Total fat** 5 g, **Saturated fat** 1 g, **Cholesterol** 0 mg, **Sodium** 90 mg, **Total carbohydrates** 4 g, **Protein** 2 g, **Iron** 10%

❸ The finished sauce.

FRESH TOMATO VINAIGRETTE FOR PASTA

Yield: 18 fl. oz. (540 ml)

Balsamic vinegar	3 fl. oz.	90 ml
Salt	2 tsp.	10 ml
Olive oil	6 fl. oz.	180 ml
Tomato concassée	8 oz.	240 g
Fresh basil, thyme or marjoram, chopped	1 oz.	30 g
Shallot, minced	2 Tbsp.	30 ml
Black pepper	½ tsp.	2 ml

1. Dissolve the salt in the vinegar in a small stainless steel bowl.
2. Whisk in the olive oil. Then stir in the tomato, fresh herbs and shallot. Season with pepper.
3. Use this vinaigrette to season up to 2 pounds (approximately 1 kilogram) of any type of cooked pasta, adjusting the seasonings before serving warm or chilled as an accompaniment to sandwiches or other foods.

Approximate values per 3-fl.-oz. (90-ml) serving: **Calories** 270, **Total fat** 27 g, **Saturated fat** 3 g, **Cholesterol** 0 mg, **Sodium** 780 mg, **Total carbohydrates** 6 g, **Protein** 0 g

ORANGE GASTRIQUE

HERBSAINT BAR AND RESTAURANT, NEW ORLEANS, LA

Chef Donald Link

Yield: 1 pt. (480 ml)

Granulated sugar	8 oz.	240 ml
Water	4 fl. oz.	120 ml
Orange zest	2 Tbsp.	30 ml
Orange juice	1 pt.	480 ml
Star anise	2	2
Brown stock	2 qt.	1.9 lt
Honey	3 Tbsp.	45 ml
Whole butter	½ oz.	15 g

1. Combine the sugar and water and cook over medium heat until lightly caramelized.
2. Add the zest, juice and star anise and stir together until the sugar is dissolved and the sauce is smooth. Add the stock and reduce until the sauce thickens and coats the back of a spoon.
3. Stir in the honey and monté au beurre.
4. Serve the sauce with grilled or roasted chicken, duck, quail or pork.

Approximate values per 1-fl.-oz. (30-ml) serving: **Calories** 100, **Total fat** 1 g, **Saturated fat** 0.5 g, **Cholesterol** 0 mg, **Sodium** 320 mg, **Total carbohydrates** 24 g, **Protein** 1 g, **Vitamin A** 60%, **Vitamin C** 30%

PESTO SAUCE

Taken from the word that means "paste" in Italian, pesto is traditionally made using basil and pine nuts pounded by hand with a heavy pestle in a mortar. Other herbs and nuts can be substituted; blanched almonds or walnuts work well, as does cilantro, mint or parsley.

Yield: 1½ pt. (720 ml)   **Method:** Puréeing

Olive oil	12 fl. oz.	360 ml
Pine nuts	3 oz.	90 g
Fresh basil leaves	6 oz.	180 g
Garlic, chopped	1 Tbsp.	15 ml
Parmesan, grated	4 oz.	120 g
Romano, grated	4 oz.	120 g
Salt and pepper	TT	TT

1 Place one-third of the oil in a blender or food processor and add all the remaining ingredients.

2 Blend or process until smooth. Add the remaining oil and blend a few seconds to incorporate.

VARIATIONS:

Walnut Pesto—Substitute walnuts for pine nuts.

Sun-Dried Tomato Pesto—Add 1 ounce (30 grams) sun-dried tomatoes that have been softened in oil or water. Add additional oil as necessary.

Approximate values per 1-fl.-oz. (30-ml) serving: **Calories** 200, **Total fat** 19 g, **Saturated fat** 4 g, **Cholesterol** 10 mg, **Sodium** 250 mg, **Total carbohydrates** 1 g, **Protein** 4 g, **Calcium** 15%

1 Combining the pesto ingredients.

2 The finished pesto sauce.

CITRUS BEURRE BLANC

VINCENT ON CAMELBACK, PHOENIX, AZ

Chef Vincent Guerithault

Yield: 4 Servings, 5 fl. oz. (150 ml) each

Orange juice	8 fl. oz.	240 ml
Lime juice	1 Tbsp.	15 ml
Lemon juice	1 Tbsp.	15 ml
White wine	8 fl. oz.	240 ml
White wine vinegar	8 fl. oz.	240 ml
Shallot, chopped fine	1 Tbsp.	15 ml
Heavy cream	1 Tbsp.	15 ml
Unsalted butter	1 lb.	480 g
Salt and pepper	TT	TT
Orange rind, grated and blanched	1 Tbsp.	15 ml
Lime rind, grated and blanched	1 Tbsp.	15 ml
Lemon rind, grated and blanched	1 Tbsp.	15 ml

1. Combine the citrus juices, wine, vinegar and shallot and reduce au sec over moderate heat.
2. Whisk in the cream, then whisk in the butter 2 ounces (60 grams) at a time.
3. Strain the sauce, season with salt and pepper and stir in the citrus rinds. Keep hot for service.

Approximate values per 5-fl.-oz. (150-ml) serving: **Calories** 890, **Total fat** 94 g, **Saturated fat** 58 g, **Cholesterol** 255 mg, **Sodium** 600 mg, **Total carbohydrates** 9 g, **Protein** 2 g, **Vitamin A** 90%

CREAM BEURRE BLANC

THE ART INSTITUTE OF WASHINGTON, ALEXANDRIA, VA

This version of beurre blanc is easier to master than a traditional beurre blanc. It is also less temperature sensitive.

Yield: 12 fl. oz. (360 ml)

Shallot, chopped fine	1 Tbsp.	15 ml
Clarified butter	2 tsp.	10 ml
White wine	6 fl. oz.	180 ml
Heavy cream	8 fl. oz.	240 ml
Unsalted butter, softened	8 oz.	240 g
Salt and white pepper	TT	TT

1. Sauté the shallot in the clarified butter until translucent but not brown. Add the wine and reduce by half.
2. Add the cream, bring to a boil and reduce by two-thirds.
3. Remove from the heat and keep warm. Whisk the butter into the sauce in several batches. Move the pan back and forth over the heat to keep the sauce from becoming too hot or too cold.
4. Season the sauce with salt and white pepper. Strain if desired. Hold in a warm place for service.

Note: Like a traditional beurre blanc, this sauce can be flavored by adding any of a wide variety of herbs and spices. Beurre rouge may be prepared by substituting red wine for the white wine.

Approximate values per 2-fl.-oz. (60-ml) serving: **Calories** 220, **Total fat** 23 g, **Saturated fat** 15 g, **Cholesterol** 70 mg, **Sodium** 10 mg, **Total carbohydrates** 1 g, **Protein** 1 g, **Vitamin A** 20%

TOMATO BUTTER SAUCE WITH THYME

NEWBURY COLLEGE, BROOKLINE, MA

Senior Instructor Scott Doughty

Yield: 1 pt. (480 ml)

Plum tomato concassée, minced	2½ lb.	1.2 kg
Olive oil	1 fl. oz.	30 ml
White wine	2 fl. oz.	60 ml
Vermouth, dry, red or white	2 fl. oz.	60 ml
Wine vinegar, red or white	2 fl. oz.	60 ml
Shallot, minced	2 Tbsp.	30 ml
Heavy cream	2 fl. oz.	60 ml
Fresh thyme, chopped	1 Tbsp.	15 ml
Salt	¾ tsp.	4 ml
Black pepper	¼ tsp.	1 ml
Whole butter, cut into pieces	4 oz.	120 g
Fresh parsley, chopped	1½ oz.	45 g

1 Sauté the tomato concassée in the oil for approximately 2 minutes. Lower the heat to a simmer and reduce the tomato until thick but not dry.

2 In a saucepan, combine the wine, vermouth, vinegar and shallot. Bring to a boil and reduce au sec. Add the cream and reduce by half.

3 Add the thyme, salt and pepper to the tomatoes. Stir in the wine, cream and shallot reduction.

4 Bring the sauce to a simmer. Add the butter pieces and stir until incorporated. Do not allow the sauce to boil or the butter will separate. Adjust the seasonings and stir in the parsley.

Approximate values per 3-fl.-oz. (90-ml) serving: **Calories** 100, **Total fat** 9 g, **Saturated fat** 4.5 g, **Cholesterol** 20 mg, **Sodium** 120 mg, **Total carbohydrates** 4 g, **Protein** 1 g, **Vitamin A** 15%, **Vitamin C** 25%

BARBECUE SAUCE

Yield: 2 qt. (1.9 lt)

Ketchup	2 qt.	1.9 lt
Water	1 pt.	480 ml
Apple cider vinegar	1 pt.	480 ml
Worcestershire sauce	8 fl. oz.	240 ml
Molasses	4 oz.	120 g
Brown sugar	6 oz.	180 g
Yellow mustard	8 oz.	240 g
Garlic powder	4 Tbsp.	60 ml
Onion, grated	2 oz.	60 g
Black pepper	1 tsp.	5 ml
Cayenne pepper	1/2 tsp.	2 ml

1 Combine all ingredients in a heavy 4-quart (4-liter) sauce pot. Bring to a simmer over medium heat, stirring often. Simmer until the sauce is reduced by half, 20 to 30 minutes.

2 Brush the sauce over grilled foods during the last 15 or 20 minutes of cooking.

Approximate values per 1-fl.-oz. (30-ml) serving: **Calories** 25, **Total fat** 1 g, **Saturated fat** 0 g, **Cholesterol** 0 mg, **Sodium** 80 mg, **Total carbohydrates** 4 g, **Protein** 0 g, **Claims**—low fat; low sodium; low calorie

SOUTHEAST ASIAN-STYLE PEANUT SAUCE

In Thailand, Vietnam and other Southeast Asian countries, peanut sauce is served with skewered and grilled foods such as chicken or pork and as an accompaniment to rice crackers.

Yield: 28 fl. oz. (840 ml)

Garlic, chopped	1 tsp.	5 ml
Onion, small dice	6 oz.	180 g
Red pepper flakes, crushed	1 tsp.	5 ml
Fragrant lime leaves (optional)	4	4
Curry powder	2 tsp.	10 ml
Lemongrass, minced	1 oz.	30 g
Vegetable oil	1 fl. oz.	30 ml
Coconut milk	8 fl. oz.	240 ml
Cinnamon sticks	2	2
Bay leaves	4	4
Lime juice	1 fl. oz.	30 ml
Rice wine vinegar	4 fl. oz.	120 ml
Chicken stock	10 fl. oz.	300 ml
Peanut butter	10 oz.	300 g

1 Sauté the garlic, onion, red pepper flakes, lime leaves, curry powder and lemongrass in the oil for 5 minutes.

2 Add the remaining ingredients and simmer for 30 minutes. Stir often, as the sauce can burn easily. Remove the cinnamon and bay leaves and serve warm.

VARIATION:

Vegetarian Peanut Sauce—Substitute vegetable stock or water for the chicken stock.

Approximate values per 1-fl.-oz. (30-ml) serving: **Calories** 100, **Total fat** 8 g, **Saturated fat** 3 g, **Cholesterol** 0 mg, **Sodium** 115 mg, **Total carbohydrates** 5 g, **Protein** 3 g

THAI MELON SALSA

Yield: 1 qt. (960 ml)

Assorted melons such as honeydew, cantaloupe and crenshaw, medium, peeled	2	2
Garlic, chopped	1 tsp.	5 ml
Brown sugar	2 Tbsp.	30 ml
Thai fish sauce	2 Tbsp.	30 ml
Serrano chiles, minced	1 Tbsp.	15 ml
Lime juice	2 fl. oz.	60 ml
Unsalted peanuts, roasted, chopped fine	4 Tbsp.	60 ml
Fresh mint	4 Tbsp.	60 ml

1 Cut the melons into small dice or shape into small balls using a parisienne scoop.

2 Combine the remaining ingredients and toss with the melon pieces. Chill thoroughly. Serve with fish, shellfish or chicken.

Approximate values per 1-fl.-oz. (30-ml) serving: **Calories** 20, **Total fat** 0.5 g, **Saturated fat** 0 g, **Cholesterol** 0 mg, **Sodium** 70 mg, **Total carbohydrates** 4 g, **Protein** 0 g, **Vitamin C** 10%, **Claims**—low fat; low sodium; low calorie

TOMATILLO SALSA

Yield: 2 qt. (1.9 lt)

Tomatillos	5 lb.	2.4 kg
Water	8 fl. oz.	240 ml
Jalapeños	3	3
Salt	1 Tbsp.	15 ml
Pepper	½ tsp.	2 ml
Garlic	2 Tbsp.	30 ml
Onion, chopped	4 oz.	120 g
Fresh cilantro, chopped	2 oz.	60 g

1. Remove the husks from the tomatillos.
2. Combine the tomatillos with the water, jalapeños, salt, pepper, garlic and onion. Bring to a boil and simmer until tender, approximately 20 minutes.
3. Chop the mixture in a food chopper or purée in a blender for a smoother sauce.
4. Add the cilantro and adjust the seasonings. The sauce may be served warm or cold.

Approximate values per 1-fl.-oz. (30-ml) serving: **Calories** 20, **Total fat** 0 g, **Saturated fat** 0 g, **Cholesterol** 0 mg, **Sodium** 120 mg, **Total carbohydrates** 3 g, **Protein** 1 g, **Claims**—fat free; low sodium; low calorie

SPANISH ROMESCO SAUCE

COLLEGE OF LAKE COUNTY, GRAYSLAKE, IL

Chef George Upton

Romesco sauce is based on key ingredients found in the Catalonian region of Spain, where red peppers, garlic, onions, tomatoes and nuts are abundant. The sauce is finished with oil and emulsified like mayonnaise. **Pimentón,** *if available, gives this sauce an authentic flavor. Serve romesco sauce with grilled foods or with toasted bread as a dip or spread.*

Yield: 22 fl. oz. (660 ml)

Red bell peppers, medium size, whole	1 lb. 12 oz.	840 g
Almonds, sliced	2 oz.	60 g
Hazelnuts	2 oz.	60 g
Garlic cloves	3	3
Fresh Italian parsley, chopped	1 Tbsp.	15 ml
Paprika or pimentón	2 tsp.	10 ml
Chilli powder or ground cumin	½ tsp.	2 ml
Sherry vinegar	4 fl. oz.	120 ml
Extra virgin olive oil	6 fl. oz.	180 ml
Salt	1 tsp.	5 ml
Black pepper	TT	TT

1. Roast the bell peppers over the open flame of a gas burner. Peel them, remove the seeds and chop them coarsely.
2. Toast the almonds and hazelnuts in a dry sauté pan. Cool them and grind them in the bowl of a food processor until they are almost a paste.
3. Add the bell peppers, garlic, Italian parsley, paprika and chilli powder to the bowl of the processor and pulse to combine the ingredients.
4. Add the vinegar and purée to a smooth paste.
5. With the processor running, add the oil in a slow stream to emulsify the sauce. Season to taste.

pimentón Spanish paprika produced from one of several varieties of *Capsicum annuum* peppers; in Extremadura, these peppers are dried over an oak fire, giving the region's *Pimentón de la Vera* a subtle smoky flavor

Approximate values per 1-fl.-oz. (30-ml) serving: **Calories** 80, **Total fat** 8 g, **Saturated fat** 1 g, **Cholesterol** 0 mg, **Sodium** 0 mg, **Total carbohydrates** 2 g, **Protein** 1 g, **Vitamin A** 15%, **Vitamin C** 50%, **Claims**—low sodium

MIGNONETTE SAUCE

This piquant vinegar sauce is traditionally served with raw shellfish such as oysters or clams on the half shell.

Yield: 1 pt. (480 ml)

White pepper	2 tsp.	10 ml
Red wine vinegar	1 pt.	480 ml
Shallot, minced	4 oz.	120 g
Salt	TT	TT

1 Combine all ingredients.

Approximate values per 1-fl.-oz. (30-ml) serving: **Calories** 5, **Total fat** 0 g, **Saturated fat** 0 g, **Cholesterol** 0 mg, **Sodium** 0.8 mg, **Total carbohydrates** 1 g, **Protein** 0 g, **Claims**—fat free; very low sodium; low calorie

---

NUOC CHAM
(VIETNAMESE DIPPING SAUCE)

Vietnam's national condiment, nuoc cham combines the pungency of fish sauce with sweetness, heat and acidity. Ideal as a dipping sauce for spring rolls or grilled foods, it is also used to dress cucumber and green salads. Grated carrots can be added for color and texture.

Yield: 10 fl. oz. (300 ml)

Granulated sugar	2 oz.	60 g
Water	1½ fl. oz.	45 ml
Fish sauce (nuoc mam)	2½ fl. oz.	75 ml
Fresh lemon or lime juice	4 fl. oz.	120 ml
Garlic clove, minced	1	1
Thai chile, seeded and minced	1	1
Shallot, minced	1	1

1 Whisk all the ingredients together in a small nonreactive bowl and allow to stand for at least 30 minutes at room temperature before serving.

Approximate values per 1-fl.-oz. (30-ml) serving: **Calories** 0, **Total fat** 0 g, **Saturated fat** 0 g, **Cholesterol** 0 mg, **Sodium** 700 mg, **Total carbohydrates** 8 g, **Protein** 1 g, **Vitamin C** 20%, **Claims**—no calories; fat free; good source of vitamin C

PERSILLADE

Although not a liquid sauce, persillade (payr-see-yade) is a classic parsley topping used to finish a dish in much the same way as a sauce. Persillade adds flavor and texture to grilled or roasted meats, especially beef and lamb, or vegetables.

Yield: 1 lb. (480 g)

Garlic, minced	1 oz.	30 g
Fresh parsley, chopped	3 oz.	90 g
Fresh bread crumbs	6 oz.	180 g
Whole butter, melted	6 oz.	180 g

1 Combine the garlic, parsley and bread crumbs. Drizzle the butter over the mixture and toss to blend.

② Sprinkle the persillade over cooked meats or vegetables as a topping, then place the dish under a broiler until lightly browned.

Approximate values per 1/2-oz. (15-g) serving: **Calories** 50, **Total fat** 4.5 g, **Saturated fat** 3 g, **Cholesterol** 10 mg, **Sodium** 30 mg, **Total carbohydrates** 3 g, **Protein** 1 g

---

BRENNAN'S LEMON BUTTER SAUCE

BRENNAN'S RESTAURANT, NEW ORLEANS, LA
Chef Michael Roussel (1938–2005)

Yield: 1 qt. (960 ml)

Brown Sauce (page 206)	4 fl. oz.	120 ml
Lemon juice	2 fl. oz.	60 ml
Whole butter, room temperature	2 lb.	960 g

① Combine the brown sauce and lemon juice in a large saucepan.

② Working the pan on and off the direct heat, add the butter a bit at a time, whisking the sauce smooth between additions.

③ Adjust the flavor with additional lemon juice if necessary. Transfer the sauce to a clean container and hold at room temperature for service. Use the sauce within 2 hours or discard it.

Approximate values per 1-fl.-oz. (30-ml) serving: **Calories** 210, **Total fat** 23 g, **Saturated fat** 14 g, **Cholesterol** 65 g, **Sodium** 20 mg, **Total carbohydrates** 1 g, **Protein** 0 g, **Vitamin A** 15%

ADDITIONAL SAUCE RECIPES IN THIS BOOK

In addition to the vinaigrettes and mayonnaise sauces found in Chapter 24, Salads and Salad Dressings, the following stocks and savory sauces appear in other chapters or in the electronic resources for this book.

Recipes shown in burgundy are available as electronic media.

CHAPTER ELEVEN

SOUPS

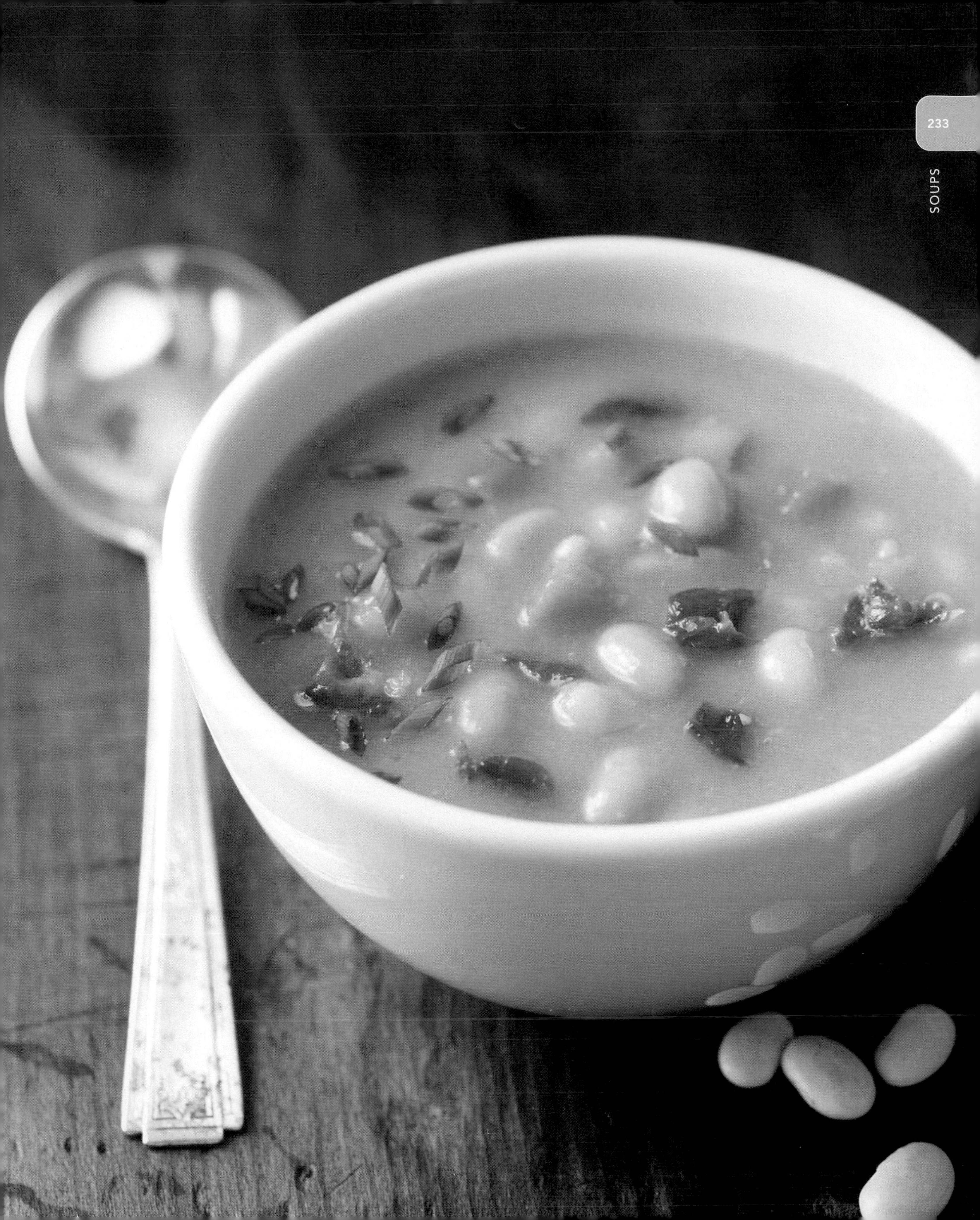

- prepare a variety of clear and thick soups
- garnish and serve soups appropriately

THE VARIETY OF INGREDIENTS, seasonings and garnishes that can be used for soups is virtually endless, provided one understands the basic procedures for making different kinds of soup. Great soups can be made from the finest and most expensive ingredients or from leftovers from the previous evening's dinner service and trimmings from the day's production. Soups are universally recognized as comfort foods in which seasonal ingredients can shine. Although fresh ingredients are preferable, wise use of leftovers means that a daily soup special can be an economical, practical menu item.

This chapter extends to soups the skills and knowledge learned in Chapter 10, Stocks and Sauces. In Chapter 10, we discussed making stocks, thickening liquids, using a liaison and skimming impurities, techniques that apply to soup making as well. Here we discuss techniques such as clarifying consommés and thickening soups with vegetable purées. This chapter also covers cream soups, cold soups and guidelines for garnishing and serving a variety of soups.

Most soups can be classified by cooking technique and appearance as either clear or thick.

Clear soups include **broths** (Fr. *bouillon*) made from meat, poultry, game, fish or vegetables as well as **consommés**, which are broths clarified to remove impurities.

Thick soups include cream soups and purée soups. The most common **cream soups** are those made from vegetables cooked in a liquid that is thickened with a starch and puréed; cream is then incorporated to add richness and flavor. **Purée soups** are generally made from starchy vegetables or legumes. After the main ingredient is simmered in a liquid, the mixture—or a portion of it—is puréed.

Some soups (notably **bisques** and **chowders** as well as **cold soups** such as gazpacho and fruit soup) are neither clear nor thick soups. Rather, they use special preparation methods or a combination of the methods mentioned before.

A soup's quality is determined by its flavor, appearance and texture. A good soup should be full-flavored, with no off or sour tastes. Flavors from each of the soup's ingredients should blend and complement, with no one flavor overpowering another. Consommés should be crystal clear. The vegetables in vegetable soups should be brightly colored, not gray. Garnishes should be attractive and uniform in size and shape. The soup's texture should be very precise. If it is supposed to be smooth, then it should be very smooth and lump-free. If the soft and crisp textures of certain ingredients are supposed to contrast, the soup should not be overcooked, as this causes all the ingredients to become mushy and soft.

Garnishing is an important consideration when preparing soups. When applied to soups, the word *garnish* has two meanings. The first is the one more typically associated with the word. It refers to foods added to the soup as decoration—for example, a broccoli floret floated on a bowl of cream of broccoli soup. The second refers to foods that may serve not only as decorations but also as critical components of the final product—for example, noodles in a bowl of chicken noodle soup. In this context, the noodles are not ingredients because they are not used to make the chicken soup. Rather, they are added to chicken soup to create a different dish. These additional items are still referred to as garnishes, however.

ESCOFFIER'S CLASSIFICATION OF SOUPS

In his 1903 culinary treatise *Le Guide culinaire*, Auguste Escoffier recognized many more categories of soups than we do today. They include the following:

Clear soups, which are always "clear consommés with a slight garnish in keeping with the nature of the consommé."

Purées, which are made from starchy vegetables and are thickened with rice, potato or soft bread crumbs.

Cullises, which use poultry, game or fish for a base and are thickened with rice, lentils, espagnole sauce or bread soaked in boiling salted water.

Bisques, which use shellfish cooked with a mirepoix as a base and are thickened with rice.

Veloutés, which use velouté sauce as a base and are finished with a liaison of egg yolks and cream.

Cream soups, which use béchamel sauce as a base and are finished with heavy cream.

Special soups, which are those that do not follow the procedures for veloutés or creams.

Vegetable soups, which are usually paysanne or peasant-type and "do not demand very great precision in the apportionment of the vegetables of which they are composed, but they need great care and attention, notwithstanding."

Foreign soups, "which have a foreign origin whose use, although it may not be general, is yet sufficiently common."

Because of changes in consumer health consciousness and kitchen operations, many of the distinctions between Escoffier's classic soups have now become blurred and, in some cases, eliminated. As discussed in this chapter, for example, clear consommés and vegetable soups are now made with stocks or broths; most cream soups use velouté as a base and are finished with milk or cream rather than a liaison. But not everything has changed: The procedures for making purées and bisques are essentially the same today as they were when Escoffier haunted the great kitchens of Europe.

CLEAR SOUPS

All clear soups start as stock or broth. Broths may be served as finished items, used as the base for other soups or refined (clarified) into consommés.

Broths

The techniques for making stocks discussed in Chapter 10 are identical to those used for making broths. Like stocks, broths are prepared by simmering flavoring ingredients in a liquid for a long time. Broths and stocks differ, however, in two ways. First, broths are made with meat instead of just bones. Second, broths (often with a garnish) can be served as finished dishes, whereas stocks are generally used to prepare other items.

Broths are made from meat, poultry, fish or vegetables cooked in a liquid. An especially full-flavored broth results when a stock and not just water is used as the liquid. Cuts of meat from the shank, neck or shoulder result in more flavorful broths, as will the flesh of mature poultry. Proper temperature, skimming and straining help produce well-flavored, clear broths.

PROCEDURE FOR **PREPARING BROTHS**

1. Truss or cut the main ingredient.
2. Brown the meat; brown or sweat the mirepoix or vegetables as necessary.
3. Place the main ingredient and mirepoix or vegetables in an appropriate stockpot and add enough cold water or stock to cover. Add a bouquet garni or sachet d'épices if desired.
4. Bring the liquid slowly to a boil; reduce to a simmer and cook, skimming occasionally, until the main ingredient is tender and the flavor is fully developed.
5. Carefully strain the broth through a china cap lined with damp cheesecloth; try to disturb the flavoring ingredients as little as possible in order to preserve the broth's clarity.
6. Cool and store following the procedures for cooling stocks. Or bring to a boil, garnish as desired and hold for service.

BEEF BROTH

MISE EN PLACE

▶ Cut beef shank into pieces.
▶ Chop onions, carrots and celery for mirepoix.
▶ Wash and peel turnips and leeks and chop into medium dice.
▶ Wash, peel and seed and then dice tomatoes.
▶ Prepare herb sachet.

Yield: 8 qt. (7.6 lt)   **Method:** Broth

Beef shank, neck or shoulder cut in 2-in.- (5-cm-) thick pieces	12 lb.	5.7 kg
Vegetable oil	8 fl. oz.	240 ml
Beef stock or water, cold	8 qt.	7.6 lt
Mirepoix	2 lb.	960 g
Turnips, medium dice	8 oz.	240 g
Leeks, medium dice	8 oz.	240 g
Tomatoes, seeded and diced	8 oz.	240 g
Sachet:		
Bay leaf	1	1
Dried thyme	½ tsp.	2 ml
Peppercorns, crushed	½ tsp.	2 ml
Parsley stems	8	8
Garlic cloves, crushed	2	2
Salt	TT	TT

1 Brown the meat in 4 fluid ounces (120 milliliters) oil, then place it in a stockpot. Add the stock or water and bring to a simmer. Simmer gently for 2 hours, skimming the surface as necessary.

2 After the meat has simmered for 2 hours, caramelize the mirepoix in the remaining oil and add it to the liquid. Add the turnips, leeks, tomatoes and sachet.

3 Simmer until full flavor has developed, approximately 1 hour. Skim the surface as necessary.

4 Carefully strain the broth through cheesecloth and season to taste. Cool and refrigerate.

Approximate values per 6-fl.-oz. (180-ml) serving: **Calories** 30, **Total fat** 1 g, **Saturated fat** 0 g, **Cholesterol** 0 mg, **Sodium** 55 mg, **Total carbohydrates** 1 g, **Protein** 4 g

1 Browning the meat.

2 Adding mirepoix to the broth.

3 Straining the broth.

Broth-Based Soups

Broths are often used as bases for such familiar soups as vegetable, chicken noodle and beef barley.

Transforming a broth into a broth-based vegetable soup, for example, is quite simple. Although a broth may be served with a vegetable (or meat) garnish, a broth-based vegetable soup is a soup in which the vegetables (and meats) are cooked directly in the broth, adding flavor, body and texture to the finished product. Any number of vegetables can be used to make a vegetable soup; it could be a single vegetable as in onion soup or a dozen different vegetables for a hearty minestrone.

When making broth-based vegetable soups, each ingredient must be added at the proper time so that all ingredients are cooked when the soup is finished. The ingredients must cook long enough to add their flavors and soften sufficiently but not so long that they lose their identity and become too soft or mushy. Soups that simmer too long can reduce in volume, concentrating seasonings, especially salt. Add additional plain broth to adjust the seasonings. A raw diced potato or carrot can also be added to a salty broth and simmered to absorb some of the excess saltiness.

Because broth-based vegetable soups are made by simmering ingredients directly in the broth, they are generally not as clear as plain broths. But appearances are still important. So when cutting ingredients for the soup, pay particular attention so that the pieces are uniform and visually appealing. Small dice, julienne, bâtonnet or paysanne cuts are recommended.

PROCEDURE FOR PREPARING BROTH-BASED VEGETABLE SOUPS

1. Sweat long-cooking vegetables in butter or fat.
2. Add the appropriate stock or broth and bring to a simmer.
3. Add seasonings such as bay leaves, dried thyme, crushed peppercorns, parsley stems and garlic, in a sachet, allowing enough time for the seasonings to fully flavor the soup.
4. Add additional ingredients according to their cooking times.
5. Simmer the soup to blend all the flavors.
6. If the soup is not going to be served immediately, cool and refrigerate it.
7. Just before service, add any garnishes that were prepared separately or do not require cooking.

HEARTY VEGETABLE BEEF SOUP

Yield: 5 qt. (4.8 lt)		**Method:** Broth

Butter or beef fat	6 oz.	180 g
Mirepoix, small dice	3 lb.	1.4 kg
Turnip, small dice	8 oz.	240 g
Garlic cloves, chopped	2	2
Beef broth or stock	4 qt.	3.8 lt
Beef, small dice	1 lb.	480 g
Sachet:		
Bay leaf	1	1
Dried thyme	½ tsp.	2 ml
Peppercorns, crushed	½ tsp.	2 ml
Parsley stems	8	8
Tomato **concassée**	12 oz.	360 g
Corn kernels, fresh, frozen or canned	12 oz.	360 g
Salt and pepper	TT	TT

MISE EN PLACE

▶ Peel and chop onions, carrots and celery for mirepoix.
▶ Wash and peel turnip and chop into fine dice.
▶ Peel and chop garlic.
▶ Cut beef into fine dice.
▶ Prepare herb sachet.
▶ While broth is simmering, peel, seed and dice tomato for concassée.

concassée peeled, seeded and diced tomato

❶ Sweating the vegetables.

❷ The finished soup.

❶ In a soup pot, sweat the mirepoix and turnip in the butter or fat until tender.
❷ Add the garlic and sauté lightly.
❸ Add the broth or stock and the diced beef; bring to a simmer. Add the sachet. Skim or degrease as necessary.
❹ Simmer until the beef and vegetables are tender, approximately 1 hour.
❺ Add the tomato concassée and corn; simmer for 10 minutes. Season to taste with salt and pepper.
❻ Cool and refrigerate or hold for service.

VARIATIONS:

A wide variety of vegetables can be added or substituted in this recipe. If leeks, rutabagas, parsnips or cabbage are used, they should be sweated to bring out their flavors before the liquid is added. Potatoes, fresh beans, summer squash and other vegetables that cook more quickly should be added according to their cooking times. Seasonal leafy greens such as turnip tops, dandelion greens or arugula can be shredded and stirred in near the end of cooking. Rice, barley and pasta garnishes should be cooked separately and added just before service.

Approximate values per 6-fl.-oz. (180-ml) serving: **Calories** 60, **Total fat** 10 g, **Saturated fat** 1.5 g, **Cholesterol** 5 mg, **Sodium** 55 mg, **Total carbohydrates** 6 g, **Protein** 1 g, **Vitamin A** 35%

Consommés

A consommé is a stock or broth that has been clarified to remove impurities so that it is crystal clear. Traditionally, all clear broths were referred to as consommés; a clear broth further refined using the process described later was referred to as a double consommé. The term *double consommé* is still used occasionally to describe any strongly flavored consommé.

Well-prepared consommés should be rich in the flavor of the main ingredient. Beef and game consommés should be dark in color; consommés made from poultry should have a golden to light amber color. They should have substantial body as a result of their high gelatin content, and all consommés should be perfectly clear with no trace of fat.

Because a consommé is a refined broth, it is absolutely essential that the broth or stock used be of the highest quality. Although the clarification process adds some flavor to the consommé, the finished consommé will be only as good as the stock or broth from which it was made.

THE CLARIFICATION PROCESS

To make a consommé, you clarify a stock or broth. The stock or broth to be clarified must be cold and grease-free. To clarify, the cold degreased stock or broth is combined with a mixture known as a clearmeat or clarification. A clearmeat is a mixture of egg whites; ground meat, poultry or fish; mirepoix, herbs and spices; and an acidic product, usually tomatoes, lemon juice or wine. (An **oignon brûlé**, also known as an onion brûlé, is also often added to help flavor and color the consommé. See Chapter 8, Mise en Place.)

The stock or broth and clearmeat are then slowly brought to a simmer. As the albumen in the egg whites and meat begins to coagulate, it traps impurities suspended in the liquid. As coagulation continues, the albumen-containing items combine with the other clearmeat ingredients and rise to the liquid's surface, forming a **raft**. As the mixture simmers, the raft ingredients release their flavors, further enriching the consommé.

After simmering, the consommé is carefully strained through several layers of cheese-cloth to remove any trace of impurities. It is then completely degreased, either by cooling and refrigerating, then removing the solidified fat, or by carefully ladling the fat from the surface. The result is a rich, flavorful, crystal-clear consommé.

oignon brûlé French for "burnt onion"; made by charring onion halves; used to flavor and color stocks and sauces

raft a crust formed during the process of clarifying consommé; it is composed of the clearmeat and impurities from the stock, which rise to the top of the simmering stock and release additional flavors

PROCEDURE FOR PREPARING CONSOMMÉS

1. In a suitable stockpot (one with a spigot makes it much easier to strain the consommé when it is finished), combine the ground meat, lightly beaten egg white and other clearmeat ingredients.

2. Add the cold stock or broth and stir to combine with the clearmeat ingredients.

3. Over medium heat, slowly bring the mixture to a simmer, stirring occasionally.

4. As the raft forms, make a hole in its center so that the liquid can bubble through, cooking the raft completely and extracting as much flavor as possible from the raft ingredients.

5. Simmer the consommé until full flavor develops, approximately 1 to 1½ hours.

6. Carefully strain the consommé through several layers of cheesecloth and degrease completely.

7. If the consommé will not be used immediately, it should be cooled and refrigerated, following the procedures for cooling stocks discussed in Chapter 10. When the consommé is completely cold, remove any remaining fat that solidifies on its surface.

8. If, after reheating the consommé, small dots of fat appear on the surface, they can be removed by blotting with a small piece of paper towel.

BEEF CONSOMMÉ

MISE EN PLACE

▶ Peel and chop onions, carrots and celery for mirepoix.
▶ Seed and dice tomato.
▶ Prepare onions brûlés and herb sachet.

Yield: 4 qt. (3.8 lt)　　　　　**Method:** Consommé

Egg whites	10	10
Ground beef, lean, preferably shank, neck or shoulder	2 lb.	960 g
Mirepoix	1 lb.	480 g
Tomatoes, seeded and diced	12 oz.	360 g
Beef broth or stock, cold	5 qt.	4.8 lt
Onions brûlés	2	2
Sachet:		
Bay leaves	2	2
Dried thyme	½ tsp.	2 ml
Peppercorns, crushed	½ tsp.	2 ml
Parsley stems	8	8
Cloves, whole	2	2
Salt	TT	TT

1. Whip the egg whites until slightly frothy.
2. Combine the egg whites, beef, mirepoix and tomatoes in an appropriate stockpot.
3. Add the broth or stock; mix well and add the onions brûlés and sachet.
4. Bring the mixture to a simmer over moderate heat, stirring occasionally. Stop stirring when the raft begins to form.
5. Break a hole in the center of the raft to allow the consommé to bubble through.
6. Simmer until full flavor develops, approximately 1½ hours.
7. Strain through several layers of cheesecloth, degrease and adjust the seasonings. Cool and refrigerate or hold for service.

Note: Guidelines for garnishing consommés as well as some classic garnishes are listed on page 252.

Approximate values per 6-fl.-oz. (180-ml) serving: **Calories** 20, **Total fat** 0 g, **Saturated fat** 0 g, **Cholesterol** 0 mg, **Sodium** 500 mg, **Total carbohydrates** 1 g, **Protein** 4 g, **Claims** low fat; low calorie

1. Combining the ingredients for the clearmeat.

2. Making a hole in the raft to allow the liquid to bubble through.

3. Degreasing the consommé with a paper towel.

4. The finished consommé.

CORRECTING A POORLY CLARIFIED CONSOMMÉ

A clarification may fail for a variety of reasons. For example, if the consommé is allowed to boil or if it is stirred after the raft has formed, a cloudy consommé can result. If the consommé is insufficiently clear, a second clarification can be performed using the following procedure. This second clarification should be performed only once, however, and only if absolutely necessary, because the eggs remove not only impurities but also some of the consommé's flavor and richness.

❶ Thoroughly chill and degrease the consommé.

❷ Lightly beat four egg whites per gallon (approximately 4 liters) of consommé and combine with the cold consommé.

❸ Slowly bring the consommé to a simmer, stirring occasionally. Stop stirring when the egg whites begin to coagulate.

❹ When the egg whites are completely coagulated, carefully strain the consommé.

THICK SOUPS

There are two kinds of thick soups: cream soups and purée soups. In general, cream soups are thickened with a roux or other starch, whereas purée soups rely on a purée of the main ingredient for thickening. But in certain ways the two soups are very similar: Some purée soups are finished with cream or partially thickened with a roux or other starch. See Tables 11.1 and 11.2.

Cream Soups

Most cream soups are made by simmering the main flavoring ingredient (for example, broccoli for cream of broccoli soup) in a white stock or thin **velouté** sauce to which seasonings have been added. The mixture is then puréed and strained. After the consistency has been adjusted, the soup is finished by adding cream. In classic cuisine, thin **béchamel** sauce is often used as the base for cream soups and can be substituted for velouté in many cream soup recipes, if desired. Properly made cream soups should have a silken texture and the thickness of heavy cream. The flavor of the soups' main ingredient should be pronounced.

Both hard vegetables (for example, celery and squash) and soft or leafy vegetables (for example, spinach, corn, broccoli and asparagus) are used for cream soups. Hard vegetables are generally sweated in butter without browning before the liquid is added. Soft and leafy vegetables are generally added to the soup after the liquid is brought to

velouté (veh-loo-tay) a leading sauce made by thickening a white stock (fish, veal, or chicken) with roux

béchamel (bay-shah-mell) a leading sauce made by thickening milk with a white roux and adding seasonings

TABLE 11.1	SOUPS, THEIR THICKENING AGENTS AND FINISHES		
CATEGORY	TYPE	THICKENING AGENT OR METHOD	FINISH
Clear soups	Broths	None	Assorted garnishes
	Consommés	None	Assorted garnishes
Thick soups	Cream soups	Roux and/or puréeing	Assorted garnishes, cream or béchamel sauce
	Purée soups	Puréeing	Assorted garnishes; cream is optional
Other soups	Bisques	Roux or rice and puréeing	Garnish of main ingredient, cream and/or butter
	Chowders	Roux	Cream
Cold soups	Cooked cold soups	Roux, arrowroot, cornstarch, puréeing, sour cream, yogurt	Assorted garnishes, cream, crème fraîche, sour cream or yogurt
	Uncooked cold soups	Puréeing	Assorted garnishes, cream, crème fraîche, sour cream or yogurt

	CREAM SOUPS	PURÉE SOUPS
TABLE 11.2 CREAM AND PURÉE SOUPS		
Technique	Cook principal ingredient in stock or velouté sauce	Cook principal ingredient in stock or water
Thickener	Roux or roux-thickened sauce	Purée of starchy ingredients
Texture	Strained; very smooth and rich	Not strained; slightly coarse and grainy

a boil. Because cream soups are puréed, it is important to cook the flavoring ingredients until they are soft and can be passed through a food mill easily.

All cream soups are finished with milk or cream. Using milk thins the soup while adding richness; using the same amount of cream adds much more richness without the same thinning effect.

Cold milk and cream curdle easily if added directly to a hot or acidic soup.

To prevent curdling:

cream sauce a sauce made by adding cream to a béchamel sauce

1. Never add cold milk or cream to hot soup. Bring the milk or cream to a simmer before adding it to the soup. Or, temper the milk or cream by gradually adding some hot soup to it and then incorporating the warmed mixture into the rest of the soup.
2. Add the milk or cream to the soup just before service, if possible.
3. Do not boil the soup after the milk or cream has been added.
4. Use béchamel or cream sauce instead of milk or cream to finish cream soups because the presence of roux or other starch helps prevent curdling.

PROCEDURE FOR **PREPARING CREAM SOUPS**

1. In a soup pot, sweat hard vegetables such as squash, onions, carrots and celery in oil or butter without browning.
2. In order to thicken the soup:
   a. add flour and cook to make a blond roux, then add the cooking liquid (that is, the stock), or
   b. add the stock to the vegetables, bring the stock to a simmer and add a blond roux that was prepared separately, or
   c. add a thin velouté or béchamel sauce (which contain roux) to the vegetables.
3. Bring to a boil and reduce to a simmer.
4. Add any soft vegetables such as broccoli or asparagus, and a sachet or bouquet garni as desired.
5. Simmer the soup, skimming occasionally, until the vegetables are very tender.
6. Purée the soup by passing it through a food mill, blender, food processor or vertical cutter/mixer (VCM). Strain through a china cap if desired. If the soup is too thick, adjust the consistency by adding hot white stock.
7. Finish the soup by adding hot milk or cream or a thin béchamel or cream sauce. Adjust the seasonings and serve.

CREAM OF BROCCOLI SOUP

Yield: 6 qt. (5.7 lt) **Method:** Cream

Whole butter	3 oz.	90 g
Onions, medium dice	12 oz.	360 g
Celery, medium dice	3 oz.	90 g
Broccoli, chopped	3 lb.	1.4 kg
Chicken velouté sauce, hot	4 qt.	3.8 lt
Chicken stock, hot	approx. 2 qt.	approx. 2 lt
Heavy cream, hot	24 fl. oz.	720 ml
Salt and white pepper	TT	TT
Broccoli florets, blanched	8 oz.	240 g

MISE EN PLACE

◀ Clean and peel onions and celery and chop into medium dice.
◀ Chop broccoli.
◀ Prepare velouté sauce and keep warm.
◀ While the soup is simmering, blanch broccoli florets.

1 Sweat the onions, celery and broccoli in the butter, without browning, until they are nearly tender.

2 Add the velouté sauce. Bring to a simmer and cook until the vegetables are tender, approximately 15 minutes. Skim the surface periodically.

3 Purée the soup, then strain it through a china cap.

4 Return the soup to the stove and thin it to the correct consistency with the stock.

5 Bring the soup to a simmer and add the cream. Season to taste.

6 Garnish with blanched broccoli florets just before service.

VARIATIONS:

To make cream of asparagus, cauliflower, corn, pea or spinach soup, substitute an equal amount of the chosen vegetable for the broccoli. If using fresh spinach, precook the leaves slightly before proceeding with the recipe.

Approximate values per 6-fl.-oz. (180-ml) serving: **Calories** 140, **Total fat** 12 g, **Saturated fat** 7 g, **Cholesterol** 40 mg, **Sodium** 340 mg, **Total carbohydrates** 5 g, **Protein** 4 g, **Vitamin A** 20%, **Vitamin C** 70%

1 Adding the velouté sauce.

2 Puréeing the soup through a food mill.

3 Garnishing the finished soup.

Purée Soups

Purée soups are hearty soups made by cooking starchy vegetables or legumes in a stock or broth, then puréeing all or a portion of them to thicken the soup. Purée soups are similar to cream soups in that they both consist of a main ingredient that is first cooked in a liquid, then puréed. The primary difference is that unlike cream soups, which are thickened with starch, purée soups generally do not use additional starch for thickening.

Rather, purée soups depend on the starch content of the main ingredient for thickening. Also, purée soups are generally coarser than cream soups and are typically not strained after puréeing. When finishing purée soups with cream, follow the guidelines discussed previously for adding cream to cream soups.

Purée soups can be made with dried or fresh beans such as peas, lentils and navy beans, or with any number of vegetables, including cauliflower, celery root, turnips and potatoes. Diced potato or rice is often used to help thicken vegetable purée soups.

PROCEDURE FOR **PREPARING PURÉE SOUPS**

1. Sweat the mirepoix in butter without browning.
2. Add the cooking liquid.
3. Add the main ingredients and a sachet or bouquet garni.
4. Bring to a boil, reduce to a simmer and cook until all the ingredients are soft enough to purée easily. Remove and discard the sachet or bouquet garni.
5. Reserve a portion of the liquid to adjust the soup's consistency. Purée the rest of the soup by passing it through a food mill, food processor, blender or VCM.
6. Add enough of the reserved liquid to bring the soup to the correct consistency. If the soup is still too thick, add hot stock as needed.
7. Return the soup to a simmer and adjust the seasonings.
8. Add hot cream to the soup if desired.

PURÉE OF SPLIT PEA SOUP

MISE EN PLACE

▶ Dice bacon.
▶ Peel onions, carrots and celery and chop into medium dice for mirepoix.
▶ Peel and chop garlic.
▶ Wash and sort split peas.
▶ Prepare herb sachet.
▶ Sauté croutons in butter while the soup is simmering.

Yield: 4 qt. (3.8 lt) **Method:** Purée

Bacon, diced	3 oz.	90 g
Mirepoix, medium dice	1 lb.	480 g
Garlic cloves, chopped	2	2
Chicken stock	3 qt.	2.8 lt
Split peas, washed and sorted	1 lb.	480 g
Ham hocks or meaty ham bones	1½ lb.	720 g
Sachet:		
Bay leaves	2	2
Dried thyme	½ tsp.	2 ml
Peppercorns, crushed	½ tsp.	2 ml
Salt and pepper	TT	TT
Croutons, sautéed in butter	as needed for garnish	

render to melt and clarify fat

1. In a stockpot, **render** the bacon by cooking it slowly and allowing it to release its fat; sweat the mirepoix and garlic in the fat without browning them.
2. Add the stock, peas, ham hocks or bones and sachet. Bring to a boil, reduce to a simmer and cook until the peas are soft, approximately 1 to 1½ hours.
3. Remove the sachet and ham hocks or bones. Pass the soup through a food mill and return it to the stockpot.
4. Remove the meat from the hocks or bones. Cut the meat into medium dice and add it to the soup.
5. Bring the soup to a simmer and, if necessary, adjust the consistency by adding hot chicken stock. Adjust the seasonings and serve, garnished with croutons.

VARIATIONS:

White beans, yellow peas and other dried beans can be soaked overnight in water and used instead of split peas.

Approximate values per 6-fl.-oz. (180-ml) serving: **Calories** 110, **Total fat** 4 g, **Saturated fat** 1.5 g, **Cholesterol** 20 mg, **Sodium** 870 mg, **Total carbohydrates** 6 g, **Protein** 11 g

① Adding peas to the stockpot.

② Puréeing the split pea soup.

③ Garnishing the finished soup.

Adjusting the Consistency of Thick Soups

Cream and purée soups tend to thicken when made in advance and refrigerated. To dilute a portion being reheated, add hot stock, broth, water or milk to the hot soup as needed.

If the soup is too thin, additional roux, beurre manié or cornstarch mixed with cool stock can be used to thicken it. If additional starch is added to thicken the soup, it should be used sparingly and the soup should be simmered a few minutes to cook out the starchy flavor. A liaison of egg yolks and heavy cream can be used to thicken cream soups when added richness is also desired. Remember, the soup must not boil after the liaison is added or it may curdle.

OTHER SOUPS

Several popular types of soup do not fit the descriptions of, or follow the procedures for, either clear or thick soups. Soups such as bisques and chowders as well as many cold soups use special methods or a combination of the methods used for clear and thick soups.

Bisques

Traditional bisques are shellfish soups thickened with cooked rice. Today, bisques are prepared using a combination of the cream and purée soup procedures. They are generally made from shrimp, lobster or crayfish and are thickened with a roux instead of rice for better stability and consistency.

Much of a bisque's flavor comes from crustacean shells, which are simmered in the cooking liquid, puréed (along with the mirepoix), returned to the cooking liquid and strained after further cooking. Puréeing the shells and returning them to the soup also adds the thickness and grainy texture associated with bisques.

Bisques are enriched with cream, following the procedures for cream soups, and can be finished with butter for additional richness. The garnish should be diced flesh from the appropriate shellfish.

PROCEDURE FOR **PREPARING BISQUES**

1. Caramelize the mirepoix and main flavoring ingredient in fat.
2. Add a tomato product and deglaze with wine.
3. Add the cooking liquid (stock or velouté sauce).
4. Incorporate roux if needed.
5. Simmer, skimming as needed.
6. Strain the soup, reserving the solids and liquid. Purée the solids in a food mill or processor and return them to the liquid. Return to a simmer.
7. Strain the soup through a fine chinois or a china cap lined with cheesecloth.
8. Return the soup to a simmer and finish with hot cream.

To add even more richness to the bisque, monté au beurre with whole butter or a compound butter such as shrimp or lobster butter just before the soup is served. Also, if desired, add 3 ounces (90 milliliters) sherry to each gallon (approximately 4 liters) of soup just before service.

SHRIMP BISQUE

MISE EN PLACE

- Peel onions, carrots and celery and chop into small dice for mirepoix.
- Peel and chop garlic.
- Prepare fish velouté with shrimp stock.
- Prepare herb sachet.
- Peel and devein shrimp.
- Wash and chop basil in chiffonade while bisque is simmering.

Yield: 4 qt. (3.8 lt) **Method:** Bisque

Clarified butter	3 fl. oz.	90 ml
Mirepoix, small dice	1 lb.	480 g
Shrimp shells and/or lobster or crayfish shells and bodies	2 lb.	960 g
Garlic cloves, chopped	2	2
Tomato paste	2 oz.	60 g
Brandy	4 fl. oz.	120 ml
White wine	12 fl. oz.	360 ml
Fish velouté (made with shrimp stock)	4 qt.	3.8 lt
Sachet:		
Bay leaf	1	1
Dried thyme	½ tsp.	2 ml
Peppercorns, crushed	½ tsp.	2 ml
Parsley stems	8	8
Heavy cream, hot	1 pt.	480 ml
Salt and white pepper	TT	TT
Cayenne pepper	TT	TT
Dry or cream sherry wine (optional)	4 fl. oz.	120 ml
Shrimp, peeled and deveined	1 lb.	480 g
Fresh basil, chiffonade	as needed for garnish	

1. Caramelize the mirepoix and shrimp shells in the butter.
2. Add the garlic and tomato paste and sauté lightly.
3. Add the brandy and flambé.
4. Add the wine. Deglaze and reduce the liquid by half.
5. Add the velouté and sachet and simmer for approximately 1 hour, skimming occasionally.
6. Strain, discarding the sachet and reserving the liquid and solids. Purée the solids and return them to the liquid. Return to a simmer and cook for 10 minutes.
7. Strain the bisque through a fine chinois or china cap lined with cheesecloth.
8. Return the bisque to a simmer and add the cream.
9. Season to taste with salt, white pepper and cayenne pepper. Add sherry, if using.
10. Cook the shrimp and slice or dice them as desired. Garnish each portion of soup with cooked shrimp and the basil chiffonade.

Approximate values per 4-fl.-oz. (120-ml) serving: **Calories** 110, **Total fat** 10 g, **Saturated fat** 6 g, **Cholesterol** 60 mg, **Sodium** 160 mg, **Total carbohydrates** 2 g, **Protein** 4 g, **Vitamin A** 10%

Chowders

Although chowders are usually associated with the eastern United States where fish and clams are plentiful, they are of French origin. Undoubtedly the word chowder is derived from the Breton phrase *faire chaudière*, which means to make a fish stew in a caldron. The procedure was probably brought to Nova Scotia by French settlers and later introduced to New England.

Chowders are hearty soups with chunks of the main ingredients (including, virtually always, diced potatoes) and garnishes. With some exceptions (notably, Manhattan clam chowder), chowders contain milk or cream. Although there are thin chowders, most chowders are thickened with roux. The procedures for making chowders are similar to those for making cream soups except that chowders are not puréed and strained before the cream is added.

SEASONINGS FOR SOUPS

The addition of herbs and spices ensures memorable soups. Tender, mild fresh herbs such as chervil, chives, cilantro, dill and parsley add a bright, clean taste to most broth, starch and vegetable combinations, especially when added just before serving. Many thick purée soups, when made without milk or cream, benefit from a splash of citrus juice or vinegar immediately before serving. The piney flavors of fresh basil or mint work well in hearty vegetable or bean soups such as minestrone. Pungent herbs such as rosemary and thyme or strong spices should be used judiciously if at all in most soups, although a delicate grating of nutmeg complements most cream soups.

PROCEDURE FOR **PREPARING CHOWDERS**

1. Render finely diced salt pork over medium heat.
2. Sweat mirepoix in the rendered pork.
3. Add flour to make a roux.
4. Add the liquid.
5. Add the seasoning and flavoring ingredients according to their cooking times.
6. Simmer, skimming as needed.
7. Add milk or cream.

MISE EN PLACE

▶ Peel and dice potatoes.
▶ Dice the salt pork.
▶ Peel and dice onions and celery.
▶ Peel and julienne carrot garnish while chowder is simmering.

NEW ENGLAND–STYLE CLAM CHOWDER

Yield: 3½ qt. (3.3 lt)   **Method:** Cream

Canned clams with juice*	2 qt.	1.9 lt
Water or fish stock	approx. 1½ qt.	approx. 1.4 lt
Potatoes, small dice	1 lb. 4 oz.	600 g
Salt pork, small dice	8 oz.	240 g
Whole butter	2 oz.	60 g
Onions, small dice	1 lb.	480 g
Celery, small dice	8 oz.	240 g
Flour	4 oz.	120 g
Milk	1 qt.	960 ml
Heavy cream	8 fl. oz.	240 ml
Salt and pepper	TT	TT
Tabasco sauce	TT	TT
Worcestershire sauce	TT	TT
Fresh thyme	TT	TT
Fresh parsley	as needed for garnish	
Carrot, julienned	as needed for garnish	

1. Drain the clams, reserving both the clams and their liquid. Add enough water or stock so that the total liquid equals 2 quarts (1.9 liters).
2. Simmer the potatoes in the clam liquid until nearly cooked through. Strain and reserve the potatoes and the liquid.
3. Render the salt pork with the butter. Add the onions and celery to the rendered fat and sweat until tender but not brown.
4. Add the flour and cook to make a blond roux.
5. Add the clam liquid to the roux, whisking away any lumps.
6. Simmer for 30 minutes, skimming as necessary.
7. Bring the milk and cream to a boil and add to the soup.
8. Add the clams and potatoes, and season to taste with salt, pepper, Tabasco sauce, Worcestershire sauce and thyme.
9. Garnish each serving with fresh parsley and julienned carrot as desired.

Note: If using fresh clams for the chowder, wash and steam approximately ½ bushel (15 liters) chowder clams in a small amount of water to yield 1¼ quarts (1.4 liters) clam meat. Chop the clams. Strain the liquid through several layers of cheesecloth to remove any sand that may be present. Add enough water or stock so that the total liquid is 2 quarts (1.9 liters). Continue with the recipe, starting at step 2.

Approximate values per 6-fl.-oz. (180-ml) serving: **Calories** 250, **Total fat** 15 g, **Saturated fat** 7 g, **Cholesterol** 45 mg, **Sodium** 930 mg, **Total carbohydrates** 17 g, **Protein** 11 g, **Vitamin A** 10%, **Vitamin C** 10%, **Calcium** 15%

SAFETY ALERT
Cooked Cold Soup

Cooked cold soups, especially those made with potatoes, beans, dairy products or other high-protein foods, are potentially hazardous foods or time/temperature controlled for safety food (PHF/TCS foods) and must be chilled quickly and held at or below 41°F (5°C). Because these soups will not be reheated for service, cross-contamination is also a concern. Keep the soup covered and store above any raw meat, poultry or seafood in the cooler.

Cold Soups

Cold soups can be as simple as a chilled version of a cream soup or as creative as a cold fruit soup blended with yogurt. Cold fruit soups have become popular on contemporary dessert menus. Other than the fact that they are cold, cold soups are difficult to classify because many of them use unique or combination preparation methods. Regardless, they are divided here into two categories: cold soups that require cooking and those that do not.

COOKED COLD SOUPS

Many cold soups are simply a chilled version of a hot soup. For example, consommé madrilène and consommé portugaise are prepared hot and served cold. Vichyssoise is a cold version of puréed potato-leek soup. When serving a hot soup cold, there are several considerations:

❶ If the soup is to be creamed, add the cream at the last minute. Although curdling is not as much of a problem as it is with hot soups, adding the cream at the last minute helps extend the soup's shelf life.

❷ Cold soups should have a thinner consistency than hot soups. To achieve the proper consistency, use less starch if starch is used as the thickener, or use a higher ratio of liquid to main ingredient if the soup is thickened by puréeing. Consistency should be checked and adjusted at service time.

❸ Cold dulls the sense of taste, so cold soups require more seasoning than hot ones. Taste the soup just before service and adjust the seasonings as needed.

❹ Always serve cold soups as cold as possible, using chilled bowls.

VICHYSSOISE (COLD POTATO-LEEK SOUP)

Yield: 4 qt. (3.8 lt) **Method:** Purée

Leeks, white part only	2 lb.	960 g
Whole butter	8 oz.	240 g
Russet potatoes, large dice	2 lb.	960 g
Chicken stock	3½ qt.	3.3 lt
Salt and white pepper	TT	TT
Heavy cream	24 fl. oz.	720 ml
Chives, snipped	as needed for garnish	
Fried sweet potato frizzles	as needed for garnish	

MISE EN PLACE
◀ Wash and trim leeks.
◀ Peel and dice potatoes.
◀ Snip chives and prepare potato garnish while soup is chilling.

❶ Split the leeks lengthwise and wash well to remove all sand and grit. Slice them thinly.

❷ Sweat the leeks in the butter without browning them.

❸ Add the diced potatoes and stock, season with salt and white pepper and bring to a simmer.

❹ Simmer until the leeks and potatoes are very tender, approximately 45 minutes.

❺ Purée the soup in a food processor, blender or food mill; strain through a fine sieve.

❻ Chill the soup well.

❼ At service time, incorporate the cream and adjust the seasonings. Serve in chilled bowls, garnished with snipped chives and sweet potato frizzles.

Approximate values per 6-fl.-oz. (180-ml) serving: **Calories** 300, **Total fat** 22 g, **Saturated fat** 13 g, **Cholesterol** 70 mg, **Sodium** 660 mg, **Total carbohydrates** 19 g, **Protein** 6 g, **Vitamin A** 20%, **Vitamin C** 20%

Many cooked cold soups use fruit juice (typically apple, grape or orange) as a base and are thickened with cornstarch or arrowroot as well as with puréed fruit. For additional flavor, wine is sometimes used in lieu of a portion of the fruit juice. Cinnamon, ginger and other spices that complement fruit are commonly added, as is lemon or lime juice, which adds acidity as well as flavor. Crème fraîche, yogurt or sour cream can be used as an ingredient or garnish to add richness.

FRESH PEACH AND YOGURT SOUP

Yield: 2 qt. (1.9 lt)   **Method:** Purée

Fresh peaches	4 lb.	1.9 kg
Dry white wine	24 fl. oz.	720 ml
Honey	4 oz.	120 g
Lemon juice	2 fl. oz.	60 ml
Cinnamon, ground	¼ tsp.	1 ml
Plain nonfat yogurt	8 oz.	240 g
Heavy cream	TT	TT
Pistachios, chopped fine	as needed for garnish	

1. Pit and coarsely chop the peaches without peeling. Place in a nonreactive saucepan. Add the wine, honey and lemon juice. Cover and simmer for 30 minutes.
2. Purée the peach mixture in a blender. Strain and chill.
3. Stir in the cinnamon, yogurt and cream.
4. Chill thoroughly. Serve in chilled bowls, garnished with finely chopped pistachio nuts.

Approximate values per 6-fl.-oz. (180-ml) serving: **Calories** 140, **Total fat** 0 g, **Saturated fat** 0 g, **Cholesterol** 0 mg, **Sodium** 20 mg, **Total carbohydrates** 32 g, **Protein** 3 g, **Vitamin A** 10%, **Vitamin C** 25%, **Claims**—fat free; very low sodium; good source of fiber

1. Simmering the peaches.

2. Straining the peach purée.

3. The finished soup.

UNCOOKED COLD SOUPS

Some cold soups are not cooked at all. Rather, they rely only on puréed fruits or vegetables for thickness, body and flavor. Cold stock is sometimes used to adjust the soup's consistency. Dairy products such as cream, sour cream and crème fraîche are sometimes added to enrich and flavor the soup.

GAZPACHO

Yield: 4 qt. (3.8 lt)	**Method:** Uncooked	
Tomatoes, peeled and diced	2 lb. 8 oz.	1.2 kg
Onions, medium dice	8 oz.	240 g
Green bell pepper, medium dice	1	1
Red bell pepper, medium dice	1	1
Cucumbers, peeled, seeded, medium dice	1 lb.	480 g
Garlic, minced	1 oz.	30 g
Red wine vinegar	2 fl. oz.	60 ml
Lemon juice	2 fl. oz.	60 ml
Olive oil	4 fl. oz.	120 ml
Salt and pepper	TT	TT
Cayenne pepper	TT	TT
Fresh bread crumbs (optional)	3 oz.	90 g
Tomato juice	3 qt.	2.8 lt
White stock	as needed	as needed
Garnish:		
Tomatoes, peeled, seeded, small dice	8 oz.	240 g
Red bell pepper, small dice	4 oz.	120 g
Green bell pepper, small dice	4 oz.	120 g
Yellow bell pepper, small dice	4 oz.	120 g
Cucumber, peeled, seeded, small dice	3 oz.	90 g
Green onion, sliced fine	2 oz.	60 g
Fresh basil	as needed for garnish	

1 Combine and purée all ingredients except the tomato juice, stock and garnish in a VCM, food processor or blender.

2 Stir in the tomato juice.

3 Adjust the consistency with the stock.

4 Stir in the vegetable garnishes and adjust the seasonings.

5 Serve in chilled cups or bowls garnished with fresh basil.

VARIATION:

Gazpacho can be made without puréeing all the ingredients. Less garnish will be required.

Approximate values per 6-fl.-oz. (180-ml) serving: **Calories** 70, **Total fat** 0.5 g, **Saturated fat** 0 g, **Cholesterol** 0 mg, **Sodium** 600 mg, **Total carbohydrates** 14 g, **Protein** 3 g, **Vitamin A** 15%, **Vitamin C** 70%, **Claims**—low fat; no cholesterol

GARNISHING SOUPS

Garnishes and toppings can range from a simple sprinkle of chopped parsley on a bowl of cream soup to tiny profiteroles stuffed with foie gras adorning a crystal-clear bowl of consommé. Some soups are so full of attractive, flavorful and colorful foods that are integral parts of the soup (for example, vegetables and chicken in chicken vegetable soup) that no additional garnishes are necessary. In others, the garnish determines the type of soup. For example, a beef broth garnished with cooked barley and diced beef becomes beef barley soup.

◄ Peel and dice the tomatoes, onions and peppers.
◄ Peel, seed and dice the cucumbers.
◄ Mince the garlic.
◄ Peel and finely slice the green onions.

SAFETY ALERT
Uncooked Cold Soup

Because uncooked cold soups are never heated, enzymes and bacteria are not destroyed and the soup can spoil quickly. Many cold soups also contain dairy products, which makes them a potentially hazardous or time/temperature controlled for safety food (PHF/TCS foods). When preparing uncooked cold soups, always prepare small batches as close to service time as possible. Keep the soup at or below 41°F (5°C) at all times. Cover and store leftovers properly.

CLASSIC CONSOMMÉS

Many classic consommés are known by their garnishes:

Consommé brunoise—blanched or sautéed brunoise of turnip, leek, celery and onion.

Consommé julienne—blanched or sautéed julienne of carrot, turnip, leek, celery, cabbage and onion.

Consommé paysanne—blanched or sautéed paysanne of leek, turnip, carrot, celery and potato.

Consommé bouquetière—assorted blanched vegetables.

Consommé madrilène—tomatoes or tomato juice; served hot or cold.

Consommé royale—cooked custard cut into tiny shapes.

Angel hair consommé—cooked angel hair (vermicelli) pasta.

Consommé with profiteroles—tiny profiteroles (pâte à choux rounds) stuffed with foie gras.

Guidelines for Garnishing Soups

Although some soups (particularly consommés) have traditional garnishes, many soups depend on the chef's imagination and the kitchen's inventory for the finishing garnish. The only rules are as follows:

1. The garnish should be attractive.
2. The meats and vegetables used should be neatly cut into an appropriate and uniform shape and size. This is particularly important when garnishing a clear soup such as a consommé, as the consommé's clarity highlights the precise (or imprecise) cuts.
3. The garnish's texture and flavor should complement the soup.
4. Starches and vegetables used as garnishes should be cooked separately, reheated and placed in the soup bowl before the hot soup is added. If they are cooked in the soup, they may cloud or thicken the soup or alter its flavor, texture and seasoning.
5. Garnishes should be cooked just until done; meat and poultry should be tender but not falling apart, vegetables should be firm but not mushy, and pasta and rice should maintain their identity. These types of garnishes are usually held on the side and added to the hot soup at the last minute to prevent overcooking.

Garnishing Suggestions

Some garnishes are used to add texture, as well as flavor and visual interest, to soups. Items such as crunchy croutons or oyster crackers, or crispy crumbled bacon on a cream soup, or diced meat in a clear broth soup add a textural variety that makes the final product more appealing.

▶ Clear soups—any combination of julienne cuts of the same meat, poultry, fish or vegetable that provides the dominant flavor in the stock or broth; vegetables (cut uniformly into any shape), pasta (flat, small tortellini or tiny ravioli), gnocchi, quenelles, barley, spaetzle, white or wild rice, croutons, crepes, tortillas or won tons.

▶ Cream soups, hot or cold—toasted slivered almonds, sour cream or crème fraîche, croutons, grated cheese or puff pastry fleurons; cream vegetable soups are usually garnished with slices or florets of the main ingredient.

▶ Purée soups—julienne cuts of poultry or ham, sliced sausage, croutons, grated cheese or bacon bits.

▶ Any soup—finely chopped fresh herbs, snipped chives, edible flowers, parsley or watercress.

SOUP SERVICE

Preparing Soups in Advance

Most soups can be made ahead of time and reheated as needed for service. To preserve freshness and quality, small batches of soup should be heated as needed throughout the meal service.

Clear soups are quite easy to reheat because there is little danger of scorching. If garnishes are already added to a clear soup, care should be taken not to overcook the garnishes when reheating the soup. All traces of fat should be removed from a consommé's surface before reheating.

Thick soups present more of a challenge. To increase shelf life and reduce the risk of spoilage, cool and refrigerate a thick soup when it is still a base (that is, before it is finished with milk or cream). Just before service, carefully reheat the soup base using a heavy-gauge pot over low heat. Stir often to prevent scorching. Then finish the soup (following the guidelines noted earlier) with boiling milk or cream, a light béchamel sauce or a liaison and adjust the seasonings. Always taste the soup after reheating and adjust the seasonings as needed.

A cream soup served in small glasses as a passed hors d'oeuvre.

Temperatures

The rule is simple: Serve hot soup hot and cold soup cold. Hot clear soups should be served near boiling; 210°F (99°C) is ideal. Hot cream soups should be served at slightly lower temperatures; 190°F–200°F (88°C–93°C) is acceptable. Cold soups should be served at a temperature of 41°F (5°C) or below, and are sometimes presented in special serving pieces surrounded by ice.

QUESTIONS
FOR DISCUSSION

1 What are the differences between a stock and a broth?

2 What are the differences between a beef consommé and a beef-based broth? How are they similar?

3 What are the differences between a cream soup and a purée soup? How are they similar?

4 Create a recipe for veal consommé.

5 Discuss several techniques for serving soup. What can be done to ensure that soups are served at the correct temperature?

6 Explain how and why soups are garnished. Why is it sometimes said that the noodles in a chicken noodle soup are actually a garnish?

7 Create a cream soup recipe using seasonal ingredients available in your local market. Discuss the changes required when adapting the recipe on page 243 for the chosen ingredient.

Terms to Know

clear soup	finish
thick soup	purée soup
broth	bisque
double	chowder
consommé	garnish
clearmeat	scorch
clarification	

CHICKEN AND SAUSAGE GUMBO

HERBSAINT BAR AND RESTAURANT, NEW ORLEANS, LA
Chef Donald Link

Gumbo, a thick, spicy stew, is traditional fare in the delta region of the American South. Gumbo is usually made with poultry, fish, shellfish or sausage and is thickened with dark roux. Okra or filé powder (ground sassafras leaves) may also be added for thickening. Filé powder is sometimes added at the time of service for additional flavor. Gumbo is traditionally served over white rice.

Yield: 5 qt. (4.8 lt)　　　　　　　　　　　　**Method:** Broth

Cayenne pepper	1 Tbsp.	15 ml
Paprika	1 Tbsp.	15 ml
White pepper	1 Tbsp.	15 ml
Black pepper	1 Tbsp.	15 ml
Chicken, boneless, skinless, cut in 1-in. (2.5-cm) pieces	4 lb.	1.9 kg
Salt	3 Tbsp.	45 ml
Flour	20 oz.	600 g
Vegetable oil	28 fl. oz.	840 ml
Onions, medium dice	2½ lb.	1.2 kg
Celery, medium dice	2½ lb.	1.2 kg
Green bell peppers, medium dice	1½ lb.	720 g
Garlic, chopped	2 Tbsp.	30 ml
Filé powder	2 Tbsp.	30 ml
Bay leaves	4	4
Chicken stock	4 qt.	3.8 lt
Andouille sausage, sliced, cut in half circles	2 lb.	960 g
Okra	1 lb.	480 g
Long-grain white rice, cooked	3 c.	710 ml
Green onion tops, sliced	1 pt.	480 ml

1. Combine the cayenne pepper, paprika, white pepper and black pepper. Season the chicken with 1 tablespoon (15 milliliters) salt and 1 tablespoon (15 milliliters) of the pepper mix. Dust the chicken with some of the flour. Pan-fry the chicken in 8 fluid ounces (240 milliliters) oil until well browned. Remove the chicken from the pan and reserve.

2. Strain the oil used to brown the chicken in order to remove burnt particles. Return the strained oil to the pan. Add 16 fluid ounces (480 milliliters) fresh vegetable oil. Over medium heat, add the remaining flour while stirring with a whisk to make a roux. Cook the roux very slowly over medium heat, stirring often, until it becomes a copper-brown color, approximately 45 minutes to 1 hour.

3. Add the onions, celery, bell peppers, garlic, filé powder, bay leaves and the remaining salt and pepper mix. Cook for 5 minutes. Add the stock and bring to a simmer. Skim the fat from the surface and cook for approximately 1½ hours, skimming occasionally.

4. When the strong roux flavor fades, add the reserved chicken and the andouille. Cook the gumbo for 1 more hour, skimming regularly.

5. Sauté the okra in the remaining 4 fluid ounces (120 milliliters) oil, drain and add to the gumbo. Adjust the seasonings with the salt, pepper, cayenne, filé powder, hot sauce or other seasonings as desired.

6. Serve each portion of gumbo with 1 to 2 tablespoons (15 to 30 milliliters) cooked rice and garnish with sliced green onion tops.

Approximate values per 8-fl.-oz. (240-ml) serving: **Calories** 750, **Total fat** 52 g, **Saturated fat** 11 g, **Cholesterol** 100 mg, **Sodium** 2240 mg, **Total carbohydrates** 36 g, **Protein** 35 g, **Vitamin A** 15%, **Vitamin C** 40%, **Iron** 20%

CHICKEN SOUP WITH MATZO BALLS

Yield: 8 qt. (7.6 lt)   **Method:** Broth

Chicken pieces	8–10 lb.	3.8 to 4.8 kg
Chicken stock	10 qt.	9.6 lt
Mirepoix	1 lb.	480 g
Sachet:		
Bay leaf	1	1
Dried thyme	½ tsp.	2 ml
Peppercorns, crushed	½ tsp.	2 ml
Parsley stems	10	10
Salt and pepper	TT	TT
Fresh parsley, chopped	as needed for garnish	
Matzo Balls (recipe follows)	as needed for garnish	

1. Simmer the chicken in the stock for 2 hours, skimming as necessary.
2. Add the mirepoix and sachet. Simmer for another hour.
3. Strain and degrease the broth. Adjust seasonings.
4. Bring to a boil at service time. Portion into heated bowls and garnish with chopped parsley and one or two Matzo Balls.

1. Simmering the matzo balls.

MATZO BALLS

Yield: 24 Balls

Eggs	4	4
Water	2 fl. oz.	60 ml
Chicken fat or butter, softened	2 oz.	60 g
Matzo meal	4 oz.	120 g
Salt and white pepper	TT	TT

1. Beat the eggs with the water. Stir in the fat or butter.
2. Add matzo meal, salt and white pepper. The batter should be as thick as mashed potatoes.
3. Chill for at least 1 hour.
4. Bring 2 quarts (2 liters) water to a gentle boil. Using a #70 portion scoop, shape the batter into balls. Carefully drop each ball into the hot water. Cover and simmer until fully cooked, approximately 30 minutes. Remove the matzo balls from the water and serve in hot chicken soup.

Approximate values per 6-fl.-oz. (180-ml) serving with 2 matzo balls: **Calories** 60, **Total fat** 3 g, **Saturated fat** 1 g, **Cholesterol** 25 mg, **Sodium** 800 mg, **Total carbohydrates** 3 g, **Protein** 6 g, **Claims**—low fat

2. The finished chicken soup with matzo balls.

FRENCH ONION SOUP

Yield: 4 qt. (3.8 lt)   **Method:** Broth

Yellow onions, sliced thin	10 lb.	4.8 kg
Clarified butter	8 fl. oz.	240 ml
Beef stock	4 qt.	3.8 lt
Chicken stock	4 qt.	3.8 lt
Fresh thyme	½ oz.	15 g
Salt and pepper	TT	TT
Sherry	8 fl. oz.	240 ml
Toasted French bread slices	as needed for garnish	
Gruyère cheese, grated	as needed for garnish	

1. Sauté the onions in the butter over low heat. Carefully caramelize them thoroughly without burning.
2. Deglaze the pan with 8 fluid ounces (240 milliliters) beef stock. Cook au sec. Repeat this process until the onions are a very dark, even brown.
3. Add the remaining beef stock and the chicken stock and thyme.
4. Bring to a simmer and cook 20 minutes to develop flavor. Adjust the seasonings and add the sherry.
5. Serve in warm bowls. Top each portion with a slice of toasted French bread and a thick layer of cheese. Place under the broiler or salamander until the cheese is melted and lightly browned.

Approximate values per 6-fl.-oz. (180-ml) serving: **Calories** 280, **Total fat** 12 g, **Saturated fat** 6 g, **Cholesterol** 25 mg, **Sodium** 1370 mg, **Total carbohydrates** 34 g, **Protein** 9 g, **Vitamin A** 25%, **Vitamin C** 20%

1. Caramelize the onions thoroughly.

2. Sprinkle grated cheese on top of each serving of soup.

3. The finished French Onion Soup.

SOUTHEAST ASIAN CONSOMMÉ WITH LEMONGRASS

CONNECTICUT CULINARY INSTITUTE, FARMINGTON, CT

Chef Jamie Roraback

Yield: 2 qt. (1.9 lt)　　　　　　　　**Method:** Consommé

Egg whites	6	6
Ground chicken, duck or lean pork	1 lb.	480 g
Mirepoix, medium dice	8 oz.	240 g
Fresh lime juice	1 Tbsp.	15 ml
White chicken, duck or pork stock, cold	2½ qt.	2.4 lt
Sachet:		
Bay leaf	1	1
Dried thyme	¼ tsp.	2 ml
Peppercorns, crushed	¼ tsp.	2 ml
Parsley stems	4	4
Star anise	2	2
Fresh ginger, chopped coarse	2 Tbsp.	30 ml
Lime zest	2 tsp.	10 ml
Lemongrass, chopped	3 Tbsp.	45 ml
Shiitake mushroom stems	3 Tbsp.	45 ml
Thai chile peppers, chopped	2	2
Cilantro stems	4	4
Soy sauce	TT	TT
Salt and white pepper	TT	TT
Sugar	TT	TT
Garnish:		
Rice noodles	8 oz.	240 g
Snow peas	4 oz.	120 g
Carrots, lozenge cut	4 oz.	120 g
Shiitake mushroom caps, thinly sliced	2 oz.	60 g
Fresh cilantro leaves	3 Tbsp.	45 ml
Fresh mint leaves, chiffonade	1 Tbsp.	15 ml
Fresh basil leaves, chiffonade	2 Tbsp.	30 ml

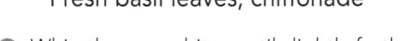

1. Whip the egg whites until slightly frothy.

2. Combine the egg whites, ground meat, mirepoix and lime juice in an appropriate stockpot and stir well.

3. Add the cold stock, mix well and add the sachet.

4. Bring the mixture to a simmer over moderate heat, stirring occasionally.

5. Break a hole in the center of the raft and allow the consommé to bubble through. Simmer until full flavor develops, approximately 1½ hours.

6. Strain the consommé through several layers of damp cheesecloth or a coffee filter, degrease and adjust the seasonings with soy sauce, salt, white pepper and sugar to taste.

7. Rehydrate the rice noodles in hot water, cool in an ice bath, drain and hold for service. Pull the strings from the snow peas, cut them on the bias, blanch, chill in an ice bath, drain and hold them for service. Blanch the carrots, chill in an ice bath and hold them for service.

8. For each serving, heat a small portion of noodles, snow peas, carrots and mushroom caps by immersing them in boiling water for a few seconds, then place them in soup bowls. Ladle the hot consommé over the vegetables and add fresh herbs to taste.

Approximate values per 8-fl.-oz. (240-ml) serving: **Calories** 130, **Total fat** 1 g, **Saturated fat** 0 g, **Cholesterol** 0 mg, **Sodium** 870 mg, **Total carbohydrates** 27 g, **Protein** 3 g, **Vitamin A** 70%, **Vitamin C** 15%, **Claims**—low fat; no saturated fat; no cholesterol; high in vitamin A; source of vitamin C

PHO BO (HANOI BEEF AND NOODLE SOUP)

Pho is the ubiquitous Vietnamese soup; it is widely eaten for breakfast and appears at meals throughout the day and into the evening. Beef (bo) is the most typical version, especially in the North. Each vendor has his or her own methods for flavoring and enriching the broth, but all allow customers to season and garnish their own bowls to taste with an assortment of chiles, fish sauces, fresh herbs and condiments. Pho is a perfect example of the Vietnamese belief that diners should be participants in preparing their food. Such rituals reinforce respect for the food and the friends with whom it is shared.

Yield: 1 qt. (960 ml)		**Method:** Broth
Oxtails or beef bones	4 lb.	1.9 kg
Water	as needed	as needed
Onion	1	1
Ginger, 3-in. (7.5-cm) piece	1	1
Salt	TT	TT
Fish sauce	3 fl. oz.	90 ml
Sachet:		
Star anise, whole	8	8
Cloves	5	5
Cinnamon stick	1	1
Bay leaves	3	3
Garnishes:		
Onions, sliced thin	as needed	as needed
Mung beans	as needed	as needed
Fresh herbs: mint, cilantro, basil	as needed	as needed
Lime wedges	as needed	as needed
Fish sauce	as needed	as needed
Fresh chiles, minced	as needed	as needed
Chile sauce	as needed	as needed
Rice vermicelli, cooked	1 lb.	480 g
Beef tenderloin, raw, sliced thin	6 oz.	180 g

1. Place the oxtails in a stockpot and add enough water to cover them by approximately 4 inches (10 centimeters). Bring it to a boil and then reduce to a simmer, skimming the surface as necessary.
2. Halve and char the onion for an onion brûlé. Split the ginger lengthwise and char its surface. Add the onion brûlé, charred ginger, salt, fish sauce and sachet to the stockpot.
3. Simmer the broth for 4 to 5 hours. Remove the sachet and strain the broth through a chinois. Adjust the seasonings and maintain the broth at a simmer.
4. Put the garnishes in bowls or trays and place them on each table.
5. Reheat the vermicelli by dropping them into boiling water for a few seconds. Divide the reheated vermicelli noodles into six large warm bowls. Place several pieces of raw beef tenderloin on top of each portion of vermicelli. Pour boiling hot broth over the meat into each bowl.
6. Serve the hot broth to the diners, allowing them to garnish their portions with onions, mung beans, herbs, lime wedges, fish sauce, chiles and chile sauce as desired. (The meat will cook when stirred into the hot broth.)

Approximate values per 8-fl.-oz. (240-ml) serving: **Calories** 360, **Total fat** 7 g, **Saturated fat** 3 g, **Cholesterol** 20 mg, **Sodium** 640 mg, **Total carbohydrates** 63 g, **Protein** 9 g

MINESTRONE

Minestrone is a rich vegetable soup of Italian heritage. Northern Italian versions are made with beef stock, butter, rice and ribbon-shaped pasta. Southern Italian versions, such as the one given here, contain tomatoes, garlic, olive oil and tube-shaped pasta. The vegetables should be fresh and varied. Substitute or change those listed as necessary to reflect the season.

Yield: 8 qt. (7.6 lt) **Method:** Broth

Dry white beans	1 lb.	480 g
Olive oil	2 Tbsp.	30 ml
Onions, diced	10 oz.	300 g
Garlic cloves, minced	2	2
Celery, diced	1 lb.	480 g
Carrots, diced	12 oz.	360 g
Zucchini, diced	1 lb.	480 g
Green beans, cut in ½-inch (1.2-cm) pieces	10 oz.	300 g
Cabbage, diced	1 lb.	480 g
Vegetable stock	5 qt.	4.8 lt
Tomato concassée	1 lb.	480 g
Tomato paste, low-sodium	12 oz.	360 g
Fresh oregano, chopped	1 Tbsp.	15 ml
Fresh basil, chopped	2 Tbsp.	30 ml
Fresh chervil, chopped	1 Tbsp.	15 ml
Fresh parsley, chopped	2 Tbsp.	30 ml
Salt and pepper	TT	TT
Elbow macaroni, cooked	4 oz.	120 g
Parmesan, grated	as needed for garnish	

1. Soak the beans in cold water overnight, then drain.
2. Cover the beans with water and simmer until tender, about 40 minutes. Reserve the beans.
3. Sauté the onions in the oil. Add the garlic, celery and carrots and cook for 3 minutes.
4. Add the zucchini, green beans and cabbage, one type at a time, cooking each briefly.
5. Add the stock, tomato concassée and tomato paste. Cover and simmer for 2½ to 3 hours.
6. Stir in the chopped herbs and season to taste with salt and pepper.
7. Add the drained beans and cooked macaroni.
8. Bring the soup to a simmer and simmer for 15 minutes. Serve in warm bowls, garnished with Parmesan.

Approximate values per 6-fl.-oz. (180-ml) serving: **Calories** 70, **Total fat** 1.5 g, **Saturated fat** 0 g, **Cholesterol** 1 mg, **Sodium** 530 mg, **Total carbohydrates** 10 g, **Protein** 3 g, **Vitamin A** 20%, **Vitamin C** 20%, **Claims**—low fat

POSOLE

NEWBURY COLLEGE, BROOKLINE, MA
Senior Instructor Scott Doughty

posole also known as hominy or samp; dried corn that has been soaked in hydrated lime or lye; posole (Sp. *pozole*) also refers to a stewlike soup made with pork and hominy served in Mexico and Central America; its name derives from the ancient Aztec *pozolli*, a corn beverage of the Aztecs and Mayans

Yield: 3 qt. (2.8 lt)   **Method:** Broth

Pork shoulder	3 lb.	1.4 kg
Chicken stock	1 qt.	960 ml
Hominy, canned	3½ lb.	1.6 kg
Onions, medium dice	1½ lb.	720 g
Garlic, chopped	1½ Tbsp.	23 ml
Fresh oregano, chopped	1½ tsp.	8 ml
Salt	1 tsp.	5 ml
Black pepper	¼ tsp.	2 ml
Cayenne pepper	¼ tsp.	2 ml
Chicken, 2½–3 lb. (1.2–1.4 kg)	1	1
Olive oil	as needed	as needed
Chilli powder	2 Tbsp.	30 ml
Canned diced tomatoes, drained	8 oz.	240 g
Anaheim chiles, medium dice	4 oz.	120 g
Fresh cilantro, chopped	½ oz.	15 g
Garnishes:		
Limes	2	2
Corn tortillas	6	6
Vegetable oil	as needed	as needed
Romaine lettuce, chiffonade	8 oz.	240 g
Cider vinegar	2 Tbsp.	30 ml
Onions, small dice	8 oz.	240 g

1 Trim the fat from the pork shoulder and cut the meat into medium dice. Place the meat in a heavy saucepot with the stock. Add more stock if necessary to just cover the meat. Bring to a simmer. Skim the scum from the surface.

2 Drain the hominy and soak it in cold water until needed.

3 After the pork has simmered for 2 minutes, add one-third of the onions, half of the garlic, and the oregano, salt, black pepper and cayenne pepper. Simmer for 1 hour.

4 Bone and skin the chicken. Cut the meat into medium dice and refrigerate until needed.

5 Sweat the remaining two-thirds of the onions in a sauté pan in a little oil until soft. Add the remaining garlic and cook an additional 2 minutes. Add the raw chicken and cook until it loses its raw look. Mix in the chilli powder, tomatoes, Anaheim chiles and drained hominy. Cook until the flavors have blended. Add the mixture to the pork in the saucepot.

6 Simmer until the chicken is cooked. Add the cilantro. Adjust the consistency of the posole with chicken stock, if necessary.

7 For service, cut the limes into wedges. Cut the tortillas in half, then cut them crosswise into thin strips and fry them in hot oil until crisp. Toss the romaine lettuce with the cider vinegar. Garnish each bowl with romaine lettuce, diced onions, fried tortilla strips and a lime wedge.

Approximate values per 8-fl.-oz. (240-ml) serving: **Calories** 550, **Total fat** 27 g, **Saturated fat** 8 g, **Cholesterol** 130 mg, **Sodium** 900 mg, **Total carbohydrates** 37 g, **Protein** 40 g, **Vitamin A** 30%, **Vitamin C** 7%, **Calcium** 10%, **Iron** 20%

CREAM OF TOMATO SOUP

THE SCHOOL OF CULINARY ARTS AT KENDALL COLLEGE, EVANSTON, IL

Chef Mike Artlip, CEC, CCE

Yield: 8 qt. (7.6 lt)　　　　**Method:** Cream

Mirepoix, small dice	2 lb. 8 oz.	1.2 kg
Olive oil	2 fl. oz.	60 ml
Whole butter	2 oz.	60 g
Tomato juice, canned	1 qt.	1 lt
Water	5 pt.	2.4 lt
Tomatoes, crushed, #10 can	1	1
Salt	2 Tbsp.	30 ml
Black pepper	2 tsp.	10 ml
Sachet:		
Parsley stems	½ oz.	15 g
Black peppercorns, crushed	10	10
Bay leaves	4	4
Fresh thyme	10 sprigs	10 sprigs
Worcestershire sauce	1 fl. oz.	30 ml
Fresh thyme, chopped	as needed	as needed
Heavy cream, scalded	24 fl. oz.	720 ml

1. Sweat the mirepoix in the oil and butter in a heavy saucepan without caramelizing.

2. Deglaze the pan with the tomato juice. Add the water, crushed tomatoes, salt, pepper and sachet. Bring to a boil, reduce to a low simmer and cook for 30 minutes.

3. Stir in the Worcestershire sauce and thyme. Continue simmering for 15 minutes.

4. Remove the sachet and purée the soup with an immersion blender until smooth. Strain the scalded cream through a china cap and add it to the soup. Simmer for 5 minutes; adjust the seasonings and serve.

Approximate values per 8-fl.-oz. (240-ml) serving: **Calories** 150, **Total fat** 12 g, **Saturated fat** 6 g, **Cholesterol** 35 mg, **Sodium** 680 mg, **Total carbohydrates** 12 g, **Protein** 3 g, **Vitamin A** 50%, **Vitamin C** 30%

CHEDDAR AND LEEK SOUP

Yield: 3 pt. (1.4 lt) **Method:** Cream

Whole butter	2 oz.	60 g
Mirepoix, chopped fine	8 oz.	240 g
Leeks, chopped fine	8 oz.	240 g
Flour	2 oz.	60 g
Chicken stock	1½ qt.	1.4 lt
Sachet:		
Bay leaf	1	1
Dried thyme	¼ tsp.	1 ml
Peppercorns, crushed	¼ tsp.	1 ml
Dry white wine or flat beer	4 fl. oz.	120 ml
Half-and-half	4 fl. oz.	120 ml
Cheddar cheese, grated	1 lb.	480 g
Salt	TT	TT
Cayenne pepper	TT	TT
Fresh parsley, chopped	as needed for garnish	
Croutons	as needed for garnish	

1. Sweat the mirepoix and leeks in the butter until tender.
2. Stir in the flour and cook to make a blond roux.
3. Stir in the stock. Add the sachet and bring to a boil, stirring frequently. Reduce the heat and simmer for 30 minutes, stirring occasionally.
4. Add the wine or beer, half-and-half and cheese. Simmer for 15 minutes, stirring occasionally.
5. Strain; adjust seasonings with salt and cayenne pepper. Thin with additional warm half-and-half, if necessary.
6. Serve in warm bowls, garnished with parsley and croutons.

Approximate values per 6-fl.-oz. (180-ml) serving: **Calories** 250, **Total fat** 18 g, **Saturated fat** 11 g, **Cholesterol** 55 mg, **Sodium** 730 mg, **Total carbohydrates** 8 g, **Protein** 14 g, **Vitamin A** 15%, **Calcium** 35%

MULLIGATAWNY SOUP

Chef Ken Morlino, CEC

Mulligatawny is a complex and substantial soup that combines chicken or lamb, apples and curry spices in a rich broth. Its name comes from the Anglicized version of the word for "pepper water" in Tamil, a dialect of south India. This soup is familiar to Britons, as it was developed during the British occupation of India from a vegetable-based sauce to which meat was added. Later the dish traveled back to England and to other British colonies, including Australia and parts of Africa.

Yield: 1 qt. (960 ml) **Method:** Cream

Unsalted butter	1 oz.	30 g
Mirepoix	12 oz.	360 g
Flour	2 Tbsp.	30 ml
Curry powder	2 tsp.	10 ml
Chicken stock	1 qt.	1 lt
Chicken meat, cooked, diced	3½ oz.	105 g
Green apple, diced	1 oz.	30 g
Mushroom, sliced	1 oz.	30 g
Milk, warm	4 fl. oz.	120 ml
Salt and white pepper	TT	TT
Fresh chives	as needed for garnish	

1. In a saucepot, heat the butter over medium heat; add the mirepoix and sauté for 5 minutes.
2. Add the flour and curry powder and cook to form a blond roux.
3. Add the stock. Bring to a simmer and cook for 15 minutes.
4. Add the chicken, apple and mushroom and cook for 15 more minutes.
5. Finish with the milk and season with salt and white pepper. Garnish with fresh chives.

Approximate values per 8-fl.-oz. (240-ml) serving: **Calories** 180, **Total fat** 10 g, **Saturated fat** 5 g, **Cholesterol** 35 mg, **Sodium** 740 mg, **Total carbohydrates** 14 g, **Protein** 8 g, **Vitamin A** 130%, **Vitamin C** 10%

POTATO CHOWDER
WITH NISQUALLY SMOKED SALMON

SOUTH PUGET SOUND COMMUNITY COLLEGE, OLYMPIA, WA

Chef William A. Wiklendt, M.Ed, CEC, CCE, AAC

Yield: 2½ qt. (2.4 lt) **Method:** Cream

Prosciutto ham, small dice	3 oz.	90 g
Onion, small dice	4 oz.	120 g
Yukon gold potatoes (or other waxy variety), medium dice	2 lb.	960 g
Chicken stock	3 pt.	1.4 lt
Roux	4 oz.	120 g
Dried dill	2 tsp.	10 ml
Dried thyme	1 tsp.	5 ml
Heavy cream	8 fl. oz.	240 ml
Nisqually smoked salmon (or other high-quality hot-smoked salmon), diced	6 oz.	180 g
Salt and pepper	TT	TT

1. Place the prosciutto in a heavy saucepot and sweat for 2 minutes. Add the onion and sauté until translucent.
2. Add the potatoes and sweat for 3 minutes. Add the stock and bring to a boil. Add the roux and simmer to thicken the soup.
3. When the potatoes are nearly tender, add the dill, thyme, cream and salmon. Gently stir to incorporate all of the flavors.
4. Simmer for 5 minutes. Do not overcook the potatoes. Adjust the seasonings and serve immediately.

VARIATION:

Nonfat, 1% or 2% milk may be substituted for the cream in the recipe to lower the fat content.

Approximate values per 6-fl.-oz. (180-ml) serving: **Calories** 270, **Total fat** 13 g, **Saturated fat** 7 g, **Cholesterol** 45 mg, **Sodium** 600 mg, **Total carbohydrates** 28 g, **Protein** 11 g, **Vitamin C** 20%

ROASTED POBLANO CHILE
AND CORN SOUP

CONNECTICUT CULINARY INSTITUTE, Farmington, CT

Chef Jamie Roraback

Yield: Approximately 4 qt. (3.8 lt.)   **Method:** Purée

Lime	1	1
Sour cream	1 pt.	480 ml
Poblano chiles	12	12
Vegetable oil	3 fl. oz.	90 ml
Fresh corn, with husks	8 ears	8 ears
Onions, medium dice	1 lb. 12 oz.	840 g
Carrots, medium dice	1 lb. 4 oz.	600 g
Garlic cloves, peeled	8	8
Chicken or vegetable stock	2 qt.	1.9 lt
Heavy cream	1 pt.	480 ml
Salt and pepper	TT	TT
Poblano chile, julienne	as needed for garnish	
Corn kernels, cooked	as needed for garnish	
Fried tortilla strips	as needed for garnish	

1. Squeeze the juice from the lime and combine it with the sour cream. Cover and refrigerate for at least 1 hour.

2. Rub the chiles with 1 fluid ounce (30 milliliters) vegetable oil and place on a sheet pan. Roast the chiles at 450°F (230°C) until well blistered, approximately 10 to 15 minutes. Remove them from the oven and cool. Peel the chiles, remove the seeds and veins, then coarsely chop them.

3. Roast the ears of corn in their husks at 450°F (230°C) for 10 to 15 minutes. Allow the ears to cool, then shuck them and cut the kernels from the cob.

4. Heat a sauté pan on the stove top until very hot. Toss the onions, carrots and garlic cloves in the remaining oil. Drop the vegetables into the hot pan and allow them to char. Stir occasionally to char them evenly. Transfer the charred vegetables to a heavy soup pot.

5. Add the roasted chiles and corn kernels to the pot. Add enough stock to cover the ingredients, then bring to a boil and reduce to a simmer. Simmer until the ingredients are tender, approximately 30 minutes. Purée the soup in a blender or food processor and strain if desired. Return the soup to the same pot, add the cream and reduce to the desired consistency. Season to taste with salt and pepper.

6. Serve the soup garnished with julienne of poblano chile, corn kernels, fried tortilla strips and the lime-flavored sour cream.

Approximate values per 8-fl.-oz. (240-ml) serving: **Calories** 430, **Total fat** 35 g, **Saturated fat** 18 g, **Cholesterol** 95 mg, **Sodium** 410 mg, **Total carbohydrates** 27 g, **Protein** 6 g, **Vitamin A** 250%, **Vitamin C** 15%, **Calcium** 10%, **Iron** 10%

ROASTED VEGETABLE SOUP

Yield: 2 qt. (1.9 lt)   **Method:** Purée

Onions, chopped coarse	1 lb.	480 g
Zucchini, chopped coarse	1 lb.	480 g
Yellow squash, chopped coarse	1 lb.	480 g
Red bell pepper, chopped coarse	6 oz.	180 g
Yellow bell pepper, chopped coarse	6 oz.	180 g
Green bell pepper, chopped coarse	6 oz.	180 g
Roma tomatoes, chopped coarse	8 oz.	240 g
Asparagus spears, chopped coarse	8 oz.	240 g
Olive oil	4 fl. oz.	120 ml
Salt	1 Tbsp.	15 ml
Black pepper	1 tsp.	5 ml
Dried thyme	1 tsp.	5 ml
Chicken stock	2 qt.	1.9 lt
Roasted garlic purée	2 oz.	60 g
Fresh parsley, chopped	as needed for garnish	
Baguette bread slices, toasted	as needed for garnish	

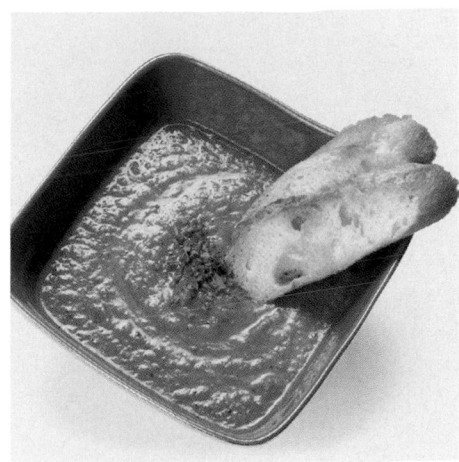

1 Combine the chopped vegetables with the oil, salt, pepper and thyme. Toss to coat the vegetables evenly with the oil and seasonings.

2 Spread the vegetables on a sheet pan and roast in a 450°F (230°C) oven until they are well browned.

3 Remove the vegetables from the oven and place them in a saucepot. Add the stock and roasted garlic purée. Bring to a boil, reduce to a simmer and cook until all of the vegetables are very tender, approximately 30 minutes.

4 Purée the soup in batches in a blender or food processor. Strain through a coarse china cap or pass through a food mill. Season to taste with salt and pepper.

5 Serve the soup garnished with chopped parsley and toasted baguette slices.

Approximate values per 8-fl.-oz. (240-ml) serving: **Calories** 210, **Total fat** 15 g, **Saturated fat** 2 g, **Cholesterol** 0 mg, **Sodium** 1570 mg, **Total carbohydrates** 19 g, **Protein** 5 g, **Vitamin A** 40%, **Vitamin C** 200%, **Iron** 10%

CALLALOO WITH CRAB

NEWBURY COLLEGE, BROOKLINE, MA

Senior Instructor Scott Doughty

Callaloo is a soup made throughout the Caribbean. Its name comes from the type of greens used to make the soup: callaloo or dasheen, the large edible leaves of the taro plant. Spinach, kale, Swiss chard or other related varieties of greens can be used to give this soup its green color, which is intensified when part or all of the broth is puréed. Called "pepperpot" in Jamaica, this soup is heavily seasoned with pepper and chiles. Ham hocks or bacon can be added as well as okra, which thickens the soup.

Yield: 2 qt. (1.9 lt)	Method: Purée	
Callaloo or spinach	1 lb.	480 g
Olive oil	1 fl. oz.	30 ml
Onions, small dice	1 lb.	480 g
Green onions, chopped fine	6 oz.	180 g
Garlic cloves, minced	2	2
Coconut milk	1 qt.	960 ml
Milk	1 pt.	480 ml
Fresh pumpkin, peeled, seeded, small dice	1 lb.	480 g
Salt	½ tsp.	2 ml
Black pepper	¼ tsp	1 ml
Crab meat	1 lb.	480 g

1. Wash the callaloo or spinach. Remove the stems and tough ribs and chop coarsely.
2. Heat the oil in a rondeau and sweat the diced onions. Add the green onions and garlic and sweat for 2 more minutes. Add the callaloo or spinach, coconut milk, milk, pumpkin, salt and pepper. Bring the soup to a boil and reduce to a simmer. Cook for 30 minutes.
3. Purée half of the soup in a blender, food processor or food mill. Return it to the pot with the remaining soup.
4. Pick over the crab meat to remove any bits of shell and add the meat to the soup. Adjust the seasonings and serve.

Approximate values per 8-fl.-oz. (240-ml) serving: **Calories** 410, **Total fat** 31 g, **Saturated fat** 23 g, **Cholesterol** 65 mg, **Sodium** 370 mg, **Total carbohydrates** 19 g, **Protein** 19 g, **Vitamin A** 50%, **Vitamin C** 70%, **Calcium** 30%, **Iron** 35%

ROASTED CORN CHOWDER

Yield: 1 qt. (960 ml)   **Method:** Purée

Corn, unshucked	10 ears	10 ears
Milk, warm	3 pt.	1.4 lt
Salt pork, small dice	4 oz.	120 g
Celery, small dice	5 oz.	150 g
Onions, small dice	10 oz.	300 g
Garlic cloves, minced	4	4
Flour	2 oz.	60 g
Chicken stock	1 qt.	960 ml
Potatoes, peeled, medium dice	12 oz.	360 g
Cream, warm	4 fl. oz.	120 ml
Worcestershire sauce	1 Tbsp.	15 ml
Fresh thyme	1 tsp.	5 ml
Nutmeg, ground	TT	TT
Salt and white pepper	TT	TT

1. Roast the ears of corn, in their husks, in a 400°F (200°C) oven for 45 minutes. Cool, shuck the corn and cut off the kernels. Purée half the corn kernels in a blender, adding a small amount of milk if necessary.
2. Render the salt pork. Add the celery, onions and garlic and sauté lightly.
3. Stir in the flour and cook to make a blond roux.
4. Add the stock and remaining milk and bring to a simmer.
5. Add the potatoes, the puréed corn and the remaining corn kernels. Simmer for 10 minutes.
6. Add the cream; adjust the seasonings with Worcestershire sauce, thyme, nutmeg, salt and white pepper and simmer for 5 minutes.
7. Serve in warm bowls.

Approximate values per 8-fl.-oz. (240-ml) serving: **Calories** 370, **Total fat** 21 g, **Saturated fat** 10 g, **Cholesterol** 55 mg, **Sodium** 520 mg, **Total carbohydrates** 38 g, **Protein** 13 g, **Vitamin A** 15%, **Vitamin C** 20%, **Calcium** 30%, **Claims**—good source of fiber, vitamin A, vitamin C, calcium

WILD MUSHROOM AND VEAL SOUP

Yield: Approximately 1 qt. (1 lt)   **Method:** Broth

Garlic, minced	2 tsp.	10 ml
Olive oil	2 fl. oz.	60 ml
Assorted wild mushrooms, such as shiitake, oyster, cèpes and morels	8 oz.	240 g
Brown veal stock	24 fl. oz.	720 ml
Fresh parsley, minced	2 Tbsp.	30 ml
Fresh mint, minced	4 Tbsp.	60 ml
Salt and pepper	TT	TT
French bread croutons	as needed for garnish	
Fresh parsley, chopped fine	as needed for garnish	

1. Briefly sauté the garlic in the oil. Add the mushrooms and cook until they are tender and any liquid given off has evaporated.
2. Add the stock, minced parsley and mint; simmer for 15 minutes. Season to taste.
3. Place one crouton in each soup bowl. Ladle in the soup and garnish with the finely chopped parsley.

Approximate values per 8-fl.-oz. (240-ml) serving: **Calories** 100, **Total fat** 7 g, **Saturated fat** 1 g, **Cholesterol** 0 mg, **Sodium** 460 mg, **Total carbohydrates** 8 g, **Protein** 3 g, **Vitamin A** 90%, **Vitamin C** 15%

HARVEST LOBSTER AND CORN CHOWDER

Yield: Approximately 48 fl. oz.　　　　　　　**Method:** Cream

Water	2 qt.	1.9 lt
White wine	8 fl. oz.	240 ml
Onions, chopped	8 oz.	240 g
Celery, chopped	4 oz.	120 g
Carrots, chopped	8 oz.	240 g
Garlic cloves	2	2
Clam juice	8 fl. oz.	240 ml
Lobster, 1 lb. (480 g)	1	1
Tomato paste	2 Tbsp.	30 ml
Black peppercorns	1 tsp.	5 ml
Bay leaf	1	1
Cognac	1 fl. oz.	30 ml
Whole butter	2 oz.	60 g
Red bell pepper, small dice	3 oz.	90 g
Onion, small dice	3 oz.	90 g
Garlic cloves, chopped	2	2
Flour	4 Tbsp.	60 ml
Fresh corn kernels	4 oz.	120 g
Heavy cream	12 fl. oz.	360 ml
Salt and pepper	TT	TT
Chives, sliced	1 Tbsp.	15 ml

1. Combine the water, wine, onions, celery, carrots, garlic and clam juice in a saucepot and bring to a boil. Add the lobster and cook for 8 minutes. Remove the lobster from the cooking liquid and remove the lobster meat from the shell.

2. Crush the shell and return it to the cooking liquid with the tomato paste, peppercorns, bay leaf and Cognac. Simmer the stock for 1 hour to extract as much flavor from the lobster shell and vegetables as possible.

3. Strain the stock through a china cap, pressing firmly with the back of a ladle to remove as much liquid as possible from the shells. This should yield approximately 24 fluid ounces (720 milliliters) liquid. Add more water should there be insufficient stock.

4. Heat the butter in a heavy saucepot. Sweat the bell pepper, onion and garlic for 1 minute. Add the flour to make a roux and cook for 5 minutes. Whisk in the stock, bring to a boil, reduce to a simmer and cook for 15 minutes.

5. Add the corn kernels. Scald the cream and add it to the soup. Bring the soup to a simmer and adjust the seasonings.

6. Dice the lobster meat and add it to the soup. Serve the soup garnished with chives.

Approximate values per 6-fl.-oz. (180-ml) serving: **Calories** 480, **Total fat** 31 g, **Saturated fat** 19 g, **Cholesterol** 155 mg, **Sodium** 450 mg, **Total carbohydrates** 29 g, **Protein** 20 g, **Vitamin A** 130%, **Vitamin C** 60%

CHILLED BEET AND BUTTERMILK SOUP

BISHOP'S RESTAURANT, Vancouver, BC

Yield: 4 Servings   **Method:** Purée

Beets, large	4	4
Red onion, sliced	1	1
Red wine vinegar	1 fl. oz.	30 ml
Sugar	1 oz.	30 g
Buttermilk	1 pt.	480 ml
Salt and pepper	TT	TT
Fresh chives, chopped	2 Tbsp.	30 ml
Sour cream or crème fraîche	1 fl. oz.	30 ml

1. In a medium saucepan, combine the beets, onion, vinegar and sugar with enough water to cover. Bring to a boil, reduce heat and simmer until tender, about 30 minutes. Strain, reserving the liquid for later use.
2. Purée the beets using a blender or food processor, adding enough of the reserved liquid to facilitate a smooth purée.
3. When cooled to room temperature, stir in the buttermilk and season to taste with salt and pepper. If the soup is too thick, dilute it with some of the reserved cooking liquid. Chill thoroughly.
4. Garnish with chopped chives and a quenelle of sour cream or crème fraîche.

Approximate values per 6-fl.-oz. (180-ml) serving: **Calories** 120, **Total fat** 3 g, **Saturated fat** 1.5 g, **Cholesterol** 7 mg, **Sodium** 170 mg, **Total carbohydrates** 19 g, **Protein** 5 g, **Vitamin C** 10%

CHILLED CHERRY SOUP

Yield: 4 qt. (3.8 lt)   **Method:** Purée

Cherries, pitted	5 lb.	2.4 kg
Apple juice	approx. 2 qt.	approx. 2 lt
Sachet:		
Cinnamon sticks	2	2
Cloves, whole	4	4
Honey	6 oz.	180 g
Cornstarch	1 oz.	30 g
Lemon juice	TT	TT
Dry champagne or sparkling wine	8 fl. oz.	240 ml
Crème fraîche	as needed for garnish	
Toasted sliced almonds	as needed for garnish	

1. Combine the cherries, apple juice, sachet and honey. Bring to a simmer and cook for 30 minutes. Remove the sachet.
2. Dilute the cornstarch with a small amount of cold apple juice. Add it to the soup for thickening. Simmer the soup for 10 minutes to cook out the starchy flavor.
3. Purée the soup in a food processor or blender and strain if desired; chill thoroughly.
4. At service, adjust the seasoning with lemon juice. Stir in chilled champagne or sparkling wine and serve garnished with crème fraîche and toasted sliced almonds.

Approximate values per 6-fl.-oz. serving: **Calories** 150, **Total fat** 0 g, **Saturated fat** 0 g, **Cholesterol** 0 mg, **Sodium** 0 mg, **Total carbohydrates** 34 g, **Protein** 1 g, **Vitamin C** 15%, **Claims**—fat free; no sodium; good source of fiber

CHAPTER TWELVE

PRINCIPLES OF MEAT COOKERY

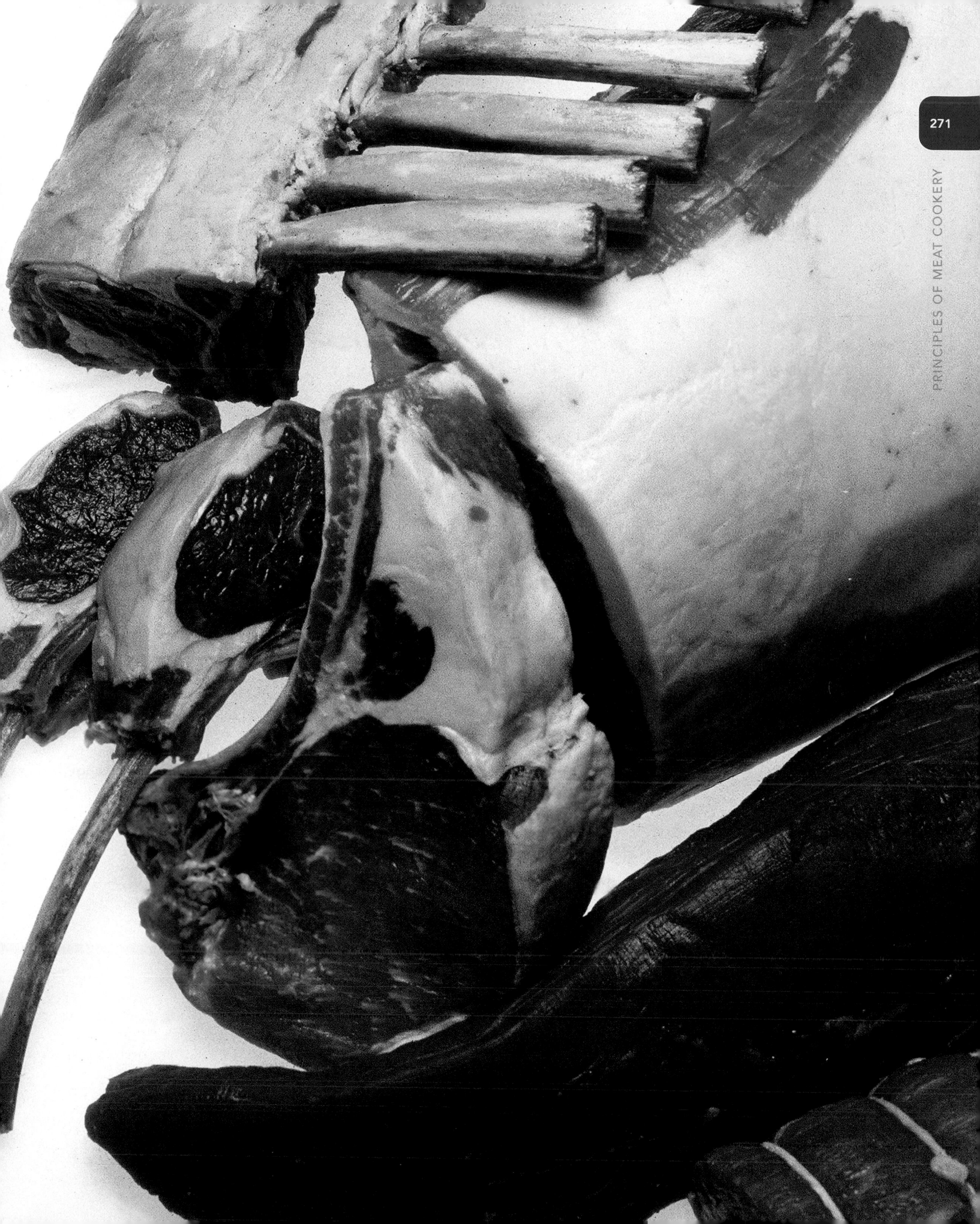

- understand the structure and composition of meats
- understand meat inspection and grading practices
- purchase meats appropriate for your needs
- store meats properly
- prepare meats for cooking
- apply various cooking methods to meats

MEATS—BEEF, VEAL, LAMB AND PORK—often consume the largest portion of a food purchasing dollar. In this chapter, we discuss how to protect that investment. Students will learn how to determine the quality of meat, how to purchase meat in the form that best suits their needs and how to store it. We also discuss several of the dry-heat, moist-heat and combination cooking methods introduced in Chapter 9, Principles of Cooking, and how they can best be used so that a finished meat item is appealing to both the eye and palate. Although each of the cooking methods is illustrated with a single beef, veal, lamb or pork recipe, the analysis is intended to apply to all meats.

In Chapters 13 through 16, students will learn about the specific cuts of beef, veal, lamb and pork typically used in food service operations, as well as some basic butchering procedures. Recipes using these cuts and applying the various cooking methods are included at the end of each of those chapters.

MUSCLE COMPOSITION

The carcasses of cattle, sheep, hogs and furred game animals consist mainly of edible lean muscular tissue, fat, connective tissue and bones. They are divided into large cuts called **primals**. Primal cuts are rarely cooked; rather, they are usually reduced to **subprimal cuts**, which in turn can be cooked as is or used to produce **fabricated cuts**. For example, the beef primal known as a short loin can be divided into subprimals, including the strip loin. The strip loin can be fabricated into other cuts, including New York steaks. The primals, subprimals and fabricated cuts of beef, veal, lamb and pork are discussed in Chapters 13 through 16, respectively; game is discussed in Chapter 18.

Muscle tissue gives meat its characteristic appearance; the amount of connective tissue determines the meat's tenderness. Muscle tissue is approximately 72 percent water, 20 percent protein, 7 percent fat and 1 percent minerals. (Meat shrinks during cooking as water evaporates and fats melt. Proper cooking helps prevent excessive **shrinkage**, which can cause the loss of finished weight and irregularly shaped meats after cooking.)

A single muscle is composed of many bundles of muscle cells or fibers held together by connective tissue. See Figures 12.1 and 12.2. The thickness of the cells, the size of the cell bundles and the connective tissues holding them together form the grain of the meat and determine the meat's texture. When the fiber bundles are small, the meat has a fine grain and texture. Grain also refers to the direction in which the muscle fibers travel. When an animal fattens, some of the water and proteins in the lean muscle tissue are replaced with fat, which appears as **marbling**. Marbling adds tenderness and flavor to meat and is a principal factor in determining meat quality.

Connective tissue forms the walls of the long muscle cells and binds them into bundles. It surrounds the muscle as a membrane and also appears as the tendons and ligaments that attach the muscles to the bone. Most connective tissue consists of either collagen or elastin. When cooked using moist heat, collagen contracts, then becomes more tender and breaks down into gelatin and water. Elastin, on the other hand, will not break down under normal cooking conditions. Because elastin remains stringy and tough, tendons and ligaments should be trimmed away before meat is cooked.

Connective tissue develops primarily in the frequently used muscles. Therefore, cuts of meat from the shoulder (also known as the chuck), which the animal uses constantly, tend to be tougher than those from the back (also known as the loin), which are used

primal cuts the primary divisions of muscle, bone and connective tissue produced by the initial butchering of the carcass

subprimal cuts the basic cuts produced from each primal

fabricated cuts individual portions cut from a subprimal

shrinkage the loss of weight in a food due to evaporation of liquid or melting of fat during cooking

marbling whitish streaks of inter- and intramuscular fat

subcutaneous fat also known as exterior fat; the fat layer between the hide and muscles

collagen a protein found in connective tissue; it is converted into gelatin when cooked with moisture

elastin a protein found in connective tissues, particularly ligaments and tendons; it often appears as the white or silver covering on meats known as silverskin

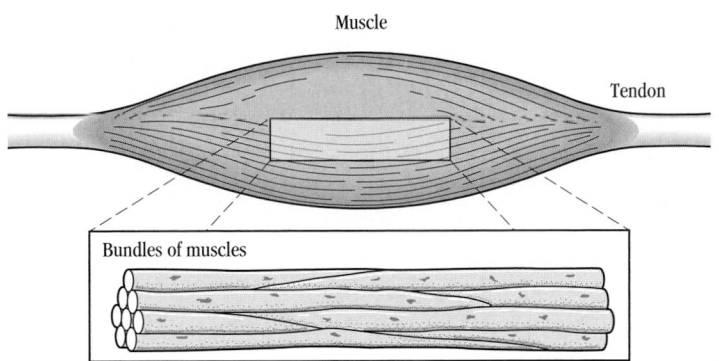

FIGURE 12.1 ▶ Muscle tissue.

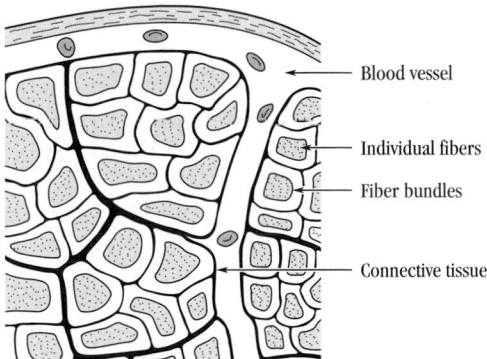

FIGURE 12.2 ▶ Crosscut of a bundle of muscle fibers.

less frequently. As an animal ages, the collagen present within the muscles becomes more resistant to breaking down through moist-heat cooking. Therefore, the meat of an older animal tends to be tougher than that of a younger one. Generally, the tougher the meat, the more flavorful it is, however.

The way that meat is fabricated also affects its tenderness. Cutting raw meat against the grain, pounding thinly sliced raw meat or grinding raw meat before cooking will tenderize tougher cuts. Butchering techniques have evolved to maximize the usability of primal cuts.

butcher to slaughter and/or dress or fabricate animals for consumption

dress to trim or otherwise prepare an animal carcass for consumption

fabricate to cut a larger portion of raw meat (for example, a primal or subprimal), poultry or fish into smaller portions

carve to cut cooked meat or poultry into portions

INSPECTION AND GRADING OF MEATS

Inspection

All meat produced for public consumption in the United States is subject to United States Department of Agriculture (USDA) inspection. Inspections ensure that products are processed under strict sanitary guidelines and are wholesome and fit for human consumption. Inspections do not indicate a meat's quality or tenderness, however. Whole carcasses of beef, pork, lamb and veal are labeled with a round stamp identifying the slaughterhouse. See Figure 12.3. The stamp shown in Figure 12.4 is used for fabricated or processed meats and is found on either the product or its packaging.

FIGURE 12.3 ▶ USDA inspection stamp for whole carcasses.

DOMESTICATION OF ANIMALS

Early humans were hunter-gatherers, dependent on what their immediate environment offered for food. As "opportunistic" meat eaters, they ate meat when they could obtain it.

Anthropologists believe that the cultivation of grains and the birth of agriculture, which took place sometime around 9000 B.C.E., led directly to the domestica-tion of animals. Sheep and goats were attracted to the fields of grain, and dogs and pigs to the garbage heaps of the new communities. Rather than allow these animals to interfere with food production, people tamed them, thus providing a steadier supply of meat. The first animals to be domesticated were most likely sheep, soon followed by goats. These an-imals—ruminants—can digest cellulose (humans cannot), so they could feed on stalks instead of valuable grains. Dogs and pigs, which prefer the same foods as humans, were tamed later, once there were more certain food supplies. Cattle were the most recently domesticated food animal, probably coming under control between 6100 and 5800 B.C.E.

FIGURE 12.4 ▶ USDA inspection stamp for fabricated or processed meats.

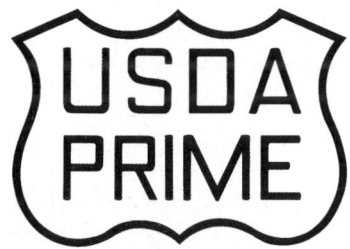

FIGURE 12.5 ▶ Quality grade stamp for USDA prime.

FIGURE 12.6 ▶ Quality grades of beef—no roll (top), Choice and Prime (bottom).

FIGURE 12.7 ▶ USDA yield grade stamp.

Grading

USDA grading provides a voluntary, uniform system by which producers, distributors and consumers can measure differences in the quality of meats and make price-quality comparisons. There are two parts to this grading system: quality grades and yield grades.

Quality grades, established in 1927, are a guide to the eating qualities of meat: its tenderness, juiciness and flavor. Based on an animal's age and the meat's color, texture and degree of marbling, the USDA quality grades are as follows:

▶ Beef—USDA Prime, Choice, Select, Standard, Commercial, Utility, Cutter and Canner
▶ Veal—USDA Prime, Choice, Good, Standard, Utility
▶ Lamb—USDA Prime, Choice, Good, Utility
▶ Pork—USDA No. 1, No. 2, No. 3, Utility

USDA Prime meats are produced in limited quantities for use in the finest restaurants, hotels and gourmet markets. They are well marbled and have thick coverings of firm fat. See Figure 12.5.

USDA Choice meat is the most commonly used grade in quality food service operations and retail markets. Choice meat is well marbled (but with less fat than Prime) and will produce a tender and juicy product.

Although lacking the flavor and tenderness of the higher grades, beef graded USDA Select or USDA Standard, and lamb and veal graded USDA Good, are also used in food service operations and retail outlets. The term "no roll" refers to beef that has not been grade-stamped (rolled) by a USDA inspector. Much of the beef sold in the United States, especially at retail, is no roll, but would have been USDA Select if graded. The lower grades of beef, lamb and veal are usually used for processed, ground or manufactured items such as meat patties or canned meat products. Figure 12.6 illustrates the three quality grades in a cut of beef.

Yield grades, established in 1965, measure the amount of usable meat (as opposed to fat and bones) on a carcass and provide a uniform method of identifying cuttability differences among carcasses. Yield grades apply only to beef and lamb and appear in a shield similar to that used for the quality grade stamp. The shields are numbered from 1 to 5, with number 1 representing the greatest yield and number 5 the smallest. See Figure 12.7. Beef and lamb can be graded for either quality or yield or both.

Grading is a voluntary program. Many processors, purveyors and retailers (especially pork and veal producers) develop and use their own labeling systems to provide quality assurance information. These private systems do not necessarily apply the USDA's standards. In fact, some pork inspection programs apply more stringent quality standards.

AGING MEATS

When animals are slaughtered, their muscles are soft and flabby. Within 6 to 24 hours, rigor mortis sets in, causing the muscles to contract and stiffen. Rigor mortis dissipates within 48 to 72 hours under refrigerated conditions. All meats should be allowed to rest, or age, long enough for rigor mortis to dissipate completely. Meats that have not been aged long enough for rigor mortis to dissipate, or that have been frozen during this period, are known as "green meats." They will be very tough and flavorless when cooked.

Typically, initial aging takes place while the meat is being transported from the slaughterhouse to the supplier or food service operation. As meat continues to rest, natural enzymes begin to break down the muscle into more tender meat. Beef and lamb are sometimes aged for longer periods to increase their tenderness and flavor characteristics. Pork is not aged further because its high fat content turns rancid easily, and veal does not have enough fat to protect it during an extended aging period.

Wet Aging

Today, most preportioned or precut meats are packaged and shipped in vacuum-sealed plastic packages (sometimes known generically by the manufacturer's trade name, Cryovac). Wet aging is the process of storing **vacuum-packaged** meats under refrigeration for up to 6 weeks. This allows the natural enzymes and microorganisms time to break down connective tissue, which tenderizes and flavors the meat. As this chemical process takes place, the meat develops an unpleasant odor that is released when the package is opened; the odor dissipates in a few minutes. Exercise great care when aging meats. Beef can be wet aged for the longest period; other meats must be consumed within a shorter time period. The shelf life for vacuum-sealed refrigerated pork is approximately 3 weeks.

Wet-Aged New York Strip

Dry Aging

Dry aging is the process of storing fresh meats in an environment of controlled temperature, humidity and air flow for up to 6 weeks. This allows enzymes and microorganisms to break down connective tissues. Dry aging is actually the beginning of the natural decomposition process. Dry-aged meats can lose from 5 to 20 percent of their weight through moisture evaporation. They can also develop mold, which adds flavor but must be trimmed off later. Moisture loss combined with additional trimming can substantially increase the cost of dry-aged meats. Dry-aged meats are prized for their rich beefy flavor, however. They are generally available only through smaller distributors and specialty butchers.

Dry-Aged Beef Short Loin

vacuum packaging a food preservation method in which fresh or cooked food is placed in an airtight container (usually plastic). Virtually all air is removed from the container through a vacuum process, and the container is then sealed.

PURCHASING AND STORING MEATS

Several factors determine the cuts of meat your food service operation should use:

1. Menu: The menu identifies the types of cooking methods used. If meats are to be broiled, grilled, roasted, sautéed or fried, more tender cuts should be used. If they are to be stewed or braised, flavorful cuts with more connective tissue can be used.
2. Menu price: Cost constraints may prevent an operation from using the best-quality meats available. Generally, the more tender the meat, the more expensive it is. But the most expensive cuts are not always the best choice for a particular cooking method. For example, a beef tenderloin is one of the most expensive cuts of beef. Although excellent grilled, it will not necessarily produce a better braised dish than the tougher, fattier brisket.
3. Quality: Often, several cuts or grades of meat can be used for a specific dish, so each food service operation should develop its own quality specifications.

Purchasing Meats

Once you have identified the cuts of meat your operation needs, you must determine the forms in which they will be bought. Meats are purchased in a variety of forms: as large as an entire carcass that must be further fabricated or as small as an individual cut (known as **portion control** or **P.C.**) ready to cook and serve. You should consider the following when deciding how to purchase meats:

1. Employee skills: Do your employees have the skills necessary to reduce large pieces of meat to the desired cuts?
2. Menu: Can you use the variety of bones, meat and trimmings that result from fabricating large cuts into individual portions?
3. Storage: Do you have ample refrigeration and freezer space so that you can be flexible in the way you purchase your meats?
4. Cost: Considering labor costs and trim usage, is it more economical to buy larger cuts of meat or P.C. units?

NO, IT DOESN'T GLOW

Fresh and frozen beef, lamb, pork and poultry can be irradiated in order to control the presence of microorganisms, such as *E. coli* and *Salmonella*, which can cause foodborne illnesses. Although the permitted dose of ionizing radiation kills significant numbers of insects, pathogenic bacteria and parasites on and in the meat, it does not make food radioactive or compromise the food's nutritional values. Nor does radiation noticeably alter a food's flavor, texture or appearance.

The Food and Drug Administration (FDA) requires that any packaged food subjected to radiation for preservation be labeled "treated with radiation" or "treated by irradiation" and display the radura symbol shown here.

freezer burn the surface dehydration and discoloration of food that results from moisture loss at below-freezing temperatures

IMPS/NAMP

The USDA publishes Institutional Meat Purchasing Specifications (IMPS) describing products customarily purchased in the food service industry. IMPS identifications are illustrated and described in *The Meat Buyers Guide*, published by the National Association of Meat Purveyors (NAMP). The IMPS/NAMP system is a widely accepted and useful tool in preventing miscommunications between purchasers and purveyors. Meats are indexed by a numerical system: Beef cuts are designated by the 100 series, lamb by the 200 series, veal by the 300 series, pork by the 400 series, and portion cuts by the 1000 series. Commonly used cuts of beef, veal, lamb and pork and their IMPS numbers, as well as applicable cooking methods and serving suggestions, are discussed in Chapters 13 through 16.

Storing Meats

Meat products are highly perishable and potentially hazardous foods, so temperature control is the most important thing to remember when storing meats. Fresh meats should be stored at temperatures between 30°F and 35°F (−1°C and 2°C). Vacuum-packed meats should be left in their packaging until they are needed. Under proper refrigeration, vacuum-packed meats with unbroken seals have a shelf life of 3 to 4 weeks. If the seal is broken, shelf life is reduced to only a few days. Ground meats have a shorter shelf life than whole-muscle meats and should be consumed within 1 or 2 days. Meats that are not vacuum packed should be wrapped tightly in air-permeable paper. Do not wrap meats tightly in plastic wrap, as this creates a good breeding ground for bacteria and will significantly shorten a meat's shelf life. Store meats on trays and away from other foods to prevent cross-contamination.

When freezing meats, the faster the better. Slow freezing produces large ice crystals that tend to rupture the muscle tissues, allowing water and nutrients to drip out when the meat is thawed (Figure 12.8). Most commercially packaged meats are frozen by blast freezing, which quickly cools by blasting −40°F (−40°C) air across the meat. Most food service facilities, however, use a slower and more conventional method known as still-air freezing. Still-air freezing is the common practice of placing meat in a standard freezer at about 0°F (−18°C) until it is frozen.

The ideal temperature for maintaining frozen meat is −50°F (−45°C). Frozen meat should not be maintained at any temperature warmer than 0°F (−18°C). Moisture- and vaporproof packaging will help prevent **freezer burn**. The length of frozen storage life varies with the species and type of meat. As a general rule, properly handled meats can be frozen for 6 months. Frozen meats should be thawed at refrigerator temperatures, not at room temperature or in warm water.

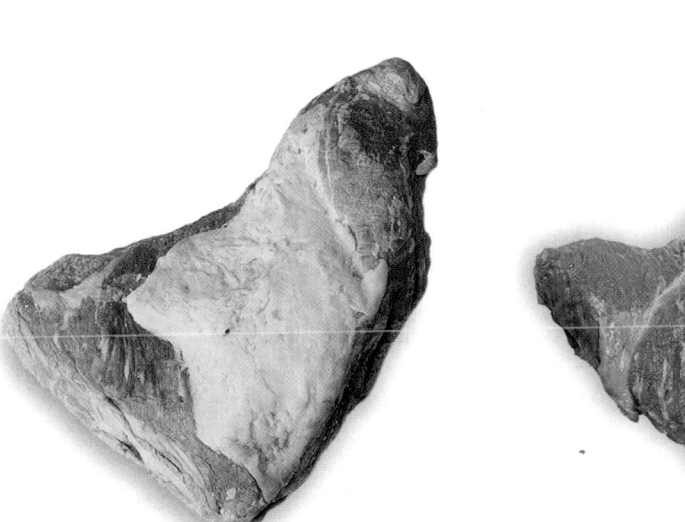

FIGURE 12.8 ▶ Meat damaged by freezer burn—freezer burned Bottom Sirloin Butt Tri Tip (left) and fresh Bottom Sirloin Butt Tri Tip (right).

MEAT LABELING: GRASS-FED

Most meat animals consume grains for some part of their lives. Even cattle, which may graze on grassland, are finished on grains for four to eight months before slaughter. The Agricultural Marketing Service of the USDA has published voluntary standards for the labeling of purely grass-fed meat. The standards state that grass and forage shall be the only feed source consumed for the lifetime of the animal except for the milk consumed prior to weaning. *Free-range*, *range-fed*, *pastured* and *pasture-raised* are some of the terms used to describe meat raised without grain-based feeds, but none of these terms are regulated. Meat from grass-fed ruminants is high in the powerful antioxidant conjugated linoleic acid, identified as a cancer preventative. Advocates for consuming grass-fed livestock also cite the environmental impact of feedlot farming as a reason to select grass-fed meat.

PREPARING MEATS

Certain procedures are often applied to meats before cooking to add flavor and/or moisture. These include marinating and rubs, discussed in Chapter 8, Mise en Place. (Marinades made with an acid, which helps break down collagen, also help tenderize meats before cooking. Trussing, barding and larding are described here.)

Loin of veal tied for roasting.

Tying and Trussing

Some meats, especially roasts and whole birds, require tying or trussing before cooking. Tying larger roasts with butcher's twine holds loose pieces of meat together during cooking and ensures that the meat retains its shape. Poultry is often trussed to protect the more delicate white breast meat during cooking. Trussing techniques are discussed along with specific cuts and types of meat in Chapters 13 through 17.

Barding

Barding is the process of covering the surface of meat or poultry with thin slices of pork fatback and tying them in place with butcher's twine. Barded meat or poultry is usually roasted. As the item cooks, the fatback continuously bastes it, adding flavor and moisture. A drawback to barding is that the fatback prevents the meat or poultry from developing the crusty exterior associated with roasting.

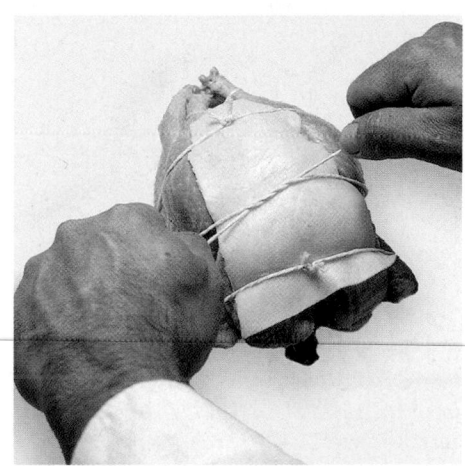

Barding a pheasant.

Larding

Larding is the process of inserting small strips of pork fat into meat with a larding needle. Larded meat is usually cooked by braising. During cooking, the added fat contributes moisture and flavor. Although once popular, larding is rarely used today because advances in selective breeding produce consistently tender, well-marbled meat.

APPLYING VARIOUS COOKING METHODS

In Chapter 9, Principles of Cooking, you learned the basic techniques for broiling, grilling, roasting, sautéing, pan-frying, deep-frying, poaching, simmering, braising and stewing. In Chapters 13 through 16, you will learn more about applying these cooking methods to beef, veal, lamb and pork. Here we apply these methods to meat cookery in general.

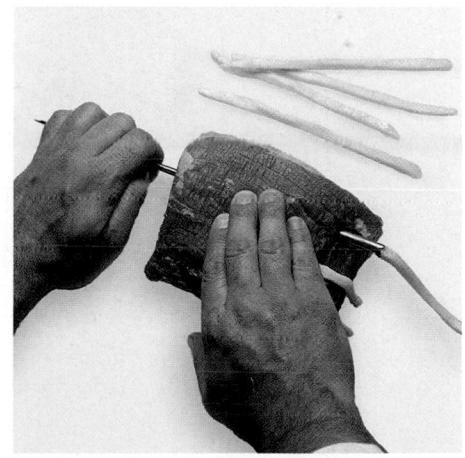

Larding meat.

COOKING GRAIN VS. GRASS-FED MEAT

Most domestic cattle, sheep and hogs are grain fed, resulting in meat with a milder flavor and higher fat content than their grass-fed counterparts. The meat from grass-fed animals tends to be leaner, requiring less cooking time. When broiled or grilled, grass-fed beef is best served cooked rare to medium rare because longer cooking would toughen and dry out the meat. When cooking meat from grass-fed animals, brush it with oil to prevent it from sticking to the pan or grill. Marinating will tenderize leaner cuts before dry-heat cooking. Select appropriate cooking methods for grass-fed meats, which may be best suited to moist-heat cooking methods.

Dry-Heat Cooking Methods

Dry-heat cooking methods subject food directly to the heat of a flame (broiling and grilling), hot air (roasting) or heated fat (sautéing and pan-frying). These cooking methods firm proteins without breaking down connective tissue. They are not recommended for tougher cuts or those high in connective tissue.

BROILING AND GRILLING

The broiling or grilling process adds flavor; additional flavors are derived from the seasonings. The broiler or grill should brown the meat, keeping the interior juicy. The grill should leave appetizing crosshatch marks on the meat's surface. To serve a good-quality broiled or grilled product, start with good-quality meat.

Selecting Meats to Broil or Grill

Only the most tender cuts should be broiled or grilled because direct heat does not tenderize. Fat adds flavor as the meat cooks, so the meat should be well marbled. Some external fat is also beneficial. Too much fat, however, will cause the broiler or grill to flare up, burning or discoloring the meat and adding objectionable flavors. Connective tissue toughens when meat is broiled or grilled, so trim away as much of it as possible.

Seasoning Meats to Be Broiled or Grilled

Meats that have not been marinated should be well seasoned with salt and pepper just before being placed on the broiler or grill. If they are preseasoned and allowed to rest, the salt will dissolve and draw out moisture, making it difficult to brown the meat properly. Some chefs feel so strongly about this that they season broiled or grilled meats only after they are cooked. Pork and veal, which have a tendency to dry out when cooked, should be basted with seasoned butter or oil during cooking to help keep them moist. (Some cuts of pork benefit from a light brining before cooking, discussed in Chapter 16, Pork.) Meats can be glazed or basted with barbecue sauce as they cook.

Cooking Temperatures

Red meats should be cooked at sufficiently high temperatures to caramelize their surface, making them more attractive and flavorful. At the same time, the broiler or grill cannot be too hot, or the meat's exterior will burn before the interior is cooked.

Because veal and pork are normally cooked to higher internal temperatures than beef and lamb, they should be cooked at slightly lower temperatures so that their exteriors are not overcooked when their interiors are cooked properly. The exterior of white meats should be a deep golden color when finished.

Degrees of Doneness

Consumers request and expect meats to be properly cooked to specific degrees of doneness. It is the chef's responsibility to understand and comply with these requests. Meats can be cooked very rare (or bleu), rare, medium rare, medium, medium well or well done. Figure 12.9 shows the proper color for some of these degrees of doneness. Use this guide for red meats cooked by any method.

Larger cuts of meat, such as a châteaubriand or thick chops, are often started on the broiler or grill to develop color and flavor and then finished to temperature in the oven to ensure complete, even cooking.

Determining Doneness

Broiling or grilling meat to the proper degree of doneness is an art. Larger pieces of meat will take longer to cook than smaller ones, but how quickly a piece of meat cooks is determined by many other

FIGURE 12.9 ▶ Degrees of doneness: Meat cooked rare, medium rare, medium, and medium well.

TABLE 12.1	DETERMINING DONENESS OF BROILED AND GRILLED ITEMS		
DEGREES OF DONENESS	**COLOR**	**DEGREE OF RESISTANCE**	**IDEAL TEMPERATURE**
Very rare (bleu)	Very red and raw-looking center (the center is cool to the touch)	Almost no resistance	115°F–120°F 46°C–49°C
Rare	Large deep-red center	Spongy; very slight resistance	125°F–130°F 52°C–54°C
Medium rare	Bright red center	Some resistance, slightly springy	130°F–140°F 54°C–60°C
Medium	Rosy pink to red center	Slightly firm; springy	140°F–150°F 60°C–66°C
Medium well	Very little pink at the center, almost brown throughout	Firm; springy	155°F–165°F 68°C–74°C
Well done	No red	Quite firm; springs back quickly when pressed	Not recommended

factors: the temperature of the broiler or grill, the temperature of the piece of meat when placed on the broiler or grill, the type of meat and the thickness of the cut. Because of these variables, timing alone is not a useful tool in determining doneness.

The most reliable method of determining doneness of a small piece of meat is by pressing the piece of meat with a finger and gauging the amount of resistance it yields. Very rare (bleu) meat will offer almost no resistance and feel almost the same as raw meat. Meat cooked rare will feel spongy and offer slight resistance to pressure. Meat cooked medium will feel slightly firm and springy to the touch. Meat cooked well done will feel quite firm and spring back quickly when pressed. See Table 12.1.

Accompaniments to Broiled and Grilled Meats

Because a broiler or grill cannot be deglazed to form the base for a sauce, compound butters or sauces such as béarnaise are often served with broiled or grilled meats. Brown sauces such as bordelaise, chasseur, périgueux or brown mushroom sauce also complement many broiled or grilled items. Additional sauce suggestions are found in Table 10.5.

PROCEDURE FOR BROILING OR GRILLING MEATS

1. Heat the broiler or grill.
2. Use a wire brush to remove any charred or burnt particles that may be stuck to the broiler or grill grate. The grate can be wiped with a lightly oiled towel to remove any remaining particles and to help season it.
3. Prepare the item to be broiled or grilled by trimming off any excess fat and connective tissue and marinating or seasoning it as desired. The meat may be brushed lightly with oil to help protect it and keep it from sticking to the grate.
4. Place the item in the broiler or on the grill. Following the example in Chapter 9, turn the meat 90 degrees to produce the attractive crosshatch marks associated with grilling. Use tongs to turn or flip the meat without piercing the surface (this prevents valuable juices from escaping).
5. Cook the meat to the desired doneness while developing the proper surface color. To do so, adjust the position of the meat on the broiler or grill, or adjust the distance between the grate and heat source.

SAFETY ALERT
Serving Meat

The Food Safety and Inspection Service of the USDA recommends the following as safe internal temperatures for serving various meats. Note that these temperatures are approximately 10–15°F (5–8°C) higher than the temperatures generally preferred by chefs and diners. Most diners would find the USDA's recommended 160°F unacceptably overcooked for a "medium" steak. Each chef or meat cook must decide for themselves whether it is more important to their clientele to cook meat to the USDA's safety standards or to diners' requests.

Fresh Beef, Veal and Lamb
Rare	not recommended
Medium rare	145°F (63°C)
Medium	160°F (71°C)
Well done	170°F (77°C)

Fresh Pork
Rare	not recommended
Medium rare	not recommended
Medium	160°F (71°C)
Well done	170°F (77°C)

Ground Meat and Meat Mixtures
Beef, veal, lamb and pork	160°F (71°C) or higher

GRILLED LAMB CHOPS WITH HERB BUTTER

Yield: 2 Servings		**Method:** Grilling
Lamb chops, loin or rib, approx. 1 in. (2.5 cm) thick	6	6
Oil	as needed	as needed
Salt and pepper	TT	TT
Herb butter	6 thin slices or 6 small rosettes	

1. Preheat the grill for 15 minutes.
2. Brush the lamb chops with oil; season with salt and pepper.
3. Place the lamb chops on the grill, turning as necessary to produce the proper crosshatching. Cook to the desired doneness.
4. Remove the lamb chops from the grill and place a slice or rosette of herb butter on each chop.
5. Serve immediately as the herb butter melts. The plate can be placed under the broiler for a few seconds to help melt the herb butter.

Approximate values per 6½-oz. (195-g) serving: **Calories** 623, **Total fat** 50 g, **Saturated fat** 27 g, **Cholesterol** 224 mg, **Sodium** 1186 mg, **Total carbohydrates** 0 g, **Protein** 42 g, **Vitamin A** 40%

1. Brushing the lamb chops with oil.

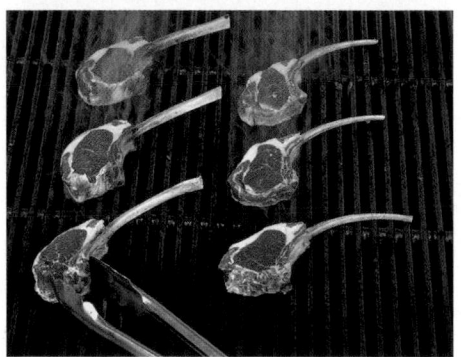

2. Placing the lamb chops on the grill.

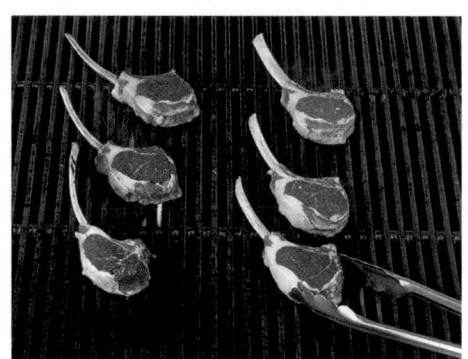

3. Rotating the lamb chops 90 degrees to create crosshatch marks.

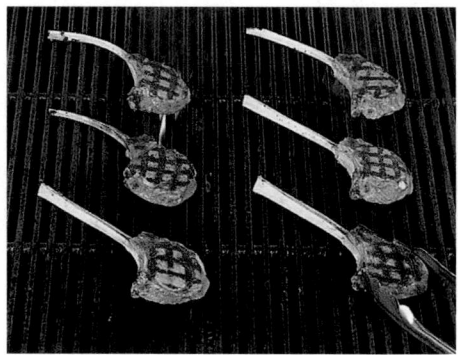

4. Turning the chops over to finish them on the other side.

ROASTING

Properly roasted meats should be tender, juicy and evenly cooked to the appropriate degree of doneness. They should have a pleasant appearance when whole as well as when sliced and plated.

Selecting Meats to Roast

Because roasting is a dry-heat cooking method and will not tenderize the finished product, meats that are to be roasted should be tender and well marbled. They are usually cut from the rib, loin or leg sections.

Seasoning Meats to Be Roasted

Seasonings are especially important with smaller roasts and roasts with little or no fat covering. With these roasts, some of the seasonings penetrate the meat while the remainder help create the highly seasoned crust associated with a good roast. A large roast with heavy fat covering (for example, a steamship round or prime rib) does not benefit from being seasoned on the surface because the seasonings will not penetrate the fat layer, which is trimmed away before service.

When practical, a roast with excess fat should be trimmed, leaving just a thin fat layer so that the roast bastes itself while cooking. A lean roast can be barded or larded before cooking to add richness and moisture. Lamb legs are sometimes studded with garlic cloves by piercing the meat with a paring knife and then pressing slivers of raw garlic into the holes.

A roast is sometimes cooked on a bed of mirepoix, or mirepoix is added to the roasting pan as the roast cooks. The mirepoix raises the roast off the bottom of the roasting pan, preventing the bottom from overcooking. This mirepoix, however, does not add any flavor to the roast. Rather, it combines with the drippings to add flavor to the jus, sauce or gravy that is made with them.

Cooking Temperatures

Small roasts such as a rack of lamb or a beef tenderloin should be cooked at high temperatures, 375°F–450°F (191°C–232°C) so that they develop good color during their short cooking times.

Traditionally, large roasts were started at high temperatures to sear the meat and seal in the juices; they were then finished at lower temperatures. Studies have shown, however, that searing does not seal in juices and that roasts cooked at constant, low temperatures provide a better yield with less shrinkage than roasts that have been seared. Temperatures between 275°F and 325°F (135°C and 163°C) are ideal for large roasts. These temperatures will produce a large, evenly cooked pink center portion.

Determining Doneness

The doneness of small roasts such as a rack of lamb is determined in much the same way as broiled or grilled meats. With experience, the chef develops a sense of timing as well as a feel for gauging the amount of resistance by touching the meat. These techniques, however, are not infallible, especially with large roasts.

Although timing is useful as a general guide for determining doneness, there are too many variables for it to be relied on exclusively. With this caution in mind, Table 12.2 lists general cooking times for roasted meats.

The best way to determine the doneness of a large roast is to use an instant-read thermometer, as shown in Figure 12.10. The thermometer is inserted into the center or thickest part of the roast and away from any bones. The proper finished temperatures for roasted meats are listed in Table 12.2.

Carryover Cooking and Resting

Cooking does not stop the moment a roast is removed from the oven. Through conduction, the heat applied to the outside of the roast continues to penetrate, cooking the center for several more minutes. Indeed, the internal temperature of a small roast can rise by as much as 5–10°F (3–6°C) after being removed from the oven. With a larger roast, such as a 50-pound steamship round, it can rise by as much as 20°F (7°C). Therefore, remove roasted meats before they reach the desired degree of doneness, and allow carryover cooking to complete the cooking process. The temperatures listed in Table 12.2 are internal temperatures after allowing for **carryover cooking**.

SAFETY ALERT
Grill Flare-Ups

Fat dripping onto a grill can cause flames to flare up and burn foods. Prevent flames by trimming excess fat from foods before cooking. Control the flame by moving the food to another section of the grill. The fat should burn off the coals within a few seconds. Should the flare-up become uncontrollable, suppress the flame with a lid or sheet tray.

carryover cooking the cooking that occurs after a food is removed from a heat source; it is accomplished by the residual heat remaining in the food

TABLE 12.2	DETERMINING DONENESS OF ROASTS	
DEGREE OF DONENESS	**IDEAL INTERNAL TEMPERATURE AFTER CARRYOVER**	**MINUTES PER POUND***
Very rare	125°F–130°F 52°C–54°C	12–15
Rare	130°F–140°F 54°C–60°C	15–18
Medium	140°F–150°F 60°C–66°C	18–20
Well done	150°F–165°F 66°C–74°C	20–25

*Assumes meat was at room temperature before roasting and cooked at a constant 325°F (163°C).

FIGURE 12.10 ▶ Proper placement of an instant-read thermometer.

As meat cooks, its juices flow toward the center. If the roast is carved immediately after it is removed from the oven, its juices will run from the meat, causing it to lose its color and become dry. Letting the meat rest before slicing allows the juices to redistribute themselves evenly throughout the roast so that the roast will retain more juices when carved. Small roasts, such as a rack of lamb, need to rest only 5 to 10 minutes; larger roasts such as a steamship round of beef require as much as an hour.

Accompaniments to Roasted Meats

Roasts may be served with a sauce based on their natural juices (called *au jus*), as described in the recipe for Roast Prime Rib of Beef au Jus (recipe follows) or with a pan gravy made with drippings from the roast. Additional sauce suggestions are found in Table 10.5.

PROCEDURE FOR **ROASTING MEATS**

1. Trim excess fat, tendons and silverskin from the meat. Leave only a thin fat covering, if possible, so that the roast bastes itself as it cooks.
2. Season the roast as appropriate and place it in a roasting pan. The roast may be placed on a bed of mirepoix or on a rack.
3. Roast the meat, uncovered, at the desired temperature (the larger the roast, the lower the temperature), usually 275°F–425°F (135°C–220°C).
4. If au jus or pan gravy is desired and a mirepoix was not added at the start of cooking, it may be added 30 to 45 minutes before the roast is done, thus allowing it to caramelize while the roast finishes cooking.
5. Cook to the desired temperature.
6. Remove the roast from the oven, allowing carryover cooking to raise the internal temperature to the desired degree of doneness. Allow the roast to rest before slicing or carving it. As the roast rests, prepare the jus, sauce or pan gravy.

ROAST PRIME RIB OF BEEF AU JUS

MISE EN PLACE

▶ Peel and chop garlic.
▶ Peel and chop onions, carrots and celery for mirepoix.

Yield: 18 Boneless Servings, 8 oz. (240 g) each   **Method:** Roasting

Oven-ready rib roast, IMPS #109, approx. 16 lb. (7.6 kg)	1	1
Salt and pepper	TT	TT
Garlic, chopped	4 oz.	120 g
Mirepoix	1 lb.	480 g
Brown stock	2 qt.	1.9 lt

1. Pull back the netting, fold back the fat cap and season the roast well with the salt, pepper and garlic. Replace the fat cap and netting; place the roast in an appropriate-sized roasting pan. Roast at 300°F–325°F (150°C–160°C).
2. Add the mirepoix to the pan approximately 45 minutes before the roast is finished cooking. Continue cooking until the internal temperature reaches 125°F (52°C), approximately 3 to 4 hours. Carryover cooking will raise the internal temperature of the roast to approximately 138°F (59°C).
3. Remove the roast from the pan and allow it to rest in a warm place for 30 minutes.
4. Drain the excess fat from the roasting pan, reserving the mirepoix and any drippings in the roasting pan.

⑤ Caramelize the mirepoix on the stove top; allow the liquids to evaporate, leaving only brown drippings in the pan.

⑥ Deglaze the pan with the stock. Stir to loosen all the drippings.

⑦ Simmer the jus, reducing it slightly and allowing the mirepoix to release its flavor; season with salt and pepper if necessary.

⑧ Strain the jus through a china cap lined with cheesecloth. Skim any remaining fat from the surface with a ladle.

⑨ Remove the netting from the roast. Trim and slice the roast as described on page 284 and serve with approximately 1 to 2 ounces (30 to 60 milliliters) jus per person.

Approximate values per 8-oz. (240-g) serving: **Calories** 951, **Total fat** 79 g, **Saturated fat** 32 g, **Cholesterol** 214 mg, **Sodium** 278 mg, **Total carbohydrates** 1 g, **Protein** 56 g, **Iron** 40%

① Draining off the excess fat.

② Caramelizing the mirepoix.

③ Deglazing the pan with brown stock.

④ Simmering the jus, reducing it slightly and allowing the mirepoix to release its flavors.

⑤ Straining the jus through a china cap and cheesecloth.

Carving Roasts

All the efforts that went into selecting and cooking a perfect roast will be wasted if the roast is not carved properly. Roasts are always carved against the grain; carving with the grain produces long stringy, tough slices. Cutting across the muscle fibers produces a more attractive and tender portion. Portions may be cut in a single thick slice, as with Roast Prime Rib of Beef, or in many thin slices. The following photographs illustrate several different carving procedures.

Carving pork tenderloin against the grain.

PROCEDURE FOR **CARVING PRIME RIB**

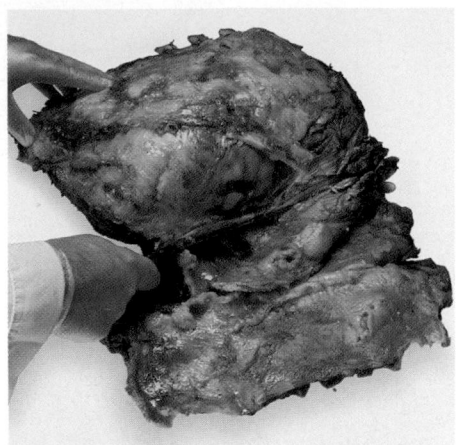

① Removing the netting, cap fat and **chine** bones.

chine the backbone or spine of an animal; a subprimal cut of beef, veal, lamb, pork or game carcass containing a portion of the backbone with some adjoining flesh.

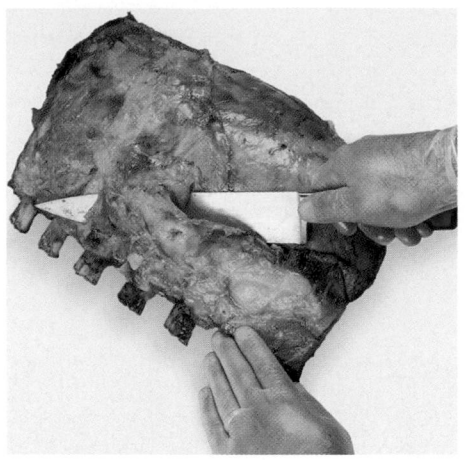

② Trimming the excess fat from the eye muscle.

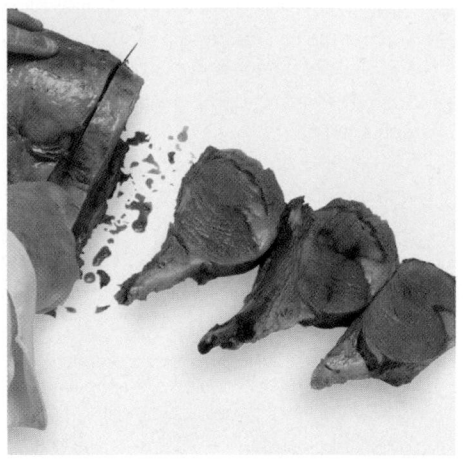

③ Slicing the rib in long, smooth strokes, the first cut (end cut) without a rib bone, the second cut with a rib bone, the third without, and so on.

PROCEDURE FOR **CARVING PRIME RIB ON THE SLICER**

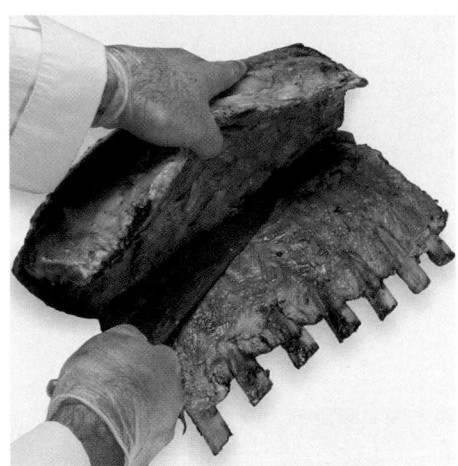

① When producing large quantities of prime rib, it is often more practical to slice it on a slicing machine. Following the steps illustrated above, remove the netting, cap fat and chine bone; trim excess fat from the eye muscle. Then use a long slicer and completely remove the rib eye from the rib bones, being careful to stay as close as possible to the bones to avoid wasting any meat.

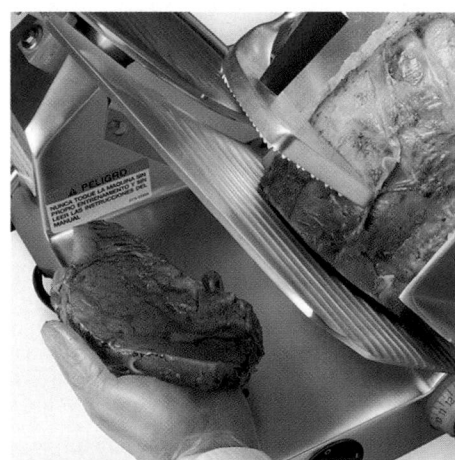

② After placing the rib on the slicing machine, set the machine to the desired thickness. The blade will have to be adjusted often because a roast's thickness fluctuates.

PROCEDURE FOR **CARVING A STEAMSHIP ROUND OF BEEF**

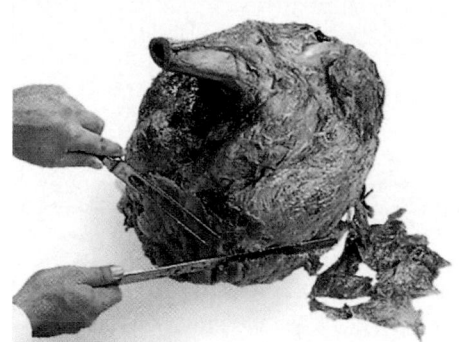

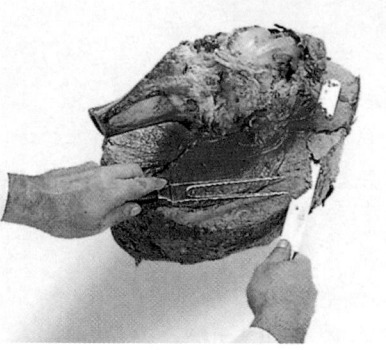

❶ After setting the roast on the cutting board with the exposed femur bone (large end of the roast) down and the tibia (shank bone) or "handle" up, trim the excess exterior fat to expose the lean meat.

❷ Begin slicing with a horizontal cut toward the shank bone, then make vertical cuts to release the slices of beef.

❸ Keeping the exposed surface as level as possible, continue carving, turning the roast as necessary to access all sides.

PROCEDURE FOR **CARVING A LEG OF LAMB**

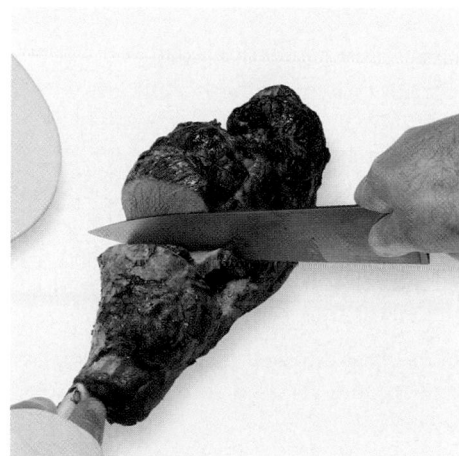

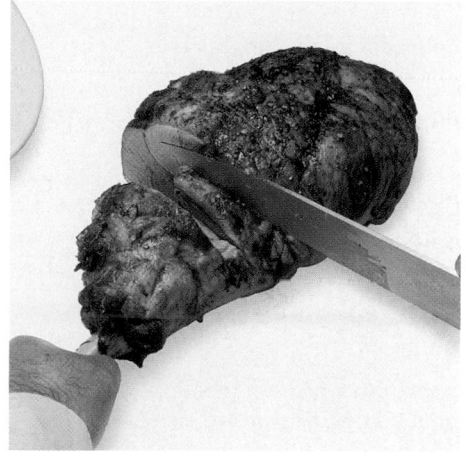

❶ Holding the shank bone firmly, cut toward the bone.

❷ Cutting parallel to the shank bone to remove the slices.

❸ Rotating the leg as needed to access the meat on all sides.

SAUTÉING

Sautéing is a dry-heat cooking method in which heat is conducted by a small amount of fat. Sautéed meats should be tender (a reflection of the quality of the raw product) and of good color (determined by proper cooking temperatures) and have a good overall flavor. Any accompanying sauce should be well seasoned and complement the meat without overpowering it.

Selecting Meats to Sauté

As with broiling, grilling and roasting, you should use tender meats of the highest quality in order to produce good results when sautéing. The cuts should be uniform in size and shape in order to promote even cooking.

Seasoning Meats to Be Sautéed

The sauces that almost always accompany sautéed meats provide much of the seasoning. The meat, however, can be marinated or simply seasoned with salt and pepper. If marinated, the meat must be patted dry before cooking to ensure proper browning. Some meats are dusted with flour before cooking to seal in juices and promote even browning.

Determining Doneness

As with broiled and grilled meats, the doneness of sautéed meats is determined by touch and timing. Red meats should be well browned; veal and pork should be somewhat lighter.

Accompaniments to Sautéed Meats

Sauces served with sautéed meats are usually made directly in the sauté pan, using the **fond**. They often incorporate a previously thickened sauce. Sauce suggestions for sautéed meats are found in Table 10.5.

fond (1) French for "stock" or "base"; (2) the concentrated juices, drippings and bits of food left in pans after foods are roasted or sautéed; it is used to flavor sauces made directly in the pans in which the foods were cooked

PROCEDURE FOR **SAUTÉING MEATS**

cutlet a relatively thick, boneless slice of meat

scallop (Fr. *escalope*; It. *scaloppa*, pl. *scaloppine*) a thin, boneless slice of meat

émincé a small, thin, boneless piece of meat

medallion a small, round, relatively thick slice of meat

mignonette a medallion

noisette a small, usually round, portion of meat cut from the rib

chop a cut of meat, including part of the rib

paillard a scallop of meat pounded until thin, usually grilled

1. Heat a sauté pan and add enough oil or clarified butter to just cover the bottom. The pan should be large enough to hold the meat in a single layer. A pan that is too large may cause the fat or meat to burn.
2. Cut the meat into **cutlets**, **scallops**, **émincés**, **medallions**, **mignonettes**, **noisettes**, **chops** or small even-sized pieces. Season the meat and dredge in flour if desired.
3. Add the meat to the sauté pan in a single layer. Do not crowd the pan.
4. Adjust the temperature so that the meat's exterior browns properly without burning and the interior cooks. The heat should be high enough to complete the cooking process before the meat begins to stew in its own juices.
5. Small items may be tossed using the sauté pan's sloped sides to flip them back on top of themselves. Do not toss the meat more than necessary, however. The pan should remain in contact with the heat source as much as possible to maintain proper temperatures. Larger items should be turned using tongs or a kitchen fork. Avoid burns by not splashing hot fat.
6. Larger items can be finished in an oven. Either place the sauté pan in the oven or transfer the meat to another pan. The latter procedure allows a sauce to be made in the original pan as the meat continues to cook.

PROCEDURE FOR **PREPARING A SAUCE IN THE SAUTÉ PAN**

1. If a sauce is to be made in the pan, hold the meat in a warm spot while preparing the sauce. When the meat is removed from the pan, leave a small amount of fat as well as the fond. If there is excessive fat, degrease the pan, leaving just enough to cover its bottom. Add ingredients such as garlic, shallots and mushrooms that will be used as garnishes and sauce flavorings; sauté them.
2. Deglaze the pan with wine or stock. Scrape the pan, loosening the fond and allowing it to dissolve in the liquid. Reduce the deglazing liquid by approximately three-fourths.
3. Add jus lié or stock to the pan. Cook and reduce the sauce to the desired consistency.
4. Add any ingredients that do not require cooking, such as herbs and spices. Adjust the seasonings with salt and pepper.

⑤ For service, the meat may be returned to the pan for a moment to reheat it and coat it with the finished sauce. The meat should remain in the sauce just long enough to reheat. Do not attempt to cook the meat in the sauce.

SAUTÉED VEAL SCALLOPS WITH WHITE WINE LEMON SAUCE

Yield: 6 Servings **Method:** Sautéing

Veal scallops, 3 oz. (90 g) each	12	12
Clarified butter	4 fl. oz.	120 ml
Flour	4 oz.	120 g
Salt and pepper	TT	TT
Shallots, chopped	2 Tbsp.	30 ml
White wine	6 fl. oz.	180 ml
Lemon juice	2 fl. oz.	60 ml
Brown veal stock	4 fl. oz.	120 ml
Unsalted butter	2 oz.	60 g
Lemon wedges	12	12

① Pound the scallops to a uniform thickness, as described in Chapter 14, Veal.
② Heat a sauté pan and add enough clarified butter to coat the bottom of the pan.
③ Dredge the scallops in flour seasoned with salt and pepper and add to the pan in a single layer. Sauté on each side for 1 to 2 minutes. As the first scallops are done, remove them to a warm platter and sauté the remaining scallops. This can be done in several batches, adding additional clarified butter as needed.
④ Add the chopped shallots to the pan and sauté.
⑤ Deglaze the pan with the wine and lemon juice.
⑥ Add the stock and reduce by half.
⑦ Swirl in the butter (monté au beurre).
⑧ Adjust the seasonings with salt and pepper.
⑨ Serve two scallops per person with approximately 1 ounce (30 milliliters) sauce. Garnish with lemon wedges.

Approximate values per 8-oz. (240-g) serving: **Calories** 537, **Total fat** 28 g, **Saturated fat** 13 g, **Cholesterol** 208 mg, **Sodium** 325 mg, **Total carbohydrates** 17 g, **Protein** 47 g, **Vitamin A** 22%

MISE EN PLACE

◄ Peel and chop shallots.

① Adding the veal scallops to the pan. Note the relationship of scallops to pan size.

② Adding the chopped shallots to the pan and sautéing them.

③ Deglazing the pan with white wine and lemon juice.

④ Adding the brown veal stock and reducing by half.

⑤ Swirling in the butter and adjusting the seasonings.

PAN-FRYING

Pan-frying uses more fat than sautéing to conduct heat. Pan-fried meats should be tender (a reflection of the quality of the raw product) and of good color (determined by proper cooking temperatures) and have a good overall flavor. Meats to be pan-fried are usually breaded. In addition to providing flavor, breading seals the meat. The breading should be free from breaks, thus preventing the fat from coming into direct contact with the meat or collecting in a pocket formed between the meat and the breading. Pan-fried items should be golden in color, and the breading should not be soggy.

Selecting Meats to Pan-Fry

As with other dry-heat cooking methods, tender meats of high quality should be used because the meat will not be tenderized by the cooking process. Meats that are pan-fried are often cut into cutlets or scallops.

Seasoning Meats to Be Pan-Fried

Pan-fried meats are usually seasoned lightly with salt and pepper either by applying them directly to the meat or by adding them to the flour and bread crumbs used in the breading procedure.

Determining Doneness

The most accurate way to determine the doneness of a pan-fried item is by timing. The touch method is difficult to use because of the large amounts of hot fat. It also may not be as accurate as with broiled or grilled meats because pan-fried meats are often quite thin. The thinness of the meat also means that thermometer readings may not be accurate.

Accompaniments to Pan-Fried Meats

Any sauce served with pan-fried meats is usually made separately because no fond is created during the pan-frying process. Sauce suggestions are listed in Table 10.5.

PROCEDURE FOR PAN-FRYING MEATS

1. Slice and pound the meat into scallops, as described in Chapter 14, Veal.
2. Bread the meat using the standard breading procedure detailed in Chapter 8, Mise en Place.
3. Heat a moderate amount of fat or oil in a heavy pan. The temperature should be slightly lower than that used to sauté so that the breading will be nicely browned when the item is fully cooked.
4. Place the meat in the pan, being careful not to splash the hot fat. The fat should come one-third to halfway up the side of the meat. Fry until brown. Turn and brown the other side. Ideally, pan-fried meats should be fully cooked when they are well browned on both sides.
5. Remove the meat from the pan; drain it on absorbent paper before serving.

BREADED VEAL CUTLETS

Yield: 10 Servings   **Method:** Pan-frying

Veal cutlets, 4 oz. (120 g) each	10	10
Salt and pepper	TT	TT
Flour	as needed for breading	
Eggs	as needed for breading	
Milk	as needed for breading	
Bread crumbs	as needed for breading	
Vegetable oil	as needed	as needed
Whole butter	6 oz.	180 g
Lemon wedges	20	20

MISE EN PLACE

◀ Set up containers with flour, eggs and milk, and bread crumbs for breading following standard breading procedure.

1. Using a mallet, pound the cutlets to an even thickness, approximately ¼ inch (6 millimeters).
2. Season the cutlets with salt and pepper.
3. Bread the cutlets using the standard breading procedure described in Chapter 8, Mise en Place.
4. Heat a heavy pan to moderate heat; add approximately ⅛ inch (3 millimeters) oil.
5. Add the cutlets in a single layer. Do not crowd the pan. Brown on one side, then the other. Total cooking time should be approximately 4 minutes.
6. Remove the cutlets and drain on absorbent paper.
7. Melt the butter in a small pan until it foams.
8. Place one cutlet on each plate and pour approximately ½ fluid ounce (15 milliliters) butter over each portion. Garnish with lemon wedges.

Approximate values per 5-oz. (150-g) serving: **Calories** 501, **Total fat** 37 g, **Saturated fat** 17 g, **Cholesterol** 193 mg, **Sodium** 338 mg, **Total carbohydrates** 5 g, **Protein** 36 g, **Vitamin A** 17%

1. Adding the breaded cutlets to the hot pan. Note the amount of oil in the pan.

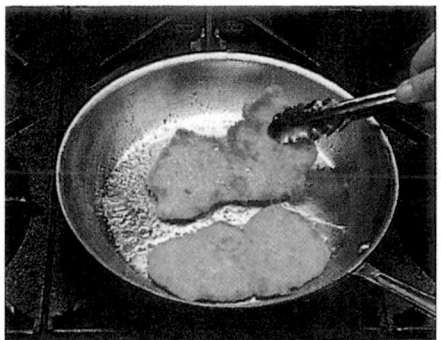

2. Turning the cutlets to brown on the second side.

3. Melting the butter in a separate pan until it foams.

4. Pouring the butter over the cutlet.

DEEP-FRYING

Deep-frying quickly cooks foods submerged in hot fat. It does not have a tenderizing effect. As even the choicest cuts of meat can always benefit from some tenderizing, deep-frying is not usually used for beef, veal, lamb or pork. There are exceptions, however. For example, commercially available frozen breaded meat cutlets are sometimes deep-fried, and some Asian dishes require deep-frying small pieces of beef or pork before finishing the meat in a sauce.

Moist-Heat Cooking Methods

Moist-heat cooking methods subject food to heat and moisture. Moist heat is often, but not always, used to tenderize tougher cuts of meat through long, slow cooking. Simmering is the only moist-heat cooking method discussed here, as it is the only one frequently used with meat.

SIMMERING

Simmering is usually associated with specific tougher cuts of meat that need to be tenderized through long, slow, moist cooking. Quality simmered meats have good flavor and texture. The flavor is determined by the cooking liquid; the texture is a result of proper cooking temperatures and time.

Selecting Meats to Simmer

Meats such as fresh or corned beef brisket, fresh or cured hams and tongue are often simmered. Beef briskets and tongues, pork butts and hams are often simmered whole.

Seasoning Meats to Be Simmered

If the meat to be simmered was cured by either smoking (as with cured hams, ham hocks and smoked pork butt) or **pickling** (as with corned beef and pickled tongue), the cooking liquid will not be used to make a sauce and should not be seasoned. Indeed, simmering cured meats helps leach out some of the excess salt, making the finished dish more palatable.

Cooking Temperatures

Moist-heat cooking methods generally use lower temperatures than dry-heat cooking methods. Meats are normally simmered at temperatures between 180°F and 200°F (82°C and 93°C). In some food service operations, meats such as hams and corned beef are cooked at temperatures as low as 150°F (66°C) for up to 12 hours. Although lower cooking temperatures result in less shrinkage and a more tender finished product, cooking times can be increased to the point that very low cooking temperatures may not be practical.

Determining Doneness

Simmered meats are always cooked well done, which is determined by tenderness. The size and quality of the raw product determines the cooking time. Undercooked meats will be tough and chewy. Overcooked meats will be stringy and may fall apart.

To test large cuts of meat for doneness, a kitchen fork should be easily inserted into the meat and the meat should slide off the fork. Smaller pieces of meat should be tender to the bite or easily cut with a table fork.

Accompaniments to Simmered Meats

Simmered meats are often served with boiled or steamed vegetables, as in the case of corned beef and cabbage. Pickled meats are usually served with mustard or horseradish sauce on the side.

pickle (1) to preserve food in a brine or vinegar solution; (2) food that has been preserved in a seasoned brine or vinegar, especially cucumbers.

PROCEDURE FOR **SIMMERING MEATS**

1. Cut, trim or tie the meat according to the recipe.
2. Bring an adequate amount of liquid to a boil. There should be enough liquid to cover the meat completely. Too much liquid will leach off much of the meat's flavor; too little will leave a portion of the meat exposed, preventing it from cooking. Because the dish's final flavor is determined by the flavor of the liquid, use plenty of mirepoix, flavorings and seasonings.
3. When simmering smoked or cured items, start them in cold water. This helps draw off some of the strong smoked or pickled flavors.
4. Add the meat to the liquid.
5. Reduce the heat to the desired temperature and cook until the meat is tender. Do not allow the cooking liquid to boil. Boiling results in a tough or overcooked and stringy product. If the simmered meat is to be served cold, a moister and juicier product can be achieved by removing the pot from the stove before the meat is fully cooked. The meat and the liquid can be cooled in a water bath like that for a stock, as described in Chapter 10, Stocks and Sauces. This allows the residual heat in the cooking liquid to finish cooking the meat.

NEW ENGLAND BOILED DINNER

Yield: 12 Servings, 6 oz. (180 g) each   **Method:** Simmering

Corned beef brisket, 8 lb. (3.8 kg)	1	1
White stock	as needed	as needed
Sachet:		
Bay leaves	2	2
Dried thyme	½ tsp.	2 ml
Peppercorns, cracked	½ tsp.	2 ml
Parsley stems	10	10
Mustard seeds	1 Tbsp.	15 ml
Cinnamon sticks	2	2
Allspice berries	4	4
Baby red beets	24	24
Baby turnips	24	24
Baby carrots	24	24
Brussels sprouts	24	24
Pearl onions	24	24
Red Bliss potatoes	24	24

1. Place the beef in a pot and add enough stock to cover it. Add the sachet, bring to a boil and reduce to a simmer.
2. Simmer until the beef is tender, approximately 3 hours. Remove the beef and hold in a hotel pan in a small amount of the cooking liquid.
3. Peel or prepare the vegetables and potatoes as needed and cook separately in a portion of the cooking liquid.
4. Carve the beef and serve with two of each of the vegetables and horseradish sauce (page 203).

Approximate values per serving: **Calories** 1067, **Total fat** 58 g, **Saturated fat** 19 g, **Cholesterol** 296 mg, **Sodium** 3844 mg, **Total carbohydrates** 73 g, **Protein** 64 g, **Vitamin A** 27%, **Vitamin C** 200%, **Iron** 66%

Combination Cooking Methods

Braising and stewing are referred to as combination cooking methods because both dry heat and moist heat are used to achieve the desired results.

BRAISING

Braised meats are first browned and then cooked in a liquid that serves as a sauce for the meat. A well-prepared braised dish has the rich flavor of the meat in the sauce and the moisture and flavor of the sauce in the meat. It should be almost **fork tender** but not falling apart. The meat should have an attractive color from the initial browning and final glazing.

Selecting Meats to Braise

Braising can be used for tender cuts (such as those from the loin or rib) or tougher cuts (such as those from the chuck or shank). Any meat to be braised should be well marbled with an ample fat content in order to produce a moist finished product.

If tender cuts such as veal chops or pork chops are braised, the finished dish has a uniquely different flavor and texture than if the meats were cooked by a dry-heat method. Tender cuts require shorter cooking times than tougher cuts because lengthy cooking is not needed to break down connective tissue.

More often, braising is used with tougher cuts that are tenderized by the long, moist cooking process. Cuts from the chuck and shank are popular choices, as they are very

MISE EN PLACE

◄ Prepare herb sachet.

1 Placing the corned beef and sachet in an appropriate pot and covering with stock.

2 Presenting the carved beef with the vegetable garnish.

fork tender describes braised meat that is so tender it shows little resistance when pierced with a fork

flavorful and contain relatively large amounts of collagen, which adds richness to the finished product.

Large pieces of meat can be braised, then carved like a roast. Portion control cuts and diced meats can also be braised.

Seasoning Meats to Be Braised

The seasoning and overall flavor of a braised dish is largely a function of the quality of the cooking liquid and the mirepoix, vegetables, herbs, spices and other ingredients that season the meat as it cooks. However, braised meats can be marinated before they are cooked to tenderize them and add flavor. The marinade is then sometimes incorporated into the braising liquid. Salt and pepper may be added to the flour if the meat is dredged before it is browned, or the meat may be seasoned directly (although the salt may draw out moisture and inhibit browning).

A standard sachet and a tomato product are usually added at the start of cooking. The tomato product adds flavor and color to the finished sauce as well as acid to tenderize the meat during the cooking process. Final seasoning should not take place until cooking is complete and the sauce will not be reduced further.

Cooking Temperatures

Braised meats are always browned before simmering. As a general rule, smaller cuts are floured before browning; larger cuts are not. Flouring seals the meat, promotes even browning and adds body to the sauce that accompanies the meat. Whether floured or not, the meat is browned in fat. After browning, white meats should be golden to amber in color; red meats should be dark brown. Do not brown the meat too quickly at too high a temperature because it is important to develop a well-caramelized surface. The caramelized surface adds color and flavor to the final product.

The meat and the braising liquid are brought to a boil over direct heat. The temperature is then reduced below boiling and the pot is covered. Cooking can be finished in the oven or on the stove top. The oven provides gentle, even heat without the risk of scorching. If braising is finished on the stove top, proper temperatures must be maintained carefully throughout the cooking process, and great care must be taken to prevent scorching or burning. Lower temperatures and longer cooking times result in more even cooking and thorough penetration of the cooking liquid, providing a more flavorful final product.

Finishing Braised Meats

Near the end of the cooking process, the lid may be removed from oven-braised meats. Finishing braised meats without a cover serves two purposes. First, the meat can be glazed by basting it often. (As the basting liquid evaporates, the meat is browned and a strongly flavored glaze is formed.) Second, removing the lid allows the cooking liquid to reduce, thickening it and concentrating its flavors for use as a sauce.

Determining Doneness

Braised meats are done when they are tender. A fork inserted into the meat should meet little resistance. Properly braised meats should remain intact and not fall apart when handled gently.

Properly browned meat to be braised or stewed is evenly well-caramelized.

Braised meats that fall apart or are stringy are overcooked. If the finished product is tough, it was probably undercooked or cooked at too high a temperature. If the entire dish lacks flavor, the meat may not have been properly browned or the cooking liquid may have been poorly seasoned.

Accompaniments to Braised Meats

Large braised items are often served like roasts. They are carved against the grain in thin slices and served with their sauce. Vegetables can be cooked with the braised meat, cooked separately and added when the main item has finished cooking or added at service. If the vegetables are cooked with the main item, they should be added at intervals based on their individual cooking times to prevent overcooking.

PROCEDURE FOR **BRAISING MEATS**

The liquid used for braising is usually thickened in one of three ways:

▶ With a roux added at the start of the cooking process; the roux thickens the sauce as the meat cooks.

▶ Prethickened before the meat is added.

▶ Thickened after the meat is cooked either by puréeing the mirepoix or by using roux, arrowroot or cornstarch.

The procedure for braising meats includes variations for whichever thickening method is selected.

1. Heat a small amount of oil in a heavy pan.
2. Dredge the meat to be braised in seasoned flour, if desired, and add it to the oil.
3. Brown the meat well on all sides and remove from the pan.
4. Add a mirepoix or the appropriate vegetables to the pan and caramelize well. If using roux, it should be added at this time.
5. Add the appropriate stock or sauce so that when the meat is returned to the pan the liquid comes approximately one-third of the way up the side of the meat.
6. Add aromatics and seasonings.
7. Return the meat to the sauce. Tightly cover the pot and bring it to a simmer. Cook slowly either on the stove top or by placing the covered pot directly in an oven at 250°F–300°F (120°C–150°C).
8. Cook the item, basting or turning it often so that all sides of the meat benefit from the moisture and flavor of the sauce.
9. When the meat is done, remove it from the pan and hold it in a warm place while the sauce is finished.
10. The sauce may be reduced on the stove top to intensify its flavors. If the meat was braised in a stock, the stock may be thickened using a roux, arrowroot or cornstarch. Strain the sauce or, if desired, purée the mirepoix and other ingredients and return them to the sauce. Adjust the sauce's consistency as desired.

AUNT RUTHIE'S POT ROAST

MISE EN PLACE
▶ Peel onions and slice thinly.
▶ Peel and mince garlic.

① Browning the brisket.

② Sautéing the onions and garlic.

③ Basting the brisket. Note the proper amount of cooking liquid.

Yield: 12 Servings, 6 oz. (180 g) meat and 4 oz. (120 g) sauce

Method: Braising

Vegetable oil	3 fl. oz.	90 ml
Beef brisket	6 lb.	2.8 kg
Onions, thinly sliced	3 lb.	1.4 kg
Garlic, minced	2 Tbsp.	30 ml
Brown veal stock	1 qt.	960 ml
Tomato sauce	1 pt.	480 ml
Brown sugar	4 oz.	120 g
Paprika	1 tsp.	5 ml
Dry mustard	2 tsp.	10 ml
Lemon juice	8 fl. oz.	240 ml
Ketchup	8 oz.	240 g
Red wine vinegar	8 fl. oz.	240 ml
Worcestershire sauce	2 fl. oz.	60 ml
Salt and pepper	TT	TT

① Heat the oil in a large rondeau. Add the beef and brown thoroughly. Remove and reserve the brisket.

② Add the onions and garlic to the pan and sauté.

③ Add the stock and tomato sauce to the pan.

④ Return the brisket to the pan, cover tightly and bring to a boil. Braise at 325°F (160°C) for 1½ hours, basting or turning the brisket often.

⑤ Combine the remaining ingredients and add to the pan.

⑥ Continue cooking and basting the brisket until tender, approximately 1 hour. Add additional stock or water as needed during braising.

⑦ Remove the brisket, degrease the sauce and adjust its consistency and seasonings. Do not strain the sauce.

⑧ Slice the brisket against the grain and serve with the sauce.

Approximate values per serving: **Calories** 803, **Total fat** 52 g, **Saturated fat** 16 g, **Cholesterol** 224 mg, **Sodium** 3290 mg, **Total carbohydrates** 40 g, **Protein** 46 g, **Vitamin A** 25%, **Vitamin C** 100%

STEWING

Stewing, like braising, is a combination cooking method. In many ways, the procedures for stewing are identical to those for braising, although stewing is usually associated with smaller or bite-sized pieces of meat.

There are two main types of stews: brown stews and white stews.

When making **brown stews**, the meat is first browned in fat; then a cooking liquid is added. The initial browning adds flavor and color to the finished product. The same characteristics apply to a good brown stew that apply to a good braised dish: It should be fork tender and have an attractive color and a rich flavor.

There are two types of **white stews**: **fricassees**, in which the meat is first cooked in a small amount of fat without coloring, then combined with a cooking liquid; and **blanquettes**, in which the meat is first blanched, then rinsed and added to a cooking liquid. A white stew should have the same flavor and texture characteristics as a brown stew, but should be white or ivory in color.

Selecting Meats to Stew
Stewing uses moist heat to tenderize meat just as braising does; therefore, many of the same cuts can be used. Meats that are to be stewed should be trimmed of excess fat and connective tissue and cut into 1- to 2-inch (2.5- to 5-cm) cubes.

STEW TERMINOLOGY

Ragoût (ra-GOO)—A general term that refers to white or brown stews in which the meat is cooked by dry heat before a liquid is added. In French, *ragoût* means "to bring back the appetite."

Fricassee (FRIHK-uh-see)—A white ragoût usually made from white meat or small game, seared without browning and garnished with small onions and mushrooms.

Navarin (nah-veh-rahng)—A brown ragoût generally made with turnips, other root vegetables, onions, peas and lamb.

Blanquette (blahn-KEHT)—A white stew in which the meat is first blanched, then added to a stock or sauce to complete the cooking and tenderizing process. Blanquettes are finished with a liaison of egg yolks and heavy cream.

Chili con carne—A ragoût of ground or diced meat cooked with onions, chile peppers, cumin and other spices. Despite the objections of purists, chili sometimes contains beans.

Goulash—A beef stew with Hungarian origins made with onions and paprika and garnished with potatoes.

Tagine—(tah-GEEN) A North African stew in which meat, poultry, fish or vegetables are flavored with onions, cilantro, spices and aromatics and then braised over a fire in a covered earthenware vessel of the same name.

Adobo—A stew of Spanish origin in which meats are simmered with onions and spices in a savory red chili sauce. In the Philippines, *adobo* refers to a stew in which ingredients such as meats, poultry or fish are pickled in vinegar, oil and spices before cooking.

Seasoning Meats to Be Stewed

Stews, like braised meats, get much of their flavor from their cooking liquid. A stew's seasoning and overall flavor is a direct result of the quality of the cooking liquid and the vegetables, herbs, spices and other ingredients added during cooking.

Cooking Temperatures

Meats for brown stews are first cooked at high temperatures over direct heat until well browned. Meats for fricassees are first sautéed at low temperatures so that they do not develop color.

Once the cooking liquid has been added and the moist-heat cooking process has begun, do not allow the stew to boil. Stews benefit from low-temperature cooking. If practical, stews can be covered and finished in the oven.

Determining Doneness

Stewed meats are done when they are fork tender. Test them by removing a piece of meat to a plate and cutting it with a fork. Any vegetables that are cooked with the meat should be added at the proper times so that they and the meat are completely cooked at the same time.

Accompaniments to Stewed Meats

Stews are often complete meals in themselves, containing meat, vegetables and potatoes in one dish. Stews that do not contain a starch are often served with pasta or rice.

PROCEDURE FOR STEWING MEATS—BROWN STEWS

Red meats, lamb and game are used in brown stews. The procedure for making a brown stew is very similar to braising.

1. Trim the meat of excess fat and silverskin and cut into 1- to 2-inch (2.5- to 5-cm) pieces.
2. Dredge the meat in flour if desired. Heat an appropriate-sized pan and add enough oil to cover the bottom. Cook the meat in the oil, browning it well on all sides. Onions and garlic can be added at this time and browned.
3. Add flour to the meat and fat and cook to make a brown roux.
4. Gradually add the liquid to the roux, stirring to prevent lumps. Bring the stew to a boil and reduce to a simmer.

⑤ Add a tomato product and a sachet or a bouquet garni. Cover and place in the oven or continue to simmer on the stove top until the meat is tender. Add other ingredients such as vegetables or potatoes at the proper time so that they will be done when the meat is tender.

⑥ When the meat is tender, remove the sachet or bouquet garni. The meat may be strained out and the sauce thickened with roux, cornstarch or arrowroot or reduced to concentrate its flavors.

⑦ If not added during the cooking process, vegetables and other garnishes may be cooked separately and added to the finished stew.

BROWN BEEF STEW

MISE EN PLACE

▶ Cube trimmed beef.
▶ Peel onions and chop into fine dice.
▶ Peel and chop garlic.
▶ Prepare herb sachet.

Yield: 8 Servings, 8 oz. (240 g) each   **Method:** Stewing

Oil	2 fl. oz.	60 ml
Beef chuck or shank, trimmed and cut into 1½-in. (3.5-cm) cubes	4 lb. 8 oz.	2.1 kg
Salt	2 tsp.	10 ml
Black pepper	½ tsp.	2 ml
Onions, small dice	10 oz.	300 g
Garlic, chopped	1 tsp.	5 ml
Flour	1½ oz.	45 g
Red wine	8 fl. oz.	240 ml
Brown stock	1 qt.	960 ml
Tomato purée	4 oz.	120 g
Sachet:		
Bay leaves	2	2
Dried thyme	½ tsp.	2 ml
Peppercorns, crushed	½ tsp.	2 ml
Parsley stems	10	10

① Heat a heavy pot until very hot and add the oil.

② Season the beef with salt and pepper and add it to the pot, browning it well on all sides. Do not overcrowd the pot. If necessary, cook the beef in several batches.

③ Add the onions and garlic and sauté until the onions are slightly browned.

④ Add the flour and stir to make a roux. Brown the roux lightly.

⑤ Add the wine and stock slowly, stirring to prevent lumps.

⑥ Add the tomato purée and the sachet.

⑦ Bring to a simmer and cook until the beef is tender, approximately 1½ to 2 hours.

⑧ If desired, remove the cooked beef from the sauce and strain the sauce. Return the beef to the sauce.

⑨ Degrease the stew by skimming off the fat.

VARIATION:

Vegetables such as turnips, carrots, celery and pearl onions can be cooked separately and added to the stew as garnish.

Approximate values per 8-oz. (240-g) serving: **Calories** 590, **Total fat** 32 g, **Saturated fat** 11 g, **Cholesterol** 185 mg, **Sodium** 710 mg, **Total carbohydrates** 15 g, **Protein** 58 g, **Vitamin A** 45%, **Iron** 40%

❶ Browning the beef.

❷ Sautéing the garlic and onions until slightly browned.

❸ Adding the flour and making a roux.

❹ Adding the red wine and beef stock.

❺ Adding the tomato purée and sachet.

❻ Degreasing the stew.

PROCEDURE FOR **STEWING MEATS—BRAISED WHITE STEWS (FRICASSEES)**

The procedure for making fricassees is similar to the procedure for brown stews. The primary difference is that the meat is sautéed but not allowed to brown. The braised white stew (fricassee) procedure outlined here is the basis for Veal Fricassee (page 347).

❶ Trim the meat of excess fat and silverskin and cut into 1- to 2-inch (2.5- to 5-cm) pieces.

❷ Heat an appropriate-sized pan and add enough oil to cover the bottom. Add the meat (and often an onion) to the pan and cook without browning.

❸ Sprinkle the meat (and onion) with flour and cook to make a blond roux.

❹ Gradually add the liquid, stirring to prevent lumps. Bring the stew to a boil and reduce to a simmer.

❺ Add a bouquet garni and seasonings. Cover the stew and place in the oven or continue to simmer on the stove top, being careful not to burn or scorch the stew.

❻ Continue to cook until the meat is tender. If the sauce is too thin, remove the meat from the sauce and hold the meat in a warm place. Reduce the sauce to the proper consistency on the stove top or thicken it by adding a small amount of blond roux, cornstarch or arrowroot.

SOUS VIDE COOKING

Sous vide, a French term that means *under vacuum*, is a low-emperature, moist-heat cooking method that resembles braising or poaching. Foods are vacuum-sealed in heavy-gauge plastic pouches and then cooked in a temperature-controlled water bath. Because foods are completely sealed, flavorful juices stay within the foods. This cooking method, in use for several decades in commercial food production, is of increasing interest to restaurant chefs for its accuracy and specific results.

To prepare foods *sous vide* in the restaurant kitchen, individual portions or small quantities of meat, fish, vegetables or other foods are trimmed and seasoned and then placed in heat-resistant plastic pouches, which are then sealed in a chamber vacuum machine. The vacuum machine, which removes air and creates a slight pressure on the food, ensures that heat transfers efficiently from the water to the pouch during cooking. Removing most of the oxygen also increases the shelf life of the food cooked in each pouch. Pressure is adjusted according to the food being cooked; firmer cuts of meat are packed at a higher pressure than fragile cuts. Tougher cuts of beef, veal, lamb and other meats that benefit from braising are ideal for *sous vide* cooking. Meats for stews or braises that would conventionally be browned before simmering may be browned before packaging.

Sous vide cooking takes place in a precisely regulated hot water bath at temperatures between 125°F (51°C) and 195°F (90°C), below simmering. The temperature is determined by the desired core temperature. When braising tougher cuts of meats, for example, a temperature of 140°F (60°C) may be recommended, hot enough to dissolve connective tissues and collagen without squeezing all the moisture and fat from the meat. Short ribs of beef cooked at this temperature retain a pink color and natural juiciness.

Sous vide is also used to cook fish and tender cuts of meat such as tenderloin of beef. When roasting conventionally, a tenderloin of beef, for example, is seared and then roasted at 375°F (191°C) to 450°F (232°C) until its internal temperature reaches the desired degree of doneness. During the process, the exterior layers of the meat cook more than the center, resulting in a meat that can be well done and dry around the edges. When cooking beef tenderloin *sous vide*, the meat is vacuum packed then cooked in a water bath at 125°F (51°C) to achieve a uniformly rare piece of meat with less shrinkage. Once the meat reaches the temperature of the water bath, it cannot overcook and can be held at the desired temperature for service. To add the flavor and eye appeal of a browned surface, the meat may be seared before serving.

Food safety is of utmost concern when using *sous vide* techniques because of the low cooking temperatures. To prevent the growth of microorganisms, any food to be cooked *sous vide* must be chilled below the temperature danger zone (41°F/5°C) before cooking. Pouches of food cooked *sous vide* must be chilled after cooking before refrigerating. The Model Food Code requires that a detailed HAACP program, including time and temperature monitoring, be in place in any food service operation using *sous vide* cooking methods. Before employing *sous vide* techniques in any food service operation, consult local health authorities to learn what technical training, licensing and recordkeeping are required. Consult the Bibliography for books on the subject. Equipment for *sous vide* cooking is briefly discussed in Chapter 4, Tools and Equipment.

PROCEDURE FOR **STEWING MEATS—SIMMERED WHITE STEWS (BLANQUETTES)**

Unlike fricassees, blanquettes contain meat that was blanched, not sautéed. (Because the meat is cooked only by moist heat and never by dry heat, the blanquette cooking process is not a true combination cooking method; nevertheless, because of its striking similarities to stewing, it is included here.) The most common blanquette is made with veal and is known as blanquette de veau, but any white meat or lamb can be prepared in this manner using a variety of garnishes. The simmered white stew (blanquette) procedure outlined here is the basis for Blanquette of Lamb (page 368).

1. Trim the meat of excess fat and silverskin and cut into 1- to 2-inch (2.5- to 5-cm) pieces.
2. Blanch the cubed meat by placing the meat in an appropriate pot, covering with cool water, adding salt, and bringing it rapidly to a boil. Drain the water. Rinse the meat to remove any impurities.
3. Return the meat to the pot and add enough stock to cover. Add a bouquet garni, salt and pepper. Simmer until the meat is tender, approximately 1 to 1½ hours.
4. Strain the meat from the stock. Discard the bouquet garni. Bring the stock to a boil, thicken it with a blond roux and simmer for 15 minutes.
5. Return the meat to the thickened stock. Add a liaison of cream and egg yolks to enrich and thicken the stew. Heat the stew to a simmer. Do not boil or the egg yolks will curdle.
6. If any vegetables are to be added, they should be cooked separately and added to the thickened stock with the meat.
7. Adjust the seasonings with a few drops of lemon juice, nutmeg or salt and pepper as needed.

QUESTIONS FOR DISCUSSION

1. Explain the difference between primals, subprimals and fabricated cuts of meat. Why is it important to be skilled in meat fabrication?
2. What is connective tissue composed of, and where is it found? What happens to connective tissue at normal cooking temperatures?
3. Discuss the government's role in regulating the marketing and sale of meat.
4. At what temperature should fresh meat be stored? At what temperature should frozen meat be stored?
5. Would it be better to grill or braise a piece of meat that contains a great deal of connective tissue? Explain your answer.
6. List three ways to improve the cooking qualities of lean meats. What techniques can be used to compensate for the lack of fat?
7. List four ways that meat can be made more tender before cooking. Discuss the usefulness of each technique.
8. Describe the similarities between sautéing meats and pan-frying them. Describe the differences.
9. Describe the similarities between braising meats and stewing them. Describe the differences.
10. Use the Internet to research labeling and grading systems of several meat processors. Discuss in which ways they differ from the USDA grading system. **WWW**

Terms to Know

connective tissue	USDA Select
muscle tissue	USDA Standard
muscle fibers	hanging/aging
grain of meat	portion control
tendons	irradiated
silverskin	butcher's twine
tenderness	baste
USDA inspection	sear
USDA Prime	resting meat
USDA Choice	

“ Beef is the soul of cooking. ”
—Marie-Antoine Carême, French chef (1784–1833)

CHAPTER THIRTEEN

BEEF

After studying this chapter, you will be able to:

- identify the primal, subprimal and fabricated cuts of beef
- perform basic butchering procedures
- apply appropriate cooking methods to several common cuts of beef

BEEF IS THE MEAT OF DOMESTICATED CATTLE. Most of the beef Americans eat comes from steers, which are male cattle castrated as calves and specifically raised for beef. Although Americans are consuming less beef today than we once did, we still consume far more beef than any other meat. The beef we are eating is leaner than that of years past, thanks to advances in animal husbandry and closer trimming of exterior fat. Cattle ranchers are rediscovering older breeds of livestock and new ways to fabricate beef, bringing excitement to the assortment of beef products available to chefs and consumers.

PRIMAL AND SUBPRIMAL CUTS OF BEEF

After the steer is slaughtered, it is cut into four pieces (called quarters) for easy handling. This is done by first splitting the carcass down the backbone into two bilateral halves. Each half is divided into the forequarter (the front portion) and the hindquarter (the rear portion) by cutting along the natural curvature between the 12th and 13th ribs. The quartered carcass is then further reduced into the primal cuts and the subprimal and fabricated cuts.

The primal cuts of beef are the chuck, brisket and shank, rib, short plate, short loin, sirloin, flank and round. Figure 13.1 shows the relationship between a steer's bone structure and the primal cuts. It is important to know the location of bones when cutting or working with meats. This makes meat fabrication and carving easier and aids in identifying cuts. Figure 13.2 shows the primal cuts of beef and their location on the carcass. An entire beef carcass can range in weight from 500 to more than 800 pounds (240 to 380 kg).

Forequarter

CHUCK

The primal chuck is the animal's shoulder; it accounts for approximately 28 percent of carcass weight. It contains a portion of the backbone, five rib bones and portions of the blade and arm bones.

Because an animal constantly uses its shoulder muscles, chuck contains a high percentage of connective tissue and is quite tough. This tough cut of beef, however, is one of the most flavorful.

The primal chuck is used less frequently than other primal cuts in food service operations. If cooked whole, the chuck is difficult to cut or carve because of the large number of bones and relatively small muscle groups that travel in different directions.

The primal chuck produces several fabricated cuts: cross rib pot roast, chuck short ribs, cubed or tenderized steaks, stew meat and ground chuck. Because the meat is less tender, the fabricated cuts usually benefit from moist-heat cooking or combination cooking methods such as stewing and braising. There are exceptions, however. The beef industry is developing new products from underutilized cuts of meat. Flat iron comes from the top shoulder of the chuck and is one such cut gaining in popularity as an alternative steak suitable for dry-heat cooking.

Chuck Square Cut (Two Pieces)

Kobe beef an exclusive type of beef traditionally produced in Kobe, Japan. Wagyu cattle are fed a special diet, which includes beer to stimulate the animal's appetite during summer months. The animals are massaged with sake to relieve stress and muscle stiffness in the belief that calm, contented cattle produce better-quality meat. This special treatment produces meat that is extraordinarily tender and full-flavored, and extraordinarily expensive. Kobe Beef America introduced Wagyu cattle to the United States in 1976. KBA's cattle are raised without hormones and the meat is dry-aged for 21 days prior to sale

Certified Angus Beef a brand created in 1978 to distinguish the highest-quality beef produced from descendants of the black, hornless Angus cattle of Scotland. The meat must meet American Angus Association standards for yield, marbling and age and be graded as high choice or prime

302

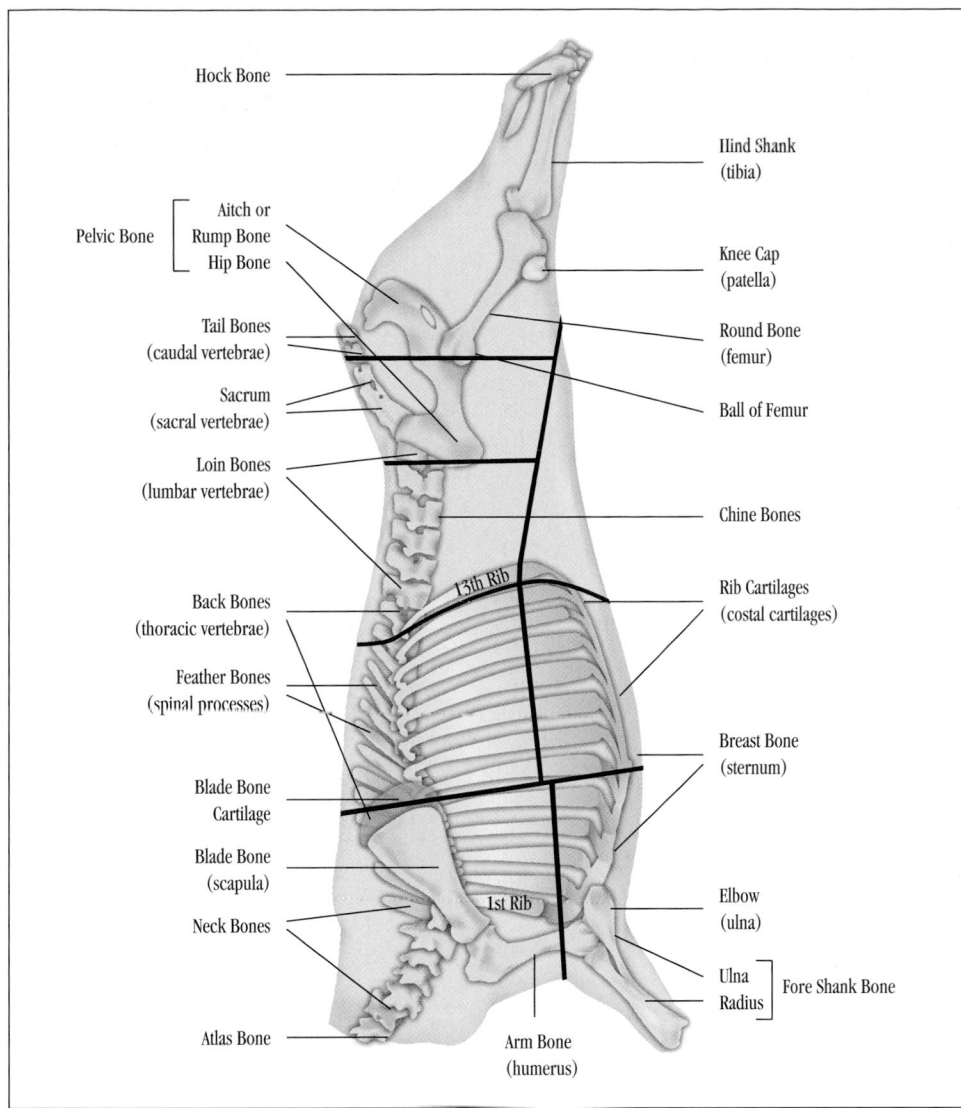

FIGURE 13.1 ▶ The skeletal structure of a steer.

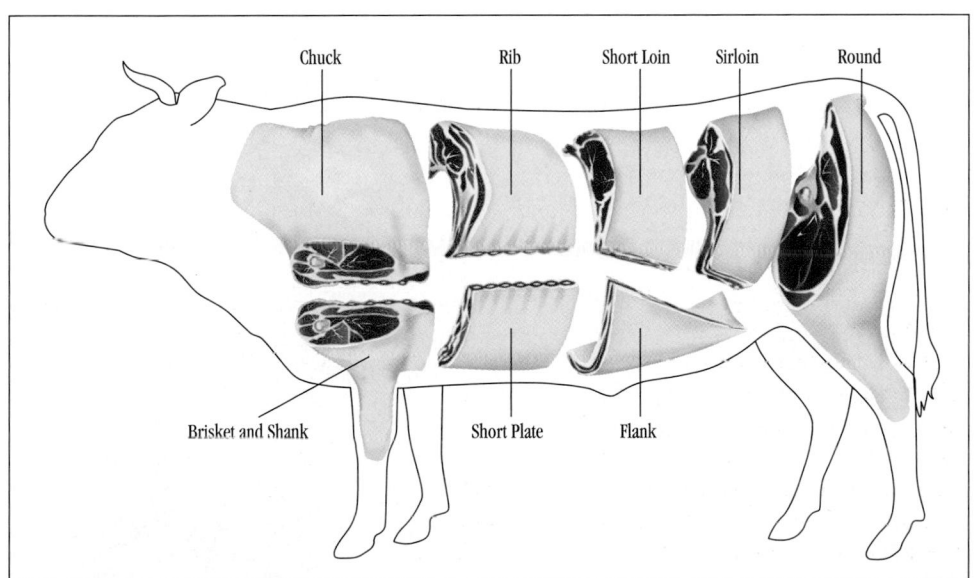

FIGURE 13.2 ▶ The primal cuts of beef.

boxed beef industry terminology for primal and subprimal cuts of beef that are vacuum sealed and packed into cardboard boxes for shipping from the packing plant to retailers and food service operations

Shoulder Top Blade

Blade Steak (Flat Iron)

Brisket

BRISKET AND SHANK

The brisket and shank are located beneath the primal chuck on the front half of the carcass. Together, they form a single primal that accounts for approximately 8 percent of carcass weight. This primal consists of the steer's breast (the brisket), which contains the ribs and breast bone, and its arm (the foreshank), which contains only the shank bone.

The ribs and breast bone are always removed from the brisket before cooking. The boneless brisket is very tough and contains a substantial percentage of fat, both intermuscular and subcutaneous. It is well suited for moist-heat and combination cooking methods such as simmering or braising. It is often pickled or corned to produce corned beef brisket, or cured and peppered to make pastrami.

Beef foreshanks are very flavorful and high in collagen. Because collagen converts to gelatin when cooked using moist heat, foreshanks are excellent for making soups and stocks. Ground shank meat is often used to help clarify and flavor consommés because of its rich flavor and high collagen content. Marrow, the soft tissue in the center of the foreshank and hindshank bones, is considered a delicacy when cooked and added to sauces or spread on toast.

RIB

The primal beef rib accounts for approximately 10 percent of carcass weight. It consists of ribs 6 through 12 as well as a portion of the backbone.

This primal is best known for yielding roast prime rib of beef. Prime rib is not named after the quality grade USDA Prime. Rather, its name reflects the fact that it constitutes the majority of the primal cut. The eye meat of the rib (the center muscle portion) is not a well-exercised muscle and therefore is quite tender. It also contains large amounts of marbling compared to the rest of the carcass and produces rich, full-flavored roasts and steaks. Although roasting the eye muscle on the rib bones produces a moister roast, the eye meat can be removed to produce a boneless rib eye roast or cut into rib eye steaks. The rib bones that are separated from the rib eye meat are quite meaty and flavorful and can be served as barbecued beef ribs. The ends of the rib bones that are trimmed off the primal rib to produce the rib roast are known as beef short ribs. They are meaty and are often served as braised beef short ribs.

Beef Rib Eye Roll

Oven-Ready Rib Roast

Skirt Steak

SHORT PLATE

The short plate is located directly below the primal rib on a side of beef; it accounts for approximately 9 percent of the overall weight of the carcass. The short plate contains rib bones and cartilage and produces the short ribs and skirt steak.

Beef Short Ribs

Short ribs are meaty, yet high in connective tissue, and are best when braised. Skirt steak is often marinated and grilled as fajitas. Other, less meaty portions of the short plate are trimmed and ground.

Porterhouse Steak

Hindquarter

SHORT LOIN

The short loin is the anterior (front) portion of the beef loin. It is located just behind the rib and becomes the first primal cut of the hindquarter when the side of beef is divided into a forequarter and hindquarter. It accounts for approximately 8 percent of carcass weight.

The short loin contains a single rib, the 13th, and a portion of the backbone. With careful butchering, this small primal can yield several subprimal and fabricated cuts, all of which are among the most tender, popular and expensive cuts of beef.

Strip Loin

The loin eye muscle, a continuation of the rib eye muscle, runs along the top of the T-shaped bones that form the backbone. Beneath the loin eye muscle on the other side of the backbone is the tenderloin, the most tender cut of all.

When the short loin is cut in cross-sections with the bone in, it produces—starting with the rib end of the short loin—club steaks (which do not contain any tenderloin), T-bone steaks (which contain only a small portion of tenderloin) and porterhouse steaks (which are cut from the sirloin end of the short loin and contain a large portion of tenderloin).

The whole tenderloin can also be removed and cut into châteaubriand, filet mignon and tournedos. A portion of the tenderloin is located in the sirloin portion of the loin. When the entire beef loin is divided into the primal short loin and primal sirloin, the large end of the tenderloin (the butt tenderloin) is separated from the remainder of the tenderloin and remains in the sirloin; the smaller end of the tenderloin (the short tenderloin) remains in the short loin. If the tenderloin is to be kept whole, it must be removed before the short loin and sirloin are separated. The loin eye meat can be removed from the bones, producing a boneless strip loin, which is very tender and can be roasted or cut into boneless strip steaks.

Tenderloin

SIRLOIN

The sirloin is located in the hindquarter, between the short loin and the round. It accounts for approximately 7 percent of carcass weight and contains part of the backbone as well as a portion of the hip bone.

The sirloin produces bone-in or boneless roasts and steaks that are flavorful and tender. With the exception of the tenderloin portion, however, these subprimals and fabricated cuts are not as tender as those from the strip loin. Cuts from the sirloin are cooked using dry-heat methods such as broiling, grilling or roasting.

Top Sirloin Butt

Bottom Sirloin Butt Tri Tip

FLANK

The flank is located directly beneath the loin, posterior to (behind) the short plate. It accounts for approximately 6 percent of carcass weight. The flank contains no bones.

Although quite flavorful, it is a less tender cut with a good deal of fat and connective tissue. Flank meat is usually trimmed and ground, with the exception of the flank steak or London broil. The flank also contains a small piece of meat known as the hanging tenderloin. Although not actually part of the tenderloin, it is very tender and can be cooked using any method.

Flank Steak

Beef Round Rump and Shank Partially Removed (Steamship Round)

ROUND

The primal round is very large, weighing as much as 200 pounds (90 kg) and accounting for approximately 24 percent of carcass weight. It is the hind leg of the animal and contains the round, aitch, shank and tail bones.

Meat from the round is flavorful and fairly tender. The round yields a wide variety of subprimal and fabricated cuts: the top round, outside round, eye round (the outside

Top (or Inside) Round

BEEF: FROM COLUMBUS TO CATTLE DRIVES

Although cattle have been domesticated for several thousand years, they have been in the New World only since 1493, when Columbus brought them along on his second expedition to the West Indies. During the succeeding decades, the Spanish brought cattle to Florida and Texas, where they thrived in the dry, hot climates.

The New World's desire for beef steadily grew from the 1500s to the early 1800s. By the mid-1800s, America's demand for beef outpaced the supply available from local family farms, and so cattle ranching was born. Based principally in the Southwest and West, ranchers used the open range to support large cattle herds. Texas longhorns, descended from the original Spanish cattle stock, were the animal of choice. Prized for the quality of their meat, longhorns are hardy animals that live off the range and demand little care. They grow rapidly on forage such as mesquite beans, prickly pear, weeds, shrubs and buffalo grass. Ranchers brought the cattle from the range to slaughterhouses near consumer markets or to places such as Kansas City with rail links to the populous East Coast.

The open range, so vital to the 19th-century cattle industry, began to disappear rapidly after the signing of the Homestead Act of 1862. Squabbles with sheep ranchers further eroded the range land available for the great cattle herds to roam. And, as the railroads expanded westward, the cattle drives shortened and the economies of scale that supported cattle ranching began to dwindle. Although there are still many large cattle ranches, by the early 20th century, great cattle drives had become nothing more than fodder for Hollywood.

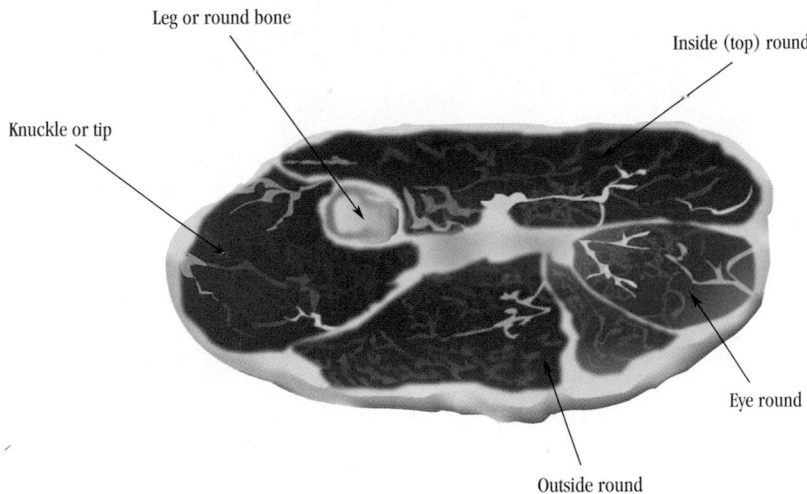

Leg or round bone

Inside (top) round

Knuckle or tip

Eye round

Outside round

FIGURE 13.3 ▶ Cross cut of muscles in a whole round.

round and the eye round together are called the bottom round), knuckle and shank. See Figure 13.3. Steaks cut from the round are less tender, but because they have large muscles and limited intermuscular fat, the top round and knuckle make good roasts. The bottom round is best when braised. The hindshank is prepared in the same fashion as the foreshank.

Organ Meats

Several organ meats are used in food service operations. This group of products is known as **offal**. It includes the heart, kidney, tongue, tripe (stomach lining) and oxtail. Offal benefit from moist-heat cooking and are often used in soup, stew or braised dishes.

offal (OFF-uhl) also called variety meats; edible entrails (for example, the heart, kidneys, liver, sweetbreads and tongue) and extremities (for example, oxtail and pig's feet) of an animal

NUTRITION

Beef is a major source of protein and the primary food source of zinc as well as B vitamins, trace minerals and other nutrients. Although well-marbled beef does contain a high percentage of saturated fat, lean cuts of beef such as eye round and top round roasts, top sirloin and shoulder pot roast have less fat than chicken thighs, a standard level of comparison. Excess fat should be trimmed as much as possible before cooking and serving.

BUTCHERING PROCEDURES

Although many food service operations buy their beef previously cut and portioned, it is still important for a cook to be able to fabricate cuts of beef and perform basic butchering tasks. Performing some basic fabrication procedures in the kitchen saves money and allows chefs to cut the meat to their exact specifications. (See Table 13.1 for a list of standard fabricated cuts.)

CLASSIC FLAVOR COMBINATIONS FOR BEEF

Antonin Carême once said that "beef is the soul of cooking." It is also the most popular meat consumed in the United States. Beef's flavor stands up well to most any sauce and seasoning. From pungent basil pesto on grilled strip steak to the assertive flavors of chili powder in a hearty stew, beef shines in robust preparations. Yet tender cuts such as the loin marry well with such subtle sauces as tarragon-scented hollandaise or red wine reductions.

PROCEDURE FOR **CUTTING A NEW YORK STEAK FROM A BONELESS STRIP LOIN**

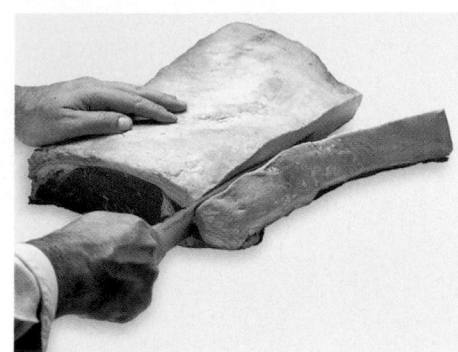

① Square up the strip loin by trimming off the lip so it extends 1 to 2 inches (2.5 to 5 centimeters) from the eye muscle.

② Turn the strip over and trim off any fat or connective tissue.

③ Turn the strip back over and trim the fat covering to a uniform thickness of ¼ inch (6 millimeters).

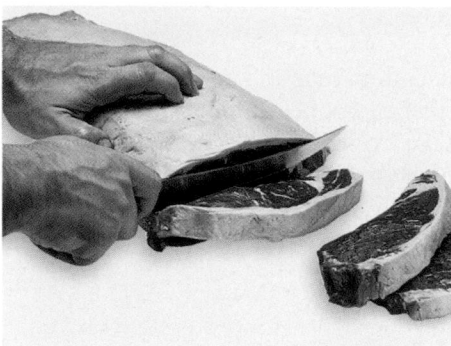

④ Cut the steaks to the thickness or weight desired.

⑤ The eye meat of steaks located on the sirloin end of the strip is divided by a strip of connective tissue. Steaks cut from this area are called vein steaks and are inferior to steaks cut from the rib end of the strip.

PROCEDURE FOR **TRIMMING A FULL BEEF TENDERLOIN AND CUTTING IT INTO CHÂTEAUBRIAND, FILET MIGNON AND TENDER TIPS**

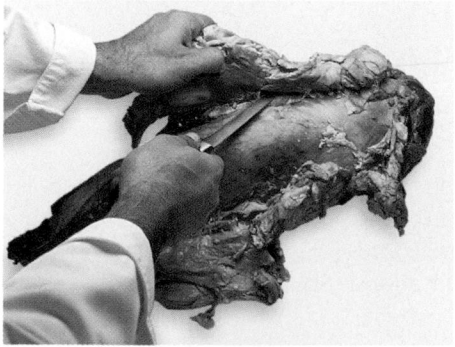

① Cut and pull the excess fat from the entire tenderloin to expose the meat.

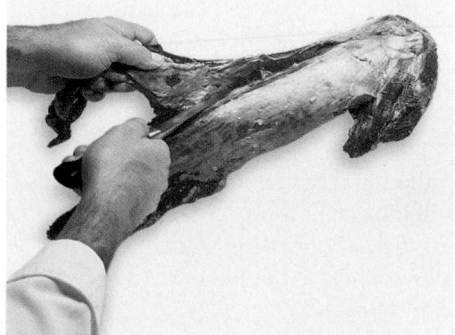

② Remove the chain muscle from the side of the tenderloin. (Although it contains much connective tissue, the chain muscle may be trimmed and the meat used as tenderloin trimmings in various dishes.)

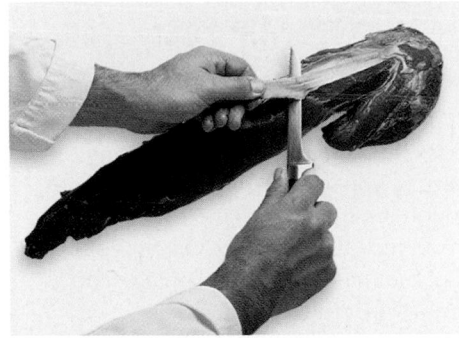

③ Trim away all of the fat and silverskin. Do so by loosening a small piece of silverskin; then, holding the loosened silverskin tightly with one hand, cut it away in long strips, angling the knife up toward the silverskin slightly so that only the silverskin is removed and no meat is wasted.

④ Cut the tenderloin as desired into (left to right) tips, châteaubriand, filet mignon, tournedos tips, and tenderloin tips.

PROCEDURE FOR **BUTTERFLYING MEATS**

Many cuts of boneless meats such as tenderloin steaks and boneless pork chops can be butterflied to create a thinner cut that has a greater surface area and cooks more quickly.

① Make the first cut nearly all the way through the meat, keeping it attached by leaving approximately ¼ inch (6 millimeters) uncut.

② Make a second cut, this time cutting all the way through, completely removing the steak from the tenderloin.

FIFTEEN SECONDS OF FLAME—A STEAK'S OWN STORY

Every cook knows that when you cook a good steak, you have to make painful compromises. You learn to blast it at high temperatures because you need more than 300°F to produce a crust with those rich, caramelized flavors that form like magic from the meat's natural sugars and amino acids. (Scientists call this process the Maillard reaction, named for the French physician who, almost a century ago, was the first to investigate similar reactions between proteins and sugars in the human body.) But you don't want the steak's interior to go much above 135°F because that's the temperature at which it stays juicy. Above that, the strands of proteins in the muscle fibers contract so much that they start to squeeze out their juices. Renowned food science author Harold McGee shocked the cooking world in 1984 when he used these principles to demonstrate that searing meat at high heat does precisely the opposite of "sealing in" those juices—it starts to dry them out.

So what usually happens when you throw your steak on the fire? You end up with a great Maillard crust, a juicy rare or rosy center—and then there's a dry, chewy "gray zone" in between.

McGee had a hunch that computers could figure out a satisfactory solution. He figured some Silicon Valley scientists could modify some mathematical simulation software to study how heat moves through meat. They could. McGee ran hundreds of simulations, in effect asking the computer: What's the best way to get the heat to diffuse through the meat so it cooks as fast and evenly as possible?

The computer told them that chefs are cooking their steaks, well, wrong. The computer simulation shows that when you throw a steak on the fire and just let it sit there, sizzling away, and then you flip the meat only once before you serve it, you're messing with the heat diffusion. There's such a huge difference between the temperatures on the side that's facing the fire and the side that's turned away that the heat inside your steak fluxes all over the place. (This applies only to beef.)

"But," McGee says, "the computer model shows that if you keep flipping the meat as you cook it, the heat diffuses through the meat much more evenly, so it cooks much more evenly. Our study suggests that the optimum flipping time is every 15 seconds."

Every 15 seconds? "Maybe that's a little extreme; it might be inconvenient," McGee says, laughing. "The computer model shows that flipping the meat every 30 seconds will work almost as well." And another recent study, at Lawrence Livermore National Laboratory, shows that frequent flipping makes steaks more healthful, too: It reduces the amount of carcinogenic compounds that can be generated when you cook over high heat by as much as 75 percent.

—DANIEL ZWERDLING is a Senior Correspondent with National Public Radio. This material originally appeared in *Gourmet Magazine*

TABLE 13.1 USING COMMON CUTS OF BEEF

PRIMAL	SUBPRIMAL OR FABRICATED CUT	IMPS	COOKING METHODS	SERVING SUGGESTIONS
Chuck	Top blade (flat iron)	114D	Dry heat (broil or grill)	Steak; fajitas
	Chuck roll, tied	116A	Combination (braise; stew)	Pot roast; beef stew
	Stew meat	135A	Combination (stew)	Beef stew
	Ground beef	136	Dry heat (broil or grill; roast) Combination (braise; stew)	Hamburgers; meatloaf Chili con carne; beef stews
Brisket and shank	Brisket	120	Moist heat (simmer)	Corned beef; New England boiled dinner
			Combination (braise)	Pot roast
	Shank	117	Combination (braise)	Shredded beef for tamales or hash
Rib	Oven-ready rib roast	109	Dry heat (roast)	Roast prime rib
	Rib eye roll	112	Dry heat (roast)	Roast prime rib
Short plate	Skirt steak	121D	Dry heat (broil or grill)	Steak; fajitas
	Short ribs	123A	Combination (braise)	Braised short ribs
Short loin	Porterhouse or T-bone steaks	173, 174	Dry heat (broil or grill)	Steaks
	Strip loin	180	Dry heat (broil or grill; roast; sauté)	New York steak; minute steak; entrecôte bordelaise
	Tenderloin	189	Dry heat (broil or grill, roast)	Tournedos Rossini; beef Wellington
Sirloin	Top sirloin butt	184	Dry heat (broil or grill; roast)	Steak; roast beef
	Tri tip	185	Dry heat (broil or grill; roast)	Steak; stir-fry; fajitas
Flank	Flank steak	193	Dry heat (broil or grill) Combination (braise)	London broil Braised stuffed flank steak
Round	Steamship round	160	Dry heat (roast)	Roast beef
	Top (inside) round	168	Dry heat (roast) Combination (braise)	Roast beef Braised beef roulade

1. List each beef primal cut and describe its location on the carcass. For each primal cut, identify two subprimal or fabricated cuts taken from it.

2. Would it be better to use the chuck for grilling or stewing? Explain your answer.

3. Which fabricated cuts contain a portion of the tenderloin? What cooking methods are best suited for these cuts? Explain your answer.

4. Most steaks are cut from the hindquarter. What popular steak is cut from the forequarter, and why is it tender when other cuts from the forequarter are relatively tough?

5. Visit the National Cattleman's Beef Association Web site to learn more. WWW Does cooking method affect the fat and cholesterol content of a beef steak? How has consumer demand for beef products changed over the past year?

6. Locate one or two restaurants in your area that participate in the Certified Angus Beef program.

7. Learn about the breeds of cattle being raised for beef in the United States WWW and other countries. How do the breeds differ in terms of fat content and finished weight? Have other countries evolved different techniques for fabricating beef?

QUESTIONS FOR DISCUSSION

Terms to Know

domesticated cattle	rib
	short plate
steer	short loin
quarters	sirloin
carcass	flank
chuck	round
brisket	marrow
shank	organ meats

FILET OF BEEF WITH COFFEE BEANS

RDG AND BAR ANNIE, HOUSTON, TX

Chef-Owner Robert Del Grande

Yield: 6 Servings   **Method:** Roasting

Beef tenderloin	1	1
Kosher salt	1 tsp.	5 ml
Black pepper	1 tsp.	5 ml
Virgin olive oil	2 Tbsp.	30 ml
Coffee beans, ground very fine	2 Tbsp.	30 ml
Cocoa powder	1 Tbsp.	15 ml
Cinnamon, ground	⅛ tsp.	0.5 ml
Pasilla chile broth:		
Whole butter	½ oz.	15 g
White onions, roughly chopped	8 oz.	240 g
Garlic cloves, whole, peeled	6	6
Pasilla chiles, stemmed, seeded, torn into large pieces	½ oz.	15 g
White corn tortilla, shredded	¾ oz.	22 g
Chicken stock	20 fl. oz.	600 ml
Heavy cream	2 fl. oz.	60 ml
Kosher salt	1 tsp.	5 ml
Brown sugar	1 tsp.	5 ml
Cooked grits, polenta or mashed potatoes	As needed for garnish	

1. Trim the beef tenderloin, removing all silverskin. Cut a 2- to 2-pound-8-ounce (0.9- to 1.2-kilogram) piece from the large (butt) end of the tenderloin. Tie this filet with butcher's twine at ½-inch (1.2-centimeter) intervals. Rub the filet with salt and pepper, then rub it with the oil.

2. Stir together the coffee, cocoa powder and cinnamon. Spread the mixture on a work surface and roll the filet in it in order to coat the beef evenly. Allow the beef to marinate for approximately 30 minutes.

3. To prepare the pasilla chile broth, heat a medium saucepan over medium-high heat. Add the butter and sauté the onions and garlic until browned. Add the pasilla chiles and tortilla pieces and sauté until golden brown.

4. Add the stock and bring to a boil. Reduce to a simmer, cover loosely and cook for 10 minutes. Remove from the heat and cool. Purée the sauce in a blender until smooth and strain through a china cap. Add the cream, salt and brown sugar and stir to combine. The sauce should not be very thick; thin it with additional stock or water if necessary. Hold for service.

5. Place the filet on a rack in a roasting pan. Roast the filet at 400°F (200°C) for 10 minutes. Lower the heat to 250°F (120°C) and cook the beef to the desired doneness, approximately 20 minutes for medium rare. Remove from the oven, remove the twine and allow to rest before carving.

6. Slice the filet to the desired thickness and serve one thick slice or several thin slices fanned on each plate. Serve with grits, polenta or mashed potatoes.

Approximate values per serving: **Calories** 500, **Total fat** 33 g, **Saturated fat** 13 g, **Cholesterol** 130 mg, **Sodium** 590 mg, **Total carbohydrates** 13 g, **Protein** 37 g, **Vitamin A** 20%

MARINATED LONDON BROIL

Yield: 6 Servings, 5–8 oz. (150–240 g) each　　　**Method:** Grilling

Marinade:		
Olive oil	4 fl. oz.	120 ml
Balsamic vinegar	4 fl. oz.	120 ml
Fresh rosemary, chopped	2 Tbsp.	30 ml
Garlic, minced	2 oz.	60 g
Black pepper	1 tsp.	5 ml
Salt	1 Tbsp.	15 ml
Beef flank steak, 2–3 lb. (1–1½ kg)	1	1

1 Combine the marinade ingredients in a hotel pan.

2 Add the flank steak to the marinade and coat completely. Allow the meat to marinate for at least 4 hours.

3 Grill the steak rare to medium rare. If cooked further, the meat will become extremely tough.

4 Carve into ¼-inch- (6-millimeter-) thick slices, cutting diagonally across the grain.

Approximate values per 8-oz. (240-g) serving: **Calories** 310, **Total fat** 16 g, **Saturated fat** 5 g, **Cholesterol** 75 mg, **Sodium** 370 mg, **Total carbohydrates** 2 g, **Protein** 38 g, **Iron** 15%

CHÂTEAUBRIAND

SIMPLICITY CATERING, Falls Church, VA

Chef Leland Atkinson

French chefs of the late 19th century began referring to the classic filet de boeuf (a very thick steak cut from the best part of the filet) as Châteaubriand in reference to the 19th-century statesman and author of the same name. The dish is traditionally served with béarnaise sauce, a bouquetière of vegetables and château potatoes.

Yield: 2–4 Servings　　　**Method:** Roasting

Beef filet, cut from the large (head) end of the tenderloin, 16–24 oz. (480–720 g)	1	1
Salt and pepper	TT	TT
Clarified butter	as needed	as needed
Béarnaise sauce (page 209)	4 fl. oz.	120 ml

1 Tie the beef with butcher's twine and season with salt and pepper.

2 Sauté the beef in clarified butter until it is well browned.

3 Transfer the beef to a 450°F (230°C) oven and roast until done, approximately 10 to 12 minutes for rare (internal temperature of 125°F/52°C), or 15 to 18 minutes for medium (140°F/60°C).

4 Remove the beef from the oven and allow it to rest for at least 5 minutes before carving.

5 At service time, slice the beef evenly on a slight diagonal bias. Serve napped with the béarnaise sauce.

Approximate values per 10-oz. (300-g) serving: **Calories** 705, **Total fat** 40 g, **Saturated fat** 18 g, **Cholesterol** 270 mg, **Sodium** 1350 mg, **Total carbohydrates** 1 g, **Protein** 80 g, **Vitamin A** 13%, **Iron** 66%

BEEF WELLINGTON

Yield: 10 Servings		Method: Roasting
Beef tenderloin, trimmed, 4 lb.–4 lb. 8 oz. (1.9–2.1 kg)	1	1
Salt and pepper	TT	TT
Vegetable oil	as needed	as needed
Pâté de foie gras	8 oz.	240 g
Truffle peelings, chopped fine	1 oz.	30 g
Puff Pastry (page 975)	2 lb.	960 g
Egg wash	as needed	as needed
Madeira sauce (page 406)	20 fl. oz.	600 ml

❶ Spreading the browned tenderloin with pâté de foie gras.

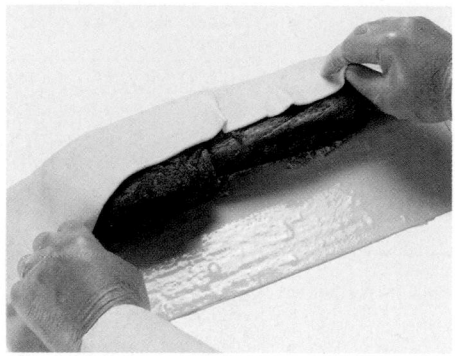

❷ Wrapping the pastry around the seared tenderloin.

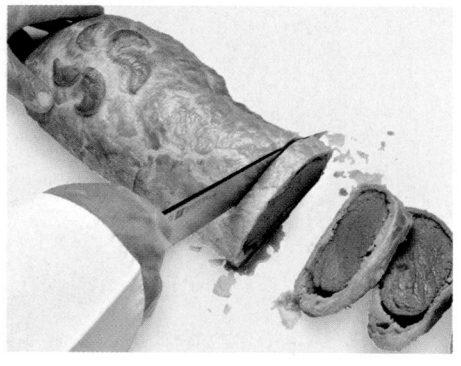

❸ Slicing the cooked Beef Wellington.

❶ Trim 3 to 4 inches (7.5 to 10 centimeters) of the tail from the tenderloin. (The small tail portion can be used for some other preparation.) Season the tenderloin with salt and pepper and sear in a small amount of oil in a large rondeau. Remove from the pan and cool.

❷ Spread the surface of the tenderloin with the pâté de foie gras. Sprinkle the truffles over the pâté.

❸ Roll the puff pastry dough into a rectangle approximately 3/16 inch (5 millimeters) thick and large enough to wrap around the entire tenderloin.

❹ Turn the tenderloin over and place it lengthwise, pâté side down, in the center of the pastry. Fold the ends over and wrap the pastry around the tenderloin, sealing it with egg wash and trimming off any excess.

❺ Transfer the Wellington to a baking sheet, placing the seam side down. Brush the surface with egg wash.

❻ Bake the Wellington in a 350°F (180°C) oven until the center reaches 125°F–130°F (52°C–54°C), approximately 40 minutes. Do not overcook; the crust holds in steam and heat, thus enhancing the effects of carryover cooking.

❼ Allow the meat to rest 5 minutes after baking. Carve the Wellington tableside or on a buffet with Madeira sauce served on the side.

VARIATION:

Individual Wellingtons can be made by cutting the tenderloin into 4- to 5-ounce (120- to 150-gram) filet mignons, using smaller pieces of puff pastry and reducing the cooking time to approximately 20 minutes.

Approximate values per serving: **Calories** 720, **Total fat** 44 g, **Saturated fat** 14 g, **Cholesterol** 160 mg, **Sodium** 700 mg, **Total carbohydrates** 29 g, **Protein** 48 g, **Vitamin A** 15%, **Iron** 40%

HOME-STYLE MEATLOAF

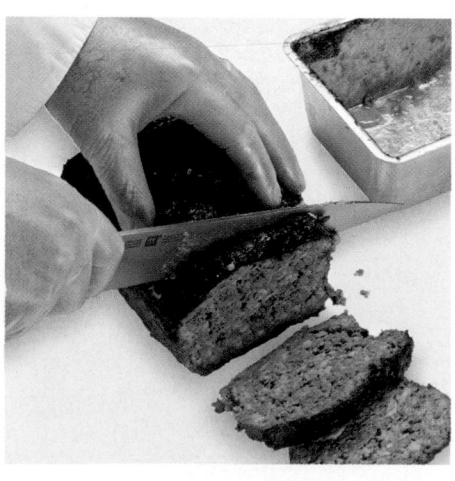

Yield: 16 Servings, 8 oz. (240 g) each		Method: Baking
Onions, small dice	1 lb.	480 g
Celery, small dice	8 oz.	240 g
Garlic, chopped	2 Tbsp.	30 ml
Vegetable oil	2 fl. oz.	60 ml
Fresh bread crumbs	6 oz.	180 g
Tomato juice	1 pt.	480 ml
Ground beef	4 lb.	1.9 kg
Ground pork	4 lb.	1.9 kg
Eggs, beaten	4	4
Salt	4 tsp.	20 ml
Black pepper	1 Tbsp.	15 ml

Fresh parsley, chopped	4 Tbsp.	60 ml
Worcestershire sauce	3 Tbsp.	45 ml
Ketchup	as needed	as needed

1. Sauté the onions, celery and garlic in the oil until tender. Remove from the heat and cool.
2. Combine all the ingredients except the ketchup and mix well.
3. Form into loaves of the desired size and place in loaf pans.
4. Brush the top of each loaf with ketchup as desired. Bake at 350°F (180°C) until the meatloaf reaches an internal temperature of 165°F (74°C), approximately 1 hour for a 9-inch × 5-inch (22-centimeter × 12-centimeter) loaf pan.
5. Allow the loaves to rest for 15 minutes before slicing. Cut slices of the desired thickness and serve with a tomato or mushroom sauce.

Approximate values per serving: **Calories** 590, **Total fat** 38 g, **Saturated fat** 13 g, **Cholesterol** 255 mg, **Sodium** 920 mg, **Total carbohydrates** 11 g, **Protein** 48 g, **Vitamin C** 20%, **Iron** 25%

HUGO'S MEATBALLS

NATIONAL CENTER FOR HOSPITALITY STUDIES, SULLIVAN UNIVERSITY, Louisville, KY

Chef Tom Hickey, CEC, CCE, CFE, CHE

Yield: 50 Meatballs, 2 oz. (60 g) each   **Method:** Roasting/Stewing

Ground beef	5 lb.	2.4 kg
Dried oregano	2 Tbsp.	30 ml
Garlic powder	2 Tbsp.	30 ml
Onion powder	2 Tbsp.	30 ml
Fresh parsley, minced	3 oz.	90 g
Salt	1 Tbsp.	15 ml
Pepper	1½ tsp.	8 ml
Parmesan cheese, grated	2½ oz.	75 g
Eggs, beaten	3	3
Worcestershire sauce	1 fl. oz.	30 ml
Bread crumbs	4½ oz.	135 g

1. Combine all ingredients and mix lightly.
2. Using a #16 portion scoop, divide into 2-ounce (60-gram) meatballs and round evenly.
3. Place the meatballs on sheet pans and bake at 325°F (160°C) until they are just set, not browned, approximately 20 minutes.
4. Drain the grease from the pan. Remove the meatballs with a slotted spoon and carefully drop into tomato sauce. Simmer for 20 minutes to allow the meatballs to finish cooking and to blend the flavors.
5. Serve the meatballs and sauce with pasta or as desired.

Approximate values per meatball: **Calories** 110, **Total fat** 5 g, **Saturated fat** 2 g, **Cholesterol** 45 mg, **Sodium** 230 mg, **Total carbohydrates** 4 g, **Protein** 11 g

MEATBALLS—A BLANK SLATE FOR CULINARY CREATIVITY

When making meatballs, the combination of meat used affects the final flavor; ground beef, lamb, pork and veal work well alone or in combination. Select meat that is 20% fat and 80% lean to ensure a juicy product. Dry bread crumbs give the meatball a firm texture; moist fresh bread crumbs yield a soft, tender meatball. Fresh herbs such as cilantro, dill, mint, rosemary, sage and tarragon and spices such as curry powder and Cajun seasoning provide the ethnic flavor profile desired. Form the meat mixture into miniature sizes for soups or larger sizes for main course portions, then chill thoroughly before baking, pan-frying or simmering.

SALISBURY STEAK

THE SCHOOL OF CULINARY ARTS AT KENDALL COLLEGE, Evanston, IL

Chef Mike Artlip, CEC, CCE

Yield: 40 Servings, 5 oz. (150 g) each   **Method:** Baking

Mirepoix, minced	5 lb. 4 oz.	2.5 kg
Olive oil	7 fl. oz.	210 ml
Dried thyme	1 tsp.	5 ml
Dried marjoram	5 tsp.	25 ml
Black pepper	1½ tsp.	8 ml
Salt	TT	TT
Cornflake crumbs	10½ oz.	315 g
Eggs, beaten	7	7
Worcestershire sauce	4 tsp.	20 ml
Milk	5 fl. oz.	150 ml
Ground beef	13 lb. 4 oz.	6.3 kg
Mushroom sauce (page 203)	as needed	as needed

1 Sauté the mirepoix in the oil until tender. Add the thyme, marjoram, pepper and salt. Remove from the pan, cool, and refrigerate until cold.

2 Combine the mirepoix with the cornflake crumbs, eggs, Worcestershire sauce and milk and mix well.

3 Add the beef, adjust the seasonings and mix well.

4 Make a small patty and cook it. Taste it to check the seasonings and adjust them if necessary.

5 Scale forty 5-ounce (150-gram) portions of the mixture. Alternatively, use a slightly rounded #8 scoop to portion the mixture. Form each portion into a flattened football-shaped patty and place on a baking sheet.

6 Bake the Salisbury steaks at 325°F (160°C) until done, approximately 10 to 15 minutes. Serve with mushroom sauce.

Approximate values per serving, without sauce: **Calories** 410, **Total fat** 25 g, **Saturated fat** 9 g, **Cholesterol** 135 mg, **Sodium** 180 mg, **Total carbohydrates** 12 g, **Protein** 32 g, **Vitamin A** 90%, **Vitamin C** 16%, **Iron** 30%

TOURNEDOS ROSSINI

A crouton or scole raises the tournedos off the plate in this classic beef preparation. This technique is frequently used to enhance the presentation of beef, veal, lamb or fish steaks that are cut into medallions.

Yield: 4 Servings   **Method:** Sautéing

Tournedos, 3 oz. (90 g) each	8	8
Clarified butter	as needed	as needed
Croutons, cut to the size of the tournedos	8	8
Foie gras, 1-oz. (30-g) slices	8	8
Truffle slices	8	8
Madeira wine	4 fl. oz.	120 ml
Demi-glace	8 fl. oz.	240 ml
Salt and pepper	TT	TT

1 Sauté the tournedos in clarified butter to the desired doneness. Place each tournedo on top of a crouton. Top each with a slice of foie gras, then a slice of truffle. Hold in a warm place.

2 Degrease the pan. Deglaze the pan with the wine and add the demi-glace.

③ Reduce the sauce to the desired consistency and adjust the seasonings.

④ Warm the tournedos briefly under a broiler or in the oven. Place two tournedos on each plate. Pour the sauce around the tournedos. Garnish with watercress, sautéed asparagus and château potatoes.

Approximate values per serving: **Calories** 890, **Total fat** 50 g, **Saturated fat** 16 g, **Cholesterol** 325 mg, **Sodium** 1880 mg, **Total carbohydrates** 45 g, **Protein** 60 g, **Vitamin A** 540%, **Iron** 40%

MINUTE STEAK DIJONAISE

Yield: 2 Servings **Method:** Sautéing

Sirloin steaks, trimmed, 6 oz. (180 g)	2	2
Dijon mustard	1 oz.	30 g
Onion, small dice	2 oz.	60 g
Clarified butter	1 fl. oz.	30 ml
Heavy cream	3 fl. oz.	90 ml
Whole butter	1 oz.	30 g
Salt and pepper	TT	TT

① Pound the steaks to a ¼-inch (6-millimeter) thickness.

② Cover one side of each sirloin first with 1½ teaspoons (8 milliliters) mustard and then half of the onion, pressing the onion firmly into the steak.

③ Sauté the steaks in the clarified butter, presentation (onion) side down first. Remove and hold in a warm place.

④ Degrease the pan. Add the cream and reduce by half. Add the rest of the mustard.

⑤ Monté au beurre. Adjust the seasonings. Serve each portion with some of the sauce.

Approximate values per serving: **Calories** 671, **Total fat** 45 g, **Saturated fat** 23 g, **Cholesterol** 255 mg, **Sodium** 2050 mg, **Total carbohydrates** 6 g, **Protein** 60 g, **Vitamin A** 36%, **Iron** 44%

BEEF STROGANOFF

Yield: 8 Servings, 8 oz. (240 g) each **Method:** Sautéing

Tenderloin tips, émincé	2 lb.	960 g
Clarified butter	3 Tbsp.	45 ml
Onion, medium dice	4 oz.	120 g
Mushrooms, halved	1 lb.	480 g
Demi-glace	10 fl. oz.	300 ml
Heavy cream	10 fl. oz.	300 ml
Sour cream	8 oz.	240 g
Dijon mustard	1 Tbsp.	15 ml
Fresh dill, chopped	1 Tbsp.	15 ml
Fresh parsley, chopped	1 Tbsp.	15 ml
Salt and pepper	TT	TT
Egg noodles, cooked	24 oz.	720 g

① Sauté the tenderloin tips in the butter, searing on all sides. Remove the meat and set aside.

② Add the onion to the pan and sauté lightly. Add the mushrooms and sauté until dry.

③ Add the demi-glace. Bring to a boil, reduce to a simmer and cook for 10 minutes.

④ Add the cream, sour cream, mustard and any meat juices that accumulated while holding the meat.

⑤ Return the meat to the sauce to reheat. Stir in the dill and parsley. Adjust the seasonings and serve over hot egg noodles.

Approximate values per serving: **Calories** 635, **Total fat** 39 g, **Saturated fat** 20 g, **Cholesterol** 201 mg, **Sodium** 510 mg, **Total carbohydrates** 32 g, **Protein** 40 g, **Vitamin A** 41%, **Iron** 46%, **Calcium** 11%

ENTRECÔTES BORDELAISE

Yield: 4 Servings　　　　**Method:** Sautéing

Beef marrow	4 oz.	120 g
Entrecôtes, 14 oz. (400 g) each	2	2
Salt and pepper	TT	TT
Clarified butter	2 fl. oz.	60 ml
Shallots, chopped	2 Tbsp.	30 ml
Red wine	8 fl. oz.	240 ml
Demi-glace	12 fl. oz.	360 ml
Whole butter	1 oz.	30 g

1. Slice the marrow into rounds and poach in salted water for 3 minutes. Drain the marrow and set it aside.
2. Season the steaks and sauté them in the clarified butter to the desired doneness. Finish in the oven if desired. Remove to a platter and hold in a warm place.
3. Sauté the shallots in the same pan.
4. Deglaze the pan with the wine and reduce by half. Add the demi-glace; simmer for 5 minutes.
5. Monté au beurre.
6. Add the marrow to the sauce. Adjust the seasonings. Divide each steak into two portions and serve the steaks with the sauce.

Approximate values per serving: **Calories** 610, **Total fat** 35 g, **Saturated fat** 17 g, **Cholesterol** 200 mg, **Sodium** 810 mg, **Total carbohydrates** 5 g, **Protein** 57 g, **Vitamin A** 21%, **Iron** 44%

PEPPER STEAK

Yield: 2 Servings　　　　**Method:** Sautéing

Boneless strip steaks, approx. 8 oz. (240 g) each	2	2
Salt	TT	TT
Peppercorns, cracked	3 Tbsp.	45 ml
Clarified butter	1 fl. oz.	30 ml
Cognac	2 fl. oz.	60 ml
Heavy cream	4 fl. oz.	120 ml
Whole butter	2 oz.	60 g

1. Season the steaks with salt. Spread the peppercorns in a hotel pan and press the steaks into them, lightly coating each side.
2. Sauté the steaks in the clarified butter over high heat for 2 to 3 minutes on each side.
3. Remove the pan from the heat. Pour the cognac over the steaks, return the pan to the heat and flambé. When the flames subside, remove the steaks from the pan and keep them warm on a plate.
4. Add the cream to the pan. Bring to a boil and reduce for 2 minutes over high heat; monté au beurre. Pour this sauce over the steaks and serve immediately.

Approximate values per serving: **Calories** 950, **Total fat** 73 g, **Saturated fat** 42 g, **Cholesterol** 300 mg, **Sodium** 1525 mg, **Total carbohydrates** 8 g, **Protein** 51 g, **Vitamin A** 72%, **Iron** 46%, **Calcium** 13%

① Press the steaks into the peppercorns.

② Flambé the cognac on the steaks.

③ Pour the finished sauce over each steak.

BEEF FAJITAS

Yield: 6 Servings **Method:** Grilling/Sautéing

Marinade:		
Garlic cloves	4	4
Salt	1½ tsp.	8 ml
Black pepper, ground coarse	1½ tsp.	8 ml
Cumin	1½ tsp.	8 ml
Onion powder	1½ tsp.	8 ml
Chilli powder	1½ tsp.	8 ml
Skirt steak	2 lb.	960 g
Vegetable oil	2 Tbsp.	30 ml
Bell peppers, mixed, red, yellow and green, sliced thin	3	3
Onion, sliced thin	1	1
Garlic cloves, chopped	2	2
Cilantro sprigs	as needed for garnish	

① Make the marinade by chopping and mashing the garlic into a paste. In a bowl, combine the garlic paste with the remaining marinade ingredients.

② Trim the fat from the skirt steak. Cut the steak into two or three pieces if necessary. Add the steaks to the marinade, turning them several times to coat all sides. Cover the steak and marinate in the refrigerator for at least 1 hour or overnight.

③ Grill the steak on a hot grill to the desired doneness. Remove the steak and allow it to rest for 10 minutes.

④ Add the oil to a heavy sauté pan, heat the pan until very hot and sauté the bell peppers, onion and garlic just until they begin to soften.

⑤ Slice the steak against the grain into thin slices. Arrange the steak and the pepper mixture on very hot cast-iron platters and garnish with the cilantro. The platters should be sizzling as they are presented to the table.

⑥ Serve the fajitas accompanied by warm flour or corn tortillas, fresh salsa, sour cream, and guacamole.

Approximate values per serving: **Calories** 630, **Total fat** 24 g, **Saturated fat** 7 g, **Cholesterol** 80 mg, **Sodium** 700 mg, **Total carbohydrates** 61 g, **Protein** 41 g, **Vitamin A** 25%, **Vitamin C** 170%, **Iron** 35%, **Claims**—good source of fiber, vitamins A and C and iron

SWISS STEAK

Yield: 10 Servings   **Method:** Braising

Beef bottom round steaks, 6 oz. (180 g) each	10	10
Flour	as needed for dredging	
Salt and pepper	TT	TT
Oil	2 fl. oz.	60 ml
Onions, small dice	1 lb.	480 g
Garlic cloves, crushed	3	3
Celery, diced	8 oz.	240 g
Flour	4 oz.	120 g
Brown stock	5 pt.	2.4 lt
Tomato purée	6 oz.	180 g
Sachet:		
Bay leaves	2	2
Dried thyme	½ tsp.	2 ml
Peppercorns, crushed	½ tsp.	2 ml
Parsley stems	8	8

1. Dredge the steaks in flour seasoned with salt and pepper.
2. Heat the oil in a roasting pan and brown the steaks well on both sides. Remove the steaks.
3. Add the onions, garlic and celery; sauté until tender.
4. Add the flour and cook to a brown roux.
5. Gradually add the stock, whisking until the sauce is thickened and smooth. Add the tomato purée and sachet.
6. Return the steaks to the braising pan, cover and cook in a 300°F (150°C) oven until tender, approximately 2 hours.
7. Remove the steaks from the sauce. Discard the sachet. Strain the sauce and adjust the seasonings. Serve the steaks with the sauce.

Approximate values per serving: **Calories** 601, **Total fat** 26 g, **Saturated fat** 7 g, **Cholesterol** 170 mg, **Sodium** 390 mg, **Total carbohydrates** 30 g, **Protein** 61 g, **Vitamin A** 49%, **Vitamin C** 12%, **Iron** 52%

BRAISED SHORT RIBS OF BEEF

Yield: 8 Servings, 8 oz. (240 g) each   **Method:** Braising

Flour	4 oz.	120 g
Salt	1 Tbsp.	15 ml
Black pepper	1 tsp.	5 ml
Dried rosemary	½ tsp.	2 ml
Short ribs of beef, cut into 2-in. (5-cm) portions	6 lb.	2.8 kg
Vegetable oil	1 fl. oz.	30 ml
Onion, chopped	6 oz.	180 g
Celery, chopped	4 oz.	120 g
Brown beef stock	24 fl. oz.	720 ml
Roux	as needed	as needed
Salt and pepper	TT	TT
Mashed potatoes (page 635)	as needed	as needed
Scallions, steamed	12	12
Cherry tomatoes	as needed	as needed

1 Straining the sauce.

1. Combine the flour, salt, pepper and rosemary. Dredge the ribs in the seasoned flour.
2. Heat the oil in a heavy brazier and brown the ribs well. Remove and hold in a warm place.
3. Add the onion and celery to the brazier and sauté lightly.
4. Return the ribs to the pan, add the stock and cook in a 300°F (150°C) oven until done, approximately 2½ hours.
5. Remove the ribs from the liquid and skim off the excess fat.
6. Bring the liquid to a boil on the stove top; thicken it with roux to the desired consistency and simmer for 15 minutes. Strain the sauce and adjust the seasonings. Return the ribs to the sauce and simmer for 5 minutes.
7. Serve the ribs with mashed potatoes garnished with the scallions, some cherry tomatoes and additional sauce.

2 The finished short ribs.

VARIATIONS:

Orange-Scented Braised Short Ribs of Beef—Omit the rosemary. Add 4 tablespoons (60 milliliters) julienned orange zest and 8 fluid ounces (240 milliliters) orange juice in step 4. Decrease the stock by 8 fluid ounces (240 milliliters).

Ginger Braised Short Ribs of Beef—Omit the rosemary. Sauté 3 ounces (90 grams) peeled and chopped fresh ginger with the onions and celery in step 3. Substitute 2 fluid ounces (60 milliliters) soy sauce for an equal amount of the beef stock and add 1 tablespoon (15 milliliters) ground ginger to the ribs before braising in step 4.

Approximate values per serving: **Calories** 1150, **Total fat** 70 g, **Saturated fat** 27 g, **Cholesterol** 320 mg, **Sodium** 1154 mg, **Total carbohydrates** 18 g, **Protein** 110 g, **Vitamin A** 18%, **Iron** 85%

BOEUF À LA FICELLE
(BEEF POACHED ON A STRING)

Yield: 8 servings   **Method:** Poaching

Beef tenderloins, center cut, 1½ lb. (720 g)	2	2
White wine	1 fl. oz.	30 ml
Carrots, tournée, 2 in. (5 cm) long	8	8
Baby white turnips, peeled	16	16
Pearl onions, blanched and peeled	16	16
Celery, peeled, 2-in. (5-cm) pieces, cut on the bias	16	16
Mushroom caps, tournée	24	24
Potatoes, tournée, 2 in. (5 cm) long	16	16
Bouquet garni:		
Carrot stick, 4 in. (10 cm)	1	1
Leek, split, 4 in. (10 cm)	1	1
Fresh thyme	1 sprig	1 sprig
Bay leaf	1	1
White veal stock, hot	3 qt.	2.8 lt
Salt and pepper	TT	TT
Port wine	1 fl. oz.	30 ml
Butter	3 Tbsp.	45 ml
Fresh chives, sliced	2 tsp.	10 ml
Dijon mustard	as needed	as needed

1. Tie the tenderloins, leaving long strings on each end.
2. Place the white wine, carrots, baby turnips, pearl onions, celery, mushroom caps, potatoes and bouquet garni in a 6-quart (6-liter) saucepot. Add the stock, bring to a simmer and cook 5 minutes.
3. Add the tenderloins to the stock and vegetables, tying the long strings to the handles of the pot so the meat is fully submerged and is not sitting on the bottom. Reduce the heat and poach the tenderloins for 15 to 20 minutes or until rare.
4. Remove the tenderloins from the cooking liquid and remove the string. Simmer the vegetables in the cooking liquid until done and remove with a slotted spoon.
5. Reduce the cooking liquid to concentrate its flavor as desired. Adjust the seasoning with salt and pepper and add the port wine. Monté au beurre.
6. Slice the tenderloin and present on plates or platters with the vegetables. Immediately before serving, ladle a portion of the hot broth over the tenderloin and vegetables. Garnish with chives. Serve additional broth and mustard separately.

Approximate values per serving: **Calories** 500, **Total fat** 19 g, **Saturated fat** 8 g, **Cholesterol** 120 mg, **Sodium** 860 mg, **Total carbohydrates** 33 g, **Protein** 47 g, **Vitamin A** 30%, **Vitamin C** 40%, **Iron** 25%

HUNGARIAN GOULASH

Yield: 9 Servings, 12 oz. (360 g) each   **Method:** Stewing

Onions, medium dice	2 lb.	960 g
Lard or vegetable oil	2 fl. oz.	60 ml
Hungarian paprika	4 Tbsp.	60 ml
Garlic, chopped	1 Tbsp.	15 ml
Caraway seeds	½ tsp.	2 ml
Salt	TT	TT
Black pepper	½ tsp.	2 ml
White stock	1 qt.	1 lt
Tomato paste	4 oz.	120 g
Beef stew meat, cut in 1½-in. (4-cm) cubes	5 lb.	2.4 kg

1. Sauté the onions in the lard or oil, browning lightly.
2. Add the paprika, garlic, caraway seeds, salt and pepper; mix well.
3. Add the stock and tomato paste. Bring to a boil, then reduce to a simmer.
4. Add the meat and continue simmering until the meat is very tender, approximately 1½ hours. Adjust the seasonings and serve with buttered egg noodles or mashed potatoes.

Approximate values per 12-oz. (360-g) serving: **Calories** 645, **Total fat** 32 g, **Saturated fat** 12 g, **Cholesterol** 235 mg, **Sodium** 910 mg, **Total carbohydrates** 13 g, **Protein** 73 g, **Vitamin A** 28%, **Vitamin C** 20%, **Iron** 63%

BEEF BOURGUIGNONNE

Yield: 10 Servings, 8 oz. (240 g) each   **Method:** Stewing

Marinade:		
Garlic cloves, crushed	3	3
Onions, sliced	3	3
Carrots, sliced	2	2
Parsley stems	10	10
Bouquet garni:		
Carrot stick, 4 in. (10 cm)	1	1
Leek, split, 4-in. (10-cm) piece	1	1
Fresh thyme	1 sprig	1 sprig
Bay leaf	1	1
Peppercorns, crushed	10	10
Salt	TT	TT
Dry red wine, preferably Burgundy	26 fl. oz.	780 ml
Beef chuck, cubed for stew	4 lb.	1.9 kg
Vegetable oil	2 fl. oz.	60 ml
Flour	2 Tbsp.	30 ml
Tomato paste	1 Tbsp.	15 ml
Tomatoes, quartered	4	4
Brown stock	1 pt.	480 ml
Mushrooms, quartered	1 lb.	480 g
Unsalted butter	1½ oz.	45 g
Pearl onions, boiled and peeled	30	30
Salt and pepper	TT	TT

1. Combine the garlic, onions, carrots, parsley, bouquet garni, peppercorns, salt and wine to make a marinade.
2. Marinate the meat for several hours under refrigeration.
3. Remove and drain the meat. Reserve the marinade.
4. Dry the beef and sauté it in the oil in a large rondeau until well browned. Do this in several batches if necessary.
5. Return all the meat to the rondeau. Sprinkle with flour and cook to make a blond roux.
6. Stir in the tomato paste and cook for 5 minutes.
7. Add the reserved marinade, tomatoes and stock. Cook in a 350°F (180°C) oven until the meat is tender, approximately 2½ hours.
8. Remove the meat from the sauce. Strain the sauce through a china cap, pressing to extract all the liquid. Discard the solids. Return the liquid and the beef to the pot.
9. Sauté the mushrooms in the butter and add them to the meat and sauce. Add the pearl onions and adjust the seasonings. Simmer for 10 minutes to blend the flavors.

Approximate values per serving: **Calories** 315, **Total fat** 15 g, **Saturated fat** 6.5 g, **Cholesterol** 97 mg, **Sodium** 640 mg, **Total carbohydrates** 8 g, **Protein** 30 g, **Vitamin A** 27%, **Vitamin C** 13%, **Iron** 26%

CHILI CON CARNE

Serve chili with cornbread, corn chips or soft rolls garnished with sour cream, shredded Monterey Jack cheese and chopped scallions. Chili works well spooned over baked potatoes or in a hollowed-out round of crusty bread.

Yield: 5 qt. (4.8 lt)   **Method:** Stewing

Onions, medium dice	1 lb.	480 g
Vegetable oil	½ fl. oz.	15 ml
Garlic, chopped	2 oz.	60 g
Ground beef	2 lb. 8 oz.	1.2 kg
Tomatoes, crushed	3 lb.	1.4 kg
Tomatoes, diced	4 lb.	1.9 kg
Brown stock	1 qt.	960 ml
Chilli powder	1 oz.	30 g
Cumin	2 tsp.	10 ml
Bay leaves	4	4
Worcestershire sauce	1½ fl. oz.	45 ml
Green chiles, diced	8 oz.	240 g
Salt and pepper	TT	TT

1. Sauté the onions in the oil until tender. Add the garlic and sauté for 1 minute.
2. Add the beef and brown, stirring occasionally. Drain off the excess fat.
3. Add the remaining ingredients, bring to a simmer, cover and cook for 1 to 1½ hours.
4. Remove the bay leaves and adjust the seasonings.

VARIATION:

Chili with Beans—Before the final adjustment of seasonings, stir in 12 ounces (360 grams) of dried red kidney beans that have been soaked, simmered until tender and drained.

Approximate values per 1½-c. (360-ml) serving: **Calories** 290, **Total fat** 13 g, **Saturated fat** 5 g, **Cholesterol** 55 mg, **Sodium** 690 mg, **Total carbohydrates** 23 g, **Protein** 22 g, **Vitamin A** 80%, **Vitamin C** 50%, **Calcium** 10%, **Iron** 25%, **Claims**—good source of fiber, vitamins A and C, iron and calcium

CARPACCIO

Carpaccio is paper-thin slices of raw beef often served drizzled with olive oil and garnished with shaved Parmesan cheese. The dish takes its name from that of the Italian Renaissance artist Vittore Carpaccio, known for his lavish use of rich red colors in his paintings. A salad of pungent greens such as arugula or watercress is a traditional accompaniment.

Yield: 8 Servings

Beef tenderloin, trimmed of all silverskin and fat	1 lb.	480 g
Fresh mayonnaise	8 oz.	240 g
Dijon mustard	1 Tbsp.	15 ml
Salt and pepper	TT	TT
Capers, chopped	4 tsp.	20 ml
Cracked black pepper	TT	TT
Onion, sliced thin	4 oz.	120 g
Olive oil	1½ fl. oz.	45 ml

1 Place the tenderloin in the freezer until nearly frozen.

2 Combine the mayonnaise with the mustard. Season with salt and pepper.

3 Slice the nearly frozen tenderloin on an electric slicer very thin, almost transparent. On eight very cold plates, arrange one slightly overlapping layer of thin slices of beef.

4 Sprinkle each plate of beef with ½ teaspoon (2.5 milliliters) capers, a generous amount of cracked black pepper, salt and ½ ounce (15 grams) sliced onions. Drizzle with 1 teaspoon (5 milliliters) oil and spoon ½ ounce (15 grams) mayonnaise in the center of each plate. Serve very cold.

Approximate values per 4-oz. (120-g) serving: **Calories** 360, **Total fat** 33 g, **Saturated fat** 7 g, **Cholesterol** 70 mg, **Sodium** 250 mg, **Total carbohydrates** 1 g, **Protein** 16 g

> "Happy and successful cooking doesn't rely only on know-how; it comes from the heart, makes great demands on the palate and needs enthusiasm and a deep love of food to bring it to life."
>
> —GEORGES BLANC, FRENCH CHEF, IN *MA CUISINE DES SAISONS*, 1984

CHAPTER FOURTEEN

VEAL

- identify the primal, subprimal and fabricated cuts of veal
- perform basic butchering procedures
- apply appropriate cooking methods to several common cuts of veal

FORMULA-FED VEAL VS. FREE-RANGE VEAL

Most veal produced today is known as formula-fed veal. Formula-fed calves are fed only nutrient-rich liquids; they are tethered in pens only slightly larger than their bodies in order to restrict their movements. Preventing the calves from eating grasses and other foods containing iron keeps their flesh white; restricting movement keeps their muscles from toughening. In recent years, controversy and allegations of cruelty have arisen concerning these methods.

An alternative to formula-fed veal is free-range veal. Free-range veal is produced from calves that are allowed to roam freely and eat grasses and other natural foods. Because they consume feed containing iron, their flesh is a reddish pink and has a substantially different flavor than meat from formula-fed calves of the same age.

Opinions differ on which has the better flavor. Some chefs prefer the consistently mild, sweet taste of formula-fed veal. Others prefer the more substantial flavor of free-range veal. The two are interchangeable in recipes. Cost, however, may be the ultimate deciding factor when determining which to use. Free-range veal is more expensive than formula-fed veal because of its limited production.

VEAL IS THE MEAT OF YOUNG, usually male, calves that are by-products of the dairy industry. Dairy cows must calve before they begin to give milk. Calves that aren't used in the dairy herds are used in today's veal industry. Although veal may come from any calf under the age of 9 months, most comes from calves slaughtered when they are 8 to 16 weeks old. Veal is lighter in color than beef, has a more delicate flavor and is generally more tender. Young veal has a firm texture, light pink color and very little fat. As soon as a calf starts eating solid food, the iron in the food begins to turn the young animal's meat red. Meat from calves slaughtered when they are older than 5 months is called calf. It tends to be a deeper red, with some marbling and external fat.

Veal's mild flavor and low fat content makes it a popular meat, especially among those looking for an alternative to beef. Its delicate flavor is complemented by both classic and modern sauces.

PRIMAL AND SUBPRIMAL CUTS OF VEAL

After slaughter, the calf carcass can be split down the backbone into two bilateral halves or, more typically, cut along the natural curvature between the 11th and 12th ribs into a foresaddle (front portion) and a hindsaddle (rear portion). The veal carcass yields five primal cuts: three from the foresaddle (the shoulder, foreshank and breast, and rib) and two from the hindsaddle (the loin and leg). The veal shoulder, rib and loin primals contain both bilateral portions; that is, a veal loin contains both sides of the animal's loin.

Figure 14.1 shows the relationship between the calf's bone structure and the primal cuts. As with all meats, it is important to know the location of bones when cutting or working with veal. This makes meat fabrication and carving easier and aids in identifying cuts. Figure 14.2 shows the primal cuts of veal and their location. A veal carcass weighs in a range of 60 to 245 pounds (27 to 110 kg).

Foresaddle

SHOULDER

Similar to the beef shoulder or chuck, the veal shoulder accounts for 21 percent of the carcass weight. It contains four rib bones (as opposed to five in the beef chuck) and portions of the backbone, blade and arm bones.

The backbone, blade and arm bones are sometimes removed and the meat roasted or stuffed and roasted. Although shoulder chops and steaks can be fabricated, they are inferior to the chops cut from more tender areas such as the loin or rib. Often the shoulder meat is ground or cubed for stew. Because of the relatively large amount of connective tissue it contains, meat from the shoulder is best braised or stewed.

FORESHANK AND BREAST

The foreshank and breast are located beneath the shoulder and rib sections on the front half of the carcass. They are considered one primal cut. Combined, they account for approximately 16 percent of the carcass weight. This primal contains rib bones and rib cartilage, breast bones and shank bones. Because the calf is slaughtered young, many of the breast bones are cartilaginous rather than bony.

This cartilage, as well as the ample fat and connective tissue also present in the breast, breaks down during long moist cooking, thus making the flavorful breast a good choice for braising. Veal breast can also be cubed for stews such as veal fricassee and veal blanquette, rolled and stuffed, or trimmed and ground.

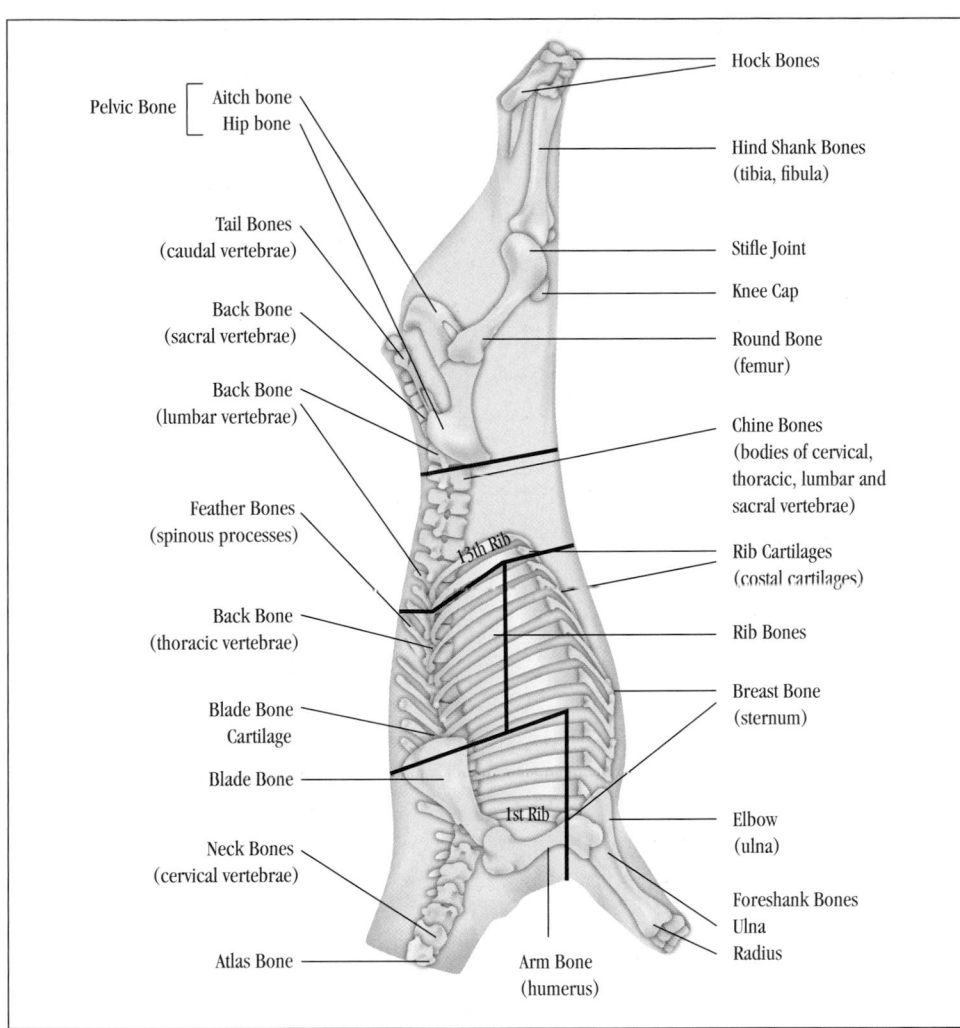

FIGURE 14.1 ▶ The skeletal structure of a calf.

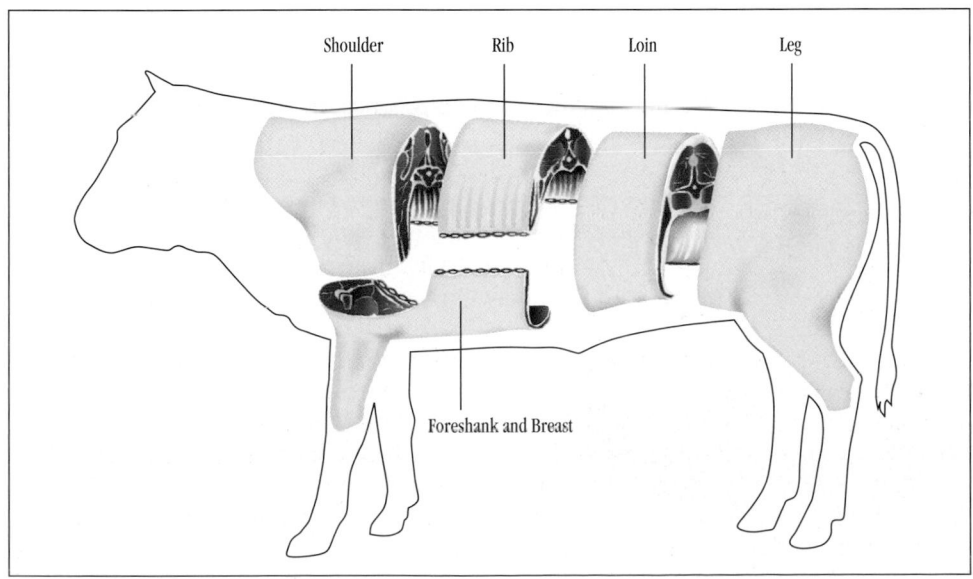

FIGURE 14.2 ▶ The primal cuts of veal.

Veal Hotel Rack, Split

Veal Loin

Loin Chops

The foreshank is also very flavorful but tough. It can be braised whole or sliced perpendicular to the shank bone and braised to produce osso buco.

RIB

The double rib, also known as a veal hotel rack, is a very tender, relatively small cut accounting for approximately 9 percent of the carcass weight. It is very popular and very expensive. The double rack consists of two racks, each with seven rib bones and a portion of the backbone.

Veal racks can be roasted either whole or split into two sides. Veal racks can be boned out; each side produces a veal rib eye and a small piece of tenderloin known as the short tenderloin, both of which make excellent roasts. More often, veal racks are trimmed and cut into chops, which can also be bone-in or boneless, to be grilled, sautéed or braised.

Hindsaddle

LOIN

The veal loin is posterior to the primal rib, contains two ribs (numbers 12 and 13) and accounts for approximately 10 percent of the carcass weight. The loin consists of the loin eye muscle on top of the rib bones and the tenderloin under them.

The veal loin eye is very tender, and the tenderloin is, without a doubt, the most tender cut of veal. If the primal veal loin is separated from the primal leg before the tenderloin is removed, the tenderloin will be cut into two pieces. The small portion (short tenderloin) remains in the primal loin, and the large portion (butt tenderloin) remains in the sirloin portion of the primal leg. The tenderloin is sometimes removed and cut into medallions. The veal loin is often cut into chops, bone-in or boneless. It is usually cooked using dry-heat methods such as broiling, grilling, roasting or sautéing.

Boneless Strip Loin

LEG

The primal veal leg consists of both the sirloin and the leg. Together, they account for approximately 42 percent of the carcass weight. The primal leg is separated from the loin by a cut perpendicular to the backbone immediately anterior to the hip bone, and it contains portions of the backbone, tail bone, hip bone, aitch bone, round bone and hindshank.

Although it is tender enough to be roasted whole, the veal leg is typically fabricated into cutlets and scallops for scallopine or schnitzel. To fabricate these cuts, the leg is first broken down into its major muscles: the top round, eye round, knuckle, sirloin, bottom round (which includes the sirloin) and butt tenderloin. Each of these muscles can be reduced to scallops by trimming all fat and visible connective tissue and slicing against the grain to the desired thickness. The scallops then should be pounded carefully to tenderize them further and to prevent them from curling when cooked.

The hindshank is somewhat meatier than the foreshank, but both are prepared and cooked in the same manner.

Veal Leg

Because the veal carcass is small enough to be handled easily, it is sometimes purchased in forms larger than the primal cuts described earlier. Depending on employee skill, available equipment and storage space and an ability to utilize fully all the cuts and trimmings that fabricating meat produces, a chef may want to purchase veal in one of the following forms:

▶ Foresaddle: The anterior (front) portion of the carcass after it is severed from the hindsaddle by a cut following the natural curvature between the 11th and 12th ribs. It contains the primal shoulder, foreshank and breast, and rib.
▶ Hindsaddle: The posterior portion of the carcass after it is severed from the foresaddle. It contains the primal loin and leg.
▶ Back: The trimmed rib and loin sections in one piece. The back is particularly useful when producing large quantities of veal chops.
▶ Veal side: One bilateral half of the carcass, produced by cutting lengthwise through the backbone.

Top Round

Organ Meats

Several calf organ meats are used in food service operations.

SWEETBREADS

Sweetbreads are the thymus glands of veal (Fr. *ris de veau*) and lamb (*ris d'agneau*). As an animal ages, its thymus gland shrinks; therefore, sweetbreads are not available from older cattle or sheep. Veal sweetbreads are much more popular than lamb sweetbreads in this country. Good-quality sweetbreads should be plump and firm, with the exterior membrane intact. Delicately flavored and tender, they are usually blanched before being sautéed or pan-fried, although sweetbreads can be prepared by almost any cooking method.

Hindshank Cut for Osso Buco

CALVES' LIVER

Calves' liver is much more popular than beef liver because of its tenderness and mild flavor. Good-quality calves' liver should be firm and moist, with a shiny appearance and without any off-odor. It is most often sliced and sautéed or broiled and served with a sauce.

KIDNEYS

Kidneys are more popular in other parts of the world than in the United States. Good-quality kidneys should be plump, firm and encased in a shiny membrane. Properly prepared kidneys have a rich flavor and firm texture; they are best prepared by moist-heat cooking methods and are sometimes used in stew or kidney pie. The hard, flavorful fat (suet) that collects on veal kidneys can be used in forcemeats, for barding and, when rendered, for deep-frying.

Sweetbreads

Calves' Liver

NUTRITION

Like beef, veal is a major source of protein as well as niacin, zinc and B vitamins. Veal has less marbling than beef. When trimmed of any visible fat, veal is lower in fat and calories than comparable beef cuts. And it is leaner than many cuts of pork and poultry.

BUTCHERING PROCEDURES

Veal quality varies greatly among purveyors. Purchase only from reputable companies to be sure of receiving a consistently high-quality product. See Table 14.1 for a list of standard fabricated cuts. Because veal carcasses are relatively small, they are sometimes purchased as primal or other large cuts and fabricated in-house to the operation's own specifications. A chef should master several important veal fabrication and butchering techniques.

Kidneys

PROCEDURE FOR **BONING A LEG OF VEAL**

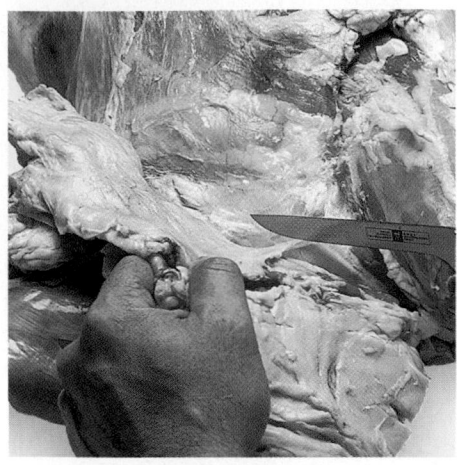

① Remove the shank by cutting through the knee joint. Remove the excess fat and flank meat.

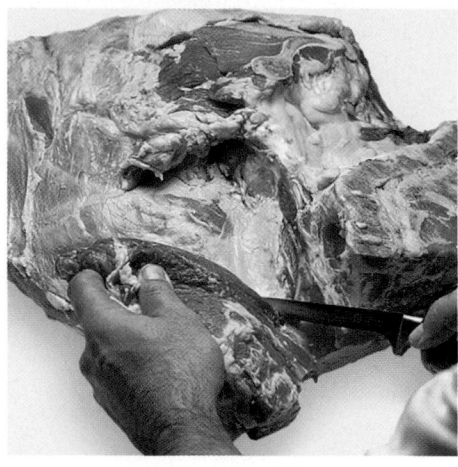

② Remove the butt tenderloin from the inside of the pelvic bone.

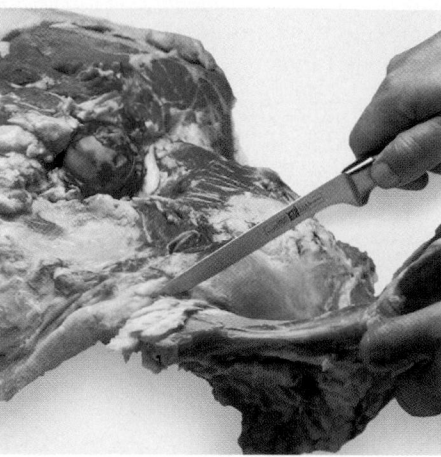

③ Remove the pelvic bone by carefully cutting around the bone, separating it from the meat. Continue until the bone is completely freed from the meat.

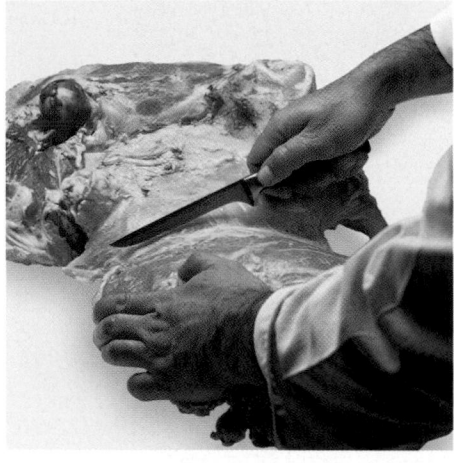

④ With the inside of the leg up, remove the top round by cutting along the natural seam.

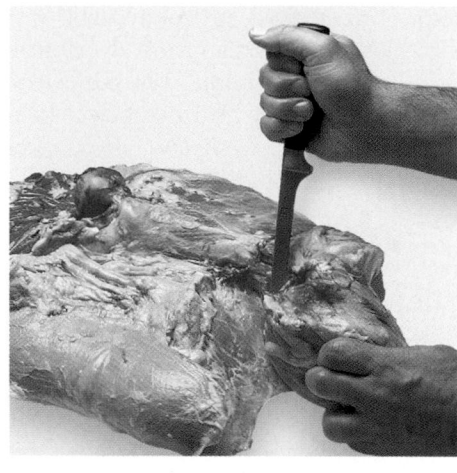

⑤ Remove the shank meat. (It is the round piece of meat lying between the eye round and the bone, on the shank end of the leg.)

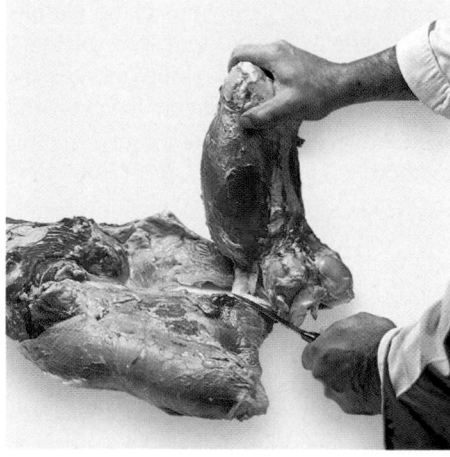

⑥ Remove the round bone and the knuckle together by cutting around the bone and through the natural seams separating the knuckle from the other muscles. Separate the knuckle meat from the bone.

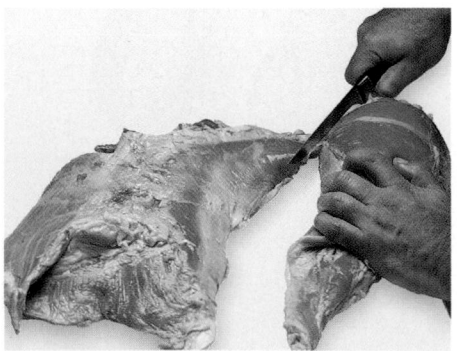

⑦ Remove the sirloin.

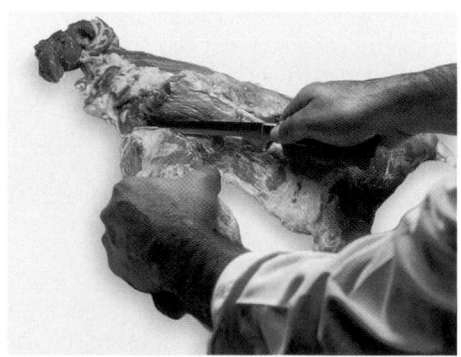

⑧ Remove the eye round from the bottom round.

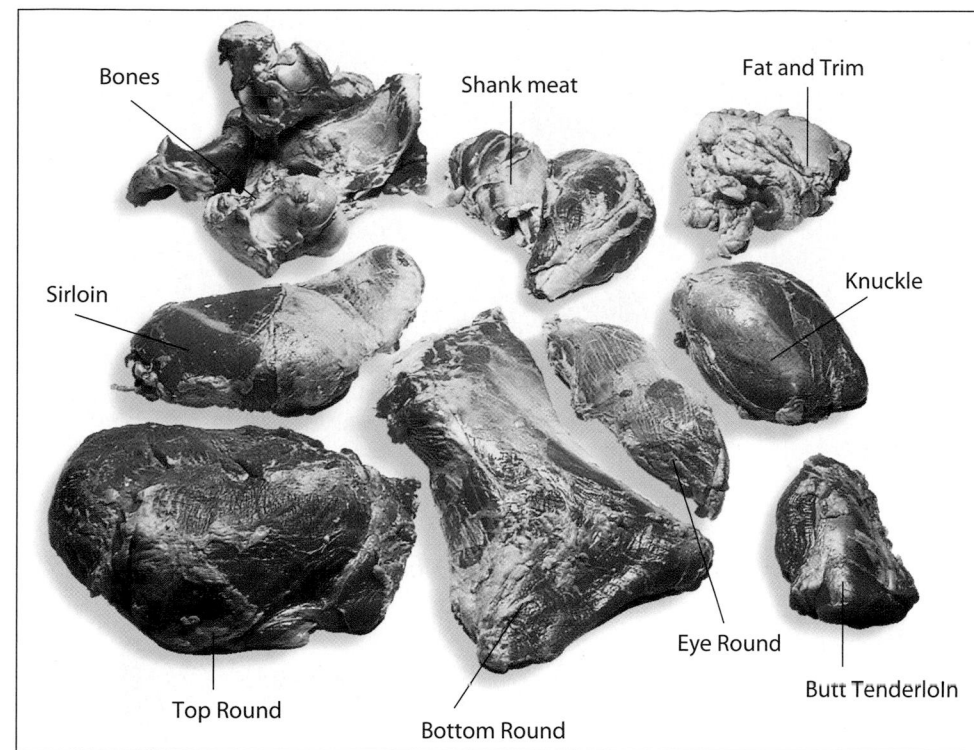

The completely boned-out veal leg, producing a top round, eye round, knuckle, shank meat, butt tenderloin, sirloin, bottom round, bones and trimmings.

PROCEDURE FOR **CUTTING AND POUNDING SCALLOPS**

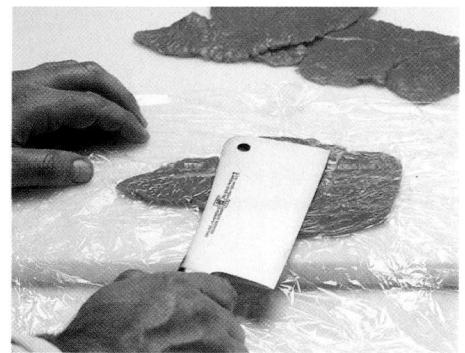

❶ Veal scallops are cut from relatively large pieces of veal (here, a portion of the top round). Trim all fat and silverskin. Going against the grain, cut slices approximately 1/4 inch (3 millimeters) thick; cut on the bias to produce larger pieces.

❷ Place the scallops between two pieces of plastic wrap and pound lightly with a spreading motion to flatten and tenderize the meat. Be careful not to tear or pound holes in the meat.

PROCEDURE FOR **CUTTING ÉMINCÉ**

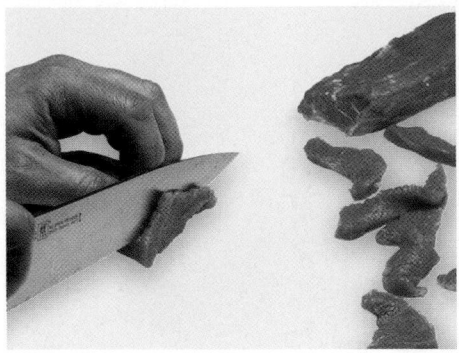

Émincé is cut from relatively small, lean pieces of meat. Here veal is cut across the grain into small, thin slices.

PROCEDURE FOR **BONING A VEAL LOIN AND CUTTING IT INTO BONELESS VEAL CHOPS**

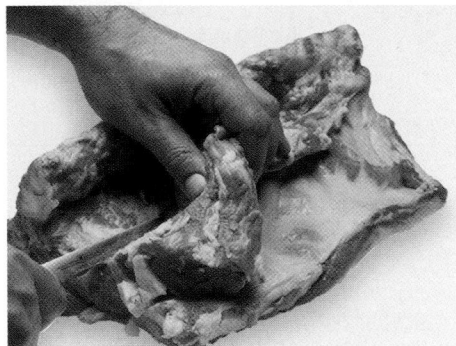

① Remove the tenderloin in a single piece from the inside of the loin by following the vertebrae and cutting completely around the tenderloin.

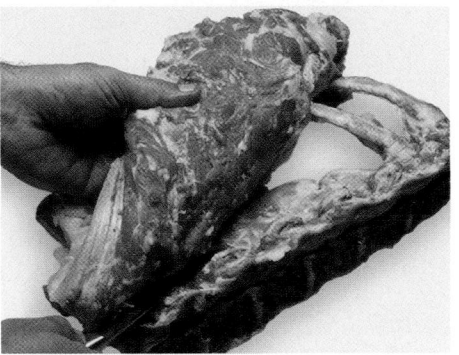

② From the backbone side, cut along the natural curve of the backbone, separating the loin meat from the backbone.

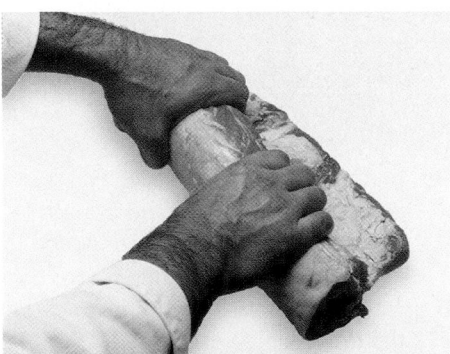

③ Trim any excess fat from the loin, and trim the flank to create a 3-inch (7.5-centimeter) lip. Tightly roll up the loin with the flank on the outside.

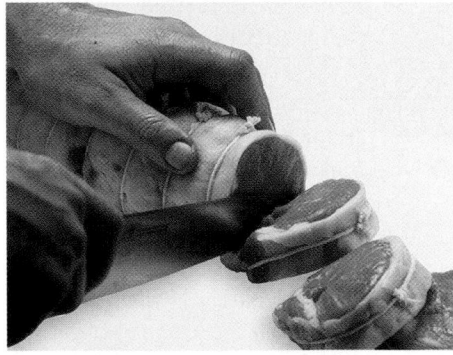

④ Tie the loin, using the procedure described next, at 1-inch (2.5-centimeter) intervals. Cut between the pieces of twine for individual boneless loin chops.

PROCEDURE FOR **TYING MEATS**

Here we apply the tying procedure to a boneless veal loin; the same procedure can be used on any type of meat.

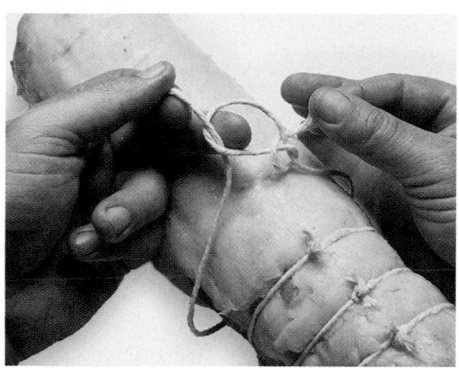

① Cut a piece of string long enough to wrap completely around the loin. Holding one end between the thumb and forefinger, pass the other end around it and across the strings. Loop the loose end of the string around your finger.

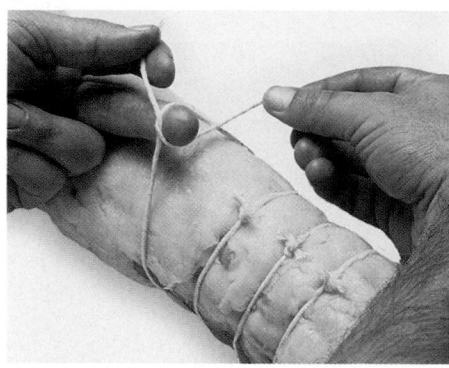

② Wrap the string around itself and pass the loose end back through the hole.

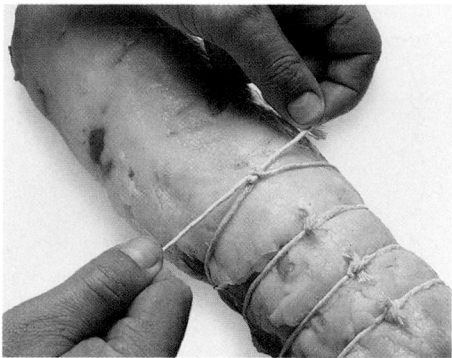

③ Pull to tighten the knot. Adjust the string so it is snug against the meat.

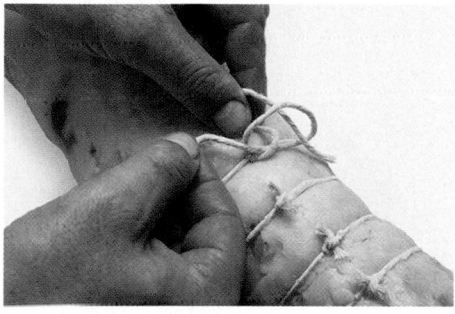

④ Loop one end of the string around your thumb and forefinger. Reach through with your thumb and forefinger and pull the other string back through the loop. Pull both strings to tighten the knot, thus preventing the first knot from loosening. Trim the ends of the strings.

⑤ Continue in this fashion until the entire loin is tied. The strings should be tied at even intervals, just snug enough to hold the shape of the loin; they should not dig into or cut the meat.

PROCEDURE FOR **CLEANING AND PRESSING SWEETBREADS**

Before fabrication, submerge the sweetbreads in cold milk or water, cover them and place in the refrigerator overnight in order to soak out any blood. Then blanch them in a court bouillon for 20 minutes.

① Remove the sweetbreads from the poaching liquid and allow them to cool.

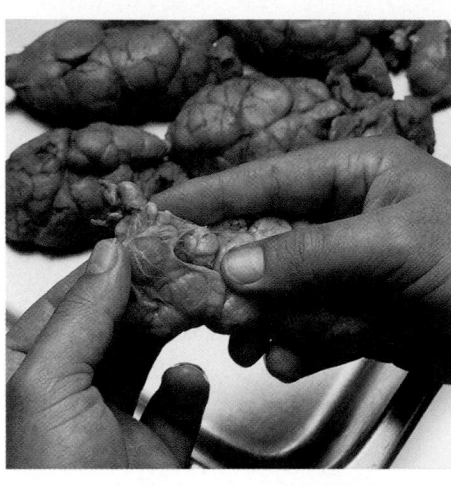

② Using your hands, pull off any sinew or membranes that may be present on the surface of the sweetbreads.

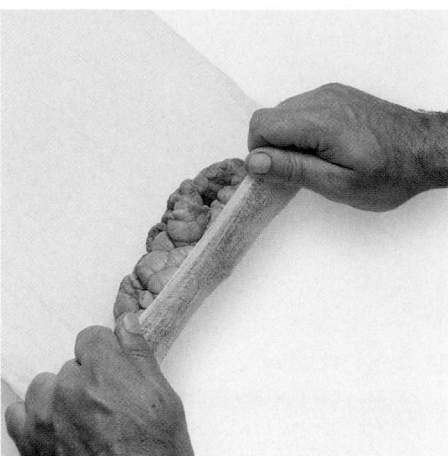

③ Wrap the sweetbreads in cheesecloth.

④ Tie the ends with butcher's twine.

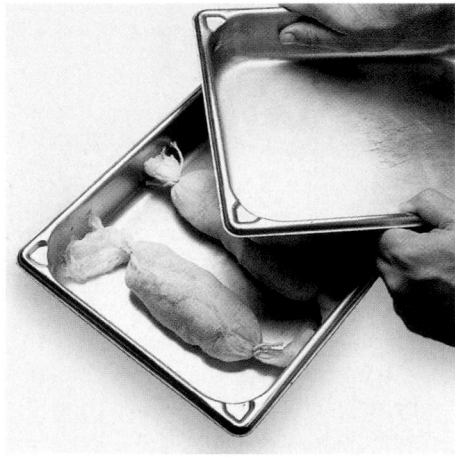

⑤ Place the wrapped sweetbreads in a half-size hotel pan or similar container.

⑥ Place another half-size hotel pan on top of the sweetbreads; place a weight in the pan to press the sweetbreads. Pressing sweetbreads in this manner improves their texture.

PROCEDURE FOR **CLEANING CALVES' LIVER**

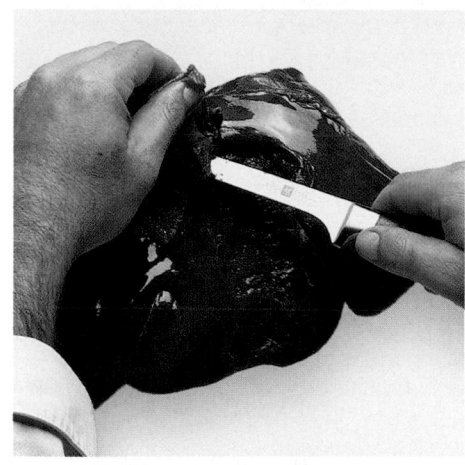

❶ Trim the large sinew and outer membrane from the bottom of the liver.

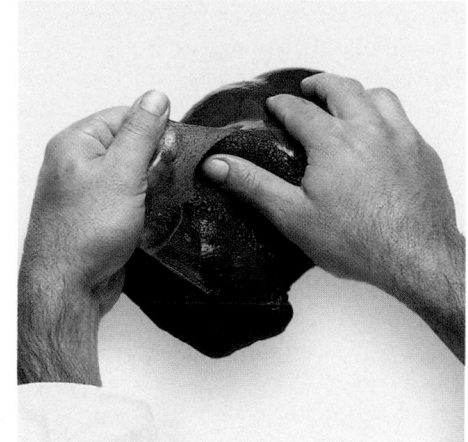

❷ Turn the liver over and peel the membrane off with your hands.

❸ The liver can be cut into thick or thin slices as needed.

PROCEDURE FOR **CLEANING VEAL KIDNEYS**

❶ Split the kidneys lengthwise, exposing the fat and sinew.

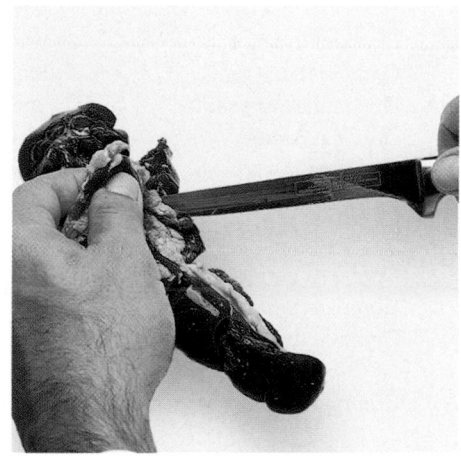

❷ With a sharp knife, trim away the fat; the kidney is now ready for cooking.

TABLE 14.1   USING COMMON CUTS OF VEAL

PRIMAL	SUBPRIMAL OR FABRICATED CUT	IMPS	COOKING METHODS	SERVING SUGGESTIONS
Shoulder	Cubed veal	1395	Combination (stew)	Blanquette or fricassee
	Ground veal	1396	Dry heat (broil or grill)	Veal patties
			Combination (braise)	Stuffing; meatballs
Foreshank and breast	Foreshank	312	Combination (braise)	Osso buco
	Breast	313	Combination (braise)	Stuffed veal breast
Rib	Hotel rack	306	Dry heat (broil or grill; roast)	Grilled veal chop; roast veal with porcini mushrooms
	Rib chops	1306	Dry heat (broil or grill)	Grilled veal chop
			Combination (braise)	Braised veal chop with risotto
	Rib eye	307	Dry heat (broil or grill; roast)	Broiled veal rib eye with chipotle sauce; roasted veal rib eye marchand de vin
			Combination (braise)	Braised rib eye
Loin	Veal loin	331	Dry heat (broil or grill; roast; sauté)	Roasted veal loin with wild mushrooms; sautéed veal medallions with green peppercorn sauce
	Loin chops	1332	Dry heat (broil or grill; sauté)	Broiled or sautéed veal chops with mushroom sauce
			Combination (braise)	Braised veal chops lyonnaise
	Boneless strip loin	344	Dry heat (broil or grill; roast; sauté)	Roasted veal loin sauce poulette
	Veal tenderloin	346	Dry heat (broil or grill; roast; sauté)	Grilled tenderloin; roasted tenderloin; sautéed tenderloin with garlic and herbs
Leg	Leg	334	Dry heat (roast; sauté)	Veal scallopini
			Combination (stew)	Blanquette
	Top round	349A	Dry heat (roast; sauté)	Veal marsala, schnitzel
	Bottom round	NA	Dry heat (sauté)	Sautéed scallops with Calvados
			Combination (braise)	Stuffed veal scallops
	Hindshank	337	Moist heat (simmer)	Veal broth
			Combination (braise)	Osso buco
Offal	Sweetbreads	715	Dry heat (pan-fry; sauté)	Sautéed sweetbreads beurre noisette
			Combination (braise)	Braised sweetbreads Madeira
	Calves' liver	704	Dry heat (broil or grill; sauté)	Broiled or sautéed calves' liver with onion and bacon
	Kidneys	NA	Combination (braise)	Kidney pie

QUESTIONS FOR DISCUSSION

1. Compare the appearance and flavor of beef and veal.

2. What are the differences between formula-fed veal and free-range veal?

3. Describe two differences between a beef carcass and a veal carcass.

4. List each veal primal and describe its location on the carcass. For each primal, identify two subprimals or fabricated cuts taken from it.

5. Would it be better to use a veal loin for grilling or braising? Explain your answer.

6. What are veal sweetbreads? Describe how sweetbreads should be prepared for cooking.

7. Certain groups oppose the use of formula-fed veal, saying that the animals are treated in an inhumane manner. What are these organizations? Are their arguments valid? What are the alternatives?

8. Use the Internet to research veal preparations from various regions of the world. Discuss the preparation techniques and ingredients used and explain the differences and similarities between them.

Terms to Know

foresaddle
hindsaddle
formula-fed veal
organ meats
veal breast

foreshank
hotel rack
loin eye
sweetbreads
émincé

GRILLED VEAL CHOP WITH WILD MUSHROOM RAGOÛT

THE BROWN PALACE HOTEL, DENVER, CO

Former Executive Chef Mark Black

Yield: 8 Servings   **Method:** Grilling

Veal chops, frenched, 8 oz. (240 g) ea.	8	8
Olive oil	4 fl. oz.	120 ml
Salt and pepper	TT	TT
Wild Mushroom Ragoût (recipe follows)	as needed	as needed

1. Brush the veal chops with oil and season with salt and pepper. Grill over a hot grill to the desired doneness.
2. Arrange each chop with side dishes as desired; top with Wild Mushroom Ragoût.

Approximate values per serving: **Calories** 580, **Total fat** 26 g, **Saturated fat** 5 g, **Cholesterol** 125 mg, **Sodium** 620 mg, **Total carbohydrates** 13 g, **Protein** 64 g, **Vitamin C** 15%, **Iron** 15%

WILD MUSHROOM RAGOÛT

Yield: 8 Servings

Bacon, diced	3 oz.	90 g
Garlic, minced	1 Tbsp.	15 ml
Shallot, minced	1 Tbsp.	15 ml
Leeks, julienne	4 oz.	120 g
Pearl onions, peeled	10 oz.	300 g
Fresh thyme, chopped	1 Tbsp.	15 ml
Wild mushrooms, mixed	12 oz.	360 g
White wine	1 pt.	480 ml
Veal demi-glace	1 qt.	960 ml
Plum tomatoes, concassée	4	4
Salt and pepper	TT	TT

1. Render the bacon in a saucepot. Add the garlic, shallot, leeks, onions and thyme and sauté until tender.
2. Add the mushrooms and sauté for 5 minutes. Deglaze with the wine and simmer for 10 to 15 minutes.
3. Add the demi-glace and reduce to the desired consistency, approximately 15 minutes.
4. Add the tomato concassée, adjust the seasonings and hold for service.

Approximate values per serving: **Calories** 240, **Total fat** 2.5 g, **Saturated fat** 1 g, **Cholesterol** 5 mg, **Sodium** 540 mg, **Total carbohydrates** 13 g, **Protein** 32 g, **Vitamin C** 15%

ROAST VEAL LOIN

Yield: 6 Servings, 6 oz. (180 g) each   **Method:** Roasting

Boneless veal loin roast, 3 lb. (1.4 kg)	1	1
Salt and pepper	TT	TT
Onions, chopped medium	2	2
Carrots, chopped medium	2	2
Garlic cloves, chopped	4	4
Fresh thyme	3 sprigs	3 sprigs
Bay leaves	2	2
Jus lié	1 pt.	480 ml

1. Tie the veal loin roast with butcher's twine.
2. Season the meat with salt and pepper and place it in a roasting pan. Scatter the onions, carrots, garlic, thyme and bay leaves around it.
3. Roast at 425°F (220°C) for approximately 45 minutes.
4. Remove the meat from the roasting pan and cut away the twine. Hold in a warm place for service.
5. Deglaze the roasting pan with the jus lié. Strain the vegetables and liquid through a chinois into a small saucepan. Discard the solids.
6. Bring the sauce to a boil and skim as much fat as possible from the surface. Season with salt and pepper. Spoon a portion of the sauce over the veal; serve the remainder on the side. Serve with any vegetable garnish such as cooked beets and beans with vinaigrette dressing.

Approximate values per serving: **Calories** 526, **Total fat** 31 g, **Saturated fat** 12 g, **Cholesterol** 209 mg, **Sodium** 509 mg, **Total carbohydrates** 6 g, **Protein** 54 g, **Vitamin A** 47%, **Iron** 16%

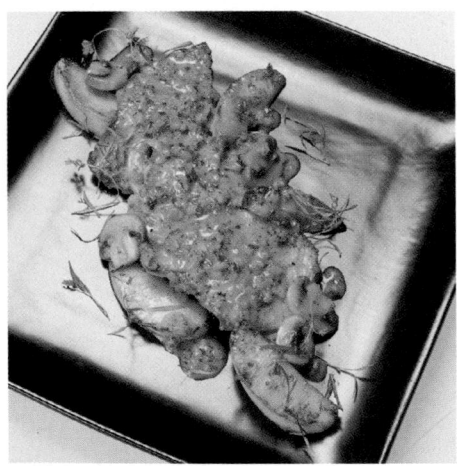

SAUTÉED VEAL SCALLOPS WITH CALVADOS

Yield: 6 Servings   **Method:** Sautéing

Mushrooms, sliced	12 oz.	360 g
Clarified butter	4 fl. oz.	120 ml
Golden Delicious apples	3	3
Veal scallops, pounded, 6 oz. (180 g) each	6	6
Salt and pepper	TT	TT
Shallots, minced	2	2
Calvados	2 fl. oz.	60 ml
Crème fraîche	8 fl. oz.	240 ml
Fresh parsley, chopped	1 Tbsp.	15 ml

1. Sauté the mushrooms in a portion of the clarified butter until dry. Remove and reserve.
2. Peel and core the apples. Cut each into 12 wedges.
3. Sauté the apple wedges in a portion of the clarified butter until slightly browned and tender. Remove and reserve.
4. Season the veal scallops with salt and pepper. Sauté in the remaining clarified butter. (This may be done in two or three batches.) Remove and reserve.
5. Add the shallots to the pan and sauté without browning.
6. Deglaze with the Calvados. Flambé the Calvados.
7. Add the sautéed mushrooms and crème fraîche. Bring to a boil and reduce until it thickens slightly.
8. Return the scallops to the pan to reheat. Serve each scallop with sauce, garnished with six apple slices and chopped parsley.

Approximate values per serving: **Calories** 650, **Total fat** 41 g, **Saturated fat** 21 g, **Cholesterol** 295 mg, **Sodium** 710 mg, **Total carbohydrates** 14 g, **Protein** 56 g, **Vitamin A** 30%

> ### SAFETY ALERT
> ### Cooking with Alcohol
>
> When alcohol comes into contact with a flame, it can ignite. In order to avoid singed eyebrows and kitchen fires, observe care when adding wine, liqueurs or liquor to a dish near the stove. When a dish calls for flambéing, follow these procedures. Stand away from the pan being flamed. Tilt the pan away from you, allowing the fumes to be ignited by the open flame. Be careful, as the flames can leap from the pan.

VEAL MARSALA

Yield: 6 servings, 7 oz. (210 g) each **Method:** Sautéing

Veal scallops, pounded, 3 oz. (90 g) each	12	12
Salt and pepper	TT	TT
Flour	as needed for dredging	
Clarified butter	2 fl. oz.	60 ml
Olive oil	2 fl. oz.	60 ml
Dry Marsala wine	6 fl. oz.	180 ml
Brown veal stock	4 fl. oz.	120 ml
Whole butter	1½ oz.	45 g

1. Season the scallops with salt and pepper. Dredge the scallops in flour and sauté them in a mixture of the clarified butter and oil, a few at a time, until all are cooked.
2. Remove the scallops and set aside. Degrease the pan and deglaze with the wine. Add the stock and reduce until it begins to thicken.
3. Return the scallops to the sauce to reheat. Remove the scallops to plates or a serving platter.
4. Reduce the sauce until it becomes syrupy; adjust the seasonings. Monté au beurre and spoon the sauce over the veal.
5. Serve the veal with mashed potatoes and cooked baby carrots or other garnishes.

Approximate values per 7-oz. (210-g) serving: **Calories** 430, **Total fat** 28 g, **Saturated fat** 12 g, **Cholesterol** 165 mg, **Sodium** 650 mg, **Total carbohydrates** 9 g, **Protein** 36 g, **Vitamin A** 15%

VEAL CORDON BLEU

THE ART INSTITUTE OF WASHINGTON, ARLINGTON, VA

Yield: 4 Servings   **Method:** Deep-frying

Veal cutlets, 4 oz. (120 g) each	4	4
Salt and white pepper	TT	TT
Parsley, chopped	4 tsp.	20 ml
Ham slices, 1 oz. (30 g) each	4	4
Swiss cheese slices, 1 oz. (30 g) each	4	4
Flour	as needed for breading	
Egg wash	as needed for breading	
Bread crumbs	as needed for breading	
Lemon wedges	as needed for garnish	

1. Place the veal cutlets on a film-covered cutting board and cover them with a layer of film wrap. Using a meat mallet, gently pound the cutlets to an even thickness of approximately ¼ inch (6 millimeters). Remove the film wrap.
2. Season the cutlets with salt and white pepper and sprinkle them with the parsley.
3. Place one slice of ham and one slice of cheese on each cutlet. If the slices are larger than the cutlet, cut the slices in half and layer them on the cutlet.
4. Begin rolling the veal cutlet. Fold the ends toward the center to close the ends of the roll and finish rolling. Refrigerate the veal rolls for 15 minutes.
5. Bread the veal rolls using the standard breading procedure described in Chapter 8, Mise en Place, and refrigerate for an additional 15 minutes.
6. Using the basket method, deep-fry the rolls at 325°F (160°C) until fully cooked, approximately 8 minutes. Serve with lemon wedges. Flavored hollandaise or béarnaise sauce may also be served with this dish.

VARIATION:

Turkey Cordon Bleu—Substitute 4-ounce (120-gram) turkey breast cutlets for the veal.

Approximate values per serving: **Calories** 470, **Total fat** 34 g, **Saturated fat** 13 g, **Cholesterol** 140 g, **Sodium** 500 mg, **Total carbohydrates** 1 g, **Protein** 40 g, **Calcium** 30%

1. Pounding the cutlets to an even thickness.

2. Rolling the veal cutlets.

3. The finished Veal Cordon Bleu.

VEAL POJARSKI

NEWBURY COLLEGE, BROOKLINE, MA
Senior Instructor Scott Doughty

Yield: 6 Servings

Method: Pan-frying

Lean veal	2 lb.	960 g
Nutmeg	¼ tsp.	1 ml
Salt	½ tsp.	2 ml
Black pepper	¼ tsp.	1 ml
Heavy cream, cold	1 pt.	480 ml
Fresh bread crumbs	9½ oz.	285 g
Clarified butter	as needed	as needed
Chasseur sauce (page 206)	as needed	as needed

1 Remove any gristle or thick fat from the veal. Pass it through a grinder once with the large die, and then once with the fine die. Spread the veal on a half-sheet pan and chill thoroughly.

2 When the veal is thoroughly chilled, transfer it to a well-chilled bowl. Add the nutmeg, salt, pepper and cream. Blend well. Then blend in 4 ounces (120 grams) bread crumbs.

3 Working quickly, divide the mixture into six portions and shape them into patties approximately 1 inch (2.5 centimeters) thick. Roll the patties in the remaining bread crumbs; chill until ready to cook.

4 Heat two large sauté pans and add a thin film of clarified butter to each one. Place half of the patties into each pan and cook until they are golden brown, approximately 5 minutes. Turn them over carefully and continue cooking until done, approximately 5 more minutes. Serve with chasseur sauce and roasted tourné potatoes and broccoli or other garnishes.

Approximate values per serving: **Calories** 560, **Total fat** 38 g, **Saturated fat** 21 g, **Cholesterol** 235 mg, **Sodium** 470 mg, **Total carbohydrates** 17 g, **Protein** 38 g, **Vitamin A** 25%, **Calcium** 10%, **Iron** 10%

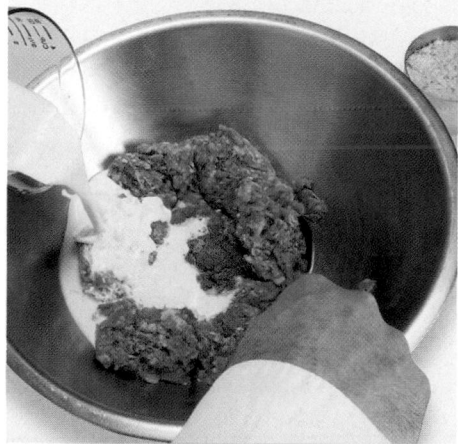

1 Combining the ingredients.

2 Pan-frying the patties.

3 The finished Veal Pojarski.

VEAL MARENGO

Yield: 6 Servings, 10 oz. (300 g) each   **Method:** Stewing

Lean boneless veal, cut in 2-in. (5-cm) cubes	2 lb. 8 oz.	1.2 kg
Salt and pepper	TT	TT
Flour	as needed for dredging	
Vegetable oil	1½ fl. oz.	45 ml
Clarified butter	3 fl. oz.	90 ml
Onions, sliced fine	12 oz.	360 g
Carrots, sliced fine	10 oz.	300 g
Garlic cloves, crushed	2	2
Tomato paste	1 oz.	30 g
Flour	2 Tbsp.	30 ml
Dry white wine	6 fl. oz.	180 ml
Brown veal stock	1 pt.	480 ml
Bouquet garni:		
Carrot stick, 4 in. (10 cm)	1	1
Leek, split, 4-in. (10-cm) piece	1	1
Fresh thyme	1 sprig	1 sprig
Bay leaf	1	1
Mushrooms, washed and quartered	8 oz.	240 g
Tomatoes, diced	1 lb.	480 g
Pearl onions, boiled and peeled	24	24
Rice pilaf	as needed	as needed

1. Season the veal cubes with salt and pepper and dredge in flour.
2. Heat a heavy-bottomed 8-quart (8-liter) sauce pan over moderate heat. Add 1 fluid ounce (30 milliliters) oil and 1 fluid ounce (30 milliliters) clarified butter to the pan. Add the veal and cook, browning well on all sides. Remove and set aside.
3. Add 1½ fluid ounces (45 milliliters) clarified butter and sauté the onions, carrots and garlic without coloring. Stir in the tomato paste and return the veal to the pan. Sprinkle with 2 tablespoons (30 milliliters) flour and cook to make a roux.
4. Add the wine, stock and bouquet garni to the pan; bring to a boil. Cover and simmer until the meat is tender, approximately 1½ hours.
5. Sauté the mushrooms until dry in the remaining oil and butter without browning. Add the tomatoes to the pan and sauté over high heat for 3 minutes. Season with salt and pepper. Remove from the heat and reserve.
6. When the veal is tender, remove it from the pan with a slotted spoon and set aside. Strain the sauce. Return the sauce to the pan and bring it to a boil. The sauce should be the consistency of a light cream sauce. Adjust the consistency of the sauce by reducing it on the stove top or by adding additional brown veal stock.
7. Return the veal to the sauce along with the mushrooms, tomatoes and pearl onions. Bring to a boil and simmer for 5 minutes. Adjust the seasonings. Serve plated with timbales of rice pilaf.

Approximate values per 10-oz. (300-g) serving: **Calories** 340, **Total fat** 16 g, **Saturated fat** 6 g, **Cholesterol** 125 mg, **Sodium** 490 mg, **Total carbohydrates** 15 g, **Protein** 32 g, **Vitamin A** 70%, **Vitamin C** 25%

SAUTÉED CALVES' LIVER WITH ONIONS

Yield: 10 Servings   **Method:** Sautéing

Onions, julienne	1 lb. 8 oz.	720 g
Clarified butter	3 fl. oz.	90 ml
Salt and pepper	TT	TT
White wine	8 fl. oz.	240 ml
Fresh parsley, chopped	1 Tbsp.	15 ml
Calves' liver, 3-oz. (90-g) slices	20	20
Flour	as needed for dredging	

1. Sauté the onions in 1 fluid ounce (30 milliliters) clarified butter until golden brown. Season with salt and pepper.
2. Add the wine, cover and braise until the onions are tender, approximately 10 minutes. Stir in the parsley.
3. Dredge the liver in flour seasoned with salt and pepper.
4. In a separate pan, sauté the liver in the remaining clarified butter until done. The liver should be slightly pink in the middle.
5. Serve the liver with a portion of the onions and their cooking liquid.

Approximate values per 6-oz. (180-g) serving: **Calories** 270, **Total fat** 9 g, **Saturated fat** 3 g, **Cholesterol** 535 mg, **Sodium** 520 mg, **Total carbohydrates** 16 g, **Protein** 30 g, **Vitamin A** 1190%, **Vitamin C** 50%

SWEETBREADS GRENOBLE

Yield: 8 Servings   **Method:** Sautéing

Sweetbreads, blanched and pressed	8	8
Salt and pepper	TT	TT
Flour	as needed for dredging	
Clarified butter	2 fl. oz.	60 ml
Dry white wine	2 fl. oz.	60 ml
Whole butter	4 oz.	120 g
Capers	3 oz.	90 g
Lemons, cut into segments, membranes removed	3	3
Veal demi-glace	2 fl. oz.	60 ml

1. Slice the sweetbreads and season with salt and pepper. Dust each piece lightly with flour.
2. Heat the clarified butter in a large sauté pan; add the sweetbreads and cook on each side for 1 to 2 minutes, until golden brown. Transfer the sweetbreads to a roasting pan and bake in a 375°F (190°C) oven for 5 minutes.
3. Deglaze the sauté pan with the wine. Add the whole butter, capers and lemon segments and cook over high heat for 1 to 2 minutes. Add the demi-glace and cook until thoroughly heated, approximately 1 more minute.
4. Arrange the sweetbreads on plates and top with the sauce.

Approximate values per serving: **Calories** 345, **Total fat** 22 g, **Saturated fat** 13 g, **Cholesterol** 512 mg, **Sodium** 461 mg, **Total carbohydrates** 4 g, **Protein** 33 g, **Vitamin A** 14%, **Vitamin C** 51%

OSSO BUCO

SIMPLICITY CATERING, Falls Church, VA
Chef Leland Atkinson

Yield: 4 Servings　　　　　　　　　　　**Method:** Braising

Veal shank, cut in 1-in. (2.5-cm) pieces	8–12 pieces	8–12 pieces
Salt and pepper	TT	TT
Flour	as needed for dredging	
Olive oil	as needed	as needed
Garlic clove, minced	1	1
Carrot, diced	4 oz.	120 g
Lemon zest, grated	1 Tbsp.	15 ml
White wine	8 fl. oz.	240 ml
Brown veal stock	1 qt.	960 ml
Tomato purée	2 Tbsp.	30 ml
Gremolada:		
Garlic clove, chopped fine	1	1
Lemon zest	1 Tbsp.	15 ml
Fresh Italian parsley, chopped	1 Tbsp.	15 ml
Risotto Milanese (page 643)	as needed for garnish	

1. Season the veal with salt and pepper and dredge the pieces in flour. Sauté them in oil until brown on both sides.
2. Add the garlic and carrot and sauté briefly.
3. Add the lemon zest, wine, stock and tomato purée. Bring to a boil and reduce to a simmer. Braise on the stove top or in a 325°F (160°C) oven until the meat is tender but not falling from the bone, 1 to 1½ hours.
4. Remove the cover and reduce the sauce until thick. Adjust the seasonings.
5. At service time, transfer the meat to a serving platter and ladle the sauce over it. Combine the gremolada ingredients and sprinkle over the meat and sauce. Serve with Risotto Milanese.

Approximate values per serving: **Calories** 350, **Total fat** 12 g, **Saturated fat** 2 g, **Cholesterol** 55 mg, **Sodium** 1500 mg, **Total carbohydrates** 41 g, **Protein** 20 g, **Vitamin A** 80%, **Vitamin C** 20%, **Iron** 20%

VEAL FRICASSEE

Yield: 16 Servings, 8 oz. (240 g) each   **Method:** Stewing

Veal stew meat, cut in 2-in. (5-cm) cubes	8 lb.	3.8 kg
Salt and white pepper	TT	TT
Whole butter	6 oz.	180 g
Onions, small dice	12 oz.	360 g
Garlic, chopped	1 tsp.	5 ml
Flour	6 oz.	180 g
White wine	4 fl. oz.	120 ml
White stock	3 qt.	2.8 lt
Bouquet garni:		
Carrot stick, 4 in. (10 cm)	1	1
Leek, split, 4-in. (10-cm) piece	1	1
Fresh thyme	1 sprig	1 sprig
Bay leaf	1	1
Heavy cream, hot	1 pt.	480 ml
Classic Rice Pilaf (page 644)	as needed	as needed

1. Season the veal with salt and white pepper and sauté in the butter without browning, approximately 2 minutes.
2. Add the onions and garlic and sauté without coloring, approximately 2 minutes.
3. Add the flour and cook to make a blond roux, approximately 3 minutes.
4. Add the wine and stock, stir well to remove any lumps of roux and bring to a boil. Add the bouquet garni, cover and simmer until the veal is tender, approximately 30 minutes.
5. Remove the veal from the sauce and reserve. Strain the sauce through a fine chinois and return it to the pan. Degrease the sauce.
6. Add the cream to the sauce. Reduce slightly to thicken if necessary. Return the veal to the sauce and adjust the seasonings.
7. Serve the fricassee with rice pilaf.

Approximate values per 8-oz. (240-g) serving: **Calories** 340, **Total fat** 18 g, **Saturated fat** 8 g, **Cholesterol** 165 mg, **Sodium** 540 mg, **Total carbohydrates** 6 g, **Protein** 40 g, **Vitamin A** 10%

1. Adding flour to the veal, onions and garlic.

2. Adding the cream to the sauce.

3. The finished Veal Fricassee.

> " I like a cook who smiles out loud when he tastes his own work. Let God worry about your modesty, I want to see your enthusiasm. "
>
> —ROBERT FARRAR CAPON, AMERICAN WRITER

CHAPTER FIFTEEN

LAMB

- identify the primal, subprimal and fabricated cuts of lamb
- perform basic butchering procedures
- apply appropriate cooking methods to several common cuts of lamb

LAMB IS THE MEAT OF SHEEP slaughtered when they are less than one year old. Meat from sheep slaughtered after that age is called *mutton*. (In Great Britain, where its strong flavor is appreciated, *mutton* refers to a sheep that is more than two years old.)

Even though lamb accounts for a small percentage of the meat consumed in the United States, many people who do not prepare lamb at home will order it at a restaurant. Because of its age, lamb meat is tender and it can be prepared by almost any cooking method. Its strong, distinctive flavor allows chefs to offer bold, robust sauces and accompaniments that might mask the flavors of other meats.

PRIMAL AND SUBPRIMAL CUTS OF LAMB

After the young sheep is slaughtered, it is usually reduced to the primal cuts: shoulder, breast, rack, loin and leg. Like some veal primals, lamb primals are crosscut sections and contain both bilateral halves (for example, the primal leg contains both hind legs). Lamb primals are not classified into a forequarter and hindquarter like beef, or a foresaddle and hindsaddle like veal.

Figure 15.1 shows the relationship between the lamb's bone structure and the primal cuts. As with all meats, it is important to know the location of bones when cutting or working with lamb. This makes meat fabrication and carving easier and aids in identifying cuts. Figure 15.2 shows the primal cuts of lamb and their location on the carcass. A lamb carcass generally weighs between 41 and 75 pounds (20 and 35 kg).

Shoulder

The primal lamb shoulder is a relatively large cut accounting for 36 percent of the carcass weight. The lamb shoulder contains four rib bones and the arm, blade and neck bones as well as many small, tough muscles whose grains travel in different directions.

All these bones and muscle groups make it nearly impossible to cook and carve a whole shoulder. Although the shoulder may be cut into chops, or boned and then roasted or braised, with or without stuffing, it is more commonly diced for stew or ground for patties.

Breast

The primal lamb breast contains the breast and foreshank portions of the carcass. Together they account for approximately 17 percent of the carcass weight and contain the rib, breast and shank bones. The primal breast is located beneath the primal rack and contains the rib tips, which are cut off to produce the rack. When separated from the rest of the breast, these small ribs are called Denver ribs and can be substituted for pork ribs when desired.

Although the breast is not used extensively in food service operations, it can be stuffed and braised, either bone-in or boneless. Lamb foreshanks are quite meaty and may be braised and served as an entrée, used for broths or ground.

Rack

The primal lamb rack is also known as the hotel rack. It is located between the primal shoulder and loin. Containing eight ribs and portions of the backbone, it accounts for approximately 8 percent of the carcass weight.

spring lamb young lamb born in the early spring and slaughtered when 3 to 5 months old; spring lamb is often served roasted whole

suckling lamb young lamb that has never been fed any grass or grains

agneau pre-salé distinctively flavored lamb that grazes on salt marshes in France

goat meat of the species *Capra hircus*, closely related to lamb; this ruminant thrives in rocky mountainous terrains, preferring scrub and bark to grass. Tender young goat is called kid. Most goats are bred for milk and cheese production. In Mediterranean countries as well as in the West Indies, goat or kid is served whole and spit-roasted or in stews and curries.

FIGURE 15.1

Pelvic Bone { Aitch Bone / Hip Bone

1st. Phalangeal Bone ⎫ Lower
Metatarsal Bone ⎬ Hindshank
Tarsal Bone ⎭ Bones
Fibula Tarsal Bone

Break Joint

Hindshank Bones
(tibia, fibula)

Tail Bones
(caudal vertebrae)

Stifle Joint

Knee Cap

Leg Bone
(femur)

Back Bone
(sacral vertebrae)

Back Bone
(lumbar vertebrae)

Chine Bones
(bodies of cervical, thoracic,
lumbar and sacral vertebrae)

13th Rib

Rib Cartilages
(costal cartilages)

Rib Bones

Feather Bones
(spinous processes)

Breast Bone
(sternum)

Back Bone
(thoracic vertebrae)

Elbow Bone
(ulna)

Blade Bone Cartilage

Blade Bone
(scapula)

Ulna ⎫ Foreshank Bones
Radius ⎭

1st Rib

Neck Bones

Break Joint

Atlas Bone

Metacarpal Bone ⎫ Lower Foreshank
Carpal Bones ⎭ Bones

Arm Bone
(humerus)

FIGURE 15.1 ▶ The skeletal structure of a lamb.

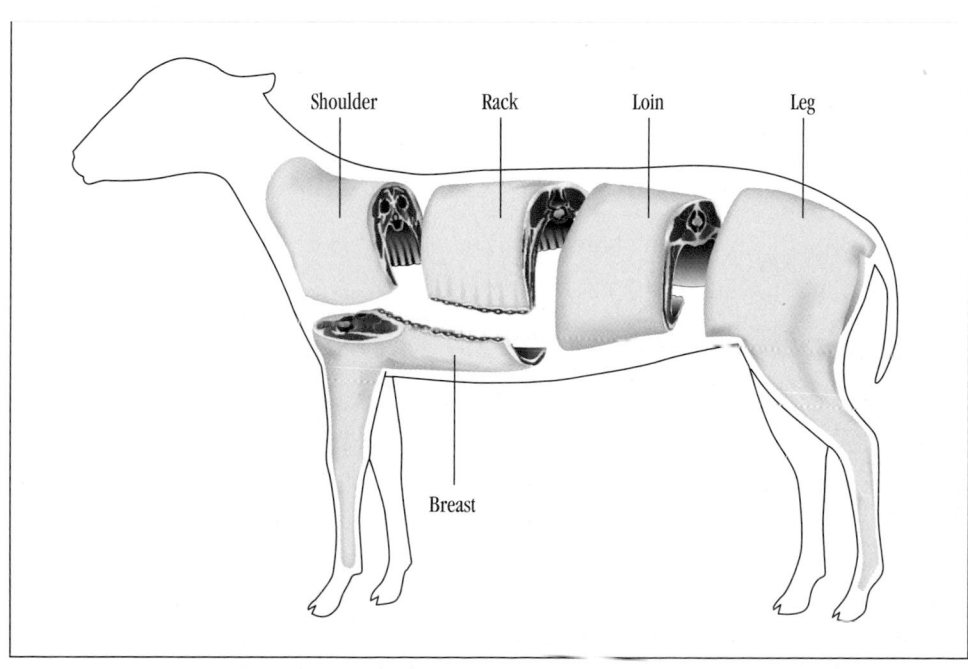

Shoulder   Rack   Loin   Leg

Breast

FIGURE 15.2 ▶ The primal cuts of lamb.

IMPERIALIST, COLONIALIST AND REVOLUTIONARY SHEEP

Columbus brought sheep to the New World on his second voyage in 1493. The Spanish soon established breeding centers in the Caribbean islands, then in Mexico and Panama. In 1565, people and livestock, including sheep, settled in St. Augustine, Florida.

During the 16th and 17th centuries, the Spanish established missions in Texas, New Mexico, Arizona and California in order to bridge their Florida and Mexico settlements. They brought sheep with them as an easily cared-for source of food and wool.

Sheep raising was not as easily established in the British colonies along the eastern seaboard. Many of the sheep brought with the early colonists were consumed for food during the harsh winters. More and more sheep had to be imported in order to satisfy the colonists' competing demands for food and clothing. By the mid-17th century, however, sheep were flourishing in the New England colonies and supplying an abundance of meat and wool.

In an attempt to maintain control of the wool trade, the British restricted the export of sheep to the American colonies and forbade the import of colonial wool and woolens. Retaliating against these restrictive trade practices, the colonists passed laws forbidding the use of sheep for food in order to preserve the flocks for wool. This protectionist scheme helped ensure a strong supply of materials for the domestic woolen industry that flourished after the Revolutionary War.

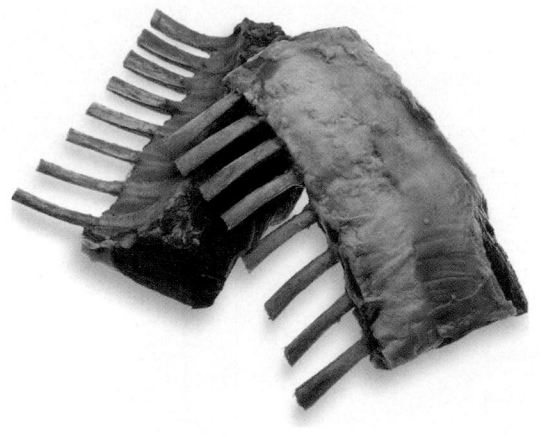

Frenched Lamb Rack

Lamb Rack

The rack is valued for its tender rib eye muscle. The hotel rack is usually split in half and trimmed so that each set of ribs can be easily cut into chops. The split racks can then be grilled, broiled or roasted as racks or cut into single or double rib chops before cooking.

Lamb Loin Trimmed

Loin

The loin is located between the primal rib and leg. It contains rib number 13 and portions of the backbone as well as the loin eye muscle, tenderloin and flank. It accounts for approximately 13 percent of the carcass weight.

Except for the flank, the loin meat is very tender and is invariably cooked using a dry-heat method such as broiling, grilling or roasting. The loin may be boned to produce boneless roasts or chops or cut into chops with the bone in. The loin eye may be removed and cut into medallions or noisettes.

Leg

The primal leg is a large section accounting for approximately 34 percent of the carcass weight. It is the posterior portion of the carcass, separated from the loin by a straight cut anterior to the hip bone cartilage. As with veal, the cut of meat that would be the sirloin on a beef carcass is separated from the lamb loin by this cut and becomes part of the primal leg. The lamb leg contains several bones: the backbone, tail, hip, aitch, round and shank bones.

The primal leg is rarely used as is. More often, it is split into two legs and partially or fully boned. Lamb legs are quite tender—the sirloin end more so than the shank end—and are well suited to a variety of cooking methods. A bone-in leg is often roasted for buffet service or braised with vegetables or beans for a hearty dish. Steaks can also be cut from the bone-in leg, with the sirloin end producing the most tender cuts. A boneless leg can be tied and roasted, with or without stuffing, or trimmed and cut into scallops. The shank end can be cut crosswise into sections containing a portion of bone, with its marrow, and the muscles alongside the bone. Shanks may be cut from the foreleg or the larger, meatier hindleg. Because they are relatively lean, lamb shanks are best prepared using moist heat, such as by braising. The meat can also be removed from the bone and diced for stew or ground for patties.

Lamb Leg

Boned, Rolled and Tied Leg
of Lamb

Lamb Shanks

Because lamb carcasses are so easily handled, purveyors often sell them whole or cut in a variety of ways to better meet their customers' needs. As well as whole-carcass, primal and fabricated cuts, lamb can be purchased in the following forms:

▶ **Foresaddle:** The anterior (front) portion of the carcass after it is severed from the hindsaddle by a cut following the natural curvature between the 12th and 13th ribs. It contains the primal shoulder, breast and foreshank and rack.

▶ **Hindsaddle:** The posterior portion of the carcass after it is severed from the foresaddle. It contains the primal loin and leg together with the kidneys.

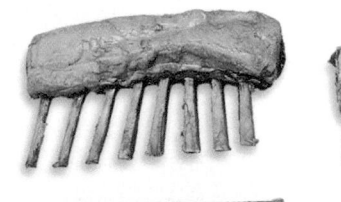
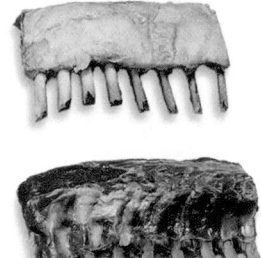

Domestic (left) and New Zealand Lamb Chops

▶ **Back:** The trimmed rack and loin sections in one piece. The back is particularly useful when producing large quantities of lamb chops.

▶ **Bracelet:** The primal hotel rack with the connecting breast sections.

frenching a method of trimming racks or individual chops of meat, especially lamb, in which the excess fat is cut away, leaving the eye muscle intact; all meat and connective tissue are removed from the rib bone

NUTRITION

Lamb, especially when purchased in subprimal cuts to be fabricated on-site, is an economical source of high-quality protein. Lean and lower in cholesterol than other red meat proteins, lamb is a good source of iron as compared with chicken, fish or poultry. Lamb has less marbling than other red meats. Its excess fat appears on the outside of many cuts and can easily be trimmed before cooking. Grass-fed lamb, like meat from other grass-fed ruminants, is high in the powerful antioxidant conjugated linoleic acid, identified as a cancer preventative.

BUTCHERING PROCEDURES

Lamb is unique among the common meat animals in that it is small enough to be handled easily in its carcass form. Thus, food service operations sometimes purchase lamb whole and fabricate the desired cuts themselves. This is practical if the operation has the necessary employee skills, equipment and storage space, as well as a need for all the various cuts and trimmings that butchering a whole carcass produces. A few important lamb fabrication and butchering techniques follow.

DOMESTIC VS. IMPORTED LAMB

Technologies that increase shelf life have made imported fresh lamb commonplace. Lamb imported from New Zealand and Australia accounts for nearly 50 percent of the lamb meat sold in the United States. Domestic lamb differs from imported lamb in a few ways. Domestic lamb is primarily grain fed and has a milder flavor than its grass-fed counterparts. And domestic lamb is raised to approximately 135 pounds, larger than imported lamb, resulting in larger cut sizes.

PROCEDURE FOR **FRENCHING A RACK OF LAMB**

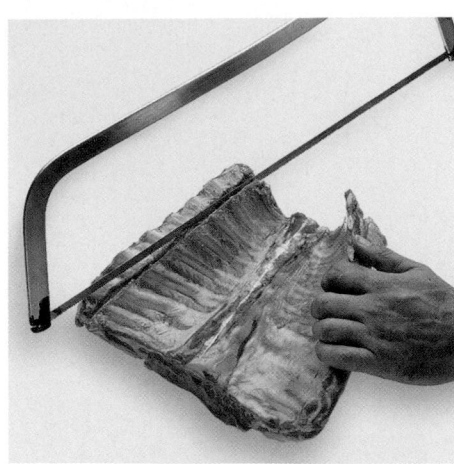

❶ With a meat saw, trim the ribs to approximately 3 inches (7.5 centimeters), measuring from the rib eye on each side of the rack.

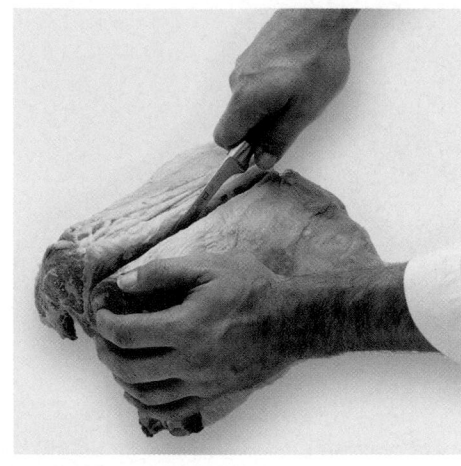

❷ Turn the rack over and cut down both sides of the feather bones, completely separating the meat from the bone.

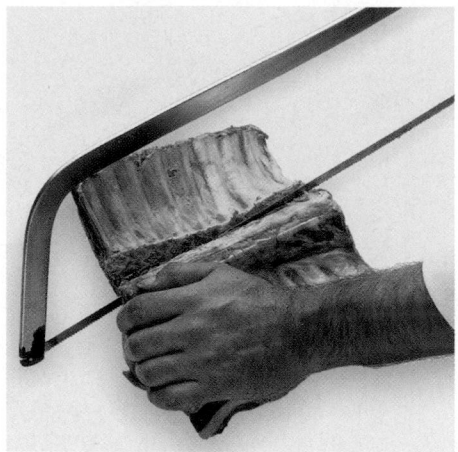

❸ Turn the rack back over. Using a meat saw, cut between the ribs and the chine bone at a 45-degree angle, exposing the lean meat between the ribs and the vertebral junctures.

❹ By pulling and cutting along the natural seam, remove the thick layers of fat and the meat between them from the rack's surface.

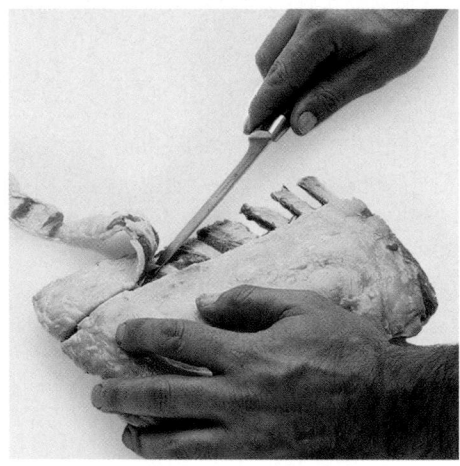

❺ Make an even cut through the fat, perpendicular to the ribs, 1 inch (2.5 centimeters) from the rib eye. Trim away all meat and fat from the rib ends. The ribs should be completely clean.

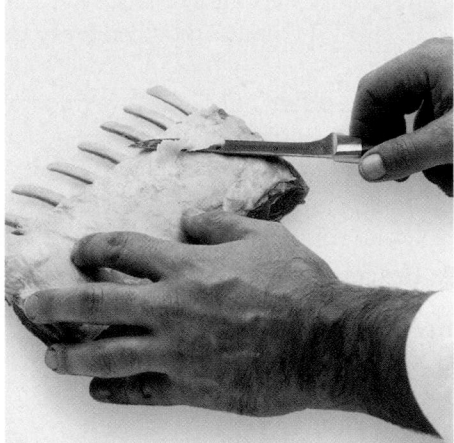

❻ Trim away the fat covering. Either leave a thin layer to protect the meat during cooking or trim the fat away completely to produce a very lean rack. The rack can also be cut into chops.

PROCEDURE FOR **TRIMMING AND BONING A LAMB LEG FOR ROASTING OR GRILLING**

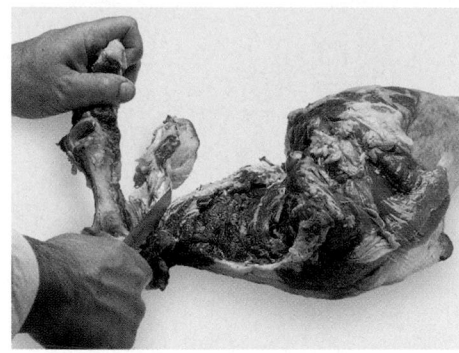

① With the tip of the knife, trim around the pelvic bone; stay close to the bone to avoid wasting any meat. Cut the sinew inside the socket and remove the bone.

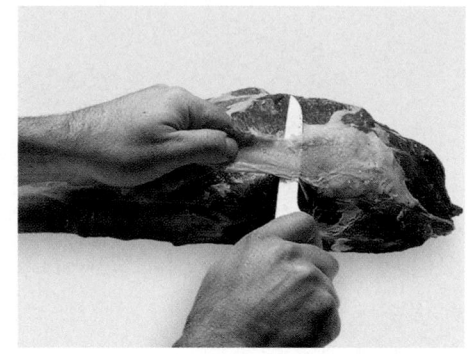

② Trim away most of the exterior fat.

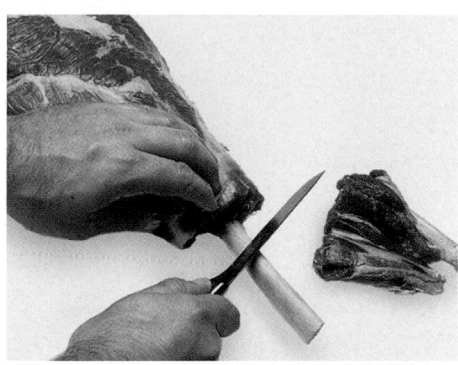

③ Cut off the shank portion completely and scrape the bone clean. This makes a handle to hold while carving the lamb.

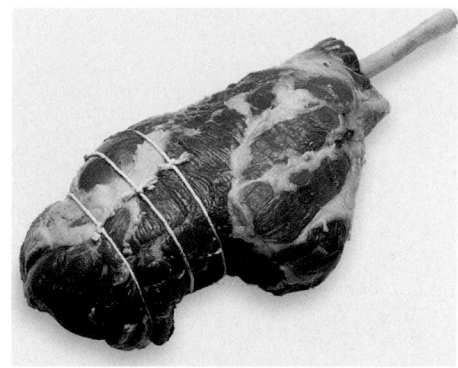

④ Fold the flap of the sirloin over on top of the ball of the leg bone and tie with butcher's twine. This helps the leg cook evenly.

CLASSIC LAMB FLAVORS

Lamb and its fat have a pronounced flavor, which lends itself to pairing with garlic and resinous herbs such as mint, oregano and rosemary. Many world cuisines incorporate some acid in their lamb preparations to balance fattiness; vinegar is the basic ingredient in mint sauce served with roasted lamb in Australia, Great Britain and New Zealand. Citrus juice, wine and yogurt are used to brighten the flavor in lamb stews and sauces served with lamb. The sweetness of dried fruits and root vegetables balances the fattiness of lamb and can be found in North African tagine, Indian curry and classic French lamb navarin.

PROCEDURE FOR **BONING A LAMB LOIN FOR ROASTING**

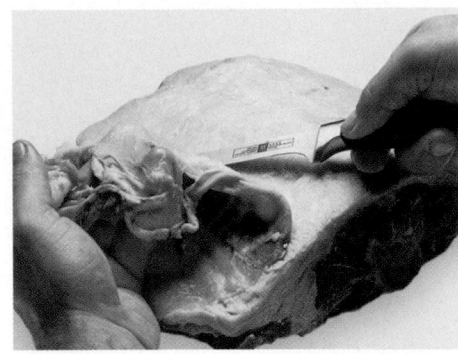

1 Start with a trimmed lamb loin (double). With the skin side up, trim the thin layer of connective tissue called the fell from the loin's surface.

2 Turn the loin over and trim the fat from around the tenderloins.

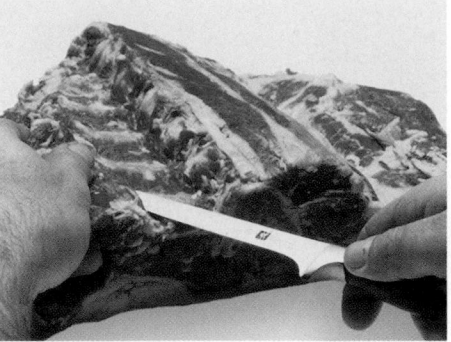

3 Starting in the middle of the backbone, cut between the tenderloin and the vertebrae, separating them but leaving the tenderloin attached to the flank. Continue until you reach the end of the vertebrae. Repeat on the other side.

4 Slide the knife under the vertebrae and the rib and cut back all the way to the backbone, separating the eye muscle from the vertebrae.

5 Pull the backbone out with your hands, keeping the loins intact.

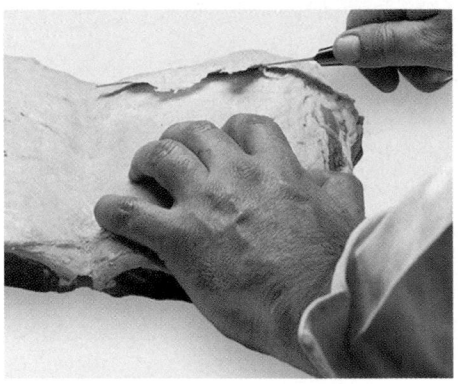

6 Turn the loins over and trim the surface fat to ¼ inch (6 millimeters).

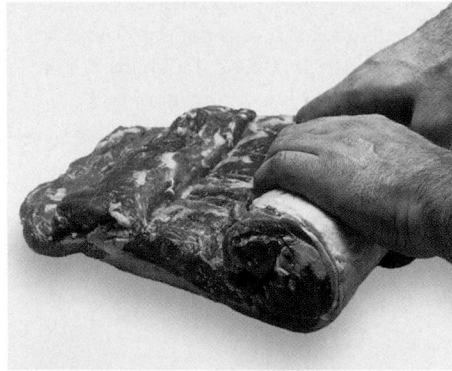

7 Roll the flank flaps under from each side.

8 Tie the roast with butcher's twine at even intervals.

PROCEDURE FOR CUTTING LAMB NOISETTES FROM A LOIN

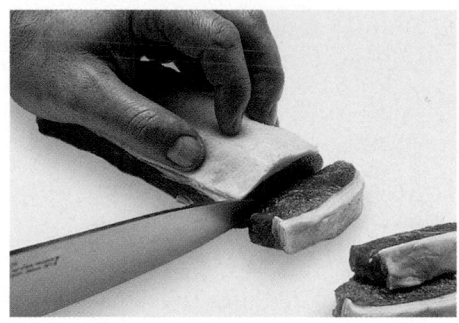

① Remove the loin eye muscle by cutting down along the backbone and along the vertebrae. Trim the eye muscle, leaving a thin layer of fat if desired.

② Cut the eye meat into noisettes of the desired thickness.

TABLE 15.1 USING COMMON CUTS OF LAMB

PRIMAL	SUBPRIMAL OR FABRICATED CUT	IMPS	COOKING METHODS	SERVING SUGGESTIONS
Shoulder	Shoulder lamb chop	1207	Dry heat (broil or grill)	Broiled or grilled lamb chops
	Diced lamb	1295	Combination (stew)	Lamb stew; lamb curry
	Ground lamb	1296	Dry heat (broil or grill; sauté)	Patties
Breast	Breast	209	Combination (braise)	Lamb breast stuffed with mushrooms
	Foreshank	210	Combination (braise)	Lamb shank braised with vegetables and white beans
Hotel rack	Lamb rack	204	Dry heat (broil or grill; roast; sauté)	Roast rack of lamb with garlic and rosemary
	Frenched lamb rack	204C	Dry heat (broil or grill; roast; sauté)	Broiled lamb with mustard and hazelnut crust
Loin	Lamb loin, trimmed	232	Dry heat (broil or grill; roast; sauté)	Noisettes of lamb with roasted garlic sauce
	Loin chops	1232	Dry heat (broil or grill; sauté)	Broiled loin chops with herb butter
Leg	Lamb leg	233A	Dry heat (broil or grill; roast)	Kebabs; roast leg of lamb
	Boned, rolled, tied leg of lamb	233B	Dry heat (roast)	Roast leg of lamb

Terms to Know

sheep	rack
mutton	bracelet
domestic lamb	fell
foreshank	noisettes
hindshank	

❶ Describe the basic differences between a lamb carcass and a beef carcass.

❷ List each lamb primal and describe its location on the carcass. Identify two subprimals or fabricated cuts taken from each primal.

❸ Which cooking methods are most appropriate for a breast of lamb? Explain your answer.

❹ Describe the procedure for preparing a frenched rack of lamb from a primal hotel rack.

❺ What is the best way to purchase lamb for a food service operation that cuts its own meat and uses large quantities of lamb chops? Explain your answer.

❻ Visit the Web site of the Agricultural Marketing Service of the USDA to learn **wWw** more about grading standards for lamb. What are the characteristics of lamb and mutton according to their grading system? What is the difference between yearling mutton and mutton? How would you prepare the different grades of lamb?

❼ Lamb was one of the first animals domesticated for human consumption. Research the historical ways in which lamb was served. Discuss how the ways of preparing lamb have changed over the centuries.

GRILLED RACK OF LAMB WITH ROSEMARY AND SPICY BELL PEPPER JELLY

VINCENT ON CAMELBACK, PHOENIX, AZ

Chef Vincent Guerithault

Yield: 8 Servings   **Method:** Grilling

Red bell peppers	2	2
Yellow bell peppers	2	2
Red serrano chiles	8	8
Sugar	8 oz	240 g
Lamb racks, frenched, 9 oz. (270 g) each	4	4
Salt and pepper	TT	TT
Dried rosemary sprigs*	8	8

1. To make the pepper jelly, julienne the bell peppers and chiles. Mix with the sugar and refrigerate overnight.
2. At service time, cook the pepper mixture (along with the liquid formed while refrigerated) over low heat for 10 to 15 minutes. Cool and keep the pepper jelly at room temperature.
3. Cut each lamb rack in half. Season with salt and pepper.
4. Grill the lamb over mesquite to the desired temperature.
5. Cut each half rack into chops and plate the lamb and pepper jelly. Garnish each plate with a dried rosemary sprig and flame. When the rosemary flames, blow it out at once and serve immediately so that the essence of rosemary is fresh.

*To dry rosemary, place fresh rosemary sprigs in a 350°F (180°C) oven for approximately 10 minutes.

Approximate values per 9-oz. (270-g) serving: **Calories** 430, **Total fat** 17 g, **Saturated fat** 6 g, **Cholesterol** 110 mg, **Sodium** 400 mg, **Total carbohydrates** 34 g, **Protein** 35 g, **Vitamin A** 45%, **Vitamin C** 280%, **Iron** 20%

SHISH KEBAB

Yield: 10 Servings　　　　　　　　　　　**Method:** Grilling or Broiling

Marinade:		
Onions, small dice	12 oz.	360 g
Garlic, chopped	1 oz.	30 g
Lemon juice	4 fl. oz.	120 ml
Salt	2 tsp.	10 ml
Black pepper	1 tsp.	5 ml
Fresh oregano, chopped	2 tsp.	10 ml
Olive oil	8 fl. oz.	240 ml
Cumin, ground	2 tsp.	10 ml
Coriander, ground	1 Tbsp.	15 ml
Fresh mint, chopped	2 tsp.	10 ml
Lamb leg or shoulder, boneless, trimmed and cut in 2-in. (5-cm) cubes	5 lb.	2.4 kg
Rice Pilaf (page 644)	as needed	as needed

1. Combine the marinade ingredients and add the lamb. Marinate for 2 hours.
2. Place three or four cubes of lamb on each of 10 skewers. Grill or broil to the desired doneness. Serve with Rice Pilaf.

Approximate values per 7.5-oz. (225-g) serving: **Calories** 410, **Total fat** 17 g, **Saturated fat** 6 g, **Cholesterol** 205 mg, **Sodium** 170 mg, **Total carbohydrates** 0 g, **Protein** 64 g, **Iron** 30%

LAMB PATTIES WITH MINT

Yield: 6 Servings, 6 oz. (180 g) each　　　　**Method:** Grilling or Broiling

Ground lamb	1 lb. 12 oz.	840 g
Fresh bread crumbs	2 oz.	60 g
Egg, beaten	1	1
Onion, minced	3 oz.	90 g
Garlic cloves, crushed	2	2
Fresh mint, chopped	3 Tbsp.	45 ml
Salt and pepper	TT	TT

1. Place the lamb in a bowl and mix in the bread crumbs, egg, onion, garlic and mint. Add salt and pepper to taste and mix well. Form the mixture into six patties.
2. Grill or broil the patties until browned on both sides. Garnish with extra mint if desired.

Approximate values per 6-oz. (180-g) serving: **Calories** 430, **Total fat** 28 g, **Saturated fat** 11 g, **Cholesterol** 165 mg, **Sodium** 590 mg, **Total carbohydrates** 9 g, **Protein** 35 g, **Iron** 20%

RACK OF LAMB WITH MUSTARD AND HAZELNUTS

Yield: 4 Servings   **Method:** Roasting

Lamb racks, frenched, 2 lb.–2 lb. 8 oz. (0.9–1.2 kg) each	2	2
Salt and pepper	TT	TT
Olive oil	2 fl. oz.	60 ml
Dijon mustard	2 oz.	60 g
Fresh bread crumbs	1 oz.	30 g
Hazelnuts, chopped fine	2 oz.	60 g
Molasses	1 fl. oz.	30 ml

1. Season the racks with salt and pepper and brown well in the oil.
2. Spread the mustard over the surface of the racks.
3. Combine the bread crumbs, hazelnuts and molasses and press this mixture into the mustard to form a crust.
4. Roast the racks at 375°F (190°C) until medium rare, approximately 30 minutes.
5. Allow the racks to rest 15 minutes. Carve into chops and serve with marchand de vin sauce made with lamb jus lié (page 205).

VARIATION:

Rack of Lamb Persillé—In Step 3, sauté 2 teaspoons (10 milliliters) chopped garlic in 2 tablespoons (30 milliliters) olive oil and 2 tablespoons (30 milliliters) butter until soft. Add 1 cup (250 milliliters) fresh bread crumbs and 2 tablespoons (30 milliliters) chopped parsley to the garlic mixture. Season with salt and pepper and toss to combine. Press this mixture into the mustard to form a crust. Proceed with Steps 4 and 5 as in original recipe.

Approximate values per serving: **Calories** 700, **Total fat** 43 g, **Saturated fat** 10 g, **Cholesterol** 195 mg, **Sodium** 880 mg, **Total carbohydrates** 14 g, **Protein** 64 g, **Iron** 35%

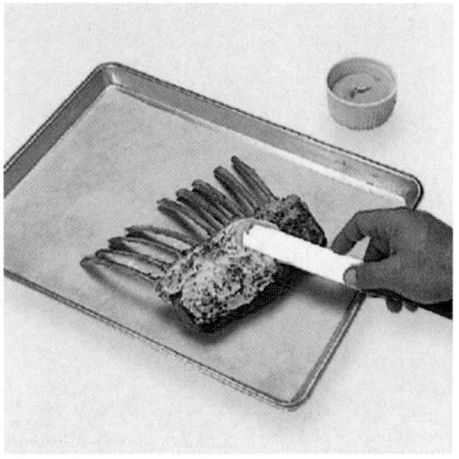

1 Spreading mustard over the rack.

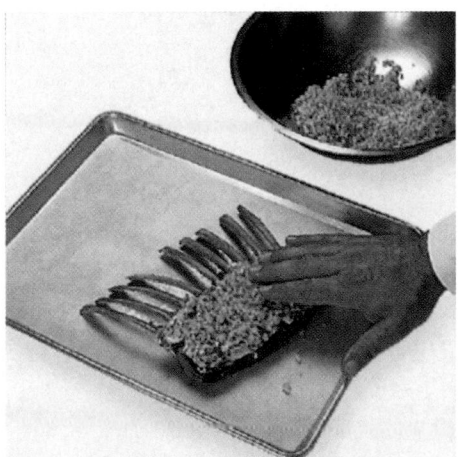

2 Pressing the bread crumb mixture into the mustard.

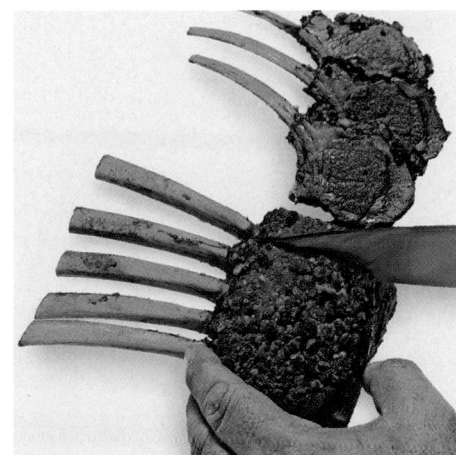

3 Slicing the cooked rack into chops.

4 Rack of lamb Persillé variation.

RACK OF SPRING LAMB WITH MINT PESTO

Yield: 8 Racks   **Method:** Grilling

Fresh mint leaves	2 oz.	60 g
Pine nuts, toasted	1 oz.	30 g
Garlic cloves, chopped	2	2
Parmesan cheese, grated	1 oz.	30 g
Chile flakes	½ tsp.	2 ml
Salt	½ tsp.	2 ml
Black pepper	½ tsp.	2 ml
Olive oil	4 fl. oz.	120 ml
Spring lamb racks, frenched	8	8

1. Combine all ingredients except the lamb in the bowl of a blender or food processor and blend to a coarse paste.
2. Spread approximately 1 tablespoon (15 milliliters) mint pesto on each lamb rack. Allow the lamb to marinate under refrigeration for at least 1 hour or preferably overnight.
3. Grill the lamb on a hot grill, browning the meat well for approximately 10 minutes while being careful not to burn the rib bones. The rib bones may be wrapped in aluminum foil to help prevent them from burning if desired.
4. Remove the lamb from the grill and brush each rack with an additional 1 tablespoon (15 milliliters) pesto. Place the lamb racks on a sheet pan and finish cooking them in a 350°F (180°C) oven to the desired doneness, approximately 15 minutes for medium rare.

Approximate values per serving: **Calories** 700, **Total fat** 43 g, **Saturated fat** 10 g, **Cholesterol** 195 mg, **Sodium** 880 mg, **Total carbohydrates** 14 g, **Protein** 64 g, **Iron** 35%

✹ STUFFED LEG OF LAMB

STUFFING

Any type of stuffing would work in this recipe. (Avoid raw meats, however, because they would not cook through in the time it takes to roast the lamb to medium rare.) For a more traditional flavor profile, substitute an equal part mirepoix for the fennel. Or use fresh mint in place of the thyme and rosemary. Season the mixture with Spanish paprika and add diced cooked chorizo to give it an Iberian flavor.

Yield: 12 Servings, 5–6 oz. (150–180 g) each   **Method:** Roasting

Bacon, fine dice	3 oz.	90 g
Fennel bulb, fine dice	1	1
Garlic cloves, chopped fine	2	2
Wild mushrooms such as shiitake, chanterelles or porcini, chopped	12 oz.	360 g
Fresh parsley, chopped	2 Tbsp.	30 ml
Fresh thyme	½ tsp.	2 ml
Fresh rosemary	½ tsp.	2 ml
Salt and pepper	TT	TT
Dry white wine	8 fl. oz.	240 ml
Fresh bread crumbs	3 oz.	90 g
Leg of lamb, 6–8 lb. (2.7–3.6 kg)	1	1
Mirepoix	1 lb.	480 g

1. To make the stuffing, sauté the bacon until crisp. Add the fennel and sauté lightly.
2. Add the garlic and sauté. Add the mushrooms, parsley, thyme, rosemary, salt and pepper and sauté for an additional 2 minutes.
3. Deglaze with the wine and reduce by three-fourths. Remove from the heat.
4. Stir in the bread crumbs.
5. Completely bone out the leg, following the natural seams in the meat. Cut off the shank meat for use in another recipe. Fill the cavity left by the bone with stuffing.
6. Season the lamb with salt and pepper. Close the leg around the stuffing and seal the opening by tying with butcher's twine.
7. Place the stuffed leg in a roasting pan on a bed of mirepoix.
8. Roast at 375°F (190°C) until medium rare, approximately 1 hour. Serve au jus or with a pan gravy.

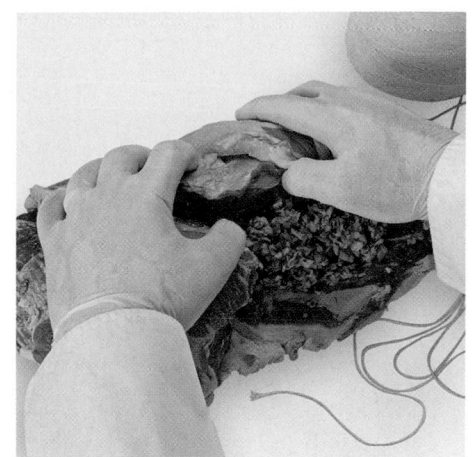

Approximate values per serving: **Calories** 540, **Total fat** 20 g, **Saturated fat** 7 g, **Cholesterol** 230 mg, **Sodium** 630 mg, **Total carbohydrates** 12 g, **Protein** 78 g, **Iron** 35%

HONEY-MUSTARD DENVER RIBS

Yield: 14 lb. (6.7 kg)　　　　　　　　**Method:** Roasting

Lamb ribs, trimmed	20 lb.	9.6 kg
Salt	4 oz.	120 g
Black pepper	2 oz.	60 g
Honey	2 lb.	960 g
Dijon mustard	1 lb. 8 oz.	720 g
Lemon juice	8 fl. oz.	240 ml

1. Rub the ribs with salt and pepper.
2. Place the ribs on a rack and roast at 375°F (190°C) for 30 minutes.
3. Combine the honey, mustard and lemon juice.
4. Baste the ribs generously with the honey-mustard mixture. Roast an additional 30 minutes, basting every 10 minutes.

Approximate values per 8-oz. (240-g) serving: **Calories** 1020, **Total fat** 47 g, **Saturated fat** 16 g, **Cholesterol** 285 mg, **Sodium** 2110 mg, **Total carbohydrates** 61 g, **Protein** 88 g, **Vitamin C** 15%, **Iron** 35%

SAUTÉED LAMB LOIN WITH STUFFED RÖSTI POTATOES AND CHERRY CONFIT

SIMPLICITY CATERING, FALLS CHURCH, VA

Chef Leland Atkinson

Yield: 6 Servings, 5 oz. (150 g) each   **Method:** Sautéing

Idaho potatoes, large	2	2
Parmesan, grated	5 oz.	150 g
Salt and pepper	TT	TT
Clarified butter	as needed	as needed
Goat cheese, room temperature	6 oz.	180 g
Black pepper, freshly ground	TT	TT
Fresh rosemary, chopped	1 tsp.	5 ml
Fresh chives, chopped	1 tsp.	5 ml
Lamb, eye of loin, trimmed, 2 lb. 4 oz. (1 kg)	1	1
Clarified butter	2 fl. oz.	60 ml
Port wine	4 fl. oz.	120 ml
Lamb jus lié	12 fl. oz.	360 ml
Whole butter	1 oz.	30 g
Cherry Confit (page 782)	as needed	as needed

1. Peel and julienne the potatoes.

2. Combine the potatoes with the Parmesan, salt and pepper.

3. Heat the clarified butter in an 8-inch (20-centimeter) nonstick pan. Add the potato mixture and pack it tightly with the back of a spoon. Cook over moderate heat until the potatoes begin to brown.

4. Flip the rösti potatoes and place the pan in a 350°F (180°C) oven. Flipping once, cook until the potatoes are crisp and evenly browned on the outside and soft in the center, approximately 20 minutes on each side.

5. Transfer the rösti potatoes to a wire cooling rack to rest.

6. Slice the rösti horizontally into two round halves. Spread the bottom half with the room-temperature goat cheese. Grind black pepper over the cheese, sprinkle the herbs evenly over the surface and carefully replace the top.

7. Season the lamb and sauté it in 2 fluid ounces (60 milliliters) clarified butter, turning frequently, until the desired doneness is achieved, approximately 8 to 12 minutes.

8. Remove the lamb and allow it to rest before slicing.

9. Deglaze the pan with the wine and add the jus lié. Reduce by half and monté au beurre.

10. At service time, ladle the sauce onto six warm plates, slice the lamb and arrange over the sauce. Cut the rösti into wedges and arrange on the plate. Spoon Cherry Confit around the lamb and serve at once.

Approximate values per serving: **Calories** 660, **Total fat** 39 g, **Saturated fat** 21 g, **Cholesterol** 215 mg, **Sodium** 1260 mg, **Total carbohydrates** 12 g, **Protein** 64 g, **Vitamin A** 60%, **Calcium** 45%

NOISETTES OF LAMB WITH GARLIC SAUCE

Yield: 4 Servings   **Method:** Sautéing

Lamb noisettes, 2–3 oz. (60–90 g) each	8	8
Salt and pepper	TT	TT
Fresh thyme	1 tsp.	5 ml
Garlic heads	3	3
Fresh rosemary	1 sprig	1 sprig
Olive oil	2 fl. oz.	60 ml
Red wine	4 fl. oz.	120 ml
Jus lié	1 pt.	480 ml

1. Season the noisettes with salt, pepper and thyme.
2. Break the garlic into cloves. Cook the cloves with the rosemary in 1 fluid ounce (30 milliliters) oil over low heat until they are very soft, approximately 10 minutes.
3. Deglaze with the wine. Add the jus lié; simmer and reduce by half.
4. Strain the sauce through a china cap, pushing to extract some of the garlic. Return the sauce to the saucepan and adjust the consistency and seasonings.
5. Sauté the noisettes to the desired degree of doneness in the remaining oil; serve with the sauce.

Approximate values per 5.5-oz. (165-g) serving: **Calories** 370, **Total fat** 26 g, **Saturated fat** 6 g, **Cholesterol** 105 mg, **Sodium** 660 mg, **Total carbohydrates** 1 g, **Protein** 32 g

CHIAPPETTI'S LAMB SHANK WITH LENTILS AND COUNTRY VEGETABLES

VIAND, CHICAGO, IL
Chef Steven Chiappetti

Yield: 2 Servings   **Method:** Braising

Vegetable oil	as needed	as needed
Lamb shanks, approx. 1 lb. 8 oz. (720 g) each	2	2
Onion, diced	4 oz.	120 g
Carrot, sliced	4 oz.	120 g
Celery, diced	4 oz.	120 g
Bay leaves	2	2
Lamb stock	1 qt.	960 ml
Soy sauce	4 fl. oz.	120 ml
Molasses	5½ oz.	165 g
Lentils, rinsed	8 oz.	240 g
Salt and pepper	TT	TT

1. Heat a small amount of oil in an ovenproof sauté pan. Sear the lamb shanks.
2. Add the onion, carrot, celery and bay leaves to the pan. Then add the stock, soy sauce and molasses to the pan and dissolve the fond with the liquid.
3. Place the pan with the lamb shanks and vegetables in a 400°F (200°C) oven and cook, uncovered, for 1½ hours.
4. Frequently baste the lamb with the molasses-soy broth.
5. Add the lentils and cook for another hour. Season to taste with salt and pepper.
6. Serve the lamb shanks, vegetables and lentils on a large platter.

Approximate values per serving: **Calories** 1660, **Total fat** 45 g, **Saturated fat** 16 g, **Cholesterol** 710 mg, **Sodium** 6300 mg, **Total carbohydrates** 92 g, **Protein** 222 g, **Vitamin A** 90%, **Calcium** 35%, **Iron** 130%

IRISH LAMB STEW

Yield: 12 Servings, 8 oz. (240 g) each		**Method:** Stewing
Lamb shoulder, 1½-in. (4-cm) cubes	4 lb.	1.9 kg
White stock	3 pt.	1.4 lt
Sachet:		
Bay leaf	1	1
Dried thyme	½ tsp.	2 ml
Peppercorns, crushed	½ tsp.	2 ml
Parsley stems	10	10
Garlic cloves, crushed	4	4
Onions, sliced	1 lb.	480 g
Leeks, sliced	8 oz.	240 g
Potatoes, peeled, large dice	1 lb. 8 oz.	720 g
Salt and white pepper	TT	TT
Carrots, tournée or bâtonnet	24	24
Turnips, tournée or bâtonnet	24	24
Potatoes, tournée or bâtonnet	24	24
Pearl onions, peeled	24	24
Fresh parsley, chopped	1 Tbsp.	15 ml

1. Combine the lamb, stock, sachet, onions, leeks and diced potatoes in a rondeau. Season with salt and white pepper. Bring to a simmer and skim the surface. Simmer the stew on the stove top or cover and cook in the oven at 350°F (180°C) until the lamb is tender, approximately 1 hour.

2. Degrease the stew; remove and discard the sachet.

3. Remove the pieces of diced potato and purée them in a food mill or ricer. Use the potato purée to thicken the stew to the desired consistency.

4. Simmer the stew for 10 minutes to blend the flavors.

5. Cook the tournée or bâtonnet vegetables and potatoes and pearl onions separately in salted water. At service, heat the vegetable garnishes and add to each portion of stew.

6. Garnish with chopped parsley and serve.

Approximate values per 8-oz. (240-g) serving: **Calories** 560, **Total fat** 26 g, **Saturated fat** 10 g, **Cholesterol** 175 mg, **Sodium** 840 mg, **Total carbohydrates** 26 g, **Protein** 54 g, **Vitamin A** 80%, **Iron** 30%

1. Skimming the surface of the stew.

2. Thickening the stew with the puréed potatoes.

3. The finished Irish Lamb Stew.

LAMB IN INDIAN COCONUT CURRY SAUCE

Yield: 3 pt. (1.4 lt)   **Method:** Stewing

Salt	1 Tbsp.	15 ml
Cumin, ground	2 Tbsp.	30 ml
Coriander, ground	2 Tbsp.	30 ml
Turmeric, ground	2 Tbsp.	30 ml
Cayenne pepper	1 tsp.	5 ml
Garam masala	2½ Tbsp.	40 ml
Black pepper	1 tsp.	5 ml
Lamb leg, 3 lb. (1.4 kg)	1	1
Ginger, 4-in. (10-cm) piece	1	1
Garlic cloves	8	8
Water	8 fl. oz.	240 ml
Vegetable oil	3 fl. oz.	90 ml
Onion, chopped fine	4 oz.	120 g
Tomatoes, peeled and chopped fine	8 oz.	240 g
Coconut milk	24 fl. oz.	720 ml
Steamed rice	as needed for garnish	
Naan or **pappadam** bread	as needed for garnish	

1. Combine the salt, cumin, coriander, turmeric, cayenne pepper, garam masala and black pepper.
2. Trim the lamb leg and then cut it into 1-inch (2.5-centimeter) pieces. Place the lamb in a stainless steel bowl and season it with approximately half of the spice mix. Marinate, refrigerated, for at least 1 hour or overnight.
3. Chop the ginger to a paste, place the paste in a double layer of cheesecloth and squeeze out as much juice as possible. Reserve the juice and discard the pulp.
4. Purée the garlic in a blender or food processor with the water and ginger juice until fairly smooth.
5. Heat the oil in a heavy-bottomed pot and add the lamb. Brown the lamb on all sides and then remove it from the pot.
6. Sauté the onion in the same pot until lightly caramelized and then add the garlic-ginger purée. Cook until all of the liquid has evaporated and only oil remains. Add the remaining spice mix and cook for approximately 20 seconds.
7. Add the tomatoes, reduce the heat and continue cooking for 3 to 4 minutes. Add the coconut milk a little at a time, incorporating it into the sauce each time before adding more. Return the lamb to the pan and simmer for 30 minutes or until the lamb is tender. Serve with steamed rice and naan or pappadam bread.

Approximate values per 1/2-c. (120-ml) serving: **Calories** 440, **Total fat** 36 g, **Saturated fat** 19 g, **Cholesterol** 75 mg, **Sodium** 660 mg, **Total carbohydrates** 7 g, **Protein** 23 g, **Vitamin C** 10%, **Iron** 30%

pappadam (PAH-pah-dahm) a thin, crisp East Indian flatbread made with chickpea, lentil or rice flour; may be flavored with black pepper, garlic or other seasonings; generally fried or toasted and served before or during meals

BLANQUETTE OF LAMB

Yield: 10 Servings, 10 oz. (300 g) each   **Method:** Stewing

White beans, dried	1 lb.	480 g
Onion piquet	2	2
Bouquets garni, for each:	2	2
Carrot stick, 4 in. (10 cm)	1	1
Leek, split, 4-in. (10-cm) piece	1	1
Fresh thyme	1 sprig	1 sprig
Bay leaf	1	1
Lamb leg or shoulder, cut in 1½-inch (4-cm) cubes	4 lb.	1.9 kg
White stock	2 qt.	1.4 lt
Sachet:		
Bay leaf	1	1
Dried thyme	½ tsp.	2 ml
Peppercorns, crushed	½ tsp.	2 ml
Parsley stems	10	10
Garlic cloves, crushed	4	4
Salt	TT	TT
Blond roux	2 oz.	60 g
Heavy cream	8 fl. oz.	240 ml
Dijon mustard	2 Tbsp.	30 ml
Egg yolks	4	4

1. Soak the beans in cold water for 12 hours. Drain, then add enough fresh water to cover the beans by 2–4 inches (5–10 centimeters).
2. Add one onion piquet and one bouquet garni and cook until the beans are tender, approximately 1½ hours. Remove and discard the onion piquet and bouquet garni.
3. Blanch the lamb cubes in boiling salted water.
4. Place the blanched lamb in an 8-quart (8-liter) saucepot. Add the stock and the second onion piquet, the second bouquet garni, the sachet and salt. Cover and simmer until the meat is tender, approximately 1½ hours.
5. Strain the meat from the liquid, reserving the meat and the liquid. Discard the onion piquet, bouquet garni and sachet. Return the liquid to the saucepot and reduce to 1 quart (approximately 1 liter). Whisk the roux into the liquid and simmer for 10 minutes.
6. Combine the cream, mustard and egg yolks in a nonreactive bowl. Whisk half of the hot sauce into the cream mixture to temper and then add it to the reduced stock as a liaison.
7. Return the lamb to the sauce and adjust the seasonings. Heat the sauce and meat thoroughly but do not allow it to boil. Serve the blanquette with the cooked beans.

Approximate values per 10-oz. (300-g) serving: **Calories** 600, **Total fat** 24 g, **Saturated fat** 11 g, **Cholesterol** 240 mg, **Sodium** 530 mg, **Total carbohydrates** 40 g, **Protein** 54 g, **Iron** 40%

1. Simmering the lamb.

2 Whisking the roux into the reduced cooking liquid.

3 Whisking a liaison into the sauce.

4 Adding the lamb to the sauce.

LAMB NAVARIN

Yield: 10 Servings, 10 oz. (300 g) each   **Method:** Stewing

Olive oil	3 Tbsp.	45 ml
Lean lamb shoulder, large dice	3 lb.	1.4 kg
Sugar, optional	1 Tbsp.	15 ml
Salt and pepper	TT	TT
Flour	3 Tbsp.	45 ml
White stock	1 qt.	960 ml
White wine	4 fl. oz.	120 ml
Tomato concassée	8 oz.	240 g
Bouquet garni:		
Carrot stick, 4 in. (10 cm)	1	1
Leek, split, 4-in. (10-cm) piece	1	1
Fresh thyme	1 sprig	1 sprig
Bay leaf	1	1
Potatoes, peeled, medium dice	1 lb. 8 oz.	720 g
Carrots, medium dice	1 lb.	480 g
White turnips, peeled, medium dice	1 lb.	480 g
Pearl onions, peeled	12	12
Fresh green peas	6 oz.	180 g

1 In a braiser, brown the meat in the oil. This can be done in several batches so that the meat browns properly.

2 Return all of the lamb to the braiser. Sprinkle the meat with the sugar (if used) and season with salt and pepper.

3 Add the flour and cook to make a blond roux.

4 Add the stock and wine. Add the tomato concassée and bouquet garni; bring to a boil. Cover and cook in the oven at 375°F (190°C) until the meat is almost tender, approximately 1 to 1½ hours.

5 Remove the meat and hold it in a warm place. Strain the sauce and skim off any excess fat.

6 Combine the sauce, meat, potatoes, carrots, turnips and onions. Cover and cook until the vegetables are almost tender, approximately 25 minutes.

7 Add the peas and cook for 10 minutes more. Adjust the seasonings before serving.

Approximate values per 10-oz. (300-g) serving: **Calories** 480, **Total fat** 24 g, **Saturated fat** 9 g, **Cholesterol** 100 mg, **Sodium** 280 mg, **Total carbohydrates** 32 g, **Protein** 31 g, **Vitamin A** 160%, **Vitamin C** 45%, **Iron** 20%

> "But I will place this carefully fed pig Within the crackling oven; and, I pray, What nicer dish can e'er be given to man.

—Aeschylus, ancient Greek poet (ca. 525–456 b.c.e.)

CHAPTER SIXTEEN

PORK

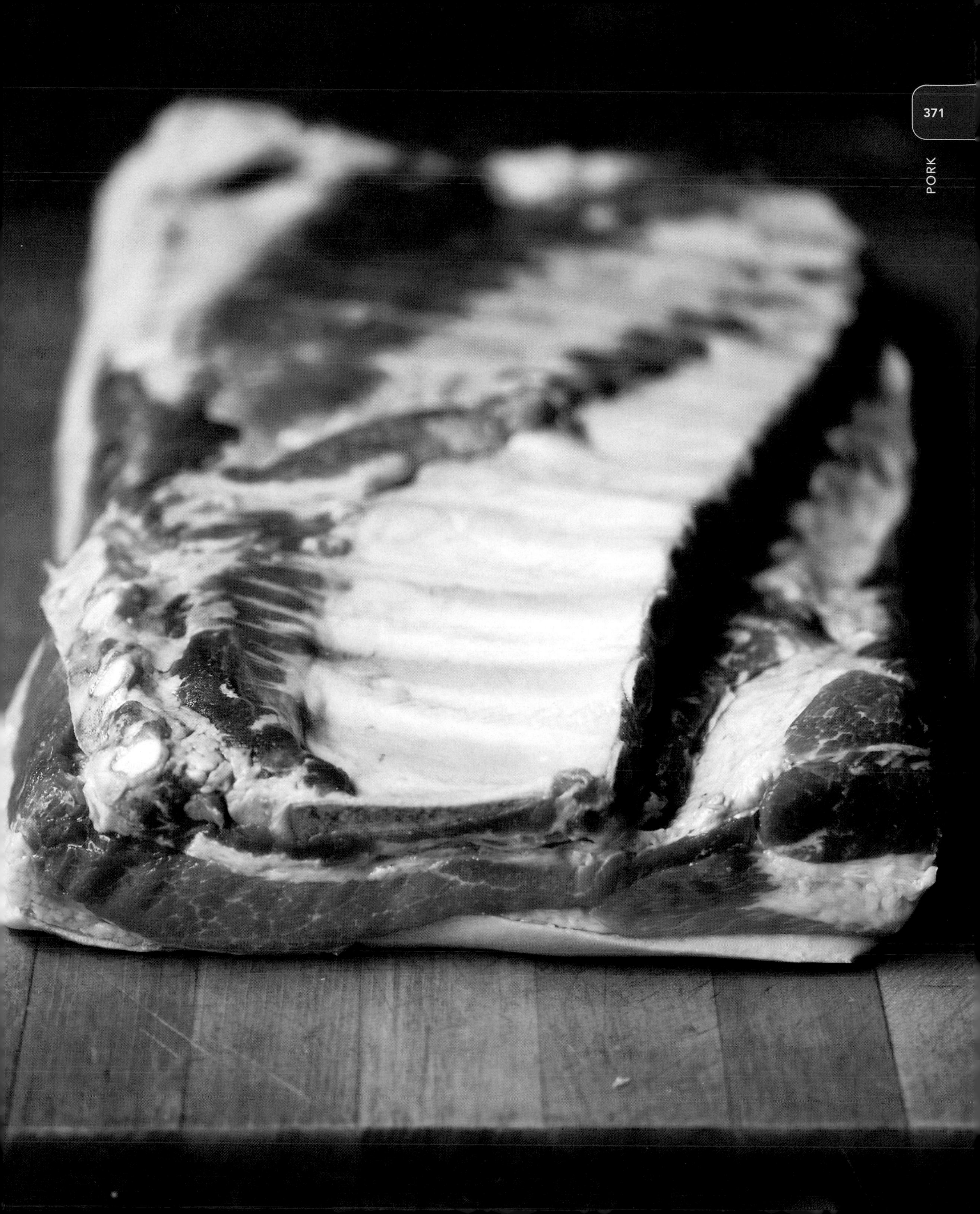

After studying this chapter, you will be able to:

- identify the primal, subprimal and fabricated cuts of pork

- perform basic butchering procedures

- apply appropriate cooking methods to several common cuts of pork

niche pork industry term for alternative or specialty pork products; meat from a specific breed such as Duroc or Tamworth hogs, or meat raised using a particular feeding method such as *free-range* or without antibiotics and hormones is considered a niche product.

PORK IS THE MEAT OF HOGS, usually butchered before they are one year old. With the exception of beef, Americans consume more pork than any other meat. The pork we eat is leaner and healthier than it once was because of advances in animal husbandry.

Because hogs are butchered at a young age, their meat is generally very tender with a delicate flavor. Pork can be enjoyed cured, processed or fresh. The mild flavor of fresh pork blends well with many different seasonings, making it a popular menu item. It is naturally tender and can be prepared by almost any dry-heat, moist-heat or combination cooking method. More than two-thirds of the pork marketed in the United States is cured to produce products such as smoked hams and smoked bacon. Cured pork products are discussed in Chapter 27, Charcuterie.

PRIMAL AND SUBPRIMAL CUTS OF PORK

After a hog is slaughtered, it is generally split down the backbone, dividing the carcass into bilateral halves. Like the beef carcass, each side of the hog carcass is then further broken down into the primal cuts: shoulder, Boston butt, belly, loin and fresh ham.

Hogs are bred specifically to produce long loins; the loin contains the highest-quality meat and is the most expensive cut of pork. Pork is unique in that the ribs and loin are considered a single primal. They are not separated into two different primals, as are the ribs and loin of beef, veal and lamb.

Figure 16.1 shows the relationship between the hog's bone structure and the primal cuts. As with all meats, it is important to know the location of bones when cutting or working with pork. This makes meat fabrication and carving easier and aids in identifying cuts. Figure 16.2 shows the primal cuts of pork and their location on the carcass. A hog carcass generally weighs in a range of 120 to 210 pounds (55 to 110 kg).

BERKSHIRE PORK

Berkshire pork is a breed of black pig named for the region of Great Britain where it was discovered. It is also known as *Kurobuta* in Japan. Considered a rare and endangered breed, Berkshire hogs produce pork that is well-marbled, moist and tender. Some producers feed the hogs sweet potatoes or beer to enhance their fat content, although this is not standard practice. Like Kobe beef, with which it is often compared, Berkshire pork is expensive and scarce.

Berkshire Hog

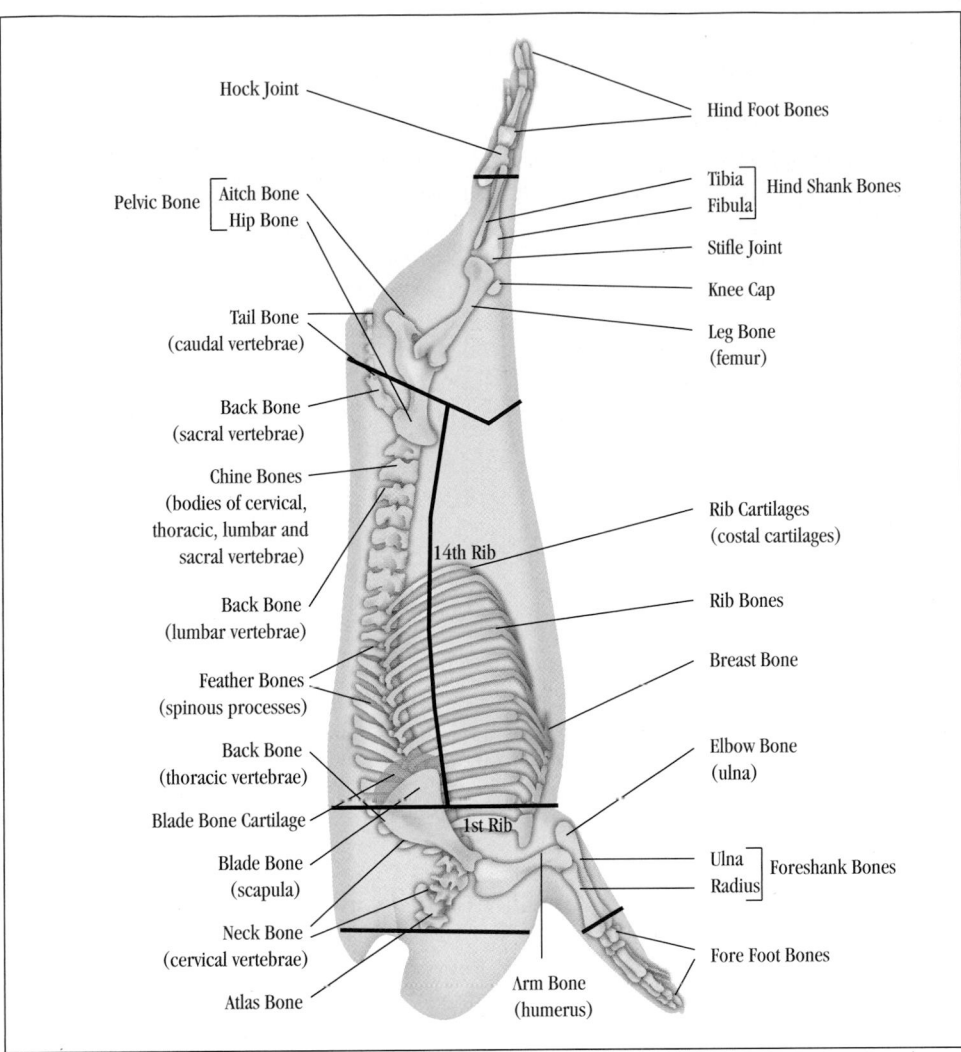

Hock Joint

Hind Foot Bones

Pelvic Bone [Aitch Bone
Hip Bone]

Tibia] Hind Shank Bones
Fibula

Stifle Joint

Knee Cap

Tail Bone
(caudal vertebrae)

Leg Bone
(femur)

Back Bone
(sacral vertebrae)

Chine Bones
(bodies of cervical,
thoracic, lumbar and
sacral vertebrae)

Rib Cartilages
(costal cartilages)

14th Rib

Back Bone
(lumbar vertebrae)

Rib Bones

Feather Bones
(spinous processes)

Breast Bone

Back Bone
(thoracic vertebrae)

Elbow Bone
(ulna)

Blade Bone Cartilage

1st Rib

Blade Bone
(scapula)

Ulna] Foreshank Bones
Radius

Neck Bone
(cervical vertebrae)

Fore Foot Bones

Atlas Bone

Arm Bone
(humerus)

FIGURE 16.1 ▶ The skeletal structure of a hog.

CLASSIC PORK FLAVORS

With a heavy layer of fat and many well-marbled cuts, pork benefits from robust seasonings. Shoulder and fresh leg roasts can be studded with garlic and strong herbs such as marjoram, oregano, rosemary or thyme before slow roasting. These cuts lend themselves to the flavors of American barbecue (smoke, whiskey, sugar and salt curing), as well as spices used in Asian grilling (lemongrass, star anise, ginger, sesame oil and soy sauce.) Lean cuts such as pork loin pair well with mild cream sauces flavored with mustard or herbs such as tarragon, as well as richer brown sauces and caramelized apples, stone fruits or mushrooms.

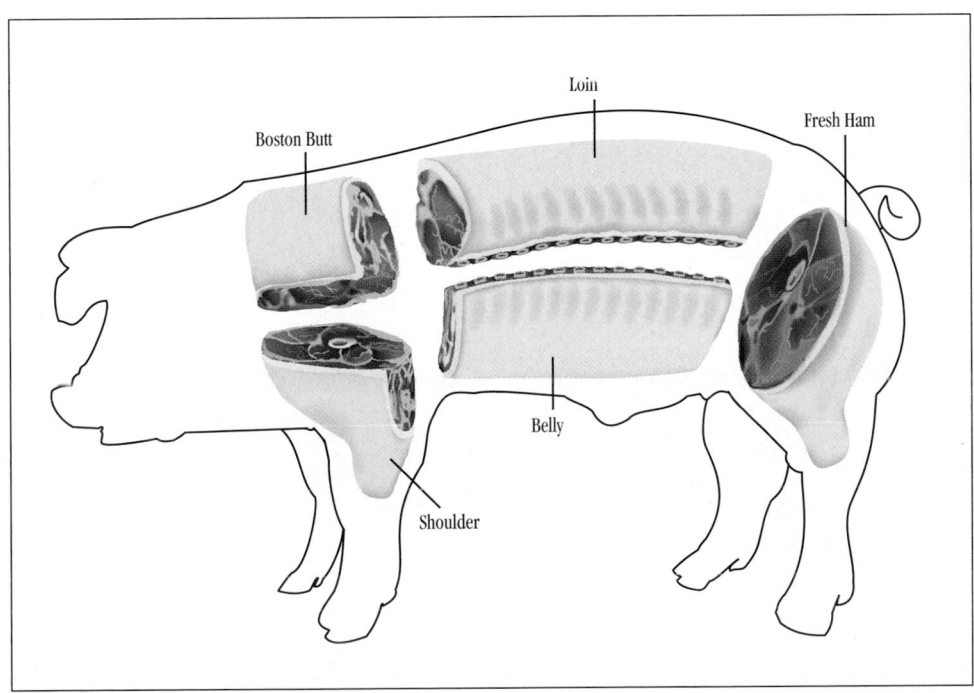

Boston Butt

Loin

Fresh Ham

Belly

Shoulder

FIGURE 16.2 ▶ The primal cuts of pork.

Boston Butt

Pork Loin

Shoulder

The primal shoulder, known as the picnic ham, is the lower portion of the hog's foreleg; it accounts for approximately 20 percent of the carcass weight. The shoulder contains the arm and shank bones and has a relatively high ratio of bone to lean meat.

Because all pork comes from hogs slaughtered at a young age, the shoulder is tender enough to be cooked by any method. It is, however, one of the least tender cuts of pork. It is available smoked or fresh. The shoulder is fairly inexpensive and, when purchased fresh, it can be cut into shoulder butt steaks or boned and cut into smaller pieces for sautéing or stewing. Whole pork shoulder is the cut preferred by many barbecue pit masters throughout the American South.

The foreshank is called the shoulder hock and is almost always smoked. Shoulder hocks are often simmered for long periods in soups, stews and braised dishes to add flavor and richness.

Boston Butt

The primal Boston butt is a square cut located just above the primal pork shoulder. It accounts for approximately 7 percent of the carcass weight.

The Boston butt is very meaty and tender, with a good percentage of fat to lean meat. Containing only a small portion of the blade bone, the Boston butt is a good choice when a recipe calls for a solid piece of lean pork. The fresh Boston butt is sometimes cut into steaks or chops to be broiled or sautéed. When the Boston butt is smoked, it is usually boneless and called a cottage ham.

Belly

The primal pork belly is located below the loin. Accounting for approximately 16 percent of the carcass weight, it is very fatty with only streaks of lean meat. It contains the spareribs, which are always separated from the rest of the belly before cooking.

Spareribs usually are sold fresh but can also be smoked. Typically, they are simmered and then grilled or baked while being basted with a spicy barbecue sauce. The remainder of the pork belly is nearly always cured and smoked to produce bacon.

Pork Belly

Loin

The loin is cut from directly behind the Boston butt and includes the entire rib section as well as the loin and a portion of the sirloin area. The primal loin accounts for approximately 20 percent of the carcass weight. It contains a portion of the blade bone on the shoulder end, a portion of the hip bone on the ham end, all of the ribs and most of the backbone.

The primal pork loin is the only primal cut of pork not typically smoked or cured. Most of the loin is a single, very tender eye muscle. It is quite lean but contains enough intramuscular and subcutaneous fat to make it an excellent choice for a moist-heat cooking method such as braising, or it can be prepared with dry-heat cooking methods such as roasting or sautéing. The loin also contains the pork tenderloin, located on the inside of the rib bones on the sirloin end of the loin.

Pork Spareribs

The tenderloin is the most tender cut of pork; it is very versatile and can be trimmed, cut into medallions and sautéed, or the whole tenderloin can be roasted or braised. The most popular cut from the loin is the pork chop. Chops can be cut from the entire loin, the choicest being center-cut chops from the primal loin after the blade bone and sirloin portions at the front and rear of the loin are removed. The pork loin can be purchased boneless or boned and tied as a roast. A boneless pork loin is smoked to produce Canadian bacon. The rib bones, when trimmed from the loin, can be served as barbecued pork back ribs.

Pork Tenderloin

Although not actually part of the primal loin, fatback is the thick layer of fat—sometimes more than an inch (2.5 centimeters) thick—between the skin and the lean eye muscle. It has a variety of uses in the kitchen, especially in the preparation of charcuterie items.

Pork Back Ribs

Pork Loin Chops

Fresh Ham

The primal fresh ham is the hog's hind leg. It is a rather large cut accounting for approximately 24 percent of the carcass weight. The ham contains the aitch, leg and hindshank bones. Fresh ham, like the legs of other meat animals, contains large muscles with relatively small amounts of connective tissue. Like many other cuts of pork, hams are often cured and smoked. But fresh hams also produce great roasts and can be prepared using almost any cooking method. When cured and smoked, hams are available in a variety of styles; they can be purchased bone-in, shankless or boneless, partially or fully cooked. Fully cooked hams are also available canned. There is a specific ham for nearly every use and desired degree of convenience. The shank portion of the ham is called the ham hock. It is used in the same manner as the shoulder hock.

NUTRITION

Like other meats, pork is a good source of protein, B vitamins and other essential nutrients, but it is also high in fat, especially saturated fats. Through new breeding and feeding techniques, the fat content of pork has been lowered in recent years. (Pork from specialty or **heritage breeds** may have a higher fat content than more widely available cuts, however.) Cuts from the loin, such as the tenderloin and boneless loin chops, are among the leaner cuts of meat available with reduced levels of saturated fat. Sodium content of smoked and preserved pork products such as bacon, ham and sausage, which are discussed in Chapter 27, Charcuterie, is high, but reduced-sodium preserved and smoked products are increasingly available.

BUTCHERING PROCEDURES

Other than **suckling pigs**, pork products generally are not purchased in forms larger than the primal cuts described earlier. Table 16.1 lists some cuts of pork commonly available. Chefs should master a few important pork fabrication and butchering techniques, however.

> ## BRINING PORK
>
> Brine is actually a very salty marinade used on meats such as ham or bacon that will be smoked for long preservation; this process is discussed in Chapter 27, Charcuterie. Lean cuts of pork or poultry can also benefit from a light brining before grilling, roasting or sautéing. Soaking the cuts in a 3–5% brine solution for a few hours or overnight increases moisture retention and tenderizes the meat. Because the meat and fond can become salty after brining, never salt brined meat before cooking. Avoid making pan gravy from brined meats. Most brine recipes include sweeteners and other seasonings to counterbalance the saltiness. The ratios of salt to water for light brine are as follows:
>
> 3% solution: 0.5 oz. (15 g) salt per 16 fl. oz. (480 ml) water
> 5% solution: 0.8 oz. (24 g) salt per 16 fl. oz. (480 ml) water

Fresh Ham

heritage or heirloom breed a loosely defined term that refers to older breeds of pork, meat or poultry less commonly raised in modern agricultural systems; many believe that protecting a genetically diverse population of livestock by raising and consuming such animals is important culturally and scientifically and will help ensure human survival

suckling pig (Fr. *cochon de lait*) very young, very small whole pigs used for roasting or barbecuing whole

PROCEDURE FOR **BONING A PORK LOIN**

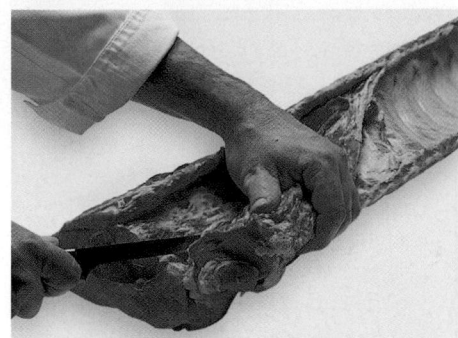

1 Starting on the sirloin end of a full pork loin, remove the tenderloin in one piece by making smooth cuts against the inside of the rib bones. Pull gently on the tenderloin as you cut.

2 Turn the loin over and cut between the ribs and the eye meat. Continue separating the meat from the bones, following the contours of the bones, until the loin is completely separated from the bones.

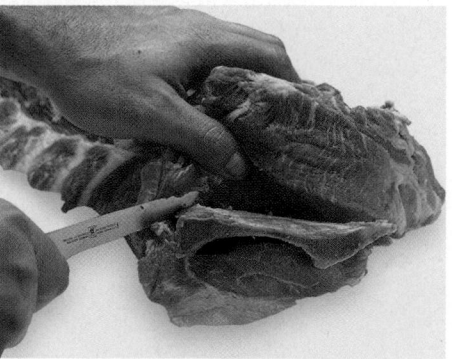

3 Trim around the blade bone on the shoulder end of the loin and remove it.

The fully boned loin consists of (from left to right) cartilage, the tenderloin, boneless loin and loin bones.

PROCEDURE FOR **TYING A BONELESS PORK ROAST WITH THE HALF-HITCH METHOD**

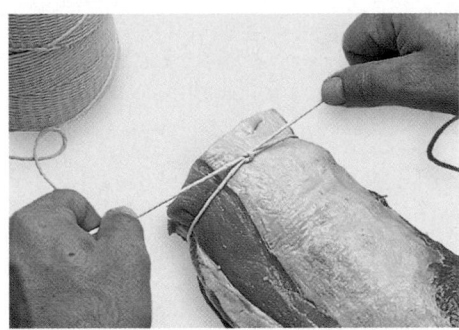

① Wrap the loose end of the string around the pork loin and tie it with a double knot.

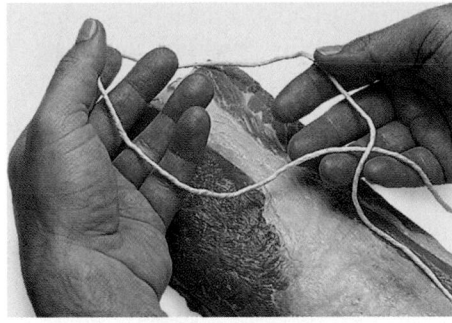

② Make a loop and slide it down over the roast to approximately 1 inch (2.5 centimeters) from the first knot.

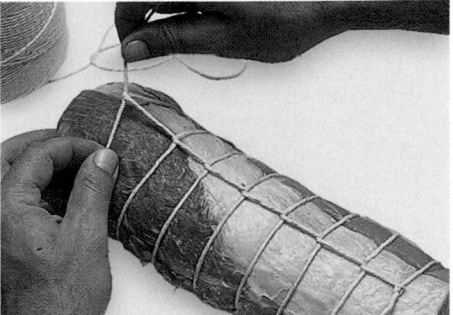

③ Make another loop and slide it down. Continue in this fashion until the whole roast has been tied.

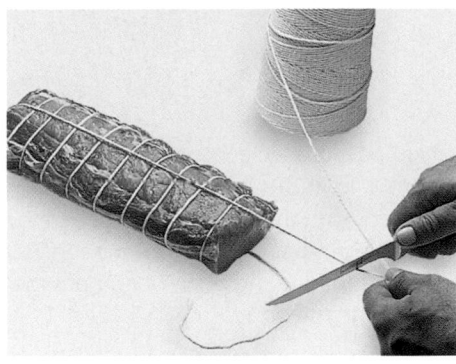

④ Turn the roast over and cut the string, leaving enough to wrap lengthwise around the roast to the original knot.

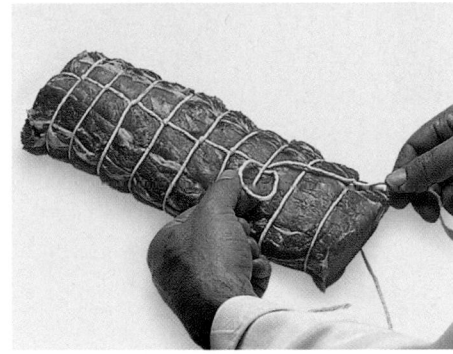

⑤ Wrap the string around the end of the roast, then around the string that formed the last loop. Continue in this fashion for the length of the roast, pulling the string tight after wrapping it around each loop.

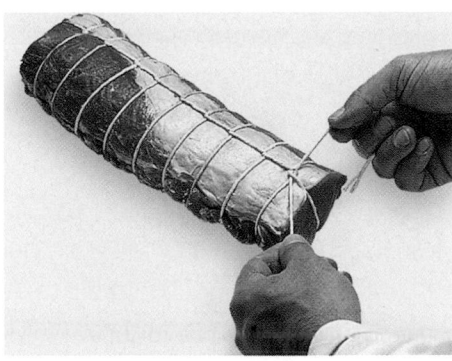

⑥ Turn the roast back over. Wrap the string around the front end of the roast and secure it to the first loop at the point where you tied the first knot.

⑦ The finished roast. Note the even intervals at which the strings are tied. They should be just snug enough to hold the shape of the roast; they should not dig in or cut the meat.

PROCEDURE FOR **CUTTING A CENTER-CUT PORK CHOP**

A center-cut pork chop can be cut from the center portion of a bone-in pork loin without the aid of a saw by using a boning knife and a heavy cleaver. Trim the excess fat from the loin, leaving a 1/4-inch (6-millimeter) layer to protect the meat during cooking.

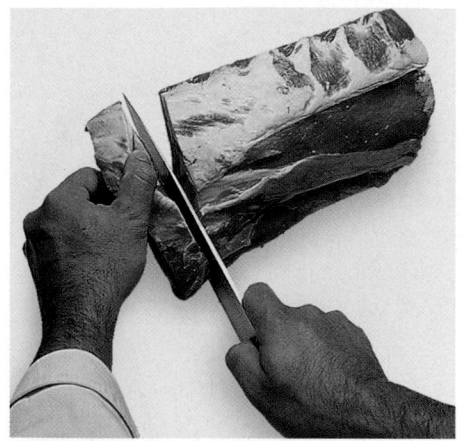

❶ Cut through the meat with the knife.

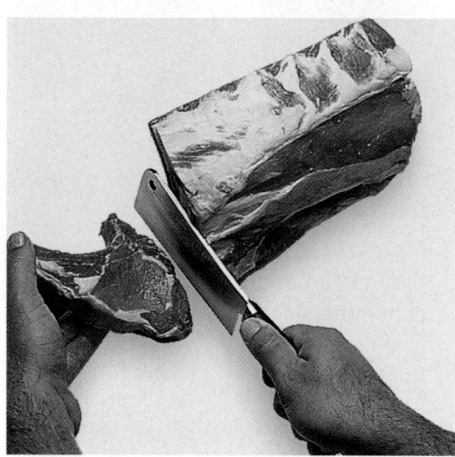

❷ Use the cleaver to chop through the chine bone.

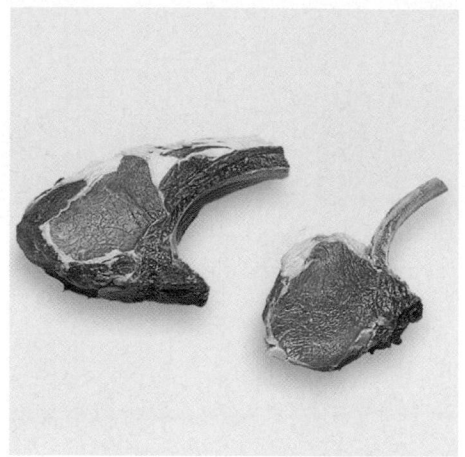

❸ To produce a cleaner chop, trim the meat from the end of the rib bone. Then, with the boning knife, separate the loin meat from the chine bones and separate the chine bone from the rib with the cleaver.

PROCEDURE FOR **CUTTING A POCKET IN A PORK CHOP**

To make a pocket in a pork chop for stuffing, start with a thick chop or a double rib chop. Cut the pocket deep enough to hold ample stuffing, but be careful not to puncture either surface of the chop.

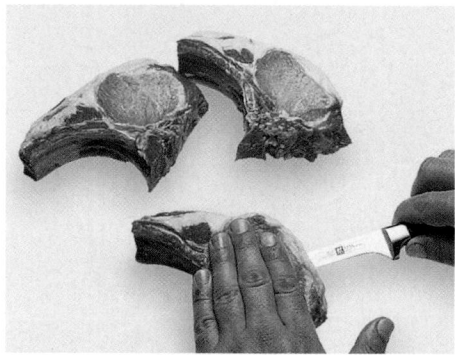

Use the tip of a boning knife to cut a pocket.

PROCEDURE FOR **TRIMMING A PORK TENDERLOIN**

As with a beef tenderloin, the pork tenderloin must be trimmed of all fat and silverskin. Follow the procedures outlined in Chapter 13, Beef, for trimming a beef tenderloin.

Use a boning knife to remove the silverskin from a pork tenderloin.

TABLE 16.1	USING COMMON CUTS OF PORK			
PRIMAL	**SUBPRIMAL OR FABRICATED CUT**	**IMPS**	**COOKING METHODS**	**SERVING SUGGESTIONS**
Shoulder	Picnic shoulder	405	Dry heat (roast or bake)	Smoked picnic shoulder
Boston butt	Boston butt	406	Dry heat (broil or grill; sauté) Moist heat (simmer)	Broiled Boston butt steaks Choucroute
Belly	Bacon	539	Dry heat (sauté) Moist heat (simmer) Combination (braise)	Breakfast meat Seasoning Seasoning
	Spareribs	416A	Combination (steam, then grill)	Barbecued spareribs
Loin	Pork loin	410	Dry heat (roast) Combination (braise)	Roast pork Braised pork chops
	Pork tenderloin	415	Dry heat (broil or grill; sauté; roast)	Roast pork tenderloin
	Pork back ribs	422	Combination (steam, then grill)	Barbecued back ribs
	Pork loin chops	1410	Dry heat (broil or grill) Combination (braise)	Broiled loin chop with mushroom sauce Braised loin chop with leeks and fennel
Fresh ham	Fresh ham	401A	Dry heat (roast)	Roast pork with apricots and almonds

QUESTIONS FOR DISCUSSION

1. List each pork primal and describe its location on the carcass. Identify two subprimals or fabricated cuts taken from each primal.

2. Discuss the characteristics of pork shoulder and explain why it is the preferred cut for Southern-style barbecue.

3. What is unique about the primal pork loin as compared to the beef or veal loin?

4. Are fatback and bacon taken from the same primal? How are they different?

5. What is the only primal cut of pork that is not typically smoked or cured? How is it best cooked? Explain your answer.

6. Research the various breeds of pork available from large-scale and niche producers. Discuss how to best prepare loin and shoulder cuts from the different processors. Explain your answers.

7. What is the World Pork Expo? How is such an event useful for chefs and restaurateurs?

Terms to Know

hogs	**spareribs**
Boston Butt	**picnic ham**
brining	**Canadian bacon**
solution	**fatback**
pork belly	

CAROLINA BARBECUED RIBS

Yield: 6 Servings, approx. 4 ribs each   **Method:** Roasting

Salt and pepper	TT	TT
Crushed red pepper flakes	1 Tbsp.	15 ml
Pork back ribs, 3–4 lb. (1.4–1.9 kg) slab	2	2
White vinegar	1 pt.	480 ml
Sauce:		
Onion, chopped coarse	5 oz.	150 g
Garlic cloves	3	3
Green bell pepper, chopped coarse	4 oz.	120 g
Plum tomatoes, canned	1 pt.	480 ml
Red Devil hot sauce	8 fl. oz.	240 ml
Brown sugar	10 oz.	300 g
Lemon juice	2 fl. oz.	60 ml

1. Combine the salt, pepper and red pepper flakes. Rub this mixture over both sides of the ribs, coating them well.
2. Place the ribs in a nonreactive pan and add the vinegar. Cover and refrigerate several hours or overnight.
3. Uncover the ribs, turn them presentation side down and bake in a 375°F (190°C) oven for 1½ hours.
4. Remove the ribs from the liquid and place on a clean sheet pan, turning them so that the presentation side is up. Increase the oven temperature to 400°F (200°C) and bake for an additional 30 minutes.
5. Prepare the sauce by puréeing the onion, garlic, bell pepper and tomatoes in a food processor or blender. Pour this mixture into a nonreactive saucepan and add the remaining sauce ingredients.
6. Simmer the sauce over low heat until it thickens, approximately 15 to 20 minutes.
7. Brush the ribs with the sauce and serve additional sauce on the side. Serve with Creamy Coleslaw (page 743) and Baked Beans (page 610).

Approximate values per serving: **Calories** 1410, **Total fat** 68 g, **Saturated fat** 23 g, **Cholesterol** 315 mg, **Sodium** 1280 mg, **Total carbohydrates** 65 g, **Protein** 134 g, **Vitamin A** 20%, **Vitamin C** 120%, **Iron** 35%

BEER-MARINATED PORK TENDERLOIN

Yield: 6 Servings, 6 oz. (180 g) each   **Method:** Grilling

Pork tenderloins, approx. 14 oz. (420 g) each	3	3
Marinade:		
Light soy sauce	4 fl. oz.	120 ml
Beer, room temperature	12 fl. oz.	360 ml
Light brown sugar	2 oz.	60 g
Fresh ginger, grated	1½ Tbsp.	22 ml

1. Clean the tenderloins, removing all visible fat and silverskin.
2. Combine the marinade ingredients, stirring until the sugar dissolves.
3. Place the tenderloins in a hotel pan and cover with the marinade. Cover the pan and refrigerate for 2 to 6 hours.
4. Remove the tenderloins from the marinade and grill over medium-hot coals, turning as needed.
5. Allow the cooked tenderloins to rest for 5 minutes, then slice thinly on the bias.

Approximate values per serving: **Calories** 592, **Total fat** 42 g, **Saturated fat** 16 g, **Cholesterol** 143 mg, **Sodium** 762 mg, **Total carbohydrates** 13 g, **Protein** 35 g, **Iron** 13%

PORK CHIMICHURRI KABOBS

Chimichurri is a thick, fresh herb sauce from Argentina, where it is traditionally served as an accompaniment to grilled meats. In this recipe it is used as both a marinade and a sauce.

Yield: 8 Servings of pork, 1 pt. (480 ml) sauce   **Method:** Grilling

Chimichurri sauce:

Garlic cloves, peeled	8	8
Onion, chopped	4 oz.	120 g
Fresh lemon juice	1½ fl. oz.	45 ml
Dried oregano, crushed	2 Tbsp.	30 ml
Fresh parsley	1 bunch	1 bunch
Olive oil	6 fl. oz.	180 ml
Sherry wine vinegar	2 fl. oz.	60 ml
Salt	1 tsp.	5 ml
Crushed red pepper flakes	½ tsp.	2 ml
Black pepper	½ tsp.	2 ml
Pork loin, boneless, trimmed	2 lb.	1.9 kg
Black beans, cooked	as needed for garnish	
Rice, cooked	as needed for garnish	

1. Combine the sauce ingredients in a food processor fitted with a metal blade and pulse until the ingredients are thoroughly blended, but not puréed. The mixture should be slightly coarse.

2. Cut the pork into 1-inch (2.5-centimeter) cubes and place them in a nonreactive pan. Add approximately three-fourths of the chimichurri sauce and stir thoroughly. Cover and refrigerate for 4 to 6 hours. Reserve the remaining sauce to serve with the kabobs.

3. Remove the pork from the marinade, discarding any marinade left in the pan. Arrange the pork on eight skewers. Cook on a hot grill, turning as necessary to cook thoroughly and brown evenly. Serve with black beans and rice and the reserved chimichurri sauce.

VARIATIONS:

Use boneless, skinless chicken or cubes of lamb shoulder meat in place of the pork.

Approximate values per serving with ½ Tbsp. (7 ml) sauce: **Calories** 200, **Total fat** 11 g, **Saturated fat** 3.5 g, **Cholesterol** 70 mg, **Sodium** 85 mg, **Total carbohydrates** 1 g, **Protein** 25 g

KEBAB AND KABOB

The *kebab* (also known as *kabob*, *shis kabab*, *shashlik* and *brochette*) refers to grilling small pieces of meat on a skewer. Historians reason that in urban centers in the Middle East and Persia where this style of cooking is thought to originate, fuel was in short supply. Therefore, smaller cuts of meats were preferred because they could be cooked more easily over portable charcoal-fired grills or braziers. Threading the meat on skewers made turning the meat to cook it evenly feasible. Meat, poultry, fish and vegetables all lend themselves to this style of cooking. Because of the short cooking time, tender cuts should be used. Marinating preserves moisture and adds flavor. When using bamboo skewers, soak them in water first to keep them from burning on the grill.

FRESH ROASTED HAM

THE SCHOOL OF CULINARY ARTS AT KENDALL COLLEGE, EVANSTON, IL

Chef Mike Artlip, CEC, CCE

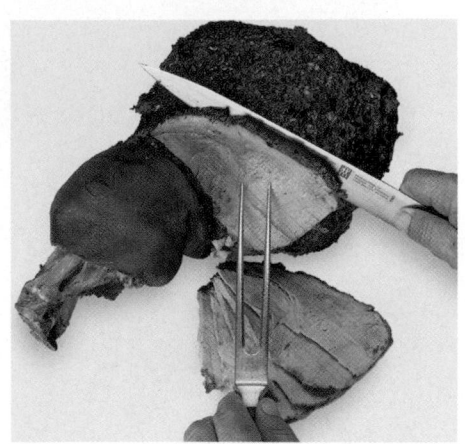

Yield: 25–30 Servings		**Method:** Roasting
Fresh ham, approx. 22 lb. (10.5 kg)	1	1
Garlic heads, minced	3	3
Dried oregano	½ oz.	15 g
Adobo seasoning	TT	TT
Salt and pepper	TT	TT
Mojo criollo	10 fl. oz.	300 ml

1. Using a skewer or meat fork, poke holes over the entire surface of the ham approximately 1 to 2 inches (2.5 to 5 centimeters) deep.
2. Combine the garlic, oregano, adobo seasoning, salt and pepper and rub the ham with the mixture, being sure to push the garlic and seasonings into the holes. Pour the mojo criollo over the ham. Marinate the ham under refrigeration for 24 hours.
3. Remove the ham from the marinade and place on a rack in a roasting pan. Roast at 325°F (160°C) until the center reaches 155°F (68°C), approximately 4 hours.
4. Allow the ham to rest for 30 minutes before carving.

adobo seasoning a commercial spice blend; although several brands are available, most include dried chiles, Mexican oregano, cumin, black pepper, garlic powder and onion powder

mojo criollo a citrus and herb marinade used in Latino cuisines; bottled brands are available in Hispanic markets

Approximate values per serving: **Calories** 550, **Total fat** 31 g, **Saturated fat** 11 g, **Cholesterol** 205 mg, **Sodium** 135 mg, **Total carbohydrates** 2 g, **Protein** 62 g, **Vitamin C** 10%, **Iron** 15%

CHINESE BARBECUED SPARERIBS

Yield: Approximately 24 ribs		**Method:** Roasting
Sparerib racks, 2 lb. 8 oz. (1.2 kg) each	2	2
Garlic cloves, crushed	2	2
Tomato ketchup	1 fl. oz.	30 ml
Soy sauce	1 fl. oz.	30 ml
Hoisin sauce	1 fl. oz.	30 ml
Red wine	1 fl. oz.	30 ml
Fresh ginger, grated	1 Tbsp.	15 ml
Honey	1 Tbsp.	15 ml

1. Cut the sparerib racks into individual ribs and arrange them on a rack in a baking pan. Roast for 45 minutes at 300°F (150°C).
2. Combine the remaining ingredients into a sauce. Brush the spareribs lightly with the sauce. Roast for 30 minutes more.
3. Turn the spareribs and brush with more sauce. Roast until the ribs are well browned, approximately 30 minutes.

Approximate values per rib: **Calories** 181, **Total fat** 11 g, **Saturated fat** 4 g, **Cholesterol** 49 mg, **Sodium** 118 mg, **Total carbohydrates** 1 g, **Protein** 21 g, **Iron** 4%

PORK LOIN WITH PRUNES

Yield: 6 Servings, 6 oz. (180 g) each   **Method:** Roasting

Boneless pork loin roast, 3 lb. (1.4 kg)	1	1
Salt and pepper	TT	TT
Prunes, pitted	1 lb. 8 oz.	720 g
Carrot, chopped coarse	3 oz.	90 g
Onion, chopped coarse	6 oz.	180 g
Vegetable oil	1 Tbsp.	15 ml
Clarified butter	1 Tbsp.	15 ml
Fresh rosemary	1 tsp.	5 ml
Fresh thyme	1 tsp.	5 ml
Bay leaf, crushed	1	1
Garlic cloves	2	2
Apple juice	8 fl. oz.	240 ml
White stock	8 fl. oz.	240 ml
Sugar	2 oz.	60 g
Vinegar	2 fl. oz.	60 ml

1. Trim and butterfly the pork loin; reserve the trimmings. (To butterfly the loin, slice it partway through the center and open it like a book, then flatten it into a rectangular shape.) Season with salt and pepper.

2. Reserve 12 prunes and arrange the remaining prunes along the length of the loin. Roll up the loin and tie with butcher's twine.

3. Brown the pork roll and pork trimmings, carrot and onion in the oil and butter.

4. Add the herbs and garlic and roast the pork on the bed of trimmings and vegetables at 350°F (180°C), basting frequently with the fat that accumulates in the pan, until done, approximately 45 to 60 minutes.

5. Poach the reserved prunes in the apple juice until plump; set aside.

6. Remove the roast from the pan and keep it warm. Degrease the pan and deglaze with the stock. Simmer for 15 minutes, then strain.

7. Combine the sugar and vinegar in a saucepan. Bring to a boil and cook without stirring until the mixture turns a caramel color. Immediately remove from the heat and add the juices from the roasting pan. When the sputtering stops, return the pan to the heat and skim any fat from the surface; keep the sauce warm over low heat.

8. Drain the prunes. Remove the twine from the roast. Slice and serve the meat with the sauce and poached prunes.

Note: Dried apricots can be substituted for the prunes in this recipe.

Approximate values per serving: **Calories** 850, **Total fat** 16 g, **Saturated fat** 5 g, **Cholesterol** 185 mg, **Sodium** 530 mg, **Total carbohydrates** 110 g, **Protein** 66 g, **Vitamin A** 45%, **Vitamin C** 15%, **Iron** 30%

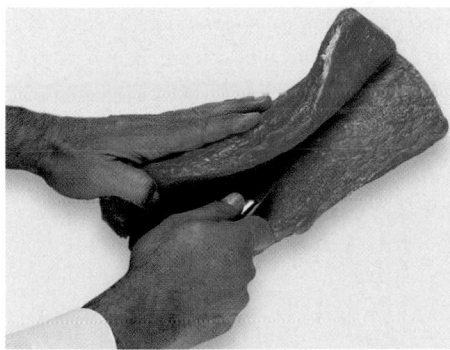

1. Butterflying the pork loin.

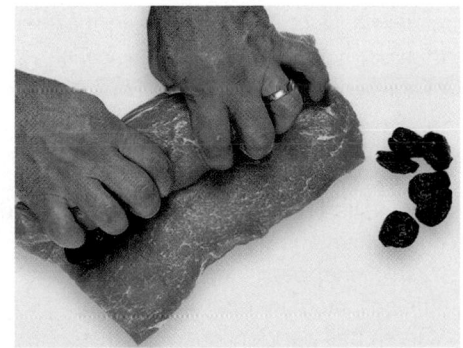

2. Rolling the pork loin around the filling.

3. The finished sliced Pork Loin with Prunes.

SAUTÉED PORK MEDALLIONS WITH RED PEPPER AND CITRUS

Yield: 8 Servings, 6 oz. (180 g) each   **Method:** Sautéing

Pork loin, boneless, 3 lb. (1.4 kg)	1	1
Salt and pepper	TT	TT
Olive oil	6 fl. oz.	180 ml
Orange juice	6 fl. oz.	180 ml
Lemon juice	1 fl. oz.	30 ml
Green onions, sliced	4 oz.	120 g
Oranges	4	4
Flour	as needed for dredging	
Red bell peppers, julienne	12 oz.	360 g
Grand Marnier	4 fl. oz.	120 ml
Demi-glace	1 pt.	480 ml

1. Season the pork with salt and pepper and marinate overnight in 4 fluid ounces (120 milliliters) olive oil, 4 fluid ounces (120 milliliters) orange juice, 1 tablespoon (15 milliliters) lemon juice and 2 ounces (60 grams) green onions.
2. Zest the oranges. Blanch and refresh the zest. Peel and section the oranges.
3. Cut the pork into 3-ounce (90-gram) medallions and pound lightly.
4. Dredge the medallions in flour seasoned with salt and pepper.
5. Sauté the medallions in the remaining olive oil until done, approximately 5 minutes. Remove from the pan and reserve.
6. Add the bell peppers and remaining green onions to the pan and sauté lightly.
7. Remove the pan from the flame and deglaze with the Grand Marnier.
8. Add the demi-glace, orange zest, and remaining orange and lemon juices. Adjust the seasonings.
9. Serve two medallions of pork per portion with sauce. Garnish with the orange sections.

Approximate values per 6-oz. (180-g) serving: **Calories** 275, **Total fat** 15 g, **Saturated fat** 3 g, **Cholesterol** 68 mg, **Sodium** 195 mg, **Total carbohydrates** 11 g, **Protein** 25 g, **Vitamin C** 60%

JAMBALAYA

THE SCHOOL OF CULINARY ARTS AT KENDALL COLLEGE, EVANSTON, IL
Chef Mike Artlip, CEC, CCE

A centerpiece of Louisiana Creole cooking, jambalaya is a rich stew of crab, shrimp, duck, chicken, pork, beef and vegetables in myriad combinations. Some historians claim that its name derives from the word jamón, Spanish for "ham," because ham and rice are the two key ingredients that are found in all such stews. Tasso ham is a heavily smoked ham made from lean pork and flavored with seasonings characteristic of Louisiana cooking. Use Canadian bacon or smoked ham if tasso ham is unavailable.

Yield: 40 Servings   **Method:** Stewing

Andouille or smoked sausage, medium dice	2 lb. 8 oz.	1.2 kg
Tasso ham, medium dice (optional)	1 lb. 4 oz.	600 g
Garlic, chopped	4 oz.	120 g
Onions, medium dice	1 lb. 4 oz.	600 g
Green bell peppers, medium dice	12 oz.	360 g
Red bell pepper, medium dice	4 oz.	120 g
Celery, medium dice	12 oz.	360 g
Green onions, chopped	1 bunch	1 bunch

Olive oil	as needed	as needed
Cajun Spice Mix (recipe follows)	TT	TT
Long-grain white rice	1 lb. 8 oz.	720 g
Tomatoes, diced, canned	56 fl. oz.	1.7 lt
Chicken stock	20 fl. oz.	600 ml
Shrimp, peeled and deveined	2 lb. 8 oz.	1.2 kg
Salt and pepper	TT	TT

1. In a large rondeau, sauté the andouille and tasso (if using) to render their fat. Remove the meat and reserve. Add the garlic, onions, bell peppers, celery and green onions to the fat and sauté. If there is not enough fat, add a small amount of olive oil.
2. As the vegetables soften, season them with a little Cajun Spice Mix.
3. Add the rice and toss until all the rice is coated with the fat. Add the tomatoes and their liquid and stir to combine.
4. Add the stock, shrimp and reserved andouille and tasso and bring to a simmer.
5. Cook at a low simmer until the rice is done, approximately 15 minutes, checking the seasoning periodically. Add more Cajun Spice Mix, salt and pepper as necessary. There will be little to no liquid left in the pan when the rice is done.

VARIATION:

Vegetarian Jambalaya—Substitute assorted cooked beans and vegetables for the shrimp, andouille and tasso and use vegetable stock instead of chicken stock.

Approximate values per serving: **Calories** 210, **Total fat** 9 g, **Saturated fat** 3 g, **Cholesterol** 65 mg, **Sodium** 390 mg, **Total carbohydrates** 20 g, **Protein** 12 g, **Vitamin C** 30%, **Iron** 10%

CAJUN SPICE MIX

Yield: 6 oz. (180 g)

Salt	1 oz.	30 g
Garlic powder	1 oz.	30 g
White pepper	½ oz.	15 g
Dried oregano, ground	⅓ oz.	10 g
Onion powder	1 oz.	30 g
Black pepper	½ oz.	15 g
Cayenne pepper	¼ oz.	7 g
Dried thyme, ground	⅓ oz.	10 g
Paprika	1 oz.	30 g

1. Combine all ingredients and mix well.

Approximate values per ½-oz. (15-g) serving: **Calories** 35, **Total fat** 0.5 g, **Saturated fat** 0 g, **Cholesterol** 0 mg, **Sodium** 920 mg, **Total carbohydrates** 8 g, **Protein** 1 g, **Vitamin A** 35%, **Iron** 15%

ESCALOPE DE PORC À LA NORMANDE
(PORK SCALLOPS WITH APPLES)

JOLIET JUNIOR COLLEGE, JOLIET, IL

Chef Keith G. Vonhoff, CEPC, CEC, CCP

Yield: 2 Servings   **Method:** Sautéing

Pork scallops, 3 oz. (90 g) each, pounded thin	4	4
Flour	as needed for dredging	
Clarified butter	1 fl. oz.	60 g
Apple, peeled, julienned	3 oz.	90 g
Veal stock	2 fl. oz.	60 ml
Apple juice	2 fl. oz.	60 ml
Heavy cream	3 fl. oz.	90 ml
Nutmeg, freshly ground	TT	TT
Salt and pepper	TT	TT

1. Dredge the pork scallops in flour and shake off the excess.
2. Heat the butter in a medium sauté pan over medium-high heat. Add the pork scallops to the pan without overcrowding.
3. Lightly brown the pork scallops on one side. Turn and brown on the other side. Remove the pork scallops from the pan and keep warm.
4. Add the apple and sauté until tender without browning.
5. Add the stock and juice and reduce au sec.
6. Add the cream and nutmeg. Reduce until the sauce reaches nappé consistency. Adjust the seasonings.
7. Return the pork scallops to the pan along with any accumulated juices. Warm the pork scallops in the sauce for a few seconds.
8. Serve two pork scallops per portion, garnished with the sauce.

Approximate values per serving: **Calories** 530, **Total fat** 40 g, **Saturated fat** 22 g, **Cholesterol** 190 mg, **Sodium** 160 mg, **Total carbohydrates** 7 g, **Protein** 35 g, **Vitamin A** 20%

PORK TENDERLOIN AU POIVRE

NATIONAL CENTER FOR HOSPITALITY STUDIES, SULLIVAN UNIVERSITY, LOUISVILLE, KY

Chef Tom Hickey, CEC, CCE, CFE, CHE

Yield: 4 Servings   **Method:** Sautéing

Pork tenderloin, 2-oz. (60-g) medallions	12	12
Kosher salt	2 tsp.	10 ml
Green peppercorns, crushed	2 fl. oz.	60 ml
Olive oil	1 fl. oz.	30 ml
White wine	2 fl. oz.	60 ml
Champagne vinegar	1 fl. oz.	30 ml
Heavy cream	4 fl. oz.	120 ml
Salt and pepper	TT	TT
Fettuccine, cooked	8 oz.	240 g

1. Flatten the medallions with the palm of your hand. Press both sides of each medallion into the kosher salt and crushed peppercorns.
2. Heat the olive oil in a sauté pan over medium-high heat. Add the medallions and sauté until browned, approximately 2 minutes. Turn the medallions and sauté on the other side until browned.
3. Remove the medallions from the pan and keep warm. Deglaze the pan with the wine and vinegar. Reduce until a few tablespoons remain.
4. Add the cream and reduce to the desired consistency. Adjust the seasonings.
5. Serve three medallions per portion, dressed with the sauce and accompanied with the cooked fettuccine.

Approximate values per serving: **Calories** 360, **Total fat** 22 g, **Saturated fat** 9 g, **Cholesterol** 135 mg, **Sodium** 840 mg, **Total carbohydrates** 3 g, **Protein** 35 g

---

NATAING
(CAMBODIAN-STYLE RED PORK)

Yield: 4 Servings, 6 oz. (180 g) each   **Method:** Sautéing

Vegetable oil	1 fl. oz.	30 ml
Ground pork	8 oz.	240 g
New Mexico chile, ground	2 Tbsp.	30 ml
Cayenne pepper	½ tsp.	2 ml
Garlic cloves, sliced very thin	6	6
Fresh ginger, minced	2 tsp.	10 ml
Shallot, sliced very thin	1	1
Granulated sugar	2 Tbsp.	30 ml
Coconut milk, unsweetened	8 fl. oz.	240 ml
Fish sauce	1 Tbsp.	15 ml
Peanuts, chopped	2 oz.	60 g
Cilantro sprigs	as needed for garnish	
Rice, cooked	as needed for garnish	
Rice crackers	as needed for garnish	

1. In a sauté pan, heat the oil and sauté the pork with the chile and cayenne pepper until the meat is browned.
2. Add the garlic, ginger and shallot and sauté until soft.
3. Add the sugar, coconut milk and fish sauce. Cook for approximately 10 minutes or until the pork is fully cooked and the flavors are well blended. Add the peanuts.
4. Garnish with the cilantro sprigs and serve warm with plain or jasmine rice. Serve rice crackers for dipping in the sauce.

VARIATION:

Cambodian-Style Red Vegetarian Stir-Fry   Substitute tofu or seitan for the ground pork. Use an additional 2 tablespoons (30 milliliters) vegetable oil when sautéing and cook until browned. Substitute light soy sauce for the fish sauce.

Approximate values per serving: **Calories** 450, **Total fat** 39 g, **Saturated fat** 17 g, **Cholesterol** 40 mg, **Sodium** 430 mg, **Total carbohydrates** 15 g, **Protein** 15 g, **Vitamin A** 25%, **Iron** 20%

CRISPY SWEET AND SOUR PORK

THE SCHOOL OF CULINARY ARTS AT KENDALL COLLEGE, EVANSTON, IL

Chef Mike Artlip, CEC, CCE

Yield: 40 Servings　　　　　　　**Method:** Deep-frying

Marinade:		
Chinese rice wine	3½ fl. oz.	105 ml
Salt	1 tsp.	5 ml
Cornstarch	3 Tbsp.	45 ml
White pepper	1 tsp.	5 ml
Garlic, minced	1½ Tbsp.	23 ml
Fresh ginger, minced	1 Tbsp.	15 ml
Sesame oil	1½ Tbsp.	23 ml
Soy sauce	1½ Tbsp.	23 ml
Eggs, beaten	6	6
Pork butt, lean, 2-in. (5-cm) dice	5 lb.	2.4 kg
Cornstarch	6 oz.	180 g
Green bell peppers, large dice	7	7
Tomatoes, chopped into 2-in. (5-cm) pieces	6 lb.	2.8 kg
Sauce:		
Cornstarch	10 oz.	300 g
Water, cold	40 fl. oz.	1.2 lt
Garlic heads, minced	5	5
Vegetable oil	1 fl. oz.	30 ml
Granulated sugar	2 lb.	960 g
Ketchup	12 fl. oz.	360 ml
Soy sauce	3 fl. oz.	90 ml
Cider vinegar	22 fl. oz.	660 ml
Pineapple chunks, #10 can, drained, juice reserved	½ can	½ can
Rice, cooked	as needed for garnish	

1. Combine the ingredients for the marinade. Add the diced pork and marinate for 30 minutes.

2. Add the cornstarch to the pork and mix well. The mixture should look like a batter. Add more cornstarch if the mixture is too thin. Allow the mixture to rest until it becomes sticky, approximately 15 minutes.

3. Using the swimming method, deep-fry the pork cubes until fully cooked, dark brown and crisp, approximately 2 to 3 minutes. Stir with a spider to prevent the pieces from sticking together while deep-frying. Drain well and reserve.

4. Steam the bell peppers until they begin to soften slightly. Add the tomatoes to the steamer and cook until they begin to soften. Remove the vegetables from the steamer and reserve.

5. To make the sauce, combine the cornstarch and water to form a slurry. Sauté the garlic in the vegetable oil without browning. Add the remaining sauce ingredients and the reserved pineapple juice and bring to a simmer. Thicken the sauce with the slurry, using just enough of the slurry to achieve the desired consistency.

6. Add the bell pepper and tomato mixture and the pineapple chunks. Bring the sauce to a simmer. Reheat the pork in a hot oven and add to the sauce immediately before service. Serve with white rice.

Approximate values per serving: **Calories** 300, **Total fat** 6 g, **Saturated fat** 2 g, **Cholesterol** 70 mg, **Sodium** 420 mg, **Total carbohydrates** 47 g, **Protein** 14 g, **Vitamin A** 15%, **Vitamin C** 60%, **Iron** 10%

STUFFED PORK CHOPS

Yield: 10 Servings	**Method:** Braising	
Thick-cut pork chops, approx. 8 oz. (240 g) each	10	10
Celery, small dice	4 oz.	120 g
Onion, small dice	6 oz.	180 g
Whole butter, melted	6 oz.	180 g
Fresh bread cubes, ½ in. (1.2 cm)	8 oz.	240 g
Parsley, chopped	1 Tbsp.	15 ml
Salt and pepper	TT	TT
White stock	approx. 8 fl. oz.	approx. 240 ml
Olive oil	2 fl. oz.	60 ml
Demi-glace	1 qt.	960 ml

1. Cut pockets in the chops.
2. Sauté the celery and onion in 2 ounces (60 grams) butter until tender.
3. Combine the celery, onion and remaining butter with the bread cubes, parsley, salt and pepper. Add enough stock to moisten the dressing.
4. Stuff the mixture into each of the pork chops. Seal the pockets with toothpicks and tie with butcher's twine.
5. Heat the olive oil in a braiser; brown the stuffed chops well on each side.
6. Add the demi-glace. Bring to a simmer, cover and place in a 325°F (160°C) oven. Cook until tender, approximately 45 minutes.
7. Remove the chops from the pan. Degrease the sauce and reduce to the desired consistency. Strain the sauce and adjust the seasonings.

Approximate values per 10-oz. (300-g) serving: **Calories** 650, **Total fat** 38 g, **Saturated fat** 16 g, **Cholesterol** 225 mg, **Sodium** 390 mg, **Total carbohydrates** 5 g, **Protein** 70 g, **Vitamin A** 15%, **Iron** 15%

1. Stuffing the pork chops.

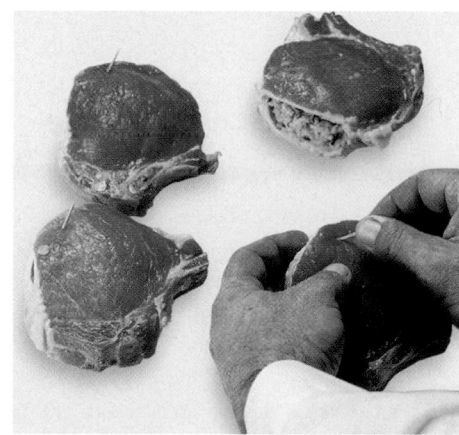

2. Closing the stuffed chops with toothpicks.

3. The finished chops

CHOUCROUTE

The French province of Alsace shares its eastern border with Germany, a country frequently associated with sauerkraut. Choucroute is the name for both the pickled cabbage and a dish containing it. French-style sauerkraut is prepared with bacon, onion, garlic, wine and spices. Once the cabbage is flavored, rich cuts of pork braise in the mixture until tender.

Yield: 12 Servings, 4 oz. (120 g) sauerkraut, 1 sausage and 7 oz. (210 g) pork each

Method: Braising

Bacon, medium dice	8 oz.	240 g
Onions, medium dice	12 oz.	360 g
Garlic, chopped fine	1½ oz.	45 g
Granny Smith apples, medium dice	8 oz.	240 g
Sauerkraut	2 lb. 8 oz.	1.2 kg
Dry white wine	4 fl. oz.	120 ml
White wine vinegar	4 fl. oz.	120 ml
Chicken stock	1 pt.	480 ml
Sachet:		
Juniper berries	6	6
Bay leaves	3	3
Cloves	2	2
Caraway seeds	1 tsp.	5 ml
Boneless pork butt, 4 lb. (1.8 kg)	1	1
Smoked pork loin	2 lb.	960 g
Red potatoes, peeled and quartered	3 lb.	1.4 kg
Bratwurst	12 links	12 links
Salt and pepper	TT	TT

1. Render the bacon.
2. Sauté the onions, garlic and apples in the bacon fat without browning.
3. Rinse the sauerkraut and squeeze out the liquid. Add the sauerkraut to the pan.
4. Stir in the wine, vinegar, stock and sachet.
5. Place the pork butt on the sauerkraut. Cover and braise in a 325°F (160°C) oven for 1 hour 45 minutes, adding additional stock if necessary during the cooking process.
6. Add the smoked pork loin and potatoes and braise an additional 45 minutes.
7. Add the bratwurst and braise until all the meats are tender and the potatoes are done, approximately 45 minutes, adding additional stock if necessary. Remove and discard the sachet. Season to taste with salt and pepper.
8. Carve the meats and serve with a portion of the sauerkraut and potatoes.

Approximate values per serving: **Calories** 940, **Total fat** 50 g, **Saturated fat** 18 g, **Cholesterol** 255 mg, **Sodium** 1910 mg, **Total carbohydrates** 33 g, **Protein** 90 g, **Vitamin C** 35%, **Iron** 30%

CASSOULET

SIMPLICITY CATERING, FALLS CHURCH, VA
Chef Leland Atkinson

Yield: 8 Servings, 8 oz. (240 g)
pork stew, 1½ oz. (45 g) sausage
and 1 piece of duck each
        Method: Stewing

White beans	1 lb.	480 g
White stock	2 qt.	1.9 lt
Smoked ham, large dice	8 oz.	240 g
Bouquet garni:		
Carrot stick, 4 in. (10 cm)	1	1
Leek, split, 4-in. (10-cm) piece	1	1
Fresh thyme	1 sprig	1 sprig
Bay leaf	1	1
Lamb or other sausage	1 lb.	480 g
Onion, medium dice	6 oz.	180 g
Garlic, chopped	½ oz.	15 g
Pork butt, cut in 2-in. (5-cm) cubes	1 lb. 8 oz.	720 g
Salt and pepper	TT	TT
Olive oil	1 fl. oz.	30 ml
Mirepoix	8 oz.	240 g
White wine	6 fl. oz.	180 ml
Tomato concassée	1 lb.	480 g
Demi-glace	1 pt.	480 ml
Brown stock	8 fl. oz.	240 ml
Sachet:		
Bay leaf	1	1
Dried thyme	½ tsp.	2 ml
Peppercorns, cracked	½ tsp.	2 ml
Parsley stems	8	8
Garlic cloves, crushed	2	2
Duck Confit (page 439)	8 pieces	8 pieces

1. To make the bean stew, soak the beans overnight in water. Drain and combine with the white stock, ham and bouquet garni. Bring to a simmer and cook for 30 minutes. Add the sausage, onion and garlic; simmer until the beans are tender.

2. Remove and reserve the sausage.

3. Drain the beans, reserving both the beans and the cooking liquid. Reduce the cooking liquid by half and combine with the beans.

4. To make the meat stew, season the pork with salt and pepper and brown it in the olive oil. Remove and reserve the meat.

5. Add the mirepoix to the pan and sauté. Deglaze with the wine and add the tomato concassée, demi-glace, brown stock and sachet. Cover and simmer the pork until tender, approximately 45 minutes.

6. Remove the meat from the sauce and reserve. Discard the sachet. Reduce the sauce until thick; return the meat to the sauce.

7. To serve, scrape the excess fat from the Duck **Confit**. Place the duck in a roasting pan and roast at 350°F (180°C) until the meat is hot and the skin is crisp, approximately 20 minutes.

8. Place a portion of hot beans in a soup plate. Place a portion of the Duck Confit in the plate. Arrange a portion of the meat stew on top of the beans and around the duck.

9. Slice the sausage and add it to the plate. Garnish with fresh herbs.

Approximate values per serving: **Calories** 630, **Total fat** 37 g, **Saturated fat** 12 g, **Cholesterol** 130 mg, **Sodium** 2360 mg, **Total carbohydrates** 23 g, **Protein** 53 g, **Vitamin C** 25%, **Iron** 30%

Southwestern France is known for quality goose and duck products such as foie gras and a variety of fine pork sausage. One specialty is **confit**, *pieces of these rich fowl salted and then simmered in rendered fat. A centerpiece of the fragrant white bean and meat stew called* cassoulet *is the chunk of meltingly tender duck or goose confit served to each guest.*

confit (kohn-FEE) meat or poultry (often lightly salt-cured) slowly cooked and preserved in its own fat and served hot

> "The fact is that it takes more than ingredients and technique to cook a good meal. A good cook puts something of himself into the preparation—he cooks with enjoyment, anticipation, spontaneity, and he is willing to experiment."
>
> —PEARL BAILEY, AMERICAN ENTERTAINER (1918–1990) IN *PEARL'S KITCHEN*, 1973

CHAPTER SEVENTEEN

POULTRY

- understand the structure and composition of poultry
- identify various kinds and classes of poultry
- understand poultry inspection and grading practices
- purchase poultry appropriate for your needs
- store poultry properly
- prepare poultry for cooking
- apply various cooking methods to poultry

POULTRY IS THE COLLECTIVE TERM FOR domesticated birds bred for eating. They include chickens, ducks, geese, guineas, pigeons and turkeys. (Game birds such as pheasant, quail and partridge are described in Chapter 18, Game; farm-raised ratites—ostrich, emu and rhea—are discussed here.) The renowned French gastronome and author Jean-Anthelme Brillat-Savarin (1755–1826) once observed that "poultry is for the cook what canvas is for the painter." He meant, of course, that poultry can be cooked by almost any method, and its mild flavor goes well with a wide variety of sauces and accompaniments. Poultry is generally the least expensive and most versatile of all main-dish foods.

In this chapter, we discuss the different kinds and classes of poultry and how to choose those that best suit your needs. You will learn how to store poultry properly to prevent food-borne illnesses and spoilage, how to butcher birds to produce the specific cuts you need and how to apply a variety of cooking methods properly.

Many of the cooking methods discussed here have been applied previously to meats. Although there are similarities with these methods, there are also many distinct differences. As you study this chapter, review the corresponding cooking methods for meats and note the similarities and differences.

MUSCLE COMPOSITION

The muscle tissue of poultry is similar to that of mammals in that it contains approximately 72 percent water, 20 percent protein, 7 percent fat and 1 percent minerals; it consists of bundles of muscle cells or fibers held together by connective tissue. Unlike red meat, poultry does not contain the intramuscular fat known as marbling. Instead, a bird stores fat in its skin, its abdominal cavity and the fat pad near its tail. Poultry fat is softer and has a lower melting point than other animal fats. It is easily rendered during cooking.

As with red meats, poultry muscles that are used more often tend to be tougher than those used less frequently. Also, the muscles of an older bird tend to be tougher than those of a younger one. Because the majority of poultry is marketed at a young age, however, it is generally very tender.

The breast and wing flesh of chickens and turkeys is lighter in color than the flesh of their thighs and legs. For this reason it is often referred to as "white meat." This color difference is due to a higher concentration of the protein myoglobin in the thigh and leg muscles. Myoglobin is the protein that stores oxygen for the muscle tissues to use. More-active muscles require more myoglobin and tend to be darker than less-active ones. Because chickens and turkeys generally do not fly, their breast and wing muscles contain little myoglobin and are therefore a light color. Birds that do fly have only dark meat. Dark meat also contains more fat and connective tissue than light meat, and its cooking time is longer.

Skin color may vary from white to golden yellow, depending on what the bird was fed. Such color differences are not an indication of overall quality.

	TABLE 17.1	USDA CHICKEN CLASSES			
CLASS	**DESCRIPTION**		**AGE**	**WEIGHT**	**COOKING METHOD**
Game hen	Young or immature progeny of Cornish chickens or of a Cornish chicken and a White Rock chicken; very flavorful		5–6 weeks	2 lb. (1 kg) or less	Split and broil or grill; roast
Broiler/fryer	Young with soft, smooth-textured skin; relatively lean; flexible breastbone		13 weeks	3 lb. 8 oz. (1.5 kg) or less	Any cooking method; very versatile
Roaster	Young with tender meat and smooth-textured skin; breastbone is less flexible than broiler's		3–5 months	3 lb. 8 oz.–5 lb. (1.5–2 kg)	Any cooking method
Capon	Surgically castrated male; tender meat with soft, smooth-textured skin; bred for well-flavored meat; contains a high proportion of light to dark meat and a relatively high fat content		Under 8 months	6–10 lb. (2.5–4.5 kg)	Roast
Hen/stewing	Mature female; flavorful but less tender meat; nonflexible breastbone		Over 10 months	2 lb. 8 oz.–8 lb. (1–3.5 kg)	Stew or braise

IDENTIFYING POULTRY

The USDA recognizes six categories or kinds of poultry: chicken, duck, goose, guinea, pigeon and turkey. Each poultry kind is divided into classes based predominantly on the bird's age and tenderness. The sex of young birds is not significant for culinary purposes. It does matter, however, with older birds; older male birds are tough and stringy and have less flavor than older female birds. Tables 17.1 and 17.2 list identifying characteristics and suggested cooking methods for each of the various kinds and classes of poultry.

Chicken

Chicken (Fr. *poulet*; Sp. *pollo*) is the most popular and widely eaten poultry in the world. It contains both light and dark meat and has relatively little fat. A young, tender chicken can be cooked by almost any method; an older bird is best stewed or braised. Chicken is extremely versatile and may be seasoned, stuffed, basted or garnished with almost anything. Chicken is inexpensive and readily available, fresh or frozen, in a variety of forms.

The French *poulet de Bresse* is a special category of chicken, frequently touted as the world's finest. The first certified-origin chicken in the world, it is a blue-legged variety raised near the village of Bresse in southeastern Burgundy. These are free-range birds fed a special diet of milk products plus sweet corn and other grains. An identifying leg band is attached to each young chick, and authentic birds will be sold with the banded leg attached. They are available in the United States, at a premium price, from specialty food importers.

Rock Cornish Game Hen

Chicken Broiler/Fryer

Capon

poussin a French term for a small, immature chicken; in the United States, *poussin* is another name for a small chicken such as a Rock Cornish game hen

TABLE 17.2   USDA DUCK, GOOSE, GUINEA, PIGEON AND TURKEY CLASSES

USDA DUCK CLASSES

CLASS	DESCRIPTION	AGE	WEIGHT	COOKING METHOD
Broiler/fryer	Young bird with tender meat; a soft bill and windpipe	8 weeks or less	3 lb. 8 oz.–4 lb. (1.5–1.8 kg)	Roast at high temperature
Roaster	Young bird with tender meat; rich flavor; easily dented windpipe	16 weeks or less	4–6 lb. (1.8–2.5 kg)	Roast
Mature	Old bird with tough flesh; hard bill and windpipe	6 months or older	4–6 lb. (1.8–2.5 kg)	Braise

USDA GOOSE CLASSES

CLASS	DESCRIPTION	AGE	WEIGHT	COOKING METHOD
Young	Rich, tender dark meat with large amounts of fat; easily dented windpipe	6 months or less	6–12 lb. (2.5–5.5 kg)	Roast at high temperature, accompany with acidic sauces
Mature	Tough flesh and hard windpipe	Over 6 months	10–16 lb. (4.5–7 kg)	Braise or stew

USDA GUINEA CLASSES

CLASS	DESCRIPTION	AGE	WEIGHT	COOKING METHOD
Young	Tender meat; flexible breastbone	3 months	12 oz.–1 lb. 8 oz. (0.3–0.7 kg)	Bard and roast; sauté
Mature	Tough flesh; hard breastbone	Over 3 months	1–2 lb (0.5–1 kg)	Braise or stew

USDA PIGEON CLASSES

CLASS	DESCRIPTION	AGE	WEIGHT	COOKING METHOD
Squab	Immature pigeon; very tender, dark flesh and a small amount of fat	4 weeks	12 oz.–1 lb. 8 oz. (0.3–0.7 kg)	Broil, roast or sauté
Pigeon	Mature bird; coarse skin and tough flesh	Over 4 weeks	1–2 lb (0.5–1 kg)	Braise or stew

USDA TURKEY CLASSES

CLASS	DESCRIPTION	AGE	WEIGHT	COOKING METHOD
Fryer/roaster	Immature bird of either sex (males are called *toms*); tender meat with smooth skin; flexible breastbone	16 weeks or less	4–9 lb. (2–4 kg)	Roast or cut into scallops and sauté or pan-fry
Young	Tender meat with smooth skin; less-flexible breastbone	8 months or less	8–22 lb. (3.5–10 kg)	Roast or stew
Yearling	Fully mature bird; reasonably tender meat and slightly coarse skin	15 months or less	10–30 lb. (4.5–13 kg)	Roast or stew
Mature	Older bird with coarse skin and tough flesh	15 months or older	10–30 lb. (4.5–13 kg)	Stew; ground or used in processed products

Duck

The duck (Fr. *canard*) used most often in commercial food service operations is a roaster duckling of the Pekin or Long Island breed. It contains only dark meat and large amounts of fat. In order to make the fatty skin palatable, it is important to render as much fat as possible. Duck has a high percentage of bone and fat to meat; for example, a 4-pound duck will serve only two people, whereas a 4-pound roasting chicken will serve four people.

For a larger duck breast with a richer, meatier flavor, chefs prefer the Moulard, also known as Mullard, a hybrid of the Pekin and Muscovy breeds. (The Muscovy is a lean, thin-skinned South American breed with a strong, musky flavor.) Moulards are used for producing foie gras (see page 398). The Moulard's large breast, called a **magret**, has a rich flavor and a texture similar to beef. It is often aged for several days and may be smoked whole or cooked by grilling, roasting or pan-searing.

Goose

A goose (Fr. *oie*) contains only dark meat and has very fatty skin. It is usually roasted at high temperatures to render the fat. Roasted goose is popular at holidays and is often served with an acidic fruit-based sauce to offset the fattiness.

Guinea

A guinea or guinea fowl (Fr. *pintade*) is the domesticated descendant of a game bird. It has both light and dark meat and a flavor similar to pheasant. Guinea is tender enough to sauté. Because it contains little fat, a guinea is usually barded before roasting. Guinea, which is relatively expensive, is not as popular in the United States as it is in Europe.

Pigeon

The young pigeon (Fr. *pigeon*) used in commercial food service operations is referred to as squab. Its meat is dark, tender and well suited for broiling, sautéing or roasting. Squab has very little fat and benefits from barding.

Turkey

Turkey (Fr. *dinde*) is the second most popular category of poultry in the United States. It has both light and dark meat and a relatively small amount of fat. Younger turkey is economical and can be prepared in almost any manner.

Ratites

Ratites are a family of flightless birds with small wings and flat breastbones. They include the ostrich (which is native to Africa), the emu (native to Australia) and the rhea (native to South America). Ratite meat, which is classified as red meat even though it is poultry flesh, is a dark, cherry-red color with a flavor similar to beef, but a little sweeter, and a soft texture. It is low in fat and calories. Most ratite meat is from birds slaughtered at 10 to 13 months of age. It is generally cut from the back

Roaster Duckling

Young Goose

Young Guinea

Turkey

duckling a duck slaughtered before it is eight weeks old

magret (may-gray) a duck breast, traditionally taken from the ducks that produce foie gras; it is usually served boneless but with the skin intact

Moulard Duck Breast

Squab

A TURKEY BY ANY OTHER NAME . . .

In *Food in History*, Reay Tannahill explains why we call a turkey a turkey and not a peru. Turkeys were known as *uexolotl* to 16th-century native Central Americans. They were first brought to Europe by returning Spanish explorers early in the 1500s. Turkish merchants visiting Seville, Spain, on their journeys to and from the eastern Mediterranean brought these exotic birds to England, where the English dubbed them "turkie-cocks." This was eventually shortened to "turkeys." The Turks called these birds *hindi*, suggesting that they believed the birds originated in India (as opposed to the Indies). This was a belief shared by the French, who called the bird *coq d'Inde*, which was later corrupted to *dinde* or *dindon*. The Germans followed suit, calling the bird *indianische Henn*, as did the Italians, who called it *galle d'India*. Meanwhile, in India, the bird was called a *peru*—which was a little closer to the geographical mark.

Ostrich Fan

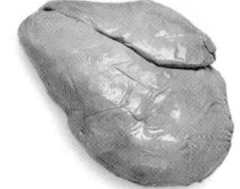

Chicken Giblets

Duck Foie Gras

FIGURE 17.1 ▶ USDA inspection stamp for poultry.

Grade Mark

FIGURE 17.2 ▶ Grade stamps for USDA Grade A poultry.

(which contains the very tender tenderloin), the thigh (also known as the fan) and the leg, and is available as steaks, filets, medallions, roasts, cubes or ground.

Ratite meat is often prepared like veal. The more tender cuts, such as those from the back or thigh, can be marinated and then cooked by dry-heat cooking methods, especially broiling, grilling, roasting and pan-frying. Because it has little fat, care must be taken to avoid overcooking, and these products are usually served medium rare to medium. Allowing these products to rest after cooking helps ensure tenderness. Tougher cuts, such as those from the leg, are best ground or prepared with combination cooking methods.

Livers, Gizzards, Hearts and Necks

Livers, gizzards, hearts and necks are commonly referred to as giblets and can be used in a variety of ways. Gizzards (a bird's second stomach), hearts and necks are often used to make giblet gravy. Gizzards are sometimes trimmed and deep-fried; hearts are sometimes served sautéed and creamed. Necks are very flavorful and can be added to stocks for flavor and richness. Livers, hearts and gizzards are not added to stocks, however, because of their strong flavors.

Chicken livers are often used in pâtés, sautéed or broiled with onions and served as an entrée.

FOIE GRAS

Foie gras is the enlarged liver of a duck or goose. Considered a delicacy since Roman times, it is now produced in many parts of the world, including the United States. Foie gras is produced by methodically fattening the birds by force-feeding them specially prepared corn while limiting their activity. Fresh foie gras consists of two lobes that must be separated, split and deveined. Good foie gras will be smooth, round and putty-colored. It should not be yellow or grainy. Goose foie gras is lighter in color and more delicate in flavor than that of duck. Duck foie gras has a deeper, winy flavor and is more frequently used than goose foie gras. Fresh foie gras can be grilled, roasted, sautéed or made into pâtés or terrines. No matter which cooking method is used, care must be taken not to overcook the liver. Foie gras is so high in fat that overcooking will result in the liver actually melting away. Most foie gras is pasteurized or canned and may consist of solid liver or small pieces of liver compacted to form a block. Canned foie gras mousse is also available, often with truffles, which are a natural accompaniment.

NUTRITION

Poultry is an economical source of high-quality protein. Poultry's nutritional values are similar to those of other meats, except that chicken and turkey breast meat is lower in fat and higher in niacin than other lean meats. Generally, dark meat contains more niacin and riboflavin than white meat.

INSPECTION AND GRADING OF POULTRY

Inspection

All poultry produced for public consumption in the United States is subject to USDA inspection. Inspections ensure that products are processed under strict sanitary guidelines and are wholesome and fit for human consumption. Inspections do not indicate a product's quality or tenderness. The round inspection stamp illustrated in Figure 17.1 can be found either on a tag attached to the wing or included in the package labeling.

Grading

Grading poultry is voluntary but virtually universal. Birds are graded according to their overall quality, with the grade (USDA A, B or C) shown on a shield-shaped tag affixed to the bird or on a processed product's packaging. See Figure 17.2.

FREE-RANGE CHICKENS

Chicken has become increasingly popular in recent years, in part because it is inexpensive, versatile and considered healthier than meat. Indeed, more than 150 million chickens are processed weekly in this country. To meet an ever-increasing demand, chickens are raised indoors in huge chicken houses that may contain as many as 20,000 birds. They are fed a specially formulated mixture composed primarily of corn and soybean meal. Animal protein, vitamins, minerals and small amounts of antibiotics are added to produce quick-growing, healthy birds.

Many consumers feel that chickens raised this way do not have the flavor of chickens that are allowed to move freely and forage for food. Some consumers are concerned about the residual effects of the vitamins, minerals and antibiotics added to the chicken feed. To meet the demand for

chickens raised the old-fashioned way, some farmers raise (and many fine establishments offer) free-range chickens.

Although the USDA has not standardized regulations for free-range chicken, generally the term free-range applies to birds

that are allowed unlimited access to the area outside the chicken house. Often they are raised without antibiotics, fed a vegetarian diet (no animal fat or by-products), processed without the use of preservatives and raised under more humane growing methods than conventionally grown birds. Most free-range chickens are marketed at 9–10 weeks old and weigh 4½–5 pounds (2–2½ kilograms)—considerably more mature and heavier than conventional broilers. They are generally sold with heads and feet intact and are more expensive than conventionally raised chickens.

Many consumers (in both the dining room and the kitchen) feel that free-range chicken is superior in flavor and quality. Others find no perceptible differences. As a consumer, you will have to decide whether any difference is worth the added expense.

According to the USDA, Grade A poultry is free from deformities, with thick flesh and a well-developed fat layer; free of pinfeathers, cuts or tears and broken bones; free from discoloration and, if it is frozen, free from defects that occur during handling or storage. Nearly all poultry used in wholesale and retail outlets is Grade A. Grade B and C birds are used primarily for processed poultry products.

Quality grades have no bearing on the product's tenderness or flavor. A bird's tenderness is usually indicated by its class (for example, a young turkey is younger and more tender than a yearling). Its grade (USDA A, B or C) within each class is determined by its overall quality.

PURCHASING AND STORING POULTRY

Purchasing Poultry

Poultry can be purchased in many forms: fresh or frozen, whole or cut up, bone-in or boneless, portion controlled (P.C.), individually quick-frozen (IQF) or ground. Chicken and turkey are also widely used in prepared and convenience items and are available fully cooked and vacuum-wrapped or boned and canned. Although purchasing poultry in a ready-to-use form is convenient, it is not always necessary; poultry products are easy to fabricate and portion. Whole fresh poultry is also less expensive than precut or frozen products.

As with meats, you should consider your menu, labor costs, storage facilities and employee skills when deciding whether to purchase whole fresh poultry or some other form.

Storing Poultry

Poultry is a potentially hazardous food. It is highly perishable and particularly susceptible to contamination by salmonella bacteria. It is critical that poultry be stored at the correct temperatures.

Fresh chickens and other small birds can be stored on ice or at 32°F–34°F (0°C–2°C) for up to 2 days; larger birds can be stored up to 4 days at these temperatures. Frozen poultry should be kept at 0°F (–18°C) or below (the colder the better) and can be held for up to 6 months. It should be thawed gradually under refrigeration, allowing two days for chickens and as long as four days for larger birds. Never attempt to cook poultry that is still partially frozen; it will be impossible to cook the product evenly, and the areas that were still frozen may not reach the temperatures necessary to destroy harmful bacteria. Never partially cook poultry one day and finish cooking it later; bacteria are more likely to grow under such conditions.

BUTCHERING PROCEDURES

Poultry is easier to butcher than meats and is often processed on-site. You should be able to perform the following commonly encountered procedures. Because the different kinds of poultry are similar in structure, these procedures apply to a variety of birds.

PROCEDURE FOR **CUTTING A BIRD IN HALF**

Often the first step in preparing poultry is to cut the bird in half. Broiler and fryer chickens are often split to make two portions. This procedure removes the backbone and breast bone (also known as the keel bone) for a neat finished product.

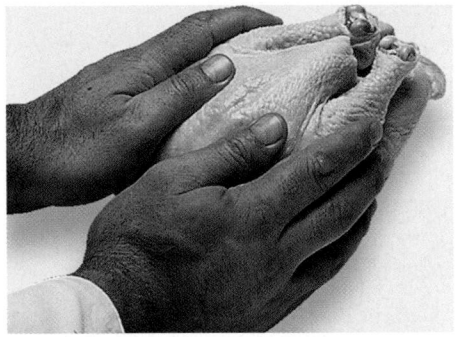

❶ Square up the bird by placing it on its back and pressing on the legs and breast to create a more uniform appearance.

❷ Place the bird on its breast and hold the tail tightly with the thumb and forefinger of one hand. Using a rigid boning knife and in a single swift movement, cut alongside the backbone from the bird's tail to the head.

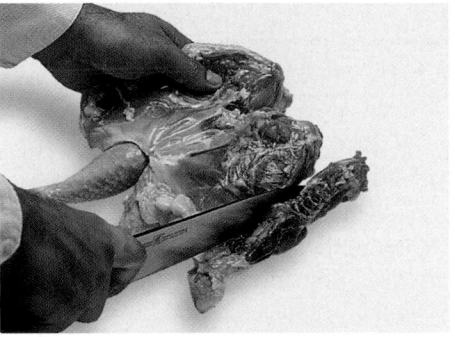

❸ Lay the bird flat on the cutting board and remove the backbone by cutting through the ribs connecting it to the breast.

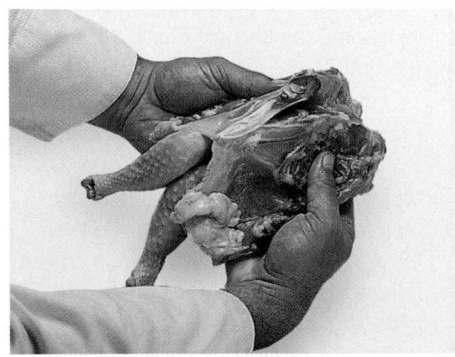

❹ Bend the bird back, breaking the breast bone free.

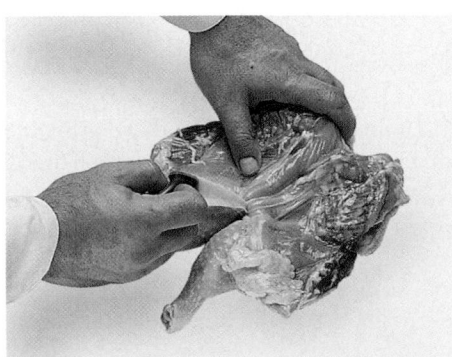

❺ Run your fingers along the keel bone to separate the breast meat from it; pull the bone completely free. Be sure to remove the flexible cartilage completely.

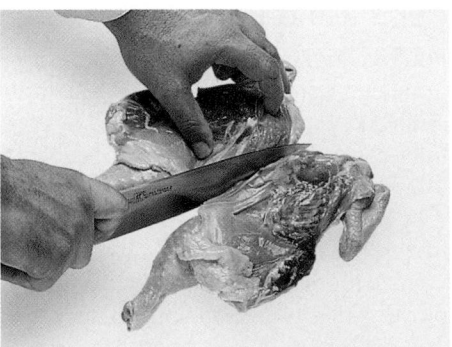

❻ Cut through the skin to separate the bird into two halves. The halves are ready to be cooked; for a more attractive presentation, follow Steps 7 and 8.

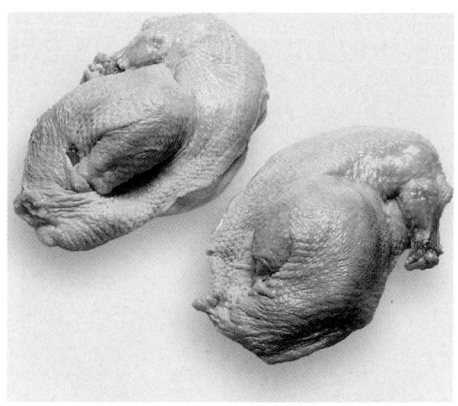

7 Trim off the wing tips and the ends of the leg bone.

8 Make a slit in the skin below the leg and tuck the leg bone into the slit.

PROCEDURE FOR **CUTTING A BIRD INTO PIECES**

This is one of the most common butchering procedures. It is also very simple once you understand the bird's structure and are able to find each of its joints.

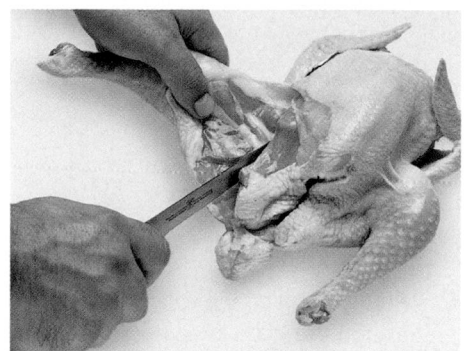

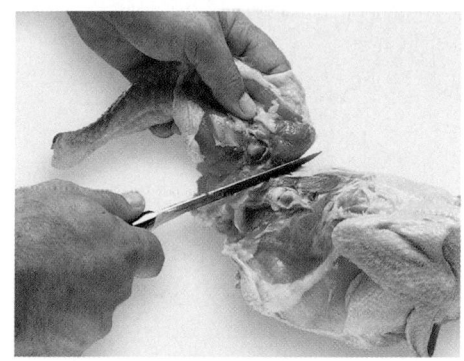

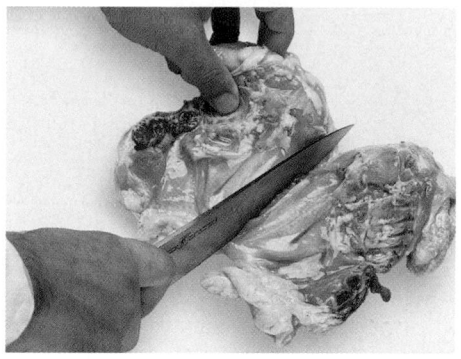

1 Remove the leg by pulling the leg and thigh away from the breast and cutting through the skin and flesh toward the thigh joint.

2 Cut down to the thigh joint, twist the leg to break the joint and cut the thigh and leg from the carcass. Be careful to trim around the oyster meat (the tender morsel of meat located next to the backbone); leave it attached to the thigh. Repeat with the other leg.

3 To split the breast, follow Steps 2 through 6 for cutting a bird in half. Cut the breast into two halves.

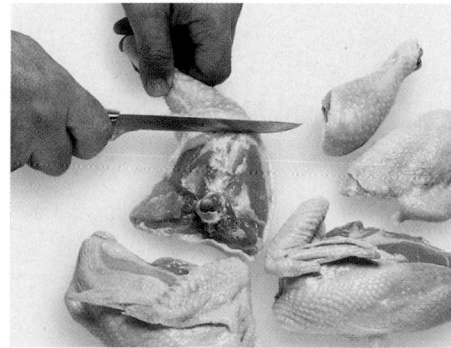

4 The bird is now cut into four quarters.

5 To cut the bird into six pieces, separate the thigh from the leg by making a cut guided by the line of fat on the inside of the thigh and leg.

6 To cut the bird into eight pieces, separate the wing from the breast by cutting the joint, or split the breast, leaving a portion of the breast meat attached to the wing.

PROCEDURE FOR **PREPARING A SUPRÊME OR AIRLINE BREAST**

A chicken suprême or airline breast is half of a boneless chicken breast with the first wing bone attached. The tip of the wing bone is removed, yielding a neat and attractive portion that can be prepared by a variety of cooking methods. The skin can be left on or removed.

❶ Remove the legs following Steps 1 and 2 for cutting a bird into pieces. Place the chicken on its back. Locate the wishbone, trim around it and remove it.

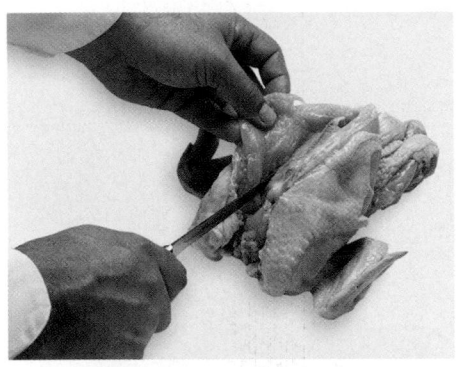

❷ Cut along one side of the breast bone, separating the meat from the bone.

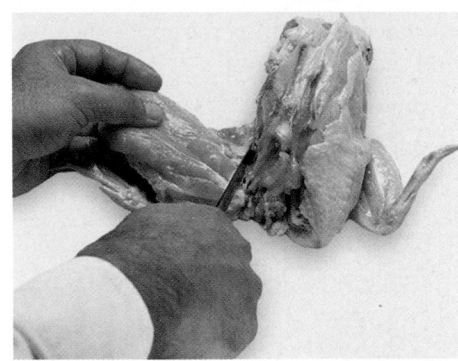

❸ Following the natural curvature of the ribs, continue cutting to remove the meat from the bones.

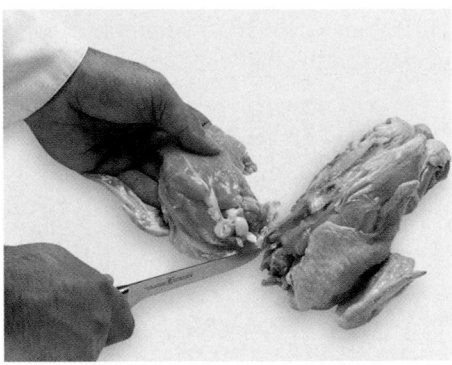

❹ When you reach the wing joint, cut through the joint, keeping the wing attached to the breast portion. Cut the breast free from the carcass.

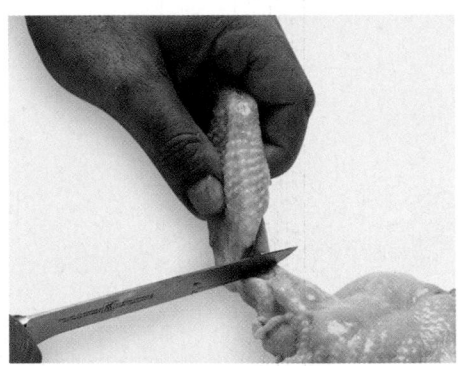

❺ Make a cut on the back of the joint between the first and second wing bones.

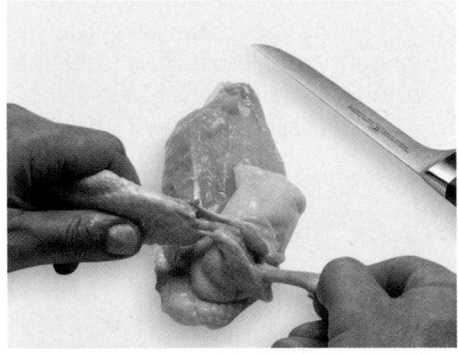

❻ Break the joint and pull the meat and skin back to expose a clean bone. Trim the wing bone.

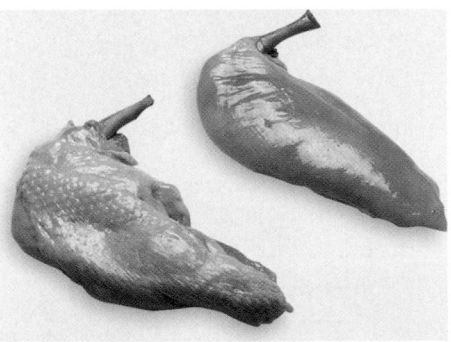

❼ The suprême can be prepared skin-on or skinless.

PROCEDURE FOR **PREPARING A BONELESS BREAST**

A boneless chicken breast is one of the most versatile and popular poultry cuts. It can be broiled, grilled, baked, sautéed, pan-fried or poached. Boneless turkey breast can be roasted or sliced and sautéed as a substitute for veal. The skin can be removed or left intact.

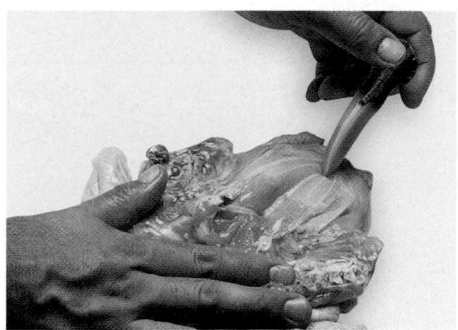

❶ Place the chicken on its back. Remove the legs following Steps 1 and 2 for cutting a bird into pieces. Remove the backbone following Steps 2 and 3 for cutting a bird in half. Remove the keel bone from the bone-in breast, following Steps 4 and 5 for cutting a bird in half.

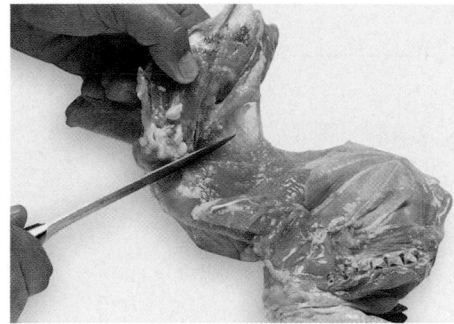

❷ With the chicken breast lying skin side down, separate the rib bones, wing and wishbone from the breast. Leave the two tender pieces of meat known as the tenderloins attached to the breast. Repeat the procedure on the other side, being sure to remove the small wishbone pieces from the front of the breast.

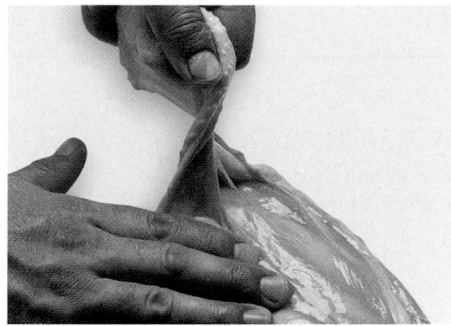

❸ Cut through the meat and skin to separate the chicken breast into two pieces. The skin may be left intact or removed to produce a skinless boneless breast.

PROCEDURE FOR **BONING A CHICKEN LEG AND THIGH**

Chicken breasts are usually more popular than legs and thighs. There are, however, uses for boneless, skinless leg and thigh meat; they can be stuffed or used for ballotines, for example.

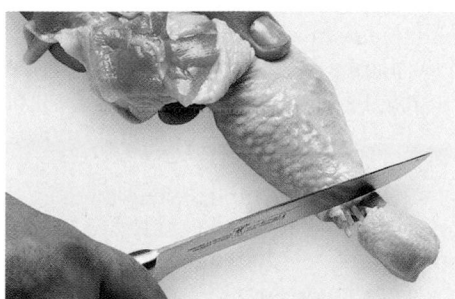

❶ Carefully cut through the skin, meat and tendons at the base of the leg. Be sure to cut through completely to the bone.

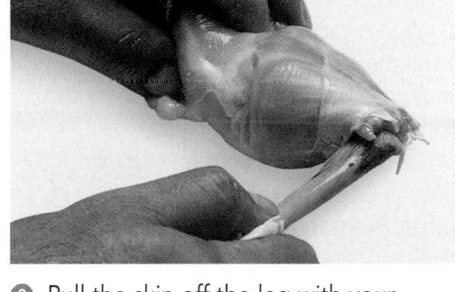

❷ Pull the skin off the leg with your hands, then break the joint between the leg and thigh. Twist and pull out the leg bone.

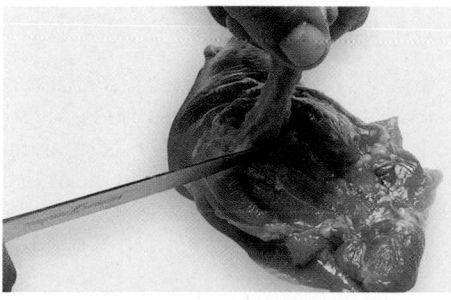

❸ Working from the inside of the thigh bone, separate it from the meat.

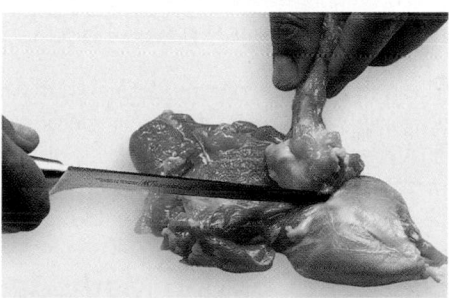

❹ Cut around the cartilage at the joint between the leg and thigh and remove the thigh bone and cartilage.

MARINATING POULTRY

Most poultry is quite mild in flavor, so a marinade is often used to add flavor and moisture, especially to poultry that will be broiled or grilled. Barbecued chicken is a simple and popular example of marinated poultry. Other poultry marinades can be a mixture of white wine or lemon juice, oil, salt, pepper, herbs and spices, such as that given in the following recipe.

MISE EN PLACE

▶ Peel and mince garlic.
▶ Peel onions and chop into small dice.

Marinating chicken breasts.

WHITE WINE MARINADE

Yield: 1 qt. (960 ml)

Garlic, minced	2 tsp.	10 ml
Onion, small dice	5 oz.	150 g
Dry white wine	24 fl. oz.	720 ml
Bay leaves	2	2
Dried thyme	2 tsp.	10 ml
White pepper	1 tsp.	5 ml
Salt	1 Tbsp.	15 ml
Lemon juice	1 fl. oz.	30 ml
Vegetable oil	4 fl. oz.	120 ml

1. Combine all ingredients. Use approximately 8 fluid ounces (240 milliliters) marinade for each double breast of chicken.

Approximate values per fluid ounce (30 ml): **Calories** 35, **Total fat** 3.5 g, **Saturated fat** 0 g, **Cholesterol** 0 mg, **Sodium** 220 mg, **Total carbohydrates** 1 g, **Protein** 0 g, **Claims**—no saturated fat; no cholesterol; no sugar; low calorie

Poultry absorbs flavors quickly, so if pieces are left too long in an acidic marinade, they may take on undesirable flavors. Two hours is often sufficient, with smaller pieces requiring less time in the marinade than larger ones. The texture of the protein will be affected by the acid in the marinade; marinating for more than a few hours can overly tenderize meats and poultry. Avoid using excess marinade because it will become contaminated and must be discontinued after using. To help calculate the quantity of marinade to make, figure on using approximately 8 fluid ounces (240 milliliters) marinade for each double breast of chicken.

If the marinade contains oil, drain the poultry well to avoid flare-up when the item is placed on the broiler or grill. Use a clean kitchen towel or a paper towel to wipe excess moisture from the poultry's surface so that it browns more easily. The marinade can be used to baste the item during cooking, but leftover marinade should not be served uncooked or reused because of the danger of bacterial contamination from the raw poultry.

As discussed in Chapter 16, Pork, poultry, especially whole chickens, can be lightly brined before cooking.

APPLYING VARIOUS COOKING METHODS

The principles of cooking discussed in Chapter 9 and applied to meats in earlier chapters also apply to poultry. Dry-heat methods are appropriate for young, tender birds. Moist-heat methods should be used with older, less tender products. Regardless of the cooking method, poultry should be rinsed under cold running water, then dried with clean disposable paper towels before cooking to remove any collected juices.

Dry-Heat Cooking Methods

Cooking poultry with dry-heat methods—broiling and grilling, roasting, sautéing, pan-frying and deep-frying—presents some unique challenges. Large birds such as turkeys benefit from low-heat cooking but are better when served with the crispy skin gained through higher temperatures. Duck and goose skins contain a great deal of fat that must be rendered during the cooking process. Small birds such as squab must be cooked at sufficiently high temperatures to crisp their skins but can be easily overcooked. Boneless chicken breasts, particularly flavorful and popular when broiled or grilled, are easily overcooked and become dry because they are lean and do not contain bones to help retain moisture during cooking. Chicken legs, although fattier than breast meat, require longer cooking time to tenderize them. Proper application of the following dry-heat cooking methods will help meet these challenges and ensure a good-quality finished product.

BROILING AND GRILLING

Broiled and grilled poultry should have a well-browned surface and can show crosshatched grill marks. It should be moist, tender and juicy throughout. It may be seasoned to enhance its natural flavors or marinated or basted with any number of flavored butters or sauces.

Selecting Poultry to Broil or Grill

Smaller birds such as Cornish hens, chickens and squab are especially well suited for broiling or grilling. Whole birds should be split or cut into smaller pieces before cooking; their joints may be broken so that they lie flat. Quail and other small birds can be skewered before being broiled to help them cook evenly and retain their shape. Be especially careful when cooking breast portions or boneless pieces; the direct heat of the broiler or grill can overcook the item very quickly.

Seasoning Poultry to Be Broiled or Grilled

Poultry is fairly neutral in flavor and responds well to marinating. Poultry may also be basted periodically during the cooking process with flavored butter, oil or barbecue sauce. At the very least, broiled or grilled poultry should be well seasoned with salt and pepper just before cooking.

Determining Doneness

With the exception of duck breasts and squab, which are sometimes left pink, broiled or grilled poultry is always cooked well done. This makes the poultry particularly susceptible to becoming dry and tough because it contains little fat and is cooked at very high temperatures. Particular care must be taken to ensure that the item does not become overcooked.

Four methods are used to determine the doneness of broiled or grilled poultry:

1. Touch—When the item is done, it will have a firm texture, resist pressure and spring back quickly when pressed with a finger.
2. Temperature—Use an instant-read thermometer to determine the item's internal temperature. This may be difficult, however, because of the item's size and the heat from the broiler or grill. Insert the thermometer in the thickest part of the item away from any bones. It should read 165°F–170°F (74°C–77°C) at the coolest point.
3. Looseness of the joints—When bone-in poultry is done, the leg will begin to move freely in its socket.
4. Color of the juices—Poultry is done when its juices run clear or show just a trace of pink. This degree of doneness is known in French as **à point**.

Accompaniments to Broiled and Grilled Poultry

If the item was basted with an herb butter, it can be served with additional butter; if the item was basted with barbecue sauce, it should be served with the same sauce. Be careful, however, that any marinade or sauce that came in contact with the raw poultry is not served unless it is cooked thoroughly to destroy harmful bacteria. Additional sauce suggestions are found in Table 10.5.

Broiled or grilled poultry is very versatile and goes well with almost any side dish. Seasoned and grilled vegetables are a natural accompaniment, and deep-fried potatoes are commonly served.

CLASSIC POULTRY FLAVORS

Ever versatile, chicken can be flavored with delicate herbs or robust, fiery spices. When roasted, chicken benefits from a simple grating of salt and pepper. Light sauces made from pan juices or velouté accented with tender herbs, lemon and white or black pepper are common accompainments that enhance the pure flavor of the poultry. But skin-on chicken pieces withstand marinating in wet or dry spice mixtures before grilling, roasting or stewing. Spice blends from adobo to garum masala can be used with any type of poultry. The versatility of poultry may account for its popularity. Dark meat from turkey legs can masquerade as lamb or pork in kebabs or stews. And boneless skinless chicken or turkey breast, when sliced thinly and pounded, makes excellent cutlets.

à point (ah PWEN) (1) French term for cooking to the ideal degree of doneness; (2) when applied to meat, refers to cooking it medium rare

PROCEDURE FOR **BROILING OR GRILLING POULTRY**

As with meats, broiled or grilled poultry can be prepared by placing it directly on the grate. Poultry is also often broiled using a rotisserie.

1. Heat the broiler or grill.

2. Use a wire brush to remove any charred or burnt particles that may be stuck to the broiler or grill grate. The grate can be wiped with a lightly oiled towel to remove any remaining particles and help season it.

3. Prepare the item to be broiled or grilled by marinating or seasoning as desired; it may be brushed lightly with oil to keep it from sticking to the grate.

4. Place the item on the grate, presentation side (skin side) down. Following the example in Chapter 9, turn the item to produce the attractive crosshatch marks associated with grilling. Baste the item often. Use tongs to turn or flip the item without piercing the surface so that juices do not escape.

5. Develop the proper surface color while cooking the item until it is done *à point*. To do so, adjust the position of the item on the broiler or grill, or adjust the distance between the grate and heat source. Large pieces and bone-in pieces that are difficult to cook completely on the broiler or grill can be finished in the oven.

A commonly used procedure to cook a large volume of poultry is to place the seasoned items in a broiler pan or other shallow pan and then place the pan directly under the broiler. Baste the items periodically, turning them once when they are halfway done. Items begun this way can be easily finished by transferring the entire pan to the oven.

MISE EN PLACE

▸ Bone and skin chicken breast.
▸ Peel and chop garlic.

1. Season the chicken breasts.

GRILLED CHICKEN BREAST WITH RED PEPPER BUTTER

Yield: 4 Servings   **Method:** Grilling

Whole chicken breasts, boneless, skinless, from 2 chickens	2	2
Salt and pepper	TT	TT
Garlic, chopped	1 tsp.	5 ml
Vegetable oil	1 Tbsp.	15 ml
Red pepper butter (page 212)	2 oz.	60 g

1. Trim any excess fat from the breasts. Split each breast into two pieces by removing the small piece of cartilage that joins the halves.

2. Season the breasts with the salt, pepper and garlic. Coat the breasts on all sides with the vegetable oil.

3. Heat and prepare the grill.

4. Grill the chicken breasts until done, turning them 90 degrees to produce attractive crosshatch markings.

5. Remove the chicken from the grill and place on a plate for service. Place a ½-ounce (15-gram) slice of red pepper butter on top of each breast. If necessary, place the plate under a broiler or salamander for a few seconds so that the butter begins to melt.

② Place the chicken on the grill at a 45-degree angle to the grates.

③ Using tongs, turn the chicken to cook the other side.

④ The cooked chicken is topped with red pepper butter.

VARIATION:

Grilled Marinated Chicken Breasts—Omit the garlic. Marinate the chicken breasts in 8 fluid ounces (240 milliliters) White Wine Marinade (page 101) for up to 1 hour. Blot excess marinade from the chicken with a paper towel before grilling.

Approximate values per serving: **Calories** 240, **Total fat** 14 g, **Saturated fat** 6 g, **Cholesterol** 95 mg, **Sodium** 60 mg, **Total carbohydrates** 1 g, **Protein** 28 g, **Vitamin A** 10%, **Vitamin C** 15%

ROASTING

Properly roasted (or baked) poultry is attractively browned on the surface and tender and juicy throughout. Proper cooking temperatures ensure a crisp exterior and juicy interior. Most roasted poultry is cooked until the juices run clear. Squab and duck breasts are exceptions; they are often served medium rare or pink.

Selecting Poultry to Roast

Almost every kind of poultry is suitable for roasting, but younger birds produce a more tender finished product. Because of variations in fat content, different kinds of poultry require different roasting temperatures and procedures.

Seasoning Poultry to Be Roasted

Although the mild flavor of most poultry is enhanced by a wide variety of herbs and spices, roasted poultry is often only lightly seasoned with salt and pepper. Poultry that is roasted at high temperatures should never be seasoned with herbs on its surface because the high cooking temperatures will burn them. If herbs or additional spices are used, they should be stuffed into the cavity. A mirepoix or a bouquet garni may also be added to the cavity for additional flavor. The cavities of dark-meated birds such as ducks and geese are often stuffed with fresh or dried fruits.

PROCEDURE FOR **TRUSSING POULTRY**

Trussing is tying a bird into a more compact shape with thread or butcher's twine. Trussing allows the bird to cook more evenly, helps the bird retain moisture and improves the appearance of the finished product. When a bird is trussed before roasting, the lean breast meat is kept from drying out in the time it takes the darker leg meat to cook. There are many methods for trussing poultry, some of which require a special tool called a trussing needle. Here we show a simple method using butcher's twine.

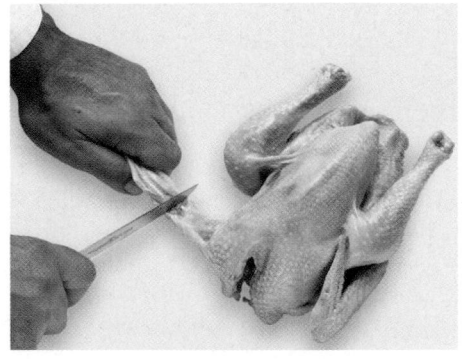

① Square up the bird by pressing it firmly with both hands. Tuck the first joint of the wing behind the back or trim off the first and second joints as shown.

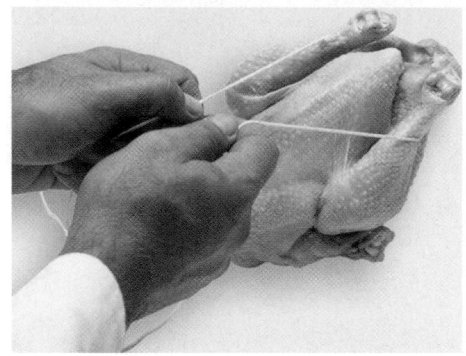

② Cut a piece of butcher's twine approximately three times the bird's length. With the breast up and the neck toward you, pass the twine under the bird approximately 1 inch (2.5 centimeters) in front of the tail.

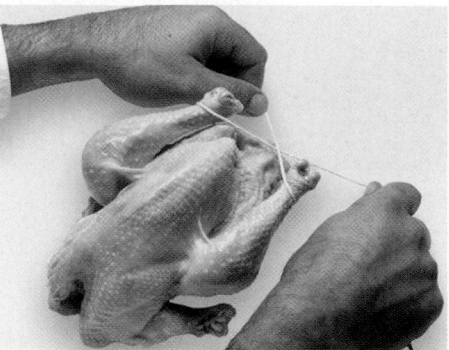

③ Bring the twine up around the legs and cross the ends, creating an X between the legs. Pass the ends of the twine below the legs.

④ Pull the ends of the twine tightly across the leg and thigh joints and across the wings if the first and second joints are trimmed off, or just above the wings if they are intact.

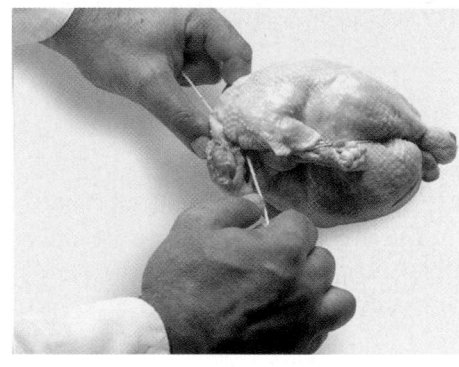

⑤ Pull the string tight and tie it securely just above the neck.

⑥ Two examples of properly trussed birds: one with the wings intact and one with the first and second wing joints removed.

Barding Poultry to Be Roasted

Guineas, squabs or any skinless birds without an adequate fat covering to protect them from drying out during roasting can be barded. Bard the bird by covering its entire surface with thin slices of fatback, securing them with butcher's twine. See page 408.

Cooking Temperatures

Small birds such as squab and Cornish game hens should be roasted at the relatively high temperatures of 375°F–400°F (190°C–200°C). These temperatures help produce crisp, well-colored skins without overcooking the flesh. Chickens are best roasted at temperatures between 350°F and 375°F (180°C and 190°C). This temperature range allows the skin to crisp and the flesh to cook without causing the bird to stew in its own juices. (Some chefs prefer to roast small unstuffed squab, Cornish game hens or chickens at higher temperatures, between 450°F and 500°F (230°C–260°C). These temperatures crisp the skin and cook the meat quickly before the lean meat dries out, but finishing the cooking at a lower temperature may be necessary.)

Large birds such as capons and turkeys are started at high temperatures of 400°F–425°F (200°C–220°C) to brown the skin, then finished at lower temperatures of 275°F–325°F

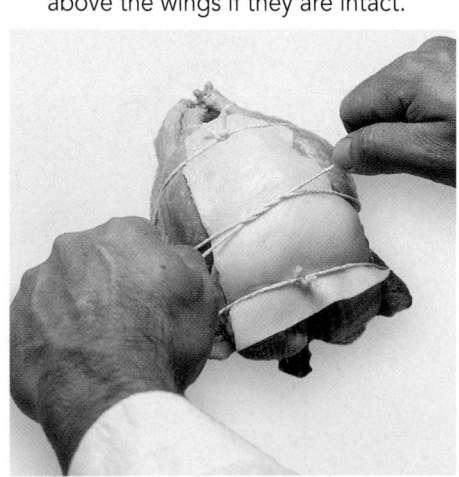

Barding a pheasant.

(135°C–160°C) to promote even cooking and produce a moister product. Ducks and geese, which are very high in fat, must be roasted at the high temperatures of 375°F–425°F (190°C–220°C) to render as much fat from the skin as possible. Duck and goose skins are often pricked before roasting so that the rendered fat can escape; this helps create a crispy skin.

Basting Roasted Poultry

With the exception of fatty birds such as ducks and geese, all poultry items should be basted while they roast in order to help retain moisture. To baste a bird, spoon or ladle the fat that collects in the bottom of the roasting pan over the bird at 15-to-20-minute intervals. Lean birds that are not barded will not produce enough fat for basting and may be brushed with butter or oil in the same manner.

Determining Doneness

Four methods are used to determine the doneness of roasted poultry. It is best to use a combination of these methods.

❶ **Temperature**—Test the internal temperature of the bird with an instant-read thermometer. The thermometer should be inserted in the bird's thigh, which is the last part to become fully cooked. It should not touch the bone and should read 165°F–170°F (74°C–77°C) at the coolest point. This method works best with large birds such as capons and turkeys. Large birds are subject to some degree of carryover cooking. This is not as much of a concern with poultry as it is with meat because large birds are always cooked well done.

❷ **Looseness of the joints**—The thigh and leg will begin to move freely in their sockets when the bird is done.

❸ **Color of juices**—This method is used with birds that are not stuffed. Use a kitchen fork to tilt the bird, allowing some of the juices that have collected in the cavity to run out. Clear juices indicate that the bird is done. If the juices are cloudy or pink, the bird is undercooked.

❹ **Time**—Because there are so many variables, timing alone is less reliable than other methods. It is useful, however, for planning production when large quantities are roasted and as a general guideline when used with other methods. Table 17.3 gives some general timing guidelines for roasting several kinds of poultry.

Accompaniments to Roasted Poultry

The most common accompaniments to roasted poultry are bread stuffing and gravy. Large birds, such as capons and turkeys, produce adequate drippings for making sauce or pan gravy. Small birds, such as squab and Cornish game hens, are often stuffed with wild rice or other ingredients and served with a sauce that is made separately.

Ducks and geese are complemented by stuffings containing rice, fruits, berries and nuts. They are very fatty, and if stuffed, they should be roasted on a rack or mirepoix bed to ensure that the fat that collects in the pan during roasting does not penetrate the cavity, making the stuffing greasy. Ducks and geese are often served with a citrus- or fruit-based sauce. Its high acid content complements these rich, fatty birds.

> ## CHICKEN WISDOM
>
> "To know how to cook is to understand a recipe so that it can be expressed in different terms, at changing levels of sophistication for different occasions," writes Chef Jacques Pépin of preparing roast chicken. When served with a plain green salad, he calls it *cuisine bourgeoise*, home-style cooking. Garnished with a sauce made from its pan juices, the chicken becomes casual dinner fare. When the roasting pan is deglazed with cognac and sautéed mushrooms and cream are added, the bird is transformed into *haute cuisine*, for more formal occasions. "This ability to extend or vary a basic dish is essential to the work of good cooks and enables them to change the cost of a meal or alter the calorie count at will," he writes. What does not vary is the skill needed to properly roast a chicken, a technique by which chefs are often judged.

dressing another name for a bread stuffing used with poultry

TABLE 17.3   ROASTING TEMPERATURES AND TIMES

POULTRY KIND OR CLASS	COOKING TEMPERATURES		MINUTES PER LB. (450 G)
Capons	350°F–375°F	180°C–190°C	18–20 min.
Chickens	375°F–400°F	190°C–200°C	15–18 min.
Ducks and geese	375°F–425°F	190°C–220°C	12–15 min.
Game hens	375°F–400°F	190°C–200°C	45–60 min. total
Guineas	375°F–400°F	190°C–200°C	18–20 min.
Squab	400°F	200°C	30–40 min. total
Turkeys (large)	325°F	160°C	12–15 min.

PROCEDURE FOR **STUFFING POULTRY**

Small birds such as Cornish game hens, small chickens and squab can be stuffed successfully. Stuffing larger birds, especially for volume production, is impractical and can be dangerous for the following reasons:

1. Stuffing is a good bacterial breeding ground, and because it is difficult to control temperatures inside a stuffed bird, there is a risk of food-borne illness.
2. Stuffing poultry is labor intensive.
3. Stuffed poultry must be cooked longer to cook the stuffing properly; this may cause the meat to be overcooked, becoming dry and tough.

When stuffing any bird, use the following guidelines:

1. Always be aware of temperatures when mixing the raw ingredients. All ingredients should be cold when they are mixed together, and the mixture's temperature should never be allowed to rise above 45°F (7°C).
2. Stuff the raw bird as close to roasting time as possible.
3. The neck and main body cavities should be loosely stuffed. The stuffing will expand during cooking.
4. After the cavities are filled, their openings should be secured with skewers and butcher's twine or by trussing.
5. After cooking, remove the stuffing from the bird and store separately.

PROCEDURE FOR **ROASTING POULTRY**

1. Season, bard, stuff and/or truss the bird as desired.
2. Place the bird in a roasting pan. It may be placed on a rack or a bed of mirepoix in order to prevent scorching and promote even cooking.
3. Roast uncovered, basting every 15 minutes.
4. Allow the bird to rest before carving to allow even distribution of juices. As the bird rests, prepare the pan gravy or sauce.

ROAST TURKEY WITH CHESTNUT DRESSING AND GIBLET GRAVY

MISE EN PLACE

- Peel and chop onions, carrots and celery for mirepoix.
- While turkey is roasting peel and chop the onion and celery into small dice for the dressing. Beat the eggs.
- Chop parsley.
- Cook, peel and coarsely chop chestnuts for the dressing.

Yield: 16 Servings, 4 oz. (120 g) turkey, 3 oz. (90 g) dressing and 4 oz. (120 ml) gravy each

Method: Roasting

Young turkey, 12–15 lb. (5.5–6.5 kg) with giblets	1	1
Salt and pepper	TT	TT
Mirepoix	20 oz.	600 g
Onions, small dice	8 oz.	240 g
Celery, small dice	6 oz.	180 g
Whole butter	4 oz.	120 g
Dried bread cubes	2 lb.	960 g
Eggs, beaten	2	2
Fresh parsley, chopped	1 Tbsp.	15 ml
Chicken stock	2¼ qt.	2.1 lt
Chestnuts, cooked and peeled, chopped coarse	8 oz.	240 g
All-purpose flour	3 oz.	90 g

1. Remove the giblets from the turkey's cavity and set aside. Season the turkey inside and out with salt and pepper. Truss the turkey.

2. Place the turkey in a roasting pan. Roast at 400°F (200°C) for 30 minutes. Reduce the temperature to 325°F (160°C) and continue cooking the turkey to an internal temperature of 165°F (74°C), approximately 2½ to 3 hours. Baste the turkey often during cooking. Approximately 45 minutes before the turkey is done, add the mirepoix to the roasting pan. If the turkey begins to overbrown, cover it loosely with aluminum foil.

3. To make the dressing, sauté the onions and celery in the butter until tender.

4. In a large bowl, toss together the bread cubes, salt, pepper, eggs, parsley, sautéed onions and celery, 4 fluid ounces (120 milliliters) stock and the chestnuts.

5. Place the dressing in a buttered hotel pan and cover with aluminum foil or buttered parchment paper. Bake at 350°F (180°C) until done, approximately 45 minutes.

6. As the turkey roasts, simmer the giblets (neck, heart and gizzard) in 1 quart (1 liter) stock until tender, approximately 1½ hours.

7. When the turkey is done, remove it from the roasting pan and set it aside to rest. Degrease the roasting pan, reserving 3 fluid ounces (90 milliliters) of the fat to make a roux.

8. Place the roasting pan on the stove top and brown the mirepoix.

9. Deglaze the pan with a small amount of stock. Transfer the mirepoix and stock to a saucepot and add the remaining stock and the broth from the giblets. Bring to a simmer and degrease.

10. Make a blond roux with the reserved fat and the flour. Add the roux to the liquid, whisking well to prevent lumps. Simmer 15 minutes. Strain the gravy through a china cap lined with cheesecloth.

11. Remove the meat from the turkey neck. Trim the gizzard. Finely chop the neck meat, heart and gizzard and add to the gravy. Adjust the seasonings.

12. Carve the turkey and serve with a portion of chestnut dressing and giblet gravy.

Approximate values per serving: **Calories** 720, **Total fat** 23 g, **Saturated fat** 9 g, **Cholesterol** 250 mg, **Sodium** 700 mg, **Total carbohydrates** 41 g, **Protein** 87 g, **Vitamin A** 6%, **Iron** 40%

1. Placing the trussed turkey in the roasting pan.

2. Adding the mirepoix to the roasting pan.

3. Tossing the dressing ingredients together.

4. Browning the mirepoix.

5. Deglazing the roasting pan.

6. Transferring the mirepoix and stock to a saucepot.

7. Straining the gravy through a china cap and cheesecloth.

Carving Roasted Poultry

Poultry can be carved in the kitchen, at tableside or on a buffet in a variety of manners. The carving methods described next produce slices of both light and dark meat.

PROCEDURE FOR CARVING A TURKEY, CAPON OR OTHER LARGE BIRD

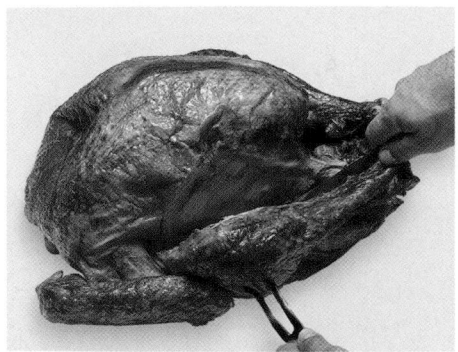

① After roasting, allow the turkey to stand for 20 minutes so that the juices can redistribute themselves. Holding the turkey firmly with a carving fork, pry a leg outward and locate the joint. Remove the leg and thigh in one piece by cutting through the joint with the tip of a knife.

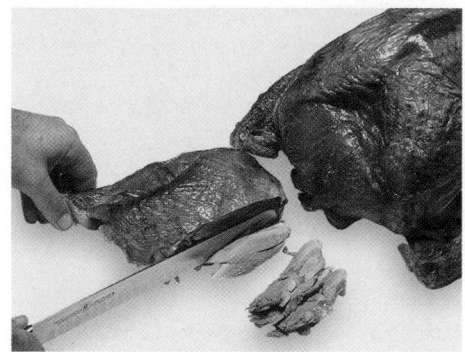

② Repeat the procedure on the other side. Once both legs and thighs have been removed, slice the meat from the thigh by holding the leg firmly with one hand and slicing parallel to the bone.

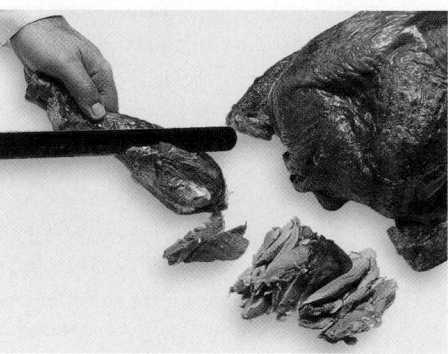

③ Separate the thigh from the leg bone by cutting through the joint. Slice the meat from the leg by cutting parallel to the bone.

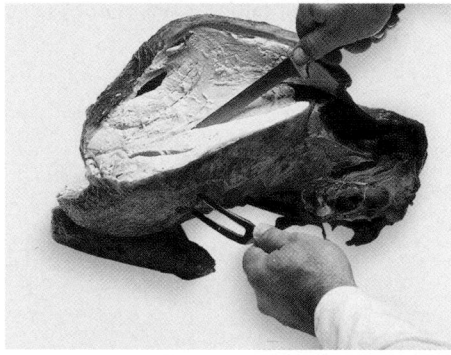

④ Cut along the backbone, following the natural curvature of the bones separating the breast meat from the ribs.

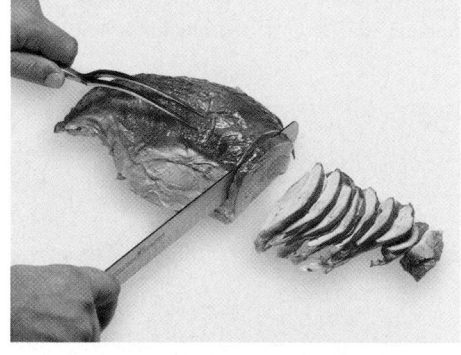

⑤ Remove an entire half breast and slice it on the cutting board as shown. Cut on an angle to produce larger slices.

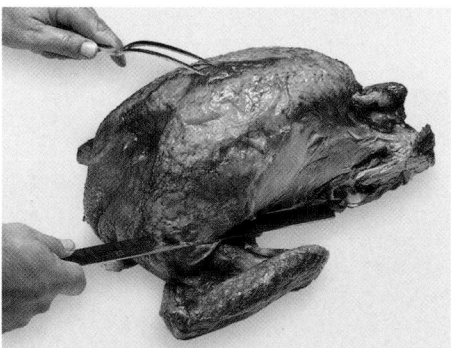

⑥ Alternatively, the breast can be carved on the bird. Make a horizontal cut just above the wing in toward the rib bones.

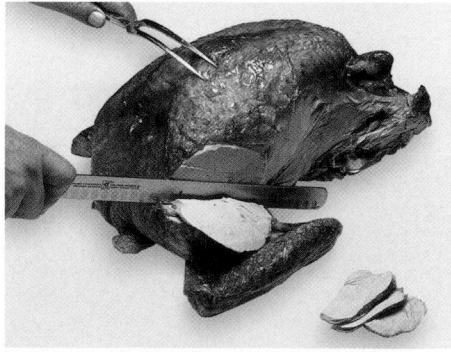

⑦ Slice the breast meat as shown.

PROCEDURE FOR **CARVING A CHICKEN OR OTHER SMALL BIRD**

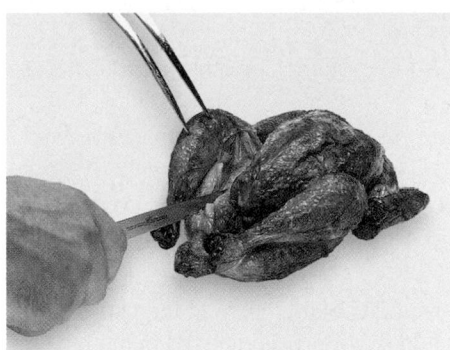

❶ After allowing the roasted chicken to rest for 15 minutes so that the juices can redistribute themselves, cut through the skin between the leg and breast.

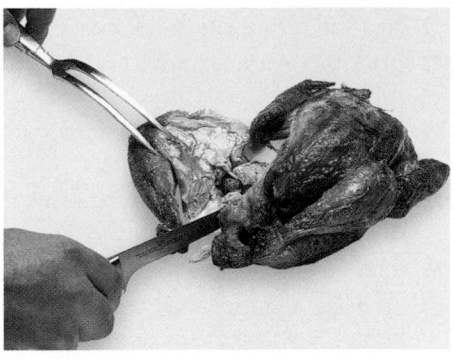

❷ Use a kitchen fork to pry the leg and thigh away from the breast. Locate the thigh's ball joint and cut through it with the knife tip, separating it completely from the rest of the chicken. Be sure to cut around the delicate oyster meat, leaving it attached to the thigh.

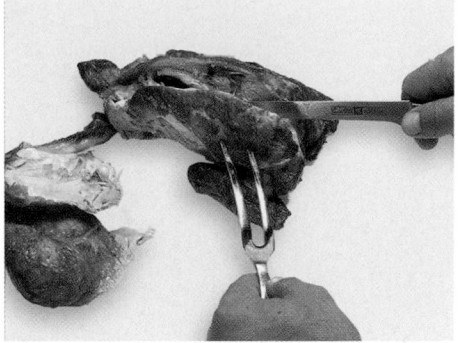

❸ With the knife tip, cut through the skin and meat on one side of the breast bone. Cut and pull the meat away from the bones with the knife.

❹ Cut through the wing joint, separating the breast meat and wing from the carcass. Repeat this procedure on the other side of the bird.

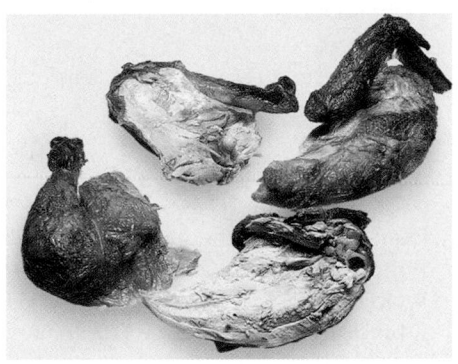

❺ The chicken is now quartered.

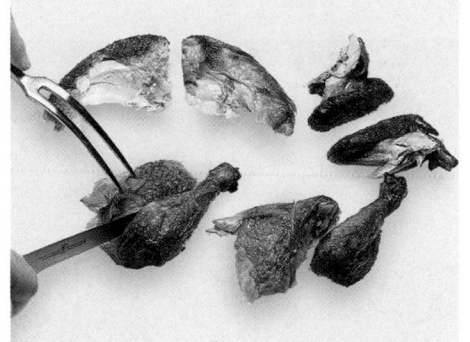

❻ To cut it into eight pieces, separate the wings from the breasts and the thighs from the legs.

POÊLÉING

Poêléing (pwah-lay-ing) is a cooking method similar to both roasting and braising. The item is cooked in the oven in a covered pot so that it cooks in its own juices and steam. Although this is a moist-heat cooking technique (because the item steams in its own juices), it is used only for tender cuts, not those that need long, slow braising. The cooking time is usually shorter than that needed for dry roasting.

The item to be poêléed can first be browned in hot fat and then laid on a bed of matignon, covered and cooked in the oven. If the item was not first browned in hot fat, it can later be browned by removing the lid toward the end of cooking. Doneness is determined using the same techniques as those used for roasting.

Vegetables to be served with the dish can be added to the poêlé as it cooks or cooked separately and plated with the finished item.

The sauce for a poêlé is made from the flavorful cooking juices left in the pan. They are mixed with a liquid (stock, jus lié or demi-glace) and finished using the same techniques as those for a braised dish. The matignon can be left in the finished sauce or strained out.

PROCEDURE FOR **POÊLÉING POULTRY**

❶ Sear the main item in hot butter or oil, if desired.

❷ Place the main item on a bed of matignon. Add vegetables or other ingredients as called for in the recipe.

❸ Cover and cook in the oven until done. Baste periodically with pan juices or with additional butter.

❹ If the main item was not first browned in hot fat, it can be browned by removing the lid toward the end of the cooking period, if desired.

❺ Remove the main item when done.

❻ To make a sauce, add a liquid to the matignon and cooking juices in the pan and reduce. Remove the matignon if desired and add flavorings as directed in the recipe.

POÊLÉ OF CHICKEN WITH PEARL ONIONS AND MUSHROOMS

MISE EN PLACE

▶ Dice bacon and peel and chop onions, celery, carrots and garlic for matignon.
▶ Blanch and peel pearl onions.
▶ Stem mushrooms.
▶ Chop fresh herbs.

❶ Place the chicken on the matignon.

Yield: 4 Servings		Method: Poêléing
Chickens, 2 lb. 8 oz.–3 lb. (1.2–1.4 kg) each	2	2
Salt and pepper	TT	TT
Fresh herbs, assorted stems and sprigs	2 oz.	60 g
Clarified butter	4 fl. oz.	120 ml
Matignon:		
Slab bacon or smoked ham, small dice	3 oz.	90 g
Onions, small dice	6 oz.	180 g
Celery, small dice	3 oz.	90 g
Carrots, small dice	3 oz.	90 g
Garlic, chopped	2 tsp.	10 ml
Pearl onions, blanched and peeled	4 oz.	120 g
Button mushrooms, stemmed	8 oz.	240 g
White wine	4 fl. oz.	120 ml
Demi-glace	1 qt.	960 ml
Tomato concassée	4 oz.	120 g
Fresh herbs, assorted, chopped	2 tsp.	10 ml

❶ Season the chicken cavities with salt and pepper and stuff them with the herb stems and sprigs. Truss the birds and season the outside with salt and pepper.

❷ Heat half the butter in a roasting pan that is just large enough to hold the birds without crowding. Sauté the bacon until most of the fat is rendered. Add the diced onions, celery and carrots and sauté until they begin to brown. Add the garlic and cook for 1 more minute.

❷ Baste the chicken with fat from the pan during cooking.

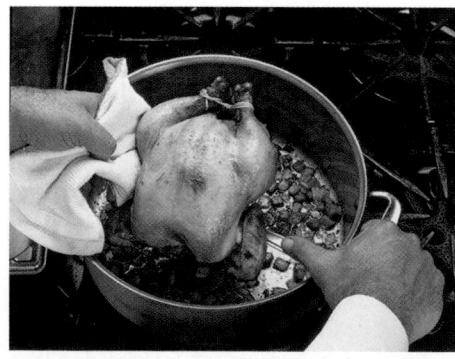

❸ Carefully remove the cooked chicken from the pan.

❹ The finished dish.

3️⃣ Place the trussed chickens on top of the matignon. Baste them with the remaining butter. Cover the roasting pan with its lid and place in a 325°F (160°C) oven until done, approximately 1½ hours, basting the chickens with fat from the pan every 20 minutes. Remove the lid for the last 30 minutes of cooking to allow the chickens to brown lightly.

4️⃣ Remove the chickens from the pan and allow them to rest in a warm place. Place the roasting pan on the stove top. Remove a small amount of the accumulated fat from the roasting pan to a sauté pan and sauté the pearl onions and mushrooms in the sauté pan until nearly tender.

5️⃣ Bring the liquid in the roasting pan to a boil; remove any excess fat or scum with a ladle. Add the wine and reduce by half. Add the demi-glace and bring to a simmer. Adjust the thickness of the sauce. If desired, strain the sauce. Add the pearl onions, mushrooms, tomato concassée and chopped herbs to the sauce. Bring to a simmer and adjust the seasonings.

6️⃣ Carve the chickens and serve them with a portion of the sauce and vegetables.

Approximate values per serving: **Calories** 1670, **Total fat** 106 g, **Saturated fat** 39 g, **Cholesterol** 475 mg, **Sodium** 2110 mg, **Total carbohydrates** 48 g, **Protein** 129 g, **Vitamin A** 170%, **Vitamin C** 50%, **Calcium** 10%, **Iron** 45%

SAUTÉING

Sautéed poultry should be tender and juicy, its flavor developed by proper browning. Additional flavors come from a sauce made by deglazing the pan, usually with wine, and adding garnishes, seasonings and liquids. Stir-frying is a popular method of sautéing poultry; boneless pieces are cut into strips and quickly cooked with assorted vegetables and seasonings.

Selecting Poultry to Sauté

Most poultry is quite tender and well suited for sautéing. Although small birds such as squab can be sautéed bone-in, large pieces and bone-in cuts from larger birds should not be sautéed. Boneless breasts, suprêmes, scallops and cutlets are the most common and practical cuts for sautéing. Because they are high in fat, boneless duck breasts can be sautéed without additional fat.

Seasoning Poultry to Be Sautéed

Poultry has a delicate flavor that is enhanced by a wide variety of herbs, spices, condiments and marinades. Flavor combinations are limited only by your imagination. When poultry items are dusted with flour before sautéing, the seasonings may first be added to the flour.

Cooking Temperatures

The sauté pan and the cooking fat must be hot before the poultry is added. The temperature at which the poultry is then sautéed is determined by its thickness and the desired color of the finished product. A thin, boneless slice requires relatively high temperatures so that its surface is browned before the center is overcooked. A thicker cut such as a suprême requires lower temperatures so that neither its surface nor the fond are burned before the item is fully cooked. Adjust the temperature throughout the cooking process in order to achieve the desired results, never letting the pan become too cool.

If the pan is overcrowded or otherwise allowed to cool, the poultry will cook in its own juices and absorb oil from the pan, resulting in a poor-quality product.

Determining Doneness

Thin cuts of poultry cook very quickly, so timing is a useful tool; it is less useful with thicker cuts. Experienced cooks can tell the doneness of an item by judging the temperature of the sauté pan and the color of the item being cooked.

A more practical method is to press the item with your finger and judge the resistance. Very undercooked poultry will offer little resistance and feel mushy. Slightly underdone poultry will feel spongy and will not spring back when your finger is removed. Properly cooked poultry will feel firm to the touch and will spring back when your finger is removed. Overcooked poultry will feel very firm, almost hard, and will spring back quickly when your finger is removed.

Accompaniments to Sautéed Poultry

Sautéed poultry is usually served with a sauce made directly in the pan in which the item was cooked. The sauce uses the fond for added flavor. A wide variety of ingredients, including garlic, onions, shallots, mushrooms and tomatoes, are commonly added to the pan as well as wine and stock. Table 10.5 suggests several sauces for sautéed poultry.

Sautéed items are often served with a starch such as pasta, rice or potatoes.

PROCEDURE FOR **SAUTÉING POULTRY**

1. Heat a sauté pan and add enough fat or oil to just cover the bottom.
2. Add the poultry item, presentation side down, and cook until browned.
3. Turn the item, using tongs or by tossing the item back on itself using the pan's sloped sides.
4. Larger items can be finished in an oven. Either place the sauté pan in the oven or transfer the poultry to another pan. The latter procedure allows a sauce to be made in the original pan while the poultry cooks in the oven. Hold smaller pieces that are thoroughly cooked in a warm place so that the pan can be used for making the sauce.

PROCEDURE FOR **PREPARING A SAUCE IN THE SAUTÉ PAN**

1. Pour off any excess fat or oil from the sauté pan, leaving enough to sauté the sauce ingredients.
2. Add ingredients such as garlic, shallots and mushrooms that will be used as garnishes and sauce flavorings; sauté them.
3. Deglaze the pan with wine, stock or other liquids. Scrape the pan, loosening the fond and allowing it to dissolve in the liquid. Reduce the liquid.
4. Add any ingredients that do not require long cooking times such as herbs and spices. Adjust the sauce's consistency and seasonings.
5. For service, the poultry can be returned to the pan for a moment to reheat it and to coat it with the sauce. The poultry should remain in the sauce just long enough to reheat. Do not attempt to cook the poultry in the sauce.
6. Serve the poultry with the accompanying sauce.

CHICKEN SAUTÉ WITH ONIONS, GARLIC AND BASIL

MISE EN PLACE

▶ Bone and skin chicken breasts.
▶ Peel onion and garlic and chop into fine dice.
▶ Slice basil in chiffonade.

Yield: 6 Servings, 5 oz. (150 g) each   **Method:** Sautéing

Whole chicken breasts, boneless, skinless, approx. 10 oz. (300 g) each	3	3
Salt and pepper	TT	TT
Flour	as needed for dredging	
Clarified butter	1 fl. oz.	30 ml
Onion, small dice	2 oz.	60 g
Garlic cloves, chopped	6	6
Dry white wine	4 fl. oz.	120 ml
Lemon juice	1 Tbsp.	15 ml
Tomato concassée	6 oz.	180 g
Chicken stock	4 fl. oz.	120 ml
Fresh basil leaves, chiffonade	6	6

1. Trim any excess fat from the breasts. Split each breast into two pieces by removing the small piece of cartilage that joins the halves.
2. Season the chicken with salt and pepper; dredge in flour.
3. Sauté the breasts in the butter, browning them and cooking à *point*. Hold in a warm place.
4. Add the onion and garlic to the fond and butter in the pan; sauté until the onion is translucent.
5. Deglaze the pan with the wine and lemon juice.
6. Add the tomato concassée and stock. Sauté to combine the flavors; reduce the sauce to the desired consistency.
7. Add the basil to the sauce and return the chicken breasts for reheating. Adjust the seasonings and serve one half breast per portion with a portion of the sauce.

Approximate values per 5-oz. (150-g) serving: **Calories** 230, **Total fat** 8 g, **Saturated fat** 3.5 g, **Cholesterol** 90 mg, **Sodium** 580 mg, **Total carbohydrates** 9 g, **Protein** 30 g, **Vitamin C** 10%, **Iron** 10%

1. Sautéing the breasts in butter.

2. The fond left in the pan after sautéing the chicken.

3. Sautéing the onions and garlic.

4. Deglazing the pan with white wine and lemon juice.

5. Adding tomatoes and chicken stock and sautéing to combine flavors.

6. Returning the chicken to the pan to reheat.

PAN-FRYING

Pan-fried poultry should be juicy. Its coating or batter should be crispy, golden brown, not excessively oily and free from any breaks that allow fat to penetrate. Both the poultry and the coating should be well seasoned.

Selecting Poultry to Pan-Fry

The most common pan-fried poultry is fried chicken. Young tender birds cut into small pieces produce the best results. Other cuts commonly pan-fried are boneless portions such as chicken breasts and turkey scallops.

Seasoning Poultry to Be Pan-Fried

Pan-fried poultry is usually floured, breaded or battered before cooking. (Breadings and batters are discussed in Chapter 8, Mise en Place.) Typically, the seasonings are added to the flour, breading or batter before the poultry is coated. Seasonings can be a blend of any number of dried herbs and spices. But often only salt and pepper are required because the poultry will be served with a sauce or other accompaniments for additional flavors.

Cooking Temperatures

The fat should always be hot before the poultry is added. The temperature at which it is cooked is determined by the length of time required to cook it thoroughly. Pan-frying generally requires slightly lower temperatures than those used for sautéing. Within this range, thinner items require higher temperatures to produce good color in a relatively short time. Thicker items and those containing bones require lower cooking temperatures and longer cooking times.

Determining Doneness

Even the largest pan-fried items may be too small to be accurately tested with an instant-read thermometer, and using the touch method can be difficult and dangerous because of the amount of fat used in pan-frying. So timing and experience are the best tools to determine doneness. Thin scallops cook very quickly, so it is relatively easy to judge their doneness. On the other hand, fried chicken can take as long as 30–45 minutes to cook, requiring skill and experience to determine doneness.

Accompaniments to Pan-Fried Poultry

Because pan-frying does not produce fond or drippings that can be used to make a sauce, pan-fried poultry is usually served with lemon wedges, a vegetable garnish or a separately made sauce. Fried chicken is an exception; it is sometimes served with a country gravy made by degreasing the pan, making a roux with a portion of the fat and adding milk or stock and seasonings.

PROCEDURE FOR **PAN-FRYING POULTRY**

1. Heat enough fat in a heavy sauté pan to cover the item to be cooked one-fourth to halfway up its side. The fat should be at approximately 325°F (160°C).
2. Add the floured, breaded or battered item to the hot fat, being careful not to splash. The fat must be hot enough to sizzle and bubble when the item is added.
3. Turn the item when the first side is the proper color; it should be half cooked at this point. Larger items may need to be turned more than once to brown them properly on all sides.
4. Remove the browned poultry from the pan and drain it on absorbent paper.

PAN-FRIED CHICKEN WITH PAN GRAVY

MISE EN PLACE

▶ Cut chicken into eight pieces.
▶ Season flour with salt and pepper.
▶ Peel onion and chop into small dice.

Yield: 8 Servings, 2 pieces each   **Method:** Pan-frying

Frying chickens, 2 lb. 8 oz.–3 lb. (1.2–1.4 kg) each, cut into 8 pieces	2	2
Salt and pepper	TT	TT
Garlic powder	2 tsp.	10 ml
Onion powder	2 tsp.	10 ml
Dried oregano	1 tsp.	5 ml
Dried basil	1 tsp.	5 ml
Flour, seasoned	9½ oz.	285 g
Buttermilk	8 fl. oz.	240 ml
Oil	as needed	as needed
Onion, small dice	4 oz.	120 g
Half-and-half or chicken stock	1½ pt.	720 ml

1. Season the chicken with salt and pepper.
2. Add the herbs and spices to 8 ounces (240 grams) of the flour.
3. Dip the chicken pieces in the buttermilk.
4. Dredge the chicken in the seasoned flour.

5. Pan-fry the chicken in oil until done, approximately 40 minutes, turning so that it cooks evenly. Reduce the heat as necessary to prevent the chicken from becoming too dark. Or remove the chicken when well browned, drain it and finish cooking it in the oven.

6. To make the pan gravy, pour off all but 3 tablespoons (45 milliliters) oil from the pan, carefully reserving the fond.

7. Add the diced onion and sauté until translucent.

8. Add 1½ ounces (45 grams) flour and cook to make a blond roux.

9. Whisk in the liquid and simmer approximately 15 minutes.

10. Strain through cheesecloth and adjust the seasonings.

11. Serve 2 pieces of chicken per person with 4 fluid ounces (120 milliliters) gravy.

Approximate values per 2-piece serving (6–7 ounces), before frying: **Calories** 650, **Total fat** 31 g, **Saturated fat** 12 g, **Cholesterol** 190 mg, **Sodium** 190 mg, **Total carbohydrates** 32 g, **Protein** 57 g, **Vitamin A** 15%, **Vitamin C** 4%, **Calcium** 15%, **Iron** 20%

1 Dipping the chicken pieces in the buttermilk.

2 Dredging the chicken in the flour mixture.

3 Adding the chicken to the oil. The bubbling fat indicates the proper cooking temperature.

4 Turning the chicken so that it cooks evenly.

5 Sautéing the diced onions until translucent.

6 Adding the liquid to the roux.

DEEP-FRYING

Young, tender poultry is an excellent and popular choice for deep-frying. The pieces should be golden brown on the outside and moist and tender on the inside. They should be neither greasy nor tough. Chopped cooked poultry can also be mixed with a heavy béchamel or velouté sauce and seasonings, breaded and deep-fried as croquettes, which are discussed in Chapter 19, Fish and Shellfish.

Selecting and Seasoning Poultry to Be Deep-Fried

Portioned chickens and whole small birds, such as Rock Cornish game hen, are best for deep-frying. Although they can be marinated or seasoned directly, it is more common to season the batter or breading that will coat them. Additional flavors come from the sauces and accompaniments served with the deep-fried poultry. Lemon wedges, sweet and sour sauce and tangy barbecue sauces are popular accompaniments to deep-fried poultry.

PROCEDURE FOR **DEEP-FRYING POULTRY**

1. Cut, trim or otherwise prepare the poultry to be deep-fried. Season and bread or batter it, as desired.
2. Heat the fat to the desired temperature, usually around 350°F (177°C). Breaded or battered poultry cooks quickly, and the fat must be hot enough to cook the food's interior without burning its surface.
3. Carefully place the poultry in the hot fat using the basket method.
4. Deep-fry the food until done. It should have a crispy, golden brown surface.
5. Remove the deep-fried poultry from the fat and hold it over the fat, allowing the excess fat to drain. Transfer the food to a hotel pan either lined with absorbent paper or fitted with a rack. Season with salt, if desired.
6. If the deep-fried poultry is to be held for later service, place it under a heat lamp.

SPICY FRIED CHICKEN TENDERS WITH CHIPOTLE DIPPING SAUCE

MISE EN PLACE
▶ Remove tendons from chicken.

Yield: 4 Servings	**Method:** Deep-frying	
Chicken tenders (or tenderloins), tendons removed	24	24
Seasoned flour:		
Flour	8 oz.	240 g
Chilli powder	3 Tbsp.	45 ml
Paprika	3 Tbsp.	45 ml
Granulated garlic	2 Tbsp.	30 ml
Black pepper	2 tsp.	10 ml
Cayenne pepper	1 Tbsp.	15 ml
Dried thyme	1 Tbsp.	15 ml
Dried oregano	1 Tbsp.	15 ml
Salt	3 Tbsp.	45 ml
Egg wash:		
Eggs	4	4
Milk	4 Tbsp.	120 ml
Bread crumbs	as needed	as needed
Sauce:		
Barbecue Sauce (page 227)	8 fl. oz.	240 ml
Chipotle peppers, canned, puréed	1 Tbsp.	15 ml
Honey	1 oz.	60 g

1. Lightly pound the chicken pieces to an even thickness.
2. Combine the ingredients for the seasoned flour.
3. Beat the eggs and milk.
4. Bread the chicken tenders using the standard breading procedure described in Chapter 8, Mise en Place, placing each fully breaded piece on a parchment-lined sheet pan. Refrigerate until ready to cook.
5. Place the sauce ingredients in a small saucepan and simmer until the flavors blend, approximately 5 minutes.
6. Using the basket method, deep-fry the chicken pieces at 325°F (160°C) until done, approximately 4 minutes. Drain and serve with the warm sauce.

Approximate values per serving: **Calories** 380, **Total fat** 12 g, **Saturated fat** 2.5 g, **Cholesterol** 160 mg, **Sodium** 2680 mg, **Total carbohydrates** 33 g, **Protein** 34 g, **Vitamin A** 60%, **Vitamin C** 15%, **Iron** 25%

Moist-Heat Cooking Methods

The moist-heat cooking methods most often used with poultry are poaching and simmering. Poaching is used to cook tender birds for short periods. Simmering is used to cook older, tougher birds for longer periods in order to tenderize them. Poaching and simmering are similar procedures, the principal differences being the temperature of the cooking liquid and the length of cooking time.

POACHING AND SIMMERING

Poached or simmered poultry should be moist, tender and delicately flavored. Although the poultry is cooked in water, overcooking will cause it to become dry and tough. During cooking, some of the poultry's flavor is transferred to the cooking liquid, which can be used to make a sauce for the finished product.

Selecting Poultry to Poach or Simmer

Young birds are best suited for poaching; boneless chicken breast pieces are the most commonly used parts. Older, tougher birds are usually simmered. Duck and geese are rarely poached or simmered because of their high fat content.

Seasoning Poultry to Be Poached or Simmered

When poaching poultry, it is especially important to use a well-seasoned and highly flavored liquid in order to infuse as much flavor as possible into the item being cooked. Either strong stock with a sachet or a mixture of stock or water and white wine with a bouquet garni or onion piquet produces good results. The poultry should be completely covered with liquid so that it cooks evenly. However, if too much liquid is used and it is not strongly flavored, flavors may be leached out of the poultry, resulting in a bland finished product.

Poultry is often simmered in water instead of stock. A sachet and a generous mirepoix should be added to help flavor it. Typically, simmering birds results in a strong broth that may be used to complete the recipe or reserved for other uses.

Cooking Temperatures

For best results, poultry should be poached at low temperatures, between 160°F and 175°F (71°C and 79°C). Cooking poultry to the proper doneness at these temperatures produces a product that is moist and tender.

Simmering is done at slightly higher temperatures, between 185°F (85°C) and the boiling point. When simmering, do not allow the liquid to boil, as this may result in a dry, tough and stringy finished product.

Determining Doneness

Poached poultry, whether whole or boneless, is cooked just until done. An instant-read thermometer inserted in the thigh or thicker part of the bird should read 165°F (74°C). Any juices that run from the bird should be clear or show only a trace of pink.

Simmered poultry is usually cooked for longer periods to allow the moist heat to tenderize the meat. A chicken that weighs 3 pounds 8 ounces (1.5 kilograms), for example, may take 2½ hours to cook.

Accompaniments to Poached or Simmered Poultry

Poached or simmered poultry can be served hot or cold. The meat from these birds can be served cold in salads, served hot in casseroles or used in any dish that calls for cooked poultry.

Poached items are typically served with a flavored mayonnaise or a sauce made from the reduced poaching liquid, such as sauce suprême. Poultry is also often poached as a means of producing a low-calorie dish. If so, a vegetable coulis makes a good sauce, or the poultry can be served with a portion of its cooking liquid and a vegetable garnish.

Simmered poultry to be served cold will be moister and more flavorful if it is cooled in its cooking liquid. To do so, remove the pot containing the bird and the cooking liquid from the heat when the bird is still slightly undercooked. Cool the meat and broth in a water bath following the procedure in Chapter 10, Stocks and Sauces. Once cooled, remove the meat and wipe off any congealed broth before proceeding with the recipe.

PROCEDURE FOR **POACHING OR SIMMERING POULTRY**

1. Cut or truss the item to be cooked as directed in the recipe.

2. Prepare the cooking liquid and bring it to a simmer. Submerge the poultry in the cooking liquid, or arrange the items to be poached in an appropriate pan and add the poaching liquid to the pan.

3. Poach or simmer the item to the desired doneness in the oven or on the stove top. Maintain the proper cooking temperature throughout the process.

4. Remove the poultry and hold it for service in a portion of the cooking liquid or, using an ice bath, cool the item in its cooking liquid.

5. The cooking liquid may be used to prepare an accompanying sauce or reserved for use in other dishes.

MISE EN PLACE

▶ Bone and skin the chicken breasts.

1. Arranging the breasts in an appropriate pan.

2. Adding the white wine, chicken stock and seasonings to the pan.

POACHED BREAST OF CHICKEN WITH TARRAGON SAUCE

Yield: 8 Servings, 4 oz. (120 g) each   **Method:** Poaching

Whole chicken breasts, boneless, skinless, approx. 10 oz. (300 g) each	4	4
Whole butter	1½ oz.	45 g
Salt and white pepper	TT	TT
White wine	4 fl. oz.	120 ml
Chicken stock	1 pt.	480 ml
Bay leaf	1	1
Dried thyme	¼ tsp.	1 ml
Dried tarragon	1 tsp.	5 ml
Flour	1 oz.	30 g
Heavy cream	4 fl. oz.	120 ml
Fresh tarragon sprigs	as needed for garnish	

1. Trim any rib meat and fat from the breasts. Cut the breasts into two pieces, removing the strip of cartilage that joins the halves.

2. Select a pan that will just hold the breasts when they are placed close together. Rub the pan with approximately ½ ounce (15 grams) butter.

3. Season the chicken breasts with salt and white pepper and arrange them in the buttered pan, presentation side up.

4. Add the wine, stock, bay leaf, thyme and dried tarragon.

5. Cut and butter a piece of parchment paper and cover the chicken breasts.

6. Bring the liquid to a simmer and reduce the temperature to poach the chicken.

7. Make a blond roux with 1 ounce (30 grams) butter and the flour; set aside to cool.

8. When the breasts are done, remove them from the liquid. Thicken the liquid with the roux. Add the cream. Simmer and reduce to the desired consistency.

9. Strain the sauce through cheesecloth and adjust the seasonings.

10. Serve each half breast napped with approximately 2 fluid ounces (60 milliliters) sauce; garnish each portion with a sprig of fresh tarragon.

Approximate values per 4-oz. (120-g) serving: **Calories** 250, **Total fat** 13 g, **Saturated fat** 7 g, **Cholesterol** 105 mg, **Sodium** 590 mg, **Total carbohydrates** 4 g, **Protein** 29 g, **Vitamin A** 10%

③ Covering the breasts with a piece of buttered parchment paper.

④ Adding the cream to the thickened sauce.

⑤ Plating the poached chicken breast.

Combination Cooking Methods

Braising and stewing use both dry and moist heat to produce a moist, flavorful product. The principal difference between braising and stewing when applied to meats is the size of the cut being cooked: Large cuts of meat are braised; smaller ones are stewed. Because most poultry is relatively small, this distinction does not readily apply in poultry cookery; therefore, the two cooking methods are discussed together here.

BRAISING AND STEWING

Braised or stewed poultry should be moist and fork tender. The poultry is always served with the liquid in which it was cooked. Ducks and geese are braised or stewed in much the same way as red meats. Chicken cacciatore, coq au vin and chicken fricassee are examples of braised or stewed chicken dishes.

Selecting Poultry to Braise or Stew

Braising and stewing, being slow, moist cooking processes, are often thought of as a means to tenderize tough meats. Although they can be used to tenderize older, tougher birds, these cooking methods are more often selected as a means of adding moisture and flavor to poultry that is inherently tender, such as young ducks and chickens. Typically, the birds are disjointed and cooked bone-in, just until done, so that they retain their juiciness.

Seasoning Poultry to Be Braised or Stewed

Braised or stewed items obtain much of their flavor from the cooking liquid and other ingredients added during the cooking process. The main item and the cooking liquid should be well seasoned. If other seasonings such as an onion piquet, sachet, bouquet garni or dried herbs and spices are required, they should be added at the beginning of the cooking process rather than at the end. This allows the flavors to blend and penetrate the larger pieces of poultry. If the poultry is dredged in flour before browning, seasonings may be added directly to the flour. As with all dishes using combination cooking methods, the finished dish should have the flavor of the poultry in the sauce and the moisture and flavor of the sauce in the poultry.

Cooking Temperatures

Some recipes, such as chicken cacciatore and coq au vin, require the main item to be thoroughly browned during the initial stages; others, such as chicken fricassee, do not. In either case, after the liquid is added, it is important to maintain a slow simmer rather than a rapid boil. This can be done on the stove top or in the oven. Low temperatures control the cooking and produce a tender, juicy finished product.

Determining Doneness

Tenderness is the key to determining doneness. It can be determined by inserting a kitchen fork into the poultry. There should be little resistance, and the poultry should freely fall off the fork. The pieces should retain their shape, however; if they fall apart, they are overdone. Small boneless pieces can be tested by cutting into them with a fork.

Accompaniments to Braised or Stewed Poultry

All braises and stews are cooked in a liquid that results in a sauce or broth served as part of the finished dish. Rice, pasta and boiled potatoes are natural accompaniments to almost any braised or stewed dish, as are boiled vegetables.

PROCEDURE FOR BRAISING OR STEWING POULTRY

1. Sear the main item in butter or oil, developing color as desired.
2. Add vegetables and other ingredients as called for in the recipe and sauté.
3. Add flour or roux if used.
4. Add the appropriate liquid.
5. Cover and simmer on the stove top or in the oven until done.
6. Add seasonings and garnishes at the appropriate times during the cooking process.
7. Finish the dish by adding cream or a liaison to the sauce or by adjusting its consistency. Adjust the seasonings.
8. Serve a portion of the poultry with the sauce and appropriate garnish.

CHICKEN FRICASSEE

MISE EN PLACE

▶ Cut chickens into 8 pieces.
▶ Peel onions and chop into medium dice.
▶ Prepare herb sachet.

Yield: 8 Servings, 2 pieces each **Method:** Braising

Frying chickens, 2 lb. 8 oz.–3 lb. (1.2–1.4 kg) each, cut into 8 pieces	2	2
Salt and white pepper	TT	TT
Clarified butter	3 fl. oz.	90 ml
Onions, medium dice	10 oz.	300 g
Flour	3 oz.	90 g
Dry white wine	8 fl. oz.	240 ml
Chicken stock	1 qt.	960 ml
Sachet:		
Bay leaf	1	1
Dried thyme	½ tsp.	2 ml
Peppercorns, cracked	½ tsp.	2 ml
Parsley stems	8	8
Garlic clove, crushed	1	1
Heavy cream	8 fl. oz.	240 ml
Nutmeg	TT	TT

1. Season the chicken with salt and white pepper.
2. Sauté the chicken in the butter without browning. Add the onions and continue to sauté until they are translucent.
3. Sprinkle the flour over the chicken and onions and stir to make a roux. Cook the roux for 2 minutes without browning.
4. Deglaze the pan with the wine. Add the stock and sachet; season with salt. Cover and simmer until done, approximately 30 to 45 minutes.

5 Remove the chicken from the pan and hold in a warm place. Strain the sauce through cheesecloth and return it to a clean pan.

6 Add the cream and bring the sauce to a simmer. Add the nutmeg and adjust the seasonings. Return the chicken to the sauce to reheat it for service.

Approximate values per 8-oz. (240-g) serving: **Calories** 700, **Total fat** 20 g, **Saturated fat** 12 g, **Cholesterol** 60 mg, **Sodium** 795 mg, **Total carbohydrates** 113 g, **Protein** 15 g, **Vitamin A** 20%

1 Sautéing the chicken and onions in butter.

2 Sprinkling the flour over the chicken.

3 Deglazing the pan with white wine.

4 Removing the chicken from the pot.

5 Straining the sauce through cheesecloth.

6 Returning the chicken to the sauce to reheat it for service.

1 List the six categories or kinds of poultry recognized by the USDA. How are these categories then divided into classes?

2 How should fresh poultry be stored? Discuss several procedures that should be followed carefully when working with poultry to prevent cross-contamination.

3 What is a suprême? Describe the step-by-step procedure for preparing a chicken suprême.

4 What is trussing? Why is this technique used with poultry?

5 Which poultry items are best suited for broiling or grilling? Explain your answer.

6 Describe the characteristics of properly roasted poultry. Which classes of poultry are recommended for roasting?

7 What is foie gras? Why must you be extremely careful when cooking foie gras?

QUESTIONS FOR DISCUSSION

Terms to Know

white meat	suprême
myoglobin	airline breast
dark meat	presentation side
tenderloin	trussing
giblets	poêléing
free-range	
breast bone or keel bone	

APRICOT AND BOURBON GRILLED CHICKEN

PENNSYLVANIA COLLEGE OF TECHNOLOGY, WILLIAMSPORT, PA

Chef Mary G. Trometter, Assistant Professor

Yield: 4 Servings　　　　　　　　　　　　　　**Method:** Grilling

Marinade:		
Dijon mustard	2 oz.	60 g
Dark brown sugar	2 oz.	60 g
Soy sauce	1 fl. oz.	30 ml
Bourbon	1 fl. oz.	30 ml
Worcestershire sauce	1 tsp.	5 ml
Whole chicken breasts, boneless, skinless, approx. 8 oz. (240 g) each	2	2
Basting sauce:		
Apricot preserves	2 oz.	60 g
White wine vinegar	1 fl. oz.	30 ml
Worcestershire sauce	2 tsp.	10 ml
Dijon mustard	2 tsp.	10 ml
Honey	2 tsp.	10 ml
Crushed red pepper flakes	¼ tsp.	2 ml
Onions, sliced into thin rings	4 oz.	120 g
Flour	2 oz.	60 g
Salt and pepper	TT	TT
Grilled vegetables	as needed	as needed

1. Combine the marinade ingredients and transfer to a shallow stainless steel pan.

2. Trim any excess fat from the chicken breasts. Split each breast into two pieces by removing the small piece of cartilage that joins the halves. Place the chicken in the marinade and turn several times to coat it well. Cover the pan with plastic wrap and refrigerate for 1 to 3 hours.

3. Combine the basting sauce ingredients in a small saucepan and simmer for 10 minutes to blend the flavors. Strain if desired and refrigerate until needed.

4. A few minutes before service, place the flour in a shallow pan and season with salt and pepper. Toss the onion rings in the seasoned flour to coat well. Shake off the excess flour and deep fry the rings at 350°F (180°C) until browned. Drain the rings on a paper towel-lined pan and hold in a warm place.

5. Remove the chicken from the marinade, pat dry and place on a preheated grill, presentation side down. Grill for approximately 2 minutes, then brush with the basting sauce. Carefully loosen the chicken from the grill with a spatula, then turn and brush with more basting sauce. Continue to baste frequently and grill until done. Serve with grilled vegetables. Garnish with the fried onion rings at service time.

Approximate values per serving: **Calories** 300, **Total fat** 11 g, **Saturated fat** 1.5 g, **Cholesterol** 95 mg, **Sodium** 400 mg, **Total carbohydrates** 31 g, **Protein** 36 g, **Iron** 10%

CHICKEN YAKITORI

Yakitori is a popular Japanese dish consisting of small pieces of chicken threaded on wooden skewers and grilled over hardwood aromatic charcoal. Yakitori stands and restaurants are ubiquitous in Japan, where quality is judged by the sauce in which the chicken is dipped before grilling.

Yield: 8 Servings	**Method:** Grilling	
Dark soy sauce	8 fl. oz.	240 ml
Sake	8 fl. oz.	240 ml
Granulated sugar	2 oz.	60 g
Chicken breast halves, boneless, skinless, approximately 5 ounces (150 grams) each	8	8
Cornstarch	1 Tbsp.	15 ml
Sesame seeds	1 Tbsp.	15 ml

1. Combine the soy sauce, sake and sugar. Set aside 8 fluid ounces (240 milliliters) of the mixture for making the sauce in Step 3.
2. Brush the chicken with the remaining soy sauce mixture and grill over hot charcoal until done, basting regularly.
3. To make the sauce, combine 2 fluid ounces (60 milliliters) of the soy sauce mixture set aside for this purpose with the cornstarch. Bring the remainder to a boil in a small saucepan and stir in the cornstarch slurry. Stirring constantly, continue boiling until the sauce thickens. Simmer 1 minute.
4. Serve each breast sliced and fanned with a small amount of the sauce accompanied with short-grain white rice. Garnish with sesame seeds.

Approximate values per 6-oz. (180-g) serving: **Calories** 240, **Total fat** 4.5 g, **Saturated fat** 1 g, **Cholesterol** 95 mg, **Sodium** 1700 mg, **Total carbohydrates** 12 g, **Protein** 37 g

ROMAN-STYLE FREE-RANGE CHICKEN

CHEF ODETTE FADA, New York, NY

Yield: 4 Servings	**Method:** Sautéing	
Free-range chicken breast halves, suprême cut	4	4
Extra virgin olive oil	1 fl. oz.	30 ml
Salt	TT	TT
Vegetable or chicken broth	8 fl. oz.	240 ml
Garlic cloves, chopped fine	4	4
Anchovy fillets in oil, chopped fine	3	3
Fresh rosemary, chopped fine	TT	TT
White wine vinegar	1 fl. oz.	30 ml.

1. Sauté the chicken breasts in the olive oil, skin side down. Season with salt.
2. Cook until the chicken begins to brown, then turn it and cook for an additional 2 minutes.
3. Add the broth and reduce by two-thirds, approximately 5 minutes.
4. Combine the garlic, anchovies, rosemary and vinegar.
5. When the chicken is done, add the vinegar mixture to the cooking liquid.
6. Remove the chicken from the heat, slice each breast into six pieces and arrange on a hot plate. Pour the sauce over the sliced chicken.

Approximate values per 7.5-oz. (225 g) serving: **Calories** 360, **Total fat** 19 g, **Saturated fat** 4.5 g, **Cholesterol** 125 mg, **Sodium** 820 mg, **Total carbohydrates** 3 g, **Protein** 46 g, **Vitamin A** 15%

GRILLED CORNISH GAME HENS WITH BASIL BUTTER

Yield: 4 Servings		**Method:** Grilling
Rock Cornish Game hens, whole	4	4
Fresh basil leaves	16	16
White Wine Marinade (page 404)	1 pt.	480 ml
Basil butter (page 211)	6 oz.	180 g

1. Remove the backbone and breast bone from each game hen. The birds will lie flat and remain in one piece.
2. Make a slit below each leg and tuck the leg bone into the slit.
3. Carefully slide two basil leaves under the skin over each breast to cover the meat.
4. Marinate the game hens in the White Wine Marinade for 1 to 2 hours.
5. Heat and prepare the grill.
6. Remove the game hens from the marinade and pat dry.
7. Melt approximately 4 ounces (120 grams) basil butter, leaving enough for eight thin slices to be served with the finished dish.
8. Brush the game hens with the melted butter and place them on the grill, skin side down. Grill the game hens, turning once and basting periodically with the melted basil butter. Finish in the oven until the hens reach an internal temperature of 165°F (74°C), if necessary.
9. Serve the game hens with a slice of basil butter melting over each breast.

Approximate values per serving: **Calories** 690, **Total fat** 50 g, **Saturated fat** 26 g, **Cholesterol** 260 mg, **Sodium** 1070 mg, **Total carbohydrates** 0 g, **Protein** 60 g, **Vitamin A** 40%

1. Marinating the game hens in white wine marinade.

2. Drying the game hens.

3. Brushing the game hens with melted basil butter.

4. Grilling the game hens.

5. Serving the game hens with a slice of basil butter.

ROAST CORNISH GAME HEN
WITH WILD RICE STUFFING

Yield: 6 Servings   **Method:** Roasting

Stuffing:

Onion, fine dice	3 oz.	90 g
Mushrooms, chopped	6 oz.	180 g
Whole butter, melted	6 oz.	180 g
Wild rice, cooked	12 oz.	360 g
Dried thyme, crushed	½ tsp.	2 ml
Dried marjoram, crushed	½ tsp.	2 ml
Salt and pepper	TT	TT
Rock Cornish game hens	6	6

1 Sauté the onion and mushrooms in 2 ounces (60 grams) of the melted butter until tender. Cool.

2 Stir in the rice and herbs and season to taste with salt and pepper. Stuffing can be made up to 2 days ahead and refrigerated before using.

3 Stuff the cavity of each hen loosely with the rice mixture. Truss and place in a roasting pan.

4 Brush the hens with the remaining butter and season with salt and pepper. Roast at 400°F (200°C) for 15 minutes.

5 Reduce the oven temperature to 300°F (150°C) and roast until the internal temperature reaches 165°F (74°C), approximately 30 minutes. Baste two or three times with melted butter.

6 Serve the hens with a pan gravy or a sauce made separately, such as mushroom sauce.

Approximate values per 14-oz. (420-g) serving: **Calories** 970, **Total fat** 65 g, **Saturated fat** 26 g, **Cholesterol** 330 mg, **Sodium** 1580 mg, **Total carbohydrates** 12 g, **Protein** 86 g, **Vitamin A** 35%, **Iron** 25%

1 Loosely stuff each hen with some of the wild rice mixture.

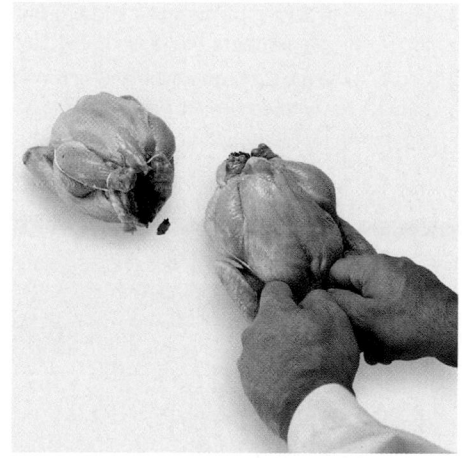

2 Truss the hens.

3 The game hens plated for service.

CHICKEN LEG STUFFED WITH MUSHROOMS AND PROSCIUTTO

Yield: 6 Servings   **Method:** Roasting

Chicken leg and thigh quarters, whole	6	6
Whole butter	1 oz.	30 g
Green onions, sliced	3	3
Prosciutto, small dice	4 oz.	120 g
Mushrooms, chanterelles, morels or other varieties as desired, sliced	6 oz.	180 g
Leek, small dice	2 oz.	60 g
Heavy cream	6 fl. oz.	180 ml
Bread crumbs, fresh	4 oz.	120 g
Salt and pepper	TT	TT
Whole butter, melted	1 oz.	30 g
Suprême Sauce (page 204)	12 fl. oz.	360 ml
Sautéed vegetables	as needed for garnish	

1. Bone the chicken legs and thighs as described on page 403, leaving the skin attached.
2. Heat the butter in a large sauté pan. Add the onions and prosciutto and sauté for 30 seconds. Add the mushrooms and leek and sauté for 2 minutes or until the mushrooms are tender.
3. Add the cream and reduce by half. Remove the pan from the heat. Add the bread crumbs and toss to combine all ingredients. Season the stuffing with salt and pepper.
4. Divide the stuffing into six portions. Open the chicken legs on a cutting board with the flesh side up. Season the legs with salt and pepper. Stuff each leg with a portion of the stuffing. Close the chicken legs around the stuffing. Tie the stuffed legs with butcher's twine at close intervals so the legs keep their shape during cooking.
5. Place the legs in a roasting pan and brush with melted butter. Roast the legs at 375°F (190°C) until the internal temperature reaches 164°F (74°C), approximately 30 minutes.
6. Remove the legs from the oven and remove the twine. Slice the chicken into ½-inch- (12-millimeter-) thick slices. Nap each plate with Suprême Sauce and fan the slices of stuffed chicken on the sauce. Serve with an appropriate accompaniment such as sautéed vegetables.

Approximate values per serving: **Calories** 540, **Total fat** 37 g, **Saturated fat** 17 g, **Cholesterol** 185 mg, **Sodium** 610 mg, **Total carbohydrates** 13 g, **Protein** 38 g, **Vitamin A** 20%

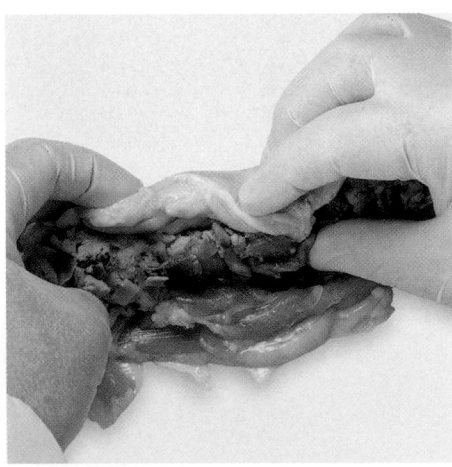

1. Closing the chicken leg around the stuffing.

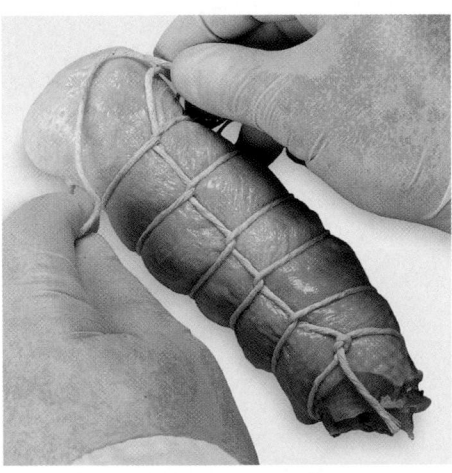

2. Tying the chicken leg with butcher's twine.

3. The sliced chicken leg.

CHICKEN BREAST SAUTÉ
WITH ROASTED RED PEPPER SAUCE

NASHVILLE STATE TECH CULINARY, NASHVILLE, TN

Yield: 4 Servings   **Method:** Sautéing

Olive oil	1 fl. oz.	30 ml
Chicken breast halves, boneless, skinless, 6–8 oz. (180–240 g) each	4	4
Salt and pepper	TT	TT
Flour	as needed for dredging	
Onion, medium dice	1 oz.	30 g
Garlic cloves, minced	2	2
White wine	2 fl. oz.	60 ml
Chicken stock	4 fl. oz.	120 ml
Roma tomato concassée	8 fl. oz.	240 ml
Red bell pepper, roasted, seeded, medium dice	1	1
Mushrooms, sliced	2 oz.	60 g
Unsalted butter	1 oz.	30 g
Heavy cream	6 fl. oz.	180 ml
Green onion, sliced	2 Tbsp.	30 ml
Parmesan, grated	as needed	as needed

1. Heat the olive oil in a sauté pan. Season the chicken breasts with salt and pepper and dredge them in flour. Sear the chicken breasts in the hot oil. Remove the chicken from the sauté pan and hold on a plate in a warm oven, preheated to 200°F (94°C).

2. Add the onion and garlic to the hot oil and sauté for 2 minutes. Deglaze the pan with the wine and then add the stock, tomato concassée and bell pepper. Bring to a simmer and reduce the liquid by half.

3. In a separate pan, sauté the mushrooms in the butter and keep warm.

4. Warm the cream slightly and add it to the sauce. Simmer the sauce until it starts to thicken. Return the chicken breasts and the juice that has accumulated on the plate to the pan and simmer until the chicken is done, approximately 2 minutes. Season the sauce with salt and pepper.

5. Serve garnished with the sautéed mushrooms and green onion. Sprinkle with Parmesan.

Note: If a smoother sauce is desired, purée the sauce before adding the chicken.

Approximate values per serving: **Calories** 480, **Total fat** 29 g, **Saturated fat** 16 g, **Cholesterol** 185 mg, **Sodium** 210 mg, **Total carbohydrates** 8 g, **Protein** 42 g, **Vitamin A** 60%, **Vitamin C** 110%, **Iron** 10%

CHICKEN STUFFED WITH SPINACH AND RICOTTA CHEESE IN SAFFRON SAUCE

SIMPLICITY CATERING, FALLS CHURCH, VA

Chef Leland Atkinson

Yield: 4 Servings **Method:** Sautéing

Spinach, stemmed	1 lb.	480 g
Ricotta	4 oz.	120 g
Egg whites, lightly beaten	2	2
Salt and pepper	TT	TT
Airline chicken breasts, skin on, 9 oz. (270 g) each	4	4
Clarified butter	1 fl. oz.	30 ml
White wine	1 pt.	480 ml
Saffron	1 pinch	1 pinch
Chicken velouté	8 fl. oz.	240 ml
Heavy cream, hot	2 fl. oz.	60 ml

1. Blanch, refresh and drain the spinach. Squeeze it tightly to remove as much moisture as possible, then chop it finely.
2. To make the stuffing, combine the ricotta, egg whites and spinach in a mixing bowl; season to taste.
3. Place the chicken breasts on a cutting board, skin side down. Using a boning knife, carefully make a pocket that runs the length of each breast.
4. Put the stuffing in a pastry bag and pipe the stuffing into each pocket. Do not overfill the chicken breasts because the stuffing will expand as it cooks.
5. Sauté the chicken in the butter until well browned. Transfer the chicken to a sheet pan and finish in a 350°F (180°C) oven, approximately 10 to 12 minutes.
6. Deglaze the sauté pan with the wine.
7. Add the saffron, bring to a boil and reduce by half.
8. Add the velouté and the cream. Adjust the seasonings and consistency; strain.
9. Ladle the sauce onto four warm plates. Slice the chicken and arrange it in the sauce; garnish as desired.

Approximate values per 17-oz. (510-g) serving: **Calories** 700, **Total fat** 33 g, **Saturated fat** 16 g, **Cholesterol** 215 mg, **Sodium** 560 mg, **Total carbohydrates** 13 g, **Protein** 65 g, **Vitamin A** 230%, **Vitamin C** 50%, **Iron** 30%

CHICKEN AND SNOW PEAS IN BLACK BEAN SAUCE

Yield: 4 Servings **Method:** Stir-frying

Chicken breasts, boneless, skinless	2 lb.	960 g
Egg white	1	1
Chinese rice wine	6 fl. oz.	180 ml
Cornstarch	2 Tbsp.	30 ml
Soy sauce	2 fl. oz.	60 ml
Granulated sugar	2 tsp.	10 ml
Onions, 6–8 oz. (120–240 g) each	2	2
Peanut oil	4 fl. oz.	120 ml
Garlic, minced	1 Tbsp.	15 ml
Fresh ginger, minced	2 tsp.	10 ml
Fermented black beans, mashed	3 Tbsp.	45 ml
Snow peas, fresh	4 oz.	120 g

1. Slice the chicken into thin strips, approximately 1½ inches × ¼ inch (4 centimeters × 0.6 centimeter).
2. Combine the egg white, one-third of the wine and 1 tablespoon (15 milliliters) cornstarch. Add the chicken and refrigerate for 2 hours.
3. For the sauce, mix the soy sauce, sugar and the remaining wine and cornstarch.
4. Quarter the onions and separate the layers.
5. Stir-fry the chicken in 3 fluid ounces (90 milliliters) oil. Remove and set aside.
6. If necessary, add all the remaining oil and stir-fry the garlic and ginger for 30 seconds. Add the onions and mashed beans and stir-fry for 30 seconds. Add the snow peas and cook for 1 minute.
7. Return the chicken to the wok, add the sauce mixture and stir-fry until hot and the sauce has thickened.
8. Serve immediately with short-grain white rice and a colorful vegetable garnish.

VARIATION:

Add 2 ounces (60 grams) sliced mushrooms and reduce the amount of snow peas by half.

Approximate values per serving: **Calories** 750, **Total fat** 46 g, **Saturated fat** 10 g, **Cholesterol** 190 mg, **Sodium** 1050 mg, **Total carbohydrates** 14 g, **Protein** 71 g, **Vitamin C** 25%

CHICKEN AND MUSHROOM CRÊPES WITH SAUCE MORNAY

PENNSYLVANIA COLLEGE OF TECHNOLOGY, WILLIAMSPORT, PA
Chef Mary G. Trometter, Assistant Professor

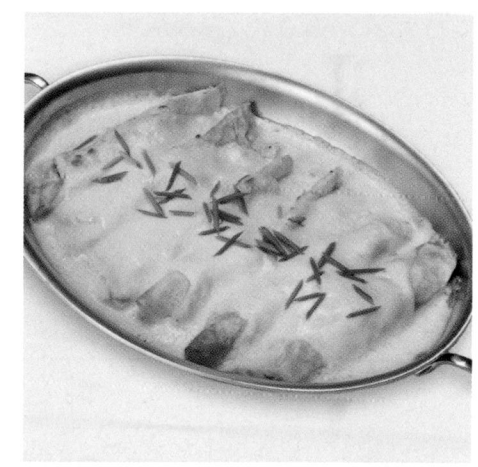

Yield: 6 Crêpes   **Method:** Poaching

Chicken stock	1 pt.	480 ml
Salt	TT	TT
Chicken, boneless, skinless	1 lb.	480 g
Mushrooms, sliced	5 oz.	150 g
Clarified butter	½ fl. oz.	15 ml
Fresh thyme, tarragon and parsley, minced	1 Tbsp.	15 ml
Black pepper	TT	TT
Savory Crêpes (page 549), 9 in. (22 cm) each	6	6
Mornay sauce (page 202)	1 pt.	480 ml
Paprika	as needed for garnish	
Fresh chives, sliced	as needed for garnish	

1. Bring the stock to a simmer and season with the salt.
2. Poach the chicken in the stock until done. Remove the chicken from the stock, reserving the stock. Allow the chicken to cool slightly and then cut it into julienne strips.
3. Sauté the mushrooms in the butter with the herbs until the mushrooms are tender. Season the mixture with salt and pepper. Combine the chicken with the mushrooms and refrigerate until cold.
4. Divide the chicken and mushrooms into six portions. Spoon one portion of the mixture into the center of each crêpe. Roll the crêpe around the mixture and place in a buttered baking dish, seam side down.
5. Heat the Mornay sauce over medium heat; thin with a portion of the reserved poaching liquid if necessary. Sprinkle with paprika if desired. Bake at 350°F (180°C) until hot and lightly brown, approximately 20 minutes. Garnish with sliced chives.

Approximate values per crêpe: **Calories** 420, **Total fat** 27 g, **Saturated fat** 15 g, **Cholesterol** 185 mg, **Sodium** 960 mg, **Total carbohydrates** 23 g, **Protein** 25 g, **Vitamin A** 15%, **Calcium** 15%

CHICKEN CURRY

Yield: 4 Servings	**Method:** Simmering	
Onions, small dice	8 oz.	240 g
Garlic, crushed	2 tsp.	10 ml
Ghee or clarified butter	1 fl. oz.	30 ml
Wet masala:		
Fresh ginger, fine dice	2 oz.	60 g
Turmeric, ground	1½ tsp.	8 ml
Coriander seeds, ground	1½ tsp.	8 ml
Cumin seeds, ground	1 tsp.	5 ml
Cayenne pepper	1 tsp.	5 ml
Fenugreek, ground	½ tsp.	2 ml
Coconut milk	20 fl. oz.	600 ml
Roasting chicken, 3 lb. (1.4 kg), cut in 8 pieces	1	1
Salt	1 tsp.	5 ml
Green chiles, slit lengthwise	3	3
Lemon juice	1 fl. oz.	30 ml

1. Stir-fry the onions and garlic in the ghee or butter until the onions are golden brown.
2. To make the wet masala, mix the ginger, turmeric, coriander, cumin, cayenne pepper and fenugreek; add just enough of the coconut milk to form a paste.
3. Add the wet masala to the onions and stir-fry for 8 minutes.
4. Add the chicken pieces and cook, turning them frequently, for 6 to 8 minutes.
5. Add the remaining coconut milk, salt and chiles. Bring to a boil, cover and reduce to a simmer. Cook until the chicken is done, approximately 45 minutes.
6. Just before service, stir in the lemon juice and adjust the seasonings. Serve with Saffron Rice (page 667) and a chutney.

Approximate values per serving: **Calories** 1130, **Total fat** 64 g, **Saturated fat** 39 g, **Cholesterol** 285 mg, **Sodium** 1070 mg, **Total carbohydrates** 32 g, **Protein** 107 g, **Vitamin C** 25%, **Iron** 70%

COQ AU VIN

lardons diced, blanched, fried bacon

Yield: 8 Servings, 2 pieces each	**Method:** Braising	
Chickens, 2 lb. 8 oz.–3 lb. (1.2–1.4 kg) each	2	2
Flour	as needed for dredging	
Salt and pepper	TT	TT
Clarified butter	2 fl. oz.	60 ml
Brandy	4 fl. oz.	120 ml
Bouquet garni:		
Carrot stick, 4 in. (10 cm)	1	1
Leek, split, 4-in. (10-cm) piece	1	1
Fresh thyme	1 sprig	1 sprig
Bay leaf	1	1
Garlic cloves, peeled and crushed	6	6
Red wine	24 fl. oz.	720 ml
Chicken stock	16 fl. oz.	480 ml
Bacon **lardons**	4 oz.	120 g
Pearl onions, peeled	18	18
Mushrooms, medium, quartered	10	10
Beurre manié	as needed	as needed

1. Cut each chicken into eight pieces and dredge in flour seasoned with salt and pepper.
2. Heat the clarified butter in a 12-inch (30-centimeter) braiser; brown the chicken in two or three batches.
3. Add the brandy and ignite. When the flame dies, add the bouquet garni, garlic, wine and stock. Bring to a boil, then reduce to a simmer.
4. Cover the pan and simmer until the chicken is tender, approximately 40 minutes.
5. In a separate pan, sauté the bacon until the fat begins to render. Add the onions and sauté until they begin to brown. Cook the bacon and onions covered, over low heat, until the onions are tender. Add the mushrooms and cook them until tender.
6. Remove the chicken from the pan and adjust the sauce's consistency with the beurre manié. Strain the sauce through a china cap and adjust the seasonings.
7. Spoon the bacon, onions and mushrooms onto a serving platter, place the chicken over them and ladle the sauce over the finished dish.

Approximate values per 12-oz. (360-g) serving: **Calories** 860, **Total fat** 51 g, **Saturated fat** 17 g, **Cholesterol** 330 mg, **Sodium** 910 mg, **Total carbohydrates** 17 g, **Protein** 83 g, **Vitamin A** 60%, **Iron** 35%

CHICKEN WITH 40 CLOVES OF GARLIC

Yield: 4 Servings, 2 pieces each   **Method:** Braising

Chicken, 2 lb. 8 oz. (1.2 kg), cut in 8 pieces	1	1
Dry white wine	26 fl. oz.	780 ml
Flour	as needed for dredging	
Salt and pepper	TT	TT
Olive oil	2 Tbsp.	30 ml
Garlic cloves, unpeeled	40	40
Fresh thyme	4 sprigs	4 sprigs
Fresh rosemary	1 sprig	1 sprig
French bread croutons	8	8
Fresh parsley, chopped	as needed for garnish	

1. Marinate the chicken pieces in the wine for 1 to 2 hours under refrigeration. Remove and pat dry.
2. Dredge the chicken in flour and season lightly with salt and pepper. Sauté the chicken in the oil.
3. Remove the chicken from the pan and sauté the garlic until it begins to brown. Place the chicken on top of the garlic in a single layer. Add the wine marinade and herbs and cover.
4. Braise in a 325°F (160°C) oven until tender, approximately 45 minutes.
5. Remove the chicken and garlic from the pan and reserve. Remove and discard the herbs. Place the pan on the stove top and reduce the sauce until slightly thick. Season with salt and pepper.
6. Serve two pieces of chicken and several of the garlic cloves resting on two French bread croutons. Top with a portion of the sauce and garnish with chopped parsley.

Approximate values per 12½-oz. (375-g) serving: **Calories** 600, **Total fat** 18 g, **Saturated fat** 4 g, **Cholesterol** 240 mg, **Sodium** 820 mg, **Total carbohydrates** 20 g, **Protein** 91 g, **Vitamin C** 15%, **Iron** 25%

COUNTRY BRAISED CHICKEN

NEWBURY COLLEGE, BROOKLINE, MA

Senior Instructor Scott Doughty

Yield: 8 Servings　　　　　　　　　　　　　**Method:** Braising

Flour	6 oz.	180 g
Salt	1 Tbsp.	15 ml
Black pepper	1 tsp.	5 ml
Paprika	1 tsp.	5 ml
Cayenne pepper	1 tsp.	5 ml
Chickens, 3 lb. (1.4 kg) each, cut into 8 pieces	2	2
Whole butter	1 oz.	30 g
Vegetable oil	1 fl. oz.	30 ml
Tomatoes	2 lb.	960 g
Onions, small dice	3	3
Green bell peppers, chopped	4	4
Garlic cloves, chopped	3	3
Curry powder	1 Tbsp.	15 ml
Mace, ground	1 tsp.	5 ml
Chicken stock	as needed	as needed
Almonds, toasted	2 oz.	60 g
Green onions, thinly sliced	as needed for garnish	

1. Combine the flour, salt, black pepper, paprika and cayenne pepper. Dredge the chicken in the seasoned flour.
2. Pan-fry the chicken in the butter and oil, skin side down, until evenly browned. Turn and cook on the other side for 30 seconds. Remove the chicken and hold.
3. Prepare tomato concassée. Sweat the onions and bell peppers with the garlic, curry powder and mace in a sauté pan. Add the tomato concassée.
4. Place the browned chicken on top of the vegetables, cover and braise to an internal temperature of 165°F (74°C), approximately 25 minutes. Remove the chicken pieces as they are done, beginning with the breast pieces. Continue cooking until all of the chicken is done.
5. Degrease the sauce if necessary, and adjust its consistency with the stock. Then adjust the seasonings and pour the sauce into a serving pan. Place the chicken on top of the sauce and garnish with the toasted almonds and slivered green onions.

Approximate values per serving: **Calories** 340, **Total fat** 23 g, **Saturated fat** 6 g, **Cholesterol** 30 mg, **Sodium** 470 mg, **Total carbohydrates** 24 g, **Protein** 11 g, **Vitamin A** 30%, **Vitamin C** 130%, **Iron** 15%

CHICKEN POT PIE

Yield: 16 Servings, 2 biscuits each

Ingredient	US	Metric
Whole butter	1 oz.	30 g
White mushrooms, quartered	8 oz.	240 g
Salt and pepper	TT	TT
Red potatoes, medium dice	6 oz.	180 g
Carrots, medium dice	6 oz.	180 g
Pearl onions	6 oz.	180 g
Peas	6 oz.	180 g
Corn kernels	6 oz.	180 g
Chicken velouté	3 pt.	1.4 lt
Heavy cream	8 fl. oz.	240 ml
Chicken, cooked, large dice	2 lb. 8 oz.	1.2 kg
Biscuit dough, cut into small discs	as needed	as needed
Egg wash	as needed	as needed

1. Heat the butter in a small sauté pan and sauté the mushrooms. Season with salt and pepper.
2. Blanch or steam the potatoes, carrots, onions, peas and corn separately until tender.
3. Bring the velouté to a simmer. Add the cream and simmer for 5 minutes.
4. Add the chicken, potatoes and vegetables to the sauce, season with salt and pepper and ladle into a shallow half-size hotel or other pan.
5. Cover the pan with the biscuit dough. Egg-wash the top of the dough. Bake at 400°F (200°C) until the top is well browned, approximately 15 minutes.

VARIATIONS:

Substitute a sheet of flaky pie dough or puff pastry for the biscuit dough. Do not cut. Brush the edges of the pan with egg wash, then cover the pan with the dough. Egg wash the top of the pastry. Make one or two small slices in the top of the dough to allow steam to escape as the pie cooks.

Turkey Pot Pie—Substitute an equal amount of turkey for the chicken.

Approximate values per serving, without crust: **Calories** 330, **Total fat** 18 g, **Saturated fat** 9 g, **Cholesterol** 110 mg, **Sodium** 530 mg, **Total carbohydrates** 16 g, **Protein** 27 g, **Vitamin A** 70%

WARM DUCK BREAST SALAD WITH ASIAN SPICES AND HAZELNUT VINAIGRETTE

CHEF JOHN ASH, SANTA ROSA, CA

Yield: 4 Servings	**Method:** Sautéing	
Whole boneless duck breasts, 12 oz. (360 g) each	2	2
Marinade:		
Garlic, minced	1 tsp.	5 ml
Green onion, minced	2 Tbsp.	30 ml
Oyster sauce	2 tsp.	10 ml
Light soy sauce	1 tsp.	5 ml
Rice wine or dry sherry	1 tsp.	5 ml
Sugar	1 tsp.	5 ml
Five-spice powder	½ tsp.	2 ml
Hazelnut vinaigrette:		
Garlic, minced	1 Tbsp.	15 ml
Hazelnut oil	3 fl. oz.	90 ml
Walnut or light olive oil	3 fl. oz.	90 ml
Fresh chives, minced	1 Tbsp.	15 ml
Balsamic vinegar	2 Tbsp.	30 ml
Light soy sauce	1 tsp.	5 ml
Sugar	¼ tsp.	1 ml
Mixed baby greens	4–6 oz.	120–180 g
Hazelnuts, toasted, skinned and chopped coarse	2 oz.	60 g

1. Trim the excess fat from the duck breasts and separate the breasts into two halves.
2. Combine the marinade ingredients. Thoroughly coat the duck with the marinade and marinate for at least 2 hours.
3. Combine the hazelnut vinaigrette ingredients at least 2 hours before service so that the flavors develop.
4. Wipe the marinade from the breasts and sauté them, skin side down first, in a dry sauté pan until medium rare, approximately 2½ minutes per side. Do not overcook.
5. Arrange a mixture of baby greens on four plates. Slice the breasts on the diagonal and arrange on the plates with the greens. Drizzle the hazelnut vinaigrette over the greens, sprinkle with hazelnuts and serve.

Approximate values per 9-oz. (270-g) serving: **Calories** 820, **Total fat** 68 g, **Saturated fat** 10 g, **Cholesterol** 230 mg, **Sodium** 240 mg, **Total carbohydrates** 7 g, **Protein** 44 g, **Vitamin C** 20%, **Iron** 35%

DUCK CONFIT

Yield: 4 Servings

Duck, 4 lb. (1.9 kg), cut in 4 pieces	1	1
Kosher salt	2 Tbsp.	30 ml
Black pepper, cracked	1 tsp.	5 ml
Bay leaves, crumbled	4	4
Fresh thyme	6 sprigs	6 sprigs
Garlic cloves, crushed	6	6
Duck or goose fat, melted	2 lb.	960 g

confit (kohn-FEE) meat or poultry (often lightly salt-cured) slowly cooked and preserved in its own fat and served hot

1. Rub the duck with the salt. Place it skin side down in a roasting pan just large enough to hold the pieces in one layer; season with the pepper, bay leaves, thyme and garlic. Cover and refrigerate overnight.

2. Dry the duck with clean paper towels. Place it, skin side up, in a clean roasting pan, just large enough to hold the pieces in one layer. Bake the duck at 325°F (160°C) until brown, approximately 15 to 20 minutes. Add enough melted duck or goose fat to cover the pieces completely.

3. Cover the pan and cook in a 300°F (150°C) oven until the duck is very tender, approximately 2 hours.

4. Remove the duck from the fat and place in a deep hotel pan. Ladle enough of the cooking fat over the pieces to cover them completely. Be careful not to add any of the cooking juices.

5. Cover the pan and refrigerate for 2 days to allow the flavors to mellow.

6. To serve, remove the duck from the fat and scrape off the excess fat. Bake at 350°F (180°C) until the skin is crisp and the meat is hot, approximately 30 minutes.

Approximate values per serving: **Calories** 670, **Total fat** 16 g, **Saturated fat** 4.5 g, **Cholesterol** 700 mg, **Sodium** 3960 mg, **Total carbohydrates** 6 g, **Protein** 125 g, **Vitamin C** 25%, **Iron** 130%

1. Season the duck.

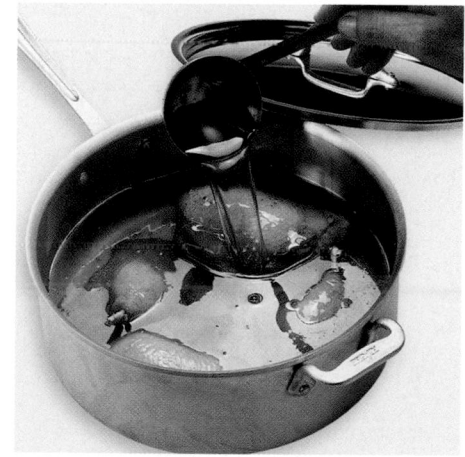

2. After the duck browns, cover it with melted fat and return it to the oven.

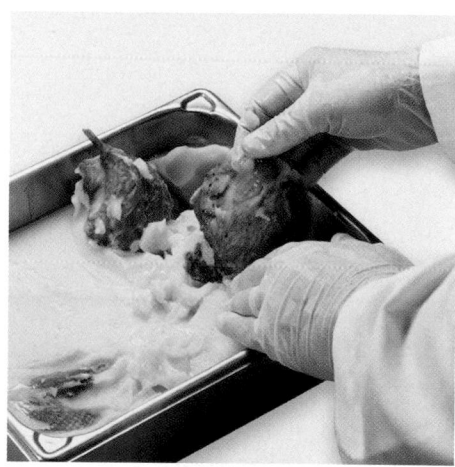

3. Remove the duck from the congealed fat, scraping off the excess.

DUCK À L'ORANGE

SIMPLICITY CATERING, FALLS CHURCH, VA
Chef Leland Atkinson

Yield: 4 Servings **Method:** Roasting

Duckling, 5–6 lb. (2.4–2.8 kg)	1	1
Salt and pepper	TT	TT
Duck or chicken stock	8 fl. oz.	240 ml
Sugar	1 Tbsp.	15 ml
Champagne vinegar	1 Tbsp.	15 ml
Brandy	2 Tbsp.	30 ml
Orange juice	12 fl. oz.	360 ml
Lemon juice	from 1 lemon	from 1 lemon
Whole butter	1 tsp.	5 ml
Orange zest, julienne	4 Tbsp.	60 ml
Oranges, peeled and sectioned	4	4

1. Prick the duck with a fork and season well with salt and pepper.
2. Roast the duck at 400°F (200°C) for 15 minutes. Reduce the heat to 350°F (180°C) and cook until the internal temperature reaches 165°F (74°C) and the meat is tender, approximately 45 to 60 minutes. Remove the duck from the roasting pan and hold in a warm place.
3. Degrease the roasting pan. Place the pan on the stove top and deglaze with the stock.
4. Melt the sugar and vinegar together in a saucepan and lightly caramelize the mixture.
5. Remove the caramelized sugar from the stove top and add the brandy.
6. Add the stock, pan drippings and fruit juices to the pan of sugar and reduce until the sauce is slightly thickened, approximately 10 to 15 minutes. Monté au beurre. Strain and degrease the sauce.
7. Blanch the orange zest in boiling water.
8. Place the duck on a warm serving platter. Arrange the orange sections around it. Sprinkle the zest over the duck. Pour the sauce over the duck and serve additional sauce on the side.

Approximate values per 28-oz. (840-g) serving: **Calories** 1810, **Total fat** 147 g, **Saturated fat** 54 g, **Cholesterol** 475 mg, **Sodium** 1050 mg, **Total carbohydrates** 30 g, **Protein** 91 g, **Vitamin A** 60%, **Vitamin C** 190%, **Iron** 50%

TURKEY BURGERS

Yield: 4 Servings **Method:** Grilling

Fresh ginger, minced	2 tsp.	10 ml
Garlic, chopped	1 tsp.	5 ml
Sesame oil	1 tsp.	5 ml
White mushrooms, chopped	4 oz.	120 g
Green onion, chopped fine	1	1
Ground turkey	20 oz.	600 g
Salt	½ tsp.	2 ml
Black pepper	¼ tsp.	1 ml
Glaze:		
Soy sauce	4 tsp.	20 ml
Sesame oil	2 tsp.	10 ml
Fresh ginger, minced	½ tsp.	2 ml
Garlic, chopped	1 tsp.	5 ml
Soft bagels, flatbread or other bread as desired	4 pieces	4 pieces
Sesame seeds	4 tsp.	20 ml
Lettuce and tomato	as needed for garnish	

1. Sauté the ginger and garlic in the sesame oil for 1 minute. Add the mushrooms and onion and sauté approximately 1 minute longer. Do not fully cook the mushrooms; allow them to retain most of their liquid in order to add moisture to the finished burgers. Remove the mushroom mixture from the heat, spread on a sheet pan and refrigerate until cold.

2. Combine the cold mushroom mixture with the ground turkey, salt and pepper and mix well. Form the mixture into four patties.

3. Stir the glaze ingredients together.

4. Oil the grate of a hot grill. Brush the burgers with the glaze and grill to an internal temperature of 165°F (74°C), basting occasionally with the glaze.

5. Serve each burger open-faced on a toasted bagel or warm flatbread. Sprinkle with sesame seeds and serve accompanied by lettuce leaves, tomato slices or other garnishes as desired.

Approximate values per serving: **Calories** 370, **Total fat** 17 g, **Saturated fat** 4 g, **Cholesterol** 110 mg, **Sodium** 960 mg, **Total carbohydrates** 22 g, **Protein** 30 g, **Iron** 20%

TURKEY MEATLOAF

Yield: 8 Servings, 7 oz. (210 g) each   **Method:** Baking

Onions, small dice	8 oz.	240 g
Celery, small dice	3 oz.	90 g
Olive oil	1 fl. oz.	30 ml
Garlic cloves, minced	3	3
Dried thyme	2 tsp.	10 ml
Dried sage	1 tsp.	5 ml
Salt	1 tsp.	5 ml
Black pepper, freshly ground	½ tsp.	2 ml
Ground turkey	2½ lb.	1.2 kg
Wheat bran	2 oz.	60 g
Ketchup	2 oz.	60 g
Worcestershire sauce	1 Tbsp.	15 ml
Italian parsley, chopped fine	1 Tbsp.	15 ml
Egg whites, beaten	2	2

1. Sauté the onions and celery in oil until translucent but not brown. Add the garlic, herbs, salt and pepper and sauté for 2 minutes. Remove from the pan and cool.

2. Place the turkey in a bowl and add the bran, ketchup, Worcestershire sauce, parsley and egg whites and mix well. Stir in the cooled onion mixture and adjust the seasonings.

3. Spray a 9-inch × 5-inch × 3-inch (22.5-centimeter × 12.5-centimeter × 7.5-centimeter) loaf pan with nonstick cooking spray and fill the pan with the turkey mixture.

4. Bake the loaf at 350°F (180°C) to an internal temperature of 165°F (74°C), approximately 1 hour 20 minutes.

5. Allow the meatloaf to cool in the pan for 15 minutes. Remove from the pan, slice and serve.

VARIATION:

The turkey meatloaf mixture can be formed into meatballs of the desired size, browned in a sauté pan, finished in the oven and used in place of traditional meatballs in any recipe.

Approximate values per serving: **Calories** 290, **Total fat** 16 g, **Saturated fat** 3.5 g, **Cholesterol** 110 mg, **Sodium** 560 mg, **Total carbohydrates** 11 g, **Protein** 27 g, **Vitamin C** 15%, **Iron** 20%

TURKEY SCALLOPINE WITH CAPERS AND LEMON

Yield: 4 Servings   **Method:** Sautéing

Turkey breast, cut in ⅛-in. (3-mm) scallops, 3 oz. (90 g) each	8	8
Salt and white pepper	TT	TT
Flour	as needed for dredging	
Clarified butter	2 fl. oz.	60 ml
Dry white wine	4 fl. oz.	120 ml
Fresh lemon juice	2 fl. oz.	60 ml
Capers	3 Tbsp.	45 ml
Cooked rice	as needed	

1. Gently pound each turkey slice with a meat mallet. Season with salt and white pepper and dredge in flour.
2. Sauté the turkey in the butter until golden brown. Remove and hold in a warm place.
3. Deglaze the pan with the wine, then add the lemon juice and capers. Return the turkey to the pan to coat with the sauce and reheat.
4. Serve two slices with a portion of the sauce accompanied with cooked rice and vegetables.

Approximate values per 6-oz. (180-g) serving: **Calories** 390, **Total fat** 13 g, **Saturated fat** 8 g, **Cholesterol** 180 mg, **Sodium** 910 mg, **Total carbohydrates** 13 g, **Protein** 56 g, **Vitamin A** 10%

SAUTÉED CHICKEN LIVERS

Yield: 4 Appetizer Servings, 4 oz. (120 g) each   **Method:** Sautéing

Chicken livers, trimmed	1 lb.	480 g
Salt and pepper	TT	TT
Flour	as needed for dredging	
Vegetable oil	1 fl. oz.	30 ml
Shallots, minced	2 Tbsp.	30 ml
Raspberry vinegar	4 fl. oz.	120 ml
Raspberry jam	2 Tbsp.	30 ml
French bread croutons	4	4
Watercress	as needed for garnish	

1. Rinse the livers and pat dry. Season with salt and pepper and dredge in flour.
2. Sauté the livers in the oil until just barely pink, approximately 3 to 4 minutes. Remove the livers from the pan and hold in a warm place.
3. Using the fat remaining in the pan, sauté the shallots until tender. Deglaze with the vinegar.
4. Add the jam. Simmer until thickened. Return the livers to the pan and toss to coat with the sauce.
5. Serve on warm plates with French bread croutons; garnish with watercress.

Approximate values per 4-oz. (120-g) serving: **Calories** 330, **Total fat** 14 g, **Saturated fat** 3 g, **Cholesterol** 715 mg, **Sodium** 660 mg, **Total carbohydrates** 22 g, **Protein** 30 g, **Vitamin A** 560%, **Iron** 60%

SPICED OSTRICH TENDERLOIN

Yield: 2 Servings   **Method:** Broiling

Cumin seeds	1 Tbsp.	15 ml
Fennel seeds	1 Tbsp.	15 ml
Black peppercorns	2 tsp.	10 ml
White peppercorns	2 tsp.	10 ml
Garlic cloves, minced	2	2
Ostrich tenderloins, 4 oz. (120 g) each	2	2
Olive oil	1 Tbsp.	15 ml
Salt	TT	TT

1. Grind the cumin, fennel and peppercorns together in a spice grinder. Combine the ground spices with the garlic.
2. Brush the tenderloins with the oil, coat with the spice mixture and season lightly with salt.
3. Cook the ostrich under a broiler to an internal temperature of at least 155°F (68°C).
4. Remove from the broiler, allow the meat to rest for 5 minutes then slice against the grain for service.

Approximate values per 4-oz. (120 g) serving: **Calories** 169, **Total fat** 5 g, **Saturated fat** 1 g, **Cholesterol** 91 mg, **Sodium** 106 mg, **Total carbohydrates** 5 g, **Protein** 27 g, **Iron** 46%

SQUAB SALAD WITH MELON

CHEF ODETTE FADA, NEW YORK, NY

Yield: 6 Servings   **Method:** Sautéing

Squab	3	3
Salt and pepper	TT	TT
Extra virgin olive oil	as needed	as needed
Dry black currants	2 Tbsp.	30 ml
Tahitian squash, thin slices	18	18
Mâche lettuce, small bunches	6	6

1. Bone the squab breasts and remove the thighs and legs. Season with salt and pepper and sauté in oil until done, approximately 10 to 15 minutes.
2. Place the currants in a bowl and cover with hot water.
3. Cook the squash slices in boiling water for 40 seconds. Cut the slices in half and arrange them on each of six plates as fans opening toward the plate's border.
4. Arrange some mâche lettuce on each plate; season with salt and pepper.
5. Slice the breasts; arrange the meat with the legs on the squash.
6. Drain the currants and sauté in 2 tablespoons (30 milliliters) oil. Sprinkle the currants around the plates and serve.

Approximate values per serving: **Calories** 230, **Total fat** 10 g, **Saturated fat** 2.5 g, **Cholesterol** 85 mg, **Sodium** 460 mg, **Total carbohydrates** 3 g, **Protein** 31 g, **Vitamin A** 20%, **Vitamin C** 30%.

TORCHON OF FOIE GRAS WITH APPLE AND DUCK GELÉES

HERBSAINT BAR AND RESTAURANT, NEW ORLEANS, LA

Chef Donald Link

Torchon (tour-shahn) is French for a cloth or towel, such as a dishcloth. The term is sometimes used to refer to dishes in which the item has been shaped into a cylinder by being wrapped in a cloth or towel.

Yield: 10 Servings		**Method:** Poaching
Whole foie gras, A grade, approximately 1.5 pounds (720 grams)	1	1
Cognac	1 Tbsp.	15 ml
Salt	1½ tsp.	8 ml
Allspice	½ tsp.	2 ml
Fennel, ground	½ tsp.	2 ml
Black pepper, ground	TT	TT
Juniper berries, chopped	2	2
Rich duck stock, clear	as needed	as needed
Apple Gelée (recipe follows), cubed	as needed	as needed

1. Immerse the foie gras in ice water for 2 to 3 hours. Then remove it from the ice water and hold at room temperature for approximately 30 minutes to allow it to soften slightly. Bisect the lobes of the foie gras and carefully remove all evident veins.

2. Place the foie gras pieces in a hotel pan without letting them overlap. Season them with the cognac, salt, allspice, fennel, pepper and juniper berries.

3. Lay a 12-inch × 12-inch (30-centimeter × 30-centimeter) piece of plastic wrap on a work surface. Divide the foie gras in half and place half of it on the plastic wrap and roll into a tight cylinder. Repeat with the other half. Refrigerate both rolls overnight.

4. Remove the foie gras from the refrigerator and hold at room temperature for 30 minutes. Lay a 12-inch × 12-inch (30-centimeter × 30-centimeter) piece of cheesecloth on a work surface. Remove one roll of foie gras from the plastic and transfer it to the cheesecloth. Roll the foie gras very tightly in the cheesecloth, twist the ends of the cloth very tightly and tie with kitchen twine. Then tie the roll at two even intervals to prevent the foie gras from becoming misshapen during cooking. Repeat with the second foie gras roll.

5. Prepare an ice bath large enough to hold the rolls. Heat 4 quarts (4 liters) water in a wide shallow pot to 185°F (85°C). Working with one roll at a time, poach the rolls for 1 minute and transfer them directly to the ice bath. Chill the foie gras in the ice bath for 15 minutes.

6. Remove the foie gras rolls from the ice water, wrap them in absorbent kitchen towels and hang in the refrigerator for 12 to 24 hours.

7. To make the duck gelée, reduce the duck stock to 1 to 2 cups (250 to 500 milliliters) of liquid. (The greater the gelatin content, the less reduction is necessary.) Pour into a shallow pan and refrigerate. The finished duck gelée should be gelled and firm enough to hold its shape when plated.

8. To serve, remove the towel and the cheesecloth from the foie gras. Using a hot knife, smooth the sides of the foie gras torchon and cut slices of the desired thickness. Serve with toasted bread, the Apple Gelée and the duck gelée.

Approximate values per serving: **Calories** 270, **Total fat** 29 g, **Saturated fat** 9 g, **Cholesterol** 255 mg, **Sodium** 850 mg, **Total carbohydrates** 3 g, **Protein** 7 g, **Vitamin A** 640%, **Iron** 25%

APPLE GELÉE

Yield: 24 fl. oz. (720 ml)

Star anise	½ tsp.	2 ml
Apple juice, pure	3 pt.	1.4 lt
Salt	TT	TT
Green apple	½	½
Lemon juice	1 tsp.	5 ml
Gelatin sheets	4	4

1. Add the star anise to the apple juice. Bring the juice to a boil and reduce by half. Season with salt.
2. Cut the apple brunoise and toss with the lemon juice.
3. Soak the gelatin sheets in cold water for approximately 5 minutes. Squeeze out the water and dissolve them in the hot apple juice.
4. Pour the mixture into a shallow pan. Cool over an ice bath. When the mixture begins to set, stir in the brunoise apple so that the apple pieces become suspended in the gelée and are evenly dispersed. Refrigerate until firm.

Approximate values per 1-fl.-oz. (30-ml) serving: **Calories** 10, **Total fat** 0 g, **Saturated fat** 0 g, **Cholesterol** 0 mg, **Sodium** 10 mg, **Total carbohydrates** 15 mg, **Protein** 2 g, **Claims**—fat free, low sodium

SAUTÉED FOIE GRAS ON WILD MUSHROOM DUXELLES WITH TOASTED BRIOCHE

SIMPLICITY CATERING, FALLS CHURCH, VA
Chef Leland Atkinson

Yield: 4 Servings   **Method:** Sautéing

Fresh foie gras, A grade	1 lb.	480 g
Wild mushrooms	1 lb.	480 g
Shallots, chopped	2 Tbsp.	30 ml
Garlic, chopped	1 tsp.	5 ml
Whole butter	1 Tbsp.	15 ml
Tomato paste	1 tsp.	5 ml
Brandy	1 Tbsp.	15 ml
Fresh thyme	1 tsp.	5 ml
Salt and pepper	TT	TT
Madeira sauce (page 206)	8 fl. oz.	240 ml
Brioche (page 950)	8 slices	8 slices

1. Allow the foie gras to come to near room temperature. With a sharp knife, scrape the thin membrane from the outside of the liver. Gently pull the pieces apart. Gently pull out any visible veins. Slice the liver on a slight bias into slices approximately 1 inch (2.5 centimeters) thick. Cover and chill until service.
2. To make the duxelles, clean and chop the mushrooms.
3. Sauté the shallots and garlic in the butter.
4. Add the mushrooms and cook until they first release their moisture and then begin to dry, approximately 5 minutes.
5. Add the tomato paste and brandy and cook until dry, stirring often.
6. Add the thyme and adjust the seasonings with salt and pepper. Remove the duxelles from the heat.
7. Quickly sauté the foie gras in a hot dry pan until it is browned on both sides but still bright pink in the middle, approximately 2 minutes.
8. Portion the duxelles onto four warm serving plates. Ladle the Madeira sauce around the duxelles. Blot the foie gras on a dry towel and arrange it over the top of the duxelles. Serve with toasted brioche.

Approximate values per serving: **Calories** 790, **Total fat** 69 g, **Saturated fat** 25 g, **Cholesterol** 535 mg, **Sodium** 1280 mg, **Total carbohydrates** 37 g, **Protein** 22 g, **Vitamin A** 1100%, **Iron** 50%

ROAST GOOSE WITH CABBAGE AND APPLES

Yield: 8 Servings, 6 oz. (180 g) each   **Method:** Roasting

Goose, approx. 12 lb. (6 kg)	1	1
Salt and pepper	TT	TT
Caraway seeds	1 Tbsp.	15 ml
Onions, large dice	6 oz.	180 g
Carrots, large dice	3 oz.	90 g
Celery, large dice	3 oz.	90 g
Green cabbage, shredded	1 lb.	480 g
Potatoes, large dice	3 lb.	1.4 kg
Tart apples, cored and diced	1 lb.	480 g
Apple cider	1 qt.	1 lt.

1. Remove the giblets from the goose; remove the fat from its cavity. Rinse the goose and pat dry. Sprinkle its interior and exterior with salt, pepper and caraway seeds. Truss the goose and place it breast side up on a rack in a roasting pan.

2. Roast in a 425°F (220°C) oven for 30 minutes. Prick the skin all over with a fork to release fat.

3. Reduce the oven temperature to 350°F (180°C) and continue roasting for another 45 minutes. Baste the bird occasionally with the fat accumulating in the pan.

4. Meanwhile, combine the vegetables and apple, and season with salt and pepper.

5. After roasting for a total of 1¼ hours, remove the goose from the pan and drain off all but 3 tablespoons (45 milliliters) of fat. Place the vegetable mixture in the roasting pan and toss to coat with the fat.

6. Place the goose on top of the vegetable mixture and pour the apple cider over all. Return to the oven and continue roasting until done, approximately 1½ hours.

7. Remove the bird from the roasting pan and allow it to rest for 20 to 30 minutes before carving. Serve with the cooked vegetable-and-apple mixture.

Approximate values per serving: **Calories** 1230, **Total fat** 62 g, **Saturated fat** 18 g, **Cholesterol** 205 mg, **Sodium** 670 mg, **Total carbohydrates** 101 g, **Protein** 66 g, **Vitamin A** 35%, **Vitamin C** 60%, **Iron** 60%

FRIED FROG LEGS IN FINES HERBES BUTTER

HERBSAINT BAR AND RESTAURANT, New Orleans, LA
Chef Donald Link

Yield: 24 Legs   **Method:** Deep-frying

Fines herbes butter:		
Unsalted butter, soft	8 oz.	240 g
Parsley, chopped	1 Tbsp.	15 ml
Fresh tarragon, chopped	1 tsp.	5 ml
Fresh chervil, chopped	1 tsp.	5 ml
Fresh chives, sliced	1 tsp.	5 ml
Garlic, minced	½ tsp.	2 ml
Cayenne pepper	½ tsp.	2 ml
Salt	1 tsp.	5 ml
Frog leg pairs, cut in half	12	12
Salt and pepper	TT	TT
Flour	1 lb.	480 g
Buttermilk	8 fl. oz.	240 ml

1. Combine all the ingredients for the fines herbes butter and mix well.
2. Pat the frog legs dry and season them with salt and pepper. Dredge the frog legs in flour, dip them in buttermilk, drain and dredge in flour again.
3. Deep-fry the frog legs until golden brown and done, approximately 5 to 7 minutes. Drain, place in a stainless steel bowl and coat generously with the fines herbes butter.
4. Arrange the legs attractively on a plate, garnish as desired and serve hot.

Approximate values per leg: **Calories** 170, **Total fat** 10 g, **Saturated fat** 5 g, **Cholesterol** 35 mg, **Sodium** 125 mg, **Total carbohydrates** 15 g, **Protein** 6 g

FROGS

Frogs are amphibians that can be prepared like poultry or fish. Their texture and flavor are similar to those of chicken. Most of the frogs used in food service operations are farm-raised, so their meat is quite tender. Typically, only the legs are eaten. They are sold frozen, in pairs, attached by a small portion of backbone.

Frog Legs

> "One can never know too much; the more one learns, the more one sees the need to learn more and that study as well as broadening the mind of the craftsman provides an easy way of perfecting yourself in the practice of your art.
>
> —AUGUSTE ESCOFFIER, FRENCH CHEF (1846–1935)

CHAPTER EIGHTEEN

GAME

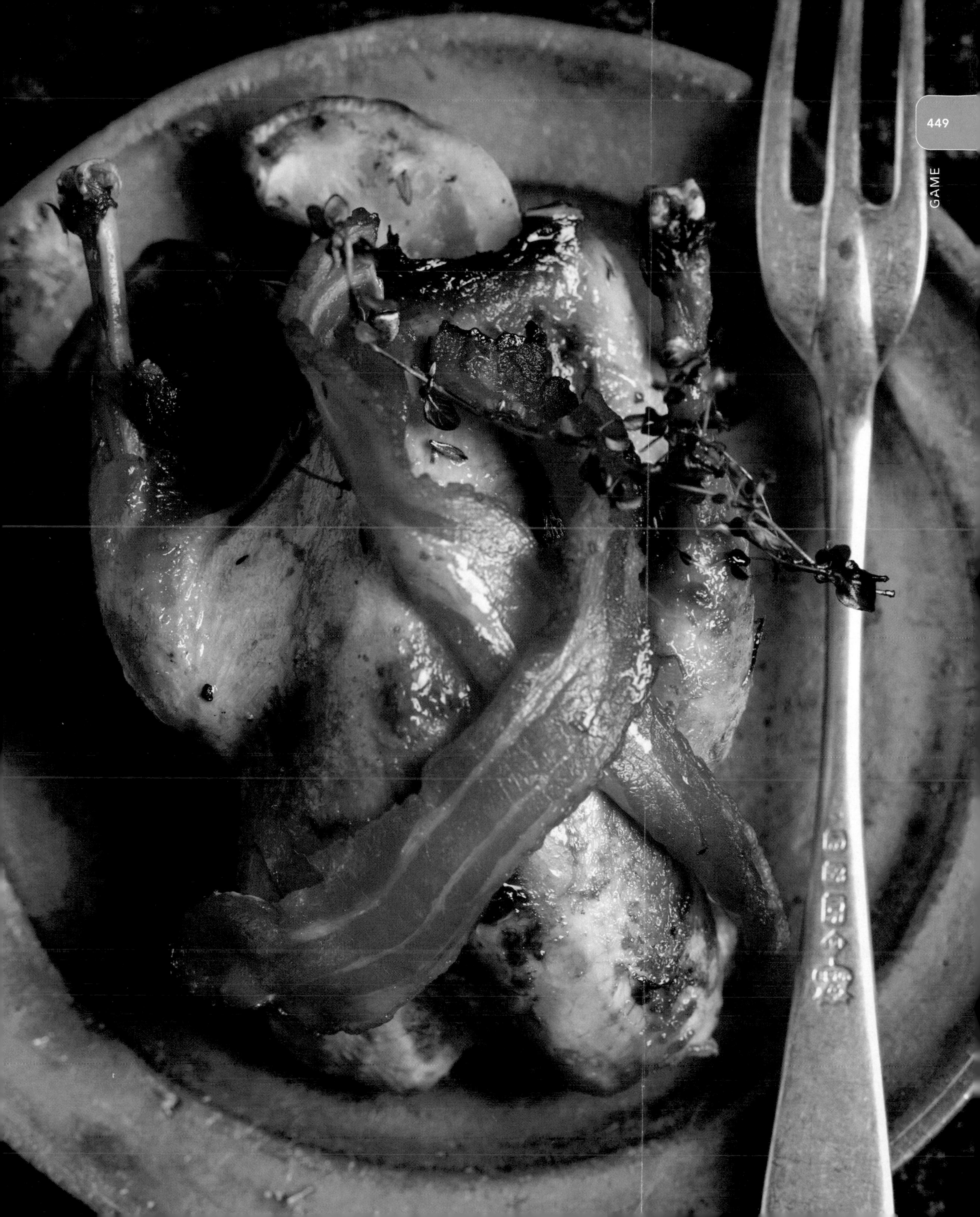

After studying this chapter, you will be able to:

- identify a variety of game
- understand game inspection practices
- purchase game appropriate for your needs
- store game properly
- prepare game for cooking
- apply various cooking methods to game

GAME (FR. *GIBIER*) ARE ANIMALS HUNTED for sport or food. Traditionally, game supplies depended on the season and the hunter's success. But game's increasing popularity in food service operations has led to farm-raising and animal husbandry techniques. As a result, pheasant, quail, deer, rabbit and other animals, although still considered game, are now farm- or ranch-raised and commercially available throughout the year.

The life of game creatures is reflected in their flesh's appearance, aroma, flavor and texture. Generally, game flesh has a dark color and a strong but not unpleasant aroma. It has a robust flavor and less fat than other meats or poultry and is more compact, becoming quite tough in older animals.

Selecting the best cooking methods for game depends on the animal's age and the particular cut of flesh. Generally, game flesh has a dark color, a strong but not unpleasant aroma and a robust flavor. Younger animals will, of course, be more tender than older ones. Flesh from the loin or less-used muscles will also be tender and therefore can be prepared with dry-heat cooking methods. Flesh from much-used muscles, such as the leg and shoulder, will be tougher and should be prepared with combination cooking methods. Less-tender cuts can also be used in sausages, pâtés and forcemeats, as discussed in Chapter 27, Charcuterie.

Game is becoming increasingly popular because of consumer desires for leaner, healthier meats. Only farm-raised game can be used in food service operations. Luckily, many popular game items are now farm-raised, government-inspected and readily available. Table 18.1 lists some common cuts of game discussed in this chapter.

IDENTIFYING GAME

Furred or Ground Game

Furred game includes large animals such as deer, moose, bear, wild boar and elk as well as smaller animals such as rabbit, squirrel, raccoon and opossum. Although these animals (and many others) are hunted for sport and food, only a few species are widely available to food service operations.

Although venison, boar and elk may seem unusual to many Americans, even rarer meats are available to the daring diner. Zebra, bear, wildebeest and other "big game" animals are sometimes available through exotic game purveyors. Most often these meats are grilled, roasted or stewed.

Reptiles, particularly rattlesnake and alligator, are now also being raised on farms to meet increased demand. Reptiles are usually braised, or sliced and deep-fried. They have a mild flavor with a texture similar to lobster.

Large game animals are rarely sold whole or in primal portions. Instead, the meat is available precut into subprimals or portions. So, except for those that are used for rabbits, this chapter does not provide butchering techniques.

ANTELOPE

The blackbuck antelope, about half the size of a large deer, is ranch-raised in the United States. Although it has almost no body fat, the meat retains a high amount of moisture. The meat is fine-grained, with a flavor that is only slightly stronger than that of deer meat (venison). It should be butchered and cooked in a manner similar to venison.

GAME FLAVORS

The tart sweetness of fruit such as apricots, blueberries, cranberries, peaches, pears, plums or raspberries balances the assertive flavor of furred game. Spiced fruit compotes discussed in Chapter 25, Fruits, are a great foil for game preparations. Some acidity in the form of citrus juice or rind, other acidic fruit juices, vinegar or wine tames the flavor of most furred game, whether used in the marinade, sauce or accompaniment.

BISON (AMERICAN BUFFALO)

Once found in huge herds roaming the plains states, bison or buffalo were hunted into near-extinction during the 19th century. Buffalo now live on reservations or ranches, where they are raised like beef cattle. Their meat is juicy and flavorful and may be prepared in the same manner as lean beef.

Buffalo Steak

DEER

The deer family includes elk, moose, reindeer, red-tailed deer, white-tailed deer (Fr. *chevreuil*) and mule deer. Meat from any of these animals is known as **venison** (Fr. *venaisan*). Farm-raised venison, particularly from the Scottish red deer bred in New Zealand and the United States, is commercially available all year. Axis deer, a species originally from India and Nepal, provides some of the finest-quality venison. Like cattle, axis deer graze on grass, so their meat is especially mild and tender. Venison is typically dark red with a mild aroma. It is leaner than other meats, having almost no intramuscular fat or marbling.

venison flesh from any member of the deer family, including antelope, elk, moose, reindeer, red-tailed deer, white-tailed deer, mule deer and axis deer

The most popular commercial venison cuts are the loin, leg and rack. The loin is tender enough to roast, sauté or grill to medium rare. It is often barded with bacon before roasting. It can be left attached along the backbone to form a cut known as the saddle. The leg is often marinated in red wine and prepared with combination cooking methods. Other cuts can also be stewed or braised or used in sausages and pâtés. Butchering procedures for venison are similar to those for lamb discussed in Chapter 15.

RABBIT

Rabbits (Fr. *lapin*) are small burrowing animals that have long been raised for food. Rabbit has mild, lean and relatively tender flesh. Its flavor and texture are similar to chicken. Ranch-raised rabbit is available all year, either whole or cut, fresh or frozen. The average weight of a whole dressed rabbit is 2 pounds 8 ounces to 3 pounds (1.2 to 1.4 kilograms). Hare (Fr. *lièvre*) are a species of larger rabbits weighing up to 14 pounds with lean, dark and strongly flavored meat. Although hare have not been domesticated, they are available from importers of wild game. Young rabbit can be roasted, pan-fried, stewed or braised and is popular in rustic "country-style" dishes, especially casseroles and pâtés. Hare are usually marinated with vinegar or wine before stewing with aromatics and spices.

Venison Saddle

MEAT OF THE FUTURE: BEEFALO

Beefalo is produced by cross-breeding a bison with a domestic beef animal. To be a registered full-blooded beefalo, the animal has to be three-eighths bison and five-eighths domestic beef. The five-eighths domestic beef portion is not restricted to any breed; it is often a combination of two or more breeds such as Hereford, Angus or Charolais. In 1985, the USDA approved a special label for beefalo; it is labeled either "Beef from Beefalo" or "Beefalo Beef."

Beefalo looks and tastes much like modern beef. The animal itself is hard to distinguish from any other beef animal. Beefalo meat is tender because the animals gain weight faster and go to market at younger ages. The meat is slightly sweeter in taste than beef.

Beefalo is lower in cholesterol than beef, fish or chicken and lower in calories and fat than beef. It offers a great alternative to beef for the diet- and health-conscious guest. The per-pound cost of beefalo may be slightly higher than beef cuts, but its low amount of interior and exterior fat gives it a higher yield with a price per usable pound comparable to beef.

Because of beefalo's finer fiber and low fat content, it cooks in one-third to one-half the time of beef and should be cooked to either rare or medium rare.

—JAMES J. MUTH, MBA, CFBE,
is a Chef Instructor at Grand Rapids
Community College, Grand Rapids, MI.

PROCEDURE FOR **BUTCHERING A RABBIT**

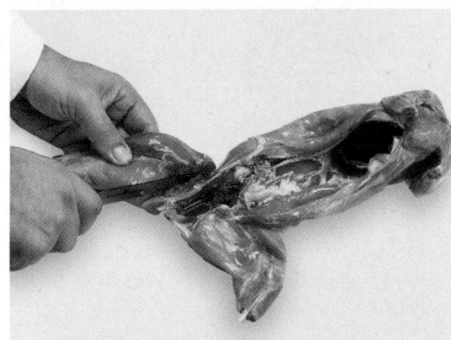

① Place the rabbit on its back. Remove the hind legs by cutting close to the backbone and through the joint on each side. Each thigh and leg can be separated by cutting through the joint.

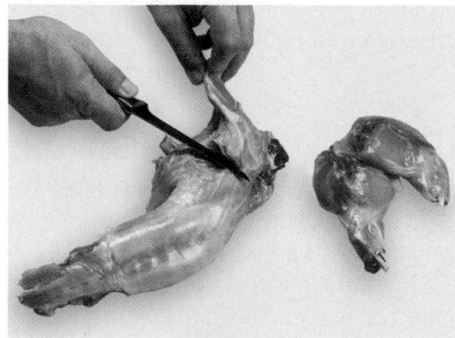

② Remove the forelegs by cutting beneath the shoulder blades.

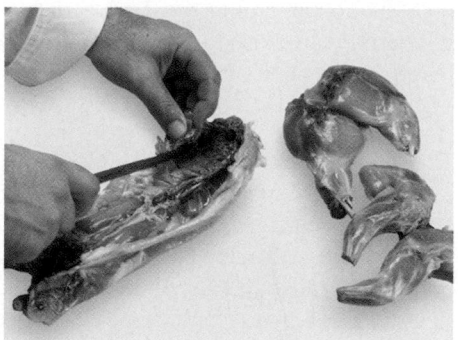

③ Cut through the breast bone and spread open the rib cage. Using a boning knife, separate the flesh from the rib bones and remove the bones.

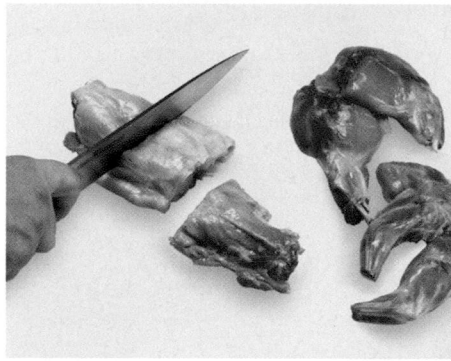

④ Cut through the backbone to divide the loin into the desired number of pieces.

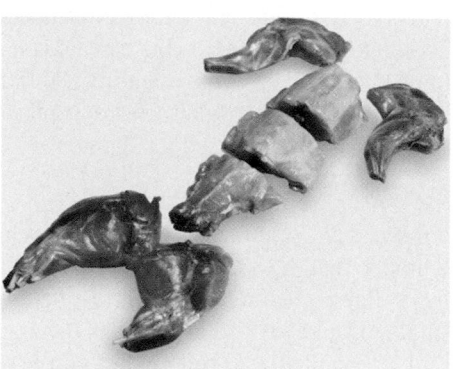

⑤ The cut-up rabbit: hind legs, thighs, loin in three pieces, forelegs.

WILD BOAR

A close relative of the domesticated hog, wild boar (Fr. *sanglier*) is leaner, with a stronger flavor. Though plentiful in Europe and parts of America, wild boar is available only during autumn. A limited supply of farm- or ranch-raised boar is available all year, however. Baby boar (under 6 months old) is considered a delicacy, but mature animals (1–2 years old) have the best flavor. The meat is most often roasted and may be used in sausages or terrines. Boar can often be substituted in recipes for venison or pork.

Boar Saddle

Feathered or Winged Game

Feathered game includes upland birds such as wild turkeys, pheasants, quails, doves and woodcocks; songbirds such as larks; and waterfowl such as wild geese and ducks. Wild birds cannot be sold in the United States. An ever-increasing number of these birds are being farm-raised to meet consumer demand, however.

Game birds are available whole or precut into pieces, fresh or frozen. Butchering techniques will not be shown in this chapter, as they are the same as those for domesticated poultry discussed in Chapter 17.

TABLE 18.1 USING FURRED GAME

ANIMAL	COMMONLY PURCHASED CUTS	COOKING METHODS	SUGGESTED USE
Antelope	Purchased and prepared in the same manner as deer		
Bison	Purchased and prepared in the same manner as lean beef		
Deer	Loin	Dry heat (roast; sauté; grill)	Sautéed medallions; whole roast loin; grilled steaks
	Leg	Combination (braise; stew)	Marinate and braise; pot roast with cranberries; chili; sausage; forcemeat
	Rack	Dry heat (roast; grill)	Grilled chops
Rabbit	Full carcass	Dry heat (sauté; pan-fry; roast; grill) Combination (braise; stew)	Pan-fried rabbit with cream gravy Braised rabbit with mushrooms
Wild boar	Loin Chops	Dry heat (roast) Combination (braise)	Roast loin with mustard crust Marinate and braise; stew with red wine and sour cream; sausage; forcemeat

Because game birds tend to have less fat than other poultry, they are often barded with fat and cooked to medium rare. If cooked well done, they become dry and stringy.

PARTRIDGE

The Hungarian and chukar partridges (Fr. *perdrix*) of Europe were introduced into the United States and Canada during the 19th century. Now found principally in the prairie and western mountain states, partridges are widely raised on game preserves and farms, producing a good commercial supply. The flavor of partridge is less delicate than that of pheasant, and the meat tends to be tougher. Partridge may be roasted or cut into pieces and sautéed or braised. Each bird weighs about 1 pound (450 grams) dressed.

Chukar Partridge

PHEASANT

The most popular of game birds, the pheasant (Fr. *faisan*) was introduced into Europe from Asia during the Middle Ages. Its mild flavor is excellent for roasting, stewing or braising. The hen is smaller and more tender than the cock. Stock made from the carcass is often used for consommé or sauce. Farm-raised birds are available fresh or frozen. A dressed bird weighs about 1 pound 8 ounces to 2 pounds 4 ounces (680 grams to 1 kilogram) and serves two people.

Pheasant

Quail

QUAIL

The quail (Fr. *caille*) is a migratory game bird related to the pheasant. The more popular European and Californian species are farm-raised and available all year.

Quail are very small, with only about 1 to 2 ounces (30 to 60 grams) of breast meat each. Quail may be grilled (especially on skewers), roasted, broiled or sautéed and are often boned and served whole with a stuffing of forcemeat or rice. Because they are so lean, roasted quail benefit from barding.

WILD GAME—DELICIOUS, NUTRITIOUS AND AVAILABLE

Wild game is now widely available for use in restaurants and at home. The best of wild game provides a safe, delicious and nutritious dining experience.

In almost all states, our native game animals are protected from harvesting for commercial purposes. It is a violation of state wildlife laws to kill and sell the meat from native species such as the whitetail deer, mule deer, pronghorn antelope, and so on. These laws were written when only native game was present in America. Since then, a growing number of nonnative species of deer and antelope have been introduced to ranches in America, and this has made it possible to harvest deer and antelope legally for meat production.

Oddly enough, however, meats such as antelope, venison, rabbit, and most other game meats are not subject to inspection under federal and most state meat inspection regulations. This is not because the authorities do not believe the meat should be inspected. When the meat inspection laws were written, these meats were not legally available and therefore were not included in the Federal Meat Act. County and city health codes, however, do require that any meat served to the public must be from an "approved source," which is interpreted as "inspected." Therefore, any game meat served in a restaurant should be certified as inspected by either state or federal meat inspection authorities.

Game meat is available from farmed (domesticated) deer and from free-ranging (ranched) deer and antelope. Most farmed deer are taken to a fixed conventional slaughterhouse where they are slaughtered and processed in the same way as cattle, sheep and goats. Ranched deer can be properly harvested only by an elaborate procedure that involves taking a mobile slaughter facility and meat inspector to the field, where the animals are killed by shooting them with a high-powered rifle under the supervision of the meat inspector. The carcass is then processed inside the mobile facility to avoid any contamination of the meat. This field harvesting eliminates any stress that might occur in transport of ranched deer to the slaughterhouse.

Farmed deer tend to be relatively more uniform in size and flavor. Free-ranging deer and antelope produce meat of more complex flavor due to the variety of their diet. The difference is somewhat like the difference in cultivated mushrooms and wild mushrooms, or pen-raised chickens compared with free-range chickens. Meat from free-range animals is more expensive due to higher labor and inspection costs.

Meat from both deer and antelope can be legally labeled "venison." All venison is relatively lean when compared with conventional red meats and requires special attention when cooking to avoid drying out the meat and toughening it. Tender cuts should be cooked as little as possible (rare to medium rare) to retain the maximum amount of moisture. Quick sautéing, grilling or roasting to retain a medium-rare center is most satisfactory for tender cuts such as the loin, tenderloin, and leg.

Braising is the most effective method for cooking the less tender cuts such as the shoulder, ribs and shanks. Beef broth and red wine are good liquids for braising. The toughest cut of meat will be very satisfactorily tenderized if braised for a sufficient period of time (which may be as long as two or three hours). When properly cooked, these cuts can surpass the more tender cuts in flavor.

—MIKE HUGHES is the owner of the Broken Arrow Ranch in Ingram, TX.

NUTRITION

Even ranch-raised game animals live in the wild and are generally more active and less well fed than domesticated animals. This lifestyle produces animals whose meat has less fat than that of domesticated animals. Most game is also lower in cholesterol and has approximately one-third fewer calories than beef. Game is also generally high in protein and minerals.

INSPECTION OF GAME

The USDA and most states restrict the sale of wild game. Truly wild game can be served only by those who hunt and share their kill.

Domestic Game

Unlike meat and poultry from domesticated animals, game is not graded for quality. Farm- or ranch-raised game is subject only to voluntary inspections for wholesomeness. Generally, however, game is processed under the same federal inspection requirements as domesticated meats and poultry. State regulations vary and are constantly being expanded and improved in response to consumer demands.

Imported Game

Only USDA-approved countries are permitted to export game to the United States. On arrival in this country, game shipments are subject to USDA spot inspections.

PURCHASING AND STORING GAME

Purchasing Game

Furred game meats are available fresh or frozen. Game birds are available cleaned and boned, fresh or frozen. Use the same criteria to determine the freshness of game as you would any other meat or poultry: The flesh should be firm, without slime or an off-odor.

Fresh game is sometimes hung before cooking to allow the meat to mature or age.② During hanging, carbohydrates (glycogen) stored in muscle tissues are converted to lactic acid. This process tenderizes the flesh and strengthens its flavor. But hanging is not necessary, especially if you object to "gamy" flavors. Commercially sold game is generally fully aged and ready to use when delivered. It does not need, nor will it benefit from, hanging.

Storing Game

As with any fresh or frozen meat, game should be well wrapped and stored under refrigeration at temperatures below 41°F (5°C). Because the flesh is generally dry and lean, frozen game should be used within 4 months. Thaw frozen game slowly under refrigeration to prevent moisture loss.

MARINATING FURRED GAME

Tradition calls for marinating game, particularly furred game, in strong mixtures of red wine, herbs and spices. Commercially raised game does not necessarily have to be marinated. Modern animal husbandry techniques used at game ranches assure the chef of receiving meat from young, tender animals. Farm-raised game animals also have a naturally milder flavor than their truly wild cousins.

For those preferring the flavors imparted by traditional marinades, the following Red Wine Marinade, suitable for most game such as antelope, elk, rabbit, venison or wild boar, is included. After the meat is removed, the marinade may be added to the cooking liquid or reduced and used in a sauce. Do not serve uncooked marinade.

HOW TO HANG GAME

The following information may be useful if you find yourself with a need to hang freshly killed game. Most game should be eviscerated (drawn or gutted) as soon as possible, then suspended by either the hind legs or the head in a dry, well-ventilated place. Because the fur or feathers help prevent bacterial contamination, they should be left intact during hanging; game should be skinned or plucked just before butchering. The length of time necessary for hanging depends on the species and age of the animal. Two days may be sufficient for a rabbit, whereas up to 3 weeks may be necessary for a deer or boar. Hanging is generally complete when the first whiff of odor is detected (although traditionalists prefer pheasant to be hung until extremely ripe).

Hanging Game Birds

RED WINE MARINADE

MISE EN PLACE

▸ Peel and finely chop the carrot and onion.
▸ Peel and mince the garlic.

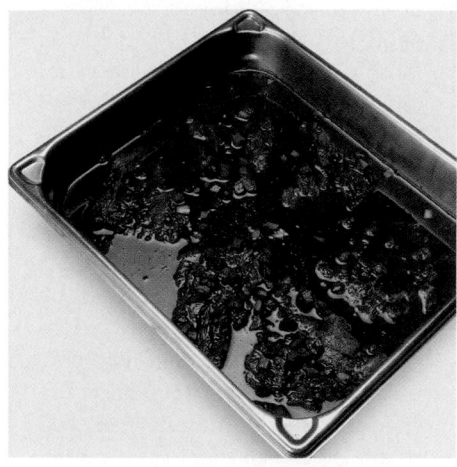

Yield: 1½ qt. (1.4 lt)

Carrot, chopped fine	2 oz.	60 g
Onion, chopped fine	2 oz.	60 g
Garlic, minced	1 Tbsp.	15 ml
Dried thyme	1 tsp.	5 ml
Bay leaves	2	2
Juniper berries, whole	2 tsp.	10 ml
Peppercorns, whole	1 Tbsp.	15 ml
Sage, ground	½ tsp.	2 ml
Red wine	1 qt.	960 ml
Red wine vinegar	4 fl. oz.	120 ml

1 Combine all ingredients.

2 Place the meat in the marinade and marinate for the desired time. Tender, farm-raised game may need only 30 minutes; older, wild animals may need 1 to 2 days.

Approximate values per fluid ounce (30 ml): **Calories** 5, **Total fat** 0 g, **Saturated fat** 0 g, **Cholesterol** 0 mg, **Sodium** 0 mg, **Total carbohydrates** 1 g, **Protein** 0 g, **Vitamin A** 6%, **Claims**—fat free; no saturated fat; no cholesterol; no sodium; low calorie

QUESTIONS FOR DISCUSSION

1 Explain the differences between truly wild game and ranch-raised game.

2 What is hanging? Is it necessary for modern food service operations to hang game?

3 Which cuts of furred game are best suited to dry-heat cooking methods? Which are best for combination cooking methods?

4 Can game birds be purchased whole? How are they fabricated?

5 What degree of doneness is best suited for game birds? Explain your answer.

6 Texas is home to several large game ranches. Explore their Internet sites to learn more about the operation of game ranches and the varieties of venison available.

Terms to Know

furred game	wild boar
feathered or	elk
winged game	rabbit
domestic game	antelope
hanging	beefalo
deer	hare
moose	partridge
bear	quail

CHILLI-RUBBED VENISON WITH CARAMELIZED BERRY SAUCE

K RESTAURANT AND WINE BAR, ORLANDO, FL

Chef Kevin Fonzo

Yield: 4 Servings		**Method:** Sautéing
Chilli powder	2 Tbsp.	30 ml
Salt	1 tsp.	5 ml
Black pepper	1 tsp.	5 ml
Venison leg, 5-oz. (150-g) portions	4	4
Olive oil	1 Tbsp.	15 ml
Mashed potatoes	as needed	as needed
Caramelized Berry Sauce (recipe follows)	8 fl. oz.	240 ml

1. In a small bowl, combine the chilli powder, salt and pepper to make a dry rub. Rub the venison with this mixture until well coated.
2. Heat the oil in a medium-sized sauté pan. Cook the venison to medium rare, making sure to brown all sides of the meat.
3. Remove the venison from the pan and allow it to rest for 1 minute, then slice into medallions.
4. Mound the mashed potatoes in the center of each plate. Arrange the venison in a fan around the potatoes. Ladle on the Caramelized Berry Sauce and garnish as desired.

Approximate values per serving: **Calories** 330, **Total fat** 13 g, **Saturated fat** 4 g, **Cholesterol** 116 mg, **Sodium** 1654 mg, **Total carbohydrates** 10 g, **Protein** 43 g, **Vitamin A** 26%, **Vitamin C** 14%, **Iron** 51%

CARAMELIZED BERRY SAUCE

Yield: 2 qt. (1.9 lt)		
Granulated sugar	6 oz.	180 g
Water	4 fl. oz.	120 ml
Strawberries, sliced	7 oz.	210 g
Raspberries	11 oz.	330 g
Blackberries	14 oz.	420 g
Blueberries	7 oz.	210 g
Veal stock	4 qt.	3.4 lt

1. Combine the sugar and water in a large saucepot. Bring to a boil and cook to a rich, golden brown.
2. Add all the berries to the caramelized sugar. Cook for 1 minute.
3. Add the veal stock and bring to a boil. Lower the heat to a simmer and reduce by half. Strain the sauce through a fine chinois and keep warm for service.

Approximate values per 2-fl.-oz. (60-ml) serving: **Calories** 39, **Total fat** 0 g, **Saturated fat** 0 g, **Cholesterol** 0 mg, **Sodium** 580 mg, **Total carbohydrates** 9 g, **Protein** 1 g, **Vitamin C** 13%

VENISON MEDALLIONS
WITH BLACK CURRANT SAUCE

Yield: 6 Servings   **Method:** Sautéing

Venison loin medallions, 5 oz. (150 g) each	6	6
Red Wine Marinade (page 456)	1 pt.	480 ml
Clarified butter	2 fl. oz.	60 ml
Salt and pepper	TT	TT
Black currant jelly	4 oz.	120 g
Demi-glace	8 fl. oz.	240 ml
Whole butter	1 oz.	30 g

1. Pound the venison medallions with a meat mallet to a uniform shape. Place them in a stainless container and cover with the Red Wine Marinade. Cover the pan and refrigerate for at least 1 hour or overnight.
2. Remove the medallions from the marinade and pat them dry with a paper towel. Strain the marinade and reserve the liquid.
3. Heat the butter in a sauté pan. Season the venison medallions with salt and pepper, add them to the pan and sauté them for 2 to 3 minutes on each side or until they are cooked rare to medium rare. Remove them from the pan and hold in a warm spot.
4. Degrease the pan and deglaze it with the reserved marinade. Reduce the marinade by half.
5. Add the jelly and demi-glace, bring to a boil and reduce the sauce until it is the correct consistency.
6. Monté au beurre. Adjust the seasonings. Serve each medallion with a portion of the sauce.

Approximate values per serving: **Calories** 630, **Total fat** 42 g, **Saturated fat** 13 g, **Cholesterol** 155 mg, **Sodium** 720 mg, **Total carbohydrates** 26 g, **Protein** 33 g, **Vitamin C** 10%, **Iron** 25%

VENISON MEDALLIONS GRAND VENEUR

Yield: 2 Servings   **Method:** Sautéing

Venison medallions, 3 oz. (90 g) each	4	4
Salt and pepper	TT	TT
Clarified butter	1 fl. oz.	30 ml
White wine	1 fl. oz.	30 ml
Poivrade sauce (page 206)	6 fl. oz.	180 ml
Red currant jelly	2 tsp.	10 ml
Heavy cream	1 fl. oz.	30 ml

1. Season the medallions with salt and pepper and sauté in the butter to the desired doneness. Remove and reserve.
2. Degrease the pan and deglaze with the wine.
3. Add the poivrade sauce and bring to a simmer. Stir in the jelly, add the cream and adjust the seasonings.
4. Return the medallions to the sauce to reheat. Serve two medallions per person with a portion of the sauce.

Approximate values per 6-oz. (180-g) serving: **Calories** 410, **Total fat** 21 g, **Saturated fat** 12 g, **Cholesterol** 195 mg, **Sodium** 1250 mg, **Total carbohydrates** 15 g, **Protein** 39 g, **Vitamin A** 15%

BRAISED RABBIT WITH CAVATELLI PASTA

CHEF JOHN ASH, SANTA ROSA, CA

Yield: 4 Servings

Method: Braising

Rabbit, 4 lb. (1.9 kg), cut into quarters	1	1
Salt and pepper	TT	TT
Olive oil	2 fl. oz.	60 ml
Chanterelle or shiitake mushrooms, stemmed and sliced	8 oz.	240 g
Yellow onion, sliced	6 oz.	180 g
Garlic, slivered	3 Tbsp.	45 ml
Carrot, small dice	3 oz.	90 g
Celery, sliced thin	3 oz.	90 g
Sun-dried tomatoes, sliced	1 pt.	480 ml
Zinfandel wine	1 pt.	480 ml
Tomato concassée	1 pt.	480 ml
Fresh thyme	1 tsp.	5 ml
Fresh sage, minced	1 tsp.	5 ml
Rabbit or chicken stock	1 qt.	960 ml
Fresh parsley, chopped fine	4 Tbsp.	60 ml
Fresh basil, chopped	4 Tbsp.	60 ml
Cavatelli, cooked, hot	24 oz.	720 g
Fresh basil sprigs	as needed for garnish	
Asiago, Parmesan or Dry Jack cheese, shaved	as needed for garnish	

1. Season the rabbit pieces with salt and pepper.
2. In a large heavy sautoir, heat the oil and quickly brown the rabbit in several batches if necessary. Remove and reserve.
3. Add the mushrooms, onion, garlic, carrot and celery and sauté until very lightly browned.
4. Return the rabbit to the pan and add the sun-dried tomatoes, wine, tomato concassée, thyme, sage and stock. Cover and simmer until the rabbit is tender and begins to pull away from the bones, approximately 45 to 50 minutes.
5. Remove the rabbit, separate the meat from the bones, discard the bones, and cut the meat into bite-sized pieces.
6. Strain the sauce, reserving the vegetables, and return the sauce to the saucepan. Bring to a boil and cook over high heat to reduce and thicken slightly, approximately 8 to 10 minutes.
7. Adjust the seasonings. Add the reserved meat and vegetables and heat. Stir in the parsley and chopped basil just before serving.
8. Toss the hot pasta with the rabbit sauce. Garnish with basil sprigs and cheese.

Approximate values per serving: **Calories** 1270, **Total fat** 47 g, **Saturated fat** 11 g, **Cholesterol** 285 mg, **Sodium** 2220 mg, **Total carbohydrates** 90 g, **Protein** 122 g, **Vitamin A** 60%, **Iron** 100%

BRAISED RABBIT WITH CHORIZO

CHEF JIM FITZGERALD, Ph.D., CCP

Yield: 4 Servings   **Method:** Braising

Rabbit, 2–3 lb. (1–1.4 kg)	1	1
Salt and pepper	TT	TT
Oil or clarified butter	8 fl. oz.	240 ml
Yellow onion, medium dice	1	1
Garlic clove, minced	1	1
Celery stalks, medium dice	2	2
Carrot, grated	1 oz.	30 g
Cloves, ground	⅛ tsp.	1 ml
Cayenne pepper	⅛ tsp.	1 ml
Port wine	4 fl. oz.	120 ml
Chorizo sausages, sliced	4 oz.	120 g
Unsweetened chocolate, chopped	1 oz.	30 g
All-purpose flour	2 oz.	60 g
Veal or chicken stock	2 pt.	960 ml

1. Cut the rabbit into seven pieces and season with salt and pepper. In a rondeau, brown the rabbit in the oil or butter. Remove from the pan and reserve.

2. In the same pan, brown the onion and then add the garlic and cook for 1 minute. Add the celery, carrot, cloves and cayenne pepper and cook for 2 more minutes.

3. Deglaze the pan with the wine and reduce au sec. Add the chorizo and chocolate, stirring well to prevent the chocolate from scorching.

4. Sprinkle the flour into the pan and cook to make a roux.

5. Whisk in 1 pint (480 milliliters) stock and cook until it thickens.

6. Add the remaining stock and the rabbit and bring to a simmer. Cover and place in a 325°F (160°C) oven and braise, basting the rabbit pieces with the braising liquid as needed, until fork tender, approximately 45 minutes. Adjust the seasonings to taste with salt and pepper.

Approximate values per 11-oz. (330-g) serving: **Calories** 610, **Total fat** 46 g, **Saturated fat** 9 g, **Cholesterol** 85 mg, **Sodium** 560 mg, **Total carbohydrates** 14 g, **Protein** 31 g, **Vitamin A** 25%, **Iron** 15%

ROAST PHEASANT WITH COGNAC AND APPLES

Yield: 2 Servings   **Method:** Roasting

Pheasant	1	1
Salt and pepper	TT	TT
Fatback	as needed	as needed
Mirepoix	12 oz.	360 g
Tart apples	2	2
Whole butter	1 oz.	30 g
Cognac	3 fl. oz.	90 ml
Crème fraîche	4 fl. oz.	120 ml

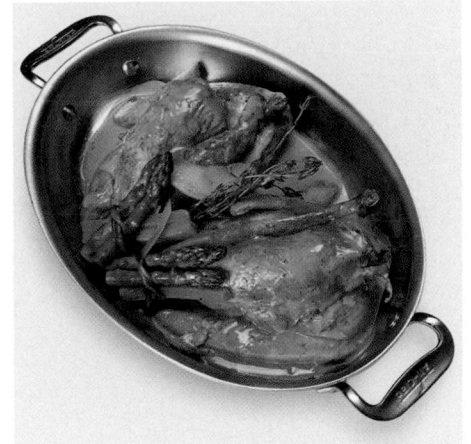

1. Season the pheasant with salt and pepper. Bard the body with the fatback.
2. Roast on a bed of mirepoix at 350°F (180°C) until done, approximately 1½ hours.
3. Peel and core each apple and slice into eight pieces. Sauté the apples in the butter just until tender.
4. When the pheasant is done, remove it from the pan and reserve in a warm place. Deglaze the pan with the cognac, add the crème fraîche and bring to a simmer. Strain the sauce and adjust the seasonings.
5. Serve one half pheasant per person, accompanied by the sliced apples and sauce.

Approximate values per serving: **Calories** 630, **Total fat** 40 g, **Saturated fat** 23 g, **Cholesterol** 220 mg, **Sodium** 1360 mg, **Total carbohydrates** 21 g, **Protein** 46 g, **Vitamin A** 45%

BRAISED ANTELOPE IN SOUR CREAM

Yield: 8 Servings, 6–8 oz. (180–250 g) each   **Method:** Braising

Salt pork	3 oz.	90 g
Bottom round of antelope, 4–5 lb. (1.9–2.4 kg)	1	1
Onions, small dice	12 oz.	360 g
Garlic cloves, sliced	2	2
Carrots, sliced	8 oz.	240 g
Red wine	24 fl. oz.	720 ml
Veal or game stock	3 pt.	1.4 lt
Bay leaves	2	2
Fresh rosemary, chopped	1 tsp.	5 ml
Fresh thyme	1/2 tsp.	2 ml
Juniper berries, crushed	10	10
Tomato paste	2 Tbsp.	30 ml
Clarified butter	1 fl. oz.	30 ml
Flour	1 Tbsp.	15 ml
Sour cream	1 pt.	480 ml
Salt and pepper	TT	TT

1. Render the salt pork. Brown the antelope meat well in the fat.
2. Add the onions, garlic and carrots; sauté until the vegetables are tender.
3. Add the wine, stock, herbs, juniper berries and tomato paste. Braise in a 325°F (160°C) oven until the meat is tender, approximately 1½ to 2 hours.
4. Remove the meat from the pan and hold in a warm place. If necessary, make a blond roux with the butter and flour and use it to thicken the sauce. Bring to a simmer, then strain the sauce.
5. Add the sour cream, heat the sauce thoroughly and season to taste with salt and pepper. Slice the meat thinly and top with sauce for service.

Approximate values per 8-oz. (240-g) serving: **Calories** 580, **Total fat** 21 g, **Saturated fat** 11 g, **Cholesterol** 320 mg, **Sodium** 1110 mg, **Total carbohydrates** 24 g, **Protein** 72 g, **Vitamin A** 80%

> "In the hands of an able cook, fish can become
> an inexhaustible source of perpetual delight."
>
> —JEAN-ANTHELME BRILLAT-SAVARIN (1755–1826)

CHAPTER NINETEEN

FISH AND SHELLFISH

After studying this chapter, you will be able to:

- understand the structure and composition of fish and shellfish

- identify a variety of fish and shellfish

- purchase fish and shellfish appropriate for your needs

- store fish and shellfish properly

- prepare fish and shellfish for cooking

- apply various cooking methods to fish and shellfish

FISH ARE AQUATIC VERTEBRATES WITH FINS for swimming and gills for breathing. Of the more than 30,000 species known, most live in the seas and oceans; freshwater species are far less numerous. Shellfish are aquatic invertebrates with shells or carapaces. They are found in both fresh and salt water.

Always an important food source, fish and shellfish have become increasingly popular in recent years, due in part to demands from health-conscious consumers. Because of increased demand and improved preservation and transportation techniques, good-quality fish and shellfish, once found only along seacoasts and lakes, are now readily available to almost every food service operation.

Many fish and shellfish species are very expensive; all are highly perishable. Because their cooking times are generally shorter and their flavors more delicate than meat or poultry, special attention must be given to fish and shellfish to prevent spoilage and to produce high-quality finished products.

In this chapter, you will learn how to identify a large assortment of fish and shellfish as well as how to properly purchase and store them, fabricate or prepare them for cooking and cook them by a variety of dry-heat and moist-heat cooking methods. This chapter presents many of the cooking methods applied to meats and poultry in the previous chapters. Review the corresponding procedures for meats and poultry, and note the similarities and differences.

STRUCTURE AND MUSCLE COMPOSITION

The fish and shellfish used in food service operations can be divided into three categories: fish, mollusks and crustaceans.

Fish (Fr. *poisson*) include both fresh- and saltwater varieties. They have fins and an internal skeleton of bone and cartilage. Based on shape and skeletal structure, fish can be divided into two groups: round fish and flatfish. **Round fish** swim in a vertical position and have eyes on both sides of their heads (Figure 19.1). Their bodies may be truly round, oval or compressed. **Flatfish** have asymmetrical, compressed bodies, swim in a horizontal position and have both eyes on top of their heads (Figure 19.2). Flatfish are bottom dwellers; most are found in deep ocean waters around the world. The skin on top of their bodies is dark, to camouflage them from predators, and can change color according to their surroundings. Their scales are small, and their dorsal and anal fins run the length of their bodies.

Mollusks (Fr. *mollusque*) are shellfish characterized by soft, unsegmented bodies with no internal skeleton. Most mollusks have hard outer shells. Single-shelled mollusks such as abalone are known as **univalves**. Those with two shells, such as clams, oysters and mussels, are known as **bivalves**. Squid and octopus, which are known as **cephalopods**, do not have a hard outer shell. Rather, they have a single thin internal shell called a *pen* or *cuttlebone*.

Crustaceans (Fr. *crustacés*) are also shellfish. They have a hard outer skeleton or shell and jointed appendages. Crustaceans include lobsters, crabs and shrimp.

The flesh of fish and shellfish consists primarily of water, protein, fat and minerals. Fish flesh is composed of short muscle fibers, pleated in shape and separated by delicate sheets of connective tissue. See Figure 19.3. Unlike the connective tissue in meat, the connective

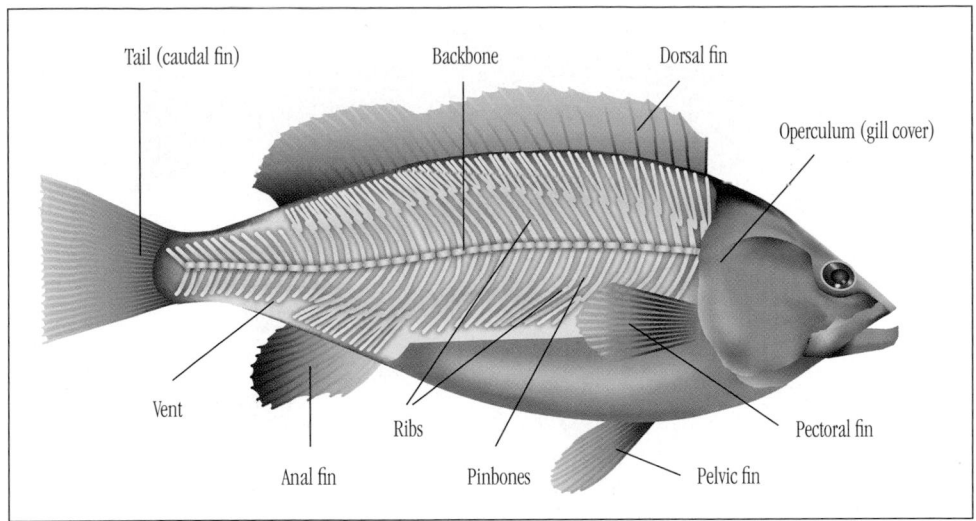

FIGURE 19.1 ▶ Bone structure of a round fish.

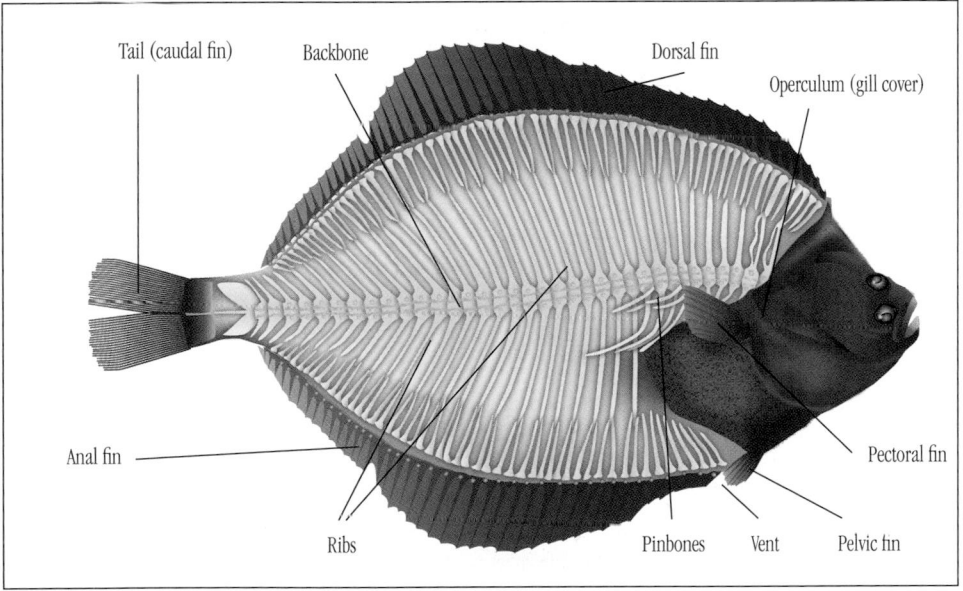

FIGURE 19.2 ▶ Bone structure of a flatfish.

SEAFOOD

Seafood means different things to different people. For some, the term applies only to shellfish or to shellfish and other small edible marine creatures. For others, it is limited to saltwater shellfish or to saltwater shellfish and fish. For yet others, it refers to all fish and shellfish, both freshwater and saltwater. Because of the term's vagueness, it is not used here.

tissue in fish is weak and does not require long cooking to break it down. Fish, as well as most shellfish, are naturally tender, so the purpose of cooking is to firm proteins and enhance flavor. The absence of the oxygen-carrying protein myoglobin makes fish flesh very light or white in color. (The orange color of salmon and some trout comes from pigments found in their food.) Compared to meats, fish do not contain large amounts of intermuscular fat. But the amount of fat a fish does contain affects the way it responds to cooking. Fish containing a relatively large amount of fat, such as salmon and mackerel, are known as fatty or oily fish. Fish such as cod and haddock contain very little fat and are referred to as lean fish. Shellfish are also very lean.

IDENTIFYING FISH AND SHELLFISH

Identifying fish and shellfish properly can be difficult because of the vast number of similar-appearing fish and shellfish that are separate species within each family. Adding confusion are the various colloquial names given to the same fish or the same name given to different

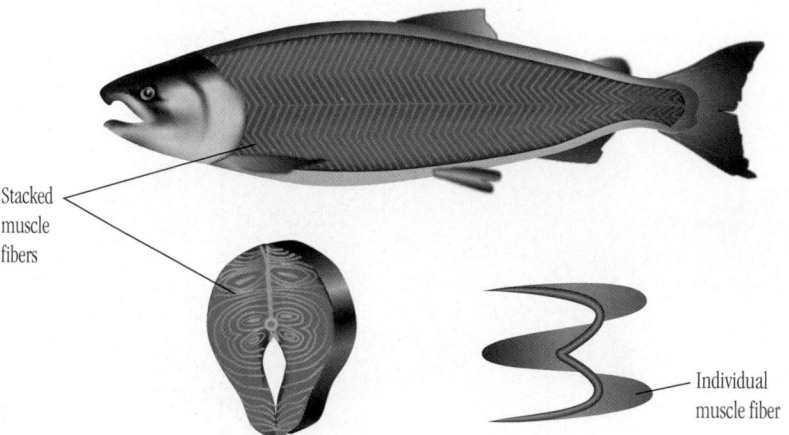

FIGURE 19.3 ▶ Muscle fibers in a round fish.

fish in different localities. Fish with an unappealing name may also be given a catchier name or the name of a similar but more popular item for marketing purposes. Moreover, some species are referred to by a foreign name, especially on menus.

The FDA publishes a list of approved market names for food fish in *The Seafood List: FDA Guide to Acceptable Market Names for Food Fish Sold in Interstate Commerce 2009.* The list is updated regularly and available on the FDA's Web site at the Center for Food Safety and Applied Nutrition. Deviations from this list are strongly discouraged but difficult to enforce. We attempt to use the most common names for each item, whether they are zoologically accurate or not.

Fish

ROUND FISH

Bass (Fr. *bar*) commonly refers to a number of unrelated spiny-finned fish. The better-known freshwater bass varieties (largemouth, smallmouth, redeye and black) are actually members of the sunfish family. They are lean and delicate but, as game, not commercially available in the United States. The saltwater bass varieties (black sea bass and striped bass) are popular commercial items.

Black sea bass are sometimes referred to as rock sea bass. They have a lean, firm white flesh with a mild flavor and flaky texture. They usually weigh from 1½ to 3 pounds (720 to 1360 grams) and are most prevalent in the Atlantic Ocean between New York and North Carolina. Black sea bass can be prepared by almost any cooking method and are often served whole in Chinese and Italian cuisines.

Striped bass, often erroneously referred to as rockfish, are **anadromous**. True striped bass cannot be marketed because pollution and overfishing have damaged the supply. A hybrid of striped bass and either white bass or white perch is **aquafarmed** for commercial use, however. It is this hybrid that food service operations receive as striped bass. Whole fish weigh from 1 to 5 pounds (450 grams to 2.2 kilograms). Striped bass have a rich, sweet flavor and firm texture. They can be steamed, baked, poached or broiled.

Striped Bass

Catfish are scaleless freshwater fish common in southern lakes and rivers and now aquafarmed extensively. Aquafarm raising eliminates the "muddy" flavor once associated with catfish and ensures a year-round supply. The flesh is pure white with a moderate fat content; a mild, sweet flavor; and a firm texture. Channel catfish are the most important commercially. They usually weigh from 1½ to 5 pounds (720 grams to 2.2 kilograms). The smaller of these fish are known as **fiddlers**; they are often deep-fried and served whole. Catfish may be prepared by almost any cooking method, but are especially well suited to frying. Note that other species are often imported to the United States under the generic

Black Sea Bass

anadromous describes a fish that migrates from a saltwater habitat to spawn in fresh water

aquafarming also known as aquaculture; the business, science and practice of raising large quantities of fish and shellfish in tanks, ponds or ocean pens

name *catfish*. Only products labeled "U.S. Farm-Raised Catfish" provide the consistent high quality and flavor that consumers have come to expect, however.

The **cod** (Fr. *cabillaud*) family includes Atlantic and Pacific cod as well as pollock, haddock, whiting and hake. Cod have a mild, delicate flavor and lean, firm white flesh that flakes apart easily. Cod can be prepared by most cooking methods, although grilling is not recommended because the flesh is too flaky.

Catfish

drawn a market form for fish in which the viscera is removed

Atlantic cod are the best-selling fish in America. They are available fresh, whole or **drawn**, or cut into fillets or steaks. They are also available frozen and are often used for precooked or prebreaded sticks or portions. Smoked cod and dried

Atlantic Cod

salt cod (Sp. *bacalao*) are also available. Although cod may reach 200 pounds (90 kilograms), most market cod weigh 10 pounds (4.4 kilograms) or less. **Scrod** is a marketing term for cod or haddock weighing less than 2½ pounds (1.1 kilograms) or less than 20 inches (50 centimeters) in length.

Haddock look like thin, small Atlantic cod and weigh about 2 to 5 pounds (900 grams to 2.3 kilograms). They have a stronger flavor and more delicate texture than Atlantic cod.

Pacific cod, also known as gray cod, are found in the northern Pacific Ocean and are not as abundant as their Atlantic cousins. Pacific cod are most often available frozen; they should be labeled "true cod" to distinguish them from rock cod and black cod, which are unrelated.

Pollock, also known as Boston bluefish or blue cod, are plentiful in the northern Atlantic and Pacific Oceans. Their flesh is gray-pink when raw, turning white when cooked. Pollock are often frozen at sea, then reprocessed into surimi. They can also be salted or smoked.

Pollock

Eels (Fr. *anguilles*) are long, snakelike freshwater fish with dorsal and anal fins running the length of their bodies. (The conger eel is from a different family and is used in Japanese cooking.) American and European eels are available live, whole, gutted or as fillets. Eels have a high fat content and firm flesh; they are sweet and mildly flavored. Their tough skin should be removed before cooking. Eels may be steamed, baked, fried or used in stews. Baby eels are a springtime delicacy, especially in Spain, where they are pan-fried in olive oil and garlic with hot red peppers. Smoked eels are also available.

Eel

The **grouper** family includes almost four hundred varieties found in temperate waters worldwide. The more common Atlantic Ocean varieties are the yellowfin grouper, black grouper, red grouper and gag; the Pacific Ocean varieties are the sea bass (also known as jewfish and different from the black sea bass) and spotted cabrilla. Although some species can reach 800 pounds or more, most commercial varieties are sold in the 5- to 20-pound (2.2- to 8.8-kilogram) range. They have lean white flesh with a mild to sweet flavor and very firm texture. Their skin, which is tough and strongly flavored, is generally removed before cooking. Grouper fillets may be baked, deep-fried, broiled or grilled.

Grouper

Herring (Fr. *hareng*) are long, silvery-blue fish found in both the northern Atlantic and Pacific Oceans. Their strongly flavored flesh has a moderate to high fat content. Whole herring weigh up to 8 ounces (225 grams). Fresh herring may be butterflied or filleted and roasted, broiled or grilled. But because herring are very soft and tend to spoil quickly, they are rarely available fresh in the United States. More often, they are smoked (and known as kippers) or cured in brine.

Very young, small herring are known as **sardines** (Fr. *sardine*). They have fatty, oily flesh with a flaky texture. Sardines are usually sold canned, whole or as skinned and boned fillets, or fried or smoked and packed in oil or sauce. Sardines are used primarily for sandwiches and salads.

Sardines

John Dory (Fr. *St. Pierre*), also known as St. Peter's fish, have a distinctive round, black spot with a yellow halo on each side of the body. Their flesh is white, firm and finely flaked. They may be filleted and prepared like flounder and are a classic bouillabaisse ingredient.

John Dory

Mackerel (Fr. *maquereau*) of culinary importance include king and Spanish mackerel as well as tuna and wahoo, which are discussed separately later. The species known as Atlantic and Pacific mackerel are not generally used for food because of their small size and high fat content. Mackerel flesh has a high fat content, gray to pink coloring, a mild flavor and flaky texture. The flesh becomes firm and off-white when cooked. Mackerel are best broiled, grilled, smoked or baked.

Mackerel

Mahi-Mahi

Mahi-mahi is the more commonly used name for dolphin or dolphinfish; this Hawaiian name is used to distinguish them from the marine mammal of the same name. (Dolphins and porpoises are marine mammals.) Also known by their Spanish name, *dorado*, mahi-mahi are brilliantly colored fish found in tropical seas. Mahi-mahi weigh about 15 pounds (6.6 kilograms) and are sold whole or as fillets. Their flesh is off-white to pink, lean and firm with a sweet flavor. Dolphinfish can be broiled, grilled or baked. The meat may become dry when cooked, however, so a sauce or marinade is recommended.

Monkfish are also known as angler fish, goosefish, rape and lotte. These extraordinarily ugly fish are rarely seen whole, for the large head is usually discarded before reaching market. Only the tail is edible; it is available in fillets, fresh or frozen. The scaleless skin must be removed. The flesh is lean, pearly white and very firm. Its texture and flavor have earned monkfish the nickname of "poor man's lobster." Monkfish absorb flavors easily and are baked, steamed, fried, grilled or broiled. They are also used for stews and soups.

Monkfish Tail

Orange roughy are caught in the South Pacific off the coasts of New Zealand and Australia. They have bright orange skin and firm, pearly-white flesh with a low fat content and extremely bland flavor. Orange roughy are almost always marketed as skinless, boneless frozen fillets, averaging 6 to 8 ounces (170 to 225 grams) each. Widely available year-round, they can be broiled, steamed, grilled or prepared in the same manner as cod.

Orange Roughy

Red snapper is also known as the American or northern red snapper. Although there are many members of the snapper family, only one is the true red snapper. Red-skinned rockfish are often mislabeled as the more popular red snapper or Pacific snapper, a practice that is currently legal only in California. True red snapper have lean, pink flesh that becomes white when cooked; it is sweet-flavored and flaky. They are sold whole or as fillets with the skin left on for identification. Red snapper may reach 35 pounds, but most are marketed at only 4 to 6 pounds (1.8 to 2.7 kilograms) or as 1- to 3-pound (450-gram to 1.3-kilogram) fillets. Red snapper can be prepared using almost any cooking method. The head and bones are excellent for stock.

Red Snapper

Salmon (Fr. *saumon*) live in both the northern Atlantic and Pacific Oceans, returning to the freshwater rivers and streams of their birth to spawn. Salmon flesh gets its distinctive pink-red color from fat-soluble carotenoids found in the crustaceans on which they feed.

SURIMI

Surimi is made from a highly processed fish paste colored, flavored and shaped to resemble shrimp, lobster, crab or other shellfish. Most surimi is based on Alaskan pollock, but some blends include varying amounts of real crab, shrimp or other items. Available chilled or frozen, surimi is already fully cooked and ready to add to salads, pasta, sauces or other dishes. Surimi is very low in fat and relatively high in protein. Because of processing techniques, however, it has more sodium and fewer vitamins and minerals than the real fish or shellfish it replaces. Americans now consume more than 100 million pounds of surimi each year, and its popularity continues to grow. The FDA no longer requires that all surimi products be labeled "imitation."

Atlantic salmon is the most important commercially, accounting for one-fourth of all salmon produced worldwide. Extensive aquafarms in Norway, Canada and Scotland produce a steady supply of Atlantic salmon. For marketing purposes, the fish's point of origin is often added to the name (for example, Norwegian, Scottish or Shetland Atlantic salmon). Atlantic salmon have a rich pink color and moist flesh. Their average weight is from 4 to 12 pounds (1.8 to 5.4 kilograms). Wild Atlantic salmon are almost never available.

Atlantic Salmon

Chinook or **king salmon** from the Pacific are also highly desirable. They average from 5 to 30 pounds (2.2 to 13.2 kilograms) and have red-orange flesh with a high fat content and rich flavor. Like other salmon, their flesh separates into large flakes when cooked. Chinooks are often marketed by the name of the river from which they are harvested (for example, Columbia, Yukon or Copper Chinook salmon). They are distinguished by the black interior of their mouth.

Chinook or King Salmon

Coho or **silver salmon** have a pinkish flesh and are available fresh or frozen, wild or from aquafarms. Wild coho average from 3 to 12 pounds (1.3 to 5.4 kilograms), whereas aquafarmed coho are much smaller, usually less than 1 pound (450 grams).

Other varieties, such as chum, sockeye, red, blueback and pink salmon, are usually canned but may be available fresh or frozen.

Salmon can be prepared by many cooking methods: broiling, grilling, poaching, steaming or baking. Frying is not recommended, however, because of their high fat content. Salmon fillets are often cured or smoked. **Gravlax** is salmon that has been cured for one to three days with salt, sugar and dill. **Lox** is salmon that has been cured in a salted brine and then, typically, cold-smoked. **Nova** is used in the eastern United States to refer to a less-salty, cold-smoked salmon.

Mini Coho Salmon

Sea bream is the name given to a large family of fish found in the Mediterranean (gilthead bream), the Caribbean (porgy), the Atlantic (black sea bream) and the Indo-Pacific (emperor and snapper). Because the marketing term *bream* is applied to so many different fish, it is difficult to generalize about their characteristics. Some have very few bones, others have quite a few; some have a rich flavor, others are very mild; some weigh up to 20 pounds (9.6 kilograms), others rarely exceed 5 pounds (2.2 kilograms). Black sea bream, for example, is a good pan fish, reaching only 35 centimeters in length and weighing less than 6 pounds (2.9 kilograms). Their flesh is firm, mild and low in fat. Also marketed as Thai snapper, they are good for baking, grilling or frying.

Black Sea Bream

Sharks provide delicious eating, despite their less-than-appealing appearance and vicious reputation. Mako and blue sharks are the most desirable, with mako often being sold as swordfish. Sand shark, sharp-nose, blacktip, angel and thresher are also available commercially. Most sharks have lean flesh with a mild flavor and firm texture. The flesh is white with tinges of pink or red when raw, turning off-white when cooked. Makos weigh from 30 to 250 pounds (13.5 to 112.5 kilograms); other species may reach as much as 1000 pounds (450 kilograms). All sharks have cartilaginous skeletons and no bones; therefore, they are not actually fish, but rather marine invertebrates. Sharks are usually cut into loins or wheels, then into steaks or cubes. They can be broiled, grilled, baked or fried. An ammonia smell indicates that the shark was not properly treated when caught. Do not buy or eat it.

Blacktip Shark

Swordfish take their name from the long, swordlike bill extending from their upper jaw. These popular fish average about 250 pounds (112.5 kilograms). Their flesh is lean and sweet with a very firm, meatlike texture; it may be gray, pink or off-white when raw, becoming white when cooked. Swordfish are most often available cut into wheels or portioned into steaks perfect for grilling or broiling.

Swordfish Wheel

Tilapia is the name given to several species of freshwater, aquafarm-raised fish bred worldwide. They grow quickly in warm water, reaching about 3 pounds (1.3 kilograms); they are available whole or filleted, fresh or frozen. The flesh is similar to catfish—lean, white and sweet, with a firm texture. Tilapia are sometimes marketed as cherry snapper or sunshine snapper, even though they are not members of the snapper family.

Tilapia

Red Mountain Trout

Rainbow Trout

Trout (Fr. *truite*) are members of the salmon family. Most of the freshwater trout commercially available are aquafarm-raised rainbow trout, although brown trout and brook trout are also being aquafarmed. Some trout species spend part of their lives at sea, returning to fresh water to spawn. On the West Coast, these are called salmon trout or steelhead. Trout have a low to moderate fat content, a flaky texture and a delicate flavor that can be easily overwhelmed by strong sauces. The flesh may be white, orange or pink. Trout are usually marketed at 8 to 10 ounces (225 to 280 grams) each, just right for an individual portion. Lake trout, sometimes known as char or Arctic char (Fr. *alose*) resemble trout and salmon. They are fresh or saltwater fish and are widely aquafarmed. Trout and char can be baked, pan-fried, smoked or steamed.

Tuna (Fr. *thon*) varieties include the bluefin, yellowfin, bonito, bigeye and blackfin. Ahi is the popular market name for either yellowfin or bigeye tuna. All are members of the mackerel family and are found in tropical and subtropical waters around the world. Tuna are large fish, weighing up to several hundred pounds each. Bluefin, the finest and most desirable for sashimi, are becoming very scarce because of overfishing. Regular canned tuna is usually prepared from yellowfin or skipjack; canned white tuna is prepared from albacore, also known as longfin tuna. Pacific tuna that is frozen at sea to preserve its freshness is referred to as clipper fish. Any of these species may be found fresh or frozen, however. Tuna is usually cut into four boneless loins for market. The loins are then cut into steaks, cubes or chunks. The flesh has a low to moderate fat content (a higher fat content is preferred for sashimi) and a deep red color. The dark, reddish-brown muscle that runs along the lateral line is very fatty and can be removed. Tuna flesh turns light gray when cooked and is very firm, with a mild flavor. Tuna work well for grilling or broiling and may be marinated or brushed with seasoned oil during cooking. Tuna are often prepared medium rare to prevent dryness.

Yellowfin Tuna

Wahoo, also known as *ono*, are found throughout tropical and subtropical waters, but are particularly associated with Hawaii (*ono* even means "good to eat" in Hawaiian). They are actually a type of mackerel and are cooked like any other mackerel.

Whitefish species inhabit the freshwater lakes and streams of North America. Lake whitefish, the most important commercially, are related to salmon. They are marketed at up to 7 pounds (3.2 kilograms) and are available whole or filleted. The flesh is firm and white, with a moderate amount of fat and a sweet flavor. Whitefish may be baked, broiled, grilled or smoked and are often used in processed fish products.

Wahoo

FLATFISH

Whitefish

Flounder (Fr. *flet*) have lean, firm flesh that is pearly or pinkish-white with a sweet, mild flavor. Although they are easily boned, most are deheaded and gutted at sea and sold as fresh or frozen fillets. These fillets are very thin and can dry out or spoil easily, so extra care should be taken in handling, preparing and storing them. Recipes that preserve moisture work best with flounder; poaching, steaming and frying are recommended. Many types of flounder are marketed as sole, perhaps in an attempt to cash in on the popularity of true sole. The FDA permits this practice (see Table 19.1).

English sole are actually flounder caught off the West Coast of the United States. They are usually marketed simply as "fillet of sole." They are a plentiful species of fair to average quality.

English Sole

Petrale sole, another West Coast flounder, are generally considered the finest of the domestic "soles." They are most often available as fillets, which tend to be thicker and firmer than other sole fillets.

Domestic Dover sole are also Pacific flounder. They are not as delicate or flavorful as other species of sole or flounder. Moreover, they are often afflicted with a parasite that causes their flesh to have a slimy, gelatinous texture. Domestic Dover sole are not recommended if other sole or flounder are available.

Petrale Sole

TABLE 19.1 FLOUNDER (A.K.A. SOLE)	
ATLANTIC OCEAN	**PACIFIC OCEAN**
Blackback/Winter flounder/Lemon sole	Arrowtooth
Fluke/Summer flounder	Petrale sole
Starry flounder	Rex sole
Yellowtail flounder	English sole
Windowpane flounder	Rock sole
Gray sole/Witch flounder	Sand sole
	Yellowfin sole
	Domestic Dover sole/Pacific flounder
	Butter sole

Lemon sole are the most abundant and popular East Coast flounder. They are also known as blackback or winter flounder (during the winter, they migrate close to shore from the deeper, colder waters). They average 2 pounds (900 grams) in weight.

Halibut are among the largest flatfish; they often weigh up to 300 pounds (135 kilograms). The FDA recognizes only two halibut species: Atlantic (eastern) and Pacific (northern, Alaskan, western) halibut. Both have lean, firm flesh that is snow-white with a sweet, mild flavor. California halibut, which are actually flounder, are similar in taste and texture but average only 12 pounds (5.4 kilograms) each. Halibut may be cut into boneless steaks or skewered on brochettes. The flesh, which dries out easily, can be poached, baked, grilled or broiled and is good with a variety of sauces.

Sole (Fr. *sole*) are probably the most flavorful and finely textured flatfish. Indeed, because of the connotations of quality associated with the name, "sole" is widely used for many species that are not members of the *Soleidae* family. Even though the FDA allows many species of flatfish to be called "sole" for marketing purposes, no true sole is commercially harvested in American waters. Any flatfish harvested in American waters and marketed as sole is actually flounder.

True **Dover sole**, a staple of classic cuisine, are a lean fish with pearly-white flesh and a delicate flavor that can stand up to a variety of sauces and seasonings. They are a member of the *Soleidae* family and come only from the waters off the coasts of England, Africa and Europe. They are imported into the United States as fresh whole fish or fresh or frozen fillets.

Turbot are a Pacific flatfish of no great culinary distinction. In Europe, however, the species known as turbot (Fr. *turbot*) are large diamond-shaped fish highly prized for their delicate flavor and firm, white flesh. They are also marketed as brill.

Lemon Sole

Halibut

True Dover Sole

Turbot

Mollusks

UNIVALVES

Univalves are mollusks with a single shell in which the soft-bodied animal resides. They are actually marine snails with a single foot, used to attach the creature to fixed objects such as rocks.

Abalone have brownish-gray, ear-shaped shells. They are harvested in California, but California law does not permit canning abalone or shipping it out of state, although abalone farms

SNAILS

Although snails (more politely known by their French name, *escargots*) are univalve land animals, they share many characteristics with their marine cousins. They can be poached in court bouillon or removed from their shells and boiled or baked briefly with a seasoned butter or sauce. They should be firm but tender; overcooking makes snails tough and chewy. The most popular varieties are the large white Burgundy snail and the small garden variety called *petit gris*. Fresh snails are available from snail ranches through specialty suppliers. The great majority of snails, however, are purchased canned; most canned snails are produced in France or Taiwan.

Snail (left) and Snail Shell (right)

are making them more readily available. Some frozen abalone is available from Mexico; canned abalone is imported from China and Japan. Abalone are lean with a sweet, delicate flavor similar to that of clams. They are too tough to eat unless tenderized with a mallet or rolling pin. They may then be eaten raw or prepared seviche-style. Great care must be taken when grilling or sautéing abalone, as the meat becomes very tough when overcooked.

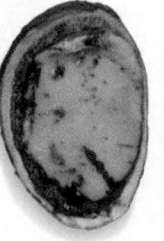 

Abalone

Conch are found in warm waters off the Florida Keys and in the Caribbean. The beautiful peachy-pink shell of the queen conch is prized by beachcombers. Conch meat is lean, smooth and very firm with a sweet-smoky flavor and chewy texture. It can be sliced and pounded to tenderize it, eaten raw with lime juice or slow-cooked whole.

BIVALVES

Bivalves are mollusks with two bilateral shells attached by a central hinge.

Clams (Fr. *palourdes*) are harvested along both the East and West Coasts, with Atlantic clams being more significant commercially. Atlantic Coast clams include hard-shell, soft-shell and surf clams. Clams are available all year, either live in the shell or fresh-shucked (meat removed from the shell). Canned clams, whether minced, chopped or whole, are also available.

Atlantic hard-shell clams or **quahogs** have hard, blue-gray shells. Their chewy meat is not as sweet as other clam meat. Quahogs have different names, depending on their size. **Littlenecks** are generally under 2 inches (5 centimeters) across the shell and usually are served on the half shell or steamed. They are the most expensive clams. **Cherrystones** are generally under 3 inches (7.5 centimeters) across the shell and are sometimes eaten raw but are more often cooked. **Topnecks** are usually cooked and are often served as stuffed clams. **Chowders**, the largest quahogs, are always eaten cooked, especially minced for chowder or soup.

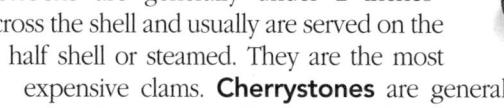

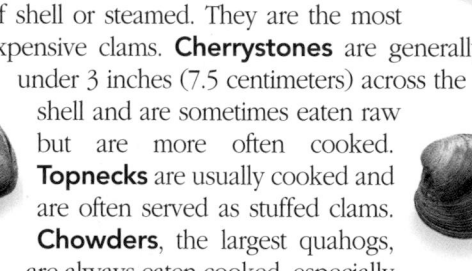

Littlenecks

Cherrystones

Topnecks

Soft-shell clams, also known as Ipswich, steamer and long-necked clams, have thin, brittle shells that do not completely close because of the clam's protruding black-tipped siphon. Their meat is tender and sweet. They are sometimes fried but are more often served steamed.

Surf clams are deep-water clams that reach sizes of 8 inches (20 centimeters) across. They are most often cut into strips for frying or are minced, chopped, processed and canned.

Soft-Shell Clams

Pacific clams are generally too tough to eat raw. The most common is the **Manila clam**, which was introduced along the Pacific coast during the 1930s. Resembling a quahog with a ridged shell, it can be served steamed or on the half shell. **Geoducks** are the largest Pacific clam, sometimes weighing up to 10 pounds (4.5 kilograms) each. They look like huge soft-shell clams with a large, protruding siphon. Their tender, rich bodies and briny flavor are popular in Asian cuisines.

Manila Clams

Cockles are small bivalves, about 1 inch (2.5 centimeters) long, with ridged shells. They are more popular in Europe than the United States and are sometimes used in dishes such as paella and fish soups or stews.

Mussels (Fr. *moules*) are found in waters worldwide. They are excellent steamed in wine or seasoned broth and can be fried or used in soups or pasta dishes.

Cockles

Blue mussels are the most common edible mussel. They are found in the wild along the Atlantic Coast and are aquafarmed on both coasts. Their meat is plump and sweet with a firm, muscular texture. The orangish-yellow meat of cultivated mussels tends to be much larger than that of wild mussels and therefore worth the added cost. Blue mussels are sold live in the shell and average from 10 to 20 per pound. Although available all year, the best-quality blue mussels are harvested during the winter months.

Blue Mussels

Greenshell (or greenlip) mussels from New Zealand and Thailand are much larger than blue mussels, averaging 8 to 12 mussels per pound. Their shells are paler gray, with a distinctive bright-green edge.

Oysters (Fr. *huitres*) have a rough gray shell. Their soft, gray, briny flesh can be eaten raw directly from the shell. They can also be steamed or baked in the shell or shucked and fried, sautéed or added to stews or chowders. Most oysters available in the United States are commercially grown and sold either live in the shell or shucked. There are four main domestic species.

Greenshell Mussels

Atlantic oysters, also called American or Eastern oysters, have darker, flatter shells than other oysters.

European flat oysters are often incorrectly called Belon (true Belon oysters live only in the Belon river of France); they are very round and flat and look like giant brownish-green Olympias.

Olympias are the only oysters native to the Pacific Coast; they are tiny (about the size of a 50-cent coin).

Pacific oysters, also called Japanese oysters, are aqua farmed along the Pacific Coast; they have curly, thick striated shells and silvery-gray to gold to almost-white meat.

European Flat Oysters

Gulf Oysters

Although it may seem as though there are hundreds of oyster species on the market, only two are commercially significant: the Atlantic oyster and the Pacific oyster. These two species yield dozens of different varieties, however, depending on their origin. For example, Atlantic oysters may be referred to as bluepoints, Chesapeake Bay, Florida Gulf, Long Island and so on, whereas Pacific oysters include Penn Cove Select, Westcott Bay, Hamma-Hamma, Kumamoto and Portuguese, among others. An oyster's flavor reflects the minerals, nutrients and salts in its water and mud bed, so a Bristol from Maine and an Apalachicola from Florida will taste very different, even though they are the same Atlantic species.

Olympia Oysters

Bluepoint Oysters

Scallops (Fr. *coquilles Saint Jacques*) contain an edible white adductor muscle that holds together the fan-shaped shells. Because they die quickly, they are almost always shucked and cleaned on board the ship. The sea scallop and the bay scallop, both cold-water varieties, and the calico scallop, a warm-water variety, are the most important commercially. Sea scallops are the largest, with an average count of 20 to 30 per pound. Larger sea scallops are also available. Bay scallops average 70 to 90 per pound; calico scallops average 70 to 110 per pound. Fresh or frozen shucked, cleaned scallops are the most common market form, but live scallops in the shell and shucked scallops with roe attached (very popular in Europe) are also available. Scallops are sweet, with a tender texture. Raw scallops should be a translucent ivory color and nonsymmetrically round and should feel springy. They can be steamed, broiled, grilled, fried, sautéed or baked. When overcooked, however, scallops quickly become chewy and dry. Only extremely fresh scallops should be eaten raw.

Hamma-Hamma Oysters

Sea Scallops

Octopus

CEPHALOPODS

Cephalopods are marine mollusks with distinct heads, well-developed eyes, a number of arms that attach to the head near the mouth and a saclike fin-bearing mantle. They do not have an outer shell; instead, there is a thin internal shell called a **pen** or **cuttlebone**.

Octopus is generally quite tough and requires mechanical tenderization or long, moist-heat cooking to make it palatable. Most octopus is imported from Portugal, though fresh ones are available on the East Coast during the winter. Octopus is sold by the pound, fresh or frozen, usually whole. Octopus skin is gray when raw, turning purple when cooked. The interior flesh is white, lean, firm and flavorful.

Squid, known by their Italian name, *calamari*, are becoming increasingly popular in the United States. Similar to octopuses but much smaller, they are harvested along both American coasts and elsewhere around the world (the finest are the East Coast loligo or winter squid). They range in size from an average of 8 to 10 per pound to the giant South American squid, which is sold as tenderized steaks. The squid's tentacles, mantle (body tube) and fins are edible. Squid meat is white to ivory in color, turning darker with age. It is moderately lean, slightly sweet, firm and tender, but it toughens quickly if overcooked. Squid are available either fresh or frozen and packed in blocks.

Squid

Crustaceans

Crustaceans are found in both fresh and salt water. They have a hard outer shell and jointed appendages, and they breathe through gills.

Crayfish (Fr. *écrevisses*), generally called *crayfish* in the North and *crawfish* or *crawdad* in the South, are freshwater creatures that look like miniature lobsters. They are harvested from the wild or aquafarmed in Louisiana and the Pacific Northwest. They are from 3½ to 7 inches (8 to 17.5 centimeters) in length when marketed and may be purchased live or precooked and frozen. The lean meat, found mostly in the tail, is sweet and tender. Crayfish can be boiled whole and served hot or cold. The tail meat can be deep-fried or used in soups, bisque or sauces. Crayfish are a staple of Cajun cuisine, often used in gumbo, étouffée and jambalaya. Whole crayfish become brilliant red when cooked and may be used as a garnish.

Crayfish

Crabs (Fr. *crabes*) are found along the North American coast in great numbers and are shipped throughout the world in fresh, frozen and canned forms. Crab meat varies in flavor and texture and can be used in a range of prepared dishes, from chowders to curries to casseroles. Crabs purchased live should last up to 5 days; dead crabs should not be used.

King crabs are very large crabs (usually around 10 pounds [4.5 kilograms]) caught in the very cold waters of the northern Pacific. Their meat is very sweet and snow-white. King crabs are always sold frozen, usually in the shell. In-shell forms include sections or clusters, legs and claws or split legs. The meat is also available in "fancy" packs of whole leg and body meat, or shredded and minced pieces.

King Crab Legs

Dungeness Crab

Dungeness crabs are found along the West Coast. They weigh 1½ to 4 pounds (680 grams to 1.8 kilograms) and have delicate, sweet meat. They are sold live, precooked and frozen, or as picked meat, usually in 5-pound (2.2-kilogram) vacuum-packed cans.

Blue crabs are found along the entire eastern seaboard and account for approximately 50 percent of the total weight of all crab species harvested in the United States. Their meat is rich and sweet. Blue crabs are available as hard-shell or soft-shell. Hard-shell crabs are sold live, precooked and frozen, or as picked meat. Soft-shell crabs are those harvested within 6 hours after molting and are available live (generally only from May 15 to September 15)

Soft-Shell Crabs

Blue Crab

or frozen. They are often steamed and served whole. Soft-shells can be sautéed, fried, broiled or added to soups or stews. Blue crabs are sold by size, with an average diameter of 4 to 7 inches (10 to 18 centimeters).

Snow or **spider crabs** are an abundant species, most often used as a substitute for the scarcer and more expensive king crab. They are harvested from Alaskan waters and along the eastern coast of Canada. Snow crab is sold precooked, usually frozen. The meat can be used in soups, salads, omelets or other prepared dishes. Legs are often served cold as an appetizer.

Stone crabs are generally available only as cooked claws, either fresh or frozen (the claws cannot be frozen raw because the meat sticks to the shell). In stone crab fishery, only the claw is harvested. After the claw is removed, the crab is returned to the water, where in approximately 18 months it regenerates a new claw. Claws average 2½ to 5½ ounces (75 to 155 grams) each. The meat is firm, with a sweet flavor similar to lobster. Cracked claws are served hot or cold, usually with cocktail sauce, lemon butter or other accompaniments.

Lobsters have brown to blue-black outer shells and firm, white meat with a rich, sweet flavor. Lobster shells turn red when cooked. They are usually poached, steamed, simmered, baked or grilled, and can be served hot or cold. Picked meat can be used in prepared dishes, soups or sautés. Lobsters must be kept alive until just before cooking. Dead lobsters should not be eaten. The Maine, also known as American or clawed lobster, and the spiny lobster are the most commonly marketed species.

Maine lobsters have edible meat in both their tails and claws; they are considered superior in flavor to all other lobsters. They come from the cold waters along the northeast coast and are most often sold live. Maine lobsters may be purchased by weight (for example, 1¼ pounds [525 grams], 1½ pounds [650 grams] or 2 pounds [900 grams] each), or as chix (that is, a lobster weighing less than 1 pound [450 grams]). Maine lobsters may also be purchased as culls (lobsters with only one claw) or bullets (lobsters with no claws). They are available frozen or as cooked, picked meat.

Figure 19.4 shows a cross-section of a Maine lobster and identifies the stomach, tomalley (the olive-green liver) and coral (the roe). The stomach is not eaten; the tomalley and coral are very flavorful and are often used in the preparation of sauces and other items.

Spiny lobsters, harvested in many parts of the world, have very small claws and are valuable only for their meaty tails, which are notched with short spines. Nearly all spiny lobsters marketed in the United States are sold as frozen tails, often identified as rock lobster. Those found off Florida and Brazil and in the Caribbean are marketed as warm-water tails; those found off South Africa, Australia and New Zealand are called cold-water tails. Cold-water spiny tails are considered superior to their warm-water cousins.

Slipper lobster, **lobsterette** and **squat lobster** are all clawless species found in tropical, subtropical and temperate waters worldwide. Although they are popular in some countries, their flavor is inferior to that of both Maine and spiny lobsters. **Langoustines** are small North Atlantic lobsters.

Shrimp (Fr. *crevettes*) are found worldwide and are widely popular. Gulf whites, pinks, browns and black tigers are just a few of the dozens of shrimp varieties used in food service operations. Although fresh, head-on shrimp are available, the most common

Snow Crab Legs

Stone Crab Claws

Maine Lobster

Tiger Shrimp

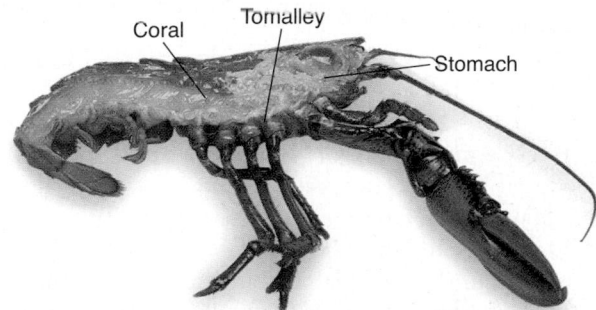

FIGURE 19.4 ▶ Parts of a Maine lobster.

Shrimp

Prawn

FIGURE 19.5 ▶ PUFI mark and statements.

FIGURE 19.6 ▶ Product inspection stamp.

form is raw, head-off (also called green headless) shrimp with the shell on. Most shrimp are deheaded and frozen at sea to preserve freshness. Shrimp are available in many forms: raw, peeled and deveined; cooked, peeled and deveined; and individually quick-frozen, as well as in a variety of processed, breaded or canned products. Shrimp are graded by size, which can range from 400 per pound (titi) to 8 per pound (extra-colossal), and are sold in counts per pound. For example, shrimp marketed as "21–26 count" means that there is an average of 21 to 26 shrimp per pound; shrimp marketed as "U-10" means that there are fewer than 10 shrimp per pound.

Green Headless Shrimp

Prawn is often used interchangeably with the word *shrimp* in English-speaking countries. Although it is perhaps more accurate to refer to freshwater species as prawns and saltwater species as shrimp, in commercial practice, prawn refers to any large shrimp. Equally confusing, *scampi* is the Italian name for the Dublin Bay prawn (which is actually a species of miniature lobster), but in the United States *scampi* refers to shrimp sautéed in garlic butter.

NUTRITION

Fish and shellfish are low in calories, fat and sodium, and are high in protein and vitamins A, B and D. Fish and shellfish are also high in minerals, especially calcium (particularly in canned fish with edible bones), phosphorus, potassium and iron (especially mollusks). Fish are high in a group of polyunsaturated fatty acids called omega-3, which may help combat high blood cholesterol levels and aid in preventing some heart disease. Shellfish are not as high in cholesterol as was once thought. Crustaceans are higher in cholesterol than mollusks, but both have considerably lower levels than red meat or eggs.

The cooking methods used for fish and shellfish also contribute to their healthfulness. The most commonly used cooking methods—broiling, grilling, poaching and steaming—add little or no fat.

INSPECTION AND GRADING OF FISH AND SHELLFISH

Inspection

Unlike mandatory meat and poultry inspections, fish and shellfish inspections are voluntary. They are performed in a fee-for-service program supervised by the United States Department of Commerce (USDC).

Type 1 inspection services cover plant, product and processing methods from the raw material to the final product. The "Packed under Federal Inspection" (PUFI) mark or statement shown in Figure 19.5 can be used on product labels processed under Type 1 inspection services. It signifies that the product is safe and wholesome, is properly labeled, has reasonably good flavor and odor and was produced under inspection in an official establishment.

Type 2 inspection services are usually performed in a warehouse, processing plant or cold storage facility on specific product lots. See Figure 19.6. A lot inspection determines whether the product complies with purchase agreement criteria (usually defined in a spec sheet) such as condition, weight, labeling and packaging integrity.

Type 3 inspection services are for sanitation only. Fishing vessels or plants that meet the requirements are recognized as official establishments and are included in the *USDC Approved List of Fish Establishments and Products.* The list is available to governmental and institutional purchasing agents as well as to retail and restaurant buyers. Updated copies of the list are published on the Internet.

Grading

Only fish processed under Type 1 inspection services are eligible for grading. Each type of fish has its own grading criteria, but because of the great variety of fish and shellfish, the USDC has been able to set grading criteria for only the most common types.

The grades assigned to fish are A, B or C. Grade A products are top quality and must have good flavor and odor and be practically free of physical blemishes or defects. The great majority of fresh and frozen fish and shellfish consumed in restaurants is Grade A. See Figure 19.7. Grade B indicates good quality; Grade C indicates fairly good quality. Grade B and C products are most often canned or processed.

FIGURE 19.7 ▶ Grade A stamp.

PURCHASING AND STORING FISH AND SHELLFISH

Determining Freshness

Because fish and shellfish are highly perishable, an inspection stamp does not necessarily ensure top quality. A few hours at the wrong temperature or a couple of days in the refrigerator can turn high-quality fish or shellfish into garbage. It is important that chefs be able to determine for themselves the freshness and quality of the fish and shellfish they purchase or use. Freshness should be checked before purchasing and again just before cooking.

Freshness can be determined by the following criteria:

1. **Smell**—This is by far the easiest way to determine freshness. Fresh fish should have a slight sea smell or no odor at all. Any off-odors or ammonia odors are a sure sign of aged or improperly handled fish.

2. **Eyes**—The eyes should be clear and full. Sunken eyes mean that the fish is drying out and is probably not fresh.

3. **Gills**—The gills should be intact and bright red. Brown gills are a sign of age.

4. **Texture**—Generally, the flesh of fresh fish should be firm. Mushy flesh or flesh that does not spring back when pressed with a finger is a sign of poor quality or age.

5. **Fins and scales**—Fins and scales should be moist and full without excessive drying on the outer edges. Dry fins or scales are a sign of age; damaged fins or scales may be a sign of mishandling.

6. **Appearance**—Fish cuts should be moist and glistening, without bruises or dark spots. Edges should not be brown or dry.

7. **Movement**—Shellfish should be purchased live and should show movement. Lobsters and other crustaceans should be active. Clams, mussels and oysters that are partially opened should snap shut when tapped with a finger. (Exceptions are geoduck, razor and steamer clams whose siphons protrude, preventing the shell from closing completely.) Ones that do not close are dead and should not be used. Avoid mollusks with broken shells or heavy shells that may be filled with mud or sand.

HOW FRESH IS FROZEN FISH?

- *Fresh*—The item is not and has never been frozen.

- *Chilled*—Now used by some in the industry to replace the more ambiguous "fresh"; indicates that the item was refrigerated, that is, held at 30°F to 34°F (−1°C to 1°C).

- *Flash-frozen*—The item was quickly frozen on board the ship or at a processing plant within hours of being caught.

- *Fresh-frozen*—The item was quick-frozen while still fresh but not as quickly as flash-frozen.

- *Frozen*—The item was subjected to temperatures of 0°F (−18°C) or lower to preserve its inherent quality.

- *Glazed*—A frozen product dipped in water; the ice forms a glaze that protects the item from freezer burn.

- *Fancy*—Code word for "previously frozen."

Whole or Round

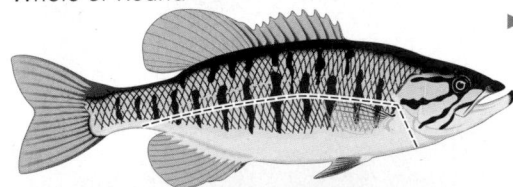

Drawn

Dressed or Pan-Dressed

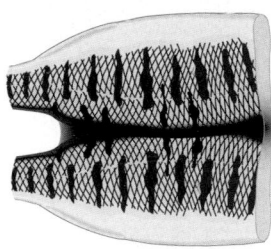

Butterflied Fillets

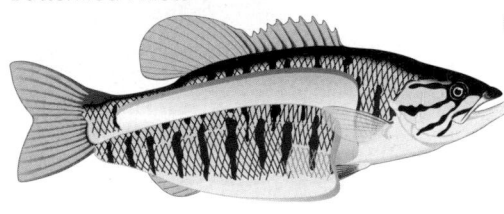

Fillets

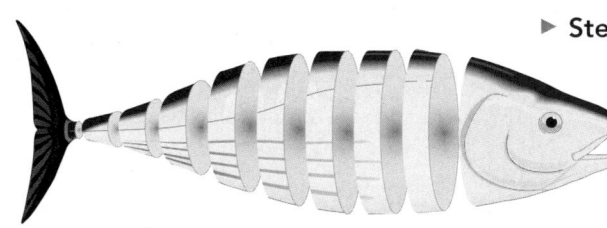

Steaks

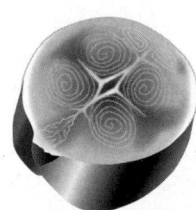

Wheel or Center-Cut

Purchasing Fish and Shellfish

Fish are available from wholesalers in a variety of market forms:

▶ **Whole** or **round**—As caught, intact.

▶ **Drawn**—Viscera (internal organs) are removed; most whole fish are purchased this way.

▶ **Dressed**—Viscera, gills, fins and scales are removed.

   ▶ **Pan-dressed**—Viscera and gills are removed; fish is scaled and fins and tail are trimmed. The head is usually removed, although small fish, such as trout, may be pan-dressed with the head still attached. Pan-dressed fish are then pan-fried.

▶ **Butterflied**—A pan-dressed fish, boned and opened flat like a book. The two sides remain attached by the back or belly skin.

▶ **Fillet**—The side of a fish removed intact, boneless or semiboneless, with or without skin.

▶ **Steak**—A cross-section slice, with a small section of backbone attached known as *darne* in French; usually prepared from large round fish such as salmon, swordfish or tuna.

▶ **Wheel** or **center-cut**—Used for swordfish and sharks, which are cut into large boneless pieces from which steaks are then cut.

FARMING THE SEAS

Aquaculture or fish farming has been practiced in Asia for thousands of years. As wild fish and shellfish have been depleted by overfishing, aquaculture has grown into a major industry in the United States and many other non-Asian countries. More than 70 percent of the seafood consumed in the United States today is imported, and more than 40 percent of this imported seafood is farm raised.

Aquaculture can take place in closed environments, where water is constantly circulated through tanks and ponds. Net pens or cages employed offshore can also hold vast numbers of fish. Mollusks (clams, oysters and mussels) are farmed in near-shore beds or, sometimes in the case of mussels, on long lines or even on the bases of offshore oil rigs. Catfish and trout have long been farm raised in the United States, but now salmon, tilapia, hybrid striped bass, abalone, crayfish, freshwater prawns, shrimp and sturgeon are also produced. Constant experimentation is taking place with different varieties: Norwegian scientists are working with halibut, and in Ecuador sturgeon are being raised for their caviar with the help of Russian experts.

For the food service industry, aquaculture can mean that many fish are no longer seasonal; there is a constant supply, less price fluctuation and more standardized quality. Fish farming is not without its critics; environmental damage can result from poor management practices, and concerns have been raised regarding the use of chemicals and antibiotics. However, as with all industry involved in food production, aquaculture is subject to federal and state regulation for both homegrown and imported products. And in response to such concerns, there is a growing organic movement within the industry.

Chefs purchase fish in the market forms most practical for each operation. Although fish fabrication is a relatively simple chore requiring little specialized equipment, before deciding to cut fish on premises, consider the following:

1. The food service operation's ability to utilize the bones and trim that cutting whole fish produces, because yield after fabrication can vary depending on a chef's skill
2. The employees' ability to fabricate fillets, steaks or portions as needed
3. The storage facilities
4. The product's intended use

Most shellfish can be purchased live in the shell, shucked (the meat removed from the shell) or processed. Both live and shucked shellfish are usually purchased by counts (that is, the number per volume). For example, standard live Eastern oysters are packed 200 to 250 (the count) per bushel (the unit of volume); standard Eastern oyster meats are packed 350 per gallon. Crustaceans are sometimes packed by size based on the number of pieces per pound; for example, crab legs or shrimp are often sold in counts per pound. Crustaceans are also sold either by grades based on size (whole crabs) or by weight (lobsters).

Storing Fish and Shellfish

The most important concern when storing fish and shellfish is temperature. All fresh fish should be stored at temperatures between 30°F and 34°F (–1°C to 1°C). Fish stored in a refrigerator at 41°F (5°C) will have approximately half the shelf life of fish stored at 32°F (0°C).

Most fish are shipped on ice and should be stored on ice in the refrigerator as soon as possible after receipt. Whole fish should be layered directly in crushed or shaved ice in a perforated pan so that the melted ice water drains away. If crushed or shaved ice is not available, cubed ice may be used provided it is put in plastic bags and gently placed on top of the fish to prevent bruising and denting. Fabricated and portioned fish may be wrapped in moisture-proof packaging before icing to prevent the ice and water from damaging the exposed flesh. Fish stored on ice should be drained and re-iced daily.

Fresh scallops, fish fillets that are purchased in plastic trays and oyster and clam meats should be set on or packed in ice. Do not let the scallops, fillets or meats come into direct contact with the ice.

Clams, mussels and oysters should be stored at 41°F (5°C), at high humidity and left in the boxes or net bags in which they were shipped. Under ideal conditions, shellfish can be kept alive for up to 1 week. Never store live shellfish in plastic bags, and do not ice them.

If a saltwater tank is not available, live lobsters, crabs and other crustaceans should be kept in boxes with seaweed or damp newspaper to keep them moist. Most crustaceans

Whole fish properly stored in a perforated pan and covered with crushed ice.

SUSTAINABLE SEAFOOD

Within the past 50 years, the supply of seafood has declined precipitously because of damaged habitat, overfishing, specific fishing practices and increased demand. Certain fish, especially slow-growing species, face extinction.

There are choices, however, that may help ensure future supplies, whether it means sourcing farmed fish, preparing specific types of fish or catching fish in certain ways. Consult the Web sites of organizations such as the Blue Ocean Institute, the Chefs Collaborative and the Monterey Bay Aquarium's Seafood Watch Program to help inform your seafood purchasing decisions.

circulate salt water over their gills; icing them or placing them in fresh water will kill them. Lobsters and crabs will live for several days under ideal conditions.

Like most frozen foods, frozen fish should be kept at temperatures of 0°F (−18°C) or colder. Colder temperatures greatly increase shelf life. Frozen fish should be thawed in the refrigerator; once thawed, they should be treated like fresh fish.

FABRICATING PROCEDURES

As discussed, fish and shellfish can be purchased in many forms. Here we demonstrate several procedures for cutting, cleaning and otherwise fabricating or preparing fish and shellfish for cooking and serving.

PROCEDURE FOR **SCALING FISH**

This procedure is used to remove the scales from fish that will be cooked with the skin on.

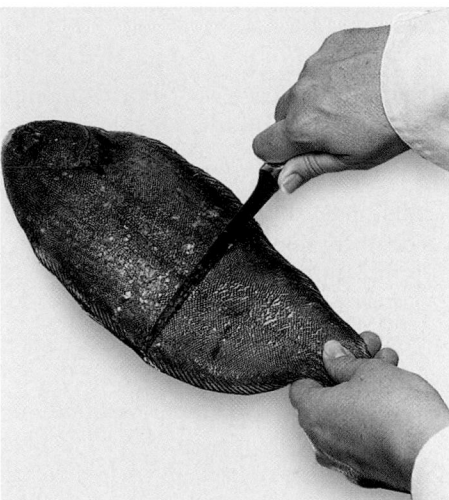

Place the fish on a work surface or in a large sink. Grip the fish by the tail and, working from the tail toward the head, scrape the scales off with a fish scaler or the back of a knife. Be careful not to damage the flesh by pushing too hard. Turn the fish over and remove the scales from the other side. Rinse the fish under cool water.

PROCEDURE FOR **PAN-DRESSING FLATFISH**

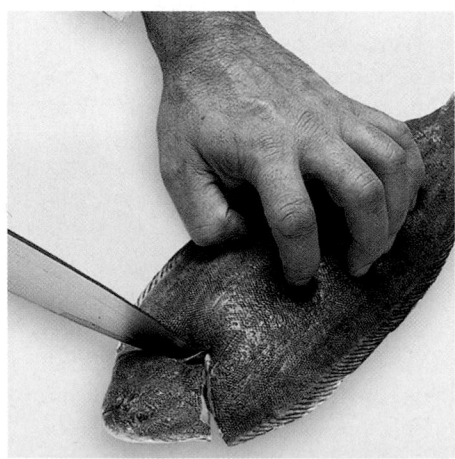

❶ Place the scaled fish on a cutting board and remove the head by making a V-shaped cut around it with a chef's knife. Pull the head away and remove the viscera.

❷ Rinse the fish under cold water, removing all traces of blood and viscera from the cavity.

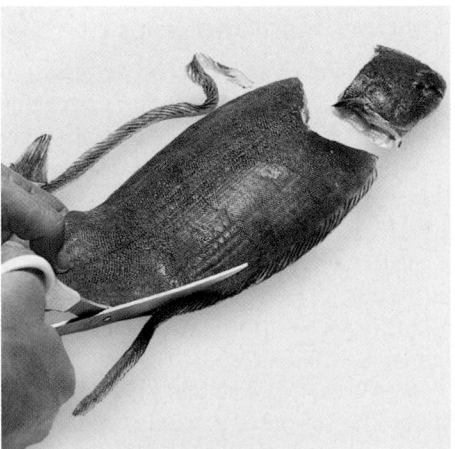

❸ Using a pair of kitchen shears, trim off the tail and all of the fins.

PROCEDURE FOR **FILLETING ROUND FISH**

Round fish produce two fillets, one from either side.

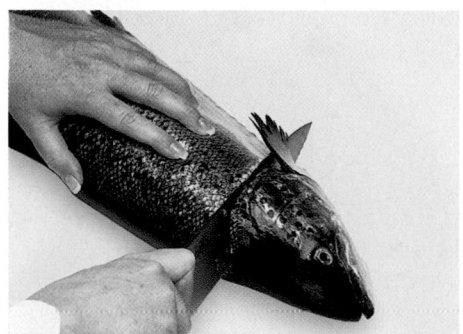

1 Using a chef's knife, cut down to the backbone just behind the gills. Do not remove the head.

2 Turn the knife toward the tail; using smooth strokes, cut from head to tail, parallel to the backbone. The knife should bump against the backbone so that no flesh is wasted; you will feel the knife cutting through the small pin bones. Cut the fillet completely free from the bones. Repeat on the other side.

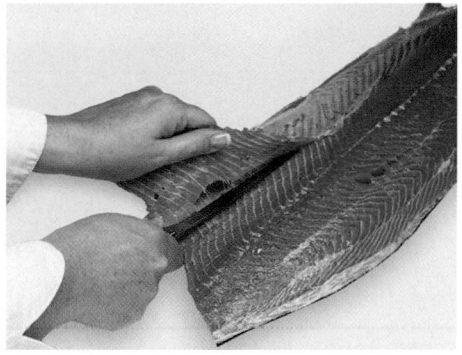

3 Trim the rib bones from the fillet with a flexible boning knife.

4 The finished fillet.

PROCEDURE FOR **FILLETING FLATFISH**

Flatfish produce four fillets: two large bilateral fillets from the top and two smaller bilateral fillets from the bottom. If the fish fillets are going to be cooked with the skin on, the fish should be scaled before cooking (it is easier to scale the fish before it is filleted). If the skin is going to be removed before cooking, it is not necessary to scale the fish.

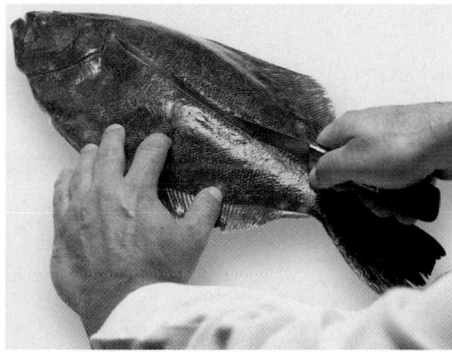

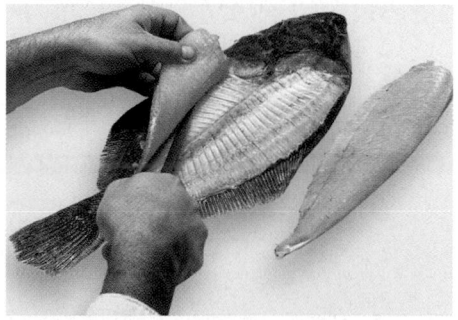

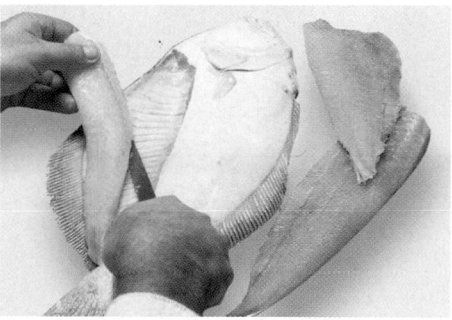

1 With the dark side of the fish facing up, cut along the backbone from head to tail with the tip of a flexible boning knife.

2 Turn the knife and, using smooth strokes, cut between the flesh and the rib bones, keeping the flexible blade against the bone. Cut the fillet completely free from the fish. Remove the second fillet, following the same procedure.

3 Turn the fish over and remove the fillets from the bottom half of the fish, following the same procedure.

PROCEDURE FOR **SKINNING DOVER SOLE**

Dover sole is unique in that its skin can be pulled from the whole fish with a simple procedure. The flesh of other small flatfish such as flounder, petrale sole and other types of domestic sole is more delicate; pulling the skin away from the whole fish could damage the flesh. These fish should be skinned after they are filleted.

Make a shallow cut in the flesh perpendicular to the length of the fish, just in front of the tail and with the knife angled toward the head of the fish. Using a clean towel, grip the skin and pull it toward the head of the fish. The skin should come off cleanly, in one piece, leaving the flesh intact.

PROCEDURE FOR **SKINNING FISH FILLETS**

Here we use a salmon fillet to demonstrate the procedure for skinning fish fillets. Use the same procedure to skin all types of fish fillets.

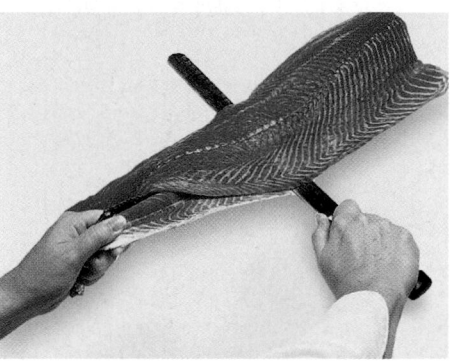

Place the fillet on a cutting board with the skin side down. Starting at the tail, use a meat slicer or a chef's knife to cut between the flesh and skin. Angle the knife down toward the skin, grip the skin tightly with one hand and use a smooth sawing motion to cut the skin cleanly away from the flesh.

PROCEDURE FOR **PULLING PIN BONES FROM SALMON FILLETS**

Round fish fillets contain a row of intramuscular bones running the length of the fillet. Known as pin bones, they are usually cut out with a knife to produce boneless fillets. In the case of salmon, they can be removed with salmon tweezers or small needle-nose pliers.

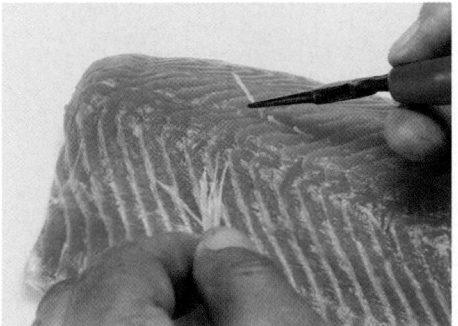

Place the fillet (either skinless or not) on the cutting board, skin side down. Starting at the front or head end of the fillet, use your fingertips to locate the bones and use the pliers to pull them out one by one.

PROCEDURE FOR **CUTTING TRANCHES**

A **tranche** is a slice cut from fillets of large flat or round fish. Usually cut on an angle, tranches look large and increase plate coverage.

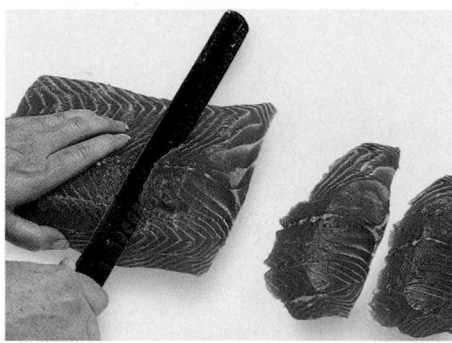

Place the fillet on the cutting board, skin side down. Using a slicer or chef's knife, cut slices of the desired weight. The tranche can be cut to the desired size by adjusting the angle of the knife. The greater the angle, the greater the surface area of the tranche.

PROCEDURE FOR **CUTTING STEAKS FROM SALMON AND SIMILARLY SIZED ROUND FISH**

Steaks are produced from salmon and similarly sized round fish by simply making cross-cuts of the whole fish. First scale, gut and remove the fins from the fish. Then:

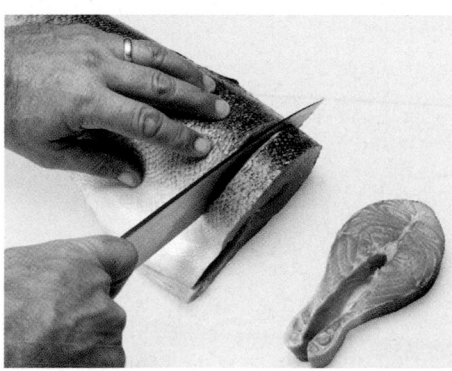

Using a chef's knife, cut through the fish, slicing steaks of the desired thickness. The steaks will contain some bones that are not necessarily removed.

PROCEDURE FOR **PEELING AND DEVEINING SHRIMP**

Peeling and deveining shrimp is a simple procedure done in most commercial kitchens. The tail portion of the shell is often left on the peeled shrimp to give it an attractive appearance or make it easier to eat. This procedure can be used on both cooked and uncooked shrimp.

1 Grip the shrimp's tail between your thumb and forefinger. Use your other thumb and forefinger to grip the legs and the edge of the shell.

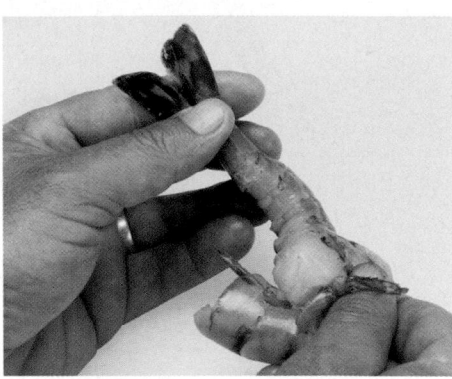

2 Pull the legs and shell away from the flesh, leaving the tail and first joint of the shell in place if desired.

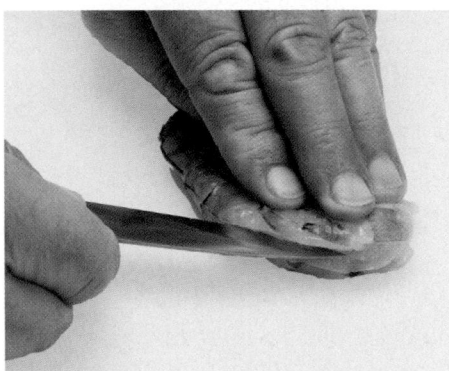

3 Place the shrimp on a cutting board and use a paring knife to make a shallow cut down the back of the shrimp, exposing the digestive tract or "vein."

4 Pull out the vein while rinsing the shrimp under cold water.

PROCEDURE FOR **BUTTERFLYING SHRIMP**

Butterflying raw shrimp improves their appearance and increases their surface area for even cooking. To butterfly shrimp, first peel them using the procedure outlined earlier. Then:

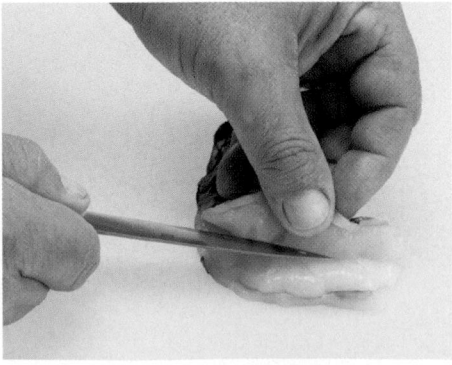

Instead of making a shallow cut to expose the vein, make a deeper cut that nearly slices the shrimp into two bilateral halves. Pull out the vein while rinsing the shrimp under cold water.

PROCEDURE FOR **PREPARING LIVE LOBSTERS FOR BROILING**

A whole lobster can be cooked by plunging it into boiling water or court bouillon. If the lobster is to be broiled, it must be split lengthwise before cooking.

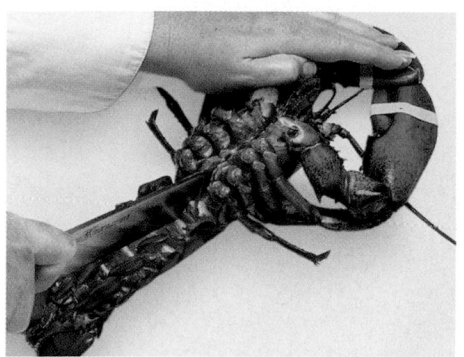

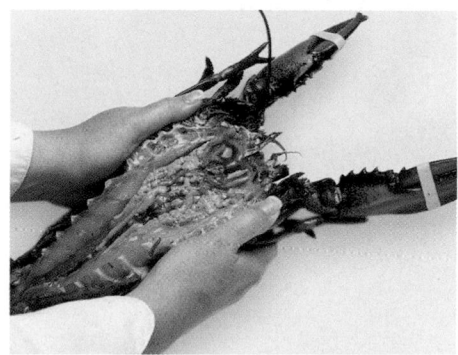

1 Place the live lobster on its back on a cutting board and pierce its head with the point of a chef's knife. Then, in one smooth stroke, bring the knife down and cut through the body and tail without splitting it completely in half.

2 Use your hands to crack the lobster's back so that it lies flat. Crack the claws with the back of a chef's knife.

3 Cut through the tail and curl each half of the tail to the side. Remove and discard the stomach. The tomalley (the olive-green liver) and, if present, the coral (the roe) can be removed and saved for a sauce or other preparation.

PROCEDURE FOR **PREPARING LIVE LOBSTERS FOR SAUTÉING**

A whole lobster may also be cut into smaller pieces for sautéing or other preparations.

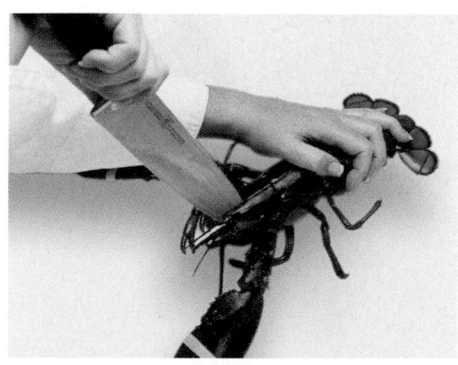

1 Using the point of a chef's knife, pierce the lobster's head.

2 Cut off the claws and arms.

3 Cut the tail into cross-sections.

4 Split the head and thorax in half. The tomalley and coral (if present) can be removed and saved for further use. The head and legs may be added to the recipe for flavor, but there is very little meat in them and they are typically discarded.

5 Crack the claws with a firm blow, using the back of a chef's knife.

PROCEDURE FOR **REMOVING COOKED LOBSTER MEAT FROM THE SHELL**

Many recipes call for cooked lobster meat. Cook the lobster by plunging it into a boiling court bouillon and simmering for 6 to 8 minutes per pound. Remove the lobster and allow it to cool until it can be easily handled. Then:

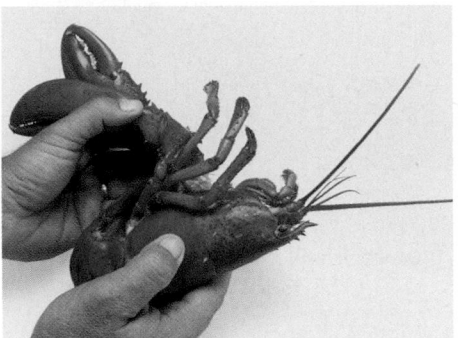

① Pull the claws and large legs away from the body. Break the claw away from the leg. Split the legs with a chef's knife and remove the meat, using your fingers or a pick.

② Carefully crack the claw with a mallet or the back of a chef's knife without damaging the meat. Pull out the claw meat in one piece.

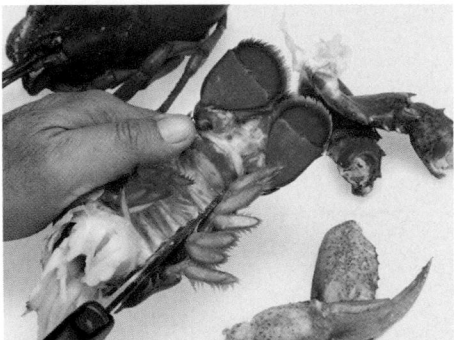

③ Pull the lobster's tail away from its body and use kitchen shears to trim away the soft membrane on the underside of the tail.

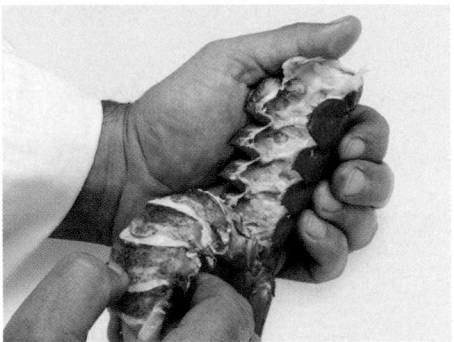

④ Pull the meat out of the shell in one piece.

PROCEDURE FOR **OPENING CLAMS**

Opening raw clams efficiently requires practice. Like all mollusks, clams should be cleaned under cold running water with a brush to remove all mud, silt and sand that may be stuck to their shells. A knife may be more easily inserted into a clam if the clam is washed and allowed to relax in the refrigerator for at least 1 hour before it is opened.

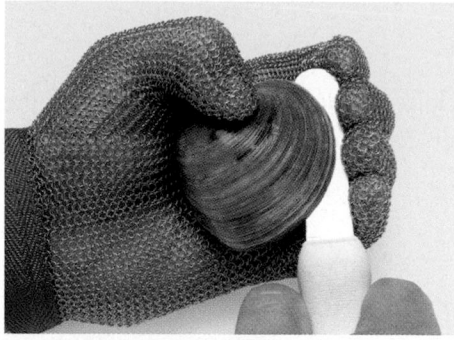

1 Wearing a mesh safety glove, hold the cleaned oyster in the palm of your hand; the notch in the edge of the shell should be toward your thumb. With the fingers of the same hand, squeeze and pull the blade of the clam knife between the clamshells. Do not push on the knife handle with your other hand; you will not be able to control the knife if it slips and you can cut yourself.

2 Wearing a mesh safety glove, pull the knife between the shells until it cuts the muscle. Twist the knife to pry the shells apart. Slide the knife tip along the top shell and cut through the muscle. Twist the top shell, breaking it free at the hinge; discard it.

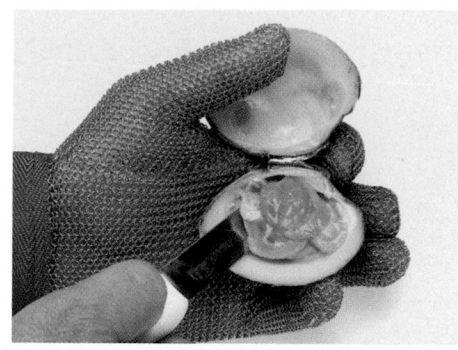

3 Use the knife tip to release the clam from the bottom shell.

PROCEDURE FOR **OPENING OYSTERS**

1 Clean the oyster by brushing it under running water.

2 Hold the cleaned oyster firmly in a folded towel in the palm of your hand. Insert the tip of an oyster knife in the hinge and use a twisting motion to pop the hinge apart. Do not use too much forward pressure on the knife; it can slip and you could stab yourself.

3 Slide the knife along the top of the shell to release the oyster from the shell. Discard the top shell.

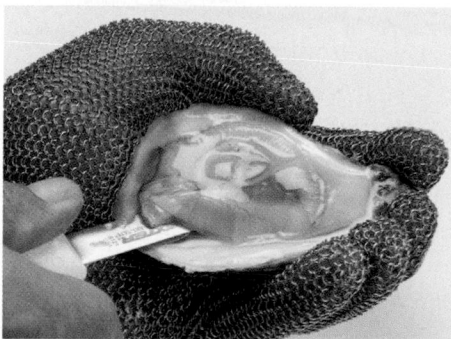

4 Use the knife tip to release the oyster from the bottom shell.

5 Fresh raw oysters on the half shell with seaweed garnish.

PROCEDURE FOR **CLEANING AND DEBEARDING MUSSELS**

Mussels are not normally eaten raw. Before cooking, a clump of dark threads called the beard must be removed. Because this could kill the mussel, cleaning and debearding must be done as close to cooking time as possible.

❶ Clean the mussel with a brush under cold running water to remove sand and grit.

❷ Pull the beard away from the mussel with your fingers or a small pair of pliers.

APPLYING VARIOUS COOKING METHODS

Fish and shellfish can be prepared by the dry-heat cooking methods of broiling and grilling, roasting (baking), sautéing, pan-frying and deep-frying, as well as the moist-heat cooking methods of steaming, poaching and simmering.

Determining Doneness

Unlike most meats and poultry, nearly all fish and shellfish are inherently tender and should be cooked just until done. Indeed, overcooking is the most common mistake made when preparing fish and shellfish. The Canadian Department of Fisheries recommends that all fish be cooked 10 minutes for every inch (2.5 centimeters) of thickness, regardless of cooking method. Although this may be a good general policy, variables such as the type and the form of fish and the exact cooking method used suggest that one or more of the following methods of determining doneness are more appropriate for professional food service operations:

❶ **Translucent flesh becomes opaque**—The raw flesh of most fish and shellfish appears somewhat translucent. As the proteins coagulate during cooking, the flesh becomes opaque.

❷ **Flesh becomes firm**—The flesh of most fish and shellfish firms as it cooks. Doneness can be tested by judging the resistance of the flesh when pressed with a finger. Raw or undercooked fish or shellfish will be mushy and soft. As it cooks, the flesh offers more resistance and springs back quickly.

❸ **Flesh separates from the bones easily**—The flesh of raw fish remains firmly attached to the bones. As the fish cooks, the flesh and bones separate easily.

❹ **Flesh begins to flake**—Fish flesh consists of short muscle fibers separated by thin connective tissue. As the fish cooks, the connective tissue breaks down and the groups of muscle fibers begin to flake, that is, separate from one another. Fish is done when the flesh begins to flake. If the flesh flakes easily, the fish will be overdone and dry.

Remember, fish and shellfish are subject to carryover cooking. Because they cook quickly and at low temperatures, it is better to undercook fish and shellfish and allow carryover cooking or residual heat to finish the cooking process.

Dry-Heat Cooking Methods

Dry-heat cooking methods are those that do not require additional moisture at any time during the cooking process. The dry-heat cooking methods used with fish and shellfish are broiling and grilling, roasting (usually referred to as baking when used with fish and shellfish), sautéing, pan-frying and deep-frying.

BROILING AND GRILLING

After brushing with oil or butter, fish can be grilled directly on the grate or placed on a heated platter under the broiler. Broiled or grilled fish should have a lightly charred surface and a slightly smoky flavor as a result of the intense radiant heat of the broiler or grill. The interior should be moist and juicy. Broiled or grilled shellfish meat should be moist and tender with only slight coloration from the grill or broiler.

Selecting Fish and Shellfish to Broil or Grill

Nearly all types of fish and shellfish can be successfully broiled or grilled. Salmon, trout, swordfish and other oily fish are especially well suited to grilling, as are lean fish such as bass and snapper. Fillets of lean flatfish with delicate textures, such as flounder and sole, are better broiled. They should be placed on a preheated broiling (sizzler) platter before being placed under the broiler.

Oysters and clams are often broiled on the half shell with flavored butters, bread crumbs or other garnishes and served sizzling hot. Squid can be stuffed, secured with a toothpick and broiled or grilled. Brushed with butter, split lobsters, king crabs and snow crabs are often broiled or grilled. Whole lobsters can be split and broiled or grilled, or their tails can be removed, split and cooked separately. Large crab legs can also be split and broiled or grilled. Shrimp and scallops are often broiled in flavored butters or grilled on skewers for easy handling.

Seasoning Fish and Shellfish to Be Broiled or Grilled

All fish should be brushed lightly with butter or oil before being placed on the grill or under the broiler. The butter or oil prevents sticking and helps leaner fish retain moisture. For most fish, a simple seasoning of salt and pepper suffices. But most fish respond well to marinades, especially those made with white wine and lemon juice. Because most fish are delicately flavored, they should be marinated for only a brief time. (Even marinated fish should be brushed with butter or oil before cooking.) Herbs should be avoided because they will burn from the intense heat of the broiler or grill, although the smoke from herbs such as fennel, lavender or thyme can impart flavor to the outside of fish when it is grilled whole.

Clams, oysters and other shellfish that are stuffed or cooked with butters, vegetables, bacon or other accompaniments or garnishes gain flavor from these ingredients. Be careful, however, not to overpower the delicate flavors of the shellfish by adding too many strong flavorings.

Accompaniments to Broiled and Grilled Fish and Shellfish

Lemon wedges are the traditional accompaniment to broiled or grilled fish and shellfish. But they can be served with sauces made separately. Butter sauces such as a beurre blanc are popular, as their richness complements the lean fish. Vegetable coulis are a good choice for a healthier, lower-fat accompaniment. Additional sauce suggestions are found in Table 10.5. If the item is cooked on a broiler platter with a seasoned butter, it is often served with that butter.

Almost any side dish goes well with broiled or grilled fish or shellfish. Fried or boiled potatoes, pasta and rice are all good choices. Grilled vegetables are a natural choice.

PROCEDURE FOR **BROILING OR GRILLING FISH AND SHELLFISH**

All fish is delicate and must be carefully handled to achieve an attractive finished product. When broiling whole fish or fillets with their skin still on, score the skin by making several diagonal slashes approximately ¼ inch (6 millimeters) deep at even intervals. This prevents the fish from curling during cooking, promotes even cooking and creates a more attractive finished product. Pat the skin dry because moisture will prevent it from browning. Be especially careful not to overcook the item. It should be served as hot as possible as soon as it is removed from the broiler or grill.

1. Heat the broiler or grill.
2. Use a wire brush to remove any charred or burnt particles that may be stuck to the broiler or grill grate. The grate can be wiped with a lightly oiled towel to remove any remaining particles and help season it.
3. Prepare the item to be broiled or grilled. For example, cut the fish into steaks or tranches of even thickness; split the lobster; peel and/or skewer the shrimp. Season or marinate the item as desired. Brush the item with oil or butter.
4. Place the item on a grill, presentation side down. If using a broiler, place the item directly on the grate or on a preheated broiler platter. Tender fish are usually broiled presentation side up on a broiler platter.
5. If practical, turn the item to produce the attractive crosshatch marks associated with grilling that are discussed in Chapter 9, Principles of Cooking. Items less than ½ inch (1.2 centimeters) thick cooked on a preheated broiler platter do not have to be turned over.
6. Cook the item to the desired doneness and serve immediately.

BROILED BLACK SEA BASS WITH HERB BUTTER AND SAUTÉED LEEKS

MISE EN PLACE

▶ Melt whole butter and keep warm.
▶ Wash, clean and julienne the leek.

Yield: 1 Serving   **Method:** Broiling

Black sea bass fillet, skin on, approx. 8 oz. (240 g)	1	1
Salt and pepper	TT	TT
Whole butter, melted	as needed	as needed
Leek, julienne	1	1
Lemon juice	2 tsp.	10 ml
Herb butter (page 211)	2 slices	2 slices

1. Score the skin of the fillet with three diagonal cuts approximately ¼ inch (6 millimeters) deep.
2. Season the fillet with salt and pepper and brush with melted butter.
3. Place the fillet on a preheated broiler platter, skin side up, and place under the broiler.
4. Blanch the leek in boiling water until nearly tender.
5. Drain the leek and sauté in 1 tablespoon (15 milliliters) whole butter until tender. Add the lemon juice; season with salt and pepper.
6. Remove the fish from the broiler when done. Top with the herb butter and serve on a bed of sautéed leeks.

Approximate values per serving: **Calories** 260, **Total fat** 15 g, **Saturated fat** 8 g, **Cholesterol** 80 mg, **Sodium** 790 mg, **Total carbohydrates** 11 g, **Protein** 21 g, **Vitamin A** 15%, **Vitamin C** 15%

❶ Scoring the fish skin.

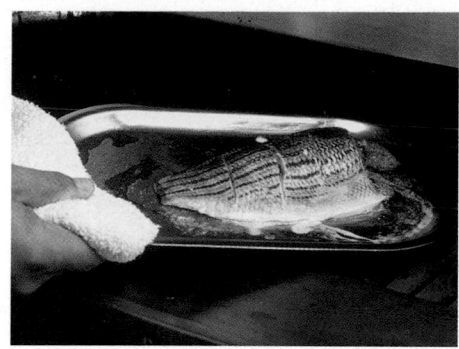

❷ Placing the fish on a broiler platter, under the broiler.

❸ Serving the fish on a bed of sautéed leeks.

BAKING

The terms *baking* and *roasting* are used interchangeably when applied to fish and shellfish. One disadvantage of baking fish is that the short baking time does not allow the surface of the fish to caramelize. To help correct this problem, fish can be browned in a sauté pan with a small amount of oil to achieve the added flavor and appearance of a browned surface, and then finished in an oven.

Selecting Fish and Shellfish to Bake

Fatty fish produce the best baked fish. Fish fillets and steaks are the best market forms to bake, as they cook quickly and evenly and are easily portioned. Although lean fish can be baked, it tends to become dry and must be basted often.

Seasoning Fish and Shellfish to Be Baked

The most popular seasonings for baked fish are lemon, butter, salt and pepper. Fish can also be marinated before baking for added flavor. But baked fish usually depend on the accompanying sauce for much of their flavor.

Shellfish are often stuffed or mixed with other ingredients before baking. For example, raw oysters on the half shell can be topped with spinach, watercress and Pernod (oysters Rockefeller) and baked. Shrimp are often butterflied, stuffed and baked; lobsters are split, stuffed and baked. Many food service operations remove clams from their shells; mix them with bread crumbs, seasonings or other ingredients; refill the shells and bake the mixture.

Accompaniments to Baked Fish and Shellfish

Baked fish is often served with a flavorful sauce such as a creole sauce (page 207) or Beurre Blanc (page 211). Additional sauce suggestions are found in Table 10.5. Almost any type of rice, pasta or potato is a good accompaniment, as is any variety of sautéed vegetable.

PROCEDURE FOR BAKING FISH AND SHELLFISH

❶ Portion the fish or shellfish and arrange on a well-oiled or buttered pan, presentation side up.

❷ Season as desired and brush the surface of the fish or shellfish generously with melted butter; add garnishes or flavorings as desired or directed in the recipe.

❸ Place the pan in a preheated oven at approximately 400°F (200°C).

❹ Baste periodically during the cooking process (more often if the fish is lean). Remove from the oven when the fish is slightly underdone.

BAKED RED SNAPPER

Yield: 4 Servings		**Method:** Baking
Red snapper fillets, 8 oz. (240 g) each	4	4
Salt and white pepper	TT	TT
Whole butter, melted	2 oz.	60 g
Fresh mint leaves, chopped	1 Tbsp.	15 ml
Garlic, minced	1 tsp.	5 ml
Tomato concassée	4 oz.	120 g
White wine	2 fl. oz.	60 ml
Lemon juice	2 fl. oz.	60 ml

1. Place the snapper on a buttered baking pan. Season the fillets with salt and white pepper; brush with butter.
2. Combine the mint, garlic and tomato concassée, and spoon on top of each portion of the fish.
3. Add the wine and lemon juice to the pan.
4. Bake at 400°F (200°C), basting once halfway through the cooking process, until done, approximately 15 minutes.

Approximate values per serving: **Calories** 600, **Total fat** 16 g, **Saturated fat** 8 g, **Cholesterol** 140 mg, **Sodium** 850 mg, **Total carbohydrates** 55 g, **Protein** 60 g, **Vitamin A** 25%, **Vitamin C** 35%

1. Brushing the fillets with butter.

2. Topping each portion with mint and tomato concassée.

3. The finished fish.

SAUTÉING

Sautéing is a very popular cooking method for fish and shellfish. It lightly caramelizes the food's surface, giving it additional flavor. Typically, other ingredients such as garlic, onions, vegetables, wine and lemon juice are added to the fond to make a sauce.

Selecting Fish and Shellfish to Sauté

Both fatty and lean fish may be sautéed. Flatfish are sometimes dressed and sautéed whole, as are small round fish such as trout. Larger fish such as salmon can be cut into steaks or filleted and cut into tranches. The portions should be relatively uniform in size and thickness and fairly thin to promote even cooking. Although clams, mussels and oysters are not often sautéed, scallops and crustaceans are popular sauté items.

Seasoning Fish and Shellfish to Be Sautéed

Many types of fish—especially sole, flounder and other delicate, lean fish fillets—are often dredged in plain or seasoned flour before sautéing. Seasoned butter is used to sauté some items, such as scampi-style shrimp. These items derive their flavor from the butter; additional seasonings should not be necessary.

FIGURE 19.9 ▶ A properly sautéed fish fillet (left) is lightly brown and holds its shape without sticking to the pan. An improperly sautéed fish fillet (right) is pale, falls apart and sticks to the pan.

Cooking Temperatures

The sauté pan and cooking fat must be hot before the fish or shellfish are added. Do not add too much fish or shellfish to the pan at one time, or the pan and fat will cool, letting the foods simmer in their own juices and cooking the fish before it browns (see Figure 19.9). Thin slices and small pieces of fish and shellfish require a short cooking time, so use high temperatures in order to caramelize their surfaces without overcooking. Large, thick pieces of fish or shellfish being cooked in the shell may require slightly lower cooking temperatures to ensure that they are cooked without overbrowning their surfaces.

Accompaniments to Sautéed Fish and Shellfish

Sautéed fish and shellfish are nearly always served with a sauce made directly in the sauté pan. This sauce may be as simple as browned butter (*beurre noisette*) or a complicated sauce flavored with the fond. In some cases, seasoned butter is used to sauté the fish or shellfish and the butter is then served with the main item. See Table 10.5 for additional sauce suggestions.

Mildly flavored rice and pasta are good choices to serve with sautéed fish or shellfish.

PROCEDURE FOR SAUTÉING FISH AND SHELLFISH

1. Cut or portion the fish or shellfish.
2. Season the item and dredge in seasoned flour if desired.
3. Heat a suitable sauté pan over moderate heat; add enough oil or clarified butter to cover the bottom to a depth of about ⅛ inch (3 millimeters).
4. Add the fish or shellfish to the pan (fish should be placed presentation side down); cook until done, turning once halfway through the cooking process. Add other foods as called for in the recipe.
5. Remove the fish or shellfish. If a sauce is to be made in the sauté pan, follow the procedures discussed in Chapter 17, Poultry.

SAUTÉED HALIBUT WITH THREE-COLOR PEPPERS AND SPANISH OLIVES

MISE EN PLACE

▸ Peel and slice onions.
▸ Peel and mince garlic.
▸ Wash, seed and julienne bell peppers.
▸ Pit and quarter olives.
▸ Wash and chop thyme.

Yield: 4 Servings

Method: Sautéing

Halibut fillets, 6 oz. (180 g) each	4	4
Salt and pepper	TT	TT
Olive oil	2 fl. oz.	60 ml
Onion, sliced	3 oz.	90 g
Garlic, minced	2 tsp.	10 ml
Green bell pepper, julienne	3 oz.	90 g
Red bell pepper, julienne	3 oz.	90 g
Yellow bell pepper, julienne	3 oz.	90 g
Tomato concassée	8 oz.	240 g
Spanish olives, pitted and quartered	2 oz.	60 g
Fresh thyme, chopped	2 tsp.	10 ml
Lemon juice	2 fl. oz.	60 ml
Fish stock	2 fl. oz.	60 ml

1 Season the fillets with salt and pepper.
2 Heat a sauté pan large enough to hold the fillets without crowding and add the oil.
3 Sauté the halibut, turning once. Remove and reserve in a warm place.
4 Add the onion and garlic to the same pan and sauté for approximately 1 minute. Add the bell peppers and sauté for 1 to 2 minutes more.
5 Add the tomato concassée, olives and thyme; sauté briefly.
6 Add the lemon juice and deglaze the pan. Add the stock, simmer for 2 minutes to blend the flavors and adjust the seasonings.
7 Return the fish to the pan to reheat. Serve each fish fillet on a bed of vegetables with sauce and an appropriate garnish.

Approximate values per serving: **Calories** 420, **Total fat** 21 g, **Saturated fat** 3 g, **Cholesterol** 70 mg, **Sodium** 870 mg, **Total carbohydrates** 10 g, **Protein** 47 g, **Vitamin A** 15%, **Vitamin C** 110%

1 Sautéing the halibut fillets.

2 Sautéing the onions, garlic and peppers.

3 Adding the fish stock.

4 Returning the fish to the pan to reheat.

PAN-FRYING

Pan-frying is very similar to sautéing, but it uses more fat to cook the main item. Pan-fried fish is always coated with flour, batter or breading to help seal the surface and prevent the flesh from coming into direct contact with the cooking fat. Properly prepared pan-fried fish and shellfish should be moist and tender with a crisp surface. If battered or breaded, the coating should be intact with no breaks.

Selecting Fish and Shellfish to Pan-Fry
Both fatty and lean fish may be pan-fried. Trout and other small fish are ideal for pan-frying, as are portioned fillets of lean fish such as halibut. Pan-fried fish and shellfish should be uniform in size and relatively thin so that they cook quickly and evenly.

Seasoning Fish and Shellfish to Be Pan-Fried
Although fish and shellfish can be marinated or seasoned directly, it is more common to season the flour, batter or breading that will coat them. Batters, for example, can contain cheese, and breadings can contain nuts and other ingredients to add different flavors to the fish or shellfish. Review the battering and breading procedures discussed in Chapter 8, Mise en Place. Additional seasonings come from sauces and other accompaniments served with the pan-fried fish or shellfish.

Cooking Temperatures
The fat should always be hot before the fish or shellfish are added. Breaded or battered fish fillets cook very quickly, and the fat should be hot enough to brown the coating without overcooking the interior. Whole pan-fried fish take longer to cook and therefore require a slightly lower cooking temperature so that the surface does not become too dark before the interior is cooked.

Accompaniments to Pan-Fried Fish and Shellfish
Lemon wedges are the classic accompaniment to pan-fried fish and shellfish. Sauces that accompany pan-fried items are made separately. Mayonnaise-based sauces such as Tartar Sauce (page 736) and Rémoulade Sauce are especially popular; rich wine-based sauces should be avoided. Vegetable coulis, such as tomato, also complement many pan-fried items. Additional sauce suggestions are found in Table 10.5.

PROCEDURE FOR **PAN-FRYING FISH AND SHELLFISH**

1. Heat enough clarified butter or oil in a heavy sauté pan so that it will come one-third to halfway up the side of the item. The fat should be at a temperature between 325°F and 350°F (163°C and 177°C).
2. Add the floured, breaded or battered item to the pan, being careful not to splash the hot fat. Cook until done, turning once halfway through the cooking process.
3. Remove the food and drain on absorbent paper.
4. Serve it promptly with an appropriate sauce.

MISE EN PLACE

▸ Wash and seed bell peppers and cut into small dice.
▸ Wash and slice green onions.
▸ Crack egg into a small bowl and beat lightly with a fork.

❶ Mixing all ingredients for the crab cakes.

❷ Forming the crab cakes.

❸ Pan-frying the crab cakes.

BLUE CRAB CAKES

Yield: 15 Cakes, 2 oz. (60 g) each | **Method:** Pan-frying

Blue crab meat	1 lb.	480 g
Heavy cream	6 fl. oz.	180 ml
Red bell pepper, small dice	2 oz.	60 g
Green bell pepper, small dice	2 oz.	60 g
Clarified butter	as needed	as needed
Green onions, sliced	1 bunch	1 bunch
Fresh bread crumbs	6 oz.	180 g
Salt and pepper	TT	TT
Dijon mustard	1 Tbsp.	15 ml
Worcestershire sauce	TT	TT
Tabasco sauce	TT	TT
Egg, slightly beaten	1	1

❶ Carefully pick through the crab meat, removing any pieces of shell. Keep the lumps of crab meat as large as possible.

❷ Place the cream in a saucepan and bring to a boil. Reduce by approximately one-half. Chill the cream well.

❸ Sauté the bell peppers in a small amount of clarified butter until tender.

❹ Combine the crab meat, reduced cream, bell peppers, green onions and approximately 3 ounces (90 grams) bread crumbs along with the salt, pepper, Dijon mustard, Worcestershire sauce, Tabasco sauce and egg. Mix to combine all ingredients, trying to keep the lumps of crab meat intact.

❺ Using a 2-ounce (60-gram) mold, form the crab mixture into cakes of the desired size.

❻ Place the remaining bread crumbs in an appropriately sized hotel pan. Place the crab cakes, a few at a time, in the hotel pan and cover with the bread crumbs. To help them adhere, press the crumbs lightly into the cakes.

❼ Heat a sauté pan over moderate heat and add enough clarified butter to cover the bottom approximately ¼ inch (6 millimeters) deep.

❽ Add the crab cakes to the pan and cook until done, turning once when the first side is nicely browned. Remove and drain on absorbent paper.

Approximate values per 2-oz. (60-g) cake serving: **Calories** 130, **Total fat** 6 g, **Saturated fat** 3.5 g, **Cholesterol** 60 mg, **Sodium** 650 mg, **Total carbohydrates** 9 g, **Protein** 10 g, **Vitamin C** 15%

DEEP-FRYING

Deep-frying is the process of cooking foods by submerging them in hot fat. Typically, fish or shellfish are breaded or battered before deep-frying. Alternatively, they can be formed into croquettes or fritters. Properly deep-fried fish and shellfish should be moist and tender, not greasy or tough. Their coating should be crispy and golden brown.

Selecting Fish and Shellfish to Deep-Fry

Whole small fish and fillets of lean fish such as catfish or halibut are excellent for deep-frying. The fillets should be of uniform size and relatively thin so that they cook quickly and evenly. Fatty fish, such as salmon, are ideal for croquettes. Peeled shrimp and shucked mollusks, especially clams and oysters, can be breaded, battered or formed into fritters and deep-fried. Deep-fried breaded or battered sliced squid or octopus served with a dipping sauce makes an excellent hors d'oeuvre.

Seasoning Fish and Shellfish to Be Deep-Fried

Typically, seasonings used for deep-fried fish or shellfish are added to the breading or batter, although salt and pepper should be added after frying. Additional flavors come from sauces or accompaniments.

Accompaniments to Deep-Fried Fish and Shellfish

As with pan-fried fish and shellfish, lemon wedges and mayonnaise-based sauces such as tartar sauce and rémoulade sauce are popular accompaniments to deep-fried fish and shellfish. Spicy tomato- or soy-based dipping sauces are also excellent choices. Traditional English fish and chips is served with malt vinegar.

PROCEDURE FOR **DEEP-FRYING FISH AND SHELLFISH**

① Shuck, peel, cut, trim or otherwise prepare the fish or shellfish to be deep-fried. Season, bread or batter it, as desired.

② Heat the fat to the desired temperature, usually around 350°F (177°C). Breaded or battered fish or shellfish cook quickly and the fat must be hot enough to cook the food's interior without burning its surface.

③ Carefully place the food in the hot fat using either the basket method or the swimming method.

④ Deep-fry the fish or shellfish until done. Doneness is usually determined by color, timing or sampling.

⑤ Remove the deep-fried food from the fat and hold it over the fryer, allowing the excess fat to drain off. Transfer the food to a hotel pan either lined with absorbent paper or fitted with a rack. Season with salt, if desired.

⑥ If the deep-fried fish or shellfish is to be held for later service, place it under a heat lamp.

DEEP-FRIED CATFISH FILLETS WITH TARTAR SAUCE

Yield: 8 Servings   **Method:** Deep-frying

Catfish fillets, cut into uniform-sized pieces	3 lb.	1.4 kg
Salt and pepper	TT	TT
Flour	as needed for breading	
Egg wash	as needed for breading	
Cornmeal	as needed for breading	
Tartar Sauce (page 736)	12 fl. oz.	360 ml

① Season the fillets with salt and pepper.
② Bread the fillets using the standard breading procedure described in Chapter 8, Mise en Place.
③ Using the basket method, deep-fry the fillets until done. Drain well and serve with the Tartar Sauce.

Approximate values per 8-oz. (240-g) serving: **Calories** 600, **Total fat** 46 g, **Saturated fat** 10 g, **Cholesterol** 160 mg, **Sodium** 910 mg, **Total carbohydrates** 16 g, **Protein** 31 g, **Iron** 15%

MISE EN PLACE

◀ Cut catfish into uniform-sized pieces.
◀ Heat deep-fat fryer.

① Flouring the seasoned fish fillets.

② Passing the floured fillets through the egg wash.

③ Coating the fillets with cornmeal.

Moist-Heat Cooking Methods

Fish and shellfish lend themselves well to moist-heat cooking methods, especially steaming, poaching and simmering. Steaming best preserves the food's natural flavors and cooks without adding fat. Poaching is also popular, especially for fish. Poached fish can be served hot or cold, whole or as steaks, fillets or portions. Boiling, which is actually simmering, is most often associated with crustaceans.

STEAMING

Steaming is a natural way to cook fish and shellfish without adding fats. Fish are steamed by suspending them over a small amount of boiling liquid in a covered pan. The steam trapped in the pan gently cooks the food while preserving its natural flavors and most nutrients. The liquid used to steam fish and shellfish can be water or a court bouillon with herbs, spices, aromatics or wine added to infuse the item with additional flavors. Mussels and clams can be steamed by placing them directly in a pan, adding a small amount of wine or other liquid and covering them. Their shells will hold them above the liquid as they cook. Fish and shellfish can also be steamed by wrapping them in parchment paper together with herbs, vegetables, butters or sauces as accompaniments and baking them in a hot oven. This method of steaming is called **en papillote**.

Steamed fish and shellfish should be moist and tender. They should have clean and delicate flavors. Any accompaniments or sauces should complement the main item without masking its flavor. Fish and shellfish cooked en papillote should be served piping hot so that the aromatic steam trapped by the paper escapes as the paper is cut open tableside.

en papillote (awn pa-pee-yote) a cooking method in which food is wrapped in paper or foil and then heated so that the food steams in its own moisture

Selecting Fish and Shellfish to Steam

Mollusks (for example, clams and mussels), fatty fish (for example, salmon and sea bass) and lean fish (for example, sole) all produce good results when steamed. The portions should be of uniform thickness and no more than 1 inch (2.5 centimeters) thick to promote even cooking.

Seasoning Fish and Shellfish to Be Steamed

Steamed fish and shellfish rely heavily on their natural flavors and often require very little seasoning. Nevertheless, salt, pepper, herbs and spices can be applied directly to the raw food before steaming. Flavored liquids used to steam fish and shellfish will contribute additional flavors. If the liquid is served with the fish or shellfish as a broth or used to make a sauce to accompany the item, it is especially important that the liquid be well seasoned. Lemons, limes and other fruits or vegetables can also be cooked with the fish or shellfish to add flavors. Clams and mussels often do not require additional salt, as the liquor released when they open during cooking is sufficiently salty.

Accompaniments to Steamed Fish and Shellfish

Steamed fish and shellfish are popular partly because they are low in fat. In keeping with this perception, a low or nonfat sauce or a simple squeeze of lemon and steamed fresh vegetables are good accompaniments. If fat is not a concern, then an emulsified butter sauce such as Beurre Blanc (page 211) or Hollandaise (page 208) may be a good choice. Table 10.5 lists several sauce suggestions.

Classic New England steamed clams are served with a portion of the steaming liquid; steamed mussels are served with a sauce that is created from the wine and other ingredients used to steam them.

PROCEDURE FOR **STEAMING FISH AND SHELLFISH**

1. Portion the fish to an appropriate size. Clean the shellfish.
2. Prepare the cooking liquid. Add seasoning and flavoring ingredients as desired and bring to a boil.
3. Place the fish or shellfish in the steamer on a rack or in a perforated pan and cover tightly.
4. Steam the fish or shellfish until done.
5. Serve the fish or shellfish immediately with the steaming liquid or an appropriate sauce.

STEAMED SALMON WITH LEMON AND OLIVE OIL

Yield: 1 Serving   **Method:** Steaming

Dressing:		
Lemon zest, blanched	1 Tbsp.	15 ml
Lemon juice	2 Tbsp.	30 ml
Salt and pepper	TT	TT
Virgin olive oil	2 Tbsp.	30 ml
White wine	8 fl. oz.	240 ml
Bay leaf	1	1
Leek, chopped	2 oz.	60 g
Fresh thyme	1 sprig	1 sprig
Peppercorns, crushed	1 tsp.	5 ml
Salmon tranche or steak, approx. 6 oz. (180 g)	1	1

1. To make the dressing, combine the lemon zest, lemon juice, salt and pepper. Whisk in the oil.
2. Combine the wine, bay leaf, leek, thyme and peppercorns in the bottom of a steamer.
3. Season the salmon with salt and pepper and place it in the steamer basket.
4. Cover the steamer and bring the liquid to a boil. Cook the fish until done, approximately 4 to 6 minutes.
5. Plate the salmon and spoon the dressing over it.

Approximate values per serving: **Calories** 620, **Total fat** 40 g, **Saturated fat** 6 g, **Cholesterol** 95 mg, **Sodium** 700 mg, **Total carbohydrates** 16 g, **Protein** 48 g, **Vitamin C** 50%

1. Placing the fish in the steamer.

2. Spooning the dressing over the fish.

RED SNAPPER EN PAPILLOTE

Yield: 6 Servings		**Method:** Steaming
Clarified butter	as needed	as needed
Leek, julienne	3 oz.	90 g
Fennel bulb, julienne	4 oz.	120 g
Carrot, julienne	3 oz.	90 g
Celery, julienne	3 oz.	90 g
Red bell pepper, julienne	3 oz.	90 g
Red snapper fillets, skin on, 6 oz. (180 g) each	6	6
Salt and pepper	TT	TT
Basil butter (page 211)	9 oz.	270 g

MISE EN PLACE

▶ Wash, clean and julienne leek.
▶ Wash, peel if necessary, and julienne fennel bulb, carrot and celery.
▶ Wash, seed and julienne bell pepper.
▶ Cut parchment paper for papillote.

① Cut six heart-shaped pieces of parchment paper large enough to contain one portion of the fish and vegetables when folded in half.

② Brush each piece of parchment paper with clarified butter.

③ Toss the vegetables together. Place one-sixth of the vegetables on half of each piece of the buttered parchment paper.

④ Place one portion of red snapper on each portion of vegetables, skin side up; season with salt and pepper.

⑤ Top each portion of fish with 1½ ounces (45 grams) basil butter.

⑥ Fold each piece of paper over and crimp the edges to seal it.

⑦ Place the envelopes (papillotes) on sheet pans and bake in a preheated oven at 450°F (230°C) for 8 to 10 minutes.

⑧ When baked, the parchment paper should puff up and brown. Remove from the oven and serve immediately. The envelope should be carefully cut open tableside to allow the aromatic steam to escape.

Approximate values per serving: **Calories** 380, **Total fat** 19 g, **Saturated fat** 11 g, **Cholesterol** 125 mg, **Sodium** 680 mg, **Total carbohydrates** 6 g, **Protein** 46 g, **Vitamin A** 50%, **Vitamin C** 30%

① Cutting heart-shaped pieces of parchment paper.

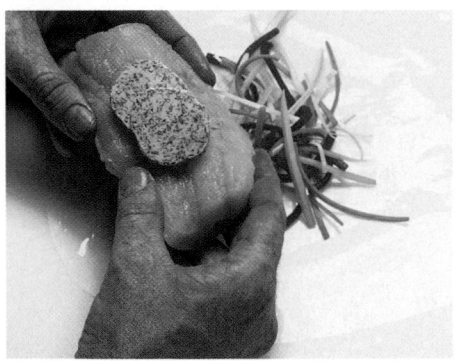

② Placing the vegetables, red snapper and compound butter on the buttered parchment paper.

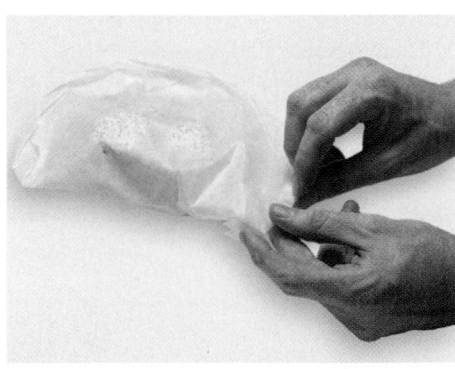

③ Crimping the edge of the parchment paper to seal it.

④ The finished papillotes.

POACHING

Poaching is a versatile and popular method for cooking fish. Shellfish are rarely poached, however. The exception is squid, which can be quickly poached and chilled for use in salads and other preparations. There are two distinct poaching methods.

The first is the **submersion method**, in which the fish is completely covered with a liquid, usually a court bouillon, fish stock or fish fumet. It is cooked until just done, reaching an internal temperature of 145°F (63°C.) The poached fish is then served (either hot or cold) with a sauce sometimes made from a portion of the cooking liquid but more often made separately. Whole fish (wrapped in cheesecloth to preserve its shape during cooking), tranches and steaks can all be cooked by submersion poaching.

The second method, called **shallow poaching**, combines poaching and steaming to achieve the desired results. The main item, usually a fillet, tranche or steak, is placed on a bed of aromatic vegetables in enough liquid to come approximately halfway up its sides. The liquid, called a **cuisson**, is brought to a simmer on the stove top. The pan is then covered with a piece of buttered parchment paper or a lid, and cooking is completed either on the stove top or in the oven. Shallow-poached fish is usually served with a sauce made with the reduced cooking liquid. (Sometimes the main item is sautéed lightly before the cooking liquid is added. If so, the cooking method is more accurately braising, as both dry- and moist-heat cooking methods are used.)

Selecting Fish to Poach

Lean white fish such as turbot, bass and sole are excellent for poaching. Some fatty fish such as salmon and trout are also excellent choices.

Seasoning Fish to Be Poached

Fish poached by either submersion or shallow poaching gain all of their seasonings from the liquid in which they are cooked and the sauce with which they are served. Therefore, it is very important to use a properly prepared court bouillon, fish fumet or good-quality fish stock well seasoned with vegetables such as shallots, onions or carrots as well as ample herbs, spices and other seasonings. Many poached fish recipes call for wine. When using wine in either the cooking liquid or the sauce, be sure to choose a wine of good quality. Most fish are very delicately flavored, and using poor-quality wine may ruin an otherwise excellent dish. Citrus, especially lemon, is a popular seasoning; lemon juice or zest may be added to the poaching liquid, the sauce or the finished dish.

Accompaniments to Poached Fish

Poached fish cooked by submersion go well with rich sauces such as hollandaise and beurre blanc. (Once coated with either sauce, the fish may be broiled briefly to lightly brown or glaze before serving.) If fat is a concern, a better choice may be a vegetable coulis (for example, broccoli or red pepper). Cold poached fish are commonly served with mayonnaise-based sauces such as sauce verte or rémoulade. Shallow-poached fish are served with sauces such as a white wine sauce or beurre blanc made from a reduction of the liquids in which the fish were poached. See Table 10.5 for additional sauce suggestions.

Poached fish are often served with rice or pasta and steamed or boiled vegetables.

PROCEDURE FOR **SUBMERSION POACHING**

1. Prepare the cooking liquid. Whole fish should be started in a cold liquid; gradually increasing the liquid's temperature helps preserve the appearance of the fish. Portioned fish should be started in a simmering liquid to preserve their flavor and more accurately estimate cooking time.

2. Use a rack to lower the fish into the cooking liquid. Be sure the fish is completely submerged.

3. Poach the fish at 175°F–185°F (79°C–85°C) until done.

4. Remove the fish from the poaching liquid, moisten with a portion of the liquid and hold in a warm place for service. Or remove the fish from the poaching liquid, cover it to prevent drying and allow it to cool, then refrigerate.

5. Serve the poached fish with an appropriate sauce.

WHOLE POACHED SALMON

MISE EN PLACE
▸ Scale and gut whole salmon.
▸ Prepare court bouillon.

Yield: 10–14 Servings

Method: Submersion poaching

Salmon, drawn, 4–5 lb. (1.9–2.4 kg)	1	1
Court bouillon (page 193)	as needed	as needed

1 Place the fish on a lightly oiled rack or screen and secure with butcher's twine.

2 Place the rack or screen in a fish poacher, tilting kettle or large pot and cover with cold court bouillon.

3 Bring the court bouillon to a simmer over moderate heat. Reduce the heat and poach the fish at 175°F–180°F (79°C–85°C) until it reaches an internal temperature of 145°F (63°C), approximately 30 to 45 minutes.

4 If the fish is to be served hot, remove it from the court bouillon, draining well, and serve immediately with an appropriate garnish. If it is to be served cold, remove it from the court bouillon, draining well, cool and refrigerate for several hours before decorating and garnishing as desired.

Approximate values per 4-oz. (120-g) serving: **Calories** 114, **Total fat** 3 g, **Saturated fat** 1 g, **Cholesterol** 29 mg, **Sodium** 80 mg, **Total carbohydrates** 0 g, **Protein** 22 g, **Calcium** 6%

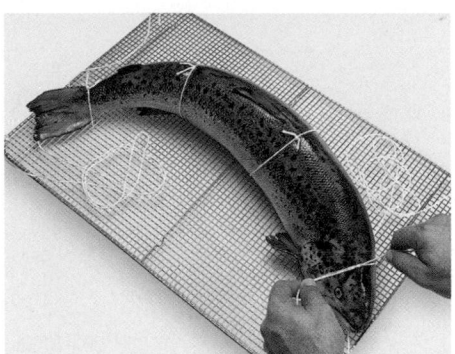

1 Arranging the whole fish on a rack.

2 Preparing the court bouillon.

3 Removing and draining the fish.

PROCEDURE FOR **SHALLOW POACHING**

1 Butter a sauteuse and add aromatic vegetables as directed in the recipe.

2 Add the fish to the pan.

3 Add the cooking liquid to the pan.

4 Cover the pan with buttered parchment paper or a lid.

5 Bring the liquid to a simmer and cook the fish on the stove top or in the oven until done.

6 Remove the fish from the pan, moisten with a portion of the liquid and hold in a warm place for service.

7 Reduce the cuisson and finish the sauce as directed in the recipe.

8 Serve the poached fish with the sauce.

FILLETS OF SOLE BONNE FEMME

Yield: 2 Servings   **Method:** Shallow poaching

Sole fillets, approx. 2½ oz. (75 g) each	4	4
Salt and pepper	TT	TT
Whole butter	1 oz.	30 g
Shallots, minced	1 tsp.	5 ml
Mushrooms, sliced	4 oz.	120 g
White wine	3 fl. oz.	90 ml
Fish stock	4 fl. oz.	120 ml
Fish velouté	4 fl. oz.	120 ml
Lemon juice	TT	TT
Fresh parsley, chopped	1 tsp.	5 ml

MISE EN PLACE
◀ Peel and mince shallots.
◀ Wash and slice mushrooms.
◀ Wash, dry and chop parsley.

1. Season the sole with salt and pepper.
2. Melt the butter in a sauté pan. Add the shallots and mushrooms. To ensure even cooking, fold the tail portion of each sole fillet under the fillet. Then arrange the sole fillets over the shallots and mushrooms in the pan. Add the wine and stock.
3. Bring the liquid to a simmer. Cover the fish with buttered parchment paper and cook on the stove top or in a 350°F (180°C) oven until done, approximately 5 to 8 minutes.
4. Remove the sole and reserve in a warm place.
5. Reduce the cuisson until approximately 1 fluid ounce (30 milliliters) remains. Add the velouté. Add lemon juice to taste and adjust the seasonings. Serve the sauce with the fish, sprinkled with chopped parsley.

Approximate values per serving: **Calories** 440, **Total fat** 14 g, **Saturated fat** 5 g, **Cholesterol** 120 mg, **Sodium** 3750 mg, **Total carbohydrates** 27 g, **Protein** 42 g

1. Arranging the sole on the bed of shallots and mushrooms.

2. Covering the fish with buttered parchment paper after the liquid is added.

3. Adding the velouté to the cuisson.

SIMMERING

"Boiled" lobster, crab and shrimp are not actually boiled; rather, they are cooked whole in their shells by simmering. Although they are not as delicate as some fish, these crustaceans can become tough and are easily overcooked if the cooking liquid is allowed to boil.

Selecting Shellfish to Simmer

Lobsters, crabs and shrimp are commonly cooked by simmering. Their hard shells protect their delicate flesh during the cooking process.

Seasoning Shellfish to Be Simmered

The shellfish being simmered are not seasoned. Rather, they gain flavor by being cooked in a seasoned or flavored liquid, typically salted water or court bouillon. A sachet of pickling spice or Old Bay seasoning is sometimes used for additional flavor.

Determining Doneness

Timing is the best method for determining the doneness of simmered shellfish. This varies depending on the size of the shellfish and how quickly the liquid returns to a simmer after the shellfish is added. Shrimp cook in as little as 3 to 5 minutes; crabs cook in 5 to 10 minutes; and it can take as little as 6 to 8 minutes for a 1-pound (450-gram) lobster to cook and 15 to 20 minutes for a 2½-pound (1.1-kilogram) lobster.

Accompaniments to Simmered Shellfish

The standard accompaniments to simmered shellfish are lemon wedges and melted butter. If the shellfish is being eaten cold, the traditional sauce is a tomato-based cocktail sauce. Nearly any type of vegetable or starch goes well with simmered shellfish, the most common being fresh corn on the cob and boiled potatoes.

PROCEDURE FOR SIMMERING OR BOILING SHELLFISH

1. Bring court bouillon or water to a boil.
2. Add the shellfish to the liquid. Bring the liquid back to a boil and reduce to a simmer. (Whenever an item is added to boiling water, it lowers the water's temperature. The greater the amount of water, however, the faster it will return to a boil. So to accelerate the time within which the water returns to a boil after the shellfish is added, use as much water as possible.)
3. Cook until done.
4. Remove the shellfish from the liquid and serve immediately, or cool by dropping them in ice water if they are to be eaten cold.

BOILED LOBSTER

MISE EN PLACE
▶ Melt butter while the lobster is boiling.

Yield: 1 Serving		Method: Boiling
Lobster, 1 lb. 8 oz. (720 g)	1	1
Boiling salted water	4 gal.	15 lt
Lemon wedges	4	4
Whole butter, melted	2 oz.	60 g

1. Drop the lobster into the boiling water. Bring the water back to a boil, reduce to a simmer and cook the lobster until done, approximately 12 minutes.
2. Remove the lobster from the pot, drain and serve immediately with lemon wedges and melted butter on the side.
3. If the lobster is to be eaten cold, drop it in a sink of ice water to stop the cooking process. When cool enough to handle, remove the meat from the shell following the procedures discussed earlier.

Approximate values per 1-lb. (450-g) serving: **Calories** 650, **Total fat** 26 g, **Saturated fat** 15 g, **Cholesterol** 390 mg, **Sodium** 1960 mg, **Total carbohydrates** 11 g, **Protein** 93 g, **Vitamin A** 35%, **Vitamin C** 45%

Combination Cooking Methods

Combination cooking methods are used with meats, game and poultry in part to tenderize them. Because fish and shellfish are inherently tender, they do not necessarily benefit from such procedures. As noted in the section on shallow poaching, fish can, on occasion, be lightly sautéed or browned and then poached. Although this procedure is a combination cooking method, it is used to enhance flavors and not to tenderize the product.

Some fish or shellfish recipes include the word *braised* or *stew* in the title. Note, however, that these recipes rarely follow the traditional combination cooking methods discussed in this book.

Serving Raw Fish and Seafood

For centuries, fresh fish and seafood have been consumed without cooking. The coastal cuisines of Japan, Sicily and South America include numerous raw fish dishes, for example. And clams and shellfish served raw on the half shell figure prominently in the classical culinary traditions in Europe and the United States. Now that chefs are exploring lighter preparations and the cuisines of Asia, serving raw fish and shellfish has become more common. Raw fish is a potentially hazardous food. Check local health department regulations for recommendations on properly serving raw fish. Sourcing the freshest products from licensed suppliers is essential. The products must be kept very cold from the moment they arrive until the moment they are prepared. Wear clean disposable gloves and observe stringent sanitary conditions when handling raw fish and seafood.

Raw fish and shellfish dishes are about texture as much as flavor. Citrus, especially lemon and lime, fresh delicate herbs and oils are popular additions to raw fish dishes. Raw fish dishes often include crisp accompaniments such as raw vegetables for textural contrast. The recipe for Seviche (page 531) at the end of this chapter is one example of a raw fish preparation, as are the recipes for sushi and sashimi in Chapter 28, Hors d'Oeuvre and Canapés.

SAFETY ALERT

Raw fish is a potentially hazardous food. Many species of fin fish carry parasites that are harmless to the fish but can cause illness in humans. To destroy these parasites, such fish should be frozen before service according to procedures outlined in the Model Food Code. Observe the strictest sanitation standards when preparing raw fish dishes to prevent cross-contamination. Many health departments enforce strict regulations to ensure that raw fish, shellfish and sashimi are properly prepared and served. Check local regulations for the most accurate information for your area.

QUESTIONS FOR DISCUSSION

1. Discuss six techniques for determining the freshness of fish and shellfish.

2. What are the physical differences between a flatfish and a round fish? How do fabrication techniques vary for these fish?

3. List four market forms for fish and discuss several factors that may determine the form most appropriate for an operation to purchase.

4. List the three categories of mollusks and give an example of a commonly used food from each category.

5. Discuss four methods for determining the doneness of fish or shellfish. Why is it important not to overcook fish and shellfish?

6. Explain the differences between shallow poaching and submersion poaching. Why is poaching a commonly used method for preparing fish and shellfish?

7. Describe the proper techniques for sautéing fish fillet. Explain how each step ensures that the fish will be crisp and browned without falling apart.

8. Why are combination cooking methods rarely used with fish and shellfish? Why is boiling rarely used?

9. Research international fish recipes and discuss the types of fish that can be substituted when regional varieties are not available.

Terms to Know

aquatic vertebrates	coral
fins	tomalley
scales	gills
freshwater fish	pin bones
round fish	tranche
flatfish	devein
mollusks	debeard
crustaceans	submersion poaching
cuttlebone	shallow poaching

ROASTED MONKFISH WITH BACON AND GARLIC

Yield: 4 Servings | **Method:** Roasting

Garlic cloves, peeled	24	24
Monkfish fillets, 6-oz. (180-g) portions	4	4
Salt and pepper	TT	TT
Flour	as needed for dredging	
Olive oil	3 Tbsp.	45 ml
Slab bacon, julienne	4 oz.	120 g
Shallots, minced	1 Tbsp.	15 ml
Sherry wine vinegar	1 Tbsp.	15 ml
Crème fraîche	4 fl. oz.	120 ml
Chicken stock	4 fl. oz.	120 ml
Whole butter	1 oz.	30 g

1. Blanch the garlic cloves for 5 to 10 minutes to soften. Drain and reserve the garlic.

2. Season the monkfish with salt and pepper and dredge in the flour. Heat a sauté pan and add the oil. Sauté the monkfish for 4 to 6 minutes, browning it well on all sides.

3. Add the garlic and bacon to the pan and coat with the oil. Place the pan in a preheated 400°F (200°C) oven for 8 to 10 minutes or until the monkfish is cooked and the bacon and garlic cloves are browned.

4. Remove the pan from the oven. Remove the monkfish, bacon and garlic from the pan and hold in a warm place while preparing the sauce.

5. Degrease the pan, leaving 1 tablespoon (15 milliliters) of fat. Add the shallots and sauté 1 minute without coloring. Deglaze the pan with the vinegar. Add the crème fraîche and the stock. Bring to a boil and reduce the sauce to nappe consistency. Adjust the seasonings with salt and pepper. Monté au beurre.

6. Slice the monkfish portions and plate with an appropriate accompaniment such as sautéed spinach. Spoon the sauce over the fish and sprinkle with garlic cloves and bacon.

Approximate values per serving: **Calories** 440, **Total fat** 29 g, **Saturated fat** 11 g, **Cholesterol** 80 mg, **Sodium** 280 mg, **Total carbohydrates** 14 g, **Protein** 32 g, **Vitamin A** 10%, **Vitamin C** 15%

TERIYAKI SALMON WITH PINEAPPLE PAPAYA SALSA

Yield: 4 Servings   **Method:** Grilling

Marinade:		
Soy sauce	8 fl. oz.	240 ml
Garlic, crushed	1 tsp.	5 ml
Ginger, minced	1 tsp.	5 ml
Brown sugar	2 oz.	60 g
Sake	4 fl. oz.	120 ml
Salmon, tranches, 4 oz. (120 g) each	4	4
Vegetable oil	as needed	as needed
Pineapple Papaya Salsa (page 779)	1 pt.	480 ml

1. To make the marinade, combine the soy sauce, garlic, ginger, brown sugar and sake.

2. Marinate the salmon in the marinade for 15 minutes.

3. Remove the salmon from the marinade and pat dry. Brush the tranches with oil and broil or grill until done.

4. Serve the salmon on a bed of warmed Pineapple Papaya Salsa.

Approximate values per serving: **Calories** 330, **Total fat** 9 g, **Saturated fat** 2 g, **Cholesterol** 65 mg, **Sodium** 3770 mg, **Total carbohydrates** 28 g, **Protein** 35 g, **Vitamin C** 60%

OVEN-FRIED PECAN CATFISH

Yield: 12 Servings   **Method:** Baking

Dijon mustard	8 fl. oz.	240 ml
Milk	6 fl. oz.	180 ml
Pecans, ground	14 oz.	420 g
U.S. farm-raised catfish fillets	12	12

1. Mix the mustard and milk in a shallow dish. Spread the pecans out on a piece of parchment paper.

2. Dip each fillet into the mustard mixture. Scrape off any excess mustard, then carefully roll the fillets in the ground pecans. Coat each fillet thoroughly, shaking off any excess. Place the fillets on a lightly oiled baking sheet.

3. Bake at 450°F (230°C) until the catfish flakes easily when tested with a fork, approximately 10 to 12 minutes.

VARIATION:

Tropical Oven-Fried Catfish—Combine 4 fluid ounces (120 milliliters) low-fat buttermilk with 1 teaspoon (5 milliliters) each of black pepper, salt and ginger and 1/8 teaspoon (1 milliliter) ground cinnamon. Crush 9 ounces (270 grams) cornflakes into crumbs. Bread 12 catfish fillets using the standard breading procedure described in Chapter 8, Mise en Place. Cover and refrigerate for at least 30 minutes to set the coating, and then bake as directed in Step 3.

Approximate values per serving: **Calories** 410, **Total fat** 31 g, **Saturated fat** 4.5 g, **Cholesterol** 75 mg, **Sodium** 600 mg, **Total carbohydrates** 6 g, **Protein** 29 g, **Iron** 10%

CHA CA (HANOI-STYLE FISH WITH DILL)

Although it is prepared by frying, cha ca means "braised fish" in Vietnamese; the marinade adds some moisture to the fish as it cooks. This dish is so popular in Hanoi that a street has been named in its honor.

Yield: 4 Servings		**Method:** Sautéing/Stir-frying
Marinade:		
Fresh ginger, 1-in. (2.5-cm) piece, peeled and chopped	1	1
Fresh Thai or serrano chiles	2	2
Granulated sugar	1 Tbsp.	15 ml
Nuoc mam (fish sauce)	2 Tbsp.	30 ml
Turmeric, ground	4 Tbsp.	60 ml
Water	2 fl. oz.	60 ml
Fresh lemon juice	2 Tbsp.	30 ml
Catfish fillets	1 lb.	480 g
Vegetable oil	2 fl. oz.	60 ml
Shallot, thinly sliced	1	1
Garlic cloves, thinly sliced	2	2
Fresh dill	6 oz.	180 g
Green onions, chopped	4	4
Rice vermicelli, cooked	as needed	as needed
Peanuts, chopped	4 Tbsp.	60 ml
Nuoc Cham (page 230)	as needed	as needed

1. Prepare the marinade by grinding the ginger, chiles and sugar into a paste. Add the remaining marinade ingredients and stir until dissolved.
2. Cut the catfish into 1-inch (2.5-centimeter) pieces. Toss the catfish in the marinade. Cover and refrigerate for 1 hour.
3. Heat a sauté pan or wok and add the oil. Sauté the shallot and garlic until translucent, but not brown. Add the fish and any remaining marinade to the hot pan and cook, stirring carefully until the fish is almost done, approximately 2 minutes.
4. Cut the dill into 1½-inch (3.75-centimeter) pieces. Add half of the dill and half of the green onions to the fish and cook until they wilt.
5. Arrange the remaining dill and green onions on a warm serving platter. Pour the fish and wilted herbs on top.
6. Reheat the vermicelli by dropping it in boiling water for a few seconds. Drain well.
7. Serve the sautéed fish and herbs with individual bowls of rice vermicelli. Each diner then places some of the herbs and fish on top of the noodles, adds a sprinkle of chopped peanuts and drizzles with Nuoc Cham.

Approximate values per serving: **Calories** 320, **Total fat** 23 g, **Saturated fat** 4 g, **Cholesterol** 55 mg, **Sodium** 770 mg, **Total carbohydrates** 6 g, **Protein** 19 g, **Vitamin A** 30%, **Vitamin C** 60%, **Iron** 10%

RED SNAPPER VERACRUZ

Yield: 4 Servings		**Method:** Sautéing
Red snapper fillets, skinless, 6 oz. (170 g) each	4	4
Salt and pepper	TT	TT
Flour	as needed for dredging	
Olive oil	2 fl. oz.	60 ml
Onions, medium dice	6 oz.	180 g
Garlic cloves, minced	4	4
Lemon juice	2 Tbsp.	30 ml

Fish or chicken stock	8 fl. oz.	240 ml
Jalapeño, seeded, small dice	1	1
Tomato concassée	1 lb. 8 oz.	720 g
Pimento-stuffed green olives, quartered	20	20
Sugar	1 tsp.	5 ml
Cinnamon stick	1	1
Dried thyme	½ tsp.	2 ml
Dried marjoram	½ tsp.	2 ml
Capers	2 Tbsp.	30 ml
Fresh cilantro	as needed for garnish	

1 Season the fillets with salt and pepper and dredge in flour. Sauté the fillets in oil until done. Remove and reserve in a warm place.

2 Add the onions and garlic to the pan and sauté until tender. Deglaze the pan with the lemon juice and add the stock, jalapeño, tomato concassée, olives, sugar, cinnamon stick, thyme and marjoram.

3 Simmer for 10 minutes. Remove the cinnamon stick and add the capers. Season to taste.

4 Return the fish to the pan to reheat. Serve on warm plates garnished with fresh cilantro.

VARIATION:

Substitute bass or halibut fillets for the red snapper.

Approximate values per serving: **Calories** 570, **Total fat** 22 g, **Saturated fat** 3 g, **Cholesterol** 80 mg, **Sodium** 1820 mg, **Total carbohydrates** 41 g, **Protein** 51 g, **Vitamin C** 70%

TROUT NANCY

BRENNAN'S RESTAURANT, NEW ORLEANS, LA
Chef Michael Roussel (1938–2005)

Yield: 8 Servings   **Method:** Sautéing

Trout fillets	8	8
Salt and pepper	TT	TT
Flour	as needed for dredging	
Whole butter	4 oz.	120 g
Lump crab meat, picked	1½ lb.	720 g
Capers	3 oz.	90 g
Brennan's Lemon Butter Sauce (page 231), prepared up to 2 hours ahead	12 fl. oz.	360 ml
Fresh parsley, chopped	4 Tbsp.	60 ml

1 Season the trout on both sides with salt and pepper, then dredge in flour.

2 Melt the butter in a large sauté pan. Cook the trout over medium heat until flaky, approximately 3 to 4 minutes per side. Remove the trout from the pan and hold in a warm oven for service.

3 Heat the crab meat and the capers briefly in the same sauté pan.

4 For service, place each trout fillet on a warm plate and top with the crab meat and capers. Spoon Brennan's Lemon Butter Sauce over the fish, garnish with parsley and serve. (Alternatively, beurre noisette could be served with the trout.)

Approximate values per serving: **Calories** 630, **Total fat** 52 g, **Saturated fat** 30 g, **Cholesterol** 255 mg, **Sodium** 560 mg, **Total carbohydrates** 5 g, **Protein** 35 g, **Vitamin A** 40%, **Vitamin C** 15%, **Calcium** 15%

MACADAMIA NUT–CRUSTED HALIBUT WITH RED ONION, TOMATO AND BALSAMIC SALSA

NEWBURY COLLEGE, Brookline, MA

Senior Instructor Scott Doughty

Yield: 4 Servings	**Method:** Sautéing	
Macadamia nuts	4 oz.	120 g
Flour	8 oz.	240 g
Halibut fillet	2 lb.	960 g
Salt and pepper	TT	TT
Egg, slightly beaten	1	1
Olive oil	as needed	as needed
Red Onion, Tomato and Balsamic Salsa (recipe follows)	1 pt.	480 ml
Herb sprigs	as needed for garnish	

1. Place the nuts on a half-sheet pan and toast them lightly in the oven. Combine the toasted nuts with 4 ounces (120 grams) of the flour in a food processor. Process until the nuts are chopped finely, but not pulverized.

2. Cut the halibut into four portions.

3. Season the fillets with salt and pepper and then bread them using the remaining flour and egg, following the standard breading procedure described in Chapter 8, Mise en Place. The nut-flour mixture is the final coating.

4. Heat a sautoir and add a thin film of oil. Place the breaded fillets in the oil, leaving some space between each fillet so that they will cook properly. Sauté the fillets until they are a deep golden brown and crusty, then turn them over and cook until the fish is medium rare to medium. Remove the fillets from the pan. Residual heat will complete the cooking.

5. Spoon some of the Red Onion, Tomato and Balsamic Salsa onto a serving platter and place the fillets on top of the salsa. Spoon a small dollop of salsa on each fillet and place a small herb sprig next to it. Serve the remaining salsa on the side.

Approximate values per serving: **Calories** 740, **Total fat** 42 g, **Saturated fat** 6 g, **Cholesterol** 125 mg, **Sodium** 300 mg, **Total carbohydrates** 36 g, **Protein** 55 g, **Vitamin A** 25%, **Vitamin C** 40%, **Calcium** 15%, **Iron** 30%

RED ONION, TOMATO AND BALSAMIC SALSA

Yield: 8 Servings		
Red onion, small dice	1	1
Tomato concassée, medium dice	8	8
Balsamic vinegar	2 fl. oz.	60 ml
Olive oil	2 fl. oz.	60 ml
Salt	½ tsp.	2 ml
Cayenne pepper	⅛ tsp.	1 ml

1. Combine all of the ingredients in a bowl. Cover and chill until ready to serve.

Approximate values per serving: **Calories** 100, **Total fat** 7 g, **Saturated fat** 1 g, **Cholesterol** 0 mg, **Sodium** 160 mg, **Total carbohydrates** 8 g, **Protein** 1 g, **Vitamin A** 15%, **Vitamin C** 40%

SESAME SWORDFISH

Yield: 1 Serving   **Method:** Sautéing

Leeks, julienne	4 oz.	120 g
Swordfish steak, 6 oz. (180 g)	1	1
Sesame oil	1 fl. oz.	30 ml
Sesame seeds	1 oz.	30 g
Fish stock	2 fl. oz.	60 ml
Tamari sauce	1 Tbsp.	15 ml

1. Deep-fry the leeks at 280°F (138°C) until golden brown. Drain well.
2. Brush both sides of the fish with oil. Coat both sides of the fish with the sesame seeds, pressing to make a solid, even coating.
3. In a very hot pan, sauté the fish in the remaining oil. Turn the fish and finish cooking it in a 375°F (190°C) oven.
4. Remove the fish from the pan and hold on a warm plate. Deglaze the pan with the stock. Add the tamari sauce and heat thoroughly.
5. Place the fish on a bed of fried leeks, then pour the sauce over the fish and serve immediately.

VARIATION:

Substitute a tuna or shark steak for the swordfish steak.

Approximate values per serving: **Calories** 780, **Total fat** 52 g, **Saturated fat** 9 g, **Cholesterol** 85 mg, **Sodium** 1410 mg, **Total carbohydrates** 24 g, **Protein** 53 g, **Vitamin C** 25%, **Calcium** 35%

SEARED TUNA WITH JASMINE RICE AND WASABI PONZU

RESTAURANT KEVIN TAYLOR, Denver, CO

Chef Kevin Taylor

Yield: 4 Servings   **Method:** Sautéing

Ponzu sauce:		
Soy sauce	2 fl. oz.	60 ml
Chicken stock	2 fl. oz.	60 ml
Fresh lemon juice	2 fl. oz.	60 ml
Olive oil	2 fl. oz.	60 ml
Wasabi powder	2 Tbsp.	30 ml
Vegetable oil	2 Tbsp.	30 ml
Tuna portions, sushi grade, 4 oz. (120 g) each	4	4
Jasmine rice, freshly cooked	1 pt.	480 ml

1. Combine the soy sauce, stock, lemon juice and olive oil in a medium saucepot and bring to a simmer. In a small bowl combine the wasabi powder with just enough water to make a paste. Combine the wasabi paste with the soy sauce mixture and hold in a warm spot.
2. Heat the vegetable oil in a sauté pan over high heat. Place the tuna in the pan and sear on all sides. Remove the tuna and drain well on a towel.
3. Place a large spoonful of rice in the middle of each of four serving bowls. Slice the tuna and fan five to seven slices around each bowl of rice. Spoon 2–3 fluid ounces (60–90 milliliters) of the ponzu sauce over the tuna. Garnish with additional wasabi paste and herbs or baby greens as desired.

ponzu (pon-zoo) Japanese dipping sauce traditionally made with lemon juice or rice wine vinegar, soy sauce, mirin or sake, seaweed and dried bonito flakes

Approximate values per serving: **Calories** 420, **Total fat** 22 g, **Saturated fat** 3 g, **Cholesterol** 50 mg, **Sodium** 1110 mg, **Total carbohydrates** 26 g, **Protein** 30 g, **Vitamin C** 20%, **Iron** 10%

PAN-SEARED SEA BASS WITH BEET VINAIGRETTE

STOUFFER STANFORD COURT HOTEL, SAN FRANCISCO, CA

Former Chef Ercolino Crugnale

Yield: 10 Servings	**Method:** Sautéing	
Chilean sea bass, diamond-cut fillets, 3 oz. (90 g) each	20	20
Salt and pepper	TT	TT
Olive oil	as needed	as needed
Shiitake mushrooms, sliced	10 oz.	300 g
Zucchini, julienne	10 oz.	300 g
Yellow squash, julienne	10 oz.	300 g
Red bell pepper, julienne	5 oz.	150 g
Chicken stock	10 fl. oz.	300 ml
Beet Vinaigrette (recipe follows)	3 fl. oz.	90 ml
Potatoes, peeled, julienne and deep-fried crisp	20 oz.	600 g

1 Season the fish on both sides. Sauté in oil until fully cooked.

2 Meanwhile, sauté the shiitake mushrooms in oil for 30 seconds. Add the zucchini, squash and bell pepper.

3 Deglaze the pan with the stock and adjust the seasonings.

4 To serve, pool the Beet Vinaigrette onto 10 warm plates. For an interesting effect, drizzle the deglazed pan juices drop by drop into the middle of the plate from a height of 3 feet (1 meter), then pool the remaining pan juices on the plate. Place the vegetables in the center with the fried potatoes on top. Arrange the fish on the vegetables.

Approximate values per serving: **Calories** 430, **Total fat** 15 g, **Saturated fat** 4 g, **Cholesterol** 90 mg, **Sodium** 610 mg, **Total carbohydrates** 29 g, **Protein** 44 g, **Vitamin A** 10%, **Vitamin C** 30%

BEET VINAIGRETTE

Yield: 1 qt. (960 ml)		
Beet juice	3 pt.	1.4 lt
Fresh horseradish, grated	3 Tbsp.	45 ml
Shallot, minced	2 Tbsp.	30 ml
Garlic, minced	1 Tbsp.	15 ml
Fresh thyme	1 bunch	1 bunch
Black peppercorns	10	10
Apple cider vinegar	8 fl. oz.	240 ml
White wine	4 fl. oz.	120 ml
Poultry demi-glace	4 fl. oz.	120 ml
Cornstarch	2 Tbsp.	30 ml
Water	1 fl. oz.	30 ml
Salt	TT	TT

1 Combine the beet juice, horseradish, shallot, garlic, thyme and black peppercorns. Reduce to 1½ pints (720 milliliters).

2 Add the vinegar, wine and demi-glace; simmer for 20 minutes.

3 Combine the cornstarch and water until smooth. Whisk the slurry into the sauce and bring to a boil. Strain through a fine-mesh china cap and season to taste.

Approximate values per 1-fl.-oz. (30-ml) serving: **Calories** 20, **Total fat** 0 g, **Saturated fat** 0 g, **Cholesterol** 0 mg, **Sodium** 100 mg, **Total carbohydrates** 4 g, **Protein** 1 g, **Claims**—fat free; low sodium; low calorie

PAN-FRIED TROUT WITH TOASTED GARLIC

Yield: 1 Serving   **Method:** Pan-frying

Trout, pan-dressed	1	1
Salt and pepper	TT	TT
Flour	as needed for dredging	
Clarified butter	1 fl. oz.	30 ml
Whole butter	½ oz.	15 g
Garlic cloves, sliced thin	2	2
Lemon juice	1 fl. oz.	30 ml
Fresh parsley, chopped	½ tsp.	2 ml

1. Season the trout with salt and pepper; dredge in flour.
2. Pan-fry the trout in the clarified butter until lightly browned and cooked through. Remove and reserve.
3. Degrease the pan, add the whole butter and cook until it begins to brown.
4. Add the garlic and sauté a few seconds, until the garlic begins to brown.
5. Add the lemon juice and parsley and swirl to combine with the butter.
6. Top the fish with the sauce and serve.

Approximate values per serving: **Calories** 650, **Total fat** 47 g, **Saturated fat** 23 g, **Cholesterol** 165 mg, **Sodium** 1600 mg, **Total carbohydrates** 28 g, **Protein** 28 g, **Vitamin A** 45%, **Vitamin C** 30%

CRAB MEAT FLAN

THE WHITE HOUSE, Washington, DC
Former Executive Sous Chef John Moeller

Yield: 6 Servings   **Method:** Baking

Lump crab meat	8 oz.	240 g
Fresh chives, chopped	1 bunch	1 bunch
Salt and white pepper	TT	TT
Eggs	5	5
Heavy cream	1 pt.	480 ml
Sherry	1 fl. oz.	30 ml
Whole butter, melted	as needed	as needed
Beurre Blanc (page 211)	18 fl. oz.	540 ml
Red Pepper Coulis (page 214)	3 fl. oz.	90 ml
Fresh chive stems	12	12
Caviar or lumpfish roe	as needed for garnish	

1. Clean the crab meat and toss with the chopped chives. Season with salt and white pepper.
2. Beat the eggs together lightly and add the cream. Add the sherry and the crab meat mixture. Adjust the seasonings.
3. Coat six ramekins with melted butter and fill with the flan mixture. Place the ramekins in a water bath and bake at 350°F (180°C) until set, approximately 45 to 50 minutes.
4. Pool the Beurre Blanc on six serving plates. Unmold the flans and place in the center of each plate. Decorate the plates with the Red Pepper Coulis and garnish with the chive stems and caviar.

Approximate values per serving: **Calories** 460, **Total fat** 43 g, **Saturated fat** 25 g, **Cholesterol** 350 mg, **Sodium** 750 mg, **Total carbohydrates** 4 g, **Protein** 14 g, **Vitamin A** 50%, **Vitamin C** 15%

flan a firm savory or sweet egg custard; dessert variety is baked over a layer of caramelized sugar and inverted for service

SALMON CROQUETTES

Croquettes are made from cooked meats, poultry, vegetables, fish, shellfish or potatoes, usually bound with a heavy béchamel or velouté sauce and seasoned. They are shaped into cones or patties, then breaded and deep-fried.

Yield: 14 Croquettes		**Method:** Deep-frying
Onion, small dice	2 oz.	60 g
Whole butter	2 oz.	60 g
Flour	2 oz.	60 g
Milk	5 fl. oz.	150 ml
Salmon, poached and flaked	1 lb.	480 g
Fresh dill, chopped	2 tsp.	10 ml
Salt and pepper	TT	TT
Lemon juice	4 tsp.	20 ml
Flour, seasoned with salt and pepper	as needed for breading	
Egg wash	as needed for breading	
Fine bread crumbs	as needed for breading	

1. Sauté the onion in the butter until translucent.
2. Add the flour and cook to make a white roux.
3. Add the milk to make a heavy béchamel sauce. Cook the sauce until very thick, approximately 5 minutes.
4. Remove the sauce from the heat and transfer it to a mixing bowl. Add the flaked salmon. Season with dill, salt, pepper and lemon juice and mix well.
5. Spread the mixture in a hotel pan, cover and refrigerate until cold.
6. Portion the mixture using a #20 portion scoop. Form each portion into a cone shape. Bread the croquettes using the standard breading procedure described in Chapter 8, Mise en Place.
7. Using the basket method, deep-fry the breaded croquettes until done.

Approximate values per croquette: **Calories** 140, **Total fat** 9 g, **Saturated fat** 4.5 g, **Cholesterol** 40 mg, **Sodium** 470 mg, **Total carbohydrates** 7 g, **Protein** 9 g, **Vitamin A** 8%, **Calcium** 10%

1. Portioning the croquette mixture with a portion scoop.

2. Forming the mixture into cone shapes.

3. Deep-frying the breaded croquettes using the basket method.

POACHED ORANGE ROUGHY FILLETS WITH WHITE WINE, TOMATO AND BASIL CREAM

CONNECTICUT CULINARY INSTITUTE, FARMINGTON, CT

Chef Jamie Roraback

Yield: 1 Serving　　　　　　　　　　**Method:** Shallow poaching

Whole butter, softened	2 tsp.	10 ml
Shallot, minced	1 Tbsp.	15 ml
Orange roughy fillets, 4 oz. (120 g) each	2	2
Salt and white pepper	TT	TT
White wine	4 fl. oz.	120 ml
Fish stock	4 fl. oz.	120 ml
Heavy cream (optional)	2 fl. oz.	60 ml
Tomato concassée	2 Tbsp.	30 ml
Fresh basil, chopped	1 Tbsp.	15 ml

1. Rub the bottom of an 8-inch (20-centimeter) sauté pan with the softened butter. Sprinkle the shallot into the pan.
2. Season the orange roughy fillets with salt and white pepper. Place the fillets in the sauté pan, presentation side up.
3. Add enough of the wine and stock so that the liquid just covers the fish. Cover the pan and heat the poaching liquid to approximately 185°F (85°C). Do not let it boil. Poach the fillets until slightly underdone, approximately 3 to 4 minutes.
4. Remove the fish from the pan to a warm plate, cover and hold in a warm place.
5. Bring the poaching liquid to a boil and reduce until approximately 2 fluid ounces (60 milliliters) remain. If desired, add the cream and reduce until the sauce is slightly thickened, approximately 1 minute. Add the tomato concassée and basil and cook only until they are warm. Adjust the seasonings with salt and white pepper. Plate the fish fillets and serve the sauce over the fish.

Approximate values per serving: **Calories** 340, **Total fat** 10 g, **Saturated fat** 5 g, **Cholesterol** 65 mg, **Sodium** 340 mg, **Total carbohydrates** 4 g, **Protein** 37 g, **Vitamin A** 15%, **Vitamin C** 10%, **Calcium** 10%

STEAMED BLACK BASS WITH SANSHO PEPPER

THE FOUR SEASONS, New York, NY

Chef Christian Albin (1947–2009)

Yield: 6 Servings		**Method:** Steaming
Black bass fillets, skin on, approx. 5 oz. (150 g) each	6	6
Leek, large, cut into strips	1	1
Sansho pepper and sea salt	TT	TT
Vinaigrette:		
Lime	1	1
Lemon	1	1
Olive oil	3 Tbsp.	45 ml
Pommery mustard	1 tsp.	5 ml
Salt and pepper	TT	TT

sansho dried berries of the prickly ash tree, ground into a powder that is also known as Szechuan pepper, fagara and Chinese pepper; generally used in Japanese cooking to season fatty foods

1. Lightly score the fish skin, then place the fillets, skin side up, and the leek in a steamer basket. Season with sansho pepper and sea salt. Steam for approximately 5 minutes.
2. To make the vinaigrette, zest and juice the lime and lemon. Blanch the zests in water. Drain and mix the zests and juices with the oil and mustard; season to taste with salt and pepper.
3. Plate the fish fillets and garnish with the leek. Drizzle the vinaigrette over the fish and leek.

Approximate values per serving: **Calories** 220, **Total fat** 7 g, **Saturated fat** 1.5 g, **Cholesterol** 125 mg, **Sodium** 530 mg, **Total carbohydrates** 5 g, **Protein** 35 g, **Vitamin C** 20%, **Claims** low fat, low saturated fat, good source of Vitamin C

PAUPIETTES OF SOLE WITH MOUSSELINE OF SHRIMP

paupiette a thin slice of meat or fish that is rolled around a filling of finely ground meat or vegetables, then fried, baked or braised in wine or stock

Yield: 6 Servings		**Method:** Poaching
Mousseline:		
Raw shrimp meat	12 oz.	360 g
Egg white	1	1
Heavy cream	6 fl. oz.	180 ml
Salt and white pepper	TT	TT
Lemon sole fillets, skinless, 4 oz. (120 g) each	12	12
Whole butter	as needed	as needed
Shallot, chopped	2 oz.	60 g
Parsley stems, chopped	6	6
White vermouth	6 fl. oz.	180 ml
Shrimp stock	12 fl. oz.	360 ml
Beurre manié	approx. 1½ oz.	approx. 45 g

1. To make the mousseline, purée the shrimp meat in a food processor. Add the egg white and pulse to incorporate. Slowly add 2 fluid ounces (60 milliliters) cream to the shrimp while pulsing the processor. Season the mousseline with salt and white pepper.
2. Place the sole fillets, skin side up, on a cutting board. Pat them dry and cover them with plastic wrap. Then flatten the fillets slightly with a mallet.
3. Spread each fillet with a portion of the mousseline. Roll up the fillets, starting with the thickest part and finishing with the tail portion.
4. Butter a sauteuse and sprinkle with the shallot and parsley stems. Place the sole paupiettes in the sauteuse and add the vermouth and stock. Bring the liquid to a boil, cover with a piece of buttered parchment paper and place in a 350°F (180°C) oven. Poach until nearly done.

1 Using a mallet to flatten a fillet slightly.

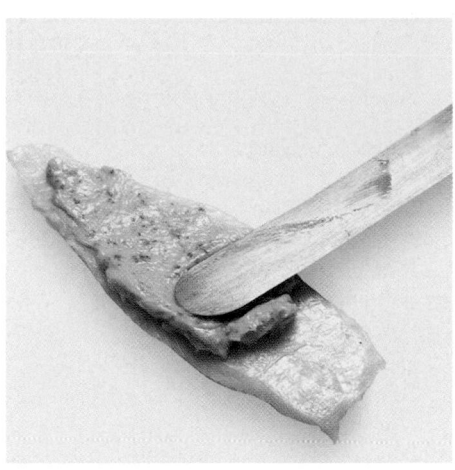

2 Spreading the fillet with the mousseline.

3 Rolling the paupiettes.

5 Remove the sole from the sauteuse and reserve in a warm place.

6 Return the sauteuse to the heat and reduce the cuisson slightly. Thicken the cuisson to the desired consistency with the beurre manié. Add the remaining cream, bring the sauce to a boil and strain through a fine chinois. Adjust the seasonings.

7 Serve two paupiettes per portion on a pool of sauce.

Approximate values per serving: **Calories** 450, **Total fat** 18 g, **Saturated fat** 9 g, **Cholesterol** 310 mg, **Sodium** 970 mg, **Total carbohydrates** 4 g, **Protein** 69 g, **Vitamin A** 35%

ROSEMARY GRILLED SHRIMP

NEWBURY COLLEGE, BROOKLINE, MA
Senior Instructor Scott Doughty

Yield: 6 Servings

Method: Grilling

Fresh rosemary sprigs, 6 in. (15 cm) each	2 sprigs	2 sprigs
Shrimp, 16–20 count, peeled and deveined	2 lb.	960 g
Salt and black pepper	TT	TT
Olive oil	as needed	as needed

1 Strip the rosemary leaves from the stems and chop the leaves.

2 Season the shrimp with salt. Coat the shrimp with pepper as desired.

3 Toss the shrimp with the rosemary and a small amount of oil until the shrimp are lightly and evenly coated with oil and the rosemary is evenly distributed. Allow the shrimp to marinate for 10 to 15 minutes.

4 Preheat the grill. Arrange the shrimp on the grill and cook until the shrimp are cooked one-third of the way through and have attractive grill marks, approximately 1 to 2 minutes. Turn them and repeat. Remove the shrimp from the grill when they are still slightly underdone in the middle; residual heat will continue cooking them. Do not overcook the shrimp or they will be tough and dry.

Approximate values per serving: **Calories** 200, **Total fat** 7 g, **Saturated fat** 1 g, **Cholesterol** 230 mg, **Sodium** 220 mg, **Total carbohydrates** 1 g, **Protein** 31 g, **Iron** 20%

LOBSTER THERMIDOR

THE ART INSTITUTE OF WASHINGTON, ARLINGTON, VA

Yield: 4 Servings   **Method:** Sautéing/Baking

Whole butter	3 oz.	90 g
Shallots, fine dice	3 oz.	90 g
Mushrooms, quartered	1 pt.	480 ml
Salt and pepper	TT	TT
Lobster or shellfish stock	8 fl. oz.	240 ml
Heavy cream	1 pt.	480 ml
Brandy	3 fl. oz.	90 ml
Dry sherry	3 fl. oz.	90 ml
Worcestershire sauce	½ tsp.	2 ml
Cayenne pepper or hot sauce	½ tsp.	2 ml
Lobster meat, cooked, medium dice	24 oz.	720 g
Fresh bread crumbs	2½ oz.	75 g
Fresh parsley, chopped	1 Tbsp.	15 ml
Lobster body shells or pastry shells	4	4
Parmesan, grated	4 Tbsp.	60 ml
Pimentos, julienne	as needed	as needed

1. Heat a heavy sautoir. Add the butter and the shallots and cook until the shallots are translucent. Add the mushrooms and cook until they soften. Season the mixture with salt and pepper.

2. Add the stock and cream. Bring to a boil and reduce by half. Stir in the brandy, sherry, Worcestershire sauce and cayenne pepper. Return to a boil and cook for 1 minute.

3. In a separate bowl, mix together the lobster, bread crumbs and parsley. Gently combine the lobster mixture with the mushrooms and sauce. Adjust the seasonings with salt and pepper.

4. Fill four lobster body shells or pastry shells with the lobster mixture. Sprinkle with Parmesan and bake at 350°F (180°C) until hot, approximately 10 to 15 minutes. Garnish with the pimentos and serve.

Approximate values per serving: **Calories** 880, **Total fat** 65 g, **Saturated fat** 40 g, **Cholesterol** 340 mg, **Sodium** 960 mg, **Total carbohydrates** 16 g, **Protein** 44 g, **Vitamin A** 60%, **Calcium** 30%, **Iron** 10%

CLAMS CASINO

Yield: 36 Clams   **Method:** Baking

Bacon slices, diced	4	4
Onion, minced	1 oz.	30 g
Red bell pepper, minced	1 oz.	30 g
Green bell pepper, minced	1 oz.	30 g
Whole butter	6 oz.	180 g
Lemon juice	1 Tbsp.	15 ml
Worcestershire sauce	2 tsp.	10 ml
Tabasco sauce	TT	TT
Littleneck clams, scrubbed	36	36
Fresh bread crumbs	2 oz.	60 g

1. Fry the bacon until well done. Drain the fat, reserving 2 tablespoons (30 milliliters).
2. Sauté the onion and bell peppers in the bacon fat until tender; remove from the heat and cool.
3. Combine 4 ounces (120 grams) of the butter with the lemon juice, Worcestershire sauce, Tabasco sauce, bacon pieces and sautéed vegetables and chill.
4. Open the clams, leaving the meat in the bottom shell. Top each clam with 1 teaspoon (5 milliliters) of the seasoned butter.
5. Melt 2 ounces (60 grams) of butter in a sauté pan and toss the bread crumbs in the butter. Top each clam with a portion of the bread crumbs.
6. Bake at 400°F (200°C) until light brown and bubbling, approximately 10 minutes. Serve immediately.

Approximate values per clam: **Calories** 45, **Total fat** 4 g, **Saturated fat** 2.5 g, **Cholesterol** 10 mg, **Sodium** 65 mg, **Total carbohydrates** 1 g, **Protein** 0 g

---

OYSTERS ROCKEFELLER

Food historians credit Antoine's Restaurant in New Orleans, in operation since the 1840s, with the invention of this classic American dish. Chef Jules Alciatore, son of the restaurant's founder, sought a replacement for European snails in a popular dish. He experimented using cooked oysters, until then more commonly served raw on the half shell. He called the results Oysters Rockefeller, the richness of the sauce reflected in its name.

Yield: 36 Oysters		**Method:** Baking
Unsalted butter	8 oz.	240 g
Fresh parsley, chopped	1 oz.	30 g
Celery, chopped	2 oz.	60 g
Fennel bulb, chopped	2 oz.	60 g
Shallots, chopped	2 oz.	60 g
Garlic, chopped	1 tsp.	5 ml
Watercress, chopped	4 oz.	120 g
Pernod	2 fl. oz.	60 ml
Fresh bread crumbs	2½ oz.	75 g
Salt and pepper	TT	TT
Oysters, on the half shell	36	36
Rock salt	as needed	as needed

1. Heat the butter in a sauté pan. Add the parsley, celery, fennel, shallots and garlic and cook for 5 minutes.
2. Add the watercress and cook for 1 minute.
3. Add the Pernod and bread crumbs; season with salt and pepper.
4. Transfer the mixture to a food processor and purée.
5. Top each oyster with approximately 2 teaspoons (10 milliliters) of the vegetable mixture; it should coat the oyster's entire surface.
6. Bake the oysters on a bed of rock salt at 450°F (230°C) until the mixture bubbles, approximately 6 to 7 minutes.

Approximate values per oyster: **Calories** 170, **Total fat** 9 g, **Saturated fat** 4.5 g, **Cholesterol** 105 mg, **Sodium** 450 mg, **Total carbohydrates** 9 g, **Protein** 13 g, **Vitamin A** 15%, **Iron** 60%

SEARED DIVER SCALLOP WITH CHANTERELLES, POTATO GAUFRETTES AND BLOOD ORANGE CREAM

RESTAURANT KEVIN TAYLOR, DENVER, CO

Chef Kevin Taylor

diver scallops scallops that are harvested from the ocean by divers who hand-pick each one; diver scallops tend to be less gritty than those harvested by dragging, and hand-harvesting is more ecologically friendly

Yield: 4 Servings   **Method:** Sautéing

Russet potato	1	1
Blood oranges	5	5
Heavy cream	2 fl. oz.	60 ml
Unsalted butter	4 oz.	120 g
Salt and pepper	TT	TT
Granulated sugar	as needed	as needed
Diver scallops, U-8	4	4
Canola oil	as needed	as needed
Fresh chanterelle mushrooms, trimmed	1 pt.	480 ml
Olive oil	as needed	as needed

1. Peel the potato and trim into a cylinder shape. Using a mandoline and the ridged cutting blade, cut thin slices of potato, turning the potato 60 to 90 degrees between each slice and adjusting the thickness of the slices until a waffle pattern (gaufrette) is produced. Using the swimming method, deep-fry the potato slices at 325°F (163°C) until crisp and lightly browned. Drain on a paper towel.

2. Juice the blood oranges. Strain the juice. Place the juice in a small saucepot and reduce by two-thirds. Add the cream and reduce this mixture by one-third. Reduce the heat and slowly whisk in the butter to form a sauce. Season with salt and pepper. If the sauce is too tart, adjust the flavor with a small amount of sugar. Hold the sauce in a warm place.

3. Season the scallops with salt and pepper. In a medium sauté pan over high heat, sear the scallops in a little canola oil until browned on one side. Turn the scallops and place the pan in a 400°F (200°C) oven until cooked to the desired doneness, approximately 3 to 5 minutes.

4. Sauté the chanterelles in a small amount of olive oil until tender. Season with salt and pepper.

5. Place a portion of the blood orange sauce in the bottom of each of four small soup plates. Place a portion of the chanterelles in the middle of each bowl on top of the sauce. Place a seared scallop on top of the chanterelles and garnish each plate with two or three gaufrette potatoes.

Approximate values per serving: **Calories** 350, **Total fat** 32 g, **Saturated fat** 18 g, **Cholesterol** 85 mg, **Sodium** 35 mg, **Total carbohydrates** 13 g, **Protein** 5 g, **Vitamin A** 25%, **Vitamin C** 60%

SHRIMP AND CORN SAUTÉ

SOUTH PUGET SOUND COMMUNITY COLLEGE, OLYMPIA, WA

Chef William A. Wiklendt, M.Ed., CEC, CCE, AAC

Yield: 5 Servings   **Method:** Sautéing

Shrimp, 16–20 count, peeled, deveined and tails removed	12 oz.	360 g
Whole butter	2 oz.	60 g
Red bell pepper, small dice	2 oz.	60 g
Green bell pepper, small dice	2 oz.	60 g
Corn kernels	12 oz.	360 g
Heavy cream	4 fl. oz.	120 ml
Salt and pepper	TT	TT
Paprika	as needed	as needed

1 Sauté the shrimp in 1 ounce (30 grams) of the butter until tender. Remove the shrimp and set aside. Sauté the bell peppers in the remaining butter until tender.

2 Add the corn and the cream and sauté until hot.

3 Return the shrimp to the pan and cook until all ingredients are hot. Adjust the seasonings with salt and pepper. Serve with rice or pasta as an appetizer or entrée.

Approximate values per serving: **Calories** 240, **Total fat** 19 g, **Saturated fat** 12 g, **Cholesterol** 110 mg, **Sodium** 70 mg, **Total carbohydrates** 11 g, **Protein** 9 g, **Vitamin A** 25%, **Vitamin C** 60%

SHRIMP WITH OLIVE OIL AND GARLIC

Yield: 4 Servings   **Method:** Sautéing

Garlic, chopped	4 Tbsp.	60 ml
Extra virgin olive oil	4 fl. oz.	120 ml
Shrimp, 26–30 count, in shell	2 lb. 4 oz.	1 kg
Coarse sea salt	1 Tbsp.	15 ml
Lemon juice	2 Tbsp.	30 ml

1 Sauté the garlic in the oil until translucent.

2 Add the shrimp and salt. Toss to coat the shrimp with the oil and cook just until the shrimp are pink, approximately 5 minutes. Add the lemon juice.

3 Arrange the shrimp on warm serving plates; top with the oil, garlic and lemon juice left in the pan. Serve immediately.

Approximate values per serving: **Calories** 530, **Total fat** 31 g, **Saturated fat** 4.5 g, **Cholesterol** 555 mg, **Sodium** 2380 mg, **Total carbohydrates** 2 g, **Protein** 60 g, **Vitamin A** 20%, **Vitamin C** 20%, **Iron** 50%

THAI CRAB CAKE

FLYING FISH, Seattle, WA

Chef-Owner Christine Keff

Yield: 4 Servings   **Method:** Sautéing

Crab meat	1 lb.	480 g
Panko (Japanese bread crumbs)	8 oz.	240 g
Lemongrass Mayonnaise (recipe follows)	8 fl. oz.	240 ml
Green onions, chopped fine	4	4
Fresh basil, chopped fine	2 Tbsp.	30 ml
Fresh cilantro, chopped fine	2 Tbsp.	30 ml
Fresh mint, chopped fine	2 Tbsp.	30 ml
Fish sauce	TT	TT
Clarified butter	as needed	as needed
Mixed baby greens	as needed for garnish	
Orange supremes	as needed for garnish	
Lemongrass Mayonnaise	as needed for garnish	

1 Gently stir together the crab meat, panko, Lemongrass Mayonnaise, green onions, herbs and fish sauce. Divide into four portions and form into cakes.

2 Heat a little butter and then sauté each cake for 3 minutes on each side over medium heat, until golden brown.

3 Serve on a plate garnished with baby greens, orange supremes and additional Lemongrass Mayonnaise.

Approximate values per 6-oz. (180-g) serving: **Calories** 544, **Total fat** 31 g, **Saturated fat** 6 g, **Cholesterol** 124 mg, **Sodium** 1006 mg, **Total carbohydrates** 45 g, **Protein** 21 g

LEMONGRASS MAYONNAISE

Yield: 1 pt. (480 ml)

Egg yolks	2	2
Rice wine vinegar	1½ Tbsp.	23 ml
Mirin	1 Tbsp.	15 ml
Soy sauce	1 tsp.	5 ml
Fish sauce	1 tsp.	5 ml
Lemongrass Oil (recipe follows)	10 fl. oz.	300 ml

1 Place all of the ingredients except the Lemongrass Oil into a food processor or blender and process for 30 seconds or until well blended.

2 With the processor running, drizzle in the oil to form an emulsion.

Approximate values per 1-fl.-oz. (30-ml) serving: **Calories** 146, **Total fat** 15 g, **Saturated fat** 3 g, **Cholesterol** 33 mg, **Sodium** 113 mg, **Total carbohydrates** 2 g, **Protein** 1 g

LEMONGRASS OIL

Yield: 10 fl. oz. (300 ml)

Fresh ginger, peeled, sliced thin	1¼ oz.	38 g
Lemongrass, chopped	2 oz.	60 g
Peanut oil	10 fl. oz.	300 ml

1. Place all of the ingredients in a small saucepan and bring to a simmer over low heat. Simmer for 5 minutes.
2. Remove from the heat and allow the flavored oil to stand overnight at room temperature. Strain before using.

Approximate values per 1-fl.-oz. (30-ml) serving: **Calories** 186, **Total fat** 21 g, **Saturated fat** 4 g, **Cholesterol** 0 mg, **Sodium** 0 g, **Total carbohydrates** 1 g, **Protein** 0 g

---

FRIED OYSTERS WITH HERBED CRÈME FRAÎCHE

Yield: 4 Appetizer Servings   **Method:** Deep-frying

Leeks, julienne	3	3
Oysters, scrubbed	24	24
Flour	4 oz.	120 g
Eggs	2	2
Egg yolks	2	2
Fresh bread crumbs	8 oz.	240 g
Sauce:		
Cornichons, chopped fine	1 Tbsp.	15 ml
Capers, chopped fine	2 Tbsp.	30 ml
Dijon mustard	1 tsp.	5 ml
Paprika	½ tsp.	2 ml
Fresh parsley, minced	2 Tbsp.	30 ml
Crème fraîche	4 fl. oz.	120 ml

1. Deep-fry the leeks at 280°F (138°C) until golden brown. Drain and set aside.
2. Open the oysters. Strain and reserve the liquor.
3. Poach the oysters in the liquor for 30 seconds. Drain, reserving the liquid. Cool the liquid and oysters separately.
4. Bread the oysters using the standard breading procedure described in Chapter 8, Mise en Place.
5. Deep-fry the oysters at 375°F (190°C) until browned, approximately 1 minute.
6. Prepare the sauce by combining all of the sauce ingredients except the crème fraîche. Whip the crème fraîche until stiff. Fold in the cornichon mixture. Chill until service.
7. Serve the oysters on a nest of leeks with the sauce.

Approximate values per serving: **Calories** 1220, **Total fat** 44 g, **Saturated fat** 17 g, **Cholesterol** 785 mg, **Sodium** 2870 mg, **Total carbohydrates** 118 g, **Protein** 89 g, **Vitamin A** 50%, **Vitamin C** 70%, **Iron** 380%

SPICY CALAMARI SALAD

Yield: 4 Servings, 6 oz. (180 g) each   **Method:** Deep-frying

Marinade:		
Lemon juice	4 fl. oz.	120 ml
Red wine vinegar	1 pt.	480 ml
Garlic powder	1 Tbsp.	15 ml
Squid, cleaned and cut into rings	1 lb.	480 g
Red bell pepper, sliced thin	3 oz.	90 g
Green bell pepper, sliced thin	3 oz.	90 g
Oyster mushrooms, sliced	12 oz.	360 g
Whole butter	½ oz.	15 g
Garlic, chopped	1 Tbsp.	15 ml
Oyster sauce	2 fl. oz.	60 ml
Chile flakes	TT	TT
Flour	6 oz.	180 g
Baking powder	1½ Tbsp.	22 ml
Cornstarch	1½ Tbsp.	22 ml
Boston lettuce, torn into small pieces	as needed for garnish	
Fresh cilantro or Italian parsley	as needed for garnish	

1 Combine the marinade ingredients. Marinate the squid in the marinade for 3 days.

2 Sauté the bell peppers and mushrooms in the butter. Add the garlic, oyster sauce and chile flakes. Set aside.

3 Drain the squid, pressing out as much liquid as possible. Combine the flour, baking powder and cornstarch; toss with the squid until well coated.

4 Deep-fry the squid at 350°F (177°C) until crispy and golden brown. Drain and toss with the bell peppers and mushrooms. Serve on a bed of lettuce, garnished with cilantro or Italian parsley.

Approximate values per 6-oz. (180-g) serving: **Calories** 450, **Total fat** 13 g, **Saturated fat** 4 g, **Cholesterol** 305 mg, **Sodium** 720 mg, **Total carbohydrates** 55 g, **Protein** 29 g, **Vitamin A** 20%, **Vitamin C** 100%, **Calcium** 35%

SOFT-SHELL CRAB PO' BOY SANDWICH

K RESTAURANT WINE BAR, ORLANDO, FL

Chef Kevin Fonzo

Yield: 6 Sandwiches   **Method:** Deep-frying

Soft-shell crabs, cleaned	6	6
Salt and pepper	TT	TT
Flour	as needed for breading	
Egg wash	as needed for breading	
Blue cornmeal	as needed for breading	
Creole Rémoulade Sauce (page 737)	1½ pt.	720 ml
Mini-baguettes, sliced in half and toasted	6	6
Lettuce, shredded	3 c.	720 ml
Tomato slices	18	18

1 Season the crabs with salt and pepper. Bread each crab using the standard breading procedure described in Chapter 8, Mise en Place.

2 Using the basket method, deep-fry the crabs until done.

3 Spread the Creole Rémoulade Sauce evenly over the baguettes.

4 Divide the shredded lettuce over the bottoms of the baguettes, then top with the tomato slices, crab and the tops of the baguettes. Serve with sautéed potatoes or potato salad.

Approximate values per sandwich: **Calories** 530, **Total fat** 21 g, **Saturated fat** 5 g, **Cholesterol** 45 mg, **Sodium** 1440 mg, **Total carbohydrates** 66 g, **Protein** 18 g, **Vitamin A** 20%, **Vitamin C** 50%

SHRIMP POACHED IN ORANGE JUICE, GINGER AND SAUTERNES

ALLEN SUSSER'S NEW WORLD CUISINE AND COOKERY BY ALLEN SUSSER, NORTH MIAMI BEACH, FL

Yield: 4 Servings   **Method:** Poaching

Jumbo shrimp, 21–25 count	16	16
Orange juice, fresh squeezed	1 pt.	480 ml
Fresh ginger, julienne	2 Tbsp.	30 ml
Sauternes wine	4 fl. oz.	120 ml
Shallots, julienne	13 oz.	390 g
Carrots, julienne	10 oz.	300 g
Kosher salt	1 tsp.	5 ml
Black pepper	1 tsp.	5 ml
Green onion, julienne	as needed for garnish	

1 Peel, clean and butterfly the shrimp.
2 Place all of the ingredients except the green onion in a low-sided pan with a lid and slowly warm over low heat to just about a simmer. Cover the pan and poach the shrimp for 3 to 4 minutes. The shrimp should be rosy pink and firm to the touch.
3 Remove from the heat and serve the shrimp with the vegetables and broth, garnished with the green onion.

Approximate values per serving: **Calories** 410, **Total fat** 4 g, **Saturated fat** 1 g, **Cholesterol** 665 mg, **Sodium** 1360 mg, **Total carbohydrates** 21 g, **Protein** 73 g, **Vitamin A** 190%, **Vitamin C** 130%, **Iron** 60%

STEAMED MUSSELS WITH LEEKS AND CARROTS

SIMPLICITY CATERING, FALLS CHURCH, VA
Chef Leland Atkinson

Yield: 2 Servings   **Method:** Steaming

Mussels, debearded and scrubbed	2 lb.	960 g
Dry white wine	8 fl. oz.	240 ml
Garlic, chopped	1 oz.	30 g
Black pepper	½ tsp.	2 ml
Fresh thyme	4 sprigs	4 sprigs
Bay leaves	2	2
Leek, julienne	2 oz.	60 g
Carrot, julienne	2 oz.	60 g
Whole butter	4 oz.	120 g
Fresh parsley, chopped	1 Tbsp.	15 ml

1 Combine the mussels, wine, garlic, pepper, thyme, bay leaves, leek and carrot in a large sautoir.
2 Cover the pan and bring to a boil. Steam until the mussels open.
3 Remove the mussels and arrange them in two large soup plates.
4 Reduce the cooking liquid by half, monté au beurre and pour the sauce over the mussels. The carrot and leek should remain on top of the mussels as garnish.
5 Sprinkle with chopped parsley and serve with French bread.

Approximate values per serving: **Calories** 1220, **Total fat** 67 g, **Saturated fat** 33 g, **Cholesterol** 375 mg, **Sodium** 2170 mg, **Total carbohydrates** 44 g, **Protein** 110 g, **Vitamin A** 140%, **Vitamin C** 120%, **Iron** 200%

PAELLA

SIMPLICITY CATERING, FALLS CHURCH, VA

Chef Leland Atkinson

Paella (pah-AY-lyah) is one of the classic dishes of Spain. The word paella *refers to both a shallow, black steel pan and the dish made in it; paella is a combination of poultry, meats, shellfish, game, chorizo, vegetables and short-grain rice with saffron. Traditionally this dish is cooked over an open wood fire. The most well-known paella is from Valencia and consists of a colorful mixture of shellfish, poultry and saffron rice.*

Yield: 4 Servings   **Method:** Steaming

Chicken thighs	4	4
Salt and pepper	TT	TT
Olive oil	2 fl. oz.	60 ml
Onion, medium dice	2 oz.	60 g
Garlic, chopped	1 Tbsp.	15 ml
Red bell pepper, medium dice	2 oz.	60 g
Green bell pepper, medium dice	2 oz.	60 g
Long-grain rice	12 oz.	360 g
Saffron	1 pinch	1 pinch
Chicken stock, well seasoned, hot	26 fl. oz.	780 ml
Chorizo, cooked, sliced	4 oz.	120 g
Clams, scrubbed	12	12
Cockles, scrubbed	12	12
Shrimp, 16–20 count	12	12
Lobster, cut up	1	1
Mussels, debearded and scrubbed	12	12

1. Season the chicken with salt and pepper. Pan-fry it in the oil, browning it well. Cook until done, approximately 20 minutes. Remove the chicken and reserve.
2. Add the onion, garlic and bell peppers to the pan and sauté until tender.
3. Add the rice and sauté until it turns translucent.
4. Add the saffron to the chicken stock. Stir the chicken stock into the rice and bring to a boil.
5. Add the chorizo, clams and cockles to the pan. Cover and place in a 375°F (190°C) oven for 20 minutes.
6. Add the shrimp, lobster and cooked chicken to the pan. Cover and cook for an additional 15 minutes.
7. Add the mussels to the pan and cook until the shrimp and lobster are done, the chicken is hot and all the shellfish are opened, approximately 5 minutes.

Approximate values per serving: **Calories** 930, **Total fat** 41 g, **Saturated fat** 10 g, **Cholesterol** 650 mg, **Sodium** 2050 mg, **Total carbohydrates** 31 g, **Protein** 110 g, **Vitamin A** 25%, **Vitamin C** 60%, **Iron** 70%

SEAFOOD FRICASSEE

PESCE RESTAURANT, HOUSTON, TX

Chef Mark Holley

Yield: 1 Serving   **Method:** Sautéing/Steaming

Barramundi fillet, 6 oz. (180 g)	1	1
Sea scallops, U-10	2	2
Salt and pepper	TT	TT
Olive oil	as needed	as needed
Shallot, minced	1 tsp.	5 ml

Greenlip mussels, cleaned	3	3
White wine	2 fl. oz.	60 ml
Champagne Cream Sauce (recipe follows)	2 fl. oz.	60 ml
Champagne grapes	1 Tbsp.	15 ml
Fresh chives, sliced	¼ tsp.	2 ml
Asparagus spears, trimmed, steamed, hot	3	3
Roasted red bell pepper strips, hot	1 oz.	30 g
Leek, julienne, fried	as needed for garnish	

1. Season the barramundi and sea scallops with salt and pepper. Heat a small amount of oil in a sauté pan, add the fish and scallops and sear over high heat. Remove the fish and scallops from the pan and reserve.

2. In the same sauté pan, sauté the shallot and mussels briefly and deglaze with the wine. Add the Champagne Cream Sauce and simmer until the mussels are open and the sauce has thickened slightly. Add the grapes and chives.

3. Place the fish and scallops in a 350°F (180°C) oven for approximately 5 minutes to reheat.

4. Season the asparagus spears and bell pepper with salt and pepper and arrange them at the top of the plate. Remove the fish and scallops from the oven and place the fish in the center of the plate. Arrange the scallops and mussels around the fish. Spoon or pour the sauce around the fish and garnish with the fried leek.

Approximate values per serving: **Calories** 740, **Total fat** 49 g, **Saturated fat** 29 g, **Cholesterol** 250 mg, **Sodium** 630 mg, **Total carbohydrates** 14 g, **Protein** 42 g, **Vitamin A** 70%, **Vitamin C** 100%, **Calcium** 15%, **Iron** 20%

CHAMPAGNE CREAM SAUCE

Yield: 1 qt. (1 lt.)

Unsalted butter	1 tsp.	5 ml
Yellow onion, medium dice	3 oz.	120 g
Bay leaves	2	2
Chardonnay wine	8 fl. oz.	240 ml
Champagne	8 fl. oz.	240 ml
Crab, whole, dressed, crushed	1 lb.	480 g
Heavy cream	1 qt.	1 lt
Kosher salt	1 tsp.	5 ml
Black pepper	¼ tsp.	1 ml
Sour cream	1 Tbsp.	15 ml

1. Heat the butter in a small saucepan over medium heat. Add the onion and bay leaves and sauté until the onion is translucent, approximately 3 minutes.

2. Add the wine, champagne and crab and reduce by half. Add the cream and reduce by half, or until the sauce is thick enough to coat the back of a spoon. Add the salt and pepper.

3. Strain the sauce through a china cap, pressing well to remove all liquid from the shells, and then add the sour cream.

4. Blend the sauce with a few pulses of an immersion blender just enough to froth the sauce. Keep warm for service.

Approximate values per 1-fl.-oz. (30-ml) serving: **Calories** 230, **Total fat** 22 g, **Saturated fat** 14 g, **Cholesterol** 85 mg, **Sodium** 170 mg, **Total carbohydrates** 2 g, **Protein** 1 g, **Vitamin A** 20%

BOUILLABAISSE (PROVENÇAL FISH STEW)

Note: This dish appears in the chapter opening photograph.

Yield: 8 servings   **Method:** Simmering

Olive oil	2 fl. oz.	60 ml
Leek, trimmed, chopped fine	4 oz.	120 g
Onion, chopped fine	4 oz.	120 g
Fennel bulb, chopped fine	1	1
Garlic, chopped	1 Tbsp.	15 ml
Salt and pepper	TT	TT
Orange zest	2 tsp.	10 ml
Fennel seeds	¼ tsp.	1 ml
Dry white wine	4 fl. oz.	120 ml
Tomatoes, crushed	1 lb.	480 g
Fish stock or clam juice	8 fl. oz.	240 ml
Saffron, soaked in 1 oz. (30 ml) hot water	¼ tsp.	1 ml
Pernod, Ricard or other anise liqueur	2 fl. oz.	60 ml
Assorted flat fish, mackerel, bass, perch, pike, whole or filleted, cut into 2 -inch- (5-cm-) thick chunks	3 lbs.	1.4 k
Lobsters, 1 lb. 4 oz. (600 g) each, cut into pieces	2	2
Clams	8	8
Shrimp, 21–25 count, peeled	16	16
Mussels	16	16
Parsley sprigs	as needed for garnish	
Garlic croutons	8	8
Rouille (recipe follows)	as needed	

1. Heat the olive oil in a large rondeau over medium heat. Add the leek, onion, fennel and garlic. Cook until the vegetables soften, approximately 5 minutes. Season to taste. Add the orange zest, fennel seeds, wine, tomatoes, stock, saffron and Pernod. Bring to a boil, then simmer to combine the flavors, approximately 10 minutes. Sauce may be prepared up to 2 days ahead to this point.

2. To make the bouillabaisse, place the firmest flatfish, lobster and clams in the bottom of the rondeau. Cook over high heat for 5 minutes, then add the remaining fish, shrimp and mussels. Cover and boil rapidly until all of the clams are opened and the fish is well cooked, approximately 10 to 15 minutes.

3. Divide the fish and shellfish evenly among eight serving bowls. Adjust the seasoning of the broth, then ladle it into each bowl and top with a toasted garlic crouton. Serve a bowl of Rouille on the table for each guest to add as desired.

Approximate values per serving: **Calories** 1030, **Total fat** 71 g, **Saturated fat** 14 g, **Cholesterol** 350 mg, **Sodium** 1960 mg, **Total carbohydrates** 29 g, **Protein** 71 g, **Vitamin A** 20%, **Vitamin C** 70%, **Calcium** 20%, **Iron** 30%

ROUILLE

Yield: 8 fl. oz. (240 ml)

White bread	1 slice	1 slice
Garlic, chopped	2 tsp.	10 ml
Cayenne pepper	¼ tsp.	1 ml
Olive oil	8 fl. oz.	240 ml
Salt	TT	TT

1 Tear the bread and place in the bowl of a food processor. Process for 40 seconds to make fresh bread crumbs.

2 Add the garlic and cayenne pepper and process to blend.

3 Slowly drizzle in the oil until the mixture resembles mayonnaise. Add a small amount of warm water if necessary to thin the sauce and make it creamier.

4 Adjust the seasoning with salt.

Approximate values per serving: **Calories** 470, **Total fat** 35 g, **Saturated fat** 5 g, **Cholesterol** 0 mg, **Sodium** 770 mg, **Total carbohydrates** 20 g, **Protein** 7 g

CRAWFISH ÉTOUFFÉE

Yield: 4 Servings

Method: Simmering

Corn oil	4 fl. oz.	120 ml
Flour	4 oz.	120 g
Onion, large, chopped fine	1	1
Celery stalk, chopped fine	1	1
Green bell pepper, chopped	½	½
Garlic cloves, minced	2	2
Shrimp broth or clam juice	1¼ pt.	600 ml
Lemon juice	1 Tbsp.	15 ml
Crawfish fat (optional)	2 oz.	60 g
Salt	1 tsp.	5 ml
Black pepper	½ tsp.	2 ml
Cayenne pepper	½ tsp.	2 ml
Dried thyme	½ tsp.	2 ml
Bay leaf	1	1
Louisiana hot sauce	1 Tbsp.	15 ml
Crawfish tails, frozen	1 lb.	480 g
Green onions, sliced	2	2
White rice, cooked	1 qt.	1 lt.

1 Heat the oil in a large sauté pan. Whisk in the flour and cook, stirring constantly, to make a medium-dark roux.

2 Add the onion, celery, bell pepper and garlic and sauté over medium-low heat until the vegetables are tender, approximately 10 minutes.

3 Slowly add the broth or clam juice and bring to a boil. Reduce the heat to a simmer and add the lemon juice, crawfish fat (if using), salt, black pepper, cayenne pepper and herbs. Simmer for 15 minutes to thicken.

4 Add the hot sauce and the crawfish tails and simmer for approximately 10 minutes. Add the green onions and adjust the seasonings. Serve over cooked rice.

Approximate values per serving: **Calories** 880, **Total fat** 32 g, **Saturated fat** 4 g, **Cholesterol** 130 mg, **Sodium** 1190 mg, **Total carbohydrates** 107 g, **Protein** 40 g, **Vitamin A** 300%, **Vitamin C** 480%, **Calcium** 45%, **Iron** 90%

INSALATA DI MARE
(ITALIAN SEAFOOD SALAD)

Yield: 8 Servings　　　　　　　　　　　　　**Method:** Poaching

Court bouillon (page 193)	1 qt.	960 ml
Sea scallops	8 oz.	240 g
Shrimp, 21–25 count, peeled, deveined	8 oz.	240 g
Squid, cleaned, bodies cut into rings	8 oz.	240 g
Mussels, cleaned	2 lb.	960 g
White wine	2 fl. oz.	60 ml
Dressing:		
Virgin olive oil	6 fl. oz.	180 ml
Lemon juice	2 Tbsp.	30 ml
Fresh parsley, chopped	4 Tbsp.	60 ml
Salt and pepper	TT	TT
Fennel, sliced thin	4 oz.	120 g
Celery, julienne	4 oz.	120 g
Carrot, julienne	4 oz.	120 g
Garlic cloves, chopped	½ oz.	15 g
Green olives, pitted	4 oz.	120 g
Crushed red pepper flakes	TT	TT

1. In a medium saucepan, bring the court bouillon to a boil. Add the sea scallops and poach for 2 to 3 minutes or until they are just cooked. Remove from the court bouillon, spread on a sheet pan and refrigerate until cold.

2. Cook the shrimp in the same court bouillon using the same method. Spread on a sheet pan and refrigerate until cold.

3. Cook the squid in the same court bouillon using the same method. Spread on a sheet pan and refrigerate until cold.

4. Place the mussels in a large saucepan and add the wine. Cover and cook over high heat for 1 to 2 minutes until the mussels open. Remove the mussels from the pan; reserve the cooking liquid. Spread the mussels on a sheet pan and refrigerate until cold. Chill the mussel cooking liquid. Remove the mussel meats from the shells and discard the shells.

5. Combine the ingredients for the dressing and 2 fluid ounces (60 milliliters) of the mussel cooking liquid. Season with salt and pepper.

6. In a stainless steel bowl, combine the sea scallops, shrimp, squid, mussels, dressing, fennel, celery, carrot, garlic, green olives and red pepper flakes. Season with salt and pepper and toss to combine. Refrigerate the salad at least 2 hours before serving to allow the flavors to blend.

Approximate values per serving: **Calories** 370, **Total fat** 26 g, **Saturated fat** 3.5 g, **Cholesterol** 85 mg, **Sodium** 660 mg, **Total carbohydrates** 9 g, **Protein** 25 g, **Vitamin A** 45%, **Vitamin C** 30%, **Iron** 30%

SEVICHE

In a seviche, the fish and shellfish are "cooked" by the acids in the citrus juice. Although a variety of fish or shellfish may be used, it is extremely important that the products be absolutely fresh. Use a nonreactive container such as stainless steel or plastic for mixing or storing the seviche. Aluminum and other metals may react with the acids in the lime juice, giving the food a metallic flavor.

Yield: 3 lb. (1.4 kg)

Raw scallops and/or shrimp	1 lb.	480 g
Raw firm white fish	1 lb.	480 g
Fresh lime juice	8 fl. oz.	240 ml
Serrano chiles, minced	4	4
Red onion, fine dice	6 oz.	180 g
Fresh cilantro, minced	4 Tbsp.	60 ml
Olive oil	1 fl. oz.	30 ml
Tomato concassée	8 oz.	240 g
Garlic, chopped	2 tsp.	10 ml
Salt and pepper	TT	TT

1. Chop the scallops, shrimp and fish coarsely but evenly. Place in a nonreactive container and add the lime juice. Cover and marinate in the refrigerator for 4 hours. The fish should turn opaque and become firm.

2. Toss in the remaining ingredients and season to taste with salt and pepper. Chill thoroughly and serve as a salad or with tortilla chips.

3. If the seviche is going to be held for more than 2 hours, drain the liquid and refrigerate separately. The reserved liquid can then be tossed with the other ingredients at service time.

Approximate values per 4-oz. (120-g) serving: **Calories** 120, **Total fat** 4.5 g, **Saturated fat** 0.5 g, **Cholesterol** 30 mg, **Sodium** 250 mg, **Total carbohydrates** 5 g, **Protein** 13 g, **Vitamin A** 10%, **Vitamin C** 20%, **Claims—** low saturated fat

SAFETY ALERT

Raw fish is a potentially hazardous food. Many species of fin fish carry parasites that are harmless to the fish but can cause illness in humans. To destroy these parasites, such fish should be frozen before service according to procedures outlined in the Model Food Code. Observe the strictest sanitation standards when preparing raw fish dishes to prevent cross-contamination. Many health departments enforce strict regulations to ensure that raw fish, shellfish and sashimi are properly prepared and served. Check local regulations for the most accurate information for your area.

CHAPTER TWENTY

EGGS AND BREAKFAST

After studying this chapter, you will be able to:

- understand the composition of eggs
- purchase and store eggs properly
- apply various cooking methods to eggs
- prepare pancakes and other griddlecakes
- understand various beverages typically served at breakfast
- offer customers a variety of breakfast foods

NATURE DESIGNED EGGS AS THE FOOD SOURCE for developing chicks. Eggs, particularly chicken eggs, are also an excellent food for humans because of their high protein content, low cost and ready availability. They are extremely versatile and are used throughout the kitchen, either served alone or as ingredients in a prepared dish. Eggs are used to provide texture, flavor, structure, moisture and nutrition in everything from soups and sauces to breads and pastries.

Egg dishes are, of course, most often associated with the meals breakfast and brunch. But food service operations must offer a variety of breakfast options to appeal to a wide range of consumers.

Breakfast cookery is often one of the first line positions a new cook will be offered. This important duty requires speed, timing and precision and can help an apprentice or beginning cook develop organized, efficient work habits.

This chapter discusses cooking methods used for eggs as well as breakfast meats, griddlecakes, crêpes, cereals and the beverages coffee and tea. Other foods typically served at breakfast, such as quick breads, fruit and cheese, are discussed elsewhere in this text.

EGGS

Composition

The primary parts of an egg are the shell, yolk and albumen. See Figure 20.1.

The **shell**, composed of calcium carbonate, is the outermost covering of the egg. It prevents microbes from entering and moisture from escaping, and also protects the egg during handling and transport. The breed of the hen determines shell color; for chickens, it can range from bright white to brown. Shell color has no effect on quality, flavor or nutrition.

The **yolk** is the yellow portion of the egg. It constitutes just over one-third of the egg and contains three-fourths of the calories, most of the minerals and vitamins and all the fat. The yolk also contains lecithin, the compound responsible for emulsification in products such as hollandaise sauce and mayonnaise. Egg yolk solidifies (coagulates) at temperatures between 149°F and 158°F (65°C and 70°C). Although the color of a yolk may vary depending on the hen's feed, color does not affect quality or nutritional content.

AVERAGE WEIGHT OF LARGE EGG, SHELLED

Whole 1.6 ounces (50 grams)
White 1 ounce (30 grams)
Yolk 0.6 ounce (20 grams)

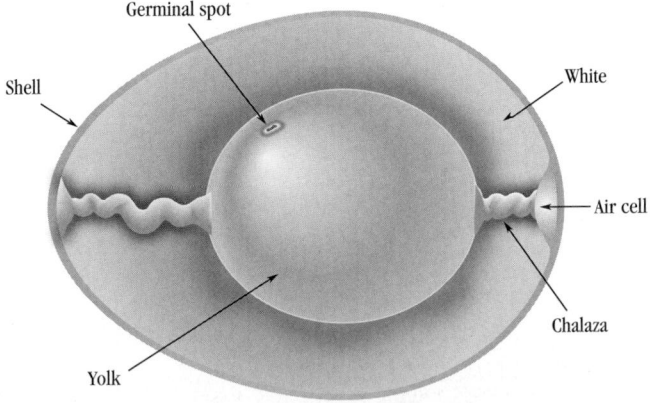

FIGURE 20.1 ▶ An egg.

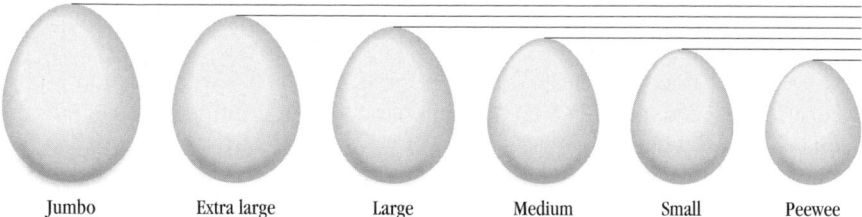

FIGURE 20.2 ▶ Egg sizes.

The **albumen** is the clear portion of the egg and is often referred to as the **egg white**. It constitutes about two-thirds of the egg and contains more than half of the protein and riboflavin. Egg white coagulates, becoming firm and opaque, at temperatures between 144°F and 149°F (62°C and 65°C).

An often-misunderstood portion of the egg is the **chalazae cords**. These thick, twisted strands of egg white anchor the yolk in place. They are neither imperfections nor embryos. The more prominent the chalazae, the fresher the egg. Chalazae do not interfere with cooking or with whipping egg whites.

Eggs are sold in Jumbo, Extra Large, Large, Medium, Small and Peewee sizes, as determined by weight per dozen. See Figure 20.2. Food service operations generally use Large eggs, which weigh 24 ounces per dozen. Other sizes are based on plus or minus 3 ounces per dozen; Medium eggs weigh 21 ounces per dozen whereas Extra Large eggs weigh 27 ounces per dozen.

Grading

Eggs are graded by the USDA or a state agency following USDA guidelines. The grade AA, A or B is given to an egg based on interior and exterior quality, not size. The qualities for each grade are described in Table 20.1. Grade has no effect on nutritional values.

Storage

Improper handling quickly diminishes egg quality. Eggs should be stored at temperatures below 45°F (7°C) and at a relative humidity of 70 to 80 percent. Eggs will age more during 1 day at room temperature than they will during 1 week under proper refrigeration. As eggs age, the white becomes thinner and the yolk becomes flatter. This changes the appearance of poached or fried eggs, making it important to use very fresh eggs for these

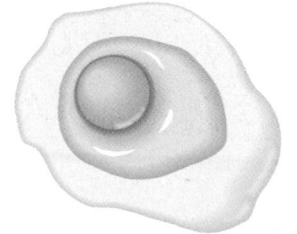

Grade AA

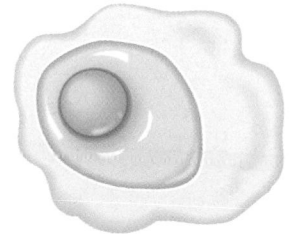

Grade A

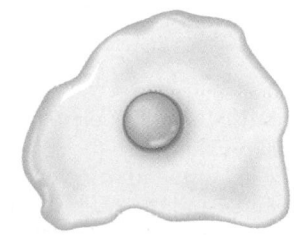

Grade B

TABLE 20.1 EGG GRADES

	GRADE AA	GRADE A	GRADE B
Spread*	Remains compact	Spreads slightly	Spreads over wide area
Albumen	Clear, thick and firm; prominent chalazae	Clear and reasonably firm; prominent chalazae	Clear; weak or watery
Yolk	Firm; centered; stands round and high; free from defects	Firm; stands fairly high; practically free from defects	Enlarged and flattened; may show slight defects
Shell	Clean; of normal shape; unbroken		Slight stains permissible; abnormal shape; unbroken
Use	Any use, especially frying, poaching and cooking in shell		Baking; scrambling, used in bulk egg products

*Spread refers to the appearance of the egg when first broken onto a flat surface.

pasteurization the process of heating something to a certain temperature for a specific period in order to destroy pathogenic bacteria

soufflé (soo-flay) either a sweet or savory fluffy dish made with a custard base lightened with whipped egg whites and then baked; the whipped egg whites cause the dish to puff when baked

cooking techniques. Older eggs, however, should be used for hard-cooking, as their shells will be easier to remove.

Cartons of fresh, uncooked eggs will keep for at least 4 to 5 weeks beyond the pack date if kept refrigerated at 36°F (2°C). Hard-cooked eggs left in their shells and refrigerated should be used within 1 week.

Store eggs away from strongly flavored foods to reduce odor absorption. Rotate egg stock to maintain freshness. Do not use dirty, cracked or broken eggs, as they may contain bacteria or other contaminants. Frozen eggs should be thawed in the refrigerator and used only in dishes that will be thoroughly cooked, such as baked products.

Sanitation

Eggs are a potentially hazardous food. Rich in protein, they are an excellent breeding ground for bacteria. Salmonella is of particular concern with eggs and egg products because the bacteria are commonly found in a chicken's intestinal tract. Although shells are cleaned at packinghouses, some bacteria may remain. Therefore, to prevent contamination, it is best to avoid mixing a shell with the liquid egg.

Inadequately cooking or improperly storing eggs may lead to food-borne illnesses. USDA guidelines indicate that **pasteurization** is achieved when the whole egg stays at a temperature of 140°F (60°C) for 3½ minutes. Hold egg dishes below 41°F (5°C) or above 135°F (57°C). Never leave an egg dish at room temperature for more than 1 hour, including preparation and service time. Never reuse a container after it has held raw eggs without thoroughly cleaning and sanitizing it. Pasteurized shell eggs are also available in some parts of the country. The convenience of using individual eggs without the risk of salmonella may outweigh the increased cost for some operations.

Egg Products

Food service operations often want the convenience of buying eggs out of the shell in the exact form needed: whole eggs, yolks only or whites only. These processed items are called *egg products* and are subject to strict pasteurization standards and USDA inspections. Egg products can be frozen, refrigerated or dried. Pasteurized egg products are also useful for environments where sanitation is a particular concern, such as schools or hospitals. Dried egg products are often used in baking but are not recommended for breakfast cookery. Concerns about the cholesterol content of eggs have increased the popularity of **egg substitutes**. There are two general types of substitutes. The first is a complete substitute made from soy or milk proteins. It should not be used in recipes in which eggs are required for thickening. The second substitute contains real albumen, but the egg yolk has been replaced with vegetable or milk products. Egg substitutes have a different flavor from real eggs, but may be useful for people on a restricted diet.

NUTRITION

Eggs contain vitamins A, D, E and K and the B-complex vitamins. They are rich in minerals and contain less cholesterol now than previously. Research indicates that the cholesterol in whole eggs does not impact serum cholesterol as much as was once feared. In fact, the American Heart Association now suggests that it is acceptable to consume up to four egg yolks per week as part of a balanced diet. Egg whites do not contain cholesterol and are often added to egg dishes such as omelets to reduce total fat content.

WHIPPED EGG WHITES

Egg whites are often whipped into a foam that is then incorporated into cakes, custards, **soufflés**, pancakes and other products. The air beaten into the egg foam gives products lightness and assists with leavening.

PROCEDURE FOR **WHIPPING EGG WHITES**

❶ Use fresh egg whites that are completely free of egg yolk and other impurities. Warm the egg whites to room temperature before whipping; this helps a better foam to form.

❷ Use a clean bowl and whisk. Even a tiny amount of fat can prevent the egg whites from foaming properly.

❸ Whip the whites until very foamy, then add salt or cream of tartar as directed.

❹ Continue whipping until soft peaks form, then gradually add granulated sugar as directed.

❺ Whip until stiff peaks form. Properly whipped egg whites should be moist and shiny; overwhipping will make the egg whites appear dry and spongy or curdled.

❻ Use the whipped egg whites immediately. If liquid begins to separate from the whipped egg whites, discard them; they cannot be rewhipped successfully.

❶ Egg whites whipped to soft peaks.

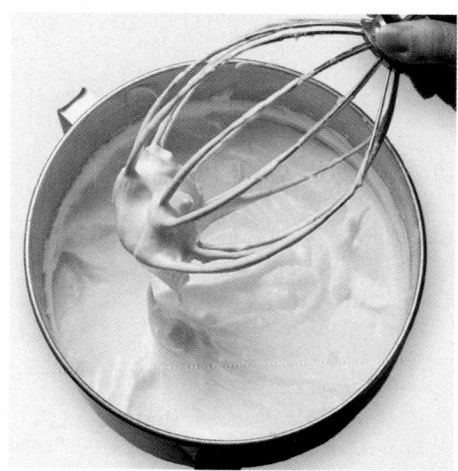

❷ Egg whites whipped to stiff peaks.

❸ Spongy, overwhipped egg whites.

APPLYING VARIOUS COOKING METHODS

No other food is as popular for breakfast, or as versatile, as the egg. Eggs can be cooked by almost any method and served with a wide array of seasonings, accompaniments and garnishes. Whatever cooking method is selected, be sure to prepare the eggs carefully: Overcooked eggs and those cooked at too high a temperature will be tough and rubbery. Undercooked eggs may transmit pathogenic bacteria and pose a risk of food-borne illness.

The following cooking methods are those most often used for egg-based dishes. They include dry-heat cooking methods (baking, sautéing and pan-frying) and moist-heat cooking methods (in-shell cooking and poaching).

DRY-HEAT COOKING METHODS

Baking

SHIRRED EGGS

Baked eggs, also referred to as shirred eggs, are normally prepared in individual ramekins or baking dishes. The ramekins can be lined or partially filled with ingredients such as bread, ham, creamed spinach or artichokes. The eggs are often topped with grated cheese, fresh herbs or a sauce. When properly cooked, the egg whites should be set while the yolks are soft and creamy.

PROCEDURE FOR **PREPARING SHIRRED EGGS**

❶ Coat each ramekin with melted butter. Add flavoring ingredients as desired.

❷ Break one or two eggs into each ramekin. Do not break the yolks. Season with salt and pepper.

❸ Bake the eggs until the white is firm, approximately 12 to 15 minutes. Approximately 3 to 5 minutes before the eggs are done, add cream or top the eggs with grated cheese, diced ham, fresh herbs or other ingredients as desired.

SHIRRED EGGS WITH HAM

MISE EN PLACE

▶ Melt butter.
▶ Slice ham.
▶ Heat cream.
▶ Grate cheese.

Yield: 1 Serving   **Method:** Baking

Whole butter, melted	as needed	as needed
Baked ham, sliced thin	½ oz.	15 g
Eggs	2	2
Salt and pepper	TT	TT
Heavy cream, hot	1 Tbsp.	15 ml
Swiss cheese, grated	1 Tbsp.	15 ml

❶ Brush the interior of a 6-fluid-ounce (180-milliliter) ramekin with melted butter. Line the ramekin with the ham.

❷ Break the eggs into a cup and pour them carefully into the ramekin on top of the ham. Season with salt and pepper.

❸ Bake at 325°F (160°C) until the eggs begin to set, approximately 8 to 10 minutes. Remove from the oven, then add the cream and cheese. Return to the oven until the eggs are cooked and the cheese is melted. Serve immediately.

Approximate values per serving: **Calories** 280, **Total fat** 22 g, **Saturated fat** 10 g, **Cholesterol** 470 mg, **Sodium** 300 mg, **Total carbohydrates** 2 g, **Protein** 17 g, **Vitamin A** 30%

❶ Adding the eggs to the ramekin on top of the ham.

❷ The finished shirred eggs with ham.

QUICHE

Quiche is a classic breakfast and brunch entrée. It consists of an egg custard (eggs, cream or milk and seasonings) and fillings baked in a crust.

The filling usually includes at least one type of cheese and can also include any number of other ingredients such as cooked, diced meats or blanched vegetables. The flavor and texture of these ingredients should complement one another without overpowering the delicate egg custard. Quiche is a good way of using leftovers, but the ingredients should still be fresh and of good quality. A recipe for quiche dough is given on page 985.

PROCEDURE FOR **PREPARING QUICHE**

❶ Prepare and bake a pie shell.

❷ Prepare the garnishes and flavoring ingredients and add them to the pie shell.

❸ Prepare a custard and add it to the pie shell. Ratios of eggs to milk or heavy cream vary depending on the specific recipe, but 6 to 8 eggs to 1 quart (1 liter) of liquid is usually sufficient to bind the custard.

❹ Bake the quiche until set and it reaches 160°F (71°C) on an instant-read thermometer; allow it to cool slightly before cutting.

QUICHE LORRAINE

Yield: 1 Quiche, 10 in. (25 cm) **Method:** Baking

Bacon, diced and cooked	4 oz.	120 g
Swiss or Gruyère cheese, shredded	2 oz.	60 g
Pie shell, 10-in. (25-cm) diameter, baked	1	1
Eggs	4	4
Milk	1 pt.	480 ml
Heavy cream	4 fl. oz.	120 ml
Salt and pepper	TT	TT
Nutmeg	TT	TT

❶ Place the bacon and cheese in the pie shell.

❷ To make the custard, combine the eggs, milk and cream, and season with salt, pepper and nutmeg.

❸ Pour the custard over the bacon and cheese and bake at 350°F (180°C) until the custard is set and it reaches an internal temperature of 160°F (71°C), approximately 1 hour.

Approximate values per ⅛-quiche serving: **Calories** 330, **Total fat** 25 g, **Saturated fat** 11 g, **Cholesterol** 105 mg, **Sodium** 420 mg, **Total carbohydrates** 14 g, **Protein** 12 g, **Vitamin A** 10%, **Calcium** 15%

MISE EN PLACE
◀ Dice, cook and drain the bacon.
◀ Shred cheese.
◀ Bake pie shell.

Sautéing

SCRAMBLED EGGS

Scrambled eggs are eggs whisked with seasonings and then sautéed. They are stirred nearly constantly during cooking. The finished eggs should be light and fluffy with a tender, creamy texture. A small amount of milk or cream may be added to the eggs to provide a more delicate finished product. Overcooking or cooking at too high a temperature causes the eggs to become tough and rubbery.

Scrambled eggs are often flavored by sautéing other foods (for example, onions, mushrooms or diced ham) in the pan before adding the eggs or by adding other foods (for example, grated cheeses or herbs) to the eggs just before cooking is complete.

Scrambled eggs can also be prepared using only egg whites. Because all of an egg's fat is stored in the yolk, no-yolk scrambled egg dishes are lower in fat, cholesterol and calories. Water or nonfat milk can be used in place of whole milk or cream to further reduce the fat and calorie content of the finished dish. Remember that egg whites coagulate at a lower temperature than yolks, so adjust the cooking time and temperature accordingly.

THE VERSATILE EGG

For versatility, the egg has few rivals. Poached eggs work in breakfast and brunch dishes but also complement tender green salads. When stuffed, hard-boiled eggs become simple hors d'oeuvre. Finely chopped and bound with mayonnaise, hard-boiled eggs fill sandwiches and canapés. Omelets, quiches and scrambled eggs benefit from countless additions, including finely diced bell peppers, onions, mushrooms, zucchini or tomatoes; cottage cheese, creamy goat cheese or any variety of shredded firm cheese; crumbled bacon or pancetta; diced ham, turkey or beef; bits of smoked salmon, cooked shrimp or cooked sausage; and fresh herbs.

PROCEDURE FOR **PREPARING SCRAMBLED EGGS**

1. Break the eggs into a mixing bowl. Season lightly with salt and pepper. Add 1 scant tablespoon (12 milliliters) milk or cream per egg and whisk everything together.
2. Heat a sauté pan, add clarified butter or oil and heat until the fat begins to sizzle.
3. Sauté any additional ingredients in the hot fat.
4. Pour the eggs into the pan all at once. As the eggs begin to set, slowly stir the mixture with a spatula. Lift cooked portions to allow uncooked egg to flow underneath.
5. Sprinkle on additional ingredients such as cheese or herbs.
6. Cook just until the eggs are set, but still shiny and moist. Remove from the pan and serve immediately.

SCRAMBLED EGGS

Yield: 6 Servings, 4 oz. (120 g) each   **Method:** Sautéing

Eggs	12	12
Heavy cream	2 fl. oz.	60 ml
Salt and pepper	TT	TT
Clarified butter	2 fl. oz.	60 ml

1. Combine the eggs, cream, salt and pepper in a mixing bowl. Whisk until well blended.
2. Heat the butter in a sauté pan.
3. Pour the egg mixture into the hot pan and cook, stirring frequently, until set, approximately 2 minutes. The eggs should be set, but still shiny and moist.

Approximate values per 4-oz. (120-g) serving: **Calories** 250, **Total fat** 21 g, **Saturated fat** 10 g, **Cholesterol** 460 mg, **Sodium** 210 mg, **Total carbohydrates** 1 g, **Protein** 13 g, **Vitamin A** 30%

1. Stirring the scrambled eggs.

2. The properly cooked eggs.

OMELETS

Omelets are needlessly intimidating egg creations that begin as scrambled eggs. They are usually prepared as individual servings using two or three eggs. The cooked eggs are either folded around or filled with a warm savory mixture.

The filling may contain vegetables, cheeses and/or meats. Any filling ingredient that needs cooking should be cooked before being added to the omelet. A shallow, well-seasoned or nonstick pan with gently sloping sides is used for cooking omelets. Should an omelet stick to the pan, run a spatula under the omelet to loosen it.

PROCEDURE FOR **PREPARING FOLDED OMELETS**

❶ Fully cook any meats and blanch or otherwise cook any vegetables that will be incorporated into the omelet.

❷ Heat an omelet pan over moderately high heat, then add clarified butter.

❸ Whisk the eggs together in a small bowl. Season with salt and pepper if desired.

❹ Pour the eggs into the pan and stir until they begin to set, approximately 10 seconds.

❺ Pull cooked egg from the sides of the pan toward the center, allowing raw egg to run underneath. Continue doing so for 20 to 30 seconds.

❻ Spoon any fillings on top of the eggs or add any other garnishes.

❼ When cooked as desired, flip one side of the omelet toward the center with a spatula or a shake of the pan. Slide the omelet onto the serving plate so that it lands folded in thirds with the seam underneath.

❽ Spoon any sauce or additional filling on top, garnish as desired, and serve immediately.

SHRIMP AND AVOCADO OMELET

Yield: 1 Serving   **Method:** Sautéing

Shrimp, peeled, deveined and cut into pieces	3 oz.	90 g
Green onion, sliced	1 Tbsp.	15 ml
Clarified butter	2 Tbsp.	30 ml
Eggs	3	3
Salt and pepper	TT	TT
Avocado, peeled and diced	¼	¼
Fresh cilantro, chopped	2 tsp.	10 ml

MISE EN PLACE
◄ Peel, devein and cut up shrimp.
◄ Wash, peel and slice green onions.
◄ Peel and dice avocado.
◄ Chop cilantro.

❶ Sauté the shrimp and onion in half of the butter until the shrimp is firm and the onion is translucent, approximately 2 minutes. Remove from the heat and set aside.

❷ Heat an omelet pan and add the remaining butter.

❸ Whisk the eggs together in a small bowl, season with salt and pepper and pour into the omelet pan.

❹ Stir the eggs as they cook. Stop when they begin to set. Lift the edges as the omelet cooks to allow the raw eggs to run underneath.

❺ When the eggs are nearly set, add the shrimp filling, avocado and cilantro. Fold the front of the eggs over and roll the omelet onto a plate.

Approximate values per serving: **Calories** 590, **Total fat** 47 g, **Saturated fat** 19 g, **Cholesterol** 865 mg, **Sodium** 620 mg, **Total carbohydrates** 4 g, **Protein** 39 g, **Vitamin A** 60%, **Vitamin C** 20%, **Iron** 30%

❶ Lifting the edge of the eggs to allow them to cook evenly.

❷ Adding the filling to the eggs.

❸ Folding the eggs.

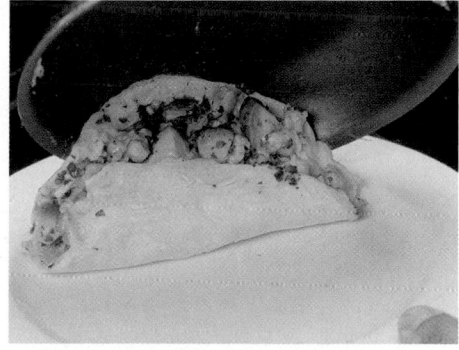

❹ Rolling the omelet onto the plate.

French-style omelets are similar, but the eggs are cooked while constantly shaking the pan to keep them light and fluffy. French omelets are tightly rolled onto a plate for service. For an elegant presentation, the filling may be added after cooking. A cut is made into the finished omelet and the filling is spooned in.

PROCEDURE FOR **PREPARING FRENCH-STYLE OMELETS**

1. Heat an omelet pan over moderately high heat and add clarified butter.
2. Whisk the eggs together in a small bowl. Season with salt and pepper if desired.
3. Pour the eggs into the pan. Stir the eggs while shaking the pan, pulling cooked eggs from the sides of the pan toward the center, allowing raw egg to run underneath. Continue doing so for 30 to 40 seconds.
4. When cooked as desired, flip one side of the omelet toward the center with a spatula or a shake of the pan. Roll the omelet onto the serving plate so that it lands with the seam underneath.

1. Shaking the pan while stirring the eggs.

2. Rolling the omelet onto the serving plate.

3. Using a paring knife to cut into the center of the omelet.

4. Spooning in the filling.

FRITTATAS

Frittatas are essentially open-faced omelets of Spanish-Italian heritage. They may be cooked in small pans as individual portions or in large pans, then cut into wedges for service. A relatively large amount of hearty ingredients is mixed directly into the eggs. The eggs are first cooked on the stove top, then the pan is transferred to an oven or placed under a salamander or broiler to finish cooking.

PROCEDURE FOR **PREPARING FRITTATAS**

❶ Fully cook any meats and blanch or otherwise prepare any vegetables that will be incorporated into the frittata.

❷ Heat a sauté pan and add clarified butter.

❸ Whisk the eggs, flavorings and any other ingredients together; pour into the pan.

❹ Stir gently until the eggs begin to set. Gently lift cooked egg at the edge of the frittata so that raw egg can run underneath. Continue cooking until the eggs are almost set.

❺ Place the pan in a hot oven or underneath a salamander or broiler to finish cooking and lightly brown the top.

❻ Slide the finished frittata out of the pan onto a serving platter.

GARDEN FRITTATA

Yield: 1 Serving   **Method:** Sautéing

Chicken breast meat, boneless, skinless	2 oz.	60 g
Garlic, chopped	1 tsp.	5 ml
Cumin, ground	TT	TT
Salt and pepper	TT	TT
Mushrooms, sliced	1 oz.	30 g
Unsalted butter	½ fl. oz.	15 g
Jalapeño, seeded, minced	1 tsp.	5 ml
Red bell pepper, roasted, peeled, seeded, julienned	1 oz.	30 g
Green onions, sliced	1 oz.	30 g
Fresh cilantro	2 tsp.	10 ml
Eggs, beaten	3	3
Monterey Jack or Cheddar cheese, shredded	1 oz.	30 g

MISE EN PLACE

◀ Skin and bone chicken.
◀ Peel and chop garlic.
◀ Wash and slice mushrooms and green onions.
◀ Seed and mince jalapeño.
◀ Roast, peel, seed and julienne red peppers.
◀ Beat eggs.
◀ Shred cheese.

❶ Rub the chicken breast with the garlic, cumin, salt and pepper. Grill or broil the chicken until done. Allow it to rest briefly, then cut it into strips.

❷ In a well-seasoned 9-inch (22-centimeter) sauté pan, sauté the mushrooms in the butter until tender. Add the jalapeño and sauté for 30 seconds. Add the chicken, bell pepper, green onions and cilantro and sauté until hot.

❸ Add the eggs and season with salt and pepper. Cook the mixture, stirring and lifting the eggs to help them cook evenly, until they begin to set.

❹ Sprinkle the cheese over the eggs and place under a salamander or broiler to melt the cheese and finish cooking the eggs. Slide the frittata onto a plate or cut into wedges for smaller portions.

Approximate values per serving: **Calories** 590, **Total fat** 39 g, **Saturated fat** 18 g, **Cholesterol** 755 mg, **Sodium** 400 mg, **Total carbohydrates** 8 g, **Protein** 51 g, **Vitamin A** 60%, **Vitamin C** 90%, **Calcium** 35%, **Iron** 20%, **Claims**—good source of fiber, vitamins A and C, calcium and iron

Pan-Frying

Pan-fried eggs are commonly referred to as **sunny side up** or **over easy**, **over medium** or **over hard**. These are visibly different products produced with proper timing and technique. Very fresh eggs are best for pan-frying, as the yolk holds its shape better and the white spreads less.

Sunny-side-up eggs are not turned during cooking; their yellow yolks remain visible. They should be cooked over medium-low heat long enough to firm the whites and partially firm the yolks: approximately 4 minutes if cooked on a 250°F (120°C) cooking surface.

For "over" eggs, the egg is partially cooked on one side, then gently flipped and cooked on the other side until done. The egg white should be firm, and its edges should not be brown. The yolk should never be broken regardless of the degree of doneness. Not only is a broken yolk unattractive, but the spilled yolk will coagulate on contact with the hot pan, making it difficult to serve.

For over-easy eggs, the yolk should remain very runny; on a 250°F (120°C) cooking surface, the egg should cook for about 3 minutes on the first side and 2 minutes on the other. Over-medium eggs should be cooked slightly longer, until the yolk is partially set. For over-hard eggs, the yolk should be completely cooked.

PROCEDURE FOR **PAN-FRYING EGGS**

1. Select a sauté pan just large enough to accommodate the number of eggs being cooked. (An 8-inch- [20-centimeter-] diameter pan is appropriate for up to three eggs.)
2. Add a small amount of clarified butter and heat until the fat just begins to sizzle.
3. Carefully break the eggs into the pan.
4. Continue cooking over medium-low heat until the eggs reach the appropriate degree of firmness. Sunny-side-up eggs are not flipped during cooking; "over" eggs are flipped once during cooking.
5. When done, gently flip the "over" eggs once again so that the first side is up, then gently slide the cooked eggs out of the pan onto the serving plate. Serve immediately.

1. Pouring the eggs into the sauté pan.

2. Flipping the eggs.

3. Sliding the eggs onto a plate for service.

Basted eggs are a variation of sunny-side-up eggs. Basted eggs are cooked over low heat with the hot butter from the pan spooned over them as they cook. Another version of basted eggs is made by adding 1 to 2 teaspoons (5 to 10 milliliters) water to the sauté pan and then covering the pan. The steam cooks the top of the eggs.

MOIST-HEAT COOKING METHODS

In-Shell Cooking (Simmering)

The difference between **soft-cooked eggs** (also called **soft-boiled**) and **hard-cooked eggs** (also called **hard-boiled**) is time. Both styles refer to eggs cooked in their shell in hot water. Despite the word *boiled* in their names, eggs cooked in the shell should never be boiled. Boiling toughens eggs and causes a green discoloration, which is from sulfur in the whites reacting with iron in the yolks. (See Figure 20.3.)

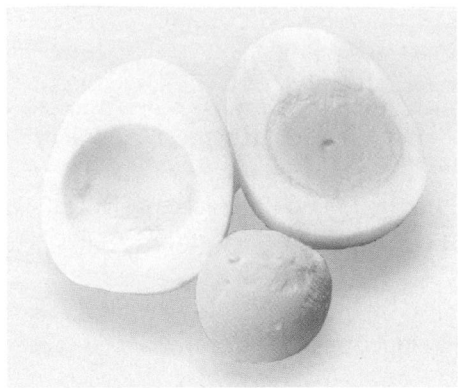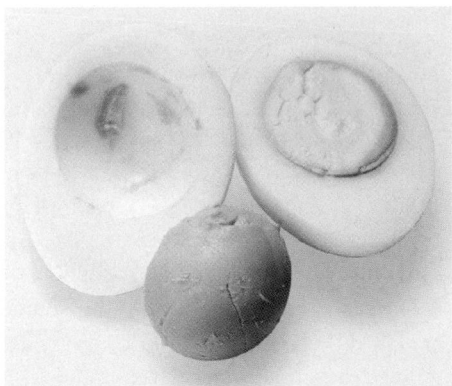

FIGURE 20.3 ▶ Properly hard-boiled eggs (left) are uniformly cooked through and gold colored. A green discoloration covers the yolk when in-shell eggs are overcooked (right).

Instead, the eggs should be simmered. Soft-cooked eggs are usually simmered for 4 to 6 minutes; hard-cooked eggs may be simmered for as long as 12 to 15 minutes. In either case, running the eggs under water immediately after simmering helps stop carryover cooking.

Sometimes it is difficult to remove the shell from very fresh eggs. Eggs that are a few days old are better for cooking in the shell.

PROCEDURE FOR **PREPARING SOFT-COOKED EGGS**

1. Fill a saucepan or stockpot with sufficient water to cover the eggs. Bring the water to a simmer.
2. Gently stir the water in a circular motion. Carefully lower each egg into the simmering water. Simmer uncovered for 3 to 5 minutes, depending on the firmness desired.
3. Lift each egg out of the water with a slotted spoon or spider. Crack the large end of the shell carefully and serve immediately.

PROCEDURE FOR **PREPARING HARD-COOKED EGGS**

1. Repeat Steps 1 and 2 for soft-cooked eggs, simmering the eggs for 12 to 15 minutes.
2. Lift each egg out of the water with a slotted spoon or spider and place in an ice bath. When the eggs are cool enough to handle, peel them and use as desired or cover and refrigerate for up to 5 days.

Poaching

Eggs that are to be poached should always be very fresh. They should also be kept very cold until used, as cold egg whites stay together better when dropped into hot water. The water for poaching eggs is held at approximately 200°F (90°C), a gentle simmer. Poached eggs should be soft and moist; the whites should be firm enough to encase the yolk completely, but the yolk should still be runny.

Some chefs add salt to the poaching water for flavor; others believe that the salt causes the egg whites to separate. To help the egg whites cling together, add 2 tablespoons (30 milliliters) white vinegar per quart (liter) of water.

PROCEDURE FOR **POACHING EGGS**

❶ Fill a saucepan or stockpot with at least 3 inches (7.5 centimeters) water. Add salt and vinegar if desired. Bring the water to a simmer and hold at a temperature of approximately 200°F (90°C).

❷ One at a time, crack the eggs into a small ramekin or cup. If a piece of shell falls into the egg, it should be removed; if the yolk breaks, the egg can be set aside for some other use.

❸ Gently slide each egg into the simmering water and cook for 3 to 5 minutes.

❹ Lift the poached egg out of the water with a slotted spoon. Trim any ragged edges with a paring knife. Serve immediately.

For quantity service, eggs can be poached in advance and held for up to 1 day. To do so, cook the eggs as described. As each egg is removed from the hot water, set it in a hotel pan filled with ice water to stop the cooking process. The eggs can then be stored in the ice water until needed. For banquet-style service, all the eggs can be reheated at once by placing the entire pan on the stove top. Or the eggs can be reheated one or two at a time by placing them in a pan of barely simmering water until they are hot.

❶ Adding an egg to a pot of simmering water.

❷ Lowering the eggs into ice water to cool them for future use.

POACHED EGGS

Yield: 1 Serving   **Method:** Poaching

Water	as needed	as needed
Salt	1 tsp.	5 ml
Vinegar	1 fl. oz.	30 ml
Eggs	2	2

❶ Bring the water to a simmer; add the salt and vinegar.

❷ Crack one egg into a cup and carefully add it to the water. Repeat with the other egg.

❸ Cook the eggs to the desired doneness, approximately 3 to 5 minutes. Remove them from the water with a slotted spoon and serve as desired or carefully lower them into ice water and refrigerate for later use.

Approximate values per 3½-oz. (105-g) serving: **Calories** 140, **Total fat** 10 g, **Saturated fat** 3 g, **Cholesterol** 425 mg, **Sodium** 280 mg, **Total carbohydrates** 1 g, **Protein** 12 g, **Vitamin A** 20%

BREAKFAST AND BRUNCH

Breakfast is often an on-the-go, rushed experience; hence the popularity of breakfast sandwiches, jumbo muffins and disposable coffee cups. Brunch, on the other hand, is a leisurely experience, combining breakfast and lunch into a social occasion. Brunch menus include traditional breakfast foods along with almost anything else. Unlike breakfast, brunch is often accompanied by champagne or other alcoholic beverages and concludes with a pastry or dessert.

Food service operations must offer a variety of breakfast options to appeal to a wide range of consumers. Hotels and resorts may offer a complimentary **continental-style breakfast** of coffee, juice and sweet rolls; a full-service à la carte dining room; a room service menu and a casual snack bar. The grand hotel Sunday and holiday brunch buffet is an American institution for celebrations and special occasions.

The foods served at breakfast include most of the foods served at other times during the day. A diner's perceptions of a proper breakfast depends on his or her cultural, ethnic, economic and geographic background as well as sleep patterns and work schedule.

Breakfast menus typically include the following items:

- ▶ Coffee, tea or other hot beverages
- ▶ Fruits or fruit juices
- ▶ Eggs
- ▶ Breads, including sweet breads
- ▶ Cereals and grains
- ▶ Potatoes
- ▶ Pancakes, waffles and French toast
- ▶ Meats or fish
- ▶ Dairy products, including milk, cheese and yogurt

Although few people could sit down to a breakfast including all of these components even occasionally, most food service operations find it necessary to offer some items from each category in order to meet their customers' expectations.

Breakfast Meats

At other meals, meat is typically the principal food, but at breakfast it is usually an accompaniment. Breakfast meats tend to be spicy or highly flavored. A hearty breakfast menu may include a small beef steak (usually sirloin and often pan-fried) or pork chop. Corned beef, roast beef or roast turkey can be diced or shredded, then sautéed with potatoes and other ingredients for a breakfast hash. Fish, particularly smoked products, are also served at breakfast.

But the most popular breakfast meats are bacon (including Canadian-style bacon), ham and sausages. They are all discussed in Chapter 27, Charcuterie. **Bacon** can be cooked on a flat griddle or in a heavy skillet or baked on a sheet pan. Regardless of the method used, the cooked bacon should be drained on absorbent paper towels to remove excess fat. **Canadian-style bacon** is very lean and requires little cooking, although slices are usually sautéed briefly before serving. The round slices may be served like ham and are essential for eggs Benedict. A **ham steak** is simply a thick slice ideal for breakfast. Fully cooked ham needs to be heated only briefly on a griddle or in a sauté pan before service. The most popular **breakfast sausages** are made from uncured, uncooked meats. They can be mild to spicy, slightly sweet or strongly seasoned with sage. Recipes for country-style and other sausages are at the end of Chapter 27, Charcuterie. Breakfast sausage is available in bulk, links or preformed patties. Link sausage is often partially cooked by steam, then browned by sautéing at service time. It should be drained on absorbent paper towels to remove excess fat before service.

Griddlecakes

Pancakes and waffles are types of griddlecakes or griddle breads. They are usually leavened with baking soda or baking powder and are quickly cooked on a very hot griddle or waffle iron with very little fat. Griddlecakes should be more than just an excuse for eating butter and maple syrup, however. They should have a rich flavor and a light, tender, moist interior.

Pancake and waffle batters may be flavored with tangy buckwheat flour, fruits, whole grains or nuts. Both pancakes and waffles are usually served with plain or flavored butter and fruit compote or syrup. Waffles must be cooked in a special waffle iron, which gives the cakes a distinctive gridlike pattern and a crisp texture. Electric waffle irons are available with square, round and even heart-shaped grids. The grids should be seasoned well, then never washed. (Follow the manufacturer's directions for seasoning.) Belgian waffles are especially light and crisp because of the incorporation of whipped egg whites and/or yeast. They are often made in a waffle iron with extra deep grids and are served for breakfast or as a dessert, topped with fresh fruit, whipped cream or ice cream.

BREAKFAST AROUND THE WORLD

In the 21st century North Americans traveling abroad will more than likely be able to order a breakfast similar to that which they would eat at home. However, in many countries residents still consume their traditional breakfast foods.

- Japan: tea; *asa-gohan*, morning rice, with side dishes of pickles, dried seaweed, tofu, fish; miso soup
- China: tea; *congee*, rice porridge, topped with meat, seafood and/or vegetables; *you tiao*, a type of fried cruller that is dipped in soy milk
- France: *café au lait*; baguette, butter and jam
- Southern Italy/Sicily: coffee *granita* served in brioche bread
- Australia: tea; steak and eggs; toast
- Egypt: *ful medames*, slow-cooked beans seasoned with olive oil, lemon and garlic
- India: tea; *khichiri*, a Hindi dish of rice, lentils and spices; *appam*, a thin rice pancake with spiced meat and vegetables; *vada pavs*, deep-fried mashed potatoes wrapped in flatbread and seasoned with chutney or chilli powder
- Costa Rica: coffee or *aqua dulce*, warm water flavored with concentrated sugarcane juice; *gallo pinto*, rice and beans with cilantro and onions
- Spain: milk, coffee, rolls and jam; *chocolate y churros*, hot chocolate with a cinnamon-sugar coated donut
- Greece: Greek coffee or instant coffee with milk; sesame bread; yogurt with honey and/or fruit
- Eastern Europe/Germany/Holland: coffee or tea; cold cuts; a variety of cheeses and breads
- Argentina: coffee or hot chocolate; *facturas*, sweet pastries with *dulce de leche*, a paste made with milk and sugar

PROCEDURE FOR **MAKING PANCAKES**

① Prepare the batter.

② Heat a flat griddle or large sauté pan over moderately high heat. Add clarified butter.

③ Portion the pancake batter onto the hot griddle using a portion scoop, ladle or adjustable batter dispenser. Pour the portioned batter in one spot; it should spread into an even circle. Drop the batter so that no two pancakes will touch after the batter spreads.

④ Cook until bubbles appear on the surface, and the bottom of the cake is set and golden brown. Flip the pancake using an offset spatula.

⑤ Cook the pancake until the second side is golden brown. Avoid flipping the pancake more than once, as this causes it to deflate.

MISE EN PLACE

▶ Melt butter.
▶ Beat eggs.

BUTTERMILK PANCAKES

Yield: 24 Pancakes

Flour	1 lb.	480 g
Granulated sugar	2 Tbsp.	30 ml
Baking powder	1 Tbsp.	15 ml
Salt	1½ tsp.	7 ml
Buttermilk	1½ pt.	720 ml
Unsalted butter, melted	2 oz.	60 g
Eggs, beaten	3	3
Clarified butter	as needed	as needed

① Sift the flour, sugar, baking powder and salt together.

② Combine the buttermilk, melted butter and eggs and add them to the dry ingredients. Mix just until the ingredients are combined.

③ If the griddle is not well seasoned, coat it lightly with clarified butter. Once its temperature reaches 375°F (190°C), drop the batter onto it in 2-fluid-ounce (60-milliliter) portions using a ladle, portion scoop or batter portioner.

④ When bubbles appear on the pancake's surface and the bottom is browned, flip the pancake to finish cooking.

VARIATIONS:

Blueberry Pancakes—Gently stir 1 pint (480 milliliters) fresh or frozen blueberries into the batter. If using frozen berries, drain them thoroughly, then pat dry with paper towels before adding them to the batter. Serve with blueberry syrup or compote.

Apple-Pecan Pancakes—Gently fold 4 ounces (120 grams) chopped cooked apples, ¼ teaspoon (2 milliliters) cinnamon and 1 ounce (30 grams) finely chopped pecans into the batter.

Approximate values per pancake: **Calories** 120, **Total fat** 4 g, **Saturated fat** 2.5 g, **Cholesterol** 35 mg, **Sodium** 250 mg, **Total carbohydrates** 17 g, **Protein** 4 g

Crêpes

Crêpes are thin, delicate, unleavened pancakes. They are made with a very liquid egg batter cooked in a small, very hot sauté pan or crêpe pan. Crêpe batter can be flavored with buckwheat flour, cornmeal or other grains. Crêpes are not eaten plain, but are usually filled and garnished with sautéed fruits, scrambled eggs, cheese or vegetables. Crêpes can be prepared in advance, then filled and reheated in the oven.

Blintzes are crêpes that are cooked on only one side, then filled with cheese, browned in butter and served with sour cream, fruit compote or preserves. A recipe for cheese blintzes is provided at the end of this chapter.

PROCEDURE FOR **PREPARING CRÊPES**

❶ Prepare the batter at least 1 hour before using and keep refrigerated.

❷ Heat a well-seasoned crêpe pan or small sauté pan over moderately high heat. Add a small amount of clarified butter.

❸ Ladle a small amount of batter into the pan. Tilt the pan so that the batter spreads and coats the bottom evenly.

❹ Cook until the crêpe is set and the bottom begins to brown, approximately 1 minute. Flip the crêpe over with a quick flick of the wrist or by lifting it carefully with a spatula.

❺ Cook the crêpe for an additional 30 seconds. Slide the finished crêpe from the pan. Crêpes can be stacked between layers of parchment paper for storage.

CRÊPES

Yield: 30 Crêpes, 6 in. (15 cm) each

Whole eggs	6	6
Egg yolks	6	6
Water	12 fl. oz.	360 ml
Milk	18 fl. oz.	540 ml
Granulated sugar	6 oz.	180 g
Salt	1 tsp.	5 ml
Flour	14 oz.	420 g
Unsalted butter, melted	5 oz.	150 g
Clarified butter	as needed	as needed

❶ Whisk together the eggs, egg yolks, water and milk. Add the sugar, salt and flour; whisk together. Stir in the melted butter. Cover and set aside to rest for at least 1 hour before cooking.

❷ Heat a small sauté or crêpe pan; brush lightly with clarified butter. Pour in 1 to 1½ fluid ounces (30 to 45 milliliters) of batter; swirl to coat the bottom of the pan evenly.

❸ Cook the crêpe until set and light brown, approximately 30 seconds. Flip it over and cook a few seconds longer. Remove from the pan. Repeat this process until all the batter is used.

❹ Cooked crêpes may be used immediately or covered and held briefly in a warm oven. Crêpes can also be wrapped well in plastic wrap and refrigerated for 2 to 3 days or frozen for several weeks.

VARIATIONS:

Savory Crêpes—Reduce the sugar to 1 tablespoon (15 milliliters). Substitute up to 5 ounces (150 grams) buckwheat flour or whole-wheat flour for an equal amount of the all-purpose flour if desired.

Savory Crêpes Florentine—Fill Savory Crêpes with creamed spinach topped with Mornay sauce.

Approximate values per 2-oz. (60-g) crêpe: **Calories** 140, **Total fat** 7 g, **Saturated fat** 3.5 g, **Cholesterol** 95 mg, **Sodium** 100 mg, **Total carbohydrates** 17 g, **Protein** 4 g

Cereals and Grains

Oats, rice, corn and wheat are perhaps the most widely eaten breakfast foods. Processed breakfast cereals are ready-to-eat products made from these grains. Most consumers now think of breakfast cereal as a cold food, but not so long ago only hot grains were breakfast staples. Oatmeal served as a **hot porridge** is still popular, especially with toppings such as cream, brown sugar, fresh or dried fruit or fruit preserves. Grits, made from ground corn, are another grain product served hot at breakfast. **Grits** may be topped with butter and presented as a starch side dish or served in a bowl as a porridge with cream and brown sugar. Oats and oatmeal, grits and other grains are discussed in Chapter 22, Potatoes, Grains and Pasta.

MISE EN PLACE
◀ Prepare batter at least 1 hour before needed.
◀ Melt butter.

❶ Coating the bottom of the pan evenly with the batter.

❷ Flipping the crêpe. Notice the proper light brown color.

muesli (MYOOS-lee) a breakfast cereal made from raw or toasted cereal grains, dried fruits, nuts and dried milk solids and usually eaten with milk or yogurt; sometimes known as granola

Ready-to-eat (cold) cereal is usually topped with milk or light cream and sugar. Creative cooks can avoid overly sweet, artificially flavored commercial products by making their own ready-to-eat breakfast cereals such as **muesli** or granola, a toasted blend of whole grains, nuts and dried fruits. The results are less expensive, more nutritious and far more interesting.

Tossing granola

Granola topping berries and yogurt

CRUNCHY GRANOLA

Yield: 3 qt. (3 lt)

Brown sugar	8 oz.	240 g
Water, hot	4 fl. oz.	120 ml
Canola oil	6 fl. oz.	180 ml
Old-fashioned oats	18 oz.	540 g
Wheat germ	4 oz.	120 g
Coconut, shredded	2½ oz.	75 g
Salt (optional)	1 Tbsp.	15 ml
Whole-wheat flour	2 oz.	60 g
Amaranth flour	2 oz.	60 g
Unbleached all-purpose flour	2 oz.	60 g
Yellow cornmeal	2 oz.	60 g
Pecans, chopped	4 oz.	120 g

1. Dissolve the brown sugar in the hot water. Add the oil.
2. Combine the dry ingredients in a large bowl. Mix thoroughly by hand.
3. Add the brown-sugar-and-oil mixture to the dry ingredients; toss to combine.
4. Spread out the granola in a thin layer on a sheet pan. Bake at 200°F (90°C) until crisp, approximately 1½ to 2 hours. Toss lightly with a metal spatula every 30 minutes.
5. Cool completely at room temperature, then store in an airtight container. Chopped dried fruits, additional nuts or fresh fruits can be added at service time. Serve plain or as a topping on fresh berries and yogurt.

Approximate values per 1-oz. (30-g) serving: **Calories** 140, **Total fat** 7 g, **Saturated fat** 1 g, **Cholesterol** 0 mg, **Sodium** 5 mg, **Total carbohydrates** 17 g, **Protein** 3 g

FROM HEALTH FOOD TO SUGAR SNACK

The century-old, multibillion-dollar-a-year American breakfast cereal industry, unlike any other in the world, is rooted in health foods. During the 1890s, Dr. John Harvey Kellogg directed a sanitarium in Battle Creek, Michigan. Among the healthful foods prescribed for his patients was his special mixture of whole grains called "granula." John, along with his brother Will, next created and began marketing wheat flakes as a nutritious breakfast food. They were not an immediate success, however; people found a cold breakfast unappealing. Undeterred, Will continued toying with cold cereals, eventually creating flakes made from toasted corn and malt. Thanks to a massive advertising campaign, the American public finally embraced corn flakes and a financial empire was born.

Charles W. Post was a patient of Dr. Kellogg's Battle Creek Sanitarium in 1891. He adopted the principles of healthful eating espoused by the Kellogg brothers and soon opened his own spa, complete with a factory producing his "Post Toasties" and "Grape-Nuts." He promoted them as a cure for appendicitis, consumption and malaria.

Soon Battle Creek became a boomtown, home to more than 40 breakfast cereal companies. Unfortunately for the consumer, not all manufacturers—then and now—were as concerned about health as John, Will and C. W. The addition of sugar, sometimes totaling more than half the cereal's weight, makes some of today's breakfast products more sugary than candy bars. Even some of the granola cereals touted as healthier alternatives to other breakfast cereals and snacks contain 20 percent sugar or more. But at least they no longer claim to cure malaria.

BEVERAGES

Coffee and tea are the staples of most beverage menus. Despite their relatively low price, a good cup of coffee or tea can be extremely important to a customer's impression of a food service operation. A cup of coffee is often either the very first or the very last item consumed by a customer. Tea, whether iced or hot, is often consumed throughout the meal. Consequently, it is important to learn to prepare and serve these beverages properly.

Coffee

Coffee (Fr. *café*) begins as the fruit of a small tree grown in tropical and subtropical regions throughout the world. The fruit, referred to as a cherry, is bright red with translucent flesh surrounding two flat-sided seeds. These seeds are the coffee beans. When ripe, the cherries are harvested by hand, then cleaned, fermented and hulled, leaving the green coffee beans. The beans are then roasted, blended, ground and brewed. Note that any coffee bean can be roasted to any degree of darkness, ground to any degree of fineness and brewed by any number of methods.

Only two species of coffee bean are routinely used: **arabica** and **robusta**. Arabica beans are the most important commercially and the ones from which the finest coffees are produced. Robusta beans do not produce as flavorful a drink as arabica. Nevertheless, robusta beans are becoming increasingly significant commercially, in part because robusta trees are heartier and more fertile than arabica trees. The conditions in which the beans are grown have almost as much effect on the final product as subsequent roasting, grinding and brewing. Because coffee takes much of its flavor and character from the soil, sunlight and air, the beans' origin is critical to the product's final quality. Each valley and mountain produces coffee distinct from all others, so geographic names are used to identify the beans whether they are from arabica or robusta trees. Thus, purveyors may offer beans known as Colombian, Chanchamayo (from Peru), Kilimanjaro (from Tanzania), Blue Mountain (from Jamaica), Java and Sumatra (from Indonesia) or Kona (from Hawaii), to name a few.

ROASTING COFFEE

Roasting releases and enhances the flavors in coffee. It also darkens the beans and brings natural oils to the surface. In general, roasts fall into four categories based on their color—light, medium, medium-dark or dark. The following descriptions are based on the most common terminology:

▶ **City roast**—Also called American or brown roast, city roast is the most widely used coffee style in the United States. City roast, which is medium brown in color, produces a beverage that may lack brilliance or be a bit flat, yet it is the roast most Americans prefer because it is the roast most often used in mass-market blends.

▶ **Brazilian**—Somewhat darker than a city roast, Brazilian roast should begin to show a hint of dark-roast flavor. The beans should show a trace of oil. In this context, the word *Brazilian* has no relationship to coffee grown in Brazil.

▶ **Viennese**—Also called medium-dark roast, Viennese roast generally falls somewhere between a standard city roast and French roast.

▶ **French roast**—French roast, also called New Orleans or dark roast, approaches espresso in flavor without sacrificing smoothness. The beans should be the color of semisweet chocolate, with apparent oiliness on the surface.

▶ **Espresso roast**—Espresso roast, also called Italian roast, is the darkest of all. The beans are roasted until they are virtually burnt. The beans should be black with a shiny, oily surface.

GRINDING COFFEE

Unlike roasting, which is best left to the experts, the grinding of coffee beans is best left to the consumer or food service operation. Whole coffee beans stay fresh longer than ground coffee. Ground coffee kept in an airtight container away from heat and light will stay fresh for 3 or 4 days. Whole beans will stay fresh for a few weeks and may be kept

Green Unroasted Coffee Beans

City-Roast Beans

French-Roast Beans

frozen for several months, as long as they are dry and protected from other flavors. Frozen coffee beans do not need to be thawed before grinding and brewing.

The fineness of the grind depends entirely on the type of coffee maker being used. The grind determines the length of time it takes to achieve optimum (19 percent) extraction from the beans. The proper grind is simply whatever grind allows this to happen in the time it takes a specific coffee maker to complete its brewing cycle. As a general rule, the finer the grind, the more quickly the coffee should be prepared. Follow the directions for your coffee maker or ask your specialty coffee purveyor for guidance.

BREWING COFFEE

Coffee is brewed by one of two methods: decoction or infusion. **Decoction** means boiling a substance until its flavor is removed. Boiling is the oldest method of making coffee, but is no longer used except in preparing extremely strong Turkish coffee. **Infusion** refers to the extraction of flavors at temperatures below boiling. Infusion techniques include steeping (mixing hot water with ground coffee), filtering (slowly pouring hot water over ground coffee held in a disposable cloth or paper filter) and dripping (pouring hot water over ground coffee and allowing the liquid to run through a strainer). Percolating is undesirable, as the continuous boiling ruins the coffee's flavor.

The secrets to brewing a good cup of coffee are knowing the exact proportion of coffee to water as well as the length of time to maintain contact between the two. This varies depending on the type of coffee brewing equipment being used.

Drip Brewing

Drip coffee is most commonly made from a machine that operates on the principle of gravity. Water is placed in a reservoir, heated and released slowly over the coffee grounds, which are contained in a filter.

For drip coffee, the best results are nearly always achieved by using 2 level tablespoons of ground coffee per ¾ cup (6 fluid ounces) water. (A standard cup of coffee is three-fourths the size of a standard measuring cup; 1 pound of coffee yields approximately 80 level tablespoons or enough for 40 "cups" of coffee.) Premeasured packages of ground coffee are generally used with commercial brewing equipment. These packages are available in a range of sizes for making single pots or large urns of coffee. If stronger coffee is desired, use more coffee per cup of water, not a longer brewing time. For weaker coffee, prepare regular-strength coffee and dilute it with hot water. Never reuse coffee grounds.

Espresso Brewing

Espresso is made with a pump-driven machine that forces hot water through compressed, finely ground coffee. An espresso machine also has a steaming rod to froth milk for espresso-based beverages.

Finely ground coffee to be used in espresso coffee machines is sold in bulk or in premeasured packets, or pods, that enable a consistent level of quality. A single serving of espresso uses about ¼ ounce (7 grams) coffee to 1½ fluid ounces (45 milliliters) water.

Drip Coffee Maker

Espresso Machine

Americans tend to prefer a larger portion, known as *espresso lungo*, made with 2 to 3 fluid ounces (60 to 90 milliliters) water. It is important that the espresso be made quickly: If the machine pumps water through the coffee for too long, too much water will be added to the cup and the intense espresso flavor will be ruined.

Conditions That Affect the Quality of Brewed Coffee

Most coffees are affected by the quality of the water used to brew them. Many commercial establishments have their machines tied into their water supply, so water quality may be beyond the maker's control. Unless equipment is properly cleaned, oils from coffee form an invisible film on the inside of the maker and pots, imparting a rancid or stale flavor to each subsequent batch. Coffeepots and carafes should be cleaned well with hot water between each use; coffee makers should be disassembled and cleaned according to the manufacturer's directions. Calcification on heating elements can also reduce their effectiveness.

Finally, all coffee should be served as soon as it is brewed. Oxidation takes a toll on the aroma and flavor, which soon becomes flat and eventually bitter. Drip coffee may be held for a short time on the coffee maker's hot plate at temperatures of 185°F to 190°F (85°C to 88°C). A better holding method, however, is to use a thermal carafe or air pot. Never attempt to reheat cold coffee, as drastic temperature shifts destroy flavor.

TASTING COFFEE

Coffee can be judged on four characteristics: aroma, acidity, body and flavor. As a general rule, coffee will taste the way it smells. Some coffees, particularly Colombian, are more fragrant than others, however.

Acidity, also called *wininess*, refers to the tartness of the coffee. Acidity is a desirable characteristic that indicates snap, life or thinness. Kenyan and Guatemalan are examples of particularly acidic coffees.

Body refers to the feeling of heaviness or thickness that coffee provides on the palate. Sumatran is generally the heaviest, with Mexican and Venezuelan being the lightest.

Flavor, of course, is the most ambiguous as well as the most important characteristic. Terms such as *mellow*, *harsh*, *grassy* and *earthy* are used to describe the rather subjective characteristics of flavor.

cupping testing coffee or tea for taste and quality, often performed by a professional taster trained to identify key coffee or tea characteristics

SERVING COFFEE

Coffee beverages can be made with specific additions and provide value-added menu alternatives. The most common ways of serving coffee are described here.

Drip Coffee or Filtered Coffee

Drip or filter coffee is the most common style of coffee served in the United States. It is served unadorned, unsweetened and black (without milk or cream). The customer then adds the desired amount of sweetener and/or milk.

▶ **Café au lait**—The French version of the Italian *caffè latte*, *café au lait* (or *café crème*) is made with strong coffee instead of espresso and hot, not steamed, milk. It is traditionally served in a handleless bowl.

▶ **Demitasse**—A small cup of strong black coffee or espresso; also refers to the small cup in which it is served.

▶ **Iced coffee**—Strong coffee served over ice. If desired, it is best to add sweetener before the coffee is poured over ice or shaken. Iced coffee can also be served with milk or cream. In Australia, a dollop of vanilla ice cream is often added. In Vietnam it is made with a small Vietnamese filter pot using condensed milk as a sweetener. Under no circumstances should leftover coffee be used to make iced coffee.

Espresso

Espresso refers to a unique brewing method in which hot water is forced through finely ground and packed coffee under high pressure. Properly made espresso is strong, rich and smooth, not bitter or acidic. As the coffee drains into the cup it will be golden brown, forming a *crema* or foam that lies on top of the black coffee underneath. It is important that the small espresso cups be prewarmed.

Espresso

steamed milk milk that is heated with steam generated by an espresso machine; it should be approximately 150°F to 170°F (66°C to 77°C)

foamed milk milk that is heated and frothed with air and steam generated by an espresso machine; it will be slightly cooler than steamed milk

barista Italian for "bartender"; now used to describe someone who has been professionally trained in the art of preparing espresso and espresso-based beverages

Cappuccino

Caffé Latte

TYPES OF ESPRESSO COFFEE

▶ **Espresso**—A single or double shot served black in a demitasse cup.

▶ **Espresso machiatto**—Espresso "marked" with a tiny portion of **steamed milk**.

▶ **Cappuccino**—One-third espresso, one-third steamed milk and one-third **foamed milk**; the total serving is still rather small, about 4 to 6 ounces (120 to 180 milliliters).

▶ **Caffè latte**—One-third espresso and two-thirds steamed milk without foam; usually served in a tall glass.

▶ **Caffè mocha**—One-third espresso and two-thirds steamed milk, flavored with chocolate syrup; usually topped with whipped cream and chocolate shavings or cocoa.

▶ **Espresso con panna**—Espresso with a dollop of whipped cream.

▶ **Breve**—Espresso with steamed half-and-half.

Any type of milk can be used to make cappuccino and other espresso beverages. Customer preference determines whether whole, skim or even soy milk is used. A higher fat content will, of course, produce a creamier tasting beverage, but will be more difficult to froth with steam. To froth milk, pour it into a metal pitcher, then position it under the steam spout of the espresso machine. Activate the steam control only when the head of the spout is under the surface of the milk. Moving the pitcher around while keeping the spout just under the surface of the milk creates foam.

FLAVORED COFFEES

Dried, ground chicory root has long been added to coffee, particularly by the French, who enjoy its bitter flavor. Toasted barley, dried figs and spices have also been used by various cultures for years. Coffees flavored with vanilla, chocolate, liquors, spices and nuts are now widely popular. These flavors are added to roasted coffee beans by tumbling the beans with special flavoring oils. The results are strongly aromatic flavors such as vanilla hazelnut, chocolate raspberry or maple walnut.

DECAFFEINATED COFFEE

Caffeine is an alkaloid found in coffee beans (as well as in tea leaves and cocoa beans). It is a stimulant that can improve alertness or reduce fatigue. In excess, however, caffeine can cause some people to suffer palpitations or insomnia. Regular filtered coffee contains 85 to 100 milligrams of caffeine per cup. Robusta beans contain more caffeine than the better-quality arabica beans. Decaffeinated coffee (with 97 percent or more of the caffeine removed) is designed to meet consumer desires for a caffeine-free product.

A CUP OF COFFEE HISTORY

Some anthropologists suggest that coffee was initially consumed by central African warriors in the form of a paste made from mashed coffee beans and animal fat rolled into balls. Eaten before battle, the animal fat and bean protein provided nourishment; the caffeine provided a stimulant.

A hot coffee drink may first have been consumed sometime during the ninth century C.E. in Persia. Made by a decoction of ripe beans, the drink was probably very thick and acrid. Nevertheless, by the year 1000, the elite of the Arab world were regularly drinking a decoction of dried coffee beans. The beans were harvested in Abyssinia (Ethiopia) and brought to market by Egyptian merchants. Within a century or so, *kahwa* became immensely popular with members of all strata of Arab

society. Coffeehouses opened throughout the Levant, catering to customers who sipped the thick, brown brew while discussing affairs of heart and state.

Coffee did not become popular in Europe until the 17th century. Its popularity is due in great part to Suleiman Aga, the Grand Panjandrum of the Ottoman Empire. In 1669, he arrived at the court of King Louis XIV of France as ambassador, bringing with him many exotic treasures, including coffee. Offered at his opulent parties, coffee soon became the drink of choice for the French aristocracy.

Coffee became popular in Vienna as a fortune of war. By 1683, the Turks were at the gates of Vienna. A decisive battle was fought, and the Turks fled, leaving behind stores of gold, equipment, supplies and a

barely known provision—green coffee beans. One of the victorious leaders, Franz George Kolschitzky, recognized the treasure, took it as his own and soon opened the first coffeehouse in Vienna, The Blue Bottle.

Despite its growing popularity, coffee was exorbitantly expensive, in part the result of the sultan's monopoly on coffee beans. His agents, principally in Marseilles, controlled the sale of beans. But the monopoly was not to survive. By the end of the 17th century, the Dutch had stolen coffee plants from Arabia and began cultivating them in Java. By the early 18th century, the French had transported seedlings to the West Indies; from there coffee plantations spread throughout the New World.

Tea and Tisanes

Tea and tisanes are made from dried leaves, herbs, spices, flowers or fruits that are prepared by infusion, which is steeping in fresh boiling water.

Tea is the beverage of choice for more than half the world's population and may be served hot or cold. Eighty-five percent of the tea consumed in the United States is iced, a uniquely American preference. **Tisanes**, or herbal infusions, have long been popular in Europe and Asia for their perceived health benefits and healing properties. As customers in the United States have become familiar with herbal teas, demand for them is growing.

Variety of cups of brewed tea (from left): Chinese tea, Japanese tea, Moroccan mint tea and black tea with milk

TEA

Tea (Fr. *thé*) is the name given to the leaves of *Camellia sinensis*, a tree or shrub that grows at high altitudes in damp tropical regions. Although tea comes from only one species of plant, there are three general types of tea—black, green and oolong. The differences among the three are the result of the manner in which the leaves are treated after picking.

Tea Varieties

Black tea is amber-brown and strongly flavored. Its color and flavor result from fermenting the leaves. Black tea leaves are named or graded by leaf size. Because larger leaves brew more slowly than smaller ones, teas are sorted by leaf size for efficient brewing. *Souchong* denotes large leaves, *pekoe* denotes medium-sized leaves and *orange pekoe* denotes the smallest whole leaves. (Note that orange pekoe does not refer to any type of orange flavor.) Broken tea is smaller, resulting in a darker, stronger brew, and is most often used in tea bags.

Black teas may be served hot or iced and are usually accompanied by lemon or milk and sweeteners, depending on customer preference.

Green tea is yellowish-green in color with a bitter flavor. Leaves used for green tea are not fermented. The finest green tea is Gunpowder, followed by Imperial and Hyson. Green tea is most often served hot, without milk, lemon or sweeteners.

Oolong tea is partially fermented to combine the characteristics of black and green teas. Oolong is popular in China and Japan, often flavored with jasmine flowers. Oolong tea is most often served hot, usually without milk or lemon.

As with coffee, tea takes much of its flavor from the geographic conditions in which it is grown. Teas are named for their place of origin—for example, Darjeeling, Ceylon (now Sri Lanka) or Assam.

Many popular and commercially available teas are actually blends of leaves from various sources. Blended and unblended teas may also be flavored with oils, dried fruit, spices, flowers or herbs; they are then referred to as **flavored teas**. Spices such as allspice, cinnamon, nutmeg and black pepper are often used to create teas flavored for cold-weather drinking. Bright herbs such as mint and citrus rind or oil, especially bergamot, which gives Earl Grey tea its flavor, add complexity to brewed teas and are also popular additions. **Chai** refers to a popular black tea and milk beverage that is sweetened and flavored with cinnamon, cardamom, vanilla or other spices. It may be served hot or iced and takes its name from the Chinese word for tea.

Tea Flavors

Tea can be described according to three key characteristics: astringency or briskness, body and aroma. *Astringency* is not bitterness, which is undesirable, but a sharp, dry feeling on the tongue that contributes to the refreshing taste of a tea. *Body* refers to the feeling of thickness on the tongue. Teas range from light to full bodied. *Aroma* is the smell and flavors of the tea when brewed.

The following descriptions apply to some of the teas frequently available through wholesalers or gourmet suppliers. Taste several different ones to determine the best choice. Remember that the same tea from different blenders or distributors may taste different, and that different flavors will be more or less appropriate for different times of the day.

BLACK TEAS

▶ **Assam**—A rich black tea from northeastern India with a reddish color. It is valued by connoisseurs, especially for breakfast.

TEA BAGS

The invention of the tea bag was apparently inadvertent. According to the Tea Association of America, in 1904, Thomas Sullivan, a New York tea merchant, sent potential customers samples of tea in small muslin or silk bags. Finding that they could make tea by simply pouring boiling water over the bags, Sullivan's new customers clamored for more.

Throughout the 20th century tea companies experimented and claimed supremacy for their bags, but the quality of the tea within is more important than the shape of the bag.

flavored tea tea to which flavorings such as oils, dried fruit, spices, flowers and herbs have been added

Fruit Tea

Gunpowder

Darjeeling

▸ **Ceylon**—A full-flavored black tea with a golden color and delicate fragrance. Ideal for serving iced, it does not become cloudy when cold.

▸ **Darjeeling**—The champagne of teas, grown in the foothills of the Himalayas in northeastern India. It is a full-bodied, black tea with a muscat flavor.

▸ **Earl Grey**—A blend of black teas, usually including Darjeeling, flavored with oil of bergamot. A popular choice for afternoon tea.

▸ **English Breakfast**—An English blend of Indian and Sri Lankan black teas; it is full-bodied and robust, with a rich color.

▸ **Keemum**—A mellow black Chinese tea with a strong aroma. It is less astringent than other teas and is delicious iced.

▸ **Lapsang Souchong**—A large-leafed (souchong) tea from the Lapsang district of China. It has a distinctive tarry, smoky flavor and aroma, appropriate for afternoon tea or dinner.

GREEN TEAS

▸ **Gunpowder**—A green Chinese tea with a tightly curled leaf and gray-green color. It has a pungent flavor and a light straw color. It is often served after the evening meal.

▸ **Sencha** (common)—A delicate Japanese green tea that has a light color with a pronounced aroma and a bright, grassy taste.

▸ **White tea**—A delicate green tea made from new buds picked before they open. Allowed to wither so that natural moisture evaporates, these leaves are lightly dried to a pale silvery color. White tea has a subtle flavor.

OOLONG TEAS

▸ **Formosa Oolong**—A unique and expensive large-leafed oolong tea with the flavor of ripe peaches. It is appropriate for breakfast or afternoon tea.

TISANES (HERB TEAS)

Tisanes are herbal infusions that do not contain any "real" tea. They are commonly made from fresh or dried flowers, herbs, seeds or roots; chamomile, mint, ginseng, linden flowers (Fr. *tilleul*) and lemon balm are among the more popular tisanes. In most countries there is a tradition of indigenous herbal medicine often administered in an infused form, as a tea. In Europe, a tisane may be served after a meal to aid digestion or taken before bed as an aid to sleep. (Herbal teas usually contain no caffeine, so they do not act as stimulants.) In a professional food service establishment herbal teas are prepackaged blends and require no mixing.

BREWING TEA

Hot tea may be brewed by the cup or the pot. In either case, it is important to use the following procedure:

① Always begin with clean equipment and fresh cold water. Water that has been sitting in a kettle or hot water tank contains less air and will taste flat or stale.

② Warm the teapot by rinsing its interior with hot water. This will help relax the tea leaves and ensure that the water will stay hot when it comes in contact with the tea.

③ Place 1 teaspoon (5 milliliters) loose tea or one tea bag per ¾ cup (6 fluid ounces/180 milliliters) of water capacity in the warmed teapot.

④ As soon as the water comes to a boil, pour the appropriate amount over the tea. Do not allow the water to continue boiling as this removes the oxygen, leaving a flat taste. The water should be at a full boil when it comes in contact with the tea so that the tea leaves will uncurl and release their flavor.

⑤ Replace the lid of the teapot and allow the tea to infuse for 3 to 5 minutes. Time the brew. Color is not a reliable indication of brewing time; tea leaves release color before flavor, and different types of tea will be different colors when properly brewed.

⑥ Remove the tea bags or loose tea from the water when brewing is complete. This can be accomplished easily if the teapot is fitted with a removable leaf basket or if a tea bag or a perforated tea ball is used. Otherwise, decant the tea through a strainer into a second warmed teapot.

SOUTHERN SWEET TEA

Sweet tea is an iced beverage traditionally offered in the American South. It is now making its way into many bottled tea drinks, fast-food menus and even vodka flavorings and cocktails. Sweet tea is not merely iced tea plus sugar. To achieve the desired flavor, a large quantity of granulated sugar is dissolved in strong, hot black tea—typically 1½ to 2 cups of sugar per gallon of tea. Adding sugar to chilled tea will not produce the same "sweet tea" flavor, which most closely resembles a tea-flavored soft drink. Lemon may be added, depending on personal preference.

A CUP OF TEA HISTORY

Some believe that the Chinese emperor Shen Nung discovered tea drinking in 2737 B.C.E. Legend holds that the emperor was boiling his drinking water beneath a tree when some leaves fell into the pot. Enchanted with the drink, he began to cultivate the plant. Whether this is myth or truth, it is known that a hot drink made from powdered dried tea leaves whipped into hot water was regularly consumed in China sometime after the fourth century. But it was not until the Ming dynasty (1368–1644) that infusions of tea leaves became commonplace.

By the ninth century, tea drinking had spread to Japan. In both Chinese and Japanese cultures, tea drinking developed into a ritual. For the Chinese, a cup of tea became the mirror of the soul. For the Japanese, it was the drink of immortality.

Tea was first transported from China to Europe by Dutch merchants during the early 1600s. By midcentury, it was introduced into England. In 1669, the British East India Company was granted a charter by Queen Elizabeth I to import tea, a monopoly it held until 1833. To ensure a steady supply, the English surreptitiously procured plants from China and started plantations throughout the Indian subcontinent, as did the Dutch.

Tea drinking became fashionable in England, at least in court circles, through Charles II (raised in exile at The Hague in Holland, he reigned from 1660 to 1685) and his Portuguese wife, Catherine of Braganza. Queen Anne of England (who reigned from 1702 to 1714) introduced several concepts that eventually became part of the English tea custom. For example, she substituted tea for ale at breakfast and began using large silver pots instead of tiny china pots.

The social custom of afternoon tea began in the late 1700s, thanks to Anna, Duchess of Bedford. Historians attribute to her the late-afternoon ritual of snacking on sandwiches and pastries accompanied by tea. She began the practice in order to quell her hunger pangs between breakfast and dinner (which was typically served at 9:30 or 10:00 P.M.).

Eventually, two distinct types of teatime evolved. Low tea was aristocratic in origin and consisted of a snack of pastries and sandwiches, with tea, served in the late afternoon as a prelude to the evening meal. High tea was bourgeois in origin, consisting of leftovers from the typically large middle-class lunch, such as cold meats, bread and cheeses. High tea became a substitute for the evening meal.

❼ Serve immediately, accompanied with sugar, lemon, milk (not cream) and honey as desired. Dilute the tea with hot water if necessary.

❽ Do not reuse tea leaves. One pound of tea yields 200 cups, making it the most inexpensive beverage after tap water.

For iced tea, prepare regular brewed tea using 50 percent more tea. Then pour the tea into a pitcher or glass filled with ice. The stronger brew will hold its flavor better as the ice melts. If iced tea is not to be used immediately, it should be brewed at room or refrigerator temperature for several hours to prevent clouding.

QUESTIONS FOR DISCUSSION

❶ Explain the difference between an omelet and a frittata.

❷ Describe four different types of pan-fried eggs, and explain how each is prepared.

❸ What is the difference between a soft-cooked egg and a hard-cooked egg? Why are these eggs simmered instead of boiled?

❹ Describe the method for making an egg-white omelet. Compare this with the methods used for making an omelet with whole eggs. Explain why different ingredients or techniques may be used when using only egg whites.

❺ Explain the differences between a typical breakfast and a typical brunch. Create a sample menu for each of these meals.

❻ List three types of griddlecakes and explain how they are prepared.

❼ Describe the difference between drip coffee and espresso coffee.

❽ Name the three principal varieties of tea.

❾ Research egg dishes from several different countries. Describe the different preparations and compare them with traditional American egg dishes. Discuss the primary ingredients used and when these dishes are served. www

Terms to Know

shell	griddlecakes
yolk	Belgian waffles
albumen	blintzes
chalazae cord	hot porridge
spread	grits
shirred eggs	espresso
sunny side up	arabica
over easy	robusta
basted eggs	decoction
continental-style	infusion
breakfast	tisanes

GREEK-STYLE SCRAMBLED EGGS

Yield: 6 Servings, 5 oz. (150 g) each   **Method:** Sautéing

Eggs	12	12
Heavy cream	2 fl. oz.	60 ml
Salt and pepper	TT	TT
Onion, diced fine	2 oz.	60 g
Clarified butter	3 fl. oz.	90 ml
Spinach, chiffonade	2 oz.	60 g
Feta, crumbled	4 oz.	120 g
Greek olives, pitted and chopped	3 Tbsp.	45 ml

1. Combine the eggs, cream, salt and pepper in a mixing bowl. Whisk until well blended.
2. Sauté the onion in the butter until translucent but not brown.
3. Pour the egg mixture into the pan and cook, stirring frequently, until half cooked, approximately 1 minute.
4. Add the spinach to the eggs and continue cooking. Just before the eggs are fully cooked, sprinkle on the feta.
5. Spoon the cooked egg mixture onto serving plates and garnish with the olives. Serve immediately.

Approximate values per 5-oz. (150-g) serving: **Calories** 290, **Total fat** 23 g, **Saturated fat** 11 g, **Cholesterol** 465 mg, **Sodium** 380 mg, **Total carbohydrates** 4 g, **Protein** 16 g, **Vitamin A** 30%, **Calcium** 15%, **Iron** 10%

ROLLED SOUFFLÉ

NEWBURY COLLEGE, BROOKLINE, MA

Senior Instructor Scott Doughty

Yield: 22 Slices, 1 oz. (30 g) each   **Method:** Baking

Whole butter, softened	as needed	as needed
Flour	1 Tbsp.	15 ml
Milk, cold	8 fl. oz.	240 ml
Eggs, separated	6	6
Parmesan, grated	4 oz.	120 g
Duxelles (page 221), warm	12 oz.	360 g
Aurora sauce (page 203)	1 qt.	960 ml
Watercress	1 bunch	1 bunch
Fresh parsley, chopped	2 Tbsp.	30 ml

1. Grease a half-sheet pan with butter and line it with parchment paper.
2. Heat 1 tablespoon (15 milliliters) butter in a small saucepan. Add the flour and cook to make a blond roux. Slowly add the milk to the roux to form a paste. Bring slowly to a simmer and continue to cook for 10 minutes, stirring constantly. Transfer the sauce to a stainless steel bowl.
3. Beat the egg yolks into the sauce. In a separate bowl, beat the egg whites with a balloon whisk until stiff, shiny peaks form. Stir approximately one-third of the whites into the sauce and yolk mixture. Gently fold in another one-third of the whites and repeat with the last one-third of the whites. Fold in the Parmesan.

4. Spread the mixture onto the prepared half-sheet pan. Bake at 350°F (180°C) until done, approximately 15 minutes. Keep the oven door closed during cooking.

5. Remove the soufflé from the oven and separate it from the edges of the pan with a paring knife. Turn the soufflé out onto a clean surface. Spread the Duxelles over the entire surface of the soufflé. Roll it up into a tight log, making sure the paper does not get rolled up with the soufflé. Trim the ends from the soufflé.

6. For buffet service, slice three or four pieces from the soufflé and place the remaining soufflé on a platter. Nappe with Aurora sauce and garnish with the watercress and parsley.

Approximate values per slice: **Calories** 130, **Total fat** 10 g, **Saturated fat** 6 g, **Cholesterol** 105 mg, **Sodium** 350 mg, **Total carbohydrates** 4 g, **Protein** 6 g

---

EGGS BENEDICT

Yield: 1 Serving   **Method:** Poaching

English muffin, split	1	1
Canadian bacon slices, ¼ in. (6 mm) thick	2	2
Salt	TT	TT
Vinegar	1 fl. oz.	30 ml
Eggs	2	2
Hollandaise (page 208)	4 fl. oz.	120 ml
Truffle slices or black olive halves	2	2

1. Toast the English muffin.
2. Sauté or griddle the bacon slices until hot.
3. Bring 1 quart (1 liter) water to a boil and add the salt and vinegar.
4. Reduce the heat to a strong simmer. Add the eggs and poach until done.
5. Place the muffins on a plate and top with the bacon slices. Place an egg on each slice of bacon and cover with the Hollandaise.
6. Garnish each egg with a truffle slice or black olive half and serve.

VARIATIONS:

Poached Eggs Florentine—Serve poached eggs on an English muffin or pastry shell over creamed spinach with hollandaise or béchamel sauce.

Poached Eggs Norwegian Style—Serve poached eggs on an English muffin with smoked salmon and hollandaise sauce.

Poached Eggs Princess Style—Serve poached eggs on an English muffin with asparagus tips and hollandaise sauce.

Poached Eggs Sardou—Serve poached eggs and creamed spinach on an artichoke bottom with hollandaise sauce.

Approximate values per serving: **Calories** 970, **Total fat** 69 g, **Saturated fat** 33 g, **Cholesterol** 610 mg, **Sodium** 2480 mg, **Total carbohydrates** 53 g, **Protein** 33 g, **Vitamin A** 80%, **Iron** 25%

EGG, BACON, LETTUCE AND TOMATO BREAKFAST SANDWICH

Yield: 1 Serving   **Method:** Pan-frying

Rustic white bread	2 slices	2 slices
Mayonnaise	1 Tbsp.	15 ml
Butter lettuce leaves	2	2
Bacon slices, cooked crisp, warm	3	3
Tomato slices	3	3
Cheddar cheese	2 slices	2 slices
Unsalted butter	1 tsp.	5 ml
Egg	1	1
Salt and pepper	TT	TT

1. Toast the bread slices. Lay them out facing each other on a cutting board. Spread one slice with the mayonnaise. Position the lettuce on the bread and top with the bacon and the tomato slices. Place the Cheddar cheese on the other slice.
2. Heat a small nonstick sauté pan over medium heat. Add the butter. Crack the egg into the pan, season with salt and pepper and cook, turning once, until the white is cooked and the yolk is still runny. Place the egg on top of the tomatoes.
3. Close the sandwich and serve immediately.

Approximate values per serving: **Calories** 710, **Total fat** 41 g, **Saturated fat** 15 g, **Cholesterol** 285 mg, **Sodium** 1440 mg, **Total carbohydrates** 52 g, **Protein** 33 g, **Vitamin A** 35%, **Calcium** 30%, **Iron** 30%

SCOTCH EGGS

A popular snack or picnic food in Great Britain, Scotch eggs consist of hard-cooked eggs wrapped in breakfast sausage, then deep-fried. They make an excellent breakfast buffet or brunch item because of their good keeping properties. Use peewee or quail eggs for a more refined presentation.

Yield: 4 Servings   **Method:** Hard-cooked

Breakfast sausage, bulk	8 oz.	240 g
Fresh sage, chopped	½ tsp.	2 ml
Fresh thyme, chopped	½ tsp.	2 ml
Worcestershire sauce	½ tsp.	2 ml
Salt and pepper	TT	TT
All-purpose flour	as needed	as needed
Eggs, hard cooked, peeled	4	4
Egg, beaten	1	1
Bread crumbs, dry	as needed	as needed

1. Combine the breakfast sausage, herbs, Worcestershire sauce, salt and pepper in a small bowl.
2. With lightly floured hands, divide the sausage mixture into four equal portions. Flatten each portion into a thin patty. Dust the eggs with flour and wrap each egg in a portion of the sausage meat. Be sure the meat is of even thickness and there are no cracks.
3. Bread the sausage-covered eggs using the standard breading procedure described in Chapter 8, Mise en Place.
4. Deep-fry the eggs approximately 7 to 8 minutes at 350°F (180°C) or until the sausage meat is fully cooked. The eggs may be finished in the oven if they begin to get too dark in the fryer.
5. Serve the eggs halved or quartered lengthwise, hot or cold, with Dijon mustard.

Approximate values per serving: **Calories** 200, **Total fat** 130 g, **Saturated fat** 5 g, **Cholesterol** 280 mg, **Sodium** 440 mg, **Total carbohydrates** 2 g, **Protein** 13 g

CORNED BEEF HASH

Yield: 12 Servings　　　　　　　　**Method:** Pan-Frying

Potatoes, waxy	1 lb. 8 oz.	720 g
Onions, large dice	8 oz.	240 g
Carrots, medium dice	2 oz.	60 g
Parsnips, peeled, medium dice	4 oz.	120 g
Vegetable oil or bacon fat	2 fl. oz.	60 ml
Corned beef, cooked, large dice	2 lb.	960 g
Eggs, beaten	2	2
Salt and pepper	TT	TT

1. Peel and quarter the potatoes. Simmer them in a saucepan of salted water until tender. Drain the potatoes, allow them to cool completely then coarsely chop them.
2. Sauté the onions, carrots and parsnips in 1 ounce (30 milliliters) oil over medium heat until tender. Remove the vegetables from the pan and let them cool.
3. Combine the cubed potatoes, sautéed vegetables and corned beef and grind through the medium die of a meat grinder.
4. Combine the ground mixture with the eggs. Season with salt and pepper. (The hash may be prepared to this point and refrigerated until needed.)
5. Form the mixture into 6-ounce (180-gram) patties or divide the mixture between 12 greased ring molds.
6. Heat the remaining oil in a large sauté pan over medium heat. Add the hash patties or the ring molds of hash. Cook until heated through, turning once when well browned on the first side. (Slide off the ring molds, if using, before serving.) Serve with fried or poached eggs.

Approximate values per serving: **Calories** 300, **Total fat** 20 g, **Saturated fat** 5 g, **Cholesterol** 110 mg, **Sodium** 880 mg, **Total carbohydrates** 13 g, **Protein** 16 g

STRAWBERRY CRÊPES FITZGERALD

BRENNAN'S RESTAURANT, NEW ORLEANS, LA
Chef Michael Roussel (1938–2005)

Yield: 8 Servings

Cream cheese, room temperature	1 lb.	480 g
Sour cream	2½ fl. oz.	75 ml
Vanilla extract	1 Tbsp.	15 ml
Granulated sugar	5 oz.	150 g
Crêpes (page 549)	16	16
Whole butter	½ oz.	15 g
Fresh strawberries, sliced	35 oz.	1 kg
Fresh lemon juice	1 Tbsp.	15 ml
Maraschino liqueur	1 fl. oz.	30 ml

1. Combine the cream cheese, sour cream, vanilla extract and 1 ounce (30 grams) sugar in a mixing bowl and beat until smooth.
2. Place 3 tablespoons (45 milliliters) of the filling on one end of each crêpe; roll the crêpes around the filling and then refrigerate them while preparing the topping.
3. To make the topping, heat the butter and the remaining sugar in a large saucepan. Cook over medium heat, stirring until the sugar dissolves. Add the strawberries and lemon juice.
4. Bring the mixture to a boil, then reduce the heat and simmer until the liquid thickens, approximately 10 to 12 minutes. Add the maraschino liqueur and flambé as described on page 341.
5. To serve, place two crêpes on each of eight plates and spoon approximately 6 fluid ounces (180 milliliters) of warm strawberry topping over the crêpes.

Approximate values per serving: **Calories** 630, **Total fat** 37 g, **Saturated fat** 22 g, **Cholesterol** 260 mg, **Sodium** 380 mg, **Total carbohydrates** 65 g, **Protein** 13 g, **Vitamin A** 20%, **Vitamin C** 100%

CHEESE BLINTZES

Yield: 16 Blintzes

Eggs	3	3
Milk	8 fl. oz.	240 ml
Vegetable oil	1 fl. oz.	30 ml
Salt	¾ tsp.	3 ml
Flour	4 oz.	120 g
Clarified butter	as needed	as needed
Ricotta	12 oz.	360 g
Egg yolk	1	1
Lemon juice	1 tsp.	5 ml
Vanilla extract	1 tsp.	5 ml
Whole butter	2 oz.	60 g

1. To make the batter, whisk together the eggs, milk and oil. Add ½ teaspoon (2 milliliters) salt. Stir in the flour and mix until smooth. Allow the batter to rest for 30 minutes.
2. Heat a crêpe pan and add a small amount of clarified butter.
3. Pour 1 fluid ounce (30 milliliters) of the batter into the pan. Tip the pan so that the batter coats the entire surface in a thin layer.
4. Cook the pancake until browned on the bottom. Remove it from the pan.
5. Repeat this procedure until all of the pancakes are made.
6. To make the filling, drain the ricotta in a china cap, discarding the liquid. Place the drained cheese in a bowl with the remaining salt and the egg yolk, lemon juice and vanilla extract and mix well.
7. To assemble, place a pancake on the work surface with the browned side up. Place 1 ounce (30 grams) of the filling in the center of the pancake. Fold the opposite ends in and then roll up to form a small package.
8. Sauté each blintz in butter until hot. Serve with sour cream or fruit compote as desired.

Approximate values per 2-oz. (60-g) serving: **Calories** 110, **Total fat** 7 g, **Saturated fat** 3.5 g, **Cholesterol** 65 mg, **Sodium** 170 mg, **Total carbohydrates** 7 g, **Protein** 5 g

WAFFLES

Yield: 20 Waffles

All-purpose flour	18 oz.	540 g
Salt	2 tsp.	10 ml
Baking powder	2 Tbsp.	30 ml
Granulated sugar	2 oz.	60 g
Eggs	4	4
Milk, warm	24 fl. oz.	720 ml
Unsalted butter, melted	5 oz.	150 g
Vanilla extract	2 tsp.	10 ml

1. Mix the dry ingredients together in a large bowl.
2. Whisk the eggs together in a separate bowl; add the milk, butter and vanilla extract,, stirring to combine.
3. Pour the liquid mixture into the dry ingredients, stirring to blend. Keep refrigerated until ready to use. Batter may be made up to 1 day in advance.
4. Cook in a preheated waffle iron according to the manufacturer's directions. Serve waffles immediately with your choice of toppings.

VARIATION:

Pecan Waffles—Sprinkle 1 tablespoon (15 milliliters) chopped pecans over the batter as soon as it is poured onto the waffle iron. Substitute 1 teaspoon (5 milliliters) pecan flavoring for the vanilla extract if desired.

Approximate values per waffle: **Calories** 190, **Total fat** 8 g, **Saturated fat** 4.5 g, **Cholesterol** 65 mg, **Sodium** 480 mg, **Total carbohydrates** 25 g, **Protein** 5 g, **Calcium** 20%

CINNAMON FRENCH TOAST

French toast begins with slices of day-old bread. (It is known in France as pain perdu, meaning "lost bread," probably because it provided a way to use bread that would otherwise have been discarded.) French bread, sourdough bread, raisin bread, challah, whole-wheat bread and even stale croissants can be used. The bread is dipped into a batter of eggs, sugar, milk or cream and flavorings, then sautéed in butter and served very hot. It may be topped with powdered sugar, fresh fruit, fruit compote or maple syrup as desired.

Yield: 6 Servings

Eggs, beaten	10	10
Heavy cream	4 fl. oz.	120 ml
Salt	TT	TT
Cinnamon, ground	TT	TT
Thick-sliced bread such as sourdough, cinnamon, banana or brioche	12 slices	12 slices
Unsalted butter	as needed	as needed
Powdered sugar	as needed	as needed

1. Whisk together the eggs, cream, salt and cinnamon.
2. Place the egg mixture in a shallow pan. Place the slices of bread in the egg mixture and let soak for 2 to 3 minutes, turning them over after the first minute or so.
3. Cook the slices of French toast in a lightly buttered, preheated sauté pan or griddle set at 350°F (180°C) until well browned. Turn the slices and cook on the second side until done.
4. Cut each slice of bread into two triangles.
5. Arrange four triangles on each plate and dust with powdered sugar.

Approximate values per 5-oz. (150-g) serving: **Calories** 320, **Total fat** 17 g, **Saturated fat** 7 g, **Cholesterol** 380 mg, **Sodium** 420 mg, **Total carbohydrates** 28 g, **Protein** 15 g, **Vitamin A** 25%, **Iron** 15%

CHAPTER TWENTY-ONE

VEGETABLES

After studying this chapter, you will be able to:

- identify a variety of vegetables
- purchase vegetables appropriate for your needs
- store vegetables properly
- understand how vegetables are preserved
- prepare vegetables for cooking or service
- apply various cooking methods to vegetables

LONG OVERCOOKED AND UNDERRATED, VEGETABLES ARE enjoying a welcome surge in popularity. Gone are the days when a chef included vegetables as an afterthought to the "meat and potatoes" of the meal. Now properly prepared fresh vegetables are used to add flavor, color and variety to almost any meal. Many restaurants are featuring vegetarian entrées, an extensive selection of vegetable side dishes or an entire vegetarian menu. This trend reflects the demands of more knowledgeable and health-conscious consumers as well as the increased availability of high-quality fresh produce. (Cooking for those on a meatless diet using vegetables as well as other ingredients is discussed in Chapter 23, Healthy Cooking.)

In this chapter, we identify many of the vegetables typically used by food service operations. (Potatoes, although they are vegetables, are discussed in Chapter 22, Potatoes, Grains and Pasta; salad greens are discussed in Chapter 24, Salads and Salad Dressings.) Here we also discuss how fresh and preserved vegetables are purchased, stored and prepared for service or cooking. Many of the cooking methods analyzed in Chapter 9, Principles of Cooking, are then applied to vegetables.

The term **vegetable** refers to any herbaceous plant that can be partially or wholly eaten. An herbaceous plant has little or no woody tissue. The portions we consume include the leaves, stems, roots, tubers, seeds and flowers. Vegetables contain more starch and less sugar than fruits. Therefore vegetables tend to be savory, not sweet. Also unlike fruits, vegetables are most often eaten cooked, not raw.

IDENTIFYING VEGETABLES

This book presents fruits and vegetables according to the ways most people view them and use them, rather than by rigid botanical classifications. Although produce such as tomatoes, peppers and eggplants are botanically fruits, they are prepared and served like vegetables and are included here under the category we call "fruit-vegetables." Potatoes, although botanically vegetables, are discussed with other starches in Chapter 22, Potatoes, Grains and Pasta.

We divide vegetables into nine categories based on either botanical relationship or edible part: cabbages, fruit-vegetables, gourds and squashes, greens, mushrooms and truffles, onions, pods and seeds, roots and tubers, and stalks. A vegetable may have several names, varying from region to region or on a purveyor's whim. The names given here follow generally accepted custom and usage.

Cabbages

The *Brassica* or cabbage family includes a wide range of vegetables used for their heads, flowers or leaves. They are generally quick-growing, cool-weather crops. Many are ancient plants with unknown origins. They are inexpensive, readily available and easy to prepare.

BOK CHOY

Bok choy, also known as pok choy, is a white-stemmed variety of southern Chinese cabbage. The relatively tightly packed leaves are dark green, with long white ribs at-

Bok Choy

tached at a bulbous stem. The stalks are crisp and mild with a flavor similar to romaine lettuce. Although bok choy may be eaten raw, it is most often stir-fried or used in soups.

Choose heads with bright white stalks and dark green leaves; avoid those with brown, moist spots. Fresh bok choy is available all year. Jars of pickled and fermented bok choy (known as Korean kim chee) are also available.

BROCCOLI

Broccoli, a type of flower, has a thick central stalk with grayish-green leaves topped with one or more heads of green florets. Broccoli may be eaten raw or steamed, microwaved or sautéed and served warm or cold. Broccoli stalks are extremely firm and benefit from blanching. Stems are often slow-cooked for soups. Generally, broccoli leaves are not eaten.

Broccoli

Choose firm stalks with compact clusters of tightly closed dark green florets. Avoid stalks with yellow flowers. Broccoli is available all year.

PROCEDURE FOR CUTTING BROCCOLI SPEARS

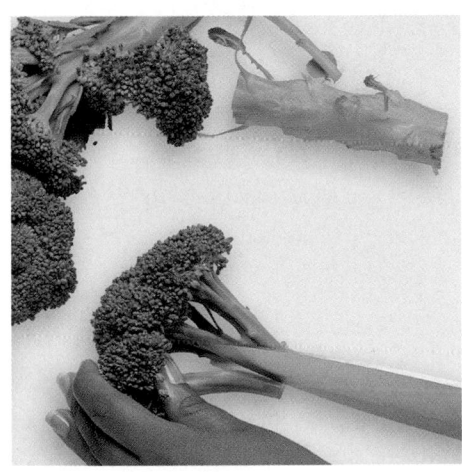

Cut off the thick, woody portion of the stalk, then cut the florets and stems into spears.

BROCCOLI RABE

Broccoli rabe, also known as raab (rob) and rapini (rah-PEE-nee) (It. *broccoli di rape, cime di rapa*) is a leafy green with small florets that look similar to broccoli. The entire plant is eaten, although some prefer to separate the spiky leaves and green florets from the more bitter stems. It may be boiled, steamed, roasted or sautéed, and its peppery, bitter flavor is a popular ingredient in both Chinese and Mediterranean, especially Italian, cuisine. It is available fresh year-round, with peak seasons in the fall and spring. Select rabe with bright green leaves and unopened buds; avoid any with wilted or yellow leaves.

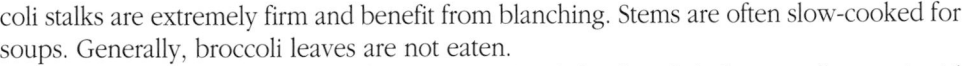

Broccoli Rabe

BRUSSELS SPROUTS

Brussels sprouts (Fr. *choux de Bruxelles*) were first cultivated around 1700. The plant produces numerous small heads arranged in neat rows along a thick stalk. The tender young sprouts are similar to baby cabbages and are usually steamed or roasted. Brussels sprouts have a strong, nutty flavor that blends well with game, ham, duck or rich meats.

Brussels Sprouts

Cauliflower

Choose small, firm sprouts that are compact and heavy. The best size is ¾ to 1½ inches (2 to 4 centimeters) in diameter. They should be bright green and free of blemishes. Their peak season is from September through February.

CAULIFLOWER

Cauliflower (Fr. *chou-fleur*) is the king of the cabbage family. Each stalk produces one flower or head surrounded by large green leaves. The head, composed of creamy white florets, can be cooked whole or cut into separate florets for steaming, blanching or stir-frying.

Choose firm, compact heads. Any attached leaves should be bright green and crisp. A yellow color or spreading florets indicate that the vegetable is overly mature. Cauliflower is available all year, especially from the late fall through the spring.

PROCEDURE FOR **CUTTING CAULIFLOWER FLORETS**

Green and Red Cabbages

1 Cut off the stem and leaves.

2 Cut the florets off the core.

HEAD CABBAGES (GREEN AND RED)

Cabbage (Fr. *chou*) has been a staple of northern European cuisine for centuries. The familiar green cabbage has a large, firm, round head with tightly packed pale green leaves. Flat and cone-shaped heads are also available. Red (or purple) cabbage is a different strain and may be tougher than green cabbage. Cabbage can be eaten raw (as in coleslaw) or used in soups or stews; it can be braised, steamed or stir-fried. The large, waxy leaves can also be steamed until soft, then wrapped around a filling of seasoned meat.

Choose firm heads without dried cores. Cabbages are available all year.

KALE

Kale

Kale has large ruffled, curly or bumpy leaves. Its rather bitter flavor goes well with rich meats such as game, pork or ham. Kale is typically boiled, stuffed or used in soups.

Choose leaves that are crisp, with a grayish-green color. Kale is available all year; its peak season is during the winter months.

Ornamental or flowering kale, sometimes marketed as "savoy," is edible, but its pink, purple, yellow or white-and-green variegated leaves are best used for decoration and garnish.

Ornamental Kale

KOHLRABI

Although it looks rather like a round root, kohlrabi is actually a bulbous stem vegetable created by crossbreeding cabbages and turnips. Both the leaves (which are attached directly to the bulbous stem) and the roots are generally removed before sale. Depending on the variety, the skin may be light green, purple or green with a hint of red. The interior flesh is white, with a sweet flavor similar to that of turnips. (Kohlrabi can be substituted for turnip in many recipes.) Younger plants are milder and more tender than large, mature ones. The outer skin must be removed from mature stems; young stems need only to be well scrubbed before cooking. Kohlrabi can be eaten raw, or it can be cooked (whole, sliced or diced) with moist-heat cooking methods such as boiling and steaming. Kohlrabi may also be hollowed out and stuffed with meat or vegetable mixtures.

Choose small, tender stems with fresh, green leaves. Peak season for kohlrabi is from June through September.

Kohlrabi

NAPA CABBAGE

Napa cabbage, also known as Chinese cabbage, is widely used in Asian cuisines. It has a stout, elongated head with relatively tightly packed, firm, pale green leaves. It is more moist and more tender than common green and red cabbages, with a milder, more delicate flavor. Napa cabbage may be eaten raw but is particularly well suited for stir-frying or steaming.

Choose heads with crisp leaves that are free of blemishes. Napa cabbage is available fresh all year.

SAVOY

Savoy cabbage has curly or ruffled leaves, often in variegated shades of green and purple. (The term *savoyed* is used to refer to any vegetable with bumpy, wavy or wrinkled leaves.) Savoy cabbage tends to be milder and more tender than regular cabbages and can be substituted for them, cooked or uncooked. Savoy leaves also make an attractive garnish.

Choose heads that are loose or tight, depending on the variety, with tender, unblemished leaves. Peak season is from August through the spring.

Napa Cabbage

Savoy

Fruit-Vegetables

Botanists classify avocados, eggplants, peppers and tomatoes as fruits because they develop from the ovary of flowering plants and contain one or more seeds. Chefs, however, prepare and serve them like vegetables; therefore they are discussed here.

AVOCADOS

Avocados include several varieties of pear-shaped fruits with rich, high-fat flesh. This light golden-green flesh surrounds a large, inedible, oval-shaped seed (pit). Some varieties have smooth, green skin; others have pebbly, almost black skin. Avocados should be used at their peak of ripeness, a condition that lasts only briefly. Firm avocados lack the desired flavor and creamy texture. Ripe avocados should be soft to the touch but not mushy. Ripe Hass avocados have almost-black skins; the skins of the other varieties remain green when ripe. Firm avocados can be left at room temperature to ripen, then refrigerated for 1 or 2 days. Avocados are most often used raw to garnish salads, mashed or puréed for sauces, sliced for sandwiches or diced for omelets. Avocado halves are popular containers for chilled meat, fish, shellfish or poultry salads. Because avocado flesh turns brown very quickly once cut, dip avocado halves or slices in lemon juice and keep unused portions tightly covered with plastic wrap.

Choose avocados that are free of blemishes or moist spots. The flesh should be free of dark spots or streaks. Avocados are available all year. The peak season for Hass avocados is April through October; for Fuertes avocados, it is November through April.

Avocados

PROCEDURE FOR **CUTTING AND PITTING AVOCADOS**

① Cut the avocado in half lengthwise. Separate the two halves with a twisting motion.

② Insert a chef's knife into the pit and twist to remove.

③ Scoop the flesh out of the skin with a large spoon.

Japanese Eggplant

Asian Eggplants

EGGPLANTS

Two types of eggplants (Fr. *aubergine*) are commonly available: Asian and western. Asian varieties are either round or long and thin, with skin colors ranging from creamy white to deep purple. Western eggplants, which are more common in the United States, tend to be shaped like a plump pear with a shiny lavender to purple-black skin. Both types have a dense, khaki-colored flesh with a rather bland flavor that absorbs other flavors well during cooking. Eggplants can be grilled, baked, steamed, fried or sautéed. They are commonly used in Mediterranean and Indian cuisines (especially in vegetarian dishes), but also appear in European and North American dishes. The skin may be left intact or removed before or after cooking, as desired. Sliced eggplants may be salted and left to drain for 30 minutes to remove moisture and bitterness before cooking.

Choose plump, heavy eggplants with a smooth, shiny skin that is not blemished or wrinkled. Asian varieties tend to be softer than western. Eggplants are available all year; their peak season is during the late summer.

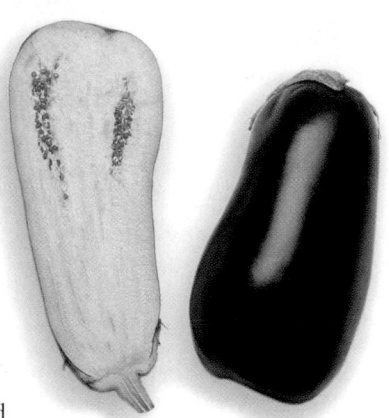

Western Eggplant

PEPPERS

Members of the *Capsicum* family are native to the New World. When "discovered" by Christopher Columbus, he called them "peppers" because of their sometimes fiery flavor. These peppers, which include sweet peppers and hot peppers (chiles), are unrelated to peppercorns, the Asian spice for which Columbus was actually searching. Interestingly, New World peppers were readily accepted in Indian and Asian cuisines, in which they are now considered staples.

Fresh peppers are found in a wide range of colors—green, red, yellow, orange, purple and white—as well as shapes, from tiny teardrops to cones to spheres. They have dense flesh and a hollow central cavity. The flesh is lined with placental ribs (the white internal veins), to which tiny yellowish-white seeds are attached. A core of seeds is also attached to the stem end of each pepper.

Chile peppers get their heat from capsaicin, which is found not in the flesh or seeds, but in the placental ribs. Thus a pepper's heat can be greatly reduced by carefully removing the ribs and attached seeds. Generally, the smaller the chile, the hotter it is. The amount of heat varies from variety to variety, however, and even from one pepper to another depending on growing conditions. Hot, dry conditions result in hotter peppers than do cool, moist conditions.

When selecting peppers, choose those that are plump and brilliantly colored with smooth, unblemished skins. Avoid wrinkled, pitted or blistered peppers. A bright green

---

EGGPLANT: TO SALT OR NOT TO SALT?

Eggplants are filled with cells that contain water and are surrounded by tiny air pockets. The presence of heat will squeeze the air out of the pockets. If the eggplant has not been salted, oil is then free to seep into these pockets and the eggplant becomes soggy when fried.

But when salt is sprinkled on an eggplant, it draws the water out of the cells. The cells then collapse, which in turn makes the air pockets collapse. As a result, no oil can seep into the tiny pockets during the frying process.

—DANIEL ZWERDLING is a senior correspondent with National Public Radio. This text originally appeared in *Gourmet*

stem indicates freshness. The searing heat of a Scotch bonnet or habañero can burn. Wearing gloves is recommended when working with these chile peppers.

Sweet Peppers

Common sweet peppers, known as bell peppers, are thick-walled fruits available in green, red, yellow, purple, orange and other colors. They are heart-shaped or boxy, with a short stem and crisp flesh. Their flavor is warm, sweet (red peppers tend to be the sweetest) and relatively mild. Raw bell peppers may be sliced or diced and used in salads or sandwiches. Bell peppers can also be stuffed and baked, grilled, fried, sautéed or puréed for soups, sauces or condiments. Green bell peppers are available all year; other colors are more readily available during the summer and fall.

Green Bell Peppers

Red and Yellow Bell Peppers

PROCEDURE FOR **CUTTING PEPPERS JULIENNE**

❶ Trim off the ends of the pepper; cut away the seeds and core.

❷ Cut away the pale ribs, trimming the flesh to the desired thickness.

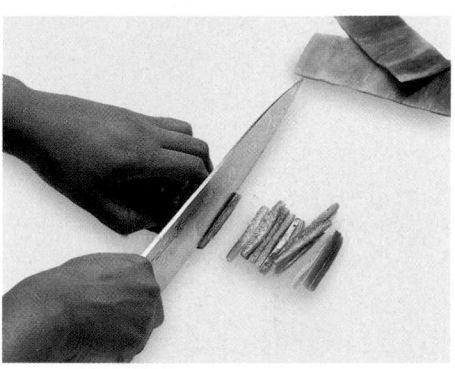

❸ Slice the flesh in julienne.

Hot Peppers

Hot peppers, also known as chiles, are also members of the *Capsicum* family. Although a chile's most characteristic attribute is its pungency, each chile actually has a distinctive flavor, from mild and rich to spicy and sweet to fiery hot.

Chiles are commonly used in Asian, Indian, Mexican and Latin American cuisines. The larger (and milder) of the hot peppers, such as Anaheim and poblano, can be stuffed and baked or sautéed as a side dish. Most chiles, however, are used to add flavor and seasoning to sauces and other dishes. Fresh chiles are available all year and are also available canned in a variety of processed forms such as whole or diced, roasted, pickled or marinated.

Habañero

(clockwise from bottom left) Red and Green Serrano, Green and Red Jalapeño, Yellow Hot, Poblano and Anaheim Chiles

---

CHILE PEPPER PUNGENCY

A pepper's heat can be measured by Scoville heat units, a subjective rating created to measure the perception of capsaicin when tasting chile peppers. The higher the rating, the larger the concentration of capsaicin and the hotter the pepper will taste. Some of the ranges of heat of common chile peppers as measured in this system are listed here.

Pepper	Pungency (Scoville)
Bell, sweet Italian	0
New Mexico, pimento	500–1000
Anaheim, ancho, pasilla, poblano	1000–1500
Chipotle, jalapeño	2500–10,000
Serrano	5000–23,000
De árbol	15,000–30,000
Aji, cayenne, piquin, tabasco	30,000–50,000
Habañero, Scotch bonnet	80,000–300,000
Pure capsaicin	16,000,000

PROCEDURE FOR **CORING JALAPEÑOS**

Cut the jalapeño in half lengthwise. Push the core and seeds out with your thumb. You can avoid burning your fingers by wearing rubber gloves when working with hot chiles.

Dried chiles are widely used in Mexican, Central American and southwestern cuisines. They can be ground to create a powdered spice called *chilli*, or soaked in a liquid and then puréed for sauces or condiments. Drying radically alters the flavor of chiles, making them stronger and more pungent. Just as one type of fresh chile cannot be substituted for another without altering a dish's flavor, so too dried chiles cannot be substituted without flavor changes.

Choose dried chiles that are clean and unbroken, with some flexibility. Avoid any with white spots or a stale aroma.

Dried Chiles (top to bottom): California, Ancho, De Árbol

PROCEDURE FOR **ROASTING PEPPERS**

A PEPPER BY ANY OTHER NAME

The popularity of southwestern cuisine, hot condiments and salsas has brought with it a new appreciation and respect for chiles. Diners and chefs may find the names given to the various chiles confusing, however. Most chiles can be used either fresh or dried; drying changes not only the pepper's flavor, but also its name. Regional variations in chile names also add to the confusion. Several of the more frequently encountered chiles are listed here according to the names most commonly used for both their fresh and dried forms:

Fresh (Fresco)	Dried (Seco)
Anaheim	Mild red or California
Ancho	Ancho or pastilla
Chilaca	Pastilla or negro
Jalapeño	Chipotle (smoked)
Mirasol	Guajillo
New Mexico green	New Mexico red
New Mexico red	Chile Colorado
Pimento	Paprika
Poblano	Mulato

❶ Roast the pepper over an open flame until completely charred.

❷ Place the pepper in a plastic bag to sweat for a few minutes, then remove the burnt skin and rinse under running water.

TOMATILLOS

Tomatillos, also known as Mexican or husk tomatoes, grow on small, weedy bushes. They are bright green, about the size of a small tomato, and are covered with a thin, papery husk. They have a tart, lemony flavor and crisp, moist flesh. Although they are an important ingredient in southwestern and northern Mexican cuisines, tomatillos may not be readily available in other areas. Tomatillos can be used raw in salads, puréed for salsa or cooked in soups, stews or vegetable dishes.

Choose tomatillos whose husks are split but still look fresh. The skin should be plump, shiny and slightly sticky. They are available all year; their peak season is during the summer and fall.

Tomatillos

TOMATOES

Tomatoes (Fr. *tomate* or *pomme d'amour*; It. *pomodoro*) are available in a wide variety of colors and shapes. They vary from green (unripe) to golden yellow to ruby red; from tiny spheres (currant tomatoes) to huge, squat ovals (beefsteak). Some, such as the plum tomato, have lots of meaty flesh with only a few seeds; others, such as the slicing tomato, have lots of seeds and juice, but only a few meaty membranes. Older varieties such as Brandywine, German Green and Golden Queen are irregularly shaped and may be prone to cracking. All tomatoes have a similar flavor, but the levels of sweetness and acidity vary depending on the species, growing conditions and ripeness at harvest.

Older Tomato Varieties

Because tomatoes are highly perishable, they are usually harvested when mature but still green (unripe), then shipped to wholesalers who ripen them in temperature- and humidity-controlled rooms. The effect on flavor and texture is unfortunate.

Tomatoes are used widely in salads, soups, sauces and baked dishes. They are most often eaten raw but can be grilled, pickled, pan-fried, roasted or sautéed as a side dish.

Sun-Dried Tomatoes

Choose fresh tomatoes that are plump with a smooth, shiny skin. The color should be uniform and true for the variety. Tomatoes are available all year; most varieties have a summer peak season. Many canned tomato products are also available (for example, purée, paste, sauce or stewed whole). Sun-dried and air-dried tomatoes are available in crumbs, pieces, slivers or halves, dry or packed in oil. The dry-pack version can be soaked in oil or steeped in hot water to soften before use.

(clockwise from lower right) Pear, Cherry, Plum and Beefsteak Tomatoes

THREE TREASURES OF THE NEW WORLD

In lieu of many spices, golden treasures and precious gems, early Spanish explorers returned to Spain with items of much greater significance: tomatoes, potatoes and corn. Unfortunately for those who financed the voyagers, the value of this produce was not immediately appreciated.

The Spanish and the Italians hailed the tomato (whose name comes from the Aztec name *tomatl*) as an aphrodisiac—perhaps because of its resemblance to the human heart—when it arrived from the New World during the 16th century. But even though tomatoes soon became part of Spanish and Italian cuisines, most other Europeans, New World colonists and, later, Americans considered tomatoes poisonous. (There is some truth to this notion: tomato vines and leaves contain tomatine, an alkaloid that can cause health problems.) Thus for many years and in many societies, only the adventurous ate tomatoes.

The potato, first delivered to Europe from its native Peru by Francisco Pizarro in the 16th century, did not win wide acceptance in haute cuisine until Antoine-Augustin Parmentier (1737–1813), a French army pharmacist, induced King Louis XVI of France (who reigned from 1775 to 1793) to try one. The king and his courtiers liked them so much they even began wearing potato blossom boutonnières. Parmentier was ultimately honored for his starchy contribution to French cuisine by having several potato dishes named for him, such as *potage Parmentier* (potato soup). Not only did Parmentier lobby for the acceptance of the potato as a food fit for a king, he also prophesied that the potato would make starvation impossible. Potatoes ultimately did become a staple of many diets. But, sadly, the converse of Parmentier's prophecy came true during the Irish potato famine of 1846–1848, when a terrible blight destroyed the potato crop. Nearly 1.5 million people died, and an equal number emigrated to the United States. They brought with them a cuisine that incorporated potatoes; thus an appreciation of the common potato was reintroduced to its native land.

When returning from his second voyage to the New World, Columbus took corn with him. Called *mahiz* or *maize* by West Indian natives, corn had been a staple of Central American diets for at least 5000 years. Although Europeans did not actively shun corn as they did tomatoes and potatoes, corn never really caught on in most of Europe. (As with another famous New World import, corn's origin was mistakenly attributed by the British, Dutch, Germans and Russians to Turkey. They called corn "Turkish wheat"; the Turks simply called it "foreign grain.") Grown for human consumption mostly in Italy, Spain and southwestern France, corn was and still is usually eaten ground and boiled as polenta. But despite an unenthusiastic European reception, corn's popularity quickly spread well beyond Europe: Within 50 years of Columbus's journey, corn was being cultivated in lands as distant from the New World as China, India and sub-Saharan Africa.

PROCEDURE FOR **PREPARING TOMATO CONCASSÉE**

① With a paring knife, mark an X on the bottom of the tomato just deep enough to penetrate the skin.

② Blanch the tomato in boiling water for 20 seconds; refresh in ice water.

③ Using a paring knife, cut out the core and peel the tomato.

④ Cut the tomato in half horizontally and squeeze out the seeds and juice.

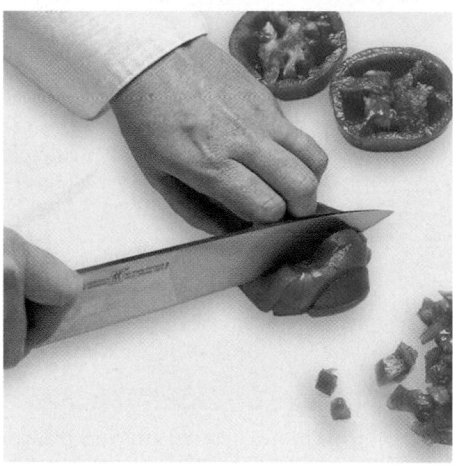

⑤ Chop or dice the tomato as desired for the recipe.

Gourds and Squashes

The *Cucurbitaceae* or gourd family includes almost 750 species; its members are found in warm regions worldwide. Gourds are characterized by large, complex root systems with quick-growing, trailing vines and large leaves. Their flowers are often attractive and edible. Although some members of the gourd family originated in Africa, chayotes and most squashes are native to the Americas.

CHAYOTES

The chayote, also known as the merliton or vegetable pear, is a food staple throughout Central America. The vine bears slightly lumpy, pear-shaped fruits with a smooth, light green skin and a paler green flesh. There is a single white, edible seed in the center. Chayotes are starchy and very bland and are usually combined with more flavorful ingredients. They may be eaten raw, but their flavor and texture benefit from roasting, steaming, sautéing or grilling.

Choose chayotes that have well-colored skin with few ridges. Avoid those with very soft spots or bruises. Their peak season is the late fall and winter.

Chayotes

CUCUMBERS

Cucumbers can be divided into two categories: pickling and slicing. The two types are not interchangeable. Pickling cucumbers include the cornichon, dill and gherkin. They are recognizable by their sharp black or white spines and are quite bitter when raw. Slicing cucumbers include the burpless, the seedless English (or hothouse), the lemon (which is round and yellow) and the common green market cucumber. Most have relatively thin skins and may be marketed with a wax coating to prevent moisture loss and improve appearance. Waxed skins should be peeled. All cucumbers are valued for their refreshing cool taste and astringency. Slicing cucumbers are usually served raw, in salads or mixed with yogurt and dill or mint as a side dish, especially for spicy dishes. Pickling cucumbers are generally served pickled, with no further processing.

Choose cucumbers that are firm but not hard. Avoid those that are limp or yellowed or have soft spots. The common varieties are available all year, although peak season is from April through October.

(from left to right) Pickling, Green and Hothouse Cucumbers

PROCEDURE FOR **SEEDING A CUCUMBER**

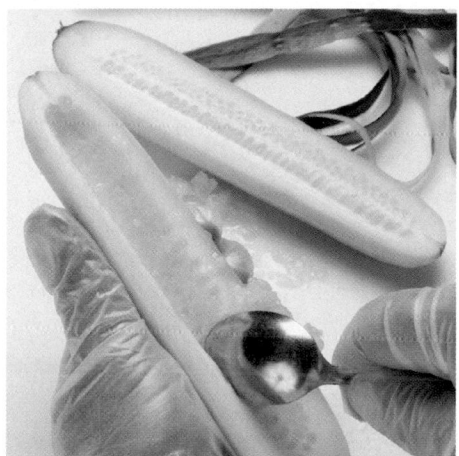

Remove the seeds from a cucumber by slicing it in half lengthwise, then scrape out the seeds with a spoon or melon ball cutter.

PROCEDURE FOR **MAKING DECORATIVE CUCUMBER SLICES**

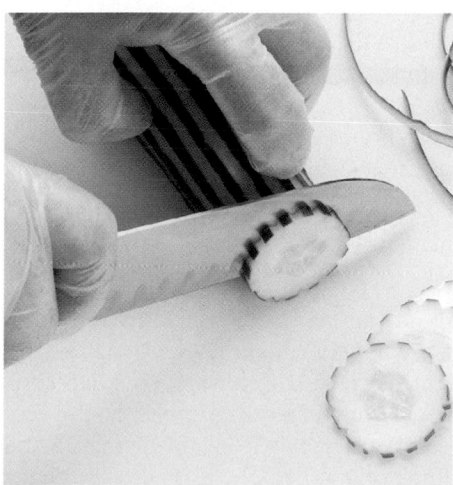

Use a zester or fork to score the rind of a cucumber before slicing.

Acorn

Butternut

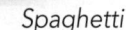

SQUASHES

Squashes are the fleshy fruits of a large number of plants in the gourd family. Many varieties are available in a range of colors, shapes and sizes. Squashes can be classified as winter or summer based on their peak season and skin type. All squashes have a center cavity filled with many seeds, although in winter varieties the cavity is more pronounced. Squash blossoms are also edible; they may be added to salads raw, dipped in batter and deep-fried or filled with cheese or meat and baked.

Spaghetti

Choose squashes with unbroken skins and good color for the variety. Avoid any squash with soft, moist spots.

Pumpkin

Winter Squashes

Winter squashes include the acorn, butternut, Hubbard, pumpkin and spaghetti varieties. They have hard skins (shells) and seeds, neither of which is generally eaten. The flesh, which may be removed from the shell before or after cooking, tends to be sweeter and more strongly flavored than that of summer squash. Winter squashes are rarely used raw; they can be baked, steamed or sautéed. Most winter squashes can also be puréed for soups or pie fillings. Their peak season is October through March.

Summer Squashes

Summer squashes include the pattypan, yellow crookneck and zucchini varieties. They have soft edible skins and seeds that are generally not removed before cooking. Most summer squashes may be eaten raw, but are also suitable for grilling, sautéing, steaming or baking. Although summer squashes are now available all year, their peak season is April through September.

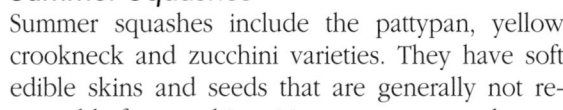

Zucchini

Yellow Crookneck

Greens

The term *greens* refers to a variety of leafy green vegetables that may be served raw, but are usually cooked. Greens have long been used in the cuisines of India, Asia and the Mediterranean and are an important part of regional cuisine in the southern United States. Most have strong, spicy flavors. The milder varieties of greens that are almost always eaten raw include the lettuces discussed in Chapter 24, Salads and Salad Dressings.

Greens have an extremely high water content, which means that cooking causes drastic shrinkage. As a general rule, allow 8 ounces (240 grams) per portion before cooking.

Choose young, tender greens with good color and no limpness. Avoid greens with dry-looking stems or yellow leaves. Most greens are available fresh all year, especially from November through June. The more popular greens are also available canned or frozen.

COLLARDS

Collard greens, often simply referred to as collards, are a type of cabbage with loose, leafy heads of bright green leaves. Collards have a sharp, tangy flavor and look like a cross between mustard greens and kale. Considered a staple ingredient in poverty cooking of the American South, collards are typically slow-simmered with ham hocks or bacon until very tender, then served with their cooking liquid. Collards are high in iron and vitamins A and C and are best if picked young or after the first frost of autumn.

Collard Greens

MUSTARD

Mustard, a member of the cabbage family, was brought to America by early European immigrants. Mustard has large, dark green leaves with frilly edges. It is known for its assertive, bitter flavor. Mustard greens can be served raw in salads or used as garnish. They can also be cooked, often with white wine, vinegar and herbs.

Choose crisp, bright green leaves without discoloration.

Mustard

SORREL

Sorrel is an abundant and rather ordinary wild member of the buckwheat family. Its tartness and sour flavor are used in soups and sauces and to accent other vegetables. It is particularly good with fatty fish or rich meats. Sorrel leaves naturally become the texture of a purée after only a few minutes of moist-heat cooking.

Choose leaves that are fully formed, with no yellow blemishes.

Sorrel

SPINACH

Spinach (Fr. *épinard*) is a versatile green that grows rapidly in cool climates. It has smooth, bright green leaves attached to thin stems. Spinach may be eaten raw in salads, cooked by almost any moist-heat method, microwaved or sautéed. It can be used in stuffings, baked or creamed dishes, soups or stews. Spinach grows in sandy soil and must be rinsed repeatedly in cold water to remove all traces of grit from the leaves. It bruises easily and should be handled gently during washing. Stems and large midribs should be removed.

Choose bunches with crisp, tender, deep green leaves; avoid yellow leaves or those with blemishes.

Spinach

SWISS CHARD

Chard—the reference to "Swiss" is inexplicable—is a type of beet that does not produce a tuberous root. It is used for its wide, flat, dark green leaves. Chard can be steamed, sautéed or used in soups. Its tart, spinachlike flavor blends well with sweet ingredients such as fruit.

Choose leaves that are crisp, with some curliness or savoying. Ribs should be an unblemished white or red.

TURNIP GREENS

The leaves of the turnip root have a pleasantly bitter flavor, similar to peppery mustard greens. The dark green leaves are long, slender and deeply indented. Turnip greens are best eaten steamed, sautéed, baked or microwaved.

Turnip Greens

Swiss Chard

Mushrooms and Truffles

MUSHROOMS

Mushrooms (Fr. *champignons*; It. *funghi*) are members of a broad category of plants known as fungi. (Fungi have no seeds, stems or flowers; they reproduce through spores.) Mushrooms have a stalk with an umbrellalike top. Although not actually a vegetable, mushrooms are used and served in much the same manner as vegetables.

Several types of cultivated mushroom are available. They include the common (or white), shiitake, crimini (also known as the Italian brown), straw, enokidake (also called enoki) and cloud ear (also known as wood ear or Chinese black). Button

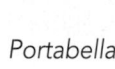

Portabella

Pom Pom Blanc

Porcini (cèpe or cep)

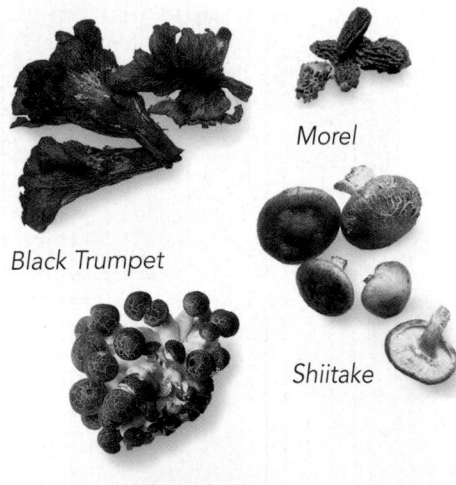

Black Trumpet

Morel

Shiitake

Clam Shell

Hen of the Woods

Oyster

White

Enokidake

mushrooms are the smallest, most immature form of the common mushroom. The largest cultivated mushroom is the portabella, which is actually an overgrown crimini; it can grow up to 6 inches (15 centimeters) in diameter.

Many wild mushrooms are gathered and sold by specialty purveyors. Because wild mushroom spores are spread around the world by air currents, the same item may be found in several areas, each with a different common name. Wild mushrooms have a stronger earthy or nutty flavor than cultivated mushrooms and should generally be cooked before eating.

Mushrooms, whether cultivated or gathered from the wild, are available fresh, canned or dried. Because mushrooms are composed of up to 80 percent water, dried products are often the most economical, even though they may cost hundreds of dollars per pound. Dried mushrooms can be stored in a cool, dry place for months. When needed, they are rehydrated by soaking in warm water until soft, approximately 10 to 20 minutes.

Choose fresh mushrooms that are clean, without soft or moist spots or blemishes. Fresh cultivated mushrooms are generally available all year; fresh wild mushrooms are available seasonally, usually during the summer and fall. Cultivated mushrooms with exposed gills (the ridges on the underside of the umbrellalike top) are old and should be avoided. Fresh mushrooms can be refrigerated in an open container for up to 5 days. Normally, it is not necessary to peel mushrooms; if they are dirty, they should be quickly rinsed (not soaked) in cool water just before use.

PROCEDURE FOR **FLUTING MUSHROOMS**

Use the sharp edge of a straight paring knife to cut thin curves into the mushroom cap. Fluted mushrooms may be baked or poached, then used as garnish.

Black Truffles

TRUFFLES

Truffles are actually tubers that grow near the roots of oak or beech trees. They can be cultivated only to the extent that oak groves are planted to encourage truffle growth. The two principal varieties are the Périgord (black) and the Piedmontese (white). Fresh truffles are

THE OLIVE

Olives (*Olea europaea*) are the fruit of a tree native to the Mediterranean area. Green olives are those harvested unripened; black olives are fully ripened. The raw fruit is inedibly bitter and must be washed, soaked and cured or pickled before eating. Green olives should have a smooth, tight skin. Ripe olives will be glossy but softer, with a slightly wrinkled skin. Many varieties and flavors are available, from the tiny black French niçoise to the large purplish Greek Kalamata. Ripe black olives are packaged in a range of seven sizes, from small to supercolossal. Unripe green olives are available in 11 sizes, from subpetite to supercolossal. Both black and green olives are available whole (with the pit), pitted, sliced, halved or in pieces. Pitted green olives are often stuffed with strips of pimento, jalapeño pepper, almonds or other foods for flavor and appearance.

Olives are used as a finger food for snacks or hors d'oeuvre, or added to salads or pasta. They may even be cooked in breads, soups, sauces, stews and casseroles. A paste made of minced ripe olives, known as tapenade, is used as a dip or condiment.

Jumbo Spanish Olives

Ripe California Olives

Kalamata Olives

Niçoise Olives

gathered in the fall and are rarely marketed outside their locale. Truffles, especially white ones, have a strong aroma and flavor, requiring only a small amount to add their special flavor to soups, sauces, pasta and other items. Black truffles are often used as a garnish or to flavor pâtés, terrines or egg dishes. Because fresh imported truffles can cost several hundred dollars per pound, most kitchens purchase truffles canned, dried or processed.

Onions

Onions are strongly flavored, aromatic members of the lily family. Most have edible grasslike or tubular leaves. Almost every culture incorporates them into its cuisine as a vegetable and for flavoring.

BULB ONIONS

Common or bulb onions (Fr. *oignons*) may be white, yellow (Bermuda or Spanish) or red (purple). Medium-sized yellow and white onions are the most strongly flavored. Larger onions tend to be sweeter and milder. Widely used as a flavoring ingredient, onions are indispensable in mirepoix. Onions are also prepared as a side dish by deep-frying, roasting, grilling, steaming or boiling.

Pearl onions are small, about ½ inch (1.25 centimeters) in diameter, with yellow or white skins. They have a mild flavor and can be grilled, boiled, roasted or sautéed whole as a side dish, or used in soups or stews.

Sweet onion varieties include the Vidalia, Maui, Walla-Walla, Texas 1015 SuperSweet and OSO Sweet. These bulb onions have a higher water content, more sugar and less sulfuric compounds than other onions. They are best for eating raw, making them good choices for sandwiches, salads, hamburgers and the like. Cooking destroys much of their perceived sweetness and special flavor. Each sweet onion variety is available for a brief period from January through August. All have a very short shelf life and should not be stored more than a few weeks.

Choose onions that are firm and dry and feel heavy. The outer skins should be dry and brittle. Avoid onions that have begun to sprout. Store onions in a cool, dry, well-ventilated area. Do not refrigerate onions until they are cut. With the exception of sweet onions, most varieties are available all year.

Red Onion
Yellow Onion
Shallots
Pearl Onion

White Onions
Walla-Walla Sweet Onions

Garlic

GARLIC

Garlic (Fr. *ail*; It. *aglio*; Sp. *ajo*) is also used in almost all the world's cuisines. A head of garlic is composed of many small cloves. Each clove is wrapped in a thin husk or peel; the entire head is encased in several thin layers of papery husk. Of the three hundred or so types of garlic known, only three are commercially significant. The most common is pure white, with a sharp flavor. A Mexican variety is pale pink and more strongly flavored. Elephant garlic is apple-sized and particularly mild. Black garlic is not a variety, but the result of a detailed heating and aging process applied to common white garlic. Long used in Korea for its purported health benefits, black garlic is chewy, with a mild, sweet, molasses-like flavor. Although whole bulbs can be baked or roasted, garlic is most often separated into cloves, peeled, sliced, minced or crushed and used to flavor a wide variety of dishes. When using garlic, remember that the more finely the cloves are crushed, the stronger the flavor will be. Cooking reduces garlic's pungency; the longer it is cooked, the milder it becomes.

Choose firm, dry bulbs with tightly closed cloves and smooth skins. Avoid bulbs with green sprouts. Store fresh garlic in a cool, well-ventilated place; do not refrigerate. Fresh garlic is available all year. Jars of processed and pickled garlic products are also available. Scapes are the vibrant green aboveground tendril of the garlic plant. This thin, soft shoot appears before the garlic bulb is fully developed and is cut away to allow the bulb to mature properly. Scapes can be used cooked or uncooked; their flavor and aroma is similar to garlic, but mild, fresh and clean. Fresh scapes are available only during a limited season in late spring.

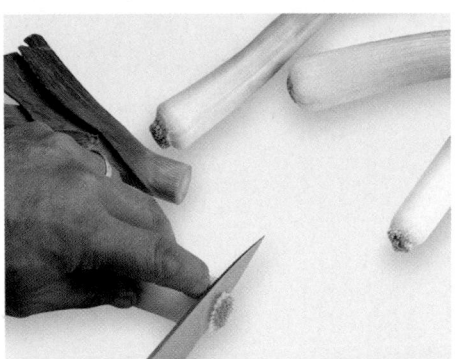

Leeks

LEEKS

Leeks (Fr. *poireaux*) look like large, overgrown scallions with a fat white tip and wide green leaves. Their flavor is sweeter and stronger than scallions, but milder than common bulb onions. Leeks must be carefully washed to remove the sandy soil that gets between the leaves. Leeks can be baked, braised or grilled as a side dish, or used to season stocks, soups or sauces.

Choose leeks that are firm, with stiff roots and stems. Avoid those with dry leaves, soft spots or browning. Leeks are available all year.

PROCEDURE FOR **CLEANING LEEKS**

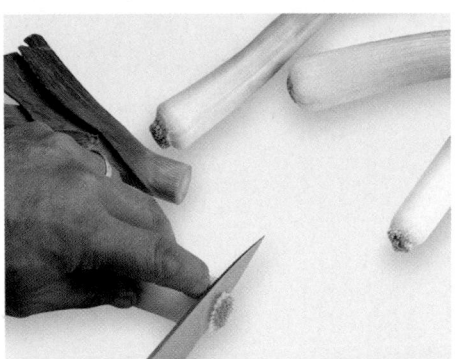

❶ Trim the root end from the leek.

❷ Cut away the dark green top and slice the white portion in half lengthwise.

❸ Rinse the leek thoroughly under running water to remove soil.

Scallions

SCALLIONS

Scallions, also known as green onions or bunch onions, are the immature green stalks of bulb onions. The leaves are bright green with either a long and slender or slightly bulbous white base. Green onions are used in stir-fries and as a flavoring in other dishes. The green tops can also be sliced in small rings and used as a garnish.

Choose scallions with bright green tops and clean white bulbs. Avoid those with limp or slimy leaves. Scallions are available all year; their peak season is the summer.

SHALLOTS

Shallots (Fr. *échalotes*) are shaped like small bulb onions with one flat side. When peeled, a shallot separates into multiple cloves, similar to garlic. They have a mild, yet rich and complex flavor. Shallots are the basis of many classic sauces and meat preparations; they can also be sautéed or baked as a side dish.

Choose shallots that are plump and well shaped. Avoid those that appear dry or have sprouted. Store shallots in a cool, dry, unrefrigerated place. Shallots are available all year.

Shallots

Pods and Seeds

Pod and seed vegetables include corn, legumes and okra. They are grouped together here because the parts consumed are all the seeds of their respective plants. In some cases, only the seeds are eaten; in others, the pod containing the seeds is eaten as well. Seeds are generally higher in protein and carbohydrates (starch and fiber) than other vegetables.

CORN

Sweet corn (Fr. *maïs*; Sp. *maíz*) is actually a grain, a type of grass. Corn kernels, like peas, are plant seeds. (Dried corn products are discussed in Chapter 22, Potatoes, Grains and Pasta.) The kernels, which may be white or yellow, are attached to a woody, inedible cob. The cob is encased by strands of hairlike fibers called silks and covered in layers of thin leaves called husks. Shuck the ears (remove the silks and husks) before cooking; the husks may be left on for roasting or grilling. Shucked ears can be grilled, boiled, microwaved or steamed. The kernels can be cut off of the cob before or after cooking. Corn on the cob is available fresh or frozen; corn kernels are available canned or frozen.

Choose freshly picked ears with firm, small kernels. Avoid those with mold or decay at the tip of the cob or brownish silks. Summer is the peak season for fresh corn. Seek out the freshest corn on the cob and serve it promptly because its sugar turns to starch once it is picked.

Yellow and White Corn

PROCEDURE FOR **CUTTING KERNELS OFF EARS OF CORN**

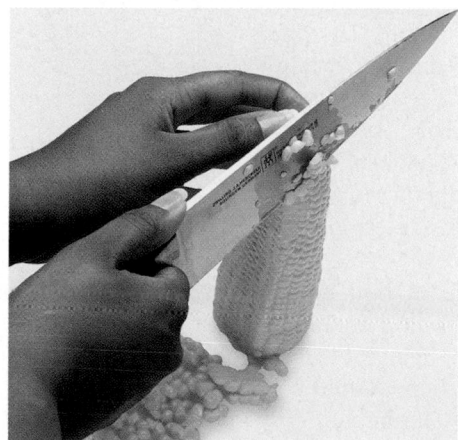

Hold the cob upright and use a chef's knife to slice off the kernels.

LEGUMES

Beans (Fr. *haricots*; It. *fagioli*) and peas (Fr. *pois*) are members of the legume family, a large group of vegetables with double-seamed pods containing a single row of seeds. Of the hundreds of known varieties of beans, some are used for their edible pods, others for shelling fresh and some only for their dried seeds. Dried beans are actually several varieties of seeds or peas left in the pod until mature, then shelled and dried.

Fava Beans

Fresh Beans

Beans used for their edible pods, commonly referred to as green beans, string beans, runner beans or snap beans, are picked when immature. Except for the stem, the entire pod can be eaten. This category includes the American green bean, the yellow wax bean and the French haricot vert, a long, slender pod with an intense flavor and tender texture. Any strings along the pod's seams should be pulled off before cooking. Beans may be left whole, cut lengthwise into thin slivers (referred to as French cut) or cut crosswise on the diagonal.

Green Beans

Shelling beans are those grown primarily for the edible seeds inside the pod. Common examples are flageolets, lima beans and fava (broad) beans. Their tough pods are not usually eaten.

All beans can be prepared by steaming, microwaving or sautéing. They can be added to soups or stews, and they blend well with a variety of flavors, from coconut milk to garlic and olive oil. Cooked beans can be chilled and served as a salad or crudité.

Choose beans that have a bright color without brown or soft spots. Large pods may be tough or bitter. The peak season for fresh beans is from April through December. Most bean varieties are available frozen or canned, including pickled and seasoned products.

Haricots Verts

Dried Beans

Black Beans

Anthropologists report that for thousands of years, cultures worldwide have preserved some members of the legume family by drying. Common dried beans include kidney beans, pinto beans, chickpeas, lentils, black beans, black-eyed peas and split green peas. Shape is the clearest distinction among these products: Beans are oval or kidney-shaped; lentils are small, flat disks; peas are round.

Black-Eyed Peas

Beans and peas destined for drying are left on the vine until they are fully matured and just beginning to dry. They are then harvested, shelled and quickly dried with warm air currents. Some dried legumes are sold split, which means the skin is removed, causing the seed's two halves to separate.

Red Kidney Beans

Most dried beans need to be soaked in water before cooking. Soaking softens and rehydrates the beans, thus reducing cooking time. Lentils and split peas generally do not require soaking, however, and will cook faster than beans. After soaking, beans are most often simmered or baked in a liquid until soft and tender. One type may be substituted for another in most recipes, although variations in color, starch content and flavor should be considered.

Lentils

Pinto Beans

Dried beans and peas are available in bulk or in 1-pound (450-gram) poly bags. They should be stored in a cool, dry place, but not refrigerated. Many of these beans are also available fully cooked, then canned or frozen. Some dried beans may be fermented or processed into flour, oil or bean curd.

Great Northern Beans

PROCEDURE FOR **SOAKING DRIED BEANS**

❶ Pick through the dried beans and remove any grit, pebbles or debris.

❷ Place the beans in a bowl and cover with cold water; remove any skins or other items that float to the surface.

③ Drain the beans in a colander, then rinse under cold running water.

④ Return the beans to a bowl and cover with fresh cold water. Allow approximately 3 cups (750 milliliters) water for each cup of beans.

⑤ Soak the beans in the cold water for the time specified in the recipe, usually several hours or overnight. Drain through a colander, discarding the water.

PROCEDURE FOR QUICK-SOAKING DRIED BEANS

The soaking procedure can be accelerated by the following technique:

① Rinse and pick through the beans.

② Place the beans in a saucepan and add enough cool water to cover them by 2 inches (5 centimeters).

③ Bring to a boil and simmer for 2 minutes.

④ Remove from the heat, cover and soak for 1 hour.

⑤ Drain and discard the soaking liquid. Proceed with the recipe.

Fresh Shelling Peas

Of the shelling peas that are prepared fresh, the most common are green garden peas (English peas) and the French petit pois. Because they lose flavor rapidly after harvest, most shelling peas are sold frozen or canned. Shelling peas have a delicate, sweet flavor best presented by simply steaming until tender but still al dente. Peas may also be braised with rich meats such as ham or used in soups. Cooked peas are attractive in salads or as garnish.

Fresh Shelling Peas

Choose small fresh pea pods that are plump and moist. Peak season is April and May.

Fresh green **soybeans (soya)** (Ja. *edamame*) are becoming a popular shelling pea in the United States. When picked before maturity, soybeans have a light green, fuzzy pod and a tender, sweet pea. Fresh green soybeans are delicious steamed in the pod, then chilled, popped open and eaten out of hand as a snack. Often served in sushi restaurants or with other Asian cuisines, they are extremely high in protein, fiber and phytochemicals. When allowed to mature and then prepared like other dried beans, however, soybeans become extremely tough, hard to digest and bitter. Mature soybeans are best used for processing into oil, tofu, sauce and other foodstuffs.

Soybeans

Edible Pea Pods

Snow peas, also known as Chinese pea pods, are a common variety of edible pea pod. They are flat and have only a few very small green peas. Snow peas have a string along their seams that can be removed by holding the leafy stem and pulling from end to end. The pods can be eaten raw, lightly blanched or steamed, or stir-fried.

Snow Peas

Another variety of edible pea pod is the sugar snap pea, a cross between the garden pea and snow pea, which was developed during the late 1970s. They are plump, juicy pods filled with small, tender peas. The entire pod is eaten; do not shell the peas before cooking.

Choose pea pods that are firm, bright green and crisp. Avoid those with brown spots or a shriveled appearance. Pea pods are available all year; their peak season is in March and April.

Pea shoots are the delicate tendrils that form before the plant bears pods. In Chinese cuisine, the shoots are harvested and stir-fried like spinach or other leafy greens.

Pea Shoots

OKRA

Okra, a common ingredient in African and Arab cuisines, was brought to the United States by slaves and French settlers. It is now integral to Creole, Cajun, southern and southwestern cuisines. Its mild flavor is similar to that of asparagus. Okra is not eaten raw; it is best pickled,

Okra

boiled, steamed or deep-fried. Okra develops a gelatinous texture when cooked for long periods, so it is used to thicken gumbos and stews. To avoid the slimy texture some find objectionable, do not wash okra until ready to cook, then trim the stem end only. Cook okra in stainless steel because other metals cause discoloration.

Choose small to medium pods (1½ to 2 inches [3.75 to 5 centimeters]) that are deep green, without soft spots. Pale spears with stiff tips tend to be tough. Okra's peak season is from June through September. Frozen okra is widely available.

Roots and Tubers

Taproots (more commonly referred to as roots) are single roots that extend deep into the soil to supply the aboveground plant with nutrients. Tubers are fat underground stems. Most roots and tubers can be used interchangeably. All store well at cool temperatures, without refrigeration. Potatoes, the most popular tuber, are discussed in Chapter 22, Potatoes, Grains and Pasta.

BEETS

Although records suggest that they were first eaten in ancient Greece, beets are most often associated with the colder northern climates, where they grow for most of the year. Beets can be boiled, then peeled and used in salads, soups or baked dishes. Choose small to medium-sized beets that are firm, with smooth skins. Avoid those with hairy root tips, as they may be tough. Beets are available all year; their peak season is March to October.

Carrots

Celery Root

Sunchokes

Beets

CARROTS

Carrots (Fr. *carottes*), among the most versatile of vegetables, are large taproots. Although several kinds exist, the Imperator is the most common. It is long and pointed, with a medium to dark orange color and a mild, sweet flavor. Carrots can be cut into a variety of shapes and eaten raw, used for a mirepoix or prepared by moist-heat cooking methods, grilling, microwaving or roasting. They are also grated and used in baked goods, particularly cakes and muffins.

Choose firm carrots that are smooth and well shaped, with a bright orange color. If the tops are still attached, they should be fresh-looking and bright green. Carrots are available all year.

CELERY ROOT

Celery root, also known as celeriac, is a large, round root, long popular in northern European cuisines. It is a different plant from stalk celery, and its stalks and leaves are not eaten. Celery root has a knobby brown exterior; a creamy white, crunchy flesh; and a mild, celerylike flavor. Its thick outer skin must be peeled away; the flesh is then cut as desired. Often eaten raw, celery root can be baked, steamed or boiled. It is used in soups, stews or salads and goes well with game and rich meats. Raw celery root may be placed in acidulated water to prevent browning.

Choose small to medium-sized roots that are firm and relatively clean, with a pungent smell. Their peak season is October through April.

JERUSALEM ARTICHOKE

Despite their name, Jerusalem artichokes are actually tubers from a variety of sunflower unrelated to artichokes. Consequently, growers are now marketing these vegetables as *sunchokes*. Their lumpy brown skin is usually peeled away (even though it is edible) to reveal a crisp, white interior with a slightly nutty flavor. Although they may be eaten raw, it is preferable to cook them before serving to make them easier to digest. Jerusalem artichokes are eaten chopped or grated into salads, or boiled or steamed for a side dish or soup.

JICAMA

Jicama is actually a legume that grows underground as a tuber. It is becoming increasingly popular because of its sweet, moist flavor; crisp texture; low calorie content; and long shelf life. After its thick brown skin is cut away, the crisp, moist white flesh can be cut as desired. Jicama is often eaten raw in salads, with salsa or as a crudité. It is also used in stir-fried dishes.

Choose firm, well-shaped jicamas that are free of blemishes. Size is not an indication of quality or maturity. They are available all year; their peak season is January through May.

Jicama   *Parsnips*

PARSNIPS

Parsnips (Fr. *panais*) are taproots that look and taste like white carrots and have the texture of sweet potatoes. Parsnips should be 5 to 10 inches (12.5 to 25 centimeters) in length, with smooth skins and tapering tips. Parsnips, peeled like carrots, can be eaten raw or cooked by almost any method. When steamed until very soft, they can be mashed like potatoes.

Choose small to medium-sized parsnips that are firm, smooth and well shaped; avoid large, woody ones. Parsnips are available all year; their peak season is December through April.

RADISHES

Radishes (Fr. *radis*) are used for their peppery flavor and crisp texture. Radishes are available in many colors, including white, black and all shades of red; most have a creamy to pure white interior. Asian radishes, known as daikons, produce roots 2 to 4 inches (5 to 10 centimeters) in diameter and 6 to 20 inches (15 to 20 centimeters) long. Radishes can be steamed or stir-fried, but most often are eaten raw or in salads or used as garnish. Radish leaves can be used in salads or cooked as greens.

Choose radishes that are firm, not limp. Their interior should be neither dry nor hollow. Radishes are available all year.

Daikon

Red Radishes

PROCEDURE FOR **MAKING RADISH ROSETTES**

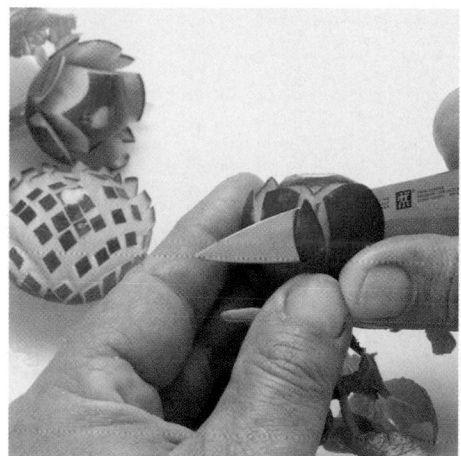

Using a straight paring knife, make parallel horizontal and vertical cuts three quarters of the way through the root end of a cleaned radish.

RUTABAGAS

Rutabagas are a root vegetable and a member of the cabbage family. Their skin is purple to yellow, and they have yellow flesh with a distinctive starchy, cabbagelike flavor. Rutabagas and turnips are similar in flavor and texture when cooked and may be used interchangeably. Rutabaga leaves are not eaten. Rutabagas should be peeled with a vegetable peeler

Rutabagas

Turnips

Fresh Water Chestnuts

cellulose a complex carbohydrate found in the cell wall of plants; it is edible but indigestible by humans

or chef's knife, then cut into quarters, slices or cubes. They are often baked, boiled and then puréed, or sliced and sautéed. They are especially flavorful when seasoned with caraway seeds, dill or lemon juice.

Choose small to medium-sized rutabagas that are smooth and firm and feel heavy. Their peak season is January through March.

TURNIPS

Also a root vegetable from the cabbage family, turnips have white skin with a rosy-red or purple blush and a white interior. Their flavor, similar to that of a radish, can be rather hot. Turnips should be peeled, then diced, sliced or julienned for cooking. They may be baked or cooked with moist-heat cooking methods, and are often puréed like potatoes.

Choose small to medium-sized turnips that have smooth skin and feel heavy. They should be firm, not rubbery or limp. Any attached leaves should be bright green and tender. Spring is their peak season.

WATER CHESTNUTS

Water chestnuts are the tuber of an Asian plant that thrives in water. The brownish-black skin is peeled away to reveal a moist, crisp, white interior, which can be eaten raw or cooked. When cooked, water chestnuts retain their crunchy texture, making them a popular addition to stir-fried dishes. They are also used in salads and casseroles or wrapped in bacon for rumaki hors d'oeuvre.

Stalks

Stalk vegetables are plant stems with a high percentage of **cellulose** fiber. These vegetables should be picked while still young and tender. Tough fibers should be trimmed before cooking.

ARTICHOKES

Artichokes (Fr. *artichauts*) are the immature flowers of a thistle plant introduced to America by Italian and Spanish settlers. Young, tender globe artichokes can be cooked whole, but more mature plants need to have the fuzzy center (known as the choke) removed first. Whole artichokes can be simmered, steamed or microwaved; they are often served with lemon juice, garlic butter or hollandaise sauce. The heart may be cooked separately, then served in salads, puréed as a filling or served as a side dish. Artichoke hearts and leafless artichoke bottoms are both available canned.

Choose fresh artichokes with tight, compact heads that feel heavy. Their color should be solid green to gray-green. Brown spots on the surface caused by frost are harmless. Artichokes' peak season is March through May.

Artichokes

PROCEDURE FOR **PREPARING FRESH ARTICHOKES**

❶ Using kitchen shears or scissors, trim the barbs from the large outer leaves of the artichoke.

❷ With a chef's knife, cut away the stem and the top of the artichoke. Steam or boil the artichoke as desired.

PROCEDURE FOR **CLEANING ARTICHOKE HEARTS**

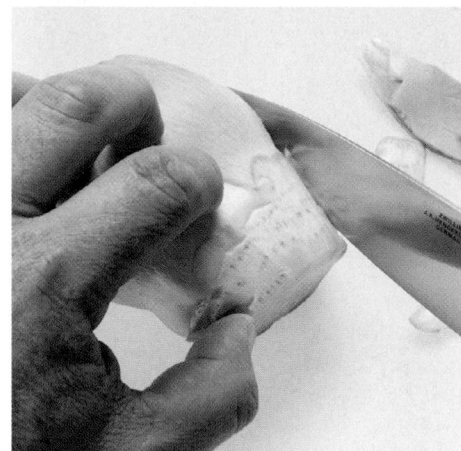

❶ Cut off the stem and the outer leaves from the artichoke.

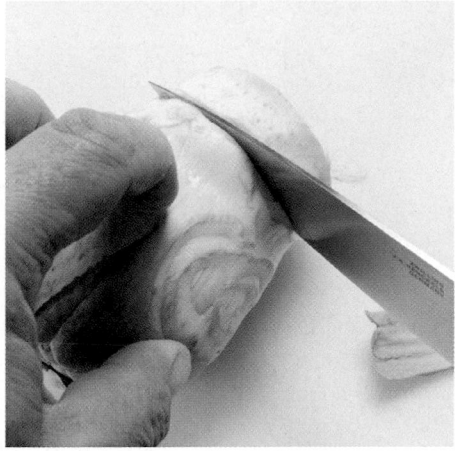

❷ Trim the inner stem from the base with a chef's knife.

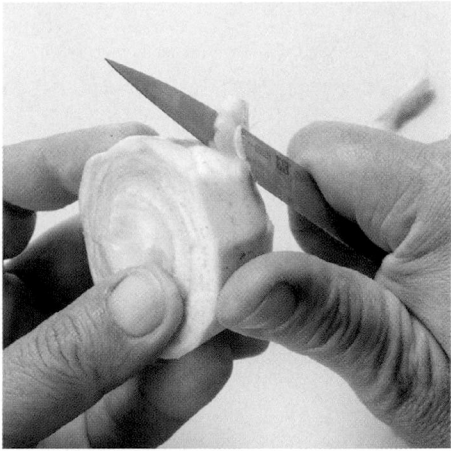

❸ Using a paring knife, trim the edges into a neat cup with no tough leaves remaining.

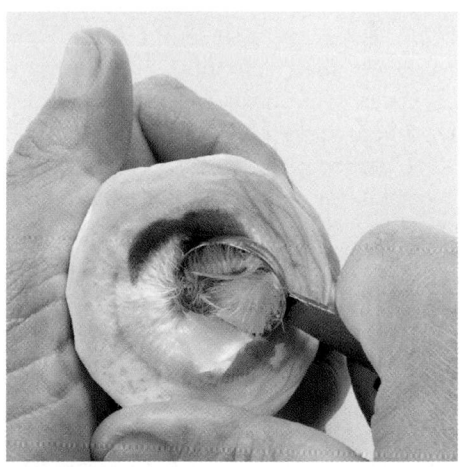

❹ Scoop out the fuzzy choke with a melon ball cutter.

❺ The cleaned artichoke bottoms are ready to cook.

ASPARAGUS

Asparagus (Fr. *aspèrges*), a member of the lily family, has bright green spears with a ruffle of tiny leaves at the tip. Larger spears tend to be tough and woody, but can be used in soups or for purée. Asparagus is eaten raw or steamed briefly, stir-fried, microwaved or grilled. Fresh spring asparagus is excellent with nothing more than lemon juice or clarified butter; asparagus with hollandaise sauce is a classic preparation.

Asparagus

Choose firm, plump spears with tightly closed tips and a bright green color running the full length of the spear. Asparagus should be stored refrigerated at 40°F (4°C), upright in ½ inch (1.25 centimeters) of water or with the ends wrapped in moist paper toweling. The stalks should not be washed until just before use. Canned and frozen asparagus are also available. Peak season is March through June.

A European variety of white asparagus is sometimes available fresh, or readily available canned. It has a milder flavor and soft, tender texture. It is produced by covering the stalks

Using a vegetable peeler to remove the tough outer skin from large asparagus spears.

with soil as they grow; this prevents sunlight from reaching the plant and retards the development of chlorophyll.

BAMBOO SHOOTS

Stripped of their tough brown outer skins, the tender young shoots of certain varieties of bamboo are edible. They make excellent additions to stir-fried dishes or can be served like asparagus. Although fresh shoots are available in Asia, canned peeled shoots packed in brine or water are more common in the United States. Canned shoots should be rinsed well before use.

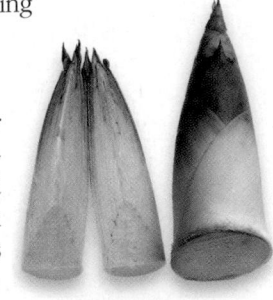

Fresh Bamboo Shoots

CELERY

Once a medicinal herb, stalk celery (Fr. *céleri*) is now a common sight in kitchens worldwide. Stalk celery is pale green with stringy curved stalks. Often eaten raw in salads or as a snack, it can be braised or steamed as a side dish. Celery is also a mirepoix component.

Choose stalks that are crisp, without any sign of dryness. Celery is available all year.

Celery

FENNEL

Fennel (Fr. *fenouil*, It. *finocchio*) is a Mediterranean favorite used for thousands of years as a vegetable (the bulb), an herb (the leaves) and a spice (the seeds). The bulb (often incorrectly referred to as sweet anise) has short, tight, overlapping celerylike stalks with feathery leaves. The flavor is similar to that of anise or licorice, becoming milder when cooked. Fennel bulbs may be eaten raw or grilled, steamed, sautéed, baked or microwaved.

Choose a fairly large, bright white bulb on which the cut edges appear fresh, without dryness or browning. The bulb should be compact, not spreading. Fresh fennel's peak season is September through May.

Fennel

HEARTS OF PALM

Hearts of palm are the tender interiors of stems from cabbage palm trees. They are ivory-colored and slender, with a delicate flavor similar to that of asparagus. Fresh hearts of palm are sometimes available in Florida (where they are grown); canned ones are widely available everywhere. Hearts of palm are generally used uncooked in salads or marinated in herb vinaigrette.

Hearts of Palm

NOPALES

The pads of a prickly pear cactus can be prepared as a vegetable known as nopales. Cactus pads have a flavor similar to that of green bell peppers. Their texture tends to be rather gelatinous or mucilaginous, making them good for stews or sauces. To prepare fresh nopales, hold the pad with tongs and cut off the thorns and "eyes" with a sharp knife or vegetable peeler. Trim off the edge all the way around. Slice the pad into julienne strips or cubes. The pieces can be boiled or steamed and served hot, or chilled and added to salads. Nopales can also be sautéed with onions, peppers and seasonings for a side dish or added to southwestern-style casseroles.

Some cultivated varieties have thin, thornless pads. Choose pads that are stiff and heavy without blemishes. They should not be dry or soggy. Fresh cactus pads are available all year, with peak season in the late spring. Canned and pickled nopales are also available.

Nopales

Baby Vegetables

Many fine restaurants serve baby vegetables: tiny turnips, finger-length squash, miniature carrots and petite heads of cauliflower. First cultivated in Europe but now widely available throughout the United States, baby vegetables include both hybrids bred to be true

Chioggi Beets

miniatures as well as regular varieties that are picked before maturity. Baby vegetables are often marketed with blossoms or greens still attached. They tend to be easily bruised and are highly perishable. Many baby vegetables can be eaten raw, but they are usually left whole, then steamed or lightly sautéed and attractively presented as an accompaniment to meat, fish or poultry entrées.

Baby Globe Carrots

Baby Zucchini with Blossoms

Baby Yellow Squash with Blossoms

NUTRITION

Most vegetables are more than 80 percent water; the remaining portions consist of carbohydrates (primarily starches) and small amounts of protein and fat. The relative lack of protein and fat makes most vegetables especially low in calories.

Much of a vegetable's physical structure is provided by generally indigestible substances such as cellulose and lignin, also known as fiber. This fiber produces the characteristic stringy, crisp or fibrous textures associated with vegetables.

Vegetables are also a good source of vitamins and minerals. Care must be taken during preparation to preserve their nutritional content, however. Once peeled or cut, vegetables lose nutrients to the air or to any liquid in which they are allowed to soak. Vitamins are concentrated just under the skin, so peel vegetables thinly, if at all.

PURCHASING AND STORING FRESH VEGETABLES

Fresh vegetables should be selected according to seasonal availability. Using a vegetable at the peak of its season has several advantages: Price is at its lowest, selection is at its greatest and the vegetable's color, flavor and texture are at their best.

ANCIENT PLANTS AND ANCIENT WAYS VANISH

Since the days of Columbus, half of all native American crop varieties have become extinct. If this trend continues, several hundred more will become extinct in our lifetimes. Similarly, ancient farming practices have all but been abandoned. As late as the 1920s, the Tohono O'odham Indians of Arizona still used traditional methods to cultivate more than 10,000 acres without pumping groundwater. Today, only a few scattered floodwater fields remain.

When species disappear we lose an irreplaceable source of genetic diversity—a source of extraordinary genes that could someday improve modern hybrid crops. When native desert crops vanish, so does the ancient tradition of native agriculture, which has selected these crops over millennia to thrive in extreme temperatures, in alkaline soils without millions of gallons of precious water and without expensive, ecologically destructive chemicals.

Today, six highly bred species—wheat, rice, corn, sorghum, potatoes and cassava—supply most of the world's nutrition. As food crops become more and more homogeneous, they often lose their natural ability to tolerate pests, disease and drought. In the past, farmers grew thousands of food crop varieties. These traditional crop varieties contain a storehouse of genetic diversity that enables them to flourish in the most difficult environments. This broad spectrum of genetic variability is a cushion against natural predators and diseases. Wild chiles from the Sierra Madre, for example, are highly disease resistant. Their virus-tolerant genes have been bred into commercial varieties of bell pepper and jalapeños.

Native Seeds/SEARCH, one of the country's first regional seed banks, was founded to keep ancient desert plants and traditional farming methods from disappearing forever. Since 1983 we've ridden mules into remote areas and made more than 1200 collections of desert-adapted crops and wild relatives. We've gathered the seeds of chapalote (a brown popcorn), blue indigo (used for dyes), tepary (a heat- and drought-tolerant bean), teosinte (a wild relative of corn), wild chiles and other plants. These seeds are available to researchers, gardeners, farmers and seed banks. Seeds are offered free to Native Americans.

Each loss of biological and cultural diversity alters and damages the balance of life on earth, often in ways we do not understand. Each loss of leaf, stem and flower diminishes our earth's richness and beauty in ways we often don't appreciate until they're gone.

—DR. GARY PAUL NABHAN, Native Seeds/SEARCH, Tucson, AZ

BACK TO BASICS

Great strides in agriculture have been made during the past two centuries. Pesticides, fungicides and herbicides now eliminate or control pests that once would have devoured, ruined or choked crops. Chemical fertilizers increase yields of many of the world's staples. But not everyone has greeted these developments with open arms.

During the past few decades, scientific and medical investigators have documented, or at least suggested, health risks associated with certain synthetic pesticides, fertilizers and other products. These findings have led to a renewed interest in a now multibillion-dollar-a-year back-to-the-basics approach to farming: organic farming. Specialty farms, orchards and even wineries now offer organically grown prod-

ucts (or, in the case of wineries, wines made from organically grown grapes). These products come with few, if any, intentional additives and should be free of any incidental additives. Proponents argue that these products are better for you and better for the health of the farm workers.

The U.S. Department of Agriculture regulates the production and labeling of or-

ganically grown foods. It requires that any natural food labeled "100 percent organic" must contain only organic ingredients—that is, those grown and manufactured without the use of added hormones, pesticides, synthetic fertilizers, and so on; soil cannot have been treated with unapproved synthetics for 3 years for a crop to be called organic. To be labeled organic or to display the USDA organic seal, processed foods must contain at least 95 percent organic ingredients by weight. Processed foods with 70 to 95 percent organic ingredients may be labeled "made with organic ingredients"; processed foods with less than 70 percent organic ingredients may list those ingredients on the information panel but may not use the term *organic* anywhere on the front of the package.

Grading

The USDA has a voluntary grading system for fresh vegetables traded on wholesale markets. The system is based on appearance, condition and other factors affecting waste or eating quality. Grades for all vegetables include, in descending order of quality, U.S. Extra Fancy, U.S. Fancy, U.S. Extra No. 1 and U.S. No. 1. There are also grades that apply only to specific vegetables, for example, U.S. No. 1 Boilers for onions.

Consumer or retail grading is currently required only for potatoes, carrots and onions. It uses alphabetical listings, with Grade A being the finest.

Purchasing

Fresh vegetables are sold by weight or count. They are packed in cartons referred to as cases, lugs, bushels, flats or crates. The weight or count packed in each of these containers varies depending on the size and type of vegetable as well as the packer. For example, celery is packed in 55-pound cartons containing 18 to 48 heads, depending on the size of each head.

Some of the more common fresh vegetables (for example, onions, carrots, celery and lettuces) can be purchased from wholesalers trimmed, cleaned and cut according to your specifications. Although the unit price will be higher for diced onions than for whole onions, for example, the savings in time, labor, yield loss and storage space can be substantial. Processed vegetables may suffer a loss of nutrients, moisture and flavor, however.

Ripening

Although vegetables do not ripen in the same manner as fruits, they do continue to breathe (respire) after harvesting. The faster the respiration rate, the faster the produce ages or decays. This decay results in wilted leaves and dry, tough or woody stems and stalks. Respiration rates vary according to the vegetable variety, its maturity at harvest and its storage conditions after harvest.

Ripening proceeds more rapidly in the presence of ethylene gas. Ethylene gas is emitted naturally by fruits and vegetables and can be used to encourage further ripening in some produce, especially fruit-vegetables such as tomatoes. Items harvested and shipped when mature but green (unripe) can be exposed to ethylene gas to induce color development (ripening) just before sale.

Storing

Some fresh vegetables are best stored at cool temperatures, between 40°F and 60°F (4°C and 16°C), ideally in a separate produce refrigerator. These include winter squash, potatoes, onions, shallots and garlic. If a produce refrigerator is not available, store these vegetables at room temperature in a dry area with good ventilation. Do not store them in a refrigerator set at conventional temperatures. Colder temperatures convert the starches in these vegetables to sugars, changing their texture and flavor.

Most other vegetables benefit from cold storage at temperatures between 34°F and 40°F (2°C and 4°C) with relatively high levels of humidity. Greens and other delicate vegetables should be stored away from apples, tomatoes, bananas and melons, as the latter give off a great deal of ethylene gas.

PURCHASING AND STORING PRESERVED VEGETABLES

Preservation techniques are designed to extend the shelf life of vegetables. These methods include irradiation, canning, freezing and drying. Except for drying, these techniques do not substantially change the vegetable's texture or flavor. Canning and freezing can also be used to preserve cooked vegetables.

Irradiated Vegetables

The irradiation process uses ionizing radiation (usually gamma rays of cobalt 60 or cesium 137) to sterilize foods. When foods are subjected to radiation, parasites, insects and bacteria are destroyed, ripening is slowed and sprouting is prevented. Irradiation works without a noticeable increase in temperature; consequently, the flavor and texture of fresh foods are not affected. Some nutrients, however, may be destroyed. Irradiated vegetables do not need to be sprayed with post-harvest pesticides, and they have an extended shelf life.

The FDA classifies irradiation as a food additive. Although irradiation is not yet approved for all foods, grains, fruits and vegetables may be treated with low-dose radiation. Irradiated foods must be labeled "Treated with radiation" or "Treated by irradiation." The symbol shown in Figure 21.1 may also be used.

Irradiated produce is purchased, stored and used like fresh produce.

FIGURE 21.1 ▶ Irradiation symbol.

Canned Vegetables

Canned vegetables are the backbone of menu planning for many food service operations. In commercial canning, raw vegetables are cleaned and placed in a sealed container, then subjected to high temperatures for a specific period. Heating destroys the microorganisms that cause spoilage, and the sealed environment created by the can eliminates oxidation and retards decomposition. But the heat required by the canning process also softens the texture of most vegetables and alters their nutritional content; many vitamins and minerals may be lost through the canning process. Green vegetables may also suffer color loss, becoming a drab olive hue.

Canned vegetables are graded by the USDA as U.S. Grade A or Fancy, U.S. Grade B or Extra-Select, and U.S. Grade C or Standard. U.S. Grade A vegetables must be top quality, tender and free of blemishes. U.S. Grade C vegetables may lack uniformity or flavor, but can be used in casseroles or soups if cost is a concern.

Combinations of vegetables as well as vegetables with seasonings and sauces are available canned. For example, corn kernels are available canned in water, in seasonings and sauces, combined with other vegetables or creamed. Canned vegetables are easy to serve because they are essentially fully cooked during the canning process.

Canned vegetables are purchased in cases of standard-sized cans (see Appendix II). Canned vegetables can be stored almost indefinitely at room temperature. Once a can is opened, any unused contents should be transferred to an appropriate storage container and refrigerated. Cans with bulges should be discarded immediately, without opening.

HYDROPONICS: WORKING WATER

Hydroponics is the science of growing plants without soil in water. Plants are grown in an inert medium such as gravel, peat, sand or other sterile material. Nutrients are distributed in water that is circulated over the plant's roots. In a hydroponic farm, the temperatures and light are controlled to maximize production. Because hydroponic farms are indoors, plants can be grown in any climate; both Canada and Holland are major producers of vegetables grown under such conditions.

Frozen Vegetables

Frozen vegetables are almost as convenient to use as canned. However, they often require some cooking, and expensive freezer space is necessary if an inventory is to be maintained. Regardless, freezing is a highly effective method for preserving vegetables. It severely inhibits the growth of microorganisms that cause spoilage without destroying many nutrients. Generally, green vegetables retain their color, although the appearance and texture of most vegetables may be somewhat altered because of their high water content: Ice crystals form from the water in the cells and burst the cells' walls.

Some vegetables are available individually quick-frozen (IQF). This method employs blasts of cold air, refrigerated plates, liquid nitrogen, liquid air or other techniques to chill the vegetables quickly. Speeding the freezing process can greatly reduce the formation of ice crystals.

Combinations of vegetables as well as vegetables with seasonings and sauces are available frozen. Some frozen vegetables are raw when frozen; others are blanched before freezing so that final cooking time is reduced and their color is preserved. Many others are fully cooked before freezing and need only to be thawed or heated for service. Frozen vegetables generally do not need to be thawed before being heated. Once thawed or cooked, they should be stored in the refrigerator and reheated in the same manner as fresh vegetables. Do not refreeze previously frozen vegetables.

Frozen vegetables are graded in the same manner as canned vegetables. They are usually packed in cases containing 1- to 2-pound (450- to 900-gram) boxes or bags. All frozen vegetables should be sealed in moisture-proof wrapping and kept at a constant temperature of 0°F (−18°C) or below. Temperature fluctuations can draw moisture from the vegetables, causing poor texture and flavor loss. Adequate packaging also prevents freezer burn, an irreversible change in the color, texture and flavor of frozen foods.

Dried Vegetables

Except for beans, peas, peppers, mushrooms and tomatoes, few vegetables are commonly preserved by drying. Unlike other preservation methods, drying dramatically alters flavor, texture and appearance. The loss of moisture concentrates flavors and sugars and greatly extends shelf life.

APPLYING VARIOUS COOKING METHODS

Vegetables are cooked in order to break down their cellulose and gelatinize their starches. Cooking gives vegetables a pleasant flavor; creates a softer, more tender texture; and makes them more digestible. Ideally, most vegetables should be cooked as briefly as possible in order to preserve their flavor, nutrients and texture. Unfortunately, sometimes one must choose between emphasizing appearance and maintaining nutrition because cooking methods that preserve color and texture often remove nutrients.

Acid/Alkali Reactions

The acid or alkali content of the cooking liquid affects the texture and color of many vegetables. This is of greater concern with moist-heat cooking methods, but it is also a consideration with dry-heat cooking methods, as they often call for blanched or parboiled vegetables.

TEXTURE

The acidity or alkalinity of the vegetable's cooking liquid influences the finished product's texture. If an acid such as lemon juice, vinegar or wine is added to the liquid for flavoring, the vegetable will resist softening and will require a longer cooking time. On the other hand, an alkaline cooking medium will quickly soften the vegetable's texture and may cause it to become mushy. Alkalinity also causes nutrient loss (especially thiamin) and may impart a bitter flavor. Alkalinity can be caused by tap water, detergent residue on utensils or the addition of baking soda (a base) to the cooking liquid. (You could add, for example, ⅛ teaspoon [0.6 milliliter] baking soda per cup [225 milliliters] of beans to speed the softening of dried beans.)

COLOR

The acidity or alkalinity of the liquid also affects the plant's pigments, causing both desirable and undesirable color changes. There are three principal pigment categories: chlorophyll, carotenoid and flavonoid. A plant's unique color is the result of a combination of these pigments. Chlorophyll pigments predominate in green vegetables such as spinach, green beans and broccoli. Carotenoid pigments predominate in orange and yellow vegetables such as carrots, tomatoes, red peppers and winter squashes. Flavonoid pigments predominate in red, purple and white vegetables such as red cabbage, beets and cauliflower.

Initially, as vegetables are cooked, their original colors intensify. Exposure to heat makes pigments, especially chlorophyll, appear brighter. Exposure to acids and bases affects both chlorophyll and flavonoid pigments. Acids will gradually turn green vegetables an olive-drab color, whereas a slight alkalinity promotes chlorophyll retention. The opposite occurs with vegetables containing flavonoids: They retain desirable colors in a slightly acidic environment but lose colors in an alkaline one. (Carotenoids are not affected by either acidity or alkalinity.) Color changes alone do not affect flavor, but the altered appearance can make the product so visually unappealing as to become inedible (Table 21.1).

Colors also change as the naturally occurring acids in vegetables are released during cooking. If the cooking pan is kept covered, the acids can concentrate, creating richer flavonoid pigments but destroying chlorophyll pigments.

Thus, if color is the one and only concern, vegetables with a high amount of chlorophyll should be cooked in an alkaline liquid, and vegetables with a high amount of flavonoids should be cooked in an acidic liquid. But remember, the improvement in color usually comes at the expense of texture and nutrients.

TABLE 21.1 ACID/ALKALI REACTIONS

VEGETABLE	PIGMENT FAMILY	EFFECT OF ACID ON:		EFFECT OF ALKALI ON:*		COOK COVERED?
		COLOR	TEXTURE	COLOR	TEXTURE	
Spinach, broccoli	chlorophyll	drab olive green	firm	bright green	mushy	no
Carrots, rutabagas	carotenoid	no change	firm	no change	mushy	no difference
Cauliflower	flavonoid	white	firm	yellow	mushy	yes
Red cabbage	flavonoid	red	firm	blue	mushy	yes

*Alkalinity always causes a loss of thiamin and other nutrients.

❶ Spinach cooked with an alkali (left) and an acid.

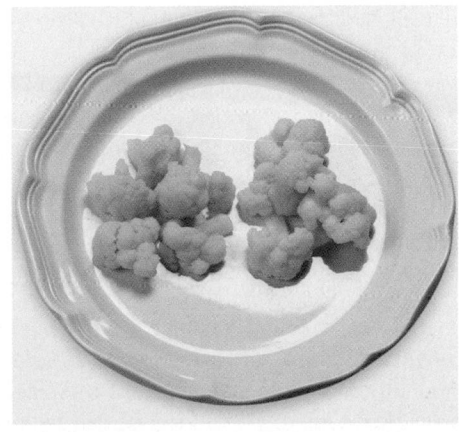

❷ Cauliflower cooked with an alkali (left) and an acid.

❸ Red cabbage cooked with an alkali (left) and an acid.

Guidelines for Vegetable Cookery

The following general guidelines for vegetable cookery should be considered regardless of the cooking method used:

❶ Vegetables should be carefully cut into uniform shapes and sizes to promote even cooking and provide an attractive finished product.

❷ Cook vegetables for as short a time as possible to preserve texture, color and nutrients.

❸ Cook vegetables as close to service time as possible. Holding vegetables in a steam table continues to cook them.

❹ When necessary, vegetables may be blanched in advance, refreshed in ice water and refrigerated. They can then be reheated as needed.

❺ White and red vegetables (those with flavonoid pigments) may be cooked with a small amount of acid such as lemon juice, vinegar or white wine to help retain their color.

❻ When preparing an assortment of vegetables, cook each type separately, then combine them. Otherwise, some items would become overcooked in the time required to properly cook others.

Determining Doneness

There are so many types of vegetables, with such varied responses to cooking, that no one standard for doneness is appropriate. Each item should be evaluated on a recipe-by-recipe basis. Generally, however, most cooked vegetables are done when they are just tender when pierced with a fork or the tip of a paring knife. Leafy vegetables should be wilted but still have a bright color.

Avoid overcooking vegetables by remembering that some carryover cooking will occur through the residual heat contained in the foods. Always rely on subjective tests—sight, feel, taste and aroma—rather than the clock.

Dry-Heat Cooking Methods

BROILING AND GRILLING

Broiling and grilling use high heat to cook vegetables quickly. This preserves their nutritional content and natural flavors. The radiant heat of the broiler or grill caramelizes the vegetables, creating a pleasant flavor that is not generally achieved when vegetables are cooked by other methods.

Selecting and Preparing Vegetables to Broil or Grill

Broiling is often used to cook soft vegetables such as tomatoes or items that might not rest easily on a grill rack. Broiling is also used to warm and brown items just before service. If necessary, the vegetables can be basted to prevent them from drying out under the broiler's direct heat. Sometimes a cooked vegetable is napped with sauce or clarified butter and placed briefly under the broiler as a finishing touch at service time.

A large range of vegetables can be grilled. Carrots, peppers, squashes, eggplants and similar vegetables should be cut into broad, thin slices. They can then be placed on the grill in the same manner as a portion of meat or fish to create attractive crosshatchings. (See Chapter 9, Principles of Cooking.) Smaller vegetables such as mushrooms, cherry tomatoes and pearl onions can be threaded onto skewers for easy handling. (Bamboo or wooden skewers should be soaked in cold water for 15 minutes before using to help prevent them from burning on the grill.)

Seasoning Vegetables to Be Broiled or Grilled

Vegetables contain little fat and therefore benefit greatly from added fat when being broiled or grilled. The added fat can be a brushing of clarified butter or a marinade such as one made from olive oil and herbs. Some vegetables may be brushed with butter and coated with bread crumbs or Parmesan before broiling.

PROCEDURE FOR **BROILING OR GRILLING VEGETABLES**

1. Heat the grill or broiler.
2. Use a wire brush to remove any charred or burnt particles that may be stuck to the broiler or grill grate. The grate may be wiped with a lightly oiled towel to remove any remaining particles and help season it.
3. Prepare the vegetables to be broiled or grilled by cutting them into appropriate shapes and sizes, then seasoning, marinating or otherwise preparing them as desired or directed in the recipe.
4. Place the vegetables on the broiler grate, broiler platter or grill grate and cook to the desired doneness while developing the proper surface color.

GRILLED VEGETABLE SKEWERS

Yield: 12 Skewers **Method:** Grilling

Marinade:		
Rice wine vinegar	4 fl. oz.	120 ml
Vegetable oil	8 fl. oz.	240 ml
Garlic, chopped	1 oz.	30 g
Dried thyme	2 tsp.	10 ml
Salt	1 Tbsp.	15 ml
Black pepper	½ tsp.	2 ml
Zucchini	6 oz.	180 g
Yellow squash	6 oz.	180 g
Broccoli florets, large	12	12
Cauliflower florets, large	12	12
Onion, large dice	24 pieces	24 pieces
Red bell pepper, large dice	12 pieces	12 pieces
Mushroom caps, medium	12	12

1. Combine all the marinade ingredients and set aside.
2. Cut the zucchini and yellow squash into ½-inch- (1.2-centimeter-) thick semicircles.
3. Blanch and refresh the zucchini, yellow squash, broccoli florets, cauliflower florets, onion and bell pepper as discussed later under Moist-Heat Cooking Methods.
4. Drain the vegetables well and combine them with the marinade. Add the mushroom caps to the marinade. Marinate the vegetables for 30 to 45 minutes, remove and drain well.
5. Skewer the vegetables by alternating them on 6-inch (10-centimeter) bamboo skewers.
6. Place the vegetable skewers on a hot grill and cook until done, turning as needed. The vegetables should brown and char lightly during cooking. Serve hot.

MISE EN PLACE

◄ Peel and chop garlic.
◄ Wash broccoli and cauliflower and cut into large florets.
◄ Peel and dice onion.
◄ Wash and seed bell pepper and cut into large dice.
◄ Wash mushroom caps.

Grilling skewers of marinated vegetables.

VARIATION:

Grilled Sliced Vegetables—Slice the zucchini, yellow squash, onion and bell pepper into large pieces. Marinate and then grill these vegetables along with the broccoli, cauliflower and mushroom caps without skewering.

Approximate values per serving: **Calories** 60, **Total fat** 2.5 g, **Saturated fat** 0 g, **Cholesterol** 0 mg, **Sodium** 610 mg, **Total carbohydrates** 8 g, **Protein** 2 g, **Vitamin C** 90%, **Claims**—low fat; no cholesterol; good source of fiber

ROASTING AND BAKING

The terms *roasting* and *baking* are used interchangeably when referring to vegetables. Roasting or baking is used to bring out the natural sweetness of many vegetables while preserving their nutritional values. The procedures are basically the same as those for roasting meats.

Grilled sliced vegetables as an accompaniment to an entrée plate.

Selecting and Preparing Vegetables to Roast or Bake

Hearty vegetables such as winter squash and eggplant are especially well suited for roasting or baking. Vegetables such as onions, carrots and turnips are sometimes cooked alongside roasting meats or poultry. The vegetables add flavor to the finished roast and accompanying sauce, and the fats and juices released from the cooking roast add flavor to the vegetables.

Vegetables can be baked whole or cut into uniform-sized pieces. Squash, for example, is usually cut into large pieces. Vegetables may be peeled or left unpeeled, depending on the desired finished product.

Seasoning Vegetables to Be Roasted or Baked

Vegetables may be seasoned with salt and pepper and rubbed with butter or oil before baking, or they may be seasoned afterward with a wide variety of herbs and spices. Oiling the vegetables helps them brown and crisp in the hot oven. Some vegetables, such as winter squashes and sweet potatoes, may be seasoned with brown sugar or honey as well.

PROCEDURE FOR **ROASTING OR BAKING VEGETABLES**

1. Wash the vegetables. Peel, cut and prepare them as desired or directed in the recipe.
2. Season the vegetables and rub or toss with oil or butter if desired.
3. Place the vegetables in a baking dish and bake in a preheated oven until done.

BAKED BUTTERNUT SQUASH

MISE EN PLACE

▶ Wash and peel butternut squash and cut into medium dice.
▶ Melt whole butter and keep warm.

Yield: 4 Servings, 4 oz. (120 g) each **Method:** Baking

Butternut squash, medium dice	1 lb.	480 g
Clarified butter	as needed	as needed
Salt and pepper	TT	TT
Cinnamon	¼ tsp.	1 ml
Cardamom, ground	⅛ tsp.	0.5 ml
Brown sugar	2 Tbsp.	30 ml
Lemon juice	2 Tbsp.	30 ml
Whole butter, melted	2 oz.	60 g

1. Place the squash in a buttered pan. Season with salt, pepper, cinnamon, cardamom and sugar.
2. Drizzle the lemon juice and melted butter over the top of the squash.
3. Bake, uncovered, in a 350°F (180°C) oven until tender, approximately 50 minutes.

Approximate values per 4-oz. (120-g) serving: **Calories** 190, **Total fat** 12 g, **Saturated fat** 7 g, **Cholesterol** 30 mg, **Sodium** 700 mg, **Total carbohydrates** 20 g, **Protein** 1 g, **Vitamin A** 90%, **Vitamin C** 35%

SAUTÉING

Sautéed vegetables should be brightly colored and slightly crisp when done and show little moisture loss. When sautéing vegetables, all preparation must be complete before cooking begins because timing is important and cooking progresses rapidly. Have all vegetables, herbs, spices, seasonings and sauces ready before beginning.

Selecting and Preparing Vegetables to Sauté

A wide variety of vegetables can be sautéed. Whatever vegetables are used, they should be cut into uniform-sized pieces to ensure even cooking.

Quick-cooking vegetables such as summer squashes, onions, greens, stalks, fruit-vegetables and mushrooms can be sautéed without any preparation except washing and cutting. Other vegetables such as Brussels sprouts, green beans, winter squashes, broccoli, cauliflower and most root vegetables are usually first blanched or otherwise partially cooked by baking, steaming or simmering. They are then sautéed to reheat and finish. Carrots, squash and other vegetables are sometimes finished by sautéing in butter and then adding a small amount of honey or maple syrup to glaze them. Some cooked vegetables are reheated by simply sautéing them in a small amount of stock or sauce.

Seasoning Vegetables to Be Sautéed

Sautéed vegetables can be seasoned with a great variety of herbs and spices. Seasonings should be added toward the end of the cooking process after all other ingredients have been incorporated in order to accurately evaluate the flavor of the finished dish.

Because sautéing vegetables uses slightly lower temperatures than sautéing meats and poultry, usually whole butter can be used instead of clarified butter. For additional flavors, fats such as bacon fat, olive oil, nut oils or sesame oil can be used in place of butter.

> ## VEGETABLE SAUNA
>
> "Sweating vegetables" in a little oil over low heat in a covered pot is, in effect, a vegetable sauna. All of the flavors of the vegetables emerge slowly in a juicy tangle, in a much more intense manner than if you simply added them just-cut to a stock. Like roasting garlic, it is a way to enlarge the natural flavors very dramatically.
>
> —*China Moon Cookbook*
> by BARBARA TROPP

PROCEDURE FOR SAUTÉING VEGETABLES

1. Wash the vegetables and cut into uniform shapes and sizes.
2. Heat a sauté pan and add enough fat to just cover the bottom. The pan should be large enough to hold the vegetables without overcrowding.
3. When preparing an assortment of vegetables, add the ingredients according to their cooking times (first add the vegetables that take the longest to cook). Plan carefully so that all vegetables will be done at the same time. Do not overcrowd the pan; maintain high enough heat so that the vegetables do not cook in their own juices.
4. Toss the vegetables using the sloped sides of the sauté pan or wok to flip them back on top of themselves. Do not toss more than necessary. The pan should remain in contact with the heat source as much as possible to maintain proper temperatures.
5. Add any sauces or vegetables with high water content, such as tomatoes, last.
6. Season the vegetables as desired with herbs or spices, or add ingredients for a glaze.

STIR-FRIED ASPARAGUS WITH SHIITAKE MUSHROOMS

Yield: 4 Servings, 4 oz. (120 g) each   **Method:** Sautéing

Asparagus	1 lb.	480 g
Fresh shiitake mushrooms	6 oz.	180 g
Vegetable oil	1 Tbsp.	15 ml
Sesame oil	1 Tbsp.	15 ml
Garlic, chopped	2 tsp.	10 ml
Oyster sauce	4 fl. oz.	120 ml
Crushed red chiles (optional)	TT	TT

MISE EN PLACE
◄ Peel and chop garlic.

1. Wash the asparagus, trim the ends and slice on the bias into 1- to 2-inch (2.5- to 5-centimeter) pieces.
2. Wash the mushrooms, trim off the stems and slice the caps into ½-inch- (1.2-centimeter-) thick slices.
3. Heat the oils in a wok or sauté pan.
4. Add the garlic and stir-fry for a few seconds.
5. Add the asparagus and mushrooms and stir-fry for 1 minute.
6. Add the oyster sauce and crushed red chiles (if using) and continue to stir-fry until the asparagus is nearly tender, approximately 3 minutes.

Approximate values per 4-oz. (120-g) serving: **Calories** 140, **Total fat** 8 g, **Saturated fat** 1 g, **Cholesterol** 10 mg, **Sodium** 1130 mg, **Total carbohydrates** 13 g, **Protein** 5 g, **Vitamin C** 50%

PAN-FRYING

Pan-frying is not as popular as other techniques for cooking vegetables. Green tomatoes, however, are sometimes seasoned, floured and pan-fried; eggplant slices are seasoned, floured, pan-fried and used for eggplant Parmesan. When pan-frying vegetables, follow the procedures outlined in Chapter 9, Principles of Cooking.

DEEP-FRYING

Deep-frying is a popular method of preparing vegetables such as potatoes, squashes and mushrooms. They can be served as hors d'oeuvre, appetizers or accompaniments to a main dish. Vegetables can also be grated or chopped and incorporated into fritters or croquettes. Any deep-fried item should have a crisp, golden exterior with a tender, nongreasy center.

Selecting and Seasoning Vegetables to Be Deep-Fried

Except for potatoes (which are discussed in Chapter 22, Potatoes, Grains and Pasta), most vegetables are breaded, battered or floured before deep-frying. Slow-cooking vegetables such as broccoli and cauliflower should be blanched in boiling water before breading or battering. Blanching speeds cooking and allows the interior to cook completely before the surface burns.

Although vegetables that will be deep-fried can be marinated or seasoned directly, it is more common to season the batter, flour or breading that will coat them. Additional flavors come from the sauces and accompaniments served with the deep-fried vegetables. Creamy herb dressings or spicy tomato or soy-based dipping sauces are popular accompaniments.

PROCEDURE FOR **DEEP-FRYING VEGETABLES**

1. Slice, trim or otherwise prepare the vegetables to be deep-fried. Cut them into uniform shapes and sizes to ensure even frying. Blanch them if necessary. Season and bread or batter them, as desired.

2. Heat the fat to the desired temperature, usually between 325°F and 350°F (160°C and 180°C). Breaded, battered or floured vegetables cook quickly and the fat must be hot enough to cook the food's interior without burning its surface.

3. Carefully place the vegetables in the hot fat using either the basket method or swimming method as appropriate.

4. Deep-fry the vegetables until done. They should have a crispy, golden brown surface.

5. Remove the deep-fried vegetables from the fat and hold them over the fryer, allowing the excess fat to drain off. Transfer the food to a hotel pan either lined with absorbent paper or fitted with a rack. Season with salt, if desired.

6. If the deep-fried vegetables are to be held for later service, place them under a heat lamp.

BEER-BATTERED ONION RINGS

Yield: Approximately 1 qt. (1 lt) Batter, enough for approx. 4 lb. (1.9 kg) rings   **Method:** Deep-frying

Flour	10 oz.	300 g
Baking powder	2 tsp.	10 ml
Salt	2 tsp.	10 ml
White pepper	¼ tsp.	1 ml
Egg	1	1
Beer	1 pt.	480 ml
Onions, whole	4 lb.	1.9 kg
Flour	as needed for dredging	

① Sift the dry ingredients together.

② Beat the egg in a separate bowl. Add the beer to the beaten egg.

③ Add the egg-and-beer mixture to the dry ingredients; mix until smooth.

④ Peel the onions and cut in ½-inch- (1.2-centimeter-) thick slices.

⑤ Break the slices into rings and dredge in flour.

⑥ Dip the rings in the batter a few at a time. Using the swimming method, deep-fry at 375°F (191°C) until done. Drain on absorbent paper, season with additional salt and white pepper and serve hot.

Approximate values per 1-oz. (30-g) serving: **Calories** 230, **Total fat** 10 g, **Saturated fat** 2.5 g, **Cholesterol** 5 mg, **Sodium** 460 mg, **Total carbohydrates** 31 g, **Protein** 4 g

① Dredging the onion rings in flour.

② Dipping the floured rings in batter.

③ Frying the onion rings using the swimming method.

Moist-Heat Cooking Methods

BLANCHING AND PARBOILING

Blanching and parboiling are variations on boiling; the difference between them is the length of cooking time. Blanched and parboiled vegetables are often finished by other cooking methods such as sautéing.

Blanching is the partial cooking of foods in a large amount of boiling water for a very short time, usually only a few seconds. Besides preparing vegetables for further cooking, blanching is used to remove strong or bitter flavors, soften firm foods, set colors or loosen skins for peeling. Kale, chard, snow peas and tomatoes are examples of vegetables that are sometimes blanched for purposes other than preparation for further cooking.

Parboiling is the same as blanching, but the cooking time is longer, usually several minutes. Parboiling is used to soften vegetables and shorten final cooking times. Parboiling is commonly used for preparing root vegetables, cauliflower, broccoli and winter squashes.

BOILING

Vegetables are often boiled. Boiled vegetables can be served as they are, or they can be further prepared by quickly sautéing with other ingredients, puréeing or mashing. Boiled vegetables are also chilled, then used in salads.

Starchy root vegetables are generally not boiled but rather simmered slowly so that the heat penetrates to their interiors and cooks them evenly. Green vegetables should be boiled quickly in a large amount of water in order to retain their color and flavor.

REFRESHING

refreshing submerging a food in cold water to quickly cool it and prevent further cooking, also known as shocking; usually used for vegetables

Unless the boiled, blanched or parboiled vegetables will be eaten immediately, they must be quickly chilled in ice water after they are removed from the cooking liquid. This prevents further cooking and preserves (sets) their colors. This process is known as **refreshing** or **shocking** the vegetables. The vegetables are removed from the ice water as soon as they are cold. Never soak or hold the vegetables in the water longer than necessary, or valuable nutrients and flavor will be leached away.

PROCEDURE FOR **REFRESHING VEGETABLES**

❶ Blanch, parboil or boil the vegetables to the desired doneness.

❷ Remove the vegetables from the cooking liquid and submerge them in ice water just until they are cold.

Selecting and Preparing Vegetables to Boil

Nearly any type of vegetable can be boiled. Carrots, cabbages, green beans, turnips and red beets are just a few of the most common ones. Vegetables can be large or small, but they should be uniform in size to ensure even cooking. Some vegetables are cooked whole and require only washing before boiling. Others must be washed, peeled and trimmed or cut into smaller or more manageable sizes.

Seasoning Vegetables to Be Boiled

Often vegetables are boiled in nothing more than salted water. Lemon juice, citrus zest, wine and other acidic ingredients are sometimes added to white and red vegetables; if so, they should be added to the liquid before the vegetables. Herbs and spices in a sachet or a bouquet garni are often used to add flavor to boiled vegetables and should be added according to the recipe.

After boiling, vegetables are sometimes finished with herbs, spices, butter, cream or sauces.

PROCEDURE FOR **BOILING VEGETABLES**

❶ Wash, peel and trim the vegetables and cut into uniform shapes and sizes.
❷ Bring an adequate amount of water, stock, court bouillon or other liquid to a boil. The liquid should cover the vegetables, and they should be able to move around freely without overcrowding.

3 Add seasonings if desired or directed in the recipe.

4 Add the vegetables to the boiling liquid. If more than one vegetable is to be cooked and they have different cooking times, they should be cooked separately to ensure that all are cooked to the proper doneness. The pot may be covered if cooking white, red or yellow vegetables. Do not cover the pot when boiling green vegetables.

5 Cook the vegetables to the desired doneness. Vegetables to be reheated before serving should be slightly undercooked and firm.

6 Remove the vegetables from the water with a slotted spoon or a spider or drain through a colander.

7 Refresh the vegetables in ice water, drain and refrigerate until needed or finish the hot boiled vegetables as desired and serve immediately.

BRUSSELS SPROUTS IN PECAN BUTTER

Yield: 6 Servings, 3 oz. (90 g) each   **Method:** Boiling

Brussels sprouts	1 lb.	480 g
Whole butter	2 oz.	60 g
Pecans, chopped	4 oz.	120 g
Salt and pepper	TT	TT

MISE EN PLACE
◀ Chop pecans.

1 Trim the Brussels sprouts and mark an X in the bottom of each with a paring knife to promote even cooking.

2 Boil the sprouts in salted water until tender, approximately 10 minutes.

3 Drain and hold the sprouts in a warm place.

4 Heat the butter in a sauté pan until noisette. Add the pecans and toss to brown them.

5 Add the Brussels sprouts and toss to reheat and blend flavors. Adjust the seasonings and serve.

VARIATION:

Substitute asparagus, green beans or fingerling potatoes for the Brussels sprouts in this recipe.

Approximate values per 3-oz. (90-g) serving: **Calories** 240, **Total fat** 21 g, **Saturated fat** 6 g, **Cholesterol** 20 mg, **Sodium** 480 mg, **Total carbohydrates** 10 g, **Protein** 4 g, **Vitamin A** 15%, **Vitamin C** 80%

1 Marking an X in the bottom of each Brussels sprout.

2 Boiling the Brussels sprouts in the appropriate amount of water.

3 Tossing the Brussels sprouts with the butter and pecans.

PROCEDURE FOR **COOKING DRIED BEANS**

Dried beans are best rehydrated by soaking as discussed earlier and then cooking in a boiling (actually simmering) liquid. After rehydration and cooking, the beans can be served or further cooked in baked, sautéed or puréed dishes.

1 After soaking, place the drained beans in a heavy saucepan and cover with cold water or stock. Allow approximately three times as much liquid as there are beans. Add flavoring ingredients as directed in the recipe, but do not add acids or salt until the beans have reached the desired tenderness. Acids and salt cause the exterior of beans to toughen and resist any further efforts at tenderizing.

2 Slowly bring the liquid to a boil. Boil uncovered for 10 minutes or as directed in the recipe. Use a ladle to remove any scum that rises to the surface.

3 Cover and reduce the heat. Allow the mixture to simmer until the beans are tender. Whole beans generally require 1 to 2½ hours, lentils 20 to 35 minutes and split peas 30 to 60 minutes. Add additional hot liquid if necessary. Do not stir the beans during cooking.

4 Drain the cooked beans through a colander.

WHITE BEAN SALAD

Yield: 3 pt. (1.4 lt)

White beans	12 oz.	360 g
Water	as needed	as needed
Carrot, small dice	4 oz.	120 g
Celery, small dice	2 oz.	60 g
Leek, sliced	2 oz.	60 g
Dressing:		
Red wine vinegar	3 Tbsp.	45 ml
Fresh lemon juice	2 tsp.	10 ml
Dijon mustard	1 Tbsp.	15 ml
Shallot, minced	1 Tbsp.	15 ml
Olive oil	6 fl. oz.	180 ml
Salt and pepper	TT	TT
Green onions, minced	2	2
Fresh parsley, chopped	1 Tbsp.	15 ml
Fresh thyme, chopped	1 Tbsp.	15 ml

1 Pick through the beans to remove any grit, pebbles or debris. Place the beans in a bowl of water and remove any skins or other items that float to the top. Drain and rinse the beans. Place the beans in a clean bowl and soak them for at least 1 hour or overnight.

2 Drain the beans and place them in a saucepot with 1½ quarts (1.4 liters) water. Bring to a boil, reduce to a simmer and cook until the beans are tender, approximately 1 hour. Drain the beans, spread on a sheet pan, cool and refrigerate.

3 Blanch and refresh the carrot, celery and leek. Drain and chill.

4 To make the dressing, combine the vinegar, lemon juice and mustard. Add the shallot and whisk in the oil a little bit at a time. Season with salt and pepper.

5 Toss the beans with the blanched vegetables, green onions, parsley and thyme. Add the dressing and toss together. Adjust the seasonings and serve chilled.

Approximate values per ½-c. (120-ml) serving: **Calories** 250, **Total fat** 15 g, **Saturated fat** 2 g, **Cholesterol** 0 mg, **Sodium** 40 mg, **Total carbohydrates** 23 g, **Protein** 8 g, **Vitamin A** 50%, **Calcium** 10%, **Iron** 20%

MISE EN PLACE

▶ Wash and peel carrot and celery and cut into small dice.
▶ Wash, peel and slice leek.
▶ Wash, peel and mince shallot.
▶ Wash and mince green onions.
▶ Wash and chop parsley and thyme.

1 Draining the beans.

2 Blanching the vegetables.

3 Tossing the salad ingredients together.

4 The finished salad ready for buffet service.

STEAMING

Vegetables can be steamed in a convection steamer or by placing them in a basket or on a rack and suspending them over boiling liquid in a wok, saucepan or hotel pan. Vegetables can also be pan-steamed by cooking them in a covered pan with a small amount of liquid; most of the cooking is done by steam because only a small portion of the food is submerged in the liquid. Steamed vegetables can be eaten plain, partially cooked and sautéed lightly to finish, incorporated into casseroles or puréed. If they are not served immediately, they must be refreshed and refrigerated until used.

Properly steamed vegetables should be moist and tender. They generally retain their shape better than boiled vegetables. Vegetables cook very rapidly in steam, and over-cooking is a common mistake.

Selecting and Preparing Vegetables to Steam

Nearly any vegetable that can be boiled can also be steamed successfully. All vegetables should be washed, peeled and trimmed if appropriate and cut into uniform-sized pieces. Pan-steaming is appropriate for vegetables that are small or cut into fairly small pieces such as peas and beans or broccoli and cauliflower florets.

Seasoning Vegetables to Be Steamed

Steaming produces vegetables with clean, natural flavors. Foods cooked in convection steamers can be seasoned with herbs and spices; convection steamers use plain water to produce steam, so the foods being cooked do not gain flavor from the cooking liquid. Vegetables steamed over liquids or pan-steamed in small amounts of liquids can be flavored by using stocks or court bouillon as the cooking liquid. Herbs, spices and aromatic vegetables can be added to any liquid for additional flavor.

Procedure for Steaming Vegetables

1 Wash, peel and trim the vegetables and cut into uniform shapes and sizes.

2 If a convection steamer is not being used, prepare a steaming liquid and bring it to a boil in a covered pan or double boiler.

3 Place the vegetables in a perforated pan in a single layer; do not crowd the pan. Place the pan over the boiling liquid or add the vegetables to the liquid.

4 Cover the pan and cook to the desired doneness.

5 Remove the vegetables from the steamer and serve, or refresh and refrigerate until needed.

MISE EN PLACE
▶ Peel and mince garlic.

Yield: 6 Servings, 6 oz. (180 g) each   **Method:** Steaming

Fresh broccoli	2 lb.	960 g
Salt and pepper	TT	TT
Whole butter	2 oz.	60 g
Almonds, sliced	1 oz.	30 g
Garlic clove, minced	1	1
Lemon juice	2 fl. oz.	60 ml

1 Cut the broccoli into uniform spears. Rinse and sprinkle lightly with salt and pepper.

2 Place the broccoli in a single layer in a perforated hotel pan and cook in a convection steamer until tender but slightly crisp, approximately 3 minutes.

3 Melt the butter in a sauté pan. Add the almonds and garlic and cook just until the nuts are lightly browned.

4 Arrange the broccoli on plates for service and sprinkle with the lemon juice. Drizzle the almonds and butter over the broccoli and serve immediately.

Approximate values per 6-oz. (180-g) serving: **Calories** 160, **Total fat** 10 g, **Saturated fat** 5 g, **Cholesterol** 20 mg, **Sodium** 500 g, **Total carbohydrates** 10 g, **Protein** 6 g, **Vitamin A** 35%, **Vitamin C** 110%

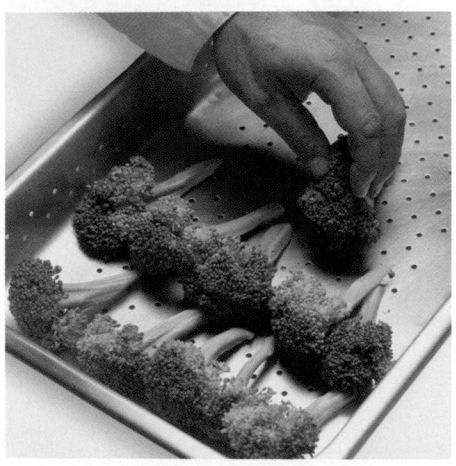

1 Placing the broccoli spears in a perforated pan.

2 Drizzling the browned almonds and butter over the broccoli.

Combination Cooking Methods

BRAISING AND STEWING

Braised and stewed vegetables are cooked slowly in a small amount of liquid. The liquid, including any given off by the vegetables, is reduced to a light sauce, becoming part of the finished product. Generally, a braised dish is prepared with only one vegetable; a stew is a mixture of several vegetables. The main ingredients are sometimes browned in fat before the liquid is added in order to enhance flavor and color.

Both braises and stews can be exceptionally flavorful because they are served with all of their cooking liquid. (Boiled vegetables lose some of their flavor to the cooking liquid.) Braised and stewed vegetables generally can be held hot for service longer than vegetables prepared by other cooking methods.

Selecting and Preparing Vegetables to Braise or Stew

Various lettuces, especially romaine and Boston, are often braised. Cabbages, Belgium endive, leeks and many other vegetables are also commonly braised. Stews may contain a wide variety of vegetables such as summer squashes, eggplant, onions, peppers, tomatoes, carrots, celery and garlic. Leafy green vegetables and winter squashes are less commonly braised or stewed.

The vegetables should be washed and peeled or trimmed if appropriate. Vegetables to be braised may be left whole, cut into uniform pieces or shredded, as desired. Lettuces are usually cut into halves or quarters; cabbage is usually shredded.

Seasoning Vegetables to Be Braised or Stewed

Both braises and stews usually include flavoring ingredients such as garlic, herbs, bacon or mirepoix. The liquid may consist of water, wine, stock or tomato juice. Vegetables can even be braised in butter and sugar or honey to create a glazed dish.

Both braises and stews can be seasoned with a variety of herbs and spices. Add the seasonings before covering the pot to finish the cooking process. Strongly flavored vegetables such as celery root and turnips are usually parboiled first in order to reduce their strong presence.

PROCEDURE FOR **BRAISING AND STEWING VEGETABLES**

❶ Wash, peel, trim and cut the vegetables.

❷ Sauté or sweat the flavoring ingredients in fat to release their flavors. Or sauté or sweat the main ingredients in fat.

❸ For a braise, add the main ingredient in a single layer. For a stew, add the ingredients according to their cooking times or as directed in the recipe.

❹ Add the cooking liquid; it should partially cover the vegetables. Bring the liquid to a boil, reduce to a simmer, cover and cook in the oven or on the stove top until done.

❺ If desired, remove the main ingredients from the pan and reduce the sauce or thicken it with beurre manié, cornstarch or arrowroot. Then return the main ingredients to the sauce.

BRAISED CELERY WITH BASIL

Yield: 12 Servings, 3 oz. (90 g) each   **Method:** Braising

Celery heads	3	3
Onions, small dice	8 oz.	240 g
Garlic, minced	2 tsp.	10 ml
Whole butter	2 oz.	60 g
Olive oil	2 Tbsp.	30 ml
Fresh thyme	1 tsp.	5 ml
Fresh basil leaves, chiffonade	20	20
Dry white wine	8 fl. oz.	240 ml
Chicken stock	1 pt.	480 ml
Salt and pepper	TT	TT

MISE EN PLACE

◀ Wash and peel onions and cut into small dice.
◀ Wash, peel and mince garlic.
◀ Slice basil in chiffonade.

❶ Trim the outer ribs from the celery heads, leaving only the tender hearts. Trim the heads to 6-inch (15-centimeter) lengths. Trim the root slightly, leaving each head together. Cut each head lengthwise into quarters.

❷ Sauté the onions and garlic in the butter and oil, without coloring, until tender. Add the celery quarters to the pan and sauté, turning occasionally.

❸ Add the thyme, basil, wine and stock. Bring to a boil, reduce to a simmer, cover and braise in the oven at 350°F (180°C) until tender, approximately 1 hour.

❹ Remove the celery and reserve. Reduce the cooking liquid on the stove top until it thickens. Adjust the liquid's seasonings and return the celery to the pan to reheat. Serve the celery with a portion of the sauce.

Approximate values per 3-oz. (90-g) serving: **Calories** 60, **Total fat** 4.5 g, **Saturated fat** 1.5 g, **Cholesterol** 5 mg, **Sodium** 170 mg, **Total carbohydrates** 2 g, **Protein** 1 g

❶ Trimming the celery.

❷ Adding the liquid to the celery.

❸ Reducing the sauce.

Microwaving

Fresh vegetables are among the few foods that can be consistently well prepared in a microwave oven. Often microwave cooking can be accomplished without any additional liquid, thus preserving nutrients. With microwaving, colors and flavors stay true, and textures remain crisp.

Microwave cooking is actually a form of steaming. As explained in Chapter 9, Principles of Cooking, microwaves agitate water molecules, thus creating steam. The water may be the moisture found naturally in the food or may be added specifically to create the steam.

Cooking time depends on the type of microwave oven as well as on the freshness, moisture content, maturity and quantity of vegetables being prepared.

Selecting and Preparing Vegetables to Microwave

Any vegetable that can be steamed successfully can be microwaved with good results. Because typical microwave ovens are relatively small, they are impractical for producing large quantities of food. They are most useful for reheating small portions of vegetables that have been blanched or partially cooked using another cooking method.

Seasoning Vegetables to Be Microwaved

Microwaving, like steaming, brings out the natural flavors of food. Herbs and spices can be added to the vegetables before they are microwaved. Or, after microwaving, the vegetables can be tossed with butter, herbs and spices or combined with a sauce.

PROCEDURE FOR MICROWAVING VEGETABLES

1. Wash, peel and trim the vegetables and cut into uniform shapes and sizes.
2. Place the vegetables in a steamer designed for microwave use or arrange the vegetables in a microwavable dish. Cover the vegetables with the lid or plastic wrap. If using plastic wrap, puncture it to allow some steam to escape during cooking.
3. Cook the vegetables to the desired doneness, allowing for some carryover cooking, or reheat the previously cooked vegetables until hot. Stir or turn the vegetables as necessary to promote even cooking.
4. Serve the vegetables or refresh and refrigerate until needed.

Puréeing

Puréeing is a technique often used with vegetables. Cooked vegetable purées can be served as is, or they can be used as an ingredient in other preparations such as pumpkin pie, mashed potatoes or vegetable soufflés. Purées can also be bound with eggs, seasoned and used to make vegetable timbales and terrines.

Puréed vegetables are generally first cooked by baking, boiling, steaming or microwaving. White, red and yellow vegetables should be cooked until quite soft. They are more easily puréed when hot or warm; this also helps ensure a smooth finished purée. For most preparations, green vegetables must be refreshed after cooking and puréed while cold, or they will overcook and become discolored.

Seasoning Vegetables to Be Puréed

Vegetables for purées can be seasoned before they are puréed following the guidelines for the cooking procedure used. They can also be seasoned after they are puréed with a wide variety of ingredients such as herbs, spices, cheese, honey or brown sugar.

Finishing Puréed Vegetables

Purées can be finished with stocks, sauces, butter or cream to add richness and flavor. First purée the main ingredient, then add additional liquids to obtain the desired consistency.

PROCEDURE FOR **PURÉEING VEGETABLES**

1 Cook the vegetables. White, red and yellow vegetables should be cooked until very soft. Green vegetables should be cooked until tender but not overcooked to the point of being discolored.

2 Purée the vegetables in a VCM, food processor or blender or by passing them through a food mill.

3 Season or finish the puréed vegetables as desired or directed in the recipe, or use them in another recipe.

PARSNIP PURÉE

Yield: 2 qt. (1.9 lt) **Method:** Boiling/Puréeing

Parsnips	4 lb.	1.9 kg
Russet potatoes	1 lb. 8 oz.	720 g
Heavy cream, hot	8 fl. oz.	240 ml
Whole butter, melted	4 oz.	120 g
Salt and white pepper	TT	TT

1 Peel the parsnips and potatoes and cut into large pieces of approximately the same size.

2 Boil the vegetables separately in salted water until tender.

3 Drain the vegetables well. Purée them together through a food mill.

4 Add the cream and butter and mix to combine. Adjust the consistency by adding cream as desired. Season the mixture with salt and white pepper and serve hot.

VARIATIONS:

Turnip Purée—Substitute turnips for the parsnips.

Winter Squash Purée—Select approximately 6½ pounds (3 kilograms) winter squash (such as acorn, butternut, pumpkin) and cut them in halves or quarters. Scoop out the seeds and then roast the squash, cut side down, in a 375°F (190°C) oven until tender. Scoop the flesh from the shells and substitute it for the parsnips.

Approximate values per ½-c. (120-ml) serving: **Calories** 240, **Total fat** 12 g, **Saturated fat** 7 g, **Cholesterol** 35 mg, **Sodium** 220 mg, **Total carbohydrates** 31 g, **Protein** 3 g, **Vitamin A** 10%, **Vitamin C** 35%

MISE EN PLACE
◀ Heat the cream and melt the butter while the parsnips and potatoes are cooking.

1 Passing the parsnips and potatoes through a food mill.

2 The finished Parsnip Purée.

Fermented and Pickled Vegetables (from left): Kosher Dill Pickles, Sauerkraut and Kim Chee

Preserving

For millennia people have preserved vegetables in times of plenty in order to have food available in times of need. Modern preservation techniques of canning and freezing aim to maintain vegetables in a state as close to fresh as possible. Ancient preservation techniques, such as drying, fermenting and pickling, alter the flavor and texture of vegetables dramatically, but are still used today. Drying, also known as dehydration, uses air and gentle heat to remove moisture from foods, so that bacteria can no longer cause spoilage or decay. Foods such as dried mushrooms and sun-dried tomatoes are then rehydrated in water or a flavorful liquid before use. Fermenting involves aging foods with salt to draw out moisture while simultaneously reducing the food's contact with air. Examples include kim chee and sauerkraut, both of which are made with cabbage. Pickling uses an acid, usually vinegar, to prevent the bacterial process of deterioration. Flavorings are added to a vinegar solution in which the vegetables are stored, sometimes after first being slightly cooked. Examples include the wide variety of cucumber pickles available, as well as pickled onions, cauliflower, carrots, and okra.

QUESTIONS FOR DISCUSSION

Terms to Know

Capsicum	hydroponics
Scoville heat units	pigments
	chlorophyll
mycologist	carotenoid
taproots	flavonoid
genetic diversity	

❶ Explain how the season affects the price, quality and availability of vegetables.

❷ List and describe three processing techniques commonly used to extend the shelf life of vegetables.

❸ What special concerns exist regarding the storage of fresh vegetables? Explain why some vegetables should not be refrigerated.

❹ Discuss proper ways to wash vegetables before using them and why.

❺ Why is it important to cut vegetables into a uniform size before cooking?

❻ Discuss several techniques used for determining the doneness of vegetables. Is carryover cooking a concern when preparing vegetables? Explain your answer.

❼ Discuss the role of acid in a cooking liquid used for preparing vegetables. Which vegetables, if any, benefit from an acidic cooking environment?

❽ Describe the necessary mise en place and procedure for refreshing vegetables.

❾ Locate information on farmer's markets in your area. What are the advantages and disadvantages of purchasing vegetables from a local grower?

❿ Many people are concerned about the use of genetically modified organisms (GMOs) and bioengineered products in the foods they eat. What is the federal government's position on these foodstuffs? What organizations are working to prohibit the use of GMOs? Why? Do you agree or disagree with their arguments? **WWW**

BROILED TOMATO

RUTH'S CHRIS STEAK HOUSE, PHOENIX, AZ

Yield: 1 Serving   **Method:** Broiling

Tomato, large	1	1
Granulated sugar	2 tsp.	10 ml
Whole butter, melted	1 oz.	30 g
Fresh parsley, chopped	1 Tbsp.	15 ml

1. Core and halve the tomato.
2. Sprinkle sugar on top of each half. Place on a broiler platter and broil until tender.
3. Drizzle with butter and garnish with parsley.

Approximate values per serving: **Calories** 170, **Total fat** 12 g, **Saturated fat** 7 g, **Cholesterol** 30 mg, **Sodium** 130 mg, **Total carbohydrates** 14 g, **Protein** 1 g, **Vitamin A** 20%, **Vitamin C** 40%

GRILLED PORTABELLA MUSHROOMS

Yield: 3 Servings, 4 oz. (120 g) each   **Method:** Grilling

Portabella mushroom caps	1 lb.	480 g
Olive oil	3 Tbsp.	45 ml
Garlic, chopped	1 tsp.	5 ml
Salt and pepper	TT	TT
Fresh thyme	1 tsp.	5 ml

1. Wipe the mushroom caps clean with a damp towel. Scrape out the gills from the underside of the mushroom caps.
2. Combine the oil and garlic and brush the mixture on the mushroom caps.
3. Season the mushrooms with salt, pepper and thyme.
4. Grill or broil the mushrooms until tender, approximately 8 minutes, depending on the size of the caps.

Approximate values per 4-oz. (120-g) serving: **Calories** 140, **Total fat** 10 g, **Saturated fat** 1.5 g, **Cholesterol** 0 mg, **Sodium** 790 mg, **Total carbohydrates** 8 g, **Protein** 6 g, **Claims**—no cholesterol; high fiber

ARIZONA BAKED CORN

NEWBURY COLLEGE, BROOKLINE, MA
Senior Instructor Scott Doughty

Yield: 8 Servings | | **Method:** Baking |

Onions, minced	10 oz.	300 g
Vegetable oil	2 Tbsp.	30 ml
Celery, minced	2 Tbsp.	30 ml
Chilli powder	5 Tbsp.	75 ml
Chipotle peppers, canned, seeded and minced	5 tsp.	25 ml
Tomato sauce, canned	6 fl. oz.	180 ml
Chicken stock, hot	8 fl. oz.	240 ml
Fresh corn kernels	3 lb.	1.4 kg
Salt	¾ tsp.	4 ml
Monterey Jack, grated	4 oz.	120 g

1. Sweat the onions in the vegetable oil for 8 minutes without browning. Add the celery and cook for an additional 2 minutes.
2. Stir in the chilli powder, chipotle peppers, tomato sauce, stock, corn and salt.
3. Pour the mixture into a buttered 2-inch- (5-centimeter-) deep one-third-size hotel pan. Cover and bake at 350°F (180°C) for 1 hour 15 minutes. Uncover, spread the cheese over the top and return to the oven until the cheese melts and begins to brown.

Approximate values per serving: **Calories** 310, **Total fat** 11 g, **Saturated fat** 3.5 g, **Cholesterol** 15 mg, **Sodium** 600 mg, **Total carbohydrates** 51 g, **Protein** 11 g, **Vitamin A** 40%, **Vitamin C** 35%, **Calcium** 15%, **Iron** 10%, **Claims**—high in vitamins A and C; source of calcium and iron

BAKED BEANS

Yield: 1½ qt. (1.4 lt) | | **Method:** Baking |

Great Northern beans, soaked	1 lb.	480 g
Onion, small dice	4 oz.	120 g
Anaheim chile, small dice	1 oz.	30 g
Molasses	3 oz.	90 g
Brown sugar	3 oz.	90 g
Ketchup	8 oz.	240 g
Prepared mustard	2 Tbsp.	30 ml
Cider vinegar	1 Tbsp.	15 ml
Worcestershire sauce	2 Tbsp.	30 ml
Tabasco sauce	TT	TT
Salt and pepper	TT	TT

1. Simmer the beans in water until almost tender, approximately 45 minutes. Drain well.
2. Combine the remaining ingredients, blending well.
3. Add the sauce to the beans, tossing to coat thoroughly. Adjust the seasonings.
4. Place the beans in a hotel pan or a 2-quart (2-liter) baking dish. Cover and bake in a 350°F (180°C) oven until the beans are completely tender, approximately 30 to 40 minutes.

VARIATION:

Boston-Style Baked Beans—Omit the chile and Tabasco sauce. Arrange 12 slices of bacon over the beans in Step 4 before baking.

Approximate values per 3-oz. (90-g) serving: **Calories** 120, **Total fat** 0 g, **Saturated fat** 0 g, **Cholesterol** 0 mg, **Sodium** 490 mg, **Total carbohydrates** 26 g, **Protein** 4 g, **Vitamin C** 15%, **Claims**—fat free; good source of fiber

OVEN-ROASTED GARLIC

Yield: 9 Servings

Method: Baking

Garlic, whole heads	9	9
Olive oil	3 fl. oz.	90 ml
Salt and pepper	TT	TT

1 Cut the top from each head of garlic and discard. Place the garlic, cut side up, in a half-size hotel pan. Brush the tops of the garlic with oil, then season generously with salt and pepper.

2 Cover the pan and bake at 300°F (150°C) until the garlic softens, approximately 1 hour. Remove the cover and continue baking until any moisture has evaporated and the garlic develops a deep golden color, approximately 15 minutes.

3 Serve the garlic heads whole or squeeze out the softened pulp to use in sauces and purées.

Approximate values per serving: **Calories** 120, **Total fat** 0 g, **Saturated fat** 0 g, **Cholesterol** 0 mg, **Sodium** 490 mg, **Total carbohydrates** 26 g, **Protein** 4 g, **Vitamin C** 15%, **Claims**—fat free; good source of fiber

1 Seasoning the heads of garlic to roast.

2 The finished Oven-Roasted Garlic.

GARLIC TIMBALES

Yield: 8 Timbales, 2 fl. oz. (60 ml) each

Method: Baking

Garlic cloves, peeled	10	10
Milk	3 fl. oz.	90 ml
Heavy cream	8 fl. oz.	240 ml
Eggs	2	2
Dried thyme	1 tsp.	5 ml
Salt and pepper	TT	TT

1 Butter eight small ramekins or timbales.

2 Place the garlic in a small saucepan, add enough water to cover and bring to a boil. Drain. Repeat this blanching procedure two more times.

3 Place the garlic in a blender with the milk and blend. Add the cream, eggs and thyme; blend until smooth. Season with salt and pepper.

4 Divide the custard among the timbales and place in a water bath. Bake for 30 to 45 minutes at 325°F (160°C).

5 Run a paring knife around the rim and unmold onto the serving plate.

VARIATION:

Broccoli or Cauliflower Timbales—Place 1 ounce (30 grams) blanched broccoli or cauliflower in each buttered timbale before adding the garlic custard mixture.

Approximate values per timbale: **Calories** 130, **Total fat** 12 g, **Saturated fat** 7 g, **Cholesterol** 95 mg, **Sodium** 320 mg, **Total carbohydrates** 3 g, **Protein** 3 g, **Vitamin A** 15%

VEGETABLE STRUDEL

UNIVERSITY OF WISCONSIN, STOUT, MENOMONIE, WI

Associate Professor Phillip H. McGuirk

Yield: 12 Servings		**Method:** Sautéing/Baking
Garlic, minced	3 oz.	90 g
Olive oil	1 fl. oz.	30 ml
Snow pea pods, julienne	1 lb.	480 g
Carrots, julienne	1 lb.	480 g
Yellow squash, julienne	1 lb.	480 g
Zucchini, julienne	1 lb.	480 g
Yellow bell peppers	1 lb.	480 g
Red bell peppers	1 lb.	480 g
Ricotta cheese	1 lb.	480 g
Fresh basil, chopped	6 Tbsp.	90 ml
Salt and pepper	TT	TT
Phyllo sheets	18	18
Whole butter, melted	6 fl. oz.	180 ml
Dry bread crumbs	1 lb.	480 g
Fresh Tomato Sauce for Pasta (page 222)	as needed for garnish	

1. Sauté the garlic in the oil without coloring for approximately 2 minutes. Remove from the pan and cool.
2. Combine all of the vegetables with the sautéed garlic, cheese and basil. Season to taste with salt and pepper and mix well.
3. Lay out a sheet of phyllo and brush it with melted butter. Sprinkle it with approximately 1 ounce (30 grams) dry bread crumbs. Lay another sheet of phyllo on top of the first, brush it with butter and sprinkle it with dry bread crumbs. Repeat until you have a stack of six sheets of phyllo.
4. Divide the vegetable-and-cheese mixture into three equal portions. Spread one portion of the mixture along the long side of the phyllo stack. Roll the phyllo up around the mixture to form a log. Place the log on a parchment-lined sheet pan, seam side down. Brush the log with melted butter and score the top of the log with a sharp knife. Repeat with the remaining phyllo sheets and vegetable mixture until you have three logs.
5. Bake the strudel at 400°F (200°C) until golden brown, approximately 15 to 20 minutes. Cut each log into four portions and serve with Fresh Tomato Sauce for Pasta or other appropriate sauce.

Approximate values per serving: **Calories** 490, **Total fat** 23 g, **Saturated fat** 12 g, **Cholesterol** 50 mg, **Sodium** 1060 mg, **Total carbohydrates** 30 g, **Protein** 9 g, **Vitamin A** 20%, **Vitamin C** 120%, **Claims**—high in fiber, vitamins A and C, calcium and Iron

MUSHROOM AND LEEK TART

Yield: 8 Tarts		**Method:** Sautéing/Baking
Clarified butter	2 fl. oz.	60 ml
Leeks, white part only, sliced thin	24 oz.	720 g
Garlic, chopped	1 tsp.	5 ml
White mushrooms, trimmed and sliced	1 lb.	480 g
Shiitake mushrooms, trimmed and sliced	1 lb.	480 g
Salt	1 Tbsp.	15 ml
Pepper	½ tsp.	2 ml
Havarti, shredded	6 oz.	180 g
Fresh thyme, chopped	1 Tbsp.	15 ml

Dried basil	½ tsp.	2 ml
Heavy cream	8 fl. oz.	240 ml
Puff pastry	4 lb.	1.9 kg
Egg wash	as needed	as needed
Parmesan, grated	8 oz.	240 g

1. Heat the butter in a large sauté pan. Add the leeks, garlic and mushrooms and sauté until tender.
2. Add the salt, pepper, Havarti, herbs and cream, bring to a boil and reduce until the mixture is thick. Adjust the seasonings. Remove from the heat and cool.
3. Roll the puff pastry approximately ¼ inch (6 millimeters) thick and cut eight circles approximately 9 inches (22 centimeters) in diameter from the pastry. Brush a 1-inch (6-millimeter) band of egg wash around the edge of each circle. Fold the edge of the pastry in toward the center to form a 1-inch (6-millimeter) rim and crimp.
4. Fill each tart shell with 6 ounces (180 grams) of the leek-and-mushroom filling. Spread the filling to the edge of the tart and sprinkle the top with Parmesan. Brush the edge of each tart with egg wash and bake in a 400°F (200°C) convection oven until the pastry is well browned, approximately 10 to 12 minutes.

VARIATION:

Any type of mushroom or mixture of mushrooms can be used in place of the white and shiitake mushrooms and any variety of cheese that melts well can be substituted for the Havarti. The tarts can also be formed into other shapes or sizes as desired.

Approximate values per tart: **Calories** 1710, **Total fat** 119 g, **Saturated fat** 42 g, **Cholesterol** 100 mg, **Sodium** 213 mg, **Total carbohydrates** 123 g, **Protein** 38 g, **Vitamin A** 25%, **Vitamin C** 20%, **Calcium** 60%, **Iron** 50%

STUFFED CUBANELLE PEPPERS

SOUTHERN NEW HAMPSHIRE UNIVERSITY, MANCHESTER, NH

John C. Knorr

Yield: 12 Peppers   **Method:** Blanching/Baking

Cubanelle peppers	12	12
Chicken breasts, boneless, skinless	24 oz.	720 g
Salt and pepper	TT	TT
Vegetable oil	2 tsp.	10 ml
Cream cheese, soft	12 oz.	360 g
Salsa	2½ pt.	1.2 lt
Monterey Jack, shredded	12 oz.	360 g

1. Cut ½ inch (1.5 centimeters) from the top of each pepper and reserve the tops. Remove the membranes and seeds from the body and blanch the peppers in boiling water for 30 seconds. Remove from the water, drain and cool.
2. Season the chicken breasts with salt and pepper. Brush them with oil and grill until done. Cool the chicken and slice into thin strips.
3. Combine the chicken, cream cheese and 1¼ cups (300 milliliters) salsa in a small mixer. Season with salt and pepper and mix well but do not purée.
4. Fill the peppers with the chicken mixture and replace the tops. Place the peppers in a baking dish and cover with the remaining salsa and shredded cheese. Bake the peppers at 375°F (190°C) until hot, approximately 30 minutes.

Note: If Cubanelle peppers are not available, fresh de agua, pimento (chile pimiento) or small poblano chiles can be substituted.

Approximate values per serving: **Calories** 320, **Total fat** 21 g, **Saturated fat** 12 g, **Cholesterol** 90 mg, **Sodium** 730 mg, **Total carbohydrates** 12 g, **Protein** 23 g, **Vitamin A** 35%, **Vitamin C** 140%, **Calcium** 30%, **Iron** 15%

MAPLE-GLAZED CARROTS

Yield: 16 Servings, 4 oz. (120 g) each | **Method:** Sautéing

Carrots, full-size or baby	4 lb.	1.9 kg
Whole butter	4 oz.	120 g
Salt and pepper	TT	TT
Maple syrup	4 fl. oz.	120 ml
Fresh parsley, chopped	2 Tbsp.	30 ml

1. If using full-size carrots, peel them and cut into a shape such as oblique, tournée or rondelle. If using baby carrots, wash, trim and cut them as necessary or desired.
2. Parboil the carrots in salt water and refresh. The carrots should be very firm.
3. Sauté the carrots in the butter until nearly tender.
4. Season with salt and pepper and add the maple syrup. Cook briefly, tossing the carrots so that they are coated with the maple syrup. Garnish with the parsley.

Approximate values per 4-oz. (120-g) serving: **Calories** 120, **Total fat** 6 g, **Saturated fat** 3.5 g, **Cholesterol** 15 mg, **Sodium** 260 mg, **Total carbohydrates** 16 g, **Protein** 1 g, **Vitamin A** 220%, **Vitamin C** 15%

---

duxelles a coarse paste made of finely chopped mushrooms sautéed with shallots in butter used in sauces and stuffing

DUXELLES

Yield: 12 oz. (360 g) | **Method:** Sautéing

Mushrooms	1 lb.	480 g
Shallots, minced	2 Tbsp.	30 ml
Garlic, chopped	1 tsp.	5 ml
Whole butter	½ oz.	15 g
Salt and pepper	TT	TT
Fresh parsley, chopped	1 Tbsp.	15 ml

1. Chop the mushrooms very finely.
2. Sauté the shallots and garlic in the butter until tender. Add the mushrooms and sauté until dry.
3. Season with salt and pepper and add the parsley. Cool and then use the duxelles as a stuffing for vegetables or as a flavoring ingredient in other recipes.

Approximate values per 1-oz. (30-g) serving: **Calories** 20, **Total fat** 1 g, **Saturated fat** 0.5 g, **Cholesterol** 5 mg, **Sodium** 210 mg, **Total carbohydrates** 2 g, **Protein** 1 g, **Claims**—low fat; low cholesterol; low calorie

1. Sautéing the mushrooms and shallots.

2. The finished Duxelles.

RATATOUILLE

Yield: 16 Servings, 4 oz. (120 g) each   **Method:** Sautéing

Onions, medium dice	12 oz.	360 g
Garlic, chopped	1 Tbsp.	15 ml
Olive oil	4 fl. oz.	120 ml
Green bell pepper, medium dice	6 oz.	180 g
Red bell pepper, medium dice	6 oz.	180 g
Eggplant, medium dice	12 oz.	360 g
Zucchini, medium dice	8 oz.	240 g
Tomato concassée	24 oz.	720 g
Fresh basil leaves, chiffonade	1 oz.	30 g
Salt	1 oz.	30 g
Black pepper	TT	TT

1. Sauté the onion and garlic in the oil.
2. Add the bell peppers, eggplant and zucchini and sauté until tender, approximately 10 minutes.
3. Add the tomato concassée, basil and seasonings. Sauté for 5 minutes. Adjust the seasonings.

Approximate values per 4-oz. (120-g) serving: **Calories** 90, **Total fat** 7 g, **Saturated fat** 1 g, **Cholesterol** 0 mg, **Sodium** 690 mg, **Total carbohydrates** 6 g, **Protein** 1 g, **Vitamin C** 35%, **Claims**—low saturated fat; no cholesterol

1. Sautéing the onions and garlic.

2. Adding the peppers, eggplant and zucchini.

3. The finished Ratatouille.

BEET AND CORN SALAD

DUO RESTAURANT, DENVER, CO

Chef John Broening

Yield: 8 Servings   **Method:** Boiling

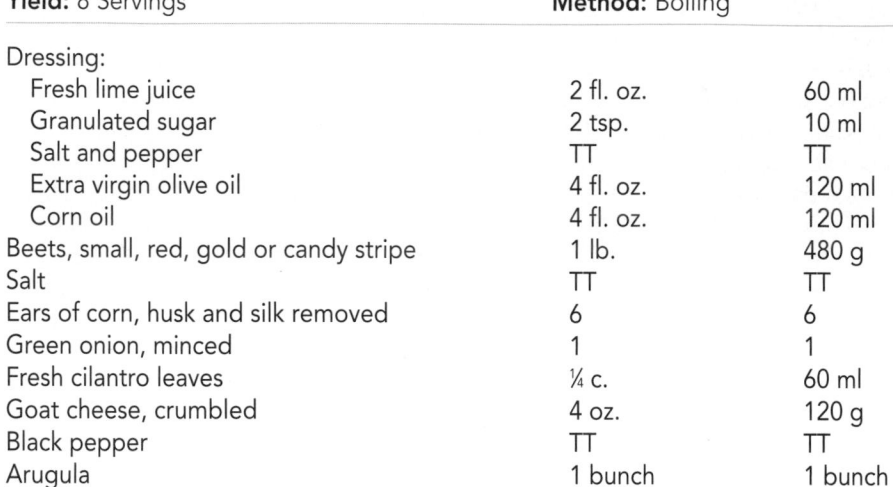

Dressing:		
Fresh lime juice	2 fl. oz.	60 ml
Granulated sugar	2 tsp.	10 ml
Salt and pepper	TT	TT
Extra virgin olive oil	4 fl. oz.	120 ml
Corn oil	4 fl. oz.	120 ml
Beets, small, red, gold or candy stripe	1 lb.	480 g
Salt	TT	TT
Ears of corn, husk and silk removed	6	6
Green onion, minced	1	1
Fresh cilantro leaves	¼ c.	60 ml
Goat cheese, crumbled	4 oz.	120 g
Black pepper	TT	TT
Arugula	1 bunch	1 bunch

1. To make the dressing, whisk together the lime juice, sugar, salt and pepper. Slowly whisk in the oils to emulsify.
2. Boil the beets in salted water until tender, approximately 15 minutes. Drain, cool, peel, dice and reserve.
3. Boil the ears of corn in salted water until tender, approximately 3 minutes. Drain, cool, cut the kernels from the cobs and reserve.
4. In a stainless steel bowl, mix together the corn, green onion, cilantro and cheese. Toss with the dressing and adjust the seasoning with salt and pepper. Divide the corn mixture evenly between eight ring molds on eight plates. Top with some of the beets. Remove the rings. Garnish with the arugula and serve.

Approximate values per serving: **Calories** 370, **Total fat** 31 g, **Saturated fat** 6 g, **Cholesterol** 5 mg, **Sodium** 110 mg, **Total carbohydrates** 21 g, **Protein** 6 g, **Vitamin A** 15%, **Vitamin C** 20%

SAUTÉED BROCCOLI RABE

Turnip, beet, escarole, arugula or other tender greens can be cooked using this same preparation method.

Yield: 4 Servings   **Method:** Sautéing

Broccoli rabe	1¼ lbs.	600 g
Olive oil	2 fl. oz.	60 ml
Garlic cloves, sliced thin	2	2
Red pepper flakes	¼ tsp.	1 ml
Chicken stock	8 fl. oz.	240 ml
Salt and pepper	TT	TT

1. Wash the broccoli rabe and cut off the stems. Leave on any excess water.
2. In a large sauté pan over medium heat, heat the oil, garlic and red pepper flakes. Sauté until the garlic softens without browning. Add the broccoli rabe and sauté for 5 minutes. Add the chicken stock, cover and cook until tender and cooked through, approximately 6 to 8 more minutes.
3. Season with salt and pepper before serving.

Approximate values per serving: **Calories** 170, **Total fat** 15 g, **Saturated fat** 2 g, **Cholesterol** 0 mg, **Sodium** 125 mg, **Total carbohydrates** 6 g, **Protein** 5 g, **Vitamin A** 60%, **Vitamin C** 40%

PAN-FRIED EGGPLANT WITH TOMATO SAUCE

NEWBURY COLLEGE, BROOKLINE, MA

Senior Instructor Scott Doughty

Yield: 8 Servings   **Method:** Pan-frying

Eggplant, large	1	1
Tomato sauce	1 pt.	480 ml
Flour	4 oz.	120 g
Salt	TT	TT
White pepper	1 tsp.	5 ml
Egg wash	8 fl. oz.	240 ml
Fresh bread crumbs, crustless	8 oz.	240 g
Vegetable oil	as needed	as needed

1 Trim the ends from the eggplant. Remove strips of peel, lengthwise, with a chef's knife, leaving narrow strips of peel between the cuts. Cut into round slices ¼ inch (6 millimeters) thick.

2 Warm the tomato sauce.

3 Season the flour with salt and add the white pepper. Bread the eggplant slices using the standard breading procedure described in Chapter 8, Mise en Place (finishing with the bread crumbs), and arrange them in a single layer on a sheet pan. Separate the layers with parchment.

4 Heat two sautoirs and add a ¼-inch (6-millimeter) layer of oil in each. When the oil is hot, pan-fry the eggplant slices until golden brown, then turn and cook until tender. Remove and drain on clean paper towels or a rack. Repeat until all the slices are cooked, adding more oil as necessary.

5 Arrange the slices on a large serving platter and ladle the tomato sauce attractively over the eggplant.

Approximate values per serving: **Calories** 220, **Total fat** 10 g, **Saturated fat** 1.5 g, **Cholesterol** 55 mg, **Sodium** 530 mg, **Total carbohydrates** 29 g, **Protein** 6 g, **Vitamin A** 15%, **Vitamin C** 15%, **Iron** 10%

1 Turning the eggplant slices to brown on the other side.

2 The platter of pan-fried eggplant.

TEMPURA VEGETABLES WITH DIPPING SAUCE

Yield: Approximately 1 qt. (1 lt) Batter, enough for 4 lb. (1.9 kg) vegetables

Method: Deep-frying

Dipping sauce:		
Mirin	2 fl. oz.	60 ml
Soy sauce	4 fl. oz.	120 ml
Rice wine vinegar	2 fl. oz.	60 ml
Lemon juice	1 Tbsp.	15 ml
Wasabi powder	1 tsp.	5 ml
Tempura batter:		
Eggs	2	2
Sparkling water, cold	1 pt.	480 ml
Flour	10 oz.	300 g
Sweet potato, approx. 8 oz. (240 g)	1	1
Broccoli florets	8 oz.	240 g
Mushrooms, small, whole	1 lb.	480 g
Zucchini, bâtonnet	8 oz.	240 g

1. Combine all of the dipping sauce ingredients. Set aside.
2. To prepare the batter, beat the eggs and add the cold water.
3. Add the flour to the egg-and-water mixture and mix until the flour is incorporated. There should still be small lumps in the batter. Overmixing develops gluten, which is undesirable.
4. Peel the sweet potato and cut it into ¼-inch- (6-millimeter-) thick slices. If the potato is large, cut each slice in half to make semicircles.
5. Blanch the broccoli florets briefly in boiling water. Drain and pat dry with paper towels.
6. Drop the vegetables in the batter a few at a time. Remove them from the batter one at a time and drop them into the deep-fryer using the swimming method. Cook until done. Remove and drain.
7. Arrange the tempura vegetables on a serving platter. Serve the dipping sauce on the side.

VARIATION:

Shrimp Tempura—Substitute peeled and deveined shrimp for some of the vegetables in this dish.

Approximate values per 4-oz. (120-g) serving: **Calories** 240, **Total fat** 15 g, **Saturated fat** 2.5 g, **Cholesterol** 25 mg, **Sodium** 530 mg, **Total carbohydrates** 22 g, **Protein** 5 g, **Vitamin A** 50%, **Vitamin C** 30%, **Iron** 10%

1. Mixing the tempura batter.

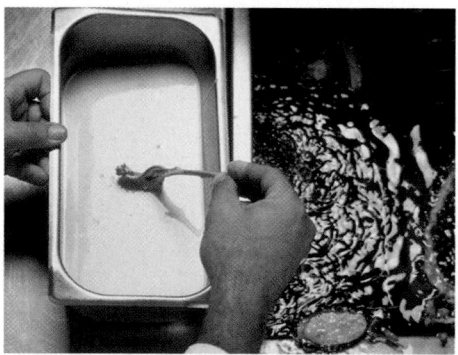

2. Battering the vegetables.

3. Frying the vegetables using the swimming method.

COLLARD GREENS

JOLIET JUNIOR COLLEGE, JOLIET, IL

Keith G. Vonhoff, CCE, CEPC, CHA, CHE, FMP, CCP

Yield: 8 Servings　　　　　　　　　**Method:** Simmering

Ham hocks, smoked	6	6
Chile flakes	½ tsp.	2 ml
Water	as needed	as needed
Collard greens	4 lb.	1.9 kg
Green onions, small dice	2	2
Brown sugar	2 tsp.	10 ml
Cider vinegar	2 fl. oz.	60 ml
Salt and pepper	TT	TT

1. In a medium saucepot, combine the ham hocks and chile flakes. Cover with 1 inch (2.5 centimeters) water, bring to a boil, reduce to a simmer and cook until the hocks are tender, approximately 1 hour. Remove the hocks from the pot, reserving the cooking liquid, which is known as pot liquor.

2. Wash, trim and cut the collard greens. Add them to the pot liquor and simmer until tender, approximately 15 minutes to 1 hour.

3. Add the green onions, sugar and vinegar to the greens. Bring to a simmer and reduce the liquid until it coats the collard greens. Season to taste with salt and pepper.

4. Remove the meat from the ham hocks and cut into medium dice. Stir the diced ham into the greens and serve.

Approximate values per serving: **Calories** 200, **Total fat** 10 g, **Saturated fat** 3.5 g, **Cholesterol** 40 mg, **Sodium** 60 mg, **Total carbohydrates** 15 g, **Protein** 16 g, **Vitamin A** 170%, **Vitamin C** 80%, **Calcium** 30%, **Iron** 10%

CALABACITAS
(SOUTHWESTERN-STYLE VEGETABLES)

Yield: 8 Servings　　　　　　　　　**Method:** Simmering

White onion, large, chopped coarse	1	1
Red bell pepper, seeded, chopped fine	1½ oz.	45 g
Garlic cloves, minced	2	2
Corn oil	1 Tbsp.	15 ml
Corn kernels	8 oz.	240 g
Yellow squash, chopped	1 lb.	480 g
Zucchini, chopped	1 lb.	480 g
Anaheim chiles, roasted, peeled, seeded and diced	2	2
Water, hot	4 fl. oz.	120 ml
Cumin, ground	1 tsp.	5 ml
Salt and pepper	TT	TT

1. In a large, deep pan sauté the onion, bell pepper and garlic in the oil. Add the corn and cook until very lightly browned.

2. Add the squash, zucchini and chiles along with the water, cumin and seasonings. Cover, reduce the heat and simmer until tender, approximately 15 minutes. Adjust the seasonings.

Approximate values per ½-c. (120-ml) serving: **Calories** 70, **Total fat** 2.5 g, **Saturated fat** 0 g, **Cholesterol** 0 mg, **Sodium** 10 mg, **Total carbohydrates** 13 g, **Protein** 2 g, **Vitamin A** 15%, **Vitamin C** 80%, **Claims**—low fat; low sodium; no saturated fat; no cholesterol; good source of vitamins A and C

SPINACH AU GRATIN

RUTH'S CHRIS STEAK HOUSE, PHOENIX, AZ

Yield: 8 Servings, 8 oz. (240 g) each		**Method:** Boiling/Broiling
Clarified butter	1 fl. oz.	30 ml
Flour	1 oz.	30 g
Half-and-half	1 pt.	480 ml
Frozen chopped spinach, thawed	2 lb. 8 oz.	1.2 kg
Salt and pepper	TT	TT
Cheddar cheese, shredded	1 lb. 8 oz.	700 g

1. Heat the butter in a medium saucepan. Add the flour and cook to make a blond roux.
2. Add the half-and-half, whisking to remove any lumps of roux. Bring to a simmer and cook for 15 minutes.
3. Drop the spinach into boiling salted water and cook for 2 minutes. Remove from the heat and drain well.
4. Combine the hot spinach with the cream sauce and adjust the seasonings.
5. Fill eight 10-ounce gratin dishes with the creamed spinach. Top each with 3 ounces (90 grams) cheese and place under the broiler until the cheese is melted and browned and the spinach is very hot. Serve immediately.

Approximate values per 8-oz. (240-g) serving: **Calories** 510, **Total fat** 38 g, **Saturated fat** 24 g, **Cholesterol** 120 mg, **Sodium** 960 mg, **Total carbohydrates** 14 g, **Protein** 28 g, **Vitamin A** 140%, **Calcium** 90%

GLAZED PEARL ONIONS

Yield: 1 lb. (480 g)		**Method:** Boiling
Pearl onions, peeled	1 lb.	480 g
Whole butter	1½ oz.	45 g
Granulated sugar	1 Tbsp.	15 ml
Salt and pepper	TT	TT

1. Place the onions, butter and sugar in a sauté pan and add enough water to barely cover.
2. Boil the onions, allowing the water to evaporate. As the water evaporates, the butter-and-sugar mixture will begin to coat the onions. When the water is nearly gone, test the doneness of the onions. If they are still firm, add a small amount of water and continue to boil until the onions are tender.
3. Sauté the onions in the butter-and-sugar mixture until they are glazed. Season to taste.

1. Boiling the pearl onions.

2. Glazing the onions in butter and sugar.

VARIATIONS:

Vegetables such as carrots, turnips, zucchini and other squashes can also be glazed with this procedure. They should be cut into appropriate shapes such as a tournée and be large enough so that they glaze properly without overcooking. When preparing a mix of glazed vegetables, cook each type separately because each has a different cooking time.

Approximate values per 2-oz. (60-g) serving: **Calories** 70, **Total fat** 4.5 g, **Saturated fat** 2.5 g, **Cholesterol** 10 mg, **Sodium** 340 mg, **Total carbohydrates** 8 g, **Protein** 1 g

---

RED BEANS AND RICE WITH ANDOUILLE

Yield: 10 Servings, 8 oz. (240 g) beans each   **Method:** Simmering

Red kidney beans, dry	1 lb.	480 g
Water	as needed	as needed
Spice mix:		
Bay leaves	5	5
Dried thyme	2 tsp.	10 ml
Dried oregano	2 tsp.	10 ml
Cayenne pepper	½ tsp.	2 ml
Black pepper	½ tsp.	2 ml
Water	1 gal.	3.8 lt
Smoked ham hocks	2	2
Celery, small dice	8 oz.	240 g
Onions, small dice	13 oz.	390 g
Green bell pepper, small dice	5 oz.	150 g
Garlic cloves	1 oz.	30 g
Andouille, sliced on the bias ¼ in. (6 mm) thick	1 lb.	480 g
Salt and pepper	TT	TT
Simmered Rice (page 642)	2 pt.	960 ml

1. Soak the beans in water overnight and drain.
2. Combine the spice mix ingredients and reserve.
3. In a heavy-bottomed saucepot, combine 1 gallon (3.8 liters) water with the ham hocks, beans, celery, onions, bell pepper, garlic and spice mix. Bring to a boil, reduce to a simmer and cook for 1 hour.
4. Remove the ham hocks from the pot. Separate the meat from the bones and discard the skin, bones and cartilage. Cut the meat into medium dice. Add the meat and the andouille slices to the pot and simmer, stirring often, until the beans are very tender and begin to break up, approximately 30 minutes. Add more water if necessary to prevent the beans from burning. Remove the bay leaves and adjust the seasonings.
5. To serve, mound a portion of the Simmered Rice on a soup plate and ladle the bean mixture around it.

Approximate values per serving: **Calories** 430, **Total fat** 17 g, **Saturated fat** 6 g, **Cholesterol** 45 mg, **Sodium** 460 mg, **Total carbohydrates** 48 g, **Protein** 21 g, **Vitamin C** 30%, **Calcium** 10%, **Iron** 30%

ORIENTAL STUFFED CABBAGE ROLLS

Yield: 8 Rolls   **Method:** Steaming

Savoy cabbage leaves, large	8	8
Ground pork	8 oz.	240 g
Carrot, grated	4 oz.	120 g
Onion, minced	4 oz.	120 g
Fresh ginger, chopped	2 Tbsp.	30 ml
Garlic cloves, chopped	3	3
Soy sauce	½ tsp.	2 ml
Sesame oil	½ tsp.	2 ml
Cellophane noodles, soaked, drained	4 oz.	120 g
Soy Dipping Sauce (recipe follows)	6 fl. oz.	180 ml

1 Trim the thick stem from each of the savoy cabbage leaves. Steam the leaves for 5 minutes and allow them to cool.

2 Combine the pork, carrot, onion, ginger, garlic, soy sauce, oil and noodles and mix well.

3 Lay the cabbage leaves out on a work surface. Divide the filling among the leaves. Fold one end of each leaf over the filling. Fold in each side, then roll into a log shape. Chill the stuffed leaves for at least 1 hour before cooking.

4 Steam the cabbage rolls until tender and they reach an internal temperature of 155°F (68°C), for approximately 15 minutes or until fully cooked. Serve with Soy Dipping Sauce.

Approximate values per serving: **Calories** 140, **Total fat** 4.5 g, **Saturated fat** 1.5 g, **Cholesterol** 20 mg, **Sodium** 550 mg, **Total carbohydrates** 18 g, **Protein** 7 g, **Vitamin A** 35%, **Vitamin C** 15%

SOY DIPPING SAUCE

Yield: 6 fl. oz. (180 ml)

Soy sauce	2 fl. oz.	60 ml
Cider vinegar	3 Tbsp.	45 ml
Hot chile oil	TT	TT
Green onion, sliced thin	2 oz.	60 g
Water	2 fl. oz.	60 ml

1 Combine all ingredients.

Approximate values per ½-fl.-oz. (15-ml) serving: **Calories** 5, **Total fat** 0 g, **Saturated fat** 0 g, **Cholesterol** 0 mg, **Sodium** 340 mg, **Total carbohydrates** 1 g, **Protein** 1 g

BRAISED RED CABBAGE WITH APPLES

Yield: 16 Servings, 4 oz. (120 g) each   **Method:** Braising

Red cabbage	3 lb.	1.4 kg
Bacon, medium dice	12 oz.	360 g
Onions, medium dice	8 oz.	240 g
Salt and pepper	TT	TT
Red wine	8 fl. oz.	240 ml
White stock	8 fl. oz.	240 ml
Cinnamon sticks	2	2
Apples, tart, cored and diced	12 oz.	360 g
Brown sugar	1 oz.	30 g
Cider vinegar	2 fl. oz.	60 ml

1. Shred the cabbage.
2. Render the bacon. Add the onions and sweat in the bacon fat until tender.
3. Add the cabbage and sauté for 5 minutes. Season with salt and pepper. Add the wine, stock and cinnamon sticks. Cover and braise until the cabbage is almost tender, approximately 20 minutes.
4. Add the apples, sugar and vinegar and mix well.
5. Cover and braise until the apples are tender, approximately 5 minutes. Remove the cinnamon sticks before service.

Approximate values per 4-oz. (120-g) serving: **Calories** 170, **Total fat** 11 g, **Saturated fat** 4 g, **Cholesterol** 20 mg, **Sodium** 540 mg, **Total carbohydrates** 11 g, **Protein** 8 g, **Vitamin C** 50%

ARTICHOKES STUFFED WITH ITALIAN SAUSAGE

Yield: 8 Servings

Method: Braising

Artichokes	8	8
Bulk sausage meat	1 lb.	480 g
Onions, chopped fine	1 lb.	480 g
Garlic, chopped fine	2 Tbsp.	30 ml
Cumin, ground	1 tsp.	5 ml
Fresh cilantro, chopped	4 oz.	120 g
Fresh thyme	2 tsp.	10 ml
Fresh bread crumbs	4 oz.	120 g
Tabasco sauce	TT	TT
Salt and pepper	TT	TT
Olive oil	2 fl. oz.	60 ml
Chicken stock	1 qt.	960 ml

1. Trim the stem and barbs from the artichokes. Using a tablespoon, scoop out the choke from the center of each artichoke.
2. Cook the sausage meat, breaking it up into small pieces. Pour off the fat. Add the onions and garlic and sauté until tender.
3. Add the cumin, cilantro, thyme and bread crumbs. Season with Tabasco sauce, salt and pepper.
4. Stuff the artichokes with the sausage mixture.
5. Place the artichokes in a braising pan and drizzle with oil. Add the stock.
6. Bring the stock to a boil. Cover and braise until the artichokes are tender, approximately 1 hour.

Approximate values per serving: **Calories** 420, **Total fat** 26 g, **Saturated fat** 7 g, **Cholesterol** 45 mg, **Sodium** 1270 mg, **Total carbohydrates** 29 g, **Protein** 18 g, **Vitamin C** 30%, **Calcium** 15%, **Iron** 20%

CHAPTER TWENTY-TWO

POTATOES, GRAINS AND PASTA

POTATOES, GRAINS (CORN, RICE, WHEAT AND OTHERS) and pastas are collectively known as starches. Some of these foods are vegetables; others are grasses. Pastas, of course, are prepared products made from grains. Starches are, for the most part, staple foods: foods that define a cuisine and give it substance. All are high in starchy carbohydrates, low in fat and commonly used as part of a well-balanced meal.

Today's chefs are rediscovering traditional and ethnic dishes that rely on grains seldom used in typical American food service operations. Pasta, made from a variety of grains in numerous shapes and flavors and accompanied by countless sauces and garnishes, now regularly appears on many menus alongside the ubiquitous potato prepared for many classic and modern dishes.

POTATOES

Potatoes (Fr. *pommes de terre*) are one of the few vegetables native to the New World, probably originating in the South American Andes. Botanically, potatoes are succulent, nonwoody annual plants. The portion consumed is the tuber, the swollen fleshy part of the underground stem. Potatoes are hardy and easy to grow, making them inexpensive and widely available. Americans eat nearly 60 pounds of potatoes annually, making potatoes one of the top 20 vegetables in the United States.

Identifying Potatoes

Discussed here are some of the more commonly used types of potatoes. Other varieties are regularly being developed or rediscovered and tested in the market place.

Choose potatoes that are heavy and very firm with clean skin and few eyes. Avoid those with many eyes, sprouts, green streaks, soft spots, cracks or cut edges. Most varieties are available all year. When ordering potatoes, note that size A is larger than size B, which must be between 1½ and 2¼ inches (3.75 and 5.5 centimeters) in diameter. Size C potatoes, or creamers, are the smallest size, measuring ¾ inch to 1⅝ inches (2 to 4 centimeters) in diameter.

New potatoes are small, immature potatoes (of any variety) that are harvested before their starches develop. Although red potatoes can be "new," not all new potatoes are necessarily red-skinned. Conversely, not all red-skinned potatoes are new. True new potatoes are waxy with a high moisture content and a thin, delicate skin.

FINGERLINGS

Fingerlings

Fingerling potatoes are typically heirloom varieties, related to the original potato varieties from the Andes. They are generally small, long and oblong with good flavor. The Russian Banana looks like a small banana and has a firm texture and rich, buttery flavor. The red-streaked French Fingerling has a nutty flavor; the red Ruby Crescent has a strong, earthy flavor. All fingerling varieties tend to be low in starch and are good for roasting and in potato salads.

PURPLE POTATOES

Purple Potatoes

Purple (or blue) potatoes have a deep purple skin. The flesh is bright purple, becoming lighter when cooked. They are mealy, with a flavor and texture similar to russets. The most common varieties are All Blue and Caribe, which were also quite popular in the mid-19th century.

RED POTATOES

Red potatoes have a thin red skin and crisp, white, waxy flesh, best suited to boiling or steaming. They do not have the dry, mealy texture that successful baking requires. Red potatoes are round, instead of long or oblong; popular varieties are Red Pontiac and Norland.

Red Potatoes

RUSSET (BURBANK) POTATOES

Russet potatoes, commonly referred to as Idaho potatoes, are the standard baking potato. They are long with rough, reddish-brown skin and mealy flesh. Russets are excellent baked and are the best potatoes for frying. They tend to fall apart when boiled. They are marketed in several size categories. Select those in the size most appropriate for their intended use.

Russet Potatoes

WHITE POTATOES

White potatoes are available in round or long varieties. They have a thin, tender skin with a tender, waxy yellow or white flesh. Round white potatoes are also referred to as chef or all-purpose potatoes. White potatoes are usually cooked with moist heat or used for sautéing. White Rose and Finnish Yellow (or Yellow Finn) are popular varieties.

White Potatoes

Another variety of white potato known as the **Yukon Gold** is a medium-sized, slightly flattened, oval potato. They have a delicate pale yellow skin with shallow pink eyes. Their pale yellow flesh has a creamy texture and rich, buttery, nutty flavor. Yukon Gold potatoes are suitable for most cooking methods and will retain their yellow color when baked, boiled or fried. First bred by botanists in Canada, Yukon Golds are now grown throughout the United States. Other lesser-known gold-fleshed varieties include Michigold, Donna, Delta Gold, Banana and Saginaw Gold.

Yukon Gold Potatoes

SWEET POTATOES

Sweet potatoes are from a different botanical family than ordinary potatoes, although they are also tubers that originated in the New World. Two types are commonly available. One has yellow flesh and a dry, mealy texture; it is known as a boniato, white or Cuban sweet potato. The other has a darker orange, moister flesh and is high in sugar; it is known as a red sweet potato. Both types have thick skins ranging in color from light tan to brownish red. (Sometimes dark-skinned sweet potatoes are erroneously labeled yams.) Sweet potatoes should be chosen according to the desired degree of sweetness. They are best suited for boiling, baking and puréeing, although the less sweet varieties can be deep-fried. The cooked flesh can also be used in breads, pies and puddings. Sweet potatoes are available canned, often in a spiced or sugary sauce.

Sweet Potatoes

YAMS

Yams are a third type of tuber, botanically different from both sweet and common potatoes. Yams are less sweet than sweet potatoes, but they can be used interchangeably. The flesh of yams ranges from creamy white to deep red. Yams are Asian in origin and are now found in Africa, South America and the southern United States.

NUTRITION

Potatoes contain a high percentage of easily digested complex carbohydrates and little or no fat. They are also a good source for minerals and vitamins, especially vitamin B_6, vitamin C and potassium, although much of the vitamin C can be destroyed when potatoes are cooked in liquid.

Red Yams

TABLE 22.1 COMPARISON OF MEALY AND WAXY POTATOES

	CONTENT OF			BEST TO			
	STARCH	MOISTURE	SUGAR	BAKE	BOIL	SAUTÉ	DEEP-FRY
Mealy: russet, white rose, purple	high	low	low	✓			✓
Waxy: red, new (red), Finnish yellow	low	high	high		✓	✓	

Purchasing and Storing Potatoes

MEALY VERSUS WAXY

One of the most important considerations in selecting potatoes is choosing between the mealy and waxy varieties. It is important to understand the differences and purchase the type of potatoes best suited to the type of dish being prepared. A comparison of mealy and waxy potatoes and their uses is presented in Table 22.1.

Mealy potatoes (also known as starchy potatoes) have a high starch content and thick skin. They are best for baking and are often ordered from suppliers simply as "bakers." Their low sugar content also allows them to be deep-fried long enough to fully cook the interior without burning the exterior. Mealy potatoes tend to fall apart when boiled, making them a good choice for whipped or puréed potatoes.

Waxy potatoes have a low starch content and thin skin. They are best for boiling. They will not develop the desired fluffy texture when baked. They tend to become limp and soggy when deep-fried because of their high moisture content.

GRADING

Like other vegetables, potatoes are subject to the voluntary USDA grading system. Select U.S. No. 1 potatoes, the top grade, when perfect appearance is required. U.S. Commercial or U.S. No. 2 potatoes work in applications requiring peeling and cutting.

PURCHASING

Potatoes are usually packed in 50-pound cartons. Counts vary depending on average potato size. For example, in a 100-count carton, each potato would weigh an average of 8 ounces. Eighty-, 90- and 100-count cartons are the most common. Generally, larger-sized potatoes (that is, smaller counts) are more expensive. Size does not affect quality, however, so the size selected should be determined by intended use.

STORING

Temperatures between 50°F and 65°F (10°C and 18°C) are best for storing potatoes. Do not store potatoes in the refrigerator. At temperatures below 40°F (4°C), potato starch turns to sugar, making the cooked product too sweet and increasing the risk that the potato will turn gray or streaky when cooked. Potatoes with a high sugar content also burn more easily when fried.

Potatoes should be stored in a dark room, as light promotes chlorophyll production, turning them green and bitter. A green patch indicates the possible presence of solanine, a toxin harmful if eaten in large amounts, and should be peeled away. Solanine is also present in the eyes and sprouts, and they, too, should be removed and discarded before cooking.

Under proper conditions, fresh baking or general-purpose potatoes should last for 2 months; new potatoes will keep for several weeks. Do not wash potatoes until ready to use, as washing promotes spoilage.

Once peeled, potatoes should be stored covered in water and refrigerated to prevent enzymatic browning.

Applying Various Cooking Methods

Potatoes have a relatively neutral flavor, making them a perfect accompaniment to many savory dishes. They can be prepared with almost any dry- or moist-heat cooking method: baking, sautéing, pan-frying, deep-frying, boiling or steaming. They can be combined with other ingredients in braises and stews. Potatoes are used in soups (vichyssoise), dumplings (gnocchi), breads, pancakes (latkes), puddings, salads and even vodka.

Many potato dishes, both classic and modern, employ more than one cooking method. For example, lorette potatoes require boiling and deep-frying; hash browns require par-boiling, then sautéing. Even French fries are best when first blanched in hot oil before final deep frying.

DETERMINING DONENESS

Most potatoes are considered done when they are soft and tender or offer little resistance when pierced with a knife tip. Fried potatoes should have a crisp, golden-brown surface; the interior should be moist and tender.

ROASTING AND BAKING

Potatoes are often roasted with meat or poultry, becoming coated with the fat and drippings released from the main item as it cooks. Either mealy or waxy potatoes, peeled or unpeeled, can be roasted successfully.

Mealy potatoes such as russets are ideal for baking. The skin is left intact, although it may be pierced with a fork to allow steam to escape. A true baked potato should not be wrapped in foil or cooked in a microwave; this changes the cooking method to steaming and prevents a crisp skin from forming. A properly baked potato should be white and fluffy, not yellowish or soggy. Once baked, potatoes can be eaten plain (or with butter, sour cream and other garnishes) or used in other recipes.

> **SAFETY ALERT**
>
> Cooked potato dishes, especially those with cream, butter or custard, are potentially hazardous foods. They must be held for service at 135°F (57°C) or higher. Be sure to reheat potato dishes to 165°F (74°C) or higher.

PROCEDURE FOR BAKING POTATOES

1. Scrub the potatoes well.
2. Using a fork, pierce the potato skins.
3. Rub the potatoes with oil and salt if desired. Do not wrap them in foil.
4. Bake the potatoes until done. A paring knife should penetrate them easily.

① Piercing the potatoes.

② Seasoning the potatoes with salt.

BAKED POTATOES

Yield: 8 Servings   **Method:** Baking

Russet potatoes	8	8
Vegetable oil	3 Tbsp.	45 ml
Kosher salt	3 Tbsp.	45 ml

① Scrub the potatoes well, but do not peel them. Pierce the skin of each potato to allow steam to escape.

② Rub the potatoes with oil, then sprinkle with salt.

③ Place the potatoes on a rack over a sheet pan. Bake in a 400°F (200°C) oven until done, approximately 1 hour. The potatoes should yield to gentle pressure, and a paring knife inserted in the thickest part should meet little resistance.

④ Hold uncovered in a warm spot and serve within 1 hour.

VARIATION:

Twice-Baked Potatoes (Yield: 16 Servings)—Cut baked potatoes in half lengthwise. Carefully scoop out the flesh, leaving the skins intact. Whip the potato flesh with 8 ounces (240 grams) sour cream, 2 ounces (60 grams) butter and 2 ounces (60 grams) cooked, crumbled bacon and then add salt and pepper to taste. Thin with hot milk if necessary. The mixture should be light and fluffy, not lumpy. Pile the filling back into the skins, mounding the tops. Brush the mounded potatoes with clarified butter and sprinkle with Parmesan. Arrange on a sheet pan and bake at 425°F (220°C) until thoroughly reheated and lightly browned.

Approximate values per 7.5-oz. (225-g) potato: **Calories** 270, **Total fat** 5 g, **Saturated fat** 0.5 g, **Cholesterol** 0 mg, **Sodium** 2630 mg, **Total carbohydrates** 51 g, **Protein** 5 g, **Vitamin C** 45%, **Claims**—low saturated fat; no cholesterol; good source of fiber

Baking en Casserole

Many classic potato dishes require baking either raw or parboiled potatoes with sauce, cheese, meat or other seasonings in a baking dish or casserole. Well-known examples include scalloped potatoes, which are baked in béchamel sauce, and potatoes au gratin, which are topped with cheese and baked. These dishes usually develop a crisp, brown crust, which is part of their appeal.

The casserole should hold its shape when cut; the potatoes should be tender, and the sauce should be smooth, not grainy.

Potato casseroles can be fully baked, then held loosely covered in a steam table for service. Portions can be reheated or browned briefly under a broiler or salamander at service time.

PROCEDURE FOR BAKING POTATOES EN CASSEROLE

① Prepare the potatoes by washing, peeling, slicing or partially cooking as desired or as directed in the recipe.

② Add the potatoes to the baking pan in layers, alternating with the sauce, cream, cheese or other ingredients. Or combine the potatoes with the other ingredients and place in a buttered baking pan.

③ Bake the potatoes until done.

GRATIN DAUPHINOISE

Yield: 4–5 lb. (1.9–2.4 kg) **Method:** Baking en casserole

Russet potatoes	3 lb.	1.4 kg
Whole butter	as needed	as needed
Salt and white pepper	TT	TT
Nutmeg	¼ tsp.	2 ml
Gruyère, grated	8 oz.	240 g
Half-and-half	24 fl. oz.	720 ml
Egg yolks	3	3

1. Peel the potatoes and cut into very thin slices.
2. Place a single layer of potatoes in a well-buttered, full-size hotel pan.
3. Season with salt, white pepper and a small amount of nutmeg. Sprinkle on a thin layer of cheese.
4. Add another layer of potatoes, seasonings and cheese and repeat until all the potatoes and about three-fourths of the cheese are used.
5. Heat the half-and-half to a simmer. Whisk the egg yolks together in a bowl, then gradually add the hot half-and-half.
6. Pour the cream-and-egg mixture over the potatoes. Top with the remaining cheese.
7. Bake uncovered at 350°F (180°C) until the potatoes are tender and golden brown, approximately 50 to 60 minutes.

Approximate values per 4-oz. (120-g) serving: **Calories** 160, **Total fat** 8 g, **Saturated fat** 5 g, **Cholesterol** 55 mg, **Sodium** 160 mg, **Total carbohydrates** 15 g, **Protein** 6 g, **Vitamin C** 15%, **Calcium** 15%

SAUTÉING AND PAN-FRYING

Waxy potatoes, such as red- and white skinned varieties, are best for sautéing or pan-frying. Often they are first parboiled or even fully cooked—a convenient way to use left-over boiled potatoes. They are then cooked in fat following the general procedures for sautéing and pan-frying discussed in Chapter 9, Principles of Cooking.

The fat can be clarified butter, oil, bacon fat or lard, depending on the desired flavor of the finished dish. The fat must be hot before the potatoes are added so that they will develop a crust without absorbing too much fat. Sautéed potatoes should have a crisp, well-browned crust and tender interior. They should be neither soggy nor greasy.

Potatoes can be sautéed or pan-fried by two methods: tossing and still-frying. The **tossing method** is used to cook relatively small pieces of potatoes in a small amount of fat. The potatoes are tossed using the pan's sloped sides so that they brown evenly on all sides. The **still-frying method** is used to create a disc-shaped potato product. The shredded or sliced potatoes are added to the pan, usually covering its bottom, and allowed to cook without stirring or flipping until they are well browned on the first side. The entire mass is then turned and cooked on the second side. When the potatoes are done, they can be cut into wedges for service.

MISE EN PLACE
◀ Grate Gruyère cheese.

1. Layering gratin potatoes.

2. The finished gratin potatoes.

PROCEDURE FOR **SAUTÉING AND PAN-FRYING POTATOES**

1. Wash, trim, peel, cut and/or cook the potatoes as desired or as directed in the recipe.
2. Heat the pan, add the fat and heat the fat. Add the potatoes to the hot fat. Do not overcrowd the pan. Use enough fat to prevent the potatoes from sticking to the pan. Depending on the recipe, use either the tossing method or the still-frying method.
3. Add garnishes, seasonings and other ingredients as desired or as directed in the recipe.
4. Cook the potatoes until done.

MISE EN PLACE
▶ Peel and julienne onions.

LYONNAISE POTATOES

Yield: 8 Servings, 4 oz. (120 g) each   **Method:** Sautéing

Potatoes, waxy	2 lb.	960 g
Onions, sliced thin	8 oz.	240 g
Clarified butter	4 fl. oz.	120 ml
Salt and pepper	TT	TT

1. Partially cook the potatoes by baking, boiling or steaming. Allow them to cool.
2. Peel the potatoes and cut into ¼-inch- (½-centimeter-) thick slices.
3. Sauté the onions in half of the butter until tender but not brown. Remove the onions from the pan with a slotted spoon and set aside.
4. Add the remaining butter to the pan. Add the potatoes and sauté, tossing as needed, until well browned on all sides.
5. Return the onions to the pan and sauté to combine the flavors. Season to taste with salt and pepper.

Approximate values per 4-oz. (120-g) serving: **Calories** 170, **Total fat** 12 g, **Saturated fat** 7 g, **Cholesterol** 30 mg, **Sodium** 650 mg, **Total carbohydrates** 16 g, **Protein** 1 g, **Vitamin A** 10%

DEEP-FRYING

Potato chips and French fries (Fr. *pommes frites*) are extremely popular in a variety of shapes, sizes and seasonings. Although a wide range of shapes, sizes and preseasoned frozen products are available, fresh fried potatoes can be a delicious, economical menu item.

Top-quality russet potatoes are recommended for deep-frying. The peel may be removed or left attached. If peeled, the potatoes should be soaked in clear, cold water until ready to cut and cook. This keeps them crisp and white by leaching some of the starch that might otherwise make the potatoes gummy or cause smaller cuts to stick together when cooked.

Deep-fried potatoes are usually blanched in oil ranging in temperature from 250°F to 300°F (120°C to 150°C) until tender and translucent. They are then drained and held for service, at which time they are finished in hotter oil, usually at a temperature between 350°F and 375°F (180°C and 190°C) until they are uniformly golden brown. (See Figure 22.1.)

Deep-frying is also used to finish cooking several classic potato dishes such as croquettes and dauphine, in which fully cooked potatoes are puréed, seasoned, shaped and fried.

Deep-fried potatoes should be drained on absorbent paper briefly and served immediately. See Table 22.2 for solutions to common problems when deep-frying potatoes.

PROCEDURE FOR **DEEP-FRYING POTATOES**

1. Wash, peel or trim the potatoes as desired.
2. Cut the potatoes into uniform-sized pieces.
3. Using the basket method, blanch the potatoes in deep fat at 250°F (121°C) for 2 to 3 minutes, depending on the size of the pieces.
4. Drain the potatoes and spread them out in a single layer on a baking sheet or in a hotel pan.
5. Just before service, submerge the potatoes in deep fat at 350°F–375°F (177°C–191°C), using the basket method, shaking the basket occasionally while the potatoes cook.
6. Cook until golden brown. Remove from the fat, drain, salt to taste and serve immediately.

DEEP-FRIED POTATOES

RUTH'S CHRIS STEAK HOUSE, PHOENIX, AZ

MISE EN PLACE
◄ Wash and chop parsley.

Yield: Varies　　　　　　　　　　**Method:** Deep-frying

Mealy potatoes, such as Idaho 70 count	as needed	as needed
Hot fat	as needed	as needed
Salt and pepper	TT	TT
Parsley, chopped	as needed for garnish	

1. Peel if necessary, then cut each potato into the desired shape; for example:
   Cottage fries—circles ¼ inch (6 millimeters) thick
   Shoestring potatoes—long juliennes (allumettes)
   French fries—sticks ⅜ inch × ⅜ inch × 3 inches (1 centimeter × 1 centimeter × 7 centimeters)
   Steak fries—four large wedges
2. Using the basket method, deep-fry the potatoes in 250°F (120°C) fat until blanched and lightly browned, approximately 2 to 3 minutes. Remove and drain. Hold the partially cooked potatoes in a single layer on a baking sheet or in a hotel pan.
3. For service, deep-fry the partially cooked potatoes in 350°F (180°C) fat until golden in color and done. Season to taste with salt and pepper.
4. Garnish with parsley if desired.

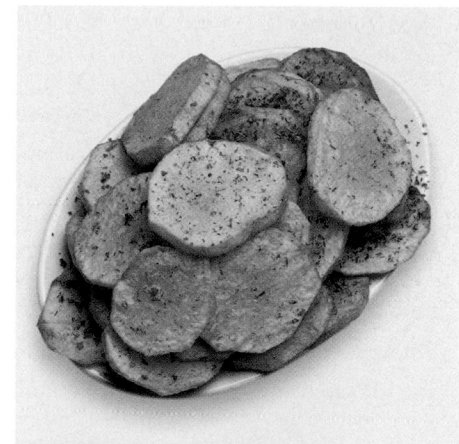

Cottage Fries

Approximate values per 1-oz. (30-g) serving: **Calories** 90, **Total fat** 4.5 g, **Saturated fat** 1.5 g, **Cholesterol** 0 mg, **Sodium** 60 mg, **Total carbohydrates** 11 g, **Protein** 1 g

Shoestring Potatoes

French Fries

Steak Fries

Blanched fried potatoes are soft and pale in color.

When properly fried, the potatoes are evenly golden brown and crisp.

Overcooked fried potatoes are dark and bitter tasting.

TABLE 22.2 TROUBLESHOOTING CHART FOR DEEP-FRIED POTATOES

PROBLEM	CAUSE	SOLUTION
Color too dark	Cooked too long Dirty oil Oil too hot Excessive sugar in potato	Reduce fry time Change oil Check thermostat; reduce temperature Fry longer at a lower temperature
Color too light	Oil too cold New oil Poor recovery time	Check thermostat; increase temperature Oil will darken with use Fry smaller batch
Excessive color variation	Fried twice Excessive sugar in potatoes Potatoes not completely submerged in fat	Fry only once Fry longer at a lower temperature Fill basket less; add more oil
Potatoes stick together	Basket overfilled	Fill basket less; shake while frying
Too greasy	Potatoes moist Dirty or old oil Oil too cold Basket overfilled	Dry potatoes completely before frying Change oil Check thermostat; increase temperature Fill basket less

BOILING

Waxy potatoes are best for all moist-heat cooking methods. Boiled potatoes (which are actually simmered) may be served as is or used in multistep preparations such as purées, salads, soups and baked casseroles. Potatoes are usually boiled in water, although stock may be used or milk added for flavor. Always begin cooking potatoes in cold liquid to ensure even cooking. Unlike other vegetables, potatoes should not be refreshed in cold water; it makes them soggy.

PROCEDURE FOR **BOILING POTATOES**

1. Wash, peel or trim the potatoes as desired.
2. Cut the potatoes into uniform-sized pieces to promote even cooking. The pieces should not be too small, or they will absorb a large amount of water as they cook, making the final product soggy.
3. Add the potatoes to enough cool liquid to cover them by several inches. Bring to a boil, reduce to a simmer and cook until done. If a slightly firm finished product is

desired, remove and drain the potatoes when they are slightly underdone and allow carryover cooking to finish cooking them.

❹ Drain the potatoes in a colander and serve or use for further preparation.

MASHED POTATOES

Yield: 4 lb. (1.9 kg)		**Method:** Boiling
Potatoes, mealy	5 lb.	2.4 kg
Salt	1 Tbsp.	15 ml
Whole butter, melted, hot	4 oz.	120 g
Milk, hot	8 fl. oz.	240 ml
Salt	2 tsp.	10 ml
White pepper	¼ tsp.	2 ml

❶ Wash and peel the potatoes. Cut each potato into four to six uniform-sized pieces.

❷ Place the potatoes in a pot, cover them with water and add 1 tablespoon (15 milliliters) salt to the water. Bring the water to a boil, reduce to a simmer and cook until the potatoes are tender. Do not overcook the potatoes.

❸ When the potatoes are cooked, drain them well in a colander. The potatoes must be very dry. Transfer them to the bowl of an electric mixer. Using the whip attachment, whip the potatoes for 30 to 45 seconds. Scrape the sides and bottom of the bowl and whip for another 15 seconds or until the potatoes are smooth and free of lumps. The potatoes must be smooth before adding any liquids or they will remain lumpy.

❹ Add the butter, milk and seasonings. Whip on low speed to incorporate all of the ingredients. Scrape the sides and bottom of the bowl and whip again for several seconds. Adjust consistency and seasoning.

VARIATIONS:

Garlic Mashed Potatoes—Sweat 1 ounce (30 grams) chopped garlic in the melted butter for 5 to 10 minutes without browning. Strain the butter if desired. Add the hot garlic butter in place of the melted butter in the recipe.

Horseradish Mashed Potatoes—Add 1 ounce (30 grams) freshly grated horseradish to the potatoes with the seasonings.

Truffle Mashed Potatoes—Add 1½ fluid ounces (45 milliliters) truffle oil to the potatoes with the seasonings.

Approximate values per 4-oz. (120-g) serving: **Calories** 190, **Total fat** 7 g, **Saturated fat** 4.5 g, **Cholesterol** 20 mg, **Sodium** 350 mg, **Total carbohydrates** 29 g, **Protein** 3 g, **Vitamin C** 20%

MISE EN PLACE

◄ Melt butter and heat milk while potatoes are cooking.

❶ Adding water to the uniformly cut potatoes.

❷ Checking the consistency of the mashed potatoes.

POTATO CLASSICS

Anna—Thin potato slices are arranged in several circular layers in a round pan coated with clarified butter; additional butter is brushed on, and the potatoes are baked until crisp, then cut into wedges for service.

Boulangère—Onions and potatoes are sautéed in butter, then transferred to a baking pan or added to a partially cooked roast in a roasting pan; stock is added, and the potatoes are cooked uncovered until done.

Château—Tournéed potatoes are sautéed in clarified butter until golden and tender.

Parisienne—Small spheres are cut from raw, peeled potatoes with a Parisienne scoop; they are seasoned and sautéed in clarified butter, then tossed with a meat glaze and garnished with chopped parsley.

Rösti—Potatoes are shredded, seasoned and pan-fried in the shape of a pie, then cut into wedges for service.

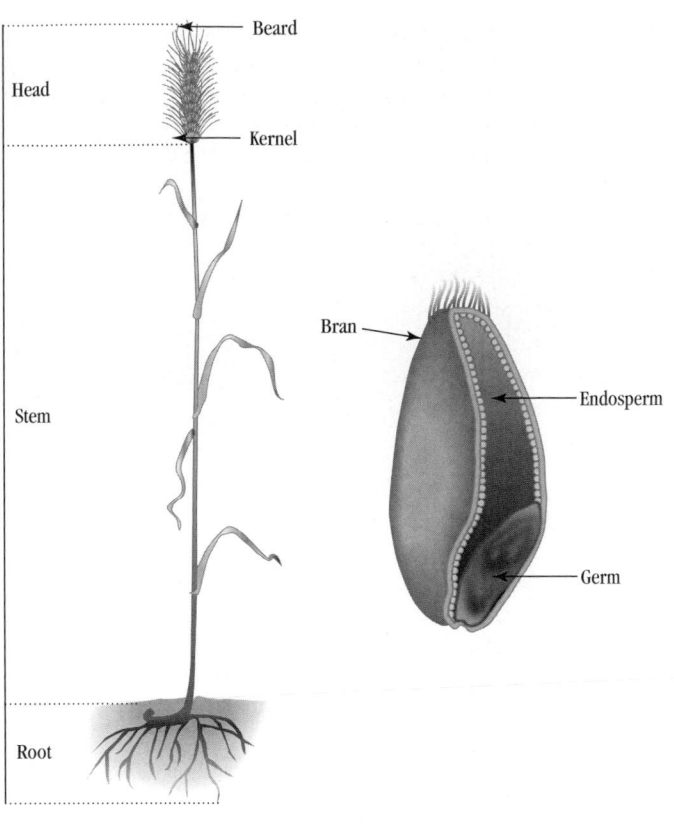

A wheat plant.   A kernel of wheat.

FIGURE 22.1 ▶ Wheat.

GRAINS

Botanically, grains are grasses that bear edible seeds. Corn, rice and wheat are the most significant. Both the fruit (that is, the seed or kernel) and the plant are called a grain.

Most grain kernels are protected by a **hull** or husk. All kernels are composed of three distinct parts: the **bran**, **endosperm** and **germ**. (See Figure 22.1.) The bran is the tough outer layer covering the endosperm. Bran is a good source of fiber and B-complex vitamins. The endosperm is the largest part of the kernel and is a source of protein and carbohydrates (starch). It is the part used primarily in milled products such as flour. The germ is the smallest portion of the grain and is the only part that contains fat. It is also rich in thiamin. The bran, endosperm and germ can be separated by milling.

Identifying Grains

This section presents information on corn, rice and wheat as well as several minor grains that are nutritionally significant and gaining popularity.

Some products are available in a stone-ground form. This means that the grains were ground with a stone mill rather than by the steel blades typically used for **cracking**, **grinding**, **hulling** and **pearling**. Stone grinders are gentler and more precise, so they are less likely to overgrind the grain. Stone-ground products will always be labeled as such and are usually more expensive than steel-ground ones.

CORN

Corn (Sp. *maíz*; It. *granturco*) is the only grain that is also eaten fresh as a vegetable. (Fresh corn is discussed in Chapter 21, Vegetables.) Its use as a dried grain dates back several thousand years in Central America and long preceded its use as a vegetable.

cracking a milling process in which grains are broken open

grinding a milling process in which grains are reduced to a powder; the powder can be of differing degrees of fineness or coarseness

hulling a milling process in which the hull or husk is removed from grains

pearling a milling process in which all or part of the hull, bran and germ are removed from grains

Cornmeal

Cornmeal is made by drying and grinding a special type of corn known as dent, which may be yellow, white or blue. Cornmeal is most often used in breads, as a coating for fried foods or cooked as polenta or mush. Products made with cornmeal have a gritty texture and a sweet but starchy flavor.

Cornmeal

Hominy

Hominy, also known as posole or samp, is dried corn that has been soaked in hydrated lime or lye. This causes the kernels to swell, loosening the hulls. The hulls and germs are removed and the kernels dried. These white or yellow kernels resemble popcorn, but with a soft, chewy texture and smoky-sour flavor. Hominy is available dried or cooked and canned. It may be served as a side dish or used in stews or soups. **Masa harina**, a finely ground flour made from dried hominy, is used for making breads, tortillas, tamales and other Mexican and southwestern dishes.

Hominy

Grits

Grits are traditionally made by grinding dried hominy. These tiny white granules may be used in baked dishes but are most often served as a hot breakfast cereal, usually topped with butter or cheese. Quick-cooking and instant grits are available.

Grits

RICE

Rice (Fr. *riz*; It. *riso*; Sp. *arroz*) is the starchy seed of a semiaquatic grass. Probably originating on the Indian subcontinent or in Southeast Asia, rice is used as a staple by more than half the world's population.

Rice can be incorporated into almost any cuisine, from Asian to Spanish to classic French. Its flavor adapts to the foods and seasonings with which the rice is cooked or served. Its texture adds an appealing chewiness to meat and poultry dishes, salads, breads and puddings. Rice is not limited to a side dish, but may be used in stews or curries; for stuffing vegetables or game birds; and in puddings, salads, beverages (such as Mexican horchata) and breads.

Rice is divided into three types based on seed size: **long-grain**, **medium-grain** and **short-grain**. Long-grain rice is the most versatile and popular worldwide. The grains remain firm, fluffy and separate when cooked. (Long-grain rice can, however, become sticky if overcooked or stirred frequently during cooking.) Short-grain rice has more starch and becomes quite tender and sticky when cooked. Italian risotto, Japanese sushi and Spanish paella are all traditionally made with short-grain rice. The appearance and starch content of medium-grain rice falls somewhere in between. Medium-grain rice becomes sticky when cool, so it is best eaten freshly made and piping hot.

Long-grain, medium-grain and short-grain rice are available in different processed forms. All rice is originally brown. The grains can be left whole, with the bran attached, for **brown rice**. Or they can be pearled for the more familiar polished **white rice**. Both brown rice and white rice can be processed into converted rice and instant rice.

Converted rice is parboiled to remove the surface starch. This procedure also forces nutrients from the bran into the grain's endosperm. Therefore, converted rice retains more nutrients than regular milled white rice, although the flavor is the same. Converted rice is neither precooked nor instant; in fact, it cooks more slowly than regular milled white rice.

Instant or **quick-cooking rice** is widely available and useful if time is a concern. Instant rice is created by fully cooking and then flash-freezing milled rice. Unfortunately, this processing removes some of the nutrients and flavor.

Converted Rice

Arborio Rice

Arborio is a round, short-grain rice used primarily in Italian dishes such as risotto. It is very sticky, with a white color and mild flavor.

Arborio Rice

Basmati Rice

Basmati is one of the finest long-grain rices in the world. It grows in the Himalayan foothills and is preferred in Indian cuisine. It is highly aromatic, with a sweet, delicate flavor and a creamy yellow color. Basmati rice is usually aged to improve its aromatic qualities and

Basmati Rice

Brown Rice

Wild Rice

Wild Pecan Rice

should be washed well before cooking. **Jasmine rice** is another aromatic long-grain rice. Similar to basmati, it is grown in Thailand and used throughout Southeast Asia.

Brown Rice

Brown rice is the whole natural grain of rice. Only the husk has been removed. Brown rice has a nutty flavor; its chewy texture is caused by the high-fiber bran. Brown rice absorbs more water and takes longer to cook than white rice.

Sticky Rice

Sticky rice is a short-grain rice used in many Asian cuisines. The short grains are fat and round with a high starch content and a pearly white color. When cooked, the grains tend to clump together, forming a sticky mass. Sticky rice must be soaked for several hours before being cooked. Also known as glutinous rice or sweet rice, it can be ground into flour and used for dumplings and pastries. Japanese sake and mirin and Chinese shaoxing are made from fermented sticky rice, as is rice vinegar.

Wild Rice

Wild rice is prepared in the same manner as traditional rice, although it is actually the seed of an unrelated reedlike aquatic plant. Wild rice has long, slender grains with a dark brown to black color. It has a nuttier flavor and chewier texture than traditional rice. Three grades are available: giant (the best quality, with very long grains); fancy (a medium-sized grain, suitable for most purposes); and select (a short grain, suitable for soups, pancakes or baked goods). Cultivated in California, Idaho and Washington, it is generally served with game, used as a stuffing for poultry or combined with regular rice for a side dish. Wild rice is expensive, but small quantities are usually sufficient.

Wild Pecan Rice

Wild pecan rice is neither wild nor made with pecans. It is a unique long-grain rice grown only in the bayou country of southern Louisiana. Wild pecan rice has a nutty flavor and exceptionally rich aroma.

GUIDELINES FOR COOKING RICE   Rice may be rinsed before cooking to remove dirt and debris, but doing so also removes some of its nutrients. It is not necessary to rinse most American-grown rice, which is generally clean and free of insects. Rice may also be soaked before cooking. Soaking softens the grains, removes some starch and speeds cooking.

The standard ratio for cooking rice is two parts liquid to one part rice. The actual ratio varies, however, depending on the type of rice. Guidelines for cooking rice are found in Table 22.3.

SAFETY ALERT

Once cooked, rice is highly perishable. Because of its neutral pH and high protein content, cooked rice is a potentially hazardous food. To avoid the risk of food-borne illnesses, be sure to hold hot rice at 135°F (57°C) or higher. Leftover rice must be quickly cooled and stored at 41°F (5°C) or below. Leftover rice must be reheated to 165°F (74°C) or higher.

TABLE 22.3   GUIDELINES FOR COOKING RICE

TYPE OF RICE	RATIO OF RICE TO WATER (BY VOLUME)	PREPARATION	COOKING TIME (SIMMERING)	YIELD FROM 1 CUP RAW RICE
Arborio	1:2.5–3	Do not rinse or soak	15–20 min.	2½–3 c. (560–675 ml)
Basmati	1:1.75	Rinse well; soak	15 min.	3 c. (675 ml)
Brown, long-grain	1:2.5	Do not rinse; may soak	45–50 min.	3–4 c. (675–900 ml)
Converted	1:2.5	Do not rinse	20–25 min.	3–4 c. (675–900 ml)
White, long-grain (regular milled)	1:2	Do not rinse	15 min.	3 c. (675 ml)
Wild	1:3	Rinse	35–60 min., depending on grade	3–4 c. (675–900 ml)

WHEAT

Wheat (Fr. *blé*) is most often milled into the wide range of flours discussed in Chapter 29, Principles of the Bakeshop. But wheat and products derived from it are also used as starchy side dishes or ingredients in soups, salads, ground meat dishes and breads. These products include cracked wheat, bulgur and couscous. When cooked, they are slightly chewy with a mild flavor. All should be fluffy; none should be soggy or sticky.

Wheat germ and **wheat bran** are widely available and highly touted for their nutritional values. Bran and germ are not generally used plain, but may be added to bread or other cooked dishes.

Cracked Wheat

Cracked wheat is the whole wheat kernel (known as a **berry**) broken into varying degrees of coarseness. It is not precooked, and the kernel's white interior should be visible. The bran and germ are still intact, so cracked wheat has a great deal of fiber but a short shelf life. Whole wheat berries must be soaked for several hours before cooking. Cracked wheat can be fully cooked by long, gentle simmering.

Bulgur

Bulgur is a wheat berry that has had the bran removed; it is then steam-cooked, dried and ground into varying degrees of coarseness. Bulgur has a nutlike flavor and texture; it is a uniform golden-brown color (uncooked cracked wheat is not) and requires less cooking time than cracked wheat. Generally, cracked wheat and bulgur cannot be substituted for one another in recipes.

Bulgur needs only to be soaked in water, then drained, for use in salads, or briefly cooked when used in stews or pilafs. Bulgur is good with grilled meats and as an alternative to rice in stuffings and other dishes. The fine grind is most often used in packaged mixes such as tabouli; the medium grind is most often available in bulk.

Bulgur

Couscous

Couscous is made from coarsely ground semolina flour ground from hard **durum wheat** berries. The semolina is moistened and rolled until small pellets form, then dried. Couscous is available in varying degrees of coarseness; medium-fine is the most popular. Couscous is prepared by steaming over water or stock in a pot called a couscousière. Couscous, traditionally served with North African stews, can be used or served like rice.

Couscous

durum wheat a species of very hard wheat with a particularly high amount of protein; it is used to make couscous or milled into semolina, which is used for making pasta

OTHER GRAINS

Barley

Barley is one of the oldest culinary grains, used by humans since prehistoric times. Barley is extremely hardy, growing in climates from the tropics to the near-Arctic. Although much of the barley crop is used to make beer or feed animals, some does find its way into soups, stews and stuffings. The most common type is pearled to produce a small, round white nugget of endosperm. It has a sweet, earthy flavor similar to oats and goes well with onions, garlic and strong herbs. Barley's texture ranges from chewy to soft, depending on the amount of water in which it is cooked. Its starchiness can be used to thicken soups or stews.

Buckwheat/Kasha

Buckwheat is not a type of wheat; it is not even a grain. Rather, it is the fruit of a plant distantly related to rhubarb. Buckwheat is included here, however, because it is prepared and served in the same manner as grains.

The whole buckwheat kernel is known as a **groat**. The product most often sold as buckwheat is actually kasha, which is a hulled, roasted buckwheat groat. Kasha is reddish brown with a strong, nutty, almost scorched flavor. It is available whole or ground to varying degrees of coarseness. Whole kasha remains in separate grains after cooking; the finer grinds become rather sticky. Kasha can be served as a side dish, usually combined with pasta or vegetables, or it can be chilled and used in salads.

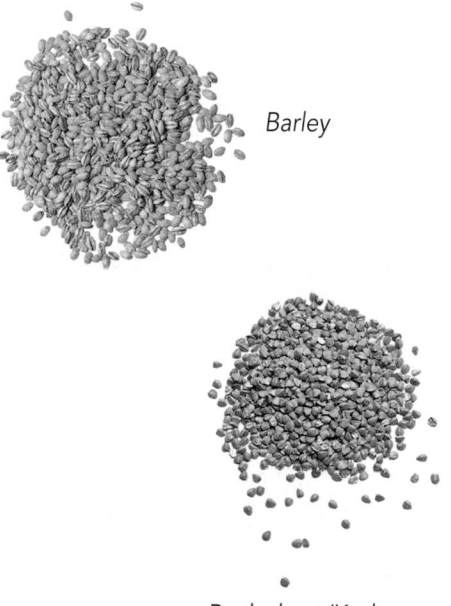

Barley

Buckwheat/Kasha

Millet

ANCIENT GRAINS FOR MODERN TIMES

As an awareness of the nutritional benefits of eating whole grains grows, long-neglected grains are re-gaining popularity with chefs and consumers. Farro (*Triticum dicoccum*) is one of the oldest forms of wheat; it was a staple in the diet of ancient Roman armies. Farro is still eaten cooked as a whole grain in Tuscany, where it is prized for its chewy, nutty flavor. Spelt (*Triticum aestivum* var. *spelta*), a related sub-species of common wheat, is also prized for its taste and consistency. Farro must be soaked like beans be-fore cooking, whereas spelt may be cooked without soaking. Treat these grains like barley. Use them to add texture to soups or cook them to add to salads and vegetable dishes.

Farro

Quinoa

Raw buckwheat groats are ground into flour typically used in pasta, blini and other pancakes. Buckwheat flour contains no gluten-forming proteins, and it tends to remain grainy, with a sandy texture. Therefore, it should not be substituted for all the wheat flour in breads or baked goods.

Millet

Millet is a high-protein cereal grain with a bland, slightly nutty flavor and a white color. Used principally as animal fodder in the United States, millet can be cooked and eaten like rice or toasted like buckwheat and cooked like kasha. It can also be ground for flour (when used for baking, it is best combined with wheat flour). Millet is usually sold hulled, as the husk is extremely hard.

Oats

After rice, oats are probably the most widely accepted whole-grain product in the American diet. Oats are con-sumed daily as a hot breakfast cereal (oatmeal) and are used in breads, muffins, cookies and other baked goods.

An oat groat is the whole oat kernel with only the husk removed. It contains both the bran and germ. *Steel-cut oats*, sometimes known as Irish oats, are groats that are toasted and then cut into small pieces with steel blades. *Rolled oats*, marketed as "old-fashioned oats," are groats that have been steamed, then rolled into flat flakes. *Quick-cooking oats* are simply rolled oats cut into smaller pieces to reduce cooking time. *Instant oats* are partially cooked and dried before rolling so that they need only to be rehydrated in boiling water. Rolled oats and quick-cooking oats can be used interchangeably, but instant oats should not be substituted in most recipes.

Oat bran is the outer covering of a hulled oat. It is available as a separate product, al-though rolled and cut oats do contain some oat bran.

The term *oatmeal* is commonly used to refer to both processed groats and the cooked porridge made from them. The processed groats known as oatmeal are a gray-white color with a starchy texture and sweet flavor. They cook into the soft, thick porridge with a ro-bust flavor called oatmeal.

Oats

Quinoa

Quinoa (keen-wa) is native to the South American Andes and was a common food of the Incas, who referred to it as the "mother grain." Although not botanically a true grain, quinoa's tiny seeds are treated as such. The grains (seeds) are small, flattened spheres, ap-proximately $\frac{1}{16}$ inch (1.5 millimeters) in diameter, ringed with the germ. They become translucent when cooked and have a slightly smoky or sesamelike flavor. Several varieties of quinoa are available, ranging in color from dark brown to almost white. The larger whiter varieties are most common and are considered superior.

Quinoa seeds have a natural, bitter-tasting coating, which protects them from birds and insects. Consequently, they should be placed in a fine-meshed colander and rinsed well with cool water for several minutes before use. Quinoa can then be cooked like rice, and will ab-sorb about twice its volume of water. For a nuttier taste, toast the grain in a hot dry pan for about 5 minutes before adding the liquid. Quinoa can also be eaten as a hot breakfast ce-real served in lieu of rice or used as a thickener for soups or stews and in salads, casseroles, breads and desserts. Quinoa flour, ground from whole seeds, has a delicate nutty flavor. A gluten-free product, it is suitable for anyone bothered by wheat allergies. Quinoa is marketed as the world's "supergrain" because the seeds form a complete protein (with all of the es-sential amino acids) and contain important vitamins and minerals as well as carbohydrates and fat. Quinoa should be kept in the refrigerator or freezer for long-term storage. The leaves of the quinoa plant are similar to spinach and can be eaten as a vegetable.

Nutrition

Grains are an excellent source of vitamins, minerals, proteins and fiber. The amount of milling or refining and the method of preparation affect their nutritional values, however. Unrefined and less-refined grains are excellent sources of dietary fiber. Rice is also quite nutritious: It is low in sodium and calories and contains all the essential amino acids. Some grains, especially white rice and oats, are usually enriched with calcium, iron and B-complex vitamins.

Purchasing and Storing Grains

PURCHASING

When buying grains, look for fresh, plump ones with a bright, even color. Fresh grains should not be shriveled or crumbly; there should be no sour or musty odors.

Grains are sold by weight. They come in bags or boxes ranging from 1 to 100 pounds. Ten-, 25- and 50-pound units are usually available.

STORING

All grains should be stored in airtight containers placed in a dark, cool, dry place. Airtight containers prevent dust and insects from entering. Airtight containers and darkness also reduce nutrient loss caused by oxidation or light. Coolness inhibits insect infestation; dryness prevents mold.

Vacuum-sealed packages will last for extended periods. Whole grains, which contain the oily germ, can be refrigerated to prevent rancidity.

Applying Various Cooking Methods

Three basic cooking methods are used to prepare grains: simmering, risotto and pilaf. Unlike simmered grains, those cooked by either the risotto or pilaf method are first coated with hot fat. The primary distinction between the pilaf and risotto methods is the manner in which the liquid is then added to the grains. See Figure 22.2. When grains are used in puddings, breads, stuffings and baked casseroles, they are almost always first fully cooked by one of these methods.

DETERMINING DONENESS

Most grains should be cooked until tender, although some recipes do require a chewier (al dente) product. Doneness can usually be determined by cooking time and the amount of liquid remaining in the pan. Some grains, such as wild rice, are fully cooked when they puff open.

In general, grains will be fully cooked when almost all the cooking liquid has been absorbed. This is indicated by the appearance of tunnel-like holes between the grains. Grains can be cooked until almost all of the liquid is absorbed, then removed from the heat and left to stand, covered, for 5 to 10 minutes. This allows the cooked grains to absorb the remaining moisture without burning.

SIMMERING

The most commonly used method for preparing grains is simmering. To do so, simply stir the grains into a measured amount of boiling salted water in a saucepan on the stove top. When the liquid returns to a boil, lower the heat, cover and simmer until the liquid is absorbed and the grains are tender. The grains are not stirred during cooking.

The grains can be flavored by using stock as the cooking liquid. Herbs and spices can also be added.

PROCEDURE FOR SIMMERING GRAINS

1. Bring the cooking liquid to a boil.
2. Stir in the grains. Add herbs or spices as desired or as directed in the recipe.
3. Return the mixture to a boil, cover and reduce to a simmer.
4. Simmer the grains until tender and most of the liquid is absorbed.
5. Remove the grains from the heat.
6. Drain if appropriate or keep covered and allow the excess moisture to evaporate, approximately 5 minutes. Fluff the grains with a fork before service.

SIMMERING	=	Grain	→	Boiling liquid	→	Cover and simmer
RISOTTO	=	Sauté grain	→	Hot liquid added gradually	→	Stir constantly
PILAF	=	Sauté grain	→	All liquid added at once	→	Cover and simmer

FIGURE 22.2 ► Cooking methods for grains.

SIMMERED RICE

Yield: 6 Servings   **Method:** Simmering

Water	1 pt.	480 ml
Salt	½ tsp.	2 ml
White rice	8 oz.	240 ml

1. Bring the water and salt to a boil in a heavy saucepan. Slowly add the rice.
2. Cover the pan and reduce the heat so that the liquid simmers gently. Cook until the rice is tender and the water is absorbed, approximately 15 to 20 minutes.
3. Remove from the heat and transfer to a hotel pan. Do not cover. Allow any excess moisture to evaporate for approximately 5 minutes.
4. Fluff the rice and serve, or refrigerate for use in another recipe.

Approximate values per ½-c. (120-ml) serving: **Calories** 150, **Total fat** 0 g, **Saturated fat** 0 g, **Cholesterol** 0 mg, **Sodium** 192 mg, **Total carbohydrates** 34 g, **Protein** 3 g, **Iron** 8%, **Claims**—fat free; no sugar

RISOTTO METHOD

Risotto is a classic northern Italian rice dish in which the grains remain firm but merge with the cooking liquid to become a creamy, almost puddinglike dish. True risotto is made with a short-grain starchy rice such as Arborio, but the risotto method can also be used to cook other grains such as barley and oats.

The grains are not rinsed before cooking, as this removes the starches needed to achieve the desired consistency. The grains are coated, but not cooked, in a hot fat such as butter or oil. A hot liquid is then gradually added to the grains so that the mixture is kept at a constant simmer. The cooking liquid should be a rich, flavorful stock. Unlike simmering and the pilaf method, the risotto method requires frequent, sometimes constant, stirring.

When finished, the grains should be creamy and tender, but still al dente in the center. Grated cheese, heavy cream, cooked meat, poultry, fish, shellfish, herbs and vegetables can be added to create a flavorful side dish or a complete meal.

PROCEDURE FOR **PREPARING GRAINS BY THE RISOTTO METHOD**

1. Bring the cooking liquid (usually a stock) to a simmer.
2. Heat the fat in a heavy saucepan over moderate heat. Add any onions, garlic or other flavoring ingredients and sauté for 1 to 2 minutes without browning.
3. Add the grains to the saucepan. Stir well to make sure the grains are well coated with fat. Do not allow the grains to brown.
4. Add any wine and cook until it is fully absorbed.
5. Begin to add the simmering stock, 4 fluid ounces (120 milliliters) at a time, stirring frequently. Wait until each portion of cooking liquid is almost fully absorbed before adding the next.
6. Test for doneness after the grains have cooked for approximately 18 to 20 minutes.
7. Remove from heat and stir in butter, grated cheese, herbs or other flavoring ingredients as directed. Garnish and serve immediately.

RISOTTO MILANESE

In Italy, risotto and pasta dishes are usually served as a separate course (primo piatto) preceding the main dish (secondo piatto) and following the appetizer (antipasto). Like pasta, risotto is a vehicle for many flavors; it can be made with lemon juice or red wine and include bitter greens, seafood or wild mushrooms. This saffron-flavored risotto breaks with tradition, however, and is often paired with Osso Buco (page 346), rich stewed veal shank.

MISE EN PLACE
◄ Heat water.
◄ Peel and mince onions.
◄ Grate cheese.

Yield: 12 Servings, 4 oz. (120 g) each   **Method:** Risotto

Chicken stock	2 qt.	1.9 lt
Saffron threads, crushed	½ tsp.	2 ml
Water, hot	2 fl. oz.	60 ml
Whole butter	6 oz.	360 g
Onions, minced	5 oz.	150 g
Arborio rice	1 lb. 8 oz.	720 g
Dry white wine	8 fl. oz.	240 ml
Parmesan, grated	4 oz.	120 g

1. Bring the stock to a simmer. Soak the saffron threads in the hot water.
2. Heat 3 ounces (90 grams) butter in a large, heavy saucepan. Add the onions and sauté until translucent.
3. Add the rice to the onions and butter. Stir well to coat the grains with butter, but do not allow the rice to brown. Add the wine and stir until it is completely absorbed.
4. Add the saffron and soaking liquid. Add the simmering stock, 4 fluid ounces (120 milliliters) at a time, stirring frequently. Wait until the stock is absorbed before adding the next 4-fluid-ounce (120-milliliter) portion.
5. After approximately 18 to 20 minutes, all the stock should be incorporated and the rice should be tender. Remove from the heat and stir in the remaining 1 ounce (30 grams) butter and the grated cheese. Serve immediately.

❶ Sautéing the rice and onions in butter.

VARIATIONS:

Risotto with Radicchio (al Radicchio)—Omit the saffron and Parmesan. Just before the risotto is fully cooked, stir in 4 fluid ounces (120 milliliters) heavy cream and 3 ounces (90 grams) finely chopped radicchio leaves.

Risotto with Four Cheeses (al Quattro Formaggi)—Omit the saffron. When the risotto is fully cooked, remove from the heat and stir in 2 ounces (60 grams) each grated Parmesan, Gorgonzola, Fontina and mozzarella. Garnish with toasted pine nuts and chopped parsley.

Risotto with Smoked Salmon (al Salmone Affumicato)—Omit the butter, saffron and Parmesan. Sauté the onions in 3 fluid ounces (90 milliliters) corn or safflower oil instead of butter. When the risotto is fully cooked, remove from the heat and stir in 8 fluid ounces (240 milliliters) half-and-half, 3 fluid ounces (90 milliliters) fresh lemon juice and 8–10 ounces (240–300 grams) good-quality smoked salmon. Garnish with chopped fresh parsley and dill. Serve with lemon wedges.

❷ Adding the stock gradually while stirring frequently.

Approximate values per 4-oz. (120-g) serving: **Calories** 110, **Total fat** 6 g, **Saturated fat** 3.5 g, **Cholesterol** 15 mg, **Sodium** 470 mg, **Total carbohydrates** 9 g, **Protein** 5 g

❸ Stirring in the butter and grated cheese.

PILAF METHOD

For the pilaf method, the raw grains are lightly sautéed in oil or butter, usually with onions or seasonings for additional flavor. Hot liquid, often a stock, is then added. The pan is covered and the mixture is left to simmer until the liquid is absorbed.

PROCEDURE FOR **PREPARING GRAINS BY THE PILAF METHOD**

1. Bring the cooking liquid (either water or stock) to a boil.
2. Heat the fat in a heavy saucepan over moderate heat. Add any onions, garlic or other flavorings and sauté for 1 to 2 minutes without browning.
3. Add the grains to the saucepan. Stir well to make sure the grains are well coated with fat. Do not allow the grains to brown.
4. All at once, add the hot cooking liquid to the sautéed grains.
5. Return the liquid to a boil, reduce to a simmer and cover.
6. Allow the mixture to simmer, either in the oven or on the stove top, until the liquid is absorbed.

MISE EN PLACE

▶ Peel onion and chop into fine dice.
▶ Heat chicken stock.

CLASSIC RICE PILAF

Yield: 3 lb. (1.4 kg)		**Method:** Pilaf
Clarified butter	1 fl. oz.	30 ml
Olive oil	1 fl. oz.	30 ml
Onion, fine dice	3 oz.	90 g
Bay leaf	1	1
Long-grain rice	1 lb.	480 g
Chicken stock, boiling	1 qt.	960 ml
Salt	TT	TT

1. Heat the butter and oil in a heavy sautoir or saucepot.
2. Add the onion and bay leaf and sauté until the onion is tender, but not brown.
3. Add the rice and stir to coat it completely with the hot fat. Do not allow the rice to brown.
4. Pour in the boiling stock and season with salt.
5. Cover the pot tightly and place it in a 350°F (180°C) oven. Bake until the liquid is absorbed and the rice is fluffy and tender, approximately 18 to 20 minutes.
6. Transfer the cooked rice to a hotel pan and fluff the rice with a fork. Remove the bay leaf and keep the rice hot for service.

1. Sautéing the rice in butter.

2. Adding the hot stock to the rice.

3. Fluffing the finished rice.

VARIATION:

Spanish Rice—Substitute 2 ounces (60 grams) bacon fat for the butter. Add three chopped garlic cloves and 1 tablespoon (15 milliliters) pure ground chilli powder with the diced onion. In Step 3, sauté the rice until it browns slightly. In place of the chicken stock, use half chicken stock and half chopped canned tomatoes with juice. Add 1 tablespoon (15 milliliters) chopped cilantro when adding the liquids.

Approximate values per 6-oz. (180-g) serving: **Calories** 130, **Total fat** 7 g, **Saturated fat** 3 g, **Cholesterol** 7.5 mg, **Sodium** 440 g, **Total carbohydrates** 12 g, **Protein** 4 g

PASTA

Pasta is made from an unleavened dough of wheat flour mixed with a liquid. The liquid is usually egg and/or water. The flour can be from almost any grain: wheat, buckwheat, rice or a combination of grains. The dough can be colored and flavored with puréed vegetables, herbs or other ingredients, and it can be cut or **extruded** into a wide variety of shapes and sizes.

Pasta can be cooked fresh while the dough is still moist and pliable, or the dough can be allowed to dry completely before cooking. Pasta can be filled or sauced in an endless variety of ways. It can stand alone or be used in salads, desserts, soups or casseroles.

Pasta is widely used in the cuisines of Asia, North America and Europe. In Italy, pasta dishes are usually served as a separate course, often referred to as the *minestre*; in other European countries, Asia and the United States, pasta dishes may be served as an appetizer, entrée or side dish.

> **extrusion** the process of forcing pasta dough through perforated plates to create various shapes; pasta dough that is not extruded must be rolled and cut

Identifying Pastas

The better-known pastas are based on the Italian tradition of kneading wheat flour with water and eggs to form a smooth, resilient dough. This dough is then rolled very thin and cut into various shapes before being boiled in water or dried for longer storage.

Commercially prepared dried pasta products are usually made with semolina flour. Semolina flour, ground from hard durum wheat and available from specialty purveyors, has a rich cream color and produces a very smooth, durable dough. Semolina dough requires a great deal of kneading, however, and bread flour is an acceptable substitute when preparing fresh pasta by hand.

Asian pasta, generally known as noodles, is made from wheat, rice, bean or buckwheat flour. It is available fresh or dried from commercial purveyors and at specialty markets.

Semolina

ITALIAN-STYLE PASTA

Although all Italian-style pasta is made from the same type of dough, the finest commercial pastas are those made with pure semolina flour, which gives the dough a rich, yellow color. Gray or streaked dough probably contains softer flours. Dried pasta should be very hard and break with a clean snap. The surface should be lightly pitted or dull. (A smooth or glossy surface will not hold or absorb sauces as well.)

Dried pasta, both domestic and imported, is available in a wide range of flavors and shapes. In addition to the traditional white (plain), green (spinach) and red (tomato) pastas, manufacturers are now offering flavor combinations such as lemon-peppercorn, whole wheat–basil and carrot-ginger. Small pieces of herbs or other flavorings are often visible in these products.

There are hundreds of recognized shapes of pasta, but only two or three dozen are generally available in the United States. When experimenting with unusual flavors and shapes, be sure to consider the taste and appearance of the final dish after the sauce and any garnishes are added.

THE MACARONI MYTH

The popular myth holds that noodles were first invented in China and discovered there by the Venetian explorer Marco Polo during the 13th century. He introduced the food to Italy and from there the rest of Europe. Although there is little doubt that the Chinese were making noodles by the first century C.E., it is now equally clear that they were not alone.

Middle Eastern and Italian cooks were preparing macaroni long before Marco Polo's adventures. A clear reference to boiled noodles appears in the *Jerusalem Talmud* of the fifth century C.E. There, rabbis debate whether noodles violate Jewish dietary laws (they do, but only during Passover). Tenth-century Arabic writings refer to dried noodles purchased from vendors. Literary references establish that dishes called *lasagna*, *macaroni* and *ravioli* were all well known (and costly) in Italy by the mid-13th century.

Pasta's current popularity dates from the 18th century, when mass production by machine began in Naples, Italy. English gentlemen on their "grand tours" of the European continent developed a fondness for pasta; the word *macaroni* became a synonym for a dandy or a vain young man. Macaroni arrived in America with English colonists, who preferred it with cream sauce and cheese or in a sweet custard. Domestic factories soon opened, and by the Civil War (1861–1865), macaroni was available to the working class. Pasta became a staple of the American middle-class diet following the wave of Italian immigrants in the late 19th century.

During the 1980s pasta became ubiquitous. Restaurants began serving it in ways previously unimagined. Corner grocery stores and local supermarkets began offering at least a dozen different shapes, often fresh and sometimes flavored. Dedicated cooks began to make pasta from scratch, though they sometimes tossed it with bottled sauce. Many also became interested in Asian noodles. Chinese, Japanese, Korean and Thai restaurants expanded their menu offerings to include traditional noodle dishes that were eagerly ordered by curious consumers. Pasta's popularity continues to grow as chefs discover the versatility of this inexpensive, nutritious food.

Italian-style pasta can be divided into three groups based on the shape of the final product: ribbons, tubes and shapes. There is no consistent English nomenclature for these pastas; the Italian names are recognized and applied virtually worldwide. (A specific shape or size may be given different names in different regions of Italy, however. These distinctions are beyond the scope of this text.)

Ribbons

Pasta dough can be rolled very thin and cut into strips or ribbons of various widths. All ribbon shapes work well with tomato, fish and shellfish sauces. Thicker ribbons, such as spaghetti and fettuccine, are preferred with cream or cheese sauces. Sheets of fresh pasta dough can be filled and shaped to create ravioli, cappelletti and tortellini. Filled pasta is usually served with a light cream- or tomato-based sauce that complements the filling's flavors.

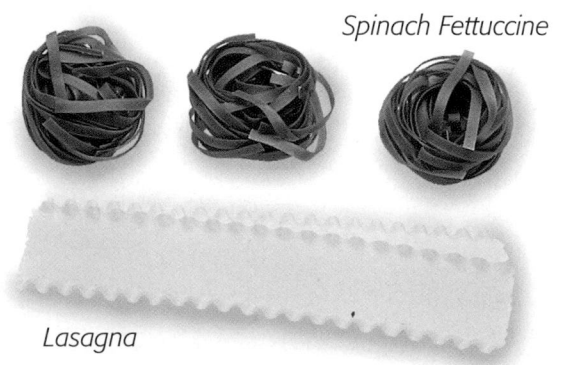

Spinach Fettuccine

Lasagna

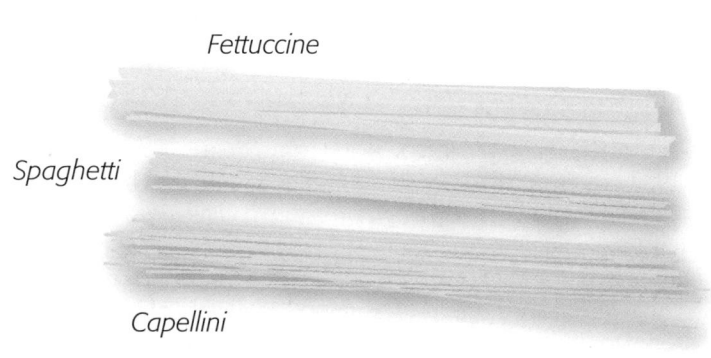

Fettuccine

Spaghetti

Capellini

Tubes

Cylindrical forms or tubes are made by extrusion. The hollow tubes can be curved or straight, fluted or smooth. Tubes are preferred for meat and vegetable sauces and are often used in baked casseroles.

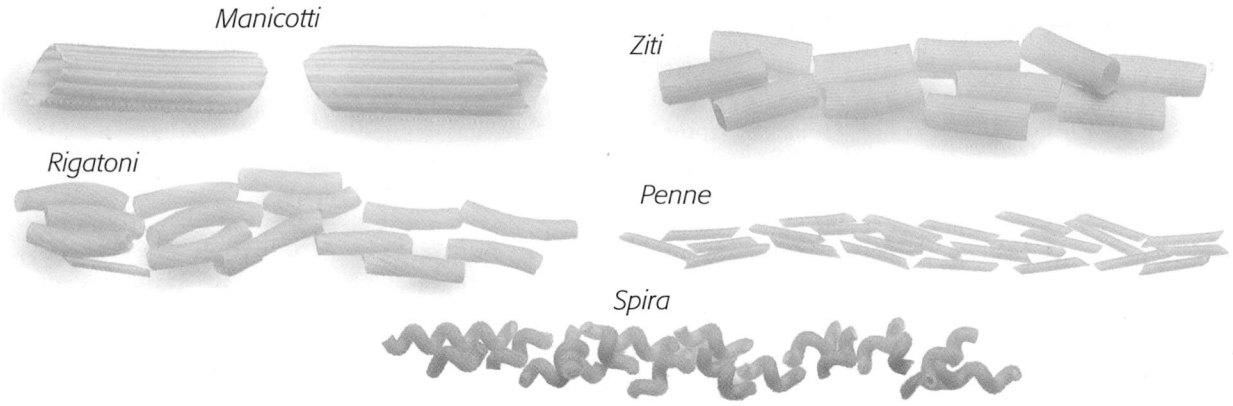

Manicotti

Ziti

Rigatoni

Penne

Spira

Shapes

The extrusion process can also be used to shape pasta dough into forms. The curves and textures produced provide nooks and crevices that hold sauces well. Shaped pastas, such as conchiglie, farfalle and fusilli, are preferred with meat sauces and oil-based sauces such as pesto. Larger shaped pastas can be cooked, then stuffed with meat or cheese fillings and baked or served as a casserole.

Conchiglie

Farfalle

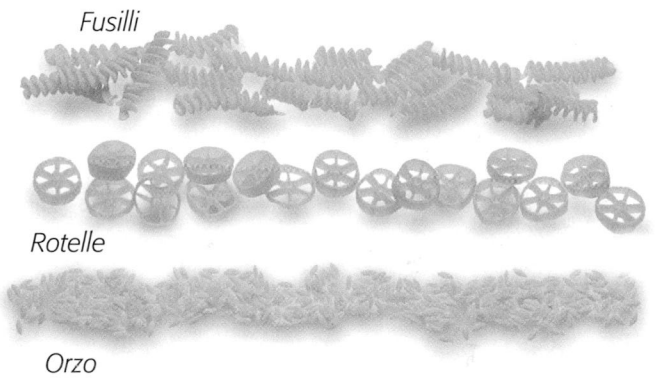

Fusilli

Rotelle

Orzo

ASIAN NOODLES

Asian noodles are not cut into the same wealth of shapes and sizes as Italian-style pasta, nor are they flavored or colored with vegetable purées, herbs or other ingredients.

Virtually all Asian noodles are ribbons—some thin, some thick—folded into bundles and packaged. Differences arise because of the flours used for the dough.

Most dried Asian noodles benefit by soaking in hot water for several minutes before further preparation. The water softens the noodle strands; the bundles separate and the noodles cook more evenly.

Wheat Noodles

Wheat noodles, also known as egg noodles, are the most popular and most widely available of the Asian noodles. They are thin, flat noodles with a springy texture; they are available fresh or dried. Dried egg noodles can be deep-fried after boiling to create crisp golden noodles (chow mein) used primarily as a garnish.

Flour Stick Wheat Noodles (without egg)

Fresh Wheat and Egg Noodles

Rice Vermicelli

Cellophane Noodles

Japanese Wheat Somen

DUMPLINGS

A **dumpling** is a small mound of dough cooked by steaming or simmering in a flavorful liquid. Dumplings are found in many cuisines: Italian gnocchi, Jewish matzo balls, German spaetzle, Chinese wontons, Belorussian pelmeni and Polish pierogi. Dumplings can be sweet or savory, plain or filled.

Plain or **drop dumplings** are made with a breadlike dough, often leavened with yeast or chemical leavening agents. They should be light and tender, but firm enough to hold their shape when cooked. Drop dumplings may be served with stews or broths, or coated with butter or sauce as an appetizer or side dish.

Filled dumplings are made by wrapping noodle dough around seasoned meat, vegetables, cheese or fruit. These parcels are then steamed, fried or baked and served as a snack food, appetizer or side dish. A recipe for deep-fried wontons is included in Chapter 28, Hors d'Oeuvre and Canapés.

Japanese wheat noodles, known as *somen* (if thin) and *udon* (if thick), may be round, square or flat. They are eaten in broth or with a dipping sauce.

Rice Noodles

Rice noodles are thin dried noodles made with rice flour. They should be soaked in hot water before cooking and rinsed in cool running water after boiling to remove excess starch and prevent sticking. Rice noodles are often served in soups or sautéed.

Rice vermicelli, which has very fine strands, can be fried in hot oil without presoaking. In only a few seconds, the strands will turn white, puff up and become crunchy. Mounds of crunchy rice noodles can be used as a base for sautéed dishes or for presenting hors d'oeuvre.

Bean Starch Noodles

Bean starch noodles are also known as spring rain noodles, bean threads, bean noodles or cellophane noodles. They are thin, transparent noodles made from mung beans. Dried bean noodles can be fried in the same manner as rice vermicelli. Otherwise, they must be soaked in hot water before using in soups, stir-fries or braised dishes.

Buckwheat Noodles

Buckwheat flour is used in the noodles of northern Japan and the Tokyo region, where they are also known as soba noodles. Soba noodles are available fresh or dried and do not need soaking before cooking. They are traditionally served in broth or with a dipping sauce, but may be substituted for Italian-style pasta if desired.

Nutrition

Pastas are very low in fat and are an excellent source of vitamins, minerals, proteins and carbohydrates. Also, the processed products are sometimes enriched with additional nutrients.

Purchasing and Storing Pasta Products

Pasta products are purchased by weight, either fresh or dried. Tubes and shapes are not generally available fresh. Dried products, by far the most common, are available in boxes or bags, usually in 1-, 10- and 20-pound units. They can be stored in a cool, dry place for several months. Fresh pasta can be stored in an airtight wrapping in the refrigerator for a few days or in the freezer for a few weeks.

Preparing Fresh Pasta

MAKING FRESH PASTA

Fresh pasta is easy to make, requiring almost no special equipment and only a few staples. The dough can be mixed by hand for small batches or in the bowl of a mixer. Mixing by hand allows the chef to get a feel for the dough, adjusting the amount of flour added as needed.

PROCEDURE FOR **MIXING PASTA DOUGH BY HAND**

① Mound the flour on a workbench. Make a well in the center. Add the eggs and whip them with a fork.

② Using your fingers, stir the eggs, gradually bringing more flour into the center.

③ Using a dough scraper, add more flour to the egg mixture, stirring constantly until a firm dough is formed.

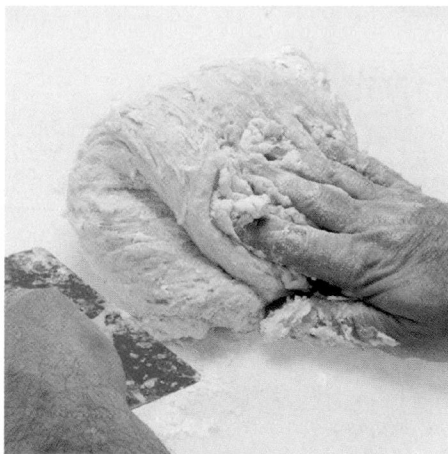

④ Knead the stiff dough until smooth.

BASIC PASTA DOUGH

Yield: 4 lb. (1.9 kg)

Eggs	15	15
Olive oil	1 fl. oz.	30 ml
Salt	1 Tbsp.	15 ml
Bread flour*	2 lb. 8 oz.	1.2 kg

1 Adding the flour to the mixing bowl and using the paddle until the mixture forms a firm dough.

1 Place the eggs, oil and salt in a large mixer bowl. Use the paddle attachment to combine.

2 Add one-third of the flour and stir until the mixture begins to form a soft dough. Remove the paddle attachment and attach the dough hook.

3 Gradually add more flour until the dough is dry and cannot absorb any more flour.

4 Remove the dough from the mixer, wrap it well with plastic wrap and set it aside at room temperature for 20 to 30 minutes.

5 After the dough has rested, roll it into flat sheets by hand or with a pasta machine. Work with only a small portion at a time, keeping the remainder well covered to prevent it from drying out.

6 While the sheets of dough are pliable, cut them into the desired width with a chef's knife or pasta machine. Sheets can also be used for making ravioli, as illustrated next.

*Semolina flour can be substituted for all or part of the bread flour in this recipe, although it makes a stronger dough that is more difficult to work with by hand.

VARIATIONS:

Garlic-Herb—Roast one head of garlic. Peel and purée the cloves and add to the eggs. Add up to 2 ounces (60 grams) finely chopped assorted fresh herbs just before mixing is complete.

Spinach—Add 8 ounces (240 grams) cooked, puréed and well-drained spinach to the eggs. Increase the amount of flour slightly if necessary.

Tomato—Add 4 ounces (120 grams) tomato paste to the eggs; omit the salt. Increase the amount of flour slightly if necessary.

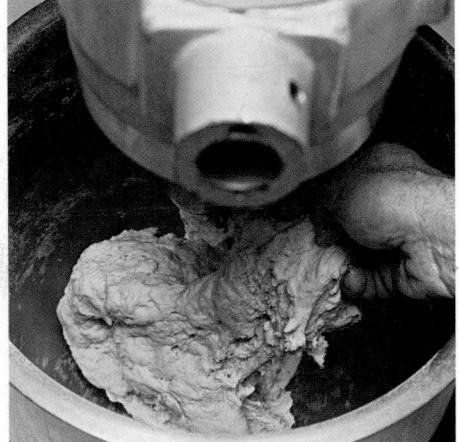

2 The finished dough.

Approximate values per 1-oz. (30-g) serving: **Calories** 80, **Total fat** 2 g, **Saturated fat** 0.5 g, **Cholesterol** 50 mg, **Sodium** 125 mg, **Total carbohydrates** 13 g, **Protein** 3 g

The basic form for pasta dough is the **sfoglia**, a thin, flat sheet of dough that is cut into ribbons, circles or squares. Although pasta dough can be kneaded by hand, stretched and rolled with a rolling pin and cut with a chef's knife, pasta machines make these tasks easier. Pasta machines are either electric or manual. Some electric models mix and knead the dough, then extrude it through a cutting disk. An extrusion machine is most practical in a food service operation that regularly serves large quantities of pasta. The pasta machine more often encountered is operated manually with a hand crank. It has two rollers that knead, press and push the dough into a thin, uniform sheet. Adjacent cutting rollers slice the thin dough into various widths for fettuccine, spaghetti, capellini and the like.

PROCEDURE FOR **ROLLING AND CUTTING PASTA DOUGH**

1 Work with a small portion of the dough. Leave the rest covered with plastic wrap to prevent it from drying out.

2 Flatten the dough with the heel of your hand.

❸ Set the pasta machine rollers to their widest setting. Insert the dough and turn the handle with one hand while supporting the dough with the other hand. Pass the entire piece of dough through the rollers.

❹ Dust the dough with flour, fold it in thirds and pass it through the pasta machine again.

❺ Repeat the folding and rolling procedure until the dough is smooth. This may require four to six passes.

❻ Tighten the rollers one or two marks, then pass the dough through the machine. Without folding it in thirds, pass the dough through the machine repeatedly, tightening the rollers one or two marks each time.

❼ When the dough is thin enough to see your hand through it, but not so thin that it begins to tear, it is ready to use or cut into ribbons. This sheet is the *sfoglia*.

❽ To cut the sfoglia into ribbons, gently feed a manageable length of dough through the desired cutting blades.

❾ Lay out the pasta in a single layer on a sheet pan dusted with flour to dry. Layers of pasta ribbons can be separated with parchment paper.

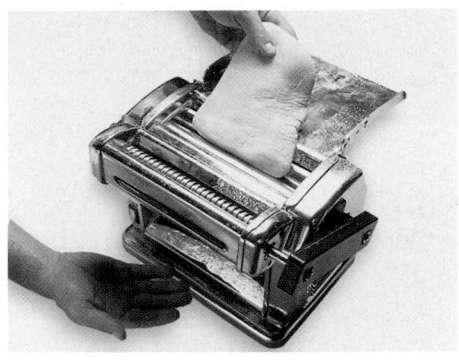

❶ Passing the entire piece of dough through the pasta machine.

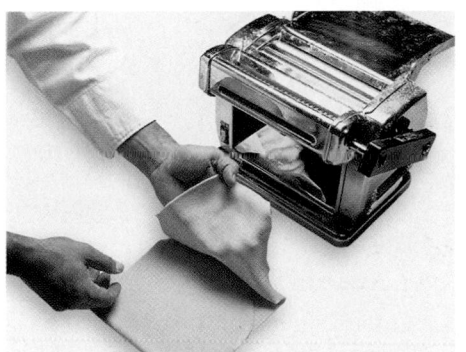

❷ Folding the dough in thirds.

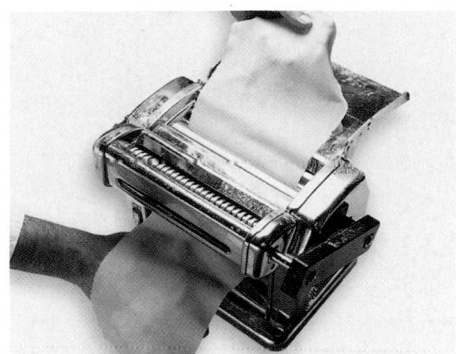

❸ Passing the dough through the pasta machine to achieve the desired thickness.

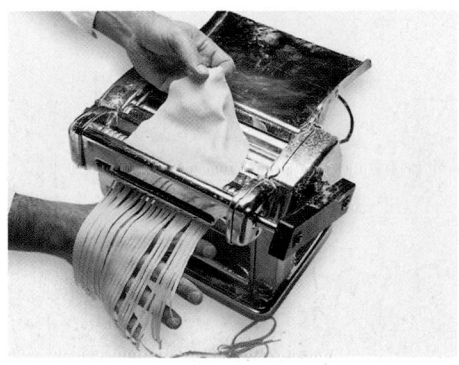

❹ Using the pasta machine to cut the dough to the desired width.

FILLING PASTA

Sheets of raw pasta dough can be filled or folded to create ravioli (squares), tortellini (round "hats" with a brim of dough), lunettes (circles of dough folded into half-moons), agnolotti (squares of dough folded into rectangles), cappelletti (squares of dough folded and shaped into rings) and other shapes. The filled pieces of dough are then cooked in boiling water using the procedure for cooking pasta ribbons discussed later. The filling can include almost anything—cheese, herbs, vegetables, fish, shellfish, meat or poultry. It can be uncooked or precooked. But any meat filling should be fully cooked before the pasta is assembled, as the time it takes for the dough to cook may not be sufficient to cook the filling.

Cannelloni is a different type of filled pasta: A large square of cooked dough is wrapped around a meat or cheese filling and baked. Popular lasagna dishes are similar. Lasagna are wide, flat sheets of pasta that are cooked and then layered with cheese, tomato sauce and meat or vegetables as desired. The finished casserole is baked and cut into portions.

Some of the larger, commercially prepared pasta shapes such as large shells (conchigloni or rigate) or large tubes (manicotti) can be partially cooked in boiling water, then filled, sauced and baked as a casserole.

Asian noodle dough is also made into filled items such as dumplings, wontons, egg rolls (made with egg noodle dough) and spring rolls (made with rice paper). These items are usually steamed, pan-fried or deep-fried. When making filled pasta, consider the flavors and textures of the filling, dough and sauce. Each should complement the others.

PROCEDURE FOR **PREPARING RAVIOLI**

1. Prepare a basic pasta dough of the desired flavor.
2. Prepare and chill the desired filling.
3. Roll out two thin sheets of dough between the rollers of a pasta machine. Gently lay the dough flat on the work surface.
4. Using a piping bag or a small portion scoop, place small mounds of filling on one of the dough pieces. Space the filling evenly, allowing approximately 2 inches (5 centimeters) between each mound.
5. Brush the exposed areas of dough with water.
6. Gently place the second sheet of dough over the mounds and press firmly around each mound to remove air pockets and seal the dough.
7. Cut between the mounds with a chef's knife, pastry wheel or circular cutter.

1. Piping the filling onto the dough.

2. Pressing around the mounds of filling to seal the dough and remove any air pockets.

3. Cutting around the mounds with a circular cutter.

Cooking Method

DETERMINING DONENESS

al dente (al DEN-tay) Italian for "to the tooth"; used to describe a food, usually pasta, that is cooked only until it gives a slight resistance when one bites into it

Italian-style pastas are properly cooked when they are **al dente**, firm but tender. Cooking times vary depending on the shape and quantity of pasta, the amount of water used, the hardness of the water and even the altitude. Fresh pasta cooks rapidly, sometimes in seconds. Noodles and dried pasta may require several minutes.

Although package or recipe directions offer some guidance, the only way to accurately test doneness is to bite into a piece. When the pasta is slightly firmer than desired, remove it from the stove and drain. It will continue to cook through residual heat.

Unlike Italian pasta, Asian noodles are not served al dente. Rather, they are either boiled until very soft or stir-fried until very crisp.

BOILING

All Italian-style pasta and most Asian noodles are cooked by just one method: boiling. The secret to boiling pasta successfully is to use ample water. Allow 1 gallon (4 liters) of water for each pound (450 grams) of pasta.

Use a saucepan or stockpot large enough to allow the pasta to move freely in the boiling water; otherwise, the starch released by the dough will make the pasta gummy and sticky. The water should be brought to a rapid boil, then all the pasta should be added at once.

Salt should be added to the water. Pasta absorbs water and salt during cooking. Adding salt to the pasta after it is cooked will not provide the same seasoning effect.

Chefs disagree on whether to add oil to the cooking water. Purists argue against adding oil, on the theory that it makes the dough absorb water unevenly. Others think oil should be added to reduce surface foam. Another theory is that oil keeps the pasta from sticking, although this works only when added to cooked, drained pasta.

Asian noodles may be prepared by boiling until fully cooked, or they may be parboiled and then stir-fried with other ingredients to finish cooking.

PROCEDURE FOR **COOKING PASTA TO ORDER**

1. Bring the appropriate amount of water to a boil over high heat.
2. Add oil to the water if desired.
3. Add the pasta and salt to the rapidly boiling water.
4. Stir the pasta to prevent it from sticking together. Bring the water back to a boil and cook until the pasta is done.
5. When the pasta is properly cooked, immediately drain it through a colander. A small amount of oil may be gently tossed into the pasta if desired to prevent it from sticking together.
6. Serve hot pasta immediately, or refresh it in cold water for later use in salads or other dishes. (Do not rinse pasta that is to be served hot.)

PROCEDURE FOR **COOKING DRIED PASTA IN ADVANCE**

Fresh pasta is so delicate and cooks so rapidly (sometimes in as little as 15 seconds) that it should be cooked to order. Dried pasta, however, can be cooked in advance for quantity service.

1. Follow the preceding directions for cooking pasta, but stop the cooking process when the pasta is about two-thirds done.
2. Drain the pasta, rinse it lightly and toss it in a small amount of oil.
3. Divide the pasta into appropriate-sized portions. Individual portions can be wrapped in plastic or laid on a sheet pan and covered. Refrigerate until needed.
4. When needed, place a portion in a china cap and immerse in boiling water to reheat. Drain, add sauce and serve immediately.

ACCOMPANIMENTS TO PASTA

Pasta is widely accepted by consumers and easily incorporated in a variety of cuisines—from Italian and Chinese to Eastern European and spa. It is used in broths; as a bed for stews, fish, shellfish, poultry or meat; or tossed with sauce. Today's creative chefs are constantly developing nontraditional but delicious ways of serving pasta.

Pasta and Broths

Small shapes can be cooked in the broth with which they are served, or cooked separately, then added to the hot liquid at service time. Soups such as *cappelletti in brodo* and chicken noodle are examples of these techniques.

Pasta Sauces

There are hundreds of Italian pasta sauces as well as sauces for Italian-style pasta, but most can be divided into six categories: ragus, seafood sauces, vegetable sauces, cream sauces, garlic-oil sauces and uncooked sauces. Recipes for a selection of pasta sauces are included in Chapter 10, Stocks and Sauces.

Although there are no firm rules governing the combinations of sauces and pasta, Table 22.4 offers some of the more common combinations.

TABLE 22.4 COMBINING SAUCES, PASTA AND GARNISHES

SAUCE	DESCRIPTION	PASTA SHAPE	GARNISH
Ragu	Braised dishes used as sauce; flavorings, meat or poultry are browned, then a tomato product and stock, wine, water, milk or cream are added	Ribbons, tubes, shapes, filled	Grated cheese
Seafood	White seafood sauces are flavored with herbs and made with white wine or stock; red seafood sauces are tomato-based	Ribbons (fettuccine and capellini)	Fish or shellfish
Vegetable	Includes both traditional sauces made with tomatoes and stock, flavored with garlic and red pepper, and modern sauces such as primavera	Ribbons, tubes, filled	Meatballs, sausage, grated cheese
Cream	Uses milk or cream and sometimes roux; usually cheese is added	Thick ribbons (spaghetti and fettuccine), filled	Ham, peas, sausage, mushrooms, smoked salmon, nuts, grated cheese
Garlic-oil	(It. *aglio-olio*) Olive oil flavored with garlic and herbs, usually parsley; can be hot or cold, cooked or uncooked (pesto is an uncooked, cold sauce)	Ribbons, shapes, filled	Grated cheese (if uncooked or cold), herbs
Uncooked	A variety of dressings and garnishes such as fresh tomatoes, basil and olive oil; or olive oil, lemon juice, parsley, basil and hot red pepper flakes; capers, anchovies, olives, fresh herbs, fresh vegetables, flavored oils and cubed cheeses can also be used	Ribbons, shapes	Cubed or grated cheese, fresh vegetables, herbs

QUESTIONS FOR DISCUSSION

Terms to Know

eyes	dent corn
creamers	posole
solanine	masa harina
gnocchi	groats
latkes	steel-cut oats
pommes frites	rolled oats
hull	sfoglia
bran	ravioli
endosperm	tortellini
germ	cannelloni

1. Explain the differences between mealy and waxy potatoes. Give two examples of each.

2. Describe the two methods of sautéing or pan-frying potatoes.

3. Discuss the steps required to prepare deep-fried potatoes and some of the techniques to use to ensure the best results.

4. All grains are composed of three parts. Name and describe each of these parts.

5. Describe and compare the three general cooking methods used to prepare grains.

6. What type of rice is preferred for making true Italian risotto? Explain the reason for this choice.

7. Name the three categories of Italian-style pasta shapes and give an example of each.

8. Why is it necessary to use ample water when cooking pasta? Should pasta be cooked in salted water? Should oil be added to the cooking water? Explain your answers.

9. Discuss the differences between cooking fresh pasta and cooking dried, factory-produced pasta.

10. Different names are given to Italian pasta shapes from one region of Italy to another. Research the various regional Italian cuisines to determine other names for some of the pastas shown on pages 646–647. **WWW**

11. Each of the types of sauce listed in Table 22.4 comes from a specific region of Italy. Which region is most closely associated with each type of sauce? Why? **WWW**

GOAT CHEESE RAVIOLI WITH ROASTED RED PEPPERS AND BABY SPINACH

Yield: 6 Servings

Fresh goat cheese	6 oz.	180 g
Cream cheese	4 oz.	120 g
Fresh parsley, chopped	3 Tbsp.	45 ml
Fresh basil, chopped fine	3 Tbsp.	45 ml
Fresh thyme, chopped fine	2 tsp.	10 ml
Black pepper	TT	TT
Basic Pasta Dough (page 650)	1 lb.	480 g
Heavy cream	24 fl. oz.	720 ml
Parmesan, grated	2 oz.	60 g
Salt	TT	TT
Roasted red bell peppers, bâtonnet	6 oz.	180 g
Baby spinach leaves, cleaned	4 oz.	120 g

1. To make the cheese filling, combine the goat and cream cheeses with the parsley, 2 tablespoons (30 milliliters) basil and 1 teaspoon (5 milliliters) thyme; season to taste with pepper.
2. Make ravioli using the cheese mixture and the Basic Pasta Dough.
3. To make the sauce, combine the cream with the remaining herbs and bring to a boil. Reduce by one-third and add the Parmesan. Season with salt and pepper.
4. Boil the ravioli until done and drain well.
5. Add the hot ravioli and roasted red bell peppers to the sauce and toss to combine. Add the baby spinach leaves to the sauce and toss to wilt the leaves.
6. Divide the pasta sauce and vegetables among six plates and serve.

Approximate values per 8-oz. (240-g) serving: **Calories** 580, **Total fat** 48 g, **Saturated fat** 30 g, **Cholesterol** 185 mg, **Sodium** 510 mg, **Total carbohydrates** 23 g, **Protein** 15 g, **Vitamin A** 60%, **Calcium** 25%

CHÂTEAU POTATOES

Yield: 10 Servings **Method:** Boiling/Sautéing

Potatoes, waxy	5 lb.	2.4 kg
Salt	TT	TT
Clarified butter	6 fl. oz.	180 ml
White pepper	TT	TT
Whole butter	2 oz.	60 g

1. Peel the potatoes if desired. Cut the potatoes into 2-inch (5-centimeter) lengths and tournée.
2. Place the potatoes in a pan of salted water. Bring to a simmer and parcook the potatoes for approximately 5 minutes. They should still be raw in the middle.
3. Remove the potatoes from the water and spread on a pan so that the steam is released and the potatoes dry completely.
4. Heat an appropriately sized sauté pan over medium heat. Add enough clarified butter to cover the bottom of the pan approximately ¼ inch (6 millimeters) deep. Sauté the potatoes in batches, adding more butter as necessary and turning them often until all sides are golden brown. If the potatoes are properly browned but not yet fully cooked, place them in a 350°F (180°C) oven for a few minutes until tender.
5. Season the potatoes with salt and white pepper and toss in a small amount of whole butter at service time.

VARIATIONS:

Parisienne Potatoes and Noisette Potatoes—Parisienne and noisette potatoes are prepared in the same manner as château potatoes but the potatoes are cut into balls with a Parisienne scoop or melon ball cutter. Parisienne potatoes are generally larger than 1 inch (2.5 centimeters) and noisette potatoes are generally smaller than 1 inch (2.5 centimeters). Parcooking time is greatly reduced; the potatoes can also be cooked from the raw state without parcooking.

Approximate values per serving: **Calories** 280, **Total fat** 20 g, **Saturated fat** 12 g, **Cholesterol** 50 mg, **Sodium** 5 mg, **Total carbohydrates** 23 g, **Vitamin C** 25%, **Claim**—high in vitamin C

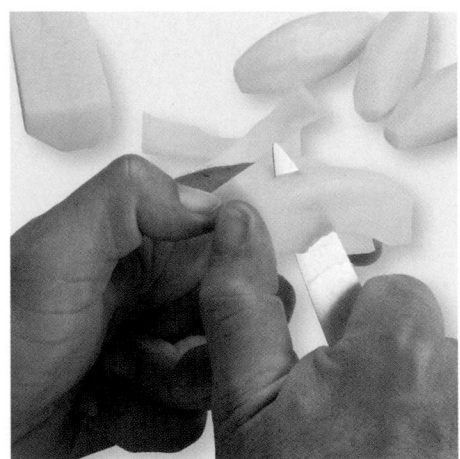

1. Tournéeing the potatoes.

2. Parcooking the potatoes.

3. Sautéing the potatoes.

ROASTED FINGERLING POTATOES

Yield: 4 Servings, 4 oz. (120 g) each   **Method:** Roasting

Fingerling potatoes, assorted	1 lb.	480 g
Fresh lemon juice	from 2 lemons	from 2 lemons
Italian herb blend	1 Tbsp.	15 ml
Salt	1 tsp.	5 ml
Black pepper	⅛ tsp.	1 ml
Olive oil	3 Tbsp.	45 ml

1. Cut the potatoes in halves or quarters and place in a bowl. Add the lemon juice, seasonings and oil and then toss to coat the potatoes thoroughly.
2. Place the seasoned potatoes in a shallow baking pan and roast at 425°F (220°C). Stir or turn the potatoes two or three times during cooking to promote even browning. Cook until the potatoes are tender, approximately 30 minutes.

Approximate values per serving: **Calories** 200, **Total fat** 10 g, **Saturated fat** 1.5 g, **Cholesterol** 0 mg, **Sodium** 590 mg, **Total carbohydrates** 27 g, **Protein** 2 g, **Vitamin C** 45%, **Iron** 10%, **Claim**—good source of fiber, vitamin C and iron

CANDIED SWEET POTATOES

Yield: 6 Servings, 4 oz. (120 g) each   **Method:** Baking

Sweet potatoes	2 lb.	960 g
Brown sugar	5 oz.	150 g
Water	2 fl. oz.	60 ml
Whole butter	2 oz.	60 g
Vanilla extract	1 tsp.	5 ml

1. Wash the sweet potatoes and cut as necessary to promote even cooking.
2. Bake the sweet potatoes on a sheet pan at 350°F (180°C) until cooked but still firm, approximately 30 minutes.
3. Combine the sugar, water and butter and bring to a boil. Add the vanilla extract and remove from the heat.
4. Peel the potatoes and slice or cut as desired. Arrange the potatoes in a baking dish and pour the sugar mixture over them.
5. Sprinkle the potatoes with additional sugar if desired and bake for 20 minutes, basting occasionally with the sugar mixture.

Approximate values per 4-oz. (120-g) serving: **Calories** 320, **Total fat** 8 g, **Saturated fat** 5 g, **Cholesterol** 20 mg, **Sodium** 105 mg, **Total carbohydrates** 60 g, **Protein** 3 g, **Vitamin A** 340%, **Vitamin C** 60%

SCALLOPED POTATOES

Yield: 1 Pan, 9 in. × 12 in. (22 cm × 30 cm) **Method:** Baking

Potatoes, mealy russet	5 lb.	2.4 kg
Béchamel (page 201)	36 fl. oz.	1 lt
Salt and white pepper	TT	TT
Nutmeg	TT	TT
Whole butter	as needed	as needed

1. Peel the potatoes and hold them in water to prevent browning. Pour the béchamel into a stainless steel bowl. Slice the potatoes thinly (a mandoline works well for this purpose) directly into the béchamel. Stir occasionally so that the sauce coats the potatoes.
2. Season as desired with the salt, white pepper and nutmeg.
3. Layer the potatoes and sauce in a buttered half-size hotel pan. Pour any remaining sauce over the top of the potatoes.
4. Bake covered at 350°F (180°C) for approximately 30 minutes. Uncover and bake until the potatoes are cooked and brown on top, approximately 20 to 30 minutes.

Approximate values per 4-oz. (120-g) serving: **Calories** 110, **Total fat** 3.5 g, **Saturated fat** 2 g, **Cholesterol** 10 mg, **Sodium** 25 mg, **Total carbohydrates** 18 g, **Protein** 3 g

1. Layering the potatoes in a hotel pan.

2. Pouring the remaining cream sauce over the potatoes.

3. The finished Scalloped Potatoes.

DELMONICO POTATOES

INLAND NORTHWEST CULINARY ACADEMY, SPOKANE, WA

Instructor Peter Tobin, CEC, CCE

Yield: Approximately 10 lb. (4.8 kg)   **Method:** Steaming/Baking

Potatoes, mealy, peeled, medium dice	6 lb.	2.8 kg
Green bell peppers, small dice	4	4
Pimentos, small dice	12 oz.	360 g
Béchamel (page 201)	3 pt.	1.4 lt
Salt and pepper	TT	TT
Nutmeg	TT	TT

1. Steam the potatoes until cooked through but firm, approximately 7 minutes. Spread them on sheet pans and refrigerate.
2. Blanch and chill the bell peppers.
3. Combine all ingredients in a large bowl. Mix carefully so as not to break up the potatoes.
4. Place the potatoes in a shallow full-size hotel pan, cover and bake at 350°F (180°C) until the internal temperature reaches at least 165°F (74°C).

Approximate values per 4-oz. (120-g) serving: **Calories** 100, **Total fat** 4 g, **Saturated fat** 2 g, **Cholesterol** 10 mg, **Sodium** 340 mg, **Total carbohydrates** 15 g, **Protein** 2 g, **Vitamin C** 35%

GERMAN-STYLE POTATO SALAD

JOLIET JUNIOR COLLEGE, JOLIET, IL

Keith G. Vonhoff, CEPC, CEC, CCP

Yield: 8 lb. (3.8 kg); 32 Servings, 4 oz. (120 g) each   **Method:** Boiling or Steaming

Bacon, paysanne	8 oz.	240 g
Onions, small dice	8 oz.	240 g
Green onions, sliced thin	2 oz.	60 g
Flour	2 oz.	60 g
Granulated sugar	5 oz.	150 g
Cider vinegar	6 fl. oz.	180 ml
Chicken stock	1 pt.	480 ml
Russet potatoes, cooked, peeled, sliced ¼ in. (6 mm) thick	5 lb.	2.4 kg
Eggs, hard cooked, peeled, sliced	6	6
Salt and pepper	TT	TT

1. In a heavy saucepan large enough to hold all of the ingredients, cook the bacon, rendering the fat without browning the bacon. Remove the bacon and set aside.
2. Add the onions and green onions and cook until tender without browning, approximately 2 minutes.
3. Stir in the flour to make a roux. Add the sugar, vinegar and stock. Stir, bring to a boil and reduce to a simmer.
4. Carefully fold in the potatoes, eggs and cooked bacon. Season to taste with salt and pepper. Serve warm.

Approximate values per serving: **Calories** 110, **Total fat** 2 g, **Saturated fat** 0.5 g, **Cholesterol** 40 mg, **Sodium** 95 mg, **Total carbohydrates** 19 g, **Protein** 4 g, **Vitamin C** 15%

POTATO PANCAKES

Yield: 12 Pancakes, 2½ oz. (75 g) each   **Method:** Pan-frying

Potatoes, all-purpose	2 lb.	960 g
Eggs, beaten	3	3
Onion, minced	4 oz.	120 g
Flour	2 oz.	60 g
Baking powder	1 Tbsp.	15 ml
Nutmeg	TT	TT
Salt and pepper	TT	TT
Vegetable oil	4 fl. oz.	120 ml
Applesauce	as needed	as needed

1 Peel and coarsely grate the potatoes.

2 Transfer the grated potatoes to a bowl and add the eggs, onion, flour and baking powder. Season with nutmeg, salt and pepper. Blend well.

3 Heat the oil. Form the potato mixture into 12 uniform-sized pancakes and pan-fry them until tender, turning once when well browned on the first side. Remove them from the pan and drain well. Serve hot with applesauce, if desired.

Approximate values per pancake: **Calories** 140, **Total fat** 6 g, **Saturated fat** 1 g, **Cholesterol** 55 mg, **Sodium** 140 mg, **Total carbohydrates** 18 g, **Protein** 3 g, **Vitamin C** 10%

RÖSTI POTATOES

THE FOUR SEASONS, New York, NY

Chef Christian Albin (1947–2009)

Yield: 6 Servings   **Method:** Pan-frying

Potatoes, all-purpose, large	4	4
Bacon fat	2 oz.	60 g
Lard	2 oz.	60 g
Kosher salt and pepper	TT	TT
Whole butter	1 oz.	30 g

1 Partially cook the potatoes in salted water until almost done. Drain and cool the potatoes, then peel and coarsely grate them.

2 Heat the bacon fat and lard in a heavy, shallow 10-inch (25-centimeter) skillet with sloping sides until quite hot. Spread half the potatoes over the bottom of the pan; sprinkle with salt and pepper. Cover with the remaining potatoes and cook over medium-high heat until the bottom turns brown and crusty, approximately 10 minutes.

3 Turn the potatoes in one piece. This is easiest to do by placing a large plate over the pan and turning both together so that the potatoes fall onto the plate. Slip the turned-over potatoes off the plate back into the pan, browned side up. Cook until the bottom is browned.

4 Before serving, smooth the edges of the potatoes with a spatula. Sprinkle with salt and brush the edge of the pan with whole butter. It will melt and run into the potatoes.

Rösti, a rich potato cake, is a mainstay of the hearty alpine cuisine of Switzerland. On menus in restaurants that cater to mountaineers and skiers, rösti frequently appears with various garnishes such as mit spiegeleier (with fried eggs), mit speck (with bacon) or mit schinken (with ham).

VARIATION:

Cheddar Cheese Rösti Potatoes—Make two thin cakes from the coarsely grated potatoes. Top one with a layer of 7 ounces (210 grams) sour cream, 2 ounces (60 grams) cubed sharp Cheddar cheese and 2 tablespoons (30 milliliters) chopped chives. Top with the other cake. Dot with 1 tablespoon (15 milliliters) whole butter and bake in a 400°F (200°C) oven for 15 minutes.

Approximate values per serving: **Calories** 290, **Total fat** 23 g, **Saturated fat** 10 g, **Cholesterol** 30 mg, **Sodium** 430 mg, **Total carbohydrates** 19 g, **Protein** 2 g, **Vitamin C** 20%

DUCHESSE POTATOES

Yield: Approximately 2 lb. (1 kg)　　**Method:** Boiling

Potatoes, mealy	2 lb.	1 kg
Whole butter	1 oz.	30 g
Nutmeg	⅛ tsp.	½ ml
Salt and pepper	TT	TT
Eggs	1	1
Egg yolks	2	2
Clarified butter	as needed	as needed

1 Peel and quarter the potatoes. Then boil them in salted water until tender. Drain and immediately turn them out onto a sheet pan to allow the moisture to evaporate.

2 While still warm, press the potatoes through a grinder or food mill, or grind through a grinder's medium die. Blend in the butter and season to taste with nutmeg, salt and pepper.

3 Mix in the eggs and egg yolks, blending well.

4 Transfer the duchesse mixture to a piping bag fitted with a large star tip. Pipe single portion-sized spirals onto a parchment-lined sheet pan. Brush with clarified butter and bake at 375°F (190°C) until the edges are golden brown, approximately 8 to 10 minutes. Serve immediately.

Note: Duchesse potatoes are often used to decorate platters used for buffets or tableside preparations or to present châteaubriand. To create borders and garnishes, the standard mixture for duchesse potatoes is forced through a piping bag while still very hot and relatively soft.

VARIATION:

Potato Croquettes—Shape the duchesse mixture into short cylinders resembling fat corks. Coat the cylinders with bread crumbs using the standard breading procedure described in Chapter 8, Mise en Place. Using the basket method, deep-fry at 360°F (182°C) until golden brown.

Approximate values per 3-oz. (90-g) serving: **Calories** 120, **Total fat** 3.5 g, **Saturated fat** 2 g, **Cholesterol** 65 mg, **Sodium** 250 mg, **Total carbohydrates** 18 g, **Protein** 3 g, **Vitamin C** 20%

MORE THAN A FRENCH FRY

Thanks to the genius of Carême, Escoffier and others, few vegetables have as extensive a classic repertoire as potatoes. Some of these dishes begin with the duchesse (duh-SHEES) potatoes mixture; in this regard, duchesse potatoes can be considered the mother of many classic potato preparations. For example,

Duchesse + Tomato concassée = *Marquis*

Duchesse + Chopped truffles + Almond coating + Deep-frying = *Berny*

Duchesse + Shaping + Breading + Deep-frying = *Croquettes*

Duchesse + Pâte à choux = *Dauphine*

Dauphine + Grated Parmesan + Piped shape + Deep-frying = *Lorette*

1 Passing the boiled potatoes through a food mill.

2 Piping the potatoes.

3 The finished Duchesse Potatoes.

DAUPHINE POTATOES

Yield: 3 lb. (1.4 kg)   **Method:** Boiling

Duchesse Potatoes (page 661)	2 lb.	960 g
Éclair Paste (page 979)	20 oz.	600 g

1. Combine the Duchesse Potatoes with the Éclair Paste while both mixtures are still warm.
2. Pipe the mixture into the desired shapes onto strips of parchment paper. Chill until ready to cook. At service, deep-fry by carefully sliding the pieces of paper into the fryer; remove the paper with tongs when the potatoes float loose. Cook until golden brown.

VARIATION:

Lorette—Add 4 ounces (120 grams) grated Parmesan in Step 2. Pipe the mixture into small crescents on pieces of parchment paper. Deep-fry by carefully sliding the pieces of paper into the fryer; remove the paper with tongs when the potatoes float loose.

Approximate values per 4-oz. (120-g) serving: **Calories** 270, **Total fat** 18 g, **Saturated fat** 8 g, **Cholesterol** 140 mg, **Sodium** 470 mg, **Total carbohydrates** 23 g, **Protein** 5 g, **Vitamin C** 15%

1. Deep-frying the potatoes using the swimming method.

2. The finished potatoes.

POTATO GNOCCHI

Yield: 5 lb. (2.4 kg); 10 Servings, 8 oz. (240 g) each   **Method:** Boiling

Potatoes, mealy, peeled	4 lb.	1.9 kg
Salt	2 tsp.	10 ml
Egg, beaten	1	1
Egg yolks, beaten	3	3
Salt	1 tsp.	5 ml
Pepper	½ tsp.	2 ml
Clarified butter	2 fl. oz.	60 ml
Nutmeg, ground	TT	TT
Flour	1 lb.	480 g
Whole butter	as needed	as needed
Parmesan, grated	4 oz.	120 g
Fontina, sliced	6 oz.	180 g

Gnocchi served with tomato sauce.

1. Cut the potatoes into uniform-sized pieces. Cover with water. Add the salt and simmer the potatoes until tender. Drain the potatoes well and spread on a sheet pan. Place the pan in a 300°F (150°C) oven for 5 minutes to dry them well. Remove the potatoes from the oven and immediately pass them through a ricer or food mill into a stainless steel bowl.

2. Add the beaten egg and yolks, salt, pepper, clarified butter and nutmeg and mix until incorporated. Add half the flour to the bowl and mix well.

3. Spread a portion of the remaining flour on a work surface. Place the dough on the work surface and knead additional flour into the dough until it is firm and workable. Divide the dough into eight equal pieces. Roll each piece into a cylinder approximately 2 feet (60 centimeters) long. With a dough knife, cut the dough into ¼- to ½-ounce (7- to 15-gram) pieces. Round each piece into a ball. Flour the tines of a dinner fork and draw the fork firmly across each ball to form ridges around the surface of the gnocchi and create an indentation on one side. Place the formed gnocchi on a floured sheet pan. Cover and refrigerate until service.

4. Boil the gnocchi in salted water for 2 to 3 minutes. A few seconds after they begin to float, remove the gnocchi from the water with a spider or slotted spoon and drain well.

5. Sauté the gnocchi in small batches in whole butter, browning them slightly. Portion them into serving dishes, top with grated Parmesan and Fontina slices and place under the broiler for 1 to 2 minutes to melt the cheese. Serve immediately.

VARIATION:

As an alternative to broiling the gnocchi with a cheese topping, they can be sautéed and served accompanied by traditional pasta sauces such as tomato sauce, pesto sauce or any number of cream sauces. Hold and reheat gnocchi as for any stuffed pasta such as tortellini or ravioli.

Approximate values per 8-oz. (240-g) serving: **Calories** 560, **Total fat** 22 g, **Saturated fat** 13 g, **Cholesterol** 145 mg, **Sodium** 560 mg, **Total carbohydrates** 72 g, **Protein** 18 g, **Vitamin A** 15%, **Vitamin C** 40%, **Calcium** 25%, **Iron** 15%, **Claims**—good source of vitamin A and iron; high in fiber, vitamin C and calcium

POLENTA

Yield: 1 lb. 12 oz. (840 g)   **Method:** Simmering

Shallots, chopped	2 tsp.	10 ml
Whole butter	as needed	as needed
Milk, white stock or water	1 qt.	960 ml
Cornmeal, yellow or white	6 oz.	180 g
Salt and pepper	TT	TT

1. Sauté the shallots in 1 tablespoon (15 milliliters) butter for 30 seconds. Add the milk, stock or water and bring to a boil.
2. Slowly add the cornmeal while stirring constantly to prevent lumps, then simmer for 30 minutes. Season with salt and pepper.
3. Scrape the polenta into a buttered nonaluminum dish; spread to an even thickness with a spatula that has been dipped in water. Refrigerate the polenta until well chilled.
4. To serve, unmold the polenta and cut into shapes. Sauté or grill the polenta for service, or sprinkle with grated Parmesan and heat under a broiler or salamander.

Approximate values per 4-oz. (120-g) serving: **Calories** 190, **Total fat** 7 g, **Saturated fat** 3.5 g, **Cholesterol** 20 mg, **Sodium** 55 mg, **Total carbohydrates** 25 g, **Protein** 6 g, **Calcium** 15%

1. Spreading the cooked polenta into a stainless steel pan.

2. Cutting the polenta into the desired shape.

3. Grilling the polenta.

CREAMY POLENTA WITH WILD MUSHROOMS

CHEF JOHN ASH, SANTA ROSA, CA

Yield: 8 Servings   **Method:** Simmering

Yellow onions, chopped coarse	12 oz.	340 g
White mushrooms, chopped coarse	4 oz.	120 g
Garlic, chopped fine	2 Tbsp.	30 ml
Dried porcini or cèpe mushrooms, rinsed, soaked in water and chopped coarse	2 oz.	60 g
Olive oil	5 fl. oz.	150 ml
Chicken or vegetable stock	2 qt.	1.9 lt
Coarse polenta	12 oz.	360 g
Salt and pepper	TT	TT
Fresh basil, chopped fine	4 tsp.	20 ml
Fresh oregano, chopped fine	1 tsp.	5 ml
Heavy cream	1 pt.	480 ml
Aged Asiago or Fontina, grated fine	4 oz.	120 g
Fresh wild mushrooms	8–10	8–10
Fresh basil sprigs	as needed for garnish	

1 Sauté the onions, white mushrooms, garlic and porcini or cèpes in 4 fluid ounces (120 milliliters) oil until lightly colored. Add the stock; bring to a boil.

2 Slowly stir in the polenta. Simmer for 10 minutes, stirring regularly. The polenta should be thick and creamy. Add more stock if necessary. Adjust the seasonings and keep warm.

3 Just before serving, add the chopped basil, oregano, cream and cheese and stir vigorously.

4 Sauté the fresh wild mushrooms in the remaining oil until tender. Spoon the polenta onto warm plates and garnish with the wild mushrooms and a sprig of fresh basil.

Approximate values per 8-oz. (240-g) serving: **Calories** 550, **Total fat** 46 g, **Saturated fat** 19 g, **Cholesterol** 95 mg, **Sodium** 1090 mg, **Total carbohydrates** 21 g, **Protein** 13 g, **Vitamin A** 35%, **Vitamin C** 15%, **Calcium** 20%, **Iron** 15%

GRITS AND CHEDDAR SOUFFLÉ

Yield: 8 Servings   **Method:** Simmering/Baking

Grits	8 oz.	240 g
Water	1½ pt.	720 ml
Milk	1½ pt.	720 ml
Unsalted butter	4 oz.	120 g
Salt	TT	TT
Tabasco sauce	½ tsp.	2 ml
Sharp Cheddar cheese, grated	8 oz.	240 g
Eggs, separated	6	6
Granulated sugar	2 tsp.	10 ml

1. Combine the grits, water, milk, butter and salt in a heavy saucepan. Bring to a simmer and cook, stirring constantly, until thick, approximately 5 to 10 minutes.
2. Remove from the heat and stir in the Tabasco sauce and 6 ounces (180 grams) cheese.
3. Whisk the egg yolks together, then stir them into the grits mixture.
4. Whip the egg whites to soft peaks, add the sugar and whip to stiff peaks. Fold the egg whites into the grits mixture.
5. Pour the soufflé into a well-buttered 2-quart (2-liter) casserole or soufflé dish. Top with the remaining 2 ounces (60 grams) cheese. Bake at 350°F (180°C) until set and browned, approximately 30 minutes. Serve immediately.

Approximate values per serving: **Calories** 410, **Total fat** 25 g, **Saturated fat** 9 g, **Cholesterol** 215 mg, **Sodium** 640 mg, **Total carbohydrates** 32 g, **Protein** 16 g, **Vitamin A** 40%, **Calcium** 30%

SAFFRON RICE

Yield: 6 Servings   **Method:** Pilaf

Basmati rice	1 lb.	480 g
Saffron threads	1 tsp.	5 ml
Boiling water	1 qt.	1 lt
Ghee or clarified butter	3 fl. oz.	90 ml
Cinnamon stick, 2 in. (5 cm) long	1	1
Cloves, whole	4	4
Onions, fine dice	5 oz.	150 g
Dark brown sugar	1 Tbsp.	15 ml
Salt	2 tsp.	10 ml
Cardamom seeds	¼ tsp.	2 ml

1. Wash the rice and drain thoroughly.
2. Steep the saffron in 2 fluid ounces (60 milliliters) boiling water.
3. In a saucepan, heat the ghee, then add the cinnamon and cloves. Add the onions and stir-fry until the onions are soft and slightly brown.
4. Add the rice and stir until it is well coated with the ghee and the grains are a light golden color.
5. Stirring constantly, add the remaining boiling water, sugar, salt and cardamom. Bring to a boil and reduce to a simmer.
6. Gently stir in the saffron and its water, cover and simmer until the rice has absorbed all the liquid.
7. Fluff with a fork and serve at once.

Approximate values per 4-oz. (120-g) serving: **Calories** 370, **Total fat** 16 g, **Saturated fat** 9 g, **Cholesterol** 35 mg, **Sodium** 780 mg, **Total carbohydrates** 51 g, **Protein** 4 g

BROWN RICE WITH SPICED PECANS

NEWBURY COLLEGE, BROOKLINE, MA
Senior Instructor Scott Doughty

Yield: 10 Servings   **Method:** Simmering

Chicken stock, hot	2½ pt.	1.2 lt
Salt	1½ tsp.	7 ml
Brown rice	1 lb.	480 g
Green onions	3	3
Whole butter	4 oz.	120 g
Spiced Pecans (recipe follows)	6 oz.	180 g

1. Bring the stock to a boil in a 2-quart (2-liter) saucepan. Add the salt and rice. Return to a boil, cover, reduce to a simmer and cook until the rice is tender, approximately 50 to 60 minutes.
2. Thinly slice the green onions on the diagonal. Then quickly sweat them in the butter. Add the green onions to the rice. Chop the Spiced Pecans and fold them into the rice mixture. Stir to combine and hold for service.

Approximate values per serving: **Calories** 350, **Total fat** 24 g, **Saturated fat** 8 g, **Cholesterol** 30 mg, **Sodium** 720 mg, **Total carbohydrates** 32 g, **Protein** 5 g, **Claims**—good source of fiber

SPICED PECANS

Yield: 6 oz. (180 g)

Whole butter	1 Tbsp.	15 g
Cayenne pepper	⅛ tsp.	1 ml
Cinnamon	⅛ tsp.	1 ml
Salt	½ tsp.	2 ml
Worcestershire sauce	1 Tbsp.	15 ml
Hot sauce	1–2 drops	1–2 drops
Pecan halves and pieces	6 oz.	180 g

1. Combine the butter, cayenne pepper, cinnamon, salt, Worcestershire sauce and hot sauce. Add the pecan halves and blend well.
2. Spread the nuts onto a sheet pan and bake at 300°F (150°C) for 10 minutes. Toss with a spatula and bake for an additional 5 to 10 minutes. Remove from the oven and cool.

Approximate values per 1-oz. (30-g) serving: **Calories** 160, **Total fat** 17 g, **Saturated fat** 2 g, **Cholesterol** 5 mg, **Sodium** 170 mg, **Total carbohydrates** 3 g, **Protein** 2 g

PILAU (INDIAN-STYLE RICE PILAF)

Yield: 2.2 lb. (1 kg) **Method:** Pilaf

Saffron	¼ tsp.	2 ml
Water, hot	2 fl. oz.	60 ml
Ghee or clarified butter	2 fl. oz.	60 ml
Onion, chopped fine	1	1
Fresh ginger, minced	2 tsp.	10 ml
Cumin, ground	1 tsp.	5 ml
Coriander, ground	½ tsp.	2 ml
Turmeric, ground	½ tsp.	2 ml
Cinnamon, ground	½ tsp.	2 ml
Cloves, ground	¼ tsp.	1 ml
Red pepper, dried, crushed	¼ tsp.	1 ml
Black pepper	⅛ tsp.	0.5 ml
Long-grain rice	8 oz.	240 g
Chicken stock, hot	1 pt.	480 ml
Raisins	3 oz.	90 g
Green peas, frozen	3 oz.	90 g
Slivered almonds or cashews, unsalted	2 oz.	60 g
Salt and pepper	TT	TT

1. Soak the saffron in the hot water for 30 minutes.
2. Heat the ghee or butter in a medium saucepot. Add the onion, ginger and all of the spices and sauté for 5 minutes. Add the rice and cook, stirring, until the rice is golden and all of the fat is absorbed.
3. Add the saffron water and stock to the rice. Reduce the heat to a simmer, cover and cook until all of the liquid is absorbed and the rice is tender, approximately 15 to 20 minutes.
4. Add the raisins, peas and nuts. Let stand for 5 minutes, adjust the seasonings and serve.

Approximate values per 1-c. (240-ml) serving: **Calories** 400, **Total fat** 19 g, **Saturated fat** 8 g, **Cholesterol** 30 mg, **Sodium** 250 mg, **Total carbohydrates** 53 g, **Protein** 7 g, **Vitamin A** 10%, **Vitamin C** 10%, **Iron** 15%

In parts of India, Iran and the Middle East where cooking rice pilau (or pilaf) is common, attentive cooks wrap the lid in a cloth to prevent drops of condensed steam from entering the rice. This ensures that the grains remain separate and fluffy after cooking.

THAI FRIED RICE

Yield: 8 Servings **Method:** Stir-frying

Vegetable oil	4 fl. oz.	120 ml
Fresh ginger, grated	1 Tbsp.	15 ml
Garlic, mashed	3 Tbsp.	45 ml
Assorted vegetables such as carrots, peppers, mushrooms, medium dice	1½ pt.	720 ml
Long-grain white rice, cooked and thoroughly chilled	17 oz.	510 g
Eggs, slightly beaten	6	6
Tomato concassée	1 pt.	480 ml
Hot chile paste	2 Tbsp.	30 ml
Fish sauce	3 fl. oz.	90 ml
Fresh lime juice	1 Tbsp.	15 ml
Fresh cilantro, chopped	as needed	as needed

1. Heat the oil in a wok or rondeau. Add the ginger and garlic and stir-fry until lightly browned. Remove from the pan.
2. Stir-fry the vegetables and remove from the pan.
3. Stir-fry the rice until warmed through.
4. Make a well in the center of the rice and pour in the eggs. Cook the eggs until almost set before mixing them into the rice.
5. Add the tomato concassée, garlic, ginger and vegetables. Mix in the chile paste, fish sauce and lime juice. Stir-fry to a temperature of 165°F (74°C). Garnish with chopped cilantro.

VARIATIONS:

Chinese-Style Fried Rice—Omit the hot chile paste, fish sauce, and lime juice. Add ½ cup (120 ml) chopped green onions to the assorted vegetables. Season with 1 tablespoon (15 milliliters) sesame oil and 4–6 tablespoons (120–180 milliliters) soy sauce. Omit the cilantro garnish.

House-Special Fried Rice—Prepare Chinese-Style Fried Rice, but add 4 ounces (120 grams) diced, cooked pork; 2 ounces (60 grams) thinly sliced, cooked chicken; and 2 ounces (60 grams) cooked shrimp in Step 5.

Note: Prepare the rice a day ahead and cool thoroughly. This separates the grains and keeps the fried rice from becoming sticky during cooking.

Approximate values per serving: **Calories** 310, **Total fat** 18 g, **Saturated fat** 3.5 g, **Cholesterol** 160 mg, **Sodium** 1100 mg, **Total carbohydrates** 30 g, **Protein** 9 g, **Vitamin A** 110%, **Vitamin C** 35%

WILD RICE AND CRANBERRY STUFFING

Yield: 5 pt. (2.5 lt)   **Method:** Simmering

Dried morels	1 oz.	30 g
Wild rice	12 oz.	360 g
Onions, minced	8 oz.	240 g
Butter or chicken fat	2 oz.	60 g
Chicken stock, hot	approx. 1 qt.	approx. 1 lt
Dried cranberries	6 oz.	180 g
Salt and pepper	TT	TT
Fresh parsley, chopped fine	4 Tbsp.	60 ml

1. Soak the dried morels overnight in lightly salted water. Drain, reserving the liquid. Rinse well, drain again and chop coarsely.
2. Rinse the wild rice well in cold water.
3. Sauté the onions in the butter or chicken fat until tender. Add the mushrooms and wild rice.
4. Strain the reserved liquid from the mushrooms through several layers of cheesecloth to remove all sand and grit. Add enough chicken stock so that the liquid totals 3 pints (1.5 liters). Add the stock mixture and cranberries to the rice. Cover and simmer until the rice is dry and fluffy, approximately 45 minutes.
5. Season to taste with salt and pepper and stir in the parsley. This rice may be served as a side dish or used for stuffing duck or game hens.

Approximate values per 4-oz. (120-g) serving: **Calories** 190, **Total fat** 6 g, **Saturated fat** 3 g, **Cholesterol** 10 mg, **Sodium** 380 mg, **Total carbohydrates** 28 g, **Protein** 7 g

This dish of the American South, a combination of black-eyed peas and rice, is traditionally served on New Year's Day to bring good luck and prosperity in the coming year.

HOPPIN' JOHN

Yield: 12 Servings		**Method:** Simmering
Dried black-eyed or field peas	1 lb.	480 g
Bacon slices, chopped	3	3
Onions, chopped	8 oz.	240 g
Chicken stock	as needed	as needed
Long-grain rice	1 lb.	480 g
Salt and pepper	TT	TT

① Rinse, sort and soak the peas. Cook until tender, according to the procedures found on page 602. Drain the peas, reserving the cooking liquid.

② Fry the bacon in a large sauté pan. Add the onions and cook until tender. Add 28 fluid ounces (840 milliliters) of the reserved cooking liquid from the peas. If there is not enough cooking liquid available, use stock as necessary.

③ Stir in the rice and the cooked peas. Bring to a boil, reduce the heat, cover and simmer without stirring until the rice is cooked and the liquid is absorbed, approximately 20 minutes.

④ Season to taste with salt and pepper. Stir well before serving.

Approximate values per serving: **Calories** 270, **Total fat** 3 g, **Saturated fat** 1 g, **Cholesterol** 5 mg, **Sodium** 80 mg, **Total carbohydrates** 48 g, **Protein** 11 g, **Iron** 20%, **Claims**—low fat; low saturated fat; low cholesterol; good source of fiber and iron

QUINOA

PRAIRIE GRASS CAFÉ, Northbrook, IL

Chef/Co-Owner George Bumbaris

Yield: 5 Servings		**Method:** Pilaf
Onion, diced	3 oz.	90 g
Olive oil	1 Tbsp.	30 ml
Quinoa, rinsed	4 oz.	120 g
Water or vegetable stock	12 fl. oz.	360 ml
Kosher salt and pepper	TT	TT

① In a small saucepot, sauté the onion in the oil over medium heat until softened.

② Add the quinoa and allow it to brown slightly.

③ Add the water or stock and season with salt and pepper. Bring to a full simmer. Lower the heat and cook until tender and each grain has burst open, approximately 12 to 15 minutes.

④ Remove from the stove and cover the pot. Allow the quinoa to rest until any remaining liquid is absorbed, approximately 10 minutes.

Approximate values per ½-c. (120-ml) serving: **Calories** 270, **Total fat** 10 g, **Saturated fat** 1.5 g, **Cholesterol** 0 mg, **Sodium** 1010 mg, **Total carbohydrates** 36 g, **Protein** 8 g, **Iron** 22%, **Claims**—no cholesterol; high fiber

BULGUR PILAF

Yield: 8 Servings, 4 oz. (120 g) each		**Method:** Pilaf
Whole butter	2 oz.	60 g
Onion, fine dice	4 oz.	120 g
Bulgur	10 oz.	300 g
Bay leaf	1	1
Chicken stock, hot	1 qt.	960 ml
Salt and pepper	TT	TT

1. Melt the butter in a large, heavy saucepan over moderate heat. Add the onion and sauté until translucent.
2. Add the bulgur and bay leaf. Sauté until the grains are well coated with butter.
3. Add the stock and season to taste with salt and pepper. Reduce the heat until the liquid barely simmers.
4. Cover and continue cooking until all the liquid is absorbed and the grains are tender, approximately 18 to 20 minutes.
5. Fluff with a fork and adjust the seasonings before service.

VARIATION:

Barley Pilaf—Substitute 2 cups (500 milliliters) pearled barley for the bulgur. Cooking time may increase by 10 to 15 minutes.

Approximate values per 4-oz. (120-g) serving: **Calories** 110, **Total fat** 7 g, **Saturated fat** 4 g, **Cholesterol** 15 mg, **Sodium** 470 mg, **Total carbohydrates** 9 g, **Protein** 4 g

1. Sautéing the bulgur in butter.

2. Adding the hot stock to the bulgur.

3. Fluffing the finished bulgur.

ORZO AND HERB SALAD

Yield: 24 oz. (720 g)   **Method:** Boiling

Orzo	1 lb.	480 g
Extra virgin olive oil	3 Tbsp.	45 ml
Fresh or frozen green peas	8 oz.	240 g
Celery, small dice	4 oz.	120 g
Plum tomatoes, small dice	12 oz.	360 g
Fresh oregano, chopped	½ oz.	15 g
Fresh chives, chopped	½ oz.	15 g
Fresh parsley, chopped	½ oz.	15 g
Garlic cloves, minced	3	3
Red wine vinegar	2 Tbsp.	30 ml
Fresh lemon juice	4 Tbsp.	60 ml
Salt and white pepper	TT	TT

orzo a rice-shaped pasta

1. Cook the orzo in lightly salted boiling water until al dente. Drain in a colander and rinse well with cold water. Remove the orzo to a large bowl and drizzle 1 tablespoon (15 milliliters) of olive oil around the orzo and toss well.
2. Cook the peas in slightly salted boiling water for 1 to 2 minutes, drain, and rinse with cold water. Toss the peas, celery, tomatoes and orzo together.
3. Combine the remaining oil with the herbs, garlic, vinegar, lemon juice, salt and white pepper. Pour over the salad and toss gently to combine. Serve chilled.

Approximate values per 4-oz. (120-g) serving: **Calories** 140, **Total fat** 3 g, **Saturated fat** 0 g, **Cholesterol** 0 mg, **Sodium** 10 mg, **Total carbohydrates** 25 g, **Protein** 5 g, **Vitamin C** 15%, **Claims**—low fat; no saturated fat; no cholesterol; low sodium

FETTUCCINE ALFREDO

Yield: 4 Servings, 6 oz. (180 g) each

Fresh fettuccine	8 oz.	240 g
Whole butter	2 oz.	60 g
Heavy cream	12 fl. oz.	360 ml
Parmesan, grated	2 oz.	60 g
Salt and white pepper	TT	TT

1. Boil the pasta, keeping it slightly undercooked. Refresh and drain.
2. To make the sauce, combine the butter, cream and Parmesan in a sauté pan. Bring to a boil and reduce slightly.
3. Add the pasta to the pan and boil the sauce and pasta until the sauce is thick and the pasta is cooked. Adjust the seasonings and serve.

Approximate values per 6-oz. (180-g) serving: **Calories** 630, **Total fat** 49 g, **Saturated fat** 29 g, **Cholesterol** 170 mg, **Sodium** 1000 mg, **Total carbohydrates** 33 g, **Protein** 14 g, **Vitamin A** 50%, **Calcium** 25%

FETTUCCINE CARBONARA

Yield: 4 Servings

Carbonara is a dish from Rome; visitors often call it "spaghetti and egg pasta." The heat of the hot pasta and pancetta set the eggs, creating a creamy sauce. Traditionally this dish is rather salty; blanch the chopped pancetta before cooking to reduce the salty taste if desired.

Eggs, pasteurized	2	2
Parmesan, grated	3 oz.	90 g
Whole butter	1 oz.	30 g
Olive oil	1½ fl. oz.	45 ml
Pancetta or salt pork, chopped	3 oz.	90 g
Garlic cloves, minced	2	2
Fresh fettuccine	9 oz.	270 g
Freshly ground black pepper	TT	TT
Salt	TT	TT
Red pepper flakes (optional)	as needed	as needed

1. Beat the eggs and Parmesan together. Set aside.
2. Heat the butter and oil in a sauté pan large enough to hold the cooked pasta. Add the pancetta and garlic. Cook gently for 8 to 10 minutes until the pancetta is lightly browned and the fat is rendered. Remove from the heat and set aside.
3. Boil the fettuccine in salted water until almost done.
4. Drain the pasta, then add it to the oil and pancetta. Toss over low heat, then add the egg mixture, tossing to coat the pasta evenly and gently cook the eggs without scrambling. Add freshly ground black pepper, then adjust the seasonings with salt and red pepper flakes, if using. Serve immediately.

Approximate values per serving: **Calories** 680, **Total fat** 49 g, **Saturated fat** 28 g, **Cholesterol** 300 mg, **Sodium** 770 mg, **Total carbohydrates** 35 g, **Protein** 26 g, **Vitamin A** 35%, **Calcium** 45%, **Iron** 15%

FETTUCCINE CON PESTO ALLA TRAPANESE

CHEF ODETTE FADA, NEW YORK, NY

Yield: 4 Servings, 8 oz. (240 g) each

Fresh fettuccine	1 lb.	480 g
Salt	TT	TT
Fresh basil leaves	½ oz.	15 g
Garlic cloves, chopped fine	4	4
Bread crumbs	2 Tbsp.	30 ml
Almonds, chopped	1 oz.	30 g
Extra virgin olive oil	approx. 3 fl. oz.	approx. 90 ml
Roma tomatoes	8 oz.	240 g

1. Boil the pasta in salted water until almost done.
2. Lightly sauté the basil, garlic, bread crumbs and almonds in the oil.
3. Peel and seed the tomatoes and julienne. Add them to the pan and sauté to blend the flavors.
4. Drain the pasta, add it to the pan and sauté for 1 minute over a low flame.
5. Add more oil and salt as needed.

Approximate values per 8-oz. (240-g) serving: **Calories** 590, **Total fat** 29 g, **Saturated fat** 3.5 g, **Cholesterol** 20 mg, **Sodium** 640 mg, **Total carbohydrates** 68 g, **Protein** 15 g, **Vitamin C** 20%, **Iron** 15%

PENNE WITH ASPARAGUS AND TOMATOES

Yield: 5 lb. (2.4 kg)

Asparagus spears	12 oz.	360 g
Salt	TT	TT
Extra virgin olive oil	2 fl. oz.	60 ml
Onion, small dice	2 oz.	60 g
Garlic cloves, chopped	12	12
Italian plum tomatoes, canned, drained and chopped	2½ lb.	1.2 kg
Salt	1 Tbsp.	15 ml
Red pepper flakes	TT	TT
Penne pasta, dry	1 lb.	480 g
Fresh basil leaves, chopped	1 oz.	30 g
Parmesan, grated	as needed for garnish	

1. Cook the asparagus spears in boiling salted water and refresh in ice water. Drain the spears and cut on the bias into 1-inch (2.5-centimeter) pieces.
2. Heat the oil in a sauté pan and sauté the onion and garlic until translucent. Add the tomatoes, salt and red pepper flakes. Increase the heat and cook 5 minutes, stirring occasionally. Keep warm.
3. Boil the penne in salted water until al dente, then drain well. Stir the asparagus into the warm sauce. Toss the pasta with the sauce and the chopped basil. Serve with freshly grated Parmesan.

Approximate values per 4-oz. (120-g) serving: **Calories** 130, **Total fat** 3 g, **Saturated fat** 0 g, **Cholesterol** 0 g, **Sodium** 460 mg, **Total carbohydrates** 21 g, **Protein** 4 g, **Vitamin C** 15%

MACARONI AND CHEESE

Yield: 24 Servings, 6 oz. (180 g) each

Elbow macaroni	2 lb.	960 g
Salt	TT	TT
Cheese Sauce (page 202)	2 qt.	1.9 lt
Worcestershire sauce	TT	TT
Tabasco sauce	TT	TT
Cheddar cheese, grated	2 lb.	960 g
Whole butter	3 oz.	90 g
Bread crumbs	8 oz.	240 g

1. Cook the macaroni in salted water until done. Drain, refresh in cold water, drain and reserve.
2. Season the Cheese Sauce with the Worcestershire and Tabasco sauces. Mix the macaroni with the Cheese Sauce and the Cheddar.
3. Butter a full-sized hotel pan using approximately 1 ounce (30 grams) whole butter. Pour the macaroni mixture into the pan.
4. Melt the remaining butter in a small sauté pan. Add the bread crumbs and toss to coat. Sprinkle the bread crumbs evenly over the macaroni.
5. Bake uncovered at 350°F (180°C) until hot, approximately 30 minutes.

VARIATION:

Macaroni and Cheese with Ham and Tomato—Stir 2 pounds (1 kilogram) each diced cooked ham and tomato concassée into the macaroni and cheese before pouring it into the hotel pan.

Approximate values per 6-oz. (180-g) serving: **Calories** 490, **Total fat** 28 g, **Saturated fat** 17 g, **Cholesterol** 80 mg, **Sodium** 430 mg, **Total carbohydrates** 39 g, **Protein** 21 g, **Vitamin A** 20%, **Calcium** 45%, **Iron** 15%

BAKED ZITI WITH FRESH TOMATO SAUCE

Yield: 30 Servings

Eggs	3	3
Ricotta	2 lb.	960 g
Fresh thyme, chopped	1 Tbsp.	15 ml
Fresh oregano, chopped	1 Tbsp.	15 ml
Fresh basil, chopped	1 Tbsp.	15 ml
Salt and pepper	TT	TT
Italian sausage links	2 lb. 8 oz.	1.2 kg
Ziti, cooked, refreshed and drained	3 lb.	1.4 kg
Parmesan, grated	4 oz.	120 g
Fresh Tomato Sauce for Pasta (page 222)	2 qt.	1.9 lt
Mozzarella, shredded	1 lb.	480 g

1. Combine the eggs, ricotta, thyme, oregano, basil, salt and pepper. Mix well and refrigerate.
2. Place the sausage links in a 2-inch- (5-centimeter-) deep full-size hotel pan; cook in a 350°F (180°C) oven for 20 minutes. Remove and drain the sausage. Slice the links into rounds and reserve.
3. Pour off the sausage fat, then place the ziti in the hotel pan. Top with an even coating of the cheese mixture, sausage slices and Parmesan.
4. Pour the Fresh Tomato Sauce for Pasta over the top layer and stir slightly to distribute the sauce.

⑤ Bake at 375°F (190°C) for 1 hour. Sprinkle the mozzarella evenly over the pasta and return to the oven for 10 minutes. Serve.

Note: Ziti may also be prepared in individual casseroles. Decrease baking time as necessary.

Approximate values per serving: **Calories** 450, **Total fat** 23 g, **Saturated fat** 10 g, **Cholesterol** 130 mg, **Sodium** 1290 mg, **Total carbohydrates** 27 g, **Protein** 35 g, **Vitamin A** 40%, **Calcium** 70%, **Iron** 15%, **Claims**—good source of fiber, vitamin C and iron; high in vitamin A and calcium

SPINACH AND RICOTTA LASAGNA WITH BOLOGNESE SAUCE

Yield: 28 Servings, 7 oz. (210 g) each

Fresh spinach pasta dough, rolled into sheets	2 lb.	960 g
Spinach, stemmed	2 lb.	960 g
Whole butter	2 oz.	60 g
Ricotta	1 lb.	480 g
Parmesan, grated	6 oz.	180 g
Eggs	2	2
Salt and pepper	TT	TT
Bolognese Sauce (page 222)	3 qt.	2.8 lt
Béchamel (page 201)	1 qt.	960 ml

① Cut the pasta dough into 4-inch (10-centimeter) strips. Boil in salted water until done and drain well.

② Sauté the spinach in the butter. Drain well and cool.

③ Combine the spinach with the ricotta, 4 ounces (120 grams) Parmesan and the eggs. Season to taste with salt and pepper.

④ Ladle a small amount of the Bolognese Sauce into the bottom of a standard full-size hotel pan. Cover the sauce with a layer of cooked pasta. Spread a thin layer of the spinach-and-cheese mixture on the pasta. Ladle a portion of the Béchamel over the spinach and spread in a thin even layer. Ladle a portion of the Bolognese Sauce over the béchamel and spread in an even layer.

⑤ Add another layer of pasta and repeat the process until all the ingredients are used, finishing with a layer of béchamel. Sprinkle the remaining Parmesan on top and bake covered at 350°F (180°C) until heated through, approximately 40 minutes. Uncover the lasagna for the last 15 minutes so that it browns.

Approximate values per 7-oz. (210-g) serving: **Calories** 270, **Total fat** 8 g, **Saturated fat** 3.5 g, **Cholesterol** 200 mg, **Sodium** 1110 mg, **Total carbohydrates** 12 g, **Protein** 37 g, **Vitamin A** 30%, **Vitamin C** 20%, **Calcium** 20%, **Iron** 40%

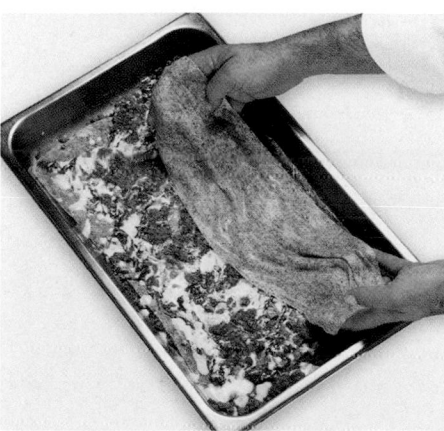

① Layering the sauces, pasta and cheese mixture in a hotel pan.

② Pouring a layer of béchamel over the lasagna.

③ The finished lasagna.

CHILLED CHINESE NOODLE SALAD

Yield: 8 Servings, 4 oz. (120 g) each

Dressing:		
Dark soy sauce	2 Tbsp.	30 ml
White vinegar	2 Tbsp.	30 ml
Salt	1 tsp.	5 ml
Granulated sugar	1 Tbsp.	15 ml
Peanut oil	1 Tbsp.	15 ml
Sesame oil	1 Tbsp.	15 ml
Orange zest	1 tsp.	5 ml
Red chile flakes	½ tsp.	2 ml
Chinese egg noodles, fresh	8 oz.	240 g
Salt	TT	TT
Bean sprouts, blanched	8 oz.	240 g
Carrots, finely shredded	6 oz.	180 g
Daikon, finely shredded	3 oz.	90 g
Green onions, sliced	2 oz.	60 g
Black sesame seeds	1 Tbsp.	15 ml
Fresh cilantro leaves	as needed for garnish	

1. Combine the dressing ingredients and whisk thoroughly.

2. Cook the egg noodles in rapidly boiling salted water until tender, approximately 2 minutes. Drain and refresh; drain again.

3. Toss the noodles with the bean sprouts, carrots, daikon, green onions and sesame seeds. Add the dressing and toss gently until the noodles and vegetables are thoroughly coated.

4. Chill well. Serve mounds of this noodle salad as an appetizer or an accompaniment for grilled fish or chicken. Garnish with cilantro.

Approximate values per 4-oz. (120-g) serving: **Calories** 110, **Total fat** 4.5 g, **Saturated fat** 0.5 g, **Cholesterol** 10 mg, **Sodium** 570 mg, **Total carbohydrates** 14 g, **Protein** 3 g, **Vitamin A** 40%, **Claims**—low cholesterol; low saturated fat

SPAETZLE

In Austria, Germany and Switzerland, spaetzle is a traditional accompaniment to roasted meats and game stews.

Yield: 30 Servings, 3 oz. (90 g) each

Eggs	12	12
Water	1 qt.	960 ml
Flour	3 lb.	1.4 kg
Salt	2 tsp.	10 ml
Nutmeg	½ tsp.	2 ml
Whole butter	8 oz.	240 g
Salt and white pepper	TT	TT
Fresh parsley, chopped	as needed for garnish	

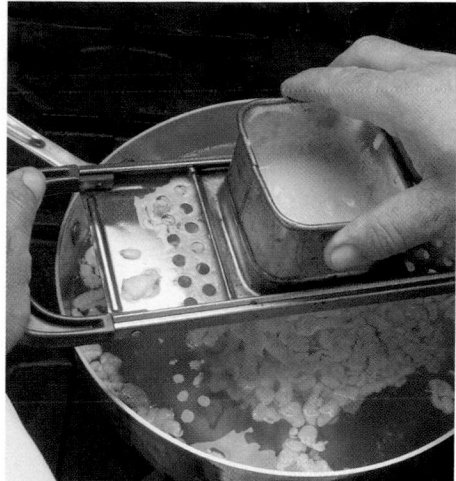

❶ Pushing the batter into the boiling water through the holes in a spaetzle maker.

❶ Whisk the eggs to blend. Add the water, flour, salt and nutmeg. Mix by hand until well blended; the batter should be a smooth, gooey paste. Cover and refrigerate the batter.

❷ Place the batter in a spaetzle maker, perforated steam table pan or colander suspended over a large pot of boiling water. Work the batter through the colander's holes using a plastic bowl scraper or rubber spatula. The batter should drop into the boiling water. Lower the water temperature to a simmer.

❸ Cook the dumplings in the simmering water until they float to the surface, approximately 3 to 4 minutes. Remove them with a skimmer and refresh in a bowl of ice water.

❹ For service, sauté the dumplings in butter to heat through. Season with salt and white pepper; garnish with chopped parsley.

Approximate values per 3-oz. (90-g) serving: **Calories** 250, **Total fat** 9 g, **Saturated fat** 4.5 g, **Cholesterol** 100 mg, **Sodium** 250 mg, **Total carbohydrates** 35 g, **Protein** 7 g, **Vitamin A** 10%, **Iron** 15%

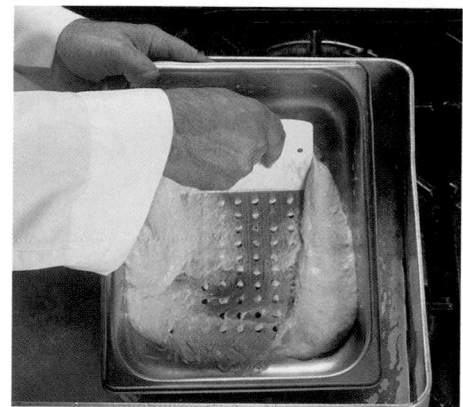

❷ Alternatively, the batter may be forced through a perforated hotel pan.

❸ Sautéing the spaetzle in butter.

CHAPTER TWENTY-THREE

HEALTHY COOKING

After studying this chapter, you will be able to:

- identify categories of nutrients and explain their importance in a healthy diet

- identify the characteristics of a nutritious diet for healthy adults

- describe diet-planning tools available to consumers and chefs

- understand the effects of storage and preparation techniques on the nutritional value of food

- appreciate the use of alternative ingredients and substitutes in developing recipes and menus to provide guests with healthy foods and dishes for special dietary needs

- understand the range of vegetarian diets and use a variety of protein products as alternatives to meat, poultry, fish or dairy

nutrition the science that studies nutrients

ENERGY FROM ESSENTIAL NUTRIENTS

1 gram pure fat = 9 calories

1 gram pure carbohydrate = 4 calories

1 gram pure protein = 4 calories

SINCE THE DAYS OF PREHISTORIC HUNTERS and gatherers, people have understood that some animals and plants are good to eat and others are not. For thousands of years, cultures worldwide have attributed medicinal and beneficial effects to certain foods, particularly plants, and have recognized that foods that might otherwise be fine to eat may be unhealthy if improperly prepared or stored. But not until the past few decades have people become increasingly concerned about how foods affect their health and which foods promote good health and longevity. Because of national health concerns about over-consumption leading to obesity, cardiovascular disease and diabetes, Americans are looking to dine out in a healthier way. At the same time, people with certain health conditions that limit the intake of sugar, fat or wheat are looking for foods that will taste good and meet their diet regimens.

This chapter sets forth basic information about nutrients and guidelines for planning a diet for healthy people. The chapter also introduces the framework for understanding ingredient substitution for those following a particular diet because of personal preference or allergies. Guidelines for chefs seeking to incorporate healthy dishes into their menus are provided. Vegetarian eating patterns and ingredients are discussed. And a selection of vegetarian recipes concludes this chapter.

BASICS OF NUTRITION

The foundation of cooking is an understanding of ingredients, culinary techniques and the nutritive values of foods. All foods are composed of nutrients, the (chemical) substances that promote the growth, maintenance and repair of the body. Some nutrients also provide energy (calories).

There are six categories of nutrients: carbohydrates, lipids (fats and cholesterol), proteins, vitamins, minerals and water. Essential nutrients are those that must be provided by food because the body does not produce them in sufficient quantities to satisfy the needs of the body or cannot make them at all. See Table 23.1. Some nutritional components are considered nonessential because healthy, well-nourished bodies can make them in sufficient quantities to satisfy their needs. Scientists, however, are beginning to understand that even some nonessential nutrients may be needed in amounts greater than formerly thought in order to provide protection against chronic diseases such as cancer, diabetes and heart disease.

The human body depends on the various nutrients for different purposes and requires different amounts of each depending on age, gender and health status. In addition, some nutrients depend on one another for proper functioning. For example, calcium and vitamin D work together in the body: Vitamin D promotes the absorption of the calcium that the body utilizes for proper bone growth. A deficiency of one will affect the working of the other. Because foods differ with regard to their nutritional content, it is important to eat a variety of foods in order to achieve proper nutritional balance.

Essential Nutrients

Three of the essential nutrients provide calories or energy needed in larger quantities than other nutrients. These essential **macronutrients** are carbohydrates, lipids (fats) and proteins.

TABLE 23.1   ESSENTIAL NUTRIENTS

Essential nutrients are those that must be provided because the human body does not produce them in sufficient quantities. They are the following:

▶ Carbohydrates (starches and sugars)

▶ Fats (linoleic and linolenic acids)

▶ Proteins (the amino acids: histidine, isoleucine, leucine, lysine, methionine, phenylalanine, threonine, tryptophan and valine)

▶ Vitamins (thiamine, riboflavin, niacin, pantothenic acid, biotin, vitamin B_6, vitamin B_{12}, folate, vitamin C, vitamin A, vitamin D, vitamin E and vitamin K)

▶ Minerals (calcium, chloride, magnesium, phosphorus, potassium, sodium, sulfur, selenium, zinc, chromium, copper, fluoride, iodide, iron, manganese and molybdenum)

▶ Water

A **calorie** (often abbreviated kcal) is the way to describe the amount of energy in food. One gram of pure fat supplies 9 kcal; one gram of pure carbohydrate supplies 4 kcal, as does one gram of pure protein. Most foods are a combination of carbohydrates, proteins and fats; hence their calorie content may not be easily determined unless we know how much of each nutrient the food contains. Calorie tables help provide that information.

Vitamins and minerals, sometimes referred to as **micronutrients** because they are needed in small quantities, are essential nutrients and must be provided through the diet because the body cannot manufacture them in quantities adequate to ensure good health. Although they provide no calories, vitamins and minerals are important to the body in generating energy from the foods we eat.

calorie the unit of energy measured by the amount of heat required to raise 1000 grams of water one degree Celsius; it is also written as kilocalorie or kcal

Carbohydrates

Carbohydrates are made up of molecules of carbon, hydrogen and oxygen and are found exclusively in plant foods. There is one exception—the sugar in milk (lactose) is also a carbohydrate. **Simple carbohydrates** include monosaccharides (single sugars such as glucose, fructose and maltose) and disaccharides (double sugars such as sucrose, galactose and lactose). See Table 23.2. Simple carbohydrates are found in the naturally occurring sugars in fruit, vegetables and milk, as well as sweeteners such as honey, corn syrup and table sugar. **Complex carbohydrates** are composed of long chains of the monosaccharide glucose. Starch and fiber are complex carbohydrates. Complex carbohydrates are found in fruits, vegetables and cereal grains such as wheat, barley and oats. The body digests (breaks down) the sugars and starches into the single sugar glucose. Glucose, also known as blood sugar, is an important source of energy for the body.

Fiber is a unique carbohydrate because humans cannot digest fiber, so they do not derive calories from it. **Dietary fiber**, which generally comes from the seeds and cell walls of fruits, vegetables and cereal grains, plays an important role in health because it is not digested. There are two types of fiber: **soluble** and **insoluble**. Fiber-containing foods are usually composed of both kinds, with one kind predominating. Because the body cannot

---

TABLE 23.2   SUGARS

MONOSACCHARIDES	DISACCHARIDES
Glucose (blood sugar)	Lactose (milk sugar composed of glucose and galactose)
Fructose (fruit sugar)	Maltose (malt sugar composed of two glucose molecules)
Galactose (part of milk sugar)	Sucrose (table sugar composed of glucose and fructose)

digest dietary fiber, it passes through the digestive system almost completely unchanged. This helps keep the digestive tract running smoothly. Insoluble fiber, such as that found in whole wheat, encourages proper elimination of waste products from the large intestines and helps avoid some forms of gastrointestinal distress. Soluble fiber, which forms a gel-type substance in the digestive tract, helps reduce serum cholesterol by helping to remove the cholesterol from the body, thereby lessening the risk for heart disease.

Lipids

Lipids, like carbohydrates, are composed of carbon, hydrogen and oxygen. The differences between carbohydrates and lipids are the number and arrangement of the carbon, hydrogen and oxygen atoms. Fats and cholesterol are considered lipids. Fats are found in both animal and plant foods, although fruits contain very little fat. Fats provide calories, help carry fat-soluble vitamins and give food a creamy, pleasant mouth feel. A healthy diet contains a moderate amount of fat; in fact, some forms of fat are considered essential.

Cholesterol, also a lipid, is found only in foods of animal origin. Cholesterol is not considered an essential nutrient, and it does not contribute calories. Cholesterol is, however, an important component of the body, although it is not necessary to eat foods containing cholesterol because the body can manufacture all it needs from the fat in the diet. Cholesterol is an important component of many regulatory substances in the body as well as a component of structural parts.

Depending on their structure, the fats in foods can be classified as saturated, monounsaturated or polyunsaturated. Most foods contain a combination of the three kinds of fats, although one kind may predominate. If **saturated fat** is the most abundant kind (as in the fat surrounding muscle meats), the food is classified as being high in saturated fat even though it contains a mixture of all three kinds of fats.

Saturated fats are found mainly in animal products such as milk, eggs and meats, as well as in tropical oils such as coconut and palm. Monounsaturated fats come primarily from plants and plant foods such as avocados and olives and the oils made from them. Polyunsaturated fats are found in plants (soy and corn, for example) and fish. Vegetable oils such as rapeseed (canola) and olive are high in monounsaturated fat. Cottonseed, sunflower, corn and safflower oils are high in polyunsaturated fat. All oils, however, are a combination of the three kinds of fat. All vegetable oils are cholesterol-free, however, because cholesterol is not found in plants.

Saturated fats such as butter, lard and other animal fats are usually solid at room temperature. Monounsaturated and polyunsaturated fats are usually soft or liquid at room temperature. Hydrogenation is a process by which a liquid fat is made more solid (or saturated) by the addition of hydrogen atoms. Hydrogenation increases the percentage of saturated fatty acids, resulting in a more solid product (such as margarine made from a liquid polyunsaturated oil such as corn oil). Hydrogenation also has the positive effect on the resulting oil of reducing the tendency to rancidity, thus increasing shelf life. Because the process results in these positive properties, **hydrogenated fats** have been used in abundance in the food manufacturing industry. The hydrogenation process also results in the formation of **trans fats**. Trans fats are considered a risk factor for heart disease and possibly other diseases such as cancer. The food service industry is working hard to find ways to provide the same functional benefits to fats as hydrogenation without adding the harmful trans fats in the process. Food manufacturers have eliminated trans fats in most widely produced products. Lower-trans-fat cooking oil is standard at fast-food restaurants, and cities such as New York and Philadelphia have banned the use of artificial trans fats in restaurants. (Natural trans fats occur in butter, cheese, milk and other animal products.)

Research suggests that high-fat diets, especially diets high in saturated fat and trans fats, may be linked to heart disease, obesity and certain forms of cancer. Saturated fats are also linked to high levels of blood cholesterol, which is associated with arteriosclerosis (hardening of the arteries). Although the liver can produce all the cholesterol the body needs, additional cholesterol is often provided in the diet from meats, poultry, fish, eggs and dairy products. The combination of a diet high in saturated fat and a diet high in dietary cholesterol may increase the risk of heart disease.

saturated fat fats found mainly in animal products such as milk, butter, cheese, eggs and meat as well as in tropical oils such as coconut and palm; usually solid at room temperature. Research suggests that high-fat diets, especially those high in saturated fat, may be linked to heart disease, obesity and certain forms of cancer.

unsaturated fat fats from plants and plant foods such as avocados, corn, cottonseed, olives, rapeseed (canola), safflower and sunflower; liquid at room temperature

hydrogenated fat unsaturated, liquid fats that are chemically altered to remain solid at room temperature, such as solid shortening or margarine

trans fats a type of fat created when vegetable oils are solidified through hydrogenation

Proteins

Proteins are found in both animal and plant foods. They differ from carbohydrates and lipids in that they contain nitrogen as well as carbon, hydrogen and oxygen. Protein chains consist of **amino acids**, the building blocks of protein. There are 20 amino acids, 9 of which are essential for healthy adults. People who eat a varied diet with adequate calories and protein can easily get all the essential amino acids even if they do not eat any animal foods. The specific combination of amino acids gives each protein its unique characteristics and properties.

Proteins are necessary for manufacturing, maintaining and repairing body tissues. They are essential for the periodic replacement of the outer layer of skin as well as for blood clotting and scar tissue formation. Hair and nails, which provide a protective cover for the body, are composed of proteins.

Vitamins

Vitamins are vital dietary substances needed for regulation of **metabolism** and for normal growth and body functions. They are essential and noncaloric and are needed in the body in small amounts.

There are 13 vitamins divided into two categories: **fat-soluble** and **water-soluble**. (See Appendix IV.) The fat-soluble vitamins are A, D, E and K and are found in foods containing fat. Excess supplies of these vitamins may be stored in fatty tissues and the liver. Water-soluble vitamins are vitamin C and the B-complex vitamins, including thiamin (B_1), riboflavin (B_2), niacin (B_3), cyano-cobalamin (B_{12}), pyridoxine (B_6), pantothenic acid, biotin and folate. Vitamins B_1 and B_2 are commonly referred to by their names (thiamin and riboflavin, respectively), whereas cobalamin and pyridoxine are commonly referred to by their letter designations (B_{12} and B_6, respectively). Water-soluble vitamins are not stored to the extent that fat-soluble vitamins are, and excesses may be excreted in the urine. Because of these differences, deficiencies in water-soluble vitamins develop more rapidly when intake is not sufficient.

Virtually all foods contain some vitamins. Many factors contribute to a particular food's vitamin concentration. An animal's feed; the manner by which the produce is harvested, stored or processed; and even the type of soil, sunlight, rainfall and temperature have significant effects on a food's vitamin content. For example, tomatoes have a higher concentration of vitamin C when picked ripe from the vine than when picked green. Furthermore, different varieties of fruits and vegetables have different vitamin contents. A Wegener apple, for example, has 19 mg of vitamin C, whereas a Red Delicious has only 6 mg.

In cooking, the chef can control vitamin concentration and retention through careful food preparation:

❶ Try to prepare vegetables as close to service time as possible; vegetables cut long before service lose more vitamins than those cut immediately before cooking.

❷ Whether a vegetable is boiled, steamed or microwaved also determines the amount of vitamins it retains. Because the B-complex vitamins and vitamin C are water-soluble, they are easily leached (washed out) or destroyed by food processing and preparation techniques involving high temperatures and water. Steaming and microwaving help retain nutrients (when steaming, keep the water level below the vegetables).

❸ In general, roasting and grilling meats, poultry, fish and shellfish preserve more vitamins than stewing and braising. The temperatures to which foods are cooked and the length of time they are cooked may affect vitamin retention as well.

❹ Storage affects vitamin concentrations. For example, long exposure to air may destroy vitamin C. Using airtight containers prevents some of this loss. Vitamin C is also lost when the fruit or vegetable becomes shriveled from water loss during long or improper storage. Riboflavin is sensitive to light, so milk products (which are good sources of riboflavin) should be stored in opaque containers.

Cooking does not always render a food less nutritious. Cooking, besides making the food more palatable in many cases, can help make the food more digestible, thereby making nutritious substances in the food more readily available to the body. Heating foods to appropriate temperatures also makes them safer to eat by destroying harmful bacteria.

metabolism all the chemical reactions and physical processes that occur continuously in living cells and organisms

flavonoids plant pigments that dissolve readily in water; they are found in red, purple and white vegetables such as blueberries, red cabbage, onions and tea

Minerals

Minerals cannot be manufactured by the body. They are obtained by eating plants that have drawn minerals from the ground or the flesh of animals that have eaten such plants. Minerals are a critical component in hard and soft tissues (for example, the calcium, magnesium and phosphorus present in bones and teeth). Minerals also regulate certain necessary body functions. For example, nerve impulses are transmitted through an exchange of sodium and potassium ions in the nerve cells.

Minerals are divided into two categories: **trace minerals** and **major minerals**. (See Appendix IV.) Trace minerals such as iron are needed in only very small amounts. Major minerals such as calcium are needed in relatively larger quantities. As with vitamins, food processing and preparation can reduce a food's mineral content. Soaking or cooking in large amounts of water can leach out small quantities of water-soluble minerals. Processing or refining grains, such as the wheat used to make white flour, also removes important minerals.

Water

The human body is approximately 60 percent water. Water is necessary for transporting nutrients and wastes throughout the body. It cushions the cells, lubricates the joints, maintains stable body temperatures and assists in waste elimination. It also promotes functioning of the nervous system and muscles. Although the principal sources of water are beverages, water is also the predominant nutrient by weight in most foods. Some foods such as tomatoes, oranges, watermelon and iceberg lettuce are particularly high in water. Others such as dried fruits, nuts and seeds are lower, but even dried fruits still contain some water. Foods such as chicken and bread also surprisingly provide some water. The body produces water when other nutrients are metabolized for energy.

Phytochemicals

Recent scientific research has identified nonnutritive components of plant foods called phytochemicals, which may be important in preventing some forms of cancer, diabetes, Alzheimer's disease, heart disease and other degenerative diseases. More than nine hundred of these chemicals have been identified, including plant estrogens, carotenoids and flavonoids. The health benefits of these substances appear to depend on consumption of a varied diet that includes plenty of grains, fruits and vegetables. The importance of phytochemicals to human health and well-being should not be minimized even though they do not constitute a nutrient category. Phytochemicals such as **flavonoids** and other compounds found in blueberries, pomegranates, green tea and cooked tomato products may act as antioxidants in the body to help eliminate free radicals (unstable potentially harmful substances produced naturally in the body during metabolism). It is believed that antioxidants can reduce the potential for developing certain forms of cancer and heart disease as well as slowing down the aging process. Eating more plant foods such as fruits and vegetables and whole grains that provide a variety of phytochemicals will go a long way to preventing the incidence of many of the debilitating diseases of modern humans.

TOOLS FOR HEALTHY EATING

It is generally recognized that a nutritious diet is an important component of a healthy lifestyle. Eating well and exercising, getting adequate sleep and living moderately all can contribute to a longer, healthier life. Planning a diet and lifestyle to enhance health is made simpler by following recommendations from organizations such as the American Heart Association, the American Cancer Society, the USDA, the FDA and the U.S. Department of Health and Human Services, to name a few. These organizations stress the importance of controlling the amount of fat in the diet; consuming plant foods such as vegetables, fruits and whole grains in greater quantities; and moderating the amount of sugar and alcohol consumed.

A useful diet planning tool is the Dietary Guidelines for Americans, jointly published every five years by the USDA and the U.S. Department of Health and Human Services. The key messages in the 2005 Dietary Guidelines include the following:

▶ Consume a wide variety of foods while staying within calorie needs. Limit added sugars, solid fats, alcoholic beverages and sources of calories that are poor sources of essential nutrients.

▶ Control calorie intake to manage body weight.

▶ Be physically active every day. Include at least 30 minutes of moderate physical activity as a baseline, increasing to 60 to 90 minutes for weight loss.

▶ Increase daily intake of fruits and vegetables, whole grains and nonfat or low-fat dairy products. Consume 2½ to 6½ cups of a combination of fruits and vegetables from various sources a day. Emphasize brightly colored—dark green, orange, red or purple—fruits and vegetables for optimum health.

▶ Choose fats wisely. Keep fat intake to a minimum and choose foods with predominantly monounsaturated fats over foods high in saturated fats.

▶ Choose carbohydrates wisely by focusing on whole fruits (instead of fruit juices) and whole grains while limiting the intake of added sugar.

▶ Consume less than 1 teaspoon of sodium a day.

▶ Drink alcoholic beverages in moderation—one drink per day for women, two drinks per day for men.

▶ Follow safe food-handling practices when preparing, serving and storing food.

The Food Guide Pyramid

The Food Guide Pyramid is an educational tool to help Americans select a healthy balanced diet using the recommendations from the Dietary Guidelines. In 2005, the pyramid was revised to reflect the changes in recommendations and philosophy. The MyPyramid food guidance system offers consumers numerous options for making healthy food choices, including recommending daily exercise. (See Figure 23.1.) An interactive Web site allows consumers to customize eating plans according to their age, sex and daily physical activity.

FIGURE 23.1 ▶ MyPyramid food guidance system.

HEALING FOODS

Those who think of food first as a pleasurable experience may be averse to also thinking of it as medicine or having curative powers, yet there is scientific evidence to support that idea. Interestingly, scientific findings suggest that positive benefits may be derived from many foods thought only to have deleterious effects on the body. The findings, although preliminary, hold out some hope for those who do not want to give up the pleasures of the table. Some of the findings include the following:

Avocados, although very high in fat, are good sources of antioxidants.

Beer may increase bone density.

Dark chocolate contains antioxidants that may be beneficial in preventing heart disease.

Coffee may offer some beneficial effects in reducing the risk of cancer and diabetes.

Eggs are a source of lutein, a phytochemical implicated in reducing the incidence of degenerative eye diseases.

Red wine may reduce the incidence of heart disease.

Avocados

THE FEDERAL GOVERNMENT GUARDS OUR LARDER

The federal government plays an important role in the way various foodstuffs are grown, raised, slaughtered, processed, marketed, stored and transported. The principal actors are the Food and Drug Administration (FDA) of the U.S. Department of Health and Human Services and the U.S. Department of Agriculture (USDA).

The FDA's activities are directed toward protecting the nation's health against impure and unsafe foods, as well as drugs, cosmetics, medical devices and other things. It develops and administers programs addressing food safety. For example, the FDA must approve any new food additive before a manufacturer markets it to food producers and processors. To gain FDA approval, the manufacturer must prove to the FDA's satisfaction that the additive (1) is effective for the intended purpose, (2) can be detected and measured in the final product and (3) is safe. The FDA holds public hearings during which experts and consumers provide evidence and opinions before it decides to grant or deny approval. If it grants approval, the FDA issues regulations identifying the amount of the additive that can be used and the foods to which it can be added. The FDA also sets standards for labeling foods, including nutrition labels. Labeling regulations not only address the type of information that must be conveyed, but also the way it is presented.

The USDA's principal responsibility is to make sure that individual food items are safe, wholesome and accurately labeled. It attempts to meet these responsibilities through inspection and grading procedures. The USDA also provides consumer services. It conducts and publishes research on nutrition and assists those producing our food to do so efficiently and effectively.

Other federal agencies that have a role in the nation's health and food supply include the U.S. Centers for Disease Control and Prevention (CDC), which tracks illnesses, including those caused by foodborne pathogens; the National Institutes of Health (NIH), which does basic biological and nutritional research; and the Department of the Interior, which sets environmental and land-use standards.

Serving Size: The FDA has defined standard serving sizes for approximately 150 food categories, making it easier for consumers to compare different brands. The serving sizes reflect familiar units, not necessarily the amounts people actually eat.

Percent Daily Value: This section shows how the food fits into the daily diet. Most people are concerned about getting too much fat, saturated fat, transfat, cholesterol and sodium in their daily diet. This section identifies the grams per serving for each of these nutrients and the percent of the daily recommended amount of that nutrient each serving provides. The percentage is based on a 2000-calorie daily diet. For example, a person on a 2000-calorie daily diet (the FDA standard) should consume no more than 65 grams of fat. The 12 grams of total fat per serving of this product is 18% of the person's recommended daily intake of fat. (No daily value for trans fats has yet been established.)

Calories from Fat: Current dietary recommendations provide that no more than 30% of a person's daily caloric intake come from fat. To help consumers meet these dietary guidelines, the number of calories per serving from fat is identified.

Recommended Daily Intake or RDI: These values represent the percentage of the daily recommended intake of important vitamins and minerals per serving. They were selected from the Recommended Dietary Allowances (RDA), set by the Food and Nutrition Board of the National Academy of Sciences. But unlike the RDA, the RDI sets the recommended amount of each vitamin and mineral for a so-called standard adult; it does not account for sex, age, health or other attributes. The RDI was formerly known as the U.S. RA but was changed because of the confusion with the RDA.

Daily Values: This outlines the basics of a good diet and is used to show how the food fits into such a daily diet. Some of the recommended intakes are maximums. For example, someone on a 2000-calorie-per-day diet should consume 65 grams or less of fat; someone on a 2500-calorie-per-day diet should consume 80 grams or less of fat. Other intakes are minimums; for example, 300 grams or more of carbohydrates for someone on a 2000-calorie-daily diet. This section remains the same on all labels and is intended as a guide for the consumer when reading the Percent Daily Value information.

Nutrition Facts

Serving Size 1 cup (228g)
Servings Per Container 2

Amount Per Serving

Calories 250   Calories from Fat 110

% Daily Value*

Total Fat 12g	18%
Saturated Fat 3g	15%
Trans Fat 1.5g	
Cholesterol 30mg	10%
Sodium 470mg	20%
Total Carbohydrate 31g	10%
Dietary Fiber 0g	0%
Sugars 5g	
Protein 5g	

Vitamin A	4%
Vitamin C	2%
Calcium	20%
Iron	4%

* Percent Daily Values are based on a 2,000 calorie diet. Your Daily Values may be higher or lower depending on your calorie needs.

	Calories:	2,000	2,500
Total Fat	Less than	65g	80g
Sat Fat	Less than	20g	25g
Cholesterol	Less than	300mg	300mg
Sodium	Less than	2,400mg	2,400mg
Total Carbohydrate		300g	375g
Dietary Fiber		25g	30g

FIGURE 23.2 ▶ Label illustrating nutritional information requirements.

AUTHORIZED HEALTH CLAIMS

The FDA requires that terms such as *low fat* and *fat-free* be used according to the following specific standards:

- *Free*—The food contains no or only "physiologically inconsequential" amounts of fat, saturated fat, cholesterol, sodium, sugars or calories.
- *Low, little, few* and *low source of*—The food can be eaten frequently without exceeding dietary guidelines for fat, saturated fat, cholesterol, sodium or calories.

Specific uses include the following:

- *Low fat*—The food has 3 grams or less of fat per serving.
- *Low saturated fat*—The food has 1 gram or less of saturated fat per serving; not more than 15 percent of a serving's calories are from saturated fat.
- *Low sodium*—The food has 140 milligrams or less of salt per serving.
- *Very low sodium*—The food has 35 milligrams or less of salt per serving.
- *Low cholesterol*—The food has 20 milligrams or less of cholesterol per serving.
- *Low calorie*—The food has 40 calories or fewer per serving.
- *Reduced, less* and *fewer*—The nutritionally altered product contains at least 25 percent fewer calories than the regular or reference (that is, FDA standard) food product.
- *Light* or *lite*—The nutritionally altered product contains at least one-third fewer calories or 50 percent less fat than the reference product. *Light in sodium* means that the nutritionally altered product contains 50 percent or less sodium than the regular or reference product. *Light* may still be used to describe color, as in light brown sugar.
- *High*—The food contains 20 percent or more of the daily value for a desirable nutrient per serving.
- *More*—The food contains at least 10 percent more of the daily value for protein, vitamins, minerals, dietary fiber or potassium compared to the reference product.
- *Good source*—The food contains 10–19 percent of the daily value per serving for the specific nutrient such as calcium or dietary fiber.
- *Lean*—The meat, poultry, game, fish or shellfish item contains less than 10 grams of fat, less than 4 grams of saturated fat and less than 95 milligrams of cholesterol per serving and per 100 grams.
- *Extra lean*—The meat, poultry, game, fish or shellfish item contains less than 5 grams of fat, less than 2 grams of saturated fat and less than 95 milligrams of cholesterol per serving and per 100 grams.

Nutrition Labeling

In an effort to provide consumers with greater information about the nutritional values of foods they purchase, the FDA requires that most food products be clearly labeled. All packaged food products must include the Nutrition Facts label (see Figure 23.2).

The FDA closely regulates the language used on all food labels. Terms such as *low fat* and *lite* have specific legal definitions. The FDA also closely monitors health claims on food labels. A cereal, for instance, may claim that its fiber content may reduce the incidence of heart disease only if it meets the criteria set forth by the FDA. The FDA has approved a number of qualified health claims that may legally be used on food labels and in the advertising of certain foods if they meet criteria. One example of a qualified health claim that is acceptable concerns nuts: "Scientific evidence suggests, but does not prove, that eating 1.5 ounces per day of some nuts, as part of a diet low in saturated fat and cholesterol, may reduce the risk of heart disease."

The FDA sets standards for the nutrition claims that can be made on restaurant menus. The language for menus is the same as that for product labels. Restaurateurs, however, are required to supply nutrition information only if they make a claim about a specific dish. For example, if a menu selection is described as "low fat," the dish must have 3 grams or less of fat per serving and the nutrition information (nutrient analysis) should be available to anyone who requests it. Restaurateurs and chefs should consult the FDA and the National Restaurant Association for guidance in complying with these labeling regulations.

INGREDIENT SUBSTITUTES AND ALTERNATIVES

More and more people are becoming health-conscious consumers. Many are trying to cut down on foods high in salt, fat, added sugar, starch and cholesterol. For others, specific physical conditions prevent them from enjoying a traditional recipe. Many Americans are

allergens substances that may cause allergic reactions in some people

on low-cholesterol and low-fat diets as well as sodium- (salt-) controlled diets to treat cardiovascular disease. Others must pay attention to their intake of calories and carbohydrates because they have diabetes.

Allergies to wheat, dairy, nuts, eggs, soy and shellfish are widespread, affecting millions of consumers; 4 percent of the American population has food allergies. To a degree, people can accomplish their goals—and chefs can assist them—by turning to ingredient substitutes and alternatives where possible.

In the case of peanut allergy, mise en place should be considered as well as removing peanuts from a given recipe. No peanuts or peanut products should even be near the area where the preparation is taking place. Avoiding peanut oil or peanut oil–containing products means that pans must be prepared with an alternative oil and utensils may not come in contact with peanut products or even peanut dust. Another common food component of concern to the public is lactose. **Lactose** is a natural sugar found in milk and dairy products. People who are lactose intolerant have a digestive problem that causes intestinal discomfort if the milk sugar is consumed, sometimes even in small amounts.

Here we use the term **ingredient substitute** to mean the replacement of one ingredient with another of presumably similar—although not necessarily identical—flavor, texture, appearance and other sensory characteristics. In some cases the substitute ingredient may be more nutritious than the ingredient or preparation technique it replaces. Instead of thickening a soup with a roux or cornstarch slurry, the chef may add puréed potatoes as a thickener or, in the case of a vegetable soup, purée some of the cooked vegetables to thicken the soup. In either case, the soup thickened with potatoes or puréed vegetables would be more nutritious than one made with a roux or slurry. Those seeking to avoid fats can use reduced-fat or nonfat sour cream in place of regular sour cream when baking quick breads. The differences in flavor, texture, appearance and baking quality should be minimal.

We use the term **ingredient alternative** to mean the replacement of one ingredient with another of different flavor, texture, appearance or other characteristic, but one that will not compromise—although it may change—the flavor of the dish. As with the ingredient substitute, the ingredient alternative may be more nutritious. Lemon juice and herbs, for instance, can be used as flavoring alternatives to salt; a salsa of fresh vegetables can replace a cream-based sauce. The dishes will not taste the same but they will still taste good.

In attempting to modify a recipe, the chef should first identify the ingredient(s) or cooking method(s) that may need to be changed. He or she can then use the following principles—reduce, replace or eliminate—to make a dish healthier or more acceptable to the customer:

1. *Reduce* the amounts of the ingredient(s) if doing so will not change the structure, taste or appearance of the dish so as to make it unrecognizable as the original dish. In many recipes (not baking) reducing the amount of oil, butter or other fat will not alter the dish to a great extent.
2. *Replace* the ingredient(s) with a substitute that will do the least to change the flavor and appearance of the dish.
3. *Eliminate* the ingredient(s) if doing so will not destroy the integrity of the dish. This may be necessary when serving a customer who is allergic to a particular ingredient for which there is no suitable substitute.

Salt Substitutes and Alternatives

A concern in the American diet is excessive sodium (salt). The average American consumes 3000 to 7000 milligrams of sodium per day, well in excess of daily needs. Research has linked excessive amounts of sodium to hypertension (high blood pressure), heart and kidney diseases and strokes.

Chefs are sometimes taught to use salt liberally to enhance flavors. Most salt substitutes (which are potassium chloride instead of sodium chloride), however, neither enhance flavors like salt nor are even palatable to many people. In trying to moderate the amount of salt in a dish, the chef should reduce the quantity of salt used, reduce the quantity of sodium-containing ingredients or use a lower-sodium alternative. Soy sauce is a good example; often the quantity can be reduced, and excellent low-sodium soy prod-

additives substances added to many foods to prevent spoilage or improve appearance, texture, flavor or nutritional value; they may be synthetic materials copied from nature (for example, sugar substitutes) or naturally occurring substances (for example, lecithin). Some food additives may cause allergic reactions in sensitive people.

ucts are available. In addition, pepper, lemon, herbs, spices, fruit and flavored vinegars can be used as salt alternatives to heighten flavor. Reducing or eliminating salt is usually successful in baked goods. Chemical leavening has sodium, but there are few sodium-free alternatives; use natural leaveners such as eggs or yeast instead.

Sugar Substitutes and Alternative Sweeteners

Sugar and other sweeteners add flavor and help in browning and caramelization. In baked goods, they add structure, texture and volume. Natural sweeteners such as honey, date or maple syrup are natural sugars suitable for those who prefer not to consume refined white sugar. Because these are usually in liquid form, appropriate adjustments should be made to the recipe. Several noncarbohydrate low-calorie sweeteners are available. Saccharin (brand name Sweet'N Low, Sweet Twin or Necta Sweet), the oldest artificial sugar substitute, has been used for more than a century. It has no calories and tastes 200–700 times as sweet as table sugar. At one time, saccharin was linked to cancer in laboratory animals, but scientific evidence for safety in humans was convincing enough to permit the use of saccharin in food. Saccharin has a bitter aftertaste, however, and many people find it unpalatable.

Aspartame (brand name NutraSweet, Equal or SugarTwin), approved by the FDA in 1981, is made up of the amino acids aspartic acid and phenylalanine. Unlike saccharin, aspartame does not have an aftertaste. It is 180–200 times as sweet as table sugar. Aspartame breaks down when heated, so it cannot be used in cooked foods. It is now widely used in soft drinks, frozen yogurts, fruit spreads, candies and similar products. According to the FDA, aspartame is a safe substitute for sugar, although it is a risk for those people with the rare disorder phenylketonuria (PKU), who cannot metabolize the phenylalanine in aspartame. Appropriate warnings are printed on all aspartame-sweetened foods. People mistakenly think that aspartame is a "natural" substance because it is made up of amino acids. By itself, aspartame as a sweetener is not found in any natural foodstuff; it is made in the laboratory and as such it is not a "natural" substance.

Another sugar substitute, acesulfame-K (brand name Sunnette or Sweet One), which the FDA approved in 1988, is 200 times as sweet as table sugar. Like aspartame, it has no aftertaste. The body cannot metabolize acesulfame-K, so it passes through the digestive system unchanged. Acesulfame-K can be used successfully in cooking and baking. Acesulfame-K is used in chewing gum, dry beverage mixes, instant coffees and teas, gelatins and nondairy creamers.

Sucralose (brand name Splenda) is 600 times as sweet as sugar and can be used like sugar in some baked goods. Sucralose, a derivative of table sugar, is virtually calorie-free because its sweetness is so intense that only minute amounts are needed to replace the sweetness of sugar. Original Splenda could be used in baking, but the resulting product would not brown like a product made with table sugar. Its manufacturer recently introduced a refined version (Splenda plus sugar) designed for improved baking results. It can be used measure for measure like regular table sugar.

The latest alternative sweetener approved by the FDA is rebaudioside A, a sweet-tasting compound found in the stevia plant (also known as sweetleaf and honey leaf). It is the extract of an herb not metabolized by the body. It is used as a sweetener for beverages where manufacturers employ it in place of aspartame. PureVia and Truvia are two brands in wide distribution.

Fat Substitutes and Alternatives

The simplest solution to reducing fat content is to reduce the amount of fat used. The fat in many recipes can often be reduced by 20–30 percent without significant negative results. Alternative types of fat—substituting olive oil for dairy butter, for example—will improve the health profile of a recipe but will not reduce the amount of fat. Oils made from nuts including almonds, hazelnuts or walnuts will also add a unique flavor and can work well in some recipes. Low-fat ingredients such as low-fat cream cheese can work well to reduce fat. Be wary of using margarines in place of butter, however. Substituting margarine for butter will reduce the kind of fat (saturated) but will not reduce the calories.

MENU LABELING LAWS

Numerous health experts believe that menu labeling will promote health and help slow the spread of obesity. Across the country, many states and cities are mandating that nutritional information be made available to consumers. In New York City, for example, multi-unit chain restaurants must publish calorie content on menus and menu boards.

California is the first state to require that all nutritional information—calories, saturated fat, carbohydrates and sodium—be available for standard menu items. The ruling pertains to chain restaurants with 20 or more locations. Federal legislation is being considered to enforce menu labeling nationwide, although how this would be applied is still under debate. Consult your local state restaurant association to stay informed of new regulations.

Choose a margarine that does not contain hydrogenated fats because hydrogenated fats are not considered a healthy alternative to butter. Fat-free margarines usually do not perform well in baked goods.

Consumer interest in reduced-fat and fat-free products has waned as Americans have become more intrigued with low-carbohydrate eating styles; however, the use of fat substitutes still remains important in the food manufacturing industry as well as in the restaurant and home kitchen. Several types of FDA-approved fat substitutes have been used with varying degrees of success in the commercial food industry. For the most part, they are not available for the restaurant or home cook. The approved fat replacements include olestra (brand name Olean), Simplesse, caprenin, salatrim (brand name Benefat) and oatrim (hydrolyzed oat flour; brand name Replace). Some are synthetic; others are derived from naturally occurring food substances but made in the laboratory.

Of the fatty-acid-based substitutes, olestra is probably the best known. It is made by the chemical combination of sucrose (sugar) and fat. The two are bonded together, and the resulting product consists of molecules too large to be digested. Because it cannot be digested, olestra does not provide any calories. Health concerns have kept olestra from being widely used, however. Olestra can cause abdominal distress in some people. Also, it can interfere with the absorption of fat-soluble vitamins and possibly remove them from the body when the olestra is eliminated in the feces.

Dairy Substitutes and Alternatives

REDUCING DAIRY FAT

Low-fat or fat-free dairy substitutes are usually good alternatives to their full-fat cousins in most applications. To find an appropriate substitute, first determine whether the fat in the dairy food is necessary for the success of the end product. If it is, try a low-fat or fat-free substitute combined with additional ingredients to substitute for some of the fat lost by using a fat-free dairy product. If the formula calls for whole milk, cream, sour cream, cream cheese or other cheese, a low-fat dairy alternative will usually work.

Reduced fat milk such as 2%, 1% or skim milk can often be substituted on an equal basis for whole or regular milk. In some instances, evaporated skim milk may be a better choice, although it could add an off-flavor; evaporated milk often imparts a "burnt" flavor because of the way it is processed. Light cream cheese (Neufchâtel) can be undetectable in baked goods when it replaces full-fat cream cheese. Using it to replace mascarpone cheese may require some other manipulation such as beating until light and fluffy with the addition of milk and/or a small amount of sour cream. Fat-free cream cheese is not usually a suitable substitute for full-fat cream cheese.

Buttermilk, a by-product of churning cream into butter, is a naturally low-fat dairy product and a good substitute for other full-fat dairy products. Low-fat and fat-free sour cream make suitable substitutions for full-fat sour cream in most preparations. Fat-free yogurt, made without gelatin, can be drained to remove excess liquid and used in place of sour cream. If the mixture is to be heated for a sauce or custard, adding a small amount of cornstarch will prevent curdling. Low-fat cottage cheese that has been blended in the food processor until smooth and creamy can be substituted for some of the full-fat cream cheese in a spread or cheesecake formula. Use low-fat cream cheese for the remainder.

LACTOSE INTOLERANCE

For those allergic to lactose (milk sugar), both true dairy products and plant sources of "milk" may be suitable. Commercially available lactose-free dairy products will work well in most preparations. Lactose is not usually a necessary ingredient for the successful outcome of a formula. Some lactose-reduced and lactose-free dairy products may taste a bit sweeter to the sensitive palate.

Soy milk, either unflavored or flavored, may be substituted for milk, although there may be a detectable flavor difference. Soy milk tends to brown prematurely; moderate temperatures should be used and cooking times shortened when soy milk is used. A milky substance can be made from nuts such as almonds or walnuts that are ground in water. However, those with a nut allergy would not be able to consume this product.

Egg Substitutes and Alternatives

Egg substitutes, discussed in Chapter 20, Eggs and Breakfast, can work for those on a restricted diet but have limited applications. When looking to reduce cholesterol in recipes, substitute egg whites for whole eggs. Two ounces (60 grams) or two egg whites can substitute for one whole egg in many recipes. It is best, however, to include some whole eggs for both color and texture. When eggs are used for leavening in baked goods, a recipe that uses chemical leavening in place of eggs may be more suitable. Commercial egg substitutes may not be lower in fat. Read the label to determine the suitability of the egg substitute.

Gluten Substitutes and Alternatives

Gluten allergies and intolerances affect as many as 15 million people in the United States; approximately 3 million have celiac disease, the most severe form of gluten intolerance; 2 million have wheat and gluten allergies and the remainder are sensitive to wheat products. Physicians are increasingly recommending gluten-free diets for children with autism and hyperactivity disorders. Substituting rice flour noodles for pasta or thickening with starch in place of roux are some of the easier solutions to common challenges when cooking for the

Millet and Amaranth Flours

celiac diner. But because wheat flour is the basis for all bakeshop products, making gluten-free cookies, muffins, cakes and bread poses specific challenges. Baked goods will be less elastic and may crumble. Developing recipes that do not use gluten-forming flours involves making a number of changes to basic formulas. Alternative flours made from non-gluten-forming proteins combined with starches can make satisfactory gluten-free baked goods.

Gluten-free substitutes for wheat flour include flours made from arrowroot, **buckwheat**, corn, potato, rice, tapioca, soy, **amaranth**, **beans** such as chickpeas, **flax meal**, **millet**, **quinoa**, **sorghum** and ground nuts. Commercially available gluten-free baking flours ease the preparation of suitable gluten-free products.

Other Ingredient Substitutes and Alternatives

There are many other ingredient substitutes, some of which are identified in Table 23.3. Often ingredient substitutes and alternatives will have a dramatic impact on the nutritional

amaranth tiny oval seeds of a type of annual herb plant native to South America; used as a cooked grain and flour

bean flour cooked beans including chickpeas, soybeans and white beans that are dried, then ground into a fine powder. Many bean flours, especially soy flour with a 50% protein content, are added to wheat flour mixtures to boost protein content.

buckwheat flour a dark, nutty-tasting flour milled from the seeds of the buckwheat plant; used for centuries in Middle Eastern and Asian countries to make bread, cereals and baked goods

flax a grain plant also known as linseed; rich in omega-3 fatty acids, a compound in oily fish found to be beneficial for promoting heart and arterial health. Flax hulls and seeds are crushed into a meal or flour to release beneficial compounds.

millet a high-protein cereal grain cooked and eaten like rice; used in combination with wheat flour in conventional baking when it is ground

quinoa tiny, spherical seeds of a plant native to South America; cooked like grain or ground and used like flour

sorghum grain harvested from a plant that resembles corn, used primarily for animal feed and food processing applications; also called milo. When ground, sorghum may be blended with other flours to make gluten-free preparations.

GLUTEN ALLERGY

Celiac disease, the inability to digest gluten, is one of the few diseases that is treated exclusively with diet. By removing all wheat, rye, and barley from the diet, people with celiac disease return to living a normal, healthy life. However, the most minute amount of gluten can cause symptoms to return. The problem is the gluten protein that is present in wheat, rye, and barley.

Staying gluten-free is quite a challenge and requires a quick education about foods and ingredients. Gluten is hidden in many places including soy sauce (fermented with wheat), sauces, soups, even some spice blends. Wheat is also used in the glue on most envelopes. Many different flours are

safe: rice flour, corn flour, cornstarch, potato flour and potato starch, tapioca starch, quinoa, soy, sorghum, bean flours, buckwheat, millet, and amaranth. Teff and oats can be safe as long as the source is free of cross-contamination from wheat.

Baking without gluten defies most of the principles of food chemistry. It's best to use a blend of two to three different gluten-free flours and starches, usually rice flour, sorghum, buckwheat, or millet with the addition of at least 30 percent starch—corn, potato, or tapioca. Some of the protein and elasticity of gluten can be replaced with gums—xanthan, guar, or locust bean gum. Usually one teaspoon per

cup is used for pastries and 3 teaspoons per cup is recommended for creating a blend that is used for bread flour. The addition of eggs helps build up the protein in the mixture. Also, adding a small amount of a flour that is high in protein (amaranth, soy, or other bean flour) helps to produce moisture in the final product.

Although gluten-free baking takes a bit of extra effort, the rewards outweigh the challenges as gluten-free consumers are very appreciative and will remain customers for life!

—BETH HILLSON, Founder, The Gluten-Free Pantry

TABLE 23.3	INGREDIENT SUBSTITUTES
INSTEAD OF	**USE**
Bacon	Canadian bacon or well-cooked, drained bacon
Butter	Powdered butter granules plus liquid (either fat-free milk or water) or butter-flavored oil sprays
Chocolate	Cocoa (vegetable oil may be added as needed)
Cream cheese	Reduced-fat or fat-free cream cheese
Emulsified salad dressing	Start with a base of reduced-fat or nonfat yogurt, sour cream or mayonnaise, then thin with fat-free milk; or use a slurry-thickened broth or juice as the oil and add vinegar and other seasonings; or blend silken tofu with other ingredients for a creamy dressing
Granulated sugar	Other natural granular sugars, date sugar, unrefined cane sugar
Ground beef	Textured soy protein; tempeh; seitan, a form of wheat gluten
Light cream	Equal portions of low-fat milk and fat-free evaporated milk
Mayonnaise	Reduced-fat mayonnaise (it can be mixed with reduced-fat or nonfat sour cream)
Sour cream	Reduced-fat or nonfat sour cream; drained reduced-fat or nonfat plain yogurt without gelatin
Wheat flour	Blends of non-gluten-forming flour and starches including rice flour, corn flour, cornstarch, potato flour and potato starch, tapioca starch, quinoa, soy, sorghum, bean flours, buckwheat, millet and amaranth
Whipped cream	Whipped chilled evaporated fat-free milk; the milk and beaters need to be very cold (needs to be stabilized)
Whole eggs	Liquid egg substitutes; use 1 egg white for every third whole egg called for in a batter; fruit purées alone or combined with starches in quick-bread batters

values of a completed dish. Ingredient substitutes and, especially, ingredient alternatives change the nutritional values of a dish; they may also change its flavor, texture or appearance. Sometimes these changes are acceptable; sometimes they are not. Because some changes result in unsatisfactory flavors, textures or appearance, many recipes are not suitable for substitution or alteration. Use your judgment. Understanding the function of the ingredients in your recipe will help adapt the recipe to meet dietary needs. Become familiar with some of the newer products available that can be used to alter or modify your recipes. Most manufacturers of commercial products have valuable information on their Web sites. In researching techniques for healthier cooking, the Internet is a good place to start.

NUTRITION, EATING OUT AND THE CHEF

On a typical day, almost half of all American adults eat at least one meal in a food service establishment. Even though eating out has become an integral part of everyday life, Americans still treat a restaurant meal as a special occasion. The portion size and menu choices offered by many restaurants have been blamed for the epidemic of obesity in this country. Restaurant meals typically have more calories, sodium, fat and cholesterol and less fiber, vitamins and minerals than meals prepared at home. A recent study found that people who eat out most often tend to weigh more than those who usually eat at home.

Many Americans are following eating patterns specifically designed to reduce body weight and/or prevent disease states associated with excess body weight. As such, the chef may be called on to make modifications to the dishes served to guests. Patrons concerned with calories and fat may choose to order appetizers in place of entrées to control quantity and thereby reduce calories and fat. They may request half-orders or split a full order with a companion. They may ask that dressings and sauces be served on the side or that a different cooking method be used—for instance, that a fish be broiled or baked instead of deep-fried or sautéed. Consumers who are concerned about ingredients may ask about how a dish is prepared. Waiters, cooks and other food service workers should take the guests' inquiries seriously. Failure to do so could result in severe illness or death. Chefs and restaurateurs should be flexible and willing to accommodate these patrons.

The U.S. Dietary Guidelines and recommendations from the American Cancer Society and the American Heart Association have all been designed to guide food consumption for a more healthful life. They present patterns for a healthful diet. Chefs can use them to plan balanced healthy menus as well. Chefs should consider using ingredients other than meat as the center of the plate presentation. Vegetables and whole grains as well as other protein foods such as beans, soy products and nuts can take the place of animal protein on the plate. In keeping with recommendations to consume more fiber, a variety of whole-grain breads, whole-grain pastas and rice as well as more exotic whole grains such as quinoa and spelt can be included on the menu along with a varied selection of fruit and vegetable dishes. Although not every food service operation can (or should) be devoted to "health food," to the extent appropriate the chef should offer healthful dining alternatives. The chef's ability to do so depends, of course, on the facility. Chefs at hospitals, prisons and schools have much greater control over the foods their guests consume. Therefore, they have a far greater opportunity and responsibility to provide selections for a well-balanced diet. Chefs at most restaurants, however, do not have such captive audiences. The chef can assist customers by doing the following:

➊ Use proper purchasing and storage techniques in order to preserve nutrients.

➋ Offer a variety of foods from each food group in the food pyramid so that customers have a choice.

➌ Offer entrées that emphasize plant instead of animal foods.

➍ Offer reduced-salt and reduced-fat dishes.

➎ Use cooking procedures that preserve rather than destroy nutrients.

➏ Use cooking procedures that minimize the use of added fat (for example, stocks, sauces and soups can be cooled and the congealed fats removed; foods can be browned in the oven instead of being sautéed in hot fat).

➐ Use equipment that minimizes the use of added fat (such as nonstick pans).

➑ Train the wait staff to respond properly to nutritional questions diners may have about menu items.

➒ Post notices or label products that may contain allergens on menus.

➓ Use ingredient alternatives or substitutes where appropriate. If a dish does not lend itself to ingredient alternatives or substitutes, consider creating a new dish that replaces less-nutritious traditional foods or preparations with more-nutritious ones. For example, instead of serving a sauce made with butter, flour and cream, you can reduce an appropriately seasoned wine, stock or juice and then thicken it with fruit or vegetable purées or cornstarch.

Sample Healthy Restaurant Meal

Chefs are increasingly challenged to create healthy menus for their establishments, menus that conform to current nutritional guidelines. Because health intakes vary by individual based on their age, gender, level of physical activity and other variables, this cannot easily be determined. As a general guideline, an overall healthy meal comprising a first course, entrée and dessert should offer the following components:

▶ The meal should consist of a total of 1000 calories.

▶ Fifteen to 25 percent of the calories should be from protein, which can be from an animal or plant-based source.

▶ Forty-five to 65 percent of the calories should come from carbohydrates, including whole grains and sugars from natural sources such as fruits.

▶ Twenty to 35 percent of the calories should be from fat. Of the total fat, less than 10 percent of the total calories should be from saturated fats such as that found in butter and animal fats. More of the fat should be from monounsaturated sources such as olive oil, fatty fish or nuts.

Apricot and Bourbon Grilled Chicken, a low-fat, low-calorie entrée.

FIGURE 23.3 ▶ Symbol for a healthy recipe.

▶ The meal should offer 8 to 12 grams of fiber.

▶ The total meal should contain no more than 1000 milligrams of sodium.

▶ As a reference, a healthy meal should include 1 to 1½ cups fresh vegetables.

These are approximate recommendations to help you plan a menu and the appropriate portion sizes within established health guidelines. Throughout this book various recipes are marked with the symbol illustrated in Figure 23.3. This symbol identifies dishes that are particularly low in calories, fat, saturated fat or sodium; if appropriate, they may also be a good source of vitamins, protein, fiber or calcium. Menus that meet these guidelines can be created using many of these recipes and other recipes.

The tremendous public interest in nutrition presents a special challenge to chefs. Ultimately it is the consumer's responsibility to choose wisely and eat properly. But chefs should be able to prepare and serve food that meets the high standards for health demanded by some patrons, while maintaining the flavor and appearance important to everyone.

VEGETARIANISM

Vegetarianism has become more mainstream over the last century. Approximately six million people in the United States today are choosing to forgo some or all animal products in their diets. The Dietary Guidelines for Americans 2005, as well as recommendations from the major health groups (American Cancer Society, American Heart Association, American Dietetic Association), stress the importance of fruits, vegetables, legumes and whole grains—the foundation of a plant-based diet. Studies have shown that the incidence of chronic diseases such as obesity, cardiovascular disease, cancer and type 2 diabetes are lower for vegetarians than for nonvegetarians. It is important to note that other

KEEPING KOSHER

To one degree or another, many observant Jews keep kosher; that is, they adhere to dietary laws rooted in the Torah (the first five books of the Old Testament) and developed over the centuries by Jewish scholars. These laws (1) categorize foods and (2) define basic dietary principles.

Kosher foods—Only meat from animals that chew their cud and have split hooves can be eaten. These include cattle, goats, deer and other game; swine are not a kosher species. Poultry can be kosher, provided it is not from a bird of prey; thus, chicken, duck, goose and turkey are allowed, but hawk and eagle are not. Even if the species is kosher, the animal must still be slaughtered and butchered according to religious rules. For fish to be kosher, it must have both scales and gills; this eliminates catfish and eel, and no shellfish can be kosher. Dairy products are kosher if the species from which they come is kosher; for cheese to be kosher, it must be made without ren-

net. Fresh fruits and vegetables are always kosher, as are baked goods, provided they are not made with animal fats. Commercially prepared foods marked with U, K or a similar symbol (often in a circle) indicates that the food product is kosher, the producer having used appropriate ingredients and met certain standards and its facilities having been inspected and approved by a rabbi.

Kosher dietary principles—All foods are either (1) meat, (2) dairy, or (3) pareve (parve). The principal dietary rule for keeping kosher is that meat and dairy foods cannot be cooked or eaten together. Over the centuries, this rule has been refined to the point that people keeping kosher will have two sets of cooking utensils, dishes and even dishcloths, one devoted to meat, the other to dairy, so that there is no accidental mixing. Particularly observant Jews will even wait for one to six hours after eating a meat dish before consuming a dairy dish. Pareve

refers to neutral (neuter) foods such as fruits, vegetables, breads, fish, eggs and certain commercially prepared foods that can be eaten with either meat or dairy items.

Not all Jews keep strictly kosher. Those who do will dine out only in a restaurant that regularly observes the same religious laws that they do at home, or in one that has been specially inspected and approved by a rabbi for the particular occasion (an option often used by catering facilities to accommodate kosher weddings, bar mitzvahs, bat mitzvahs and other Jewish celebrations). Other Jews will keep kosher by not eating any shellfish, meat, poultry or fish from nonkosher species or mixing dairy and meat, but they will not insist that separate meat and dairy cooking and eating utensils be used. They will generally dine in nonkosher restaurants, provided that the menu (sometimes referred to as "kosher-style") offers appropriate selections from kosher species.

healthy lifestyle factors (not smoking, moderate use or abstinence from alcohol, and exercise) that vegetarians typically follow may also be responsible for the lower disease rates. All of these factors together probably account for the decreased incidence of disease among vegetarians.

The vegetarian diet has many variations. A person who follows a vegetarian diet can be any of the following:

▶ **Vegan** (VEE-gun)—A person who eats no meat, fish or poultry or any products derived from animals such as milk, cheese, eggs, honey or gelatin; also referred to as a **strict** or **pure vegetarian**.

▶ **Raw foodist**—Typically, a vegan who eats only raw or slightly warmed plant products (adherents believe that cooking foods to a temperature of 116°F [47°C] or higher destroys enzymes and nutrients). A person on a raw foods diet, also referred to as a **living foodist**, may soak certain foods such as nuts and sprouts to soften them and increase nutrient absorption.

▶ **Fructarian** or **fruitarian**—A person who eats only fruits, nuts, seeds and other plant products that can be gathered without harming the plant (some eat only plant matter that has already fallen off the plant).

▶ **Ovo-vegetarian**—A vegetarian who eats eggs but not dairy products.

▶ **Ovo-lacto-vegetarian** or **lacto-ovo-vegetarian**—A person who eats plant products as well as dairy products and eggs (although some may not eat cheeses made with animal-based enzymes such as rennet, or eggs produced by factory farms). This diet is one of the most typical of vegetarian diets, and these terms are often used interchangeably with the term *vegetarian*.

▶ **Lacto-vegetarian**—A vegetarian who eats dairy products but not eggs.

INGREDIENTS FOR VEGETARIAN COOKING

Given the growing interest in vegetarianism, a chef needs to know how to cater to a vegetarian diner. A chef needs to understand that it is not necessarily enough to simply remove the meat from the center of the plate and replace it with pasta. Nor is it always sufficient to offer a plate composed of several starch and vegetable side dishes as if it were a balanced and inviting meal. A diet rich in a variety of fruits, vegetables, starches and grains, well prepared and properly seasoned, will satisfy even those adhering to the more strict vegetarian diets. Chefs can prepare flavorful, visually stimulating vegetarian dishes with a traditional range of ingredients available in most restaurant kitchens. Potatoes, grains, starches, vegetables and fruits—discussed in Chapter 21, Vegetables; Chapter 22, Potatoes, Grains, and Pasta; Chapter 24, Salads and Salad Dressings; and Chapter 25, Fruits—form the backbone of vegetarian cooking. To help chefs in planning vegetarian dishes, Table 23.4 lists foods that are eaten by the most common types of vegetarians.

Although the professional kitchen offers hundreds of foods appropriate for all vegetarian diets, chefs can use a number of ingredients to enhance the complexity of their vegetarian cooking. Some foods that replace the protein found in animal products are featured here, as well as other ingredients that may mimic more traditional animal-based foods.

Soybean-Based Ingredients

The versatile and protein-rich soybean forms the basis for a wide range of products used in vegetarian and traditional ethnic cuisines worldwide. Soy-based foods have been favorites in Asian cooking for centuries. Although there are brown, black and green varieties, most soybeans are yellow. Fresh green soybeans (edamame) are steamed and eaten as a snack. According to the United Soybean Board, soy protein is the only plant protein that is equivalent to animal protein; it is a rich source of phytochemicals, making soy an ideal ingredient for vegetarian cooking. Soy can be made into a diverse range of foods, including flour, "milk," cheese and oil.

KEEPING HALAL

Many Muslims follow dietary laws based on the Qur'an (the revealed book), the Hadith (the sayings or traditions of the prophet Muhammad) and the collective wisdom of Muslim scholars. *Halal*, which means "allowed" or "lawful," refers to foods and beverages that can be consumed by observant Muslims. Foods and beverages that are *haram* are not allowed, and those that are of a questionable or suspect nature are referred to as *mushbooh*.

As all fruits and vegetables are halal, the majority of Muslim dietary laws address permitted and prohibited meats. Cooked (not raw) beef, lamb and chicken are halal, provided the animals are slaughtered and butchered according to certain rituals and methods. Fish and shellfish are also halal. Pork, game, carnivorous animals, birds of prey, carrion (the meat of animals that died of natural causes), and blood are haram, as are products derived from them. Eggs and dairy products from permitted animals are halal, as are baked goods made with ingredients from permitted animals. Any halal food contaminated with blood, pork or other haram product is deemed haram and cannot be eaten. Alcohol, whether consumed as a beverage, used as a flavoring or even present in a cleaning solution for dishes, is haram. Gelatin, emulsifiers, animal-based fats and certain dairy products are considered mushbooh unless certified as halal. Halal certification is often denoted as a capital H inside a triangle.

In food service operations, it is best if equipment dedicated solely to halal cooking is used. If this is impractical and the same equipment is used to cook halal and haram foods, the equipment must be thoroughly sanitized before it can be used for halal products. Normally, a careful visual inspection of the equipment suffices.

MOTIVATIONS FOR VEGETARIANISM

For millennia, people have followed vegetarian diets for a variety of reasons, including religious and ethical beliefs. Religion has long played a leading role in defining how and what people eat. Although few religions mandate a complete vegetarian diet for their followers, many of the world's major religions promote meatless diets, in part as a spiritual ideal and in part in recognition of humans' kinship with animals. Many followers of Buddhism adhere to some form of vegetarian diet as do strict observers of Hinduism, the predominant religion of India practiced in cities worldwide by Indian immigrants and their families, as many as 800 million people worldwide.

Some Jews and Christians believe that God originally intended humans to be vegetarians, even though the consumption of meat is allowed. Ellen White, one of the founders of the Seventh-Day Adventist Church, was a vegetarian activist; today approximately half of the practicing Adventists in the United States follow a vegetarian diet.

More recently, environmental and health concerns have become the major motivations for adopting some sort of vegetarian diet. Some vegetarians refuse to eat meat because of an emotional aversion to inflicting pain and harm on other living creatures or an objection to the manner in which animals are raised and slaughtered. Many vegetarians cite environmental concerns as one of the principal reasons why they chose to forgo animal products in their diet. Some people strongly believe that the production of meat and animal products at current and likely future levels is environmentally unsustainable. They argue that modern industrial agriculture is changing ecosystems faster than they can adapt.

TABLE 23.4 DIET PATTERNS OF MAJOR FORMS OF VEGETARIAN DIETS

FOOD GROUPS CONSUMED	TYPE OF VEGETARIAN				
	OVO-LACTO	OVO-	LACTO-	VEGAN	FRUITARIAN
Grains	Yes	Yes	Yes	Yes	No
Legumes	Yes	Yes	Yes	Yes	No
Nuts, seeds	Yes	Yes	Yes	Yes	Yes
Vegetables	Yes	Yes	Yes	Yes	No
Fruits	Yes	Yes	Yes	Yes	Yes
Dairy	Yes	No	Yes	No	No
Eggs	Yes	Yes	No	No	No

Soy milk is made from dried soybeans that are soaked and then finely ground and pressed to extract a milky liquid. Soy milk comes in liquid or powdered form. Liquid soy milk resembles skim milk and has a slight nutty flavor. Most liquid soy milk is sold in aseptic packaging, giving it a one-year shelf life if unopened. Like other dairy products, once opened, liquid soy milk requires refrigeration and lasts approximately 5 to 7 days. Powdered soy milk is shelf-stable and lasts for a year at room temperature. Soy cheese, soy yogurt and flavored soy beverages are dairy substitutes made from soy milk.

Use soy milk measure-for-measure in any recipe that calls for dairy milk. Manufacturing technologies have evolved to produce soy milk products with a richer texture and flavor, more suitable for enriching sauces. At high temperatures, soy milk can separate; simmer foods with soy milk gently and add the soy milk near the end of the cooking time to prevent it from separating.

Tofu or bean curd (Fr. *fromage de soja*) is a staple of Japanese and Chinese cuisines now appreciated internationally for its high nutritional value, low cost and flavor adaptability. Tofu is made by processing soybeans into soy milk, which is then coagulated or cultured and formed into a cake. The result is a soft, creamy-white substance similar to cheese. Tofu is easy to digest and is a good source of protein, low in fat and sodium with no cholesterol.

Tofu may be eaten fresh; added to soup, broth or noodle dishes; tossed in cold salads; grilled, deep-fried or sautéed; or puréed to make a creamy spread. Its flavor is bland, but it readily absorbs flavors from other ingredients.

Two types of tofu are widely available: cotton (or traditional) and silken. **Cotton tofu** is the most common. The soy milk is coagulated (nowadays with calcium sulfate). The curds are then placed in a perforated mold lined with cloth and pressed with a weight to remove the liquid. Cotton tofu is solid, with an irregular surface caused by the weave of the cotton fabric in which it is wrapped for pressing. This traditional tofu comes in three styles: soft, firm and extra firm, each style being progressively drier and firmer. Select the style of tofu suited to the preparation. Firmer tofu is solid enough to be grilled or sautéed. It absorbs the flavors of rubs and marinades. Softer tofu may be scrambled like eggs or processed to form a smooth spread.

Silken tofu (Ja. *kinugoshi*) has a silky-smooth appearance and texture and a somewhat more delicate flavor than cotton tofu. Silken tofu is made in a process similar to the way yogurt is cultured. No curds are formed, nor is whey produced. This makes a tofu with a custardlike texture suitable for processing into a creamy substance,

Silken Tofu

good to use as a base for dips or in spreads or smoothies. Because the water has not been pressed out of silken tofu, it should not be cooked at high temperatures or for a long time, as it falls apart easily. Silken tofu can also be drained to make a thicker spread with a consistency similar to mascarpone or cream cheese.

Fresh tofu is usually packaged in water. It should be refrigerated and kept in water until used. If the water is drained and changed daily, the tofu should last for 1 week. Tofu can be frozen for several months, though its texture may be slightly altered after thawing. Weight down the firm tofu while it is thawing to create a denser, firmer product, suitable for grilling. Place a sheet pan on top of the tofu, then place a heavy object such as a #10 can on top of the sheet pan. Drain the liquid from the tofu before using.

Miso (MEE-so) is a thick paste made by salting and fermenting soybeans and rice or barley. After soaking, the soybeans are steamed, then crushed. The mixture is blended with water. Rice or barley is added along with salt before the mixture is inoculated with a living culture, koji or aspergillis mold. After fermenting and aging, often in large wooden barrels for as long as a year, the paste is ready to use. In Japan, where the manufacture of miso is a fine art akin to cheese making in France, there are countless styles of miso ranging in color from pale to rust and in taste from sweet to salty. In the United States, two types of miso are commonly available: sweet **white miso** (shiro miso) and dark or **red miso**. Creamy-colored white miso contains a high percentage of rice and has a mild, somewhat sweet flavor. Dark or red miso, which contains a higher percentage of soybeans, is aged longer and has a stronger, saltier flavor.

Miso can be used in cold and warm preparations but should never be boiled; it contains beneficial enzymes and bacteria that can be killed at high temperatures. A pungent seasoning, miso should be used judiciously so as not to overpower a dish. As little as 1 teaspoon (5 milliliters) per portion can be adequate to flavor a simple broth. With its high salt content, miso will keep indefinitely under refrigeration.

Tempeh (TEHM-pay) is a type of bean cake made from fermented whole soybeans mixed with a grain such as rice or millet. The mixture is inoculated with rhizopus mold, which binds the grains into a firm cake. The traditional food of Indonesia, tempeh has a chewy consistency and a yeasty, nutty flavor.

With its chunky texture, tempeh makes a pleasant meat substitute. It lends itself to being marinated for grilling or sautéing. When crumbled, tempeh can be added to soups or stews to replace ground beef, poultry or pork. A firm cake, tempeh is easily sliced or cut into cubes. Because of the type of live culture used to make it, tempeh should be cooked before eating. Proper cooking also tempers its pronounced flavor. Tempeh is sold both fresh and frozen. It lasts for approximately 1 week in the refrigerator or several months when frozen.

Textured soy protein, also known as textured soy flour or TSP, a proprietary name, is a defatted soy protein that is dried and then compressed into granules or chunks or extruded into shapes. Food manufacturers use it as a meat extender and in commercially produced meat replacements. Granulated textured soy protein must be rehydrated before cooking, which causes it to take on a texture similar to that of meat. Larger forms of textured soy protein benefit from simmering after rehydration. Adding some vinegar or lemon juice to the simmering liquid helps speed rehydration. A shelf-stable dry product, textured soy protein can be stored for up to a year when tightly sealed at room temperature. Once it has been rehydrated, textured soy protein must be refrigerated and should be used within a few days.

Other Popular Ingredients in Vegetarian Cooking

Seitan (SAY-tan), often referred to as "wheat meat," is a form of wheat gluten, the insoluble protein in wheat. A staple in the diets of Buddhist monks for centuries, seitan has a firm, chewy texture and a bland flavor. Seitan is made by preparing a dough from wheat gluten or wheat flour and water. The dough is repeatedly rinsed to remove any remaining starch or bran. The spongy pieces of seitan are then simmered in a broth of soy sauce

White Miso

Red Miso

Tempeh

Textured Soy Protein

Seitan

or tamari with ginger, garlic and kombu (seaweed). Cooking tenderizes seitan and imbues it with the flavors of the cooking liquid. As it absorbs flavors, seitan can be flavored to mimic many foods. Using seasonings associated with poultry such as thyme and sage brings out a more chickenlike flavor in the seitan, whereas using dark soy sauce and meaty mushrooms can give it a meatlike flavor. Seitan should be added to a dish near the end of cooking, as it is already fully cooked. Fully cooked fresh seitan is sold refrigerated in irregularly sized chunks. Once opened, it should be consumed within a few days. Powdered seitan mix is also available.

GRAIN BEVERAGES

Many grains and nuts can be used to produce beverages that can be used in place of stock or dairy products when making soups, sauces and custards. Almond, hazelnut, oat and rice milks are commercially available. These ingredients tend to be lower in fat but higher in carbohydrates than their dairy counterparts—and they are cholesterol-free.

ANALOGOUS FOODS

Numerous products made from soy, wheat, grains, or other plant materials are designed to mimic the appearance and texture of popular animal-based products. These commercially prepared products offer a texture and appearance similar to that of their animal-protein-based counterparts. Although their flavors are less successful in imitating the actual flavor of their fish, meat or poultry counterparts, many offer consumers the pleasure of eating familiar foods in traditional dishes. Plant-based products are available in the form of "nuggets," "burgers," "sausage," "hot dogs," "ground meat," "bacon," "cold cuts" and even "pastrami." Soy protein extract and judicious use of appropriate seasonings, such as sage in a turkey stuffing analogue, help mimic the flavor of their meat counterparts.

In most cases, these analogous food products may be prepared in the same way as their meat, poultry or fish counterparts. Steaming, sautéing, simmering, grilling and baking work well. Follow the manufacturer's directions, keeping in mind that these products are usually fully cooked, requiring only crisping and heating, and could suffer in overcooking.

VEGETARIAN CUISINE: REBALANCING THE CENTER OF THE PLATE

The principles of vegetarian cuisine are no different from those of the classic kitchen. When creating an appetizing and satisfying vegetarian dish, chefs use the same professional judgment as when preparing a roast or steak. Flavors must be in balance. Ingredients must be thoughtfully selected and skillfully prepared. Only the ingredients themselves vary. Chefs need to understand the basic principles of cooking and work with the textures and flavors offered by plant-based ingredients.

Chefs also need to understand the unique role played by animal products in specific recipes they are considering adapting for a vegetarian diner. As discussed in Chapter 12, Principles of Meat Cookery, the muscle fibers in different cuts of meat, poultry and game yield foods with a chewy texture not easily mimicked by vegetable or soy analogues.

Well-marbled meat has fat throughout. When cooked, this fat melts, adding tenderness and flavor to the finished dish. It may be necessary to add fat to enhance flavor and add moisture to dishes cooked without meats. Replacing animal protein in a main dish with an equal amount of tofu, texturized soy protein, grain, bean purée or plant food may not result in a dish with the same appearance and depth of flavor as the original made with meat. Chefs must carefully choose the ingredients they use. Vegetables should be chosen for their flavor and texture. The mouth feel each ingredient contributes to a finished dish should also be considered. Ripe avocados, for example, have a rich, creamy texture that can mimic the mouth feel of a soft cream cheese.

Baking without eggs poses a number of challenges because of the function eggs perform in many baked goods. Quick-bread formulas using chemical leavening may be better suited to adapting to vegetarian preparation than creaming-style cakes.

With these considerations in mind, here are some suggestions on how to plan and prepare to add vegetarian dishes to a restaurant menu.

▶ **Use or adapt items from the regular menu.** Many items on existing menus may be vegetarian or can easily be adapted for a vegetarian diner. Soups, salads, stir-fried vegetables and pasta dishes lend themselves to vegetarian ingredients.

▶ **Grains and beans add texture and satiation.** Think about these versatile starches as the center-of-the-plate offerings when planning a vegetarian menu. Chewy grains such as cooked bulgur, barley and millet offer a good textural appeal that can be lacking in plant-based cuisine. Ensuring that a customer feels sufficiently fed is another consideration, something that a plate of steamed vegetables may not offer.

▶ **Take advantage of meaty vegetables and soy products as main attractions in a vegetarian dish.** Eggplant, mushrooms (especially portabellas), okra, sweet potatoes and parsnips have flavor and body that mimics that of meat. Pan-fried breaded eggplant slices or grilled whole portabella mushroom caps offer hearty vegetable alternatives to a slice of chicken or beef.

▶ **Compose dishes with an eye to balancing color.** We eat with our eyes as well as our taste buds. When combining grains and beans on a plate, consider using different colors, such as black beans and red rice or yellow lentils and black-eyed peas.

▶ **Balance textures on the same plate.** Look for complementary and contrasting textures in a vegetarian plate. When serving a creamy purée, such as mashed sweet potatoes, for example, balance the texture with something crunchy or crisp such as fried zucchini or a risotto cake.

▶ **Layer flavors for complexity of taste.** A dish prepared with few ingredients need not be bland or boring. Combine cooking methods in one dish to bring out a complex taste. Sun-dried tomatoes added to a fresh tomato sauce add a rich dimension of taste that might otherwise be lacking.

▶ **Create a vegetarian pantry stocked with ingredients that help enhance plant-based cooking.** Without base flavor notes created from rich meat stocks, vegetarian dishes can lack depth of flavor. Varieties of fresh and dried mushrooms help enrich flavorful stocks, soups and stews. Dried seaweed such as kombu (sea kelp) adds a briny flavor mimicking seafood stock. Soy sauce and miso can give a vegetable broth a savory taste and appealing dark color, as can wine reductions. Richly flavored nut oils such as sesame oil, hazelnut oil and walnut oil can add complex tastes to dishes prepared without rich meat stocks or butter. Olives and dried fruit have intense flavors and pleasing textures that can add variety to a vegetarian dish. Toasted sesame and other seeds and nuts add bursts of flavor and a textural contrast to a dish.

▶ **Seek inspiration from ethnic cuisines in which vegetarian food is traditional.** Asian, Indian, Mexican, Middle Eastern and South American cuisines offer many exciting vegetarian options. Recipes in this book for Cambodian-Style Red Pork and Samosas are just as frequently prepared without meat or poultry in their native countries as we have done in our recipe variations on the listed pages.

The recipes at the end of this chapter are suitable for most vegetarian diets and do not include animal proteins or eggs. Throughout this book are many vegetarian dishes, indicated with the symbol shown in Figure 23.4. These recipes do not contain any meat, fish, shellfish or poultry but may contain dairy products and/or eggs. Vegetarian dishes are not necessarily low in calories, fat or sodium, nor are they automatically good sources of vitamins, protein, fiber or calcium, as defined by government standards.

FIGURE 23.4 ▶ Symbol for a vegetarian recipe.

TABLE 23.5 VEGETARIAN INGREDIENT SUBSTITUTES

INSTEAD OF	IN THIS APPLICATION	USE	COMMENTS
Butter	Sautéing	Vegetable oil or vegetable oil spray	
	Flavoring	Nut oil: hazelnut, pecan or walnut; nut butter: almond, cashew, peanut or sesame butter	Additional oil or liquid may be needed; thin nut butters with oil, fruit juices or nut, rice or soy milks
	Spreading	Ground nut spread: almond, cashew, peanut or sesame butter; vegetable purées: bean, roasted eggplant, red pepper	
	Baking	Dried fruit or cooked vegetable purées	Quick breads, cookies and general baking; may affect color, taste and texture
Cream	Hot soups, sauces	Soy or rice milk; puréed silken tofu	Add at last moment, heating gently to prevent separation
	Cold creams or spreads	Enriched soy milk	Oil may be needed to improve mouth feel
Sour cream, yogurt	Beverage or custard Cold creams or spreads	Soy coffee creamer Puréed silken tofu	
Eggs	Leavening	Chemical leavening	Consider loss of color from lack of egg yolk; texture will be denser than product containing eggs
	Emulsifier in sauces such as mayonnaise	Form a temporary emulsion; form emulsion using ground nuts or soaked bread	
Beef, fish or poultry stock	Sauces, soups, stews	Vegetable stock; broth made from miso or seaweed	
Demi-glace	Sauces, stews	Rich vegetable stock made with a larger proportion of vegetables, reduced and thickened with starch	
Gelatin	Thickening, gelling	Agar	Gels more firmly than gelatin
Prepared sauces made with fish such as nuoc mam, oyster or Worcestershire	Flavoring	Soy sauce, balsamic or red wine vinegar	

SHARON SALOMON, MS, RD

This chapter was researched and written with the assistance of Sharon Salomon, a registered dietitian with a master of science degree in clinical nutrition. As an undergraduate at Queens College in Flushing, New York, Ms. Salomon majored in cultural anthropology and traveled to Mexico, Turkey and Europe as part of her education. On these trips she enjoyed the benefits of living with local people in their homes, where she spent most of her free time in the families' kitchens learning authentic preparation of their native cuisines. Ms. Salomon has also studied at La Varenne Cooking School in France and attended the Culinary Institute of America for certification in nutritional cuisine. Ms. Salomon received her master's degree in clinical nutrition from Arizona State University in Tempe, Arizona.

Ms. Salomon has combined her love of food and cooking with her nutrition education in a variety of ways. She has taught nutrition and culinary nutrition courses and has worked as a caterer as well as a spokesperson for the Arizona Beef Council, the National Pork Producers Council and the California Kiwi Association. In addition to this chapter, Ms. Salomon contributed the Healthy Baking chapter in *On Baking: A Textbook of Baking and Pastry Fundamentals*, Prentice Hall, 2009.

HAUTE VEGETABLES

Today, America's most respected chefs are elevating plant-based cuisine to the highest culinary art. Internationally acclaimed chefs Thomas Keller of the French Laundry in Yountville, California, and Per Se in New York City and Charlie Trotter of the eponymous restaurant in Chicago both offer a vegetable tasting menu each evening in their respective restaurants. Although the menu is not strictly vegetarian—dairy products are used in abundance—Chef Keller explores the flavors and versatility of vegetables in his multicourse menu. Chef Trotter regularly offers a strictly raw food menu, demonstrating that vegetarian dining can have a place in the finest restaurant.

The following are some dishes from one of Chef Keller's vegetable tasting menus:

- Creamed Ramp Top "Pierogis," French Laundry Garden Shallots, Cipollini Onion "Rissolée," Glazed Ramp Bulbs with "Sauce Soubise" and Chive-Infused Extra Virgin Olive Oil
- "Fricassée" of Roasted Marble Potatoes, California Grey Morel Mushrooms, Split English Peas and English Pea "Purée"

The following are some dishes from one of Chef Trotter's raw vegetable tasting menus:

- Root Vegetable Salad with Eggplant and Purple Tomatillo Vinaigrette
- Green and White Cauliflower with Shaved Asparagus Salad, Date Purée and Garlic Blossoms

---

1. Identify the six categories of nutrients and list two sources for each.

2. List four ways to reduce mineral and vitamin loss when storing or preparing foods.

3. Describe the key messages in the 2005 U.S. Dietary Guidelines.

4. What other diet-planning tools can be used along with the Dietary Guidelines to plan a nutritious diet? Use the Internet to visit the MyPyramid Web site at http://mypyramid.gov and report on your findings. **WWW**

5. Consult the nutritional information panel on a jar of prepared mayonnaise or salad dressing. Compare this with the nutritional information provided with a similar recipe in this book. Discuss the differences.

6. Create a three-course menu following the health guidelines discussed in this chapter. Discuss the ways you might adapt and combine recipes in this book to conform to the guidelines.

7. What procedures should a restaurant and its chef put in place for serving customers with food allergies? What menu substitutions should be available for those allergic to nuts or wheat protein?

8. Identify three popular recipes that use meat, fish or poultry. Discuss how you would adapt such recipes for the vegetarian customer.

9. Vegetarian restaurants and restaurants that offer vegetarian menu options exist in every state. Schools, corporations, airlines and hospitals even offer vegetarian menu options. Use the Internet to research vegetarian menus. Analyze two or three such menus and discuss how they address the concerns of their customers. **WWW**

QUESTIONS FOR DISCUSSION

Terms to Know

essential nutrients
soluble fiber
insoluble fiber
cholesterol
saturated fat
hydrogenated fat
trans fat
amino acids
registered dietitian
fat soluble vitamins

water soluble vitamins
allergies
celiac disease
kosher
halal
vegan
ovo-vegetarian
lacto-ovo vegetarian

RICH BROWN VEGETABLE STOCK

Yield: Approximately 4 qt. (4 lt)

Vegetable oil	2 fl. oz.	60 ml
Garlic cloves, chopped	10	10
Mirepoix, small dice	4 lb.	1.9 kg
Leeks, whites and greens, chopped	1 lb.	480 g
Turnip, diced	4 oz.	120 g
Tomato, diced	4 oz.	120 g
Red wine	1 pt.	480 ml
Tomato paste	2 oz.	60 g
Onion brûlée	1	1
Water	4 qt.	3.8 lt
Sachet:		
Bay leaf	1	1
Dried thyme	½ tsp.	2 ml
Peppercorns, crushed	¼ tsp.	1 ml
Parsley stems	8	8

1. Heat the oil. Add the garlic and vegetables and sweat for 10 minutes. Increase heat to medium-high and cook the vegetables until lightly caramelized, approximately 10 more minutes.
2. Add the wine, tomato paste, onion brûlée, water and sachet.
3. Bring the mixture to a boil, reduce to a simmer and cook for 1 hour 30 minutes.
4. Strain. Reduce to make a glace or cool and refrigerate.

Approximate values per 1-fl.-oz. (30-ml) serving: **Calories** 5, **Total fat** 0 g, **Saturated fat** 0 g, **Cholesterol** 0 mg, **Sodium** 0 mg, **Total carbohydrates** 0 g, **Protein** 0 g, **Claims**—fat free; low calorie

VEGETABLE DEMI-GLACE

Yield: Approximately 1½ qt. (1.4 lt)

Carrots, chopped	8 oz.	240 g
Celery, chopped	8 oz.	240 g
Leeks, whites and greens, chopped	4 oz.	120 g
Onions, coarsely chopped	6 oz.	120 g
Olive oil	2 Tbsp.	30 ml
Tomato paste	4 oz.	120 g
Garlic cloves, minced	6	6
Red wine	12 fl. oz.	360 ml
Bay leaf	1	1
Vegetable stock	2 qt.	1.9 lt
Fresh thyme, chopped	1 tsp.	5 ml
Cornstarch or arrowroot	as needed	as needed

1. Sauté the vegetables in the oil until well browned, approximately 10 minutes. Stir in the tomato paste and garlic. Cook, stirring until the vegetables are well coated with the tomato paste.
2. Add 6 fluid ounces (180 milliliters) wine and reduce by half. Add the remaining wine and reduce by half.
3. Add the bay leaf, stock and thyme and cook until the liquid is reduced by half. Strain.
4. Adjust the thickness of the sauce by thickening it with a cornstarch slurry as needed. Cool and refrigerate.

Approximate values per 1-fl.-oz. (30-ml) serving: **Calories** 6, **Total fat** 0 g, **Saturated fat** 0 g, **Cholesterol** 0 mg, **Sodium** 0 mg, **Total carbohydrates** 0 g, **Protein** 0 g, **Claims**—fat free; low calorie

SOUTHWESTERN BLACK BEAN SOUP

Yield: Approximately 3 qt. (2.8 lt) **Method:** Purée

Dried black beans, soaked	1 lb.	480 g
Vegetable stock	4 qt.	3.8 lt
Sachet:		
Bay leaves	2	2
Dried thyme	½ tsp.	2 ml
Peppercorns, cracked	10	10
Canola oil	1 Tbsp.	15 ml
Onion, diced	4 oz.	120 g
Garlic cloves, minced	2	2
Anaheim chile, diced	1 oz.	30 g
Jalapeño or serrano chile, minced	1 Tbsp.	15 ml
Cumin, ground	1 tsp.	5 ml
Coriander, ground	1 tsp.	5 ml
Dried oregano	1 tsp.	5 ml
Salt and pepper	TT	TT
Lime wedges	as needed for garnish	
Fresh cilantro, chopped	as needed for garnish	

1. Combine the beans and stock or water in a medium stockpot and bring to a simmer. Add the sachet.
2. Sauté the onion, garlic and chiles in the oil. Add to the stockpot.
3. Stir in the cumin, coriander and oregano.
4. Simmer the soup, uncovered, approximately 2½ to 3½ hours. The beans should be very soft, just beginning to fall apart. Add additional stock if necessary.
5. Purée about half of the soup, then stir it back into the remaining soup. Season to taste with salt and pepper.
6. Serve in warmed bowls garnished with lime wedges and chopped cilantro.

Approximate values per 6-fl.-oz. (180-ml) serving: **Calories** 70, **Total fat** 2 g, **Saturated fat** 0 g, **Cholesterol** 0 mg, **Sodium** 1010 mg, **Total carbohydrates** 9 g, **Protein** 4 g, **Claims**—low fat; no saturated fat; no cholesterol

GRILLED BBQ PORTABELLA MUSHROOM SANDWICH ON FOCACCIA

K RESTAURANT WINE BAR, ORLANDO, FL

Chef Kevin Fonzo

Yield: 6 Sandwiches

Focaccia, cut into 6-in. (15-cm) squares	6	6
Portabella mushrooms	6	6
Barbecue Sauce (page 227)	2 fl. oz.	60 ml
Red bell peppers, roasted, peeled, julienne	2	2
Fresh basil leaves	30	30
Soy or other vegetarian cheese, crumbled	6 Tbsp.	90 ml

1. Slice the focaccia squares horizontally and toast.
2. Brush the mushrooms with the Barbecue Sauce and grill until hot and tender.
3. To assemble each sandwich, place one mushroom on the bottom of a focaccia square and top with one-sixth of the bell pepper strips, five basil leaves and 1 tablespoon (15 milliliters) cheese. Top with the remaining focaccia, cut in half and serve.

Approximate values per sandwich: **Calories** 230, **Total fat** 9 g, **Saturated fat** 3.5 g, **Cholesterol** 15 mg, **Sodium** 660 mg, **Total carbohydrates** 45 g, **Protein** 11 g, **Vitamin C** 80%, **Iron** 15%, **Claims**—good source of fiber

FALAFEL

Yield: 12 Sandwiches

Chickpeas, dried	1 lb.	480 g
Garlic cloves, minced	6	6
Fresh parsley, chopped	½ oz.	15 g
Chives, minced	½ oz.	15 g
Cumin, ground	1 Tbsp.	15 ml
Coriander, ground	2 tsp.	10 ml
Cayenne pepper	TT	TT
Eggs	3	3
Salt	TT	TT
Flour	5 oz.	150 g
Silken tofu, puréed	6 oz.	180 g
Lemon juice	2 fl. oz.	60 ml
Pita breads	12	12
Iceberg lettuce, shredded	6 oz.	180 g
Tomatoes, diced	6 oz.	180 g

1. To make the falafel, soak the chickpeas following the procedures for dried beans outlined in Chapter 22, Vegetables. Drain the chickpeas, place them in a pot and cover with cool water. Simmer until tender, approximately 2 to 3 hours; remove from the heat and drain well.
2. Process the chickpeas in a food processor or a food chopper until coarsely chopped. Add the garlic, parsley, chives, cumin, coriander and cayenne pepper and process for a few seconds.
3. Add the eggs, salt and flour and process briefly. Remove the falafel from the machine and chill in the refrigerator for 1 hour.
4. Combine the tofu and lemon juice and mix well. Set aside.
5. Portion the falafel using a #50 scoop (there should be approximately 60 balls) and deep-fry the balls using the swimming method at 375°F (190°C) until crisp and hot. Drain well and hold in a warm place.
6. To assemble each sandwich, cut a pita bread in half or open it to form a pocket and stuff with several balls of falafel and ½ ounce (15 grams) each of the shredded lettuce and diced tomatoes and then dress with the tofu sauce. Arrange the sandwiches as desired and serve hot.

Approximate values per sandwich: **Calories** 290, **Total fat** 3 g, **Saturated fat** 0.5 g, **Cholesterol** 55 mg, **Sodium** 470 mg, **Total carbohydrates** 55 g, **Protein** 12 g, **Claims**—low fat; low saturated fat; good source of fiber

VEGGIE WRAP

Yield: 1 Sandwich

Spinach-flavored tortilla	1	1
Garlic Yogurt Dressing (recipe follows)	2 Tbsp.	30 ml
Jasmine rice, cooked	3 oz.	90 g
Roma tomato, diced	2 Tbsp.	30 ml
Cucumber, julienne	1 oz.	30 g
Alfalfa sprouts	as needed	as needed
Broccoli florets, blanched	1 oz.	30 g
Red onion, sliced thin	1 oz.	30 g
Capers	1 Tbsp.	15 ml

1. Place the tortilla on a piece of parchment paper and spread it with 1 tablespoon (15 milliliters) of the Garlic Yogurt Dressing.
2. Arrange the rice in a mound across the center of the tortilla. Top the rice with the vegetables and capers.

SAFFRON VEGETABLE RISOTTO

UNIVERSITY OF WISCONSIN–STOUT, MENOMINEE, WI
Associate Professor Philip McGuirk

Yield: 12 Servings, 8 oz. (240 g) each   **Method:** Risotto

Vegetable oil	8 fl. oz.	240 ml
Garlic, chopped	1 oz.	30 g
Onions, medium dice	8 oz.	240 g
Arborio rice	1 lb.	480 g
Vegetable stock, hot	3 pt.	1.4 lt
Bay leaves	2	2
Saffron threads, crushed	1 tsp.	5 ml
Red bell peppers, medium dice	1 lb.	480 g
Green bell peppers, medium dice	1 lb.	480 g
Asparagus, cut into 1-in. (2.5-cm) pieces	12 oz.	360 g
Fresh parsley, chopped	2 Tbsp.	30 ml
Salt and white pepper	TT	TT

1 Heat 5 fluid ounces (150 milliliters) oil in a heavy saucepot. Add the garlic and onions and sweat for 1 minute. Add the rice and stir to combine with the oil. Cook over low heat for 20 minutes.

2 Add 1 pint (480 milliliters) of the stock, the bay leaves and saffron. Stir and cook the rice until it has absorbed the stock. Add the remaining stock and cook until the rice is creamy, stirring often.

3 Sauté the bell peppers and asparagus in the remaining oil until tender.

4 Add the bell peppers, asparagus and parsley to the rice and stir to combine. Adjust the seasonings with salt and white pepper.

Approximate values per serving: **Calories** 330, **Total fat** 10 g, **Saturated fat** 0 g, **Cholesterol** 0 mg, **Sodium** 190 mg, **Total carbohydrates** 32 g, **Protein** 10 g, **Vitamin A** 45%, **Vitamin C** 180%, **Claims**—good source of fiber, calcium and iron; high in vitamins A and C

SWEET AND SOUR TEMPEH

Yield: 6 Servings, 7 oz. (210 g) each   **Method:** Sautéing

Vegetable stock	8 fl. oz.	240 ml
Soy sauce	3 Tbsp.	45 ml
Tempeh, large dice	8 oz.	240 g
Pineapple chunks, canned, 20 oz. (600 g)	1	1
Vegetable oil	2 Tbsp.	30 ml
Green bell pepper, bâtonnet	5 oz.	150 g
Red bell pepper, bâtonnet	5 oz.	150 g
Onions, bâtonnet	6 oz.	180 g
Garlic, chopped	½ tsp.	2 ml
Fresh ginger, chopped	1 tsp.	5 ml
Ketchup	1 Tbsp.	15 ml
Honey	2 Tbsp.	30 ml
Cornstarch	2 Tbsp.	30 ml
White wine vinegar	2 fl. oz.	60 ml
Steamed rice	as needed for garnish	

1. Combine the stock and soy sauce in a saucepan and bring to a simmer. Add the tempeh and simmer 10 minutes. Strain the tempeh, reserving the sauce.
2. Strain the pineapple chunks and reserve the juice.
3. Dry the tempeh well. Heat the oil in a sauté pan. Add the tempeh and brown lightly. Add the bell peppers, onions, garlic and ginger. Sauté until the vegetables are nearly tender. Add the pineapple chunks to the pan.
4. Combine the tempeh cooking liquid with the reserved pineapple juice, ketchup and honey. Add enough water to total 1 pint (480 milliliters). Add the liquid to the tempeh-and-vegetable mixture and bring to a simmer.
5. Combine the cornstarch and vinegar to form a slurry. Stir the slurry into the tempeh and vegetables, bring to a simmer and cook for 2 minutes.
6. Serve the Sweet and Sour Tempeh with steamed rice.

Approximate values per serving: **Calories** 220, **Total fat** 9 g, **Saturated fat** 1.5 g, **Cholesterol** 0 mg, **Sodium** 1060 mg, **Total carbohydrates** 30 g, **Protein** 9 g, **Vitamin A** 20%, **Vitamin C** 120%, **Claims**—no cholesterol; good source of iron; high in vitamins A and C

SEITAN STROGANOFF

Yield: 4 Servings, 10 oz. (300 g) each   **Method:** Sautéing

Vegetable oil	1 Tbsp.	15 ml
Onions, small dice	8 oz.	240 g
Garlic clove, chopped	1	1
Seitan, sliced	12 oz.	360 g
Carrot, small dice	4 oz.	120 g
Mushrooms, sliced	3 oz.	90 g
Shiitake mushrooms, trimmed, sliced	3 oz.	90 g
Miso	1 oz.	30 g
Soy sauce	2 Tbsp.	30 ml
Vegetable stock	4 fl. oz.	120 ml
Silken tofu	8 oz.	240 g
Lemon juice	1 Tbsp.	15 ml
Soy cream	4 fl. oz.	120 ml
Salt and pepper	TT	TT
Wide noodles, cooked	as needed for garnish	
Fresh parsley, chopped	2 Tbsp.	60 ml

1 Heat the oil in a large sauté pan. Add the onions and garlic and sauté for 1 minute. Add the seitan, carrot and mushrooms and cook until the mushrooms release their liquid and the liquid is nearly evaporated.

2 Stir the miso and soy sauce into the vegetable stock and add it to the seitan. Bring to a simmer and remove from the heat.

3 Combine the tofu, lemon juice and soy cream in the bowl of a food processor and process until smooth.

4 Stir the tofu mixture into the seitan mixture until smooth. Do not bring to a boil or the sauce will curdle. Season to taste with salt and pepper.

5 Serve over noodles and garnish with chopped parsley.

Approximate values per serving: **Calories** 320, **Total fat** 9 g, **Saturated fat** 1 g, **Cholesterol** 0 mg, **Sodium** 1560 mg, **Total carbohydrates** 21 g, **Protein** 40 g, **Vitamin A** 70%, **Vitamin C** 20%, **Calcium** 15%, **Claims**— no cholesterol; good source of fiber, calcium and iron; high in vitamins A and C

PAN-SEARED TOFU PROVENÇAL

Yield: 4 Servings   **Method:** Sautéing

Extra-firm tofu, drained	24 oz.	720 g
Canola oil	2 Tbsp.	30 ml
Extra virgin olive oil	3 Tbsp.	45 ml
Red onions, sliced into rings	6 oz.	90 g
Garlic, chopped	2 tsp.	10 ml
White wine	8 fl. oz.	240 ml
Lemon juice	2 Tbsp.	30 ml
Kalamata olives, pitted	4 oz.	120 g
Capers	1 Tbsp.	15 ml
Salt and pepper	TT	TT
Red teardrop tomatoes, halved	6 oz.	180 g
Yellow teardrop tomatoes, halved	6 oz.	180 g
Fresh basil, chopped	4 Tbsp.	120 ml
Fresh oregano, chopped	1 Tbsp.	15 ml

1 Cut the tofu into eight 3-ounce (90-gram) triangles and pat dry on paper towels. Heat the canola oil in a large sauté pan. Sear the tofu on both sides until brown. Remove the tofu to a platter and keep warm.

2 Add the olive oil to the pan. Add the onions and garlic to the pan and sauté for 3 to 4 minutes. Deglaze the pan with the wine and lemon juice.

3 Add the olives and capers to the pan and simmer in the wine sauce until it begins to thicken slightly.

4 Add the tomatoes to the pan and reduce the sauce to the desired consistency. Stir in the basil and oregano. Return the tofu to the sauce to reheat it. Adjust the seasonings. Serve the tofu with some of the sauce spooned over it.

Approximate values per serving: **Calories** 460, **Total fat** 35 g, **Saturated fat** 3.5 g, **Cholesterol** 0 mg, **Sodium** 550 mg, **Total carbohydrates** 15 g, **Protein** 19 g, **Vitamin A** 15%, **Vitamin C** 30%, **Calcium** 35%, **Iron** 20%

CHAPTER TWENTY-FOUR

SALADS AND SALAD DRESSINGS

THIS CHAPTER DISCUSSES ALL TYPES OF SALADS: the small plate of crisp iceberg lettuce with tomato wedges, cucumber slices and ranch dressing; the dinner plate of sautéed duck breast fanned across bright red grilled radicchio and toothy green arugula, sprayed with a vinaigrette dressing; the scoop of shredded chicken, mango chutney and seasonings, bound with mayonnaise; and the bowl of artichokes and mushrooms marinated in olive oil and lemon juice.

Each of these dishes fits the definition of a salad: a single food or a mix of different foods accompanied or bound by a dressing. A salad can contain meat, grains, fruits, nuts or cheese and absolutely no lettuce. It can be an appetizer, a second course served after the appetizer, an entrée (especially at lunch), a course following the entrée in the European manner or even dessert.

The color, texture and flavor of each salad ingredient should complement those of the others, and the dressing should complement all the ingredients. Harmony is critical to a salad's success—no matter what type of salad is being prepared.

This chapter opens with a section identifying greens commonly used in salads. A discussion of salad dressings follows. Finally, techniques for preparing green salads (both tossed and composed), bound salads, vegetable salads and fruit salads are discussed.

SALAD GREENS

Identifying Salad Greens

Salad greens are not necessarily green: Some are red, yellow, white or brown. They are all, however, leafy vegetables. Many are members of the lettuce or chicory family.

LETTUCE

Lettuce (Fr. *laitue*; It. *lattuga*) has been consumed for nearly as long as people have kept records of what they and others ate. Archaeologists found that Persian royalty were served lettuce at their banquets more than 2500 years ago. Now grown and served worldwide, lettuces are members of the genus *Lactuca*. The most common types of lettuce are butterhead, crisp head, leaf and romaine.

Boston

Iceberg

Boston

Boston and bibb are two of the most popular butterhead lettuces. Their soft, pliable, pale green leaves have a buttery texture and flavor. Boston is larger and paler than bibb. Both Boston and bibb lettuce leaves form cups when separated from the heads; these cups make convenient bases for holding other foods on cold plates.

Iceberg

Iceberg lettuce is the most common of all lettuce varieties in the United States; it outsells all other varieties combined, although its appeal is declining as more types of greens become widely available. Its tightly packed spherical head is composed of crisp, pale green leaves with a very mild flavor. Iceberg lettuce remains crisp for a relatively long time after being cut or prepared. Select heads that are firm but not hard and leaves that are free of burnt or rusty tips.

Leaf

Leaf lettuce grows in bunches. It has separate, ruffle-edged leaves branching from a stalk. Because it does not grow into a firm head, it is easily damaged during harvest and transport. Both red and green leaf lettuce have bright colors, mild flavors and tender leaves. Good-quality leaf lettuce should have nicely shaped leaves free of bruises, breaks or brown spots.

Romaine

Romaine lettuce, also known as **cos**, is a loosely packed head lettuce with elongated leaves and thick midribs. Its outer leaves are dark green and although they look coarse, they are crisp, tender and tasty without being bitter. The core leaves are paler and more tender but still crisp. Romaine has enough flavor to stand up to strongly flavored dressings such as the garlic and Parmesan cheese used in a Caesar salad. A good-quality head of romaine has dark green outer leaves that are free of blemishes or yellowing.

Red and Green Leaf Lettuces

Baby Lettuces

Baby greens have similar but more subtle flavors than their mature versions. They are often less bitter and are always more tender and delicate. Because of their size and variety, they are perfect for composed salads and as delicate garnish on light entrées. **Mesclun** is a mixture of several kinds of baby lettuces.

Brune d'Hiver

Lola Rosa

Red Sails

Romaine

Baby Red Bibb

Baby Red Oak Leaf

Pirate

Baby Green Bibb

Baby Red Romaine

Micro greens are even smaller than baby lettuces. They are the first true leaves of virtually any edible greens, such as lettuce, spinach, kale and so on. Micro greens are very fragile and must be handpicked and carefully packaged for delivery. Chefs enjoy using them as garnish, especially on entrée and appetizer plates.

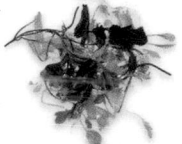

Micro Greens

CHICORY

Chicories come in a variety of colors, shapes and sizes; most are slightly bitter. Chicories are quite hearty and can also be cooked, usually grilled or braised.

Belgian Endive

Belgian endive grows in small, tight heads with pointed leaves. It is actually the shoot of a chicory root. The small sturdy leaves are white at the base with yellow fringes and tips. (A purple-tipped variety is sometimes available.) Whole leaves can be separated, trimmed and filled with soft butters, cheeses or spreads and served as an hors d'oeuvre, or they can be used for composed salads. The leaves, cut or whole, can also be added to cold

Belgian Endive

Curly Endive

Radicchio

Arugula

Dandelion

Sorrel

salads. Heads of Belgian endive are often braised or grilled and served with meat or poultry. As the name suggests, Belgian endive is imported from Belgium, but a commercial crop is now produced in California as well.

Curly Endive

In the United States, curly endive is often called by its family name, chicory, or its French name, frisée (free-ZAY). The dark green outer leaves are pointed, sturdy and slightly bitter. The yellow inner leaves are more tender and less bitter. Curly endive has a strong flavor that goes well with strong cheeses, game and citrus. It is often mixed with other greens to add texture and flavor.

Escarole

Escarole (es-kah-ROLE), sometimes called broadleaf endive, has thick leaves and a slightly bitter flavor. It has green outer leaves and pale green or yellow center leaves. Escarole is very sturdy and is often mixed with other greens for added texture. Its strong flavor stands up to full-flavored dressings and is a good accompaniment to grilled meats and poultry.

Escarole

Radicchio

Radicchio (rah-DEE-kee-oh) resembles a small red cabbage. It retains its bright reddish color when cooked and is popular braised or grilled and served as a vegetable side dish. Because of its attractive color, radicchio is popular in cold salads, but it has a very bitter flavor and should be used sparingly and mixed with other greens in a tossed salad. The leaves form cups when separated and can be used to hold other ingredients when preparing composed salads. Radicchio is quite expensive, and availability is sometimes limited.

OTHER SALAD GREENS AND INGREDIENTS

Leafy vegetables besides lettuce and chicory, as well as other ingredients, are used to add texture, flavor and color to salads. A partial listing follows.

Arugula

Arugula (ah-ROO-guh-lah), also known as rocket, is a member of the cabbage family. Arugula leaves are somewhat similar to broad dandelion leaves in size and shape. The best are 2 to 4 inches (5 to 10 centimeters) long. Arugula has a very strong, spicy, peppery flavor—so strong, in fact, that it is rarely served by itself. It is best when used to add zip to salads by combining it with other greens or with a garnish of cheese.

Dandelion

Dandelion grows as a weed throughout most of the United States. It has long, thin, toothed leaves with a prominent midrib. When purchasing dandelion for salads, look for small leaves; they are more tender and less bitter. Older, tougher leaves can be cooked and served as a vegetable.

Mâche

Mâche (mahsh) or lamb's lettuce is very tender and very delicately flavored. Its small, curved, pale to dark green leaves have a slightly nutty flavor. Because its flavor is so delicate, mâche should be combined only with other delicately flavored greens such as Boston or bibb lettuce and dressed sparingly with a light vinaigrette dressing.

Mâche

Sorrel

Sorrel, sometimes called sourgrass, has leaves similar to spinach in color and shape. Sorrel has a very tart, lemony flavor that goes well with fish and shellfish. It should be used sparingly and combined with other greens in a salad. Sorrel can also be made into soups, sauces and purées.

Spinach

Like sorrel, spinach can be cooked or used as a salad green. As a salad green, it is popularly served tossed with hot bacon dressing. Spinach is deep green with a rich flavor and tender texture. Good-quality spinach should be fairly crisp. Avoid wilted or yellowed bunches.

Spinach

Sprouts

Sprouts are not salad greens but are often used as such in salads and sandwiches. Sprouts are very young alfalfa, daikon or mustard plants. Alfalfa sprouts are very mild and sweet. Daikon and mustard sprouts are quite peppery.

Sprouts

Watercress

Watercress has tiny, dime-sized leaves and substantial stems. It has a peppery flavor and adds spice to a salad. Good-quality fresh watercress is dark green with no yellowing. To preserve its freshness, watercress must be kept very cold and moist. It is normally packed topped with ice. Individual leaves are plucked from the stems and rinsed just before service.

Watercress

Edible Flowers

Many specialty produce growers offer edible, pesticide-free blossoms. They are used for salads and as garnishes wherever a splash of color would be appreciated. Some flowers such as nasturtiums, calendulas and pansies are grown and picked specifically for eating. Others, such as yellow cucumber flowers and squash blossoms, are by-products of the vegetable industry.

Nasturtiums

Squash blossoms and other very large flowers should be cut in julienne strips before being added to salads. Pick petals from large and medium-sized flowers. Smaller whole flowers can be tossed in a salad or used as a garnish when composing a salad. Very small flowers or petals should be sprinkled on top of a salad so that they are not hidden by the greens.

Fresh Herbs

Basil, thyme, tarragon, oregano, dill, cilantro, marjoram, mint, sage, savory and even rosemary are used to add interesting flavors to otherwise ordinary salads. Because many herbs have strong flavors, use them sparingly so that the delicate flavors of the greens are not overpowered. Leafy herbs such as basil and sage can be cut chiffonade. Other herbs can be picked from their stems or chopped before being tossed with the salad greens. Flowering herbs such as chive blossoms are used like other edible flowers to add color, flavor and aroma. Refer to Chapter 6, Flavors and Flavorings, for more information on herbs.

Pansies

Calendulas

Nutrition

Salad greens are an especially healthful food. Greens contain virtually no fat and few calories and are high in vitamins A and C, iron and fiber. But when greens are garnished with meat and cheese and tossed with a dressing (many of which are oil based), fat and calories are added. In an attempt to maintain the healthful nature of greens, low-fat or fat-free dressings should be available to customers.

Purchasing and Storing Salad Greens

PURCHASING

Lettuces are grown in nearly every part of the United States; nearly all types are available year-round. Other important salad greens such as spinach are available all year; many of the specialty greens are seasonal.

Lettuce is generally packed in cases of 24 heads with varying weights. Other salad greens are packed in trays or boxes of various sizes and weights.

> ### SAFETY ALERT
> #### Flowers
>
> Many flowers and blossoms are toxic, especially those grown from bulbs. Even flowers that would otherwise be edible may contain pesticides that can be harmful if ingested. Use only flowers grown specifically for use as food; purchase edible flowers only from reputable purveyors.

Remove wilted leaves and trim discolorations on lettuce before using.

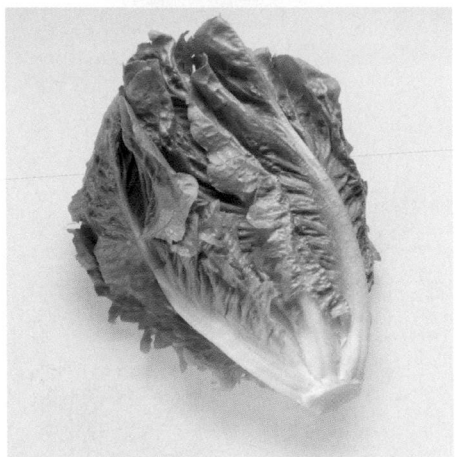

Trimmed head of romaine lettuce ready for tearing or cutting.

Because salad greens are simply washed and eaten, it is extremely important that they be as fresh and blemish-free as possible. Try to purchase salad greens daily. All greens should be fresh looking, with no yellowing. Heads should be heavy, with little or no damage to the outer leaves.

Many types of salad greens are available precut and prewashed. These greens are often vacuum packed to increase shelf life, although delicate greens are sometimes loosely packaged in 5- to 10-pound (2- to 5-kilogram) boxes. Precut and prewashed greens are relatively expensive but can reduce labor costs dramatically.

STORING

Although some types of salad greens are hearty enough to keep for a week or more under proper conditions, all salad greens are highly perishable. Generally, softer-leaved varieties such as Boston and bibb tend to perish more quickly than the crisper-leaved varieties such as iceberg and romaine. Frequently, greens that have wilted slightly can be revived by soaking them in chilled water for up to an hour. The greens should then be drained and refrigerated until crisp.

Greens should be stored in their original protective cartons in a specifically designated refrigerator. Ideally, greens should be stored at temperatures between 34°F and 38°F (1°C and 3°C). (Most other vegetables should be stored at warmer temperatures of 40°F to 50°F [4°C to 10°C].) Greens should not be stored with tomatoes, apples or other fruits that emit ethylene gas, which causes greens to wilt and accelerates spoilage.

Do not wash greens until needed as excess water causes them to deteriorate quickly.

Preparing Salad Greens

All salad greens, even those purchased precut and prewashed, will need to undergo some preparation before service, principally tearing, cutting, washing and drying.

TEARING AND CUTTING

Some chefs want all salad greens torn by hand. Delicate greens such as butterhead and baby lettuces look nicer, and it is less likely that they will be bruised if hand-torn. But often it is not practical to hand-tear all greens. It is perfectly acceptable to cut hardy greens with a knife. And it can be more practical to snip small lettuce leaves and fresh herbs with kitchen scissors.

PROCEDURE FOR **CUTTING ROMAINE LETTUCE**

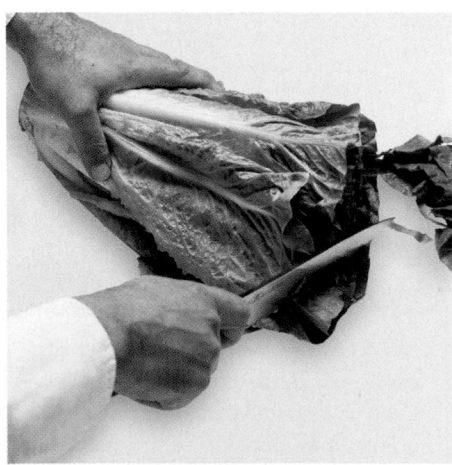

❶ To cut romaine lettuce, trim the outer leaves and damaged tips with a chef's knife and split the head lengthwise.

❷ Make one or two cuts along the length of the head, leaving the root intact, then cut across the width of the head.

❸ Alternative method: Trim the outer leaves and damaged tips with a chef's knife. Pull the leaves from the core and cut the rib out of each leaf. The leaf can then be cut to the desired size.

PROCEDURE FOR **CORING ICEBERG LETTUCE**

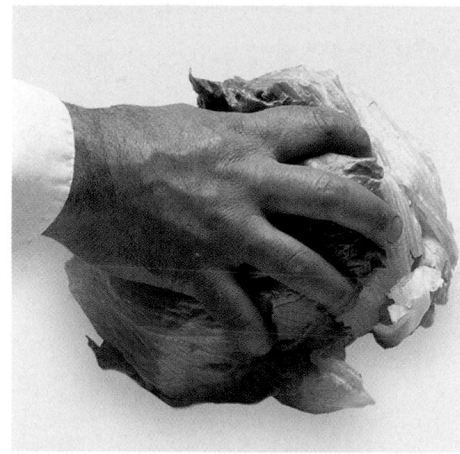

1 Loosen the core by gripping the head and smacking the core on the cutting board. (Do not use too much force or you may bruise the lettuce.)

2 Remove the core and cut the lettuce as desired.

PROCEDURE FOR **REMOVING THE MIDRIB FROM SPINACH**

Fold the leaf in half and pull off the stem and midrib. Only the tender leaf should remain.

SAFETY ALERT
Hand Washing

Because salads are not cooked, it is especially important to be extra careful about proper hand washing when preparing them. Remember that many health departments require single-use gloves to be worn—and changed frequently—whenever working with products that will not be cooked before service.

WASHING

All lettuces and other salad greens should be washed before use. Even though they may look clean, greens may harbor hidden insects, sand, soil and pesticides. Pay special attention to greens sourced from local farms that may not have facilities to preclean their produce. All greens should be washed after they are torn or cut. Whole heads can be washed by repeatedly dipping them in cold water and allowing them to drain. But washing whole heads is not recommended: It will not remove anything trapped near the head's center, and water trapped in the leaves can accelerate spoilage.

PROCEDURE FOR **WASHING SALAD GREENS**

1 Clean and sanitize a sink, then fill it with cold water, which should be slightly warmer than the temperature of the greens. Place the cut or torn greens in the water.

2 Gently stir the water and greens with your hands and remove the greens. Do not allow the greens to soak. Using fresh water each time, repeat the procedure until no grit can be detected on the bottom of the sink after the greens are removed.

DRYING

Salad greens should be dried after washing. Wet greens do not stay as crisp as thoroughly dried ones. Also, wet greens tend to repel oil-based dressings and dilute their flavors. Greens may be dried by draining them well in a colander and blotting them with absorbent cloth or paper towels, or, preferably, they can be dried in a salad spinner, which uses centrifugal force to remove the water. Sanitize the spinner after each use.

PROCEDURE FOR **DRYING GREENS**

After washing the greens, place them in the basket of a salad spinner and spin for approximately 30 seconds.

SALAD DRESSINGS

A dressing is a sauce for a salad. Just as sauces for hot foods should complement rather than mask the flavor of the principal food, the sauce (dressing) for a salad should complement rather than mask the flavors of the other ingredients. Although a great many ingredients can be used to make salad dressings, most are based on either a mixture of oil and vinegar, called a vinaigrette, or a mayonnaise or other emulsified product.

Vinaigrette-style dressings can be made without oil; creamy dressings similar to mayonnaise-based dressings can be made with sour cream, yogurt or buttermilk instead of mayonnaise. Nevertheless, for all practical purposes these dressings are still prepared like vinaigrettes and mayonnaise-based dressings, and they are treated that way here.

Vinaigrette Dressings

The simple vinaigrette, also known as basic **French dressing**, is a temporary emulsion of oil and vinegar seasoned with salt and pepper. The standard ratio is three parts oil to one part vinegar. The ratio can vary, however. When using strongly flavored oils, less than three parts oil to one part vinegar generally suffices. In some recipes, all or part of the vinegar is replaced with citrus juice, in which case it may take more than one part vinegar and citrus juice to three parts oil to achieve the proper acidity level. Mild or sweet vinegars such as balsamic may require less oil to balance the flavors in the dressing. The best way to determine the correct ratio of oil to vinegar is to taste the dressing, preferably on the food it will dress.

Oils and vinegars have unique flavors that can be mixed and matched to achieve the correct balance for a particular salad. Olive oil goes well with red wine vinegar; nut oils go well with white wine or sherry vinegars. Neutral-flavored oils such as canola, corn or safflower can be mixed with a flavored vinegar.

Oil and vinegar repel each other and will separate almost immediately when mixed. They should be whisked together immediately before use.

OILS

Many types of oil can be used to make salad dressings. Light, neutral-flavored oils such as canola, corn, cottonseed, soybean and safflower are relatively low priced and used extensively for this purpose. Other oils can be used to add flavor. Olive oil is very popular; both mild-flavored pure olive oil and full-flavored extra virgin olive oil are used. Nut oils such as hazelnut and walnut are expensive, but they add unique and interesting flavors. Infused oils are also popular. (See pages 214–215.)

VINEGARS

Many different vinegars can be used to make salad dressings. Red wine vinegar is the most common because it is inexpensive and its flavor blends well with many foods. But other vinegars such as cider, balsamic and white wine are also used. Fruit-flavored vinegars are extremely popular and widely available, as are herb- and garlic-flavored ones.

Flavored vinegars are easy to make. Fruit, herbs or garlic are added to a wine vinegar (either red or white) and left for several days for the flavors to blend. The vinegar is then strained and used as desired.

Acidic juices such as lemon, orange and lime are sometimes substituted for all or part of the vinegar in a salad dressing.

OTHER FLAVORING INGREDIENTS

Herbs, spices, shallots, garlic, mustard and sugar are only a few of the many flavoring ingredients used to enhance a vinaigrette dressing. Items such as herbs, shallots and garlic should be minced or chopped before being added to the dressing. If dried herbs are used, the dressing should rest for at least 1 hour to allow the flavors to develop. Other ingredients may be added at any time.

French dressing classically, a vinaigrette dressing made from oil, vinegar, salt and pepper; in the United States, the term also refers to a commercially prepared dressing that is creamy, tartly sweet and red-orange in color

NOT JUST FOR SALADS

With its light taste and texture, vinaigrette dressing makes an appealing sauce where a light touch is desired. It is quick to make and versatile; changing the taste of a vinaigrette is only a matter of switching the type of oil and vinegar used. Its balanced acidity makes vinaigrette a good foil for fish dishes, as shown in Pan-Seared Sea Bass with Beet Vinaigrette (page 512).

PROCEDURE FOR **PREPARING A VINAIGRETTE**

① Choose an oil and vinegar that complement each other as well as the foods they will dress.

② Combine the vinegar, seasonings and any other flavorings in a bowl.

③ Whisk in the oil gradually.

④ Allow the finished dressing to rest a few hours at room temperature before using so that the flavors can blend.

⑤ Rewhisk immediately before use.

Whisking together the vinaigrette dressing.

emulsion a uniform mixture of two unmixable liquids; it is often temporary (for example, oil in water)

BASIC VINAIGRETTE DRESSING

Yield: Approximately 1 qt. (1 lt)

Wine vinegar	8 fl. oz.	240 ml
Salt	2 tsp.	10 ml
Pepper	TT	TT
Salad oil	24 fl. oz.	720 ml

① Combine the vinegar, salt and pepper and mix well. Whisk in the oil gradually. Store at room temperature.

VARIATIONS:

Dijon Vinaigrette—Add 4 ounces (120 grams) Dijon-style mustard to the vinegar and proceed with the recipe.

Herb Vinaigrette—Add 2 tablespoons (30 milliliters) fresh herbs or 1 tablespoon (15 milliliters) dried herbs such as basil, tarragon, thyme, marjoram and chives to the vinaigrette.

Approximate values per 1-fl.-oz. (30-ml) serving: **Calories** 190, **Total fat** 22 g, **Saturated fat** 3 g, **Cholesterol** 0 mg, **Sodium** 75 mg, **Total carbohydrates** 0 g, **Protein** 0 g, **Claims**—no cholesterol; low sodium; no sugar

Mayonnaise

Although most food service operations buy commercially made mayonnaise, every chef should know how it is made to more fully understand how to use it and why it reacts the way it does when used. Knowing how to make mayonnaise also allows the chef to create a mayonnaise with the exact flavorings desired.

Mayonnaise is an **emulsion**. An emulsion, or emulsified sauce, is formed when two liquids that would not ordinarily form a stable mixture are forced together and held in suspension, as discussed in Chapter 10, Stocks and Sauces. To make mayonnaise, oil is whisked together with a very small amount of vinegar. (It is the water in the vinegar that does not normally mix with oil.) As the oil and vinegar are whisked together, the oil breaks into microscopic droplets that are separated from each other by a thin barrier of vinegar. If left alone, the droplets would quickly regroup, forming a large puddle of oil and a small puddle of vinegar. To prevent the oil droplets from regrouping, an emulsifier is added. For mayonnaise, the emulsifier is lecithin, a protein found in egg yolks. (The acid in the vinegar also helps form the emulsion.) Lecithin has the unique ability to combine with both oil and water. It surrounds the oil droplets, preventing them from coming in contact with each other and regrouping.

The balance of vinegar, oil, lecithin and agitation (whipping) is crucial to achieve a proper emulsion. The higher the proportion of oil to vinegar, the thicker the sauce will be. The higher the proportion of vinegar to oil, the thinner the sauce will be. (For example, the Emulsified Vinaigrette Dressing on page 724 is a thin emulsion.) Some chefs add ½ fluid ounce (15 milliliters) boiling water to each 7 fluid ounces (210 milliliters) finished mayonnaise to help maintain the emulsion.

MAYONNAISE VS. SALAD DRESSING

Commercially prepared salad dressing is often used as a substitute for "real" mayonnaise. Although it may look, smell and spread like the real thing, salad dressing tends to be sweeter than mayonnaise. Salad dressing costs less than real mayonnaise because it is made without egg yolks, relying instead on chemical thickening agents. The cost is reduced further because the FDA requires salad dressing to contain only 30 percent oil, whereas mayonnaise must contain at least 65 percent oil.

TABLE 24.1	TROUBLESHOOTING MAYONNAISE	
PROBLEM	**CAUSE**	**SOLUTION**
Too thin	Not enough oil added	Continue adding oil until mixture thickens
	Too much lemon juice or vinegar added	Adjust formula
Too thick	Too much oil added for the amount of yolks	Adjust formula
	Insufficient vinegar used	Add more vinegar
Sauce breaks or curdles	Inadequate emulsification when mixing	Whisk vigorously, adding oil slowly; use electric mixer to make a more stable emulsion; attempt repairing the mayonnaise
	Oil too cold when added	Use room-temperature oil; attempt repairing the mayonnaise
	Oil added too quickly	Attempt repairing the mayonnaise
	Too much oil added	Adjust formula using additional egg yolks or less oil; attempt repairing the mayonnaise

There is a limit to how much oil each egg yolk can emulsify, however. One yolk contains enough lecithin to emulsify approximately 7 fluid ounces (210 milliliters) of oil. If more than that amount of oil per egg yolk is added, the sauce will break; that is, the oil and vinegar will separate, and the mayonnaise will become very thin. Often mayonnaise that has broken can be repaired by beating the broken mayonnaise into additional egg yolks or prepared mayonnaise until the emulsion re-forms. To repair a broken mayonnaise, slowly beat 7 fluid ounces (210 milliliters) broken mayonnaise into one egg yolk or 4 fluid ounces (120 milliliters) prepared mayonnaise. Adjust the amount of egg yolk or prepared mayonnaise to be used according to the batch that has broken. Table 24.1 lists common problems that can occur when making mayonnaise and some solutions.

INGREDIENTS

A neutral-flavored vegetable oil is most often used for a standard mayonnaise. Other oils are used to contribute their special flavors. For example, olive oil is used to make a strong garlic mayonnaise called *aïoli*.

Wine vinegar is used for a standard mayonnaise. Flavored vinegars such as tarragon vinegar are often used to create unique flavors.

Seasonings vary according to the intended use but typically include dry mustard, salt, pepper and lemon juice.

Broken mayonnaise is thin and separated or curdled.

CONVENIENCE PRODUCTS

A great many prepared and dry-mix salad dressings are available. Although they vary greatly in quality, they can be very economical; they offer consistency, reduced labor costs and, sometimes, reduced food costs. Some of these products use stabilizers, artificial flavorings and colors; nearly all contain preservatives. When considering the advantages of prepared or dry-mix salad dressings, always keep quality in mind.

PROCEDURE FOR **PREPARING MAYONNAISE**

SAFETY ALERT
Mayonnaise

The raw eggs in freshly prepared mayonnaise make it a potentially hazardous food. Use pasteurized eggs if possible, chill the ingredients before mixing and keep the finished mayonnaise at 41°F (5°C) or below. Although there is sufficient acid in commercially prepared mayonnaise to serve as a deterrent to bacterial growth, homemade mayonnaise should not be handled in the same manner, as it does not necessarily have the same protection.

1. Gather all ingredients and hold at room temperature. Room-temperature ingredients emulsify more easily than cold ones.
2. By hand or in an electric mixer or food processor, whip the egg yolks on high speed until frothy.
3. Add the seasonings to the yolks and whip to combine. Salt and other seasonings will dissolve or blend more easily when added at this point rather than to the finished mayonnaise.
4. Add a small amount of the liquid (for example, vinegar) from the recipe and whip to combine.
5. With the mixer on high or whisking vigorously by hand, begin to add the oil very slowly until an emulsion forms.
6. After the emulsion forms, the oil can be added a little more quickly but still in a slow, steady stream. The mayonnaise can now be whipped at a slightly slower speed.
7. The mayonnaise will become very thick as more oil is added. A small amount of liquid can be added if it becomes too thick. Alternate between oil and liquid two or three times until all the oil is added and the correct consistency is reached. Important: A large egg yolk can emulsify up to 7 fluid ounces (210 milliliters) oil; adding more oil may cause the mayonnaise to break.
8. Adjust the seasonings and refrigerate immediately.

MAYONNAISE

Yield: Approximately 1 qt. (1 lt)

Egg yolks, pasteurized	4	4
Salt	1 tsp.	5 ml
White pepper	TT	TT
Dry mustard	1 tsp.	5 ml
Wine vinegar	3 Tbsp.	45 ml
Salad oil	28 fl. oz.	840 ml
Lemon juice	TT	TT

1. Place the egg yolks in the bowl of a mixer and whip on high speed until thick and lemon-colored.
2. Add the dry ingredients and half the vinegar to the yolks; whisk to combine.
3. Begin to add the oil a drop at a time until the mixture begins to thicken and an emulsion begins to form.
4. Add the remaining oil in a slow steady stream, thinning the mayonnaise occasionally by adding a little vinegar. Continue until all the oil and vinegar have been incorporated.
5. Adjust the seasonings and add lemon juice to taste.
6. Refrigerate until needed.

Approximate values per 1-fl.-oz. (30-ml) serving: **Calories** 230, **Total fat** 26 g, **Saturated fat** 3.5 g, **Cholesterol** 25 mg, **Sodium** 75 mg, **Total carbohydrates** 0 g, **Protein** 0 g

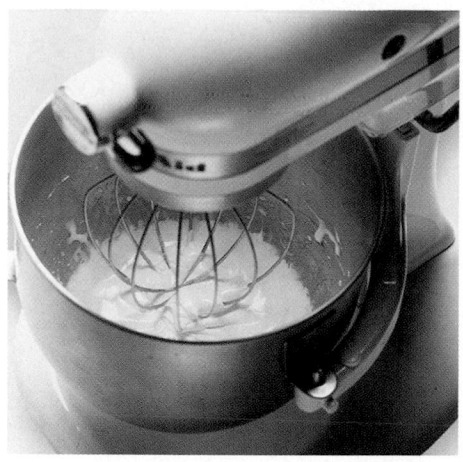

❶ Whipping the egg yolks until frothy.

❷ Adding the oil very slowly, allowing the emulsion to form.

❸ The finished mayonnaise.

Mayonnaise-Based Dressings

Mayonnaise-based salad dressings are salad dressings that use mayonnaise as a base, with other ingredients added for flavor, color and texture. These ingredients include dairy products (especially buttermilk and sour cream), vinegar, fruit juice, vegetables (either puréed or minced), tomato paste, garlic, onions, herbs, spices, condiments, capers, anchovies and boiled eggs. Recipes for several mayonnaise-based salad dressings appear at the end of this chapter.

Emulsified Vinaigrette Dressings

An emulsified vinaigrette is a standard vinaigrette dressing emulsified with whole eggs. An emulsified vinaigrette dressing is thinner and lighter than a mayonnaise-based dressing and heavier than a basic vinaigrette. Its flavor is similar to a basic vinaigrette, but it will not separate and it clings to greens quite easily.

PROCEDURE FOR **PREPARING AN EMULSIFIED VINAIGRETTE DRESSING**

❶ Gather all ingredients and hold at room temperature. Room-temperature ingredients emulsify more easily than cold ones.

❷ Whip the eggs until frothy.

❸ Add the dry ingredients and any flavorings such as garlic, shallots and herbs.

❹ Add a small amount of the liquid from the recipe and whip to incorporate the ingredients.

❺ With the mixer on high or whisking vigorously by hand, begin adding the oil very slowly until the emulsion forms.

❻ After the emulsion is formed, add the oil a little more quickly, but still in a slow, steady stream.

❼ Alternate between oil and liquid two or three times until all the oil is added. The dressing should be much thinner than mayonnaise. If it is too thick, it can be thinned with a little water, vinegar or lemon juice. Determine which to use by first tasting the dressing.

EMULSIFIED VINAIGRETTE DRESSING

Yield: Approximately 1 qt. (1 lt)

Eggs, pasteurized	2	2
Salt	1 Tbsp.	15 ml
White pepper	½ tsp.	2 ml
Paprika	1 Tbsp.	15 ml
Dry mustard	1 Tbsp.	15 ml
Granulated sugar	1 Tbsp.	15 ml
Herbes de Provence	1 Tbsp.	15 ml
Cayenne pepper	TT	TT
Wine vinegar or cider vinegar	4 fl. oz.	120 ml
Salad oil	24 fl. oz.	720 ml
Lemon juice	3 fl. oz.	90 ml

1 Place the eggs in the bowl of a mixer and whip at high speed until frothy.

2 Add the dry ingredients and approximately 1 fluid ounce (30 milliliters) vinegar to the eggs; whip to combine.

3 While whipping at high speed, begin adding the oil very slowly until an emulsion forms.

4 Add the remaining oil in a slow, steady stream. Occasionally thin the dressing by adding a little vinegar and lemon juice. Continue until all the oil, vinegar and lemon juice have been incorporated.

5 Adjust the flavor and consistency.

6 Refrigerate until needed.

Approximate values per 1-fl.-oz. (30-ml) serving: **Calories** 200, **Total fat** 22 g, **Saturated fat** 3 g, **Cholesterol** 15 mg, **Sodium** 220 mg, **Total carbohydrates** 1 g, **Protein** 1 g

1 Whipping the whole eggs.

2 Adding the oil drop by drop to establish the emulsion.

3 The finished emulsified vinaigrette dressing.

PREPARATION METHODS

There are two types of **green salads**: tossed and composed. The more informal **tossed salad** is prepared by placing the greens, garnishes and dressing in a large bowl and tossing to combine. A **composed salad** usually has a more elegant look. It is prepared by arranging each of the ingredients on plates in an artistic fashion.

Other types of salads include **bound salads**, which are cooked meats, poultry, fish, shellfish, pasta or potatoes bound with a dressing; **vegetable salads**; and **fruit salads**.

TABLE 24.2 MATCHING DRESSINGS AND SALAD GREENS	
DRESSING	**GREENS**
Vinaigrette dressing made with vegetable oil and red wine vinegar	Any greens: iceberg, romaine, leaf lettuce, butterhead lettuce, escarole, curly endive, Belgian endive, radicchio, baby lettuces, sorrel, arugula, dandelion, micro greens
Vinaigrette dressing made with a nut oil and white wine or sherry vinegar	Delicate greens: butterhead lettuce, bibb lettuce, Belgian endive, baby lettuces, mâche, watercress, micro greens
Vinaigrette dressing made with vegetable oil and balsamic vinegar	Any greens: romaine, leaf lettuce, radicchio, arugula
Emulsified vinaigrette dressing	Any greens: romaine, leaf lettuce, butterhead lettuce, escarole, curly endive, Belgian endive, radicchio, baby lettuces, sorrel, arugula, watercress
Mayonnaise-based dressing such as blue cheese or green goddess	Hardy greens: iceberg, romaine, leaf lettuce, escarole, curly endive, sorrel, dandelion

Green Salads

TOSSED SALADS

Tossed salads are made from leafy vegetables such as lettuce, spinach, watercress, arugula or dandelion greens. They may consist only of greens and dressing, or they can be garnished with fruits, vegetables, nuts or cheese. They can be dressed with many different types of dressings, from a light oil and vinegar to a hearty hot bacon. It is important that salad dressings be added at the last possible moment before service. Acidic dressings cause most greens to wilt and become soggy. Salting greens lightly before dressing with vinaigrette helps keep them crisp.

Matching Dressings and Salad Greens

There is a simple rule to follow when choosing dressings for salads: The more delicate the texture and flavor of the greens or other ingredients, the lighter and more subtle the dressing should be. Vinaigrette-based dressings are much lighter than mayonnaise-based or similar dressings and should be used with butterhead lettuces, mâche or other delicate greens. Crisp head lettuce such as iceberg and hardy lettuce such as romaine can stand up to heavier, mayonnaise-based or similar dressings. Vinaigrette dressings coat greens evenly, whereas thicker dressings tend to clump. When making a tossed salad, begin with a portion of the dressing, adding more only as needed to prevent the greens from wilting. Table 24.2 lists some popular greens and dressing combinations. Whichever combinations are selected, cold salads should always be served on chilled plates.

Salad Garnishes

It is impossible to make a complete list of the garnishes that can be combined with salad greens for a tossed salad. The following is a partial list:

▶ Vegetables—nearly any vegetable (raw, blanched or fully cooked) cut into appropriate sizes and uniform shapes

▶ Fruits—citrus segments, apples or pears; dried fruits such as raisins, currants or apricots

▶ Eggs, meats, poultry, fish and shellfish—poached or hard-boiled eggs; cooked meats and poultry sliced or diced neatly and uniformly; poached, grilled or cured fish, diced or flaked; small, whole cooked shellfish such as shrimp and scallops; lobster or crab sliced, diced or chopped

▶ Cheeses—grated hard cheeses such as Parmesan, Romano or Asiago; semihard cheeses such as Cheddar or Swiss, cut julienne or shredded

▶ Nuts—nearly any are appropriate, roasted, candied or smoked

▶ Croutons—assorted breads, seasoned in various ways and toasted

CROUTONS

A crouton is simply a piece of bread that is toasted, sautéed or dried. Two types are often used.

The more familiar ones are small seasoned cubes of bread that are baked or toasted and sprinkled over soups or salads.

A more classic variety is made by sautéing slices of bread in clarified butter or olive oil until brown and crisp. The bread may be rough slices from a baguette, or shapes (such as hearts, diamonds or circles) cut from larger slices. Sautéed croutons have two advantages over the toasted variety: They stay crisp longer after coming in contact with moist foods, and they gain flavor from the butter or olive oil in which they are cooked. Sautéed croutons can be used to decorate the border of a serving dish, as a base for canapés, as a garnish for soups, as an accompaniment to spreads or caviar or as a base under some meat and game dishes.

PROCEDURE FOR **MAKING TOSSED SALADS**

1. Select greens with various colors, textures and flavors.
2. Carefully cut or tear, wash and dry the greens.
3. Prepare the garnishes as directed or desired.
4. Prepare the dressing.
5. Combine the greens, garnishes and dressing by tossing them together, or toss the greens and garnishes and, using a spray bottle, spray the greens with the dressing.

MESCLUN SALAD WITH RASPBERRY VINAIGRETTE

Yield: 6 Servings   **Method:** Tossed

Baby lettuces, assorted	approx. 8 heads	approx. 8 heads
Mâche	4 oz.	120 g
Fresh herbs	2 Tbsp.	30 ml
Edible flowers	approx. 12	approx. 12
Raspberry Vinaigrette (page 732)	4 fl. oz.	120 ml

1. Trim, wash and dry the baby lettuces and mâche.
2. Pick the fresh herbs from their stems. Leafy herbs such as basil may be cut chiffonade or left as whole leaves.
3. If desired, pick the petals from the edible flowers. Small flowers may be left whole.
4. Place the lettuces and mâche in a bowl and add the herbs. Ladle the Raspberry Vinaigrette over them and toss gently, using two spoons.
5. Transfer the salad to six cold plates. Some of the larger leaves may be used as liners if desired.
6. Garnish each salad with flowers or flower petals.

Approximate values per serving: **Calories** 150, **Total fat** 9 g, **Saturated fat** 1 g, **Cholesterol** 0 mg, **Sodium** 180 mg, **Total carbohydrates** 14 g, **Protein** 4 g, **Vitamin A** 35%, **Vitamin C** 120%

COMPOSED SALADS

Composed green salads usually use a green as a base and are built by artistically arranging other ingredients on the plate. There are usually four components: the base, body, garnish and dressing.

The **base** is usually a layer of salad greens that line the plate on which the salad will be served. Depending on the desired effect, the leaves can be cup-shaped or flat.

The **body** is the main ingredient. It can be lettuce or other greens, or another salad made from cooked or blended ingredients, such as chicken salad or fruit.

The **garnish** is added to the salad for color, texture and flavor. It can be as substantial as a grilled, sliced duck breast or as simple as a sprinkling of chopped herbs; it can be warm or cold. The choice is unlimited, but whatever is used should always complement and balance the flavor of the body.

The **dressing** should complement rather than mask the other flavors in the salad. If the body already contains a dressing, such as a bound salad, additional dressing may not be necessary.

Composed green salads are usually dressed by ladling the dressing over the salad after it is plated. Alternatively, the individual ingredients can be dressed before they are arranged on the plate. A third method that may be limited by the intricacy of the salad

Transferring composed salads to chilled plates for service.

but will save precious time during a busy period is to prepare individual salads on a sheet pan. Then, just before service, mist them with dressing using a spray bottle designated for this purpose; then transfer them to chilled plates using a spatula.

PROCEDURE FOR MAKING COMPOSED SALADS

1. Gather all ingredients for the salad and wash, trim, cut, cook, chill or otherwise prepare them as necessary or as called for in the recipe.
2. Arrange all ingredients artistically on the plates, dressing each ingredient as desired or as directed in the recipe.
3. At service time, heat or cook any items that are being served hot and add them to the salad.

SALAD NIÇOISE

Yield: 6 Servings   **Method:** Composed

Red wine vinegar	4 fl. oz.	120 ml
Salt and pepper	TT	TT
Virgin olive oil	12 fl. oz.	360 ml
Fresh basil leaves, chiffonade	12	12
Chicory	1 head	1 head
Tomatoes	6	6
Cucumbers	1 lb. 8 oz.	720 g
Green beans	12 oz.	360 g
Eggs, hard-boiled, chilled	6	6
Artichokes	6	6
Romaine lettuce, large leaves, washed	12	12
New potatoes, size B, boiled, quartered, chilled	12 oz.	360 g
Green bell peppers, bâtonnet	2	2
Tuna, fresh, grilled and chilled	1 lb. 8 oz.	720 g
Niçoise olives	4 oz.	120 g

1. Make a vinaigrette dressing using the red wine vinegar, salt, pepper, olive oil and basil.
2. Wash and dry the chicory.
3. Core each tomato and cut into eight wedges.
4. Peel and slice the cucumbers.
5. Trim the green beans and cook al dente.
6. Peel the eggs and cut into wedges.
7. Cook the artichokes. Trim the outer leaves from each artichoke, leaving only the heart. Remove the choke from the heart and cut each heart into quarters.
8. Line each cold plate with two romaine lettuce leaves, then arrange the remaining ingredients artistically. Use the contrasting shapes, colors and textures to create an attractive presentation.
9. At service time, whisk the dressing to combine the ingredients and pour approximately 2½ fluid ounces (75 milliliters) over each salad.

Approximate values per serving: **Calories** 890, **Total fat** 70 g, **Saturated fat** 11 g, **Cholesterol** 200 mg, **Sodium** 760 mg, **Total carbohydrates** 21 g, **Protein** 44 g, **Vitamin A** 130%, **Vitamin C** 60%, **Iron** 30%

BOUND SALADS

The creative chef can prepare a wide variety of salads by combining cooked meats, poultry, fish, shellfish, potatoes, pasta, grains and/or legumes with a dressing and garnishes. Although the combinations vary greatly, these salads are grouped here because their

MISE EN PLACE

◄ Wash and chop basil in chiffonade.
◄ Hard-boil eggs and chill.
◄ Wash lettuce.
◄ Boil and quarter potatoes and chill.
◄ Wash bell peppers and cut in bâtonnet.
◄ Grill tuna and chill.

1. Lining a cold salad plate with a base of lettuce leaves.

2. The composed Salad Niçoise.

ingredients are all bound. That is, each salad consists of one or more ingredients held together in a cohesive mass. The binding agent can be either a vinaigrette or a mayonnaise-based or similar dressing. The ingredients should be evenly distributed throughout, and the degree of cohesiveness can range from tightly packed to flaky and easily separated.

The foods that can be used to produce bound salads are so varied that it is impossible to list them all. Generalizing preparation techniques is also difficult. There are as many ways to prepare a bound salad as there are ingredients, dressings and garnishes.

Bound salads can be used as the body of a composed salad (for instance, a serving of egg salad on a bed of greens). Some are used in sandwiches but not ordinarily as side dishes—for example, tuna or chicken salad. Some are served as side dishes but not in sandwiches—for example, potato or pasta salad. Follow specific recipes and traditional uses for each salad to build confidence. Then use these skills and imagination to create enticing new salad combinations.

GUIDELINES FOR MAKING BOUND SALADS

❶ Preparing a salad from cooked foods is a good opportunity to use leftovers, but be sure they are fresh and of good quality. The finished salad can be only as good as each of its ingredients.

❷ When making a bound salad, choose ingredients whose flavors blend well and complement each other.

❸ Choose ingredients for color; a few colorful ingredients will turn a plain salad into a spectacular one.

❹ To improve appearance, cut all ingredients the same size.

❺ All ingredients should be cut into pieces that are small enough to be eaten easily with a fork.

❻ Be sure all meats, poultry, fish and shellfish are properly cooked before using them. Improperly cooked foods can cause food-borne illness and spoilage.

❼ Always chill cooked ingredients well before using them. Warm ingredients promote bacterial growth, especially in mayonnaise-based salads.

❽ Always use dressings sparingly. They should enhance the flavors of the other salad ingredients, not mask them.

MISE EN PLACE

▶ Cook chicken and chill.
▶ Wash and peel celery and chop into small dice.
▶ Wash and slice green onions.

Adding grapes to the chicken salad.

CHUTNEY CHICKEN SALAD

Yield: 8 lb. (3.8 kg)   **Method:** Bound

Chicken meat, cooked	5 lb.	2.4 kg
Celery, small dice	8 oz.	240 g
Green onions, sliced	3 oz.	90 g
Mango chutney	12 oz.	360 g
Mayonnaise	1 pt.	480 ml
Seedless grapes	12 oz.	360 g

❶ Remove any bones, skin and fat from the chicken and cut the meat into large dice.
❷ Combine the chicken meat, celery, green onions, mango chutney and mayonnaise in a bowl; mix well.
❸ Cut the grapes in half. Add them to the chicken mixture and toss gently to combine.

Approximate values per 4-oz. (120-g) serving: **Calories** 230, **Total fat** 14 g, **Saturated fat** 3 g, **Cholesterol** 70 mg, **Sodium** 135 mg, **Total carbohydrates** 4 g, **Protein** 22 g

Vegetable Salads

Vegetable salads are made from cooked or raw vegetables or a combination of both. They can be served on buffets, as an appetizer or as a salad course. As with other salads, vegetable salads must successfully combine color, texture and flavor. Some vegetable salads such as coleslaw and carrot-raisin salad are made with mayonnaise. Most, however, are made by either marinating the vegetables or combining them in a vinaigrette dressing.

Almost any vegetable can be successfully marinated. The amount of time depends on the vegetables and the marinade, but several hours to overnight is usually sufficient for flavors to blend. Soft vegetables such as mushrooms, zucchini and cucumbers can be added directly to a cold marinade. Hard vegetables such as carrots and cauliflower should be blanched in salted water, refreshed, drained and then added to a cold marinade. Carrots, artichokes, mushrooms, cauliflower, zucchini, pearl onions and the like are sometimes simmered quickly in a marinade flavored with lemon juice and olive oil, and then served cold. This style is called **à la grecque**.

Many marinated salads will last several days under proper refrigeration. As the salads age in the marinade, they will change in appearance and texture. This may or may not be desirable. For example, mushrooms and artichokes become more flavorful, whereas green vegetables are discolored by the acids in the marinade. If marinated salads are prepared in advance, check their appearance as well as their seasonings carefully at service time.

à la grecque (ah la grehk) a preparation style in which vegetables are marinated in olive oil, lemon juice and herbs, then served cold

PROCEDURE FOR **PREPARING VEGETABLE SALADS**

1. Gather and wash all vegetables.
2. Trim, cut, shred or otherwise prepare the vegetables as desired or as directed in the recipe.
3. Blanch or cook the vegetables if necessary.
4. Combine the vegetables with the marinade or dressing. Adjust the seasonings.

TOMATO AND ASPARAGUS SALAD WITH FRESH MOZZARELLA

Yield: 6 Servings   **Method:** Composed

Asparagus	2 lb.	960 g
Basic Vinaigrette Dressing (page 720)	12 fl. oz.	360 ml
Tomatoes	6	6
Leaf lettuce	1 head	1 head
Fresh mozzarella	12 oz.	360 g
Fresh basil leaves, chiffonade	12	12

1. Trim the asparagus and blanch in salted water. Refresh, drain and marinate in 6 fluid ounces (180 milliliters) Basic Vinaigrette Dressing for approximately 15 minutes.
2. Core each tomato and cut into six wedges.
3. Clean the lettuce and separate the leaves.
4. Slice the mozzarella into 18 slices.
5. Arrange the tomatoes, cheese and asparagus on six plates, using the lettuce as a base. Pour on the remaining dressing and garnish with the basil.

Approximate values per serving: **Calories** 410, **Total fat** 32 g, **Saturated fat** 9 g, **Cholesterol** 35 mg, **Sodium** 370 mg, **Total carbohydrates** 11 g, **Protein** 19 g, **Vitamin A** 20%, **Vitamin C** 110%, **Calcium** 40%

MISE EN PLACE
◀ Wash basil and cut in chiffonade.

Fruit Salads

There are so many different fruits with beautiful bright colors and sweet delicious flavors that preparing fruit salads is easy work. Fruit salads are a refreshing addition to buffets and can be served as the first course of a lunch or dinner. A more elaborate fruit salad can be served as a light lunch.

Always prepare fruit salads as close to service time as possible. The flesh of many types of fruit becomes soft and translucent if cut long before service. Other fruits such as apples, bananas and peaches turn brown in a matter of minutes after cutting. Refer to Chapter 25, Fruits, for more information on this browning reaction and for information on specific fruits. (Sliced apples and pears, for example, can be tossed with lemon juice to prevent enzymatic browning.) Many fruit salad recipes are found at the end of that chapter.

If a fruit salad is dressed at all, the dressing is usually sweet and made with honey or yogurt mixed with fruit juices or purées. Alternatively, Grand Marnier, crème de menthe or other liqueurs sprinkled over the salad can serve as a dressing. Fruit salads can be tossed or composed. Either should offer the diner a pleasing blend of colors, shapes, sizes, flavors and textures.

QUESTIONS FOR DISCUSSION

1. Name several factors that will cause salad greens to wilt or deteriorate.

2. Describe the proper procedure for washing and drying lettuce.

3. Raw salad greens have been the source of salmonella outbreaks. Locate information on a recent recall of salad greens and discuss why the outbreak occurred and what could have been done to prevent it from happening. **WWW**

4. Explain the difference between a vinaigrette and an emulsified vinaigrette dressing.

5. Describe the procedure for making mayonnaise. How can the flavor of a mayonnaise be altered?

6. Describe a typical bound salad. How does a bound salad differ from a dressed salad?

7. List five ways salads can be presented or offered on a menu.

8. In France and other parts of Europe, salad is traditionally served after the main course. Using the Internet and library resources, research the types of salads served after meals and the reason they come after the main course. **WWW**

Terms to Know

butterhead lettuce
head lettuce
mesclun
cos
microgreens
chicory
core
salad spinner
tossed salad
composed salad
bound salad
enzymatic browning

CAESAR SALAD FOR TABLESIDE SERVICE

Yield: 4 Servings   **Method:** Temporary emulsion

Garlic clove	1	1
Anchovy fillets	1 Tbsp.	15 ml
Lemon, cut in half	1	1
Salt	½ tsp.	2 ml
Eggs, pasteurized	2	2
Olive oil	4 fl. oz.	120 ml
Parmesan, grated	2 oz.	60 g
Black pepper, freshly ground	TT	TT
Romaine lettuce leaves, hearts only, washed, dried, chilled and cut into 2-inch (5-centimeter) lengths	1 lb.	480 g
Garlic Croutons (page 732)	4 oz.	120 g

1. Place the garlic clove in a wooden bowl, crush the garlic with a fork and rub the pieces around the bowl. Remove the pieces of garlic.
2. Place the anchovies in the bowl and mash them with the fork.
3. Squeeze the lemon juice into the bowl. Add the salt and the eggs. Beat together with the fork.
4. Begin adding the oil to the egg mixture drop by drop while mixing rapidly with the fork to form an emulsion. When the emulsion begins to form, add the remaining oil in a slow stream while continuing to mix rapidly with the fork.
5. Add the Parmesan and season with pepper.
6. Add the romaine leaves and gently toss to coat with the dressing. Serve on chilled plates garnished with Garlic Croutons.

This Caesar salad recipe is traditionally prepared tableside using coddled eggs (eggs that have been simmered in water for 1 minute, cooking them slightly). Here pasteurized eggs are substituted because of health concerns associated with the use of raw eggs. If desired, the eggs can be omitted; however, the dressing will not be emulsified.

Approximate values per serving: **Calories** 500, **Total fat** 39 g, **Saturated fat** 7 g, **Cholesterol** 110 mg, **Sodium** 1340 mg, **Total carbohydrates** 24 g, **Protein** 12 g, **Vitamin A** 140%, **Vitamin C** 50%, **Calcium** 25%, **Iron** 15%

CAESAR DRESSING

Yield: 2 qt. (2 lt)   **Method:** Emulsion

Garlic, chopped	1 Tbsp.	15 ml
Eggs, pasteurized	2	2
Parmesan, grated	4 oz.	120 g
Balsamic vinegar	2 fl. oz.	60 ml
Red wine vinegar	2 fl. oz.	60 ml
Whole-grain mustard	1 Tbsp.	15 ml
Dijon-style mustard	1 Tbsp.	15 ml
Anchovy fillets	1 oz.	30 g
Salt	1 Tbsp.	15 ml
Black pepper	1 tsp.	5 ml
Vegetable oil	12 fl. oz.	360 ml
Olive oil	12 fl. oz.	360 ml

A traditional Caesar salad is made tableside, but this food processor method is useful when larger quantities are needed.

1. Combine the garlic, eggs, Parmesan, vinegars, mustards, anchovies, salt and pepper in the bowl of a food processor and process until smooth, approximately 1 minute.
2. With the machine running slowly, begin adding the oils to form an emulsion.
3. Continue until all the oil is incorporated.

Approximate values per 1-fl.-oz. (30-ml) serving: **Calories** 180, **Total fat** 19 g, **Saturated fat** 3 g, **Cholesterol** 15 mg, **Sodium** 290 mg, **Total carbohydrates** 1 g, **Protein** 2 g

GARLIC CROUTONS

Yield: 1 lb. 14 oz. (900 g)

Whole butter	6 oz.	180 g
Garlic, chopped	1 Tbsp.	15 ml
French or sourdough bread cubes	1 lb. 8 oz.	720 g
Parmesan, grated	1 oz.	30 g
Dried basil	2 tsp.	10 ml
Dried oregano	2 tsp.	10 ml

1. Melt the butter in a small saucepan and add the garlic. Cook the garlic in the butter over low heat for 5 minutes.
2. Place the bread cubes in a bowl; add the Parmesan and herbs.
3. Pour the garlic butter over the bread cubes and immediately toss to combine.
4. Spread the bread cubes on a sheet pan in a single layer and bake at 350°F (180°C). Stir the croutons occasionally and cook until dry and lightly browned, approximately 15 minutes.

Approximate values per 1-oz. (30-g) serving: **Calories** 200, **Total fat** 9 g, **Saturated fat** 5 g, **Cholesterol** 20 mg, **Sodium** 390 mg, **Total carbohydrates** 25 g, **Protein** 5 g, **Iron** 10%, **Calcium** 10%

RASPBERRY VINAIGRETTE

Yield: 2 qt. (2 lt)   **Method:** Temporary emulsion

Red wine vinegar	8 fl. oz.	240 ml
Rice wine vinegar	8 fl. oz.	240 ml
Lemon juice	1½ fl. oz.	45 ml
Dried thyme	1 Tbsp.	15 ml
Salt	1 Tbsp.	15 ml
Black pepper	1 Tbsp.	15 ml
Garlic, minced	1 Tbsp.	15 ml
Honey	4 oz.	120 g
Raspberry preserves, without seeds	8 oz.	240 g
Olive oil	12 fl. oz.	360 ml
Salad oil	1 pt.	480 ml

1. Whisk together the vinegars, lemon juice, thyme, salt, pepper and garlic.
2. Whisk in the honey and raspberry preserves.
3. Slowly whisk in the oils, emulsifying the dressing.

Approximate values per 1-fl.-oz. (30-ml) serving: **Calories** 130, **Total fat** 12 g, **Saturated fat** 1 g, **Cholesterol** 0 mg, **Sodium** 140 mg, **Total carbohydrates** 5 g, **Protein** 0 g, **Claims**—no cholesterol

FAT-FREE VINAIGRETTE

Yield: 10 fl. oz. (300 ml)   **Method:** Temporary emulsion

White wine vinegar	2 fl. oz.	60 ml
Dijon mustard	1 oz.	30 g
Fresh herbs, assorted, chopped	3 Tbsp.	45 ml
Shallots, roasted, chopped	4 oz.	120 g
Rich chicken stock	4 fl. oz.	120 ml
Salt and pepper	TT	TT

1 Place all of the ingredients in the bowl of a blender and blend well.

VARIATION:

Vegetarian Fat-Free Vinaigrette—Use vegetable stock instead of chicken stock.

Approximate values per 1-fl.-oz. (30-ml) serving: **Calories** 20, **Total fat** 0 g, **Saturated fat** 0 g, **Cholesterol** 0 mg, **Sodium** 85 mg, **Total carbohydrates** 3 g, **Protein** 1 g, **Vitamin A** 15%, **Vitamin C** 25%, **Claims**—low calorie; fat free; high in vitamin C; source of vitamin A

BLUE CHEESE VINAIGRETTE

NEWBURY COLLEGE, Brookline, MA
Senior Instructor Scott Doughty

Yield: 24 fl. oz. (720 ml)   **Method:** Temporary emulsion

Blue cheese	8 oz.	240 g
Salt	1 tsp.	5 ml
Garlic, mashed	1 tsp.	5 ml
White wine vinegar	4 fl. oz.	120 ml
Black pepper	¼ tsp.	2 ml
Olive oil	12 fl. oz.	360 ml

1 Crumble the blue cheese and set aside 2 ounces (60 grams) of the chunks for garnish. Pass the remainder through a drum sieve or food mill fitted with a fine disk.

2 Combine the salt, garlic, vinegar and pepper. Add the oil in a slow steady stream, whisking constantly to incorporate. Gradually beat in the sieved blue cheese until smooth. Stir in the reserved blue cheese chunks.

Approximate values per 1-fl.-oz. (30-ml) serving: **Calories** 190, **Total fat** 19 g, **Saturated fat** 4.5 g, **Cholesterol** 10 mg, **Sodium** 270 mg, **Total carbohydrates** 1 g, **Protein** 2 g

POPPY SEED DRESSING

NEWBURY COLLEGE, Brookline, MA

Senior Instructor Scott Doughty

Yield: 20 fl. oz. (600 ml)   **Method:** Temporary emulsion

Cider vinegar	8 fl. oz.	240 ml
Honey	6 fl. oz.	180 ml
Salt	¾ tsp.	4 ml
Dry mustard	1 tsp.	5 ml
Celery leaves, minced	2 tsp.	10 ml
Green onion, white part only, minced	1	1
Vegetable oil	8 fl. oz.	240 ml
Poppy seeds	1½ Tbsp.	24 ml

1. Combine the vinegar, honey, salt, mustard, celery leaves and green onion.
2. Beat in the oil, by droplets at first, then in a thin stream.
3. Add the poppy seeds and beat to distribute.

Note: For a creamier texture, make the dressing in a blender or food processor.

Approximate values per 1-fl.-oz. (30-ml) serving: **Calories** 140, **Total fat** 11 g, **Saturated fat** 1 g, **Cholesterol** 0 mg, **Sodium** 90 mg, **Total carbohydrates** 11 g, **Protein** 0 g

SAUCE GRIBICHE

Yield: Approximately 1 qt. (1 lt)   **Method:** Emulsion

Hard-cooked egg yolks	4	4
Salt and pepper	TT	TT
Dijon-style mustard	1 Tbsp.	15 ml
Olive oil	1½ pt.	720 ml
White wine vinegar	3 fl. oz.	90 ml
Cornichons, chopped	1 oz.	30 g
Capers, chopped	1 Tbsp.	15 ml
Fresh mixed herbs such as parsley, chervil, tarragon or chives, chopped	1 oz.	30 g

1. Blend the egg yolks with the salt, pepper and mustard.
2. Very slowly, as for mayonnaise, whisk in the oil. Occasionally, add a few drops of vinegar to thin the sauce.
3. Add the cornichons, capers and herbs; mix well. Adjust the seasonings and acidity with the remaining vinegar.

Approximate values per 1-fl.-oz. (30-ml) serving: **Calories** 190, **Total fat** 21 g, **Saturated fat** 3 g, **Cholesterol** 25 mg, **Sodium** 95 mg, **Total carbohydrates** 0 g, **Protein** 1 g

Gribiche is a cold mayonnaise-type sauce made with hard-cooked egg yolks instead of raw egg yolks. It is traditionally flavored with capers and herbs and is served with fish or vegetables.

THOUSAND ISLAND DRESSING

Yield: 42 fl. oz. (1.2 lt) **Method:** Mayonnaise-based

Red wine vinegar	1 Tbsp.	15 ml
Granulated sugar	1 Tbsp.	15 ml
Mayonnaise	1 pt.	480 ml
Ketchup	8 oz.	240 g
Sweet pickle relish	6 oz.	180 g
Hard-cooked eggs, chopped	4	4
Fresh parsley, chopped	2 Tbsp.	30 ml
Green onions, chopped	1 bunch	1 bunch
Salt and pepper	TT	TT
Worcestershire sauce	TT	TT

1. Combine the vinegar and sugar; stir to dissolve the sugar.
2. Add the remaining ingredients and mix well.
3. Adjust the seasonings with the salt, pepper and Worcestershire sauce.

Approximate values per 1-fl.-oz. (30-ml) serving: **Calories** 100, **Total fat** 9 g, **Saturated fat** 1 g, **Cholesterol** 25 mg, **Sodium** 160 mg, **Total carbohydrates** 4 g, **Protein** 1 g

GREEN GODDESS DRESSING

Yield: Approximately 1 qt. (1 lt) **Method:** Mayonnaise-based

Fresh parsley	2 oz.	60 g
Mayonnaise	1 pt.	480 ml
Sour cream	12 oz.	360 g
Garlic, chopped	1 Tbsp.	15 ml
Anchovy fillets, minced	1 oz.	30 g
Fresh chives, chopped	1 oz.	30 g
Fresh tarragon, chopped	1 Tbsp.	15 ml
Lemon juice	2 Tbsp.	30 ml
Red wine vinegar	2 Tbsp.	30 ml
Salt and white pepper	TT	TT
Worcestershire sauce	TT	TT

1. Rinse and chop the parsley very fine. Do not wash or dry it after it has been chopped or you will remove some of the green chlorophyll that is necessary to achieve the proper color in the finished product.
2. Combine all the ingredients and mix well. Season to taste with salt, white pepper and Worcestershire sauce.

Approximate values per 1-fl.-oz. (30-ml) serving: **Calories** 80, **Total fat** 8 g, **Saturated fat** 2.5 g, **Cholesterol** 10 mg, **Sodium** 125 mg, **Total carbohydrates** 1 g, **Protein** 1 g

ROQUEFORT DRESSING

Yield: Approximately 1 qt. (1 lt)   **Method:** Mayonnaise-based

Mayonnaise	8 fl. oz.	240 ml
Red wine vinegar	1 fl. oz.	30 ml
Sour cream	8 fl. oz.	240 ml
Buttermilk	4 fl. oz.	120 ml
Garlic, chopped	1 tsp.	5 ml
Worcestershire sauce	1 tsp.	5 ml
Tabasco sauce	TT	TT
White pepper	TT	TT
Roquefort, crumbled	12 oz.	360 g

1. Combine all the ingredients except the Roquefort and mix well.
2. Add the crumbled Roquefort and combine. Thin with additional buttermilk if desired.

Approximate values per 1-fl.-oz. (30-ml) serving: **Calories** 110, **Total fat** 10 g, **Saturated fat** 4 g, **Cholesterol** 20 mg, **Sodium** 240 mg, **Total carbohydrates** 1 g, **Protein** 3 g

LOW-FAT BLUE CHEESE DRESSING

Yield: Approximately 1 qt. (1 lt)   **Method:** Temporary emulsion

Nonfat yogurt	20 oz.	600 g
Low-fat buttermilk	6 fl. oz.	180 ml
Blue cheese, crumbled	4 oz.	120 g
White pepper	¼ tsp.	1 ml
Granulated sugar	3 Tbsp.	30 ml
Worcestershire sauce	TT	TT
Dry mustard	1 tsp.	5 ml
Tabasco sauce	TT	TT

1. Combine all the ingredients in the bowl of a mixer or food processor and process until smooth.

Approximate values per 1-fl.-oz. (30-ml) serving: **Calories** 30, **Total fat** 1 g, **Saturated fat** 0.5 g, **Cholesterol** 5 mg, **Sodium** 70 mg, **Total carbohydrates** 3 g, **Protein** 2 g, **Claims**—low fat; low cholesterol; low sodium; low calorie

TARTAR SAUCE

Yield: Approximately 1 pt. (480 ml)   **Method:** Mayonnaise-based

Mayonnaise	1 pt.	480 ml
Capers, chopped	2 oz.	60 g
Sweet pickle relish	3 oz.	90 g
Onion, minced	2 Tbsp.	30 ml
Fresh parsley, minced	2 Tbsp.	30 ml
Lemon juice	1 Tbsp.	15 ml
Salt	TT	TT
Worcestershire sauce	TT	TT
Tabasco sauce	TT	TT

1. Stir all the ingredients together until well blended. Chill thoroughly before serving.

Approximate values per 1-fl.-oz. (30-ml) serving: **Calories** 220, **Total fat** 23 g, **Saturated fat** 4 g, **Cholesterol** 20 mg, **Sodium** 420 mg, **Total carbohydrates** 2 g, **Protein** 0 g

RÉMOULADE SAUCE

Chef Jim Fitzgerald, Ph.D., CCP

Yield: Approximately 1 pt. (480 ml) **Method:** Emulsion

Egg yolks, pasteurized	3	3
Salt	⅛ tsp.	0.5 ml
Lemon juice	1 Tbsp.	15 ml
Vegetable oil	12 fl. oz.	360 ml
Water, very hot	1 tsp.	5 ml
Salt and white pepper	TT	TT
Capers, drained and chopped	2 oz.	60 g
Cornichons, chopped	2 oz.	60 g
Fresh chives, chopped	3 Tbsp.	45 ml
Dijon mustard	1 Tbsp.	15 ml
Anchovy fillets, chopped	3	3
Tabasco	TT	TT
Worcestershire sauce	½ tsp.	2 ml

1. Combine the egg yolks, salt and lemon juice in a mixing bowl or a food processor. While whisking, add the oil in drops to form an emulsion. When the mixture thickens, the remaining oil can be added in a slow, steady stream. Add the hot water and mix to lighten the mayonnaise's color.

2. Adjust the seasoning with salt, white pepper and additional lemon juice as necessary.

3. Stir in the remaining ingredients by hand. If the sauce is too thick, thin it with 1 tablespoon (15 milliliters) red wine vinegar into which 1 teaspoon (5 milliliters) sugar has been dissolved.

VARIATION:

Creole Rémoulade—Omit the capers, cornichons and chives. In Step 3, add ½ cup (120 milliliters) finely chopped yellow onion, 3 ounces (90 grams) ketchup, 1 tablespoon (15 milliliters) minced garlic, ¼ teaspoon (1 milliliter) cayenne pepper and ⅓ cup (85 milliliters) finely chopped fresh parsley.

Approximate values per 1-fl.-oz. (30-ml) serving: **Calories** 200, **Total fat** 22 g, **Saturated fat** 3 g, **Cholesterol** 40 mg, **Sodium** 150 mg, **Total carbohydrates** 0 g, **Protein** 1 g

KHIRA RAITA
(CUCUMBER-YOGURT SALAD)

Yield: 10–12 Servings   **Method:** Bound

Plain yogurt	1 pt.	480 ml
Cucumber, peeled and grated	12 oz.	360 g
Cumin	1 tsp.	5 ml
Salt and pepper	TT	TT
Granulated sugar	1 Tbsp.	15 ml
Lime juice	1 Tbsp.	15 ml
Fresh cilantro, chopped	2 Tbsp.	30 ml
Jalapeño, minced	1 tsp.	5 ml
Paprika	as needed	as needed

1. Stir together all the ingredients except the paprika. Chill for several hours before service.
2. At service time, dust the top lightly with paprika.

Approximate values per 3-oz. (90-g) serving: **Calories** 40, **Total fat** 0 g, **Saturated fat** 0 g, **Cholesterol** 0 mg, **Sodium** 280 mg, **Total carbohydrates** 7 g, **Protein** 3 g, **Calcium** 10%, **Claims**—fat free; low calorie

Raita (RA-tah) are yogurt and vegetable salads typically served as condiments in Indian cuisine. Raita may be made with many types of vegetables, including eggplants, cooked potatoes, tomatoes and even bananas, and are meant as a cooling counterpoint to the spiciness of other dishes.

JAPANESE-STYLE CUCUMBER SALAD

NEWBURY COLLEGE, BROOKLINE, MA
Senior Instructor Scott Doughty

Yield: 10–12 Servings   **Method:** Tossed

Cucumbers, peeled, split and seeded	6	6
Salt	2½ tsp.	13 ml
Water chestnuts, whole	4 oz.	120 g
Green onions	1 bunch	1 bunch
Carrot	1	1
Fresh ginger, unpeeled	4 oz.	120 g
Rice wine vinegar	4 fl. oz.	120 ml
Granulated sugar	2 tsp.	10 ml
Dark sesame oil	2 tsp.	10 ml
Sesame seeds	5 Tbsp.	75 ml
Soy sauce	as needed	as needed

1. Slice the cucumbers very thin with a knife or mandoline. Sprinkle 2 teaspoons (10 milliliters) salt evenly over them and mix well. Allow them to rest in a bowl for 20 to 30 minutes.
2. Very thinly slice the water chestnuts. Slice the green onions. Peel the carrot. Cut the carrot into 2-inch (5-centimeter) sections, cut each section lengthwise into very thin slices and cut each slice lengthwise into thin shreds. Cover and refrigerate the carrot shreds.
3. Rinse the cucumbers in several changes of cold water to remove the excess salt. Squeeze them in small batches in a clean towel to extract as much liquid as possible. Combine the cucumbers, water chestnuts and green onions.
4. Mince and mash the ginger into a mushy consistency and squeeze it through several layers of cheesecloth to extract as much juice as possible. Discard the pulp. Mix 1 teaspoon (5 milliliters) of the juice with the vinegar, the remaining salt and the sugar. Beat in the sesame oil in a thin stream. Stir the dressing into the cucumber mixture and chill.

⑤ Toast the sesame seeds in a 325°F (160°C) oven until lightly browned.

⑥ To serve, place a portion of the marinated cucumbers on a plate and add some of the excess juice from the bowl. Garnish each salad with the carrot shreds and toasted sesame seeds. Serve soy sauce on the side.

Approximate values per serving: **Calories** 70, **Total fat** 3.5 g, **Saturated fat** 0 g, **Cholesterol** 0 mg, **Sodium** 170 g, **Total carbohydrates** 9 g, **Protein** 2 g, **Vitamin A** 40%

ORGANIC MICROGREENS AND SPRING VEGETABLES WITH FRAGRANT HERB VINAIGRETTE AND DRY FARMER'S CHEESE

RDG AND BAR ANNIE, Houston, TX

Chef-Owner Robert Del Grande

Yield: 8 Servings of salad and 28 fl. oz. (840 ml) of dressing

Method: Tossed

Lemon	1	1
Plum tomatoes, concassée	5	5
Shallot, minced	1	1
Garlic cloves, steamed and mashed	6	6
Serrano chile, seeded, minced	1	1
Champagne vinegar	2 Tbsp.	30 ml
Maple syrup	1 tsp.	5 ml
Virgin olive oil	4 fl. oz.	120 ml
Grapeseed oil	8 fl. oz.	240 ml
Fresh mint, chopped	4 Tbsp.	60 ml
Fresh tarragon, chopped	4 Tbsp.	60 ml
Salt	TT	TT
Assorted spring vegetables, blanched and chilled	3 c.	720 ml
Organic microgreens	8 oz.	240 g
Dry farmer's cheese, crumbled	8 Tbsp.	120 ml

① Juice the lemon.

② Combine the tomato concassée, shallot, garlic, chile, vinegar, maple syrup and lemon juice in the bowl of a small mixer. Slowly whisk in the oils until thoroughly combined. Stir in the herbs and season with salt.

③ Toss the spring vegetables in a small amount of the dressing and season with salt.

④ For each salad, toss 1 ounce (30 grams) of the greens with a small amount of the dressing and arrange on a plate. Garnish with some of the seasoned spring vegetables and sprinkle each salad with 1 tablespoon (15 milliliters) farmer's cheese.

Approximate values per serving with 1 fl. oz. (30 ml) dressing: **Calories** 180, **Total fat** 16 g, **Saturated fat** 4.5 g, **Cholesterol** 15 mg, **Sodium** 100 mg, **Total carbohydrates** 6 g, **Protein** 4 g, **Vitamin A** 20%, **Vitamin C** 25%, **Calcium** 15%

WILTED SPINACH SALAD WITH ROASTED PEPPERS

GREENS, SAN FRANCISCO, CA

Chef Annie Somerville

Yield: 2 Large or 4 Small Servings	**Method:** Tossed	
Red or yellow bell pepper, medium	1	1
Extra virgin olive oil	3 fl. oz.	90 ml
Salt and pepper	TT	TT
Red onion, sliced thin	2 oz.	60 g
Baguette, thin slices for croutons	12	12
Spinach	1 lb.	480 g
Frisée or escarole	1 head	1 head
Balsamic vinegar	3 Tbsp.	45 ml
Garlic clove, chopped fine	1	1
Niçoise or Gaeta olives, pitted	10	10
Parmesan, grated	1 oz.	30 g

1. Roast and peel the bell pepper and cut into ¼-inch (6-millimeter) strips. Toss the bell pepper strips with ½ tablespoon (8 milliliters) of the olive oil and a few pinches of salt and pepper. Set aside to marinate.
2. Cover the onion slices with cold water to leach the strong onion flavor. Set aside.
3. Place the baguette slices on a baking sheet and brush them lightly with oil. Toast in a 375°F (190°C) oven until crisp and lightly browned, approximately 5 minutes.
4. Stem, wash and dry the spinach. Trim the stem end of the frisée or escarole and discard the tough outer leaves. Wash and dry.
5. Drain the onion. In a large bowl, combine the vinegar, garlic, ½ teaspoon (2 milliliters) salt and a few pinches of pepper. Add the greens, onion, bell pepper and olives.
6. Heat the remaining oil in a small pan until it is very hot and just below the smoking point. Immediately pour it over the salad and toss with a pair of metal tongs to coat and wilt the leaves. Sprinkle on the Parmesan.
7. Add the croutons and serve immediately.

Approximate values per large serving: **Calories** 730, **Total fat** 52 g, **Saturated fat** 9 g, **Cholesterol** 10 mg, **Sodium** 1070 mg, **Total carbohydrates** 51 g, **Protein** 21 g, **Vitamin A** 480%, **Vitamin C** 330%, **Calcium** 60%, **Iron** 60%, **Claims**—high in fiber, vitamins A and C, calcium and iron

CURLY ENDIVE, APPLE AND GORGONZOLA SALAD

Yield: 6 Servings	**Method:** Composed	
Belgian endive	2 heads	2 heads
Curly endive	1 head	1 head
Granny Smith apple	1	1
Red Delicious apple	1	1
Heavy cream	4 fl. oz.	120 ml
Red wine vinegar	2 fl. oz.	60 ml
Gorgonzola, crumbled	3 oz.	90 g
Salt and pepper	TT	TT
Walnuts, toasted	1 oz.	30 g

1. Separate the leaves of the Belgian endive. Tear the curly endive into small pieces. Wash and thoroughly dry the leaves.
2. Core the apples and cut them into thin wedges.

3 Combine the cream, vinegar and Gorgonzola and season to taste with salt and pepper. Add the apple wedges to the cream mixture.

4 Divide the Belgian endive spears among six plates, forming a flower pattern. Place a portion of the curly endive in the center of each plate on top of the Belgian endive.

5 Spoon a portion of the apple mixture onto each plate, arranging the apple wedges attractively. Garnish with toasted walnuts.

Approximate values per serving: **Calories** 240, **Total fat** 17 g, **Saturated fat** 8 g, **Cholesterol** 40 mg, **Sodium** 260 mg, **Total carbohydrates** 17 g, **Protein** 8 g, **Vitamin A** 120%, **Vitamin C** 30%, **Calcium** 25%, **Iron** 15%, **Claims**—good source of iron; high in fiber, vitamins A and C and calcium

CAPRESE SALAD

Yield: 25 Servings　　　　**Method:** Composed

Fresh mozzarella	50 slices	50 slices
Tomatoes	50 slices	50 slices
Fresh basil leaves, chiffonade	4 Tbsp.	60 ml
Salt and pepper	TT	TT
Extra virgin olive oil	3 Tbsp.	45 ml

1 Arrange the mozzarella and tomato slices in overlapping circles on a serving platter, alternating slices of cheese and tomato.

2 Sprinkle the basil, salt and pepper over the salad. Drizzle with the oil. Serve two slices of tomato and two slices of cheese on each individual serving plate.

Approximate values per serving: **Calories** 190, **Total fat** 14 g, **Saturated fat** 8 g, **Cholesterol** 45 mg, **Sodium** 85 mg, **Total carbohydrates** 4 g, **Protein** 11 g, **Vitamin A** 15%, **Vitamin C** 20%, **Calcium** 35%

COBB SALAD

Yield: 10 Entrée Servings　　　　**Method:** Composed

Romaine lettuce	8 oz.	240 g
Green leaf lettuce	4 oz.	120 g
Watercress	4 oz.	120 g
Eggs	4	4
Avocados	4	4
Bacon slices	16	16
Roquefort, crumbled	1 lb.	480 g
Turkey breast, roasted, julienne	1 lb.	480 g
Tomato concassée	1 lb.	480 g
Basic Vinaigrette Dressing, Dijon variation (page 720)	24 fl. oz.	720 ml

1 Tear, wash and dry the lettuces. Pick over and wash the watercress.

2 Hard-cook the eggs, then peel and chop them.

3 Pit and peel the avocados and cut into wedges.

4 Dice the bacon and cook in a sauté pan until crisp. Remove and drain well.

5 Toss the salad greens together and arrange the eggs, avocado, bacon, cheese, turkey and tomato concassée on top in an artistic fashion. Serve the Mustard Vinaigrette Dressing on the side.

Approximate values per serving: **Calories** 1000, **Total fat** 84 g, **Saturated fat** 18 g, **Cholesterol** 215 mg, **Sodium** 1770 mg, **Total carbohydrates** 21 g, **Protein** 40 g, **Vitamin A** 45%, **Vitamin C** 60%, **Calcium** 45%, **Iron** 20%

GREEK SALAD

Yield: 3 lb. 8 oz. (1.8 kg)   **Method:** Tossed/Composed

Extra virgin olive oil	4 fl. oz.	120 ml
Lemon juice	2 fl. oz.	60 ml
Red wine vinegar	2 fl. oz.	60 ml
Garlic, minced	1 tsp.	10 ml
Fresh oregano, chopped	1 Tbsp.	30 ml
Cucumbers	2	2
Feta	12 oz.	360 g
Olives, Kalamata or other Greek variety	1 lb.	480 g
Fresh parsley, chopped	1 oz.	30 g
Green onions, sliced	1 bunch	1 bunch
Pepper	TT	TT
Romaine lettuce	1 head	1 head
Anchovy fillets	8	8
Tomatoes, cut into 6 wedges	3	3

1. To make the dressing, whisk together the oil, lemon juice, vinegar, garlic and oregano.
2. Peel the cucumbers and slice in half lengthwise. Remove the seeds and cut into bâtonnet.
3. Dice or crumble the feta into small pieces.
4. Combine the olives, cucumbers, parsley and green onions in a bowl and add the dressing. Toss to combine and season to taste with pepper.
5. Line plates or a platter with the romaine lettuce leaves. Add the olive-cucumber mixture and sprinkle on the feta cheese. Garnish as desired with the anchovies and tomato wedges.

Approximate values per 6-oz. (180-g) serving: **Calories** 280, **Total fat** 24 g, **Saturated fat** 7 g, **Cholesterol** 35 mg, **Sodium** 900 mg, **Total carbohydrates** 9 g, **Protein** 7 g, **Vitamin A** 15%, **Vitamin C** 35%, **Calcium** 25%, **Iron** 15%

NEW POTATO SALAD WITH MUSTARD AND DILL

Yield: 5 lb. (2.4 kg)   **Method:** Bound

New potatoes	4 lb.	1.9 kg
Mayonnaise	4 fl. oz.	120 ml
Sour cream	4 oz.	120 g
Garlic, chopped	1½ tsp.	7 ml
Salt	TT	TT
Black pepper	1½ tsp.	7 ml
Fresh dill, chopped	2 Tbsp.	30 ml
Dijon-style mustard	2 Tbsp.	30 ml
Green bell pepper, julienne	1	1
Red bell pepper, julienne	1	1
Red onion, julienne	6 oz.	180 g
Celery, julienne	4 oz.	120 g

1. Boil the potatoes in salted water until done but still firm. Chill well and cut into quarters.
2. Combine the mayonnaise, sour cream, garlic, salt, pepper, dill and mustard; mix well.
3. Combine all the ingredients and adjust the seasonings with salt and pepper.

Approximate values per 4-oz. (120-g) serving: **Calories** 110, **Total fat** 6 g, **Saturated fat** 1.5 g, **Cholesterol** 5 mg, **Sodium** 360 mg, **Total carbohydrates** 12 g, **Protein** 1 g, **Vitamin C** 25%

POTATO SALAD

Yield: 6 lb. 8 oz. (3.2 kg)   **Method:** Bound

Potatoes, chef	4 lb.	1.9 kg
Eggs, hard-cooked, chilled	6	6
Celery, medium dice	8 oz.	240 g
Green onions, sliced	1 bunch	1 bunch
Radishes, chopped coarse	6 oz.	180 g
Mayonnaise	1 pt.	480 ml
Dijon-style mustard	2 oz.	60 g
Fresh parsley, chopped	1 oz.	30 g
Salt and pepper	TT	TT

1. Boil the potatoes in salted water until nearly cooked. Drain the potatoes, spread them on a sheet pan and refrigerate until cold.
2. Peel the cold potatoes and cut into large dice.
3. Peel and chop the eggs.
4. Combine all the ingredients and adjust the seasonings with salt and pepper.

Approximate values per 4-oz. (120-g) serving: **Calories** 200, **Total fat** 16 g, **Saturated fat** 3 g, **Cholesterol** 65 mg, **Sodium** 390 mg, **Total carbohydrates** 11 g, **Protein** 3 g, **Vitamin C** 15%

CREAMY COLESLAW

Yield: 2 lb. (960 g)   **Method:** Bound

Mayonnaise	8 fl. oz.	240 ml
Sour cream or crème fraîche	4 oz.	120 g
Granulated sugar	1 oz.	30 g
Cider vinegar	1 fl. oz.	30 ml
Garlic clove, minced	1	1
Green cabbage, shredded	1 lb.	480 g
Red cabbage, shredded	8 oz.	240 g
Carrot, shredded	4 oz.	120 g
Salt and white pepper	TT	TT

1. Combine the mayonnaise, sour cream or crème fraîche, sugar, vinegar and garlic in a bowl; whisk together.
2. Add the shredded cabbages and carrot to the dressing and mix well. Season to taste with salt and white pepper.

Approximate values per 4-oz. (120-g) serving: **Calories** 200, **Total fat** 19 g, **Saturated fat** 4.5 g, **Cholesterol** 20 mg, **Sodium** 340 mg, **Total carbohydrates** 8 g, **Protein** 1 g, **Vitamin A** 20%, **Vitamin C** 50%

ASIAN COLESLAW

JOLIET JUNIOR COLLEGE, JOLIET, IL

Keith G. Vonhoff, CEPC, CEC, CCP

Yield: 6 lb. 8 oz. (3.2 kg)　　　　　　　**Method:** Bound

Peanut dressing:		
Peanuts, oil-roasted	2½ oz.	75 g
Garlic cloves	4	4
Peanut oil	2 fl. oz.	60 ml
Granulated sugar	1 Tbsp.	15 ml
Soy sauce	2 fl. oz.	60 ml
Rice wine vinegar	2 fl. oz.	60 ml
Hot pepper sauce	½ tsp.	2 ml
Sesame oil	1 Tbsp.	15 ml
Salt	¾ tsp.	4 ml
Red cabbage, chiffonade	6 lb.	2.8 kg
Red bell peppers, julienne	10 oz.	300 g
Yellow bell peppers, julienne	10 oz.	300 g
Orange bell peppers, julienne	10 oz.	300 g
Green onions, sliced on the bias	2 oz.	60 g
Sesame seeds, toasted	2 Tbsp.	30 ml
Salt and pepper	TT	TT

1　Purée the peanuts and garlic in a food processor.

2　Slowly add the peanut oil to emulsify.

3　Add the remaining dressing ingredients and mix well.

4　Combine the remaining ingredients in a stainless steel bowl. Pour the dressing over the vegetables and mix gently. Season to taste with salt and pepper.

Approximate values per 3-oz. (90-g) serving: **Calories** 80, **Total fat** 4.5 g, **Saturated fat** 0.5 g, **Cholesterol** 0 mg, **Sodium** 240 mg, **Total carbohydrates** 9 g, **Protein** 3 g, **Vitamin C** 160%, **Claims**—no cholesterol; high in vitamin C

COUSCOUS SALAD

Yield: 3 lb. (1.4 kg)   **Method:** Bound

Couscous	6 oz.	180 g
Red bell pepper, medium dice	1	1
Green bell pepper, medium dice	1	1
Green onions, sliced on the bias	1 bunch	1 bunch
Cucumbers, peeled, seeded, medium dice	6 oz.	180 g
Black olives, pitted	4 oz.	120 g
Red onion, julienne	6 oz.	180 g
Dressing:		
Orange juice concentrate	3 fl. oz.	90 ml
Water	2 fl. oz.	60 ml
Rice vinegar	2 fl. oz.	60 ml
Garlic, chopped	1 tsp.	5 ml
Salt	1 tsp.	5 ml
Black pepper	1 tsp.	5 ml
Fresh oregano, chopped	2 tsp.	10 ml
Salad oil	3 fl. oz.	90 ml
Honey	2 Tbsp.	30 ml
Fresh thyme, chopped	2 tsp.	10 ml

1 Steam the couscous until tender; set aside to cool.

2 Combine the couscous with the vegetables.

3 Whisk together all the dressing ingredients.

4 Combine the salad ingredients with the dressing. Chill thoroughly before serving.

Approximate values per 3-oz. (90-g) serving: **Calories** 90, **Total fat** 6 g, **Saturated fat** 0.5 g, **Cholesterol** 0 mg, **Sodium** 200 mg, **Total carbohydrates** 7 g, **Protein** 1 g, **Vitamin C** 35%, **Claims**—low saturated fat; no cholesterol

Tabouli is one of many small plate appetizers served throughout the Middle East with drinks before dinner. It also accompanies grilled fish, meat or vegetables.

TABOULI

Yield: 15 Servings, 4 oz. (120 g) each   **Method:** Bound

Bulgur	10 oz.	300 g
Green onions, finely chopped	10 oz.	300 g
Fresh parsley, chopped	6 oz.	180 g
Fresh mint, chopped	2 oz.	60 g
Lemon juice	8 fl. oz.	240 ml
Salt	TT	TT
Olive oil	8 fl. oz.	240 ml
Pepper	TT	TT
Tomatoes, seeded, medium dice	1 lb.	480 g
Pine nuts, toasted	4 oz.	120 g
Pita bread	as needed	as needed
Butterhead lettuce, washed	as needed	as needed

1. Place the bulgur in a bowl and cover with cold water. Soak the bulgur until tender, approximately 2 to 4 hours. (Timing will vary depending on freshness.)
2. Drain the bulgur and squeeze out all the excess water.
3. Add the green onions, parsley and mint. Season the lemon juice with salt. Beat in the olive oil, then mix into the bulgur.
4. Fold in the tomatoes. Adjust the seasoning with salt and pepper.
5. Garnish with the toasted pine nuts and serve with pita bread or lettuce leaves.

Approximate values per 4-oz. (120-g) serving: **Calories** 280, **Total fat** 21 g, **Saturated fat** 3 g, **Cholesterol** 0 mg, **Sodium** 280 mg, **Total carbohydrates** 17 g, **Protein** 5 g, **Vitamin A** 30%, **Vitamin C** 60%, **Iron** 70%, **Claims**—no cholesterol; good source of fiber

PANZANELLA (ITALIAN BREAD SALAD)

WILDFLOWER BREAD COMPANY, SCOTTSDALE, AZ

Yield: 20 Servings, 8 oz. (240 g) each

Method: Tossed

Crusty bread, cut into 1-in. (2.5-cm) cubes	1 gal.	4 lt
Tomatoes, diced	21 oz.	630 g
Fresh basil, chopped	2½ oz.	75 g
Fresh parsley, chopped	2½ oz.	75 g
Red bell peppers, medium dice	5 oz.	150 g
Mushrooms, quartered, marinated	5 oz.	150 g
Garlic, chopped	2 tsp.	10 ml
Garlic salt	TT	TT
Lemon pepper	TT	TT
Olive oil	5 fl. oz.	150 ml
Red wine vinegar	3½ fl. oz.	105 ml
Fresh parsley, chopped	as needed for garnish	
Parmesan, grated	as needed for garnish	

1. Spread the bread cubes out on a sheet pan and allow them to dry at room temperature for 3 to 4 hours.

2. Mix the remaining ingredients (except the garnishes) together in a large bowl until everything is evenly distributed.

3. Toss the bread cubes into the salad and coat them well with the salad liquid.

4. Serve at room temperature, garnished with a light sprinkle of chopped parsley and grated Parmesan.

Approximate values per 8-oz. (240-g) serving: **Calories** 452, **Total fat** 10 g, **Saturated fat** 2 g, **Cholesterol** 1 mg, **Sodium** 1566 mg, **Total carbohydrates** 78 g, **Protein** 12 g, **Vitamin A** 31%, **Vitamin C** 40%, **Iron** 41%

> "Talking of pleasure, this moment I was writing with one hand, and with the other holding to my mouth a nectarine— how good how fine. It went down all pulpy, slushy, oozy, all its delicious embonpoint melted down my throat like a large, beatified strawberry."
>
> —JOHN KEATS, ENGLISH POET (1795–1821)

CHAPTER TWENTY-FIVE

FRUITS

After studying this chapter, you will be able to:

- identify a variety of fruits
- purchase fruits appropriate for various needs
- store fruits properly
- understand how fruits are preserved
- prepare fruits for cooking or service
- apply various cooking methods to fruits

BOTANICALLY, A FRUIT IS AN ORGAN that develops from the ovary of a flowering plant and contains one or more seeds. Culinarily, a fruit is the perfect snack food: the basis of a dessert, colorful sauce or soup or an accompaniment to meat, fish, shellfish or poultry. No food group offers a greater variety of colors, flavors and textures than fruit.

This chapter identifies many of the fruits typically used by food service operations. It then addresses general considerations in purchasing fresh and preserved fruits. A discussion follows about some of the cooking methods presented in Chapter 9, Principles of Cooking, as they apply to fruits. Recipes in which a fruit is the primary ingredient are presented at the chapter's end.

IDENTIFYING FRUITS

This book presents fruits according to the ways most people view them and use them, rather than by rigid botanical classifications. Fruits are divided here into eight categories: berries, citrus, exotics, grapes, melons, pomes, stone fruits and tropicals, according to either their shape, seed structure or natural habitat. Botanically, tomatoes, beans, eggplant, capsicum peppers and other produce are fruits. But in ordinary thinking, they are not; they are vegetables and are discussed in Chapter 21, Vegetables.

A fruit may have several names, varying from region to region or on a purveyor's whim. Botanists are also constantly reclassifying items to fit new findings. The names given here follow generally accepted custom and usage.

Berries

Berries are small, juicy fruits that grow on vines and bushes worldwide. Berries are characterized by thin skins and many tiny seeds that are often so small they go unnoticed. Some of the fruits classified here as berries do not fit the botanical definition (for example, raspberries and strawberries), while fruits that are berries botanically (for example, bananas and grapes) are classified elsewhere.

Berries may be eaten plain or used in everything from beer to bread, soup to sorbet. They make especially fine jams and compotes.

Berries must be fully **ripened** on the vine, as they will not ripen further after harvesting. Select berries that are plump and fully colored. Avoid juice-stained containers and berries with whitish-gray or black spots of mold. All berries should be refrigerated and used promptly. Do not wash berries until just before they are needed, as washing removes some of their aroma and softens them.

BLACKBERRIES

Blackberries are similar to raspberries, but are larger and shinier, with a deep purple to black color. Thorny blackberry vines are readily found in the wild; commercial production is limited. Their peak season is mid-June through August. Loganberries, Marionberries, olallie berries and boysenberries are blackberry hybrids.

BLUEBERRIES

Blueberries (Fr. *myrtilles*) are small and firm, with a true blue to almost black skin and a juicy, light gray-blue interior. Cultivated berries (high-bush varieties) tend to be larger than wild (low-bush) ones. Blueberries are native to North America and are grown commercially from Maine to Oregon and along the Atlantic seaboard. Their peak season is short, from mid-June to mid-August.

CRANBERRIES

Cranberries, another native North American food, are tart, firm fruit with a mottled red skin. They grow on low vines in cultivated bogs (swamps) throughout Massachusetts,

ripe fully grown and developed; a ripe fruit's flavor, texture and appearance are at their peak, and the fruit is ready to use as food

Blackberries

Blueberries

Wisconsin and New Jersey. Rarely eaten raw, they are made into sauce or relish or are used in breads, pies or pastries. Cranberries are readily available frozen or made into a jelly-type sauce and canned. Although color does not indicate ripeness, cranberries should be picked over before cooking to remove those that are soft or bruised. Their peak harvesting season is from Labor Day through October, leading to the association of cranberries with Thanksgiving dinner.

Cranberries

CURRANTS

Currants are tiny, tart fruits that grow on shrubs in grapelike clusters. The most common are a beautiful, almost translucent red, but black and golden (or white) varieties also exist. All varieties are used for jams, jellies and sauces, and black currants are made into a liqueur, crème de cassis. Although rarely grown in the United States, currants are very popular and widely available in Europe, with a peak season during the late summer. (The dried fruits called currants are not produced from these berries; they are a special variety of dried grapes.)

White Currants

Red Currants

RASPBERRIES

Raspberries (Fr. *framboises*) are perhaps the most delicate of all fruits. They have a tart flavor and velvety texture. Red raspberries are the most common, with black, purple and golden berries available in some markets. When ripe, the berry pulls away easily from its white core, leaving the characteristic hollow center. Because they can be easily crushed and are susceptible to mold, most of the raspberries grown are marketed frozen. They grow on thorny vines in cool climates from Washington State to western New York and are imported from New Zealand and South America. The peak domestic season is from late May through November.

Raspberries

STRAWBERRIES

Strawberries (Fr. *fraises*) are brilliant red, heart-shaped fruits that grow on vines. The strawberry plant is actually a perennial herb; the berry's flesh is covered by tiny black seeds called achenes, which are the plant's true fruits. Select berries with a good red color and intact green leafy hull. (The hulls can be easily removed with a paring knife.) Avoid berries with soft or brown spots. Huge berries may be lovely to look at, but they often have hollow centers and little flavor or juice. Although strawberries are available to some extent all year, fresh California strawberries are at their peak from April through June.

Strawberries

The tiny wild or Alpine berries, known by their French name, *fraises des bois*, have a particularly intense flavor and aroma. They are not widely available in the United States.

PROCEDURE FOR **FANNING STRAWBERRIES**

Cut thin parallel slices into the base of the strawberry without cutting through the stem. Press lightly to fan out the strawberry, exposing the cut slices.

Citrus

Citrus fruits include lemons, limes, grapefruits, tangerines, kumquats, oranges and several hybrids. They are characterized by a thick rind, most of which is a bitter white pith (albedo) with a thin exterior layer of colored skin known as the **zest**. Their flesh is segmented and juicy. Citrus fruits are acidic, with a strong aroma; their flavors vary from bitter to tart to sweet.

Citrus fruits grow on trees and shrubs in tropical and subtropical climates worldwide. All citrus fruits are fully ripened on the tree and will not ripen further after harvesting. They should be refrigerated for longest storage.

Select fruits that feel heavy and have thin, smooth skins. Avoid those with large blemishes or moist spots.

zest the colored outer portion of the rind of citrus fruit; contains the oil that provides flavor and aroma

White Grapefruits

GRAPEFRUITS

Grapefruits (Fr. *pamplemousses*) are large and round with a yellow skin, thick rind and tart flesh. They are an 18th-century hybrid of the orange and pummelo (a large, coarse fruit used mostly in Middle and Far Eastern cuisines). Two varieties of grapefruit are widely available all year: white-fleshed and pink- or ruby-fleshed. White grapefruits produce the finest juice, although pink grapefruits are sweeter. Fresh grapefruits are best eaten raw or topped with brown sugar and lightly broiled.

Red Grapefruits

KUMQUATS

Kumquats are very small, oval-shaped, orange-colored fruits with a soft, sweet skin and slightly bitter flesh. They can be eaten whole, either raw or preserved in syrup, and may be used in jams and preserves.

Kumquats

LEMONS

The most commonly used citrus fruits, lemons (Fr. *citrons*), are oval-shaped, bright yellow fruits available all year. Their strongly acidic flavor makes them unpleasant to eat raw but perfect for flavoring desserts and confections. Lemon juice is also widely used in sauces, especially for fish, shellfish and poultry. Lemon zest is candied or used as garnish. Rubbing the skin of a lemon or other citrus fruit with a sugar cube extracts much of the aromatic oil. The cube can then be crushed or dissolved to use in formulas calling for citrus flavor.

Lemons

LIMES

Limes (Fr. *limons*) are small fruits with thin skins ranging from yellow-green to dark green. Limes are too tart to eat raw and are often substituted for lemons in prepared dishes. They are also juiced or used in cocktails, curries or desserts. Lime zest can be grated and used to give color and flavor to a variety of dishes. Limes are available all year; their peak season is during the summer. The key lime is a small tart lime variety native to South Florida and used to make key lime pie.

Limes

Key Limes

ORANGES

Oranges (Sp. *naranjas*) are round fruits with a juicy, orange-colored flesh and a thin, orange skin. They can be either sweet or bitter.

Valencia oranges and navel oranges (a seedless variety) are the most popular sweet oranges. They can be juiced for beverages or sauces, and the flesh may be eaten raw, added to salads, cooked in desserts or used as a garnish. The zest may be grated or julienned for sauces or garnish. Sweet oranges are available all year; their peak season is from December to April.

Blood oranges are also sweet but are small, with a rough, reddish skin. Their flesh is streaked with a bloodred color.

Valencia Oranges

Navel Oranges

Blood oranges are available primarily during the winter months and are eaten raw, juiced or used in salads or sauces. When selecting sweet oranges, look for fruits that feel plump and heavy, with unblemished skin. The color of the skin depends on weather conditions; a green rind does not affect the flavor of the flesh.

Bitter oranges include the Seville and bergamot. They are used primarily for the essential oils found in their zest. Oil of bergamot gives Earl Grey tea its distinctive flavor; oil of Seville is essential to curaçao, Grand Marnier and orange flower water. Seville oranges are also used in marmalades and sauces for meats and poultry.

Blood Oranges

TANGERINES

Tangerines, sometimes referred to as mandarins, are small and dark orange. Their rind is loose and easily removed to reveal sweet, juicy, aromatic segments. Tangerines are most often eaten fresh and uncooked, but are available canned as mandarin oranges.

Tangelos are a hybrid of tangerines and grapefruits. They are the size of a medium orange; they have a bulbous stem end and few to no seeds.

Tangerines

PROCEDURE FOR **SEGMENTING CITRUS FRUITS**

Citrus segments, known as supremes, are made by first carefully cutting off the entire peel (including the bitter white pith) in even slices.

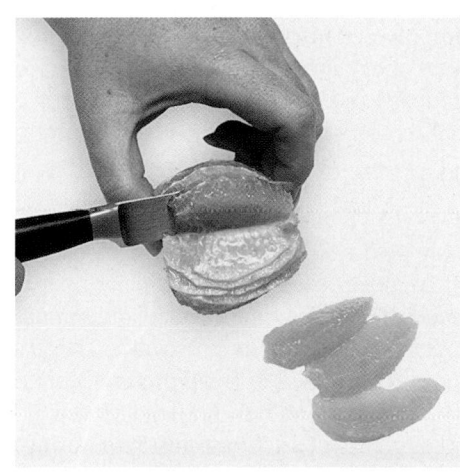

Individual segments are then removed by gently cutting alongside each membrane.

PROCEDURE FOR **ZESTING CITRUS FRUITS**

A five-hole zester is used to remove paper-thin strips of the colored rind.

PROCEDURE FOR **CUTTING CITRUS PEELS**

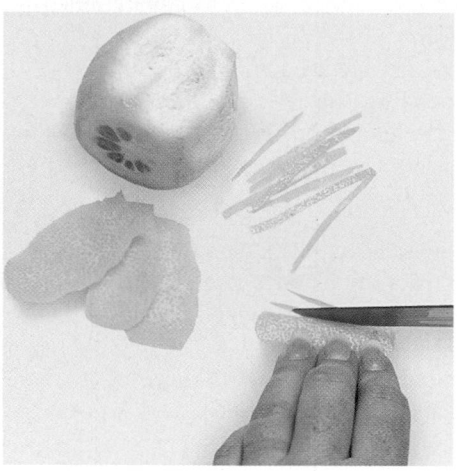

Large strips of citrus zest may be used as a garnish or to flavor soups or sauces.

Exotics

Improved transportation has led to the increasing availability (although sporadic in some areas) of exotic or unusual fresh fruits such as figs, persimmons, pomegranates, prickly pears, rhubarb and star fruits. Other exotic fruits, such as breadfruit, durian, feijoa and loquat, are still available only on a limited basis from specialty purveyors and are not discussed here.

FIGS

Figs (Fr. *figues*) are the fruit of ficus trees. They are small, soft, pear-shaped fruits with an intensely sweet flavor and rich, moist texture made crunchy by a multitude of tiny seeds. Fresh figs can be sliced and served in salads or with cured meats such as prosciutto. They can also be baked, poached or used in jams, preserves or compotes.

Dark-skinned figs, known as Mission figs, are a variety planted at Pacific Coast missions during the 18th century. They have a thin skin and small seeds and are available fresh, canned or dried. The white-skinned figs grown commercially include the White Adriatic, used principally for drying and baking, and the all-purpose Kadota. The most important domestic variety, however, is the Calimyrna. These large figs have a rich yellow color and large nutty seeds. Fresh Calimyrna figs are the finest for eating out of hand; they are also available dried.

Calimyrna Figs

For the best flavor, figs should be fully ripened on the tree. Unfortunately, fully ripened figs are very delicate and difficult to transport. Most figs are in season from June through October; fresh Calimyrna figs are available only during June.

GOOSEBERRIES

Several varieties of gooseberry (Fr. *groseille maquereau*) are cultivated for culinary purposes. One well-known variety is the European gooseberry, a member of the currant family that grows on spiny bushes in cool, moist regions of the Northern Hemisphere. Its berries can be relatively large, like a small plum, but are usually less than 1 inch (2.5 centimeters) in diameter. The skin, which is firm and smooth or only slightly hairy, can be green, white (actually gray-green), yellow or red. The tart berries contain many tiny seeds. They are eaten fresh or used for jellies, preserves, tarts and other desserts or as a traditional accompaniment to rich or fatty dishes, such as goose and mackerel. North American gooseberry varieties are smaller, perfectly round, and pink to deep red at maturity. Although more prolific, these varietals lack flavor and are generally considered inferior to European gooseberries.

HYBRIDS AND VARIETIES

Several fruits are extremely responsive to selective breeding and crossbreeding and have been toyed with by botanists and growers since at least the time of ancient Rome. Two distinct products are recognized: hybrids and varieties. **Hybrids** result from crossbreeding fruits from different species that are genetically unalike. The result is a unique product. Citrus is particularly responsive to hybridization; tangelos result from a cross between tangerines and grapefruits. **Varieties** result from breeding fruits of the same species that have different qualities or characteristics. Breeding two varieties of peaches, for example, produces a third variety with the best qualities of both parents. Nectarines are a peach variety with smooth skin that is easier to eat than that of fuzzy peach varieties.

Cape gooseberries, also known as physalis, ground cherries and poha, are unrelated to European and American gooseberries. Native to Peru, they became popular during the 19th century along the African Cape of Good Hope, for which they are named. Australia and New Zealand are currently the largest producers. Cape gooseberries are covered with a paper-thin husk or calyx. About the size of a cherry, they have a waxy, bright orange skin and many tiny seeds. Their flavor is similar to coconut and oranges, but tarter. Cape gooseberries may be eaten raw, made into jam or used in desserts. Fresh, they make an especially striking garnish, especially when dipped in chocolate.

Cape Gooseberries

GUAVA

Guava (GWAH-vah) are a small, oval or pear-shaped fruit with a strong fragrance and a mild, slightly grainy flesh. They are excellent in jams and preserves, and guava juice is available plain or blended with other tropical fruit juices. Guava paste, a thick, sliceable gel, is a popular treat throughout Central America and the Caribbean. Guava will ripen if stored at room temperature and should be slightly soft and fully ripened for the best flavor.

Guava

LYCHEES

The lychee (LEE-chee), also spelled *litchi* or *leechee*, is the fruit of a large tree native to southern China and Southeast Asia. The fruits, which grow in clusters, are oval to round, red and about 1 inch (2.5 centimeters) in diameter. The tough outer skin encloses juicy, white, almost translucent flesh and one large seed. Neither the skin nor the seed is edible. The fruit travels well and is now cultivated in Florida and Hawaii, so supplies are relatively stable. Lychees are eaten fresh out of hand or juiced and are widely available canned or dried. Fresh lychees are mild but sweet with a pleasant perfume.

Lychees

MANGOSTEENS

The mangosteen, another native of Southeast Asia, is cultivated in Java, Sumatra and the Philippines. Mangosteens (no relation to mangos) are the size of a small orange, with flattened ends. They have a thick, hard, deep reddish-purple rind with hard white petal-shaped protrusions at the stem end. The interior flesh is snow-white and segmented, looking something like a mandarin orange. The texture is juicy and delicate with a slightly astringent flavor. Because the fruit must ripen on the tree and keeps only a short time, it is rarely found fresh except in outdoor local markets. Mangosteens are usually eaten fresh, although canned fruit and mangosteen juice is available.

Mangosteens

PERSIMMONS

Persimmons, sometimes referred to as kaki or Sharon fruits, are a bright orange, acorn-shaped fruit with a glossy skin and a large papery blossom. The flesh is bright orange and jellylike, with a mild but rich flavor similar to honey and plums. Persimmons should be peeled before use; any seeds should be discarded. Select bright orange fruits and refrigerate only after they are completely ripe. When ripe, persimmons will be very soft and the skin will have an almost translucent appearance.

Persimmons

Ripe persimmons are delicious eaten raw; halved and topped with cream or soft cheese; or peeled, sliced and added to fruit salads. Persimmon bread, muffins, cakes and pies are also popular. Underripe persimmons are almost inedible, however. They are strongly tannic with a chalky or cottony texture.

Persimmons are tree fruits grown in subtropical areas worldwide, although the Asian varieties—now grown in California—are the most common. Fresh persimmons are available from October through January.

POMEGRANATES

An ancient fruit native to Persia (now Iran), pomegranates (POM-uh-gran-uhtz) have long been a subject of poetry and a symbol of fertility. Pomegranates are round, about the size of a large orange, with a pronounced calyx. The skin forms a hard shell with a pinkish-red color. The interior is filled with hundreds of small, red seeds (which are, botanically, the actual fruits) surrounded by juicy red pulp. An inedible yellow membrane separates

Pomegranates

the seeds into compartments. Pomegranates are sweet-sour, and the seeds are pleasantly crunchy. The bright red seeds make an attractive garnish. Pomegranate juice is a popular beverage in Mediterranean cuisines, and grenadine syrup is made from concentrated pomegranate juice.

Select heavy fruits that are not rock-hard, cracked or heavily bruised. Whole pomegranates can be refrigerated for several weeks. Pomegranates are available from September through December; their peak season is in October.

PRICKLY PEARS

Prickly Pears

Prickly pear fruits, also known as cactus pears and Barbary figs, are actually the berries of several varieties of cactus. They are barrel- or pear-shaped, about the size of a large egg. Their thick, firm skin is green or purple with small sharp pins and nearly invisible stinging fibers. Their flesh is spongy, sweet and a brilliant pink-red, dotted with small black seeds. Prickly pears have the aroma of watermelon and the flavor of sugar water.

Once peeled, prickly pears can be diced and eaten raw, or they can be puréed for making jams, sauces, custards or sorbets, to which they give a vivid pink color. Prickly pears are especially common in Mexican and southwestern cuisines.

Select fruits that are full-colored, heavy and tender, but not too soft. Avoid those with mushy or bruised spots. Ripe prickly pears can be refrigerated for a week or more. Prickly pears are grown in Mexico and several southwestern states and are available from September through December.

PROCEDURE FOR **PEELING PRICKLY PEARS**

❶ To avoid being stung by a prickly pear, hold it steady with a fork, then use a knife to cut off both ends.

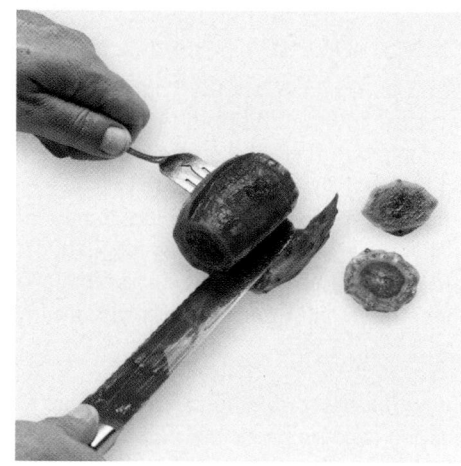

❷ Cut a lengthwise slit through the skin. Slip the tip of the knife into the cut and peel away the skin by holding it down while rolling the fruit away.

DRAGON FRUIT

Dragon Fruit

Dragon fruit are any of several species of the *Cactaceae* family native to South America now widely grown in tropical climates. About the size of an eggplant with a flavor that resembles a kiwi or melon, the fruit is eaten raw and made into a refreshing juice. Dragon fruit are peeled and handled like prickly pears, to which they are related.

RAMBUTANS

Rambutans

Rambutans (ram-BOOT-enz), the fruit of a tree in the soapberry family, are closely related to lychees. Native to

Malaysia, they are now cultivated throughout Southeast Asia. The bright-red, oval fruit is about the size of a small hen's egg and is covered with long, soft spines, hence the name "hairy" lychees. The interior has a white, lightly acidic pulp. Rambutans darken with age, so select brightly colored fruit with soft, fleshy spines. Rambutans are eaten fresh and used in preserves and ice cream; they are also available canned.

RHUBARB

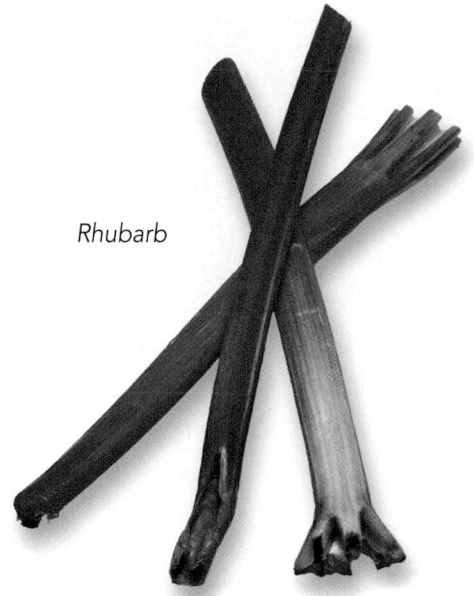

Rhubarb

Although botanically a vegetable, rhubarb (ROO-barb) is most often prepared as a fruit. It is a perennial plant that grows well in temperate and cold climates. Only the pinkish-red stems are edible; the leaves contain high amounts of oxalic acid, which is toxic.

Rhubarb stems are extremely acidic, requiring large amounts of sugar to create the desired sweet-sour taste. Cinnamon, ginger, orange and strawberry are particularly compatible with rhubarb. It is excellent for pies, cobblers, preserves or stewing. Young, tender stalks of rhubarb do not need to be peeled. When cooked, rhubarb becomes very soft and turns a beautiful light pink color.

Fresh rhubarb is sold as whole stalks, with the leaves removed. Select crisp, unblemished stalks. Rhubarb's peak season is during the early spring, from February through May. Frozen rhubarb pieces are readily available and are excellent for pies, tarts or jams.

STAR FRUITS

Star fruits, also known as carambola, are oval, up to 5 inches (12.5 centimeters) long, with five prominent ribs or wings running their length. A cross-section cut is shaped like a star. The edible skin is a waxy orange-yellow; it covers a dry, paler yellow flesh. Its flavor is similar to that of plums, sweet but bland. Star fruits do not need to be peeled or seeded. They are most often sliced and added to fruit salad or used as a garnish. Unripe fruits can be cooked in stews or chutneys.

Star Fruits

Color and aroma are the best indicators of ripeness. The fruits should be a deep golden-yellow, and there should be brown along the edge of the ribs. The aroma should be full and floral. Green fruits can be kept at room temperature to ripen, then refrigerated for up to 2 weeks. Star fruits are cultivated in Hawaii, Florida and California, though some are still imported from the Caribbean. Fresh fruits are available from August to February.

YUZU

Yuzu (YOO-zoo) is a sour citrus fruit from Japan. Its aromatic rind is used as a garnish and flavor enhancer. Tart yuzu juice is used by pastry chefs in confections and creams. Both the bottled juice and dried rind are available from specialty producers, although the fresh fruit is rarely available in the United States.

Grapes

Grapes (Fr. *raisins*; Sp. *uvas*) are the single largest fruit crop in the world, due, of course, to their use in wine making. This section, however, discusses only table grapes, those grown for eating. Grapes are berries that grow on vines in large clusters. California is the world's largest producer, with more than a dozen varieties grown for table use. Grapes are classified by color as white (which are actually green) or black (which are actually red). White grapes are generally blander than black ones, with a thinner skin and firmer flesh.

The grape's color and most of its flavor are found in the skin. Grapes are usually eaten raw, either alone or in fruit salads. They are also used as a garnish or accompaniment to desserts and cheeses. Dried grapes are known as raisins (Fr. *raisins sec*; usually made from Thompson Seedless or muscat grapes), currants (made from Black Corinth grapes and labeled Zante currants) or sultanas (made from sultana grapes).

Grapes are available all year because the many varieties have different harvesting schedules. Look for firm, unblemished fruits that are firmly attached to the stem. A surface bloom or dusty appearance is caused by yeasts and indicates recent harvesting. Wrinkled grapes or those with brown spots around the stem are past their prime. All grapes should be rinsed and drained before use.

Red Flame Grapes

RED FLAME GRAPES

Red Flame grapes are a seedless California hybrid, second only in importance to the Thompson Seedless. Red Flame grapes are large and round with a slightly tart flavor and variegated red color.

THOMPSON SEEDLESS GRAPES

The most commercially important table grapes are a variety known as Thompson Seedless, which are pale green with a crisp texture and sweet flavor. Their peak season is from June to November. Many are dried in the hot desert sun of California's San Joaquin Valley to produce dark raisins. For golden raisins, Thompson Seedless grapes are treated with sulfur dioxide to prevent browning, then dried mechanically.

Thompson Seedless Grapes

Concord Grapes

OTHER TABLE GRAPES

Of the table grapes containing seeds, the most important varieties are the Concord, Ribier and Emperor. They range from light red to deep black, and all three are in season during the autumn. Concord grapes, one of the few grape varieties native to the New World, are especially important for making juices and jellies.

Virtually all the fine wine made in the world comes from varieties of a single grape species, *Vitis vinifera*. It is grown in the United States, Europe, South Africa, South America, the Middle East, Australia and wherever fine wine is made. The variety of grapes used in any given wine determines the wine's character, which is discussed in Chapter 6, Flavor and Flavorings.

Melons

Like pumpkins and cucumbers, melons are members of the gourd family (*Cucurbitaceae*). The dozens of melon varieties can be divided into two general types: sweet (or dessert) melons and watermelons. Sweet melons have a tan, green or yellow netted or furrowed rind and dense, fragrant flesh. Watermelon has a thick, dark green rind surrounding crisp, watery flesh.

Melons are almost 90 percent water, so cooking destroys their texture, quickly turning the flesh to mush. Most are served simply sliced, perhaps with a bit of lemon or lime juice. Melons also blend well in fruit salads or with rich, cured meats such as prosciutto. Melons may be puréed and made into sorbet or chilled, uncooked soup.

Melons should be vine-ripened. A ripe melon should yield slightly and spring back when pressed at the blossom end (opposite the stem). It should also give off a strong aroma. Avoid melons that are very soft or feel damp at the stem end. Ripe melons may be stored in the refrigerator, although the flavor will be better at room temperature. Slightly underripe melons can be stored at room temperature to allow flavor and aroma to develop.

Cantaloupes

CANTALOUPES

American cantaloupes, which are actually muskmelons, are sweet melons with a thick, yellow-green netted rind; a sweet, moist, orange flesh; and a strong aroma. (European cantaloupes, which are not generally available in the United States, are more craggy and furrowed in appearance.) As with all sweet melons, the many small seeds are found in a central cavity. Cantaloupes are excellent for eating alone and are especially good with ham or rich meats.

Avoid cantaloupes with the pronounced yellow color or moldy aroma that indicates overripeness. Mexican imports ensure a year-round supply, although their peak season is summer.

Casaba Melons

CASABA MELONS

The casaba melon is a teardrop-shaped sweet melon. It has a coarse, yellow skin and a thick, ridged rind; its flesh is creamy white to yellow. Casaba melons are used like cantaloupes. Casaba melons do not have an aroma, so selection must be based on a deep skin color and the absence of dark or moist patches. Their peak season is during September and October.

CRENSHAW MELONS

Crenshaw (or cranshaw) melons have a mottled, green-yellow ridged rind and orange-pink flesh. They are large, pear-shaped sweet melons with a strong aroma. The flesh has a rich, spicy flavor and may be used like cantaloupe. Crenshaws are available from July through October; their peak season is during August and September.

Crenshaw Melons

HONEYDEW MELONS

Honeydew melons are large, oval sweet melons with a smooth rind that ranges from white to pale green. Although the flesh is generally pale green, with a mild, sweet flavor, pink- or gold-fleshed honeydews are also available. Like casaba melons, honeydew melons have little to no aroma. They are available almost all year; their peak season is from June through October.

Green Honeydews

SANTA CLAUS MELONS

Santa Claus or Christmas melons are large, elongated sweet melons with a green-and-yellow-striped, smooth rind. The flesh is creamy white or yellow and tastes like casaba. They are a winter variety, with peak availability during December, which explains the name.

Gold Honeydews

WATERMELONS

Watermelons are large (up to 30 pounds or 13.5 kilograms) round or oval-shaped melons with a thick rind. The skin may be solid green, green-striped or mottled with white. The flesh is crisp and extremely juicy with small, hard, black seeds throughout. Seedless hybrids are available. Most watermelons have pink to red flesh, although golden-fleshed varieties are becoming more common. Watermelons are of a different genus from the sweet melons described earlier. They are native to tropical Africa and are now grown commercially in Texas and several southern states.

Santa Claus Melons

Watermelons

Gold Watermelons

Rome   *Red Delicious*

Granny Smith

Golden Delicious

McIntosh

Gala

Pomes

Pomes are tree fruits with thin skin and firm flesh surrounding a central core containing many small seeds called pips or carpels. Pomes include apples, pears and quince.

APPLES

Apples (Fr. *pommes*), perhaps the most common and commonly appreciated of all fruits, grow on trees in temperate zones worldwide. They are popular because of their convenience, flavor, variety and availability.

Apples can be eaten raw out of hand, or they can be used in a wide variety of cooked or baked dishes. They are equally useful in breads, desserts or vegetable dishes and go well with game, pork and poultry. Classic dishes prepared with apples are often referred to as *à la Normande.* Apple juice (cider) produces alcoholic and nonalcoholic beverages and cider vinegar.

Of the hundreds of known apple varieties, only 20 or so are commercially significant in the United States. Several varieties and their characteristics are noted in Table 25.1. Most have a moist, creamy white flesh with a thin skin of yellow, green or red. They range in flavor from very sweet to very tart, with an equally broad range of textures, from firm and crisp to soft and mealy.

In Europe, apples are divided into distinct cooking and eating varieties. Cooking varieties are those that disintegrate to a purée when cooked. American varieties are less rigidly classified. Nevertheless, not all apples are appropriate for all types of cooking. Those that retain their shape better during cooking are the best choices when slices or appearance are important. Varieties with a higher malic acid content break down easily, making them more appropriate for applesauce or juicing. Either type may be eaten out of hand, depending on personal preference.

Although not native to North America, apples are now grown commercially in 35 states, with Washington and New York leading in production. Apples are harvested when still slightly underripe, then stored in a controlled atmosphere (temperature and oxygen are greatly reduced) for extended periods until ready for sale. Modern storage techniques make fresh apples available all year, although their peak season is during the autumn.

When selecting apples, look for smooth, unbroken skins and firm fruits, without soft spots or bruises. Badly bruised or rotting apples should be discarded immediately. They emit quantities of ethylene gas that speed spoilage of nearby fruits. (Remember the say-

TABLE 25.1	APPLE VARIETIES				
VARIETY	**SKIN COLOR**	**FLAVOR**	**TEXTURE**	**PEAK SEASON**	**USE**
Fiji	Yellow-green with red highlights	Sweet-spicy	Crisp	All year	Eating, in salads
Gala	Yellow-orange with red stripes	Sweet	Crisp	Aug.–March	Eating, in salads, sauce
Golden Delicious	Glossy, greenish-gold	Sweet	Semifirm	Sept.–Oct.	In tarts, with cheese, in salads
Granny Smith	Bright green	Tart	Firm and crisp	Oct.–Nov.	Eating, in tarts
Jonathan	Brilliant red	Tart to acidic	Tender	Sept.–Oct.	Eating, all-purpose
McIntosh	Red with green background	Tart to acidic	Soft	Fall	Applesauce, in closed pies
Pippin (Newton)	Greenish-yellow	Tart	Semifirm	Fall	In pies, eating, baking
Red Delicious	Deep red	Sweet but bland	Soft to mealy	Sept.–Oct.	Eating
Rome	Red	Sweet-tart	Firm	Oct.–Nov.	Baking, pies, sauces
Winesap	Dark red with streaks	Tangy	Crisp	Oct.–Nov.	Cider, all-purpose

ing that "one bad apple spoils the barrel.") Store apples chilled for up to 6 weeks. Apple peels (the skin) may be eaten or removed as desired, but in either case, apples should be washed just before use to remove pesticides and any wax that was applied to improve appearance. Apple slices can be frozen (often with sugar or citric acid added to slow spoilage) or dried.

PROCEDURE FOR **CORING APPLES**

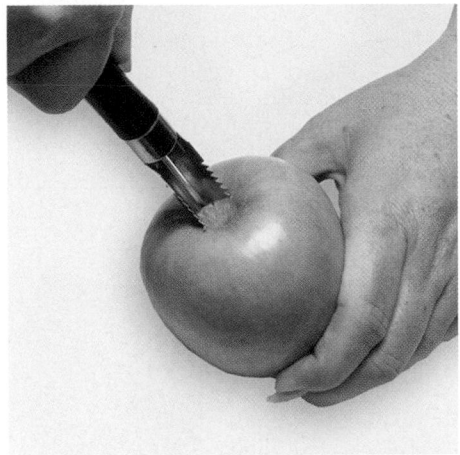

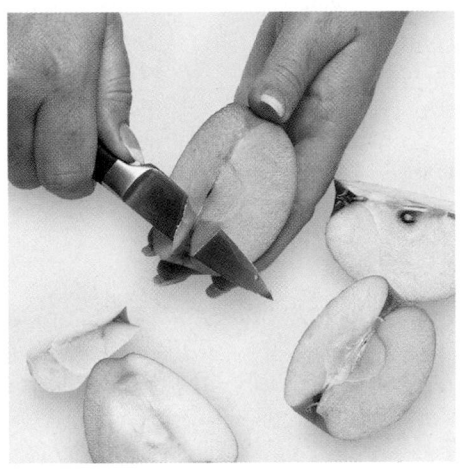

❶ Remove the core from a whole apple with an apple corer by inserting the corer from the stem end and pushing out the cylinder containing the core and seeds.

❷ Alternatively, first cut an apple into quarters, then use a paring knife to cut away the core and seeds.

PEARS

Pears (Fr. *poires*) are an ancient tree fruit grown in temperate areas throughout the world. Most of the pears marketed in the United States are grown in California, Washington and Oregon.

Although thousands of pear varieties have been identified, only a dozen or so are commercially significant. Several varieties and their characteristics are noted in Table 25.2. Pear varieties vary widely in size, color and flavor. They are most often eaten out of hand but can be baked or poached. Pears are delicious with cheese, especially blue cheeses, and can be used in fruit salads, compotes or preserves.

Asian pears, also known as Chinese pears or apple-pears, are of a different species than common pears. They have the moist, sweet flavor of a pear and the round shape and crisp texture of an apple. They are becoming increasingly popular in the United States, particularly those known as Twentieth Century or Nijisseiki.

When selecting pears, look for fruits with smooth, unbroken skin and an intact stem. Pears will not ripen properly on the tree, so they are picked while still firm and should be allowed to soften before use. Underripe pears may be left at room temperature to ripen. A properly ripened pear should have a good fragrance and yield to gentle pressure at the stem end. Pears can be prepared or stored in the same ways as apples.

Anjou

Asian Pears

Bosc

Bartlett

Red d'Anjou

TABLE 25.2 PEAR VARIETIES

VARIETY	APPEARANCE	FLAVOR	TEXTURE	PEAK SEASON	USE
Anjou (Beurre d'Anjou)	Greenish-yellow skin; egg-shaped with short neck; red variety also available	Sweet and juicy	Firm, keeps well	Oct.–May	Eating, poaching
Bartlett (Williams)	Thin yellow skin; bell-shaped; red variety also available	Very sweet, buttery, juicy	Tender	Aug.–Dec.	Eating, canning, in salads
Bosc	Golden-brown skin; long tapered neck	Buttery	Dry, holds its shape well	Sept.–May	Poaching, baking
Comice	Yellow-green skin; large and chubby	Sweet, juicy	Smooth	Oct.–Feb.	Eating
Sekel	Tiny; brown to yellow skin	Spicy	Very firm, grainy	Aug.–Dec.	Poaching, pickling

QUINCE

Common quince (kwince; Fr. *coing*) resemble large, lumpy yellow pears. Their flesh is hard, with many pips or seeds, and they have a wonderful fragrance. Too astringent to eat raw, quince develop a sweet flavor and pink color when cooked with sugar. Quince are used in meat stews, jellies, marmalades and pies. They have a high **pectin** content and may be added to other fruit jams or preserves to encourage gelling.

Quince

Fresh quince, usually imported from South America or southeast Europe, are available from October through January. Select firm fruits with a good yellow color. Small blemishes may be cut away before cooking. Quince will keep for up to a month under refrigeration.

pectin a gelatin-like carbohydrate obtained from certain fruits; used to thicken jams and jellies

Stone Fruits

Stone fruits, also known as drupes, include apricots, cherries, nectarines, peaches and plums. They are characterized by a thin skin, soft flesh and one woody stone or pit. Although most originated in China, the shrubs and trees producing stone fruits are now grown in temperate climates worldwide.

The domestic varieties of stone fruits are in season from late spring through summer. They tend to be fragile fruits, are easily bruised and difficult to transport, and have a short shelf life. Do not wash them until ready to use, as moisture can cause deterioration. Stone fruits are excellent dried and are often used to make liqueurs and brandies. (The kernel inside the pits of many stone fruits contains amygdalin, a compound that has a bitter almond flavor. Eating the raw kernel can cause digestive discomfort or more serious side effects and should be avoided. When cooked it is harmless and can add flavor to jams and creams.)

APRICOTS

Apricots (Fr. *abricots*) are small, round stone fruits with a velvety skin that varies from deep yellow to vivid orange. Their juicy orange flesh surrounds a dark, almond-shaped pit. Apricots can be eaten out of hand, poached, stewed, baked or candied. They are often used in fruit compotes or savory sauces for meat or poultry and are also popular in quick breads and fruit tarts or puréed for dessert sauces, jams, custards or mousses.

Apricots have a short season, peaking during June and July, and do not travel well. Select apricots that are well shaped, plump and fairly firm. Avoid ones that are greenish-yellow or mushy. Fresh apricots will last for several days under refrigeration, but the flavor is best at room temperature. If fresh fruits are unavailable, canned apricots are usually an acceptable substitute. Dried apricots and apricot juice (known as nectar) are readily available.

Apricots

CHERRIES

From the northern states, particularly Washington, Oregon, Michigan and New York, come the two most important types of cherry: the sweet cherry and the sour (or tart) cherry.

Sweet cherries (Fr. *cerises*) are round to heart-shaped, about 1 inch (2.5 centimeters) in diameter, with skin that ranges from yellow to deep red to nearly black. The flesh, which is sweet and juicy, may vary from yellow to dark red. The most common and popular sweet cherries are the dark red Bings. Yellow-red Royal Ann and Rainier cherries are also available in some areas.

Rainier Cherries

Sweet cherries are often marketed fresh, made into maraschino cherries or candied for use in baked goods. Fresh sweet cherries have a very short season, peaking during June and July. Cherries will not ripen further after harvesting. Select fruits that are firm and plump with a green stem still attached. There should not be any brown spots around the stem. A dry or brown stem indicates that the cherry is less than fresh. Once the stem is removed, the cherry will deteriorate rapidly. Store fresh cherries in the refrigerator and do not wash them until ready to use.

Sour cherries are light to dark red and are so acidic they are rarely eaten uncooked. The most common sour cherries are the Montmorency and Morello. Most sour cherries are canned or frozen, or cooked with sugar and starch (usually cornstarch or tapioca) and sold as prepared pastry and pie fillings.

Both sweet and sour varieties are available dried.

Bing Cherries

PROCEDURE FOR **PITTING CHERRIES**

Remove the stem and place the cherry in the pitter with the indentation facing up. Squeeze the handles together to force out the pit.

PEACHES AND NECTARINES

Peaches (Fr. *pêches*) are moderate-sized, round fruits with a juicy, sweet flesh. Nectarines are a variety of peach, the main difference between the two being their skin. Peaches have a thin skin covered with fuzz, whereas nectarines have a thin, smooth skin. The flesh of either fruit ranges from white to pale orange. Although their flavors are somewhat different, they may be substituted for each other in most recipes.

Peaches and nectarines are excellent for eating out of hand or in dessert tarts or pastries. They are also used in jams, chutneys, preserves and savory relishes, having a particular affinity for Asian and Indian dishes. Although the skin is edible, peaches are generally peeled before being used. (Peaches are easily peeled if blanched first.)

Peaches

Peaches and nectarines are either freestones or clingstones. With freestones, the flesh separates easily from the stone; freestone fruits are commonly eaten out of hand. The flesh of clingstones adheres firmly to the stone; they hold their shape better when cooked and are the type most often canned.

Select fruits with a good aroma; an overall creamy, yellow or yellow-orange color; and an unwrinkled skin free of blemishes. Red patches are not an indication of ripeness; a green skin indicates that the fruit was picked too early and it will not ripen further. Peaches and nectarines will soften but do not become sweeter after harvesting.

Nectarines

HEIRLOOM VARIETIES AND GENETIC DIVERSITY

"Sun Crest has the buttery flavor that melts in your mouth, smooth and sweet with the message of summer in each bite," writes David Mas Masumoto, a third-generation Japanese American peach farmer. But this variety, "one of the last remaining truly juice peaches," doesn't keep well when picked fully ripe. Like many older varieties of fruits and vegetables, it is less suited to the demands of commercial agriculture. In his book *Epitaph for a Peach*, Masumoto writes of the challenges faced by a small family farmer and trying to find a market for these unique peaches.

Many chefs and home gardeners now seek out older or *heirloom* varieties such as that which Masumoto grows. Despite the fact that they may bruise easily or be irregular in size and appearance, heirloom fruits and vegetables are appealing because of their unique flavor and suitability to specific growing conditions. But the term *heirloom* suggests a cherished and irreplaceable artifact that may no longer

be of use. According to botanists and farmers, these neglected varieties are essential in order to ensure a continued food supply. The intensive agriculture on which the world's food supply increasingly depends means less genetic diversity.

With less diversity, crops become more vulnerable to insect and environmental stress. Recognizing the need to protect all species, the USDA has organized the National Plant Germplasm System (NPGS), a collection of state, federal and private farms where genetically diverse assortments of plants are grown and distributed. More than 30 such repositories or farms exist across the country. There, countless species of stone fruits, berries, legumes, nuts and all manner of plants are grown to enhance breeding for future fruit and vegetable crops. Seeds of wild species are stored for future propagation.

Organizations such as the Chef's Collaborative and Slow Food USA are good resources from which to learn more about fruits, vegetables and other food products whose cultivation is in jeopardy. Slow Food's Ark of Taste is a catalog of more than 200 cherished and delicious foods in danger of extinction, including the Blenheim Apricot, the Hatcher Melon and Masumoto's beloved Sun Crest peach.

The United States, especially California, is the world's largest producer of peaches and nectarines. Their peak season is through the summer months, with July and August producing the best crop. South American peaches are sometimes available from January to May. Canned and frozen peaches are readily available.

PLUMS

Plums (Fr. *prunes*) are round to oval-shaped fruits that grow on trees or bushes. Dozens of plum varieties are known, although only a few are commercially significant. Plums vary in size from very small to 3 inches (7.5 centimeters) in diameter. Their thin skin can be green, red, yellow or various shades of blue-purple.

Plums are excellent for eating out of hand. Plums can also be baked, poached or used in pies, cobblers or tarts; they are often used in jams or preserves, and fresh slices can be used in salads or compotes.

Fresh plums are widely available from June through October; their peak season is in August and September. When selecting plums, look for plump, smooth fruits with unblemished skin. Generally, they should yield to gentle pressure, although the green and yellow varieties remain quite firm. Avoid plums with moist, brown spots near the stem. Plums may be left at room temperature to ripen, then stored in the refrigerator. Prunes, discussed later, are produced by drying special plum varieties, usually the French Agen.

Santa Rosa Plums

Damson Plums

Tropicals

Tropical fruits are native to the world's hot, tropical or subtropical regions. Most are now readily available throughout the United States thanks to rapid transportation and distribution methods. All can be eaten fresh, without cooking. Their flavors complement each other and go well with rich or spicy meat, fish and poultry dishes.

BANANAS

Common yellow bananas (Fr. *bananes*) are actually the berries of a large tropical herb. Grown in bunches called hands, they are about 7 to 9 inches (17.5 to 22.5 centimeters) long, with a sticky, soft, sweet flesh. Their inedible yellow skin is easily removed. Baby bananas (Nino, Ladyfinger or Finger Bananas) measure 4 to 5 inches long (10 to 12.5 centimeters) with yellow or red skin. Their flesh is more dense and sweeter than most larger banana varieties, and their diminutive size makes them ideal for many dessert applications.

Properly ripened bananas are excellent eaten out of hand or used in salads. Lightly bruised or overripe fruits are best used for breads or muffins. Bananas blend well with other tropical fruits and citrus. Their unique flavor is also complemented by curry, cinnamon, ginger, honey and chocolate.

Common Yellow Bananas

Fresh bananas are available all year. Bananas are always harvested when still green, because the texture and flavor will be adversely affected if the fruits are allowed to turn yellow on the tree. Unripe bananas are hard, dry and starchy. Because bananas ripen after harvesting, it is acceptable to purchase green bananas if there is sufficient time for final ripening before use. Bananas should be left at room temperature to ripen. A properly ripened banana has a yellow peel with brown flecks. The tip should not have any remaining green coloring. As bananas continue to age, the peel darkens and the starches turn to sugar, giving the fruits a sweeter flavor. Avoid bananas that have large brown bruises or a gray cast (a sign of cold damage).

Plantains, also referred to as cooking bananas, are larger than but not as sweet as common bananas. They are frequently cooked as a starchy vegetable in tropical cuisines.

Plantains

DATES

Dates (Fr. *dattes*) are the fruit of the date palm tree, which has been cultivated since ancient times. Dates are about 1 to 2 inches (2.5 to 5 centimeters) long, with a paper-thin skin and a single grooved seed in the center. Most are golden to dark brown when ripe.

Although dates appear to be dried, they are actually fresh fruits. They have a sticky-sweet, almost candied texture and rich flavor. Dates provide flavor and moisture for breads, muffins, cookies and tarts. They can also be served with fresh or dried fruits, or stuffed with meat or cheese as an appetizer.

Medjool Dates

Pitted dates are readily available in several packaged forms: whole, chopped or extruded (for use in baking). Whole unpitted dates are available in bulk. Date juice is also available for use as a natural sweetener, especially in baked goods. Although packaged or processed dates are available all year, peak season for fresh domestic dates is from October through December. When selecting dates, look for those that are plump, glossy and moist.

KIWIS

Kiwis, sometimes known as kiwifruits or Chinese gooseberries, are small oval fruits, about the size of a large egg, with a thin, fuzzy brown skin. The flesh is bright green with a white core surrounded by hundreds of tiny black seeds.

Kiwis

Kiwis are sweet, but somewhat bland. They are best used raw, peeled and eaten out of hand or sliced for fruit salads or garnish. Although kiwis are not recommended for cooking because heat causes them to fall apart, they are a perfect addition to glazed fruit tarts and can be puréed for sorbets, sauces or mousses. Kiwis contain an enzyme similar to that in fresh pineapple and papaya, which has a tenderizing effect on meat and prevents gelling.

MANGOES

Mangoes (Fr. *mangues*) are oval or kidney-shaped fruits that normally weigh between 6 ounces and 1 pound (180 and 500 grams). Their skin is smooth and thin but tough, varying from yellow to orange-red, with patches of green, red or purple. As mangoes ripen, the green disappears. The juicy, bright orange flesh clings to a large, flat pit.

Mangoes

A mango's unique flavor is spicy-sweet, with an acidic tang. Mangoes can be puréed for use in drinks or sauces, or the flesh can be sliced or cubed for use in salads, pickles, chutneys or desserts. Mangoes go well with spicy foods such as curry and with barbecued meats.

Although Florida produces some mangoes, most of those available in the United States are from Mexico and Central America. Their peak season is from May through August. Select fruits with good color that are firm and free of blemishes. Ripe mangoes should have a good aroma, and should not be too soft or shriveled. Allow mangoes to ripen completely at room temperature, then refrigerate for up to 1 week.

PROCEDURE FOR **PITTING AND CUTTING MANGOES**

1. Cut along each side of the pit to remove two sections.

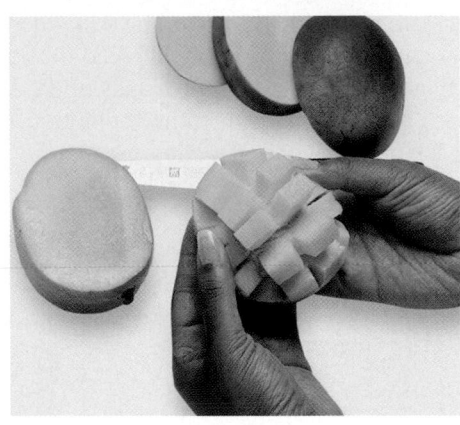

2. Each section can then be cubed using the "hedgehog" technique: Make crosswise cuts through the flesh, just to the skin; press up on the skin side of the section, exposing the cubes.

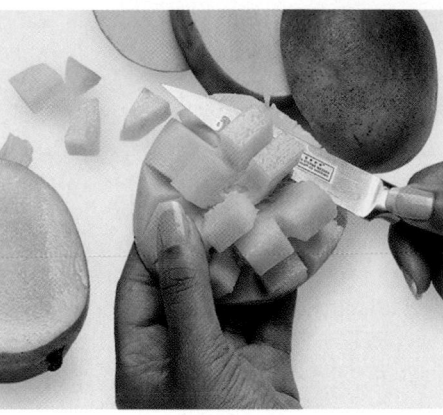

3. The mango may be served like this or the cubes can be cut off to use in salads or other dishes.

Red Papayas

papain an enzyme found in papayas that breaks down proteins; used as the primary ingredient in many commercial meat tenderizers

PAPAYAS

The papaya (puh-PIE-yuh) is a greenish-yellow fruit shaped rather like a large pear and weighing 1 to 2 pounds (500 to 1000 grams). When halved, it resembles a melon. The flesh is golden to reddish-pink; its center cavity is filled with round, silver-black seeds resembling caviar. Ripe papayas can be eaten raw, with only a squirt of lemon or lime juice. They can also be puréed for sweet or spicy sauces, chilled soups or sorbets.

Papayas contain **papain**, which breaks down proteins, and therefore papayas are an excellent meat tenderizer. Meats can be marinated with papaya juice or slices before cooking. Papain, however, makes fresh papayas unsuitable for use in gelatins because it inhibits gelling. Unripe (green) papayas are often used in pickles or chutneys and can be baked or stewed with meat or poultry.

Papayas

Papaya seeds are edible, with a peppery flavor and slight crunch. They are occasionally used to garnish fruit salads or add flavor to fruit salsas and compotes.

Papayas are grown in tropical and subtropical areas worldwide. Although they are available year-round, their peak season is from April through June. Select papayas that are plump, with a smooth, unblemished skin. Color is a better determinant of ripeness than is softness: The greater the proportion of yellow to green skin color, the riper the fruit. Papayas may be held at room temperature until completely ripe, then refrigerated for up to 1 week.

PASSION FRUITS

Passion fruits (Fr. *fruits de la passion*) have a firm, almost shell-like purple skin with orange-yellow pulp surrounding large, black, edible seeds. They are about the size and shape of large hen eggs, with a sweet, rich and unmistakable citrusy flavor. The pulp is used in custards, sauces and ice creams.

Select heavy fruits with dark, shriveled skin and a strong aroma. Allow them to ripen at room temperature, if necessary, then refrigerate. Passion fruits are now grown in New Zealand, Hawaii and California and should be available all year, although their peak season is in February and March. Bottles or frozen packs of purée are readily available and provide a strong, true flavor.

Passion Fruit

PINEAPPLES

Pineapples (Fr. *ananas*) are the fruit of a shrub with sharp spear-shaped leaves. Each fruit is covered with rough, brown eyes, giving it the appearance of a pine cone. The pale yellow flesh, which is sweet and very juicy, surrounds a cylindrical woody core that is edible but too tough for most uses. Most pineapples weigh approximately 2 pounds (1 kilogram), but dwarf varieties are also available.

Pineapples are excellent eaten raw, alone or in salads. Slices can be baked or grilled to accompany pork or ham. The cuisines of Southeast Asia incorporate pineapple into various curries, soups and stews. Pineapple juice is a popular beverage, often used in punch or cocktails. Canned or cooked pineapple can be added to gelatin mixtures, but avoid using fresh pineapple; an enzyme (bromelin) found in fresh pineapple breaks down gelatin.

Pineapples do not ripen after harvesting. They must be left on the stem until completely ripe, at which time they are extremely perishable. Most pineapples come from Hawaii. Fresh pineapples are available all year, with peak supplies in March through June. Select heavy fruits with a strong, sweet aroma and rich color. Avoid those with dried leaves or soft spots. Pineapples should be used as soon as possible after purchase. Pineapples are also available canned in slices, cubes or crushed, dried or candied.

Pineapples

PROCEDURE FOR **TRIMMING AND SLICING PINEAPPLES**

❶ Slice off the leaves and stem end. Stand the fruit upright and cut the peel off in vertical strips.

❷ Cut the peeled fruit in quarters, then cut away the woody core.

❸ The flesh can then be cut as desired.

NUTRITION

Most fruits are quite nutritious. They have a high water content (usually 75 to 95 percent) and low protein and fat contents, all of which makes them low in calories. They are also an excellent source of fiber, and the sugar content of ripe fruits is a good source of energy. Some fruits, such as citrus, melons and strawberries, contain large amounts of vitamin C (which may be destroyed, however, by cooking or processing). Deep yellow and green fruits, such as apricots, mangoes and kiwis, are high in vitamin A; bananas, raisins and figs are a good source of potassium.

PURCHASING FRESH FRUITS

Fresh fruits have not been subjected to any processing (such as canning, freezing or drying). Fresh fruits may be ripe or unripe, depending on their condition when harvested or the conditions under which they have been stored. In order to use fresh fruits to their best advantage, it is important to make careful purchasing decisions. It is important to pay attention to the size of each piece of fruit, its grade or quality, its ripeness on delivery and its nutritional content in order to serve fruit in an appropriate and cost-effective manner.

Grading

Fresh fruits traded on the wholesale market may be graded under the USDA's voluntary program. The grades, based on size and uniformity of shape, color and texture as well as the absence of defects, are U.S. Fancy, U.S. No. 1, U.S. No. 2 and U.S. No. 3. Most fruits purchased for food service operations are U.S. Fancy. Fruits with lower grades are suitable for processing into sauces, jams, jellies or preserves.

Ripening

Several important changes take place in a fruit as it ripens. The fruit reaches its full size; its pulp or flesh becomes soft and tender; its color changes. In addition, the fruit's acid content declines, making it less tart, and its starch content converts into the sugars fructose and glucose, which provide the fruit's sweetness, flavor and aroma.

Unfortunately, these changes do not stop when the fruit reaches its peak of ripeness. Rather, they continue, deteriorating the fruit's texture and flavor and eventually causing spoilage.

Depending on the species, fresh fruits can be purchased either fully ripened or unripened. Figs and pineapples, for example, ripen only on the plant and are harvested at or just before their peak of ripeness, then rushed to market. They should not be purchased unripened as they will never attain full flavor or texture after harvesting. On the other hand, some fruits, including bananas and pears, continue to ripen after harvesting and can be purchased unripened.

With most harvested fruits, the ripening time as well as the time during which the fruits remain at their peak of ripeness can be manipulated. For instance, ripening can be delayed by chilling. Chilling slows the fruit's **respiration rate** (fruits, like animals, consume oxygen and expel carbon dioxide). The slower the respiration rate, the slower the conversion of starch to sugar. For quicker ripening, fruit can be stored at room temperature.

Ripening is also affected by ethylene gas, a colorless, odorless hydrocarbon gas. Ethylene gas is naturally emitted by ripening fruits and can be used to encourage further ripening in most fruits. Apples, tomatoes, melons and bananas give off the most ethylene and should be stored away from delicate fruits and vegetables, especially greens. Fruits that are picked and shipped unripened can be exposed to ethylene gas to induce ripening just before sale. Conversely, to extend the life of ripe fruits a day or two, isolate them from other fruits and keep them well chilled.

Fresh fruits will not ripen further once they are cooked or processed. The cooking or processing method applied, however, may soften the fruits or add flavor.

respiration rate the speed with which the cells of a fruit use oxygen and produce carbon dioxide during ripening

Purchasing

Fresh fruits are sold by weight or by count. They are packed in containers referred to as crates, bushels, cartons, cases, lugs or flats. The weight or count packed in each of these containers varies depending on the type of fruit, the purveyor and the state in which the fruits were packed. For example, Texas citrus is packed in cartons equal to ⁷⁄₁₀ of a bushel; Florida citrus is packed in cartons equal to ⅘ of a bushel. Sometimes fruit size must be specified when ordering. A 30-pound case of lemons, for example, may contain 96, 112 or 144 individual lemons, depending on their size.

Some fresh fruits, especially melons, pineapples, peaches and berries, are available trimmed, cleaned, peeled or cut. Sugar and preservatives are sometimes added. They are sold in bulk containers, sometimes packed in water. These items offer a consistent product with a significant reduction in labor costs. The purchase price may be greater than that for fresh fruits, and flavor, freshness and nutritional qualities may suffer somewhat from the processing.

PURCHASING AND STORING PRESERVED FRUITS

Preservation techniques are designed to extend the shelf life of fruits in essentially fresh form. These methods include irradiation, acidulation, canning, freezing and drying. Except for drying, these techniques do not substantially change the fruits' texture or flavor. Canning and freezing can also be used to preserve cooked fruits.

Preserves such as jellies and jams are cooked products and are discussed later in this chapter.

Irradiated Fruits

As described in Chapter 21, Vegetables, some fruits can be subjected to ionizing radiation to destroy parasites, insects and bacteria. The treatment also slows ripening without a noticeable effect on the fruits' flavor and texture. Irradiated fruits must be labeled "treated with radiation," "treated by irradiation" or with the symbol shown here.

Irradiation Symbol

Acidulation

Apples, pears, bananas, peaches and other fruits turn brown when cut. Although this browning is commonly attributed to exposure to oxygen, it is actually caused by the reaction of enzymes.

Enzymatic browning can be retarded by immersing cut fruits in an acidic solution such as lemon or orange juice. This simple technique is sometimes referred to as **acidulation**. Soaking fruits in water or lemon juice and water (called acidulated water) is not recommended. Unless a sufficient amount of salt or sugar is added to the water, the fruits will just become mushy. But if enough salt or sugar is added to retain texture, the flavor will be affected.

Canned Fruits

Almost any type of fruit can be canned successfully; pineapple and peaches are the largest sellers. In commercial canning, raw fruits are cleaned and placed in a sealed container, then subjected to high temperatures for a specific amount of time. Heating destroys the microorganisms that cause spoilage, and the sealed environment created by the can eliminates oxidation and retards decomposition. But the heat required by the canning process also softens the texture of most fruits. Canning has little or no effect on vitamins A, B, C and D because oxygen is not present during the heating process. Canning also has no practical effect on proteins, fats or carbohydrates.

In solid-pack cans, little or no water is added. The only liquid is from the fruits' natural moisture. Water-pack cans have water or fruit juice added, which must be taken into account when determining costs. Syrup-pack cans have a sugar syrup—light, medium or heavy—added. The syrup should also be taken into account when determining food costs, and the additional sweetness should be considered when using syrup-packed fruits. Cooked fruit products such as pie fillings are also available canned.

Canned fruits are purchased in cases of standard-sized cans (see Appendix II). Once a can is opened, any unused contents should be transferred to an appropriate storage container and refrigerated. Cans with bulges should be discarded immediately, without opening.

Frozen Fruits

Freezing is a highly effective method for preserving fruits. It severely inhibits the growth of microorganisms that cause fruits to spoil. Freezing does not destroy nutrients, although the appearance or texture of most fruits can be affected because of their high water content. This occurs when ice crystals formed from the water in the cells burst the cells' walls.

Many fruits, especially berries and apple and pear slices, are now individually quick-frozen (IQF). This method employs blasts of cold air, refrigerated plates, liquid nitrogen, liquid air or other techniques to chill the produce quickly. Speeding the freezing process can greatly reduce the formation of ice crystals.

Fruits can be trimmed and sliced before freezing and are also available frozen in sugar syrup, which adds flavor and prevents browning. Berries are frozen whole, whereas stone fruits are usually peeled, pitted and sliced. Fruit purées are also available frozen.

Frozen fruits are graded as U.S. Grade A (Fancy), U.S. Grade B (Choice or Extra Standard), or U.S. Grade C (Standard). The "U.S." indicates that a government inspector has graded the product, but packers may use grade names without an actual inspection if the contents meet the standards of the grade indicated.

IQF fruits can be purchased in bulk by the case. All frozen fruits should be sealed in moisture-proof wrapping and kept at a constant temperature of 0°F (–18°C) or below. Temperature fluctuations can cause freezer burn. Frozen berries such as blueberries and blackberries should not be thawed before adding to batters because their juice can easily discolor the batter.

Dried Fruits

Drying is the oldest known technique for preserving fruits, having been used for more than 5000 years. When ripe fruits are dried, they lose most of their moisture. This concentrates their flavors and sugars and dramatically extends shelf life. Although most fruits can be dried, plums (prunes), grapes (raisins, sultanas and currants), apricots and figs are the fruits most commonly dried. The drying method can be as simple as leaving ripe fruits in the sun to dry naturally or the more cost-efficient technique of passing fruits through a compartment of hot, dry air to quickly extract moisture.

Dried fruits actually retain from 16 to 26 percent residual moisture, which leaves them moist and soft. They are often treated with sulfur dioxide to prevent browning (oxidation) and to extend shelf life. Dried fruits may be eaten out of hand; added to cereals or salads; baked in muffins, breads, pies or tarts; stewed for chutneys or compotes; or used as a stuffing for roasted meats or poultry. Before use, dried fruits may be softened by steeping them for a short time in a hot liquid such as water, wine, rum, brandy or other liquor. Some dried fruits should be simmered in a small amount of water before use.

Store dried fruits in airtight containers to prevent further moisture loss; keep in a dry, cool area away from sunlight. Dried fruits may mold if exposed to both air and high humidity.

Golden Raisins

Currants

Kiwis

Persimmons

Apples

Apricots

Pears

JUICING

Fruit juice is used as a beverage, alone or mixed with other ingredients, and as the liquid ingredient in other preparations. Juice can be extracted from fruits (and some vegetables) in two ways: pressure and blending.

Pressure is used to extract juice from fruits such as citrus that have a high water content. Pressure is applied by hand-squeezing or with a manual or electric reamer. All reamers work on the same principle: A ribbed cone is pressed against the fruit to break down its flesh and release the juice. Always strain juices to remove seeds, pulp or fibrous pieces.

A blender or an electric juice extractor can be used to liquefy less-juicy fruits and vegetables such as apples, carrots, tomatoes, beets and cabbage. The extractor pulverizes the fruit or vegetable, then separates and strains the liquid from the pulp with centrifugal force.

Interesting and delicious beverages can be made by combining the juice of one or more fruits or vegetables: pineapple with orange, apple with cranberry, strawberry with tangerine and papaya with orange. Color should be considered when creating mixed-juice beverages, however. Some combinations can cause rather odd color changes. Although yellow and orange juices are not a problem, those containing red and blue flavonoid pigments (such as Concord grapes, cherries, strawberries, raspberries and blueberries) can create some unappetizing colors. Adding an acid such as lemon juice helps retain the correct red and blue hues.

juice the liquid extracted from any fruit or vegetable

nectar the diluted, sweetened juice of peaches, apricots, guavas, black currants or other fruits, the juice of which would be too thick or too tart to drink straight

cider mildly fermented apple juice; nonalcoholic apple juice may also be labeled cider

APPLYING VARIOUS COOKING METHODS

Although most fruits are edible raw and typically served that way, some fruits can also be cooked. Commonly used cooking methods are broiling and grilling, baking, sautéing, deep-frying, poaching, simmering and preserving.

When cooking fruits, proper care and attention are critical. Even minimal cooking can render fruits overly soft or mushy. To combat this irreversible process, sugar can be added. When fruits are cooked with sugar, the sugar will be absorbed slowly into the cells, firming the fruits. Acids (notably lemon juice) also help fruits retain their structure. (Alkalis, such as baking soda, cause the cells to break down more quickly, reducing the fruits to mush.)

Determining Doneness

There are so many different fruits with such varied responses to cooking that no one standard for doneness is appropriate. Each item should be evaluated on a recipe-by-recipe basis. Generally, however, most cooked fruits are done when they are just tender when pierced with a fork or the tip of a paring knife. Simmered fruits, such as compotes, should be softer, cooked just to the point of disintegration. Avoid overcooking fruits by remembering that some carryover cooking will occur through the residual heat contained in the foods. Always rely on subjective tests—sight, feel, taste and aroma—rather than the clock.

Dry-Heat Cooking Methods

BROILING AND GRILLING

Fruits are usually broiled or grilled just long enough to caramelize sugars; cooking must be done quickly in order to avoid breaking down the fruits' structure. Good fruits to broil or grill are pineapples, apples, grapefruits, bananas, persimmons and peaches. The fruits may be cut into slices, chunks or halves as appropriate. A coating of sugar, honey or liqueur adds flavor, as do lemon juice, cinnamon and ginger.

When broiling fruits, use an oiled sheet pan or broiling platter. When grilling fruits, use a clean grill grate or thread the pieces onto skewers. Only thick fruit slices will need to be turned or rotated to heat fully. Broiled or grilled fruits can be served alone, as an accompaniment to meat, fish or poultry or as topping for ice creams or custards.

SAFETY ALERT
Fruit Sanitation

Remove any labels and wash fruits thoroughly before using, even if they are to be peeled or juiced. Because fruits are often served uncooked, proper hand washing is especially important when preparing them. Remember that many health departments require single-use gloves to be worn—and changed frequently—whenever working with products that will not be cooked before service.

PROCEDURE FOR **BROILING OR GRILLING FRUITS**

1 Select ripe fruits and peel, core or slice as necessary.
2 Top with sugar or honey to add flavor and aid caramelization.
3 Place the fruits on the broiler platter, sheet pan or grill grate.
4 Broil or grill at high temperatures, turning as necessary to heat the fruits thoroughly but quickly.

BROILED GRAPEFRUIT

Yield: 8 Servings		**Method:** Broiling
Ruby grapefruits	4	4
Sweet sherry	2 Tbsp.	30 ml
Brown sugar	4 Tbsp.	60 ml

1 Cut each grapefruit in half (perpendicular to the segments), then section with a sharp knife, carefully removing any visible seeds.
2 Sprinkle the grapefruit halves with the sherry and sugar.
3 Arrange on a baking sheet and place under a preheated broiler. Cook briefly, only until well heated and the sugar caramelizes. Serve immediately.

Approximate values per serving: **Calories** 70, **Total fat** 0 g, **Saturated fat** 0 g, **Cholesterol** 0 mg, **Sodium** 0 mg, **Total carbohydrates** 16 g, **Protein** 1 g, **Vitamin C** 80%, **Claims**—fat free; no sodium

BAKING

After washing, peeling, coring or pitting, most pomes, stone fruits and tropicals can be baked to create hot, flavorful desserts. Fruits with sturdy skins, particularly apples and pears, are excellent for baking alone, as their skin (peel) holds in moisture and flavor. They can also be used as edible containers by filling the cavity left by coring with a variety of sweet or savory mixtures.

Combinations of fruits can also be baked successfully; try mixing fruits for a balance of sweetness and tartness (for example, strawberries with rhubarb or apples with plums).

Several baked desserts are simply fruits (fresh, frozen or canned) topped with a crust (called a cobbler), strudel (called a crumple or crisp) or batter (called a buckle). Fruits, sometimes poached first, can also be baked in a wrapper of puff pastry, flaky dough or phyllo dough to produce an elegant dessert.

PROCEDURE FOR **BAKING FRUITS**

1. Select ripe but firm fruits and peel, core, pit or slice as necessary.
2. Add sugar or any flavorings.
3. Wrap the fruits in pastry dough if desired or directed in the recipe.
4. Place the fruits in a baking dish and bake uncovered in a moderate oven until tender or properly browned.

WARM BAKED PEACHES OR NECTARINES

Yield: 8 Servings　　　　　　　　　　**Method:** Baked

Freestone peaches or nectarines	4	4
Vanilla bean	1	1
Granulated sugar	2 oz.	60 g
Lemon juice	1 fl. oz.	30 ml
Unsalted butter	2 oz.	60 g
Pastry Cream (page 1051) or ice cream	as needed	as needed

1. Cut the peaches or nectarines in half. Remove the pits. Place them, cut side up, in a well-buttered half-size hotel pan or ovenproof dish.
2. Split the vanilla bean and scrape the seeds into the sugar. Sprinkle the fruit with the sugar and lemon juice.
3. Place a small piece of butter in the center of each fruit half and bake at 350°F (180°C) until tender and lightly browned, approximately 20 minutes. Serve warm with Pastry Cream or ice cream.

Approximate values per serving: **Calories** 100, **Total fat** 6 g, **Saturated fat** 3.5 g, **Cholesterol** 15 mg, **Sodium** 0 mg, **Total carbohydrates** 13 g, **Protein** 0 g, **Vitamin A** 10%, **Vitamin C** 10%, **Claims**—low calorie; no sodium

SAUTÉING

Fruits develop a rich, syrupy flavor when sautéed briefly in butter, sugar and, if desired, spices or liqueur. Cherries, bananas, apples, pears and pineapples are good choices. They should be peeled, cored and seeded as necessary and cut into uniform-size pieces before sautéing.

For dessert, fruits are sautéed with sugar to create a caramelized glaze or syrup. The fruits and syrup can be used to fill crêpes or to top spongecakes or ice creams. Liquor may be added and the mixture flamed (flambéed) in front of diners.

For savory mixtures, onions, shallots or garlic are often added.

In both sweet and savory fruit sautés, the fat used should be the most appropriate for the finished product. Butter and bacon fat are typical choices.

PROCEDURE FOR **SAUTÉING FRUITS**

1. Peel, pit and core the fruits as necessary and cut into uniform-size pieces.
2. Melt the fat in a hot sauté pan.
3. Add the fruit pieces and any flavoring ingredients. Do not crowd the pan, as this will cause the fruit to stew in its own juices.
4. Cook quickly over high heat.

MISE EN PLACE

▶ Wash and peel onions and cut into fine dice.
▶ Peel apples or peaches.

SAVORY FRUIT COMPOTE

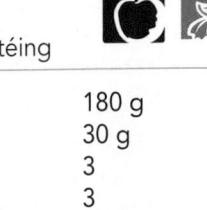

Yield: Approximately 2 lb. (1 kg) **Method:** Sautéing

Onions, fine dice	6 oz.	180 g
Whole butter or bacon fat	1 oz.	30 g
Apples (tart) or peaches, peeled	3	3
Apricots	3	3
Granulated sugar	4 oz.	120 g
Hot paprika	TT	TT
Salt and white pepper	TT	TT

1 Sweat the onions in the butter or bacon fat without browning.

2 Slice the apples or peaches and apricots into thin, even pieces. Add the apples to the onions and sauté for 1 to 2 minutes. Add the apricots.

3 Sprinkle the sugar over the fruits and cook, uncovered, over medium heat until tender. Season with paprika, salt and white pepper.

4 Serve warm as an accompaniment to roast pork, game or other meat.

Approximate values per 1-oz. (30-g) serving: **Calories** 60, **Total fat** 1.5 g, **Saturated fat** 1 g, **Cholesterol** 5 mg, **Sodium** 50 mg, **Total carbohydrates** 12 g, **Protein** 0 g, **Vitamin A** 4%, **Claims**—low fat; low cholesterol; low sodium

DEEP-FRYING

Few fruits are suitable for deep-frying. Apples, bananas, pears, pineapples and firm peaches mixed in or coated with batter, however, produce fine results. These fruits should be peeled, cored, seeded and cut into evenly sized slices or chunks. They may also need to be dried with paper towels so that the batter or coating can adhere.

Fruit fritters are also a popular snack or dessert item. Fritters contain diced or chopped fish, shellfish, vegetables or fruits bound together with a thick batter and deep-fried. Because frying time is very short, the main ingredient is usually precooked. Fritters are spooned or dropped directly into the hot fat; they form a crust as they cook. Popular examples are clam fritters, corn fritters, artichoke fritters and apple fritters.

PROCEDURE FOR **DEEP-FRYING FRUIT—FRITTERS**

1 Cut, chop and otherwise prepare the food to be made into fritters.

2 Precook any ingredients if necessary.

3 Prepare the batter as directed.

4 Scoop the fritters into deep fat at 350°F (180°C), using the swimming method.

5 Cook until done. The fritters should be golden brown on the outside and moist but set on the inside.

6 Remove the fritters from the fat and hold them over the fryer, allowing the excess fat to drain off. Transfer the food to a hotel pan either lined with absorbent paper or fitted with a rack. Serve hot.

7 If the fritters are to be held for later service, place them under a heat lamp.

APPLE FRITTERS

Yield: 100 Fritters, 2 in. (5 cm) each   **Method:** Deep-frying

Eggs, separated	6	6
Milk	1 pt.	480 ml
Flour	1 lb.	480 g
Baking powder	1 Tbsp.	15 ml
Salt	1 tsp.	5 ml
Granulated sugar	2 oz.	60 g
Cinnamon, ground	½ tsp.	2 ml
Apples, peeled, cored, medium dice	1 lb. 8 oz.	720 g
Powdered sugar	as needed	as needed

MISE EN PLACE
◂ Separate eggs.
◂ Peel and core apples and cut into medium dice.

1 Combine the egg yolks and milk.

2 Sift together the flour, baking powder, salt, sugar and cinnamon. Add the dry ingredients to the milk-and-egg mixture; whisk until smooth.

3 Allow the batter to rest 1 hour.

4 Stir the apples into the batter.

5 Just before the fritters are to be cooked, whip the egg whites to soft peaks and fold into the batter.

6 Scoop the fritters into deep fat at 350°F (180°C), using the swimming method. Cook until uniformly browned, approximately 5 minutes.

7 Dust with powdered sugar and serve hot.

VARIATION:

Banana Fritters—Omit the cinnamon and apples. Add 3 tablespoons (45 milliliters) finely grated orange zest, 4 fluid ounces (120 milliliters) orange juice and 2 large bananas, peeled and diced (not puréed).

Approximate values per fritter: **Calories** 60, **Total fat** 4 g, **Saturated fat** 1 g, **Cholesterol** 15 mg, **Sodium** 5 mg, **Total carbohydrates** 6 g, **Protein** 1 g

1 Adding the dry ingredients to the liquids.

2 Folding the egg whites into the batter.

3 Dropping the fritters into the deep fat.

4 Dusting the fritters with powdered sugar.

Moist-Heat Cooking Methods

POACHING

One of the more popular cooking methods for fruits is poaching. Poaching softens and tenderizes fruits and infuses them with additional flavors such as spices or wine. Poached fruits can be served hot or cold and used in tarts or pastries or as an accompaniment to meat or poultry dishes.

The poaching liquid can be water, wine, liquor or sugar syrup. (As noted earlier, sugar helps fruits keep their shape, although it takes longer to tenderize fruits poached in sugar syrup.) The low poaching temperature (185°F/85°C) allows fruits to soften gradually. The agitation created at higher temperatures would damage them.

Cooked fruits should be allowed to cool in the flavored poaching liquid or syrup. Most poaching liquids can be used repeatedly. If they contain sufficient sugar, they can be reduced to a sauce or glaze to accompany the poached fruits.

PROCEDURE FOR **POACHING FRUITS**

1. Peel, core and slice the fruits as necessary.
2. In a sufficiently deep, nonreactive saucepan, combine the poaching liquid (usually water or wine) with sugar, spices, citrus zest and other ingredients as desired or as directed in the recipe.
3. Submerge the fruits in the liquid. Place a circle of parchment paper over the fruits to help them stay submerged.
4. Place the saucepan on the stove top over a medium-high flame; bring to a boil.
5. As soon as the liquid boils, reduce the temperature. Simmer gently.
6. Poach until the fruits are tender enough for the tip of a small knife to be easily inserted. Cooking time depends on the type and variety of fruit used, its ripeness and the cooking liquid.
7. Remove the saucepan from the stove top and allow the liquid and fruits to cool.
8. Remove the fruits from the liquid and then refrigerate. The liquid can be returned to the stove top and reduced until thick enough to use as a sauce or glaze or refrigerated for further use.

PEARS POACHED IN RED WINE

MISE EN PLACE
▶ Chop basil.

Yield: 8 Servings		**Method:** Poaching
Ripe pears, Anjou or Bartlett	8	8
Zinfandel wine	52 fl. oz.	1.5 l
Whole peppercorns	8–10	8–10
Vanilla bean	1	1
Granulated sugar	12 oz.	360 g
Fresh basil, chopped	1 oz.	30 g
Orange zest	from 1 orange	from 1 orange

1. Peel and core the pears, leaving the stems intact.
2. Combine the remaining ingredients in a large nonreactive saucepan. Arrange the pears in the liquid in a single layer.
3. Place the pears on the stove top over a medium-high flame. Bring to just below a boil, then immediately reduce the heat and allow the liquid to simmer gently. Cover with a round of parchment paper if necessary to keep the pears submerged.
4. Continue poaching the pears until tender, approximately 1 to 1½ hours. Remove the saucepan from the stove and allow the pears to cool in the liquid.
5. Remove the pears from the poaching liquid and return the liquid to the stove top. Reduce until the liquid is thick enough to coat the back of a spoon, then strain.
6. Serve the pears chilled or at room temperature in a pool of the reduced wine syrup.

Approximate values per 7-oz. (210-g) serving: **Calories** 410, **Total fat** 1.5 g, **Saturated fat** 0 g, **Cholesterol** 0 mg, **Sodium** 35 mg, **Total carbohydrates** 91 g, **Protein** 6 g, **Vitamin A** 40%, **Calcium** 90%, **Iron** 110%, **Claims**—low fat; no cholesterol; low sodium; high fiber

SIMMERING

Simmering techniques are used to make stewed fruits and compotes. Fresh, frozen, canned and dried fruits can be simmered or stewed. As with any moist-heat cooking method, simmering softens and tenderizes fruits. The liquid used can be water, wine or the juices naturally found in the fruits. Sugar, honey and spices may be added as desired. Stewed or simmered fruits can be served hot or cold, as a first course, a dessert or an accompaniment to meat or poultry dishes.

PROCEDURE FOR **SIMMERING FRUITS**

❶ Peel, core, pit and slice the fruits as necessary.

❷ Bring the fruits and cooking liquid, if used, to a simmer. Cook until the fruit is tender.

❸ Add sugar or other sweeteners as desired or as directed in the recipe.

DRIED FRUIT COMPOTE

Yield: 3 lb. (1.4 kg)   **Method:** Simmering

Dried apricots	5 oz.	150 g
Prunes, pitted	5 oz.	150 g
Dried pears or apples	5 oz.	150 g
Dried peaches	5 oz.	150 g
Water, hot	24 fl. oz.	720 ml
Cinnamon stick	1	1
Light corn syrup	12 fl. oz.	360 ml
Cointreau	2 fl. oz.	60 ml

❶ Coarsely chop the fruits. Place the pieces in a nonreactive saucepan and add the water and cinnamon stick.

❷ Bring the mixture to a simmer, cover and cook until tender, approximately 12 to 15 minutes.

❸ Add the corn syrup and Cointreau. Simmer uncovered until thoroughly heated. Remove the cinnamon stick. Serve warm or refrigerate for longer storage.

Approximate values per 1-oz. (30-g) serving: **Calories** 60, **Total fat** 0 g, **Saturated fat** 0 g, **Cholesterol** 0 mg, **Sodium** 15 mg, **Total carbohydrates** 15 g, **Protein** 0 g, **Claims**—fat free; very low sodium

MISE EN PLACE

◀ Pit the prunes.

concentrate also known as a fruit paste or compound; a reduced fruit purée, without a gel structure, used as a flavoring

jam a fruit gel made from fruit pulp and sugar

jelly a fruit gel made from fruit juice and sugar

marmalade a citrus jelly that also contains unpeeled slices of citrus fruit

preserve a fruit gel that contains large pieces or whole fruits

Preserving

Fresh fruits can be preserved with sugar if the fruit-and-sugar mixture is concentrated by evaporation to the point that microbial spoilage cannot occur. The added sugar also retards the growth of, but does not destroy, microorganisms.

Pectin, a substance present in varying amounts in all fruits, can cause cooked fruits to form a semisolid mass known as a gel. Fruits that are visually unattractive but otherwise of high quality can be made into gels, which are more commonly known as **jams**, **jellies**, **marmalades** and **preserves**.

The essential ingredients of a fruit gel are fruit, pectin, acid (usually lemon juice) and sugar. They must be carefully combined in the correct ratio for the gel to form. For fruits with a low pectin content (such as strawberries) to form a gel, pectin must be added, either by adding a fruit with a high pectin content (for example, apples or quinces) or by adding packaged pectin.

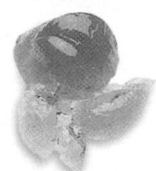
Apple Jelly

Apricot Jam

Orange Marmalade

QUESTIONS FOR DISCUSSION

Terms to Know

pith	enzymatic
supreme	browning
hybrid	acidulation
grenadine syrup	IQF
ethylene gas	juice extractor
astringency	flavonoids
freestone	fritter
cling	zest
bromelin	

① Define ripeness and explain why ripe fruits are most desirable. How does the ripening process affect the availability of some fruits?

② Describe the proper storage conditions for most fruits. Which fruits emit ethylene gas, and why is this a consideration when storing fruits?

③ Explain why some apple varieties are preferred for cooking, whereas other varieties are preferred for eating. Which variety is generally preferred for making applesauce?

④ Which types of fruits are best for dry-heat cooking methods? Explain your answer. Why is sugar usually added when cooking any type of fruit?

⑤ List and describe three ways to prepare fruits for extended storage.

⑥ Research a tropical or exotic fruit that is not available in your local area. Where is this fruit originally from? How is it eaten or used in cooking? What challenges face producers and importers in bringing this fruit to market in the United States? **WWW**

⑦ What fruits are native to your region of the country? Consult with the Cooperative State Research, Education, and Extension Service or Farm Service Agency in your state and report on one fruit grown where you live. Discuss the season when it is harvested, the number and location of farms growing the fruit and the uses for the fruit. **WWW**

FIGS WITH BERRIES AND HONEY MOUSSE

GREENS, SAN FRANCISCO, CA
Chef Annie Somerville

Yield: 4 Servings

Raspberries or blackberries	1 pt.	480 ml
Fresh figs such as Black Mission, Kadota or Calmyrna	1 pt.	480 ml
Honey	6 oz.	180 g
Egg yolks, pasteurized	4	4
Salt	TT	TT
Heavy cream	1 pt.	480 ml

1. Pick through the berries, rinse them and drain them in a colander.
2. Rinse the figs and cut them in half, leaving the stem attached.
3. To make the mousse, whisk the honey, yolks and salt together in a bowl over a pan of barely simmering water. Whisk the mixture continuously for 8 minutes. After 5 minutes, the mousse will begin to thicken and the texture will become creamy. Whisk vigorously until the mousse leaves thick ribbons on its surface when poured over itself. Set aside to cool. The texture of the cooled mousse will be stiff and sticky.
4. Whisk 1 fluid ounce (30 milliliters) cream into the mousse, working it until it loosens.
5. Whip the remaining cream until it is firm, fold it into the mousse until it is just incorporated, then whisk the two together. The texture will be light and creamy.
6. Loosely arrange the figs on a platter, sprinkle with the berries, garnish with mint and serve with the mousse.

Approximate values per serving: **Calories** 680, **Total fat** 47 g, **Saturated fat** 28 g, **Cholesterol** 370 mg, **Sodium** 200 mg, **Total carbohydrates** 57 g, **Protein** 6 g, **Vitamin A** 60%, **Vitamin C** 25%

PINEAPPLE PAPAYA SALSA

Yield: 2 qt. (2 lt)

Tomatoes	3	3
Fresh pineapple, approx. 2 lb. (960 g)	1	1
Fresh papaya, approx. 1 lb. (480 g)	1	1
Green onions, sliced	5	5
Fresh cilantro, chopped	1 bunch	1 bunch
Jalapeños, seeded, minced	2	2
Lemon juice	3 Tbsp.	45 ml
Garlic, chopped	1 tsp.	5 ml
Salt	2 tsp.	10 ml

1. Core and dice the tomatoes.
2. Peel and dice the pineapple.
3. Peel, seed and dice the papaya.
4. Combine all the ingredients and chill well.

Approximate values per 1-fl.-oz. (30-ml) serving: **Calories** 25, **Total fat** 0 g, **Saturated fat** 0 g, **Cholesterol** 0 mg, **Sodium** 330 mg, **Total carbohydrates** 5 g, **Protein** 0 g, **Vitamin C** 45%, **Claims**—fat free; low calorie

WATERMELON AND CHERRY SALAD WITH FRESH MINT SYRUP

Yield: 10 Servings

Fresh mint	1 bunch	1 bunch
Water	8 fl. oz.	240 ml
Granulated sugar	3 oz.	90 g
Watermelon	3 lb.	1.4 kg
Cherries, fresh, pitted	2 lb.	960 g
Fresh mint sprigs	as needed for garnish	

1 Pick the mint leaves and wash them.

2 Bring the water to a boil in a small saucepan. Blanch the mint leaves in the water for 20 seconds. Remove the leaves and refresh them in cold water. Reserve the blanching water.

3 Add the sugar to the blanching water, bring to a boil and cook for 2 minutes.

4 Drain the mint leaves. Squeeze all of the water out of them and chop them finely. Add the chopped mint to the sugar syrup. Refrigerate the syrup until cold.

5 Dice the watermelon or scoop balls from it with a melon ball cutter. Combine the watermelon with the pitted cherries in a stainless bowl. Pour the mint syrup over the fruit and toss gently.

6 Serve garnished with sprigs of fresh mint.

Approximate values per serving: **Calories** 140, **Total fat** 0 g, **Saturated fat** 0 g, **Cholesterol** 0 mg, **Sodium** 0 mg, **Total carbohydrates** 35 g, **Protein** 2 g, **Vitamin A** 25%, **Vitamin C** 35%, **Claims**—fat free; no saturated fat; no cholesterol; no sodium; good source of fiber; high in vitamins A and C

GRATIN OF FRESH BERRIES WITH CRÈME FRAÎCHE

Yield: 1 serving

Assorted fresh berries, such as raspberries, blueberries and blackberries	4 oz.	120 g
Crème fraîche	2 fl. oz.	60 ml
Orange liqueur	1 tsp.	5 ml
Brown sugar	1 Tbsp.	15 ml

1 Arrange the berries in an even layer in a shallow, heatproof serving dish.

2 Stir the crème fraîche and orange liqueur together. Spoon this mixture over the berries.

3 Sprinkle the sugar over the crème. Place under a broiler or salamander just until the sugar melts. Serve immediately.

Approximate values per serving: **Calories** 210, **Total fat** 7 g, **Saturated fat** 4 g, **Cholesterol** 20 mg, **Sodium** 30 mg, **Total carbohydrates** 33 g, **Protein** 3 g, **Vitamin C** 40%, **Claims**—very low sodium; high fiber

BAKED APPLES

Yield: 8 Servings   **Method:** Baking

Apples, Red or Golden Delicious	8	8
Raisins	6 oz.	180 g
Orange zest	1½ Tbsp.	23 ml
Brown sugar	4 oz.	120 g

1. Rinse and core each apple. The peels should be scored or partially removed to allow the pulp to expand without bursting the skin during baking.
2. Plump the raisins by soaking them in boiling water for 10 minutes. Drain the raisins thoroughly.
3. Combine the raisins, zest and sugar. Fill the cavity of each apple with this mixture.
4. Stand the apples in a shallow baking dish. Add enough water to measure about ½ inch (1.2 centimeters) deep.
5. Bake the apples at 375°F (190°C) for 15 minutes. Reduce the temperature to 300°F (150°C) and continue baking until the apples are tender but still hold their shape, approximately 1 hour. Occasionally, baste the apples with liquid from the baking dish.

Approximate values per apple: **Calories** 220, **Total fat** 0.5 g, **Saturated fat** 0 g, **Cholesterol** 0 mg, **Sodium** 10 mg, **Total carbohydrates** 52 g, **Protein** 1 g, **Vitamin C** 15%, **Claims**—low fat; no cholesterol; very low sodium; good source of fiber

---

GRILLED FRUIT KEBABS

Yield: 8 Skewers   **Method:** Grilling

Cantaloupe	½ melon	½ melon
Honeydew	¼ melon	¼ melon
Pineapple	½ pineapple	½ pineapple
Strawberries	8	8
Brown sugar	2 oz.	60 g
Lime juice	4 fl. oz.	120 ml
Cinnamon, ground	¼ tsp.	1 ml

1. Remove the rind and cut the melons and pineapple into 1-inch (2.5-centimeter) cubes. Hull the strawberries and leave whole.
2. To make the sugar glaze, combine the sugar, lime juice and cinnamon, stirring until the sugar dissolves.
3. Heat the grill and clean the grate thoroughly.
4. Thread the fruits onto kebab skewers, alternating colors for an attractive appearance.
5. Brush the fruits with the sugar glaze. Grill, rotating the skewers frequently to develop an evenly light brown surface.
6. Serve immediately as an appetizer, a garnish for ice cream or an accompaniment to rich meats such as pork or lamb.

Approximate values per skewer: **Calories** 70, **Total fat** 0 g, **Saturated fat** 0 g, **Cholesterol** 0 mg, **Sodium** 10 mg, **Total carbohydrates** 16 g, **Protein** 1 g, **Vitamin C** 50%, **Claims**—fat free; very low sodium

CHERRY CONFIT

Yield: 4 oz. (120 g)   **Method:** Sautéing

Red onion, small dice	2 Tbsp.	30 ml
Whole butter	2 tsp.	10 ml
Dried cherries	3 oz.	90 g
Brandy	1 Tbsp.	15 ml
Port wine	1 Tbsp.	15 ml
Sherry vinegar	½ tsp.	2 ml

1. Sauté the onion in the butter without coloring.
2. Add the cherries. Add the brandy and flambé.
3. Add the wine and vinegar; cook until almost dry. Serve warm or at room temperature with charcuterie items or grilled or roasted meats.

Approximate values per 1-oz. (30-g) serving: **Calories** 35, **Total fat** 2 g, **Saturated fat** 1 g, **Cholesterol** 5 mg, **Sodium** 20 mg, **Total carbohydrates** 3 g, **Protein** 0 g, **Claims**—low fat; very low sodium; low calorie

BRAISED RHUBARB

Yield: 10 lb. (4.8 kg)   **Method:** Braising

Tart green apples, peeled and cubed	2 lb. 8 oz.	1.2 kg
Rhubarb, IQF pieces	7 lb.	3.3 kg
Unsalted butter	4 oz.	120 g
Sweet white wine	8 fl. oz.	240 ml
Brown sugar	14 oz.	420 g
Vanilla extract	2 tsp.	10 ml
Cinnamon, ground	1 Tbsp.	15 ml
Nutmeg, ground	¼ tsp.	1 ml
Orange juice	2 fl. oz.	60 ml
Salt	½ tsp.	2 ml

1. Sauté the apples and rhubarb in the butter until they begin to soften.
2. Add the wine and reduce by half. Add the remaining ingredients. Simmer until the rhubarb is very tender.
3. Serve at room temperature in prebaked pastry cups, topped with crème chantilly or crème fraîche and fennel greens, or serve warm over ice cream.

Approximate values per 1-oz. (30-g) serving: **Calories** 60, **Total fat** 2 g, **Saturated fat** 0.5 g, **Cholesterol** 0 mg, **Sodium** 25 mg, **Total carbohydrates** 11 g, **Protein** 0 g, **Claims**—low fat; no cholesterol; very low sodium

BERRY COMPOTE

Yield: 1 pt. (480 ml) **Method:** Simmering

Berries, fresh or frozen	1 pt.	480 ml
Granulated sugar	4 oz.	120 g
Oranges	2	2
Honey	3 fl. oz.	90 ml
Cinnamon stick	1	1
Brandy	3 Tbsp.	45 ml
Ice cream	as needed for garnish	
Poundcake	as needed for garnish	

1. Select an assortment of fresh or frozen berries—strawberries, blueberries, raspberries, blackberries and cherries can be used, depending on availability.
2. Place the fruits and sugar in a nonreactive saucepan. Finely grate the zest from one orange and set aside. Add the juice from the two oranges to the saucepan. Bring to a simmer over low heat; cook until the fruits are soft but still intact.
3. Strain the mixture, saving both the fruits and the liquid. Return the liquid to the saucepan. Add the finely grated zest from one orange and the honey, cinnamon and brandy.
4. Bring to a boil and reduce until the mixture thickens enough to coat the back of a spoon. Remove from the heat and cool to room temperature.
5. Remove the cinnamon stick. Gently stir the reserved fruits into the sauce, cover and chill. Serve with ice cream or poundcake.

Approximate values per 1-fl.-oz. (30-ml) serving: **Calories** 70, **Total fat** 0 g, **Saturated fat** 0 g, **Cholesterol** 0 mg, **Sodium** 0 mg, **Total carbohydrates** 16 g, **Protein** 0 g, **Vitamin C** 15%, **Claims**—fat free; no sodium

APPLESAUCE

Yield: Approximately 1 qt. (1 lt) **Method:** Simmering

McIntosh apples	4 lb.	1.9 g
Cinnamon sticks	2	2
Granulated sugar	5 oz.	150 g
Lemon juice	1 Tbsp.	15 ml

1. Peel, core and quarter the apples. Place in a saucepan with just enough cold water to cover the bottom of the pan. Add the cinnamon sticks.
2. Bring to a simmer, cover and cook until the apples are tender, approximately 15 minutes.
3. Add the sugar and lemon juice. Simmer for 10 minutes.
4. Remove the cinnamon sticks and press the apples through a food mill.

Approximate values per 1-oz. (30-g) serving: **Calories** 50, **Total fat** 0 g, **Saturated fat** 0 g, **Cholesterol** 0 mg, **Sodium** 0 mg, **Total carbohydrates** 13 g, **Protein** 0 g, **Claims**—fat free; no sodium

FRESH CRANBERRY-ORANGE RELISH

Yield: 3 qt. (3 lt)   **Method:** Simmering

Granulated sugar	1 lb.	480 g
Orange juice	4 fl. oz.	120 ml
Water	4 fl. oz.	120 ml
Fresh or frozen cranberries	1 lb. 8 oz.	720 g
Cinnamon stick	1	1
Orange liqueur	2 fl. oz.	60 ml
Orange zest, finely grated	2 Tbsp.	30 ml
Orange segments	20	20

1. Combine the sugar, orange juice and water in a nonreactive rondeau or saucepan; bring to a boil.
2. Add the cranberries and cinnamon stick and simmer uncovered until the berries begin to burst, approximately 15 minutes. Skim off any foam that rises to the surface.
3. Add the orange liqueur and zest and simmer for another 15 to 20 minutes.
4. Remove from the heat and remove the cinnamon stick. Add the orange segments. Cool and refrigerate. Serve with roasted game, poultry or charcuterie items.

VARIATIONS:

Jalapeño-Cranberry Relish—Omit the orange liqueur, zest and segments. Add 1 fresh jalapeño pepper, minced, and ½ cup (120 milliliters) hot pepper jelly.

Approximate values per 1-fl.-oz. (30-ml) serving: **Calories** 25, **Total fat** 0 g, **Saturated fat** 0 g, **Cholesterol** 0 mg, **Sodium** 0 mg, **Total carbohydrates** 6 g, **Protein** 0 g, **Claims**—fat free; no sodium; low calorie

MANGO CHUTNEY

Yield: 1½ qt. (1.4 lt)   **Method:** Simmering

Mangoes, peeled and diced	2 lb.	960 g
Onion, fine dice	4 oz.	120 g
Garlic cloves, minced	2	2
Cider vinegar	8 fl. oz.	240 ml
Dark brown sugar	8 oz.	240 g
Golden raisins	2½ oz.	75 g
Crystallized ginger	4 oz.	120 g
Salt	½ tsp.	2 ml
Cinnamon sticks	2	2
Crushed red pepper flakes	½ tsp.	2 ml
Mustard seeds	½ tsp.	2 ml
Fresh ginger, minced	1 tsp.	5 ml
Lime juice	1 fl. oz.	30 ml

1. Combine the mangoes, onion, garlic, vinegar and sugar in a large, heavy saucepan. Cook until the sugar dissolves.
2. Stir in the raisins, crystallized ginger, salt and spices. Simmer until the onion and raisins are very soft, approximately 45 minutes. Skim foam from the surface as necessary.
3. Stir in the lime juice and adjust the seasonings.
4. Remove from the heat and cool uncovered. The chutney will thicken somewhat as it cools but should be thinner than fruit preserves.

Approximate values per 1-fl.-oz. (30-ml) serving: **Calories** 50, **Total fat** 0 g, **Saturated fat** 0 g, **Cholesterol** 0 mg, **Sodium** 30 mg, **Total carbohydrates** 12 g, **Protein** 0 g, **Vitamin C** 10%, **Claims**—fat free; very low sodium

CANDIED CITRUS RIND

Yield: 50–100 Candied Strips   **Method:** Preserving

Citrus fruit	5–10 fruits	5–10 fruits
Water	1 qt.	960 ml
Salt	½ tsp.	2 ml
Granulated sugar	1 lb.	480 g
Corn syrup	7 oz.	210 g
Granulated sugar	as needed for storage	

Orange, lemon, grapefruit, mandarins, or tangerines may be used. Organic produce is recommended.

1. Wash the fruits. With a sharp knife, cut large, thin pieces of the peel from the citrus fruits. Remove as much of the white pith as possible.
2. Cut the peel into long, thin strips, about ¼ inch (6 millimeters) wide.
3. Bring 1 pint (480 milliliters) water and the salt to boil in a saucepan large enough to hold the citrus rind. Add the rind and simmer for 2 minutes. Drain.
4. Bring the remaining water, sugar and corn syrup to a boil. Add the blanched citrus rind and reduce the heat to a low simmer. Cook the rinds for about 15 to 20 minutes until they are translucent and tender. Store the rind in the syrup in the refrigerator. Or drain the rind on a screen until cool. Sprinkle the drained rind with granulated sugar and store in an airtight container.

Approximate values per piece: **Calories** 35, **Total fat** 0 g, **Saturated fat** 0 g, **Cholesterol** 0 mg, **Sodium** 20 mg, **Total carbohydrates** 9 g, **Protein** 0 g

Drained Rind

Rind Dipped in Sugar

CHAPTER TWENTY-SIX

SANDWICHES

After studying this chapter,
you will be able to:

- select high-quality sandwich ingredients
- identify different types and styles of sandwiches
- prepare sandwiches to order

A SANDWICH IS OFTEN THE FIRST meal a person learns to prepare. Even those who claim that they cannot cook often make delicious hot and cold sandwiches without considering it cooking. Mastering a grilled cheese or assembling the quintessential BLT may not require a degree in the culinary arts, but it does require the ability to select and use ingredients wisely.

Sandwiches, which are usually quick and easy to assemble, lend themselves well to a chef's creativity. Imaginative sandwiches can become sensational menu additions in even the most formal restaurants, and amazing sandwiches can keep lunch customers visiting regularly. Sandwiches offer food service operations economical opportunities for using leftovers, and they offer customers, especially those with smaller budgets or appetites, meals to eat out of hand. Thus, the ability to correctly prepare hot and cold sandwiches to order is a fundamental skill in many food service operations.

INGREDIENTS FOR SANDWICHES

Sandwiches are constructed from bread, a spread and one or more fillings. These components should be selected and combined carefully so that the finished sandwich is flavorful and visually appealing.

Bread

Bread provides more than a convenient means for handling a sandwich. It holds or contains the spread and fillings and gives the sandwich its shape. Bread also adds flavor, texture, nutrition and color, and often determines the appearance of the finished product. Virtually any bread can be used in sandwich making: rolls, biscuits, bagels, croissants, fruit and nut breads, whole-grain breads and savory breads as well as flatbreads such as naan, lavosh and tortillas; pocket breads such as pitas; and flavorful breads such as focaccia and Swedish limpa.

Whatever bread is used and whether its flavor is mild or intense, the bread should complement the fillings and not overpower them. The bread should be fresh (although day-old bread is easier to slice and is excellent toasted) and its texture should be able to withstand moisture from the spread and fillings without becoming soggy or pasty. An overly hard or crusty bread, however, may make the sandwich difficult to eat.

Spread

A spread is used to add flavor, moisture and richness to the sandwich, and sometimes helps to hold or bind it together. Some spreads, especially plain or flavored butters, also act as a barrier to prevent the moisture in the filling from soaking into the bread.

There are three principal spreads: butter, mayonnaise and vegetable purées.

BUTTER

One of the most common spreads, plain butter adds flavor and richness; it is also an excellent moisture barrier. Flavored or compound butters, discussed in Chapter 10, Stocks and Sauces, make excellent sandwich spreads, adding flavor dimensions to the finished product. For example, try caper butter on a Cajun-style blackened beef sandwich or a red chile honey butter on a smoked turkey sandwich. Any butter spread should be softened or whipped so that it will spread easily without tearing the bread.

MAYONNAISE

Perhaps the most popular sandwich spread, mayonnaise adds moisture, richness and flavor and complements most meat, poultry, fish, shellfish, vegetable, egg and cheese fillings. Like butter, mayonnaise can be enlivened by adding flavoring ingredients. Condiments (for example, coarse-grained mustard or grated horseradish), herbs, spices and spice blends (for example, curry or chilli powder) and other ingredients such as garlic and pesto sauce can be stirred into fresh or commercially prepared mayonnaise. Fresh mayonnaise can also be prepared with assorted oils, such as olive oil, walnut oil or chile oil. See Chapter 24, Salads and Salad Dressings, for recipes and additional information on mayonnaise.

VEGETABLE PURÉES

Puréed vegetables are often used as sandwich spreads, such as roasted red pepper purée for a sandwich of Italian meats and cheeses or a well-seasoned chickpea purée with lemon and tahini paste for a vegetarian sandwich. Unlike butter, vegetable purées usually will not provide a moisture barrier between the bread and the fillings, although roasted nut butters and peanut butter will prevent bread from becoming soggy.

Filling

The filling is the body of the sandwich, providing most of its flavor. A sandwich often contains more than one filling. For example, the filling in a Reuben sandwich is corned beef, cheese and sauerkraut, whereas in a BLT it is bacon, lettuce and tomato. Fillings for cold sandwiches must be precooked and properly chilled, although some hot sandwich fillings may be cooked to order.

When choosing fillings, be sure that the flavors complement each other. Their textures may be similar or contrasting. If an ingredient, such as lettuce, is supposed to be crisp, it should be very crisp, not limp. If an ingredient is supposed to be tender and moist, make sure it is so. Improperly prepared, poor-quality or mishandled filling ingredients can ruin an otherwise wonderful sandwich.

Popular fillings include the following:

BEEF

Although the classic hot beef sandwich is the hamburger, other hot or cold beef products are commonly used. For example, hot or cold small steaks, slices of larger cuts such as the tenderloin, thin slices of roast beef and so on make excellent fillings. Also popular are hot or cold slices of cured beef products, including corned beef, pastrami and tongue as well as beef sausages such as salami, bologna and hot dogs.

PORK

Various ham and bacon products, served either hot or cold, are extremely popular. In addition, pork loin and tenderloin are light, white meats that adapt well to various flavor combinations and cooking methods. Barbecued pork, pork sausages and pork hot dogs are also popular.

POULTRY

Sliced turkey breast, either roasted or smoked, and processed turkey are often used in hot and cold sandwiches. Moreover, food substitutes such as turkey bologna, turkey pastrami, turkey hot dogs and turkey ham are popular because they generally have a lower fat content than the beef or pork original. Boneless chicken breast, either sliced or whole, can be prepared by a variety of methods and complements a broad range of sandwich flavors.

HISTORY OF SANDWICHES

One of the earliest recorded references to foods eaten between two pieces of bread tells of Rabbi Hillel, a great Jewish teacher who lived sometime between 70 B.C.E. and 70 C.E. He created the Passover custom of eating *haroseth* (chopped nuts and apples) and *mohror* (bitter herbs) between two pieces of matzo (unleavened bread). This "sandwich" was intended to represent the mortar used by the Jews to build the Egyptians' pyramids and the bitter sadness of their internment away from the land of Israel.

The term *sandwich* came into use approximately 200 years ago. The Fourth Earl of Sandwich, Sir John Montague (1718–1792), is credited with popularizing the concept of eating meats and cheeses between two slices of bread. Apparently the earl, not wanting to leave the gaming tables that he loved so much, would demand that his servants bring him meat and bread. He combined the two and ate them with one hand, allowing him a free hand to continue playing at the tables. Some historians argue that a more likely scenario is that, as the head of defense, the earl was kept busy planning British strategy for the Revolutionary War underway in the American colonies. Whichever the case, the name stuck.

Sandwiches became more popular in the United States when soft white bread became common in the early 20th century. Today, sandwiches are found on breakfast, lunch and dinner menus and are served by every type of food service operation, from the most casual diner to the fanciest four-star dining room.

FISH AND SHELLFISH

Although fried fish fillets are an old standard, grilled fish sandwiches are gaining in popularity. Canned fish products, particularly tuna and salmon, are also widely used. Often fish and shellfish, especially tuna, shrimp and crab, are used for mayonnaise-based bound salads. Sardines and anchovies are sometimes mixed into bound salads or arranged artistically on open-faced sandwiches.

VEGETABLES

Vegetables add texture, moisture, flavor and nutrition to most any sandwich. Fresh vegetables such as lettuce, onions and tomatoes are commonly used in combination with meat, cheese and other fillings. Celery or bell peppers add a nice crunchy texture to cheese or mayonnaise-based bound salad fillings. Vegetables, however, can stand on their own as sandwich fillings. Marinated, grilled vegetables can be used in hot or cold sandwiches, and a combination of sliced, fresh vegetables and a flavorful dressing wrapped in soft lavosh or a tortilla becomes a portable salad.

EGGS

Hard-cooked eggs are most often used as an ingredient in a mayonnaise-based salad, where they are chopped and combined with seasonings. Hard-cooked eggs can also be sliced thin and used as an attractive garnish on open-faced sandwiches. Fried or scrambled eggs can be layered between pieces of bread or rolled in a tortilla for a breakfast sandwich.

CHEESE

Cheese is available in such a variety of textures, flavors, colors and styles that it is a welcome addition to nearly any sandwich. Sliced cheese can be used as a filling in hot or cold sandwiches, and melted cheese or a cheese sauce makes an excellent topping for hot open-faced sandwiches. Flavored cream cheese is also used as a spread or filling, particularly with bagels and fruit or nut breads.

BOUND SALADS

Protein salads bound with mayonnaise or salad dressing are popular sandwich fillings. Examples include chicken, tuna, egg and ham salads. Bound salads are discussed in Chapter 24, Salads and Salad Dressings.

TYPES OF SANDWICHES

Sandwiches can be hot or cold, closed or open-faced, depending on the way in which the ingredients are assembled and presented.

Hot Sandwiches

Hot closed sandwiches include those in which the filling ingredients are served hot, such as a hamburger or hot dog, and those where the entire sandwich is heated for service, such as a grilled cheese or Monte Cristo. Hot closed sandwiches can be categorized as basic, grilled or deep-fried.

Basic hot closed sandwiches are generally those in which the principal filling is served hot between two pieces of bread. These sandwiches may also include fillings that are not hot, such as tomato slices and lettuce leaves. Variations of the basic hot closed sandwich include tacos, quesadillas, burros (or burritos) and wraps, in which the hot and/or cold fillings are folded or wrapped in a tortilla or other supple flatbread.

Grilled sandwiches are those in which the filling is placed between two pieces of bread, which are buttered on the outside and then browned on a griddle or in a sauté pan. In grilled sandwiches, the filling will be warmed during this procedure but will not cook. Therefore, fillings such as bacon or sliced meat should be fully cooked before the sandwich is assembled and grilled.

Cooking grilled cheese sandwiches.

PROCEDURE FOR **PREPARING WRAP SANDWICHES**

① Top the tortilla with a spread or dressing.

② Mound vegetables and meat, fish or poultry items across the tortilla.

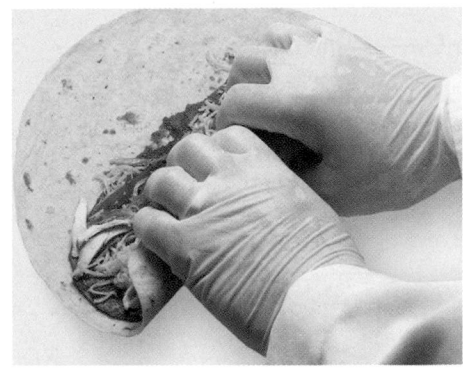

③ Roll the tortilla tightly around the filling.

A sandwich grill, also known as a panini grill, with a heated hinged lid, makes easy work of grilling sandwiches as it allows them to be toasted on each side without flipping.

PROCEDURE FOR **PREPARING SANDWICHES ON A PANINI GRILL**

① Place filled sandwich on a preheated panini grill, then close the lid.

② Remove sandwiches when heated through and visibly browned.

Deep-fried sandwiches are made by dipping a closed sandwich in egg batter or bread crumbs and then deep-frying it. The most common example is the Monte Cristo: white bread filled with sliced ham, Swiss cheese and Dijon mustard.

The hot open-faced turkey or steak sandwich proved long ago that sandwiches do not need to be eaten by hand. In the typical **hot open-faced sandwich**, bread (grilled, toasted or fresh) is placed on a serving plate, covered with hot meat or other filling and topped with an appropriate gravy, sauce or cheese. The completed dish is often browned under a broiler immediately before service. Condiments and garnishes are usually served on the side. Figure 26.1 illustrates various methods used to prepare the bread and assemble hot open-faced sandwiches.

Perhaps the ultimate hot open-faced sandwich is the **pizza**. Bread dough is topped with sauce, cheese, meat and vegetables, then baked. Small personal-sized pizzas are a popular menu item even in upscale restaurants.

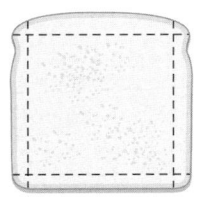

Trim crusts from two pieces of toasted bread.

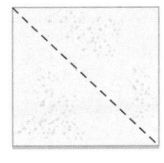

Cut one piece diagonally.

Arrange trimmed, cut toast on plate.

Lay main ingredient over toast. EX: bacon, roast beef, sliced turkey.

Cover with cheese or sauce and heat.

FIGURE 26.1 ▶ Arranging hot open-faced sandwiches.

Cold Sandwiches

Cold sandwiches are made with raw ingredients that are not intended to be cooked, such as vegetables and cheese, or with meat, poultry, fish or shellfish that is precooked and then chilled before use as a filling. Cold sandwiches may be closed or open-faced.

Cold closed sandwiches contain two or more pieces of bread with one or more fillings and one or more spreads. Cold closed sandwiches are usually eaten with the hands and come in three basic styles: basic, multidecker and tea.

Basic cold sandwiches are made with two pieces of bread or one split roll, one spread and one or more fillings. A tuna salad sandwich and an Italian-style submarine are both examples of basic cold closed sandwiches. A variation of the basic cold sandwich is a wrap with cold fillings—for example, an herb-flavored tortilla spread with peanut sauce and wrapped around spinach leaves, diced grilled chicken and cold cooked rice.

Multidecker cold sandwiches are made with three or more pieces of bread, one or more spreads and two or more fillings. The club sandwich, in which sliced turkey, bacon, lettuce and tomato are layered with three slices of toasted bread, is a classic example of a multidecker sandwich (see the recipe on page 805).

PROCEDURE FOR **PREPARING COLD MULTIDECKER SANDWICHES**

❶ The first slice of toasted bread is spread with butter or mayonnaise, then topped with meat and vegetables.

❷ The second slice of bread is added, then spread with mayonnaise.

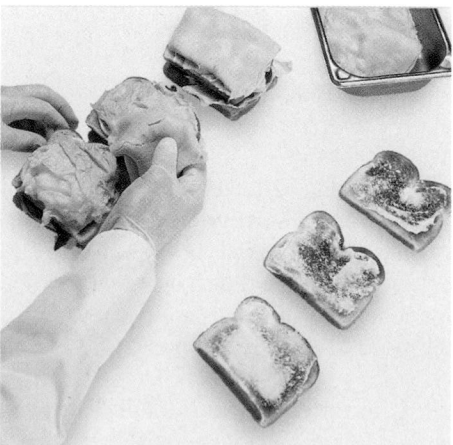

❸ A second layer of vegetables and meat is added.

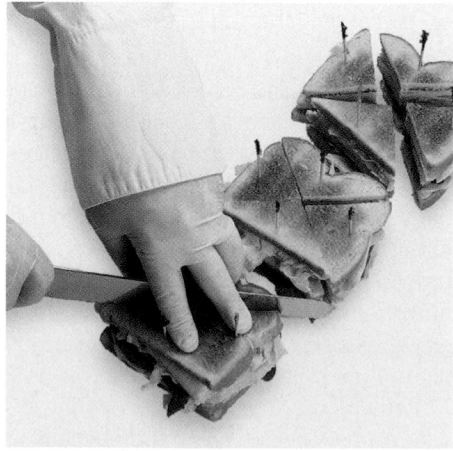

❹ The finished sandwich is cut into quarters for service.

Open-faced sandwiches featuring smoked salmon (top), roast beef and shrimp (bottom) are attractively garnished with items that complement the principal ingredient.

Tea sandwiches are small, fancy constructions made with light, soft, trimmed breads and delicate fillings and spreads. They are usually cut or rolled into shapes such as diamonds, circles or pinwheels and served as a finger food at parties and receptions. The name derives from their service at afternoon tea.

Cold open-faced sandwiches are simply larger versions of canapés, which are discussed in Chapter 28, Hors d'Oeuvre and Canapés. The most popular style is the open-faced Norwegian sandwich known as **smørbrød**. As with canapés, much emphasis is placed on visual appeal. A single slice of bread is coated with a spread, then covered with thin slices of meat, poultry or fish, or a thin layer of a bound salad. Carefully cut and arranged garnishes such as hard-cooked eggs, fresh herbs, pickles, onions and radishes are used to complete the presentation. A simple version of an open-faced cold sandwich is a delicatessen classic—a bagel with lox and cream cheese.

smørbrød (SMURR-brur) Norwegian cold open-faced sandwiches; similarly, the Swedish term *smörgåsbord* (SMORE-guhs-bohrd) refers to a buffet table of bread and butter, salads, open-faced sandwiches, pickled or marinated fish, sliced meats and cheeses

SANDWICH MISE EN PLACE

Sandwiches are generally prepared to order, and their preparation usually requires a great deal of handwork. Therefore, the goal is to assemble all ingredients and equipment within easy reach to minimize movement and ensure efficiency at the time of final assembly. Because each menu and food service operation has its own requirements, there is no one correct station setup, but there are a few basic guidelines.

1. *Prepare ingredients.* All sandwich ingredients should be cooked, mixed, sliced and prepared ahead of service to facilitate quick, efficient assembly at service time. So, before service, slice the meats, cheeses and vegetables; clean and dry lettuce and other fresh vegetable ingredients; blend the flavored spreads; mix the bound salads; and so on.

FIGURE 26.2 ▶ A typical sandwich bar.

❷ *Arrange and store ingredients.* Arrange all sandwich ingredients within easy reach of the work area. Cold items must be properly refrigerated at all times. A sandwich bar, similar to a steam table but with refrigerated compartments, is frequently used for this purpose. (See Figure 26.2.) Under-counter refrigeration can be used for backup supplies and less frequently used ingredients. Sliced meats, cheeses and vegetables must be well covered to prevent dehydration or contamination. Many ingredients can be preportioned, either by weight or count, then wrapped in individual portions for storage.

❸ *Select and arrange equipment.* The heavy equipment needed for making sandwiches can include preparation equipment such as meat slicers, griddles, grills, fryers and broilers as well as storage equipment such as refrigerated sandwich bars for cold ingredients and steam tables for hot ingredients. Even the simplest sandwich menu will require the use of basic hand tools such as spatulas, spreaders, portion scoops, knives and cutting boards. Be sure that the supply of such items is adequate to permit quick handwork and to avoid delays or cross-contamination.

PRESENTING AND GARNISHING SANDWICHES

Sandwiches, especially cold closed sandwiches, are usually cut into halves, thirds or quarters for service. Cutting makes a sandwich easier for the customer to handle and allows for a more attractive presentation; the sandwich wedges can be arranged to add height to the plate and to expose the fillings' colors and textures. For sit-down service, hot closed sandwiches such as hamburgers are often presented open-faced. Condiments, such as mustard and mayonnaise, and garnishes, such as sliced tomatoes, onions, pickles and lettuce leaves, are served on the side or on one of the open bun halves. This tends to be a more attractive presentation, and it allows the customer to assemble and add ingredients to the sandwich as desired.

Although a sandwich can be a meal unto itself, it may be served with a salad or starch accompaniment. Potato chips or French-fried potatoes are, of course, standard fare, perhaps because they are also finger foods and they provide a crunchy texture. Bound salads, such as potato and macaroni, are also common starch accompaniments. Plated sandwiches have long been served with coleslaw, fruit salad or a small mixed green salad as side dishes. Even the standard soup-and-sandwich combo—half a sandwich with a cup of soup—remains a popular lunch selection.

GREATEST HITS FROM THE SANDWICH COUNTER

Writing in his monumental *Le Guide culinaire* of 1903, Auguste Escoffier describes just two types of sandwiches: those "with two slices of buttered bread . . . covering a slice of ham or tongue, etc." and "the kind served at elaborate functions," which are much smaller, and in which the "sandwiched product (whatever this be)" is diced. Among his list of common sandwich ingredients are ham, beef, chicken, foie gras, caviar and watercress.

Today's cook must recognize a somewhat wider variety of sandwiches, however. And, as the following list shows, often a sandwich's popular name bears no connection to its ingredients.

BLT—Bacon, lettuce and tomato between two slices of toasted bread.

Croque Monsieur—Ham and cheese sandwich dipped in beaten egg and grilled; made popular by bars and bistros throughout Paris.

Deli—Contains any of various meats commonly sold in a delicatessen, such as pastrami, corned beef, turkey, ham, roast beef and so on. Usually the meat is sliced very thin and piled very high between two slices of white or rye bread.

Fluffernutter—Peanut butter and marshmallow fluff spread on—what else?—white bread; popular during the 1960s.

French Dip—Thin slices of roast beef in a crusty French-bread roll served au jus.

Gyro—Well-seasoned rotisserie-roasted lamb, thinly sliced and served wrapped in pita bread with onions and cucumber-yogurt dressing. A Greek-American creation, the gyro (YEAR-o) became popular at Greek lunch counters in New York City during the 1970s.

Panino—A crusty roll layered with cold cuts and cheese such as salami, ham, prosciutto and fontina; usually grilled and served warm. The plural form, *panini*, is often used when referring to this Italian specialty.

Po' Boy—French bread loaf split and filled with various ingredients, especially fried oysters or shrimp and rémoulade sauce. Created during the 1920s, it is New Orleans' version of a submarine sandwich.

Reuben—Corned beef, Swiss (Emmenthaler) cheese, sauerkraut and mustard or Thousand Island dressing grilled between two slices of rye bread. The Reuben was probably created during the early 1900s by Arnold Reuben, owner of New York City's Reuben's Restaurant.

QUESTIONS FOR DISCUSSION

1 List examples for each of the three primary sandwich components.

2 Explain the differences between a hot open-faced and a hot closed sandwich.

3 List several hand tools used in sandwich production, and explain the need for an ample supply of these tools.

4 Why is cross-contamination a concern when preparing sandwiches? What simple steps can be taken to avoid the spread of pathogenic microorganisms?

5 Create three sandwich concepts for a college town coffee shop. Describe the types of bread, the fillings and the accompaniments for each one. Discuss the preparation required in order to produce these sandwiches quickly during a busy lunchtime rush.

6 Sandwiches have become nearly universal, consumed in countries around the world. Use the Internet to research popular sandwiches served on three or four of the world's continents. Discuss and compare the different sandwich components and preparation methods used for each one. WWW

Terms to Know

club	croque monsieur
panini	French dip
tea sandwich	gyro
BLT	

GROUPER SANDWICH
WITH LEMON RÉMOULADE

K RESTAURANT WINE BAR, ORLANDO, FL

Chef Kevin Fonzo

Yield: 6 Sandwiches

Olive oil	1 fl. oz.	30 ml
Grouper fillets, 5 oz. (150 g) each	6	6
Salt and pepper	TT	TT
Lemon Rémoulade (recipe follows)	3 fl. oz.	90 ml
Kaiser rolls, sliced, toasted	6	6
Mixed greens	3 c.	720 ml
Tomato slices	6	6

1. Heat the oil in a large sauté pan. Season the grouper fillets with salt and pepper and then sauté the fish until golden brown and cooked through.

2. To assemble each sandwich, spread ½ fluid ounce (15 milliliters) Lemon Rémoulade on the bottom half of the roll, then top with ½ cup (120 milliliters) mixed greens, one tomato slice and one cooked fish fillet. Cover with the remaining half of the roll and serve.

Approximate values per serving: **Calories** 330, **Total fat** 8 g, **Saturated fat** 1 g, **Cholesterol** 40 mg, **Sodium** 380 mg, **Total carbohydrates** 36 g, **Protein** 28 g, **Vitamin A** 15%, **Vitamin C** 60%

LEMON RÉMOULADE

Yield: Approximately 20 fl. oz. (600 ml)

Mayonnaise	1 pt.	480 ml
Sweet pickle relish	3 oz.	90 g
Onion, chopped fine	2 Tbsp.	30 ml
Fresh parsley, chopped	2 Tbsp.	30 ml
Fresh lemon juice	2 Tbsp.	30 ml
Salt and black pepper	TT	TT
Worcestershire sauce	TT	TT
Tabasco sauce	TT	TT

1. Mix all the ingredients together until thoroughly blended.

Approximate values per 1-fl.-oz. (30-ml) serving: **Calories** 170, **Total fat** 18 g, **Saturated fat** 2.5 g, **Cholesterol** 15 mg, **Sodium** 160 mg, **Total carbohydrates** 2 g, **Protein** 0 g

HAMBURGER

Yield: 1 Sandwich

Beef, ground round	4–6 oz.	120–180 g
Salt and pepper	TT	TT
Hamburger bun or other appropriate bread	1	1
Garnishes	as desired	as desired

1. Form the ground round into a patty, handling the beef as little as possible.
2. Season the patty with salt and pepper and broil or grill to the desired doneness, turning once. While the patty is cooking, toast the bun or bread if desired.
3. Remove the patty from the broiler or grill, place on half of the bun or one slice of bread and garnish the other with a lettuce leaf, a slice of onion, a slice of tomato and/or pickles. Serve with condiments such as ketchup and mustard.

Approximate values per sandwich: **Calories** 580, **Total fat** 32 g, **Saturated fat** 9 g, **Cholesterol** 99 mg, **Sodium** 355 mg, **Total carbohydrates** 40 g, **Protein** 29 g

VARIATIONS:

Cheeseburger—Place one or two slices of American, Cheddar, Swiss or other cheese on the cooking patty approximately 1 minute before it is done.

Approximate values per sandwich: **Calories** 680, **Total fat** 42 g, **Saturated fat** 15 g, **Cholesterol** 130 mg, **Sodium** 520 mg, **Total carbohydrates** 42 g, **Protein** 36 g, **Calcium** 20%

Bacon Blue Cheeseburger—Place approximately 1 tablespoon (15 milliliters) crumbled blue cheese and two slices of crisp bacon on top of the cooking patty approximately 1 minute before it is done.

Approximate values per sandwich: **Calories** 650, **Total fat** 39 g, **Saturated fat** 12 g, **Cholesterol** 110 mg, **Sodium** 560 mg, **Total carbohydrates** 41 g, **Protein** 33 g

Mushroom Burger—Sauté 2 ounces (60 grams) sliced mushrooms in 1–2 teaspoons (5–10 milliliters) butter or olive oil. Top the cooked hamburger or cheeseburger with the cooked mushrooms.

Approximate values per sandwich, without cheese: **Calories** 660, **Total fat** 37 g, **Saturated fat** 12 g, **Cholesterol** 110 mg, **Sodium** 400 mg, **Total carbohydrates** 48 g, **Protein** 33 g

California Burger—Prepare a hamburger or cheeseburger and serve on a whole-wheat bun accompanied by 2 ounces (60 grams) guacamole, 1 ounce (30 grams) alfalfa sprouts, two slices of ripe tomato and one thin slice of red onion.

Approximate values per sandwich, without cheese: **Calories** 690, **Total fat** 40 g, **Saturated fat** 9 g, **Cholesterol** 100 mg, **Sodium** 770 mg, **Total carbohydrates** 50 g, **Protein** 33 g, **Vitamin C** 20%

Hamburger Boom

America's number one comfort food seems to be the hamburger. And chefs are responding with burgers from humble to haute. Smothered with pulled pork or studded with foie gras, hamburgers lend themselves to customization. Combine different cuts of beef to enhance flavor. Blend in fresh herbs or grated cheese. Present your creation on a homemade roll. Or serve a couple of mini patties on bite-size buns.

BLACKENED STEAK SANDWICH

Yield: 2 Sandwiches

New York strip steak, 10 oz. (300 g)	1	1
Blackened Steak Seasoning (recipe follows)	as needed	as needed
Clarified butter	1 fl. oz.	30 ml
Capers	1 Tbsp.	15 ml
Whole butter, softened	1 oz.	30 g
French bread, cut on the bias	2 slices	2 slices
Baby lettuce, cleaned	4 oz.	120 g
Roma tomatoes, sliced	2	2
Red onion, sliced	1 oz.	30 g

1. Heat a cast-iron skillet over high heat for 10 minutes. Pat the steak dry with a clean towel. Coat the steak in the Blackened Steak Seasoning.

2. Carefully place the steak into the hot pan and ladle ½ fluid ounce (15 milliliters) clarified butter over the steak. Be very careful, as the butter may flare up. There will be intense smoke and the steak will form a black crust. Cook the steak for approximately 2 minutes.

3. Turn the steak, ladle the remaining clarified butter over it and cook to the desired degree of doneness. Remove the steak from the pan and hold in a warm place.

4. Chop the capers and combine them with the softened butter. Spread each slice of bread with half of the caper butter.

5. Slice the steak on the bias.

6. To assemble each sandwich, place half of the warm steak on a slice of buttered bread and arrange half of the greens, tomatoes and onion attractively on the plate and serve.

VARIATION:

To serve this sandwich cold, allow the steak to cool after cooking, then refrigerate it until completely cold. Proceed with the recipe.

Approximate values per sandwich: **Calories** 610, **Total fat** 38 g, **Saturated fat** 20 g, **Cholesterol** 180 mg, **Sodium** 650 mg, **Total carbohydrates** 21 g, **Protein** 44 g, **Vitamin A** 30%, **Vitamin C** 40%

BLACKENED STEAK SEASONING

Yield: 3 Tbsp. (45 ml)

Paprika	1 Tbsp.	15 ml
Salt	2 tsp.	10 ml
Onion powder	1 tsp.	5 ml
Garlic powder	1 tsp.	5 ml
Cayenne pepper	1 tsp.	5 ml
White pepper	½ tsp.	2 ml
Black pepper	½ tsp.	2 ml
Dried thyme	½ tsp.	2 ml

1. Combine all ingredients and mix well.

ARUGULA, CAPICOLA HAM AND PROVOLONE PANINO

Yield: 1 Serving

Ciabatta or hard roll, 4 in. × 2½ in. (10 cm × 6 cm)	1	1
Mayonnaise	2 Tbsp.	30 ml
Pesto Sauce (page 225)	2 tsp.	10 ml
Arugula	½ oz.	15 g
Capicola, prosciutto or ham, sliced thin	2 oz.	60 g
Provolone, sliced thin	1 oz.	30 g
Oven-dried tomato wedges	1 oz.	30 g
Black pepper	TT	TT
Olives	as needed for garnish	
Tomatoes, quartered	as needed for garnish	

1. Cut the roll in half horizontally. Spread the interior of the roll generously with the mayonnaise and pesto.
2. Arrange the arugula, capicola, provolone and tomatoes in layers on the bottom portion of the roll. Season the layers with pepper as desired.
3. Place the sandwich on a preheated panini grill or on a griddle. Cook until heated through and browned, approximately 3 to 5 minutes. (If using a griddle, place a weight on the sandwich as it cooks, then flip it halfway through to brown on both sides.)
4. Cut on the diagonal and serve immediately garnished with olives and fresh tomato wedges on the side.

capicola Italian dry-cured salami made from pork shoulder that is seasoned with garlic, hot pepper, spices and wine, then smoked and cured

Approximate values per sandwich: **Calories** 670, **Total fat** 57 g, **Saturated fat** 14 g, **Cholesterol** 60 mg, **Sodium** 2200 mg, **Total carbohydrates** 16 g, **Protein** 24 g, **Vitamin C** 80%, **Calcium** 30%

CUBANO (CUBAN GRILLED HAM AND PORK SANDWICH)

Yield: 1 Serving

Sub roll, 6 in. (15 cm)	1	1
Dijon mustard	1 fl. oz.	30 ml
Ham, shaved thin	2 oz.	60 g
Pork loin, roasted, shaved thin	2 oz.	60 g
Swiss (Emmenthaler) cheese	2 slices	2 slices
Dill pickle, thinly sliced lengthwise	1	1

1. Split the sub roll in half lengthwise. Spread the cut side of the roll with mustard.
2. Arrange the ham, pork loin and cheese in layers on the roll, finishing with the pickle slices.
3. Place the sandwich in a preheated and lightly greased panini grill or on a griddle. Press down to compress the sandwich. Cook until heated through and browned, approximately 2 to 4 minutes. (If using a griddle, place a weight on the sandwich as it cooks and flip it halfway through to brown on both sides.)
4. Cut on the diagonal and serve immediately, garnished with potato or vegetable chips if desired.

Approximate values per sandwich: **Calories** 650, **Total fat** 23 g, **Saturated fat** 9 g, **Cholesterol** 105 mg, **Sodium** 2320 mg, **Total carbohydrates** 65 g, **Protein** 42 g, **Calcium** 35%, **Iron** 20%

SOUTHWESTERN GRILLED CHICKEN WRAP

Yield: 12 Sandwiches

Chicken breast, boneless, skinless	3 lb.	1.4 kg
Salt and pepper	TT	TT
Haas avocados	1 lb. 8 oz.	720 g
Red bell peppers	1 lb. 8 oz.	720 g
Red onion, peeled	1 lb. 8 oz.	720 g
Tomatoes	1 lb.	480 g
Tortillas, 12 in. (30 cm)	12	12
Black Bean Spread (recipe follows)	3 lb.	1.4 kg
Black olives, sliced	6 oz.	180 g
Fresh cilantro, chopped	2 bunches	2 bunches
Cheddar cheese, grated	1 lb. 8 oz.	720 g
Jalapeños, minced	2	2
Fresh salsa or sour cream	as needed	as needed

1. Season the chicken breast with salt and pepper and grill or broil until done. Chill and cut into strips.
2. Peel the avocados and cut each into 12 slices. Clean the bell peppers and cut into ¼-inch (6-millimeter) strips. Slice the onion thinly. Dice the tomatoes.
3. To make each sandwich, place one tortilla on a cutting board and spread with approximately 4 ounces (120 grams) Black Bean Spread.
4. Sprinkle one-twelfth of the bell peppers, onion, tomatoes, olives, cilantro, cheese and jalapeños over the bean spread.
5. Top with one-twelfth of the chicken and three slices of avocado. Drizzle each wrap with salsa or sour cream, if desired.
6. Roll the tortilla around the ingredients tightly enough so that the sandwich will hold its shape. Cut the sandwich as desired for service.

Approximate values per sandwich: **Calories** 642, **Total fat** 37 g, **Saturated fat** 16 g, **Cholesterol** 118 mg, **Sodium** 695 mg, **Total carbohydrates** 37 g, **Protein** 41 g, **Vitamin A** 37%, **Vitamin C** 76%, **Calcium** 50%, **Iron** 22%

BLACK BEAN SPREAD

Yield: 3 lb. (1.4 kg)

Black beans, soaked and drained	1 lb. 8 oz.	720 g
Water	4 qt.	4 lt
Onion, diced	4 oz.	120 g
Tomatoes, diced	6 oz.	180 g
Fresh cilantro, chopped	2 Tbsp.	30 ml
Salt and pepper	TT	TT
Cumin, ground	1 tsp.	5 ml
Chilli powder	1 tsp.	5 ml

1. Combine the beans and the water, bring to a boil, reduce to a simmer and cook until tender, approximately 1½ to 2 hours.
2. Add the remaining ingredients and simmer for 10 minutes.
3. Drain the beans, reserving the cooking liquid. Chill the beans and the liquid.
4. Purée the beans in a food processor, adding enough of the cooking liquid to make a soft, spreadable purée.

Approximate values per 2-oz. (60-g) serving: **Calories** 100, **Total fat** 0.5 g, **Saturated fat** 0 g, **Cholesterol** 0 mg, **Sodium** 51 mg, **Total carbohydrates** 37 g, **Protein** 12 g, **Claims**—low fat; no cholesterol; low sodium

REUBEN SANDWICH

Yield: 1 Sandwich

Dark rye bread	2 slices	2 slices
Thousand Island dressing	2 Tbsp.	30 ml
Cooked corned beef, hot, sliced very thin	4 oz.	120 g
Sauerkraut, hot, drained well	2 oz.	60 g
Swiss (Emmenthaler) cheese	2 slices	2 slices
Whole butter, softened	as needed	as needed

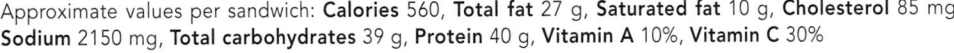

1. Spread each slice of bread with approximately 1 tablespoon (15 milliliters) Thousand Island dressing.
2. Place the corned beef, sauerkraut and cheese on one slice of bread. Top with the second slice of bread, keeping the dressing side inside the sandwich.
3. Butter the top slice of bread and place the sandwich on a hot griddle, butter side down. Carefully butter the second slice of bread.
4. Griddle the sandwich, turning once when the first side is well browned. The sandwich is done when both sides are well browned, the fillings are very hot and the cheese is melted.
5. Cut the sandwich in half diagonally and arrange as desired for service.

Approximate values per sandwich: **Calories** 560, **Total fat** 27 g, **Saturated fat** 10 g, **Cholesterol** 85 mg, **Sodium** 2150 mg, **Total carbohydrates** 39 g, **Protein** 40 g, **Vitamin A** 10%, **Vitamin C** 30%

MONTE CRISTO SANDWICH

Yield: 1 Sandwich

White bread	2 slices	2 slices
Whole butter, softened	as needed	as needed
Cooked turkey breast, sliced thin	1 oz.	30 g
Ham, sliced thin	1 oz.	30 g
Swiss (Emmenthaler) cheese	2 slices	2 slices
Egg	1	1
Milk	2 Tbsp.	30 ml

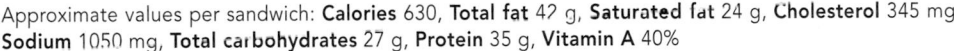

1. Spread one side of each slice of bread with butter.
2. Arrange the turkey breast, ham and cheese on top of the butter on one slice of bread.
3. Place the other slice of bread on top of the cheese, butter side against the cheese.
4. Beat the egg and milk together. Dip the sandwich in the egg batter and allow the batter to soak into the bread for approximately 4 to 5 minutes.
5. Using the swimming method, deep fry the sandwich in oil at 375°F (190°C) until it is evenly browned. Remove from the oil and drain well. Cut the sandwich into four pieces and arrange as desired.

Approximate values per sandwich: **Calories** 630, **Total fat** 42 g, **Saturated fat** 24 g, **Cholesterol** 345 mg, **Sodium** 1050 mg, **Total carbohydrates** 27 g, **Protein** 35 g, **Vitamin A** 40%

KENTUCKY HOT BROWN SANDWICH

Yield: 6 Sandwiches

Heavy cream, hot	6 fl. oz.	180 ml
Romano, grated	6 oz.	180 g
Velouté sauce, hot	1 qt.	960 ml
Dry sherry	2 Tbsp.	30 ml
White toast, crust removed	12 slices	12 slices
Turkey breast, cooked, sliced	1 lb. 8 oz.	720 g
Parmesan, grated	2 oz.	60 g
Tomato wedges	12	12
Bacon slices, lean, cooked crisp	12	12

1. To make the sauce, add the cream and the Romano to the velouté sauce and bring to a simmer. Simmer for 1 minute, then strain the sauce through a china cap. Stir in the sherry. Hold in a warm place for service.
2. Cut the toast diagonally into triangles.
3. To assemble each sandwich, arrange four toast triangles in a gratin dish and top with 4 ounces (120 grams) turkey and 4 fluid ounces (120 milliliters) sauce. Bake at 350°F (180°C) until brown, approximately 15 minutes.
4. Top each sandwich with Parmesan, two tomato wedges and two strips of bacon and serve very hot.

Approximate values per sandwich: **Calories** 720, **Total fat** 34 g, **Saturated fat** 17 g, **Cholesterol** 185 mg, **Sodium** 2180 mg, **Total carbohydrates** 45 g, **Protein** 59 g, **Vitamin A** 20%, **Calcium** 50%

MUFFULETTA SANDWICH

Yield: 1 Sandwich, 4–6 Servings

Olive Salad:		
Red bell pepper, roasted, chopped	8 oz.	240 g
Niçoise or Gaeta olives, pitted, chopped	4 oz.	120 g
Olives, green, pitted, chopped	4 oz.	120 g
Olive oil	4 fl. oz.	120 ml
Fresh Italian parsley, chopped	2 Tbsp.	30 ml
Anchovy fillets, mashed	2	2
Dried oregano	1 tsp.	5 ml
Lemon juice	1 Tbsp.	15 ml
Round Italian bread, 8-in. (18-cm) diameter	1	1
Arugula or curly endive, chiffonade	1½ oz.	45 g
Tomato concassée	6 oz.	180 g
Mortadella, sliced thin	6 oz.	180 g
Soppressata, sliced thin	4 oz.	120 g
Provolone or Fontina, sliced thin	4 oz.	120 g
Black pepper	TT	TT

1. To make the olive salad, combine the bell pepper, olives, oil, parsley, anchovies, oregano and lemon juice and marinate for several hours.
2. Cut the loaf of bread in half horizontally. Remove some of the soft interior of the bread to create a slight hollow area.
3. Drain the olive salad, reserving the oil. Brush the interior of the bread with the reserved oil, using it all.
4. Arrange the olive salad, greens, tomato concassée, mortadella, soppressata and cheese in layers on the bottom portion of the loaf of bread, finishing with a thick layer of olive salad. Season the layers with pepper as desired.

⑤ Place the top on the sandwich and wrap tightly with plastic wrap. Refrigerate the sandwich for several hours so that the layers will remain in place when the sandwich is cut.

⑥ Cut the sandwich into four to six wedges and arrange as desired for service.

Approximate values per sandwich: **Calories** 670, **Total fat** 57 g, **Saturated fat** 14 g, **Cholesterol** 60 mg, **Sodium** 2200 mg, **Total carbohydrates** 16 g, **Protein** 24 g, **Vitamin C** 80%, **Calcium** 30%

ROASTED RED BEET
AND GOAT CHEESE PITA SANDWICH

Yield: 8 Servings, ½ pita each

Goat cheese, soft variety	8 oz.	240 g
Cream cheese	8 oz.	240 g
Fresh parsley, chopped	2 Tbsp.	30 ml
Fresh thyme	1 Tbsp.	15 ml
Dressing:		
Grated horseradish	1 Tbsp.	30 ml
Dijon mustard	2 tsp.	10 ml
Rice wine vinegar	1 fl. oz.	30 ml
Olive oil	4 fl. oz.	120 ml
Salt and pepper	TT	TT
Mixed baby greens	4 oz.	120 g
Snow peas, julienne	4 oz.	120 g
Green onions, julienne	2 oz.	60 g
Cucumber, peeled, seeded, julienne	4 oz.	120 g
Red beets, roasted, peeled, julienne	8 oz.	240 g
Whole-wheat pitas	4	4

① Combine the goat cheese, cream cheese, parsley and thyme in the bowl of a mixer and blend until smooth.

② Combine the dressing ingredients and whisk together.

③ In a stainless steel bowl, combine the greens, snow peas, green onions, cucumber and beets. Add the dressing, season with salt and pepper and gently toss to combine.

④ Cut the pitas in half. Open the pockets and spread 2 ounces (60 grams) of the goat cheese mixture into each pocket.

⑤ Stuff each pita pocket with one-fourth of the lettuce-and-vegetable mixture.

⑥ Cut each sandwich in half and serve two quarters per portion with an appropriate accompaniment.

Approximate values per serving: **Calories** 380, **Total fat** 30 g, **Saturated fat** 12 g, **Cholesterol** 45 mg, **Sodium** 370 mg, **Total carbohydrates** 19 g, **Protein** 11 g, **Vitamin A** 40%, **Vitamin C** 30%, **Iron** 15%, **Claims**—good source of fiber, calcium and iron; high in vitamins A and C

EGG SALAD AND SMOKED SALMON SANDWICH

Yield: 4 Servings

Eggs, hard boiled, peeled	6	6
Mayonnaise	3 fl. oz.	180 ml
Dijon mustard	1 tsp.	5 ml
Green onion, minced	1 Tbsp.	30 ml
Tabasco sauce	¼ tsp.	1 ml
Kosher salt	½ tsp.	2 ml
Black pepper, ground	½ tsp.	2 ml
Multigrain bread, sliced, toasted	8 slices	8 slices
Bibb lettuce	4 leaves	4 leaves
Smoked salmon, sliced	8 oz.	240 g
Fresh dill	4 sprigs	4 sprigs

1. Chop the eggs coarsely.
2. Transfer the eggs to a bowl. Stir in the mayonnaise, mustard, green onion, Tabasco sauce, salt and pepper.
3. To make each sandwich, place one slice of toasted bread on a cutting board. Put a lettuce leaf on the bread. Top with one-fourth of the egg salad and a slice of smoked salmon. Place a dill sprig on top of the salmon. Top with a slice of toasted bread.

Approximate values per serving: **Calories** 590, **Total fat** 31 g, **Saturated fat** 6 g, **Cholesterol** 355 mg, **Sodium** 970 mg, **Total carbohydrates** 47 g, **Protein** 26 g, **Vitamin A** 20%, **Vitamin C** 25%, **Iron** 25%

PAN BAGNAT
(PROVENÇAL TUNA SANDWICH)

Yield: 4 Servings

French bread, 12-in. (30-cm) loaf	1	1
Garlic, chopped	1 Tbsp.	15 ml
Salt	½ tsp.	2 ml
Olive oil	2 fl. oz.	60 ml
Tomato	1	1
Red bell pepper, roasted, seeded	6 oz.	180 g
Green bell pepper, roasted, seeded	6 oz.	180 g
Tuna, canned, water-packed, undrained	12 oz.	360 g
Capers, drained	2 Tbsp.	30 ml
Green onions, minced	2	2
Red onion, sliced thin	4 oz.	120 g
Anchovy fillets (optional)	4	4

Pan bagnat means "bathed bread" in French. The juices from the tuna and vegetables soak into the crusty bread, which is already "swimming" with garlicky oil. This popular sandwich from southern France keeps well and should be made at least 30 minutes in advance of service.

1. Cut the French bread almost in half, keeping the top and bottom attached. Combine the garlic, salt and oil and brush the inside of the loaf with this mixture. Heat the loaf in a 350°F (180°C) oven until the crust is crisp, approximately 5 to 6 minutes.
2. Cut the tomato into thin slices. Cut the bell peppers into four pieces each. Combine the tuna, capers and green onions.
3. Spread the tuna mixture evenly on the loaf. Cover the tuna with the tomato, bell peppers and red onion slices. Top with anchovy fillets, if using. Press down on loaf. Secure it in four places with toothpicks, then cut into four uniform portions. Alternatively, wrap the loaf securely in parchment paper. Press down and cut into uniform portions.

Approximate values per serving: **Calories** 340, **Total fat** 9 g, **Saturated fat** 1.5 g, **Cholesterol** 20 mg, **Sodium** 1010 mg, **Total carbohydrates** 38 g, **Protein** 25 g, **Vitamin A** 30%, **Vitamin C** 150%, **Iron** 20%

CLUB SANDWICH

Yield: 1 Sandwich

Sliced bread, toasted	3 slices	3 slices
Mayonnaise	as needed	as needed
Lettuce leaves	2	2
Tomato slices	3	3
Bacon slices, cooked crisp	3	3
Salt and pepper	TT	TT
Cooked turkey breast, sliced thin	3 oz.	90 g

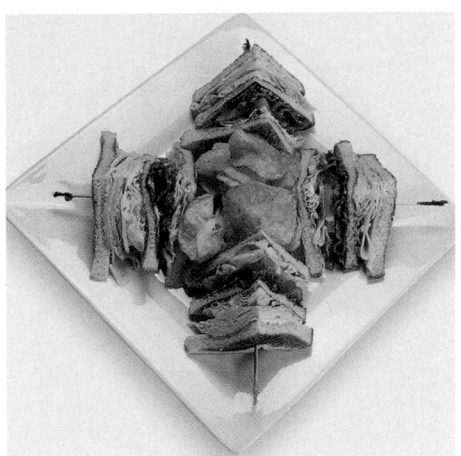

1. Spread one side of each slice of bread with mayonnaise.
2. Arrange the lettuce, tomato and bacon on one slice of toast. Season with salt and pepper.
3. Place another slice of toast on top of the bacon.
4. Arrange the turkey breast on top of the second slice of toast.
5. Place the third slice of toast on top of the turkey breast, mayonnaise side down.
6. Place 4 frilled toothpicks in the sandwich, one on each side, approximately 1 inch (2.5 centimeters) in from the edge. Cut the sandwich diagonally into quarters and arrange as desired for service.

Approximate values per sandwich: **Calories** 530, **Total fat** 24 g, **Saturated fat** 6 g, **Cholesterol** 95 mg, **Sodium** 830 mg, **Total carbohydrates** 38 g, **Protein** 39 g, **Vitamin A** 4%, **Vitamin C** 10%

CHICKEN PESTO AND FETA SANDWICH

WILDFLOWER BREAD COMPANY, Scottsdale, AZ

Yield: 8 Sandwiches

Mushrooms, sliced thin	8 oz.	240 g
Balsamic vinaigrette	1 fl. oz.	30 ml
Red bell peppers, roasted	8 oz.	240 g
Tomatoes, medium	4	4
Chicken breasts, boneless, skinless, 4 oz. (120 g) each	8	8
Italian rolls	8	8
Pesto Sauce (page 225)	8 oz.	240 g
Feta	8 oz.	240 g

1. Marinate the mushrooms in the balsamic vinaigrette for at least 24 hours under refrigeration, stirring occasionally.
2. Slice the bell peppers into ¼-inch- (6-millimeter-) wide strips.
3. Slice the tomatoes into ¼-inch- (6-millimeter-) thick slices.
4. Trim any fat or rib meat from the chicken breasts and then grill until done.
5. To assemble each sandwich, slice one roll in half lengthwise. Spread 1 ounce (30 grams) of the Pesto Sauce on the bottom of the roll, then crumble 1 ounce (30 grams) of the feta on top of the Pesto Sauce, covering the entire surface. Place a chicken breast on top of the feta, then ½ ounce (15 grams) of the mushrooms on the chicken, then 1 ounce (30 grams) of the bell pepper strips on top of the mushrooms; finish with three tomato slices and the top of the roll. Insert two toothpicks, slice and serve.

Approximate values per sandwich: **Calories** 540, **Total fat** 20 g, **Saturated fat** 7 g, **Cholesterol** 135 mg, **Sodium** 830 mg, **Total carbohydrates** 39 g, **Protein** 51 g, **Vitamin A** 20%, **Vitamin C** 60%, **Calcium** 30%, **Iron** 25%

GRILLED VEGETABLE SANDWICH

Note: This dish appears in the chapter opening photograph.

Yield: 6 Servings

Eggplant, cut into ¼-inch thick slices	1	1
Salt	1 tsp.	5 ml
Zucchini, cut lengthwise into ¼-inch- (6-millimeters-) thick	1	1
Yellow squash, cut lengthwise into ¼-inch- (6-millimeters-) thick slices	1	1
Red onion, cut into ¼-inch- (6-millimeters-) thick slices	1	1
Olive oil	3 fl. oz.	90 ml
Garlic, minced	2 Tbsp.	30 ml
Herbes de Provence	¾ tsp.	4 ml
Black pepper	as needed	as needed
Sandwich rolls, multigrain	6	6
Herb-garlic cheese (Boursin)	4 oz.	120 g
Lettuce	6 leaves	6 leaves
Red bell peppers, roasted, cut into strips	6 oz.	180 g

1. Sprinkle the eggplant with salt and set aside in a colander for 10 minutes.

2. Dry the sliced zucchini, squash and eggplant with paper towels. Place them on a sheet pan with the onion slices. Brush the vegetables with the oil and sprinkle with the garlic and herbs de Provence. Season with more salt and pepper.

3. Place the sliced vegetables on a hot grill without crowding. Grill until lightly charred and done, approximately 4 to 5 minutes on each side. (The vegetables may be prepared ahead of serving. Refrigerate until needed.)

4. Split each roll in half. Spread the herb-garlic cheese generously on the top half of each roll. Arrange one-sixth of the lettuce, onion, bell peppers, squash and eggplant in layers on each roll. Place the tops on the sandwiches and serve immediately.

Approximate values per sandwich: **Calories** 480, **Total fat** 24 g, **Saturated fat** 7 g, **Cholesterol** 25 mg, **Sodium** 970 mg, **Total carbohydrates** 59 g, **Protein** 11 g, **Vitamin A** 45%, **Vitamin C** 80%, **Calcium** 15%, **Iron** 20%

WHOLE-WHEAT CALZONE WITH SPINACH AND FETA

SPOKANE COMMUNITY COLLEGE, Spokane, WA

Instructor Peter Tobin, CEC, CCE

Yield: 12 Servings

Crust:

Water, warm	1 pt.	480 ml
Granulated sugar	2 Tbsp.	30 ml
Yeast, dry	½ oz.	15 g
Whole-wheat flour	8 oz.	240 g
Bread flour	1 lb.	480 g
Olive oil	2 fl. oz.	60 ml
Salt	2 tsp.	10 ml

Filling:

Clarified butter	2 fl. oz.	60 ml
Onion, small dice	6 oz.	180 g
Frozen spinach, thawed, drained, chopped	24 oz.	720 g
Dried thyme	1 tsp.	5 ml
Cottage cheese	2 lb.	960 g
Feta	12 oz.	360 g
Nutmeg, ground	½ tsp.	2 ml
Salt	1 tsp.	5 ml
Black pepper	1 tsp.	5 ml
Provolone or mozzarella, grated	4 oz.	120 g
Fresh Tomato Sauce for pasta (page 222)	3 pt.	1.4 lt
Egg wash	4 fl. oz.	120 ml
Cornmeal	as needed	as needed

1. In a mixing bowl, combine the water and sugar and then add the yeast, flours, oil and salt. Using a dough hook, mix the dough on medium speed until it is smooth and elastic, approximately 10 minutes.

2. Place the dough in a lightly oiled bowl, cover with a towel and remove to a warm area to proof until the dough has doubled in volume, approximately 1 hour.

3. Heat the butter in a saucepan. Add the onion and sauté lightly. Add the spinach and thyme and cook until heated through.

4. Transfer the spinach mixture to a bowl and stir in the cottage cheese, feta, nutmeg, salt, pepper and grated cheese. Spread the mixture on a sheet pan and refrigerate until completely cool.

5. To build the calzones, punch down the dough and divide into 12 equal pieces. Roll out each piece of dough into an 8-inch (20-centimeter) round. Spread the center of each round with 1 fluid ounce (30 milliliters) Fresh Tomato Sauce for Pasta. Place 4–6 ounces (120–180 grams) of the spinach mixture in the middle of each round. Brush the edges of the dough with egg wash. Fold the dough in half around the filling, forming a half circle. Seal the edges with your fingers or the tines of a fork. Dust a sheet pan with cornmeal and place the calzones on the pan.

6. Brush the calzones with egg wash and bake at 425°F (220°C) until the crust is evenly browned and the filling is hot, approximately 7 to 10 minutes. Serve the calzones hot with tomato sauce on the side.

Approximate values per serving: **Calories** 660, **Total fat** 23 g, **Saturated fat** 11 g, **Cholesterol** 75 mg, **Sodium** 2300 mg, **Total carbohydrates** 78 g, **Protein** 37 g, **Vitamin A** 100%, **Vitamin C** 25%, **Calcium** 35%, **Iron** 30%

CHAPTER TWENTY-SEVEN

CHARCUTERIE

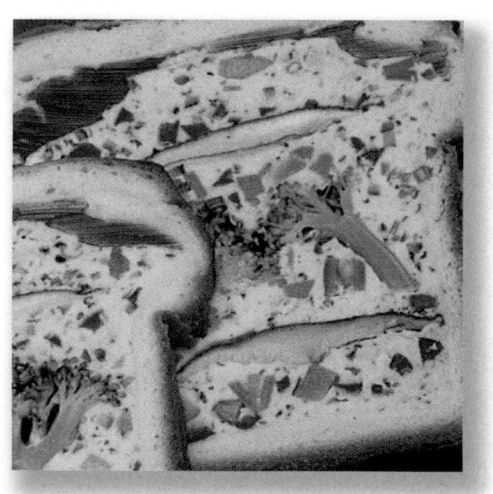

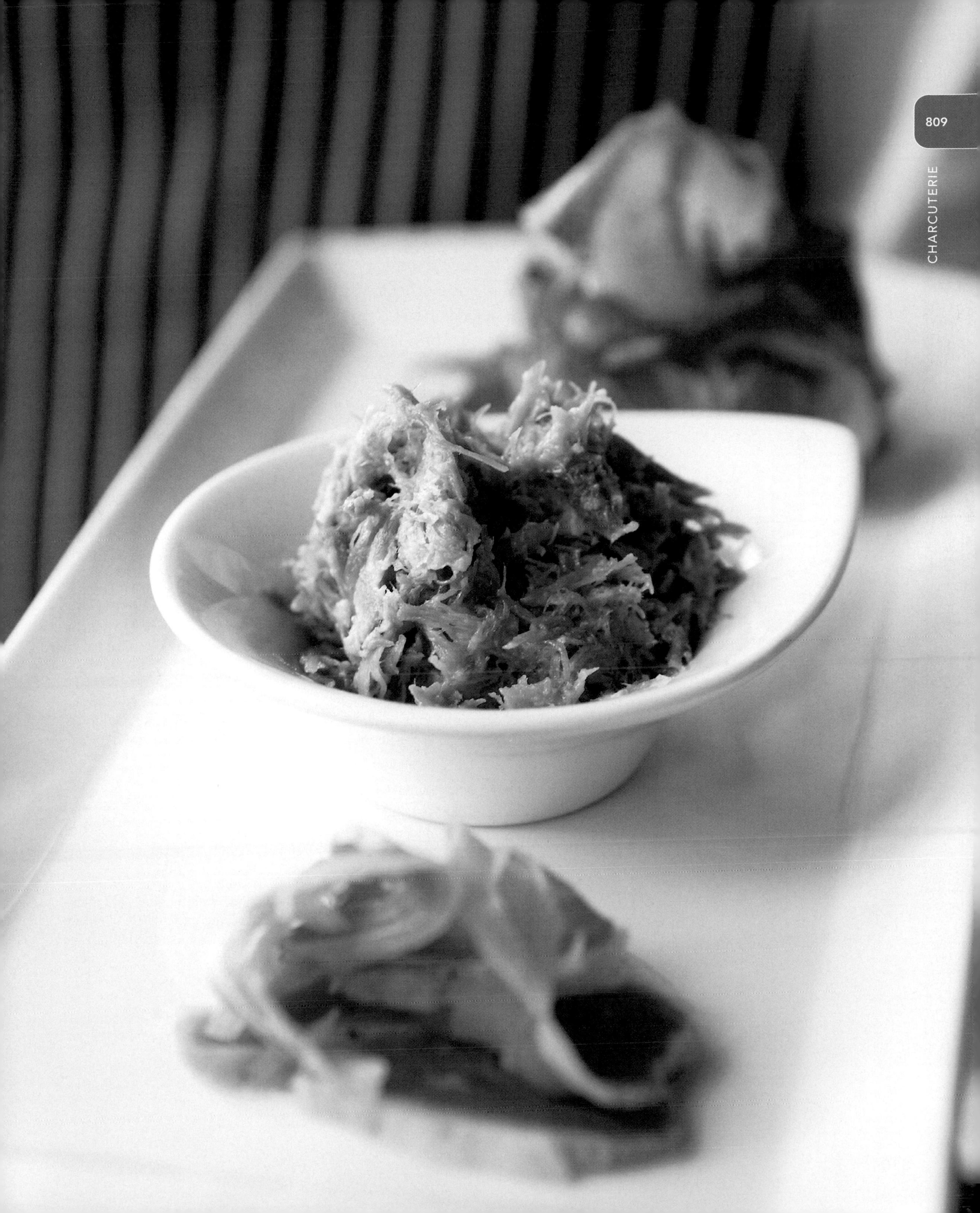

After studying this chapter, you will be able to:

- prepare a variety of forcemeats

- assemble and cook a variety of pâtés, terrines and sausages

- understand the proper methods for brining, curing and smoking meats and fish

- identify several cured pork products

THE CLASSIC ART OF CHARCUTERIE (shar-COO-tuhr-ree) is as popular today as ever. Consumers regularly enjoy high-quality pâtés, galantines, sausages and hams. Traditionally, charcuterie was limited to these products. Over the years, however, the term has come to include similar products made with game, poultry, fish, shellfish and even vegetables.

Charcuterie is an art and science in itself. This chapter is not intended to be a complete guide to the charcutier's art. Instead, this chapter focuses on procedures for making common charcuterie items that can be prepared easily in most kitchens. The preparation of sausages as well as curing methods, including salt curing, brining and both cold and hot smoking, is discussed. The chapter ends with information about several cured pork products.

FORCEMEATS AND THEIR USES

A **forcemeat** is a preparation made from uncooked ground meats, poultry, fish or shellfish that is seasoned and then emulsified with fat. Forcemeats are the primary ingredient used to make pâtés, terrines, galantines and sausages.

The word *forcemeat* is derived from the French word *farce*, meaning "stuffing." Depending on the preparation method, a forcemeat can be very smooth and velvety, well-textured and coarse, or anything in between. Regardless of its intended use, it has a glossy appearance when raw and will slice cleanly when cooked. A properly emulsified forcemeat provides a rich flavor and a comforting texture on the palate.

Forcemeats are emulsified products. Emulsification is the process of binding two ingredients that ordinarily would not combine. (Emulsified sauces are discussed in Chapter 10, Stocks and Sauces; emulsified salad dressings are discussed in Chapter 24, Salads and Salad Dressings.) The proteins present in the meat, poultry, fish and shellfish combine easily with both fat and liquids. In forcemeats, these proteins act as a stabilizer that allows the fat and liquids, which ordinarily would not combine, to bind. When improperly emulsified forcemeats are cooked, they lose their fat, shrink and become dry and grainy. To ensure proper emulsification of a forcemeat:

1. The ratio of fat to other ingredients must be precise.
2. Temperatures must be maintained below 41°F (5°C).
3. The ingredients must be mixed properly.

Forcemeat Ingredients

Forcemeats are usually meat, poultry, fish or shellfish combined with binders, seasonings and sometimes garnishes. Selections from each of these basic categories are used to make an array of forcemeats. All ingredients must be of the finest quality and added in just the right proportions.

MEATS

The **dominant meat** is the meat, poultry, fish or shellfish that gives the forcemeat its name and essential flavor. When preparing meats, poultry or fish for forcemeat, it is important to trim all silverskin, gristle and small bones so that the meat will be more easily ground and will produce a smoother finished product.

Many forcemeats contain some pork. Pork adds moisture and smoothness to the forcemeat. Without it, poultry-based forcemeats tend to be rubbery, whereas venison and other game-based forcemeats tend to be dry. The traditional ratio is one part pork to two parts dominant meat.

Many forcemeats also contain some liver. Pork liver is commonly used, as is chicken liver. Liver contributes flavor as well as binding to the forcemeat. For a finer texture, grind the livers and then force them through a drum sieve before incorporating them into the forcemeat.

FATS

Here, fat refers to a separate ingredient, not the fat in the dominant meat or pork, both of which should be quite lean in order to ensure the correct ratio of fat to meat. Usually pork fatback or heavy cream is used to add moisture and richness to the forcemeat. Because fat carries flavor, it also promotes the proper infusion of flavors and smoke.

BINDERS

There are two principal types of binders: panadas and eggs.

A **panada** (pah-nahd) is something other than fat that is added to a forcemeat to enhance smoothness (especially in fish mousselines, which tend to be slightly grainy in texture), to aid emulsification (especially in vegetable terrines, in which the protein levels are insufficient to bind on their own) or both (for example, in liver mousses). It should not make up more than 20 percent of the forcemeat's total weight. Usually a panada is nothing more than crustless white bread soaked in milk or, more traditionally, a heavy béchamel or rice.

Eggs or egg whites are used as a primary binding agent in some styles of forcemeat. If used in forcemeats that have a large ratio of liver or liquids, they also add texture.

SEASONINGS

Forcemeats are seasoned with salt, curing salt, marinades and various herbs and spices.

Salt not only adds flavor to a forcemeat but also aids in the emulsification of the meat and fat. As with other foods, a forcemeat that lacks salt will taste flat.

Curing salt is a mixture of salt and sodium nitrite. Sodium nitrite controls spoilage by inhibiting bacterial growth. Equally important, curing salt preserves the rosy pink colors of some forcemeats that might otherwise oxidize to an unappetizing gray. Although currently regarded as substantially safer than the previously used potassium nitrate (saltpeter), some studies suggest that sodium nitrite is a carcinogen. For a typical consumer, however, the amount of sodium nitrite consumed from cured meats should not pose a substantial health threat.

Traditionally, ingredients for forcemeats were marinated for long periods, sometimes days, before grinding. The trend today is for a shorter marinating time so that the true flavors of the main ingredients shine through. Both classic and contemporary marinades include herbs, citrus zest, spices and liquors, all of which lend flavor, character and nuance to the forcemeat.

Pâté spice is a mixture of spices and dried herbs that can be premixed and used as needed.

PÂTÉ SPICE

Yield: 7⅔ oz. (220 g)

Cloves	1 oz.	30 g
Dried ginger	1 oz.	30 g
Nutmeg	1 oz.	30 g
Paprika	1 oz.	30 g
Dried basil	⅔ oz.	20 g
Black pepper	⅔ oz.	20 g
White pepper	⅔ oz.	20 g
Bay leaf	⅓ oz.	10 g
Dried thyme	1 oz.	30 g
Dried marjoram	⅓ oz.	10 g

1 Grind all the ingredients in a spice grinder. Pass through a sieve to remove any large pieces.

VARIATION:

This mixture can be used as is, or mix 1 ounce (30 grams) (or any amount desired) with 1 pound (480 grams) salt. The salt-and-spice mixture can then be used to season forcemeats; ⅓ ounce (10 grams) per pound of forcemeat usually suffices for most pâtés.

Approximate values per 1-oz. (30-g) serving: **Calories** 20, **Total fat** 1 g, **Saturated fat** 0 g, **Cholesterol** 0 mg, **Sodium** 0 mg, **Total carbohydrates** 3 g, **Protein** 1 g, **Vitamin A** 6%

EQUIPMENT FOR PREPARING FORCEMEATS

To properly prepare forcemeats, certain equipment is required. A food chopper or food processor and a heavy-duty drum sieve with a metal band are essential tools used to make forcemeat. A standard meat grinder or meat-grinding attachment with various-sized grinding dies is also useful especially when preparing meats for coarse pâtés and sausage.

An X-Blade and Assorted Dies for a Standard Grinder

A forcemeat's seasoning and texture can be tested by cooking a small portion before the entire forcemeat is cooked. (Unlike sauces, stews and other dishes, a forcemeat cannot be tasted during the cooking process to adjust the seasonings.) A small portion of a hearty forcemeat can be sautéed; a small portion of a more delicate forcemeat should be poached for 3 to 5 minutes. When cooked, the forcemeat should hold its shape and be slightly firm but not rubbery. If it is too firm, add a little cream. Adjust the seasonings appropriately; keep in mind that foods served cold may require additional salt and seasonings.

GARNISHES

Forcemeat garnishes are meats, fat, vegetables or other foods added in limited quantities to provide contrasting flavors and textures and to improve appearance. The garnishes are usually diced, chopped or more coarsely ground than the dominant meat. Common garnishes include pistachio nuts, diced fatback, truffles or truffle peelings and diced ham or tongue.

Preparing Forcemeats

The three common forcemeat preparations are **country-style**, **basic** and **mousseline**. Each can be produced easily in a typical food service operation. Other types of forcemeat preparations such as the emulsified mixture used to make hot dogs and bratwurst are not commonly encountered in food service operations and are not discussed here.

When preparing any forcemeat, certain guidelines must be followed:

1. Forcemeat preparations include raw meats, liver, eggs and dairy products. If improperly handled, these potentially hazardous foods create a good environment for the growth of microorganisms. To avoid the risk of food-borne illness, temperatures must be carefully controlled, and all cutting boards and food contact surfaces must be as sanitary as possible at all times.

2. To ensure a proper emulsification, the forcemeat must be kept cold—below 41°F (5°C)—at all times. Refrigerate all moist ingredients, and keep forcemeats in progress in an ice bath. Chilling or freezing metal grinder and food processor parts helps keep the ingredients as cold as possible.

3. Cut all foods into convenient sizes that fit easily into grinder openings. Do not overstuff grinders or overfill food processors. When grinding items twice, always begin with a larger die, followed by a medium or small die. For exceptional smoothness, press the forcemeat through a sieve after grinding to remove any lumps or pieces of membrane.

COUNTRY-STYLE FORCEMEATS

A traditional country-style forcemeat is heavily seasoned with onions, garlic, pepper, juniper berries and bay leaves. It is the simplest of the forcemeats to prepare and yields the heartiest and most distinctive pâtés and sausages.

The dominant meat for a country-style forcemeat is usually ground once through the grinder's large die, then ground again through the medium die. This produces the characteristic coarse, country-style texture. As with most forcemeats, the dominant meat for a country-style forcemeat is usually marinated and seasoned before grinding and then mixed with some liver.

PROCEDURE FOR **PREPARING A COUNTRY-STYLE FORCEMEAT**

1. Chill all ingredients and equipment thoroughly. Throughout preparation, they should remain at temperatures below 41°F (5°C).
2. Cut all meats into an appropriate size for grinding.
3. Marinate, under refrigeration, the dominant meat and pork with the desired herbs, spices and liquors.
4. If using liver, grind it and force it through a sieve.
5. Cut the fatback into an appropriate size and freeze.
6. Prepare an ice bath for the forcemeat. Then grind the dominant meat, pork and fat as directed in the recipe, usually once through the grinder's largest die and a second time through the medium die.
7. If using liver, eggs, panada or garnishes, fold them in by hand, remembering to keep the forcemeat over an ice bath at all times.
8. Cook a small portion of the forcemeat; adjust the seasonings and texture as appropriate.
9. Refrigerate the forcemeat until needed.

COUNTRY-STYLE FORCEMEAT

MISE EN PLACE

▶ Chill the equipment.
▶ Dice pork and fatback.
▶ Clean and dice pork liver.
▶ Peel onion and cut into small dice.
▶ Peel and mince garlic.
▶ Wash and chop fresh parsley.

Yield: 4 lb. 8 oz. (2.1 kg)

Lean pork, diced	2 lb.	960 g
Pâté Spice (page 812)	2 Tbsp.	30 ml
Salt	1 Tbsp.	15 ml
Black pepper	TT	TT
Brandy	2 fl. oz.	60 ml
Pork liver, cleaned and diced	1 lb.	480 g
Fatback, diced	1 lb.	480 g
Onion, small dice	3 oz.	90 g
Garlic, minced	1 Tbsp.	15 ml
Fresh parsley, chopped	3 Tbsp.	45 ml
Eggs	6	6

1 Combine the diced pork with the Pâté Spice, salt, pepper and brandy; marinate under refrigeration for several hours.

2 Grind the liver or purée it in a blender, then force it through a drum sieve. Reserve.

3 Grind the marinated pork and fatback through the grinder's large die.

4 Grind half of the pork and fatback a second time through the medium die along with the onion, garlic and parsley.

5 Working over an ice bath, combine the coarse and medium ground pork with the liver and eggs.

6 Cook and taste a small portion of the forcemeat and adjust the seasonings as necessary.

The forcemeat is now ready to use as desired in the preparation of pâtés, terrines, galantines and sausages.

Approximate values per 1-oz. (30-g) serving: **Calories** 90, **Total fat** 8 g, **Saturated fat** 3 g, **Cholesterol** 50 mg, **Sodium** 105 mg, **Total carbohydrates** 1 g, **Protein** 5 g, **Vitamin A** 30%

1 Marinating the meat and fatback with herbs and spices.

2 Forcing the ground liver through a sieve.

3 Grinding half of the meat a second time.

4 Incorporating the liver and eggs into the ground meat mixture over an ice bath to keep the forcemeat cold.

BASIC FORCEMEATS

Smoother and more refined than a country-style forcemeat, a basic forcemeat is probably the most versatile of all. It should be well seasoned, but the seasonings should not mask the dominant meat's flavor. Examples of basic forcemeats are those used in most game pâtés and terrines as well as traditional pâtés en croûte.

A basic forcemeat is made by grinding the meat and fat separately—the meat twice and the fat once. The fat is then worked into the meat, either by hand or in a food processor or chopper. A quicker method involves grinding the fat and meat together and then blending them in a food processor. Whichever method is used, some recipes call for the incorporation of crushed ice to minimize friction, reduce temperature and add moisture.

PROCEDURE FOR **PREPARING A BASIC FORCEMEAT**

1. Chill all ingredients and equipment thoroughly. Throughout preparation, they should remain at temperatures below 41°F (5°C).
2. Cut all meats into an appropriate size for grinding.
3. Marinate, under refrigeration, the dominant meat and pork with the desired herbs, spices and liquors.
4. If using liver, grind it and force it through a sieve.
5. Cut the fatback into an appropriate size and freeze.
6. Grind the meats twice, once through the grinder's large die and then through the medium die; hold over an ice bath.
7. Grind the chilled or frozen fat once through the medium die and add it to the meat mixture.
8. Work the fat into the meat over an ice bath or in a well-chilled food processor or chopping machine.
9. Over an ice bath, add any required eggs, panada and/or garnishes and work them into the mixture.
10. Cook a small portion of the forcemeat in stock or water; adjust the seasonings and texture as appropriate.
11. Refrigerate the forcemeat until needed.

An alternative method for preparing a basic forcemeat replaces Steps 6 to 9 with the following procedures:

ALT6 Grind the meats and fats together twice.

ALT7 Place them in a food processor or chopper and blend until smooth.

ALT8 Add any required eggs or panada while the machine is running and blend them in with the meat and fat.

ALT9 Remove the forcemeat from the machine and, working over an ice bath, fold in any garnishes by hand.

Whichever method is used, a particularly warm kitchen or a lengthy running time in the food processor or chopping machine may necessitate the addition of small quantities of crushed ice to properly emulsify the forcemeat. Add the ice bit by bit while the machine is running.

BASIC FORCEMEAT

MISE EN PLACE

- ▶ Chill the equipment.
- ▶ Dice veal, lean pork and fatback.
- ▶ Cut ham into medium dice.
- ▶ Chop black olives coarsely.

Yield: 4 lb. 8 oz. (2.1 kg)

Veal, diced	1 lb. 8 oz.	720 g
Lean pork, diced	1 lb. 8 oz.	720 g
Brandy	2 fl. oz.	60 ml
Pâté Spice (page 812)	2 tsp.	10 ml
Salt	1½ tsp.	7 ml
White pepper	TT	TT
Fatback, diced	1 lb. 8 oz.	720 g
Eggs	4	4
Ham, medium dice	4 oz.	120 g
Pistachio nuts	2 oz.	60 g
Black olives, chopped coarse	2 oz.	60 g

1. Combine the veal and pork with the brandy, Pâté Spice, salt and white pepper; marinate under refrigeration for several hours.
2. Grind the meats through the grinder's large die and again through the small die.
3. Grind the fatback through the grinder's small die.
4. Combine the meat and fat in the bowl of a food processor and blend until they are emulsified.
5. Work in the eggs until the forcemeat is smooth and well emulsified. Do not overprocess the forcemeat.
6. Fold in the ham, pistachio nuts and olives.
7. Cook a small portion of the forcemeat by poaching or sautéing it. Taste and adjust the seasonings as necessary.

The forcemeat is now ready to use as desired in the preparation of pâtés, terrines, galantines and sausages.

Approximate values per 1-oz. (30-g) serving: **Calories** 140, **Total fat** 12 g, **Saturated fat** 4.5 g, **Cholesterol** 45 mg, **Sodium** 80 mg, **Total carbohydrates** 1 g, **Protein** 7 g

1. Grinding the meat through the chilled grinder.

2. Combining the fat with the meat in the food processor.

3. Adding the eggs to the meat.

4. Folding the garnishes into the forcemeat.

MOUSSELINE FORCEMEATS

A properly made mousseline (moos-uh-LEEN) forcemeat is light, airy and delicately flavored. It is most often made with fish or shellfish but sometimes with veal, pork, feathered game or poultry. (A mousseline forcemeat is not the same as a mousse, which usually contains gelatin and is discussed later.)

A mousseline forcemeat is prepared by processing ground meats and cream in a food processor; often egg whites are added to lighten and enrich the mixture. The proportion of fish or dominant meat to eggs to cream is very important: too many egg whites, and the mousseline will be rubbery; too few, and it may not bind together. If too much cream is added, the mousseline will be too soft or will fall apart during cooking.

A mousseline forcemeat can be served hot or cold. It can be used to make fish sausages and a variety of timbales and terrines, or it can be used to make quenelles, which are discussed later. A shrimp mousseline is used with Paupiettes of Sole (page 516).

PROCEDURE FOR **PREPARING A MOUSSELINE FORCEMEAT**

1. Chill all ingredients and equipment thoroughly. Throughout preparation, they should remain at temperatures below 41°F (5°C).
2. Cut all meats into an appropriate size for processing.
3. Grind the meat in a cold food processor until smooth. Do not overprocess.
4. Add eggs and pulse until just blended.
5. Add cream and seasonings in a steady stream while the machine is running. Stop the machine and scrape down the sides of the bowl once or twice during the processing. Do not run the machine any longer than necessary to achieve a smooth forcemeat.
6. If desired, pass the forcemeat through a drum sieve to remove any sinew or bits of bone.
7. Over an ice bath, fold in any garnishes by hand.
8. Poach a small amount of the mousseline in stock or water. Taste and adjust the seasonings and texture as necessary.
9. Refrigerate until ready for use.

MOUSSELINE FORCEMEAT

MISE EN PLACE

▶ Chill the equipment.

Yield: 4 lb. (1.9 kg)

Fish, scallops, skinless chicken breast or lean veal	2 lb.	960 g
Egg whites	4	4
Salt	1 Tbsp.	15 ml
White pepper	TT	TT
Nutmeg, ground	TT	TT
Cayenne pepper	TT	TT
Heavy cream	up to 1 qt.	up to 960 ml

1. Grind the dominant meat through a large die.
2. Process the meat in a food processor until smooth.
3. Add the egg whites one at a time and pulse the processor until they are incorporated.
4. Scrape down the sides of the processor's bowl and add the spices.
5. With the machine running, add the cream in a slow, steady stream. Check the consistency, adding only enough cream to make a firm but smooth forcemeat.
6. Scrape down the bowl again and process the mousseline until it is smooth and well mixed. Do not overprocess.
7. Remove the mousseline from the machine and hold in an ice bath. If additional smoothness is desired, force the mousseline through a drum sieve in small batches using a plastic scraper or rubber spatula.
8. Cook a small portion of the forcemeat by poaching it. Taste and adjust the seasonings and texture as necessary.

The forcemeat is now ready to cook as quenelles or use as desired in the preparation of pâtés, terrines, galantines and sausages.

Note: Forcemeat made only from fish will use the least amount of cream. Frozen meat will absorb less cream than meat that is merely chilled.

Approximate values per 1-oz. (30-g) serving: **Calories** 80, **Total fat** 7 g, **Saturated fat** 4 g, **Cholesterol** 30 mg, **Sodium** 25 mg, **Total carbohydrates** 1 g, **Protein** 4 g, **Vitamin A** 8%

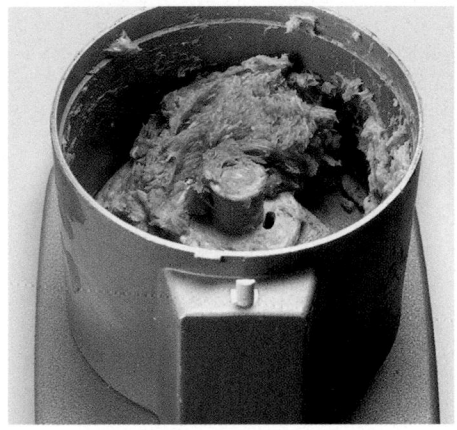

1. Processing the ground meat in a cold food processor just until smooth.

2. Adding the egg whites and pulsing until blended.

3. Adding the cream in a steady stream while the machine runs.

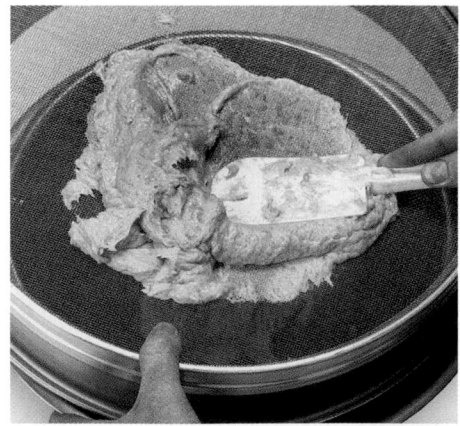

4. Passing the forcemeat through a drum sieve to ensure a smooth finished product.

QUENELLES

Quenelles (kuh-NEHL) are small dumpling-shaped portions of a mousseline forcemeat poached in an appropriately flavored stock. The technique used for making and poaching quenelles is also used for testing the seasoning and consistency of a mousseline forcemeat.

PROCEDURE FOR **PREPARING QUENELLES**

❶ Prepare a mousseline forcemeat.

❷ Bring an appropriately flavored poaching liquid to a simmer.

❸ Use two spoons to form the forcemeat into oblong-shaped dumplings. For small quenelles, use small spoons; for larger quenelles, use larger spoons.

❹ Poach the quenelles until done. Test by breaking one in half to check the center's doneness.

❺ Small soup-garnish-sized quenelles can be chilled in ice water, drained and held for service. Reheat them in a small amount of stock before garnishing the soup.

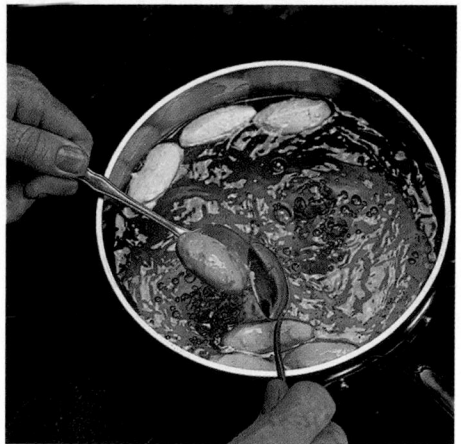

Forming the quenelles using two spoons and poaching until done.

USING FORCEMEATS

Forcemeats are used as basic components in the preparation of other foods, including terrines, pâtés, galantines and sausages. Aspic jelly is also an important component of these products.

Terrines, Pâtés and Galantines

Traditionally, a **pâté** (pah-tay) was a fine savory meat filling wrapped in pastry, baked and served hot or cold. A **terrine** was considered more basic, consisting of coarsely ground and highly seasoned meats baked in an earthenware mold and always served cold. (The mold is also called a terrine, derived from the French word *terre*, meaning "earth.") Today, many types of pâtés are baked in loaf-type pans without a crust, which according to tradition would make them terrines, whereas pâtés baked in pastry are called **pâtés en croûte** (pah-TAY awn croot). Thus, the terms *pâté* and *terrine* are now used almost interchangeably. **Galantines** (GAL-uhn-teen) are made from forcemeats of poultry, game or suckling pig wrapped in the skin of the bird or animal and poached in an appropriate stock. They are usually served cold. **Ballotines** (bahl-lo-teen) are similar, but generally use only deboned poultry legs and are served hot.

Terrines, pâtés and galantines are often made with forcemeats layered with garnishes to produce a decorative or mosaic effect when sliced. A wide variety of foods can be used as garnishes, including strips of ham, fatback or tongue; mushrooms or other vegetables; truffles and pistachio nuts. Garnishes should always be cooked before they are added to the pâté, terrine or galantine, or they will shrink during cooking, creating air pockets.

Pâté Pans, Molds and Terrines

Pâté pans, molds and terrines come in a variety of shapes and sizes. Pâtés that are not baked in a crust can be prepared in standard metal loaf pans of any shape, although rectangular ones make portioning the cooked pâté much easier. For pâtés en croûte, the best pans are collapsible or hinged, made of thin metal. They make it easier to remove the pâté after baking. Collapsible and hinged pans come in various shapes and sizes, from small plain rectangles to large intricately fluted ovals. Traditional earthenware molds and terrines as well as ones made from enameled cast iron, metal, glass or even plastic are available. Most terrines are rectangular or oval in shape. See Chapter 4, Tools and Equipment.

QUENELLES DE BROCHET

In Lyon, the gastronomic capital of France, quenelles de brochet are a classic first course. Made from pike, the quenelles are hand-formed into 4-inch- (10-centimeter-) long dumplings that are accompanied by tomato coulis or a sauce based on a fish velouté, frequently garnished with steamed crayfish.

TERRINES

Terrines are forcemeats baked in a mold without a crust. The mold can be the traditional earthenware dish or some other appropriate metal, enameled cast iron or glass mold. Any type of forcemeat can be used to make a terrine. The terrine can be as simple as a baking dish filled with a forcemeat and baked until done. A more attractive terrine can be constructed by layering the forcemeat with garnishes to create a mosaic effect when sliced. A terrine can even be layered with different forcemeats—for example, a pink salmon mousseline layered with a white pike mousseline.

PROCEDURE FOR **PREPARING TERRINES**

❶ Prepare the desired forcemeat and garnishes and keep refrigerated until needed.

❷ Line a mold with thin slices of fatback, blanched leafy vegetables or other appropriate liner. (Some chefs claim that the fatback keeps the terrine moist during cooking; most modern chefs do not agree but nevertheless use it for aesthetic purposes.) The lining should overlap slightly, completely covering the inside of the mold and extending over the edge of the mold by approximately 1 inch (2.5 centimeters). Alternatively, line the mold with plastic wrap.

❸ Fill the terrine with the forcemeat and garnishes, being careful not to leave air pockets. Tap the mold several times on a solid work surface to remove any air pockets.

❹ Fold the liner or plastic wrap over the forcemeat and, if necessary, use additional pieces to completely cover its surface.

❺ If desired, garnish the top of the terrine with herbs that were used in the preparation of the forcemeat.

❻ Cover the terrine with its lid or aluminum foil and bake in a water bath in a 350°F (180°C) oven. Regulate the oven temperature so that the water stays between 170°F and 180°F (77°C and 82°C).

❼ Cook the terrine to an internal temperature of 165°F (74°C) for poultry-based forcemeats, 155°F (68°C) for fish-based forcemeats or 145°F (63°C) for meat-based forcemeats.

❽ Remove the terrine from the oven and allow it to cool slightly. If desired, pour off any fat and liquid from around the terrine and cover it with cool liquid aspic jelly.

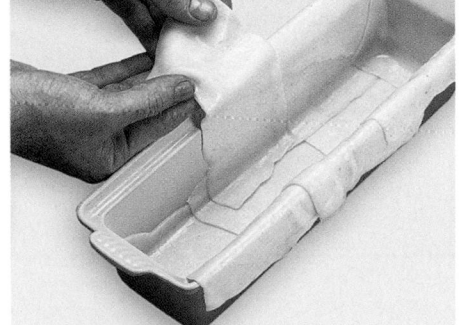

❶ Lining a mold with thin slices of fatback.

❷ Filling the terrine with the forcemeat and garnish.

❸ Placing the herb-decorated terrine in a water bath.

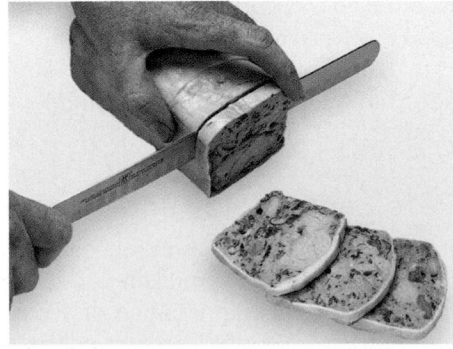

❹ Slicing the finished terrine.

Types of Terrines

Several types of terrines are not made from traditional forcemeats; many others are not made from forcemeats at all. But all are nonetheless called terrines because they are molded or cooked in the earthenware mold called a terrine. These include liver (and foie gras) terrines, vegetable terrines, brawns or aspic terrines, mousses, rillettes and confits.

Liver terrines are popular and easy to make. Puréed poultry, pork or veal livers are mixed with eggs and a panada of cream and flour, then baked in a fatback-lined terrine. Although most livers purée easily in a food processor, a smoother finished product is achieved if the livers are forced through a drum sieve after or in lieu of puréeing them in the processor.

Foie gras terrines are made with the fattened goose or duck livers called foie gras. Foie gras is unique, even among other poultry livers, in that it consists almost entirely of fat. (See Chapter 17, Poultry.) It requires special attention during cooking; if it is cooked improperly or too long, it turns into a puddle of very expensive fat.

Vegetable terrines have a relatively low fat content and stunning eye appeal. Beautiful vegetable terrines are made by lining a terrine with a blanched leafy vegetable such as spinach, then alternating layers of two or three separately prepared vegetable fillings to create contrasting colors and flavors. A different style of vegetable terrine is made by suspending brightly colored vegetables in a mousseline forcemeat to create a mosaic pattern when sliced.

Brawns or **aspic terrines** are made by simmering gelatinous cuts of meat (most notably, pigs' feet and head, including the tongue) in a rich stock with wine and flavorings. The stock is enriched with the gelatin and flavor from the meat, creating an unclarified aspic jelly. The meat is then pulled from the bone, diced and packed into the terrine mold. The stock is reduced to concentrate its gelatin content, strained through cheesecloth and poured over the meat in the terrine. After the terrine has set, it is removed from the mold and sliced for service. The finished product is a rustic and flavorful dish.

A more elegant-appearing brawn is made by lining a terrine mold with aspic jelly, arranging a layer of garnish (for example, sliced meats, vegetables or low-acid fruits) along the mold's bottom, adding aspic jelly to cover the garnish and repeating the procedure until the mold is full.

A **mousse** can be sweet or savory. Sweet mousses are described in Chapter 34, Custards, Creams, Frozen Desserts and Dessert Sauces. A savory mousse—which is not a mousseline forcemeat—is made from fully cooked meats, poultry, game, fish, shellfish or vegetables that are puréed and combined with a béchamel or other appropriate sauce, bound with gelatin and lightened with whipped cream. A mousse can be molded in a decorated, aspic-jelly-coated mold such as that described next, or it can be formed in molds lined with plastic wrap, which is peeled off after the mousse is unmolded. A small mousse can be served as an individual portion; a larger molded mousse can be displayed on a buffet.

Rillettes and **confits** are actually preserved meats. Rillettes (ree-YEHT) are prepared by seasoning and slow-cooking pork or fatty poultry such as duck or goose in generous amounts of their own fat until the meat falls off the bone. The warm meat is mashed and combined with a portion of the cooking fat. The mixture is then packed into a crock or terrine, and rendered fat is strained over the top to seal it. Rillettes are eaten cold as a spread accompanied by bread or toast.

Confit (kohn-FEE) is prepared in a similar manner except that before cooking, the meat or poultry is often lightly salt-cured to draw out some moisture. The confit is then cooked until very tender but not falling apart. Confits are generally served hot. Like rillettes, confits can be preserved by sealing them with a layer of strained rendered fat. Properly prepared and sealed rillettes and confits will keep for several weeks under refrigeration.

Although it is sometimes incorrectly called chicken liver pâté, **chopped chicken liver** is prepared in a similar fashion to a rillette. Chopped chicken liver, however, will not have the keeping qualities of traditional rillettes or confits because it is not normally sealed in a crock or terrine with rendered fat. It should be eaten within a day or two of its preparation.

Preparing Molds When Making Terrines

A mold can be lined with aspic jelly, then decorated and filled with cold mousse. The aspic-jelly-coated mousse is then unmolded for an attractive presentation.

GARNISHING SLICED TERRINES AND PÂTÉS

Cornichons sliced into decorative fans are an attractive garnish for sliced country terrines and pâtés en croûte.

	TABLE 27.1 GELATIN CONCENTRATIONS		

TYPE OF GEL	AMOUNT OF GELATIN PER GALLON (4 LITERS) WATER	TYPICAL USE
Soft	2 oz. (60 g)	Cubed aspic jelly for edible garnishes
Firm	4 oz. (120 g)	Brushing slices of pâté or galantine; glazing edible centerpieces; molding terrines, aspics and brawns that will be sliced
Very firm	8 oz. or more (240 g or more)	Nonedible purposes such as coating nonedible centerpieces or trays for presentations

PROCEDURE FOR PREPARING ASPIC-JELLY-COATED CHILLED MOUSSES

1 Set a metal mold in ice water and fill with cool liquid aspic jelly. Swirl the mold so the aspic jelly adheres to all sides. Pour out the excess. Repeat as needed to achieve the desired thickness; ¼ inch (6 millimeters) or less is usually sufficient.

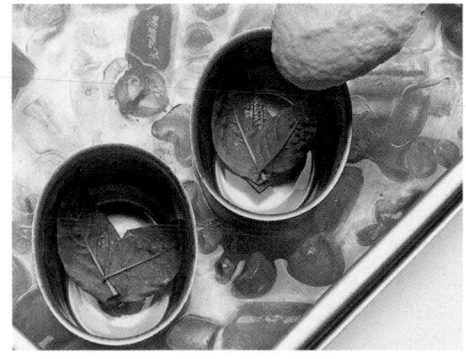

2 Garnish the mold by dipping pieces of vegetable or other foods in the liquid aspic jelly and placing them carefully inside the aspic-jelly-coated mold. The mold can now be filled with a cold filling such as a mousse.

3 Refrigerate the mold until it is well chilled. Unmold the aspic by dipping the mold in warm water, then inverting and tapping the mold on a plate.

PROCEDURE FOR GLAZING PÂTÉ SLICES WITH ASPIC JELLY

Slices of chilled terrines, pâtés en croûte or gallantines may be garnished and coated with aspic to preserve their color, prevent drying and create a more attractive presentation.

1 Cool the clarified aspic jelly by slowly stirring it over an ice bath.

2 Brush or spoon the aspic jelly over slices of chilled pâté arranged on a cooling rack. Repeat until the coating reaches the desired thickness.

ASPIC JELLY

Aspic jelly is a savory jelly produced by increasing the gelatin content of a strong stock and then clarifying the stock following the process for preparing consommé discussed in Chapter 11, Soups.

Although gelatin is a natural ingredient present in all good meat or poultry stocks, additional gelatin is usually added to the stock in order to assist gelling (setting). One way is to produce a stock with an extremely high gelatin content by using gelatinous meats and bones such as calves' feet, pigs' ears and pork skin; another is to add plain gelatin to a finished stock. An easier method of preparing aspic jelly is to add gelatin directly to a flavorful finished consommé.

In addition to adding flavor and shine, a coating of aspic jelly prevents displayed foods from drying out and inhibits the oxidation of sliced red meats. Aspic jelly is often lightly flavored with liquors such as Madeira and cut into decorative garnishes for both plated presentations and buffet displays. Decorative platters on which pâtés are displayed may be coated with aspic jelly. It is also used to bind savory mousses, glaze slices of pâté and coat molded mousses. Aspic jelly is funneled into cooked pâtés en croûte to fill the gaps created when the forcemeat shrinks during the cooking process. Aspic jelly is also the basis of aspic molds or terrines (often simply called aspics), in which layers of cooked meats or vegetables are bound together and held in place by the aspic jelly. Many of these uses are discussed later.

The gelatin content of aspic jelly varies depending on its intended use. Table 27.1 lists guidelines for quantities of gelatin to use in various applications. Aspic jelly to be used only on a display can have a very high gelatin content for easier handling. Aspic jelly to be eaten should be fairly firm when cold, gelled at room temperature but tender enough to melt quickly in the mouth when eaten. To test the gelatin content of a liquid, pour a teaspoon (5 milliliters) onto a plate and refrigerate the plate for a few minutes. If the liquid does not gel firmly, additional gelatin can be softened in a small amount of cool liquid, then added to the hot liquid.

PÂTÉS EN CROÛTE

Considered by some to be the pinnacle of the charcutier's art, pâtés en croûte are forcemeats baked in a crust. The forcemeat can be country-style, basic or mousseline, but a basic forcemeat is most commonly used. Although pâtés en croûte can be baked without using a mold, a mold helps produce a more attractive finished product.

Making Pâté Dough (Pâte au Pâté)

The crust surrounding a baking forcemeat must be durable enough to withstand the long baking process and hold in the juices produced as the pâté bakes. Unfortunately, some of the more durable crusts are tough and unpleasant to eat.

The goal is to achieve a balance so that the crust will hold the juices of the baking pâté and still be relatively pleasant to the palate. Some pâtés, especially more delicate ones such as fish mousselines, can be wrapped in brioche dough (page 950).

DOUGH FOR PÂTÉ

Yield: 1 lb. 8 oz. (720 g)

All-purpose flour	1 lb.	480 g
Shortening	7 oz.	210 g
Salt	1½ tsp.	7 ml
Water	5 fl. oz.	150 ml
Egg	1	1

1 Place the flour in the bowl of a mixer. Add the shortening and mix on low speed until smooth.

2 Combine the salt, water and egg; add them to the flour and shortening mixture.

3 Knead until smooth and refrigerate. The dough will be easier to work with if allowed to rest for at least 1 hour.

Approximate values per 1-oz. (30-g) serving: **Calories** 150, **Total fat** 9 g, **Saturated fat** 2 g, **Cholesterol** 10 mg, **Sodium** 100 mg, **Total carbohydrates** 15 g, **Protein** 2 g

Assembling, Baking and Glazing Pâté

After preparing a forcemeat and pastry dough, all that remains is to assemble and bake the pâté en croûte. The amount of pastry dough and forcemeat needed is determined by the size of the mold or pan chosen. Once the pâté is baked and cooled, aspic jelly is poured into holes in the dough to fill the space created when the pâté shrank during cooking. Slices of pâté can also be glazed with aspic for a more formal presentation.

PROCEDURE FOR ASSEMBLING AND BAKING PÂTÉS EN CROÛTE

1. Prepare the pâté dough and the forcemeat, keeping the forcemeat refrigerated until needed.
2. Roll out the dough into a rectangular shape ⅛ inch (3 millimeters) thick.
3. Using the pâté mold as a pattern, determine how much dough is needed to line its inside; allow enough dough along each side of the mold's length to cover the top when folded over. Mark the dough. Cut the dough slightly larger than the marked lines. Cut a second rectangular piece of dough that is slightly larger than the top of the mold; it will be used as a lid.
4. Lightly butter the inside of the mold.
5. Lightly dust the large rectangle of dough with flour, fold it over and transfer it to the mold.
6. Use your thumbs and a dough ball made from dough trimmings to form the dough neatly into the corners of the mold. Continue until the dough is of even thickness on all sides and in the corners.
7. Trim the dough, leaving ¾ inch (2 centimeters) on the ends and enough dough to cover the top along the sides.
8. Line the dough-covered mold with thin slices of fatback or ham, allowing ¾ inch (2 centimeters) extra around the top of the mold, or as directed in the recipe. This layer helps protect the pastry crust from coming in contact with the moist forcemeat, which would make it soggy.
9. Fill the lined mold with the forcemeat to ½ inch (1.2 centimeters) below the top of the mold, pressing it well into the corners to avoid air pockets. Layer and garnish as appropriate.
10. Fold the fatback or ham over the top of the forcemeat, using additional pieces if necessary to cover its entire surface. Fold the pastry over the forcemeat.
11. Brush the exposed surface of the pastry with egg wash; carefully cap with the top piece of dough. Press any overlapping dough down inside the sides of the mold with a small spatula.
12. Using round cutters, cut one or two holes in the top to allow steam to escape during cooking. Egg-wash the surface. Place a doughnut-shaped piece of dough around each of the holes. Egg-wash any decorations.
13. Bake the pâté in a preheated 450°F (230°C) oven for 15 minutes. Then cover the surface of the pâté with aluminum foil. Reduce the heat to 350°F (180°C) and continue baking until the internal temperature reaches 165°F (74°C) for poultry-based forcemeats, 155°F (68°C) for fish-based forcemeats or 145°F (63°C) for meat-based forcemeats.
14. Allow the pâté to cool for at least 1 hour or overnight. Using a funnel, pour cool liquid aspic jelly through the holes to fill the space created when the pâté shrank during cooking. Allow the pâté en croûte to cool overnight before slicing.

1. Cutting the dough into a large rectangle.

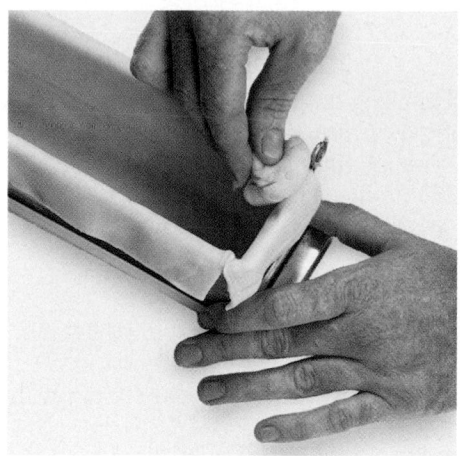

➋ Pressing the dough into the mold with a floured dough ball.

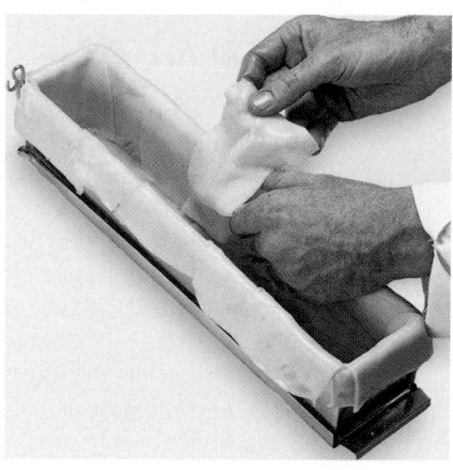

➌ Lining the dough-covered mold with thin slices of fatback.

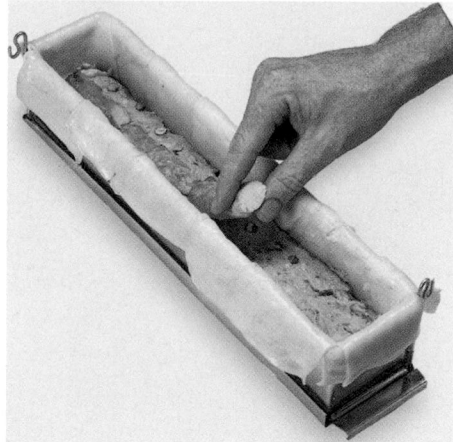

➍ Filling the lined mold with the forcemeat and garnish.

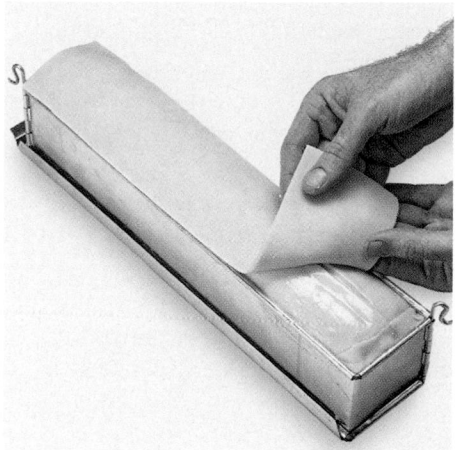

➎ Placing the top on the pâté.

➏ Pouring aspic jelly into the steam hole of the baked pâté through an aluminum foil chimney.

➐ Slicing the pâté with a thin-bladed knife.

GALANTINES

A classic galantine is a boned chicken stuffed with a chicken-based forcemeat to resemble its original shape and then poached. Today, galantines are still most often prepared from whole ducks or chickens, but they can also be made from game, veal, fish or shellfish. When appropriate, the forcemeat is stuffed in the skin, which has been removed in one piece, sometimes with flesh still attached. When the skin is not available, or in the case of fish and shellfish where there is no skin, the galantine is made by forming the forcemeat into a cylindrical shape and wrapping it in cheesecloth, or plastic wrap and foil, before poaching. Galantines are always served cold and are often displayed on buffets, sliced and glazed with aspic jelly.

A ballotine is similar to a galantine. It is made by removing the bones from a poultry leg, filling the cavity with an appropriate forcemeat and poaching or braising the leg with vegetables. Ballotines are often served hot with a sauce made from the cooking liquid.

PROCEDURE FOR **PREPARING A POULTRY GALANTINE**

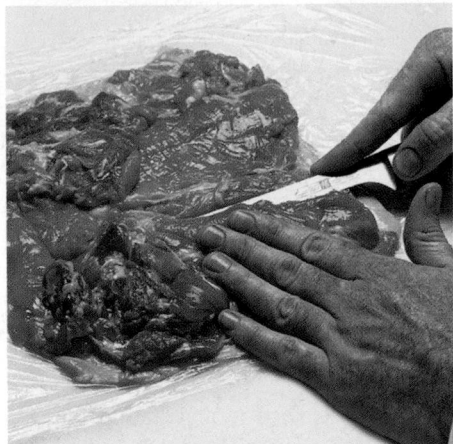

1 Butterflying the breasts and tenderloins and placing a thin layer of meat over the skin.

1 Bone the chicken by cutting through the skin along the length of the backbone and then following the natural curvature of the carcass. Keep all the meat attached to the skin. Remove the legs and wings by cutting through the joints when you reach them; leave the legs and wings attached to the skin. Then cut off the wings. Bone the thighs and legs, leaving the skin and meat attached to the rest of the bird. Trim the skin to form a large rectangle.

2 Prepare a forcemeat using the meat from the skinned bird or any other appropriate meat. Reserve a portion of the meat as garnish if desired. Prepare any other garnishes. Refrigerate the forcemeat and garnishes until needed.

3 Spread out the skin and meat on plastic wrap or several layers of cheesecloth with the skin side down and the flesh up.

4 Remove the chicken tenderloins and pull the tendon out of each. Butterfly the breasts and tenderloins and cover the entire skin with a thin layer of meat.

5 Arrange the forcemeat and garnishes in a cylindrical shape across the center of the skin.

6 Using the plastic or cheesecloth to assist the process, tightly roll the skin around the forcemeat and garnishes to form a tight cylinder.

7 Tie the ends of the cheesecloth with butcher's twine and secure the galantine at even intervals using strips of cheesecloth. If plastic wrap was used, wrap the galantine with heavy-duty aluminum foil.

8 Poach the galantine in water (or a full-flavored stock if wrapped in cheesecloth) to an internal temperature of 165°F (74°C) for poultry-based forcemeats, 155°F (68°C) for fish-based forcemeats or 145°F (63°C) for meat-based forcemeats.

9 Cool the galantine in its cooking liquid until it can be handled. Remove the cheesecloth or plastic wrap and aluminum foil and rewrap the galantine in clean cheesecloth or plastic wrap. Refrigerate overnight before decorating or slicing.

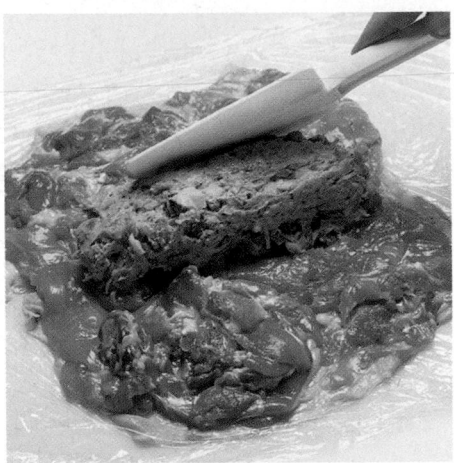

2 Arranging the forcemeat and garnishes in a cylindrical shape across the center of the skin.

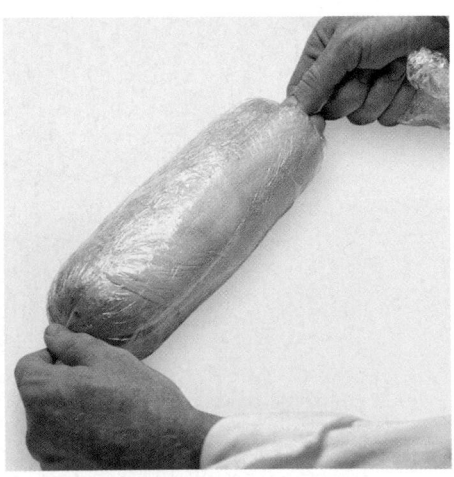

3 Using plastic wrap to roll the galantine into a tight cylinder.

4 Securing the galantine with heavy-duty aluminum foil.

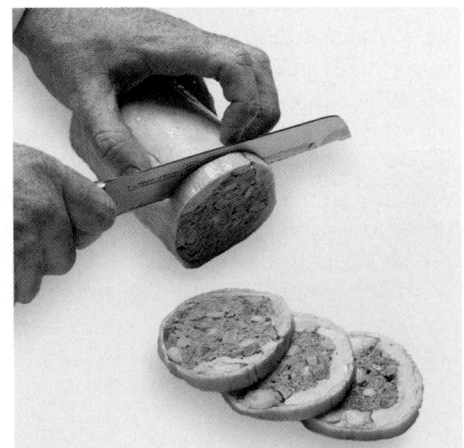

5 Slicing the finished product.

Sausages

Sausages are forcemeats stuffed into casings. For centuries, sausages consisted of ground meat, usually pork, and seasonings. Today, sausages are made not only from pork, but also from game, beef, veal, poultry, fish, shellfish and even vegetables.

There are three main types of sausages:

❶ **Fresh sausages** include breakfast sausage links and Italian sausages. They are made with fresh ingredients that have not been cured or smoked.

❷ **Smoked** and **cooked sausages** are made with raw meat products treated with chemicals, usually the preservative sodium nitrite. Examples are kielbasa, bologna and hot dogs.

❸ **Dried** or **hard sausages** are made with cured meats, then air-dried under controlled conditions. Dried sausages may or may not be smoked or cooked. Dried or hard sausages include salami, **pepperoni** and **soppressata.**

Smoked and cooked sausages and dried or hard sausages are rarely prepared in typical food service operations, although chefs are increasingly interested in these artisanal foods. Rather, they are produced by specialty shops in facilities where sanitation is ensured. (For the proper fermentation and preserving of dry-cured products, controlled temperatures under sanitary conditions are essential.) Here we discuss the ingredients and procedures for a variety of fresh sausages, the fundamentals of sausage-making that can be prepared in almost any kitchen.

SAUSAGE COMPONENTS

Sausage Meats

Sausage meats are forcemeats with particular characteristics and flavorings. Coarse Italian and lamb sausages, for example, are simply a country-style forcemeat without liver and with different seasonings, stuffed into casings and formed into links. Hot dogs, bratwurst and other fine-textured sausages are variations of basic forcemeats stuffed into casings and formed into links.

Sausage Casings

Although sausage mixtures can be cooked without casings, most sausages are stuffed into casings before cooking. Two types of sausage casings are commonly used in food service operations:

❶ **Natural casings** are portions of hog, sheep or cattle intestines sold by the bundle or hank. Their diameters are measured in millimeters, and they come in several sizes depending on the animal or portion of the intestine used. Sheep casings are considered the finest-quality small casings. Both hog and sheep casings are used to make hot dogs and many types of pork sausage. Beef casings are quite large and are used to make sausages such as ring bologna and Polish sausage. Most natural casings are purchased in salt packs. In order to rid them of salt and impurities, the casings must be carefully rinsed in warm water and allowed to soak in cool water for at least 1 hour or overnight before use.

❷ **Collagen casings** are manufactured from collagen extracted from cattle hides. They are generally inferior to natural casings in taste and texture, but they do have advantages: Collagen casings do not require any washing or soaking before use, and they are uniform in size.

PREPARING SAUSAGES

Equipment for Making Sausages

Sausage-stuffing machines are best for those who engage in large-scale sausage production. Otherwise, all that is needed is a grinder with a sausage nozzle. Nozzles are available in several sizes to accommodate the various casing sizes.

Slices of Rosette de Lyon, a dry-cured French sausage, also known as saucisson sec.

andouille (an-DOO-ee) a very spicy smoked pork sausage, popular in Cajun cuisine

mortadella (mohr-tah-DEH-lah) an Italian smoked sausage made with ground beef, pork and pork fat, flavored with coriander and white wine; it is air-dried and has a delicate flavor; also a large American bologna-type pork sausage studded with pork fat and garlic

pepperoni (peh-peh-ROH-nee) a hard, thin, air-dried Italian sausage seasoned with red and black pepper

saucisson sec (soh-see-SOHN seck) a hard, air-dried French sausage seasoned with garlic and black pepper

soppressata (soh-preh-SAH-tah) a hard, aged Italian salami, sometimes coated with cracked peppercorns or herbs

Sausage Nozzles

PROCEDURE FOR **PREPARING SAUSAGES**

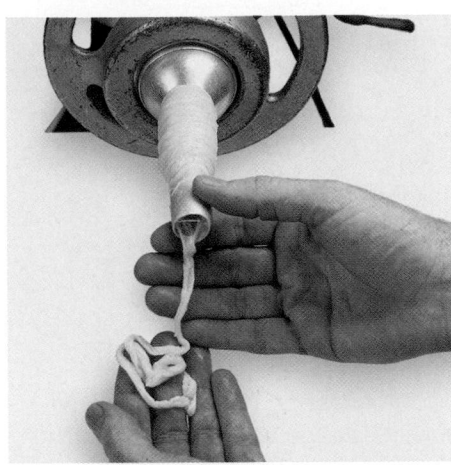

❶ Prepare a forcemeat.

❷ Thoroughly chill all parts of the sausage stuffer that will come in contact with the forcemeat.

❸ Rinse and soak the casings if using natural ones. Cut the casings into 4- to 6-foot (1.2- to 1.8-meter) lengths.

❹ Put the sausage in the sausage stuffer.

❺ Slide the entire casing over the nozzle of the sausage stuffer. Tie the end in a knot and pierce with a skewer to prevent an air pocket.

❻ Support and guide the casing off the end of the nozzle as the sausage is extruded from the nozzle into the casing.

❼ After all the sausage has been stuffed into the casing, twist or tie the sausage into uniform links of the desired size.

❶ Sliding the casing over the nozzle of the sausage stuffer.

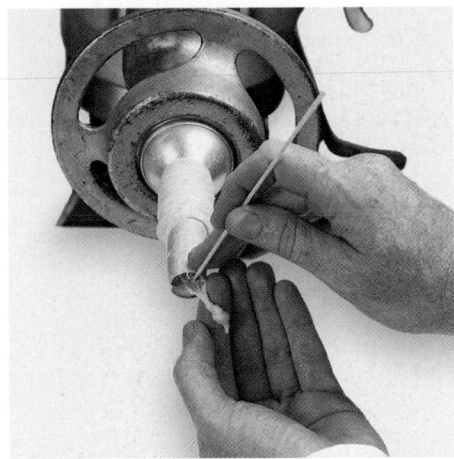

❷ Knotting and piercing the casing with a skewer.

❸ Supporting and guiding the casing off the end of the nozzle as the sausage is extruded from the machine into the casing.

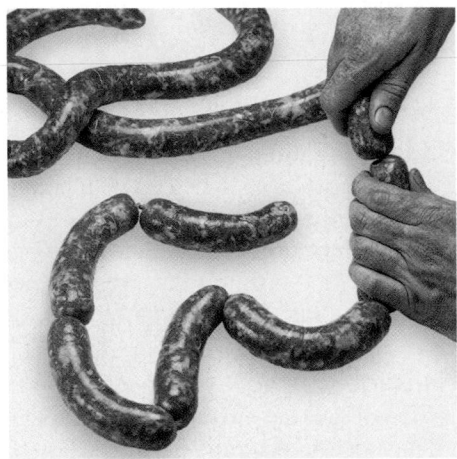

❹ Twisting the sausage into uniform links.

SALT CURING, BRINING AND SMOKING

Curing, brining and smoking are ancient techniques for preserving food. Today, foods such as hams, corned beef and smoked salmon are salt-cured, brined or smoked primarily for flavor. Cured meats have a characteristic pink color caused by the reaction of sodium nitrite, which is added during processing, with the naturally occurring myoglobin protein in the meat.

Salt Curing

Salt curing is the process of surrounding a food with salt or a mixture of salt, sugar, nitrite-based curing salt, herbs and spices. Salt curing dehydrates the food, inhibits bacterial growth and adds flavor. It is most often used with pork products and fish. Salt curing is not a quick procedure—and the time involved adds money to production costs. For example, country-style hams are salt-cured. Proper curing requires approximately one and a half days per pound of ham, which means three weeks for the average ham.

Some salt-cured hams such as Smithfield and prosciutto are not actually cooked. The curing process preserves the meat and makes it safe to consume raw. Gravlax (page 844) is a well-known salmon dish prepared by salt-curing salmon fillets with a mixture of salt, sugar, pepper and dill.

Brining

A brine is actually a very salty marinade. Most brines have approximately 20 percent salinity, which is equivalent to 1 pound (480 grams) of salt per gallon (4 liters) of water. As with dry-salt cures, brines can also contain sugar, nitrites, herbs and spices. Brining is sometimes called pickling.

Today, most cured meats are prepared in large production facilities where the brine is injected into the meat for rapid and uniform distribution. Commercially brined corned beef is cured by this process, as are most common hams. After brining, hams are further processed by smoking.

Smoking

There are two basic methods of smoking foods: cold smoking and hot smoking. The principal difference is that hot smoking actually cooks the food, while cold smoking does not.

Both are done in a **smoker** specifically designed for this purpose. Smokers can be gas or electric; they vary greatly in size and operation. But they have several things in common. All consist of a chamber that holds the food being smoked, a means of burning wood to produce smoke and a heating element.

Different types of wood can be used to smoke food. Specific woods are selected to impart specific flavors. Hickory is often used for pork products; alder is excellent for smoked salmon. Maple, chestnut, juniper, mesquite and many other woods are also used. Resinous woods such as pine give food a bitter flavor and should be avoided.

Cold smoking is the process of exposing foods to smoke at temperatures of 50°F to 85°F (10°C to 29°C). Meat, poultry, game, fish, shellfish, cheese, nuts and even vegetables can be cold-smoked successfully. Most cold-smoked meats are generally salt cured or brined first. Salt curing or brining adds flavor, allows the nitrites (which give the ham, bacon and other smoked meats their distinctive pink color) to penetrate the flesh and, most important, extracts moisture from the food, allowing the smoke to penetrate more easily. Cold-smoked foods are actually still raw. Some, such as smoked salmon (lox), are eaten without further cooking. Most, such as bacon and hams, must be cooked before eating.

Hot smoking is the process of exposing foods to smoke at temperatures of 200°F to 250°F (93°C to 121°C). As with cold smoking, a great variety of foods can be prepared by hot smoking. Meats, poultry, game, fish and shellfish that are hot-smoked also benefit from salt curing or brining. Although most hot-smoked foods are fully cooked when removed from the smoker, many are used in other recipes that call for further cooking.

Although most smoking requires specialized equipment, two affordable options exist for imparting a smoked flavor to foods. A stove top smoker, which resembles a hotel pan with a tight-fitting lid, can be used to hot-smoke small cuts of meat, fish, poultry or vegetables. Wood chips are scattered inside the bottom of the pan. Foods to be smoked sit on top of a mesh rack placed inside the box. The heat of the stove top ignites the woodchips, permeating the food with a smoky flavor. Foods smoked in this manner must reach proper internal cooking temperatures to be served without additional cooking. Liquid smoke is a flavoring made from smoke, which has been condensed from the burning of wood chips. When used judiciously it can impart a pleasant smoky taste to barbecue sauces and marinades.

Pork Products

Preparing hams and curing and smoking pork products are a traditional part of charcuterie. Here is a selection of some of the more common cured pork products available to chefs.

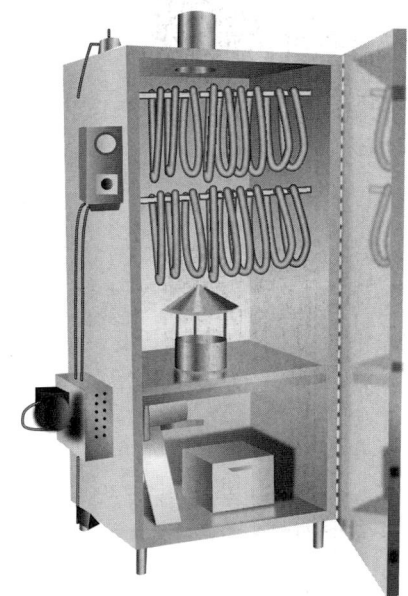

Commercial Smoker

Sliced Bacon

Pancetta

*IMPS No. 510,
Ham, Boneless,
Skinless, Cured
and Smoked,
Fully Cooked*

*IMPS No. 501, Ham Short
Shank, Cured and Smoked*

Most bacon comes from a hog's fatty belly.

Common bacon is produced by brining and cold-smoking trimmed pork belly. It is available in slab or sliced form. Sliced bacon is purchased by count (number of slices) per pound; thick-sliced bacon runs 10–14 slices per pound, whereas thin-sliced bacon may contain as many as 28–32 slices per pound.

Canadian bacon is produced from a boneless pork loin, trimmed so that only a thin layer of fat remains on its surface. It is then brined and smoked.

Pancetta (pan-CHEH-tuh) is an Italian pork-belly bacon that is not smoked. It is salt-cured, peppered and often rolled into a cylinder shape. It can be sliced into rounds and fried; it is diced, rendered and combined with sauce to make fettuccine carbonara.

A **fresh ham** is a hog's hind leg; it is a primal cut. Many processed products produced from the primal fresh ham are also called ham.

Ham, in the United States, describes a variety of processed pork products, most of which come from the primal fresh ham. **Boneless** or **formed hams** are produced by separating a primal ham into its basic muscles, defatting the meat, curing it, stuffing the meat into casings of various sizes and shapes and cooking it. Boneless or formed hams either are smoked or have chemical smoke flavoring added during the curing process. The quality of boneless or formed hams varies greatly. The best hams are formed from only one or two large muscles and have low fat content and no added water other than that used during the curing process. Hams of lesser quality are formed from many small pieces of muscle and have a higher fat and water content. Many boneless or formed hams are listed in *The Meat Buyers Guide* and are indexed by the NAMP/IMPS system.

Country ham is a specialty of the southeastern United States. Country hams are dry-cured, smoked and hung to air-dry for a period ranging from several weeks to more than a year. During drying, a mold develops on the ham rind that must be scrubbed off before the ham is cooked. It is best cooked by first soaking, then slow simmering. The most famous country hams are Virginia hams; those from Smithfield, Virginia, are considered the finest. Only hams produced in rural areas can be called country hams; others must be labeled country-style ham.

Prosciutto (proh-SHOO-toe) is the Italian word for ham. What we call prosciutto in the United States is called **Parma** in Italy. Parma ham, produced near that Italian city, is made from hogs fed on the whey of cheese processed nearby. It is salt-cured and air-dried but not smoked. The curing process makes it safe and wholesome to consume raw. Several domestic varieties of prosciutto are produced, varying widely in quality. Imported prosciuttos are much larger than the domestic varieties because Italian hogs are larger when butchered.

Jamón (AH-mohn) is the Spanish word for ham. Jamón Serrano or mountain ham is salt-cured and air-dried but not smoked. Jamón Iberico is a salted, dry-cured ham from specific breeds of hogs, a Spanish delicacy prized since Roman times. The most esteemed is that made from the Bellota breed that feed on foraged acorns. Like prosciutto, these hams are served raw, thinly sliced.

Westphalian ham is dry-cured, brined and then smoked with beechwood. Authentic Westphalian hams are produced in the Westphalia region of Germany and are quite similar to prosciutto. They are sold bone-in or boneless. Their characteristic flavor is derived from the juniper berries used in the curing process and the beechwood used for smoking.

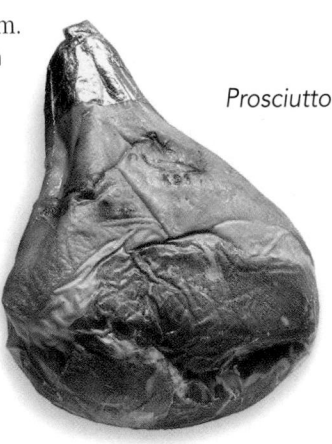

Canadian Bacon

Prosciutto

Other Cured Meat Products

Although pork is the most common meat in classic charcuterie, other meats and poultry lend themselves to preservation. Beef is used to make pastrami, pickled beef brisket that is spiced and then air-dried. It is steamed, then sliced for sandwiches. **Bresaola,** a specialty of the Lombardy region of Italy, is salted, spiced and dry-aged beef, served raw and thinly sliced. It is made from the eye round of beef and has a subtle flavor of juniper berries. The similar specialty of the Swiss Alps is known as bunderfleisch. Smoked chicken, duck and turkey are delicious alternatives to ham in sandwiches and on salads. But few cured lamb products exist, possibly because of the strong flavor of lamb fat when aged.

Bresaola, dried beef from the Lombardy region.

SAUCE CHAUD-FROID

Sauce chaud-froid (shoh-FRAWH) (French for "hot-cold") is prepared hot but served cold. Traditionally used to coat meats, poultry or fish that were eaten cold, sauce chaud-froid is now more typically used to coat a whole poached salmon or whole roasted poultry item, which is then further decorated and used as a centerpiece. As with aspic jelly, chaud-froid that is to be eaten should be fairly firm when cold, gelled at room temperature but tender enough to melt quickly in the mouth when eaten. Chaud-froid used for decorative purposes only should have a heavier gelatin content and be quite firm, which makes it easier to work with.

A classic sauce chaud-froid is a mixture of one part cream and two parts stock (veal, chicken and/or fish) strengthened with gelatin. Depending on the stock used, this coating ranges in color from cream to beige. A more modern sauce chaud-froid (also known as a mayonnaise chaud-froid or mayonnaise collée) is based on mayonnaise; it is easier to make than the classic sauce and provides a whiter product, which is more desirable when used for centerpieces.

MAYONNAISE CHAUD-FROID

Yield: Approximately 2 qt. (1.9 lt)

Aspic jelly (firm to very firm)	1 qt.	960 ml
Mayonnaise (commercially made)	1 lb.	480 g
Sour cream	1 lb.	480 g

1. Melt the aspic jelly.
2. In a stainless steel bowl, combine the mayonnaise with the sour cream and mix until smooth.
3. Stir the aspic jelly into the mayonnaise and sour cream mixture until smooth.
4. Warm the sauce over a double boiler, stirring gently with a spoon until smooth and all the air bubbles disappear.

PROCEDURE FOR **COATING FOODS WITH SAUCE CHAUD-FROID**

1. Cook (usually by poaching or roasting), trim and otherwise prepare the item to be decorated.

2. Place the item on a cooling rack over a clean sheet pan and refrigerate until ready to decorate. (Sauce that drips into the clean pan can be reused.)

3. Warm an ample amount of sauce chaud-froid in a stainless steel bowl over a double boiler until it is completely melted. Stir the sauce gently with a spoon rather than a whisk in order to prevent air bubbles from forming.

4. When the sauce is warm and smooth, remove the bowl from the double boiler and place it in an ice bath.

5. Using the back of a large ladle, stir the sauce by spinning the bowl and holding the ladle stationary. This should be done almost continuously while the sauce cools. Do not scrape the solidified chaud-froid from the sides of the bowl, as lumps will form.

6. When the sauce has cooled to room temperature, remove the item to be decorated from the refrigerator and place it on the worktable.

7. Coat the item with the sauce in a single, smooth motion. Use a ladle if the item is small; if it is large, pour the sauce directly from the bowl. The sauce should adhere to the cold food, and the coating should be free of bubbles or runs.

8. Repeat as necessary, reusing the sauce that drips onto the sheet pan, until the desired thickness is achieved.

9. Using a paring knife, carefully cut away any sauce from areas that are to be left uncoated.

10. Decorate the item as desired with vegetable flowers or other garnishes. If desired, finish the item by coating the vegetable garnishes with a layer of clear aspic jelly, using the same procedure.

1. Scoring the skin of the fish.

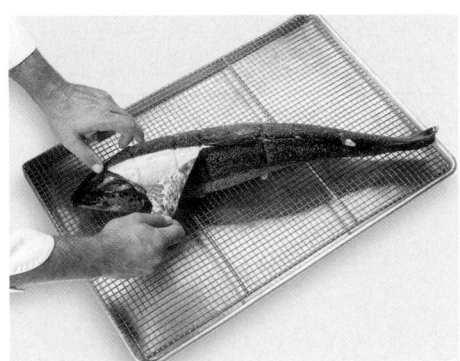

2. Removing the skin.

3. Removing the dark flesh and preparing the fish for the first coating of sauce chaud-froid.

4. Glazing the fish with the sauce chaud-froid.

5. Decorating the fish with vegetable flowers.

6. The finished salmon coated with chaud-froid sauce.

1 Explain why the art of charcuterie is relevant to the training of modern chefs.

2 Compare the three styles of forcemeat.

3 In what way is a terrine different from a pâté? How does a pâté differ from a pâté en croûte?

4 Describe the differences and the similarities between a ballotine and a galantine.

5 Describe the typical procedure for making sausages. Why is the selection of casings important?

6 Explain the difference between hot smoking and cold smoking. Describe a food typically prepared by each of these methods.

7 Discuss the types of cured products that may be consumed without further cooking. What makes these products safe to eat?

8 Describe the differences and the similarities between aspic jelly and sauce chaud-froid. In what ways are aspic jelly and sauce chaud-froid used?

9 Research the types of salts and curing agents used to make cold cuts, pâtés and forcemeats commercially. Explain when and why they are used. Discuss potential health hazards associated with consuming such ingredients and their alternatives. wWw

QUESTIONS FOR DISCUSSION

Terms to Know

forcemeat	galantine
emulsification	ballotine
dominant meat	fatback
panada	aspic
curing salt	rillette
sodium nitrite	hank
grinding die	quenelle

BASIC GAME FORCEMEAT

Yield: 4 lb. 8 oz. (2.1 kg)

Venison, cubed	1 lb. 8 oz.	720 g
Veal, cubed	1 lb. 8 oz.	720 g
Brandy	4 fl. oz.	120 ml
Salt	2 tsp.	10 ml
Pepper	½ tsp.	2 ml
Dried thyme	1 tsp.	5 ml
Pork fatback, cubed	1 lb.	480 g
Eggs	3	3
Game stock, cold	1 pt.	480 ml
Fresh parsley, chopped	1 oz.	30 g
Green peppercorns	½ oz.	15 g

1. Combine the venison and veal with the brandy, salt, pepper and thyme; marinate for several hours or overnight.

2. Grind the marinated meat and marinade ingredients in a chilled meat grinder once through a large die and then once through a small die; refrigerate.

3. Grind the fatback once through the small die.

4. Emulsify the fat with the ground meats in the bowl of a cold food processor. This can be done in several batches. Place the forcemeat in a stainless steel bowl over an ice bath.

5. Add the eggs, stock, parsley and peppercorns to the forcemeat in several batches; work them in by hand.

6. Additional garnishes may be added as desired. The forcemeat can be used to make a variety of pâtés or terrines.

Approximate values per 1-oz. (30-g) serving: **Calories** 100, **Total fat** 7 g, **Saturated fat** 3 g, **Cholesterol** 40 mg, **Sodium** 110 mg, **Total carbohydrates** 1 g, **Protein** 7 g

1. Emulsifying the fat with the ground meats.

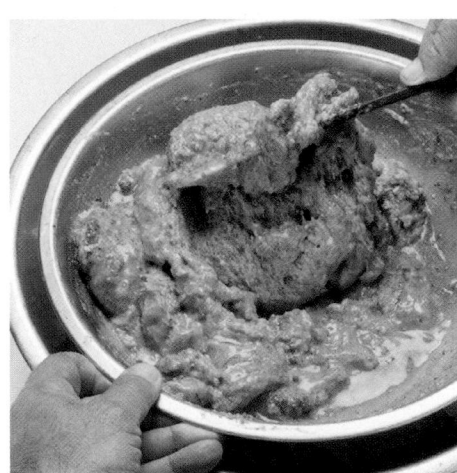

2. Folding in the eggs, stock, parsley and peppercorns.

3. Filling a terrine with the forcemeat.

LIVER TERRINE

Yield: 1 Terrine, 12 × 4 × 3 in. (30 × 10 × 7.5 cm)

Onions, diced	6 oz.	180 g
Vegetable oil	½ fl. oz.	15 ml
Pork liver	1 lb. 4 oz.	600 g
Fatback, diced	12 oz.	360 g
Eggs	2	2
Salt	1 Tbsp.	15 ml
Green peppercorns	½ tsp.	2 ml
Allspice, ground	½ tsp.	2 ml
Cloves, ground	¼ tsp.	1 ml
Ginger, ground	¼ tsp.	1 ml
Cream sauce	8 fl. oz.	240 ml
Brown veal stock	6 fl. oz.	180 ml
Fatback, sliced	as needed	as needed

❶ Filling the terrine with forcemeat.

❶ In a small sauté pan, sweat the onions in the vegetable oil until tender without coloring. Refrigerate the onions until cold.

❷ Trim and dice the liver.

❸ Grind the liver and diced fatback through a grinder with a fine die. Add the onions and pass the liver and fatback through the grinder again.

❹ Gently beat the eggs together by hand and add the salt, green peppercorns, allspice, cloves and ginger.

❺ Combine the cream sauce and brown veal stock, add the egg mixture and mix well.

❻ Add the ground liver mixture and beat until smooth.

❼ Line a terrine with slices of fatback. Fill the mold with the forcemeat and cover with the overhanging slices of fatback.

❽ Cover the terrine with its lid or aluminum foil and bake in a water bath at 350°F (180°C) to an internal temperature of 145°F (63°C), approximately 1½ hours.

❾ Allow the terrine to cool for 1 hour, then refrigerate the terrine until cold. Unmold, slice and serve with toasted French bread accompanied by condiments such as coarse mustard, cornichons, pickled onions and Cherry Confit (page 782).

❷ Slicing the finished terrine.

Approximate values per 4-oz. (120-g) serving: **Calories** 490, **Total fat** 46 g, **Saturated fat** 20 g, **Cholesterol** 265 mg, **Sodium** 800 mg, **Total carbohydrates** 5 g, **Protein** 14 g, **Vitamin A** 250%, **Iron** 45%

PORK RILLETTES

Note: This dish appears in the chapter opening photograph.

Yield: 5 lb. (2.4 kg)

Lard or pork fat	1 lb.	480 g
Onions, thinly sliced	14 oz.	420 g
Garlic	¾ oz.	22 g
Thyme sprigs	4	4
Bay leaves	2	2
White wine or meat stock	1 pt.	480 ml
Pork shoulder, fatty, boneless	3 lb.	1.4 kg
Bacon, diced	12 oz.	360 g
Salt and pepper	TT	TT
Pâté Spice (page 812) or other seasoning blend	as needed	as needed

1. Place the lard or pork fat, onions, garlic, thyme, bay leaves and white wine in a heavy saucepan large enough to hold all the ingredients. Heat over low heat until the fat melts and the liquid reduces in half, approximately 30 minutes.

2. Cut the pork shoulder into long strips approximately ½-inch (1.2-centimeters) thick.

3. Add the pork to the fat and seasonings. Cook over low heat, stirring occasionally until the meat is soft and breaks up easily, 3½ to 4 hours. Cover after 2 hours if the meat is getting too dry.

4. Transfer the cooked mixture into a large bowl and shred it into small pieces using two forks. Alternately, place the cooked pork mixture into the bowl of a food processor and pulse just until the meat is shredded.

5. Adjust the seasonings with salt, pepper and Pâté Spices or other seasoning mixture. Pack the pork rillettes into several terrines or individual serving crocks and spoon some of the cooking liquid and fat over the top. Cover and refrigerate. Serve with toasted French bread accompanied by condiments such as coarse mustard, cornichons, pickled onions and Fresh Cranberry Orange Relish (page 784).

Approximate values per 3-oz. (90-g) serving: **Calories** 367, **Total fat** 35 g, **Saturated fat** 15 g, **Cholesterol** 198 mg, **Sodium** 650 mg, **Total carbohydrates** 10 g, **Protein** 14 g

SMOKED DUCK AND FOIE GRAS GALANTINE ON A PEAR GALETTE

SIMPLICITY CATERING, FALLS CHURCH, VA

Chef Leland Atkinson

Yield: 1 Galantine

Duck breast, 10 oz. (300 g), boneless, skinless	1	1
Duck meat, lean	1 lb.	480 g
Pork butt, boneless, cubed	8 oz.	240 g
Pâté spice	2 tsp.	10 ml
Salt	1 Tbsp.	15 ml
Orange zest	1 Tbsp.	15 ml
Fresh thyme	1 tsp.	5 ml
Fresh ginger	1 tsp.	5 ml
Juniper berries, crushed	10	10
Port wine	4 fl. oz.	120 ml
Olive oil	1 fl. oz.	30 ml
Fatback, cubed	8 oz.	240 g
Foie gras pâté, diced	3 oz.	90 g
Ham, medium dice	2 oz.	60 g

Pistachios, chopped	2 oz.	60 g
Fatback, slab	as needed	as needed
Smoker marinade:		
Brown sugar	2 oz.	60 g
Garlic, chopped	1 tsp.	5 ml
Lemon juice	3 fl. oz.	90 ml
Walnut oil	6 fl. oz.	180 ml
Salt and pepper	TT	TT
Galette (per order):		
Pear	1	1
Clarified butter	1 tsp.	5 ml
Granulated sugar	½ tsp.	2 ml
Italian parsley	as needed	as needed

1. Cut the duck breast into several long strips.
2. Marinate the duck breast, duck meat and pork in the pâté spice, salt, orange zest, thyme, ginger, juniper berries and port wine for 2 days.
3. Remove the strips of duck breast from the marinade and sauté in the olive oil to brown. Remove, drain and reserve.
4. Grind the remaining duck meat, pork and marinade ingredients and the cubed fatback in a chilled grinder, first through the large die, then through the small die.
5. Place the ground meat in a stainless steel bowl over an ice bath. Fold in the foie gras, ham and pistachios.
6. Slice the fatback slab into thin sheets. Spread a piece of plastic wrap on the work surface and lay out the slices of fatback in a large rectangle with the edges overlapping slightly.
7. Place the forcemeat and duck breast strips along the length of the fatback rectangle so that when the galantine is rolled up, the strips of duck will be arranged in the center. Use plastic wrap to roll the galantine into a large cylinder.
8. Roll the cylinder in heavy-duty aluminum foil and poach until it reaches an internal temperature of 140°F (60°C). Remove and chill the galantine for at least 6 hours.
9. Combine the smoker marinade ingredients in a blender. Unwrap the galantine, brush it with the smoker marinade and chill for 1 hour. Place the galantine in a smoker and cold-smoke for 2 hours. Remove and chill before slicing.
10. For each galette, core the pear and slice ⅛ inch (3 millimeters) thick. Add the clarified butter to a warm sauté pan and arrange the pear slices in the pan by overlapping them to form a circle. Sprinkle the pear slices with the sugar. Sauté the galette, using a spatula to carefully turn it over when browned on the first side.
11. Place a pear galette on a plate and place a slice of galantine directly in the center of the galette. Garnish with Italian parsley or as desired. May be accompanied by Cherry Confit (page 782).

Approximate values per 4-oz. (120-g) serving: **Calories** 280, **Total fat** 22 g, **Saturated fat** 8 g, **Cholesterol** 100 mg, **Sodium** 290 mg, **Total carbohydrates** 5 g, **Protein** 17 g, **Vitamin C** 10%, **Iron** 20%

SALMON AND SEA BASS TERRINE
WITH SPINACH AND BASIL

Yield: 1 Terrine, 12 × 4 × 3 in. (30 × 10 × 7.5 cm)

Salmon fillet, boneless, skinless	1 lb. 8 oz.	720 g
Egg whites	3	3
Salt and white pepper	TT	TT
Cayenne pepper	TT	TT
Heavy cream	24 fl. oz.	720 ml
Fresh basil leaves	12	12
Truffles, brunoise (optional)	¾ oz.	22 g
Spinach leaves, cleaned	6 oz.	180 g
Sea bass fillet	12 oz.	350 g

1. Grind the salmon through the large die of a well-chilled meat grinder.
2. Place the salmon in the bowl of a food processor and process until smooth.
3. Add the egg whites, one at a time, pulsing the processor to incorporate. Scrape down the bowl and season with salt, white pepper and cayenne pepper.
4. With the machine running, add the cream in a steady stream. Scrape down the bowl again and process the mousseline until it is smooth and well mixed.
5. Blanch the basil leaves and refresh. Chop them finely.
6. Remove the mousseline from the bowl of the processor. Fold in the basil leaves and truffles and refrigerate.
7. Blanch and refresh the spinach leaves.
8. Spread the spinach leaves on a piece of plastic wrap, completely covering a rectangle approximately the length and width of the terrine mold.
9. Cut the sea bass fillet into strips approximately 1 inch (2.5 centimeters) wide and place end to end on the spinach leaves. Season with salt and white pepper.
10. Use the plastic wrap to wrap the spinach leaves tightly around the fish fillets.
11. Grease a terrine and line it with plastic wrap.
12. Half-fill the lined terrine with the salmon mousseline.
13. Carefully unwrap the spinach and sea bass fillets and place them down the center of the terrine. Fill the terrine with the remaining mousseline.
14. Tap the terrine mold firmly to remove any air pockets, then fold the plastic wrap over the top.
15. Cover and bake the terrine in a water bath at 300°F (150°C) to an internal temperature of 155°F (68°C), approximately 1½ hours.
16. Cool the terrine well, unmold, slice or decorate and serve with dill-flavored mayonnaise if desired.

Approximate values per 3.5-oz. (105-g) slice: **Calories** 210, **Total fat** 16 g, **Saturated fat** 8 g, **Cholesterol** 75 mg, **Sodium** 180 mg, **Total carbohydrates** 1 g, **Protein** 15 g, **Vitamin A** 25%

VEGETABLE TERRINE

Yield: 1 Terrine, 8 × 4 × 3 in. (20 × 10 × 7.5 cm)

Carrots, diced	10 oz.	300 g
Cauliflower florets	20 oz.	600 g
Broccoli florets	10 oz.	300 g
Cream cheese	3 oz.	90 g
Eggs, separated	3	3
Almonds, ground	2 Tbsp.	30 ml
Salt and pepper	TT	TT
Nutmeg, grated	¼ tsp.	1 ml
Lemon juice	1 tsp.	5 ml
Fresh mint, chopped	1 Tbsp.	15 ml

1. Cook each vegetable separately in a steamer until tender, but not mushy.
2. Purée each vegetable separately in a food processor with 1 ounce (30 grams) cream cheese and 1 egg yolk.
3. Add the ground almonds to the carrot purée and season with salt and pepper.
4. Add the nutmeg and lemon juice to the cauliflower purée and season with salt and pepper.
5. Add the mint to the broccoli purée and season with salt and pepper.
6. Whip the egg whites to stiff peaks. Fold one-third of the whipped egg whites into each of the vegetable purées.
7. Layer the three purées in a terrine mold. Place the terrine in a water bath and bake at 325°F (160°C) until firm, approximately 45 minutes. Chill for service.

Approximate values per 1-in. (2.5-cm) slice: **Calories** 114, **Total fat** 7 g, **Saturated fat** 3 g, **Cholesterol** 91 mg, **Sodium** 87 mg, **Total carbohydrates** 8.5 g, **Protein** 6 g, **Vitamin A** 171%, **Vitamin C** 87%

VEGETABLE TERRINE IN BRIOCHE

SIMPLICITY CATERING, FALLS CHURCH, VA
Chef Leland Atkinson

Yield: 1 Terrine, 12 × 4 × 3 in. (30 × 10 × 7.5 cm)

Chicken breast meat, lean	2 lb.	960 g
Egg whites	3	3
Heavy cream	4 fl. oz.	120 ml
Brandy	2 fl. oz.	60 ml
Nutmeg, ground	TT	TT
Salt and pepper	TT	TT
Carrot, medium dice	3 oz.	90 g
Broccoli florets	8 oz.	240 g
Shiitake mushrooms, trimmed	12–18	12–18
Olive oil	1 fl. oz.	30 ml
Red bell pepper, medium dice	2 oz.	60 g
Leek, white part only, medium dice	2 oz.	60 g
Fresh chives, basil and parsley, chopped	4 Tbsp.	60 ml
Brioche dough	1 lb.	480 g
Egg yolks, beaten	2	2
Eggs	2	2
Water	1 fl. oz.	30 ml
Madeira aspic	as needed	as needed

1. Dice or grind the chicken and place it in the bowl of a cold food processor and process.
2. Add the egg whites and then the cream and brandy in a steady stream while the motor is running.
3. Season the mousseline with nutmeg, salt and pepper and poach a small amount to test for texture and seasonings.
4. Adjust the seasonings and transfer to a metal mixing bowl in an ice bath.
5. Separately blanch the carrot and broccoli; drain and blot dry on a paper towel.
6. Sauté the mushrooms in oil. Drain and chill. In the same pan, sauté the bell pepper and leek. Remove from the stove and add the herbs. Fold the carrot, bell pepper, leek and herbs into the mousseline.
7. Roll the brioche dough out to approximately ⅛ inch (3 millimeters) thick and refrigerate until well chilled.
8. Line a buttered pâté mold with the chilled brioche, reserving the excess for the top and garnish.
9. Fill the mold one-fourth full with the mousseline. Layer the mushrooms over the mousseline and then cover them with another layer of mousseline, followed by the broccoli. Repeat this process until the mold is filled, finishing with a layer of mousseline.
10. Fold the ends of the brioche over the filling and brush with the beaten egg yolks.
11. Make a top from the remaining brioche and place it over the mold; cut a vent and insert a foil funnel into the vent.
12. Beat the eggs with the water to make an egg wash. Brush the exposed brioche with the egg wash and bake at 425°F (220°C) until the internal temperature reaches 125°F (52°C), approximately 35 to 40 minutes.
13. When cold, fill the pâté with Madeira aspic, if needed.

Approximate values per 3-oz. (90-g) slice: **Calories** 450, **Total fat** 20 g, **Saturated fat** 6 g, **Cholesterol** 185 mg, **Sodium** 520 mg, **Total carbohydrates** 35 g, **Protein** 34 g, **Vitamin A** 45%, **Vitamin C** 150%, **Claims**—high fiber

ROASTED RED PEPPER MOUSSE

Yield: 1 lb. 8 oz. (720 g)

Onion, small dice	3 oz.	90 g
Garlic, chopped	1 tsp.	5 ml
Olive oil	1 fl. oz.	30 ml
Red bell peppers, roasted and peeled, small dice	10 oz.	300 g
Salt and pepper	TT	TT
Chicken stock	8 fl. oz.	240 ml
Granulated gelatin	1 Tbsp.	15 ml
Dry white wine	2 fl. oz.	60 ml
Heavy cream, whipped	6 fl. oz.	180 ml

1. Sauté the onion and garlic in the oil until tender, approximately 2 minutes.
2. Add the bell peppers, salt, pepper and stock. Bring to a boil, lower to a simmer and cook for 5 minutes.
3. Soften the gelatin in the wine, then add it to the bell pepper mixture. Purée the bell pepper mixture in a blender or food processor and strain through a china cap.
4. Place the bell pepper purée over an ice bath. Stir until cool but do not allow the gelatin to set. Fold in the whipped cream. Pour the mousse into aspic-lined or well-oiled timbales or molds and refrigerate several hours or overnight.
5. Unmold the mousse and serve as desired.

VARIATIONS:

Broccoli Mousse—Substitute 8 ounces (240 grams) blanched, chopped broccoli for the red bell peppers.

Approximate values per 1-oz. (30-g) serving: **Calories** 60, **Total fat** 6 g, **Saturated fat** 2.5 g, **Cholesterol** 15 mg, **Sodium** 200 mg, **Total carbohydrates** 2 g, **Protein** 1 g, **Vitamin C** 25%

SALMON MOUSSE

Yield: 1 lb. 8 oz. (720 g)

Salmon, boneless, skinless	12 oz.	360 g
Fish velouté, warm	8 fl. oz.	240 ml
Heavy cream	8 fl. oz.	240 ml
Granulated gelatin	1½ Tbsp.	23 ml
White wine	4 fl. oz.	120 ml
Salt and white pepper	TT	TT
Cayenne pepper	TT	TT

1. Steam the salmon and transfer it to a food processor while still warm. Add the warm velouté in a steady stream while the machine is running.
2. Whip the cream to soft peaks and reserve.
3. Add the gelatin to the wine and allow it to rest for 5 minutes. Heat the gelatin mixture to a simmer.
4. Transfer the salmon and velouté to a mixing bowl and stir in the gelatin mixture. Season with salt, white pepper and cayenne pepper.
5. When the mixture has cooled to near room temperature, use a rubber spatula to fold in the whipped cream until just mixed. The mousse is now ready to be formed into timbales or molded into various shapes as desired.

Approximate values per 1-oz. (30-g) serving: **Calories** 100, **Total fat** 6 g, **Saturated fat** 3 g, **Cholesterol** 25 mg, **Sodium** 480 mg, **Total carbohydrates** 6 g, **Protein** 5 g, **Vitamin A** 4%

CHOPPED CHICKEN LIVER

Yield: 20 oz. (600 g)

Chicken livers, trimmed	1 lb.	480 g
Chicken fat or butter	2 oz.	60 g
Eggs, hard-cooked	2	2
Onions, small dice	6 oz.	180 g
Kosher salt and pepper	TT	TT

1 Sauté the livers in the chicken fat or butter until lightly browned with a slightly pink interior.

2 Chop the livers with a chef's knife, blending in the eggs and onions. Season to taste with salt and pepper.

3 The final product should be slightly coarse and peppery. Blend in additional chicken fat or butter if necessary to make the mixture hold together.

4 Pack into a serving bowl, cover well and chill for 24 hours. Serve with crackers, toast or matzos and sliced radishes.

Approximate values per 1-oz. (30-g) serving: **Calories** 60, **Total fat** 4 g, **Saturated fat** 1 g, **Cholesterol** 105 mg, **Sodium** 240 mg, **Total carbohydrates** 1 g, **Protein** 4 g, **Vitamin A** 70%

1 Sautéing the chicken livers.

2 Chopping the cooked livers.

3 The finished Chopped Chicken Liver.

BREAKFAST SAUSAGE PATTIES

Yield: 11 lb. (5.2 kg)

Salt	1¾ oz.	50 g
Ground white pepper	½ oz.	15 g
Sage	¾ oz.	22 g
Crushed red pepper flakes	¼ oz.	7 g
Pork butt, 70% lean, 30% fat, cubed	10 lb.	4.8 kg
Water, ice cold	1 pt.	480 ml

1 Combine the seasonings in a small bowl.

2 In a large stainless steel bowl, toss the pork butt with the seasonings.

3 Grind the pork and seasonings through the medium plate of a cold meat grinder into a large stainless bowl placed over an ice bath.

4 Place the ground pork and seasonings in the chilled bowl of a mixer and mix on low speed for approximately 1 minute while gradually adding the cold water. Continue to mix until the mixture becomes sticky to the touch, approximately 5 to 10 more seconds.

5 Cook a small portion of the sausage to test the flavor and texture. Adjust the seasonings if necessary.

6 Form the sausage into patties or fill casings as desired and pan-fry, broil, bake or grill as desired until done.

Approximate values per 2-oz. (60-g) serving: **Calories** 70, **Total fat** 3 g, **Saturated fat** 1 g, **Cholesterol** 30 mg, **Sodium** 250 mg, **Total carbohydrates** 0 g, **Protein** 10 g

SPICY ITALIAN SAUSAGE

Yield: 5 lb. (2.4 kg)

Pork butt	5 lb.	2.4 kg
Salt	1½ Tbsp.	23 ml
Black pepper	1½ tsp	7 ml
Fennel seeds	1½ tsp.	7 ml
Paprika	1 Tbsp.	15 ml
Crushed red pepper flakes	1½ tsp.	7 ml
Coriander, ground	¾ tsp.	4 ml
Water, cold	5 fl. oz.	150 ml

1 Cut the pork into 2-inch (5-centimeter) cubes.
2 Combine the pork with the remaining ingredients except the water.
3 Grind the meat once through the coarse die of a well-chilled grinder.
4 Add the water and mix well.
5 Stuff the sausage into casings.

Approximate values per 4-oz. (120-g) serving: **Calories** 220, **Total fat** 9 g, **Saturated fat** 3 g, **Cholesterol** 80 mg, **Sodium** 260 mg, **Total carbohydrates** 0 g, **Protein** 36 g

CHORIZO

Yield: 7 lb. 8 oz. (3.4 kg)

Pork, lean	5 lb.	2.4 kg
Fatback	2 lb. 8 oz.	1.2 kg
Crushed red pepper flakes	1 tsp.	5 ml
Garlic, chopped	1 oz.	30 g
Cumin, ground	3 Tbsp.	45 ml
Cayenne pepper	2 Tbsp.	30 ml
Salt	4 tsp.	20 ml
Paprika	5 Tbsp.	75 ml
Red wine vinegar	3 fl. oz.	90 ml

1 Cut the pork and fatback in 1-inch (2.5-centimeter) pieces. Grind the pork once using a medium die. Grind half of the pork a second time together with the fatback through a fine die.
2 Combine all the ingredients in the bowl of a mixer fitted with a paddle. The sausage may be used in bulk or formed into links as desired.

Approximate values per 1-oz. (30-g) serving: **Calories** 120, **Total fat** 10 g, **Saturated fat** 4 g, **Cholesterol** 25 mg, **Sodium** 90 mg, **Total carbohydrates** 0 g, **Protein** 5 g

chorizo (chor-EE-zoh) a coarse, spicy pork sausage flavored with ground chiles and removed from its casing before cooking; used in Mexican and Spanish cuisines

DUCK PROSCIUTTO WITH FRESH MANGO

CHEF STEVEN CHIAPPETTI, CHICAGO, IL

Yield: 2 Servings

Muscovy duck breasts	2	2
Kosher salt	8 oz.	240 g
Granulated sugar	4 oz.	120 g
Molasses	2 Tbsp.	30 ml
Red wine vinegar	2 fl. oz.	60 ml
Olive oil	2 fl. oz.	60 ml
Fresh mango	1	1
Mâche lettuce	2 bunches	2 bunches

1. Rinse the duck breasts under cold water and trim off the excess fat. Place the duck breasts on a sheet pan and refrigerate until ready to use.
2. In a medium-size bowl, combine the salt, 2 ounces (60 grams) of the sugar and the molasses. Rub this mixture on the duck breasts. Cover and refrigerate the duck for 48 hours.
3. Rinse the duck well under cold water and refrigerate another 48 hours before serving.
4. To make the dressing, boil the remaining sugar and vinegar in a small pan until thick. Remove from the heat and let cool. Whisk in the oil.
5. Peel and finely dice the mango.
6. Place a tablespoon of diced mango on each plate.
7. Slice the duck breast paper-thin and fan over the mango.
8. Arrange the mâche lettuce next to the mango and drizzle the oil-and-red-wine reduction dressing over the plate.

Approximate values per serving: **Calories** 550, **Total fat** 30 g, **Saturated fat** 4.5 g, **Cholesterol** 155 mg, **Sodium** 3610 mg, **Total carbohydrates** 41 g, **Protein** 30 g, **Vitamin A** 70%, **Vitamin C** 100%, **Iron** 40%

GRAVLAX

Gravlax is a centuries-old Scandinavian method for preserving fresh salmon. The modern technique consists of rubbing a salt-and-sugar mixture into the cut fillets of salmon. The rub extracts moisture from the fish, which firms the flesh and extends its keeping properties. As liquid is extracted, the gentle flavors of white pepper and dill permeate the fish. (Although these are the classic seasonings for gravlax, other herbs and spices can be used. Adding grated lemon rind to the rub imparts a citrus note, for example.) Paper-thin slices of gravlax are usually served with a slightly sweet mayonnaise flavored with mustard and dill.

Yield: Approximately 5 lb. (2.42 kg)

Salmon, drawn, 10–12 lb.	1	1
Kosher salt	8 oz.	240 g
White peppercorns, cracked	1 oz.	30 g
Fresh dill, chopped	2 bunches	2 bunches
Granulated sugar	8 oz.	240 g

1. Fillet the salmon, removing the pin bones but leaving the skin attached.
2. To make the salt cure, combine the salt, peppercorns, dill and sugar.
3. Coat the salmon fillets with the salt cure and wrap each fillet separately in plastic wrap.
4. Place the fillets in a hotel pan and place another hotel pan on top. Place two #10 cans in the top hotel pan to weigh it down and press the fish.
5. Refrigerate the salmon for 2 to 3 days.
6. Unwrap the gravlax, scrape off the salt cure and slice the gravlax very thin.

Approximate values per 1-oz. (30-g) serving: **Calories** 110, **Total fat** 4.5 g, **Saturated fat** 1 g, **Cholesterol** 30 mg, **Sodium** 1130 mg, **Total carbohydrates** 3 g, **Protein** 16 g, **Claims**—low saturated fat

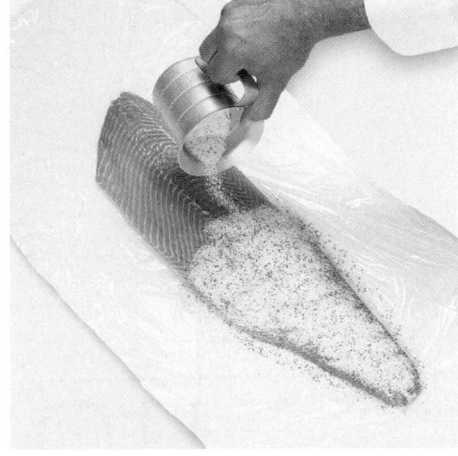

1. Coating the salmon fillet with the salt cure.

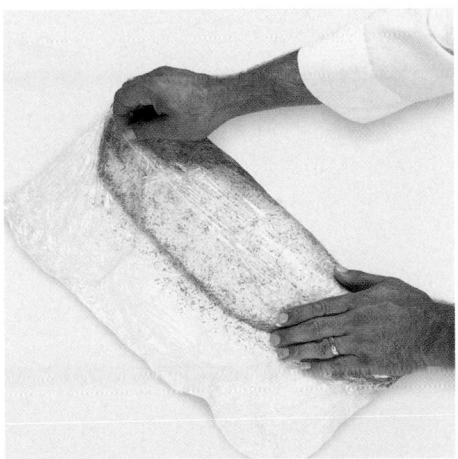

2. Wrapping the fillets in plastic wrap.

3. Weighting down a pan placed on top of the wrapped fish.

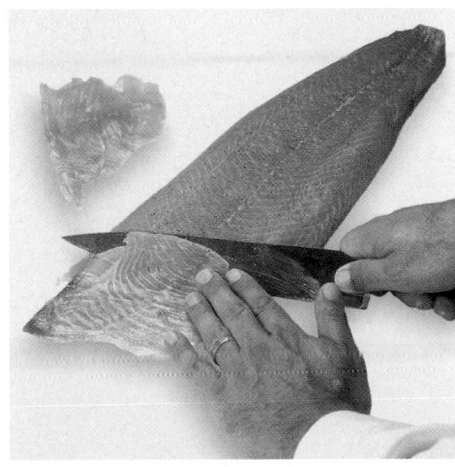

4. Slicing the cured gravlax thinly.

CHAPTER TWENTY-EIGHT

HORS D'OEUVRE AND CANAPÉS

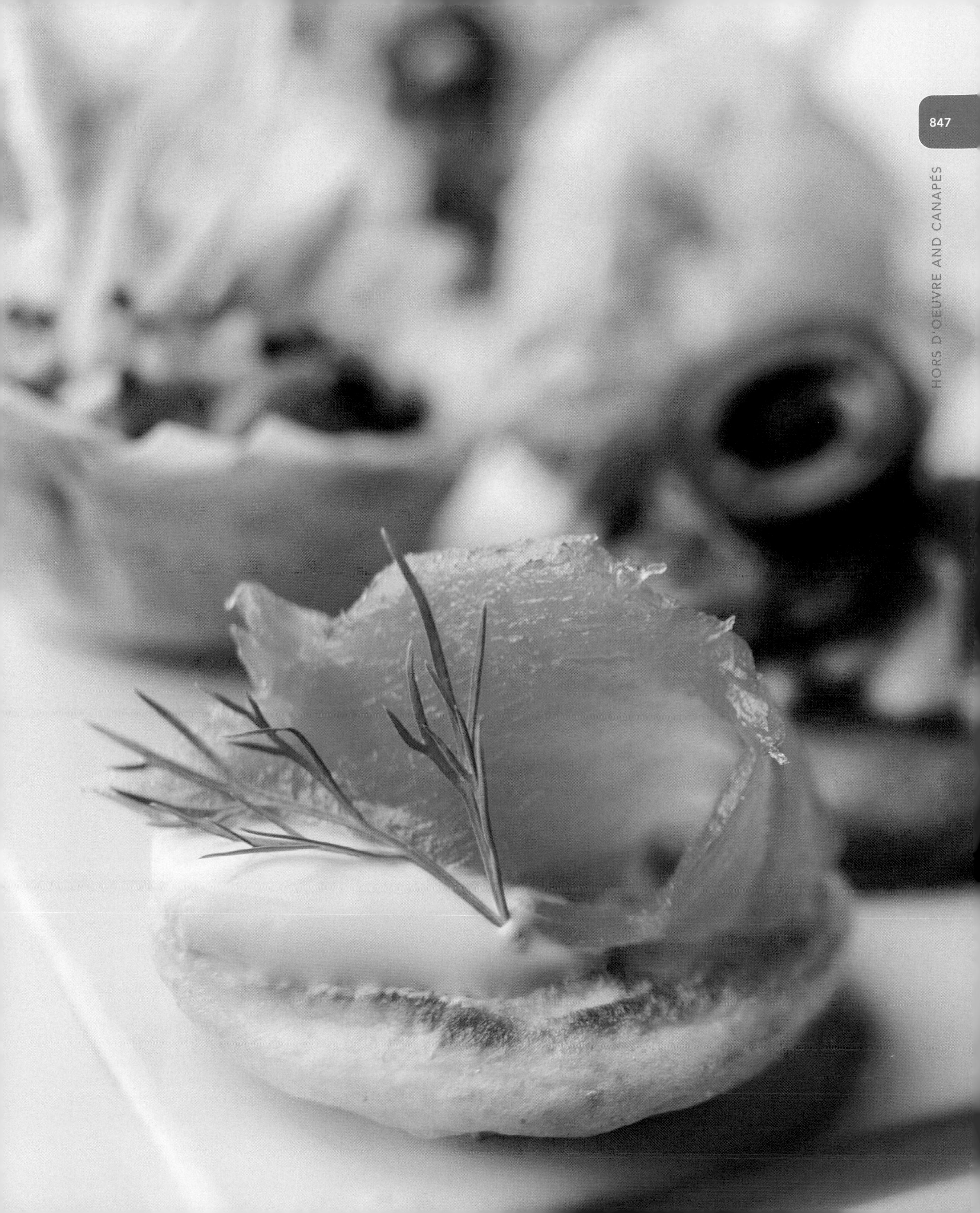

After studying this chapter, you will be able to:

After studying this chapter, you will be able to:

- prepare and serve a variety of cold and hot hors d'oeuvre, including canapés
- choose hors d'oeuvre, including canapés, that are appropriate for the meal or event

HORS D'OEUVRE, WHETHER HOT OR COLD, are very small portions of foods served before the meal to whet the appetite. Hors d'oeuvre and canapés can be passed elegantly by waiters or displayed on buffets. Appetizers, or starters, whether hot or cold, are generally the first course or introduction to a meal; they are more typically served with dinner than with lunch. Sometimes there is very little difference between an hors d'oeuvre and an appetizer.

Preparing hors d'oeuvre, including canapés, uses skills from almost every work station. Because they can consist of meat, poultry, fish, shellfish, vegetables, potatoes, grains, pasta, fruits, baked goods and sauces, they require a detailed knowledge of these foods and how they are prepared.

The French term *hors d'oeuvre* translates as "outside the work." Its usage was correct under the classic kitchen brigade system, for it was the service staff's responsibility to prepare small tidbits for guests to enjoy while the kitchen prepared the meal. Today, however, the kitchen staff prepares the hors d'oeuvre as well as the meals. Cold hors d'oeuvre (a final *s* is added as an Americanized plural) are usually prepared by the garde-manger; hot ones are prepared in the main kitchen.

There are really only two limitations on the type of food and manner of preparation that can be used for hors d'oeuvre: the chef's imagination and the foods at his or her disposal. There are, however, a few guidelines.

Guidelines for Preparing Hors d'Oeuvre

1. They should be small, one to two bites.
2. They should be flavorful and well seasoned without being overpowering.
3. They should be visually attractive.
4. They should complement whatever foods may follow without duplicating their flavors.

COLD HORS D'OEUVRE

Cold hors d'oeuvre are divided here into five broad categories based on preparation method, principal ingredient or presentation style: canapés, crudités, dips, caviar and sushi and sashimi. These categories may vary somewhat from classical teachings, but they are completely appropriate for modern menus and food service operations.

Canapés

Classic canapés are tiny open-faced sandwiches. They are constructed from a base, a spread and one or more garnishes. Many modern interpretations exist, such as those in which French bread slices, hollowed-out vegetables or mussels contain the garnish.

The most common **canapé base** is a thin slice of bread cut into an interesting shape and toasted. Although almost any variety of bread can be used, spiced, herbed or otherwise flavored breads may be inappropriate for some spreads or garnishes. Melba toasts, crackers and slices of firm vegetables such as cucumbers or zucchini are also popular canapé bases. Whatever item is used, the base must be strong enough to support the weight of the spread and garnish without falling apart when handled.

UN ARTISTE DE L'HORS D'OEUVRE

Well may it be said that a good hors d'oeuvre artist is a man to be prized in any kitchen, for, although his duties do not by any means rank first in importance, they nevertheless demand of the chef the possession of such qualities as are rarely found united in one person: reliable and experienced taste, originality, keen artistic sense, and professional knowledge.

—AUGUSTE ESCOFFIER,
Le Guide culinaire

Salami Cornet Canapés

TABLE 28.1	A SELECTION OF CANAPÉ SPREADS AND SUGGESTED GARNISHES
SPREAD	**SUGGESTED GARNISHES**
Anchovy butter	Hard-cooked eggs, capers, green or black olive slices
Blue cheese	Grape half, walnuts, roast beef roulade, pear slice, currants, watercress
Caviar butter	Caviar, lemon, egg slice, chives
Deviled ham	Cornichons, mustard butter, sliced radish
Horseradish butter	Smoked salmon, roast beef, smoked trout, marinated herring, capers, parsley
Lemon butter	Shrimp, crab, caviar, salmon, chives, parsley, black olive slices
Liver pâté	Truffle slice, cornichon
Mustard butter	Smoked meats, pâté, dry salami coronet, cornichon
Pimento cream cheese	Smoked oyster, sardine, pimento, parsley
Pesto sauce	Cooked mushrooms, dry salami, prosciutto, tomato, sliced Parmesan
Shrimp butter	Poached bay scallops, shrimp, caviar, parsley
Tuna salad	Capers, cornichons, sliced radish
Wasabi mayonnaise	Grilled tuna, smoked fish, sliced daikon, sprouts

The **canapé spread** provides much of the canapé's flavor. Spreads are usually flavored butters, cream cheese or a combination of the two. Several examples of spreads are listed in Table 28.1. Each spread is made by adding the desired amount of the main ingredient (chopped or puréed as appropriate) and seasonings to softened butter or cream cheese and mixing until combined. Quantities and proportions vary according to individual tastes. Other canapé spreads include bound salads (for example, tuna or egg), finely chopped shrimp or liver mousse. Any of a number of ingredients can be combined for spreads, using the following guidelines:

Guidelines for Preparing Canapé Spreads

1 The spread's texture should be smooth enough to produce attractive designs if piped through a pastry bag fitted with a decorative tip.

2 The spread's consistency should be firm enough to hold its shape when piped onto the base, yet soft enough to stick to the base and hold the garnishes in place.

3 The spread's flavor should complement the garnishes and be flavorful enough to stimulate the appetite without being overpowering.

A spread may be a substantial portion of the canapé as well as its distinguishing characteristic. Or it can be applied sparingly and used more as a means of gluing the garnish to the base than as a principal ingredient.

Canapés with bread bases tend to become soggy quickly from both the moisture in the spread and the moisture in the refrigerator where they are stored. Using a spread made with butter will help keep the bread bases crisper, as will buttering the base with a thin coat of softened plain butter before piping on the spread. The best way to ensure a crisp base is to make the canapés as close to service time as possible.

The variety of canapé garnishes is vast. The garnish can dominate or complement the spread, or it can be a simple sprig of parsley intended to provide visual appeal but little flavor. Although several ingredients can be used to garnish the same canapé, remember the limitations imposed by the canapé's size and purpose. Traditional garnishes can be made by shaping thinly sliced smoked salmon into rosettes, or thin slices of salami into cornets, into which additional spread can be piped. The natural shape of a boiled, peeled shrimp also makes an attractive canapé garnish.

Shrimp and Caviar Canapés

Salmon Rosette Canapés

PROCEDURE FOR **PREPARING CANAPÉS**

This procedure can be adapted and used with a variety of ingredients to produce a variety of canapés. If the canapé base is a bread crouton, begin with Step 1. If some other product is used as the base, prepare that base and begin with Step 4.

1. Trim the crust from an unsliced loaf of bread. Slice the bread lengthwise approximately ⅓ inch (8 millimeters) thick.

2. Cut the bread slices into the desired shapes using a serrated bread knife or canapé cutter. See Figure 28.1.

3. Brush the bread shapes with melted butter and bake in a 350°F (180°C) oven until they are toasted and dry. Remove and cool. Alternatively, the entire bread slice can be buttered and toasted, then cut into shapes.

4. If desired, spread each base with a thin layer of softened plain butter.

5. Apply the spread to the base. If a thin layer is desired, use a palette knife. If a thicker or more decorative layer is desired, pipe the spread onto the base using a pastry bag and decorative tip. Alternatively, the entire bread slice can be buttered, toasted, cooled, covered with a spread and then cut into the desired shapes.

6. Garnish the canapé as desired.

7. If desired, glaze each canapé with a thin coating of aspic jelly. The aspic jelly can be applied with a small spoon or a spray bottle designated for that purpose.

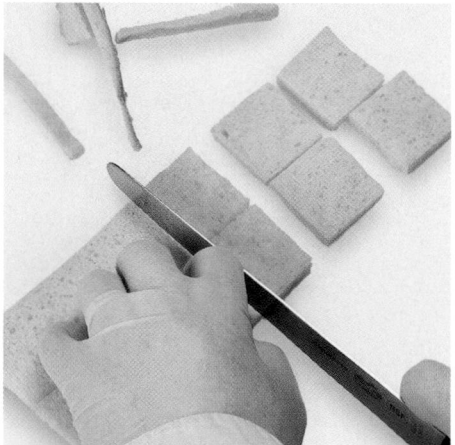

1. Slicing bread into the desired shapes.

2. Applying the spread to the base with a palette knife.

3. Piping the spread onto the base.

4. Coating the entire slice of toasted bread with a spread before cutting it into canapés.

5. Garnishing the canapés.

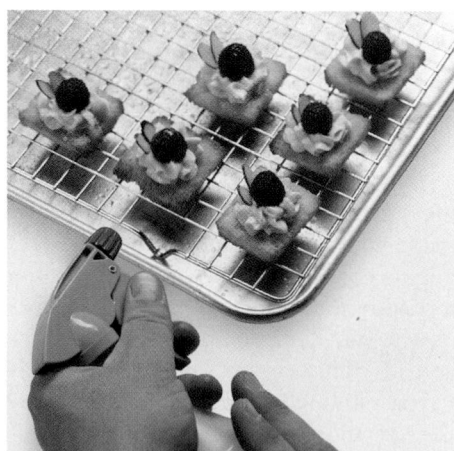

6. Spraying the finished canapés with aspic.

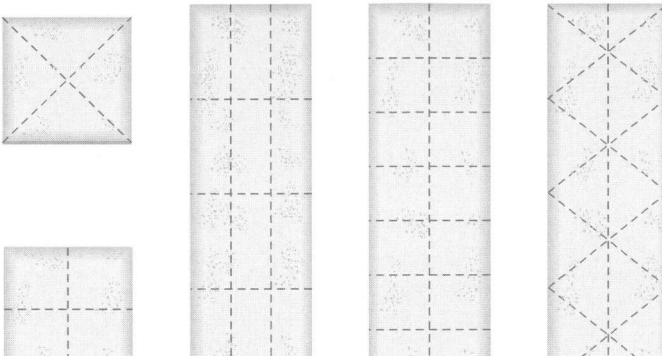

Square pieces of bread   Lengthwise cuts from a whole loaf

FIGURE 28.1 ▶ Bread can be sliced into several basic shapes to avoid waste.

BARQUETTES, TARTLETS AND PROFITEROLES

Barquettes, tartlets and profiteroles are all adaptations of the basic canapé. A barquette is a tiny boat-shaped shell made from a savory dough such as pâte brisée. A **tartlet** is simply a round version of a barquette. A **profiterole** is a small puff made from pâte à choux. These three items can be prepared like canapés by filling them with flavored spreads and garnishing as desired.

PROCEDURE FOR **PREPARING BARQUETTES**

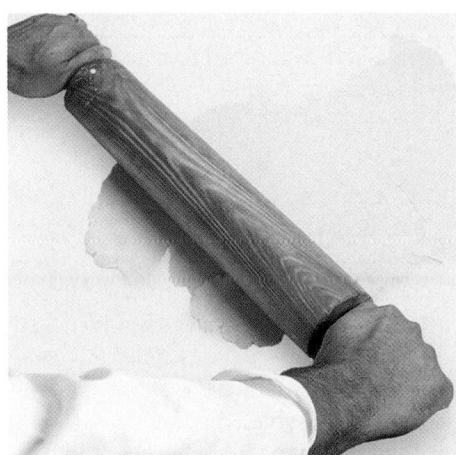

❶ Rolling out the pastry dough.

❷ Pressing the dough into the barquette shells.

❸ Pricking the dough with a fork to allow steam to escape during baking.

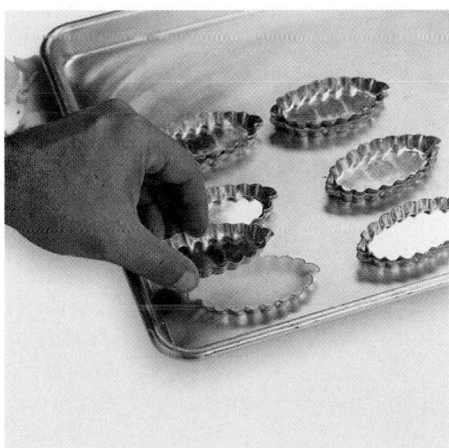

❹ Placing a second barquette shell on top of the dough to prevent it from rising as it bakes.

Bruschetta

Stuffed Egg Canapés

Steamed Mussel, Cream-Cheese-Filled
Endive and Tartlet Canapés

OTHER TYPES OF CANAPÉS

Vegetables such as cherry tomatoes, blanched snow peas, mushroom caps and Belgian endive leaves are sometimes used as canapé bases. Thickly sliced rounds of cucumber or hollowed-out small potatoes can also be used as containers for canapés, as well as hard-cooked eggs or mussel shells. They are filled and garnished in the same manner as barquettes, tartlets and profiteroles. Bruschetta or crostini are slices of country bread that are grilled, brushed with garlic and olive oil and then garnished with diced tomatoes or other toppings. These Italian-style canapés are versatile and easy to prepare.

Crudités

Crudité, a French word meaning "raw thing," generally refers to raw or slightly blanched vegetables served as an hors d'oeuvre. Although almost any vegetable will do, the most commonly used are broccoli, cauliflower, carrots, celery, asparagus and green beans, all of which are often blanched, and cucumbers, zucchini, yellow squash, radishes, green onions, cherry tomatoes, Belgian endive leaves, mushrooms, peppers and jicama, which are served raw.

When preparing crudités, use only the freshest and best-looking produce available. Because they are displayed and eaten raw, blemishes and imperfections cannot be disguised. Vegetables, both blanched and raw, should be cut into attractive shapes. Crudités are usually served with one or more dips.

Dips

Dips can be served hot or cold and as an accompaniment to crudités, crackers, chips, toasts, breads or other foods.

Cold dips often use mayonnaise, sour cream or cream cheese as a base. The methods for preparing mayonnaise-based and sour cream-based dips are identical to those for making mayonnaise-based salad dressings discussed in Chapter 24, Salads and Salad Dressings. The principal difference is that dips are normally thicker than dressings.

To use cream cheese as a base, first soften it by mixing it in an electric mixer fitted with a paddle. Then add the flavoring ingredients such as chopped cooked vegetables, chopped cooked fish or shellfish, herbs, spices, garlic or

Artful Array of Crudités and Dip

onions. Adjust the consistency of the dip by adding milk, buttermilk, cream, sour cream or other appropriate liquid.

Some cold dips such as guacamole and hummus use purées of fruits, vegetables or beans as the base. Hot dips often use a béchamel, cream sauce or cheese sauce as a base and usually contain a dominant flavoring ingredient such as chopped spinach or shellfish.

Dips can be served in small bowls or hollowed-out cabbages, squash, pumpkins or other vegetables. Hot dips are often served in chafing dishes. The combinations of ingredients and seasonings that can be used to make dips as well as the foods that are dipped in them are limited only by the chef's imagination.

HUMMUS

Yield: Approximately 1 qt. (960 ml)

Chickpeas, cooked	1 lb.	480 g
Tahini	8 oz.	240 g
Garlic, chopped	2 tsp.	10 ml
Cumin, ground (optional)	½ tsp.	2 ml
Lemon juice	4 fl. oz.	120 ml
Water or vegetable stock	as needed	as needed
Salt	1 tsp.	5 ml
Cayenne pepper	TT	TT
Paprika	TT	TT
Olive oil	2 fl. oz.	60 g
Fresh parsley, chopped	2 tsp.	10 ml

1. Combine the chickpeas, tahini, garlic, cumin, if using, and lemon juice in a food processor; process until smooth. If necessary, with the food processor running, add as much water or stock as needed to make the mixture the consistency of firm mayonnaise. Season with salt, paprika and cayenne pepper.

2. Spoon the hummus onto a serving platter and smooth the surface. Drizzle the oil over the hummus and garnish with the chopped parsley. Serve with warm pita bread that has been cut into quarters.

Note: If using canned chickpeas, drain and reserve the liquid. Use it in place of the water or stock if needed to adjust the consistency.

Approximate values per 2-fl.-oz. (60-ml) serving: **Calories** 210, **Total fat** 16 g, **Saturated fat** 1 g, **Cholesterol** 0 mg, **Sodium** 250 mg, **Total carbohydrates** 10 g, **Protein** 7 g, **Iron** 8%

MISE EN PLACE

◄ Cook chickpeas.
◄ Chop garlic.
◄ Chop parsley.

tahini (tah-HEE-nee) a thick, oily paste made from crushed sesame seeds

Caviar

Caviar, considered by many to be the ultimate hors d'oeuvre, is the salted roe (eggs) of the sturgeon fish. In the United States, only sturgeon roe can be labeled simply "caviar." Roe from other fish must be qualified as such on the label (for example, salmon caviar or lumpfish caviar).

Most of the world's caviar comes from sturgeon harvested in the Caspian Sea and imported from Russia and Iran. Imported sturgeon caviar, classified according to the sturgeon species and the roe's size and color, includes beluga, osetra and sevruga as well as pressed caviar. **Beluga** is the most expensive caviar and comes from the largest species (the sturgeon can weigh up to 1750 pounds [800 kilograms]); the dark gray and well-separated eggs are the largest and most fragile kind. **Osetra** is considered by some connoisseurs to be the best caviar; the eggs are medium-sized, golden yellow to brown and quite oily. **Sevruga** is harvested from small sturgeon; the eggs are quite small and light to dark gray. **Pressed caviar** is a processed caviar made from osetra and sevruga roes. The eggs are cleaned, packed in linen bags and hung to drain; as salt and moisture drain away, the natural shape of the eggs is destroyed and the eggs are pressed together. Approximately 3 pounds (1.3 kilograms) of roe produce only 1 pound (450 grams) of pressed caviar; pressed caviar has a spreadable, jamlike consistency.

Beluga Caviar

Sevruga Caviar

Osetra Caviar

American Salmon Roe

Most of the caviar consumed in the United States, however, comes from either domestic sturgeon or other fish and is labeled American sturgeon caviar, golden whitefish caviar, lumpfish caviar or salmon caviar. **American sturgeon caviar** is not considered to be of the same quality as Russian or Iranian caviars; nevertheless, roe from sturgeon harvested in the coastal waters of the American Northwest and the Tennessee River is becoming increasingly popular, due in part to its relatively low price. **Golden whitefish caviar** is a small and very crisp roe; it is a natural golden color and comes from whitefish native to the northern Great Lakes. **Lumpfish caviar** is readily available and reasonably priced; it is produced from lumpfish harvested in the North Atlantic. The small and very crisp eggs are dyed black, red or gold; the food coloring is not stable, however, and when used to garnish foods, colored lumpfish caviar tends to bleed. **Salmon caviar**, the eggs of the chum and silver salmon, is a very popular garnish. The eggs are large with a good flavor and natural orange color.

PURCHASING AND STORING CAVIARS

Although all caviar is processed with salt, some caviar is labeled **malassol**, which means "little salt." Caviar should smell fresh, with no off-odors. The eggs should be whole, not broken, and they should be crisp and pop when pressed with the tongue. Excessive oiliness may be caused by a large number of broken eggs. The best way to test caviar's quality is to taste it. Remember, price alone does not necessarily indicate quality.

Most caviar can be purchased fresh or pasteurized in tins or jars ranging from 1 ounce (28 grams) to more than 4 pounds (2 kilograms). Some caviars are also available frozen. (Frozen caviar should be used only as a garnish and should not be served by itself.) In order to ensure the freshest possible product, always purchase caviar in small quantities as often as possible based on the needs of the restaurant.

Fresh caviar should be stored at 32°F (0°C). Because most refrigerators are considerably warmer than that, store the caviar on ice in the coldest part of the refrigerator and change the ice often. If properly handled, fresh caviar will last 1 to 2 weeks before opening and several days after opening. Pasteurized caviar does not require refrigeration until it is opened and will last several days in the refrigerator after opening.

SERVING CAVIARS

Fine caviar should be served in its original container or a nonmetal bowl on a bed of crushed ice, accompanied only by lightly buttered toasts or blinis and sour cream. Connoisseurs prefer china, bone or other nonmetal utensils for serving caviar because metal reacts with the caviar, producing off-flavors.

Lesser-quality caviars are often served on ice, accompanied by minced onion, chopped hard-cooked egg whites and yolks (separately), lemon, sour cream and buttered toasts.

Lumpfish and other nonsturgeon caviars are usually not served by themselves. Rather, they are used as ingredients in or garnishes for other dishes.

Sushi and Sashimi

Generally, **sushi** refers to cooked or raw fish and shellfish rolled in or served on seasoned rice. **Sashimi** is raw fish eaten without rice. In Japan, the word sushi (or **zushi**) refers only to the flavored rice. Each combination of rice and another ingredient or ingredients has a specific name. These include *nigiri zushi* (rice with raw fish), *norimaki zushi* (rice rolled in seaweed), *fukusa zushi* (rice wrapped in omelet), *inari zushi* (rice in fried bean curd) and *chirashi zushi* (rice with fish, shellfish and vegetables). Although a Japanese sushi master spends years perfecting style and technique, many types of sushi can be produced in any professional kitchen with very little specialized equipment.

INGREDIENTS FOR SUSHI AND SASHIMI

Fish

The key to good sushi and sashimi is the freshness of the fish. All fish must be of the highest quality and absolutely fresh, preferably no more than one day out of the water. Ahi and yellowfin tuna, salmon, flounder and sea bass are typically used for sushi. Cooked shrimp and eel are also popular.

Rice

Sushi rice is prepared by adding seasonings such as vinegar, sugar, salt and rice wine (sake or mirin) to steamed short-grain rice. The consistency of the rice is very important. It must be sticky enough to stay together when formed into finger-shaped oblongs, but not too soft.

Seasonings

Seasonings include the following:

▶ **Shoyu** —Japanese soy sauce, which is lighter and more delicate than the Chinese variety.

▶ **Wasabi** —A strong aromatic root, purchased as a green powder. It is sometimes called green horseradish, although it is not actually related to the common horseradish.

▶ **Pickled ginger** —Fresh ginger pickled in vinegar, which gives it a pink color.

▶ **Nori** —A dried seaweed purchased in sheets; it adds flavor and is sometimes used to contain the rolled rice and other ingredients.

The procedure for making sushi and sashimi is illustrated by the recipe for Nigiri Sushi.

NIGIRI SUSHI

Yield: 24 Pieces

Sushi-quality fish fillets such as ahi, salmon, flounder or sea bass	1 lb.	480 g
Wasabi powder	1 oz.	30 g
Water	1 fl. oz.	30 ml
Sushi Rice (recipe follows)	2 lb.	960 g
Pickled ginger, sliced	2 oz.	60 g
Shoyu	3 fl. oz.	90 ml

1. Trim the fish fillets of any skin, bone, imperfections or blemishes. Cut the fillets into 24 thin slices, approximately 2 inches by 1 inch (5 centimeters by 2.5 centimeters).
2. Mix the wasabi powder and water to form a paste.
3. With your hands, form a 1½-ounce (50-gram) portion of rice into a finger-shaped mound.
4. Rub a small amount of wasabi on one side of a slice of fish.
5. Holding the rice mound in one hand, press the fish, wasabi side down, onto the rice with the fingers of the other hand.
6. Serve with additional wasabi, pickled ginger and shoyu.

Approximate values per piece: **Calories** 80, **Total fat** 2 g, **Saturated fat** 0 g, **Cholesterol** 10 mg, **Sodium** 310 mg, **Total carbohydrates** 11 g, **Protein** 5 g, **Claims**—low fat; low cholesterol; no sugar

MISE EN PLACE
◀ Prepare and chill sushi rice.

1 Slicing the fish for sushi.

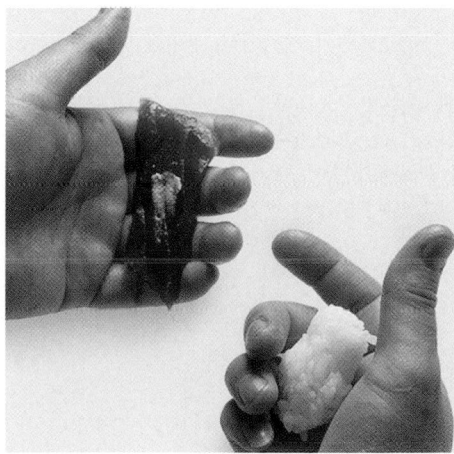

2 Forming a finger-shaped rice mound.

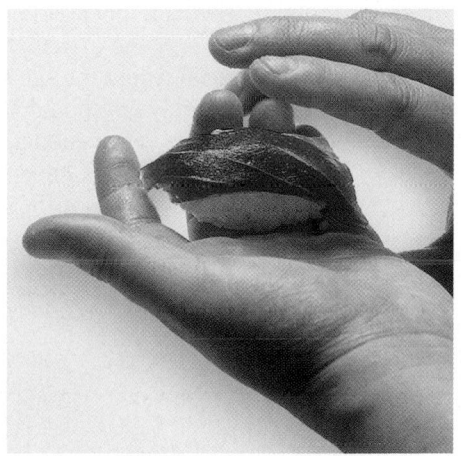

3 Pressing the fish onto the rice.

4 The finished sushi plate.

ZUSHI (SUSHI RICE)

Yield: 2 lb. (1 kg)

Short-grain rice	1 lb.	480 g
Water	20 fl. oz.	600 ml
Rice vinegar	2 fl. oz.	60 ml
Granulated sugar	3 Tbsp.	45 ml
Salt	2½ tsp.	12 ml
Mirin	1 fl. oz.	30 ml

1. Wash the rice and allow it to drain for 30 minutes.
2. Combine the rice and water in a saucepan. Bring to a boil, lower to a simmer, cover and steam for 20 minutes.
3. Combine the rice vinegar, sugar, salt and mirin and add to the rice. Mix well and cool to room temperature.

Approximate values per 1-oz. (30-g) serving: **Calories** 60, **Total fat** 0 g, **Saturated fat** 0 g, **Cholesterol** 0 mg, **Sodium** 140 mg, **Total carbohydrates** 13 g, **Protein** 1 g, **Claims**—fat free

Adding the seasonings to the cooked rice.

HOT HORS D'OEUVRE

To provide a comprehensive list of hot hors d'oeuvre would be virtually impossible; therefore, just a few of the more commonly encountered ones that can be easily made in almost any kitchen are discussed here.

Filled Pastry Shells

Because savory (unsweetened) barquettes and tartlets, éclair puffs and bouchées can hold a small amount of liquid, they are often baked and then filled with warm meat, poultry or fish purées or ragoûts, garnished and served hot. They become soggy quickly, however, and must be prepared at the last possible minute before service.

Brochettes

Hors d'oeuvre brochettes are small skewers holding a combination of meat, poultry, game, fish, shellfish or vegetables. The foods are typically marinated, then baked, grilled or broiled, and are usually served with a dipping sauce. Brochettes can be small pieces of boneless chicken breast marinated in white wine and grilled, beef cubes glazed with teriyaki sauce or lamb or chicken satay (saté) with peanut sauce.

In order to increase visual appeal, the main ingredients should be carefully cut and consistent in size and shape. The ingredients are normally diced, but strips of meat and poultry can also be threaded onto the skewers.

As hors d'oeuvre, the skewers should be very small, slightly larger than a toothpick. When assembling brochettes, leave enough exposed skewer so that diners can pick them up easily. Wooden skewers have a tendency to burn during cooking. Soaking them in water before assembling helps reduce the risk of burning.

LAMB SATAY

Yield: 16 Skewers

Lamb leg meat, boned, trimmed	2 lb.	960 g
Marinade:		
Vegetable oil	2 fl. oz.	60 ml
Lemongrass, chopped	2 Tbsp.	30 ml
Garlic, chopped	1 Tbsp.	15 ml
Crushed red pepper flakes	1 tsp.	5 ml
Curry powder	1 Tbsp.	15 ml
Honey	1 Tbsp.	15 ml
Fish sauce	1 Tbsp.	15 ml
Southeast Asian–Style Peanut Sauce (page 228)	as needed	as needed
Cilantro	as needed for garnish	
Lime, cut into wedges	as needed for garnish	

MISE EN PLACE
◀ Trim and bone lamb.
◀ Prepare the peanut sauce.
◀ Cut lime wedges.

1. Cut the lamb into 2-ounce (60-gram) strips approximately 4 inches (10 centimeters) long. Lightly pound the strips with a mallet. Thread the strips onto 6-inch (15-centimeter) bamboo skewers that have been soaked in water.

2. To make the marinade, combine the marinade ingredients in the bowl of a food processor and purée until smooth.

3. Brush the meat with the marinade and allow to marinate for 1 hour.

4. Grill the skewers until done, approximately 2 minutes. Serve with Southeast Asian–Style Peanut Sauce garnished with cilantro and lime wedges.

VARIATIONS:

Beef or chicken satay can be made by substituting well-trimmed beef or boneless, skinless chicken meat for the lamb.

Approximate values per skewer: **Calories** 118, **Total fat** 7 g, **Saturated fat** 2 g, **Cholesterol** 37 mg, **Sodium** 40 mg, **Total carbohydrates** 2 g, **Protein** 12 g

Meatballs

Meatballs made from ground beef, veal, pork or poultry and served in a sauce buffet style are a popular hot hors d'oeuvre. One of the best known is the Swedish meatball. It is made from ground beef, veal and pork bound with eggs and bread crumbs and served in a velouté or cream sauce seasoned with dill. Other sauces that can be used in the same manner are mushroom sauce, red wine sauce or any style of tomato sauce.

SWEDISH MEATBALLS

MISE EN PLACE

▶ Peel onion and chop into fine dice.
▶ Grind fresh bread for bread crumbs.
▶ Heat demi-glace and cream and chop dill while the meatballs are baking.

Yield: 4 lb. 8 oz. (2.1 kg)

Onions, small dice	8 oz.	240 g
Whole butter	2 oz.	60 g
Ground beef	2 lb.	960 g
Ground pork	2 lb.	1 kg
Bread crumbs, fresh	4 oz.	120 g
Eggs	3	3
Salt	1 Tbsp.	15 ml
Black pepper	TT	TT
Nutmeg, ground	TT	TT
Allspice, ground	TT	TT
Lemon zest, grated	1 tsp.	5 ml
Demi-glace, hot	1 qt.	1 lt
Heavy cream, hot	8 fl. oz.	240 ml
Fresh dill, chopped	2 Tbsp.	30 ml

1. Sauté the onions in the butter without coloring. Remove and cool.
2. Combine the onions with all of the ingredients except the demi-glace, cream and dill. Mix well.
3. Portion the meat with a #20 scoop; form into balls with your hands and place on a sheet pan.
4. Bake the meatballs at 400°F (200°C) until firm, approximately 15 minutes. Remove the meatballs from the pan with a slotted spoon, draining well, and place in a hotel pan.
5. Combine the demi-glace, cream and dill; pour over the meatballs.
6. Cover the meatballs and bake at 350°F (180°C) until done, approximately 20 minutes. Skim the grease from the surface and serve.

Approximate values per 5-oz. (150-g) serving: **Calories** 250, **Total fat** 16 g, **Saturated fat** 7 g, **Cholesterol** 105 mg, **Sodium** 420 mg, **Total carbohydrates** 7 g, **Protein** 20 g, **Calcium** 30%

PHYLLO DOUGH

Phyllo (fee-low), also spelled *filo* or *fillo,* is from the Greek *phyllon,* meaning "thin sheet or leaf." Although its name is Greek, its origin is unknown. Indians, Turks, Syrians, Yugoslavs and Austrians all claim it as their own. Somewhat blandly flavored, phyllo sheets are brushed with melted butter or oil, stacked and then used in many Mediterranean, Middle Eastern and Central Asian dishes as a tart crust or a wrapper for various sweet or savory fillings. Phyllo is now also used for strudels and various hors d'oeuvres. Shredded phyllo, called kataifi, is also made and used for some Mediterranean and Middle Eastern specialties.

Phyllo dough is made from flour, water, a bit of oil and eggs. The dough must be stretched tissue-paper thin, using techniques that can take years to master. Fortunately, excellent commercially prepared phyllo is available in frozen sheets. Sheets of phyllo can stick together if thawed too quickly, so thaw frozen dough slowly for a day or so in the refrigerator. Then temper the package of dough at room temperature for at least 1 hour before opening. (Unused phyllo should not be refrozen; it will keep for several days in the refrigerator if tightly wrapped.)

When ready to use, open the package and unfold the stack of leaves. Place them flat on a sheet pan or work surface and cover with a sheet of plastic wrap topped with a damp towel. Remove one leaf at a time from the stack, keeping the remainder well covered to prevent them from drying out. Brush melted butter or oil over the sheet's entire surface. Chopped nuts, sugar, cocoa powder or bread crumbs can be dusted over the butter or oil for additional flavor. Repeat with additional leaves until the desired number of layers have been prepared and stacked together. The number of layers will depend on the thickness of the sheets and their use. Cut the stacked phyllo with scissors or a very sharp knife and use as directed in the recipe.

Wrapped Hors d'Oeuvre

A slice of savory meat or roasted pepper wrapped around a complementary or contrasting slice of fruit or vegetable makes a flavorful hot hors d'oeuvre. Shrimp wrapped in bacon, asparagus spears in prosciutto or a cube of mozzarella in a slice of roasted red pepper are typical, as are the hors d'oeuvre known as rumaki. Traditionally, rumaki were made by wrapping chicken livers in bacon and broiling or baking them. Today, however, many other foods prepared in the same fashion are called rumaki. For example, blanched bacon can be wrapped around olives, pickled watermelon rind, water chestnuts, pineapple, dates or scallops. These morsels are then broiled, baked or fried and served piping hot.

RUMAKI

Yield: 60 Pieces

MISE EN PLACE
◀ Slice water chestnuts while liver is marinating in Step 2.

Chicken livers	1 lb.	480 g
Marinade:		
Brown sugar	1 Tbsp.	15 ml
Water, hot	1 Tbsp.	15 ml
Dark soy sauce	1 Tbsp.	15 ml
Garlic, minced	1 Tbsp.	15 ml
Bacon, sliced thin	30 slices	30 slices
Water chestnuts, sliced	60 slices	60 slices

1. Trim the livers and cut into 60 equal-sized pieces. Place the livers in a stainless steel bowl.
2. Combine the marinade ingredients. Pour the marinade over the livers and refrigerate for 1 hour.
3. Cut the bacon slices in half, spread them on a sheet pan and parcook at 375°F (190°C) for approximately 5 minutes. Pour off and discard the excess fat.
4. Drain the livers. Roll one piece of liver and one water chestnut slice in one piece of bacon and secure with a toothpick. Repeat with the remaining ingredients. Place on a baking rack over a sheet pan with the seam side down.
5. Bake the rumaki in a 400°F (200°C) convection oven until the bacon is crisp and the liver is cooked, approximately 10 minutes. Do not overcook or the rumaki will be dry. Serve hot.

Approximate values per piece: **Calories** 60, **Total fat** 5 g, **Saturated fat** 1.5 g, **Cholesterol** 30 mg, **Sodium** 170 mg, **Total carbohydrates** 1 g, **Protein** 4 g, **Vitamin A** 10%

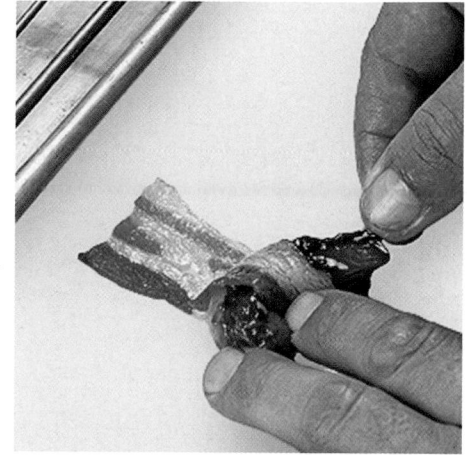

1 Rolling rumaki.

2 The finished rumaki.

Filled Dough

Phyllo dough, savory pie crust or puff pastry dough forms the base of numerous hot hors d'oeuvres. These doughs can be stuffed with a wide variety of pork, chicken, fish or vegetable stuffings before baking or deep-frying. Prepared doughs such as phyllo dough or wonton skins simplify the preparation of filled hors d'oeuvre.

Wonton skins are an Asian noodle dough used to produce a wide variety of hors d'oeuvre, such as a miniature version of the traditional egg roll or a puff filled with a mixture of seasoned cream cheese and crab. Or they can be stuffed with a wide variety of fillings before cooking. As hors d'oeuvre, stuffed wonton skins can be steamed, but they are more often pan-fried or deep-fried. (Wonton skins can also be baked and used as a canapé base, as shown in the recipe for Baked Wonton Crisps, page 864.)

MISE EN PLACE

▶ Chop garlic.
▶ Slice green onions.
▶ Prepare the sauce.

❶ Brushing the wonton edges with water.

❷ Folding the wontons and sealing the edges.

❸ The finished wontons.

STUFFED WONTONS WITH APRICOT SAUCE

Yield: 24 Pieces

Cream cheese	8 oz.	240 g
Crab meat	8 oz.	240 g
Garlic, chopped	1 tsp.	5 ml
Green onions, sliced	1 oz.	30 g
Salt and pepper	TT	TT
Worcestershire sauce	TT	TT
Sesame oil	TT	TT
Wonton skins	24	24
Apricot Sauce (recipe follows)	as needed	as needed

❶ Place the cream cheese in the bowl of a mixer and mix until soft.

❷ Add the crab meat, garlic and green onions. Season with salt and pepper, Worcestershire sauce and a drop or two of sesame oil.

❸ Place several wonton skins on a work surface. Brush the edges with water. Place 1 tablespoon (15 milliliters) of the cream cheese mixture in the center of each skin. Fold the wonton skin in half to form a triangle; seal the edges.

❹ Using the swimming method, deep-fry the wontons at 350°F (180°C) for 10 seconds. Remove the wontons, drain well and refrigerate.

❺ At service time, deep-fry the wontons at 350°F (180°C) until crisp, approximately 1 minute. Serve with Apricot Sauce.

Approximate values per piece, with sauce: **Calories** 130, **Total fat** 8 g, **Saturated fat** 2.5 g, **Cholesterol** 20 mg, **Sodium** 105 mg, **Total carbohydrates** 11 g, **Protein** 4 g

APRICOT SAUCE

Yield: 8 oz. (240 g)

Apricot preserves	8 oz.	240 g
Fresh ginger, grated	1 Tbsp.	15 ml
Dry mustard	1 tsp.	5 ml
Red wine vinegar	½ fl. oz.	15 ml

❶ Combine all ingredients and heat until the preserves melt and the flavors blend.

Approximate values per 1-oz. (30-g) serving: **Calories** 70, **Total fat** 0 g, **Saturated fat** 0 g, **Cholesterol** 0 mg, **Sodium** 10 mg, **Total carbohydrates** 19 g, **Protein** 0 g, **Claims**—fat free

Other Hot Hors d'Oeuvre

Other types of hot hors d'oeuvre include tiny red potatoes filled with sour cream and caviar or Roquefort cheese and walnuts; tiny artichoke or clam fritters or any of the hundreds of varieties of chicken wings that are seasoned or marinated, baked, fried, broiled or grilled and served with a cool and soothing or outrageously spicy sauce.

The secret is to use creativity, to keep the ingredients harmonious and, if the hors d'oeuvre are to precede dinner, not to allow them to duplicate the foods to be served or overpower them with excessively spicy flavors. Mainstays of the menu are, however, another source for interesting hors d'oeuvre. Miniature versions of main dishes such as a rich beef stew in a barquette, a cooked raviolo in tomato sauce or miniature salmon croquettes can add variety to an hors d'oeuvre assortment without taxing the kitchen staff.

SERVING HORS D'OEUVRE

Hors d'oeuvre are not served only as a precursor to dinner. At many events, the only foods served may be butlered hors d'oeuvre, an hors d'oeuvre buffet or a combination of the two. Whether the hors d'oeuvre are being served before dinner or as dinner, butler style or buffet style, they must always be attractively prepared and displayed.

All events have themes and varying degrees of formality. Long buffets with overflowing baskets of crudités and sweet potato chips with dips presented in hollowed squashes and cabbages may be appropriate for one event, whereas elegant silver trays of carefully prepared canapés passed among guests by white-gloved, tuxedoed service staff may be appropriate for another. When preparing and serving hors d'oeuvre, always keep the event's theme in mind and plan accordingly.

When choosing hors d'oeuvre, select an assortment that contrasts flavors, textures and styles. There are no limits to the variety of hors d'oeuvre that can be served, but three to four cold and three to four hot selections are sufficient for most occasions. The following is a sample selection of hot and cold hors d'oeuvre that contrast flavors, textures and styles as well as types of food.

Cold

- ▶ Canapés of smoked salmon on brioche
- ▶ Barquettes filled with Roquefort cheese and garnished with grapes
- ▶ Tiny tortilla cups filled with grilled chicken and spicy tomato salsa

Hot

- ▶ Tiny pouches of shrimp wrapped in phyllo dough (page 875)
- ▶ Stuffed mushroom caps (page 872)
- ▶ Shrimp grilled on rosemary (page 517)
- ▶ Small chèvre tarts (page 873)

Butler Service

Butler service hors d'oeuvre, or "passed" hors d'oeuvre, are presented to guests on trays by the service staff. The hors d'oeuvre can be hot or cold and should be very small to make it easier for the guests to eat them without the aid of a knife or fork. (Custom utensils such as hors d'oeuvre forks and spoons allow guests to sample one-bite appetizers while standing up.) Soups can be portioned into small cups or glasses for which no spoon is needed and passed as hors d'oeuvre.

Hot and cold hors d'oeuvre should be passed separately so that they can be kept at the correct temperatures. For a 1-hour cocktail reception before a dinner, three to five hors d'oeuvre per person is usually sufficient. If hors d'oeuvre are the only food being served, however, four to five pieces per person per hour may be more appropriate.

Buffet Service

An hors d'oeuvre buffet should be beautiful and appetizing. It may consist of a single table to serve a small group of people or several huge multilevel displays designed to feed thousands. Colors, flavors and textures must all be taken into account when planning the menu.

Both hot and cold hors d'oeuvre may be served on buffets. Hot hors d'oeuvre are often kept hot by holding them in chafing dishes. Alternatively, hot hors d'oeuvre can be displayed on trays or platters; the trays and platters, however, must be replaced frequently to ensure that the food stays hot. Cold hors d'oeuvre can be displayed on trays, mirrors, platters, baskets, leaves, papers or other serving pieces to create the desired look. Individual portions of shrimp cocktail or other appetizer can work well on buffets, especially when seating is available for guests to enjoy them.

Seared Scallops in Hors d'Oeuvre Spoons

Small Portions of Soup

Individual Servings of Beef Tenderloin and Puréed Potatoes for an Hors d'Oeuvre Buffet

Cold Canapé Presentation

Arranging Buffet Platters

When displaying hors d'oeuvre and other foods on mirrors, trays or platters, the foods should be displayed in a pattern that is pleasing to the eye and flows toward the guest or from one side to the other. An easy and attractive method for accomplishing this is to arrange the items on a mirror or tray with an attractive centerpiece. The food can be placed in parallel diagonal lines, alternating the various styles and shapes. Three alternative arrangements are shown in the following photographs. Be careful not to make the tray or mirror too fussy or cluttered, however; often the best approach is to keep it simple.

Creating interesting levels and height will also add to the visual excitement when displaying hors d'oeuvre platters.

QUESTIONS FOR DISCUSSION

1. Discuss four guidelines that should be followed when preparing hors d'oeuvre.

2. Identify and describe the three parts of a canapé.

3. Describe the differences among beluga, osetra and sevruga caviars, and explain how these differ from domestic caviars.

4. Select several recipes for sauces and fillings from other chapters in this book that would be suitable to use in the preparation of hors d'oeuvre. Describe the techniques and other ingredients you would use to adapt these recipes.

5. Create an hors d'oeuvre menu for a small cocktail party. Include three hot and three cold items and explain the reasons for your selections.

6. Discuss what is being done to protect future sturgeon fish supplies from the Caspian Sea while ensuring the world wide supply of caviar. **wWw**

Terms to Know

canapé	osetra
canapé base	sevruga
canapé spread	pressed caviar
garnish	malassol
barquette	sushi
bruschetta	sashimi
crudité	nori
caviar	brochettes
beluga	rumaki

CURRIED CHICKEN CANAPÉS

PREP CHEF, INC., PHOENIX, AZ
Chef Sidney Brodsky

Bread, thinly sliced	as needed	as needed
Chicken Curry Spread (recipe follows)	as needed	as needed
Vegetable garnishes	as desired	as desired

1 Toast the bread lightly. Top with a smooth, even layer of Chicken Curry Spread.

2 Cut the bread into the desired shapes, such as squares, circles or diamonds, being sure to wipe the knife blade clean after each cut. Garnish each canapé as desired.

CHICKEN CURRY SPREAD

Yield: 25 Servings

Chicken breasts, boneless, skinless, cooked	1 lb.	480 g
Cream of coconut	4 fl. oz.	120 ml
Mayonnaise	4 fl. oz.	120 ml
Curry powder	1½ Tbsp.	45 ml
Lemon juice	1 Tbsp.	30 ml
Salt and white pepper	TT	TT

1 Cut the chicken into small pieces and place in a food processor. Pulse until a fine texture is obtained.

2 Add the remaining ingredients and mix until blended. Refrigerate until needed, but use within 2 days.

VARIATION:

For a mixture that can be piped into barquettes or used as a garnish, process the chicken until very smooth and add 2–3 ounces (60–90 grams) plain cream cheese.

Approximate values per 1-oz. (30-g) serving: **Calories** 80, **Total fat** 6 g, **Saturated fat** 2 g, **Cholesterol** 20 mg, **Sodium** 40 mg, **Total carbohydrates** 1 g, **Protein** 6 g

BUCKWHEAT BLINI

Yield: 24 Blini

Granulated sugar	2 tsp.	10 ml
Dry yeast	¼ oz.	7 g
Milk, lukewarm	14 fl. oz.	420 ml
Buckwheat flour	4 oz.	120 g
All-purpose flour	3 oz.	90 g
Salt	½ tsp.	2 ml
Unsalted butter, melted	3 Tbsp.	45 ml
Vegetable oil	2 Tbsp.	30 ml
Egg yolks	3	3
Egg whites	2	2

1. Stir the sugar and yeast into the milk and let stand until foamy, approximately 5 minutes.
2. Whisk in the flours, salt, butter, oil and egg yolks. Beat until smooth.
3. Cover the batter and allow it to rise in a warm place until doubled, approximately 1 hour.
4. Beat the egg whites to stiff peaks, then fold them into the risen batter.
5. Lightly oil and preheat a large sauté pan. Drop 2 tablespoons (30 milliliters) of batter into the sauté pan, spacing the blini at least 1 inch (2.5 centimeters) apart. Cook until the bottom of each blini is golden, approximately 1 minute. Turn the blini and cook an additional 30 seconds. Remove from the pan and keep warm for service.

Blini may be used as a canapé base and are frequently topped with crème fraîche and garnished with caviar.

Approximate values per blini: **Calories** 70, **Total fat** 4 g, **Saturated fat** 1.5 g, **Cholesterol** 35 mg, **Sodium** 60 mg, **Total carbohydrates** 7 g, **Protein** 2 g

---

BAKED WONTON CRISPS

Yield: 64 Crisps

Wonton skins, large	16	16
Vegetable oil	6 fl. oz.	180 ml
Black sesame seeds	2 oz.	60 g
Salt and black pepper	TT	TT
Cayenne pepper	TT	TT

1. Cut the wonton skins on the diagonal to make four triangles from each sheet.
2. Brush a sheet pan with 3 fluid ounces (90 milliliters) of the oil. Position the triangles on the sheet pan. Brush the wontons with the remaining oil.
3. Sprinkle the triangles evenly with the sesame seeds, salt, black pepper and cayenne pepper. Bake in a 400°F (200°C) oven until evenly golden and crisp, approximately 8 to 10 minutes. Serve with spreads and dips such as hummus, tapenade or baba ghanoush or topped with bound salads as a canapé. Store in an airtight container for up to 1 week.

Approximate values per crisp: **Calories** 40, **Total fat** 4 g, **Saturated fat** 0 g, **Cholesterol** 0 mg, **Sodium** 60 mg, **Total carbohydrates** 7 g, **Protein** 0 g

TOSTADITAS OF GULF CRAB WITH GUACAMOLE

RDG AND BAR ANNIE, HOUSTON, TX
Chef-Owner Robert Del Grande

Yield: 36 Pieces

Gulf crab meat, fresh	1 lb.	480 g
Mayonnaise	2 Tbsp.	30 ml
Heavy cream	2 Tbsp.	30 ml
Salt	1 tsp.	5 ml
Chipotle sauce (optional)	1 Tbsp.	15 ml
Guacamole:		
Hass avocados, ripe, medium dice	2	2
White onion, minced	4 oz.	120 g
Serrano chiles, stems removed, minced	2	2
Cilantro leaves, minced	2 Tbsp.	30 ml
Olive oil	2 tsp.	10 ml
Fresh lime juice	1 tsp.	5 ml
Kosher salt	1 tsp.	5 ml
Black pepper	¼ tsp.	1 ml
Tomato, chopped	1	1
Tortilla triangles, fried crisp	36	36

1 Check the crab meat for any small pieces of shell. In a small mixing bowl, combine the mayonnaise, heavy cream, salt and chipotle sauce, if using. Mix until blended and smooth. Add the crab meat and toss to coat the crab. Do not overmix. Refrigerate until ready to use.

2 To prepare the guacamole, combine all of the guacamole ingredients except the tomato. Stir the ingredients together with a spoon to form a coarse mixture. Do not overmix; leave bits of avocado intact. At service time, stir in the tomato.

3 To serve, place a small spoonful of guacamole on each crisp tortilla chip. Top the guacamole with a small spoonful of crab meat. If desired, garnish each tostadita with a few drops of chipotle sauce.

Approximate values per piece: **Calories** 50, **Total fat** 3.5 g, **Saturated fat** 0.5 g, **Cholesterol** 10 mg, **Sodium** 180 mg, **Total carbohydrates** 2 g, **Protein** 3 g

KALAMATA OLIVE AND ASIAGO CROSTINI

LES GOURMETTES COOKING SCHOOL, PHOENIX, AZ

Barbara Fenzl, CCP

Yield: 12 Pieces

French bread	½ loaf	½ loaf
Fresh basil leaves, chopped	50	50
Tomato concassée	4 oz.	120 g
Garlic, chopped	2 tsp.	10 ml
Kalamata olives, pitted, chopped	15	15
Asiago, grated	2 oz.	60 g

1 Slice the bread ¼ inch (6 millimeters) thick.

2 Combine the remaining ingredients and mix well.

3 Spread ½ tablespoon (8 milliliters) of the mixture on each slice of bread. Place under the broiler or salamander until hot and the cheese is melted, approximately 2 minutes.

Approximate values per piece: **Calories** 60, **Total fat** 2 g, **Saturated fat** 1 g, **Cholesterol** 5 mg, **Sodium** 180 mg, **Total carbohydrates** 8 g, **Protein** 2 g, **Claims**—low fat; low cholesterol; no sugar

---

BABA GHANOUSH

Yield: Approximately 40 fl. oz. (1.2 lt)

Eggplants	3	3
Virgin olive oil	4 fl. oz.	120 ml
Salt and pepper	TT	TT
Fresh lemon juice	4 fl. oz.	120 ml
Garlic cloves	6	6
Tahini	7 oz.	210 g

1 Cut the eggplants in half and score the cut surface of each half from edge to edge in a crosshatch pattern approximately ½ inch (1.2 centimeters) deep.

2 Brush the cut surfaces with 2 fluid ounces (60 milliliters) of the oil, season with salt and pepper and place cut side down on a sheet pan. Roast in a 350°F (180°C) oven until very soft, approximately 45 minutes.

3 Cool the eggplants and scoop out the flesh. Purée the flesh in a food processor with the lemon juice, garlic, tahini, salt and pepper. Add the remaining oil and blend in. Adjust the seasonings. Serve in a bowl, drizzled with additional oil, if desired, and accompanied by pita bread or crudités.

Approximate values per 2-Tbsp. (30-ml) serving: **Calories** 60, **Total fat** 5 g, **Saturated fat** 0.5 g, **Cholesterol** 0 mg, **Sodium** 0 mg, **Total carbohydrates** 3 g, **Protein** 1 g

TAPENADE

Yield: 12 fl. oz. (360 ml)

Garlic cloves	4	4
Kalamata olives, pitted	1 pt.	480 ml
Anchovies	1 oz.	30 g
Capers	2 Tbsp.	30 ml
Fresh thyme	1 tsp.	5 ml
Fresh rosemary	1 tsp.	5 ml
Fresh oregano	1 tsp.	5 ml
Fresh lemon juice	3 Tbsp.	45 ml
Extra virgin olive oil	2 fl. oz.	60 ml

1 Place all of the ingredients in the bowl of a food processor and pulse or process until the mixture forms a coarse paste. Refrigerate.

Approximate values per tablespoon (15 ml): **Calories** 35, **Total fat** 3.5 g, **Saturated fat** 0 g, **Cholesterol** 0 mg, **Sodium** 160 mg, **Total carbohydrates** 1 g, **Protein** 0 g

MEZZE: LITTLE BITES

Mezze are small plates of assorted salads such as hummus and baba ghanoush that are served with drinks to allow guests to linger and relax before the main meal. Mezze (also spelled *meze* and *mezedes*) form part of the dining tradition in countries from North Africa, Greece and Turkey to the Middle East. Spaniards observe a similar custom. Tapas, small portions of savory foods such as shrimp in garlic sauce or deep-fried olives, are served in bars at lunch or dinner. These little bites serve two purposes; they whet the appetite and keep patrons drinking.

GUACAMOLE

Yield: Approximately 1 qt. (1 lt)

Haas avocados, ripe	6	6
Lemon juice	2½ fl. oz.	75 ml
Green onions, sliced	4 Tbsp.	60 ml
Fresh cilantro, chopped	3 Tbsp.	45 ml
Tomato, seeded, diced	3 Tbsp.	45 ml
Garlic, chopped	1 tsp.	5 ml
Dried oregano	½ tsp.	2 ml
Jalapeño, seeded, chopped	1	1
Salt	TT	TT
Tomato concassée	as needed for garnish	as needed for garnish

1 Cut each avocado in half. Remove the seed and scoop out the pulp.

2 Add the lemon juice to the avocado pulp and mix well, mashing the avocado pulp.

3 Add the remaining ingredients except the tomato concassé. Season with salt and mix well. Garnish with tomato concassée and served with assorted corn chips.

Approximate values per 2-fl.-oz. (60-ml) serving: **Calories** 120, **Total fat** 12 g, **Saturated fat** 0 g, **Cholesterol** 0 mg, **Sodium** 25 mg, **Total carbohydrates** 1 g, **Protein** 2 g, **Vitamin C** 15%, **Claims**—no saturated fat; no cholesterol; no sugar; high fiber

SPINACH AND ARTICHOKE DIP

Yield: 4 lb. 6 oz. (2 kg)

Onion, medium dice	3 oz.	90 g
Garlic, chopped	2 tsp.	10 ml
Clarified butter	1 fl. oz.	30 ml
Frozen chopped spinach, thawed	1 lb. 8 oz.	720 g
Artichoke hearts, canned, chopped coarse	1 lb.	480 g
Cream sauce	1 qt.	960 ml
Worcestershire sauce	2 tsp.	10 ml
Parmesan, grated	6 oz.	180 g
Salt and pepper	TT	TT
Tabasco sauce	TT	TT

1. Sauté the onion and garlic in the butter until tender without coloring.
2. Add the spinach and sauté until hot.
3. Add the artichoke hearts, cream sauce, Worcestershire sauce and 4 ounces (120 grams) Parmesan. Mix well.
4. Season with salt, pepper and Tabasco sauce.
5. Transfer the dip to a half-size hotel pan. Top with the remaining Parmesan and bake at 350°F (180°C) until hot and browned on top, approximately 20 minutes.

Approximate values per 2-oz. (60-g) serving: **Calories** 110, **Total fat** 6 g, **Saturated fat** 3.5 g, **Cholesterol** 15 mg, **Sodium** 250 mg, **Total carbohydrates** 8 g, **Protein** 5 g, **Vitamin A** 20%

1. Sautéing the onion, garlic and spinach.

2. Serving the dip from a chafing dish.

BRANDADE DE MORUE
(FRENCH SALT COD SPREAD)

Yield: 3 lb. (1.4 kg); 12 Servings, 4 oz. (120 g) each

Salted cod	1 lb.	480 g
Bay leaf	1	1
Fresh thyme sprig	1	1
Garlic cloves	3	3
Russet potatoes	1 lb.	480 g
Pepper	TT	TT
Olive oil	2 fl. oz.	60 ml
Milk	4 fl. oz.	120 ml
Black olives, oil-cured	3 oz.	90 g
Sautéed Garlic Croutons (recipe follows)	as needed	as needed

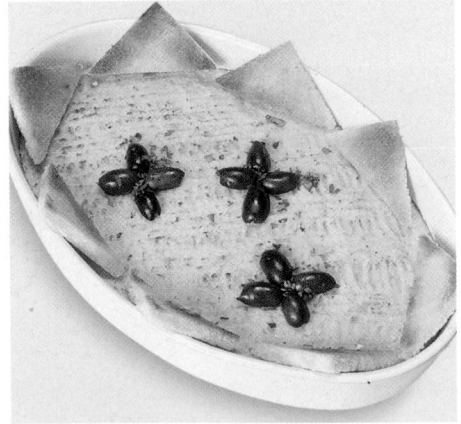

1. Rinse the cod under cold running water to remove the surface salt. Place the cod in a bowl of cold water and soak under refrigeration for 24 hours, changing the water at least once.

2. Drain the cod. Place in a saucepan and cover with cold water. Bring to a boil, drain and cover with cold water again. Add the bay leaf and thyme and bring to a simmer. Simmer the cod for 10 minutes or until it flakes easily. Drain the cod. Flake the cod into the bowl of a food processor, removing any bones or dark flesh. Add the garlic and process until the cod resembles a shaggy paste.

3. While the cod is cooking, simmer the potatoes until done. Peel them while still warm and pass them through a food mill or ricer.

4. In a mixing bowl, combine the cod and potatoes. Season with pepper and stir in the oil and milk. The mixture should resemble soft mashed potatoes. The mixture may be used immediately or refrigerated and held for up to 1 week.

5. To serve, spread the brandade mixture into a shallow casserole. Lightly score the surface in a cross-hatch pattern. Bake uncovered at 375°F (190°C) for 15 to 20 minutes or until lightly browned on top and hot. Serve garnished with black olives and Sautéed Garlic Croutons.

Approximate values per serving: **Calories** 220, **Total fat** 9 g, **Saturated fat** 1 g, **Cholesterol** 60 mg, **Sodium** 380 mg, **Total carbohydrates** 9 g, **Protein** 25 g

SAUTÉED GARLIC CROUTONS

Yield: 16 Croutons

Olive oil	1 fl. oz.	30 ml
Garlic cloves	2	2
Country bread slices, crusts removed, cut into 4 triangles	4	4

1. Heat a sauté pan and add the oil. Flatten the garlic cloves with the back of a knife and add to the oil. Cook the garlic until brown. Remove the garlic and discard.

2. Add the bread triangles to the pan and quickly toss to coat evenly with the oil.

3. Cook the croutons, browning evenly on both sides, adding a little more oil if necessary.

Approximate values per crouton: **Calories** 30, **Total fat** 2 g, **Saturated fat** 0 g, **Cholesterol** 0 mg, **Sodium** 30 mg, **Total carbohydrates** 3 g, **Protein** 0 g

DATE AND CHORIZO RUMAKI

Yield: 32 Pieces

Bacon, sliced thin	16 slices	16 slices
Chorizo (page 843)	8 oz.	240 g
Cream cheese	4 oz.	120 g
Whole dates, pitted	32	32

1. Partially cook the bacon on a sheet pan in a 350°F (180°C) oven for approximately 5 minutes.

2. Cook the chorizo to render the excess fat. If the chorizo is in links, remove the meat from the casings before cooking.

3. Remove the cooked chorizo from the pan and drain in a mesh strainer or china cap to remove excess fat. Then blend the cream cheese into the meat.

4. Cut the dates open, butterfly style. Stuff each date with a portion of the chorizo mixture.

5. Wrap each date with a half slice of bacon, securing with a toothpick.

6. Arrange the rumaki on a rack placed over a sheet pan. Bake at 350°F (180°C) until the bacon is crisp and the dates are hot, approximately 15 to 20 minutes.

Approximate values per piece: **Calories** 90, **Total fat** 5 g, **Saturated fat** 2.5 g, **Cholesterol** 15 mg, **Sodium** 150 mg, **Total carbohydrates** 7 g, **Protein** 3 g

NORIMAKI ZUSHI

Yield: 36 Pieces

Dried shiitake mushrooms	4	4
Water, hot	8 fl. oz.	240 ml
Shoyu	4 fl. oz.	120 ml
Brown sugar	1 Tbsp.	15 ml
Cucumber	½	½
Sushi-quality fish fillets such as ahi, salmon, flounder or sea bass	5 oz.	150 g
Nori	3 sheets	3 sheets
Sushi rice	18 oz.	540 g
Wasabi paste	4 Tbsp.	60 ml
Pickled ginger	2 oz.	60 g

1. Soak the mushrooms in hot water for 20 minutes. Remove the mushrooms and reserve 4 ounces (120 grams) of the liquid. Trim off the mushroom stems.
2. Julienne the mushroom caps. Combine the reserved soaking liquid with 2 tablespoons (30 milliliters) of the shoyu and the sugar. Simmer the caps in this liquid and reduce au sec. Remove from the heat and refrigerate.
3. Peel and seed the cucumber; cut it into strips the size of pencils, approximately 6 inches (15 centimeters) long.
4. Trim the fish fillets of any skin, bone, imperfections or blemishes. Cut the fillets into strips the same size as the cucumbers.
5. Cut the sheets of nori in half and place one half sheet on a napkin or bamboo rolling mat. Divide the rice into six equal portions; spread one portion over each half sheet of nori, leaving a ½-inch (1.2-centimeter) border of nori exposed.
6. Spread 1 teaspoon (5 milliliters) wasabi paste evenly on the rice.
7. Lay one-sixth of the mushrooms, cucumber and fish strips in a row down the middle of the rice.
8. Use the napkin or bamboo mat to roll the nori tightly around the rice and garnishes.
9. Slice each roll into six pieces and serve with the remaining shoyu, pickled ginger and wasabi.

Approximate values per piece: **Calories** 40, **Total fat** 0 g, **Saturated fat** 0 g, **Cholesterol** 5 mg, **Sodium** 220 mg, **Total carbohydrates** 6 g, **Protein** 2 g, **Vitamin C** 15%, **Claims**—fat free; low cholesterol; low calorie

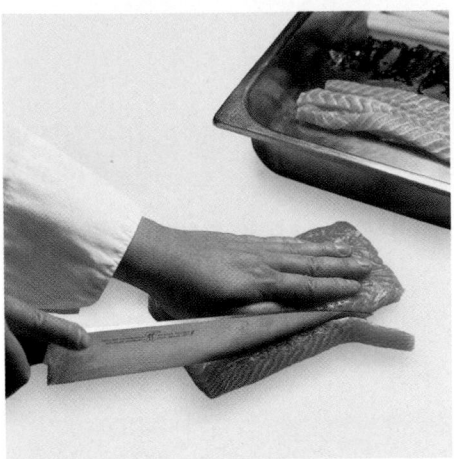

1. Preparing the garnishes for the sushi roll.

2. Spreading the rice over the nori.

3. Adding the garnishes in a row down the middle of the rice.

4. Rolling the nori around the rice and garnishes.

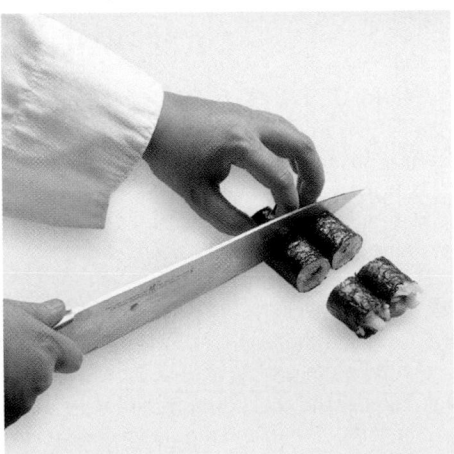

5. Slicing the roll into six pieces.

RED POTATOES WITH WALNUTS AND GORGONZOLA

Yield: 80 Pieces

New red potatoes	40	40
Salt and pepper	TT	TT
Fresh thyme	2 tsp.	10 ml
Olive oil	2 fl. oz.	60 ml
Cream cheese	8 oz.	240 g
Gorgonzola	3 oz.	90 g
Bacon, medium dice, cooked	1 oz.	30 g
Sour cream	4 oz.	120 g
Walnuts, chopped coarse	1½ oz.	45 g
Worcestershire sauce	TT	TT
Tabasco sauce	TT	TT
Chives, minced	3 Tbsp.	45 ml

1. Cut the potatoes in half and scoop out a portion of the inside with a Parisienne scoop.
2. Toss the potatoes with the salt, pepper, thyme and oil. Arrange the potatoes on a sheet pan with their flat surfaces down and bake at 400°F (200°C) until brown and cooked through, approximately 15 minutes.
3. Soften the cream cheese in the bowl of an electric mixer. Add the Gorgonzola, bacon, sour cream and walnuts. Mix until smooth. Season with the Worcestershire and Tabasco sauces.
4. Using a pastry bag and plain tip, fill each hot potato half with the cold cheese mixture and sprinkle with minced chives.

VARIATION:

Fill the cooked potatoes with crème fraîche, top with caviar and sprinkle with sliced chives instead of using the bacon-and-cheese mixture.

Approximate values per piece: **Calories** 50, **Total fat** 3 g, **Saturated fat** 1 g, **Cholesterol** 5 mg, **Sodium** 35 mg, **Total carbohydrates** 6 g, **Protein** 1 g, **Claims**—low fat; low cholesterol; low sodium; no sugar

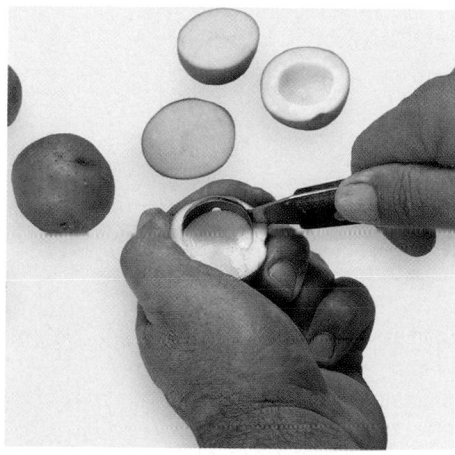

1. Scooping out the potato halves.

2. Filling the potato halves with the cheese mixture.

3. Garnishing the finished potato hors d'oeuvre.

STUFFED MUSHROOM CAPS

Yield: 48 Pieces

White mushrooms, medium	60	60
Clarified butter	2 fl. oz.	60 ml
Onion, minced	4 oz.	120 g
Flour	1 Tbsp.	15 ml
Heavy cream	4 fl. oz.	120 ml
Ham, cooked, chopped	4 oz.	120 g
Fresh parsley, chopped	2 Tbsp.	30 ml
Salt and pepper	TT	TT
Swiss cheese, shredded	2 oz.	60 g

1. Wash the mushrooms. Remove and chop the stems and 12 of the caps.
2. Sauté the whole mushroom caps in 1 ounce (30 grams) clarified butter until partially cooked but still firm. Remove from the pan and reserve.
3. Add the remaining butter to the pan. Sauté the onion and chopped mushrooms until dry.
4. Add the flour and cook for 1 minute. Add the cream; bring to a simmer and cook for 2 minutes.
5. Add the ham and parsley and season to taste with salt and pepper; stir to combine. Remove from the pan and cool slightly.
6. Stuff the mushroom caps with the ham mixture and sprinkle with shredded Swiss cheese.
7. Bake the mushrooms at 350°F (180°C) until hot, approximately 10 to 15 minutes.

Approximate values per piece: **Calories** 30, **Total fat** 2.5 g, **Saturated fat** 1.5 g, **Cholesterol** 10 mg, **Sodium** 35 mg, **Total carbohydrates** 1 g, **Protein** 1 g, **Claims**—low fat; low cholesterol; low sodium; low calorie; no sugar

ESCARGOTS IN GARLIC BUTTER

Yield: 48 Pieces

Snails, canned	48	48
Butter, softened	1 lb.	480 g
Shallots, minced	2 Tbsp.	30 ml
Garlic, chopped	2 tsp.	10 ml
Fresh parsley, chopped	3 Tbsp.	45 ml
Salt and pepper	TT	TT
Mushroom caps, medium	48	48

1. Drain and rinse the snails.
2. Combine the butter, shallots, garlic, parsley, salt and pepper in a mixer or food processor and mix or process until well blended.
3. Sauté the mushroom caps in a small amount of the garlic butter until cooked but still firm. Remove from the heat.
4. Place a snail in each cap and top with a generous amount of the garlic butter. Alternatively, place the escargots in clean shells and top each one with the garlic butter.
5. Bake the mushrooms and snails at 450°F (230°C) for 5 to 7 minutes and serve hot.

VARIATION:

Prepare 48 small bouchées from puff pastry. Sauté the snails in a generous amount of the garlic butter and place one snail in each bouchée. Drizzle the snail with the garlic butter and serve.

escargot (ays-skahr-go) French for "snail"; those used for culinary purposes are land snails (genus *Helix*); the most popular are the large Burgundy snails and the smaller but more flavorful common or garden snail known as *petit gris*

Approximate values per piece: **Calories** 63, **Total fat** 6 g, **Saturated fat** 4 g, **Cholesterol** 19 mg, **Sodium** 64 mg, **Total carbohydrates** 0.5 g, **Protein** 1 g, **Vitamin A** 6%

CHÈVRE TARTS

Yield: 12 Tarts

Tomato concassée	4 oz.	120 g
Black pepper	TT	TT
Parmesan, grated	3 oz.	90 g
Puff pastry	8 oz.	240 g
Olive oil	as needed	as needed
Pesto Sauce (page 225)	2 fl. oz.	60 ml
Goat cheese (chèvre), Montrachet style	4 oz.	120 g
Zucchini, shredded	4 oz.	120 g

> ### Latin Flavor Profile
>
> Changing the type of sauce and cheese will create a new flavor profile for this tart. Use hot salsa in place of the Pesto Sauce and queso fresco in place of the French-style goat cheese to create an appetizer suitable for a Latin-themed menu.

1 Season the tomato concassée with the pepper and sprinkle with 2 tablespoons (30 milliliters) Parmesan.

2 Roll out the puff pastry until it is approximately ¼ inch (6 millimeters) thick, then cut it into 12 circles, approximately 2½ inches (6.2 centimeters) in diameter.

3 Brush mini-muffin tins with oil and line them with the puff pastry circles.

4 Add 1 teaspoon (5 milliliters) Pesto Sauce to each tart.

5 Add ⅓ ounce (10 grams) goat cheese to each tart.

6 Add enough shredded zucchini to each tart to nearly fill it.

7 Top each tart with the tomato concassée and sprinkle with the remaining Parmesan.

8 Bake at 375°F (190°C) until the tarts are brown on top and the dough is cooked, approximately 15 to 20 minutes.

Approximate values per tart: **Calories** 210, **Total fat** 15 g, **Saturated fat** 4.5 g, **Cholesterol** 15 mg, **Sodium** 270 mg, **Total carbohydrates** 11 g, **Protein** 7 g, **Vitamin A** 20%

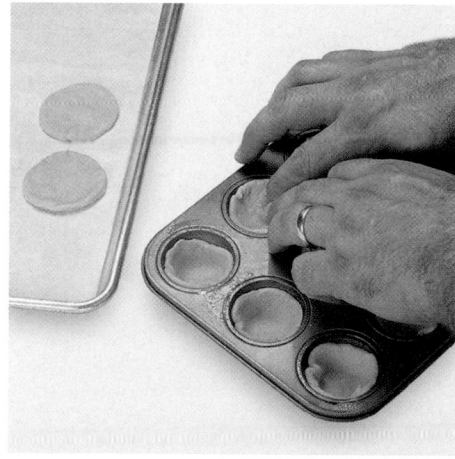

1 Lining mini-muffin tins with puff pastry dough.

2 Filling the tarts.

3 The baked tarts.

SPANAKOPITTA

Yield: 90 Pieces

Onion, small dice	4 oz.	120 g
Unsalted butter, melted	6 oz.	180 g
Fresh spinach, cooked and cooled, or frozen spinach, thawed	24 oz.	720 g
Fresh mint, chopped	1 Tbsp.	15 ml
Feta, crumbled	1 lb.	480 g
Eggs, beaten	3	3
Salt and pepper	TT	TT
Phyllo dough	1 lb.	480 g

1. Sauté the onion in 1 tablespoon (15 milliliters) butter until tender. Remove and cool.
2. Combine the cooled onion, spinach, mint, feta and eggs. Season with salt and pepper and mix well.
3. Spread one sheet of phyllo dough on the work surface; brush with melted butter. Place another sheet of phyllo on top of the first; brush it with butter. Place a third sheet of phyllo on top of the second and brush it with butter as well.
4. Cut the dough into 2-inch- (5-centimeter-) wide strips.
5. Place 1 tablespoon (15 milliliters) of the spinach mixture on the end of each strip of phyllo.
6. Starting with the end of the dough strip with the spinach mixture, fold one corner of the dough over the spinach mixture to the opposite side of the strip to form a triangle. Continue folding the dough, keeping it in a triangular shape, like folding a flag.
7. Place the phyllo triangles on a sheet pan and brush with melted butter. Bake at 375°F (190°C) until brown and crisp, approximately 20 minutes.

Approximate values per piece: **Calories** 45, **Total fat** 3 g, **Saturated fat** 2 g, **Cholesterol** 15 mg, **Sodium** 105 mg, **Total carbohydrates** 3 g, **Protein** 2 g, **Vitamin A** 8%, **Claims**—low fat; low cholesterol; no sugar

1. Stacking the layers of buttered phyllo pastry.

2. Placing the filling on the pastry.

3. Folding the pastry and filling into triangles.

SHRIMP CRUMPLE

Yield: 24 Pieces

Marinade:		
Rice vinegar	1 Tbsp.	15 ml
Cayenne pepper	TT	TT
Garlic, minced	1 tsp.	5 ml
Fresh ginger, minced	1 tsp.	5 ml
Orange juice	1 Tbsp.	15 ml
Salt and pepper	TT	TT
Fresh thyme	TT	TT
Papaya	½	½
Shrimp, 16–20 count, peeled and deveined	12	12
Phyllo dough	6 sheets	6 sheets
Whole butter, melted	as needed	as needed

1. To make the marinade, combine the vinegar, cayenne pepper, garlic, ginger and orange juice in a bowl. Stir to combine; season with salt, pepper and thyme.
2. Peel and seed the papaya and cut into medium dice. Place the papaya in a bowl and pour a small amount of marinade over it.
3. Split the shrimp and add them to the marinade.
4. Spread one sheet of phyllo dough on a work surface and brush it with butter. Lay another sheet on top of the first and brush it with butter. Place a third sheet of phyllo on top of the second and brush it with butter as well.
5. Prepare a second stack of phyllo with the three remaining sheets. Cut each stack of phyllo dough into 12 squares.
6. Place one half shrimp in the center of each square of phyllo dough and place several pieces of papaya on each shrimp. Gather the dough around the shrimp and papaya to form a small pouch.
7. Repeat with the remaining shrimp.
8. Bake the phyllo pouches at 350°F (180°C) until the phyllo is browned and the shrimp is cooked, approximately 15 to 20 minutes.

Approximate values per piece: **Calories** 60, **Total fat** 1 g, **Saturated fat** 0 g, **Cholesterol** 85 mg, **Sodium** 125 mg, **Total carbohydrates** 4 g, **Protein** 9 g, **Vitamin C** 15%

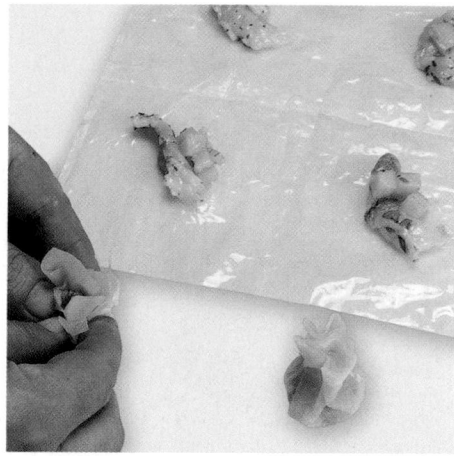

1. Forming pouches with the phyllo squares.

2. The finished hors d'oeuvre.

SAMOSAS
(DEEP-FRIED INDIAN TURNOVERS)

Yield: 30 Samosas

Pastry:		
All-purpose flour	9 oz.	270 g
Salt	1 tsp.	5 ml
Garam masala	1 tsp.	5 ml
Peppercorns, cracked	1 tsp.	5 ml
Turmeric	1 tsp.	5 ml
Vegetable oil	1½ Tbsp.	23 ml
Water, warm	7 fl. oz.	210 ml
Filling:		
Potatoes, peeled, small dice	4 oz.	120 g
Clarified butter or ghee	1 Tbsp.	15 ml
Ground lamb, lean	12 oz.	360 g
Fresh ginger juice	2 tsp.	10 ml
Garlic, minced	1 tsp.	5 ml
Onion, small dice	2 oz.	60 g
Garam masala	2 tsp.	10 ml
Chilli powder	1 tsp.	5 ml
Turmeric	1 tsp.	5 ml
Salt	1 tsp.	5 ml
Green peas	3 oz.	90 g
Fresh lemon juice	1 Tbsp.	15 ml
Fresh cilantro, chopped	2 Tbsp.	30 ml

1. In the bowl of an electric mixer fitted with a dough hook, combine the flour, salt, garam masala, peppercorns and turmeric and mix thoroughly. With the mixer at medium speed, add the oil, then add enough of the warm water to make a stiff dough. Knead the dough in the mixer until it is completely smooth and pliable. Cover the dough with a damp cloth and allow it to rest for 20 minutes.

2. Blanch the potatoes in salted water until nearly tender. Remove, refresh and reserve the potatoes.

3. Heat the clarified butter or ghee in a sauté pan and sauté the lamb until it begins to brown. Add the ginger juice, garlic and onion and sauté for approximately 5 minutes. Add the spices, salt, potatoes and peas and gently cook until the potatoes and peas are tender, approximately 5 minutes. Stir in the lemon juice and cook until the liquid evaporates. Stir in the cilantro. Transfer the filling to a sheet pan to cool completely.

4. Roll the dough into a rope and cut into 15 evenly sized pieces. Roll each piece out to a round approximately 5 inches (12 centimeters) in diameter, then cut each round in half. Place a spoonful of the filling toward one half of each piece of pastry. Run a wet finger around the edge and fold over to make a triangular pastry with one curved side. Pinch the edges together, then press the edges with the tines of a fork to seal them.

5. Using the basket method, deep-fry the turnovers at 350°F (180°C) until done, approximately 3 minutes. Drain and serve hot with chutney.

VARIATION:

Vegetarian Samosas—Omit the lamb. Add 2 ounces (60 grams) chopped unsalted peanuts and 6 ounces (180 grams) chopped mushrooms in Step 3. Increase the amount of onion to 4 ounces (120 grams).

Approximate values per samosa: **Calories** 60, **Total fat** 2 g, **Saturated fat** 0.5 g, **Cholesterol** 10 mg, **Sodium** 160 mg, **Total carbohydrates** 8 g, **Protein** 3 g

CHA GIO
(DEEP-FRIED VIETNAMESE SPRING ROLLS)

Yield: 1 lb. (480 g) Filling; approximately 32 rolls

Cellophane noodles	2 oz.	60 g
Vegetable oil	2 Tbsp.	30 ml
Garlic cloves, minced	1 Tbsp.	15 ml
Shrimp, raw, peeled, deveined and chopped	4 oz.	120 g
Pork, minced	4 oz.	120 g
Carrot, grated	1	1
Green onions, sliced	3	3
Mung bean sprouts	1 oz.	30 g
Fish sauce	2 tsp.	10 ml
Vietnamese chile sauce	1 Tbsp.	15 ml
Cornstarch	2 tsp.	10 ml
Water, cold	2 tsp.	10 ml
Spring roll wrappers	32	32

❶ Soak the cellophane noodles in boiling water for 5 minutes. Drain and cut into 1- to 2-inch (2.5- to 5-centimeter) pieces.

❷ Heat a wok or sauté pan and add the oil. Stir-fry the garlic for a few seconds. Add the shrimp and pork and stir-fry, breaking up any large lumps. Add the carrot, green onions, bean sprouts, fish sauce, chile sauce and drained noodles. Cook until the carrots are slightly softened. Remove from the heat and cool completely.

❸ Mix the cornstarch and water together in a small bowl. Moisten the spring roll wrappers with water and keep them covered with a damp towel to prevent them from drying out.

❹ Place approximately 1 tablespoon (30 milliliters) filling in the center of a wrapper. Fold the sides over toward the middle and roll up into a cigar shape. Brush the edge with the water-and-cornstarch mixture to seal.

❺ Using the swimming method, deep-fry the spring rolls at 325°F (160°C) until hot and crisp, approximately 45 seconds. Drain on absorbent paper and serve with Nuoc Cham (page 230).

Approximate values per roll: Calories 60, **Total fat** 2 g, **Saturated fat** 0 g, **Cholesterol** 10 mg, **Sodium** 70 mg, **Total carbohydrates** 7 g, **Protein** 2 g, **Vitamin A** 15%

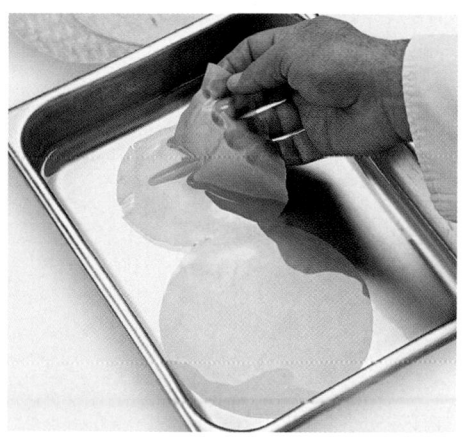

❶ Soaking the spring roll wrappers.

❷ Filling the spring roll wrappers.

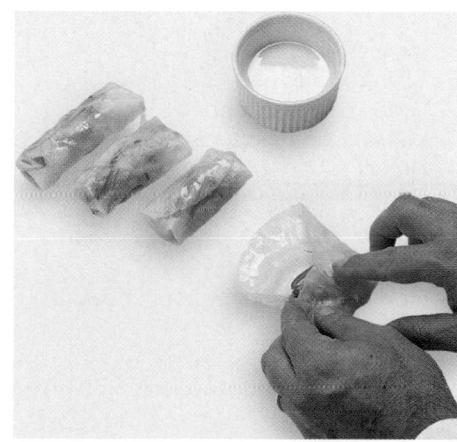

❸ Folding the wrapper around the filling.

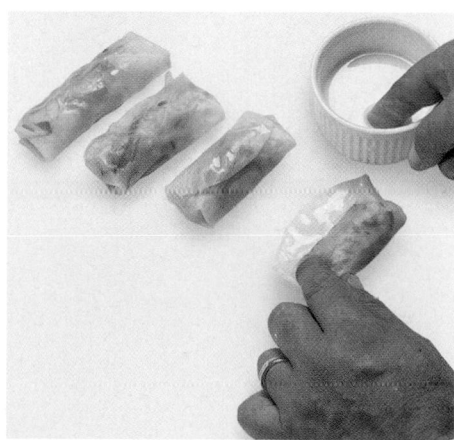

❹ Sealing the spring roll with water.

CRAB AND SOMEN SUMMER ROLLS
WITH GARLIC CILANTRO SAUCE

GROS BONNET CULINARY ACADEMY, HONOLULU, HI

Chef Craig Omori

Yield: 4 Rolls

Rice paper, large	4 sheets	4 sheets
Nori	4 sheets	4 sheets
Somen noodles, cooked	24 oz.	720 g
Imitation crab meat	8 oz.	240 g
Carrot, julienne	2 oz.	60 g
Japanese cucumber, peeled, seeded, julienne	2 oz.	60 g
Red bell pepper, julienne	2 oz.	60 g
Thai basil leaves	16	16
Mint leaves	28	28
Shiitake mushrooms, sliced thinly	8	8
Garlic Cilantro Sauce (recipe follows)	as needed	as needed

1. Soak the rice paper sheets in warm water for 10 seconds. Remove from the water and place on a damp towel and allow to rest for 1 minute.
2. Place one sheet of nori on top of the rice paper.
3. Place one-fourth of the somen noodles in a long pile along the bottom of the nori sheet. Arrange one-fourth of the crab meat, carrot, cucumber, bell pepper, basil and mint on top of the noodles.
4. Roll the rice paper around the filling like a burrito. Repeat with the remaining rice paper, nori and filling to make four rolls. Slice each roll into six slices and serve with Garlic Cilantro Sauce on the side.

Approximate values per roll: Calories 320, **Total fat** 1.5 g, **Saturated fat** 0 g, **Cholesterol** 10 mg, **Sodium** 760 mg, **Total carbohydrates** 61 g, **Protein** 15 g, **Vitamin A** 50%, **Vitamin C** 50%, **Claims—** low fat; no saturated fat; low cholesterol; good source of fiber; high in vitamins A and C

GARLIC CILANTRO SAUCE

Yield: 20 fl. oz. (600 ml)

Low-fat yogurt	1 pt.	480 g
Cilantro, chopped	3 Tbsp.	45 ml
Green onions, chopped	3 Tbsp.	45 ml
Vietnamese fish sauce	3 Tbsp.	45 ml
Honey	4 tsp.	20 ml
Garlic, chopped	2 tsp.	10 ml
Lime juice	4 tsp.	20 ml

Combine all ingredients in the bowl of a food processor and process until well blended.

Approximate values per 1-fl.-oz. (30-ml) serving: Calories 10, **Total fat** 0 g, **Saturated fat** 0 g, **Cholesterol** 0 mg, **Sodium** 110 mg, **Total carbohydrates** 2 g, **Protein** 1 g

BLUE CORN AND SHRIMP TAMALES

Yield: 16 Pieces

Fresh blue corn masa	1 lb.	480 g
Baking powder	½ tsp.	2 ml
Shortening	4 oz.	120 g
Salt	TT	TT
Onions, small dice	5 oz.	150 g
Red bell pepper, small dice	2 oz.	60 g
Green bell pepper, small dice	2 oz.	60 g
Garlic, chopped	1 tsp.	5 ml
Vegetable oil	2 Tbsp.	30 ml
Salt and pepper	TT	TT
Shrimp, 16–20 count, peeled and deveined	16	16
Dried corn husks	as needed	as needed

tamale a Mexican steamed dish consisting of seasoned meats, poultry and/or vegetables wrapped with a corn husk spread with masa

1. Combine the masa, baking powder and shortening in the bowl of an electric mixer, season with salt and mix until the masa pulls away from the sides of the bowl.

2. Sauté the onions, bell peppers and garlic in the oil until tender; season with salt and pepper. Remove from the heat and cool.

3. Cut the shrimp in half lengthwise.

4. To assemble the tamales, use a rubber spatula to spread 5 ounces (150 grams) of the masa mixture lengthwise on a 16-inch × 12-inch (40-centimeter × 30-centimeter) piece of parchment paper to form a 4-inch × 12-inch (10-centimeter × 30-centimeter) band of masa. Spread 1½ ounces (45 grams) of the vegetable mixture in a line lengthwise down the center of the masa.

5. Place eight shrimp halves, end to end, on top of each row of the vegetable mixture. Roll the parchment paper so that the masa completely encircles the shrimp and vegetable mixture. Twist the ends of the paper to seal. Repeat three more times to make four rolls. Freeze the rolls.

6. Unwrap each frozen roll and cut into four pieces. Wrap each piece tightly in dried corn husks that have been soaked in water, tying each end with thin strands of husk. Steam the tamales for 30 to 45 minutes. Allow the steamed tamales to rest for 10 minutes after cooking so that the masa becomes firm. Serve warm.

Approximate values per piece: **Calories** 280, **Total fat** 11 g, **Saturated fat** 3 g, **Cholesterol** 185 mg, **Sodium** 200 mg, **Total carbohydrates** 22 g, **Protein** 21 g, **Vitamin A** 25%, **Iron** 35%

1. Arranging the vegetables and shrimp on the masa.

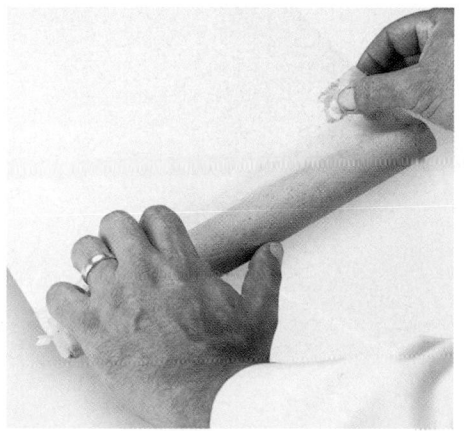

2. Rolling the tamale in parchment paper.

3. Wrapping pieces of tamale in corn husks.

CHAPTER TWENTY-NINE

PRINCIPLES OF THE BAKESHOP

FLOUR, SUGAR, EGGS, MILK, BUTTER, FLAVORINGS—with this simple list of ingredients a seemingly endless variety of sweet goods, from breads to sauces to pastries, can be made. But to produce consistently good brioche, Bavarians, biscuits or the like, careful attention must be paid to the character and quantity of each ingredient, the way the ingredients are combined and how heat is applied to them. Unlike, for example, a cut of meat that can be grilled, roasted, sautéed or braised and still be the same cut of meat, bakeshop products depend on careful, precise preparation for their very identity.

Accurate measurements are critical in the bakeshop. It is equally important to follow bakeshop **formulas** carefully and completely. Unlike other types of cooking, baking mistakes often cannot be discovered until the product is finished, by which time it is too late to correct them. For example, if salt is left out when preparing a stew, the mistake can be corrected by adding salt at service time. If salt is left out of a batch of bread dough, the mistake cannot be corrected after the bread has baked, and its texture and flavor may be ruined. It is probably more important to follow a written formula, measure ingredients precisely and combine them accurately in the bakeshop than anywhere else in the kitchen.

In order to provide a thorough introduction to the skills needed in a bakeshop, this book focuses on preparing the types of breads and desserts usually found in a small retail shop or restaurant. Because this book is not designed for large wholesale or commercial bakeries, mixes, stabilizers and mechanical preparation and shaping skills are not included.

BAKESHOP TOOLS AND EQUIPMENT

Beginning cooks may find the tools of the bakeshop a bit complex. Indeed, the tools required for a professional pâtisserie are quite specialized. A well-rounded chef need not be concerned with possessing every gadget available, but should recognize and be familiar with most of the items shown in Figure 29.1. Although many of these hand tools will make a task easier, most can be improvised by a creative chef. Several of the items shown, such as the springform pans, tartlet pans and petit four molds, are used for shaping or holding batters and doughs. The various spatulas are used for spreading icings or fillings. The piping tools and cake comb are used for decorating and finishing baked goods. When purchasing tools and equipment for the bakeshop, look for quality and durability.

Bakeshop ovens may be conventional, convection or steam injection models. Convection ovens can reduce cooking time, but the air currents may damage delicate products such as spongecake or puff pastry. Steam injection ovens use conventional heat flow but allow the baker to automatically add steam to the cooking chamber as needed to produce crisp-crusted breads. Although expensive, steam injection ovens are a necessity for commercial bakeries and most larger restaurant and hotel bakeshops. Baking instructions in the following chapters are based on the use of a conventional oven. If a convection oven is used instead, remember that the temperature and baking time may need to be reduced.

FIGURE 29.1 ▶ Bakeshop tools (clockwise from center back): cake turntable, cake pans, flan ring, tartlet pans, cannoli form, cake comb, offset spatulas, flat cake spatula, blade for scoring breads, flower nail, rectangular tartlet pans, piping bag and tips, metal spatula, dough cutter, rolling pin, springform pan, copper sugar pot (on cooling rack), nest of round cutters.

INGREDIENTS

Although substituting ingredients may have little or no effect on some dishes (carrots can be substituted for turnips in a stew, for instance), this is not the case with baked goods. Different flours, fats, liquids and sweeteners function differently. Bread flour and cake flour are not the same, nor are shortening and butter. If one ingredient is substituted for another, the results will be different.

Understanding ingredients, why they function the way they do and how to adjust for their differences will make the baking experience more successful and consistent. This chapter discusses flours, sugar and other sweeteners, fats, thickeners and flavorings such as chocolate, vanilla and nuts. Flavorings such as herbs, spices and liquors are discussed in Chapter 6, Flavors and Flavorings. Dairy products, also common in baked goods, are discussed in Chapter 7, Dairy Products, and eggs, coffee and tea are discussed in Chapter 20, Eggs and Breakfast.

Flours

Flour *provides bulk and structure* to baked goods. Some flours are *used to thicken liquids* in items such as puddings and pie fillings, or to *prevent foods from sticking during preparation and baking*. Flour is produced when grain kernels are milled or ground into a powder. Grains are grasses that bear edible seeds. Corn, rice and wheat are the most significant grains for human consumption, but the most frequently used—and therefore the most important—ingredient in the bakeshop is wheat flour.

WHEAT FLOUR

Wheat flour (Fr. *farine*) is produced by milling wheat kernels (berries). As discussed in Chapter 22, Potatoes, Grains and Pasta, a wheat kernel has an outer covering called bran. It is composed of several layers that protect the endosperm, which contains starches and proteins. The innermost part is the germ, which contains fat and serves as the wheat seed (see Figure 22.2). During milling, the kernels first pass through metal rollers to crack them, and then the bran and germ are removed through repeated stages of sifting and separation. The remaining endosperm is then ground into flour. Flour made from the portion of the endosperm closest to the germ (also known as patent flour) is finer; flour made from the portion of the endosperm nearer the bran (clear flour) is coarser and darker.

Composition of Flour

Flour consists primarily of five nutrients: fat, minerals, moisture, starches and proteins. Fat and minerals each generally account for less than 1 percent of flour's content. The moisture content of flour is also relatively low—when packaged, it cannot exceed 14 percent under government standards. But its actual moisture content varies depending on climatic conditions and storage. In damp areas, flour absorbs moisture from the atmosphere.

Starches constitute 63 to 77 percent of flour and are necessary for the absorption of moisture during baking. This process, known as gelatinization, occurs primarily at temperatures above 140°F (60°C). Starches also provide food for yeast during fermentation.

Flour proteins are of crucial importance because of their gluten-forming potential. **Gluten** is the tough, rubbery substance created when wheat flour is mixed with water. Gluten strands are both plastic (that is, they change shape under pressure) and elastic (they resume their original shape when that pressure is removed). Gluten is responsible for the volume, texture and appearance of baked goods. It provides structure and enables dough to retain the gases given off by leavening agents. Without gluten, there could be no raised breads: The gases created by yeast fermentation or chemical leaveners would simply escape if there were no network of gluten strands to trap them in the dough.

In general, the higher a flour's protein content, the greater that flour's gluten-forming potential. In some cases, however, flour with, for example, 13% protein may perform better than one with 14% protein because the proteins in the flour are of superior quality. The proteins responsible for gluten formation are *glutenin* and *gliadin*. Flour does not contain gluten; only a dough or batter can contain gluten. Gluten is produced when glutenin and gliadin are moistened and manipulated, as when they are stirred or kneaded. In order to make a chewy product such as a crusty French loaf, a flour with a high protein content must be used. Lower-protein flours are used for tender soft products such as cakes or muffins. Table 29.1 lists the protein content and uses for several common flours. Substituting one type of flour for another may be acceptable in some formulas as long as the ratio of fats, moisteners and other ingredients is adjusted accordingly. In most cases, however, substituting one type of flour for another will result in a changed and probably less desirable product.

Gluten development is affected by a number of factors, including mixing time and the presence of fat. Generally, the longer a substance is mixed, the more gluten will develop. Extreme overmixing in industrial equipment can break down the gluten structure, however. The type and balance of ingredients in a formula will also affect gluten development. Fats coat the protein in the flour, inhibiting the formation of the gluten bond. Flour needs to absorb liquid in order for the proteins to bond into gluten. Firm bread dough that can be kneaded and shaped before baking requires a high-protein flour. When this dough is made with water it will bake into a product with a solid structure. When whole milk is used in the same formula, the product will be more tender because the milkfat weakens the gluten bond.

The character of the wheat determines the character of the flour. Wheat is classified as soft or hard depending on the kernel's hardness. The harder the wheat kernel, the higher its protein content. Soft wheat yields a soft flour with a low protein content. **Soft flour**, also called **weak flour**, is best for tender products such as cakes. Hard wheat yields a

gluten an elastic network of proteins created when wheat flour is moistened and manipulated

TABLE 29.1	PROTEIN CONTENT OF FLOURS	
TYPE OF FLOUR	**PERCENT PROTEIN**	**USES**
Cake	6–8	Tender cakes
Pastry	7–9.5	Biscuits, pie crusts
All-purpose	9.5–12	General baking
Bread	11.5–14	Yeast breads
Whole-wheat	13–14	Breads
High-gluten	13.5–14.5	Bagels; used to increase protein content of weaker flour such as rye, whole-grain or specialty flours

hard flour with a high protein content. Hard flour, also known as **strong flour**, is used for yeast breads.

Various types of flour are created by mixing or blending flours from different varieties of wheat. All-purpose flour, a blend of hard and soft flours, is designed for use in a wide range of foods. It is also referred to throughout this book because it is readily available in quantities appropriate for small food service operations. Large bakeshops rarely use all-purpose flour; instead, they choose flours specifically milled and blended for specific characteristics.

Aging and Bleaching

Any flour develops better baking qualities if allowed to rest for several weeks after milling. Freshly milled flour produces sticky doughs and products with less volume than those made with aged flour. During aging, flour turns white through a natural oxidation process referred to as bleaching.

Natural aging and bleaching are somewhat unpredictable, time-consuming processes, however, so chemicals are often used to do both. Potassium bromate and chlorine dioxide gas rapidly age flour. Chlorine dioxide and other chemicals bleach flour by removing yellow pigments in order to obtain a uniform white color. Bleaching destroys small amounts of the flour's naturally occurring vitamin E. Many artisan bakers use unbleached and unbromated flours exclusively. (It should be noted, however that potassium bromate has been identified as a possible carcinogen and may not be added to flour milled and sold in Canada or Europe.)

SPECIALTY FLOURS

Whole-wheat flour is made by milling the entire wheat kernel, including the bran and nutritious germ. Whole-wheat flour has a nutty, sweet flavor and brown, flecked color. Products made with whole-wheat flour will be denser, with less volume than those made with white flour; bran particles cut through the gluten strands in the dough, resulting in a heavier crumb. Whole-wheat flour has a reduced shelf life because fats in the germ can become rancid during storage. Whole-wheat pastry and high-gluten flours are available. Though not a flour, **wheat germ** is often used in place of some flour in recipes for flavor and fiber. Wheat germ, preferably toasted, can be used in place of up to one-third of the wheat flour in a dough formula. The finished product will have a denser texture, however.

Vital wheat gluten (gluten flour) is the pure protein extracted from wheat flour. With an average protein content of 75 percent, it is used to boost the protein content of weaker flours such as rye and whole-wheat flour. It must be blended with other ingredients to form a dough or batter.

Self-rising flour is an all-purpose flour to which salt and a chemical leavener, usually baking powder, have been added. It is not recommended for professional use. Chemicals lose their leavening ability over time and may cause inconsistent results. Furthermore, different formulas call for different ratios of salt and leaveners; no commercial blend is appropriate for all purposes.

Whole-Wheat Flour

Rye Flour

Nonwheat flours, also referred to as **composite flours**, are made from grains, seeds or beans. Corn, soybeans, rice, oats, buckwheat, potatoes and other items provide flours, but none of them contain the gluten-forming proteins of wheat flour. Composite flours are generally blended with a high-protein wheat flour for baking. Substituting composite flour for wheat flour changes the flavor and texture of the product.

Rye flour is commonly used in bread baking. It is milled from the rye berry much as wheat flour is milled from the wheat berry. Rye flour comes in four grades or colors: white, medium, dark and rye meal. White rye flour is made from only the center of the rye berry. Medium and dark rye flours are made from the whole rye berry after the bran is removed and have the most intense rye flavor. Rye meal is the entire rye berry milled into a flour of different granulations, most often a coarse-textured flour. Some mills refer to their rye meal as pumpernickel flour. Others use pumpernickel to describe dark rye flour. All rye flours have a warm, pungent flavor similar to caraway and a gray-brown color. Although rye flour contains proteins, they will not form gluten, so bread made with 100% rye flour will be dense and flat. Therefore, rye flour is usually blended with a high-protein wheat flour to produce a more acceptable product.

NUTRITION

Flours are generally high in carbohydrates and low in fat. The grains from which they are milled are often rich in vitamins and minerals. Some of these nutrients, however, are lost during milling. In enriched flours, thiamin, riboflavin, niacin and iron are added at levels set by the government.

PURCHASING AND STORING

Most flours are purchased in 50- and 100-pound bags. They should be stored in a lit, ventilated room at temperatures no higher than 80°F (27°C). Flour can be stored in a refrigerator or freezer if necessary to prevent the onset of rancidity. Refrigeration may cause the flour to absorb moisture, however, which will limit the flour's ability to absorb additional moisture during actual use. An open bag of flour should be transferred to a closed container to prevent contamination. Even unopened bags of flour should not be stored near items with strong odors, as flour readily absorbs odors. Whole grains should be stored in airtight containers in cool, dry, dark conditions. Coolness inhibits insect infestations; dryness prevents mold. Using airtight containers stored in darkness helps prevent nutrient loss.

Sugar and Sweeteners

Sugar (Fr. *sucre*) and other sweeteners serve several purposes in the bakeshop: They provide flavor and color, tenderize products by weakening gluten strands, provide food for yeasts, serve as a preservative and act as a creaming or foaming agent to assist with leavening.

SUGAR

Sugars are carbohydrates. They are classified as either (1) single or simple sugars (monosaccharides), such as glucose and fructose, which occur naturally in honey and fruits, or (2) double or complex sugars (disaccharides), which may occur naturally, such as lactose in milk, or in refined sugars.

The sugar most often used in the kitchen is **sucrose**, a refined sugar obtained from both the large tropical grass called sugarcane (*Saccharum officinarum*) and the root of the sugar beet (*Beta vulgaris*). Sucrose is a disaccharide, composed of one molecule each of glucose and fructose. The chemical composition of beet and cane sugars is identical. The two products taste, look, smell and react the same. Sucrose is available in many forms: white granulated, light or dark brown granulated, molasses and powdered.

Sugar Manufacturing

Common refined or table sugar is produced from sugarcane or sugar beets. The first step in sugar production is to crush the cane or beet to extract the juice. This juice contains tannins, pigments, proteins and other undesirable components that must be removed through refinement. Refinement begins by dissolving the juice in water, then boiling it in

sucrose the chemical name for common refined sugar; it is a disaccharide, composed of one molecule each of glucose and fructose

large steam evaporators. The solution is then crystallized in heated vacuum pans. The un-crystallized liquid by-product, known as molasses, is separated out in a centrifuge. The remaining crystallized product, known as raw sugar, contains many impurities; the USDA considers it unfit for direct use in food.

Raw sugar is washed with steam to remove some of the impurities. This yields a product known as turbinado sugar. Refining continues as the turbinado is heated, liquefied, centrifuged and filtered. Chemicals may be used to bleach and purify the liquid sugar. Finally, the clear liquid sugar is recrystallized in vacuum pans as granulated white sugar.

Pure sucrose is sold in granulated and powdered forms and is available in several grades. Because there are no government standards regulating grade labels, various manufacturers' products may differ slightly.

Clockwise from top left: Demerara sugar cubes, light brown sugar, powdered sugar, sugar cubes, brown sugar crystals, granulated sugar

Types of Sugar

Turbinado sugar, sometimes called Demerara sugar, is the closest consumable product to raw sugar. It is partially refined and light brown in color, with coarse crystals and a caramel flavor. It is sometimes used in beverages and certain baked goods. Because of its high and variable moisture content, turbinado sugar is not recommended as a substitute for granulated or brown sugar.

Sanding sugar has a large, coarse crystal structure that prevents it from dissolving easily. It is used almost exclusively for decorating cookies and pastries.

Granulated sugar is the all-purpose sugar used throughout the kitchen. The crystals are a fine, uniform size suitable for a variety of purposes. **Sugar cubes** are formed by pressing moistened granulated sugar into molds and allowing it to dry. Most cubes are used for beverage service.

Brown sugar is simply regular refined cane sugar with some of the molasses returned to it. Light brown sugar contains approximately 3.5% molasses; dark brown sugar contains about 6.5%. **Molasses** adds moisture and a distinctive flavor. Brown sugar can be substituted for refined sugar, measure for measure, in any formula where its flavor is desired. Because of the added moisture, brown sugar tends to lump, trapping air into pockets. Always store brown sugar in an airtight container to prevent it from drying and hardening.

Superfine or castor sugar is granulated sugar with a smaller-sized crystal. It can be produced by processing regular granulated sugar in a food processor for a few moments. Superfine sugar dissolves quickly in liquids and produces light and tender cakes.

Powdered sugar (Fr. *sucre en poudre*) or confectioner's sugar is made by grinding granulated sugar crystals through varying degrees of fine screens. Powdered sugar cannot be made in a food processor. It is widely available in various degrees of fineness: 10X is the finest and most common; 6X and 4X are progressively coarser. Because of powdered sugar's tendency to lump, 3% cornstarch is added to absorb moisture. Powdered sugar is most often used in icings and glazes and for decorating baked products.

LIQUID SWEETENERS

Except for leavening, liquid sweeteners can be used to achieve the same benefits as sugar in baked goods. Most of these liquids have a distinctive flavor as well as sweetness. Some liquid sweeteners are made from sugarcane; others are derived from other plants, grains or bees.

Corn syrup is produced by extracting starch from corn kernels and treating it with acid or an enzyme to develop a sweet syrup. This syrup is extremely thick or viscous and less sweet tasting than honey or refined sugar. Its viscosity gives foods a thick, chewy texture. It stabilizes products made with sugar, preventing them from recrystallization. Corn syrup is available in light and dark forms; the dark syrup has caramel color and flavor added. Corn syrup is a **hygroscopic** (water-attracting) sweetener, which means it will attract water from the air on humid days and lose water through evaporation more slowly than granulated sugar. Thus, it keeps products moister and fresher longer.

Honey (Fr. *miel*) is a strong sweetener consisting of fructose and glucose. It is created by honeybees from nectar collected from flowers. Its flavor and color vary depending on the season, the type of flower the nectar came from and its age. Commercial

hygroscopic describes a food that readily absorbs moisture from the air

Honey

honey is often a blend, prepared to be relatively neutral and consistent. Like corn syrup, honey is highly hygroscopic. Its distinctive flavor is found in several ethnic foods such as baklava and halvah, and beverages such as Drambuie and Benedictine.

Maple syrup is made from the sap of sugar maple trees. Sap is collected during the spring, then boiled to evaporate its water content, yielding a sweet brown syrup. One sugar maple tree produces about 12 gallons of sap each season; 30–40 gallons of sap will produce 1 gallon of syrup. Pure maple syrup must weigh not less than 11 pounds per gallon; it is graded according to color, flavor and sugar content. The more desirable products, Grades AA and A, have a light amber color and delicate flavor. Pure maple syrup is expensive, but it does add a distinct flavor to baked goods, frostings and, of course, pancakes and waffles. Maple-flavored syrups, often served with pancakes, are usually corn syrups with artificial colorings and flavorings added.

As mentioned earlier, **molasses** (Fr. *mélasse*) is the liquid by-product of sugar refining. Edible molasses is derived only from cane sugar, as beet molasses has an unpleasant odor and bitter flavor. Unsulfured molasses is not a true by-product of sugar making. It is intentionally produced from pure cane syrup and is preferred because of its lighter color and milder flavor. Sulfured molasses is a by-product and contains some of the sulfur dioxide used in secondary sugar processing. It is darker and has a strong, bitter flavor.

The final stage of sucrose refinement yields blackstrap molasses, which is somewhat popular in the American South. Blackstrap molasses is very dark and thick, with a strong, unique flavor.

Sorghum molasses is produced by cooking down the sweet sap of a brown corn plant known as sorghum, which is grown for animal feed. The flavor and appearance of sorghum molasses are almost identical to that of unsulfured sugarcane molasses.

NUTRITION

Sweeteners are carbohydrates. They are high in calories and contain no fiber, protein, fat, vitamin A or vitamin C. They contain only trace amounts of thiamin, riboflavin and niacin.

COOKING SUGAR

Sugar can be incorporated into a prepared item in its dry form or first liquefied into a syrup. **Sugar syrups** (not to be confused with liquid sweeteners such as molasses) take two forms: **simple syrups**, which are mixtures of sugar and water, and **cooked syrups**, which are made of melted sugar cooked until it reaches a specific temperature.

Simple Sugar Syrups

Simple or stock syrups are solutions of sugar and water. They are used to moisten cakes and to make sauces, sorbets, and beverages.

The syrup's **density** or concentration is dictated by its intended purpose. Cold water will dissolve up to double its weight in sugar; heating the solution forms denser, more concentrated syrups. A hydrometer, which measures specific gravity and shows degrees of concentration on the Baumé scale, is the most accurate guide to density. The higher the number, the greater the density of the solution.

Simple syrups can be prepared without the aid of a hydrometer, however. To make a simple sugar syrup, specific amounts of water and sugar are combined in a saucepan and brought to a boil. Once the solution boils, it is important not to stir, as this may cause recrystallization or lumping. For successful simple sugar syrups, the following formulas must be followed precisely.

▶ Light syrup—Boil 2 parts water with 1 part sugar for 1 minute. This concentration would measure 17°–20° on the Baumé scale. A light syrup can be used for making sorbet or moistening spongecake.

▶ Medium syrup—Boil 1½ parts water with 1 part sugar for 1 minute. This concentration would measure 21°–24° on the Baumé scale. A medium syrup can be used for candying citrus peel.

▶ Heavy syrup—Boil equal parts water and sugar for 1 minute. This concentration would measure 28°–30° on the Baumé scale, and the solution should be at 220°F (104°C). Heavy syrup is a basic, all-purpose syrup kept on hand in many bakeshops.

Molasses

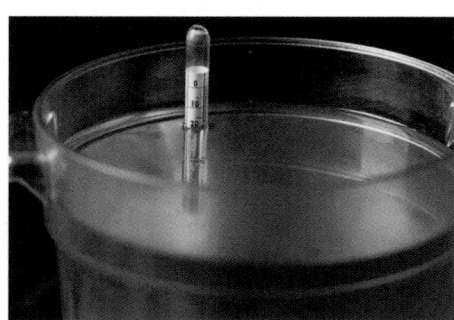

Using a Baumé hydrometer or saccharometer.

density the relationship between the mass and volume of a substance ($D = m/v$). For example, as more and more sugar is dissolved in a liquid, the heavier or denser the liquid will become. Sugar density is measured on the Baumé scale using a hydrometer or saccharometer.

Cooked Sugars

Caramel sauce, meringue, buttercream, candy and other confections often need liquid sugar that will be firm when cool or have a cooked caramel flavor. For these purposes, sugar needs to be cooked to temperatures far higher than for simple syrups. A small amount of water is generally added at the beginning to help the sugar dissolve evenly. As the mixture boils, the water evaporates, the solution's temperature rises and its density increases. The syrup's concentration depends on the amount of water remaining in the final solution: The less water, the harder the syrup will become when cool.

The sugar's temperature indicates its concentration. If a great deal of water is present, the temperature will not rise much above 212°F (100°C). As water evaporates, however, the temperature will rise until it reaches 320°F (160°C), the point at which all water is evaporated. At temperatures above 320°F (160°C), the pure sugar begins to brown or caramelize. As sugar caramelizes, its sweetening power decreases dramatically. At approximately 375°F (191°C), sugar will burn, developing a bitter flavor. If allowed to continue cooking, sugar will ignite.

Sugar solutions are unstable because of their molecular structure. They can recrystallize because of agitation or uneven heat distribution. To prevent recrystallization:

1. Always use a heavy, clean saucepan, preferably copper.
2. Stir the solution to make sure all sugar crystals dissolve before it reaches a boil. Do not stir the solution after it begins boiling, however.
3. An **interferent** may be added when the solution begins to boil. Cream of tartar, vinegar, glucose (a monosaccharide) and lemon juice are known as interferents because they interfere with the formation of sugar crystals. Some formulas specify which interferent to use, although most are used in such small quantities that their flavor cannot be detected.
4. Brush down the sides of the pan with cold water to wash off crystals that may be deposited there. These sugar crystals may seed the solution, causing more crystals (lumps) to form if not removed. Instead of using a brush to wash away crystals, the pan can be covered for a few moments as soon as the solution comes to a boil. Steam will condense on the cover and run down the sides of the pan, washing away the crystals.

The concentration of sugar syrup should be determined with a candy thermometer that measures very high temperatures. If a thermometer is not available, use the traditional but less accurate ice-water test: Spoon a few drops of the hot sugar into a bowl of very cold water. Check the hardness of the cooled sugar with your fingertips. Each stage of cooked sugar is named according to its firmness when cool—for example, soft ball or hard crack. Table 29.2 lists the various stages of cooked sugar and the temperature for each. Each stage is also identified by the ice-water test result. Note that even a few degrees makes a difference in the syrup's concentration.

Preparing cooked sugar syrups and caramel.

Brushing sugar crystals from the side of the pan.

SAFETY ALERT

Be extremely careful when working with hot sugar syrups. Because sugar can be heated to very high temperatures, these syrups can cause severe burns. Do not touch liquefied or caramelized sugar with your bare hand until it has cooled completely.

Soft ball stage.

Hard ball stage.

Hard crack stage.

TABLE 29.2	STAGES OF COOKED SUGAR	
STAGE	**TEMPERATURE**	**ICE-WATER TEST—ONE DROP**
Thread	236°F (113°C)	Spins a 2-in. (5-cm) thread when dropped
Soft ball	240°F (116°C)	Forms a soft ball
Firm ball	246°F (119°C)	Forms a firm ball
Hard ball	260°F (127°C)	Forms a hard, compact ball
Soft crack	270°F (132°C)	Separates into a hard, but not brittle, thread
Hard crack	300°F (149°C)	Separates into a hard, brittle sheet
Caramel	338°F (170°C)	Liquid turns dark brown in the pan

Fats

Fat is the general term for butter, margarine, lard, shortening and oil. Fats *provide flavor and color, add moisture and richness, assist with leavening, help extend a product's shelf life* and *shorten gluten strands*, producing tender baked goods.

The flavor and texture of a baked good depends on the type of fat used and the manner in which it is incorporated with other ingredients. In pastry doughs, solid fat shortens or tenderizes the gluten strands; in bread doughs, fat increases loaf volume and lightness; in cake batters, fat incorporates air bubbles and helps leaven the mixture. Fats should be selected based on their flavor, melting point and ability to form emulsions. See Table 29.3.

Most bakeshop ingredients combine completely with liquids; fats do not. Fats will not dissolve but will break down into smaller and smaller particles through mixing. With proper mixing, these fat particles are distributed, more or less evenly, throughout the other ingredients, causing fat and liquid to blend or emulsify.

BUTTER AND MARGARINE

Butter is prized for its flavor; however, it melts at a relatively low temperature of approximately 93°F (33°C) and burns easily. Unsalted butter is preferred for baking because it tends to be fresher, and additional salt might interfere with product formulas. Margarine melts at a slightly higher temperature than butter, making it useful for some rolled-in doughs such as puff pastry or Danish. Because they require higher temperatures to melt, margarine and other vegetable-based shortenings can leave a greasy taste on the tongue. Butter and margarine are discussed in Chapter 7, Dairy Products.

TABLE 29.3	MELTING POINT OF FATS*
Butter, whole	92°F–98°F (33°C–36°C)
Butter, clarified	92°F–98°F (33°C–36°C)
Cocoa butter	88°F–93°F (31°C–34°C)
Lard	89°F–98°F (32°C–36°C)
Margarine, solid	94°F–98°F (34°C–36°C)
Shortening, all-purpose vegetable	120°F (49°C)
Shortening, emulsified vegetable	115°F (46°C)
Shortening, heavy-duty fryer	97°F–107°F (36°F–42°C)

*The melting point of any fat depends on its specific ratio of fatty acids, its intended use and its manufacturer. Natural products such as butter and lard will vary more from one lot to the next than will manufactured products such as margarine or shortening. (This information was obtained from a variety of manufacturers and assumes that the fat is pure and previously unused.)

LARD

Lard (Fr. *saindoux*) is rendered pork fat. It is a solid white product of almost 100% pure fat; it contains only a small amount of water. Lard yields flaky, flavorful pastries, such as pie crusts, but is rarely used commercially because it turns rancid quickly.

SHORTENINGS

Any fat is a **shortening** in baking because it shortens gluten strands and tenderizes the product. What is generally referred to as shortening, however, is a type of solid, white, generally flavorless fat, specially formulated for baking. Shortenings are made from animal fats and/or vegetable oils that are solidified through hydrogenation. These products are 100% fat with a relatively high melting point. Solid all-purpose shortening is ideal for greasing baking pans because it is flavorless and odorless. When substituting shortening in a formula calling for butter, additional liquid must be added to compensate for the lack of moisture in the shortening.

Emulsifiers may be added to regular shortening to assist with moisture absorption and retention as well as leavening. **Emulsified shortenings**, also known as high-ratio shortenings, are used in the commercial production of cakes and frostings when the formula contains a large amount of sugar. If a formula calls for an emulsified shortening, use it. If you substitute any other fat, the product's texture suffers.

Lard

OIL

Unlike butter and other fats, oil blends thoroughly throughout a mixture. It therefore coats more of the proteins, and the gluten strands produced are much shorter, a desirable result in fine-textured products such as muffins or chiffon cakes. For baking, select a neutral-flavored oil unless the distinctive taste of olive oil is desired, as in some breads. Never substitute oil in a formula requiring a solid shortening. For detailed information on oil, see Chapter 6, Flavors and Flavorings.

Thickeners

STARCHES

Starches are often used as thickening agents in the bakeshop. Cornstarch, arrowroot and flour can be used as thickeners for pastry creams, sauces, custards and fruit fillings. **Cornstarch** is a grain-based starch. It must be dissolved in cold water, then added to the mixture to be thickened and then heated. Once it reaches just below the boiling point, it must be cooked until it thickens into an opaque gel. Products thickened with cornstarch should not be vigorously stirred once cooled or they can break down. Products thickened with cornstarch tend to separate when thawed after freezing.

Arrowroot is dissolved in cold water and added to a liquid to thicken it. Used primarily to thicken hot sauces, arrowroot can break down if overcooked, making it most appropriate for thickening sauces that will be served immediately.

Although less commonly encountered in professional bakeshops, tapioca can be used to thicken a variety of pastry products. **Tapioca** is a starch produced from the root of the tropical cassava (manioc) plant. It is available as a flour or as balls, referred to as pearls. Tapioca flour can be used in the same manner as cornstarch to thicken sauces and fruit mixtures. Pearl tapioca is used to thicken milk for tapioca pudding or to thicken fruit pie fillings. Most pearl tapioca must be soaked in a cold liquid for several hours before cooking. Instant tapioca, which is smaller, needs to soak for only 20 to 30 minutes before cooking.

Pearl Tapioca

GELATIN

One of the most commonly used thickeners in the bakeshop is **gelatin**, a natural product derived from collagen, an animal protein. It is available in two forms: granulated gelatin and sheet (also called leaf) gelatin. A two-step process is necessary to use either form: The gelatin must first be softened in a cold liquid, **bloomed**, then dissolved in a hot liquid.

bloom to soften granulated gelatin in a cold liquid before dissolving and using

Granulated Gelatin

Granulated gelatin is available in bulk or in ¼-ounce (7-gram) envelopes (slightly less than 1 tablespoon). One envelope is enough to set 1 pint (480 milliliters) of liquid into a firm gel for aspic or decorating, or 3 cups (720 milliliters) of liquid into a softer mousse consistency. Granulated gelatin should be softened in four times its weight of cold liquid for at least 5 minutes, then heated gently to dissolve. The initial softening in a cold liquid is necessary to separate the gelatin molecules so that they will not lump together when the hot liquid is added. Melting over a double boiler prevents scorching.

Sheet or **leaf gelatin** is available in 1-kilogram boxes, sometimes further packaged in envelopes containing five or six sheets. The sheets are produced in varying thicknesses and weights; the average weighs about ⅒ ounce (3 grams) per sheet. They must be separated and soaked in ice water until very soft, at least 15 minutes. They are then removed from the water, squeezed to remove excess moisture and stirred into a hot liquid until completely dissolved. When sheet gelatin is added to a hot liquid, it is not necessary to melt it first.

PROCEDURE FOR **USING SHEET GELATIN**

1 Gelatin sheets are submerged in ice water for several minutes to soften.

2 Softened gelatin sheets are then removed from the ice water and incorporated into a hot liquid.

SUBSTITUTING GRANULATED FOR SHEET GELATIN

Unflavored granulated and sheet gelatin can be substituted weight for weight in any recipe, but granulated gelatin must be softened or "bloomed" in a cold liquid before it is dissolved in order to avoid lumps. To calculate the amount of additional water or liquid required when substituting granulated for sheet gelatin, multiply the weight of sheet gelatin called for in the recipe by 4. Then soften the granulated gelatin in this amount of an appropriate cold liquid—water, stock or liquer, for example—before dissolving it in the hot mixture as called for in the recipe.

Granulated and sheet gelatin can be substituted weight for weight in any formula. Sheet gelatin, though more expensive, is preferred for its lack of flavor and color. It also tends to dissolve more readily and evenly and has a longer shelf life than the granulated form. Once incorporated into a product such as a Bavarian, gelatin can be frozen, or melted and reset once or twice, without a loss of thickening ability. Because it scorches easily, gelatin and mixtures containing gelatin should not be allowed to boil. Products thickened with gelatin, such as mousse or custard, can become rubbery after a few days in the refrigerator.

Flavorings

Many flavoring ingredients are used in the bakeshop. Practically any herb, spice, beverage or extract can be used to give baked goods, creams and confections their characteristic flavors. As with all baking ingredients, select flavoring components for overall quality and freshness, and combine flavorings carefully to achieve a balanced, good-tasting finished product. Recommendations for bakeshop uses for herbs and spices can be found in Chapter 6, Flavors and Flavorings.

EMULSIONS AND EXTRACTS

Emulsions and extracts are liquid flavoring agents derived from various flavoring oils (**essential oils**) taken from fruits, beans, spices or seeds.

Emulsions are flavoring oils mixed into water with the aid of emulsifiers. Lemon and orange are the most common emulsions. Emulsions are much stronger than extracts and should be used carefully and sparingly. **Extracts** are mixtures of flavoring oils or essen-

essential oils pure oils extracted from the skins, peels and other parts of plants used to give their aroma and taste to flavoring agents in foods, cosmetics and other products

tial oils and ethyl alcohol. Vanilla, almond and lemon are frequently used extracts. An extract may be made with pure flavoring oils or with artificial flavors and colors. Contents are regulated by the FDA, and package labels must indicate any artificial ingredients. Emulsions and extracts are highly volatile. They should be stored in sealed containers in a cool area away from direct light.

VANILLA

Vanilla (Fr. *vanille*) is the most frequently used flavoring in the bakeshop. It comes from the pod fruit, called a bean, of a vine in the orchid family. Vanilla beans are purchased whole, individually or by the pound. They should be soft and pliable, with a rich brown color and good aroma. The finest vanilla comes from Tahiti and Madagascar.

To use a vanilla bean, cut it open lengthwise with a paring knife. Scrape out the moist seeds with the knife's tip and stir them into the mixture being flavored. The seeds do not dissolve and will remain visible as small black or brown flecks. After all the seeds have been removed, the bean can be stored in a covered container with sugar to create vanilla sugar. Because the intensity of vanilla extract varies, it is difficult to recommend an equivalent in vanilla beans. Generally, ½ fluid ounce (15 milligrams) vanilla extract can be substituted for 1 vanilla bean; however, taste should be the ultimate guide.

Vanilla beans should be stored in an airtight container in a cool, dark place. During storage, the beans may develop a white coating. This is not mold, but rather crystals of vanilla flavor known as vanillin. It should not be removed.

Pure vanilla extract is an easy and less expensive way to give bakeshop products a true vanilla flavor. It is dark brown and aromatic, and comes in several strengths referred to as folds. The higher the number of folds, the stronger the flavor of the extract. Any product labeled "vanilla extract" must not contain artificial flavorings and must be at least 35% alcohol by volume. Vanilla extract should be stored at room temperature in a closed, opaque container. It should not be frozen.

Artificial or imitation vanilla flavoring is made with synthetic **vanillin**. Artificial flavoring is available in a clear form, which is useful for white buttercreams in which the dark brown color of pure vanilla extract would be undesirable. Although inexpensive, artificial vanilla is, at best, weaker and less aromatic than pure extract. It can also impart a chemical or bitter taste to foods.

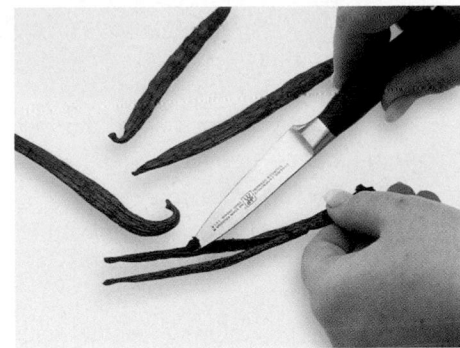

Scraping the seeds from the interior of a vanilla bean.

Chocolate

Chocolate is one of the most popular flavorings—perhaps the most popular—for candies, cookies, cakes and pastries. Chocolate is also served as a beverage and is an ingredient in the traditional spicy Mexican mole sauce. Chocolate is available in a variety of forms and degrees of sweetness.

CHOCOLATE PRODUCTION

Chocolate (Fr. *chocolat*) begins as yellow fruit pods dangling from the trunk and main branches of the tropical cacao tree. A native species of the Amazon rainforest, the cacao tree is found in the Caribbean, parts of Africa, Asia and Latin America. Each pod contains about 40 almond-sized cocoa beans. After the pods ripen, the beans are placed in the sun for several days to dry and ferment. Although time-consuming, this process helps develop the aroma and essential oils in the beans. They are then cleaned, dried, cured and roasted to develop flavor and reduce bitterness. Next, the beans are crushed to remove their shells, yielding the prized chocolate **nib**. Like coffee beans, chocolate beans are blended to the specifications of the chocolate manufacturer to obtain the desired flavor and aroma of their end product, a trade secret closely guarded unless the finest beans are used. Nibs are shipped to manufacturers worldwide where they can be further roasted. They are crushed into a thick (nonalcoholic) paste known as **chocolate liquor** or **chocolate mass**. Chocolate mass contains about 53% fat, known as **cocoa butter**. The chocolate mass is further refined depending on the desired product. If **cocoa powder** is to be produced, virtually all the cocoa butter is removed. Adding more cocoa butter, sugar, milk solids and flavorings to the chocolate mass creates a variety of other products. Most manufacturers of fine chocolates use the Swiss technique of **conching** to increase

Cocoa Beans

conching stirring melted chocolate with large stone or metal rollers to create a smooth texture in the finished chocolate

MELTING CHOCOLATE

Two important rules for melting chocolate:

❶ Chocolate must never exceed 120°F or there will be a loss of flavor.

❷ Water—even a drop in the form of steam—must never touch the chocolate.

When a droplet of water enters melted chocolate, the chocolate becomes lumpy (a process called *seizing*). There must be a minimum of 1 tablespoon water per ounce of chocolate to keep this from happening.

If seizing does occur, the addition of fat such as vegetable shortening, clarified butter, or cocoa butter will somewhat restore the chocolate to a workable condition.

For melting chocolate, unlined copper is the traditional "chocolate pot" because it is so responsive to changes in temperature.

Aluminum or heatproof glass also works well. Ideally, chocolate should be heated to 120°F, the point at which all the different fat fractions in the cocoa butter are melted.

When melting chocolate or cocoa butter, temperatures exceeding 120°F adversely affect the flavor. There are many acceptable methods for melting dark chocolate. If the heat source does not exceed 120°F it is fine to add the dark chocolate in large pieces and leave it to melt unmonitored. When the heat source is capable of bringing the chocolate over 120°F, however, the chocolate should be finely chopped or grated to ensure uniformity of melting. The chocolate must be carefully watched and stirred to avoid overheating. If using a double boiler, wa-

ter in the lower container should not exceed 140°F and the upper container should not touch the water. The chocolate should be stirred constantly.

Milk and white chocolate must always be stirred frequently while melting because they contain milk solids which seed (lump) if left undisturbed.

Remove chocolate from the heat source when it reaches 115°F as the temperature may continue to rise, and stir vigorously to prevent overheating and to distribute the cocoa butter evenly. Always melt chocolate uncovered as moisture could condense on the lid, drop back in the chocolate, and cause seizing.

—ROSE LEVY BERANBAUM, *The Cake Bible*

smoothness. Conching involves stirring large vats of blended chocolate with a heavy granite roller or paddle to smooth out sugar crystals and mellow the flavor, a process that may last from 12 hours to 3 days.

TASTING CHOCOLATES

There are three types of cocoa beans: a very hardy, abundant African variety used as a base bean, and two flavorful, aromatic varieties used for flavor. Unlike wine or coffee, it is difficult to taste processed chocolate and tell which beans were used. Most chocolates are blends, created by their manufacturer to be unique yet consistent. Varietal chocolates, those made from one type of bean grown in one specific area, have become trendy, though expensive, for both chocolate bars and baking chocolates.

Roasting greatly affects the final flavor of chocolate. Generally, German and Spanish manufacturers use a high (or strong) roast; Swiss and American makers use a low (or mild) roast.

Refining is also a matter of national taste. Swiss and German chocolate are the smoothest, followed by English chocolates. American chocolate is noticeably grainier.

Chocolate quality is actually the product of several factors besides flavor. All of the following factors should be evaluated when selecting chocolates:

❶ Appearance—color should be even and glossy, without any discoloration

❷ Smell—should be chocolatey with no off-odors or staleness

❸ Break—should snap cleanly without crumbling

❹ Texture—should melt quickly and evenly on the tongue

TYPES OF CHOCOLATE

Unsweetened chocolate is pure hardened chocolate liquor without any added sugar or milk solids. It is frequently used in baking and is sometimes referred to as "baking chocolate." Unsweetened chocolate is approximately 53% cocoa butter and 47% cocoa solids. Its flavor is pure and chocolatey, but the absence of sugar makes it virtually inedible as is.

Both **bittersweet** and **semisweet chocolates** contain at least 35% chocolate liquor plus additional cocoa butter, sugar, flavorings and sometimes emulsifiers. Generally, semisweet chocolate will be sweeter than bittersweet chocolate, but there are no precise definitions, so flavor and sweetness will vary from brand to brand. Both are excellent eating chocolates and can usually be substituted measure for measure in any formula.

Couverture (koo-vehr-TYOOR) refers to high-quality chocolate containing at least 32% cocoa butter. Professional chocolatiers generally prefer couverture chocolate, which has a higher fluidity than other chocolates when melted. It is available in a range of flavors, such as bittersweet, semisweet and milk chocolate. Couverture has a glossy appearance and can be used to create a thin, smooth coating on confections and pastries.

Government standards require that **sweet chocolate** contain not less than 15% chocolate liquor and varying amounts of sugar, milk solids, flavorings and emulsifiers. As the name implies, sweet chocolate is sweeter, and thus less chocolatey, than semisweet chocolate.

Milk chocolate is the favorite eating chocolate in the United States. It contains sugar, vanilla, perhaps other flavorings and, of course, milk solids. The milk solids that make the chocolate milder and sweeter than other chocolates also make it less suitable for baking purposes. Do not substitute milk chocolate for dark chocolate in any product that must be baked, as the milk solids tend to burn. If melted slowly and carefully, milk chocolate can be used in glazes, mousses or candies.

Chocolate chips are drops of chocolate available in count sizes from 14 to 160 per ounce (average chips are 800 to 1000 per pound). They are easy additions to cookies, muffins and cakes. Like the larger **chocolate chunks**, chips are available in many flavors including white chocolate, butterscotch, peanut butter and fruit flavors. **Pistoles** or **calets** are small round pieces of chocolate, often the finest couverture, designed to eliminate the need for chopping chocolate in the bakeshop—especially useful when tempering.

Cocoa powder is the brown powder left after the fat (cocoa butter) is removed from cocoa beans. It does not contain any sweeteners or flavorings and is used primarily in baked goods. Alkalized or Dutch-processed cocoa powder has been treated with an alkaline solution, such as potassium carbonate, to raise the powder's pH from 5.5 to 7 or 8. Alkalized powder is darker and milder than nonalkalized powder and has a reduced tendency to lump. Either can be used in baked goods, however.

Clockwise from lower left: semisweet chips, disks of chocolate liquor, block of bittersweet chocolate, block of milk chocolate, disks of white chocolate, alkalized cocoa powder

Chocolate Pistoles

Dutch-Processed Cocoa Powder (left) and American-Style Non-Alkalized Cocoa Powder

Cocoa Butter

Chocolate liquor is approximately 53% fat, known as **cocoa butter**. Cocoa butter has long been prized for its resistance to rancidity and its use as a cosmetic. Cocoa butter has a very precise melting point, just below body temperature. Fine chocolatiers use high percentages of cocoa butter to give their chocolates melt-in-the-mouth quality.

White Chocolate

This ivory-colored substance is not the product of an albino cocoa bean. It is actually a confectionery product that does not contain any chocolate solids or liquor. (Thus it is usually labeled *white confectionery* or *coating* in the United States.) The finest white chocolate couverture contains a minimum of 31% cocoa butter, a maximum of 55% sugar, 20% milk solids and vanilla or other flavors. Other products replace all or part of the cocoa butter with vegetable oils. These confectionery products will be less expensive than those containing pure cocoa butter, but their flavor and texture will be noticeably inferior. White chocolate melts at a lower temperature than dark chocolate and burns easily. It is excellent for mousses, sauces, and candy making but is less often used in baked products.

Imitation Chocolate or Chocolate-Flavored Coating

A less-expensive product substituted in many prepared foods, imitation chocolate is made with hydrogenated vegetable oils instead of cocoa butter, as little as 8% defatted cocoa powder and as much as 55% sugar, plus emulsifiers, flavorings and perhaps milk solids. The resulting product melts at a higher temperature and requires no tempering. Imitation chocolates have an inferior taste and leave a waxy feel in the mouth, though when quality

FROM CACAO TO CHOCOLATE CHIPS

To understand the history of chocolate, a chef or chocoholic must first understand the fundamental difference between its original use as a beverage and its later transformation into a candy.

The cacao tree (called *Theobroma cacao*, meaning "food of the gods") originated in the river valleys of South America and was carried into what is now Mexico by the Mayans before the seventh century A.D. It was cultivated by Mayans, Aztecs and Toltecs not only as a source of food but also as currency. Chocolate was consumed only as a treasured drink. Cacao beans were roasted, crushed to a paste and steeped in water, then thickened with corn flour to create a cold, bitter beverage. Sometimes honey, vanilla or spices, including chiles, were added. The Aztec emperor Montezuma was so enamored with the beverage that he reportedly consumed 50 cups at each meal.

Columbus brought cacao beans to Spain from his fourth voyage to the New World in 1504. (The common term *cocoa* is actually a western European mispronunciation of the proper term *cacao*, caused by confusion with another New World delicacy, the coconut.) But almost 20 years passed before Spanish conquistadors, led by Cortez, understood the beans' value. With Montezuma's encouragement, Cortez and his soldiers slowly acquired a taste for the bitter beverage, spurred on by the intoxicating effects of caffeine.

Cortez's most important contribution to the history of chocolate was to take beans with him when he left Mexico. He planted them on the islands he passed on his return to Spain: Trinidad, Haiti and Fernando Po, from which the giant African cocoa industry grew. Through Cortez's farsighted efforts, Spain controlled all aspects of the cocoa trade until well into the 18th century.

The Spanish began drinking chocolate at home during the 16th century. It was usually mixed with two other expensive imports, sugar and vanilla, and frothed with a carved wooden swizzle stick known as a *molinet*. This thick, cold drink was made from tablets of crushed cocoa beans produced and sold by monks. The Spanish believed that cocoa cured all ills and supplied limitless stamina. In the early 17th century, cocoa beverages, now served hot, crept into France via royal marriages.

Cocoa spread through the rest of Europe by different routes. The Dutch, who had poached on Spanish trade routes for many years, eventually realized the value of the unusual beans they found on Spanish ships. Holland soon became the most important cocoa port outside Spain. From there, a love of cocoa spread to Germany, Scandinavia and Italy. In 1655, England acquired Jamaica and its own cocoa plantations.

Until the Industrial Revolution, cocoa was made by hand using mortar and pestle or stone-grinding disks to crush the cocoa nibs. By the 1700s, cocoa factories had opened throughout Europe. James Baker opened the first cocoa factory in the United States in 1765.

Conrad van Houten, a Dutch chemist, patented "chocolate powder" in 1825. His work marked the beginning of a shift from drinking to eating chocolate. It also paved the way for everything we know as chocolate today. Van Houten developed a screw press that removed most of the cocoa butter from the bean, leaving a brown, flaky powder, essentially the same substance as modern cocoa powder.

Eventually, it was discovered that the extra cocoa butter resulting from the production of cocoa powder could be added to ground beans to make the paste more malleable, smoother and more tolerant of added sugar. The English firm of Fry and Sons introduced the first eating chocolate in 1847. Their recipe was the same then as today: crushed cocoa beans, cocoa butter and sugar.

In 1876, Swiss chocolatier Daniel Peter invented solid milk chocolate using the new condensed milk created by baby food manufacturer Henri Nestlé. Pennsylvania cocoa manufacturer Milton Hershey introduced his milk chocolate bars in 1894, followed by Hershey's Kisses in 1907. Nestlé Foods introduced the chocolate chip, perfect for cookies, in 1939.

Chocolate Chef, sculpted by Pastry Chef Rubin Foster

---

is no concern, they may be used in most cases when chocolate is required. Products containing imitation chocolate should be labeled "chocolate flavored."

NUTRITION

Chocolate is high in calories and fat. It contains minimal amounts of vitamin A and trace amounts of other vitamins as well as some sodium, phosphorus, potassium and other minerals.

STORING CHOCOLATE

All chocolates should be stored at a cool, consistent temperature, away from strong odors and moisture. Chocolate should never be stored under refrigeration. Dark chocolate,

TO TEMPER OR NOT TO TEMPER

The number-one mystique that surrounds chocolate has to do with tempering. From the dessert maker and pastry chef's point of view, I take a radical position: I do not think it is necessary or practical to temper. But what are we talking about anyway?

Briefly, tempering is a process of slowly raising and lowering the temperature of melted chocolate, stirring constantly, until the complex fat crystals in the cocoa butter stabilize and "behave" in concert with each other. At a cool room temperature, chocolate that has been tempered will dry rapidly to a hard and shiny piece that breaks with a snap. It shrinks slightly as it

dries, enabling it to release easily from a mold. A tempered chocolate piece keeps at room temperature for months without losing its luster or snap. Any bar of chocolate that you purchase to eat or to melt has been tempered. Once melted or exposed to heat, however, it loses its temper, though it can be retempered.

Chocolate that is melted but not tempered will dry slowly, at room temperature, to a soft, almost cakey texture. It will stick inside a mold. Untempered chocolate "blooms"—that is, it becomes dull and streaky, or it takes on a mottled appearance—unless it is refrigerated immediately.

Candy makers almost always temper the chocolate they use. But dessert chefs have little need to temper. There is no reason to temper the chocolate used in cake and torte batters, buttercreams, and most ganaches. The same is true for mousses, custards, and creams. Chocolate that will be stored in the refrigerator or consumed quickly need not be tempered. Chocolate glazes, properly handled, do not require tempering to remain shiny for the short life of the dessert.

—ALICE MEDRICH, *Cocolat: Extraordinary Chocolate Desserts*

white chocolate and cocoa powder can be kept for up to 1 year without loss of flavor. Milk chocolate will not keep as well because it contains milk solids.

Chocolate may develop grayish-white spots during storage referred to as **bloom**. Two types of bloom can develop on chocolate. **Fat bloom** occurs when cocoa butter crystals rise and crystallize on the chocolate's surface. Chocolate stored above 70°F (21°C) will develop fat bloom over time. Because fat bloom has no effect on taste, tempering the product will remedy the problem. **Sugar bloom** occurs when moisture collects on the surface of the chocolate and blends with the sugar in the chocolate, leaving a white sugar film. The result is a gritty chocolate that cannot be improved by tempering.

Nuts

Nuts (Fr. *noix*) provide texture and flavor to baked goods and are often substituted for all or part of the wheat flour in a pastry such as Linzer Tart (page 996) or a dacquoise (page 994). A nut is the edible single-seed kernel of a fruit surrounded by a hard shell. A hazelnut is an example of a true nut. The term is used more generally, however, to refer to any seed or fruit with an edible kernel in a hard shell. Walnuts and peanuts are examples of non-nut "nuts" (peanuts are legumes that grow underground; walnuts have two kernels). Nuts are high in fat, making them especially susceptible to rancidity and odor absorption. Nuts should be stored in nonmetal, airtight containers in a cool, dark place. Most nuts may be kept frozen for up to 1 year.

Nuts are often roasted in a low (275°F/135°C) oven or in a sauté pan over low heat before being used in order to heighten their flavor. Allowing roasted nuts to cool to room temperature before grinding prevents them from releasing too much oil. Some nuts such as hazelnuts, pistachios, almonds, peanuts and cashews are ground into nut butters used to flavor pastries. When sweetened, nut butter is referred to as a paste, and is used to flavor chocolates, ice creams and other baked items.

Almonds (Fr. *amandes*) are the seeds of a plumlike fruit native to western India that was first cultivated by the ancient Greeks. It is now a major commercial crop in California. Almonds are available whole, sliced, slivered or ground. Blanched almonds have had their brown, textured skins removed; natural almonds retain their skins. Unless the brown color of natural almond skin is undesirable, the two types can be used interchangeably in recipes. Almonds are frequently used in pastries and candies and are the main ingredient in almond paste and marzipan.

Almonds

Almond Paste

Brazil Nuts

Coconuts

Hazelnut Paste

coconut water the thin, slightly opaque liquid contained within a fresh coconut

coconut milk a coconut-flavored liquid made by pouring boiling water over shredded coconut; may be sweetened or unsweetened; do not substitute cream of coconut for coconut milk

coconut cream (1) a coconut-flavored liquid made like coconut milk but with less water; it is creamier and thicker than coconut milk; (2) the thick fatty portion that separates and rises to the top of canned or frozen coconut milk; do not substitute cream of coconut for true coconut cream

cream of coconut a canned commercial product consisting of thick, sweetened coconut-flavored liquid; used for baking and in beverages

Brazil nuts (Fr. *noix du Brésil*), sometimes referred to as cream nuts, are the large, oval-shaped seeds of huge trees that grow wild in the rain forests of Central and South America. Their high oil content gives them a rich, buttery flavor and a tender texture. Brazil nuts are available both in the shell and shelled, and are eaten raw, roasted, salted and in ice creams and bakery and confectionery products.

Cashews (Fr. *noix de caju*), native to the Amazon, are actually the seeds of a plant related to poison ivy. Because of toxins in the shell, cashews are always sold shelled. They are expensive and have a pronounced flavor. Cashews make a wonderful addition to cookies and candies.

Cashews

Chestnuts (Fr. *marrons*) are true nuts that must be cooked before using. Available steamed, dried, boiled or roasted, they are often sold as a canned purée, with or without added sugar. Candied or glazed chestnuts are also available. Most chestnuts are grown in Europe, primarily Italy, but new varieties are beginning to flourish in North America. Their distinctive flavor is found in many sweet dishes and pastries.

Coconuts (Fr. *noix de coco*) are the seeds from one of the largest of all fruits. They grow on the tropical coconut palm tree. The nut is a dark brown oval, covered with coarse fibers. The shell is thick and hard; inside is a layer of white, moist flesh. The interior also contains a clear liquid known as **coconut water**. (This is not the same as **coconut milk** or **coconut cream**, both of which are prepared from the flesh.) Coconut has a mild aroma, a sweet, nutty flavor and a crunchy, chewy texture. Fresh coconuts are readily available but require some effort to use. Coconut flesh is available shredded or flaked, with or without added sugar. Coconut purée is sold as a pastry ingredient and in ethnic markets. Coconut is most often used in pastries and candies and is also an important ingredient in Indian and Caribbean cuisines. A good fresh coconut should feel heavy; you should be able to hear the coconut water sloshing around inside. Avoid cracked, moist or moldy coconuts.

Chestnuts

Hazelnuts (Fr. *noisettes*) are true nuts that grow wild in the northwestern and upper midwestern states. The cultivated form, known as a filbert, is native to temperate regions throughout the Northern Hemisphere. A bit larger than the hazelnut, the filbert has a weaker flavor than its wild cousin. Both nuts look like smooth brown marbles. Filberts are more abundant, so are generally less expensive. Their distinctive flavor goes well with chocolate and coffee.

Hazelnuts

To remove the hazelnut's skin, roast whole nuts in a 275°F (135°C) oven for 12 to 15 minutes. They should give off a good aroma and just begin to darken. While they are still hot, rub the nuts in a dry towel or against a mesh sifter to remove the skin.

Hazelnut paste (Fr. *praline*) is a smooth composition made from finely ground roasted hazelnuts and sugar. It is used to flavor creams, chocolates and icings. Gianduja (zhahn-DOO-yah) refers to chocolate blended with hazelnut paste. It is used as a filling or in candies.

Macadamia nuts are small, round, creamy white nuts with a sweet, rich flavor and high fat content, native to Australia. The shell is extremely hard and must be removed by machine, so the macadamia is always sold out of the shell. Its flavor blends well with fruit, coconut and white and dark chocolate.

Macadamias

Peanuts (Fr. *arichides*), also known as groundnuts, are actually legumes that grow underground. The peanut is native to South America; it made its way into North America via Africa and the slave trade. Peanuts may be eaten raw or roasted and are available shelled or unshelled, with or without their thin red skins. Peanuts are ubiquitous ground with a bit of oil into peanut butter.

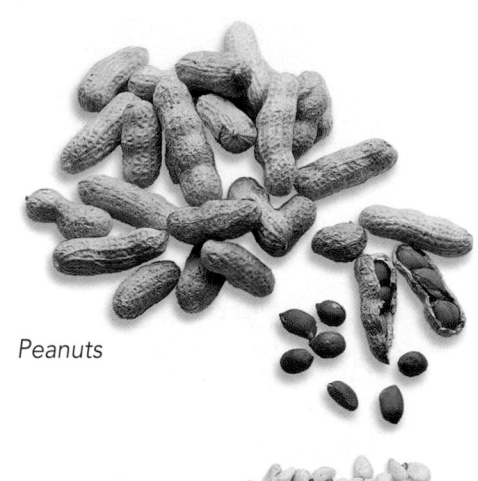

Peanuts

Pecans (Fr. *noix pacane*), native to the Mississippi River Valley, are perhaps the most popular nuts in America. Their flavor is rich and mapley and appears most often in breads, sweets and pastries. They are available whole in the shell or in various standard sizes and grades of pieces.

Pine nuts (Fr. *pignons*), also known as piñon nuts and pignole, are the seeds of several species of pine tree. The small, creamy white, teardrop-shaped nuts are commonly used in pastries from Spain, Italy and the American South-west. They are rarely chopped or ground because of their small size, and will need roasting only if being used in a dish that will not receive further cooking.

Pecans

Pistachios (Fr. *pistaches*) are native to central Asia, where they have been cultivated for more than 3000 years. California now produces most of the pistachios marketed in the United States. Pistachios are unique for the green color of their meat. When ripe, the shell opens naturally at one end, aptly referred to as "smiling," which makes shelling the nuts quite easy. Red pistachios are dyed, not natural. Pistachios are sold whole, shelled or unshelled, and are used in pastries and confections.

Pistachios

Pine Nuts

Walnuts (Fr. *noix*), relatives of the pecan, are native to Asia, Europe and North America. The black walnut, native to Appalachia, has a dark brown meat and a strong flavor. The English walnut, now grown primarily in California, has a milder flavor, is easier to shell and is less expensive. Walnuts are more popular than pecans outside the United States. They are used in baked goods and are pressed for oil.

MEASURING INGREDIENTS

The precise, accurate measurement of ingredients is extremely important for bakeshop products. As a result, baking formulas often use weight, even for liquid ingredients. Measuring ingredients by weight is more accurate, and, once the basic procedures are mastered, it will be faster than measuring by volume. It is also important to remember that most foods do not weigh their volume. In other words, 1 cup of flour equals 8 fluid ounces of flour (a measure of volume) but it does not contain 8 ounces of flour by weight. For best results, use the measurement specified in each recipe. Because accurate weights are so important, balance scales are commonly employed in the bakeshop. Procedures for using these scales are shown in Chapter 8, Mise en Place.

English Walnuts

TABLE 29.4	MIXING METHODS	
METHOD	**PURPOSE**	**EQUIPMENT**
Beating	Vigorously agitating foods to incorporate air or develop gluten	Spoon or electric mixer fitted with a paddle
Blending	Mixing two or more ingredients until evenly distributed	Spoon, rubber spatula, whisk or electric mixer fitted with a paddle
Creaming	Vigorously combining fat and sugar while incorporating air	Electric mixer fitted with a paddle on medium speed
Cutting	Incorporating solid fat into dry ingredients only until lumps of the desired size remain	Pastry cutters, fingers or electric mixer fitted with a paddle
Folding	Very gently incorporating ingredients such as whipped cream or whipped eggs with dry ingredients, a batter or cream	Rubber spatula or balloon whisk
Kneading	Working a dough to develop gluten	Hands or electric mixer fitted with a dough hook; if done by hand, the dough must be vigorously and repeatedly folded and turned in a rhythmic pattern
Sifting	Passing one or more dry ingredients through a wire mesh to remove lumps and combine and aerate	Rotary or drum sifter or mesh strainer
Stirring	Gently mixing ingredients by hand until evenly distributed and blended	Spoon, whisk or rubber spatula
Whipping	Beating vigorously to incorporate air	Whisk or electric mixer fitted with a whip

MIXING METHODS

A critical step in the production of all baked goods is the mixing of ingredients. The techniques used to mix or combine ingredients affect the baked good's final volume, appearance and texture. Mixing distributes ingredients evenly. Mixing activates the proteins in wheat flour, causing the formation of the elastic structure called gluten. Mixing incorporates air into (**aerates**) a mixture to help it rise and develop a light texture when baked. Different mixing methods ensure that ingredients are combined in the proper order to achieve the desired results.

aerate to incorporate air into a mixture through sifting and mixing

There are several mixing methods—**beating**, **blending**, **creaming**, **cutting**, **folding**, **kneading**, **sifting**, **stirring** and **whipping**. (See Table 29.4.) Learn the differences among these mixing methods, then use the designated method with the appropriate equipment or tool to ensure a good-quality finished product.

Baked goods are made from doughs and batters. A **dough** has a low water content. The water-protein complex known as gluten forms the continuous medium into which other ingredients are embedded. A dough is usually prepared by beating, blending, cutting or kneading and is often stiff enough to cut into various shapes.

A **batter** generally contains more liquids, fat, and sugar than a dough. Gluten development is minimized and liquid forms the continuous medium in which other ingredients are dispersed. A batter bakes into softer, moister products. A batter is usually prepared by blending, creaming, stirring or whipping and is generally thin enough to pour.

THE BAKING PROCESS

Many changes occur in a dough or batter as it bakes. A pourable liquid solidifies into a tender, light cake; a sticky mass becomes chewy cookies; a soft, elastic dough becomes firm, crusty French bread. These physical changes are the result of the ingredients used, the mixing methods employed and the effect of heat applied during the baking process.

TABLE 29.5	GASES THAT LEAVEN BAKED GOODS
GAS	**PRESENT IN**
Air	All products, especially those containing whipped eggs or creamed fat
Steam	All products when liquids evaporate or fats melt
Carbon dioxide	Products containing baking soda, baking powder, baking ammonia or yeast

Namely, gases form and are trapped within the dough or batter; starches, proteins and sugars cook; fats melt; moisture evaporates and staling begins.

By learning to control these changes, the student baker also learns to control the final product. Control can be exerted in the selection of ingredients and the methods by which those ingredients are combined, as well as the baking temperature and duration. Batters and dough pass through nine stages during and after the baking process.

Gases Form

A baked good's final texture is determined by the amount of leavening or rise that occurs both before and during baking. This rise is caused by the gases present in the dough or batter. These gases are carbon dioxide, air and steam. See Table 29.5. Air and carbon dioxide are present in doughs and batters before they are heated. (Air may be incorporated during the mixing process. Carbon dioxide is released as a by-product of leaveners used in the mixture.) Other gases are formed when heat is applied. For example, steam is created as the moisture in a dough is heated; yeast and baking powder rapidly release additional carbon dioxide when placed in a hot oven. These gases then expand and leaven the product. Additional information on the effects of baking powder and baking soda is found in Chapter 30, Quick Breads. Yeast is discussed in detail in Chapter 31, Yeast Breads.

Gases Are Trapped

The stretchable network of proteins created in a batter or dough, either egg proteins or gluten, traps gases in the product. Without an appropriate network of proteins, the gases would just escape without causing the mixture to rise.

Starches Gelatinize

Starches are complex carbohydrates present in plants and grains such as potatoes, wheat, rice and corn. Flour made from these and other grains is the primary ingredient in most baked goods. When starch granules in a batter or dough reach a temperature of approximately 140°F (60°C), they absorb additional moisture—up to 10 times their own weight—and expand. This contributes to the baked good's structure. (See Figure 9.3.)

Proteins Coagulate

Gluten and dairy and egg proteins begin to coagulate (solidify) when the dough or batter reaches a temperature of 160°F (71°C). This process provides most of the baked good's structure. (See Figure 9.2.)

Proper baking temperatures are important for controlling the point at which proteins coagulate. If the temperature is too high, proteins will solidify before the gases in the product have expanded fully, resulting in a product with poor texture and volume. If the temperature is too low, gases will escape before the proteins coagulate, resulting in a product that may collapse.

Fats Melt

As fats melt, steam is released and fat droplets are dispersed throughout the product. These fat droplets coat the starch (flour) granules, thus moistening and tenderizing the product by keeping the gluten strands short. Shortenings melt at different temperatures. It is important to select a fat with the proper melting point for the product being prepared.

Water Evaporates

Throughout the baking process, the water contained in the liquid ingredients will turn to steam and evaporate. This steam is a useful leavener. As steam is released, the dough or batter dries out starting from the outside, and the result is the formation of a crust.

Sugars Caramelize

As sugars are heated above 320°F (160°C), they caramelize, adding flavor and causing the product to darken. Caramelization of sugars is responsible for most of the flavors associated with baked goods. Because high temperatures are required for caramelization, most foods will brown only on the outside and only through the application of dry heat. (See Chapter 9, Principles of Cooking.)

Carryover Baking

The physical changes in a baked good do not stop when it is removed from the oven. The residual heat contained in the hot baking pan and within the product itself continues the baking process as the product cools. This is why a crisp-style cookie or biscuit may be soft and seem a bit underbaked when removed from the oven; it will finish baking as it cools.

Staling

Staling is a change in a baked good's texture and aroma caused by both moisture loss and changes in the structure of the starch granules. Stale products have lost their fresh aroma and are firmer, drier and more crumbly than fresh goods.

Staling is not just a general loss of moisture into the atmosphere; it is also a change in the location and distribution of water molecules within the product. This process, known as **starch retrogradation**, occurs as starch molecules cool, becoming more dense and expelling moisture.

In breads, this moisture migrates from the interior to the drier crust, causing the crust to become tough and leathery. If the product is not well wrapped, moisture will escape completely into the surrounding air. In humid conditions, unwrapped bread crusts absorb moisture from the atmosphere, resulting in the same loss of crispness. The flavor and texture of breads can be revived by reheating them to approximately 140°F (60°C), the temperature at which starch gelatinization occurs. Usually, products can be reheated only once without causing additional quality loss.

The retrogradation process is temperature dependent. It occurs most rapidly at temperatures of approximately 40°F (4°C). Therefore, baked products should not be refrigerated unless they contain perishable components such as cream fillings. It is better to store products frozen or at room temperature, as long as food safety is not of concern.

Products containing fats and sugars, which retain moisture, tend to stay fresh longer. Commercial bakeries usually add chemical emulsifiers, modified shortening or special sweeteners to retard staling, but these additives are not as practical for small-scale production.

starch retrogradation the process whereby starch molecules in a batter or dough lose moisture after baking; the result is baked goods that are dry or stale

1 What is the importance of protein in flour for bread making? Name the general types of flours available and their different uses in the bakeshop.

2 Discuss the four functions of sugar and sweeteners in baked goods.

3 Many varieties of fat and shortening are available to today's baker and pastry chef. Discuss which fats are preferred for various bakeshop applications.

4 Use the Internet to locate a U.S. producer of European-style pastry ingredients. What type of flavorings and nut products do they produce and market? **WWW**

5 Discuss the various mixing methods and the tools used.

6 What elements in baked goods make them rise?

7 List and describe the nine steps in the baking process.

8 Explain what process causes staling. List the ways to minimize staling of breads and cakes.

Terms to Know

formula
patent flour
gluten
soft flour
hard flour
bleached flour
wheat germ
vital wheat
  gluten
composite flours
sugarcane
molasses
hygroscopic
hydrometer
simple syrup

interferent
sheet (leaf)
  gelatin
emulsion
extract
vanillin
nib
chocolate liquor
chocolate mass
cocoa butter
couverture
fat bloom
sugar bloom
gianduja

CHAPTER THIRTY

QUICK BREADS

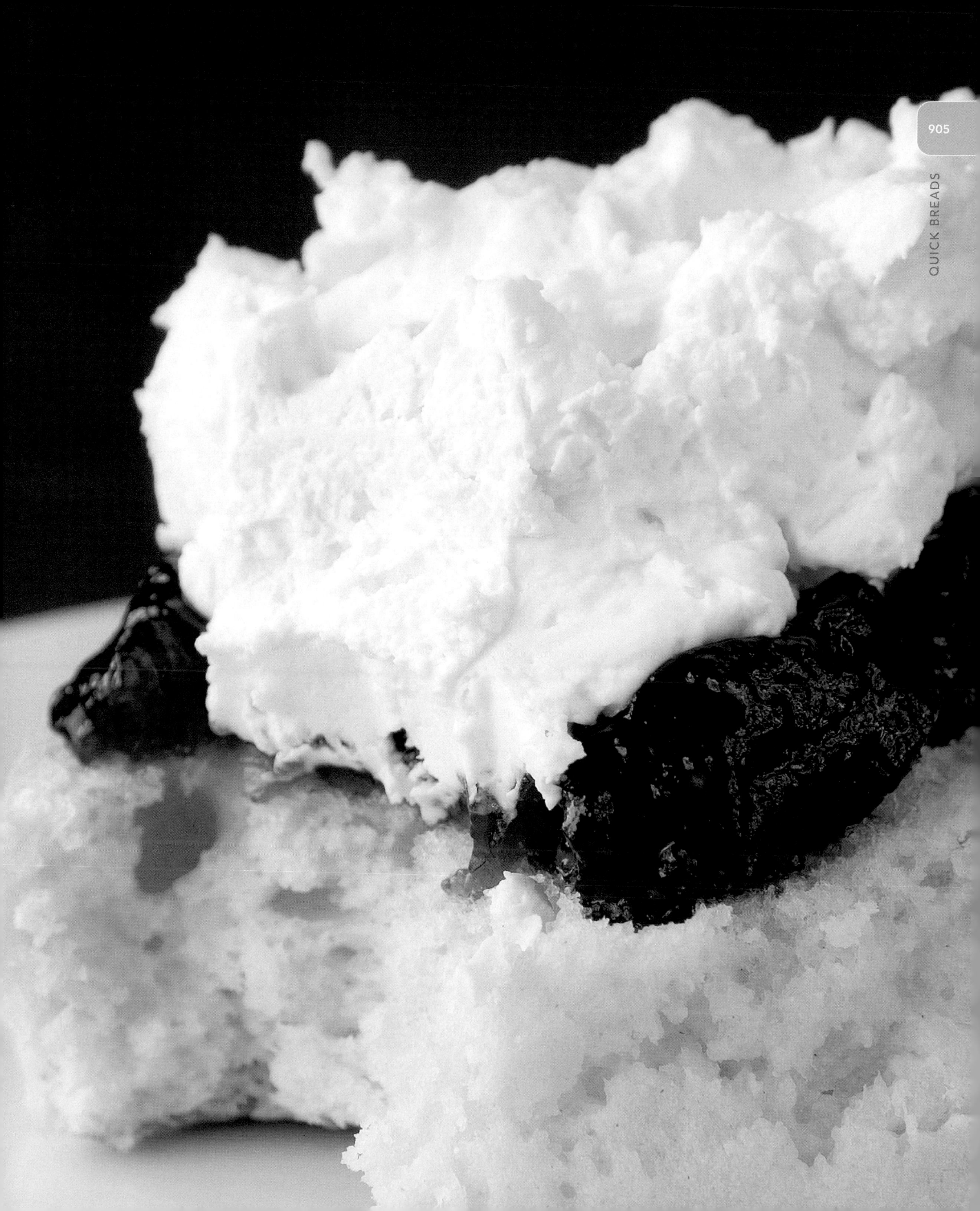

- use chemical leavening agents properly
- prepare a variety of quick breads using the biscuit method, muffin method and creaming method
- prepare a variety of griddlecakes, pancakes and waffles

BUTTERMILK BISCUITS, BLUEBERRY MUFFINS, BANANA NUT bread and currant scones are all quick breads. Why they are called quick breads is obvious: They are quick to make and quick to bake. With only a few basic ingredients and no yeast, almost any food service operation can provide its customers with fresh muffins, biscuits, scones and loaf breads.

The variety of ingredients is virtually limitless: cornmeal, whole wheat, fruits, nuts, spices and vegetables all yield popular products. And the use of these products is not limited to breakfast service—they are equally appropriate for lunch, snacks and buffets. In this chapter we look at these basic quick breads as well as recipes for griddlecakes such as pancakes and waffles.

CHEMICAL LEAVENING AGENTS

Quick breads are made with chemical leavening agents, principally baking soda and baking powder. This sets them apart from breads that are made with yeast and require additional time for fermentation and proofing, as discussed in Chapter 31, Yeast Breads. Understanding how chemical leavening agents operate is essential to successfully producing quick breads.

Chemical leavening agents release gases (primarily carbon dioxide) through chemical reactions between acids and bases contained in the recipe. These gases form bubbles or air pockets throughout the dough or batter. As the product bakes, these gases expand, causing the product to rise. The proteins in the dough or batter then set around these air pockets, giving the quick bread its rise and texture.

Baking Soda

Sodium bicarbonate ($NaHCO_3$) is more commonly known as household baking soda. Baking soda is an alkaline compound (a base), which releases carbon dioxide gas (CO_2) if both an acid and moisture are present. Heat is not necessary for this reaction to occur. Therefore, products made with baking soda must be baked at once, before the carbon dioxide has a chance to escape from the batter or dough.

Acids commonly used with baking soda are buttermilk, sour cream, lemon juice, honey, molasses and fruits high in acid such as citrus. Generally, the amount of baking soda used in a recipe is only the amount necessary to neutralize the acids present. If more leavening action is needed, baking powder, not more baking soda, should be used. Too much baking soda causes the product to taste soapy or bitter; it may also cause a yellow color and brown spots to develop.

Baking Powder

Baking powder is a mixture of sodium bicarbonate and one or more acids, generally cream of tartar ($KHC_4H_4O_6$) and/or sodium aluminum sulfate ($Na_2SO_4 \cdot Al_2[SO_4]_3$). Baking powder also contains a starch to prevent lumping and balance the chemical reactions. Because baking powder contains both the acid and the base necessary for the desired chemical reaction, the quick-bread recipe does not need to contain any acid. Only moisture is necessary to induce the release of gases.

There are two types of baking powder: single-acting and double-acting. An excess of either type produces undesirable flavors, textures and colors in baked products.

Single-acting baking powder requires only the presence of moisture to start releasing gas. The eggs, milk, water or other liquids in the recipe supply this moisture. As with baking soda, products using single-acting baking powder must be baked immediately.

Double-acting baking powder is more popular. With double-acting baking powder, there is a small release of gas on contact with moisture and a second, stronger release of gas when heat is applied. Products made with double-acting baking powder need not be baked immediately, but can sit for a short time without loss of leavening ability. All recipes in this book rely on double-acting baking powder.

Both baking soda and baking powder are sometimes used in one recipe. This is because baking soda can release CO_2 only to the extent that there is also an acid present in the recipe. If the soda/acid reaction alone is insufficient to leaven the product, baking powder is needed for additional leavening.

Baking Ammonia

Baking ammonia (ammonia bicarbonate or ammonia carbonate) is also used as a leavening agent and to add crispness in some baked goods, primarily cookies and crackers. Baking ammonia releases ammonia and carbon dioxide very rapidly when heated. The strong odor it releases as it bakes dissipates once the product is cooked above 140°F (60°C). It is suitable for low-moisture products with large surface areas that are baked at high temperatures, such as crackers and biscotti. Consequently, it is rarely used in quick breads.

Purchasing and Storing

Purchase chemical leaveners in the smallest unit appropriate for the style of the operation. Although a large can of baking powder may cost less than several small ones, if not used promptly the contents of a larger container can deteriorate, causing waste or unusable baked goods.

Chemical leavening agents should always be kept tightly covered. Not only is there a risk of contamination if left open, but they can also absorb moisture from the air and lose their effectiveness. They should be stored in a cool place, as heat deteriorates them. A properly stored and unopened container of baking powder or baking soda has a shelf life of several years.

MIXING METHODS

Quick breads are generally mixed by the **biscuit method**, the **muffin method** or the **creaming method**. The mixing method employed is directly related to the type and consistency of fat used in the recipe. Cold solid fats, such as butter, lard or vegetable shortening, are used in the biscuit method to produce flaky products. Fats that are soft but not liquid are used in the high-fat creaming method. Liquid fats, such as oil or melted butter, are used in the muffin method to produce very moist, tender products. See Table 30.1.

Quick breads are tender products with a soft **crumb**. To keep gluten development to a minimum, flour is mixed into quick breads swiftly and gently.

Biscuit Method

The biscuit method is used for biscuits, shortcakes and scones and is very similar to the technique used to make flaky pie doughs. The goal is to create a baked good that is light, flaky and tender.

TABLE 30.1	QUICK-BREAD MIXING TECHNIQUES	
MIXING TECHNIQUE	**FAT**	**RESULT**
Biscuit method	Solid (chilled)	Flaky dough
Muffin method	Liquid (oil or melted butter)	Soft, tender, cakelike texture
Creaming method	Softened (room temperature)	Rich, tender, cakelike texture

BISCUITS AND SCONES: A GENEALOGY

Biscuit is a French word used to describe any dry, flat cake, whether sweet or savory. It was, perhaps, originally coined to describe twice-baked cakes (*bis* = twice, *cuit* = cooked). Crusader chronicles, for example, mention soldiers eating a "bread called 'bequis' because it is cooked twice" and still today the Reims biscuit is returned to the oven for further baking after it is removed from its tin.

Over the centuries, the French began to use the term *biscuit* generically and appended modifiers to identify the particular type of dry, flat cake. For example, a *biscuit de guerre* was the very hard, barely risen product of flour and water used from the time of the Crusades to the era of Louis XIV as an army ration (*guerre* is French for "war"); *biscuit de Savoie* is a savory spongecake; *biscuit de pâtisserie* is a sweet biscuit.

To the British, a biscuit is what Americans call a cracker or cookie. Yet there appears to be no British quick bread quite comparable to the American biscuit—the closest relative would be the scone. But because a scone contains eggs and butter, it is much richer than a biscuit.

Elizabeth Alston, in *Biscuits and Scones*, proposes that the biscuit is an American variant of the scone. She theorizes that early British colonists in America brought with them traditional scone recipes. Unable to find or afford the necessary fresh butter and eggs, these practical bakers substituted lard and omitted the eggs. What they created, however, were not mock scones, but rather a new product, different from scones but still delicious. Alston further speculates that French cooks initially called the new American product "biscuit de something" and eventually dropped the "de something."

crumb the interior of bread or cake; may be elastic, aerated, fine grained or coarse grained

PROCEDURE FOR **PREPARING PRODUCTS WITH THE BISCUIT METHOD**

make-up the cutting, shaping and forming of dough products before baking

1. Measure all ingredients.
2. Sift the dry ingredients together.
3. Cut in the fat, which should be in a solid form.
4. Combine the liquid ingredients, including any eggs.
5. Add the liquid ingredients to the dry ingredients. Mix just until the ingredients are combined. Do not overmix, as this causes toughness and inhibits the product's rise.
6. Place the dough on the bench and knead it lightly 10 or 15 times (approximately 20 to 30 seconds). The dough should be soft and slightly elastic, but not sticky. Too much kneading toughens the biscuits. Use a slow speed and a short mixing time when kneading biscuit dough in a mixer.
7. The dough is now ready for **make-up** and baking.

MAKE-UP OF BISCUIT-METHOD PRODUCTS

1. Roll out the dough on a floured surface to a thickness of ½ to ¾ inch (1.2 to 1.8 centimeters). Be careful to roll it evenly. Biscuits should double in height during baking.
2. Cut into the desired shapes. Cut straight down; do not twist the cutters, as this inhibits rise. Space cuts as close together as possible to minimize scraps.
3. Position the biscuits on a lightly greased or paper-lined sheet pan. If placed with sides nearly touching, the biscuits will rise higher and have softer sides. Place farther apart for crusty sides.
4. Reworking and rerolling the dough may cause tough, misshapen biscuits. Nevertheless, it may be possible to reroll scraps once by pressing the dough together gently without kneading.
5. Tops may be brushed with egg wash before baking or with melted butter after baking. Bake immediately in a hot oven.
6. Cool the finished products on a wire rack.

COUNTRY BISCUITS

MISE EN PLACE

- ▶ Line sheet pan with parchment paper.
- ▶ Preheat oven to 425°F (220°C).

1. Sifting the dry ingredients together.

Yield: 36 Biscuits, 2¼ oz. (66 g) each **Method:** Biscuit

All-purpose flour	2 lb. 8 oz.	1.2 kg
Salt	¾ oz.	24 g
Granulated sugar	2 oz.	60 g
Baking powder	2 oz.	60 g
Unsalted butter, cold	14 oz.	420 g
Milk	24 fl. oz.	720 ml

1. Sift the dry ingredients together, making sure they are blended thoroughly.
2. Cut in the butter. The mixture should look mealy; do not overmix.
3. Add the milk and stir, combining only until the mixture holds together.
4. Transfer the dough to a lightly floured work surface; knead until it forms one mass, approximately five or six kneadings.
5. Roll out the dough to a thickness of ½ inch (1.2 centimeters). Cut with a floured cutter and place the biscuits on a paper-lined sheet pan.

❷ Cutting in the fat.

❸ Kneading the dough.

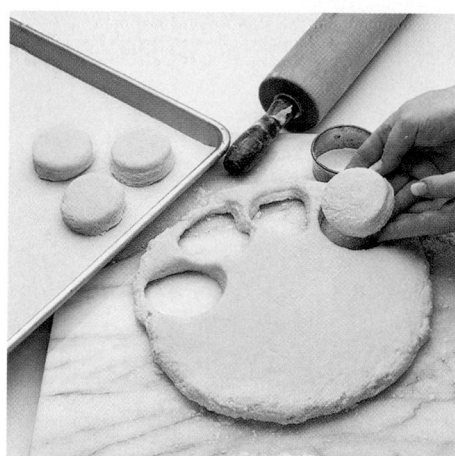

❹ Cutting the biscuits.

❻ Bake at 425°F (220°C) until the tops are light brown, the sides almost white and the interiors still moist, approximately 10 to 12 minutes. Internal heat will continue to cook the biscuits after they are removed from the oven.

❼ Remove the biscuits to a wire rack to cool.

Approximate values per biscuit: **Calories** 210, **Total fat** 10 g, **Saturated fat** 6 g, **Cholesterol** 25 mg, **Sodium** 240 mg, **Total carbohydrates** 27 g, **Protein** 4 g, **Vitamin A** 10%

Muffin Method

Muffins are any small, cakelike baked good made in a muffin tin (pan). Batters for muffins and loaf quick breads are generally interchangeable. For example, banana muffin batter may be baked in a loaf pan, provided the baking time is altered.

When preparing baked goods by the muffin method, the goal is to produce a tender product with an even shape and an even distribution of fruits, nuts or other ingredients. The most frequent problem encountered with muffin-method products is overmixing. This causes toughness and may cause holes to form inside the baked product, a condition known as **tunneling**, illustrated in Figure 30.1.

tunneling large tubular holes in muffins and cakes, a defect caused by improper mixing

FIGURE 30.1 ▶ Properly mixed corn muffins (left) rise evenly and show no signs of tunneling. Improperly mixed corn muffins (right) rise unevenly and have large irregular holes.

PROCEDURE FOR **PREPARING PRODUCTS WITH THE MUFFIN METHOD**

1. Measure all ingredients.
2. Sift the dry ingredients together.
3. Combine the liquid ingredients, including melted fat or oil. Melted butter or shortening may resolidify when combined with the other liquids; this is not a cause for concern.
4. Add the liquid ingredients to the dry ingredients and stir just until combined. Do not overmix. The batter will be lumpy.
5. The batter is now ready for make-up and baking.

MAKE-UP OF MUFFIN-METHOD PRODUCTS

1. Muffin pans and loaf pans should be greased with butter, shortening or commercial pan grease. Paper liners may be used and will prevent sticking if the batter contains fruits or vegetables. Paper liners, however, inhibit rise.
2. A portion scoop is a useful tool for ensuring uniform-sized muffins. Be careful not to drip or spill batter onto the edge of the muffin cups; it will burn and cause sticking.
3. Allow muffins and loaf breads to cool for several minutes before attempting to remove them from the pan.
4. Cool the finished products on a wire rack.

BLUEBERRY MUFFINS

MISE EN PLACE

▶ Preheat oven to 350°F (180°C).
▶ Melt butter.
▶ Grease or line muffin cups.

Yield: 12 Muffins, 2½ oz. (75 g) each   **Method:** Muffin

All-purpose flour	8 oz.	240 g
Granulated sugar	5 oz.	150 g
Baking powder	2 tsp.	10 ml
Salt	¼ tsp.	1 ml
Eggs	2	2
Milk	8 fl. oz.	240 ml
Unsalted butter, melted	2 oz.	60 g
Vanilla extract	1 tsp.	5 ml
Blueberries	5 oz.	150 g
Lemon zest	1 Tbsp.	15 ml

1. Sift together the dry ingredients (flour, sugar, baking powder, salt).
2. Stir together the liquid ingredients (eggs, milk, melted butter, vanilla extract).
3. Stir the liquid mixture into the dry ingredients. Do not overmix. The batter should be lumpy.
4. Gently fold in the blueberries and lemon zest.
5. Portion into greased or paper-lined muffin cups and bake at 350°F (180°C) until light brown and set in the center, approximately 18 minutes.
6. Cool the muffins in the pan for several minutes before removing.

VARIATIONS:

Cranberry Orange Muffins—Substitute fresh orange zest for the lemon zest and 4 ounces (120 grams) dried cranberries for the blueberries.

Pecan Spice Muffins—Omit the blueberries and lemon zest. Add 4 ounces (120 grams) chopped pecans, ½ teaspoon (2 milliliters) cinnamon and ¼ teaspoon (1 milliliter) each nutmeg and ground ginger to the batter.

Approximate values per muffin: **Calories** 180, **Total fat** 6 g, **Saturated fat** 3 g, **Cholesterol** 50 mg, **Sodium** 150 mg, **Total carbohydrates** 29 g, **Protein** 4 g

❶ Combining the liquid ingredients.

❷ Folding in the blueberries.

❸ Portioning the batter.

Creaming Method

The creaming method is comparable to the mixing method used for many butter cakes. In fact, many butter cake recipes may be baked in muffin pans and served as muffins. The softened fat and granulated sugar should be properly creamed to incorporate air, which will help leaven the product as it bakes. The final product will be cakelike, with a fine texture. There is less danger of overmixing with this method because the higher fat content shortens gluten strands and tenderizes the batter.

PROCEDURE FOR **PREPARING PRODUCTS WITH THE CREAMING METHOD**

❶ Measure all ingredients.

❷ Sift the dry ingredients together.

❸ Combine the softened fat and sugar in a mixer bowl. Cream on low speed until the color lightens and the mixture fluffs.

❹ Add eggs gradually, mixing well.

❺ Add the dry and liquid ingredients to the creamed fat alternately. In other words, a portion of the flour is added to the fat and incorporated, then a portion of the liquid is added and incorporated. These steps are repeated until all the liquid and dry ingredients are incorporated. By adding the liquid and dry ingredients alternately, you avoid overmixing the batter and prevent the butter and sugar mixture from curdling.

❻ The batter is now ready for make-up and baking. Panning and baking procedures are the same as those for quick breads prepared with the muffin method.

SOUR CREAM MUFFINS

MISE EN PLACE

▶ Allow butter and eggs to come to room temperature.
▶ Preheat oven to 350°F (180°C).
▶ Grease or line muffin cups.

Yield: 12 Muffins, 3¼ oz. (100 g) each   **Method:** Creaming

Unsalted butter, room temperature	8 oz.	240 g
Granulated sugar	8 oz.	240 g
Eggs, lightly beaten	2	2
All-purpose flour	10 oz.	300 g
Baking powder	1 tsp.	5 ml
Baking soda	1 tsp.	5 ml
Salt	1 tsp.	5 ml
Sour cream	10 oz.	300 g
Vanilla extract	1 tsp.	5 ml

1. Cream the butter and sugar until light and fluffy. Stir the eggs in one at a time.
2. Sift the dry ingredients together.
3. Stir the dry ingredients and sour cream, alternately, into the butter mixture in three additions. Stir in the vanilla extract.
4. Portion the batter into greased muffin cups and bake at 350°F (180°C) until light brown and set, approximately 20 minutes.
5. Allow the muffins to cool briefly in the pan before removing.

VARIATIONS:

Sour cream muffins can be topped with **streusel** or flavored with a wide variety of fruits or nuts by adding approximately 4–6 ounces (20–180 grams) fresh or frozen drained fruit to the batter. Blueberries, dried cherries, candied fruits, pecans and diced pears yield popular products. To make basic spice muffins, add ½ teaspoon (2 milliliters) each of cinnamon and nutmeg.

Approximate values per muffin: **Calories** 290, **Total fat** 17 g, **Saturated fat** 10 g, **Cholesterol** 70 mg, **Sodium** 260 mg, **Total carbohydrates** 31 g, **Protein** 4 g, **Vitamin A** 15%

streusel a crumbly mixture of fat, flour, sugar and sometimes nuts and spices, used to top baked goods

1. Creaming the butter and sugar.

2. Adding the sour cream.

3. Topping the muffins with the streusel.

STREUSEL TOPPING

Yield: 4 lb. 11 oz. (2.25 kg)

All-purpose flour	2 lb.	960 g
Cinnamon, ground	2 tsp.	10 ml
Salt	2 tsp.	10 ml
Brown sugar	11 oz.	330 g
Granulated sugar	8 oz.	240 g
Whole butter, cold	1 lb. 8 oz.	720 g

1 Combine the dry ingredients. Cut in the butter until the mixture is coarse and crumbly.

2 Sprinkle on top of muffins or quick breads before baking. Streusel topping will keep for several weeks under refrigeration and may be frozen for longer storage. There is no need to thaw before use.

Approximate values per 1-oz. (30-g) serving: **Calories** 190, **Total fat** 8 g, **Saturated fat** 5 g, **Cholesterol** 20 mg, **Sodium** 45 mg, **Total carbohydrates** 29 g, **Protein** 2 g

---

TABLE 30.2   TROUBLESHOOTING CHART FOR MUFFINS

PROBLEM	CAUSE	SOLUTION
Soapy or bitter flavor	Chemical leaveners not properly mixed into batter	Sift chemicals with dry ingredients
	Too much baking soda	Adjust recipe
Elongated holes (tunneling)	Overmixing	Do not mix until smooth; mix only until moistened
Crust too thick	Too much sugar	Adjust recipe
	Oven temperature too low	Adjust oven
Flat top with only a small peak in center	Oven temperature too low	Adjust oven
Cracked, uneven top	Oven temperature too high	Adjust oven
No rise; dense product	Old batter	Bake promptly
	Damaged leavening agents	Store new chemicals properly
	Overmixing	Do not overmix

---

1 Name two chemical leavening agents and explain how they cause batters and doughs to rise. Describe the purpose of leavening agents in baked goods. Explain why baking soda is used with an acid in baked goods.

2 List three common methods used for mixing quick breads. What is the significance of the type of fat used for each of these mixing methods?

3 What is the most likely explanation for discolored and bitter-tasting biscuits? What is the solution?

4 What happens when muffin batter has been overmixed?

5 Visit the Web sites for King Arthur Flour and White Lily Foods to learn more about the varieties of flours and flavoring ingredients that are available for use in biscuits and muffins. What are each of these companies famous for? How do the products of these two regional flour manufacturers differ? **WWW**

QUESTIONS FOR DISCUSSION

Terms to Know

sodium bicarbonate	base
single-acting baking powder	baking ammonia
	biscuit method
double-acting baking powder	muffin method
	creaming method
acid	

CREAM SCONES

Yield: 24 Scones, 1½ oz. (45 g) each

Method: Biscuit

All-purpose flour	1 lb.	480 g
Granulated sugar	1½ oz.	45 g
Baking powder	1 Tbsp.	15 ml
Baking soda	1 tsp.	5 ml
Salt	1 tsp.	5 ml
Unsalted butter, cold	4 oz.	120 g
Egg yolks	2	2
Half-and-half	11 fl. oz.	330 ml

1. Combine all ingredients using the biscuit method.
2. Roll out the dough to a thickness of approximately ½ inch (1.2 centimeters). Cut as desired.
3. Bake at 400°F (200°C) for approximately 10 minutes.
4. Brush the tops with butter while hot.

VARIATIONS:

Add ½ cup (125 milliliters) raisins, sultanas or currants to the dry ingredients.

Approximate values per scone: **Calories** 130, **Total fat** 6 g, **Saturated fat** 3.5 g, **Cholesterol** 35 mg, **Sodium** 160 mg, **Total carbohydrates** 17 g, **Protein** 3 g

SHORTCAKES

Yield: Approximately 48 Pieces, 2¾ oz. (83 g) each

Method: Biscuit

All-purpose flour	4 lb.	1.9 kg
Baking powder	3¾ oz.	115 g
Salt	2 tsp.	10 ml
Granulated sugar	13 oz.	390 g
Unsalted butter, cold	1 lb. 12 oz.	840 g
Eggs	7	7
Milk	18 fl. oz.	540 ml
Whole butter, melted	as needed	as needed
Granulated sugar	as needed	as needed

1. Combine ingredients using the biscuit method.
2. Cut into 3-inch (7.5-centimeter) circles and space 2 inches (5 centimeters) apart on a paper-lined sheet pan.
3. Bake at 400°F (200°C) until lightly browned, approximately 15 to 18 minutes.
4. Remove from the oven and brush the tops with melted butter, then sprinkle with granulated sugar.

Approximate values per 2¾-oz. (83-g) serving: **Calories** 310, **Total fat** 15 g, **Saturated fat** 9 g, **Cholesterol** 65 mg, **Sodium** 250 mg, **Total carbohydrates** 38 g, **Protein** 5 g, **Vitamin A** 15%

SWEET POTATO BISCUITS

SULLIVAN UNIVERSITY, NATIONAL CENTER FOR HOSPITALITY STUDIES, LOUISVILLE, KY

Chef Sam Mudd

Yield: 48 Biscuits, 2½ in. (6 cm) each   **Method:** Biscuit

Sweet potatoes	4 lb.	1.9 kg
High-gluten flour	20 oz.	600 g
Cake flour	13 oz.	390 g
Salt	4½ tsp.	23 ml
Baking powder	4 Tbsp.	60 ml
All-purpose shortening	8 oz.	240 mg
Light brown sugar, packed	8 oz.	240 g
Cinnamon, ground	1 Tbsp.	15 ml
Nutmeg, ground	1 tsp.	5 ml
Cloves, ground	½ tsp.	2 ml
Allspice, ground	¼ tsp.	1 ml
Buttermilk	1 qt.	960 ml
Eggs	2	2
Milk	4 fl. oz.	120 ml
Unsalted butter, softened	2 oz.	60 g
Honey	1 oz.	30 g

1. Peel the sweet potatoes and cut into large pieces. Steam until tender, mash or pass through a food mill and spread onto a parchment-lined sheet pan. Cool completely.

2. In a mixing bowl, sift together the flours, salt and baking powder. Cut the shortening into the dry ingredients until the mixture resembles coarse meal.

3. In a separate mixing bowl, combine the sweet potatoes, sugar, cinnamon, nutmeg, cloves and allspice.

4. Work the sweet potato mixture into the flour mixture until combined. Add 28 fluid ounces (840 milliliters) buttermilk. Mix to form a soft dough. The consistency will depend on the moisture content of the sweet potatoes. Add the remaining buttermilk if necessary.

5. Allow the dough to rest for 5 minutes.

6. Dust the work surface with high-gluten flour. Roll out the dough to a thickness of ½ inch (1.2 centimeters). Cut to the desired size with a floured cutter and place on a paper-lined sheet pan.

7. Make an egg wash with the eggs and milk and brush the tops of the biscuits. Bake at 400°F (200°C) for 12 to 15 minutes.

8. Combine the softened butter and the honey. Remove the biscuits from the oven when done and immediately brush with the honey butter.

Approximate values per serving: **Calories** 180, **Total fat** 7 g, **Saturated fat** 2 g, **Cholesterol** 10 mg, **Sodium** 380 mg, **Total carbohydrates** 26 g, **Protein** 4 g, **Vitamin A** 90%

BASIC BERRY MUFFINS

STOUFFER STANFORD COURT HOTEL, SAN FRANCISCO, CA

Former Executive Chef Ercolino Crugnale

Yield: 60 Muffins, 2½ oz. (75 g) each   **Method:** Muffin

Eggs	8	8
Heavy cream	1 qt.	960 ml
Lemon zest, finely grated	from 2 lemons	from 2 lemons
Nutmeg, ground	¼ tsp.	1 ml
Granulated sugar	1 lb. 4 oz.	600 g
Baking powder	6 Tbsp.	90 ml
Cake flour	3 lb.	1.4 kg
Kosher salt	1 Tbsp.	15 ml
Berries or nuts*	1–1½ lb.	480–720 g
Unsalted butter, melted	1 lb.	480 g

1. Whisk the eggs, cream and zest together by hand.
2. Sift the dry ingredients together. Add the berries or nuts, tossing to coat them evenly with the flour mixture.
3. Add the dry ingredients to the egg mixture and stir until about two-thirds mixed. Add the melted butter and finish mixing.
4. Portion into greased muffin tins and bake at 375°F (190°C) for approximately 15 to 18 minutes.

*Blueberries, blackberries, raspberries, chopped pecans or walnuts may be used, as desired.

Approximate values per muffin: **Calories** 260, **Total fat** 13 g, **Saturated fat** 8 g, **Cholesterol** 70 mg, **Sodium** 135 mg, **Total carbohydrates** 31 g, **Protein** 3 g, **Vitamin A** 15%, **Claims**—low sodium

MORNING GLORY MUFFINS

Yield: 18 Large Muffins, 5 oz. (150 g) each   **Method:** Muffin

All-purpose flour	1 lb.	480 g
Granulated sugar	18 oz.	540 g
Baking soda	4 tsp.	20 ml
Salt	1 Tbsp.	15 ml
Cinnamon, ground	4 tsp.	20 ml
Carrots, grated	14 oz.	420 g
Raisins	6 oz.	180 g
Pecan pieces	4 oz.	120 g
Coconut, shredded	4 oz.	120 g
Apple, unpeeled, grated	6 oz.	180 g
Eggs	6	6
Corn oil	10½ fl. oz.	315 ml
Vanilla extract	4 tsp.	20 ml

1. Sift the dry ingredients together and set aside.
2. Combine the carrots, raisins, pecans, coconut and apple.
3. Whisk together the eggs, oil and vanilla extract.
4. Toss the carrot mixture into the dry ingredients. Then add the liquid ingredients, stirring just until combined.
5. Bake in well-greased muffin tins at 350°F (180°C) until done, approximately 25 minutes.

Approximate values per muffin: **Calories** 520, **Total fat** 27 g, **Saturated fat** 5 g, **Cholesterol** 70 mg, **Sodium** 310 mg, **Total carbohydrates** 63 g, **Protein** 6 g, **Vitamin A** 45%, **Claims**—good source of fiber

BASIC BRAN MUFFINS

Yield: 24 Muffins, 2 oz. (60 g) each   **Method:** Muffin

Toasted wheat bran	6 oz.	180 g
All-purpose flour	12 oz.	360 g
Granulated sugar	4 oz.	120 g
Baking powder	4 tsp.	20 ml
Salt	1 tsp.	5 ml
Milk	12 fl. oz.	360 ml
Honey	3 oz.	90 g
Molasses	3 oz.	90 g
Eggs	2	2
Vanilla extract	1 tsp.	5 ml
Unsalted butter, melted	4 oz.	120 g

1. Combine all ingredients using the muffin method. Allow the batter to rest at least 30 minutes or up to 36 hours in the refrigerator.
2. Scoop into greased or paper-lined muffin tins. Bake at 350°F (180°C) until lightly brown and firm, approximately 20 minutes.

VARIATIONS:

Up to 6 ounces (180 grams) raisins or chopped nuts may be added to the batter if desired.

Approximate values per muffin: **Calories** 170, **Total fat** 5 g, **Saturated fat** 2.5 g, **Cholesterol** 30 mg, **Sodium** 110 mg, **Total carbohydrates** 26 g, **Protein** 4 g, **Claims**—low sodium; good source of fiber

PUMPKIN MUFFINS

Yield: 29 Muffins, approximately 4½ oz. (135 g) each   **Method:** Muffin

All-purpose flour	1 lb. 10 oz.	780 g
Baking soda	1½ tsp.	8 ml
Baking powder	1 Tbsp.	15 ml
Cinnamon, ground	2 tsp.	10 ml
Cloves, ground	1 tsp.	5 ml
Ginger, ground	2 tsp.	10 ml
Cardamom, ground	½ tsp.	2 ml
Eggs	8	8
Granulated sugar	2 lb. 10 oz.	1.2 kg
Vegetable oil	8 fl. oz.	240 ml
Salt	2½ tsp.	12 ml
Pumpkin purée	2 lb.	960 g
Orange juice	12 fl. oz.	360 ml
Streusel (optional; page 913)	as needed	as needed

1. Sift together the dry ingredients and set aside.
2. Whip the eggs in a mixer fitted with the whip attachment until well beaten. Add the sugar, oil and salt and whip for 5 minutes on medium speed. Add the pumpkin purée and mix until combined. Add the dry ingredients and mix until well blended. Pour in the orange juice and mix until smooth.
3. Scale the batter into greased and paper-lined muffin tins or paper baking cups approximately three-quarters full. Sprinkle with streusel, if using.
4. Bake at 400°F (200°C) until the muffins bounce back when lightly pressed, approximately 18 to 22 minutes.

Approximate values per muffin: **Calories** 360, **Total fat** 10 g, **Saturated fat** 1.5 g, **Cholesterol** 55 mg, **Sodium** 380 mg, **Total carbohydrates** 65 g, **Protein** 5 g, **Vitamin A** 100%

LEMON POPPY SEED MUFFINS

Yield: 48 Muffins, 2¾ oz. (83 g) each   **Method:** Creaming

Pastry flour	2 lb.	960 g
Bread flour	8 oz.	240 g
Baking soda	1 tsp.	5 ml
Baking powder	1 Tbsp.	15 ml
Poppy seeds	3 oz.	90 g
Unsalted butter, room temperature	1 lb.	480 g
Granulated sugar	1 lb. 10 oz.	780 g
Glucose or honey	4 fl. oz.	120 g
Olive oil	4 fl. oz.	120 ml
Eggs	12	12
Salt	2 tsp.	10 ml
Vanilla extract	1 fl. oz.	30 ml
Lemon zest, grated	1 Tbsp.	15 g
Sour cream	1 pt.	480 ml
Powdered sugar	as needed	as needed

1. Sift together the flours, baking soda and baking powder. Stir in the poppy seeds and set aside.
2. Using a mixer fitted with the paddle attachment, cream the butter until lump-free and fluffy. Add the sugar, glucose or honey and oil and blend until light.
3. Gradually add the eggs followed by the salt, vanilla extract, lemon zest and sour cream. Then stir in the sifted dry ingredients.
4. Portion the batter into 5-ounce (150-gram) portions using a scale or #6 scoop and place in greased or paper-lined muffin tins.
5. Bake at 425°F (220°C) until the centers of the muffins bounce back when lightly pressed, approximately 15 to 18 minutes. Dust muffins with powdered sugar.

Approximate values per muffin: **Calories** 580, **Total fat** 29 g, **Saturated fat** 14 g, **Cholesterol** 155 mg, **Sodium** 310 mg, **Total carbohydrates** 72 g, **Protein** 9 g, **Vitamin A** 15%, **Vitamin C** 15%

IRISH SODA BREAD

Yield: 1 Round Loaf, 8 in. (20 cm)   **Method:** Muffin

Currants	2 oz.	60 g
Irish whiskey	1½ fl. oz.	45 ml
All-purpose flour, sifted	12 oz.	360 g
Salt	1 tsp.	5 ml
Baking powder	1½ tsp.	7 ml
Baking soda	1 tsp.	5 ml
Brown sugar	1 Tbsp.	15 ml
Low-fat buttermilk	1 pt.	480 ml

1. Soak the currants in the whiskey until plump, at least 1 hour.
2. Sift the dry ingredients together. Stir in the currants and whiskey.
3. Stir in the buttermilk, making a stiff batter.
4. Spread the batter in a greased 8-inch (20-centimeter) round cake pan. Bake at 350°F (180°C) until well browned and firm, approximately 30 minutes.

Approximate values per 3-oz. (90-g) serving: **Calories** 150, **Total fat** 1 g, **Saturated fat** 0 g, **Cholesterol** 0 mg, **Sodium** 480 mg, **Total carbohydrates** 31 g, **Protein** 5 g, **Calcium** 10%, **Claims**—low fat; no cholesterol; no saturated fat

BASIC CORN MUFFINS

Yield: 30 Muffins, 2½ oz. (75 g) each   **Method:** Muffin

Yellow cornmeal	12 oz.	360 g
All-purpose flour	12 oz.	360 g
Granulated sugar	10 oz.	300 g
Baking powder	1 Tbsp.	15 ml
Baking soda	1 tsp.	5 ml
Salt	¾ tsp.	3 ml
Buttermilk	24 fl. oz.	720 ml
Eggs	6	6
Unsalted butter, melted	6 oz.	180 g

1 Combine ingredients using the muffin method.

2 Portion into greased muffin tins, filling two-thirds full.

3 Bake at 375°F (190°C) until done, approximately 20 to 25 minutes.

VARIATIONS:

Southern-Style Cornbread—Omit the sugar. Pour the batter into cast-iron skillets or molds that are preheated and well greased with shortening or bacon fat. Bake at 425°F (220°C) until golden.

Tijuana Cornbread—Add 1 tablespoon (15 milliliters) chilli powder and 1 teaspoon (5 milliliters) ground cumin to the dry ingredients. Add 6 ounces (180 grams) roasted Anaheim chiles and 6 ounces (180 grams) shredded Cheddar cheese to the recipe when adding the liquid ingredients.

Approximate values per muffin: **Calories** 180, **Total fat** 6 g, **Saturated fat** 3.5 g, **Cholesterol** 55 mg, **Sodium** 140 mg, **Total carbohydrates** 28 g, **Protein** 4 g

FLAVORFUL CORN BREAD

Corn muffin batter is extremely versatile. Replace some of the cornmeal with blue or white varieties. Fold in cooked meats, diced fresh corn, other vegetables or shredded basil and herbs. Any type of grated cheese is a welcome addition. Bake the bread in timbale molds or loaf pans instead of traditional muffin cups. Adjust baking time if needed.

ZUCCHINI BREAD

Yield: 2 Loaves, 9 in. × 5 in. (24 cm × 12 cm) each   **Method:** Muffin

Eggs	3	3
Corn oil	8 fl. oz.	240 ml
Granulated sugar	1 lb. 2 oz.	540 g
Vanilla extract	1 tsp.	5 ml
Cinnamon, ground	2 tsp.	10 ml
Salt	1 tsp.	5 ml
Baking soda	1 tsp.	5 ml
Baking powder	1/2 tsp.	2 ml
All-purpose flour	14 oz.	420 g
Zucchini, coarsely grated	11 oz.	330 g
Pecans, chopped	4 oz.	120 g

1 Combine all ingredients using the muffin method.

2 Bake in two greased loaf pans at 350°F (180°C), approximately 1 hour.

Approximate values per 2-oz. (60-g) serving: **Calories** 260, **Total fat** 16 g, **Saturated fat** 2 g, **Cholesterol** 30 mg, **Sodium** 190 mg, **Total carbohydrates** 27 g, **Protein** 2 g

HUSH PUPPIES (DEEP-FRIED CORNBREAD)

Yield: 60 Pieces, 2 in. (5 cm) each | **Method:** Muffin

Yellow cornmeal	1 lb.	480 g
All-purpose flour	8 oz.	240 g
Baking powder	1 Tbsp.	15 ml
Salt	1 Tbsp.	15 ml
Black pepper	1 Tbsp.	15 ml
Granulated sugar	2 oz.	60 g
Onions, minced	8 oz.	240 g
Eggs	4	4
Milk	1 pt.	480 ml

1. Combine all ingredients using the muffin method.
2. Drop small scoops (using a #60 or #70 portion scoop) into deep fat at 375°F (190°C). Using the swimming method, deep-fry until golden brown.
3. Remove from the fat and drain. Serve immediately.

Approximate values per piece: **Calories** 70, **Total fat** 3 g, **Saturated fat** 1 g, **Cholesterol** 5 mg, **Sodium** 120 mg, **Total carbohydrates** 10 g, **Protein** 1 g

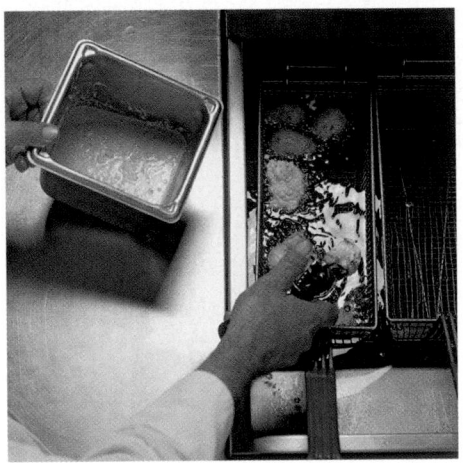

1. Scooping the hush puppy batter into the deep-fat fryer.

2. Draining the cooked Hush Puppies.

SOUR CREAM COFFEECAKE

Yield: 1 Tube Cake, 10 in. (25 cm) | **Method:** Creaming

Filling:		
All-purpose flour	1½ Tbsp.	27 ml
Cinnamon, ground	1 Tbsp.	15 ml
Brown sugar	6 oz.	180 g
Pecans, chopped	4 oz.	120 g
Unsalted butter, melted	1 oz.	30 g
Unsalted butter	4 oz.	120 g
Granulated sugar	8 oz.	240 g
Eggs	2	2
Sour cream	8 oz.	240 g
Cake flour, sifted	7 oz.	210 g
Salt	¼ tsp.	1 ml
Baking powder	1 tsp.	5 ml
Baking soda	1 tsp.	5 ml
Vanilla extract	1 tsp.	5 ml

1. To make the filling, blend all the filling ingredients together in a small bowl. Set aside.

2. To make the cake batter, cream the butter and sugar. Add the eggs one at a time, beating well after each addition. Add the sour cream. Stir until smooth.

3. Sift the sifted flour, salt, baking powder and baking soda together twice. Stir into the batter. Stir in the vanilla extract.

4. Spoon half of the batter into a greased tube pan. Top with half of the filling. Cover the filling with the remaining batter and top with the remaining filling. Bake at 350°F (180°C) for approximately 35 minutes.

Approximate values per ¹⁄₁₆-cake serving: **Calories** 240, **Total fat** 13 g, **Saturated fat** 6 g, **Cholesterol** 40 mg, **Sodium** 130 mg, **Total carbohydrates** 29 g, **Protein** 2 g

---

POPOVERS

CONNECTICUT CULINARY INSTITUTE, FARMINGTON, CT

Chef Jamie Roraback

Popovers are crisp hollow muffins made from a rich egg batter. The steam released from the eggs and milk as the popovers bake is trapped in the gluten web of the batter, causing it to rise. Popovers and other products that rely on steam for leavening are baked at a high temperature so that the steam forms quickly before the gluten bond sets. These muffins resemble products baked from éclair paste. Yorkshire pudding, a popular accompaniment to roasted rib of beef, is made from this same batter. Yorkshire pudding is baked in beef fat in a shallow pan and then served cut into squares.

Yield: 20 Popovers

Beef fat or vegetable oil	10 fl. oz.	300 ml
All-purpose flour	8 oz.	240 g
Salt	1 tsp.	5 ml
Eggs	6	6
Whole milk	1 pt.	480 ml
Whole butter, melted	3 oz.	90 g

1. Place twenty 4-ounce (120-milliliter) greased ramekins or popover tins on a sheet pan and drop 1 tablespoon (15 milliliters) of beef fat or vegetable oil in the bottom of each ramekin. Place the ramekins in a 425°F (220°C) oven until the fat smokes.

2. Sift the flour and salt together into a large bowl. In a separate bowl, whisk together the eggs, milk and butter. Pour the liquid ingredients into the dry ingredients and whip until smooth.

3. Remove the ramekins from the oven and fill each approximately two-thirds full with batter. Bake at 425°F (220°C) for 20 minutes without opening the oven door. After 20 minutes, lower the heat to 375°F (190°C) and bake until the popovers dry out inside, approximately 10 more minutes.

4. Remove the popovers from the oven, unmold and serve.

5. For crisper popovers, slit the sides of the unmolded popovers to allow the steam to escape. Place on a sheet pan and return them to the oven until the tops are firm, crisp and brown, approximately 10 minutes.

VARIATION:

Onion Popovers—Sauté 2 ounces (60 grams) finely chopped onion in 1 tablespoon (15 grams) butter until tender. Sprinkle the onions over the batter just before baking.

Approximate values per popover: **Calories** 250, **Total fat** 21 g, **Saturated fat** 11 g, **Cholesterol** 95 mg, **Sodium** 150 mg, **Total carbohydrates** 10 g, **Protein** 4 g

CHAPTER THIRTY-ONE

YEAST BREADS

- select and use yeast properly
- perform the 10 steps involved in yeast bread production
- mix yeast doughs using the straight dough method and the sponge method

BREAD MAKING IS AN ART that dates back to ancient times. Over the centuries, bakers have learned to manipulate the basic ingredients—flour, water, salt and leavening—to produce a vast variety of breads. Thin-crusted baguettes, tender Parker House rolls, crisp flatbreads and chewy bagels derive from careful selection and handling of the same key ingredients. A renewed interest in the traditional craft of baking has seen many new bread bakeries open in recent years. Customers are demanding and more restaurants are serving exciting bread assortments to their guests with each meal. Although few baked goods intimidate novice bakers as much as yeast breads, few baked goods are actually as forgiving to prepare. By mastering a few basic procedures and techniques, restaurants and bakeshops can offer their customers delicious, fresh yeast products.

Yeast breads can be divided into two major categories: lean doughs and rich doughs. Lean doughs, such as those used for crusty French and Italian breads, contain little or no sugar or fat. Traditional sourdough and rye breads are lean doughs that require special handling to bring out their unique flavor. Rich doughs, such as brioche and challah, contain significantly more sugar and fat than lean doughs. Laminated or rolled-in doughs, so called because the fat is rolled into the dough in layers, are a type of rich dough used for baked goods such as croissants and sweetened Danish pastries.

This chapter covers in detail the basic production techniques for making lean, sourdough and other yeast-raised products. Rereading the discussion of the functions of ingredients found in Chapter 29, Principles of the Bakeshop, is recommended before beginning this chapter.

YEAST

Yeast is a living organism: a one-celled fungus. Various strains of yeast are present virtually everywhere. Yeast feeds on carbohydrates present in the starches and sugars in bread dough, converting them to carbon dioxide and ethanol, an alcohol, in an organic process known as **fermentation**:

Yeast + Carbohydrates = Alcohol + Carbon Dioxide

When yeast releases carbon dioxide gas during bread making, the gas becomes trapped in the dough's gluten network. (See Chapter 29, Principles of the Bakeshop.) The trapped gas leavens the bread, providing the desired rise and texture. The small amount of alcohol produced by fermentation evaporates during baking.

As with most living things, yeast is very sensitive to temperature and moisture. It prefers temperatures between 75°F and 95°F (24°C and 35°C). At temperatures below 34°F (2°C), it becomes dormant; above 138°F (59°C), it dies. Table 31.1 lists the temperatures for yeast development. Moisture activates the yeast cells, helping the yeast convert carbohydrates in the dough into food.

Salt is used in bread making because it conditions gluten, making it stronger and more elastic. Salt also affects yeast fermentation. Because salt inhibits the growth of yeast, it helps control the dough's rise. Too little salt and not only will the bread taste bland, it

fermentation the process by which yeast converts sugar into alcohol and carbon dioxide; it also refers to the time that yeast dough is left to rise—that is, the time it takes for carbon dioxide gas cells to form and become trapped in the gluten network

TABLE 31.1	TEMPERATURES FOR YEAST DEVELOPMENT	
TEMPERATURE		**YEAST DEVELOPMENT**
34°F	(2°C)	Inactive
60°F–70°F	(16°C–21°C)	Slow action
75°F–95°F	(21°C–32°C)	Best temperature for yeast activity
85°F–100°F	(29°C–38°C)	Best water temperature for hydrating instant yeast
100°F–110°F	(38°C–4°C)	Best water temperature for hydrating active dry yeast
138°F	(59°C)	Yeast dies

will rise too rapidly. Too much salt, however, and the yeast will be destroyed. By learning to control the amount of food for the yeast and the temperatures of fermentation, bakers learn to control the texture and flavor of yeast-leavened products.

Types of Yeast

Baker's yeast, *Saccharomyces cerevisiae*, is available in three forms: compressed, active dry and instant. (Do not be confused by a product called brewer's yeast; it is a nutritional supplement with no leavening ability.)

COMPRESSED YEAST

Compressed yeast is a mixture of yeast and starch with a moisture content of approximately 70 percent. Also referred to as **fresh yeast**, compressed yeast must be kept refrigerated. It should be creamy white and crumbly with a fresh, yeasty smell. Do not use compressed yeast that has developed a sour odor, brown color or slimy film. Compressed yeast is softened in twice its weight in warm water at 100°F (38°C) before being added to bread dough. Some bakers even add compressed yeast directly to the dry mix.

Compressed yeast is available in 1-pound (450-gram) blocks. Under proper storage conditions, compressed yeast has a shelf life of 2 to 3 weeks. When fresh, it may be frozen and stored for 1 month. Frozen compressed yeast will lose about 5 percent of its activity when thawed.

Compressed Yeast

ACTIVE DRY YEAST

Active dry yeast differs from compressed yeast in that virtually all the moisture has been removed by hot air. The absence of moisture renders the organism dormant and allows the yeast to be stored without refrigeration for several months. When preparing doughs, dry yeast is generally rehydrated in a lukewarm (approximately 110°F [43°C]) liquid before being added to the other ingredients.

Dry yeast is available in ¼-ounce (7-gram) packages and 1- or 2.2-pound (500-gram or 1-kilogram) vacuum-sealed bags. It should be stored in a cool, dry place and refrigerated after opening.

INSTANT DRY YEAST

Instant dry yeast has gained popularity because of its ease of use; it is added directly to the dry ingredients in a bread formula without rehydrating. The water in the formula activates it. Like all yeasts, instant dry yeast is a living organism and will be destroyed at temperatures above 138°F (59°C). Although instant yeast can be added to flour without hydration, some bakers still prefer to hydrate instant yeast before using it in certain types of formulas. When doughs are mixed briefly or are very firm, such as bagel or croissant dough, instant dry yeast may not fully dissolve during mixing. In such cases the yeast is moistened in four to five times its weight of water. Deduct this amount of water from the total water called for in the formula.

Dry Yeast

THE RISE OF YEAST BREADS

How and when the first yeast-leavened breads came into being, no one knows. Perhaps some wild yeasts—the world is full of them—drifted into a dough as it awaited baking. Perhaps some ancient baker substituted fermented ale or beer for water one day. In any case, the resulting bread was different, lighter and more appetizing.

Based on models, images and writings found in excavated tombs, historians are fairly certain that the ancient Egyptians saved a bit of fermented dough from one day's baking to add to the next day's. This use of sourdough starter continues today, enjoying widespread popularity.

Other cultures developed their own leavening methods. The Greeks and Romans prepared a wheat porridge with wine, which caused their doughs to ferment. The Gauls and Iberians added the foamy head from ale to their doughs. Both methods resulted in lighter breads that retained their fresh textures longer. Since ancient times, bread baking has been one of the first household tasks readily turned over to professionals. The first cooks to work outside homes during the Greek and Roman Empires were bakers. The bakery trade flourished during the Middle Ages, with a wide variety of breads being produced. Yeast-leavened breads remained the exception, not the norm, until well into the 17th century, however. The first real collection of bread recipes is found in Nicolas Bonnefon's *Les Délices de la campagne*, published in 1654. Bonnefon's instructions, meant for those dissatisfied with commercial products of the time, included the use of beer yeast. By the end of the 17th century, published works included recipes for breads leavened with sourdough starter and the yeasts used in breweries.

Louis Pasteur finally identified yeast as a living organism in 1857. Soon after, a process for distilling or manufacturing baker's yeast was developed. By 1868, commercial baking yeast was available in stores.

SUBSTITUTING YEASTS

The flavors of dry and compressed yeasts are virtually indistinguishable, but dry yeasts are at least twice as strong. Because too much yeast can ruin bread, always remember to reduce the specified weight for compressed yeast when substituting dry yeast or active dry yeast in a formula. Likewise, if a formula specifies dry or active dry yeast, increase the quantity specified when substituting compressed yeast.

Any type of yeast may be used in the formulas in this book. Use the formulas in Table 31.2 to convert one type of yeast to another.

NATURAL YEAST LEAVENERS—SOURDOUGH STARTER

Before commercial yeast production, bakers relied on natural yeast leaveners, also called starters, to make bread rise. Early starters were simple mixtures of flour and a liquid (water, potato broth, milk) left to capture wild yeasts and beneficial acid-producing bacteria from the environment. Once the mixture fermented, it was used to leaven bread and contribute a distinctive flavor, from mild and buttery to sharp and tangy, to the finished product. Only a portion of the starter was used at a time. The rest was kept for later use, replenished periodically with additional flour and liquid so that the yeast activity could continue. Over time and in different regions, bakers developed numerous strategies for using natural yeast starters to create different flavors and textures in bread.

The making of a natural starter begins by combining equal parts flour and water into a wet mixture. A small amount of grapes, apple peels or orange rinds may be added to

Starter activity at three stages: just mixed (lower right), 3 hours after mixing (left) and 12 hours later (upper right).

TABLE 31.2 YEAST SUBSTITUTIONS

Use these formulas to convert from one type of yeast to another:

Compressed (fresh) yeast	×	0.5	=	Active dry yeast
Compressed (fresh) yeast	×	0.33	=	Instant yeast
Active dry yeast	×	2	=	Compressed (fresh) yeast
Active dry yeast	×	0.75	=	Instant yeast
Instant yeast	×	3	=	Compressed (fresh) yeast
Instant yeast	×	1.33	=	Active dry yeast

seed the mixture with natural yeast spores. Or some prepared yeast may be used to get the mixture going. After several hours, bubbles will appear on the surface, indicating that yeast activity has begun. Within 12 to 24 hours, yeast activity should be noticeable and the mixture will double or triple in volume. Over time, the starter will develop a mellow flavor with some noticeable acidity.

To maintain a natural starter, frequently replenish or feed it with more flour and water. When making bread in a production bakery, feed the starter as often as every 8 hours to keep the yeast active. The amount of flour and water necessary to feed a starter varies, but never add more flour and water than would double the mixture at one time. Yeast is more active in a wet starter than a dry one; add more flour when the starter will not be used for an extended period of time. More water can be added to activate the starter on the day when it will be used.

SIMPLE SOURDOUGH STARTER

Yield: 3 lb. 12 oz. (1.8 kg)

Active dry yeast	1 tsp.	5 ml
Water, warm	4 fl. oz.	120 ml
Water, room temperature	24 fl. oz.	720 ml
All-purpose flour	2 lb.	960 g

1. Combine the yeast and warm water. Let stand until foamy, approximately 10 minutes.
2. Stir in the room-temperature water, then add the flour, 2 ounces (60 grams) at a time.
3. Blend by hand or with a mixer fitted with the paddle attachment on low speed for 2 minutes.
4. Place the starter in a warmed bowl and cover with plastic wrap. Let stand at room temperature for 8 to 12 hours. The starter should triple in volume but still be wet and sticky. Refrigerate until ready to use.
5. Each time a portion of the starter is used, it must be replenished and activated. Remove the starter from the refrigerator several hours before using. Replenish the starter to activate the yeast cells, then use. To replenish the starter, stir in equal amounts by volume of flour and warm water. Then allow the mixture to ferment at room temperature for several hours or overnight before using again or refrigerating.

Note: If liquid rises to the top of the starter, it can be drained off or stirred back into the mixture. If the starter develops a pink or yellow film, it has been contaminated and must be discarded.

Approximate values per fluid ounce (30 ml): **Calories** 100, **Total fat** 0 g, **Saturated fat** 0 g, **Cholesterol** 0 mg, **Sodium** 0 mg, **Total carbohydrates** 22 g, **Protein** 3 g

PRODUCTION STAGES FOR YEAST BREADS

The production of yeast breads can be divided into 10 stages:

1. Scaling the ingredients
2. Mixing and kneading the dough
3. Fermenting the dough
4. Punching down the dough
5. Portioning the dough
6. Rounding the portions
7. Shaping the portions (make-up)
8. Proofing the products
9. Baking the products
10. Cooling and storing the finished products

absorption the ability of flour to absorb moisture when mixed into a dough; varies according to protein content, growing conditions and storage conditions of the flour

Stage 1: Scaling the Ingredients

As with any other bakeshop product, it is important to scale or measure ingredients accurately and to have all ingredients at the proper temperature when making a yeast bread. Liquids such as water, milk and eggs may all be weighed to ensure accuracy in a formula. When a minute quantity of an ingredient is required, such as for salt and spices, a volume measurement may be preferred.

The amount of flour required in yeast bread may vary depending on the humidity level, storage conditions of the flour and the accuracy with which other ingredients are measured. Flour from different mills or from different batch lots may **absorb** more or less water depending on the type of wheat used. Flour with a higher protein content will absorb more liquid than one with a lower protein content. Even switching flour batches will affect the amount of water needed in a formula. The amount of flour stated in most formulas is to be used as a guide. Have additional flour available before mixing. Experience will teach when more or less flour is actually needed.

Stage 2: Mixing and Kneading the Dough

The way ingredients are combined affects the outcome of the bread. Yeast dough must be mixed and kneaded properly in order to combine the ingredients uniformly, distribute the yeast and develop the gluten. If the dough is not mixed properly, the bread's texture and shape suffer.

Yeast breads are usually mixed by either the **straight dough method** (direct method) or the **sponge method**. Another method used for rich, flaky doughs is discussed later in the section on rolled-in doughs.

Once the ingredients are combined, the dough must be kneaded to develop gluten, the network of proteins that gives bread its shape and texture. Kneading achieves certain key results. It helps the protein hydrate, ensuring development of the gluten web in the bread dough, and it warms the dough to a temperature conducive to keeping the yeast active. Kneading can be done by hand or with a mixer fitted with a dough hook. The goal is to create a dough that is smooth and moderately elastic.

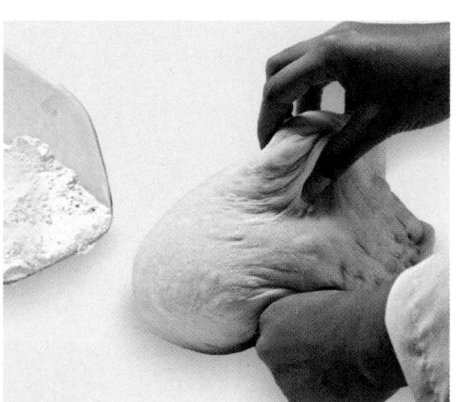

❶ First, bring a portion of the dough toward you.

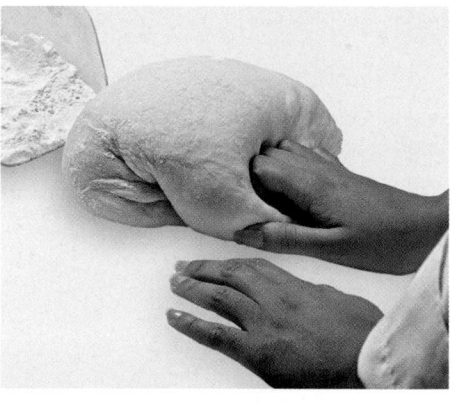

❷ Then push the dough away with your fist.

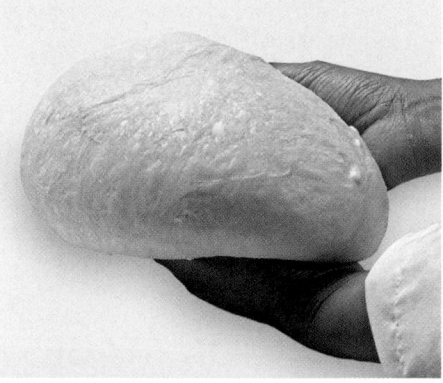

❸ Repeat until the dough is properly kneaded.

After the ingredients are combined, the dough is kneaded until it is smooth and elastic, on medium speed for approximately 5 to 10 minutes. The goal is to properly develop the gluten structure in the dough and to warm the dough so that the yeast becomes active. The dough should look smooth. In many cases, the dough will clear away from the machine bowl toward the end of the kneading process.

MIXING METHODS

Straight Dough Method

The simplest and most common method for mixing yeast dough is known as the straight dough method. With this method, all ingredients are simply combined and mixed. Once the ingredients are combined, the dough is kneaded until it is smooth and elastic. Kneading time varies according to the kneading method used and the type of dough being produced. The straight dough method is illustrated by the recipe for Soft Yeast Dinner Rolls (page 934).

Sponge Method

The sponge method of mixing yeast dough has two stages. During the first stage the yeast, the liquid and approximately half the flour are combined to make a thick batter known as a **sponge**. The sponge is allowed to rise until bubbly and doubled in size. During the second stage, the remaining ingredients are added. The dough is kneaded and allowed to rise again. These two fermentations give sponge method breads a somewhat different flavor and a lighter texture than breads made with the straight dough method.

Do not confuse sponge method breads with sourdough starters. The sponge method is often used to improve the texture of heavy doughs such as rye and some enriched yeast doughs. Unlike a sourdough starter, the first-stage sponge is prepared only for the specific formula and is not reserved for later use. The sponge method is illustrated by the recipe for Light Rye Bread (page 936).

> **sponge** a thick flour and water batter, which may or may not contain yeast, used to improve the flavor and texture of breads

Stage 3: Fermenting the Dough

As mentioned earlier, fermentation is the natural process by which yeast converts sugar into alcohol and carbon dioxide. Fermentation begins the moment the dough is finished mixing and continues until the dough is baked and reaches a temperature high enough to kill the yeast cells, 138°F (59°C).

Fermentation also refers to the period when yeast dough is left to rise—that is, the time it takes for carbon dioxide gas to form and become trapped in the gluten network. Fermentation is divided into two stages. **Bulk fermentation** refers to the rise given to the entire mass of yeast dough before the dough is shaped; **proofing** refers to the rise given to shaped yeast products just before baking.

Dough develops characteristics during fermentation that will enhance the taste and texture of the finished bread. As it feeds on the sugars and starches in the dough, the yeast converts them to flavorful enzymes and bacteria. The gluten strengthens during fermentation, ensuring a bread that will hold its structure when baked. For fermentation, place the kneaded dough into a container large enough to allow the dough to expand, or scrape the dough onto a floured workbench. The surface of the dough may be oiled to prevent drying. Cover the dough and place it in a draft-free place at a temperature between 75°F and 85°F (24°C and 29°C).

CONTROLLING FERMENTATION

The ingredients in the formula, the dough temperature and the temperature of the environment in which the dough ferments will affect the total fermentation time. Bakers use different strategies to regulate fermentation time to achieve desired results.

Ingredients—Dough with more yeast and more yeast food will ferment more quickly. Increasing the yeast in a formula will increase the rate of fermentation, thus speeding production time. Adding sugar, honey or other yeast food will speed fermentation also, although too much sugar can

actually slow yeast's activity; enriched dough formulas often include a higher percentage of yeast for this reason.

Dough Temperature—Using warmer water in the dough and fermenting it in a warm environment will speed up the fermentation process. Conversely, kneading the dough to the proper dough temperature and then letting it ferment in a cool environment will slow down this process. When mixing yeast dough, keep in mind that

wintertime baking in colder climates may require very warm water to begin yeast activity. Summertime baking in hot climates may require very cool water to keep bread dough from fermenting too quickly.

Room Temperature—Bakeries often extend the fermentation time of certain doughs in a specially designed refrigerator called a retarder. The cool temperature slows down the yeast activity, giving the dough the maximum opportunity to develop its flavor.

Rounding bread dough.

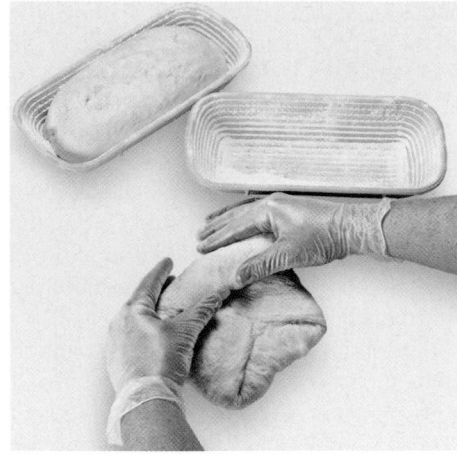

Loaves in a brotform.

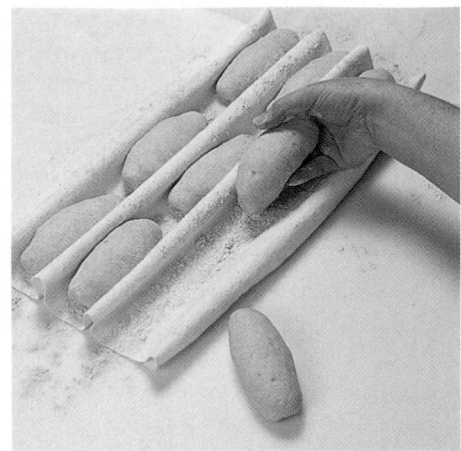

Bread dough being placed in a canvas couche before being proofed.

Fermentation is complete when the dough has approximately doubled in size and no longer springs back when pressed gently with two fingers. The time necessary varies depending on the type of dough, the temperature of the room and the temperature of the dough.

Stage 4: Punching Down the Dough

After fermentation, the dough is gently folded down to expel and redistribute the gas pockets with a technique known as **punching down**. The procedure reactivates the yeast cells, encouraging more yeast activity. Punching down dough also helps even out the dough's temperature and relaxes the gluten.

Stage 5: Portioning the Dough

The dough is now ready to be divided into portions. For loaves, the dough is scaled to the desired weight. For individual rolls, the dough can be rolled into an even log from which portions are cut off with a chef's knife or dough cutter. Weighing the cut dough pieces on a portion scale ensures even-sized portions. When portioning, work quickly and keep the dough covered to prevent it from drying out.

Stage 6: Rounding the Portions

The portions of dough must be shaped into smooth, round balls in a technique known as **rounding**. Rounding stretches the outside layer of gluten into a smooth coating. This helps hold in gases and makes it easier to shape the dough. Unrounded rolls rise unevenly and have a rough, lumpy surface.

Stage 7: Shaping the Portions: Make-Up

Lean doughs and some rich doughs can be shaped into a variety of forms: large loaves, small loaves, free-form or country-style rounds or individual dinner rolls. Table 31.3 identifies common pan sizes and the approximate weight of the dough used to fill them. Free-form loaves are often placed between the floured folds of heavy linen canvas (**couche**) to hold their shape while proofing. Or these loaves may be placed in linen-lined baskets (**bannetons**) or coiled willow or plastic baskets (**brotform**). These baskets hold the loaves' shape and leave a distinctive imprint on the loaves when they are removed from them before baking. Some shaping techniques are shown here. Other doughs, particularly brioche, croissant and Danish, are usually shaped in very specific ways. Those techniques are discussed and illustrated with their specific formulas.

bagel a dense, donut-shaped yeast roll; it is cooked in boiling water, then baked, which gives it a shiny glaze and chewy texture

bun any of a variety of small, round yeast rolls; can be sweet or savory

club roll a small oval-shaped roll made of crusty French bread

Kaiser roll a large round yeast roll with a crisp crust and a curved pattern stamped on the top; used primarily for sandwiches

TABLE 31.3 PAN SIZE		
PAN	**APPROXIMATE SIZE**	**WEIGHT OF DOUGH***
Sandwich loaf	16 in. × 4 in. × 4½ in. (40 cm × 10 cm × 11.2 cm)	4 lb. (1920 g)
Pullman	13 in. × 4 in. × 3 in. (32.5 cm × 10 cm × 7.5 cm)	3 lb. (1440 g)
Large	9 in. × 5 in. × 3 in. (22.5 cm × 12.5 cm × 7.5 cm)	2 lb. (960 g)
Medium	8 in. × 4 in. × 2 in. (20 cm × 10 cm × 5 cm)	1 lb. 8 oz. (720 g)
Small	7 in. × 3 in. × 2 in. (17.5 cm × 7.5 cm × 5 cm)	1 lb. (480 g)
Miniature	5 in. × 3 in. × 2 in. (12.5 cm × 7.5 cm × 5 cm)	8 oz. (240 g)

* Weights given are approximate; variations may occur based on the type of dough used as well as the temperature and length of proofing.

PROCEDURE FOR **FORMING A TWISTED KNOT ROLL OR LOAF**

1. Roll a portion of dough into a long rope. Form a loop by attaching the left end to the middle of the rope. Pinch to seal the dough.
2. Pass the right end of the rope through the loop.
3. Fold down the top of the loop and twist slightly.
4. Thread the loose end of the loaf through the loop.

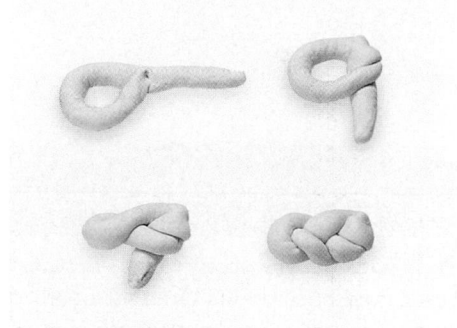

Forming a twisted knot loaf.

PROCEDURE FOR **ROLLING A LONG LOAF OR BAGUETTE**

1. Round a portion of dough into a ball by rolling it under cupped hands across the surface of the workbench.
2. Roll the ball of dough out into a short cylinder.
3. With both hands together, roll the dough until it gradually begins to lengthen.
4. Roll to the desired length.

Stage 8: Proofing the Products

Proofing is the final rise of shaped or panned yeast products before baking. For most bread, the temperature should be between 80°F and 115°F (27°C and 46°C), slightly higher than the temperature for fermentation. Some humidity is also desirable to prevent the dough from drying or forming a crust. Temperature and humidity can be controlled with a special cabinet known as a **proof box**.

Most products are proofed until the dough doubles in size and springs back slowly when lightly touched. Underproofing results in poor volume and texture. Overproofing results in a sour flavor, poor volume and a paler color after baking. Some doughs made with low-protein flours such as rye or multigrains and some enriched yeast doughs may be proofed less, until expanded only 50 to 70 percent in volume. The weaker gluten structure and the heavy weight of the fats in the dough make them fragile. Proofing these doughs until doubled in volume can result in loaves that collapse in the oven.

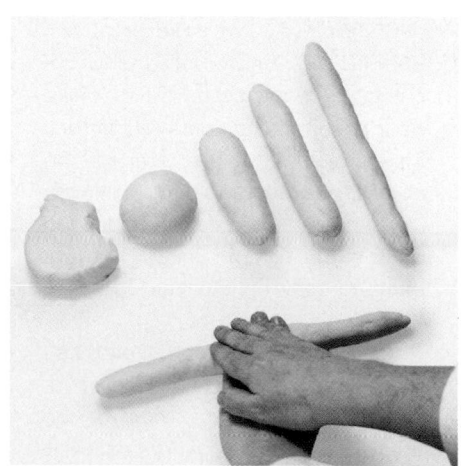

Forming and then rolling a long loaf or baguette.

oven spring the rapid rise of yeast goods in a hot oven, resulting from the production and expansion of trapped gases

Stage 9: Baking the Products

As yeast breads bake, a variety of chemical and physical changes turn the dough into an edible product. These changes are discussed in Chapter 29, Principles of the Bakeshop. Because of the expansion of gases, yeast products experience a sudden rise, referred to as **oven spring**, when first placed in a hot oven. As the dough's temperature increases, the yeast dies, the gluten fibers become firm, the starches gelatinize, the moisture evaporates and, finally, the crust forms and turns brown. To assist the rise during baking and to improve their appearance when baked, loaves may be washed and/or scored before baking.

WASHES

The appearance of yeast breads can be altered by applying a glaze or **wash** to the dough before baking. The crust is made shiny or matte, hard or soft, darker or lighter by the proper use of washes. See Table 31.4. Washes are also used to attach seeds, wheat germ, oats or other toppings to the dough's surface.

The most commonly used wash is an egg wash, composed of whole egg and water—usually one part water to three parts egg. Yeast products can also be topped with plain water, a mixture of egg and milk, plain milk or richer glazes containing sugar and flavorings. Even a light dusting of white flour can be used to top dough. (This is commonly seen with potato rolls.) Rye breads are often coated with a starch wash made from cornstarch cooked in water, which produces a dark shiny crust.

Washes may be applied before or after proofing. If applied after proofing, be extremely careful not to deflate the product. Avoid using too much wash, as it can burn or cause the product to stick to the pan. Puddles or streaks of egg wash on the dough will cause uneven browning.

Occasionally, a formula will specify that melted butter or oil be brushed on the product after baking. Do not, however, apply egg washes to already baked products, as the egg will remain raw and the desired effect will not be achieved.

SCORING AND DOCKING

The shape and appearance of some breads can be improved by cutting their tops with a sharp knife or razor (lame) just before baking. This is referred to as **scoring** or **slashing**. Hard-crusted breads are usually scored to allow for continued rising and the escape of gases after the crust has formed. Breads that are not properly scored will burst or break along the sides. Scoring can also be used to make an attractive design on the product's surface. Some flatbreads such as pizza and crackers may be **docked** or pricked with small holes to prevent the formation of irregular air bubbles in the finished product.

STEAM IN THE OVEN

The crisp crust desired for certain breads and rolls is achieved by introducing moisture into the oven during baking. Steam revitalizes the yeast in the dough and keeps the sur-

ARTISAN BREAD

The term *artisan bread* is not easily defined because the term has been adopted by small-scale independent bakers as well as industrial producers. Some generally recognized characteristics of artisan bread are handcrafted breads made with high-quality, traditional ingredients without additives or preservatives. Unbleached, unbromated and organic flours are preferred to make doughs that contain natural starters. Mixers may be used to prepare the dough, but rounding and forming is usually done by hand. And artisan breads are often baked without pans, directly on the heated stone deck of a hearth oven.

Greg Mistell, owner of Delphina's Bakery and Pearl Bakery in Portland, Oregon, and past chairman of the Bread Bakers Guild of America, has written that artisan bread is an "honest loaf," not a separate category of products. Many of the formulas in this book will produce artisan bread when made with care by those attentive to the craft of bread making.

TABLE 31.4	WASHES FOR YEAST PRODUCTS
WASH	**USE**
Whole egg and water	Shine and color
Whole egg and milk	Shine and color with soft crust
Egg white and water	Shine with a firm crust
Egg yolk and cream or milk	Shine and color with soft crust
Milk or cream	Color with a soft crust
Water	Crisp crust
Flour	Texture and contrast
Starch wash	Shine and color

face of the dough soft so that it can rise fully in the oven. Steam is introduced into the oven in the early baking stages only. Excessive steam will produce a crust that is pale and thick. Professional bakers' ovens have built-in steam injection jets to provide moisture as needed. Steam must not be present during the final stages of baking so the bread can brown.

To create steam in any oven, spray or mist the bread with water several times during baking, or place a pan on the oven's lowest rack to receive hot water. Then pour ½ to ¾ cup (120 to 180 milliliters) hot water into the pan just before placing the bread in the oven. This creates a burst of steam and a moist oven during the first few minutes of baking. Rich doughs, which do not form crisp crusts, are usually baked without steam.

DETERMINING DONENESS

Baking time is determined by a variety of factors: the product's size, the oven thermostat's accuracy and the desired crust color. Larger items require a longer baking time than smaller ones. Lean dough products bake faster and at higher temperatures than enriched dough products.

Bread loaves are commonly tested for doneness by tapping them on the bottom and listening for a hollow sound. This indicates that air, not moisture, is present inside the loaf. If the bottom is damp or heavy, the loaf probably needs more baking time. The texture and color of the crust are also a good indication of doneness, particularly with individual rolls. Browning (caramelization) on the outside of bread flavors the entire loaf. A pale loaf will have less flavor than a well-browned one. The baking times indicated in these recipes are estimates only and may vary depending on the equipment used. Experience will teach how to determine doneness without strict adherence to elapsed time.

Stage 10: Cooling and Storing the Finished Products

The quality of even the finest yeast products suffers if they are cooled or stored improperly. Yeast products should be cooled on racks at room temperature and away from drafts. Yeast breads and rolls should be removed from their pans for cooling unless indicated otherwise. Allow loaves to cool completely before slicing. This allows the internal structure to settle and evaporates any excess moisture remaining after baking.

Once cool, yeast products should be stored at room temperature or frozen for longer storage. Do not refrigerate baked goods, as refrigeration promotes staling. Do not wrap crisp-crusted breads such as Italian or French loaves, as this causes the crust to soften.

PROCEDURE FOR **PREPARING YEAST BREAD**

STRAIGHT DOUGH METHOD

1. Scale the ingredients. Adjust the water to the proper temperature and rehydrate the yeast if necessary.
2. Combine all ingredients in a mixer fitted with a dough hook on low speed to moisten.
3. Adjust the mixture with more water or flour if needed to correct dough consistency.
4. Knead the dough on medium speed to properly develop the gluten, approximately 5 to 10 minutes.
5. Ferment the dough until double in bulk, then punch it down to release gases.
6. Scrape the dough onto the workbench, then divide and scale into uniform pieces. Round each piece into a smooth ball, then rest before rolling into desired shapes. Pan the formed dough as desired.
7. Proof the dough. Apply egg wash and score the dough if necessary; then bake.

GUIDELINES FOR GAUGING BREAD DONENESS

- Uniform, rich, burnished gold to brown crust color
- Hollow sound when bottom of loaf is tapped
- The internal temperature can be gauged with great accuracy using an instant-read thermometer.

  Lean dough—internal temperature of 190°F to 210°F (88°C to 99°C).

  Rich dough—internal temperature of 180°F to 190°F (82°C to 88°C).

SOFT YEAST DINNER ROLLS

MISE EN PLACE

▶ Adjust water temperature.
▶ Soften butter.
▶ Prepare the egg wash.
▶ Line sheet pans with parchment while the dough ferments.

Yield: 64 Rolls, approximately 1¼ oz. (38 grams) each

Method: Straight dough

Water, warm	24 fl. oz.	720 ml
Active dry yeast	2 oz.	60 g
Bread flour	2 lb. 12 oz.	1320 g
Salt	1 oz.	30 g
Granulated sugar	4 oz.	120 g
Nonfat dry milk powder	2 oz.	60 g
Shortening	2 oz.	60 g
Unsalted butter, softened	2 oz.	60 g
Eggs	2	2
Egg wash	as needed	as needed

1 Combine the water and yeast in a small bowl. Combine the remaining ingredients (except the egg wash) in the bowl of a mixer.

2 Add the water-and-yeast mixture to the remaining ingredients; stir to combine.

3 Knead with a dough hook on medium speed for 10 minutes.

1 Mixing the soft yeast dough: (a) Combining the ingredients in the bowl of a mixer fitted with a dough hook.

(b) Adding the yeast-and-water mixture.

2 Kneading the dough.

3 The dough before fermenting.

4 Punching down the risen dough: (a) Pressing down on the center of the dough with your fist.

(b) Folding the edges of the dough in toward the center.

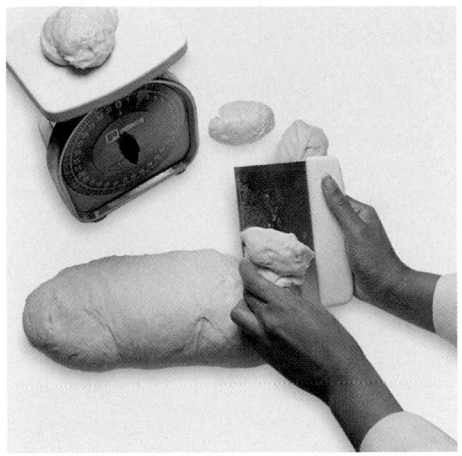

⑤ Scaling the dough.

⑥ Rounding the rolls.

⑦ Egg-washing the rolls.

④ Transfer the dough to a lightly greased bowl, cover and place in a warm spot. Ferment until doubled, approximately 1 hour.

⑤ Punch down the dough. Let it rest a few minutes to allow the gluten to relax.

⑥ Divide the dough into 1¼-ounce (38-gram) portions and round. Shape as desired and arrange on paper-lined sheet pans. Proof until doubled in size.

⑦ Carefully brush the proofed rolls with egg wash. Bake at 400°F (200°C) until medium brown, approximately 12 to 15 minutes.

Approximate values per roll: **Calories** 90, **Total fat** 1.5 g, **Saturated fat** 0.5 g, **Cholesterol** 10 mg, **Sodium** 160 mg, **Total carbohydrates** 15 g, **Protein** 3 g, **Claims**—low fat; low saturated fat; low cholesterol

PROCEDURE FOR **PREPARING YEAST BREAD**

SPONGE METHOD

① Scale the ingredients. Adjust the water to the proper temperature and rehydrate the yeast if necessary.

② Mix the sponge from a portion of the flour, the water and the yeast. Usually half the total flour weight is used.

③ Ferment the sponge until bubbly and about double in size, approximately 1 hour.

④ Add the remaining ingredients, then knead the dough on medium speed until properly developed, approximately 5 to 10 minutes.

⑤ Ferment the dough until double in bulk, then punch it down to release gases.

⑥ The dough is now ready for scaling, shaping, proofing and baking.

LIGHT RYE BREAD

Yield: 2 Large Loaves, approximately 1½ lb. (720 g) each   **Method:** Sponge

Unbleached wheat flour	1 lb.	480 g
Medium rye flour	8 oz.	240 g
Dark molasses	3 oz.	90 g
Water, warm	14 fl. oz.	420 ml
Active dry yeast	½ oz.	15 g
Nonfat dry milk powder	1½ oz.	45 g
Caraway seeds, crushed	2 Tbsp.	30 ml
Kosher salt	1 Tbsp.	15 ml
Unsalted butter, melted	1 Tbsp.	15 ml
Egg wash	as needed	as needed

MISE EN PLACE

▶ Adjust water temperature.
▶ Crush caraway seeds.
▶ Melt butter.
▶ Prepare the egg wash.
▶ Dust sheet pan with cornmeal while the dough ferments.

1 Stir the flours together and set aside.

2 To make the sponge, combine the molasses, water and yeast. Add 8 ounces (240 grams) of the flour mixture. Stir vigorously for 3 minutes. Cover the bowl and set aside to rise until doubled and very bubbly, approximately 1 hour.

3 Stir the milk powder, caraway seeds, salt and butter into the sponge.

4 Transfer the dough to a mixer fitted with a dough hook.

5 Gradually add the remaining flour to the sponge. Mix on low speed and continue adding flour until the dough is stiff but slightly tacky. Knead for 5 minutes on low speed.

6 Transfer the dough to a lightly greased bowl, cover and place in a warm place until doubled, approximately 45 to 60 minutes.

7 Punch down the dough and divide into two pieces. Shape each piece into a round loaf and place on a sheet pan that has been dusted with cornmeal or lightly oiled. Brush the loaves with egg wash and let rise until doubled, approximately 45 minutes.

8 Score the tops with a razor or knife. Bake at 375°F (190°C) until golden brown and crusty, approximately 25 minutes.

Approximate values per ⅒-loaf slice: **Calories** 160, **Total fat** 1.5 g, **Saturated fat** 0 g, **Cholesterol** 15 mg, **Sodium** 370 mg, **Total carbohydrates** 31 g, **Protein** 6 g, **Claims**—low fat; no saturated fat; low cholesterol

1 Rye bread sponge.

2 Mixing the rye dough.

3 Shaping the rye loaves.

ROLLED-IN DOUGHS

Baked goods made with rolled-in (laminated) doughs include croissants, Danish pastries and non-yeast-leavened puff pastry. (Puff pastry is discussed in Chapter 32, Pies, Pastries and Cookies.) The dough is so named because the fat is incorporated through a process of rolling and folding. Products made with a rolled-in dough have a distinctive flaky texture created by the repeated layering of fat and dough. As the dough bakes, moisture is released from the fat in the form of steam. The steam is then trapped between the layers of dough, causing them to rise and separate.

Making Rolled-In Doughs

Rolled-in doughs are made following most of the 10 production stages discussed earlier. The principal differences are (1) the butter is incorporated through a turning process after the dough base is fermented and punched down; (2) rolled-in doughs are portioned somewhat differently from other yeast doughs; and (3) the portions are shaped without rounding.

Butter is often used for rolled-in products because of its flavor. Unfortunately, butter is hard to work with because it cracks and breaks when cold and becomes too soft to roll at room temperature. Margarine, shortening or specially formulated high-moisture fats, however, can be used—sometimes in combination with butter—in order to reduce costs or to make it easier to work with the dough.

The dough base should not be kneaded too much, as gluten will continue to develop during the rolling and folding process. An electric dough sheeter can be used to roll the dough. This saves time and ensures a more consistent product.

THE CULTURED CROISSANT

A croissant brings to mind a Parisian sidewalk café and a steaming cup of café crème. It is, however, a truly international delicacy. Bakers in Budapest, Hungary, to celebrate the city's liberation from Turkey in 1686, created the croissant; its shape was derived from the crescent moon of the Turkish flag. Both the French and the Italians soon adopted the delicacy as a breakfast pastry. The first machine for mass-producing croissants was designed by a Japanese firm and manufactured in Italy. Although croissants became popular in the United States only during the late 20th century, Americans now consume millions of croissants each year.

PROCEDURE FOR PREPARING YEAST-RAISED ROLLED-IN DOUGHS

1. Mix the dough and allow it to rise.
2. Prepare the butter or shortening.
3. Roll out the dough evenly, then top it with the butter. The butter may be formed into a rectangle to be enclosed in the dough or it may be softened and spread on the dough.
4. Fold the dough around the butter, enclosing it completely.
5. Roll out the dough into a rectangle, about ¼ to ½ inch (0.6 to 1.2 centimeters) thick. Always be sure to roll at right angles; do not roll haphazardly or in a circle as you would pastry doughs.
6. Fold the dough in thirds. Be sure to brush off any excess flour from between the folds. This completes the first **turn**. Chill the dough for 20 to 30 minutes.
7. Roll out the dough and fold it in the same manner a second and third time, allowing the dough to rest between each turn. After completing the third turn, wrap the dough carefully and allow it to rest, refrigerated, for several hours or overnight before shaping and baking. (Additional turns may be given to this dough, although four are common.)

PARISIAN CROISSANTS

MISE EN PLACE
▶ Soften the butter.

Yield: 60 Rolls

Method: Rolled-in dough

Bread flour	2 lb. 4 oz.	1080 g
Salt	1 oz.	30 g
Granulated sugar	6 oz.	180 g
Milk	21 fl. oz.	630 ml
Active dry yeast	1 oz.	30 g
Unsalted butter, softened	1 lb. 8 oz.	720 g
Egg wash	as needed	as needed

1. Stir the flour, salt and sugar together in the bowl of a mixer fitted with a dough hook.
2. Warm the milk to approximately 90°F (32°C). Stir in the yeast.
3. Add the milk-and-yeast mixture to the dry ingredients. Stir until combined, then knead on medium speed for 10 minutes.
4. Place the dough in a large floured bowl, cover and let rise until doubled in size, approximately 1 hour.
5. Prepare the butter while the dough is rising. Place the butter in an even layer between two large pieces of plastic wrap and roll into a flat rectangle, approximately 8 inches × 11 inches (20 centimeters × 27.5 centimeters) and chill.
6. After the dough has risen, punch it down. Roll out the dough into a large rectangle, approximately ½ inch (1.2 centimeters) thick and large enough to enclose the rectangle of butter. Place the unwrapped butter in the center of the dough and fold the dough around the butter, enclosing it completely.
7. Roll out the block of dough into a long rectangle, approximately 1 inch (2.5 centimeters) thick. Fold the dough in thirds, a single book fold. This completes the first turn. Wrap the dough in plastic and chill for approximately 20 to 30 minutes.
8. Repeat the rolling and folding process two more times, chilling the dough between each turn. When finished, wrap the dough well and chill it overnight before shaping and baking.
9. To shape the dough into croissant rolls, cut off one-fourth of the block at a time, wrapping the rest and returning it to the refrigerator. Roll each section of dough into a large rectangle, about ¼ inch (6 millimeters) thick.
10. Cut the dough into uniform triangles. Starting with the large end, roll each triangle into a crescent and place on a paper-lined sheet pan.
11. Brush lightly with egg wash. Proof until doubled, but do not allow the dough to become so warm that the butter melts.
12. Bake at 375°F (190°C) until golden brown, approximately 12 to 15 minutes.

Approximate values per roll: **Calories** 200, **Total fat** 12 g, **Saturated fat** 7 g, **Cholesterol** 40 mg, **Sodium** 230 mg, **Total carbohydrates** 19 g, **Protein** 3 g, **Vitamin A** 10%

1. Rolling out the butter between two sheets of plastic wrap.

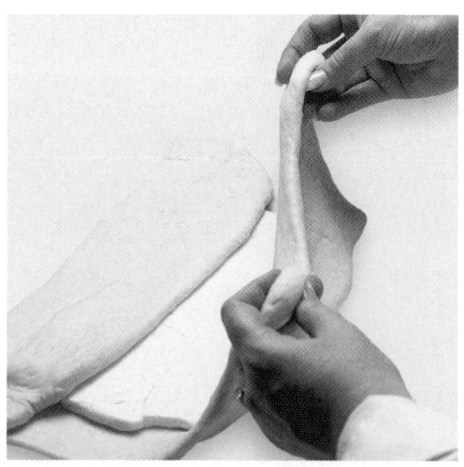

2. Folding the dough around the butter, which has been placed in the center.

3. Brushing the excess flour from the rolled-out dough.

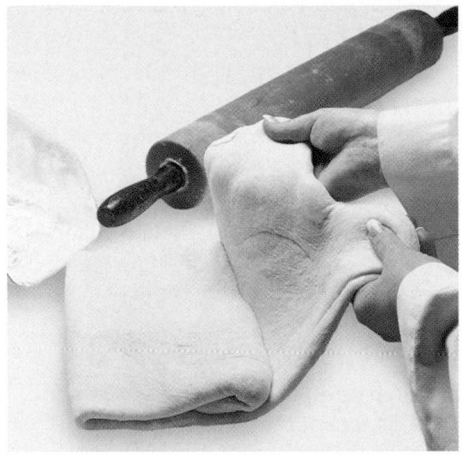

④ Folding the dough in thirds.

⑤ The finished croissant dough.

⑥ Cutting the dough into triangles.

⑦ Baked croissants.

QUALITIES OF BREAD

Bread is judged by its external and internal appearance, flavor, aroma and keeping properties. Well-crafted bread has a pleasing uniform brown surface color. The crust is neither too thick nor too thin, depending on the type of formula. The crust is crisp or tender without being leathery and excessively thick. With the exception of long-fermented sourdough, the crust should be uniform and free from surface blisters. The interior (crumb) of a tender crusted bread or enriched dough product should be even and moist without being sticky. A long-fermented country bread or sourdough may contain an irregular cell structure characteristic of this type of bread. Well-crafted bread has good keeping properties; improperly made bread will stale in a matter of hours. Table 31.5 identifies common problems when making yeast breads and possible solutions.

TABLE 31.5	TROUBLESHOOTING CHART FOR YEAST BREAD	
PROBLEM	**CAUSE**	**SOLUTION**
Dense leaden dough	Too much flour forced into the dough	Gradually add water; adjust formula
Crust too pale	Oven temperature too low	Adjust oven
	Dough overproofed	Proof only until almost doubled, then bake immediately
Crust too dark	Too much steam	Adjust steam
	Oven too hot	Adjust oven
	Too much sugar in the dough	Adjust formula or measure sugar carefully
Top crust separates from loaf	Dough improperly shaped	Shape dough carefully
	Crust not scored properly	Score dough to a depth of ½ in. (1.2 cm)
	Dough dried out during proofing	Cover dough during proofing; increase humidity in proof box
Sides of loaf are cracked	Bread expanded after crust formed in oven	Score top of loaf before baking
	Bread underproofed	Proof until loaf almost doubled
Dense texture	Not enough yeast	Adjust formula or measure yeast carefully
	Not enough fermentation time	Let dough rise until doubled or as directed
	Bread underproofed	Proof until loaf almost doubled
	Improper molding technique	Handle dough gently
	Too much salt	Adjust formula or measure salt carefully
Ropes of undercooked dough running through product	Insufficient kneading	Knead dough until it is smooth and elastic or as directed
	Insufficient rising time	Allow adequate time for proofing
	Oven too hot	Adjust oven
Free-form loaf spreads and flattens	Dough too soft	Adjust formula or measure carefully
Large holes in bread	Too much yeast	Adjust formula or measure yeast carefully
	Overkneaded	Knead only as directed
	Inadequate punch-down	Punch down properly to knead out excess air before shaping
Blisters on crust	Too much liquid	Measure ingredients carefully
	Improper shaping	Knead out excess air before shaping
	Too much steam in oven	Reduce amount of steam or moisture in oven

YEAST BREADS **941**

1 Describe the characteristics of lean and rich doughs and give an example of each.

2 Explain the differences among active dry yeast, instant dry yeast and compressed yeast. Describe the correct procedures for working with these yeasts.

3 Explain the differences between a sponge and a sourdough starter. How is each of these items used?

4 Describe the straight dough mixing method and give two examples of products made with this procedure.

5 List the 10 production stages for yeast breads. Which of these production stages would also apply to quick-bread production? Explain your answer.

6 Discuss strategies for fermenting yeast dough during the summer months when the kitchen temperature can be very hot. Which procedures might be handled differently under those conditions? How would these procedures be different in the colder winter months?

7 Briefly describe the procedure for making a rolled-in dough and give two examples of products made from rolled-in doughs.

8 What can happen when croissant dough is proofed at high temperatures or for too long?

9 Locate a professional organization for bread bakers. What services are available to its members? **WWW**

QUESTIONS FOR DISCUSSION

Terms to Know

leavening
baker's yeast
fresh yeast
sourdough
natural starter
straight dough
sponge
bulk
  fermentation
proofing
punch down

rounding
couche
banneton
brotform
proof box
wash
scoring
slashing
croissant

WHITE SANDWICH BREAD

The finished loaf.

Yield: 2 Large Loaves		Method: Straight dough
Water, warm	12 fl. oz.	360 ml
Nonfat dry milk powder	1¼ oz.	35 g
Granulated sugar	1 oz.	30 g
Salt	2 tsp.	10 ml
Active dry yeast	½ oz.	15 g
Bread flour	1 lb. 8 oz.	720 g
Unsalted butter, softened	1 oz.	30 g
Eggs	2	2

1. Combine the water, milk powder, sugar, salt, yeast and 12 ounces (340 grams) flour. Blend well. Add the butter and eggs and beat for 2 minutes.
2. Stir in the remaining flour, 2 ounces (60 grams) at a time. Knead until the dough is smooth and elastic, approximately 8 minutes.
3. Place the dough in a lightly greased bowl, cover and let it ferment at room temperature until doubled, approximately 1 to 1½ hours.
4. Shape into loaves, pan and proof until doubled.
5. Bake at 400°F (200°C) if free-form or small loaves; bake at 375°F (190°C) if larger loaves. Bake until brown and hollow sounding, approximately 35 minutes for small loaves and 50 minutes for large loaves.

Panning the dough for cloverleaf rolls.

VARIATION:

Whole-Wheat Bread—Substitute up to 12 ounces (360 grams) whole-wheat flour for an equal amount of the bread flour.

Approximate values per 2-oz. (60-g) serving: **Calories** 150, **Total fat** 2 g, **Saturated fat** 1 g, **Cholesterol** 25 mg, **Sodium** 250 mg, **Total carbohydrates** 28 g, **Protein** 6 g, **Vitamin A** 4%, **Claims**—low fat

ENGLISH MUFFIN LOAVES

Yield: 2 Large Loaves		Method: Straight dough
Active dry yeast	½ oz.	15 g
Granulated sugar	1 Tbsp.	15 ml
Baking soda	¼ tsp.	1 ml
Salt	2 tsp.	10 ml
All-purpose flour	1 lb. 8 oz.	720 g
Milk	1 pt.	480 ml
Water	4 fl. oz.	120 ml
Cornmeal	as needed	as needed

1. Stir together the yeast, sugar, baking soda, salt and 12 ounces (360 grams) flour.
2. Combine the milk and water and heat to 120°F (49°C).
3. Stir the warm liquids into the dry ingredients, beating well. Add enough of the remaining flour to make a stiff batter.
4. Spoon the batter into loaf pans that have been greased and dusted with cornmeal. Proof until doubled.
5. Bake at 400°F (200°C) until golden brown and done, approximately 25 minutes.

Approximate values per ½-loaf slice: **Calories** 119, **Total fat** 1 g, **Saturated fat** 0.5 g, **Cholesterol** 3 mg, **Sodium** 202 mg, **Total carbohydrates** 23 g, **Protein** 4 g

FRENCH OR ITALIAN BREAD

Yield: 4 Loaves, 1 lb. 7 oz. (690 g) each   **Method:** Straight dough

Water, warm	39 fl. oz.	1170 ml
Active dry yeast	1 oz.	30 g
Bread flour	3 lb. 12 oz.	1.8 kg
Salt	1¼ oz.	37 g

1 Combine the water and yeast in a mixer bowl. Add the remaining ingredients and mix on low speed with a dough hook until all the flour is incorporated.

2 Increase to medium speed and knead the dough until it is smooth and elastic.

3 Let the dough ferment until doubled. Punch down, divide, shape and score as desired. Proof the loaves until doubled.

4 Bake at 400°F (200°C) with steam during the first few minutes of baking, until the crust is well developed and golden brown and the bread is baked through, approximately 12 minutes for rolls and 20 minutes for small loaves.

Approximate values per 1½-oz. (45-g) serving: **Calories** 80, **Total fat** 0 g, **Saturated fat** 0 g, **Cholesterol** 0 mg, **Sodium** 135 mg, **Total carbohydrates** 16 g, **Protein** 3 g, **Claims**—fat free; low sodium; no sugar

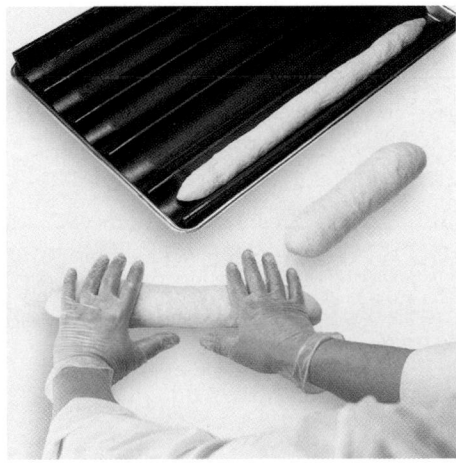

1 The dough is portioned and then rolled into baguettes in two stages.

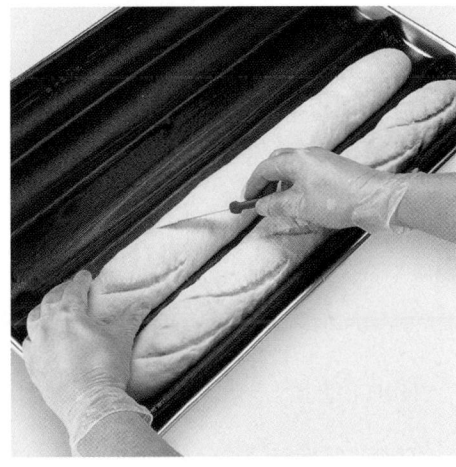

2 The proofed loaves are scored to allow steam to escape.

3 The finished baguettes.

WHOLE-WHEAT BREAD

Yield: 2 Large Loaves or 35 Dinner Rolls   **Method:** Straight dough

Salt	2 tsp.	10 ml
Nonfat dry milk powder	1¼ oz.	38 g
Whole-wheat flour	1 lb. 10 oz.	780 g
Water, warm	17 fl. oz.	510 ml
Active dry yeast	½ oz.	15 g
Honey	3 oz.	90 g
Unsalted butter, softened	1 oz.	30 g
Whole butter, melted	as needed	as needed

1 Combine the salt and milk powder with 12 ounces (360 grams) flour in a large mixer bowl.
2 Stir in the water, yeast, honey and softened butter. Beat until combined into a thick batterlike dough.
3 Add the remaining flour 2 ounces (60 grams) at a time. Knead on medium speed approximately 8 minutes until the dough is smooth and elastic.
4 Place the dough in a lightly greased bowl and cover. Let the dough ferment in a warm place until doubled.
5 Punch down, portion and shape as desired.
6 Let the shaped dough proof until doubled. Bake at 375°F (190°C) until firm and dark brown, approximately 1 hour for loaves and 20 minutes for rolls. Brush the top of the loaves or rolls with melted butter after baking.

Approximate values per 1½-oz. (45-g) serving: **Calories** 170, **Total fat** 2 g, **Saturated fat** 1 g, **Cholesterol** 5 mg, **Sodium** 250 mg, **Total carbohydrates** 32 g, **Protein** 6 g, **Claims**—low fat; low saturated fat; low cholesterol; good source of fiber

SAN FRANCISCO SOURDOUGH BREAD

STOUFFER STANFORD COURT HOTEL, SAN FRANCISCO, CA

Former Executive Chef Ercolino Crugnale

Yield: 1 Loaf   **Method:** Straight dough

Active dry yeast	½ oz.	15 g
Water, warm (120°F/49°C)	8 fl. oz.	240 ml
Sourdough starter	6 oz.	180 g
Bread flour	1 lb.	480 g
Kosher salt	1 Tbsp.	15 ml
Cornmeal	as needed	as needed
Egg white, beaten	1	1

1 Sprinkle the dry yeast over 2 fluid ounces (60 milliliters) warm water and set aside until dissolved and foamy.
2 In the bowl of a mixer fitted with a dough hook, combine the starter and the remaining warm water. Add 6 ounces (180 grams) bread flour.
3 Stir until a dough forms, then add the yeast mixture. Knead 5 minutes on medium speed.
4 Add the remaining flour and the salt. Knead until the dough is smooth and elastic, approximately 10 minutes.
5 Place the dough in a lightly greased bowl and cover with a damp cloth. Ferment the dough in a warm place, approximately 80°F to 90°F (27°C to 32°C), until doubled.
6 Punch down the dough and shape it into a round loaf. Place the loaf on a greased and cornmeal-dusted sheet pan.
7 Proof the dough in a warm place, covered with a damp cloth, until it has risen to 2½ times its original size.

8. Brush the risen loaf with the beaten egg white and score the top of the loaf with a sharp knife.

9. Bake at 450°F (230°C), with a pan of boiling water underneath the oven rack, for 10 minutes.

10. Reduce the oven temperature to 375°F (190°C), remove the water and continue baking until the loaf is well browned, approximately 35 to 45 minutes.

Approximate values per 2-oz. (60-g) serving: **Calories** 135, **Total fat** 0.5 g, **Saturated fat** 0 g, **Cholesterol** 0 mg, **Sodium** 355 mg, **Total carbohydrates** 27 g, **Protein** 4 g, **Claims**—low fat; no saturated fat; no cholesterol

---

BREADSTICKS

Yield: 24 Breadsticks

Method: Straight dough

Active dry yeast	½ oz.	15 g
Water, warm	10 fl. oz.	300 ml
Granulated sugar	1 oz.	30 g
Olive oil	4 fl. oz.	120 ml
Salt	2 tsp.	10 ml
Bread flour	1 lb. 2 oz.	540 g
Egg wash	as needed	as needed
Sesame seeds	3 Tbsp.	30 g

1. Stir the yeast, water and sugar together in a mixer bowl.

2. Blend in the oil, salt and 8 ounces (240 grams) flour.

3. Gradually add the remaining flour. Knead the dough until it is smooth and cleans the sides of the bowl, approximately 5 minutes.

4. Remove the dough from the bowl and allow it to rest for a few minutes. Roll the dough into a rectangle, about ¼ inch (6 millimeters) thick.

5. Cut the dough into 24 even pieces. Roll each piece into a rope and twist; bring the ends together, allowing the sides to curl together. Place on a paper-lined sheet pan.

6. Brush with egg wash and top with sesame seeds. Let the sticks rise until doubled, approximately 20 minutes.

7. Bake at 375°F (190°C) until golden brown, approximately 12 to 15 minutes.

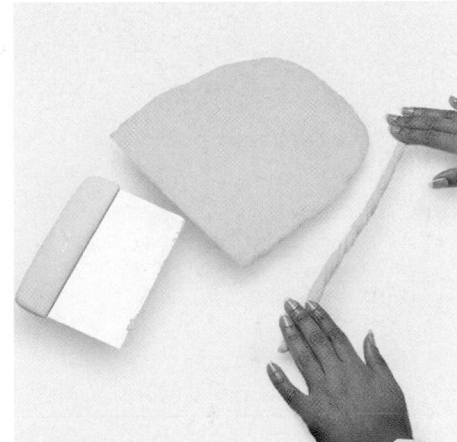

1. Rolling breadstick dough.

VARIATIONS:

Garlic Breadsticks—Knead 1 ounce (30 grams) grated Parmesan and 1 ounce (30 grams) minced garlic into the dough.

Herb Breadsticks—Knead 3 tablespoons (45 milliliters) chopped fresh herbs such as basil, parsley, dill and oregano into the dough.

Approximate values per breadstick: **Calories** 60, **Total fat** 5 g, **Saturated fat** 1 g, **Cholesterol** 10 mg, **Sodium** 190 mg, **Total carbohydrates** 2 g, **Protein** 1 g, **Claims**—low saturated fat; low cholesterol

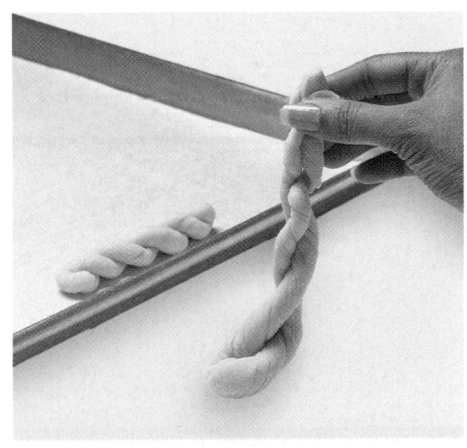

2. Twisting breadstick dough.

FOCACCIA (ROMAN FLATBREAD)

Yield: 1 Half-Sheet Pan, 12 in. × 18 in.
(30 cm × 45 cm)

Method: Straight dough

Granulated sugar	1 Tbsp.	15 ml
Active dry yeast	1 Tbsp.	15 ml
Water, lukewarm	12 fl. oz.	350 ml
All-purpose flour	1 lb. 2 oz.	540 g
Kosher salt	2 tsp.	10 ml
Onion, chopped fine	3 oz.	90 g
Olive oil	1 Tbsp.	15 ml
Fresh rosemary, crushed	2 Tbsp.	30 ml

Topping the flatbread dough with crushed rosemary.

1. Combine the sugar, yeast and water. Stir to dissolve the yeast. Stir in the flour 4 ounces (120 grams) at a time.
2. Stir in 1½ teaspoons (7 milliliters) salt and the onion. Mix well, then knead on a lightly floured board or in the bowl of a mixer fitted with a dough hook until smooth.
3. Place the dough in an oiled bowl, cover and ferment until doubled.
4. Punch down the dough, then flatten it onto an oiled sheet pan. It should be no more than 1 inch (2.5 centimeters) thick. Brush the top of the dough with the olive oil. Let the dough proof until doubled, approximately 15 minutes.
5. Sprinkle the rosemary and remaining ½ teaspoon (2 milliliters) salt on top of the dough. Bake at 400°F (200°C) until lightly browned, approximately 20 minutes.

Approximate values per 1-oz. (30-g) serving: **Calories** 100, **Total fat** 0.5 g, **Saturated fat** 0 g, **Cholesterol** 0 mg, **Sodium** 230 mg, **Total carbohydrates** 21 g, **Protein** 3 g, **Claims**—low fat; no saturated fat; no cholesterol

EGGPLANT AND SUN-DRIED TOMATO PIZZA

GREENS, SAN FRANCISCO, CA

Chef Annie Somerville

Yield: 1 Pizza, 15 in. (37 cm), or 2 Pizzas, 9 in. (22 cm) each

Japanese eggplants	2	2
Extra virgin olive oil	2 fl. oz.	60 ml
Garlic, chopped	2 tsp.	10 ml
Salt and pepper	TT	TT
Pizza Dough (recipe follows)	1 lb.	480 g
Sun-dried tomatoes, packed in oil	5	5
Provolone, grated	4 oz.	120 g
Mozzarella, grated	2 oz.	60 g
Parmesan, grated	½ oz.	15 g
Fresh basil leaves, chiffonade	12	12

1. Slice the eggplants diagonally into ½-inch (1.2-centimeter) slices.
2. Toss the eggplants with 1 fluid ounce (30 grams) olive oil and the garlic; season with salt and pepper.
3. Place the eggplant slices on a baking sheet and roast at 375°F (190°C) until soft in the center, approximately 15 to 20 minutes. Cool and slice into strips.
4. Preheat the oven to 500°F (260°C). Roll out the dough and place it on a lightly oiled pizza pan or well-floured wooden peel; brush it lightly with the remaining oil. Lay the eggplant and sun-dried tomatoes on top. Toss the Provolone and mozzarella together and sprinkle on the pizza.
5. Bake the pizza until the crust is golden and crisp, approximately 8 to 12 minutes. Remove from the oven and sprinkle with the Parmesan and basil.

Approximate values per 4-oz. (120-g) serving: **Calories** 420, **Total fat** 17 g, **Saturated fat** 5 g, **Cholesterol** 15 mg, **Sodium** 500 mg, **Total carbohydrates** 54 g, **Protein** 14 g, **Vitamin A** 100%, **Vitamin C** 30%

PIZZA DOUGH

Yield: 1 Large or 8 Individual Pizzas   **Method:** Straight dough

Active dry yeast	1 Tbsp.	15 ml
Water, warm	2 fl. oz.	60 ml
Bread flour	14 oz.	420 g
Water, cool	6 fl. oz.	180 ml
Salt	1 tsp.	5 ml
Olive oil	2 Tbsp.	30 ml
Honey	1 Tbsp.	15 ml

1. Stir the yeast into the warm water to dissolve. Add the flour.
2. Stir the remaining ingredients into the flour mixture. Knead with a dough hook or by hand until smooth and elastic, approximately 5 minutes.
3. Place the dough in a lightly greased bowl and cover. Allow the dough to ferment in a warm place for 30 minutes. Punch down the dough and divide into portions. The dough may be wrapped and refrigerated for up to 2 days.
4. On a lightly floured surface, roll the dough into very thin rounds and top as desired. Bake at 400°F (200°C) until crisp and golden brown, approximately 8 to 12 minutes.

Approximate values per 2-oz. (60-g) serving: **Calories** 220, **Total fat** 4 g, **Saturated fat** 0.5 g, **Cholesterol** 0 mg, **Sodium** 290 mg, **Total carbohydrates** 41 g, **Protein** 6 g, **Claims**—low saturated fat; no cholesterol

NAAN (INDIAN FLATBREAD)

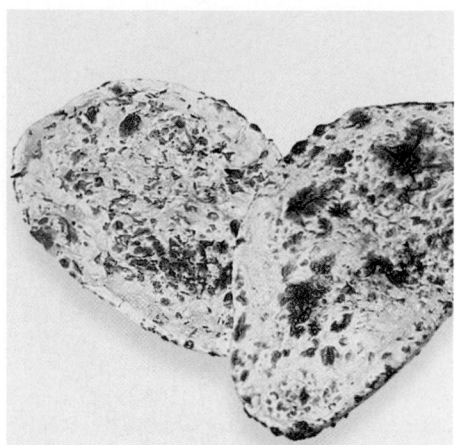

Yield: 6 Loaves, approximately 10 oz. (300 g) each   **Method:** Sponge

Compressed yeast	1 tsp.	5 ml
Water	17 fl. oz.	510 ml
Bread flour	24 oz.	720 g
Whole-wheat flour	12 oz.	360 g
Yogurt	10 oz.	300 g
Olive oil	2 Tbsp.	30 ml
Baking powder	½ tsp.	2 ml
Baking soda	½ tsp.	2 ml
Salt	3½ tsp.	20 g
Vegetable or olive oil	as needed	as needed
Black sesame seeds	as needed	as needed

1. To prepare the sponge, dissolve ½ teaspoon (2 milliliters) yeast in 6 fluid ounces (180 milliliters) water in the bowl of a mixer fitted with a dough hook. Add 8 ounces (240 grams) bread flour and mix until well incorporated. Cover and set aside. Ferment at room temperature until cracks appear on the surface of the starter, approximately 3 hours.

2. Place the sponge and the remaining 16 ounces (480 grams) bread flour, 11 fluid ounces (330 milliliters) water, whole-wheat flour, yogurt, olive oil, baking powder and baking soda in the bowl of a mixer fitted with a dough hook. Mix on low speed for 3 minutes. Stop the mixer and scrape down the bowl. Add the remaining compressed yeast and mix on high speed for an additional 3 minutes. Add the salt, then mix until the dough is smooth and elastic, approximately 5 minutes more.

3. Let the dough ferment, covered, for 3 hours.

4. Punch down the dough and divide it into 6 uniform pieces. Round the portioned dough. Cover and let rest for 30 minutes.

5. Stretch each piece of dough out until it measures 12 inches (30 centimeters) long. Place the dough on flour-dusted sheet pans and proof until doubled, approximately 50 minutes.

6. Dimple the surface of the dough with your fingertips. Brush the dough with oil and sprinkle it with black sesame seeds. Place the dough directly on the heated surface of a deck oven at 485°F (252°C) or place the sheet pan of dough on a rack in the oven. Bake until the breads are well browned and crisp, approximately 10 to 12 minutes. To prevent a soggy crust, open the oven door or vent during the last two minutes of baking to remove any excess steam that may build up in the oven. Cool the loaves on cooling racks, then serve immediately.

Approximate values per 1½-oz. (45-g) serving: **Calories** 100, **Total fat** 1 g, **Saturated fat** 0 g, **Cholesterol** 0 mg, **Sodium** 230 mg, **Total carbohydrates** 19 g, **Protein** 4 g, **Claims**—low fat; no saturated fat; no cholesterol

CHALLAH

Challah (HAH-la) is the traditional bread for Jewish Sabbath and holiday celebrations. It is rich with eggs and flavored with honey; time-honored tradition dictates that challah be braided or formed into a turban-shaped loaf and topped with poppy or sesame seeds. Challah is excellent for toast or sandwiches.

Yield: 2 Large Loaves   **Method:** Straight dough

Honey	3 fl. oz.	90 ml
Salt	1 Tbsp.	15 ml
Bread flour	1 lb. 12 oz.	840 g
Active dry yeast	½ oz.	15 g
Water, hot (90°F/32°C)	2 fl. oz	60 ml
Water, warm	5 fl. oz.	150 ml
Eggs	4	4
Unsalted butter, melted	4 oz.	120 g
Egg wash	as needed	as needed
Sesame or poppy seeds	as needed	as needed

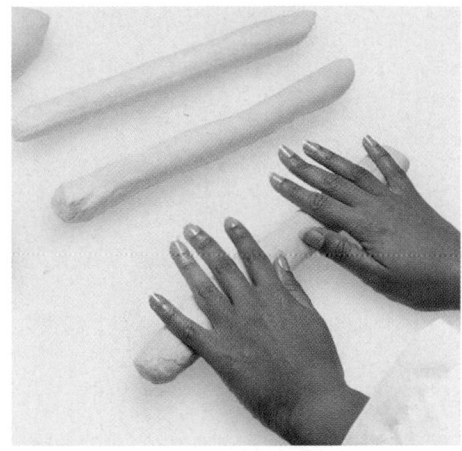

❶ Rolling challah dough into ropes.

❶ Stir together the honey, salt and 8 ounces (240 grams) flour in a mixer bowl. Dissolve the yeast in the hot water. Add the yeast mixture, warm water, eggs and butter to the mixer bowl. Stir until smooth.

❷ Using a dough hook, knead the dough on medium speed, adding the remaining flour 2 ounces (60 grams) at a time until smooth and elastic, approximately 5 minutes.

❸ Place the dough in a lightly greased bowl, cover and let the dough ferment until doubled, approximately 1 to 1½ hours.

❹ Punch down the dough and divide into six equal portions. Roll each portion into a long strip, about 1 inch (2.5 centimeters) in diameter and 12 inches (30 centimeters) long. Lay three strips side by side and braid. Pinch the ends together, then roll the ends of the braid to seal. Tuck the ends under the loaf. Place the loaf on a paper lined sheet pan. Braid the three remaining pieces of dough in the same manner.

❺ Place the loaves on a paper-lined sheet pan. Brush the loaves with egg wash and sprinkle with sesame or poppy seeds. Proof until doubled, approximately 45 minutes.

❻ Bake at 350°F (170°C) until the loaves are golden brown and sound hollow when thumped, approximately 40 minutes.

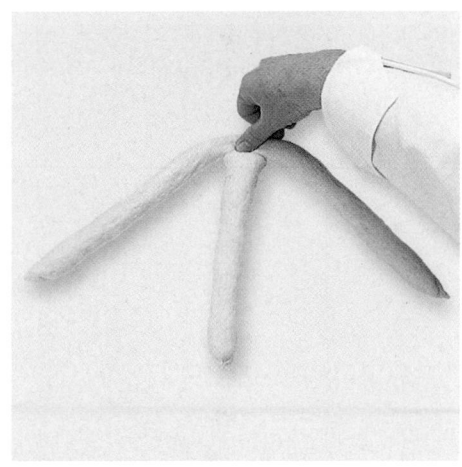

❷ Pressing three strands together.

Approximate values per 2-oz. (30-g) serving: **Calories** 156, **Total fat** 4 g, **Saturated fat** 2 g, **Cholesterol** 44 mg, **Sodium** 145 mg, **Total carbohydrates** 25 g, **Protein** 6 g

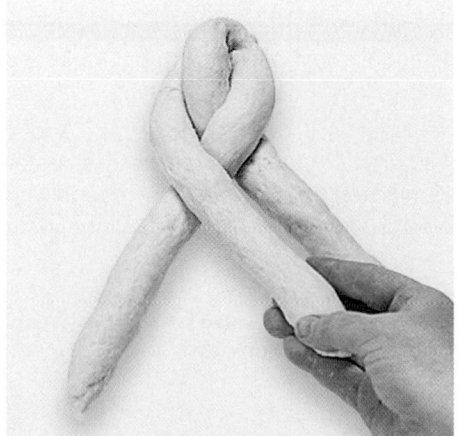

❸ Crossing the strips one over the other to make the braid.

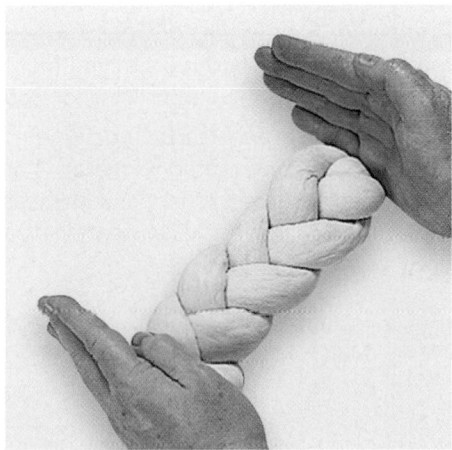

❹ Rolling the ends together to seal the braid.

BRIOCHE

Brioche (bree-ohsh) is a rich, tender bread made with a generous amount of eggs and butter. The high ratio of fat makes this dough difficult to work with, but the flavor is well worth the extra effort. Brioche is traditionally baked in fluted pans and has a cap or topknot of dough; this shape is known as brioche à tête. The molded dough is washed with beaten egg or egg yolks and milk or cream before and after proofing. It is important to keep the wash from touching the sides of the pan, where it could coagulate and prevent the dough from rising when baked. The dough may also be baked in a loaf pan, making it perfect for toast or canapés.

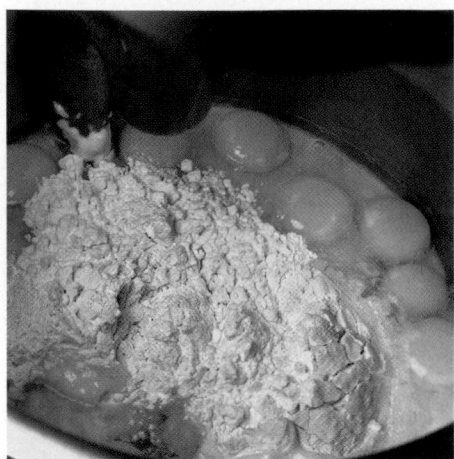

❶ Combining the ingredients for brioche.

❷ Adding the yeast-and-water mixture to the dough.

Yield: 3 Large Loaves or 60 Rolls	**Method:** Straight dough	
All-purpose flour	4 lb. 7 oz.	2.1 kg
Eggs	24	24
Salt	1¾ oz.	50 g
Granulated sugar	7 oz.	210 g
Active dry yeast	1¾ oz.	50 g
Water, warm	7 fl. oz.	210 ml
Unsalted butter, room temperature	3 lb.	1.3 kg

❶ Place the flour, eggs, salt and sugar into the bowl of a mixer fitted with a dough hook. Stir the ingredients together.

❷ Combine the yeast and water and add to the other ingredients.

❸ Knead approximately 20 minutes on medium speed. The dough will be smooth, shiny and moist. It should not form a ball.

❹ Slowly add the butter to the dough. Knead only until all the butter is incorporated. Remove the dough from the mixer and place it into a bowl dusted with flour. Cover and let the dough ferment at room temperature until doubled.

❺ Punch down the dough, cover tightly with plastic wrap and refrigerate overnight.

❻ Portion and shape the chilled dough as desired. Place the shaped dough in well-greased pans and proof at room temperature until doubled.

❼ Bake at 375°F (190°C) until the brioche is a dark golden brown and sounds hollow. Baking time will vary depending on the temperature of the dough and the size of the rolls or loaves being baked.

VARIATIONS:

Raisin Brioche—Gently warm 3 fluid ounces (90 milliliters) rum with 6 ounces (180 grams) raisins. Set aside until the raisins are plumped. Drain off the remaining rum and add the raisins to the dough after the butter is incorporated.

Brioche for Sandwiches or Coulibiac—Reduce the sugar to 3 ounces (90 grams). Ferment the dough, then retard it overnight. Mold in a rectangular loaf pan for slicing. Or use the dough to wrap salmon and fillings for Coulibiac.

Savory Cheese and Herb Brioche—Reduce the sugar to 3 ounces (90 grams). Add 4 ounces (120 grams) grated Parmesan, 4 ounces (120 grams) grated Gruyère cheese, ¼ teaspoon (1 milliliter) black pepper and ¼ teaspoon (1 milliliter) dried thyme to the dough with the flour. Mold in rectangular or conical pans. Served sliced thin with smoked salmon, pâté or other savory spreads.

Approximate values per 4-oz. (120-g) serving: **Calories** 475, **Total fat** 30 g, **Saturated fat** 17 g, **Cholesterol** 192 mg, **Sodium** 138 mg, **Total carbohydrates** 43 g, **Protein** 9 g, **Vitamin A** 30%, **Iron** 16%

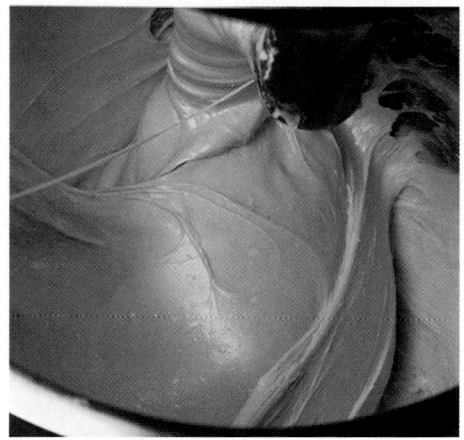

③ Brioche dough after kneading for 20 minutes.

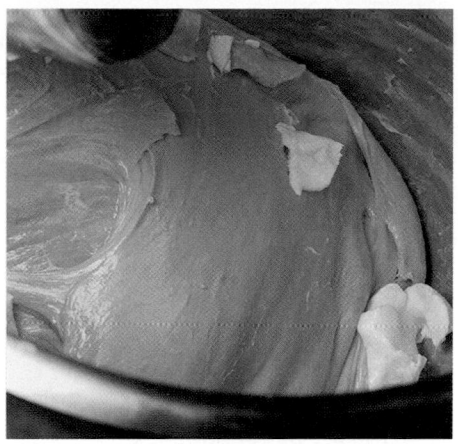

④ Adding the butter to the brioche dough.

⑤ The finished brioche dough ready for fermentation.

⑥ Shaping a brioche à tête.

⑦ Panning the rolls.

⑧ A finished brioche and slices.

JUMBO CINNAMON BUNS

Yield: 24 Large Rolls **Method:** Straight dough

Dough:		
Buttermilk	12 fl. oz.	360 ml
Instant yeast	2 oz.	60 g
Egg	1	1
Egg yolks	3	3
Vanilla extract	1 tsp.	5 ml
All-purpose flour	2 lb.	960 g
Granulated sugar	5 oz.	150 g
Salt	½ oz.	15 g
Unsalted butter, softened	18 oz.	540 g
Filling:		
Unsalted butter, melted	6 oz.	180 g
Cinnamon, ground	½ oz.	15 g
Brown sugar	6 oz.	180 g
Pecans, chopped	12 oz.	360 g
Raisins (optional)	12 oz.	360 g
Powdered Sugar Glaze (recipe follows)	as needed	as needed

1. In the bowl of a mixer fitted with a dough hook, combine the buttermilk, yeast, egg, egg yolks and vanilla. Add the flour, sugar, salt and softened butter. Mix on medium speed until well blended, until a windowpane has been obtained and the dough reaches approximately 75°F (24°C).
2. Ferment the dough until doubled, approximately 1 hour. Meanwhile, prepare the filling.
3. Whisk together the melted butter, cinnamon and brown sugar. Set aside.
4. Roll the fermented dough into a rectangle measuring 18 inches × 30 inches (45 centimeters × 75 centimeters).
5. Spread the filling evenly over the entire surface of the dough. Sprinkle with the pecans and raisins (if using).
6. Starting with the longer side, roll the dough into a spiral. Cut into 24 pieces, each approximately 1½ inches (3.7 centimeters) thick. Place the rolls close together, cut side up, on a paper-lined sheet pan and allow them to rise until the rolls have increased 70 percent in volume.
7. Bake at 350°F (180°C) until golden brown, approximately 20 to 25 minutes.
8. Cool slightly, then top with Powdered Sugar Glaze.

Approximate values per roll: **Calories** 510, **Total fat** 35 g, **Saturated fat** 16 g, **Cholesterol** 100 mg, **Sodium** 370 mg, **Total carbohydrates** 45 g, **Protein** 8 g, **Vitamin A** 15%, **Iron** 15%

POWDERED SUGAR GLAZE

Yield: 11 fl. oz. (330 ml)

Powdered sugar, sifted	1 lb.	480 g
Vanilla extract	2 tsp.	10 ml
Lemon juice	2 tsp.	10 ml
Water, warm	2 Tbsp.	30 ml

1. Combine all the ingredients in a small bowl. Stir to blend thoroughly and dissolve any lumps. Cover and store at room temperature.

Approximate values per 1-fl.-oz. (30-ml) serving: **Calories** 160, **Total fat** 0 g, **Saturated fat** 0 g, **Cholesterol** 0 mg, **Sodium** 0 mg, **Total carbohydrates** 41 g, **Protein** 0 g

PECAN STICKY BUNS

Yield: 12–15 Buns **Method:** Straight dough

Active dry yeast	1 oz.	30 g
Granulated sugar	2 oz.	60 g
Milk	1 Tbsp.	15 ml
Buttermilk	5½ fl. oz.	165 ml
Salt	2 tsp.	10 ml
Vanilla extract	1 tsp.	5 ml
Lemon zest, grated	1 Tbsp.	15 ml
Lemon juice	1 tsp.	5 ml
Egg yolks	2	2
All-purpose flour	1 lb.	480 g
Unsalted butter, very soft	8 oz.	240 g
Topping:		
Honey	3 fl. oz.	90 ml
Brown sugar	3 oz.	90 g
Pecans, chopped	2 oz.	60 g
Filling:		
Cinnamon, ground	1 tsp.	5 ml
Pecans, chopped	3 oz.	90 g
Brown sugar	4 oz.	120 g
Unsalted butter, melted	3 oz.	90 g

❶ Brushing melted butter over the sticky bun dough.

1 To make the dough, stir the yeast, sugar and milk together in a small bowl. Set aside.

2 Stir the buttermilk, salt, vanilla extract, lemon zest and lemon juice together and add to the yeast mixture.

3 Add the egg yolks, flour and softened butter to the liquid mixture. Knead until the butter is evenly distributed and the dough is smooth and fully developed, approximately 6 minutes. Cover and ferment until doubled.

4 Prepare the topping and filling mixtures while the dough is fermenting. To make the topping, cream the honey and sugar together. Stir in the pecans. This mixture will be very stiff. To make the filling, stir the cinnamon, pecans and sugar together.

5 Lightly grease muffin cups, then distribute the topping mixture evenly, about 1 tablespoon (15 milliliters) per muffin cup. Set the pans aside at room temperature until the dough is ready.

6 Punch down the dough and let it rest 10 minutes. Roll out the dough into a rectangle about ½ inch (1.2 centimeters) thick. Brush with melted butter and top evenly with the filling mixture.

7 Starting with either long edge, roll up the dough. Cut into slices about ¾ to 1 inch (1.8 to 2.5 centimeters) thick. Place a slice in each muffin cup over the topping.

8 Let the buns proof until doubled, approximately 20 minutes. Bake at 325°F (160°C) until very brown, approximately 25 minutes. Immediately invert the muffin pans onto paper-lined sheet pans to let the buns and their topping slide out.

❷ Rolling up the filling in the sticky bun dough.

❸ Cutting and panning the sticky buns.

Approximate values per bun: **Calories** 480, **Total fat** 26 g, **Saturated fat** 11 g, **Cholesterol** 75 mg, **Sodium** 100 mg, **Total carbohydrates** 55 g, **Protein** 5 g, **Vitamin A** 15%, **Iron** 15%

DANISH PASTRIES

According to baking lore, Danish pastry was actually created by a French baker more than 350 years ago. He forgot to knead butter into his bread dough and attempted to cover the mistake by folding in softened butter. This rich, flaky pastry is now popular worldwide for breakfasts, desserts and snacks. The dough may be shaped in a variety of ways and is usually filled with jam, fruit, cream or marzipan. Applying a sugar syrup wash to the pastries when they are hot from the oven adds sheen and flavor.

❶ Kneading the cold butter with the flour.

Yield: 36 Pastries

Method: Rolled-in dough

Active dry yeast	½ oz.	15 g
All-purpose flour	1 lb. 4 oz.	600 g
Granulated sugar	4 oz.	120 g
Water, warm	4 fl. oz.	120 ml
Milk, warm	4 fl. oz.	120 ml
Eggs, room temperature	2	2
Salt	1 tsp.	5 ml
Vanilla extract	1 tsp.	5 ml
Cinnamon, ground	½ tsp.	2 ml
Unsalted butter, melted	1½ oz.	45 g
Unsalted butter, cold	1 lb.	480 g
Egg wash	as needed	as needed

❶ In a large bowl, stir together the yeast and 12 ounces (360 grams) flour. Add the sugar, water, milk, eggs, salt, vanilla, cinnamon and melted butter. Stir until well combined.

❷ Add the remaining flour gradually, kneading the dough by hand or with a mixer fitted with a dough hook. Knead until the dough is smooth and only slightly tacky to the touch, approximately 2 to 3 minutes.

❸ Place the dough in a bowl that has been lightly dusted with flour. Cover and refrigerate for 1 to 1½ hours.

❹ Prepare the remaining butter while the dough is chilling. Start by sprinkling flour over the work surface and placing the cold butter on the flour. Then pound the butter with a rolling pin until the butter softens. Using a pastry scraper or the heel of your hand, knead the butter and flour until the mixture is spreadable. The butter should still be cold. If it begins to melt, refrigerate it until firm. Keep the butter chilled until the dough is ready.

❺ On a lightly floured surface, roll out the dough into a large rectangle, about ½ inch (1.2 centimeters) thick. Brush away any excess flour.

❻ Spread the chilled butter evenly over two-thirds of the dough. Fold the unbuttered third over the center, then fold the buttered third over the top. Press the edges together to seal in the butter.

❼ Roll the dough into a rectangle about 12 inches × 18 inches (30 centimeters × 45 centimeters). Fold the dough in thirds as before. This rolling and folding (called a turn) must be done a total of six times. Chill the dough between turns as necessary. After the final turn, wrap the dough well and retard for at least 4 hours or overnight.

❷ Spreading the butter over two-thirds of the rolled-out dough.

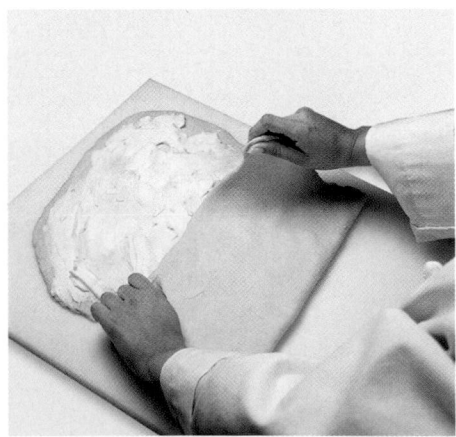

❸ Folding the dough in thirds to cover the butter.

❽ Shape and fill the Danish dough as desired. Place the shaped pastries on a paper-lined baking sheet and proof for approximately 15 to 20 minutes.

❾ Brush the pastries with egg wash and sprinkle lightly with sugar if desired. Bake at 400°F (200°C) for 5 minutes. Decrease the oven temperature to 350°F (180°C) and bake until light brown, approximately 12 to 15 minutes.

Approximate values per pastry, without filling: **Calories** 85, **Total fat** 1.5 g, **Saturated fat** 0 g, **Cholesterol** 15 mg, **Sodium** 65 mg, **Total carbohydrates** 15.5 g, **Protein** 2 g

④ Rolling out the dough.

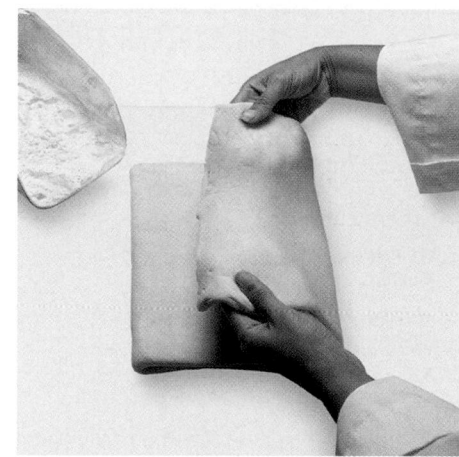

⑤ Folding the dough in thirds to complete a turn.

⑥ Cutting rectangles of Danish dough.

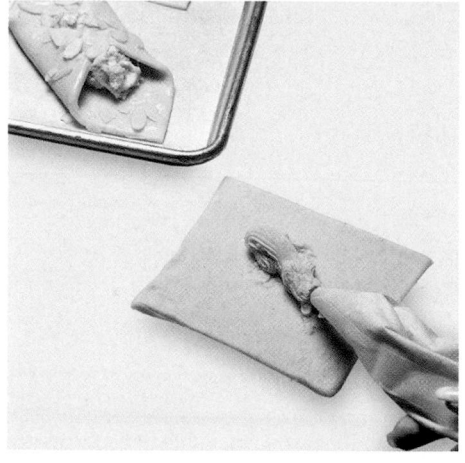

⑦ Piping cream cheese filling onto Danish dough.

⑧ Shaping snails from Danish dough.

PROCEDURE FOR SHAPING PINWHEELS OR WINDMILLS

Roll out the Danish dough approximately ⅛ to ½ inch (3 to 6 millimeters) thick and cut it into even 4-inch (10-centimeter) squares (upper left). Starting at each corner, make four diagonal cuts 1 inch (2.5 centimeters) long in the dough without cutting the dough in half (upper right). Fold one point in each triangular section of dough down toward the center to form the pinwheel shape (lower left and right).

FILLINGS FOR DANISH PASTRIES

CREAM CHEESE FILLING

Yield: 2 lb. 4 oz. (1080 g)

Cream cheese	1 lb. 8 oz.	720 g
Granulated sugar	4 oz.	120 g
Eggs	3	3
Lemon zest, grated fine	1 tsp.	5 ml
Vanilla extract	1 Tbsp.	15 ml
All-purpose or pastry flour	3 oz.	90 g

1. In the bowl of a mixer fitted with the paddle attachment, blend the cream cheese and sugar on low speed until smooth. Scrape down the bowl and gradually add the eggs.
2. Stir in the lemon zest and vanilla. Fold in the flour.
3. Fill pastries with this mixture before baking.

Approximate values per 1-oz. (30-g) serving: **Calories** 100, **Total fat** 6 g, **Saturated fat** 4 g, **Cholesterol** 25 mg, **Sodium** 75 mg, **Total carbohydrates** 10 g, **Protein** 1 g

APRICOT FILLING

Yield: 2 lb. (960 g)

Dried apricots	8 oz.	240 g
Orange juice	1 pt.	480 ml
Granulated sugar	6 oz.	180 g
Salt	¼ tsp.	1 ml
Unsalted butter	2 oz.	60 g

1. Place the apricots and orange juice in a small saucepan. Cover and simmer until the apricots are very tender, approximately 25 minutes. Stir in the sugar and salt. When the sugar is dissolved, add the butter and remove from the heat.
2. Purée the mixture in a blender until smooth. Cool completely before using.

Approximate values per 1-oz. (30-g) serving: **Calories** 60, **Total fat** 1.5 g, **Saturated fat** 1 g, **Cholesterol** 5 mg, **Sodium** 20 mg, **Total carbohydrates** 13 g, **Protein** 0 g, **Vitamin A** 20%, **Vitamin C** 15%, **Claims**—low fat; low sodium; good source of vitamins A and C

RICOTTA FILLING

Yield: 2 lb. 14 oz. (1.25 kg)

Cream cheese	1 lb. 8 oz.	720 g
Ricotta	10 oz.	300 g
Granulated sugar	5 oz.	150 g
Eggs	2	2
Vanilla extract	1 tsp.	5 ml
Pastry flour	4 oz.	120 g

1. In the bowl of a mixer fitted with a paddle, combine the cream cheese and ricotta on low speed until no lumps remain.
2. Add the sugar; gradually add the eggs and scrape down the bowl between additions.
3. Add the vanilla extract and then the flour and combine well.

Approximate values 1-oz. (30-g) serving: **Calories** 90, **Total fat** 6 g, **Saturated fat** 4 g, **Cholesterol** 25 mg, **Sodium** 50 mg, **Total carbohydrates** 6 g, **Protein** 2 g

KUGELHOPF

Yield: 4 Loaves, approximately
1 lb. 9 oz. (750 g) each   **Method:** Straight dough

Milk	10 fl. oz.	300 ml
Instant yeast	2 oz.	60 g
Eggs	16 oz.	480 g
Vanilla extract	1 tsp.	5 ml
Bread flour	2 lb. 2 oz.	1020 g
Granulated sugar	5 oz.	150 g
Salt	3/4 oz	22 g
Unsalted butter, softened	18 oz.	540 g
Raisins	1 lb.	480 g

1. In a mixer fitted with the paddle, combine the milk, yeast, eggs and vanilla. Add the bread flour, sugar and salt. Mix on medium speed until well blended.

2. Switch to the dough hook. Knead until the ingredients are thoroughly mixed and the dough is soft and smooth. Gradually add the butter, kneading until the dough is smooth. Add the raisins and gently mix them into the dough.

3. Ferment the dough, covered until doubled, approximately 1 to 1 1/2 hours. Punch down the dough and let it bench rest for 15 minutes, covered.

4. Divide the dough into four equal pieces. Round the dough and place each piece into a buttered kugelhopf mold. Proof until the loaves have gained 70% in volume, approximately 1 hour.

5. Bake at 350°F (175°C) for approximately 45 minutes. If the loaves brown too quickly, cover them with lightly buttered aluminum foil.

6. Cool the loaves in the pans for approximately 30 minutes before unmolding to prevent collapsing.

Approximate values per 1-oz. (30-g) serving: **Calories** 100, **Total fat** 5 g, **Saturated fat** 3 g, **Cholesterol** 30 mg, **Sodium** 90 mg, **Total carbohydrates** 12 g, **Protein** 2 g

CHAPTER THIRTY-TWO

PIES, PASTRIES AND COOKIES

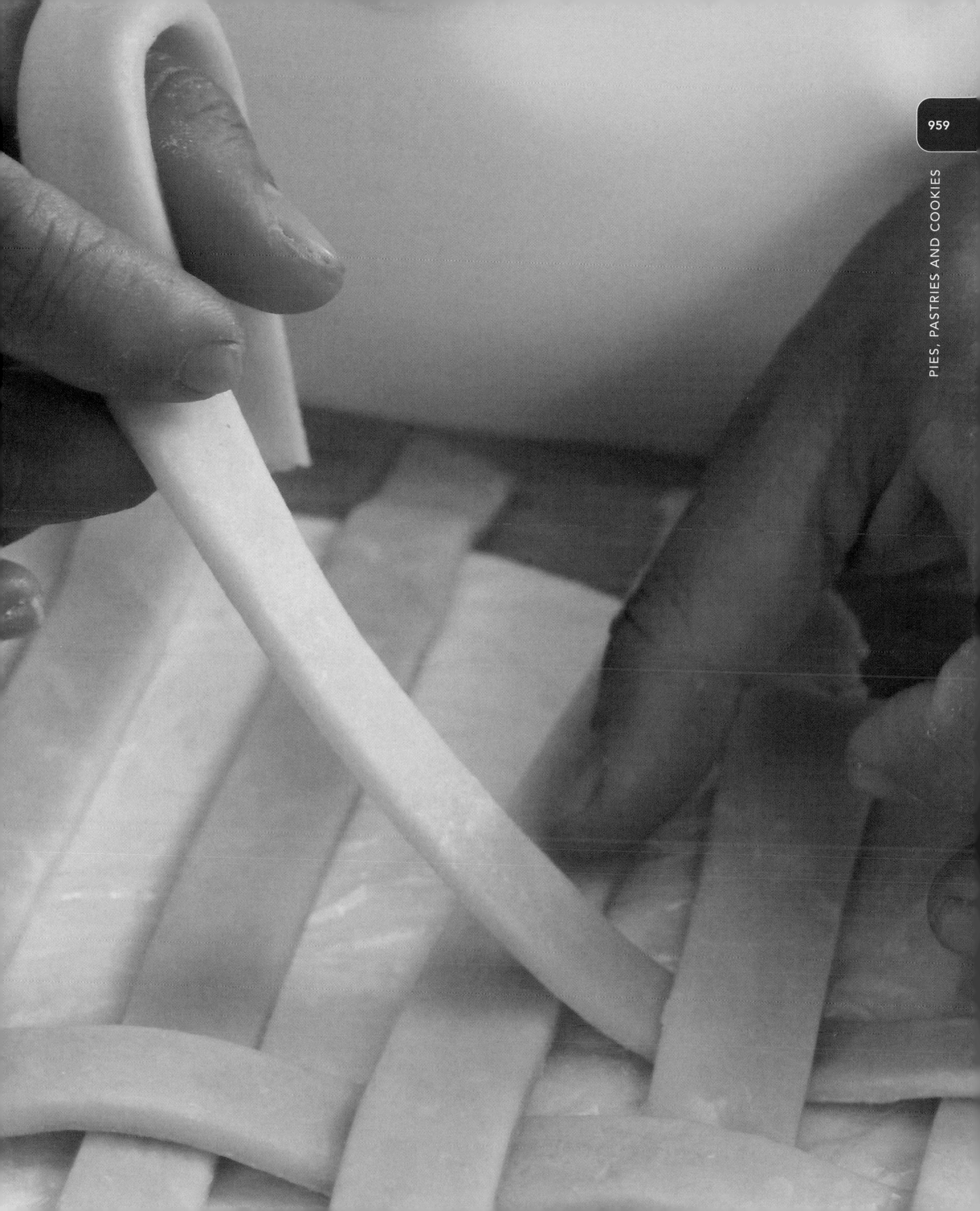

After studying this chapter, you will be able to:

- prepare a variety of pie crusts and fillings
- prepare a variety of classic pastries
- prepare a variety of meringues
- prepare a variety of cookies
- prepare a variety of dessert and pastry items, incorporating components from other chapters

MENTION PASTRIES TO DINERS AND MOST conjure up images of buttery dough baked to crisp flaky perfection and filled or layered with rich cream, ripe fruit or smooth custard. Mention pastries to novice chefs and most conjure up images of sophisticated, complex and intimidating work. Although the diners are correct, the novice chefs are not. Pastry making is the art of creating containers for various fillings. Taken one step at a time, most pastries are nothing more than selected building blocks or components assembled in a variety of ways to create traditional or unique desserts.

Perhaps the most important (and versatile) building block is the dough. Pastries can be made with flaky dough, mealy dough, sweet dough, puff pastry, éclair dough, meringue or phyllo. See Table 32.1. Because pies, tarts and cookies are constructed from some of these same doughs (principally pie dough and sweet dough), they, as well as pie fillings, are discussed in the section on pies and tarts; puff pastry, éclair paste and baked meringue are discussed in the section on classic pastries. The cream, custard and mousse fillings used in some of the recipes at the end of this chapter are discussed in Chapter 34, Custards, Creams, Frozen Desserts and Dessert Sauces. Cakes and frostings are covered in Chapter 35, Cakes and Frostings.

PIES AND TARTS

A **pie** is composed of a sweet or savory filling in a baked crust. It can be open-faced (without a top crust) or, more typically, topped with a full or lattice crust. A pie is generally made in a round, slope-sided pan and cut into wedges for service. A **tart** is similar to a pie except it is made in a shallow, straight-sided pan, often with fluted edges. A tart can be almost any shape; round, square, rectangular and petal shapes are the most common. It is usually open-faced and derives much of its beauty from an attractive arrangement of glazed fruit, piped cream or chocolate decorations.

Crusts

Pie crusts and tart shells can be made from several types of dough or crumbs. **Flaky dough**, **mealy dough** and **crumbs** are best for pie crusts; sweet dough is usually used for tart shells. A pie crust or tart shell can be shaped and completely baked before filling (known as **baked blind**) or filled and baked simultaneously with the filling.

FLAKY AND MEALY DOUGHS

Flaky and mealy pie doughs are quick, easy and versatile. Flaky dough, sometimes known as **pâte brisée**, takes its name from its final baked texture. It is best for pie top crusts and lattice coverings and may be used for prebaked shells that will be filled with a cooled filling shortly before service. Mealy dough takes its name from its raw texture. It is used whenever a soggy crust would be a problem (for example, as the bottom crust of a custard or fruit pie) because it is sturdier and resists sogginess better than flaky

TABLE 32.1 CLASSIFICATION OF PASTRY DOUGHS

DOUGH	FRENCH NAME	CHARACTERISTICS AFTER BAKING	USE
Flaky dough	Pâte brisée	Very flaky; not sweet	Prebaked pie shells; pie top crusts
Mealy dough	Pâte brisée	Moderately flaky; not sweet	Custard, cream or fruit pie crusts; quiche crusts
Sweet dough	Pâte sucrée	Very rich; crisp; not flaky	Tart and tartlet shells
Éclair paste	Pâte à choux	Hollow with crisp exterior	Cream puffs; éclairs; savory products
Puff pastry	Pâte feuilletée	Rich but not sweet; hundreds of light, flaky layers	Tart and pastry cases; cookies; layered pastries; savory products
Meringue	Meringue	Sweet; light; crisp or soft depending on preparation	Topping or icing; baked as a shell or component for layered desserts; cookies
Phyllo	Phyllo	Very thin, crisp, flaky layers; bland	Middle Eastern pastries and savory dishes, especially hors d'oeuvre; baklava

dough. Both flaky and mealy doughs are too delicate for tarts that will be removed from the pan for service. Sweet dough, described later, is better for these types of tarts.

Flaky and mealy doughs contain little or no sugar and can be prepared from the same formula with only a slight variation in mixing method. For both types of dough, a cold fat, such as butter or shortening, is cut into the flour. The amount of flakiness in the baked crust depends on the size of the fat particles in the dough. The larger the pieces of fat, the flakier the crust will be. This is because the flakes are actually the sides of fat pockets created during baking by the melting fat and steam. When preparing flaky dough, the fat is left in larger pieces, about the size of peas or peanuts. When preparing mealy dough, the fat is blended in more thoroughly, until the mixture resembles coarse cornmeal. Because the resulting fat pockets are smaller, the crust is less flaky.

The type of fat used affects both the dough's flavor and flakiness. Butter contributes a delicious flavor, but does not produce as flaky a crust as other fats. Butter is also more difficult to work with than other fats because of its lower melting point and its tendency to become brittle when chilled. Hydrogenated vegetable shortening produces a flaky crust but contributes nothing to its flavor. The flakiest pastry is made with lard. Because some people dislike its flavor for sweet pies or do not eat pork products, lard is more often used for pâté en croûte or other savory preparations. Some chefs prefer to use a combination of butter with either shortening or lard. Oil is not an appropriate substitute as it disperses too thoroughly throughout the dough; when baked, the crust will be extremely fragile but without any flakiness.

After the fat is cut into the flour, water or milk is added to form a soft dough. Less water is needed for mealy dough because more flour is already in contact with the fat, reducing its ability to absorb liquid. Cold water is normally used for both flaky and mealy doughs. The water should be well chilled to prevent softening the fat. Milk may be used to increase richness and nutritional value. It will produce a darker, less crisp crust, however. If dry milk powder is used, it should be dissolved in water first.

Hand mixing is best for small to moderate quantities of dough. The chef retains better control over the procedure when he or she can feel the fat being incorporated. It is very difficult to make flaky dough with an electric mixer or food processor, as machines tend to cut the fat in too thoroughly. (If a food processor is used, the mixing time should be brief.) Overmixing develops too much gluten, making the dough elastic and difficult to use. If an electric mixer must be used for large quantities, use the paddle at the lowest speed and be sure the fat is well chilled, even frozen. Refrigerating pie dough after mixing is recommended to allow the moisture to evenly distribute through the mixture and to firm the fat for ease of handling.

PROCEDURE FOR **PREPARING FLAKY AND MEALY DOUGHS**

1. Sift flour, salt and sugar (if used) together in a large bowl.
2. Cut the fat into the flour.
3. Gradually add a cold liquid, mixing gently until the dough holds together. Do not overmix.
4. Cover the dough with plastic wrap and chill thoroughly before using.
5. Remember that rerolled scraps will be tough and elastic.

BASIC PIE DOUGH

Yield: 2 lb. 10 oz. (1260 g)

Unsalted butter, chilled	1 lb.	480 g
Pastry flour	1 lb. 6 oz.	660 g
Buttermilk or water	4 fl. oz.	120 ml
Salt	2 tsp.	10 ml
Granulated sugar (optional)	1 Tbsp.	15 ml
Vanilla extract (optional)	1 Tbsp.	15 ml

1. Cut butter into medium dice ⅜ inch (9 millimeters) square. Sift the flour onto a work surface or into a large bowl.
2. Cut the butter into the flour mixture until the desired consistency (flaky or mealy) is reached.
3. Combine the buttermilk, salt, sugar and vanilla (if using) in a bowl with a whisk. Gradually add the buttermilk to the flour mixture. Mix gently until the dough holds together. Do not overmix or add too much liquid.
4. Cover the dough with plastic wrap and chill thoroughly before using.

Approximate values per 1-oz. (30-g) serving: **Calories** 130 **Total fat** 9 g, **Saturated fat** 6 g, **Cholesterol** 25 mg, **Sodium** 110 mg, **Total carbohydrates** 11 g, **Protein** 2 g

1. Cutting the fat into the flour coarsely for flaky dough.

2. Cutting the fat into the flour finely for mealy dough.

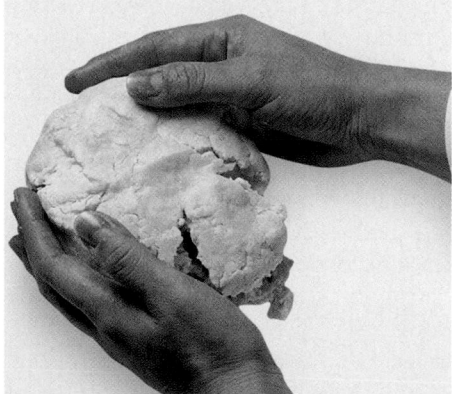

3. The finished dough.

SWEET DOUGH

Sweet dough or **pâte sucrée** is a rich, nonflaky dough used for sweet tart shells. It is sturdier than flaky or mealy dough because it contains egg yolks and the fat is blended in thoroughly. Because more fat coats the flour, less gluten is formed, making for a tender dough when baked. It is also more cookielike than classic pie dough and has the rich flavor of butter. It creates a crisp but tender crust and is excellent for tartlets as well as for straight-sided tarts that will be removed from their pans before service. The raw dough may be kept refrigerated for up to 2 weeks or frozen for up to 3 months.

PROCEDURE FOR **PREPARING SWEET DOUGH**

1 Cream softened butter. Add sugar and beat until the mixture is light and fluffy.

2 Slowly add eggs, blending well.

3 Slowly add flour, mixing only until incorporated. Overmixing toughens the dough.

4 Cover the dough with plastic wrap and chill thoroughly before using.

5 Scraps may be rerolled once or twice, provided the dough is still cool, nongreasy and pliable. If too much gluten develops, the crust will shrink and toughen.

SWEET DOUGH

Yield: 7 lb. 8 oz. (3.5 kg) Dough; approx. 10 Shells, 9 in. (22 cm) each

Unsalted butter, softened	1 lb. 8 oz.	720 g
Powdered sugar	1 lb. 5 oz.	630 g
Egg yolks	1 lb. (26 yolks)	480 g
Eggs	2	2
All-purpose flour	3 lb. 8 oz.	1680 g

1 Cream the butter and powdered sugar in the large bowl of a mixer fitted with the paddle attachment.

2 Combine the egg yolks and whole eggs. Slowly add the eggs to the creamed butter. Mix until smooth and free of lumps, scraping down the bowl as needed.

3 With the mixer on low speed, slowly add the flour to the butter-and-egg mixture. Mix only until incorporated; do not overmix. The dough should be firm, smooth and not sticky.

4 Dust a half-sheet pan with flour. Pack the dough into the pan evenly. Wrap well in plastic wrap and chill until firm.

5 Work with a small portion of the chilled dough when shaping tart shells or other products.

Approximate values per 1-oz. (30-g) serving: **Calories** 120, **Total fat** 5 g, **Saturated fat** 3 g, **Cholesterol** 15 mg, **Sodium** 0 mg, **Total carbohydrates** 16 g, **Protein** 2 g, **Vitamin A** 4%

SHAPING CRUSTS

Crusts are shaped by rolling out the dough to fit into a pie pan or tart shell (mold) or to sit on top of fillings. Mealy, flaky and sweet doughs are all easier to roll out and work with if well chilled, as chilling keeps the fat firm and prevents stickiness. When rolling and shaping the dough, work on a clean, flat surface (wood or marble is best). Lightly dust the work surface, rolling pin and dough with pastry flour before starting to roll the dough. Also, work only with a manageable amount at a time: usually one crust's worth for a pie or standard-sized tart or enough for 10 to 12 tartlet shells.

Roll out the dough from the center, working toward the edges. Periodically, lift the dough gently and rotate it. This keeps the dough from sticking and helps produce an even thickness. If the dough sticks to the rolling pin or work surface, sprinkle on a bit more flour. Too much flour, however, makes the crust dry and crumbly and causes gray streaks.

MISE EN PLACE
◄ Soften butter.

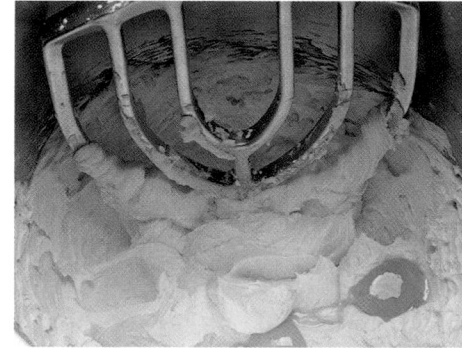

1 Mixing sweet dough.

2 The finished sweet dough.

PROCEDURE FOR ROLLING AND SHAPING DOUGH FOR DOUBLE CRUST PIES AND TART SHELLS

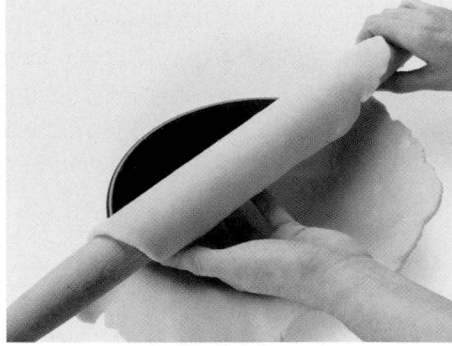

① A typical pie crust or tart shell should be rolled to a thickness of approximately ⅛ inch (3 millimeters); it should also be at least 2 inches (5 centimeters) larger in diameter than the baking pan.

② Carefully roll the dough up onto a rolling pin. Position the pin over the pie pan or tart shell and unroll the dough, easing it into the pan or shell.

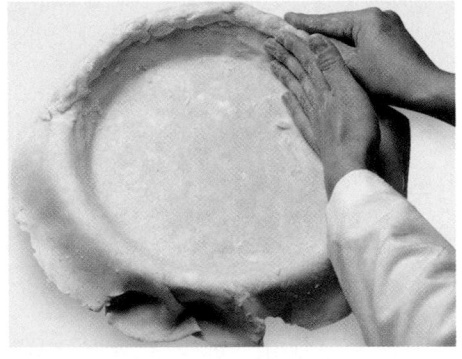

④ When making a double crust pie, roll the dough out as before, making the circle large enough to hang over the pan's edge. The dough may be lifted into place by rolling it onto the rolling pin, as with the bottom crust.

③ Press the dough into the pan and trim the edges as needed. Bake or fill as desired.

⑤ Seal the top crust to the bottom crust with egg wash or water. Crimp as desired. Slits or designs can be cut from the top crust to allow steam to escape.

PROCEDURE FOR ROLLING AND SHAPING DOUGH FOR LATTICE CRUSTS

① Roll the dough out as before. Using a ruler as a guide, cut even strips of the desired width, typically ½ inch (1.2 centimeters).

② Using an over-under-over pattern, weave the strips together on top of the filling. Be sure the strips are evenly spaced for an attractive result. Crimp the lattice strips to the bottom crust to seal. Streusel topping is also used for some pies, particularly fruit pies. A standard recipe is given in Chapter 30, Quick Breads.

OF TARTS AND TORTES

The names given to desserts can be rather confusing. One country or region calls an item a torte while another region calls the same item a gâteau. The following definitions are based on classic terms. You will, no doubt, encounter variations depending on your location and the training of those with whom you work.

Cake—In American and British usages, *cake* refers to a broad range of pastries, including layer cakes, coffee cakes and gâteaux. *Cake* may refer to almost everything that is baked, tender, sweet and sometimes frosted. But to the French, *le cake* is a loaf-shaped fruitcake, similar to an American poundcake with the addition of fruit, nuts and rum.

Gâteau—(pl. *gâteaux*) To the French, *gâteau* refers to various pastry items made with puff pastry, éclair paste, short dough or sweet dough. In America, *gâteau* often refers to any cake-type dessert.

Pastry—*Pastry* may refer to a group of doughs made primarily with flour, water and fat. *Pastry* can also refer to foods made with these doughs or to a large variety of fancy baked goods.

Tart—A tart is a pastry shell filled with sweet or savory ingredients. Tarts have straight, shallow sides and are usually prepared open-face. In France and Britain, the term *flan* is sometimes used to refer to the same items. A tartlet is a small, individual-sized tart.

Torte—In Central and Eastern European countries, a torte (pl. *torten*) is a rich cake in which all or part of the flour is replaced with finely chopped nuts or bread crumbs. Other cultures refer to any round sweet cake as a torte.

PROCEDURE FOR **ROLLING AND SHAPING DOUGH FOR TARTLET SHELLS**

❶ A typical crust for tartlets should be approximately ⅛ inch (3 millimeters) thick.

❷ Roll the dough out as described earlier. Then roll the dough up onto the rolling pin.

BAKING CRUSTS

Pie crusts can be filled and then baked, or baked and then filled. To retain their shape, pie crusts are **baked blind**—lined with parchment or buttered foil, then filled with baking (or pie) weights or dry rice or beans and baked without the filling. Unfilled baked crusts can be stored at room temperature for 2 to 3 days or wrapped in plastic wrap and frozen for as long as 3 months.

baked blind describes a pie shell or tart shell that is baked unfilled, using baking weights or beans to support the crust as it bakes

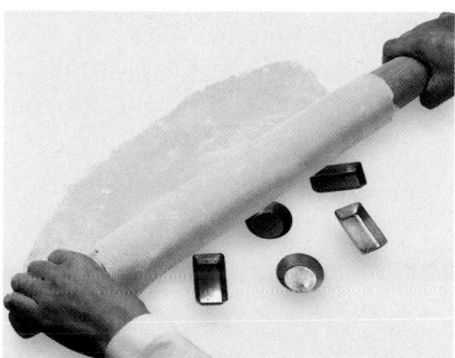

❶ Lay out a single layer of tartlet shells. Unroll the dough over the shells, pressing the dough gently into each one.

❷ Roll the rolling pin over the top of the shells. The edge of the shells will cut the dough. Be sure the dough is pressed against the sides of each shell. Bake or fill as desired.

PROCEDURE FOR **ROLLING AND BAKING UNFILLED CRUSTS (BAKED BLIND)**

1 Roll the dough out to the desired thickness.

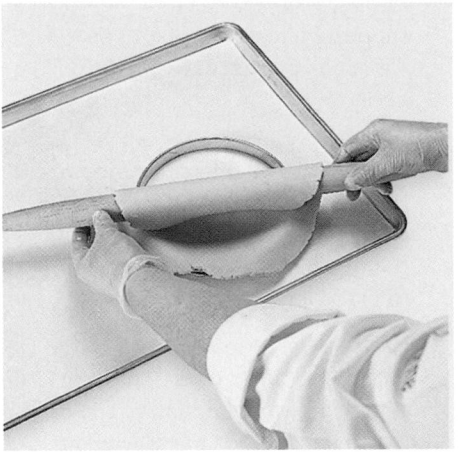

2 Place a tart ring on a paper-lined sheet pan. Carefully roll the dough up onto a rolling pin. Position the pin over the tart ring and unroll the dough.

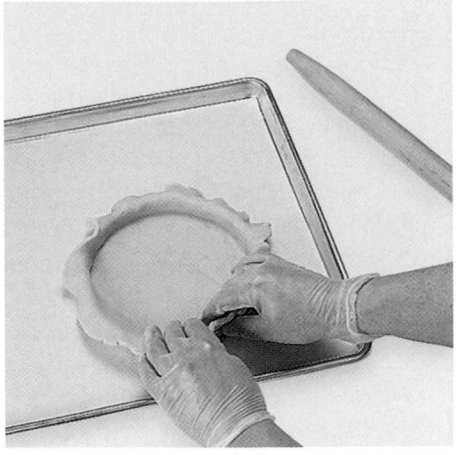

3 Ease the dough into the tart ring, pressing to make a smooth edge.

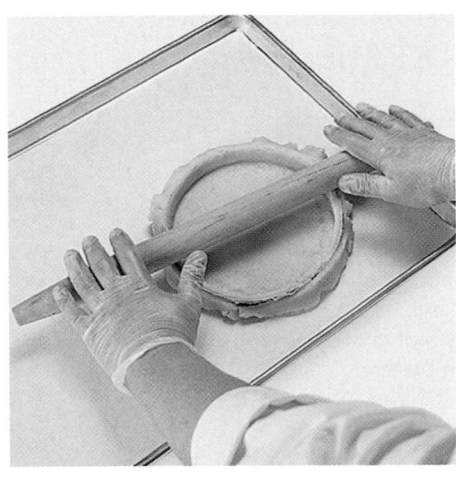

4 Run a rolling pin over the edge of the tart ring to remove excess dough and produce a level edge to the tart. **Dock** the tart dough with a fork.

dock to prick small holes in an unbaked dough or crust to allow steam to escape and to prevent the dough from rising when baked

5 Cover the dough with heat-resistant plastic, parchment paper or greased aluminum foil (greased side down). Press the plastic, paper or foil against the walls of the shell, allowing a portion of it to extend above the pan. Fill the pan with baking weights or dry rice or beans.

6 Bake the weighted crust at 350°F (180°C) for 10 to 15 minutes. Remove the weights and paper.

➐ Brush the baked crust with egg wash, then return the crust to the oven. Bake until golden brown and fully cooked, approximately 10 to 15 minutes. Allow to cool, then fill as desired.

CRUMB CRUSTS

A quick and tasty bottom crust can be made from finely ground cookie crumbs moistened with melted butter. Crumb crusts can be used for unbaked pies such as those with cream or chiffon fillings, or they can be baked with their fillings, as with cheesecakes.

Chocolate cookies, graham crackers, gingersnaps, vanilla wafers and macaroons are popular choices for crumb crusts. Some breakfast cereals such as corn flakes or bran flakes are also used. Ground nuts and spices can be added for flavor. Whatever cookies or other ingredients are used, be sure they are ground to a fine, even crumb. If packaged crumbs are unavailable, a food processor, blender or rolling pin can be used.

The typical ratio for a crumb crust is one part melted butter, two parts sugar and four parts crumbs. For example, 8 ounces (240 grams) graham crackers mixed with 4 ounces (120 grams) sugar and 2 ounces (60 grams) melted butter produces enough crust to line one 9- or 10-inch (22- or 25-centimeter) pan. The amount of sugar may need to be adjusted depending on the type of crumbs used, however; for example, chocolate sandwich cookies need less sugar than graham crackers. If the mixture is too dry to stick together, gradually add more melted butter. Press the mixture into the bottom of the pan and chill or bake it before filling.

Making a crumb crust.

Fillings

Fillings make pies and tarts distinctive and flavorful. Four types of fillings are discussed here: **cream**, **fruit**, **custard** and **chiffon**. There is no one correct presentation or filling-and-crust combination. The apples in an apple pie, for example, may be sliced, seasoned and topped with streusel; caramelized, puréed and blended with cream; chopped and covered with a flaky dough lattice; or poached, arranged over pastry cream and brushed with a shiny glaze. Only an understanding of the fundamental techniques for making fillings—and some imagination—ensures success.

CREAM FILLINGS

A cream filling is really nothing more than a flavored pastry cream. Pastry cream is a type of starch-thickened egg custard discussed in Chapter 34, Custards, Creams, Frozen Desserts and Dessert Sauces. When used as a pie filling, pastry cream should be thickened with cornstarch so that it is firm enough to hold its shape when sliced. The cornstarch must be cooked long enough so that the starch fully gelatinizes and thickens before using. Popular flavors are chocolate, banana, coconut and lemon.

A cream filling is fully cooked on the stove top, so a prebaked or crumb crust is needed. The crust can be filled while the filling is still warm, or the filling can be chilled and piped into the crust later. A cream pie is often topped with meringue, which is then browned quickly in an oven or under a broiler.

MISE EN PLACE

▶ Prepare and bake pie shells.

❶ Filling a baked pie shell with chocolate custard.

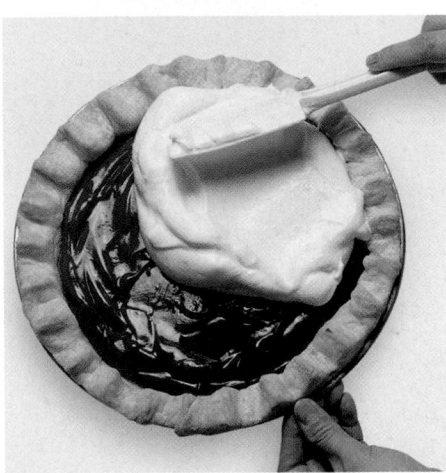

❷ Topping with Crème Chantilly.

BASIC CREAM PIE

Yield: 3 Pies, 9 in. (22 cm) each   **Method:** Cream filling

Granulated sugar	14 oz.	420 g
Milk	44 fl. oz.	1.3 lt
Heavy cream	20 fl. oz.	600 ml
Egg yolks	8	8
Cornstarch	4½ oz.	135 g
Unsalted butter	4 oz.	120 g
Vanilla extract	1 fl. oz.	30 ml
Flaky pie dough shells, baked	3	3
Crème Chantilly (page 1057) or meringue	as needed	as needed

1. In a heavy saucepan, dissolve 8 ounces (240 grams) sugar in the milk. Add the heavy cream and bring to a boil.
2. Meanwhile, whisk the egg yolks and the remaining sugar together in a small bowl. Add the cornstarch and whisk until smooth.
3. Temper the egg mixture with approximately half of the hot milk. Stir the warmed egg mixture back into the remaining milk and return it to a boil, whisking constantly.
4. Whisking constantly and vigorously, allow the cream to boil until thick, approximately 2 minutes. Remove from the heat and stir in the butter and vanilla extract. Stir until the butter is melted and incorporated.
5. Pour the cream into the pie shells. Chill the pies.
6. The pies can be topped with Crème Chantilly once the filling is very cold or with meringue while the filling is still warm. The meringue is then lightly browned in a 425°F (210°C) oven.
7. Chill the pies for service.

VARIATIONS:

Chocolate Cream Pie—Melt 12 ounces (340 grams) bittersweet chocolate. Fold the melted chocolate into the hot cream after adding the butter and vanilla extract.

Banana Cream Pie—Layer 12 ounces (340 grams) sliced bananas (about 3 medium bananas) into the baked shell with the warm cream. Do not purée the bananas, as this will make the filling runny.

Coconut Cream Pie I—Substitute 12 fluid ounces (340 milliliters) cream of coconut for 12 fluid ounces (340 milliliters) milk and 4 ounces (120 grams) sugar. Top the pie with meringue and shredded coconut.

Coconut Cream Pie II—Stir 8 ounces (250 grams) toasted coconut into the warm cream.

Approximate values per ⅛-pie serving: **Calories** 220, **Total fat** 9 g, **Saturated fat** 5 g, **Cholesterol** 130 mg, **Sodium** 55 mg, **Total carbohydrates** 29 g, **Protein** 5 g, **Vitamin A** 10%

FRUIT FILLINGS

A fruit filling is a mixture of fruit, fruit juice, spices and sugar thickened with a starch. Apple, cherry, blueberry and peach are traditional favorites. The fruit can be fresh, frozen or canned. (See Chapter 25, Fruits, for comments on selecting the best fruits for fillings.) The starch can be flour, cornstarch, tapioca or a packaged commercial instant or pregelatinized starch.

The ingredients for a fruit filling are most often combined using one of three methods: **cooked fruit**, **cooked juice** or **baked**.

Cooked Fruit Fillings

The cooked fruit filling method is often used when the fruits need to be softened by cooking (for example, apples or rhubarb) or are naturally rather dry. A cooked fruit filling should be combined with a prebaked or crumb crust.

STARCHES FOR PIES

Although flour is somewhat unreliable as a thickener, it can be used in traditional baked fruit pies in which the fruit is not excessively juicy, such as Pippin apples or Bosc pears. Cornstarch is preferred for custard and fruit fillings because it sets up into a somewhat firm, clear gel. Be aware that cornstarch loses its potency when combined with sugar or an acid such as lemon juice. When a pie is to be frozen, cornstarch is not recommended as a thickener, however. The gel formed by cornstarch when cooking breaks down during freezing. Use tapioca or tapioca starch instead. Tapioca is a good choice for fruit fillings because it thickens at a lower temperature than cornstarch, withstands freezing and cooks into a clear gel. Instant tapioca can be measured and then ground into a powder before using. Grinding makes it easier to disperse. Modified starch, also known as waxy maize, can also be used for pies that must be frozen.

PROCEDURE FOR **PREPARING COOKED FRUIT FILLINGS**

1. Combine the fruit, sugar and some juice or liquid in a heavy, nonreactive saucepan and bring to a boil.
2. Dissolve the starch (usually cornstarch) in a cold liquid, then add to the boiling fruit.
3. Stirring constantly, cook the fruit-and-starch mixture until the starch is clear and the mixture is thickened.
4. Add any other flavorings and any acidic ingredients such as lemon juice. Stir to blend.
5. Remove from the heat and cool before filling a prebaked pie or crumb crust.

APPLE-CRANBERRY PIE

Yield: 1 Pie, 9 in. (22 cm)   **Method:** Cooked fruit filling

Fresh tart apples such as Granny Smiths, peeled, cored and cut in 1-in. (2.5-cm) cubes	1 lb.	480 g
Brown sugar	4 oz.	120 g
Granulated sugar	4 oz.	120 g
Orange zest	1 Tbsp.	15 ml
Cinnamon, ground	1 tsp.	5 ml
Salt	¼ tsp.	1 ml
Cornstarch	2 tsp.	10 ml
Orange juice	3 fl. oz.	90 ml
Fresh cranberries, rinsed	8 oz.	240 g
Mealy dough pie shell, partially baked	1	1
Streusel Topping (page 913)	4 oz.	120 g

1. Combine the apples, brown sugar, granulated sugar, orange zest, cinnamon and salt in a large, nonreactive saucepan.
2. Dissolve the cornstarch in the orange juice and add it to the apples.
3. Cover and simmer until the apples begin to soften, stirring occasionally. Add the cranberries, cover and continue simmering until the cranberries begin to soften, approximately 2 minutes.
4. Place the apple-cranberry mixture in the pie shell and cover with the prepared Streusel Topping. Bake at 400°F (200°C) until the filling is bubbling hot and the topping is lightly browned, approximately 20 minutes.

VARIATION:

Apple-Rhubarb Pie—Substitute cleaned rhubarb, cut into 1-inch (2.5-centimeter) chunks, for the cranberries. Add ⅛ teaspoon (0.5 milliliter) nutmeg.

Approximate values per ⅙-pie serving: **Calories** 300, **Total fat** 10 g, **Saturated fat** 4 g, **Cholesterol** 5 mg, **Sodium** 254 mg, **Total carbohydrates** 63 g, **Protein** 3 g

Cooked Juice Fillings

The cooked juice filling method is used for juicy fruits such as berries, especially when they are canned or frozen. This method is also recommended for delicate fruits that cannot withstand cooking, such as strawberries, pineapple and blueberries. Because only the juice is cooked, the fruit retains its shape, color and flavor better. A cooked juice filling should be combined with a prebaked or crumb crust.

PROCEDURE FOR **PREPARING COOKED JUICE FILLINGS**

1. Drain the juice from the fruit. Measure the juice and add water if necessary to create the desired volume.
2. Combine the liquid with sugar in a nonreactive saucepan and bring to a boil.
3. Dissolve the starch in cold water, then add it to the boiling liquid. Cook until the starch is clear and the juice is thickened.
4. Add any other flavoring ingredients.
5. Pour the thickened juice over the fruit and stir gently.
6. Cool the filling before placing it in a precooked pie shell.

BLUEBERRY PIE FILLING

MISE EN PLACE
▶ Grate lemon zest.

Yield: 8 lb. (3.8 kg)　　　　　　　　　　**Method:** Cooked juice filling

Canned blueberries, #10 can, unsweetened	1	1
Granulated sugar	1 lb. 12 oz.	840 g
Cornstarch	4½ oz.	135 g
Water	8 fl. oz.	240 ml
Cinnamon, ground	½ tsp.	2 ml
Lemon juice	2 Tbsp.	30 ml
Lemon zest, grated fine	1 Tbsp.	15 ml

1. Drain the juice from the canned blueberries, reserving both the fruit and the juice.
2. Measure the juice and, if necessary, add enough water to provide 1 quart (1 liter) of liquid. Bring to a boil, add the sugar and stir until dissolved.
3. Dissolve the cornstarch in 8 fluid ounces (240 milliliters) water.
4. Add the cornstarch to the boiling juice and return to a boil. Cook until the mixture thickens and clears. Remove from the heat.
5. Add the cinnamon, lemon juice, lemon zest and reserved blueberries. Stir gently to coat the fruit with the glaze.
6. Allow the filling to cool to room temperature, then use it to fill prebaked pie shells or other pastry items.

Approximate values per 1-oz. (30-g) serving: **Calories** 40, **Total fat** 0 g, **Saturated fat** 0 g, **Cholesterol** 0 mg, **Sodium** 0 mg, **Total carbohydrates** 10 g, **Protein** 0 g, **Claims**—fat free; no cholesterol; no sodium; low calorie

Baked Fruit Fillings

The baked fruit filling method is a traditional technique in which the fruit, sugar, flavorings and starch are combined in an unbaked shell. The dough and filling are then baked simultaneously. Results are not always consistent with this technique, however, as thickening is difficult to control.

PROCEDURE FOR **PREPARING BAKED FRUIT FILLINGS**

1. Combine the starch, spices and sugar.
2. Peel, core, cut and drain the fruit as desired or as directed in the recipe.
3. Toss the fruit with the starch mixture, coating well.
4. Add a portion of juice to moisten the fruit. Small lumps of butter are also often added.
5. Fill an unbaked shell with the fruit mixture. Cover with a top crust, lattice or streusel and bake.

CHERRY PIE

Yield: 2 Pies, 9 in. (22 cm) each **Method:** Baked fruit filling

Tapioca, instant	1½ oz.	45 g
Salt	1 pinch	1 pinch
Granulated sugar	1 lb.	480 g
Almond extract	½ tsp.	2 ml
Canned pitted cherries, drained, liquid reserved	3 lb.	1.4 kg
Mealy dough pie shells, unbaked	2	2
Unsalted butter	1 oz.	30 g
Egg wash	as needed	as needed
Sanding sugar	as needed	as needed

1. Stir the tapioca, salt and granulated sugar together. Add the almond extract and cherries.
2. Stir in up to 8 fluid ounces (240 milliliters) of the liquid drained from the cherries, adding enough liquid to moisten the mixture thoroughly.
3. Allow the filling to stand for 30 minutes. Then stir gently and place the filling in the unbaked pie shells.
4. Cut the butter into small pieces. Dot the filling with the butter.
5. Place a top crust or a lattice crust over the filling; seal and flute the edges. If using a full top crust, cut several slits in the dough to allow steam to escape. Brush the top crust or lattice with egg wash and sprinkle with sanding sugar.
6. Place on a preheated sheet pan and bake at 400°F (200°C) for 50 to 60 minutes.

Approximate values per ⅛-pie serving: **Calories** 340, **Total fat** 9 g, **Saturated fat** 3 g, **Cholesterol** 5 mg, **Sodium** 170 mg, **Total carbohydrates** 63 g, **Protein** 2 g

CUSTARD FILLINGS

A custard pie has a soft filling that bakes along with the crust. Popular examples include pumpkin, egg custard and pecan pies. As explained in Chapter 34, Custards, Creams, Frozen Desserts and Dessert Sauces, custards are liquids thickened by coagulated egg proteins. To make a custard pie, an uncooked liquid containing eggs is poured into a pie shell. When baked, the egg proteins coagulate, firming and setting the filling.

The procedure for making custard pies is simple: Combine the ingredients and bake. But there is often a problem: baking the bottom crust completely without overcooking the filling. For the best results, start baking the pie near the bottom of a hot oven at 400°F (200°C). After 10 minutes, lower the heat to 325°F–350°F (160°C–180°C) to finish cooking the filling slowly.

To determine the doneness of a custard pie.

1. Shake the pie gently. It is done if it is no longer liquid. The center should show only a slight movement.
2. Insert a thin knife about 1 inch (2.5 centimeters) from the center. The filling is done if the knife comes out clean.

◄ Drain cherries, reserving the liquid.
◄ Prepare and shape pie shells.
◄ Make the egg wash.
◄ Preheat the oven and sheet pan to 400°F (200°C) while filling rests.

CONVENIENCE PRODUCTS

Prepared or canned pie fillings are available in a variety of fruit and custard flavors. These products offer convenience and the ability to serve fruit pies out of season. The ratio of fruit to pregelled liquid varies greatly from brand to brand, however. Most commercial fillings are stabilized to permit any additional cooking needed to assemble the final product. Shelf life tends to be extremely long, often without the need for refrigeration. Dry custard mixes are also available, needing only the addition of water or milk to produce a cream pie filling.

PUMPKIN PIE

MISE EN PLACE

▶ Beat eggs.
▶ Prepare and shape pie shells.
▶ Preheat the oven and sheet pan to 400°F (200°C) while the filling rests.

Yield: 2 Pies, 9 in. (22 cm) each   **Method:** Custard filling

Eggs, beaten slightly	4	4
Pumpkin purée	2 lb.	960 g
Granulated sugar	12 oz.	360 g
Salt	1 tsp.	5 ml
Nutmeg, ground	½ tsp.	2 ml
Cloves, ground	½ tsp.	2 ml
Cinnamon, ground	2 tsp.	10 ml
Ginger, ground	1 tsp.	5 ml
Evaporated milk	24 fl. oz.	720 ml
Flaky dough pie shells, unbaked	2	2

1 Combine the eggs and pumpkin. Blend in the sugar.

2 Add the salt and spices, and then the evaporated milk. Whisk until completely blended and smooth.

3 Allow the filling to rest for 15 to 20 minutes before filling the pie shells. This allows the starch in the pumpkin to begin absorbing liquid, making it less likely to separate after baking.

4 Pour the filling into the unbaked pie shells. Place in the oven on a preheated sheet pan at 400°F (200°C). Bake for 15 minutes. Lower the oven temperature to 350°F (180°C) and bake until a knife inserted near the center comes out clean, approximately 40 to 50 minutes.

Approximate values per ⅛-pie serving: **Calories** 210, **Total fat** 10 g, **Saturated fat** 2.5 g, **Cholesterol** 30 mg, **Sodium** 230 mg, **Total carbohydrates** 25 g, **Protein** 4 g, **Vitamin A** 6%

TABLE 32.2   TROUBLESHOOTING CHART FOR PIES

PROBLEM	CAUSE	SOLUTION
Crust shrinks	Overmixing	Adjust mixing technique
	Overworking dough	Adjust rolling technique
	Not enough fat	Adjust formula
	Dough was stretched or rolled incorrectly	Improve technique
Soggy crust	Wrong dough used	Use mealier dough
	Oven temperature too low	Adjust oven
	Not baked long enough	Adjust baking time
	Filling too moist	Adjust formula
Crumbly crust	Not enough liquid	Adjust formula
	Not enough fat	Adjust formula
	Improper mixing	Adjust mixing technique
Tough crust	Not enough fat	Adjust formula
	Overmixing	Adjust mixing technique
Runny filling	Insufficient starch	Adjust formula
	Starch insufficiently cooked	Cook longer
Lumpy cream filling	Starch not incorporated properly	Blend starch with sugar before adding liquid; stir filling while cooking
	Filling overcooked	Adjust cooking time
Custard filling "weeps" or separates	Too many eggs	Reduce egg content or add starch to the filling
	Eggs overcooked	Reduce oven temperature or baking time

TABLE 32.3 SUGGESTIONS FOR ASSEMBLING PIES AND TARTS

FILLING	CRUST	TOPPING	GARNISH
Vanilla or lemon cream	Prebaked flaky dough or crumb	None, meringue or whipped cream	Crumbs from the crust
Chocolate cream	Prebaked flaky dough or crumb	None, meringue or whipped cream	Crumbs from the crust or shaved chocolate
Banana cream	Prebaked flaky dough	Meringue or whipped cream	Dried banana chips
Coconut cream	Prebaked flaky dough	Meringue or whipped cream	Shredded coconut
Fresh fruit	Unbaked mealy dough, or sweet dough if shallow tart	Lattice, full crust or streusel	Sanding sugar or cut-out designs if lattice or top crust is used
Canned or frozen fruit	Unbaked mealy dough	Lattice, full crust or streusel	Sanding sugar or cut-out designs if lattice or top crust is used
Chiffon or mousse	Crumb or prebaked, sweetened flaky dough	None or whipped cream	Crumbs, fruit or shaved chocolate
Custard	Unbaked mealy dough	None	Whipped cream, cinnamon
Vanilla pastry cream	Prebaked sweet dough	Fresh fruit	Glaze
Lemon or citrus curd	Prebaked sweet dough	Fresh fruit, berries	Glaze, Italian meringue

CHIFFON FILLINGS

A chiffon filling is created by adding gelatin to a stirred custard or a fruit purée. Whipped egg whites are then folded into the mixture. The filling is placed in a prebaked crust and chilled until firm. These preparations are the same as those for chiffons, mousses and Bavarians discussed in Chapter 34, Custards, Creams, Frozen Desserts and Dessert Sauces.

Assembling Pies and Tarts

The various types of pie fillings can be used to fill almost any crust or shell, provided the crust is prebaked as necessary. The filling can then be topped with meringue or whipped cream as desired. Garnishes such as toasted coconut, cookie crumbs and chocolate curls are often added for appearance and flavor. Table 32.3 offers some suggestions for pie and tart filling and topping combinations.

Storing Pies and Tarts

Pies and tarts filled with cream or custard must be refrigerated to retard bacterial growth. Unbaked fruit pies or pie shells may be frozen for up to 2 months. Freezing baked fruit pies is not recommended, but they may be stored for 2 to 3 days at room temperature or in the refrigerator. Custard, cream and meringue-topped pies should be stored in the refrigerator for no more than 2 to 3 days. They should not be frozen, as the eggs will separate, making the product runny.

Arranging fresh fruit decoratively over a filled tart shell.

CLASSIC PASTRIES

Puff pastry, **éclair paste** and **meringue** are classic components of French pastries; they are used to create a wide variety of dessert and pastry items. Many combinations are traditional. Once you master the skills necessary to produce these products, however, you will be free to experiment with other flavors and assembly techniques.

Puff Pastry

Puff pastry is one of the bakeshop's most elegant and sophisticated products. Also known as **pâte feuilletée**, it is a rich, buttery dough that bakes into hundreds of light, crisp layers.

Puff pastry is used for both sweet and savory preparations. It can be baked and then filled, or filled first and then baked. Puff pastry may be used to wrap beef (for beef Wellington), pâté (for pâté en croûte) or almond cream (for an apple tart). It can be shaped into shells or cases known as vol-au-vents or bouchées and filled with shellfish in a cream sauce or berries in a pastry cream. Puff pastry is essential for napoleons, pithiviers and tartes tatin.

Like croissant and Danish dough (discussed in Chapter 31, Yeast Breads), puff pastry is a rolled-in dough. But unlike those doughs, puff pastry does not contain any yeast or chemical leavening agents. Fat is rolled into the dough in horizontal layers; when baked, the fat melts, separating the dough into layers. The fat's moisture turns into steam, which causes the dough to rise and the layers to further separate.

Butter is the preferred fat for puff pastry because of its flavor and melt-in-the-mouth quality. But butter is rather difficult to work with because it becomes brittle when cold and melts at a relatively low temperature. Therefore, specially formulated puff pastry shortenings are used to compensate for butter's shortcomings. They do not, however, provide the true flavor of butter.

MAKING PUFF PASTRY

The procedure described here for making and folding puff pastry dough is just one of several. All methods, however, depend on the proper layering of fat and dough through a series of turns to give the pastry its characteristic flakiness and rise.

Some chefs prefer to prepare a dough called blitz or quick puff pastry. It does not require the extensive rolling and folding procedure used for true puff pastry. Blitz puff pastry is less delicate and flaky but may be perfectly acceptable for some uses. A formula for it is supplied in the electronic resources for this chapter.

PROCEDURE FOR **PREPARING PUFF PASTRY**

détrempe a paste made with flour and water during the first stage of preparing a pastry dough, especially rolled-in doughs

1. Prepare the dough base (**détrempe**) by combining the flour, water, salt and a small amount of fat. Do not overmix. Overmixing results in greater gluten formation, and too much gluten can make the pastry undesirably tough.

2. Wrap the détrempe and chill for several hours or overnight. This allows the gluten to relax and the flour to absorb the liquid.

3. Shape the butter into a rectangle of even thickness; wrap and chill until ready to use.

4. Allow the détrempe and butter to sit at room temperature until slightly softened and of the same consistency.

5. Roll out the détrempe into a rectangle of even thickness.

6. Position the butter in the center of the dough. Fold each edge of the dough around the butter, enclosing it completely.

7. Roll out the block of dough and butter into a long, even rectangle. Roll only at right angles so that the layered structure is not destroyed.

8. Fold the dough like a business letter: Fold the bottom third up toward the center so that it covers the center third, then fold the top third down over the bottom and middle thirds. This is called the **single book fold**. This completes the first **turn**.

9. Rotate the block of dough one quarter turn (90 degrees) on the work surface. Roll out again into a long, even rectangle.

10. Fold the dough in thirds again, like a business letter. This completes the second turn. Wrap the dough and chill for approximately 30 minutes. The resting period allows the gluten to relax; the chilling prevents the butter from becoming too soft.

⑪ Repeat the rolling and folding process, chilling between every one or two turns, until the dough has been turned a total of five times.

⑫ Wrap well and chill overnight. Raw dough may be refrigerated for a few days or frozen for 2 to 3 months.

⑬ Shape and bake as needed. Baked, unfilled puff pastry can be stored at room temperature for 2 to 3 days.

PUFF PASTRY

Yield: 2 lb. (1 kg) **Method:** Rolled-in dough

All-purpose flour	13 oz.	390 g
Salt	1½ tsp.	7 ml
Unsalted butter, cold	3 oz.	90 g
Water, cold	7 fl. oz.	210 ml
Unsalted butter, softened	10 oz.	300 g

① To form the détrempe, sift the flour and salt together in a large bowl. Cut the cold butter into small pieces and then cut the pieces into the flour until the mixture resembles coarse cornmeal.

② Make a well in the center of the mixture and add all the water at once. Using a rubber spatula or your fingers, gradually draw the flour into the water. Mix until all the flour is incorporated. Do not knead. The détrempe should be sticky and shaggy-looking.

③ Turn the détrempe out onto a lightly floured surface. Knead the dough a few times by hand, rounding it into a ball. Wrap the dough tightly in plastic and chill overnight.

④ To roll in the butter, first prepare the softened butter by placing it between two sheets of plastic wrap. Use a rolling pin to roll the softened butter into a rectangle, approximately 5 inches × 8 inches (12.5 centimeters × 20 centimeters). It is important that the détrempe and butter be of almost equal consistency. If necessary, allow the détrempe to sit at room temperature to soften or chill the butter briefly to harden.

⑤ On a lightly floured board, roll the détrempe into a rectangle approximately 12 inches × 15 inches (30 centimeters × 37.5 centimeters). Lift and rotate the dough as necessary to prevent sticking.

⑥ Use a dry pastry brush to brush away any flour from the dough's surface. Loose flour can cause gray streaks and can prevent the puff pastry from rising properly when baked.

⑦ Peel one piece of plastic wrap from the butter. Position the butter in the center of the rectangle and remove the remaining plastic. Fold the four edges of the détrempe over the butter, enclosing it completely. Stretch the dough if necessary; it is important that none of the butter be exposed.

⑧ With the folded side facing up, press the dough several times with a rolling pin. Use a rocking motion to create ridges in the dough. Place the rolling pin in each ridge and slowly roll back and forth to widen the ridge. Repeat until all the ridges are doubled in size.

⑨ Using the ridges as a starting point, roll the dough out into a smooth, even rectangle approximately 8 inches × 24 inches (20 centimeters × 60 centimeters). Be careful to keep the corners of the dough as right angles.

⑩ Use a dry pastry brush to remove any loose flour from the dough's surface. Fold the dough in thirds, like a business letter. If one end is damaged or in worse condition, fold it in first; otherwise, start at the bottom. This completes the first turn.

⑪ Rotate the block of dough 90 degrees so that the folded edge is on your left and the dough faces you like a book. Roll out the dough again, repeating the ridging technique. Once again, the dough should be in a smooth, even rectangle of approximately 8 inches × 24 inches (20 centimeters × 60 centimeters).

⑫ Fold the dough in thirds again, completing the second turn. Cover the dough with plastic wrap and chill for at least 30 minutes.

⑬ Repeat the rolling and folding technique until the dough has had a total of five turns. Do not perform more than two turns without a resting and chilling period. Cover the dough completely and chill overnight before shaping and baking.

① Détrempe (left) and butter for puff pastry.

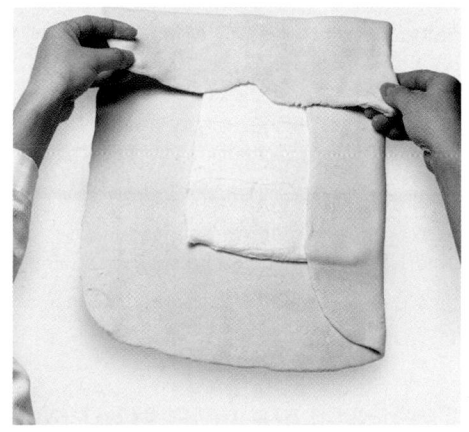

② Folding the dough around the butter.

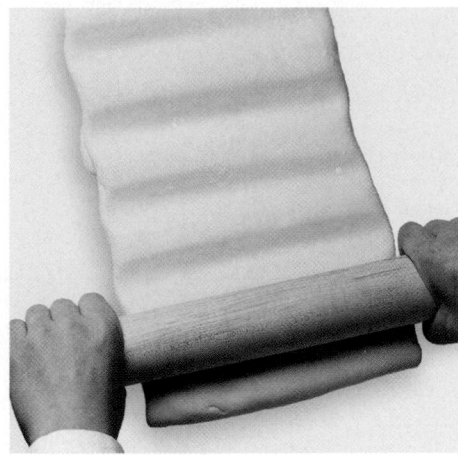

❸ Rolling out the dough.

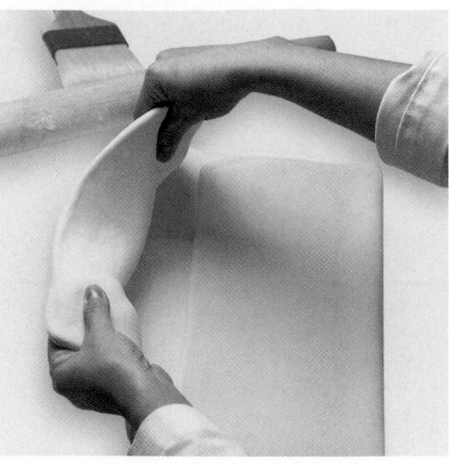

❹ Folding the dough in thirds.

Note: The détrempe can be made in a food processor. To do so, combine the flour, salt and pieces of cold butter in the bowl of a food processor fitted with a metal blade. Process until a coarse meal is formed. With the processor running, slowly add the water. Turn the machine off as soon as the dough comes together to form a ball. Proceed with the remainder of the recipe.

Approximate values per 1-oz. (30-g) serving: **Calories** 120, **Total fat** 9 g, **Saturated fat** 6 g, **Cholesterol** 25 mg, **Sodium** 110 mg, **Total carbohydrates** 9 g, **Protein** 1 g, **Vitamin A** 8%

bouchées (boo-SHAY) small puff pastry shells that can be filled and served as bite-size hors d'oeuvre or petits fours

vol-au-vents deep, individual portion–sized puff pastry shells, often shaped as a heart, fish or fluted circle; they are filled with a savory mixture and served as an appetizer or main course

feuilletées (fuh-yuh-TAY) square, rectangular or diamond-shaped puff pastry boxes; may be filled with a sweet or savory mixture

SHAPING PUFF PASTRY

Once puff pastry dough is prepared, it can be shaped into containers of various sizes and shapes. **Bouchées** are small puff pastry shells often used for hors d'oeuvre or appetizers. **Vol-au-vents** are larger, deeper shells, often filled with savory mixtures for a main course. Although they may be simply round or square, special vol-au-vent cutters are available in the shape of fish, hearts or petals. **Feuilletées** are square, rectangular or diamond-shaped puff pastry boxes. They can be filled with a sweet or savory mixture.

It is not necessary to work with the entire block of dough when making bouchées, cookies and the like. Cut the block into thirds or quarters and work with one portion at a time. When making straight cuts in puff pastry, press the tip of your knife into the dough and cut by pressing down on the handle. Do not drag the knife through the dough or you will crush the layers and prevent the dough from rising properly.

PROCEDURE FOR **SHAPING VOL-AU-VENTS AND BOUCHÉES**

❶ Roll out the puff pastry dough to a thickness of approximately ¼ inch (6 millimeters).

❷ Cut the desired shape and size using a vol-au-vent cutter or rings.

❸ Place the vol-au-vent or bouchée on a paper-lined sheet pan. If you used rings, place the base on the paper-lined sheet pan, brush lightly with water, then top it with the dough ring; score the edge with the back of a paring knife. Chill for 20 to 30 minutes to allow the dough to relax before baking.

❹ Brush with egg wash if desired and dock the center with a fork.

1 A vol-au-vent cutter looks like a double cookie cutter with one cutter about 1 inch (2.5 centimeters) smaller than the other. To cut the pastry, simply position the cutter and press down.

2 To shape with rings, use two rings, one approximately 1 inch (2.5 centimeters) smaller in diameter than the other. The larger ring is used to cut two rounds. One will be the base and is set aside. The smaller ring is then used to cut out an interior circle from the second round, leaving a border ring of dough. (Save the dough ring's center to reroll for tart shells or turnovers.)

PROCEDURE FOR **SHAPING FEUILLETÉES**

1 Roll out the puff pastry dough into an even rectangle, approximately ⅛ to ¼ inch (3 to 6 millimeters) thick. Square off the edges of the dough using a pastry cutter and a straightedge, reserving the scraps for other uses.

2 Using a sharp paring knife or chef's knife, cut squares that are about 2 inches (5 centimeters) larger than the desired interior of the finished feuilletée.

3 Fold each square in half diagonally. Cut through two sides of the dough, about ½ inch (1.2 centimeters) from the edge. Cut a V, being careful not to cut through the corners at the center fold.

4 Open the square and lay it flat. Brush water on the edges to seal the dough. Lift opposite sides of the cut border at the cut corners and cross them.

5 Place the feuilletées on a paper-lined sheet pan.

6 Score the edges with the back of a paring knife. Chill for 20 to 30 minutes to allow the dough to relax before baking.

7 Brush with egg wash if desired and dock the center with a fork.

Puff pastry scraps cannot be rerolled and used for products needing a high rise. The additional rolling destroys the layers. Scraps (known as rognures), however, can be used for cookies such as palmiers (page 991), turnovers, decorative crescents (fleurons), tart shells, napoleons (page 990) or any item for which rise is less important than flavor and flakiness. Most puff pastry products bake best in a hot oven, about 400°F–425°F (200°C–220°C).

Éclair Paste

Éclair paste, also known as **pâte à choux**, bakes up into golden brown, crisp pastries. Inside these light pastries are mostly air pockets with a bit of moist dough. They can be filled with sweet cream, custard, fruit or even savory mixtures. The dough is most often piped into rounds for **cream puffs**, fingers for **éclairs** or rings for **Paris-Brest**. Éclair paste may also be piped or spooned into specific shapes and deep-fried for doughnut-type products known as **beignets**, **churros** and **crullers**. This dough may also be flavored with cheese and sometimes herbs and spices and made into savory puffs known as **gougères**.

MAKING ÉCLAIR PASTE

Éclair paste is unique among doughs because it is cooked before baking. The cooking occurs when the flour is added to a boiling mixture of water, milk and butter. This process breaks down the starches in the flour, allowing them to absorb the liquid, speeding gelatinization. Eggs are added to the flour mixture for leavening. The dough produced is batterlike with a smooth, firm texture; it does not have the dry, crumbly texture of other doughs. Without this technique, the dough would not puff up and develop the desired large interior air pockets when baked.

PROCEDURE FOR PREPARING ÉCLAIR PASTE

1. Combine the liquid ingredients and butter cut into small cubes. Bring to a boil.
2. As soon as the water-and-butter mixture comes to a boil, add all the flour to the saucepan. If the liquid is allowed to boil, evaporation occurs; this can create an imbalance in the liquid-to-flour ratio.
3. Stir vigorously until the liquid is absorbed. Continue cooking the dough until it forms a ball that comes away from the sides of the pan, leaving only a thin film of dough on the sides of the pan.
4. Transfer the dough to a mixing bowl. Allow it to cool to below 140°F (60°C), then add the eggs one at a time, beating well after each addition. (This may be done in a mixer fitted with the paddle attachment or by hand.) The number of eggs used varies depending on the size of each egg and the moisture content of the flour mixture. Stop adding eggs when the dough just begins to fall away from the beaters.
5. The finished dough should be smooth and pliable enough to pipe through a pastry bag; it should not be runny.
6. Pipe the dough as desired and bake immediately. A high oven temperature is necessary at the start of baking; it is then lowered gradually to finish baking and drying the product. Do not open the oven door during the first half of the baking period.
7. Allow the dough to bake until completely dry. If the products are removed from the oven too soon, they will collapse. Test doneness by breaking open one pastry. If the interior is moist and eggy, continue baking.
8. Baked éclair paste can be stored, unfilled, for several days at room temperature or frozen for several weeks. Once filled, the pastry should be served within 2 or 3 hours, as it quickly becomes soggy.

Paris-Brest rings of baked éclair paste cut in half horizontally and filled with light pastry cream and/or whipped cream; the top is dusted with powdered sugar or drizzled with chocolate glaze

cream puffs baked rounds of éclair paste cut in half and filled with pastry cream, whipped cream, fruit or other filling

éclairs baked fingers of éclair paste filled with pastry cream; the top is then coated with chocolate glaze or fondant

churros a Spanish and Mexican pastry in which sticks of éclair paste flavored with cinnamon are deep-fried and rolled in sugar while still hot

beignets squares or strips of éclair paste deep-fried and dusted with powdered sugar

croquembouche a pyramid of small puffs, each filled with pastry cream; a French tradition for Christmas and weddings, it is held together with caramelized sugar and decorated with spun sugar or marzipan flowers

profiteroles small baked rounds of éclair paste filled with ice cream and topped with chocolate sauce

crullers a Dutch pastry in which a loop or strip of twisted éclair paste is deep-fried

gougère éclair pastry flavored with cheese baked and served as a savory hors d'oeuvre

ÉCLAIR PASTE (PÂTE À CHOUX)

Yield: 2–2½ lb. (1.2–1.3 kg) Dough

Milk*	8 fl. oz.	240 ml
Water	8 fl. oz.	240 ml
Salt	1½ tsp.	7 ml
Granulated sugar	2 tsp.	10 ml
Unsalted butter	7 oz.	210 g
All-purpose flour	10 oz.	300 g
Eggs	9–10	9–10

1. Preheat the oven to 425°F (220°C). Line a sheet pan with parchment. Have a pastry bag with a large plain tip ready.

2. Place the milk, water, salt, sugar and butter in a saucepan. Bring to a boil. Make sure the butter is fully melted.

3. Remove from the heat and immediately add all the flour. Vigorously beat the dough by hand. Put the pan back on the heat and continue beating the dough until it comes away from the sides of the pan. The dough should look relatively dry and should just begin to leave a film on the saucepan.

4. Transfer the dough to the bowl of a mixer fitted with the paddle attachment and beat it for a few seconds at medium speed. Then beat in the eggs one at a time.

5. Continue to add the eggs one by one until the mixture is shiny but firm. It may not be necessary to use all of the eggs. The dough should pull away from the sides of the bowl in thick threads; it will not clear the bowl.

6. Put a workable amount of dough into the pastry bag and pipe onto the parchment-lined sheet pans in the desired shapes at once.

7. Bake immediately, beginning at 425°F (220°C) for 10 minutes, then lowering the heat to 350°F (180°C). Continue baking until the shapes are brown and dry inside, approximately 25 more minutes. Open the oven door as little as possible to prevent rapid changes in the oven's temperature.

8. Cool completely, then fill as desired. Leftovers can be frozen or stored at room temperature.

*For a crisper product, replace the milk with water.

Approximate values per 1-oz. (30-g) serving: **Calories** 90, **Total fat** 7 g, **Saturated fat** 4 g, **Cholesterol** 60 mg, **Sodium** 180 mg, **Total carbohydrates** 6 g, **Protein** 2 g, **Vitamin A** 8%

MISE EN PLACE
◄ Preheat oven to 425°F (220°C).
◄ Line sheet pans with parchment paper.

1. Heating the butter and milk.

2. Adding the flour to the hot liquid.

3. Stirring the dough to dry it.

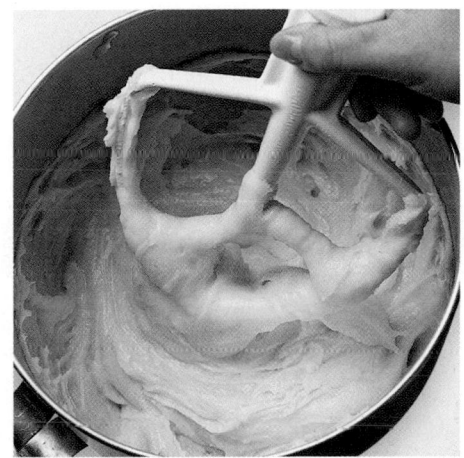

4. The finished batter after the eggs are incorporated.

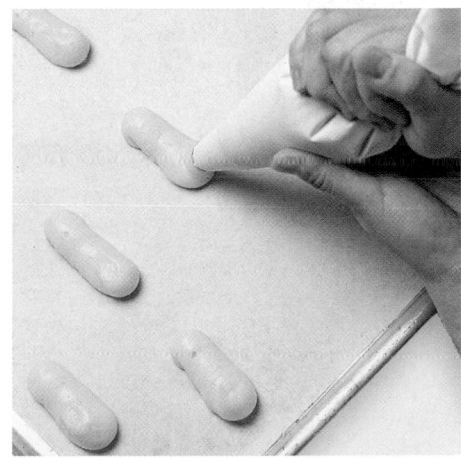

5. Piping éclairs.

Meringue

Meringue refers to both a basic mixture of egg whites whipped with sugar and a confection or cake baked from this preparation. The texture—hard or soft—depends on the ratio of sugar to egg whites. A low sugar content in comparison with the egg whites creates a soft meringue. **Soft meringue** can be folded into a mousse or Bavarian to lighten it, or used in a spongecake or soufflé. Meringues with only a small amount of sugar will always be soft; they will not become crisp no matter how they are used.

Hard meringue is made with egg whites and an equal part or more, by weight, of sugar. It can be incorporated into a buttercream or pastry cream or used to top a pie or baked Alaska. These toppings are usually placed briefly under a broiler to caramelize the sugar, creating an attractive brown surface.

With twice as much sugar, by weight, as egg whites, hard meringue can be piped into disks or other shapes and dried in an oven. A low oven temperature evaporates the eggs' moisture, leaving a crisp, sugary, honeycomb-like structure. Disks of baked meringue can be used as layers in a torte or cake. Cups or shells of baked meringue can be filled with cream, mousse, ice cream or fruit. Often baked meringues also contain ground nuts (and are then known as dacquoise), cocoa powder or other flavorings.

MAKING MERINGUE

There are three methods for making meringue: **common**, **Swiss** and **Italian**. See Table 32.4. Regardless of which preparation method is used, the final product should be smooth, glossy and moist. A meringue should never be dry or spongelike. Review the procedure for whipping egg whites given in Chapter 20, Eggs and Breakfast.

Common Meringue

Common meringue is made by first beating egg whites to a soft foam (soft peaks). Granulated sugar is then slowly beaten or folded into the egg whites. The final product may be hard or soft depending on the ratio of sugar to egg whites.

Swiss Meringue

Swiss meringue is made by combining unwhipped egg whites with sugar and warming the mixture over a bain marie to a temperature of approximately 100°F (38°C) until the sugar is dissolved. The syrupy solution is then whipped until cool and stiff. The final product may be hard or soft, depending on the ratio of sugar to egg whites. Swiss meringue is extremely stable but rather difficult to prepare. If the mixture gets too hot, it will not whip properly; the result will be syrupy and runny. Swiss meringue is often used as a topping or in buttercream.

Italian Meringue

Italian meringue is made by slowly pouring a hot sugar syrup into whipped egg whites. The heat from the syrup cooks the egg whites, adding stability. Be sure that the sugar syrup reaches the correct temperature and that it is added to the egg whites in a slow, steady stream. Italian meringue is used in buttercream (see Chapter 33, Cakes and Frostings) or folded into pastry cream to produce crème Chiboust. It may be flavored and used as a cake filling and frosting called boiled icing.

TABLE 32.4	TYPES OF MERINGUE		
TYPE	**RATIO OF SUGAR TO EGG WHITES BY WEIGHT**	**PREPARATION**	**USE**
Common—hard	Twice as much or more	Whip or fold sugar into whipped egg whites	Baked
Common—soft	Equal parts or less	Whip or fold sugar into whipped egg whites	Pie topping; soufflé; cake ingredient
Swiss	Varies	Warm egg whites to 100°F (38°C) with sugar, then whip	Buttercream; pie topping; baked
Italian	Varies	Hot sugar syrup poured into whipped egg whites	Buttercream; frosting; crème Chiboust, mousses, baked

TABLE 32.5 TROUBLESHOOTING CHART FOR MERINGUE

PROBLEM	CAUSE	SOLUTION
Weeps or beads of sugar syrup are released	Old eggs	Use fresher eggs or add starch or stabilizer
	Egg whites overwhipped	Whip only until stiff peaks form
	Not enough sugar	Increase sugar
	Not baked long enough	Increase baking time
	Browning too rapidly	Do not dust with sugar before baking; reduce oven temperature
	Moisture in the air	Avoid preparing in humid conditions
Fails to attain any volume or stiffness	Fat present	Start over with clean bowls and utensils
	Sugar added too soon	Allow egg whites to reach soft peaks before adding sugar
Lumps	Not enough sugar	Add additional sugar gradually or start over
	Overwhipping	Whip only until stiff peaks form
Not shiny	Not enough sugar	Add additional sugar gradually or start over
	Overwhipping	Whip only until stiff peaks form

ITALIAN MERINGUE

Yield: Approximately 1 lb. 7 oz. (690 g)

Granulated sugar	13 oz.	390 g
Corn syrup	2 oz.	60 g
Water	3 fl. oz.	120 ml
Egg whites, room temperature	8 oz.	240 g

1. Place 12 ounces (360 grams) sugar in a heavy saucepan with the corn syrup and water. Attach a candy thermometer to the pan and bring the sugar to a boil over high heat.

2. Place the egg whites in the bowl of an electric mixer fitted with the whip attachment. As the temperature of the boiling sugar approaches 220°F (104°C), begin whipping the egg whites. When the whites form soft peaks, gradually add the remaining 1 ounces (30 grams) sugar. Lower the mixer speed and continue whipping.

3. When the sugar reaches the soft ball stage (240°F/116°C), remove it from the heat. Pour it into the whites, with the mixer running at high speed. Pour in a steady stream between the side of the bowl and the beater. Once all the sugar is incorporated, whip 1 more minute at high speed, then reduce to medium speed and whip until the meringue is cool.

Approximate values per cup (225 ml): **Calories** 102, **Total fat** 0 g, **Saturated fat** 0 g, **Cholesterol** 0 mg, **Sodium** 16 mg, **Total carbohydrates** 25 g, **Protein** 1 g, **Claims**—fat free; no cholesterol; low sodium

COOKIES

Cookies are small, flat pastries usually eaten alone (although not singularly) as a snack or as a petit four with coffee at the end of a meal. The proliferation of cookie shops in malls and office buildings attests to the popularity of freshly baked cookies. They are indeed one of America's best-loved foods.

Part of the pleasure of cookies comes from their versatility. They may be eaten as a midmorning snack or as the elegant end to a formal dinner. Cookies also provide the finishing touch to a serving of ice cream, custard or fruit. Flavors are limited only by the baker's imagination; chocolate, oatmeal, cornmeal, fresh and dried fruit and nuts all find their way into several types of cookies. Several cookie formulas are given at the end of this chapter.

THE STORY BEHIND THE CHIP

History was made in 1930 when Ruth Wakefield, innkeeper of the Toll House Inn in Whitman, Massachusetts, cut up a semisweet chocolate bar and added the pieces to cookie dough. She was disappointed, however, that the pieces kept their shape when baked—until her first bite, that is.

Mrs. Wakefield contacted Nestlé Foods Corporation, which published her cookie recipe on the wrapper of their semisweet chocolate bars. The recipe's popularity led Nestlé to create and begin selling chocolate chips in 1939.

Today's cookie maker can now choose from milk, white, sweet or bitter chocolate chips, along with mint, butterscotch, peanut butter, cinnamon and other flavor chips, offered in several sizes from a variety of manufacturers.

Drop Cookies

Mixing Methods

Most cookies are made from a rich dough that is mixed by the **creaming method** used for quick breads and cake batters. (See Chapter 30, Quick Breads, and Chapter 33, Cakes and Frostings.) However, because cookie dough contains less liquid than these batters, the liquid and flour need not be added alternately. Cookies can be leavened with baking soda, baking powder or just air and steam. Most cookies are high in fat, which contributes flavor and tenderness and extends shelf life. In cookie formulas with a high percentage of fat and low moisture content, overdevelopment of gluten is usually not a problem. However, careless mixing can produce tough and dense cookies. When there are eggs or liquid in the dough, the flour is blended in gently to minimize gluten development. Add-ins such as chopped nuts, chocolate and pieces of fruit are stirred into the dough for this same reason.

PROCEDURE FOR **MIXING COOKIE DOUGHS**

1. Cream the fat and sugar together to incorporate air and to blend the ingredients completely.
2. Add the eggs gradually, scraping down the bowl as needed.
3. Stir in the liquid ingredients.
4. Stir in the flour, salt, spices and leaveners.
5. Fold in any nuts, chocolate chips or chunky ingredients by hand.

Make-Up Methods

Cookie varieties are usually classified by the way in which the individual cookies are prepared. This section describes eight preparation or make-up techniques: **drop**, **icebox**, **bar**, **sheet**, **cut-out**, **pressed**, **rolled** or **molded** and **wafer**. Some doughs can be made up by more than one method. For example, chocolate chip cookie dough can be (1) baked in sheets and cut into bars, (2) dropped in mounds or (3) rolled into logs, chilled and sliced like icebox cookies. Regardless of the make-up method used, uniformity of size and shape is important for appearance and baking time. Cookies should also be evenly spaced on sheet pans for proper air circulation and crust formation.

DROP COOKIES

Drop cookies are made from a soft dough that is spooned or scooped into mounds for baking. Chunky cookies such as chocolate chip, oatmeal raisin and nut jumbles are common examples. Although a uniform appearance is not as important for drop cookies as for other types, uniform size and placement results in uniform baking time. Space the dough to allow room for spread, which is common with drop cookies. A portion scoop is recommended for portioning the dough. Drop cookies tend to be thick with a soft or chewy texture.

ICEBOX COOKIES

Icebox cookies are made from dough that is shaped into logs or rectangles, chilled thoroughly, then sliced into individual pieces and baked as needed. Icebox cookies can be as simple as a log of chocolate chip dough or as sophisticated as elegant pinwheel and checkerboard cookies assembled with two colors of short dough. This method usually produces uniform, waferlike cookies with a crisp texture.

BAR COOKIES

Bar cookies are made from a stiff dough that is rolled into a log, then baked. The bars are then cut into thick slices. Biscotti (page 999) are a type of bar cookie that is baked a second time after the log has been baked. This produces a dry cookie with a long shelf life.

Icebox Cookies

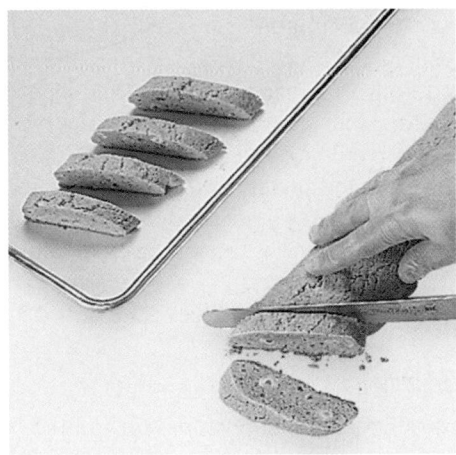

Bar Cookies

Sheet Cookies

SHEET COOKIES

Sheet cookies are made from a dough or batter that is pressed, poured or layered in shallow pans and cut into portions after baking, usually squares or rectangles to avoid waste or scraps. This category contains a wide variety of layered or fruit-filled products. Often a short dough such as that used for a fruit tart or shortbread cookie forms the base of the bar cookies, and then a topping is layered on the cookie before or after baking. See the formula for Lemon or Lime Bars (page 1001). Brownies, often considered a sheet cookie, are discussed in Chapter 33, Cakes and Frostings.

CUT-OUT COOKIES

Cut-out cookies are made from a firm dough that is rolled out into a sheet and then cut into various shapes before baking. A seemingly infinite selection of cookie cutters is available, or you can use a paring knife or pastry wheel to cut the dough into the desired shapes. Always start cutting cookies from the edge of the dough, working inward. Cut the cookies as close to each other as possible to avoid scraps. Cut-out cookies are usually baked on an ungreased pan to keep the dough from spreading.

Cut-out cookies are often garnished or decorated with nuts, glaze, fruit or candies. Raw cookies should be decorated as soon as they are placed on the pan. If the dough is allowed to stand, the surface will dry out and the garnish will not adhere properly.

PRESSED COOKIES

Also referred to as bagged or **spritz cookies**, these products are made with a soft dough that is forced through a pastry tip or **cookie press**. Pressed cookies are usually small, with a distinct, decorative shape. The task of piping out dozens of identical cookies may seem daunting, but the skill can be mastered with practice and an understanding of doughs. Doughs for pressed cookies often use eggs as their only liquid. Eggs, which are a toughener, contribute body and help the cookies retain their shape. Using too much fat or too soft a flour (that is, one low in protein) can cause the cookies to spread and lose their shape.

ROLLED OR MOLDED COOKIES

Rolled or molded cookies are made from stiff dough that is hand-shaped into spheres, crescents or other traditional shapes. Most drop cookies can also be rolled or molded. Often shortbread cookie dough is pressed into decorative carved molds before baking. Dough for molding is firm and dry so that it holds its shape and keeps the impression intact during baking. Traditional European gingerbread and Scandinavian springerle cookies are molded cookies.

Cut-Out or Rolled Cookies

Pressed Cookies

cookie press also known as a *cookie gun*, a hollow tube fitted with a plunger and an interchangeable decorative tip or plate; soft cookie dough is pressed through the tip to create shapes or patterns

Wafer Cookies

WAFER COOKIES

Wafer cookies are extremely thin and delicate. They are made with a thin batter that is poured or spread onto a baking sheet and baked. Then, while still hot, the wafer is molded into a variety of shapes. The most popular shapes are the tightly rolled cigarette, the curved tuile and the cup-shaped tulipe. Wafer batter, also known as **stencil batter**, is sweet and buttery and is often flavored with citrus zest or ground nuts.

The textures associated with cookies—crispness, softness, chewiness or spread—are affected by various factors, including the ratio of ingredients in the dough, the oven's temperature and the pan's coating. Understanding these factors allows you to adjust formulas or techniques to achieve the desired results. See Table 32.6.

Storing Cookies

Most cookies can be stored for up to 1 week in an airtight container. Do not store crisp cookies and soft cookies in the same container, however. The crisp cookies will absorb moisture from the soft cookies, ruining the texture of both. Do not store strongly flavored cookies, such as spice, with those that are milder, such as shortbread.

Most cookies freeze well if wrapped airtight to prevent moisture loss or freezer burn. Raw dough can also be frozen, either in bulk or shaped into individual portions.

TABLE 32.6		COOKIE TEXTURES				
DESIRED TEXTURE	**FAT**	**SUGAR**	**LIQUID**	**FLOUR**	**SIZE OR SHAPE**	**BAKING**
Crispness	High	High; use granulated sugar	Low	Strong	Thin dough	Well done; cool on baking sheet
Softness	Low	Low; use hygroscopic sugars	High	Weak	Thick dough	Use parchment-lined pan; underbake
Chewiness	High	High; use hygroscopic sugars	High	Strong	Not relevant; chilled dough	Underbaked; cool on rack
Spread	High	High; use coarse granulated sugar	High; especially from eggs	Weak	Not relevant; room-temperature dough	Use greased pan; low temperature

QUESTIONS FOR DISCUSSION

1. How does the type of pie filling influence the selection of a pie crust? What type of crust would be best for a pie made with fresh, uncooked fruit? Explain your answer.

2. How does rolling fat into a dough in layers (as with puff pastry) produce a flaky product? Why isn't sweet dough (which contains a high ratio of butter) flaky?

3. Explain the difference between a cream pie filling and a custard pie filling. Give two examples of each type of filling.

4. List and describe three ways of preparing fruit fillings for pies.

5. Why is it said that éclair paste is the only dough that is cooked before it is baked? Why is this step necessary? List three ways of using éclair paste in making classic desserts.

6. Explain the differences and similarities among common, Swiss and Italian meringues.

7. List and describe four make-up methods for cookie doughs.

8. When was the Oreo cookie first sold? How many are now sold annually? How can you explain their popularity? **WWW**

Terms to Know

pie
tart
flaky dough
mealy dough
pâte brisée
pâte sucrée
lattice crust
cooked fruit filling

cooked juice filling
single-book fold
turns
pâte à choux
soft meringue
hard meringue
stencil batter

Several of the formulas given in the following pages are combinations of the pastry items presented in this chapter and the creams, custards and other dessert products covered in other chapters. For example, the Strawberry Napoleon is made with the puff pastry discussed in this chapter, the pastry cream and crème Chantilly discussed in Chapter 34, Custards, Creams, Frozen Desserts and Dessert Sauces, and the fondant glaze discussed in Chapter 33, Cakes and Frostings. As a student, you should first learn to prepare a variety of pastry components. You can then combine and assemble them appropriately into both classic and modern desserts.

SHORTBREAD TART DOUGH

HOUSTON COMMUNITY COLLEGE, HOUSTON, TX

Pastry Chef Eddy Van Damme

Yield: 4 lb. 7 oz. (2.1 kg)

Egg yolks, hard-boiled	5 oz.	150 g
Unsalted butter	1 lb. 8 oz.	720 g
Powdered sugar	11 oz.	330 g
Vanilla extract	1 Tbsp.	15 ml
Salt	1½ tsp.	8 ml
Almond or hazelnut flour	4½ oz.	135 g
Pastry flour	1 lb. 10 oz.	780 g

1. Press the egg yolks through a sieve using a plastic pastry scraper. Set aside.
2. Using a mixer fitted with the paddle attachment, cream the butter. Add the sugar, combining well.
3. Add the vanilla extract, salt and almond or hazelnut flour, then the sieved egg yolks, and mix until combined.
4. Add all of the pastry flour and mix on low speed just until combined. Do not overmix.
5. Wrap the dough in plastic and chill for several hours or overnight.
6. When ready to use, roll out the chilled dough on a lightly floured board. The dough may be crumbly and difficult to work with, which is normal. Simply press the dough back together with your fingertips.

Approximate values per 2-oz. (60-g) serving: **Calories** 227, **Total fat** 19 g, **Saturated fat** 10 g, **Cholesterol** 93 mg, **Sodium** 103 mg, **Total carbohydrates** 25 g, **Protein** 4 g

QUICHE DOUGH

Yield: 7½ lb. (3.6 kg)

All-purpose flour	4 lb. 7 oz.	2 kg
Salt	1½ oz.	45 g
Unsalted butter, cold	2 lb. 4 oz.	1 kg
Eggs	12	12

1. Combine the flour and salt in the bowl of a mixer fitted with the paddle attachment. Cut in the butter until the mixture looks like coarse cornmeal.
2. Whisk the eggs together to blend, then add them slowly to the dry ingredients. Blend only until the dough comes together in a ball.
3. Remove from the mixer, cover and chill until ready to use.

Approximate values per 1-oz. (30-g) serving: **Calories** 120, **Total fat** 7 g, **Saturated fat** 4 g, **Cholesterol** 35 mg, **Sodium** 140 mg, **Total carbohydrates** 12 g, **Protein** 2 g

Topping the pie with meringue.

LEMON MERINGUE PIE

Yield: 2 Pies, 9 in. (22 cm) each   **Method:** Cream filling

Granulated sugar	1 lb. 4 oz.	600 g
Cornstarch	3 oz.	90 g
Salt	1 pinch	1 pinch
Water, cold	24 fl. oz.	720 ml
Egg yolks	10	10
Lemon juice, fresh	8 fl. oz.	240 ml
Lemon zest, grated	2 Tbsp.	60 ml
Unsalted butter	1 oz.	60 g
Flaky dough pie shells, baked	2	2
Egg whites	8 oz.	240 g
Granulated sugar	8 oz.	240 g

1. To make the filling, combine 1 pound 4 ounces (600 grams) sugar and the cornstarch, salt and water in a heavy saucepan. Cook over medium-high heat, stirring constantly, until the mixture becomes thick and almost clear.
2. Remove from the heat and slowly whisk in the egg yolks. Stir until completely blended. Return to the heat and cook, stirring constantly, until thick and smooth.
3. Stir in the lemon juice and zest. When the liquid is completely incorporated, remove the filling from the heat. Add the butter and stir until melted.
4. Set the filling aside to cool briefly. Fill the pie shells with the lemon filling.
5. To prepare the meringue, whip the egg whites until soft peaks form. Slowly add 8 ounces (240 grams) sugar while whisking constantly. The meringue should be stiff and glossy, not dry or spongy-looking.
6. Mound the meringue over the filling, creating decorative patterns with a spatula. Be sure to spread the meringue to the edge of the crust so that all of the filling is covered.
7. Place the pies in a 400°F (200°C) oven until the meringue is golden brown, approximately 5 to 8 minutes. Let cool at room temperature, then refrigerate. Serve the same day.

Approximate values per ⅛-pie serving: **Calories** 400, **Total fat** 12 g, **Saturated fat** 4 g, **Cholesterol** 135 mg, **Sodium** 310 mg, **Total carbohydrates** 67 g, **Protein** 5 g, **Vitamin C** 10%

FRESH STRAWBERRY PIE

Yield: 2 Pies, 9 in. (22 cm) each   **Method:** Cooked juice filling

Granulated sugar	1 lb. 7 oz.	710 g
Water	8 fl. oz.	240 ml
Cornstarch	2½ oz.	75 g
Water, cold	12 fl. oz.	360 ml
Salt	½ tsp.	2 ml
Lemon juice	2 fl. oz.	60 ml
Red food coloring	as needed	as needed
Fresh strawberries, rinsed and sliced in half	2 qt.	2 lt
Flaky dough pie shells, baked	2	2
Whipped cream	as needed	as needed

1. Bring the sugar and 8 fluid ounces (240 milliliters) water to a boil.
2. Dissolve the cornstarch in the cold water and add to the boiling liquid. Cook over low heat until clear, approximately 5 minutes.
3. Stir in the salt, lemon juice and enough red food coloring to produce a bright red color.

④ Pour this glaze over the strawberries and toss gently to coat them. Spoon the filling into the prepared pie shells. Chill thoroughly and top with whipped cream for service.

Approximate values per ⅛-pie serving: **Calories** 330, **Total fat** 8 g, **Saturated fat** 2 g, **Cholesterol** 0 mg, **Sodium** 200 mg, **Total carbohydrates** 63 g, **Protein** 2 g, **Vitamin C** 80%

FREEFORM APPLE PIES

CONNECTICUT CULINARY INSTITUTE, FARMINGTON, CT
Chef Jamie Roraback

Yield: 4 Pies, 6 in. (15 cm) each	**Method:** Baked fruit filling	
Dough:		
Unsalted butter	8 oz.	240 g
All-purpose flour	8 oz.	240 g
Salt	1 tsp.	5 ml
Water, ice cold	3 fl. oz.	90 ml
Filling:		
Apples, peeled, cored, large dice	1 lb.	480 g
Unsalted butter	1 oz.	30 g
Granulated sugar	2 oz.	60 g
Cinnamon, ground	¼ tsp.	2 ml
Vanilla extract	1 Tbsp.	15 ml
Apple brandy	2 fl. oz.	60 ml
Egg wash:		
Egg	1	1
Milk	2 Tbsp.	30 ml
Sanding sugar	as needed for garnish	
Ice cream and Caramel Sauce (page 1066)	as needed for garnish	

① To prepare the dough, cut the butter into medium dice and place it in the freezer for 5 minutes. Sift the flour with the salt. Toss the butter with the flour and salt and then place the mixture in the bowl of a food processor. Pulse until the butter chunks are the size of very small peas. Drizzle in the ice water and pulse just until the dough barely comes together. Do not overmix.

② Turn the dough out onto a work surface. Press it gently and quickly, then divide the dough into four rounds. Place the rounds on a sheet pan, cover them with plastic wrap and refrigerate for approximately 20 minutes before rolling out.

③ To prepare the filling, heat a sauté pan over high heat, add the apples and let them brown slightly. Add the butter and let it melt so that it loosens and frees the apples from the bottom of the pan. Then cook for approximately 1 minute, add the sugar and let it brown, stirring occasionally. Add the cinnamon and vanilla extract. Add the apple brandy and flambé. Cool the filling before assembling the pies.

④ Prepare the egg wash by whipping the egg together with the milk.

⑤ On a floured surface, roll out each round of dough into a circle approximately 8 inches (20 centimeters) in diameter. Place an appropriate-size plate or other circular object on top of the rolled-out dough and cut out a circle.

⑥ Place one-quarter of the apple filling in the center of each dough round, leaving 1½ inches (3.7 centimeters) of dough exposed along the edges. Brush the dough with egg wash and then fold the border over the filling in approximately five or six folds, each fold slightly overlapping the previous one. Place the pies on a sheet pan and brush additional egg wash over the surface. Sprinkle with sanding sugar.

⑦ Place the pies in the freezer until frozen. (Freezing will help prevent the butter running from the crust during baking.)

⑧ Preheat the oven to 400°F (200°C). Bake the frozen pies, rotating them occasionally. Bake until the apples are tender and the crust is evenly browned, approximately 20 minutes. Serve warm or at room temperature, dusted with powdered sugar and accompanied by whipped cream or ice cream and Caramel Sauce.

Approximate values per ½-pie serving: **Calories** 420, **Total fat** 27 g, **Saturated fat** 16 g, **Cholesterol** 95 mg, **Sodium** 300 mg, **Total carbohydrates** 36 g, **Protein** 4 g, **Vitamin A** 20%

BLACKBERRY COBBLER

A cobbler is a homestyle baked fruit dessert, usually made with a top crust of flaky pie dough, biscuit dough or streusel topping. The finished product will be slightly runny and is often served warm in a bowl or rimmed dish, accompanied by whipped cream or ice cream.

Yield: 10 Servings   **Method:** Baked fruit filling

Blackberries, IQF, thawed and drained	2 qt.	2 lt
Granulated sugar	8 oz.	240 g
Tapioca, instant	2 oz.	60 g
Water	10 fl. oz.	300 ml
Unsalted butter	2 oz.	60 g
Lemon zest	1 Tbsp.	15 ml
Streusel Topping (page 913)	16 oz.	480 g

1. Combine the berries, sugar, tapioca, water, butter and lemon zest, tossing the berries gently until well coated with the other ingredients.
2. Transfer to a lightly buttered half-size hotel pan, then set aside for at least 30 minutes before baking.
3. Cover the top of the cobbler with an even layer of the Streusel Topping. It can also be topped with Basic Pie Dough (page 962) or Country Biscuit dough (page 908) before baking.
4. Bake at 350°F (180°C) until the berry mixture bubbles and the crust is appropriately browned, approximately 40 to 50 minutes.

Approximate values per 6-oz. (180-g) serving: **Calories** 210, **Total fat** 5 g, **Saturated fat** 3 g, **Cholesterol** 20 mg, **Sodium** 10 mg, **Total carbohydrates** 39 g, **Protein** 1 g, **Vitamin C** 45%

FRESH BERRY TART

Yield: 1 Tart, 9 in. (22 cm)

Sweet Dough (page 963) tart shell, 9 in. (22 cm), fully baked	1	1
Pastry Cream (page 1051)	1 lb.	480 g
Fresh berries such as strawberries, blackberries, blueberries or raspberries	3 pt.	1.5 lt
Apricot glaze	as needed	as needed

1. Fill the cool tart shell with Pastry Cream.
2. Arrange the berries over the Pastry Cream in an even layer. Be sure to place the berries so that the Pastry Cream is covered.
3. Heat the apricot glaze and brush over the fruit to form a smooth coating.

Approximate values per ⅛-tart serving: **Calories** 135, **Total fat** 3 g, **Saturated fat** 1 g, **Cholesterol** 2 mg, **Sodium** 62 mg, **Total carbohydrates** 26 g, **Protein** 2 g

FRENCH APPLE TART

This procedure can be used for individual tartlets or large round, rectangular or daisy-shaped tart pans. The amount of each ingredient, the yield and the baking time will depend on the capacity and number of tart molds used.

Yield: 1 Tart, 12 in. (30 cm)

Sweet Dough (page 963)	20 oz.	600 g
Almond Cream (recipe follows)	1½ lb.	720 g
Tart apples, peeled, cored and sliced thin	5 to 6	5 to 6
Unsalted butter, melted	2 fl. oz.	60 ml
Granulated sugar	as needed	as needed
Apricot glaze, melted	as needed	as needed

1. Line the tart form with Sweet Dough. Do not dock the dough.
2. Pipe in an even layer of Almond Cream over the tart shell.
3. Arrange the apples in overlapping rows, covering the Almond Cream completely.
4. Brush the top of the apples with the melted butter and sprinkle lightly with granulated sugar.
5. Bake at 375°F (190°C) until the crust is done and the apples are light brown.
6. Allow the tart to cool to room temperature. Brush the top with apricot glaze.

Approximate values per 4-oz. (120-g) serving: **Calories** 395, **Total fat** 17 g, **Saturated fat** 7 g, **Cholesterol** 234 mg, **Sodium** 98 mg, **Total carbohydrates** 56 g, **Protein** 7 g, **Vitamin A** 12%

ALMOND CREAM

Yield: 3 lb. (1.4 kg)

Unsalted butter, softened	8 oz.	240 g
Granulated sugar	1 lb.	480 g
Eggs	5	5
All-purpose flour	5 oz.	150 g
Almonds, ground	12 oz.	360 g

1. Cream the butter and sugar. Slowly add the eggs, scraping down the bowl as necessary.
2. Stir the flour and almonds together, then add to the butter mixture. Blend until no lumps remain.
3. Almond cream may be stored under refrigeration for up to 3 weeks.

Approximate values per 1-oz. (30-g) serving: **Calories** 140, **Total fat** 8 g, **Saturated fat** 3 g, **Cholesterol** 30 mg, **Sodium** 5 mg, **Total carbohydrates** 13 g, **Protein** 2 g

TARTE TATIN

Yield: 8 Servings

All-purpose flour	as needed	as needed
Puff pastry	9 oz.	270 g
Unsalted butter, softened	4 oz.	120 g
Granulated sugar	6 oz.	180 g
Apples, firm variety, peeled, cored and quartered	7	7

1. Select a tarte tatin pan or a heavy 9- to 10-inch (22.5- to 25-centimeter) round pan. Do not use a nonstick pan.
2. Lightly flour a work surface and roll out the puff pastry dough into a circle slightly larger than the pan.
3. Press the butter onto the bottom of the pan. Sprinkle the sugar evenly over the butter.
4. Arrange the quartered apples in a circle in the pan, pressing them into the sugar and butter and packing them as closely as possible to allow for shrinkage during cooking. Place several cut pieces of apple in the center of the pan so that there is a single layer of tightly packed apples completely covering the bottom of the pan.
5. Place the pan over medium-high heat and cook for 5 minutes without stirring, until the butter begins to melt and bubble. Shake the pan from side to side to help prevent the apples from sticking. Continue cooking for another 10 to 15 minutes, repositioning the pan occasionally to be sure the sugar caramelizes evenly. Cook until the sugar is a deep amber color.
6. Place the circle of puff pastry dough over the apples and place the pan in a 425°F (220°C) oven for 15 to 20 minutes or until the crust is puffed and brown.
7. Remove the tarte tatin from the oven. Shake the pan to loosen the apples. Invert the pan onto a round serving platter, being careful not to get burned by the hot syrup. Reposition any apples that may have stuck to the pan. Cut the tart into eight wedges and serve with whipped cream or crème fraîche.

Approximate values per serving: **Calories** 420, **Total fat** 24 g, **Saturated fat** 9 g, **Cholesterol** 30 mg, **Sodium** 80 mg, **Total carbohydrates** 50 g, **Protein** 3 g

STRAWBERRY NAPOLEON

Yield: 10 Servings

Puff pastry, 4-in. × 15-in. (10-cm × 37-cm) strips, docked and baked	3	3
Pastry Cream (page 1051)	1 lb.	480 g
Fresh strawberries, sliced	1 qt.	1 lt
Crème Chantilly (page 1057)	1 pt.	500 ml
Basic Sugar Glaze (page 1028)	as needed	as needed
Dark chocolate, melted	1 oz.	30 g

1. Allow the puff pastry to cool completely before assembling.
2. Place a strip of puff pastry on a cake cardboard for support. Pipe on a layer of Pastry Cream, leaving a clean margin of almost ½ inch (1.2 centimeters) on all four sides.
3. Top the cream with a layer of berries.
4. Spread on a thin layer of Crème Chantilly and top with a second layer of puff pastry. Repeat the procedure for the second layer of puff pastry and chill.

⑤ Prepare the Basic Sugar Glaze. Place the melted chocolate in a piping cone. When ready to glaze, place the third strip of puff pastry on an icing rack, flat side up. Pour the Basic Sugar Glaze down the length of the pastry and spread evenly with a metal cake spatula. Allow the excess to drip over the sides.

⑥ Immediately pipe thin lines of chocolate across the glaze. Use a toothpick to pull a spiderweb pattern in the glaze. Chill to set the glaze, then place the top in position on the napoleon.

Approximate values per 5-oz. (150-g) serving: **Calories** 320, **Total fat** 20 g, **Saturated fat** 9 g, **Cholesterol** 115 mg, **Sodium** 65 mg, **Total carbohydrates** 29 g, **Protein** 4 g, **Vitamin A** 15%, **Vitamin C** 60%

PALMIERS

Puff pastry	as needed	as needed
Granulated sugar	as needed	as needed

① Roll out the puff pastry into a very thin rectangle. The length is not important, but the width should be at least 7 inches (17.5 centimeters).

② Using a rolling pin, gently press the sugar into the dough on both sides.

③ Make a 1-inch (2.5-centimeter) fold along the long edges of the dough toward the center. Sprinkle on additional sugar.

④ Make another 1-inch (2.5-centimeter) fold along the long edges of the dough toward the center. The two folds should almost meet in the center. Sprinkle on additional sugar.

⑤ Fold one side on top of the other. Press down gently with a rolling pin or your fingers so that the dough adheres. Chill for 1 hour.

⑥ Cut the log of dough in thin slices. Place the cookies on a paper-lined sheet pan and bake at 400°F (200°C) until the edges are brown, approximately 8 to 12 minutes.

Approximate values per 1-oz. (30-g) serving: **Calories** 130, **Total fat** 5 g, **Saturated fat** 1 g, **Cholesterol** 0 mg, **Sodium** 35 mg, **Total carbohydrates** 19 g, **Protein** 1 g

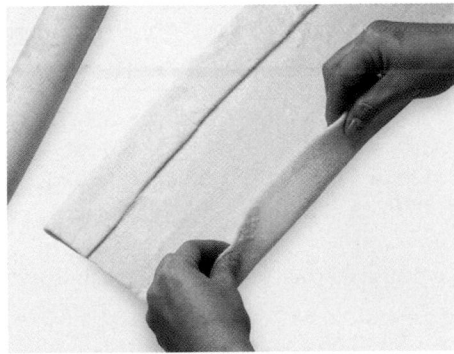

① Folding the dough toward the center from both edges.

② Slicing the log of dough into individual cookies.

❶ Using a piping bag to fill the éclairs with pastry cream.

❷ Dipping the éclairs in chocolate glaze.

CHOCOLATE ÉCLAIRS

Yield: 20 Éclairs

Baked éclair shells, 4 in. (10 cm) long, made from Éclair Paste (page 979)	20	20
Vanilla Pastry Cream (page 1051)	2 lb.	960 ml
Chocolate glaze:		
Unsweetened chocolate	4 oz.	120 g
Semisweet chocolate	4 oz.	120 g
Unsalted butter	4 oz.	120 g
Light corn syrup	4 tsp.	20 ml
White chocolate, melted (optional)	as needed	as needed

❶ Use a paring knife or skewer to cut a small hole into the end of each baked, cooled éclair shell.

❷ Pipe the Vanilla Pastry Cream into each shell using a piping bag fitted with a small plain tip. Be sure that the cream fills the full length of each shell. Refrigerate the filled éclairs.

❸ To prepare the chocolate glaze, melt all the ingredients together over a bain marie. Remove from the heat and allow to cool until slightly thickened, stirring occasionally.

❹ In a single, smooth stroke, drag the top of each filled éclair through the glaze. Only the very top of each pastry should be coated with chocolate.

❺ Melted white chocolate may be piped onto the wet glaze, then pulled into patterns using a toothpick. Keep the finished éclairs refrigerated and serve within 8 to 12 hours.

Approximate values per éclair: **Calories** 410, **Total fat** 31 g, **Saturated fat** 17 g, **Cholesterol** 110 mg, **Sodium** 230 mg, **Total carbohydrates** 27 g, **Protein** 5 g, **Vitamin A** 20%

BAKED MERINGUE

Yield: 6 lb. 8 oz. (3.1 kg)

Egg whites	2 lb. 3 oz.	1 kg
Granulated sugar	4 lb. 6 oz.	2.1 kg
Coffee extract (optional)	2½ fl. oz.	75 ml

❶ Whip the egg whites to soft peaks. With the mixer running at medium speed, slowly add the sugar and continue whipping until very stiff and glossy.

❷ If desired, whip in the coffee extract.

❸ Spread or pipe the meringue into the desired shapes on parchment-lined sheet pans.

❹ Bake at 200°F (90°C) for 5 hours or overnight in a nonconvection oven. The baked meringues should be firm and crisp but not browned.

❺ Use in assembling dessert or pastry items.

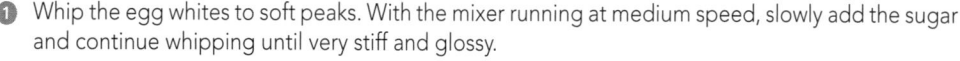

Approximate values per serving: **Calories** 80, **Total fat** 0 g, **Saturated fat** 0 g, **Cholesterol** 0 mg, **Sodium** 15 mg, **Total carbohydrates** 20 g, **Protein** 1 g, **Claims**—no fat; no saturated fat; no cholesterol; low sodium

CHOCOLATE DÉLICE

Yield: 1 Cake, 8 in. (20 cm)

Ganache (recipe follows)	7 oz.	210 g
Classic Dacquoise (recipe follows), 8-in. (20-cm) disks	3	3
Crème Chantilly (page 1057)	2 qt.	2 lt
Candied Almonds (recipe follows)	as needed	as needed

1 Spread an even layer of ganache over two of the dacquoise disks.

2 Top one disk with approximately ¾ cup (170 milliliters) Crème Chantilly. Place the second disk on top, chocolate side up. Top with another ¾ cup (170 milliliters) Crème Chantilly. Position the third disk on top, flat side up.

3 Spread the remaining Crème Chantilly over the top and sides.

4 Sprinkle Candied Almonds over the top and sides of the cake.

5 Freeze to firm the cream, approximately 1 hour. Remove from freezer and refrigerate for service.

Approximate values per ⅛-cake serving: **Calories** 490, **Total fat** 32.5 g, **Saturated fat** 13 g, **Cholesterol** 50 mg, **Sodium** 35 mg, **Total carbohydrates** 39 g, **Protein** 10 g, **Vitamin A** 16%

1 Piping out the meringue disks.

2 Layering the ganache-covered dacquoise.

3 Frosting the Chocolate Délice.

GANACHE

Yield: 7 oz. (210 g)

Semisweet chocolate	4 oz.	120 g
Heavy cream	3 fl. oz.	90 ml

1 Chop the chocolate into small pieces and place in a bowl.

2 Heat the cream just to boiling. Pour the cream over the chocolate and stir until the mixture is glossy and smooth. Allow to cool slightly before using.

Approximate values per serving: **Calories** 130, **Total fat** 10 g, **Saturated fat** 6 g, **Cholesterol** 15 mg, **Sodium** 0 mg, **Total carbohydrates** 10 g, **Protein** 1 g, **Vitamin A** 6%

CLASSIC DACQUOISE

Yield: 3 Disks, 8 in. (20 cm) each

Blanched almonds	2 oz.	60 g
Granulated sugar	6 oz.	180 g
Egg whites	3 oz.	90 g

1. Preheat oven to 225°F (110°C). Line a baking sheet with parchment. Draw three 8-inch (20-centimeter) circles on the parchment.
2. Grind the almonds in a food processor. They should be the consistency of cornmeal and as dry as possible. Combine with 2 ounces (60 grams) sugar and set aside.
3. Whip the egg whites on medium speed until foamy. Increase the speed and gradually add 1 ounce (30 grams) sugar.
4. Continue whipping until the egg whites form soft peaks. Gradually add the remaining sugar.
5. Continue whipping until smooth and glossy, approximately 2 minutes.
6. Sprinkle the almond-sugar mixture over the meringue and fold together by hand.
7. Using a pastry bag with a plain tip, pipe the meringue onto the parchment paper to form three 8-inch (20-centimeter) rounds.
8. Bake until firm and crisp but not brown, approximately 60 to 75 minutes. Cool completely.

Approximate values per serving: **Calories** 100, **Total fat** 2.5 g, **Saturated fat** 0 g, **Cholesterol** 0 mg, **Sodium** 15 mg, **Total carbohydrates** 16 g, **Protein** 2 g, **Claims**—low fat; low saturated fat; no cholesterol; very low sodium

CANDIED ALMONDS

Egg whites	2	2
Granulated sugar	2 oz.	60 g
Sliced almonds	8 oz.	240 g

1. Preheat oven to 325°F (160°C).
2. Whisk the egg whites and sugar together. Add the almonds. Toss with a rubber spatula to coat the nuts completely.
3. Spread the nuts in a thin layer on a lightly greased baking sheet. Bake until lightly toasted and dry, approximately 15 to 20 minutes. Watch closely to prevent burning.
4. Stir the nuts with a metal spatula every 5 to 7 minutes during baking.
5. Cool completely. Store in an airtight container for up to 10 days.

Approximate values per serving: **Calories** 160, **Total fat** 10 g, **Saturated fat** 1 g, **Cholesterol** 0 mg, **Sodium** 10 mg, **Total carbohydrates** 10 g, **Protein** 6 g, **Claims**—no saturated fat; no cholesterol; very low sodium

APPLE STRUDEL

Yield: 2 Rolls, 12 in. (30 cm) each

Apples, peeled, cored and slivered	1 lb. 8 oz.	720 g
Lemon juice	1 Tbsp.	15 ml
Granulated sugar	8 oz.	240 g
Raisins	2 oz.	60 g
Orange zest, grated	1 Tbsp.	15 ml
Cinnamon, ground	1 tsp.	2 ml
Phyllo dough	12 sheets	12 sheets
Clarified butter, melted	4 fl. oz.	120 ml
Ground almonds	½ oz.	15 g

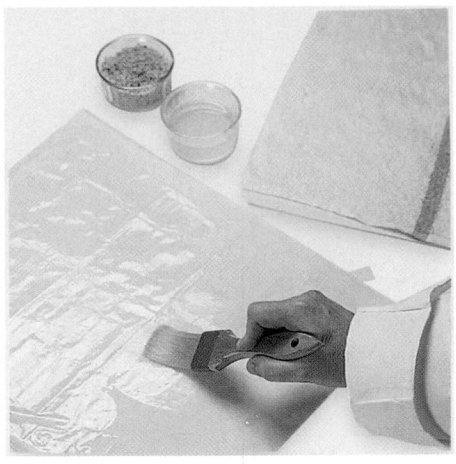

1. Toss the apples with the lemon juice and half of the sugar in a medium bowl. Let stand for 30 minutes, then drain off the liquid that forms.
2. Gently combine the drained apples with the raisins, orange zest, cinnamon and remaining sugar.
3. Prepare the phyllo dough by laying one sheet out on a piece of parchment paper. Brush lightly with butter and top with a second sheet of phyllo. Brush this sheet lightly with butter and sprinkle with about 1 teaspoon (5 milliliters) ground almonds. Top with a third sheet of dough, more butter and nuts and repeat until six sheets of phyllo are stacked.
4. Place half of the apple mixture along the long edge of the assembled dough. Using the paper to assist with rolling the dough, roll the phyllo around the filling tightly. Repeat steps 3 and 4 with the remaining phyllo sheets and filling.
5. Place the paper and the strudels, seam side down, on a baking sheet. Brush the surface lightly with melted butter. Bake at 375°F (190°C) until golden brown and crisp, approximately 18 minutes.

Approximate values per ⅙-roll serving: **Calories** 260, **Total fat** 10 g, **Saturated fat** 6 g, **Cholesterol** 20 mg, **Sodium** 0 mg, **Total carbohydrates** 42 g, **Protein** 2 g

1. Brushing phyllo sheets with clarified butter.

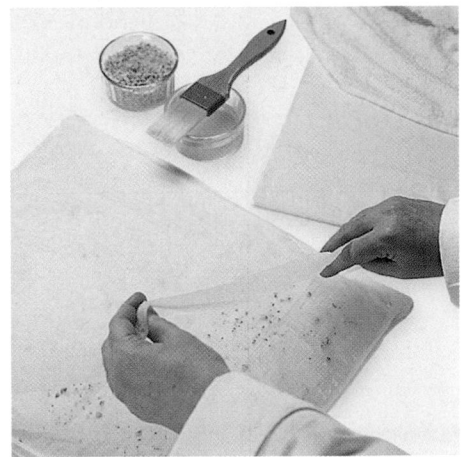

2. Sprinkling phyllo with chopped nuts before adding another layer of phyllo.

3. Topping the phyllo sheets with the apples.

4. Rolling up the strudel.

5. The finished Apple Strudel.

LINZER TART

CHEFS SUSAN FENIGER AND MARY SUE MILLIKEN

Yield: 8–10 Servings

Unsalted butter, softened	8 oz.	240 g
Granulated sugar	8 oz.	240 g
Egg yolks	2	2
Orange zest	2 Tbsp.	30 ml
Lemon zest	1 Tbsp.	15 ml
All-purpose flour	11 oz.	330 g
Hazelnuts, skins removed, ground fine	6 oz.	180 g
Baking powder	1 tsp.	5 ml
Cinnamon, ground	2 tsp.	10 ml
Cloves, ground	½ tsp.	2 ml
Salt	¼ tsp.	1 ml
Raspberry preserves	14 oz.	420 g

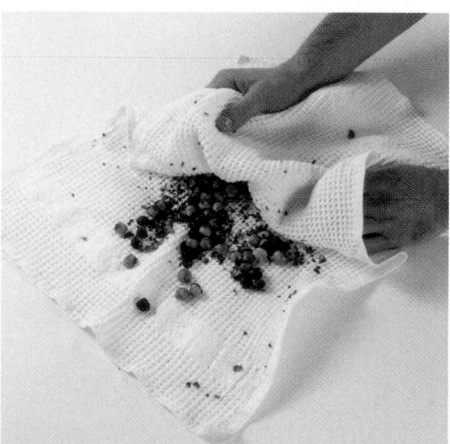

Rubbing toasted hazelnuts with a towel to remove the skin.

1. To make the dough, cream together the butter and sugar until light and fluffy. Add the egg yolks and the orange and lemon zests. Beat until well combined.

2. In another bowl, mix together all the remaining ingredients except the preserves. Add the dry mixture all at once to the creamed mixture and mix briefly, until just combined. (This dough looks more like cookie dough than pastry.) Wrap in plastic and chill until firm, at least 4 hours or overnight.

3. Divide the dough in half. On a generously floured board, briefly knead one piece of dough and flatten it with the palm of your hand. Gently roll the dough out ¼ inch (6 millimeters) thick and use it to line a 9- or 10-inch (22- or 25-centimeter) tart pan with a removable bottom. This rich dough patches easily. Chill for approximately 10 minutes.

4. Roll out the second piece of dough to form a 12-inch × 4-inch (30-centimeter × 10-centimeter) rectangle. Using a sharp knife or pastry wheel, cut lengthwise strips, approximately ⅓ inch (8 millimeters) wide.

5. Remove the lined tart shell from the refrigerator and spread the raspberry preserves evenly over it. To create the lattice pattern with the pastry strips, first lay some strips in parallel lines, ½ inch (1.2 centimeters) apart. Then lay a second row of strips at a 45-degree angle to the first. Press the strips to the edge of the crust to seal.

6. Bake at 350°F (180°C) until the crust is golden brown and the filling is bubbly in center, approximately 45 minutes. Set aside to cool.

Approximate values per ⅒-tart serving: **Calories** 300, **Total fat** 29 g, **Saturated fat** 12 g, **Cholesterol** 90 mg, **Sodium** 65 mg, **Total carbohydrates** 7 g, **Protein** 4 g, **Vitamin A** 20%, **Claims**—low sodium; good source of fiber

CHOCOLATE JUMBLE COOKIES

Yield: 34 Cookies, 1 oz. (30 g) each	**Method:** Drop cookies	
Coffee or espresso	2 fl. oz.	60 ml
Unsweetened chocolate	2 oz.	60 g
Flour, sifted	4½ oz.	135 g
Salt	¼ tsp.	1 ml
Unsalted butter	3 oz.	90 g
Vanilla extract	½ tsp.	2 ml
Granulated sugar	8 oz.	240 g
Eggs	2	2
Walnuts, chopped	6 oz.	180 g
Milk chocolate chips	6 oz.	180 g

1. Combine the coffee and chocolate and melt over a bain marie.
2. Stir the flour and salt together and set aside.
3. Cream the butter, vanilla extract and sugar together until fluffy. Add the eggs one at a time. Add the chocolate, stirring to blend well.
4. Stir the flour into the chocolate mixture, then fold in the nuts and chocolate chips. Refrigerate the dough for at least 1 hour before baking.
5. Portion into 1-ounce (30-gram) mounds using a #20 portion scoop. Place on parchment-lined baking sheets and bake at 375°F (190°C) until set, approximately 12 minutes.

Approximate values per cookie: **Calories** 130, **Total fat** 8 g, **Saturated fat** 3 g, **Cholesterol** 20 mg, **Sodium** 25 mg, **Total carbohydrates** 14 g, **Protein** 2 g

---

OATMEAL COOKIES

Yield: 32 Cookies, approximately 2 oz. (60 g) each

Method: Drop cookies

All-purpose or pastry flour	10½ oz.	315 g
Baking soda	1 tsp.	5 ml
Cinnamon, ground	1 Tbsp.	15 ml
Quick-cooking oats	9 oz.	270 g
Unsalted butter	9 oz.	270 g
Granulated sugar	9 oz.	270 g
Brown sugar	9 oz.	270 g
Eggs	2	2
Orange juice concentrate	1½ fl. oz.	45 ml
Vanilla extract	½ fl. oz.	15 ml
Salt	1 tsp.	5 ml
Raisins	12 oz.	360 g

1. Sift together the flour, baking soda and cinnamon. Stir in the oats. Set aside. Cream the butter until light and fluffy. Add the sugars and continue creaming until the mixture is lightened. Add the eggs one at a time, scraping down the bowl frequently and mixing well after each addition. Add the orange juice concentrate, vanilla and salt.
2. Fold in the dry ingredients and the raisins.
3. Portion the dough onto paper-lined sheet pans and bake at 375°F (191°C) until golden, approximately 10 to 12 minutes.

Approximate values per cookie: **Calories** 150, **Total fat** 5 g, **Saturated fat** 1.5 g, **Cholesterol** 10 mg, **Sodium** 105 mg, **Total carbohydrates** 24 g, **Protein** 2 g, **Claims**—low cholesterol; low sodium

PEANUT BUTTER SANDIES

Yield: 4½ Dozen Cookies, 1⅓ oz. (40 g) each | **Method:** Drop cookies

Pastry flour	24 oz.	720 g
Baking soda	1 tsp.	5 ml
Baking powder	1 tsp.	5 ml
Unsalted butter	1 lb.	480 g
Granulated sugar	1 lb.	480 g
Eggs	2	2
Peanut butter	10 oz.	300 g
Salt	2 tsp.	10 ml
Peanut halves (optional)	2 oz.	60 g

1. Sift together the flour, baking soda and baking powder. Set aside. Cream the butter. Add the sugar and continue creaming. Gradually add the eggs, followed by the peanut butter and salt.
2. Add the dry ingredients to the butter mixture and mix to make a firm dough.
3. Scale the dough into 1-pound (480-gram) pieces. Roll the dough into 12-inch (36-centimeter) logs. Cut into 1-inch (3-centimeter) pieces.
4. Roll each cookie into a ball and place on a sheet pan. Press each ball down using the bottom of a measuring cup to slightly less than ½ inch (1 centimeter). The edges of the cookies will develop some cracks, which is a desired look.
5. Using a fork, press crisscross markings on the surface of each cookie. Lightly brush the cookies with water. Sprinkle lightly with granulated sugar and press one peanut half, if using, into each cookie.
6. Bake at 400°F (200°F) until golden brown, approximately 12 minutes.

Approximate values per cookie: **Calories** 190, **Total fat** 12 g, **Saturated fat** 5 g, **Cholesterol** 20 mg, **Sodium** 160 mg, **Total carbohydrates** 22 g, **Protein** 3 g

CHOCOLATE CHIP COOKIES

Yield: 50 cookies, approximately 2 oz. (60 g) each | **Method:** Drop cookies

Unsalted butter	1 lb.	480 g
Granulated sugar	8 oz.	240 g
Brown sugar	12 oz.	360 g
Eggs	3	3
Vanilla extract	2 tsp.	10 ml
Salt	2 tsp.	10 ml
Pastry flour	1 lb. 4 oz.	600 g
Baking soda	1 tsp.	5 ml
Pecans or walnut pieces, chopped	8 oz.	240 g
Chocolate chips	2 lb.	960 g

1. Cream the butter and the sugars in the bowl of a mixer fitted with the paddle attachment. Beat until light, approximately 5 minutes at medium speed.
2. Add the eggs to the creamed mixture one at a time. Add the vanilla.
3. Stir the salt, flour and baking soda together and add to the creamed mixture.
4. Stir in the pecans and chocolate chips.
5. Portion the dough using a #20 scoop onto a paper-lined sheet pan and bake at 350°F (180°C) until the cookies are golden brown and cooked through, approximately 10 to 12 minutes.

Approximate values per 2-oz. (60-g) cookie: **Calories** 310, **Total fat** 20 g, **Saturated fat** 7 g, **Cholesterol** 20 mg, **Sodium** 160 mg, **Total carbohydrates** 35 g, **Protein** 3 g

BISCOTTI

Italian in origin, biscotti are twice-baked cookies served with coffee, wine or other beverages. The dough is mixed and shaped into a log. The log of dough is baked, then cut on a diagonal into individual cookies, which are returned to the oven to bake further. This twice-baked process ensures that the cookies will have a long-lasting firm, crisp texture.

Yield: 3 Dozen Biscotti, 2 oz. (60 g) each		**Method:** Bar cookies	
Cinnamon, ground		1 Tbsp.	15 ml
Ammonium carbonate or baking powder		2 tsp.	10 ml
Hazelnut flour		10 oz.	300 g
Almond flour		3 oz.	90 g
Pastry flour		1 lb.	480 g
Eggs		5	5
Granulated sugar		1 lb.	480 g
Unsalted butter, melted		8 oz.	240 g
Whole hazelnuts		10 oz.	300 g
Chocolate, melted and tempered (optional)		as needed	as needed

1. Sift together the cinnamon and ammonium carbonate or baking powder. Stir in the hazelnut, almond and pastry flours. Set aside.
2. In a large bowl, whisk together the eggs and sugar to the ribbon stage, approximately 3 minutes. Add the butter. Stir in the flour mixture with a rubber spatula, then stir in the whole hazelnuts.
3. Divide the dough into three even pieces. Refrigerate until cold.
4. Roll each piece of dough into a 12-inch (30-centimeter) log. Place on a paper-lined sheet pan, leaving at least 3 inches (7.5 centimeters) of space between each log.
5. Bake at 350°F (180°C) until golden in color, approximately 20 minutes. Cool the logs, then slice them into 1-inch- (3-centimeter-) thick slices.
6. Place the sliced cookies upright on paper-lined sheet pans.
7. Double-tray the pans. Reduce heat to 325°F (160°C) and bake until the biscotti are thoroughly crisp, approximately 40 minutes.
8. Once cool, the biscotti may be dipped in tempered chocolate.

VARIATIONS:

Orange Biscotti—Add 1 tablespoon (15 milliliters) grated orange zest to the flour mixture.

Anise Biscotti—Add 1 teaspoon (5 milliliters) chopped anise seeds to the flour mixture.

Chocolate Biscotti—Replace 5 ounces (150 grams) pastry flour with cocoa powder. Add ½ teaspoon (2 milliliters) coffee extract and ½ teaspoon (2 milliliters) cinnamon to the flour mixture.

Approximate values per cookie: **Calories** 260, **Total fat** 17 g, **Saturated fat** 4 g, **Cholesterol** 45 mg, **Sodium** 30 mg, **Total carbohydrates** 26 g, **Protein** 5 g

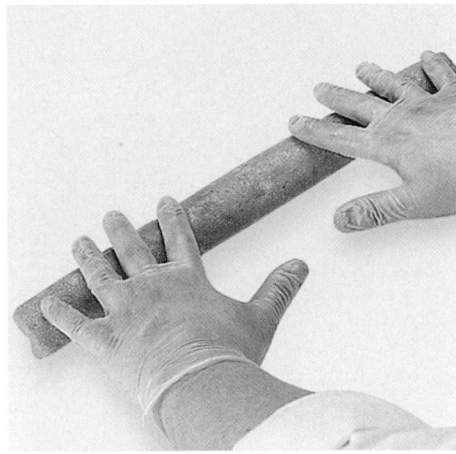

① Biscotti dough rolled into a log before the first baking.

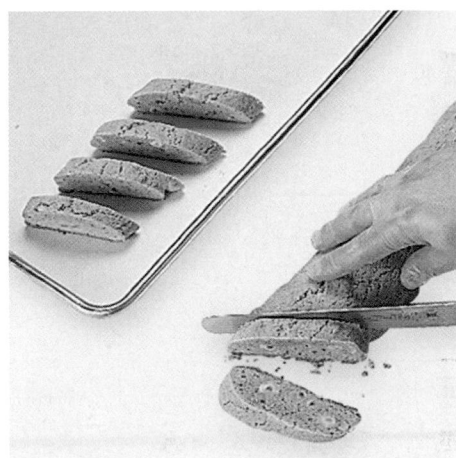

② Slicing biscotti before the second baking.

① Spreading the cherry-almond mixture over the baked dough.

② Cutting the cookies.

③ Dipping the finished cookies in chocolate.

CHERRY-ALMOND FLORENTINES

HOUSTON COMMUNITY COLLEGE, HOUSTON, TX

Pastry Chef Eddy Van Damme

Yield: 40 Cookies   **Method:** Sheet cookies

Sweet Dough (page 963), chilled	1 lb. 8 oz.	720 g
Granulated sugar	6 oz.	180 g
Glucose or corn syrup	2 fl. oz.	60 ml
Water	3 fl. oz.	90 ml
Butter, cubed	5 oz.	150 g
Honey	2½ fl. oz.	75 ml
Heavy cream, boiling	3 fl. oz.	90 ml
Vanilla extract	1 tsp.	5 ml
Almonds, sliced, toasted	11 oz.	330 g
Dried cherries	2 oz.	60 g
Semisweet couverture, tempered	as needed	as needed

① Line a half-size sheet pan with parchment paper. Roll the chilled Sweet Dough ⅛ inch (3 millimeters) thick and slightly larger than the half-size sheet pan. Line the bottom and sides of the sheet pan with the dough. Prick the dough with a fork.

② Bake blind at 375°F (190°C) until blond in color, approximately 8 to 11 minutes. Remove from the oven and set aside to cool.

③ Boil the sugar, glucose and water to a golden caramel, approximately 325°F (160°C).

④ Add the butter and honey to the caramel, then add the boiling cream. Bring the mixture to a full boil.

⑤ Remove from heat and add the vanilla extract, almonds and cherries. While still warm, spread the mixture onto the prebaked crust in a thin, even layer.

⑥ Bake at 375°F (190°C) for approximately 20 minutes or until the center has set and is golden brown.

⑦ Cool completely, trim the edges then cut into 2-inch (5-centimeter) squares. Dip one corner of each piece in tempered semisweet chocolate.

Approximate values per cookie: **Calories** 160, **Total fat** 10 g, **Saturated fat** 3.5 g, **Cholesterol** 15 mg, **Sodium** 0 mg, **Total carbohydrates** 15 g, **Protein** 3 g

LEMON OR LIME BARS

Yield: 80 Cookies, 1½ in. (4 cm) each; 1 Half-Sheet Pan   **Method:** Sheet cookies

Sweet Dough (page 963), chilled	2 lb. 8 oz.	1200 g
Egg wash	as needed	as needed
Filling:		
Granulated sugar	1 lb. 6 oz.	640 g
Eggs	8	8
Pastry flour	2 oz.	60 g
Lemon or lime juice	11 fl. oz.	330 ml
Milk	5 fl. oz.	150 ml
Salt	½ tsp.	2 ml
Powdered sugar for garnish	4 oz.	120 g

1. Roll the chilled Sweet Dough out on parchment paper cut to fit the sides and bottom of a half-sheet pan. Flip the parchment-covered dough onto a half-sheet pan. Remove the parchment. Trim uneven edges and reserve dough scraps. Prick the surface of the dough with a fork and bake at 350°F (180°C) until the dough is light golden, approximately 15 minutes. If cracks develop during the baking process, patch with the leftover dough and return briefly to the oven.
2. Brush the baked dough with egg wash and return to the oven for 3 minutes or until the egg wash has set.
3. To prepare the filling, whip the sugar and the eggs just until smooth. Whisk in the pastry flour until well combined, then add the lemon juice, milk and salt.
4. Pour the lemon filling into the prebaked shell.
5. Bake at 325°F (160°C) until set, approximately 25 minutes.
6. Cool, then cut into 1½-inch × 1½-inch (4-centimeter × 4-centimeter) squares. Dust liberally with powdered sugar.

Approximate values per cookie: **Calories** 140, **Total fat** 6 g, **Saturated fat** 3 g, **Cholesterol** 40 mg, **Sodium** 80 mg, **Total carbohydrates** 21 g, **Protein** 2 g

LINZER COOKIES

Yield: 2 Dozen Cookies, 2½ in. (6 cm.) each   **Method:** Cut-out Cookie

Shortbread Tart Dough (page 985), made with hazelnuts, chilled	4 lb. 7 oz.	2.1 kg
Raspberry jam	1 lb.	480 g

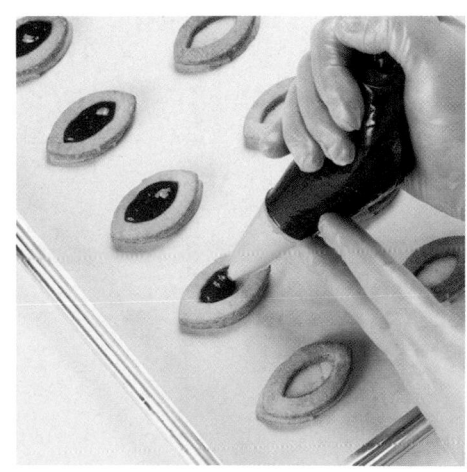

1. On a well-floured surface, roll the chilled hazelnut shortbread dough ¼ inch (6 millimeters) thick.
2. Cut the dough with a floured cutter into 2½-inch (6-centimeter) circles or ovals. Place the dough cutouts on paper lined sheet pans.
3. Using a slightly smaller cookie cutter, remove the center from half of the dough cutouts. These will be the cookie tops for the sandwich cookies. (Save these dough scraps for more cookies.)
4. Bake at 375° F (190°C) until pale blond in color, approximately 8-10 minutes. Cool the cookies completely.
5. Melt 3 ounces (120 grams) of the raspberry jam. Brush the solid cookies with the melted jam. Place the remaining cookie tops on the jam-coated cookies. Using a pastry bag fitted with a small plain tip, fill the center of each cookie with raspberry jam.

Approximate values per cookie: **Calories** 200, **Total fat** 15 g, **Saturated fat** 7 g, **Cholesterol** 65 mg, **Sodium** 75 mg, **Total carbohydrates** 24 g, **Protein** 4 g

SUGAR COOKIES

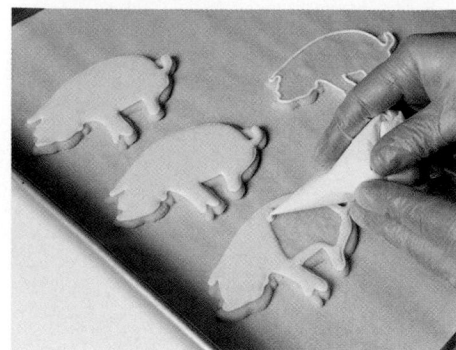

Yield: 24 Cookies   **Method:** Cut-out cookies

All-purpose flour	12 oz.	360 g
Baking powder	2 tsp.	10 ml
Mace, ground	¼ tsp.	1 ml
Unsalted butter, softened	4 oz.	120 g
Granulated sugar	8 oz.	240 g
Vanilla extract	1 tsp.	5 ml
Egg	1	1
Decorative Cookie Icing (recipe follows)	as needed	as needed

1. Stir together the flour, baking powder and mace. Set aside.
2. Cream the butter and sugar until light and fluffy. Blend in the vanilla. Add the egg and beat again until fluffy. Gradually add the flour mixture, beating just until well combined.
3. Wrap the dough in plastic wrap and refrigerate until firm, approximately 1 to 2 hours.
4. Work with half of the dough at a time, keeping the remainder refrigerated. On a lightly floured board, roll out the dough to a thickness of approximately ⅛ inch (3 millimeters). Cut as desired with cookie cutters about 3 inches (7.5 centimeters). Carefully transfer the cookies to lightly greased baking sheets.
5. Bake at 325°F (160°C) until golden brown, approximately 10 to 12 minutes. Let stand for 1 minute, then transfer to wire racks to cool.
6. To decorate the cookies, use a pastry tip fitted with a small plain tip to pipe a fine outline of Decorative Cookie Icing around the edge of each cookie. Allow the icing to set for 5 minutes. Thin the remaining icing with water until it has the texture of thick cream. Fill the center of each cookie with additional icing.

Approximate values per cookie: **Calories** 90, **Total fat** 3 g, **Saturated fat** 1.5 g, **Cholesterol** 15 mg, **Sodium** 0 mg, **Total carbohydrates** 14 g, **Protein** 1 g, **Claims**—low fat; low cholesterol; no sodium

DECORATIVE COOKIE ICING

Yield: 1 lb. 6 oz. (665 g)

Powdered sugar	1 lb.	480 g
Lemon juice or water	4 fl. oz.	120 ml
Corn syrup	2 fl. oz.	60 ml
Vanilla extract	1 tsp.	5 ml
Food coloring	as needed	as needed

1. Combine the powdered sugar, lemon juice, corn syrup and vanilla in the bowl of a mixer fitted with the paddle attachment. Blend on low speed until the sugar dissolves and the mixture is smooth. Adjust the consistency of the icing by adding more water if necessary. Color as needed.
2. Apply the icing to cookies and let them air dry until the icing hardens. Cover leftover icing and store it in the refrigerator, where it will keep about 3 weeks.

Approximate values per ¾-oz. (20-g) serving: **Calories** 60, **Total fat** 0 g, **Saturated fat** 0 g, **Cholesterol** 0 mg, **Sodium** 0 mg, **Total carbohydrates** 16 g, **Protein** 0 g

GINGERBREAD COOKIES

Yield: 1 Dozen Cookies, 2⅓ oz. (70 g) each   **Method:** Cut-out cookies

Unsalted butter, softened	4 oz.	120 g
Brown sugar	4 oz.	120 g
Molasses	6 fl. oz.	180 ml
Egg	1	1
All-purpose flour	12 oz.	360 g
Baking soda	1 tsp.	5 ml
Salt	½ tsp.	2 ml
Ginger, ground	2 tsp.	10 ml
Cinnamon, ground	1 tsp.	5 ml
Nutmeg, ground	½ tsp.	2 ml
Cloves, ground	½ tsp.	2 ml
Raspberry jam	as needed	as needed

1. Cream the butter and sugar until light and fluffy. Add the molasses and egg and beat to blend well; set aside.
2. Stir together the remaining ingredients. Gradually add the flour mixture to the butter mixture, beating until just blended. Gather the dough into a ball and wrap in plastic wrap; refrigerate for at least 1 hour.
3. On a lightly floured board, roll out the gingerbread to a thickness of ¼ inch (6 millimeters). Cut out the cookies with a floured cutter and transfer to greased baking sheets.
4. Bake at 325°F (160°C) until the cookies are lightly browned around the edges and feel barely firm when touched, approximately 10 minutes. Transfer to wire racks to cool. Decorate as desired with Royal Icing (page 1029), Decorative Cookie Icing (page 1002) or melted chocolate.

Approximate values per cookie: **Calories** 260, **Total fat** 8 g, **Saturated fat** 5 g, **Cholesterol** 40 mg, **Sodium** 220 mg, **Total carbohydrates** 41 g, **Protein** 4 g, **Vitamin A** 8%

SPRITZ COOKIES

Yield: 4 Dozen Cookies, ½ oz. (15 g) each   **Method:** Pressed cookies

Unsalted butter, softened	8 oz.	240 g
Granulated sugar	4 oz.	120 g
Salt	¼ tsp.	1 ml
Vanilla extract	1 tsp.	5 ml
Egg	1	1
Cake flour, sifted	10 oz.	300 g
Raspberry jam	as needed	as needed

1. Cream the butter and sugar until light and fluffy. Add the salt, vanilla extract and egg; beat well.
2. Gradually add the flour, beating until just blended. The dough should be firm but neither sticky nor stiff.
3. Press or pipe the dough onto an ungreased sheet pan using a cookie press or a piping bag fitted with a large star tip.
4. Bake at 350°F (180°C) until lightly browned around the edges, approximately 10 minutes. Transfer to wire racks to cool.
5. Pipe raspberry jam onto each cookie once cooled, if desired.

Approximate values per cookie: **Calories** 40, **Total fat** 2.5 g, **Saturated fat** 1.5 g, **Cholesterol** 10 mg, **Sodium** 10 mg, **Total carbohydrates** 4 g, **Protein** 0 g, **Claims**—low fat; low cholesterol; very low sodium; low calorie

LACY PECAN COOKIES

Yield: 4 Dozen Cookies, 3 in. (7.5 cm) each   **Method:** Wafer cookies

Brown sugar	6 oz.	180 g
Unsalted butter	5 oz.	150 g
Dark corn syrup	7½ oz.	225 g
Vanilla extract	1 tsp.	5 ml
Salt	¾ tsp.	3 ml
All-purpose flour	6 oz.	180 g
Pecans, finely chopped	5 oz.	150 g

1 Combine the sugar, butter, corn syrup and vanilla in a large, heavy saucepan. Bring to a boil.

2 Mix the salt, flour and nuts together.

3 As soon as the sugar mixture comes to a boil, start timing it. Let it boil for 1 minute. Remove from the heat and stir in the flour-nut mixture. Pour into a hotel pan and cool completely.

4 Use a small portion scoop to make equal-sized balls of dough. Flatten out the balls of dough and place on a silicone baking mat or paper-lined sheet pans.

5 Bake at 325°F (160°C) until very dark brown and no longer moist in center, approximately 15 to 18 minutes. Remove from oven and shape as desired.

Approximate values per serving: **Calories** 80, **Total fat** 4.5 g, **Saturated fat** 1.5 g, **Cholesterol** 5 mg, **Sodium** 45 mg, **Total carbohydrates** 10 g, **Protein** 1 g

1 Portioning the batter on a sheet pan lined with a silicone mat.

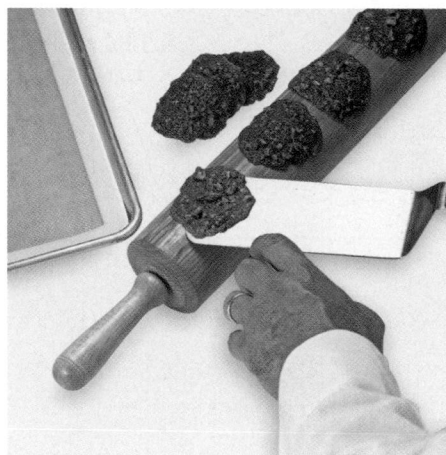

2 Shaping the baked cookies over a rolling pin while still hot.

TULIPE COOKIES

Yield: 5 Dozen Cookies, approximately 6 in.
(15 cm) each; 4 lb. 8 oz. (2 kg) Batter

Method: Wafer cookies

Unsalted butter	1 lb.	480 g
Powdered sugar	1 lb.	480 g
All-purpose flour	1 lb.	480 g
Egg whites	1 lb.	480 ml
Butter, melted	as needed	as needed

1. Melt the unsalted butter and place in the bowl of a mixer fitted with the paddle attachment. Add the sugar and blend until almost smooth.
2. Add the flour and blend until smooth. With the mixer running, add the egg whites very slowly. Beat until blended, but do not incorporate air into the batter.
3. Strain the batter through a china cap and set aside to cool completely.
4. Coat several sheet pans with melted butter or line with silicone mats. Spread the dough into 6-inch (15-centimeter) circles on the pans. Bake at 400°F (200°C) until the edges are brown and the dough is dry, approximately 12 to 18 minutes.
5. To shape into cups, lift the hot cookies off the sheet pan one at a time with an offset spatula. Immediately place over an inverted glass and top with a ramekin or small bowl. The cookies cool very quickly, becoming firm and crisp. The cookie cups can be used for serving ice cream, crème brûlée, fruit or other items.

Approximate values per 2½-oz. (75-g) cookie: **Calories** 240, **Total fat** 12 g, **Saturated fat** 8 g, **Cholesterol** 35 mg, **Sodium** 40 mg, **Total carbohydrates** 37 g, **Protein** 4 g, **Vitamin A** 10%

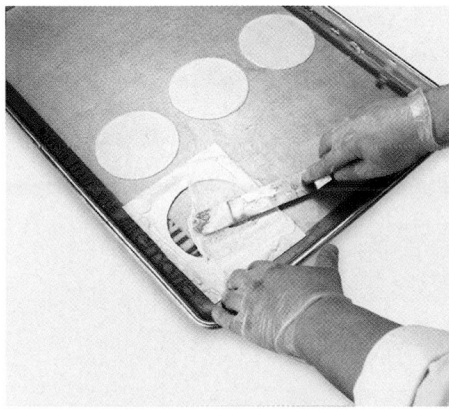

1. Spreading the batter into circles on a sheet pan lined with a silicone mat.

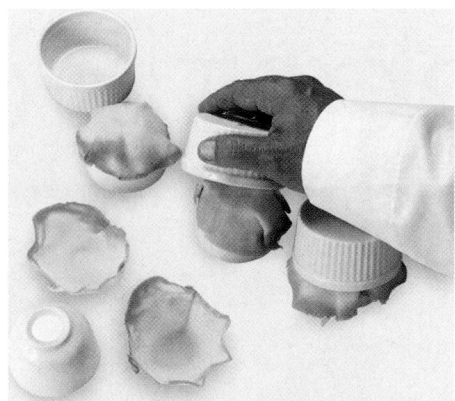

2. Shaping the baked wafer cookies into cups while still hot.

CHAPTER THIRTY-THREE

CAKES AND FROSTINGS

- prepare a variety of cakes
- prepare a variety of frostings
- assemble cakes using basic finishing and decorating techniques

CAKES ARE POPULAR IN MOST BAKESHOPS because a wide variety of finished products can be created from only a few basic cake, filling and frosting formulas. Many of these components can even be made in advance and assembled into finished desserts as needed. Cakes are also popular because of their versatility: They can be served as unadorned sheets in a high-volume cafeteria or as the elaborate centerpiece of a wedding buffet.

Cake making need not be difficult or intimidating, but it does require an understanding of ingredients and mixing methods. This chapter begins by explaining how typical cake ingredients interact. Each of the traditional mixing methods is then explained and illustrated with a recipe. Information on panning batters, baking temperatures, determining doneness and cooling methods follows. The second portion of this chapter presents mixing methods and formulas for a variety of frostings and icings. The third section covers cake assembly and presents some simple and commonly used cake-decorating techniques. A selection of popular cake formulas concludes the chapter.

CAKES

Most cakes are created from liquid batters with high fat and sugar contents. The baker's job is to combine all the ingredients to create a structure that will support these rich ingredients yet keep the cake as light and delicate as possible. As with other baked goods, it is impossible to taste a cake until it is fully cooked and too late to alter the formula. Therefore, it is extremely important to study any formula before beginning and to follow it with particular care and attention to detail.

Ingredients

Good cakes begin with high-quality ingredients (see Chapter 29, Principles of the Bakeshop); however, even the finest ingredients must be combined in the proper balance. Too much flour and the cake may be dry; too much egg and the cake will be tough and hard. Changing one ingredient may necessitate a change in one or more of the other ingredients.

Each ingredient performs a specific function and has a specific effect on the final product. Cake ingredients can be classified by function as **tougheners**, **tenderizers**, **moisteners**, **driers**, **leaveners** and **flavorings**. Some ingredients fulfill more than one of these functions. For example, eggs contain water, so they are moisteners, and they contain protein, so they are tougheners. Understanding the function of various ingredients helps the student chef understand why cakes are made in particular ways and why a preparation sometimes fails. With additional experience, chefs should be able to recognize and correct flawed formulas, one step toward developing their own cake formulas.

TOUGHENERS

Flour, milk and eggs contain protein. Protein provides structure and strengthens the cake once it is baked. Too little protein and the cake may collapse; too much protein and the cake may be tough and coarse-textured.

TENDERIZERS

Sugar, fats and egg yolks interfere with the development of the gluten structure when cakes are mixed. They shorten the gluten strands, making the cake tender and soft. These ingredients also improve the cake's keeping qualities.

MOISTENERS

Liquids such as water, milk, juice and eggs bring moisture to the mixture. Moisture is necessary for gluten formation and starch gelatinization, as well as for improving a cake's keeping qualities.

DRIERS

Flour, starches and milk solids absorb moisture, giving body and structure to the cake.

LEAVENERS

Cakes rise because gases in the batter expand when heated. Cakes are leavened by air trapped when fat and sugar are creamed together, by carbon dioxide released from baking powder and baking soda and by air trapped in beaten eggs. All cakes rely on natural leaveners—steam and air—to create the proper texture and rise. Because baking soda and baking powder are also used in some cake formulas, the material on chemical leaveners in Chapter 30, Quick Breads, should be reviewed.

FLAVORINGS

Flavorings such as extracts, cocoa, chocolate, spices, salt, sugar and butter provide cakes with the desired flavors. Acidic flavoring ingredients such as sour cream, chocolate and fruit also provide the acid necessary to activate baking soda.

Cake ingredients should be at room temperature, approximately 70°F (21°C), before mixing begins. If one ingredient is too cold or too warm, it may affect the batter's ability to trap and hold the gases necessary for the cake to rise.

Mixing Methods

Even the finest ingredients will be wasted if the cake batter is not mixed correctly. When mixing any cake batter, the goals are to combine the ingredients uniformly, incorporate air cells and develop the proper texture.

All mixing methods can be divided into two categories: *high fat*, those that create a structure that relies primarily on **creamed fat**, and *egg foam*, those that create a structure that relies primarily on **whipped eggs**. Within these broad categories are several mixing methods or types of cakes. Creamed-fat cakes include **butter cakes** (also known as **creaming method cakes**) and **high-ratio cakes**. Whipped-egg cakes include **genoise**, **spongecakes**, **angel food** cakes and **chiffon** cakes. See Table 33.1. Although certain general procedures are used to prepare each cake type, there are, of course, numerous variations. (Certain European-style cake formulas include both creaming and egg foam mixing techniques. Sacher Torte [page 1041], for example, is made from a creamed-fat batter into which whipped egg whites are folded before baking.) Follow specific formula instructions precisely.

CREAMED FAT

Creamed-fat/high-fat cakes include most of the popular American-style cakes: poundcakes, layer cakes, coffeecakes and even brownies. All are based on high-fat formulas, most containing chemical leaveners. A good high-fat cake has a fine grain, cells of uniform size and a crumb that is moist rather than crumbly. Crusts should be thin and tender. Creamed-fat/high-fat cakes can be divided into two classes: butter cakes and high-ratio cakes.

Butter Cakes

Butter cakes, also known as creaming method cakes, begin with softened butter or shortening **creamed** to incorporate air cells. Proper creaming ensures a fine even crumb and uniform rise, although because of their high fat content, these cakes usually need the assistance of a chemical leavener to achieve the proper rise.

Modern-day butter cakes—the classic American layer cakes, popular for birthdays and special occasions—are made with the creaming method. These cakes are tender yet sturdy enough to handle rich buttercreams or fillings. High-fat cakes are too soft and delicate, however, to use for roll cakes or to slice into extremely thin layers.

Equal weights of butter increase in volume when creamed thoroughly (right) and expand very little in volume when creamed insufficiently (left).

TABLE 33.1 CAKES

CATEGORY	TYPE OF CAKE/MIXING METHOD	KEY FORMULA CHARACTERISTICS	TEXTURE
Creamed fat (high fat)	Butter (creaming method)	High-fat formula; chemical leavener used	Fine grain; air cells of uniform size; moist crumb; thin and tender crust
	High-ratio (two-stage)	Emulsified shortening; two-part mixing method	Very fine grain; moist crumb; relatively high rise
Whipped egg	Genoise (egg foam)	Whole eggs are whipped with sugar; no chemical leaveners	Dry and spongy
	Sponge (egg foam)	Egg yolks are mixed with other ingredients, then whipped egg whites are folded in	Moister and more tender than genoise
	Angel food (egg foam)	No fat; large quantity of whipped egg whites; high percentage of sugar	Tall, light and spongy
	Chiffon (egg foam)	Vegetable oil used; egg yolks mixed with other ingredients, then whipped egg whites folded in; baking powder may be added	Tall, light and fluffy; moister and richer than angel food

Creaming fat mechanically leavens the cake and creates a mixture in which fats and liquid are suspended. Air cells are trapped in the fat, lightening the mixture. As eggs are mixed into the creamed fat, the mixture emulsifies. Fats and liquids, which normally would not blend, are held in suspension, ensuring that the batter will hold the additional liquids and flour necessary to produce a delectable cake.

PROCEDURE FOR **PREPARING BUTTER CAKES (CREAMING METHOD)**

1. Preheat the oven and prepare the pans. Have ingredients at room temperature, 70°F (21°C), for effective creaming
2. Sift the dry ingredients together and set aside.
3. Cream the butter or shortening on low speed until it is light and fluffy. Add the sugar and cream until the mixture is fluffy and smooth. Scrape down the bowl frequently to make certain the entire mixture is well creamed.
4. Add the eggs slowly, beating well after each addition. Scrape down the bowl after each addition.
5. Add the dry and liquid ingredients alternately to prevent development of gluten and to preserve the emulsion.
6. Divide the batter into prepared pans and bake immediately.

AMERICAN POUNDCAKE

MISE EN PLACE
▶ Soften butter.
▶ Grease pans.
▶ Preheat oven to 325°F (160°C).

Yield: 2 Loaves, 8 in. × 4 in. (20 cm × 10 cm) each; 3 lb. 10 oz. (1750 g) Batter   **Method:** Creaming

Cake flour	1 lb.	480 g
Baking powder	2 tsp.	10 ml
Salt	½ tsp.	2 g
Unsalted butter, softened	1 lb.	480 g
Granulated sugar	12 oz.	360 g
Eggs	9	9
Vanilla extract	1 tsp.	5 ml
Lemon extract	1 tsp.	5 ml

1 Creaming the butter.

2 Folding in the flour.

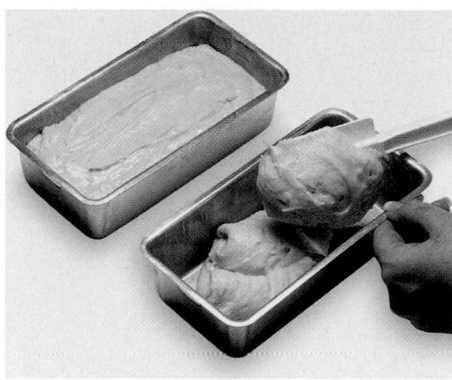

3 Panning the batter.

1 Sift the flour, baking powder and salt together. Set aside.

2 Cream the butter until light and lump-free. Add the sugar and cream until light and fluffy. Add the eggs one at a time, scraping down the bowl frequently and mixing well after each addition. Stir in the extracts.

3 Fold in the dry ingredients by hand in three stages. Divide the batter into greased loaf pans. Spread evenly with a spatula.

4 Bake at 325°F (160°C) until golden brown and springy to the touch, approximately 1 hour and 10 minutes.

VARIATION:

French-Style Fruitcake—Add 6 ounces (180 grams) finely diced nuts, raisins and candied fruit to the batter. Substitute vanilla extract for the lemon extract and add 1½ fluid ounces (45 milliliters) rum to the batter. After baking, brush the warm cake with additional rum.

Approximate values per 3-oz. (90-g) serving: **Calories** 350, **Total fat** 21 g, **Saturated fat** 12 g, **Cholesterol** 145 mg, **Sodium** 90 mg, **Total carbohydrates** 35 g, **Protein** 5 g, **Vitamin A** 20%

High-Ratio Cakes

Commercial bakeries often use a special **two-stage** mixing method to prepare large quantities of a very liquid cake batter with high sugar content. These formulas require special emulsified shortenings to help give the cake its structure. They are known as two-stage cakes because the liquids are added in two stages or portions. If emulsified shortenings are not available, do not substitute all-purpose shortening or butter, as those fats cannot absorb the large amounts of sugar and liquid in the formula.

Because they contain a high ratio of sugar and liquid to flour, these cakes are often known as high-ratio cakes. They have a very fine, moist crumb and relatively high rise. High-ratio cakes can be used interchangeably with modern butter cakes and are most common in high-volume bakeries.

PROCEDURE FOR **PREPARING HIGH-RATIO CAKES**

1 Preheat the oven and prepare the pans.

2 Place all of the dry ingredients and emulsified shortening into a mixer bowl. Blend on low speed for several minutes.

3 Add approximately half of the liquid and blend.

4 Scrape down the bowl and add the remaining liquid ingredients. Blend into a smooth batter, scraping down the bowl as necessary.

5 Pour the batter into prepared pans, using liquid measurements to ensure uniform division.

HIGH-RATIO YELLOW CAKE

MISE EN PLACE

▶ Grease pans.
▶ Preheat oven to 340°F (170°C).
▶ Allow eggs to come to room temperature.

Yield: 1½ to 2 Full-Sheet Pans **Method:** Two-stage

Cake flour	2 lb. 8 oz.	1200 g
Granulated sugar	2 lb. 10 oz.	1260 g
Emulsified shortening, room temperature	1 lb. 4 oz.	600 g
Salt	1 oz.	30 g
Baking powder	2 oz.	60 g
Dry milk powder	4 oz.	120 g
Light corn syrup	6 oz.	180 g
Water, cold	36 fl. oz.	1080 ml
Eggs, room temperature	1 lb. 4 oz.	600 g
Lemon extract	½ fl. oz.	15 ml

1 Combine the flour, sugar, shortening, salt, baking powder, milk powder, corn syrup and 1 pint (480 milliliters) cold water in a large bowl of a mixer fitted with the paddle attachment. Beat for 5 minutes on low speed, scraping down the bowl halfway through the mixing.

2 Combine the eggs, the remaining water and the lemon extract in a separate bowl. Add these liquid ingredients to the creamed-fat mixture in three additions. Scrape down the bowl after each addition.

3 Beat for 2 minutes on low speed.

4 Divide the batter into greased and floured pans. Pans should be filled only halfway. One gallon of batter is sufficient for an 18-inch × 24-inch × 2-inch (45-centimeter × 60-centimeter × 5-centimeter) sheet pan. Bake at 340°F (170°C) until a cake tester comes out clean and the cake springs back when lightly touched, approximately 12 to 18 minutes.

Approximate values per 3-oz. (90-g) serving: **Calories** 390, **Total fat** 16 g, **Saturated fat** 5 g, **Cholesterol** 60 mg, **Sodium** 320 mg, **Total carbohydrates** 57 g, **Protein** 5 g, **Calcium** 10%

WHIPPED EGG

Cakes based on whipped-egg foams include European-style genoise as well as spongecakes, angel food cakes and chiffon cakes. Some formulas contain chemical leaveners, but the air whipped into the eggs (whether whole or separated) is the primary leavening agent. Egg-foam cakes contain little or no fat. Genoise and spongecake are pliable; moisture in the eggs develops the protein in the flour, making these cakes springy and elastic. These cakes are well suited for rolling, as for a Swiss Jelly Roll (page 1015) or for cutting into thin layers or using to line a torte ring.

Genoise

Genoise is the classic European-style cake. It is based on whole eggs whipped with sugar until very light and fluffy. Chemical leaveners are not used. Slightly warming the egg mixture helps improve the volume of the egg foam. For flavor and moisture, a small amount of oil or melted butter is sometimes added to the batter after mixing. Genoise to which fat is added after mixing will bake into a cake that is more tender than a plain genoise because the fat helps shorten gluten strands. Often genoise is baked in a thin sheet and layered with buttercream, puréed fruit, jam or chocolate filling to create multilayered specialty desserts, sometimes known as torten. Because genoise is rather dry, it is usually soaked with a flavored sugar syrup (see Chapter 29, Principles of the Bakeshop) or liqueur for additional flavor and moisture. A basic genoise recipe is included here.

PROCEDURE FOR **PREPARING GENOISE**

1 Preheat the oven and prepare the pans.

2 Sift the flour with any additional dry ingredients.

③ Combine the whole eggs and sugar in a large bowl and warm over a double boiler to a temperature of 100°F (38°C).

④ Whip the egg-and-sugar mixture until very light and tripled in volume.

⑤ Fold the sifted flour into the whipped eggs carefully but quickly.

⑥ Fold in oil or melted butter if desired.

⑦ Divide into pans and bake immediately.

CLASSIC GENOISE

Yield: 1 Full-Sheet Pan	**Method:** Egg foam	
Eggs	10	10
Granulated sugar	8 oz.	240 g
Vanilla extract	2 tsp.	10 ml
Cake flour	9 oz.	270 g
Unsalted butter, melted (optional)	1½ oz.	45 g

MISE EN PLACE

◄ Melt butter, if using.
◄ Line pan with parchment paper.
◄ Preheat the oven to 425°F (220°C).

① Whisk the eggs and sugar together in a large mixer bowl. Place the bowl over a bain marie and whisk the mixture continuously to warm the eggs to approximately 105°F to 113°F (40°C to 45°C).

② When the eggs are warm, remove the bowl from the bain marie and attach it to a mixer fitted with the whip attachment. Whip the egg-and-sugar mixture at medium speed until the mixture is cool and forms thick ribbons, approximately 12 to 15 minutes.

③ If using the melted butter, remove approximately one-eighth of the batter. Place it in a small bowl and mix it with the melted butter. Set aside.

④ Using a rubber spatula or balloon whisk, delicately fold the flour into the remaining genoise batter. Carefully fold in the reserved butter-genoise mixture.

⑤ Spread the batter immediately onto a paper-lined sheet pan. Bake at 425°F (220°C) until light brown and springy to the touch, approximately 10 minutes.

VARIATION:

Chocolate Genoise—Reduce the cake flour to 7 ounces (210 grams). Sift 2 ounces (60 grams) cocoa powder with the flour.

Approximate values per 2-oz. (60-g) serving: **Calories** 140, **Total fat** 4 g, **Saturated fat** 2 g, **Cholesterol** 110 mg, **Sodium** 30 mg, **Total carbohydrates** 21 g, **Protein** 4 g, **Vitamin A** 6%

① Whipped eggs.

② Folding in the flour.

③ Adding the melted butter, if used.

④ Panning the batter.

Spongecakes

Spongecakes (Fr. *biscuits*) are made with separated eggs. A batter is prepared with egg yolks and other ingredients, and then egg whites are whipped with a portion of the sugar to firm but not dry peaks and folded into the batter. Spongecakes are leavened primarily with air, but baking powder may be included in the formula. As with genoise, oil or melted butter may be added if desired.

Spongecakes are extremely versatile. They can be soaked with sugar syrup or a liqueur and assembled with buttercream as a traditional layer cake. Or they can be sliced thinly and layered, like genoise, with a jam, custard, chocolate or cream filling.

PROCEDURE FOR **PREPARING SPONGECAKES**

ribbon stage a term used to describe the consistency of a batter or mixture, especially a mixture of beaten egg and sugar; when the beater or whisk is lifted, the mixture will fall back slowly onto its surface in a ribbonlike pattern

1. Preheat the oven and prepare the pans.
2. Sift the dry ingredients together with a portion of the sugar.
3. Separate the eggs. Whip the egg yolks with some of the sugar to the **ribbon stage**, that is, until they fall from the beater in thick ribbons that slowly disappear into the surface. Whip in any flavorings.
4. In a separate bowl with a clean whip, whip the egg whites with a portion of the sugar, then carefully fold the whipped yolks and whipped whites together with the remaining sugar.
5. Carefully fold the whipped egg whites into the batter. Then gently fold the sifted dry ingredients into the egg foam in two or three additions.
6. Pour the batter into the pans and bake immediately.

CLASSIC SPONGECAKE

MISE EN PLACE
▸ Sift flour.
▸ Preheat the oven to 375°F (190°C).

Yield: 2 Rounds, 9 in. (22 cm) each   **Method:** Egg foam

Cake flour, sifted	6 oz.	180 g
Granulated sugar	11 oz.	330 g
Eggs	10	10
Vanilla extract	1½ tsp.	7 ml
Cream of tartar	1½ tsp.	7 ml

1. Line the bottom of two springform pans with parchment. Do not grease the sides of the pans.
2. Sift the flour and 6 ounces (180 grams) sugar together and set aside.
3. Separate the eggs, placing the yolks and the whites in separate mixing bowls. Whip the yolks on high speed until thick, pale and at least doubled in volume, approximately 3 to 5 minutes. Whip in the vanilla. The yolks should be whipped until ribbons form.
4. Place the bowl of egg whites on the mixer and, using a clean whip, beat until foamy. Add the cream of tartar and 1 ounce (30 grams) sugar. Whip at medium speed until the whites are glossy and stiff but not dry.
5. Remove the bowl from the mixer. Pour the egg yolks onto the whipped whites. Quickly fold the two mixtures together by hand. Sprinkle the remaining sugar over the mixture and fold in lightly.
6. Sprinkle one-third of the sifted flour over the batter and fold in. Repeat the procedure until all the flour is incorporated. Do not overmix; fold just until incorporated.
7. Pour the batter into the prepared pans, smoothing the surface as needed. Bake immediately at 375°F (190°C) until the cake is golden brown and spongy, approximately 30 minutes. A toothpick inserted in the center will be completely clean when removed.
8. Allow the cakes to rest in their pans until completely cool, approximately 2 hours.
9. To remove the cakes from their pans, run a thin metal spatula around the edge of each pan. When the cake is completely cool, it can be frosted or wrapped in plastic wrap and frozen for 2 to 3 months.

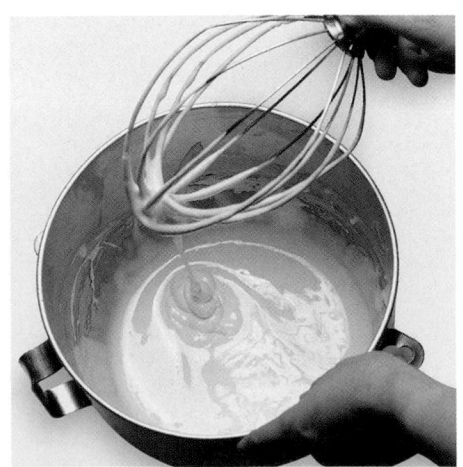

1. The eggs whipped to the ribbon stage.

❷ Folding the flour into the batter.   ❸ Panning the batter.

VARIATIONS:

Swiss Jelly Roll—Spread the cake batter onto a paper-lined half-sheet pan. Bake at 375°F (190°C) until the cake is golden brown and spongy, approximately 20 minutes. Cool the cake for 10 minutes. Invert the warm cake onto a piece of parchment dusted with powdered sugar. Carefully remove the paper on which the cake baked. Spread the warm cake with 8 ounces (240 grams) seedless raspberry or other jam. Roll the cake tightly. Trim the ends and dust with more sugar before serving.

Chocolate Spongecake—Reduce the cake flour to 5 ounces (150 grams) and sift it with 1½ ounces (45 grams) cocoa powder.

Approximate values per 2-oz. (60-g) serving: **Calories** 130, **Total fat** 2.5 g, **Saturated fat** 1 g, **Cholesterol** 105 mg, **Sodium** 30 mg, **Total carbohydrates** 23 g, **Protein** 4 g, **Claims**—low fat; low saturated fat; very low sodium

Angel Food Cakes

Angel food cakes are tall, light cakes made without fat and leavened with a large quantity of whipped egg whites. Care must be taken when whipping egg whites because egg whites will not foam properly if grease or egg yolk is present in the mixing bowl. Angel food cakes are traditionally baked in ungreased tube pans, but large loaf pans can also be used. The pans are left ungreased so that the batter can cling to the sides as it rises. The cakes should be inverted as soon as they are removed from the oven and left in the pan to cool. This technique allows gravity to keep the cakes from collapsing or sinking as they cool.

Although they contain no fat, angel food cakes are not low in calories, as they contain a high percentage of sugar. The classic angel food cake is pure white, but flavorings, ground nuts or cocoa powder may be added for variety. Although angel food cakes are usually not frosted, they may be topped with a fruit-flavored or chocolate glaze. They are often served with fresh fruit, fruit compote or whipped cream.

PROCEDURE FOR **PREPARING ANGEL FOOD CAKES**

❶ Preheat the oven.
❷ Combine the dry ingredients, including a portion of the sugar, in a bowl and set aside.
❸ Whip the egg whites with a portion of the sugar until stiff and glossy.
❹ Gently fold the dry ingredients into the egg whites.
❺ Spoon the batter into an ungreased pan and bake immediately.
❻ Allow the cake to cool inverted in its pan.

MISE EN PLACE

▶ Sift flour.
▶ Preheat the oven to 350°F (180°C).

CHOCOLATE ANGEL FOOD CAKE

Yield: 1 Tube Cake, 10 in. (25 cm); approx. 10 Servings

Method: Egg foam

Cocoa powder, alkalized	1 oz.	30 g
Water, warm	2 fl. oz.	60 ml
Vanilla extract	2 tsp.	10 ml
Granulated sugar	12 oz.	360 g
Cake flour, sifted	3½ oz.	105 g
Salt	¼ tsp.	1 ml
Egg whites	1 lb.	480 g
Cream of tartar	2 tsp.	10 ml
Powdered sugar	as needed	as needed

1. Combine the cocoa powder and water in a bowl. Add the vanilla and set aside.
2. In another bowl, combine 5 ounces (150 grams) granulated sugar with the flour and salt.
3. Whip the egg whites until foamy, add the cream of tartar and beat to soft peaks. Gradually beat in the remaining granulated sugar. Continue beating until the egg whites are stiff but not dry.
4. Whisk a very large spoonful of the whipped egg whites into the cocoa mixture. Fold this into the remaining egg whites.
5. Sift the dry ingredients over the whites and fold in quickly but gently.
6. Pour the batter into an ungreased tube pan and smooth the top with a spatula. Bake immediately at 350°F (180°C) until the cake springs back when lightly touched and a cake tester comes out clean, approximately 40 to 50 minutes. The cake's surface will have deep cracks.
7. Remove the cake from the oven and immediately invert the pan onto the neck of a bottle. Allow the cake to rest upside down until completely cool.
8. To remove the cake from the pan, run a thin knife or spatula around the edge of the pan and the edge of the interior tube. If a two-piece tube pan was used, lift the cake and tube portion out of the pan. Use a knife or spatula to loosen the bottom of the cake, then invert it onto a cake cardboard or serving platter. Dust with powdered sugar before serving. This cake may also be frosted with Basic Sugar Glaze (page 1028).

1. Folding the egg-white-and-cocoa mixture into the whipped egg whites.

2. Folding in the flour.

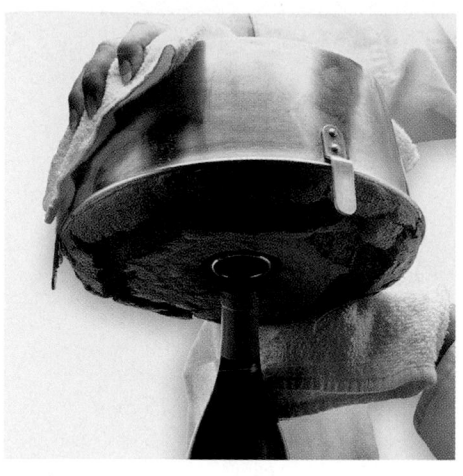

❸ Cooling the cake upside down in its pan.

❹ Removing the cake from the pan.

VARIATIONS:

Vanilla Angel Food Cake—Omit the cocoa powder and warm water. Increase the vanilla extract to 1 tablespoon (15 milliliters) and fold it in at the end of Step 5.

Lemon Angel Food Cake—Omit the cocoa powder and warm water. Add 2 teaspoons (10 milliliters) fresh lemon zest to the sugar-and-flour mixture. Add 1 teaspoon (5 milliliters) lemon extract, folding it and the vanilla extract in at the end of Step 5.

Approximate values per ⅒-cake serving: **Calories** 210, **Total fat** 0.5 g, **Saturated fat** 0 g, **Cholesterol** 0 mg, **Sodium** 150 mg, **Total carbohydrates** 44 g, **Protein** 7 g, **Claims**—low fat; no saturated fat; no cholesterol

Chiffon Cakes

Although chiffon cakes are similar to angel food cakes in appearance and texture, the addition of egg yolks and vegetable oil makes them moister and richer. Chiffon cakes are usually leavened with whipped egg whites but may contain baking powder as well. Like angel food cakes, chiffon cakes are baked in an ungreased pan to allow the batter to cling to the pan as it rises. Chiffon cakes can be frosted with a light buttercream or whipped cream or topped with a glaze. Lemon and orange chiffon cakes are the most traditional, but formulas containing chocolate, nuts or other flavorings are also common.

PROCEDURE FOR **PREPARING CHIFFON CAKES**

❶ Preheat the oven.

❷ Sift the dry ingredients together. Add the liquid ingredients, including oil.

❸ Whip the egg whites with a portion of the sugar until almost stiff.

❹ Fold the whipped egg whites into the batter.

❺ Spoon the batter into an ungreased pan and bake immediately.

❻ Allow the cake to cool inverted in its pan.

MISE EN PLACE

▶ Sift flour.
▶ Preheat oven to 325°F (160°C).

❶ Folding the whipped egg whites into the cake batter.

❷ The glazed orange chiffon cake.

Yield: 1 Tube Cake, 10 in. (25 cm)	Method: Egg foam	
Cake flour, sifted	8 oz.	240 g
Granulated sugar	12 oz.	360 g
Baking powder	1 Tbsp.	15 ml
Salt	1 tsp.	5 ml
Vegetable oil	4 fl. oz.	120 ml
Egg yolks	6	6
Water, cool	2 fl. oz.	60 ml
Orange juice	4 fl. oz.	120 ml
Orange zest, grated	1 Tbsp.	15 ml
Vanilla extract	1 Tbsp.	15 ml
Egg whites	8	8
Glaze:		
Powdered sugar, sifted	3 oz.	90 g
Orange juice	2 Tbsp.	30 ml
Orange zest, grated	2 tsp.	10 ml

❶ Sift together the flour, 6 ounces (180 grams) granulated sugar and the baking powder and salt.

❷ In a separate bowl mix the oil, yolks, water, orange juice, orange zest and vanilla. Add the liquid mixture to the dry ingredients.

❸ In a clean bowl, beat the egg whites until foamy. Slowly beat in the remaining 6 ounces (180 grams) granulated sugar. Continue beating until the egg whites are stiff but not dry.

❹ Stir one-third of the egg whites into the batter to lighten it. Fold in the remaining egg whites.

❺ Pour the batter into an ungreased 10-inch (25-centimeter) tube pan. Bake at 325°F (160°C) until a toothpick comes out clean, approximately 1 hour.

❻ Immediately invert the pan over the neck of a bottle. Allow the cake to hang upside down until completely cool, then remove from the pan.

❼ Stir the glaze ingredients together in a small bowl and drizzle over the top of the cooled cake.

VARIATION:

Lemon Chiffon Cake—Substitute 2 fluid ounces (60 milliliters) fresh lemon juice and 2 fluid ounces (60 milliliters) water for the orange juice. Substitute grated lemon zest for the orange zest. Top with Basic Sugar Glaze (page 1028).

Approximate values per ¹⁄₁₀-cake serving: **Calories** 370, **Total fat** 15 g, **Saturated fat** 2.5 g, **Cholesterol** 130 mg, **Sodium** 280 mg, **Total carbohydrates** 54 g, **Protein** 6 g, **Vitamin C** 10%

Panning, Baking and Cooling

PREPARING PANS

In order to prevent cakes from sticking, most baking pans are coated with fat, a nonstick baking parchment or both. Pans should be prepared before the batter is mixed so that they may be filled and the cakes baked as soon as the batter is finished. If the batter stands while the pans are prepared, air cells within the batter will deflate and volume may be lost.

Solid shortening is better than butter for coating pans because it does not contain any water; butter and margarine contain water and this may cause the cake to stick in places. Solid shortening is also less expensive, tasteless and odorless. Finally, solid shortening does not burn as easily as butter, and it holds a dusting of flour better.

Pan release sprays are useful but must be applied carefully and completely. Although relatively expensive, sprays save time and are particularly effective when used with parchment pan liners.

TABLE 33.2 PAN PREPARATIONS

PAN PREPARATION	USED FOR
Ungreased	Angel food and chiffon cakes
Ungreased sides; paper on bottom	Genoise layers
Greased and papered	High-fat cakes, sponge sheets
Greased and coated with flour	High-fat cakes, chocolate cakes, anything in a Bundt or shaped pan
Greased, floured and lined with paper	Cakes containing melted chocolate, fruit chunks or fruit or vegetable purées

In kitchens where a great deal of baking is done, it may be more convenient to prepare quantities of pan coating to be kept available for use as needed. Pan coating is a mixture of equal parts oil, shortening and flour that can be applied to cake pans with a pastry brush. It is used whenever pans need to be greased and floured. Pan coating will not leave a white residue on the cake's crust, as a dusting of flour often does. Apply sparingly, as a thick coating may leave a discernible taste. Pan coating is not appropriate for all cakes, however. Angel food and chiffon cakes are baked in ungreased, unlined pans because these fragile cakes need to cling to the sides of the pan as they rise. See Table 33.2.

PAN COATING

Yield: 3 lb. (1440 g)

Vegetable oil	1 lb.	480 g
All-purpose shortening	1 lb.	480 g
Bread flour	1 lb.	480 g

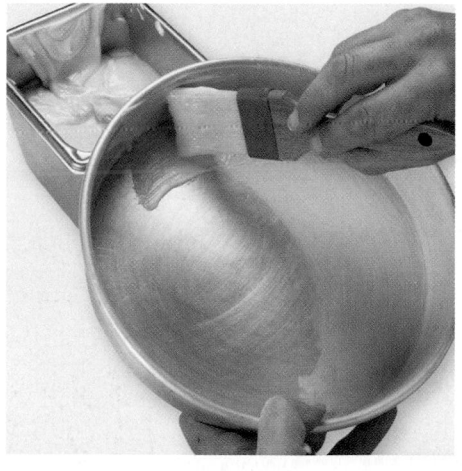

1. Place all the ingredients in the bowl of a mixer fitted with the paddle attachment. Blend on low speed for 5 minutes or until smooth.
2. Store in an opaque airtight container at room temperature for up to 1 month. Apply to baking pans in a thin, even layer using a pastry brush.

FILLING PANS

Pans should be filled no more than one-half to two-thirds full. This allows the batter to rise during baking without spilling over the edges. Pans should be filled to uniform depths. High-fat and egg-foam cake batters can be ladled into each pan according to weight. High-ratio cake batter is so liquid that it can be measured by volume and poured into each pan. Filling the pans uniformly prevents both uneven layers and over- or underfilled pans. When baking three 8-inch layers to be stacked for one presentation and the amount of batter is different in each pan, the baking times will vary and the final product will be uneven. Table 33.3 lists average quantities of batter needed to fill standard-sized baking pans.

Cake batter should always be spread evenly in the pan. Use an offset spatula. Do not work the batter too much, however, as this destroys air cells and prevents the cake from rising properly.

BAKING

Temperatures

Always preheat the oven before preparing the batter. If the finished batter must wait while the oven reaches the correct temperature, valuable leavening will be lost and the cake will not rise properly.

TABLE 33.3 CAKE PAN SIZES

PAN SHAPE AND SIZE	QUANTITY OF BATTER	BUTTER/HIGH-FAT	EGG-FOAM	NO. OF SERVINGS FOR 2-LAYER CAKE
Round, 2 in. deep				
6 in.	1 pt.	8–10 oz.	5–6 oz.	6
8 in.	3 c.	12–16 oz.	8–10 oz.	12
10 in.	1½ qt.	24–32 oz.	16–18 oz.	20
12 in.	1 qt. + 3½ c.	32–36 oz.	18–22 oz.	30
14 in.	2½ qt.	40–48 oz.	24–30 oz.	40
Square, 2 in. deep				
8 in.	1 qt.	16–18 oz.	10–12 oz.	16
10 in.	1½ qt.	24–30 oz.	16–18 oz.	20
12 in.	2½ qt.	40–48 oz.	26–30 oz.	36
14 in.	3 qt. + 1½ c.	48–52 oz.	32–40 oz.	48
Rectangular, 2 in. deep				
6 in. × 8 in.	2½ c.	10–12 oz.	6–8 oz.	12
9 in. × 13 in.	2 qt.	32–36 oz.	20–24 oz.	24
18 in. × 13 in.	2 qt. + 3 c.	56–64 oz.	28–32 oz.	48
18 in. × 26 in.	5 qt.	6–8 lb.	40–48 oz.	96

*Quantities given are approximate and are based on filling the pans two-thirds full of batter. The weight of cake batter needed to properly fill a pan will vary depending on the type of batter, additional flavor ingredients and the amount of air incorporated during mixing.

Most butter cakes are baked at temperatures between 325°F and 375°F (160°C and 190°C). The temperature must be high enough to create steam within the batter and cause that steam and other gases in the batter to expand and rise quickly. If the temperature is too high, however, the cake may rise unevenly and the crust may burn before the interior is completely baked. The temperature must also be low enough so that the batter can set completely and evenly without drying out. If the temperature is too low, however, the cake will not rise sufficiently and may dry out before baking completely. Delicate egg-foam cakes and spongecakes may be baked at slightly higher temperatures when panned in thin layers.

If no temperature is given in a formula or the dimensions of the baking pans being used are different from those specified, use common sense in setting the oven temperature. The larger the surface area, the higher the temperature can usually be. Tall cakes, such as Bundt or tube cakes, should be baked at a lower temperature than thin layer or sheet cakes. Tube or loaf cakes take longer to bake than thin sheet cakes; butter cakes, because they contain more liquid, take longer to bake than genoise or spongecake.

Altitude Adjustments

As discussed in Chapter 9, Principles of Cooking, altitude affects the temperatures at which foods cook. The decreased atmospheric pressure at altitudes above 3000 feet affects the creation of steam and the expansion of hot air in dough and cake batters. These factors must be considered when making cakes. Because gases expand more easily at higher altitudes, cakes and breads may rise so much that their structure cannot support the weight and the bread or cake collapses.

Therefore, the amount of leavening should be decreased at higher altitudes. Chemical leaveners should usually be reduced by one-third at 3500 feet and by two-thirds at altitudes over 5000 feet. Eggs should be underwhipped to avoid incorporating too much air, which would also create too much rise. In general, oven temperatures should also be increased by 25°F (−4°C) at altitudes over 3500 feet to help set the product's structure rapidly.

Because the boiling point decreases at higher altitudes, more moisture will evaporate from baked goods in the oven. This may cause dryness and an excessive proportion of sugar, which shows up as white spots on a cake's surface. Correct this by reducing every 8 ounces (240 grams) sugar by ½ ounce (15 grams) at 3000 feet and by 1½ ounces (45 grams) at 7000 feet.

Attempting to adjust typical (that is, sea-level) formulas for high altitudes is somewhat risky, especially in a commercial operation. Furthermore, different types of baked goods will need different adjustment techniques. Try to find and use formulas developed especially for the area where the baking is taking place, or contact the local offices of the region's state department of agriculture or the agricultural extension service for detailed assistance.

Determining Doneness

In addition to following the baking time suggested in a formula, several simple tests can be used to determine doneness. Whichever tests are used, avoid opening the oven door to check the cake's progress. Cold air or a drop in oven temperature can cause the cake to fall. Use a timer to note the minimum suggested baking time. Then, and only then, should the following tests be used to evaluate the cake's doneness:

▶ **Appearance**—The cake's surface should be a light to golden brown. Unless noted otherwise in the formula, the edges should just begin to pull away from the pan. The cake should not jiggle or move beneath its surface.

▶ **Touch**—Touch the cake lightly with your finger. It should spring back quickly without feeling soggy or leaving an indentation.

▶ **Cake tester**—If appearance and touch indicate that the cake is done, test the interior by inserting a toothpick, bamboo skewer or metal cake tester into the cake's center. With most cakes, the tester should come out clean. If wet crumbs cling to the tester, the cake probably needs to bake a bit longer.

If a formula provides particular doneness guidelines, they should be followed. For example, some flourless cakes are fully baked even though a cake tester will not come out clean.

COOLING

Generally, a cake is allowed to cool for 10 to 15 minutes in its pan set on a cooling rack after taking it out of the oven. This helps prevent the cake from cracking or breaking when it is removed from its pan.

To remove the partially cooled cake from its pan, run a thin knife or spatula blade between the pan and the cake to loosen it. Place a wire rack, cake cardboard or sheet pan over the cake and invert. Then remove the pan. The cake can be left upside down to cool completely or inverted again to cool top side up. Wire racks are preferred for cooling cakes because they allow air to circulate, speeding the cooling process and preventing steam from making the cake soggy.

Angel food and chiffon cakes should be turned upside down immediately after they are removed from the oven. They are left to cool completely in their pans to prevent the cake from collapsing or shrinking. The top of the pan should not touch the countertop, so that air can circulate under the inverted pan.

All cakes should be left to cool away from drafts or air currents that may cause them to collapse. Cakes should not be refrigerated to speed the cooling process, as rapid cooling can cause cracking. Prolonged refrigeration also causes cakes to dry out.

FROSTINGS

Frosting, also known as **icing**, is a sweet decorative coating used as a filling between the layers or as a coating over the top and sides of a cake. It is used to add flavor and to improve a cake's appearance. Frosting can also extend a cake's shelf life by forming a protective coating.

BROWNIES

Where do you draw the line between cakes and brownies? The decision must be a matter of texture and personal preference, for the preparation methods are nearly identical. Brownies are generally chewy and fudgy, sweeter and denser than even the richest of butter cakes. Brownies are a relatively inexpensive and easy way for a food service operation to offer its customers a fresh-baked dessert. Although not as sophisticated as an elaborate gâteau, a well-made brownie can always be served with pride (and a scoop of ice cream).

Brownies are prepared using the same procedures as those for high-fat cakes. Eggs and air incorporated during the mixing process are usually the only leaveners in a traditional brownie formula. Good brownies are achieved with a proper balance of ingredients: A high percentage of butter to flour and not too many eggs produces a dense, fudgy brownie. The fat coats the flour, preventing the protein from developing into gluten. Less butter produces a more cakelike brownie. Increasing the eggs produces a brownie with a crumb structure that more closely resembles a true cake. Likewise, the higher the ratio of sugar, the gooier the finished brownie will be. In some formulas, the fat is creamed to incorporate air, as with butter cakes. In others, the fat is first melted and combined with other liquid ingredients. Brownies are rarely made with whipped egg whites, however, as this makes their texture too light and cakelike.

Each customer and cook has his or her own idea of the quintessential brownie. Some are cloyingly sweet, with a creamy texture and an abundance of chocolate; others are bitter and crisp. Some are frosted; others need only a dusting of powdered sugar. Baked brownies can be frozen for 2 to 3 months if well wrapped.

TABLE 33.4 TROUBLESHOOTING CHART FOR CAKES

PROBLEM	CAUSE	SOLUTION
Butter curdles during mixing	Ingredients too warm or too cold Incorrect fat is used Fat inadequately creamed before liquid was added	Eggs must be at room temperature and added slowly Use correct ingredients Add a portion of the flour, then continue adding the liquid
Cake lacks volume	Flour too strong Old chemical leavener Egg foam underwhipped Oven too hot	Use a weaker flour Replace with fresh leavener Use correct mixing method; do not deflate eggs during folding Adjust oven temperature
Crust burst or cracked	Too much flour or too little liquid Oven too hot	Adjust formula; scale accurately Adjust oven temperature
Cake shrinks after baking	Weak internal structure Too much sugar or fat for the batter to support Cake not fully cooked	Adjust formula Adjust formula Test for doneness before removing from oven
Texture is dense or heavy	Too little leavening Too much fat or liquid Improper leavening Oven too cool	Adjust formula Adjust formula Cream fat or whip eggs properly Adjust oven temperature
Texture is coarse with an open grain	Overmixing Oven too cool	Alter mixing method Adjust oven temperature
Poor flavor	Poor ingredients Unclean pans	Check flavor and aroma of all ingredients Do not grease pans with rancid fats
Uneven shape	Butter not incorporated evenly Batter spread unevenly Oven rack not level Uneven oven temperature	Incorporate fats completely Spread batter evenly Adjust oven racks Adjust oven temperature

There are seven general types of frosting: **buttercream**, **foam**, **fudge**, **fondant**, **glaze**, **royal icing** and **ganache**. See Table 33.5. Each type can be produced with a number of formulas and in a range of flavorings.

Because frosting is integral to the flavor and appearance of many cakes, it should be made carefully using high-quality ingredients and natural flavors and colors. A good frosting is smooth; it is never grainy or lumpy. It should complement the flavor and texture of the cake without overpowering it.

Buttercream

A buttercream is a light, smooth, fluffy mixture of sugar and fat (butter, margarine or shortening). It may also contain egg yolks for richness or whipped egg whites for lightness. Pasteurized eggs must always be used in buttercreams to ensure food safety. A good buttercream will be sweet, but not cloying; buttery, but not greasy.

Buttercreams are popular and useful for most types of cakes and may be flavored or colored as desired. They may be stored, covered, in the refrigerator for several days but must be softened before use.

The three most popular styles of buttercream, which are discussed here, are **simple**, **Italian** and **French**.

SIMPLE BUTTERCREAM

Simple buttercream, sometimes known as **American-style buttercream**, is made by creaming butter and powdered sugar together until the mixture is light and smooth.

TABLE 33.5 FROSTINGS

FROSTING	PREPARATION	TEXTURE/FLAVOR
Simple buttercream (American)	Mixture of sugar and fat (usually butter); can contain egg yolks or egg whites	Rich but light; smooth; fluffy
Foam	Meringue made with hot sugar syrup	Light, fluffy; very sweet
Fudge	Cooked mixture of sugar, butter and water or milk; applied warm	Heavy, rich and candylike
Fondant	Cooked mixture of sugar and water; applied warm	Thick, opaque; sweet
Glaze	Powdered sugar with liquid	Thin; sweet
Royal icing	Uncooked mixture of powdered sugar and egg whites	Hard and brittle when dry; chalky
Ganache	Blend of melted chocolate and cream; may be poured or whipped	Rich, smooth; intense chocolate flavor

Cream, pasteurized eggs and flavorings may be added as desired. Simple buttercream requires no cooking and is quick and easy to prepare.

If cost is a consideration, hydrogenated all-purpose shortening can be substituted for a portion of the butter, but the flavor and mouth feel will be different. Buttercream made with shortening tends to feel greasier and heavier because shortening does not melt on the tongue like butter. It will be more stable than pure butter buttercream, however, and is necessary when a pure white frosting is desired.

PROCEDURE FOR **PREPARING SIMPLE BUTTERCREAMS**

❶ Cream softened butter or shortening until the mixture is light and fluffy.
❷ Beat in pasteurized egg, if desired.
❸ Beat in sifted powdered sugar, scraping down the sides of the bowl as needed.
❹ Beat in the flavoring ingredients.

SIMPLE BUTTERCREAM

Yield: Approximately 3 lb. (1.5 kg)

Lightly salted butter, softened	1 lb.	480 g
Pasteurized egg (optional)	2 oz.	60 g
Powdered sugar, sifted	2 lb.	960 g
Vanilla extract	2 tsp.	10 ml

❶ Using a mixer fitted with the paddle attachment, cream the butter until light and fluffy.
❷ Beat in the egg (if using). Gradually add the sugar, frequently scraping down the bowl.
❸ Add the vanilla and continue beating until the frosting is smooth and light.

MISE EN PLACE

◀ Soften butter.
◀ Sift powdered sugar.

VARIATIONS:

Light Chocolate Buttercream—Dissolve 1 ounce (30 grams) sifted cocoa powder in 2 fluid ounces (60 milliliters) cool water. Add to the buttercream along with the vanilla.

Lemon Buttercream—Decrease the vanilla extract to 1 teaspoon (5 milliliters). Add 1 teaspoon (5 milliliters) lemon extract and the finely grated zest of one lemon.

Approximate values per 1-oz. (30-g) serving: **Calories** 170, **Total fat** 6 g, **Saturated fat** 4 g, **Cholesterol** 25 mg, **Sodium** 70 mg, **Total carbohydrates** 28 g, **Protein** 0 g, **Vitamin A** 10%

ITALIAN BUTTERCREAM

Italian buttercream, also known as **meringue buttercream**, is based on an Italian meringue, which is whipped egg whites cooked with hot sugar syrup. (See Chapter 32, Pies, Pastries and Cookies.) Softened butter is then whipped into the cooled meringue, and the mixture is flavored as desired. This type of buttercream is extremely soft and light. It can be used on most types of cakes and is particularly popular for multilayered genoise and spongecakes.

PROCEDURE FOR **PREPARING ITALIAN BUTTERCREAMS**

1. Whip the egg whites until soft peaks form.
2. Beat granulated sugar into the egg whites and whip until firm and glossy.
3. Meanwhile, combine additional sugar with water and cook to the soft ball stage (240°F/116°C), brushing down the sides of the pan with clean water to prevent the sugar from crystallizing.
4. With the mixer on medium speed, pour the sugar syrup into the whipped egg whites. Pour slowly and carefully to avoid splatters.
5. Continue whipping the egg-white-and-sugar mixture until completely cool.
6. Whip softened, but not melted, butter into the cooled egg-white-and-sugar mixture.
7. Add flavoring ingredients as desired.

ITALIAN BUTTERCREAM

MISE EN PLACE
▶ Soften butter.

Yield: Approximately 5 lb. 5 oz. (2.5 kg)

Egg whites	14 oz.	420 g
Granulated sugar	1 lb. 11 oz.	810 g
Water	as needed	as needed
Lightly salted butter, softened but not melted	2 lb. 12 oz.	1320 g

1. All ingredients should be at room temperature before beginning.
2. Place the egg whites in a mixer bowl. Have 9 ounces (270 grams) sugar nearby.
3. Place 1 pound 2 ounces (540 grams) sugar in a heavy saucepan with enough water to moisten. Bring to a boil over high heat, brushing down the sides of the pan with clean water to prevent the sugar from crystallizing.
4. As the sugar syrup's temperature approaches soft ball stage (240°F/116°C), begin whipping the egg whites. Watch the sugar closely so that the temperature does not exceed 240°F (116°C).
5. When soft peaks form in the egg whites, gradually add 9 ounces (270 grams) sugar to them. Reduce the mixer speed to medium and continue whipping the egg whites to stiff peaks.
6. When the sugar syrup reaches soft ball stage, immediately pour it into the whites while the mixer is running. Pour the syrup in a steady stream between the side of the bowl and the beater. If the syrup hits the beater, it will splatter and cause lumps. Continue beating at medium speed until the egg whites are completely cool. At this point, the product is known as Italian meringue.
7. Gradually add the softened butter to the Italian meringue. When all the butter is incorporated, add flavoring ingredients as desired.

1 Adding the sugar syrup to the whipped egg whites.

2 Adding the softened butter to the cooled Italian meringue.

3 The finished Italian buttercream.

VARIATIONS:

Chocolate Italian Buttercream—Add 1 tablespoon (15 milliliters) vanilla extract to the buttercream, then stir in 10 ounces (300 grams) melted and cooled bittersweet chocolate.

Coffee Italian Buttercream—Add 2 fluid ounces (60 milliliters) coffee extract or strong coffee to the buttercream.

Approximate values per 1-oz. (30-g) serving: **Calories** 175, **Total fat** 13 g, **Saturated fat** 8 g, **Cholesterol** 34 mg, **Sodium** 140 mg, **Total carbohydrates** 16 g, **Protein** 1 g, **Vitamin A** 10%

FRENCH BUTTERCREAM

French buttercream, also known as **mousseline buttercream**, is similar to Italian buttercream except that the hot sugar syrup is whipped into beaten egg yolks (not egg whites). Softened butter and flavorings are added when the sweetened egg yolks are fluffy and cool. An Italian meringue such as the one created in the preceding formula is sometimes folded in for additional body and lightness. French buttercream is perhaps the most difficult type of buttercream to master, but it has the richest flavor and smoothest texture. Like a meringue buttercream, mousseline buttercream may be used on almost any type of cake.

PROCEDURE FOR **PREPARING FRENCH BUTTERCREAMS**

1 Prepare a sugar syrup and cook to soft ball stage (240°F/116°C), brushing down the sides of the pan with clean water to prevent the sugar from crystallizing.

2 Beat egg yolks to a thin ribbon.

3 Slowly beat the sugar syrup into the egg yolks.

4 Continue beating until the yolks are pale, stiff and completely cool.

5 Gradually add softened butter to the cooled yolks.

6 Fold in Italian meringue.

7 Stir in flavoring ingredients.

MISE EN PLACE

▶ Soften butter.

FRENCH MOUSSELINE BUTTERCREAM

Yield: Approximately 6 lb. (3 kg)

Granulated sugar	1 lb. 10 oz.	780 g
Water	8 fl. oz.	240 ml
Egg yolks	16	16
Lightly salted butter, softened but not melted	3 lb.	1.4 kg
Italian Meringue (page 981)	1 lb.	480 g
Vanilla, coffee, lemon or other flavoring extracts	2 fl. oz.	60 ml

1 Combine the sugar and water in a small saucepan and bring to a boil. Continue boiling until the syrup reaches 240°F (116°C), brushing down the sides of the pan with clean water to prevent the sugar from crystallizing.

2 Meanwhile, beat the egg yolks in the bowl of a mixer fitted with the whisk attachment on low speed. When the sugar syrup reaches 240°F (116°C), pour it slowly into the egg yolks, gradually increasing the speed at which they are whipped. Continue beating at medium-high speed until the mixture is very pale, stiff and cool, approximately 10 minutes.

3 Gradually add the softened butter to the egg mixture, frequently scraping down the bowl.

4 Fold in the Italian Meringue with a spatula. Fold in flavoring extracts just until well distributed throughout the buttercream.

VARIATION:

Chocolate Mousseline Buttercream—Add 2 fluid ounces (60 milliliters) vanilla extract to the buttercream, then stir in 10 ounces (300 grams) melted and cooled bittersweet chocolate.

Approximate values per 1-oz. (30-g) serving: **Calories** 230, **Total fat** 20 g, **Saturated fat** 12 g, **Cholesterol** 105 mg, **Sodium** 190 mg, **Total carbohydrates** 12 g, **Protein** 1 g, **Vitamin A** 20%

FLAVOR COMBINATIONS FOR CAKES

Citrus, coffee, maple, peanut butter and vanilla are popular flavorings for buttercream icings but the possible cake and filling combinations are limitless. Chocolate cakes can be filled with almond, citrus, coffee, hazelnut and red fruit-flavored icings. Dense chocolate ganache paired with apricot, cherry, raspberry or other jam works well in plain or chocolate butter cakes. Tropical fruit flavors such as kiwi, key lime and pineapple complement butter and sponge cakes as do rich custards and flavored creams.

Foam Frosting

Foam or **boiled frosting** is simply an Italian meringue (made with hot sugar syrup). Foam frosting is light and fluffy but very sweet. It may be flavored with extract, liqueur or melted chocolate. It is frequently used to ice layer cakes and complements a cake with lemon, coconut or chocolate flavor.

Foam frosting is rather unstable. It should be used immediately and served the day it is prepared. Refrigeration often makes the foam weep beads of sugar. Freezing causes it to separate or melt.

An easy foam frosting can be made by following the formula for Italian Meringue (page 981). As soon as the meringue has cooled to room temperature, it can be flavored as desired with an extract or emulsion.

Fudge Frosting

A fudge frosting is a warmed mixture of sugar, butter and water or milk. It is heavy, rich and candylike. It is also stable and holds up well. A fudge frosting should be applied warm and allowed to dry on the cake or pastry. When dry, it will have a thin crust and a moist interior. A fudge frosting can be vanilla- or chocolate-based and is used on cupcakes, layer cakes and sheet cakes.

PROCEDURE FOR **PREPARING FUDGE FROSTINGS**

1. Place sifted powdered sugar in the bowl of a mixer fitted with the paddle attachment.
2. Heat the butter or shortening, corn syrup and water.
3. Blend the hot liquids into the sugar. Add extracts or flavorings.
4. Use fudge frosting while still warm.

BASIC FUDGE FROSTING

Yield: 2 lb. 12 oz. (1.3 kg)

Powdered sugar, sifted	2 lb.	960 g
Unsalted butter	3 oz.	90 g
Shortening	2 oz.	60 g
Corn syrup	3 oz.	90 g
Water	4 fl. oz.	120 ml
Salt	⅛ tsp.	0.5 ml
Vanilla extract	1 tsp.	5 ml

1. Place the powdered sugar in the bowl of a mixer fitted with the whisk attachment.
2. Bring the butter, shortening, corn syrup, water and salt to a boil in a saucepan over medium high heat. Remove the pan from heat.
3. With the machine running, pour the hot mixture over the powdered sugar. Whip until the mixture is smooth and fluffy. Stir in the vanilla.
4. The icing can be used immediately.

VARIATION:

Cocoa Fudge Frosting—Sift 3 ounces (90 grams) cocoa powder with the powdered sugar. Add 2 ounces (60 grams) melted unsalted butter with the shortening.

Approximate values per 1-oz. (30-g) serving: **Calories** 140, **Total fat** 2.5 g, **Saturated fat** 0.5 g, **Cholesterol** 0 mg, **Sodium** 15 mg, **Total carbohydrates** 30 g, **Protein** 0 g, **Claims**—low fat; low saturated fat; no cholesterol; very low sodium

Fondant

Fondant is a thick, opaque sugar paste commonly used for glazing napoleons, petits fours and other pastries as well as some cakes. It is a cooked mixture of sugar and water, with **glucose** or corn syrup added to encourage the correct type of sugar crystallization. Poured over the surface being coated, fondant quickly dries to a shiny, nonsticky coating. It is naturally pure white and can be tinted with food coloring. Fondant can also be flavored with melted chocolate.

Fondant is rather tricky to make, so it is usually purchased prepared either as a ready-to-use paste or a powder to which water is added. To use **prepared fondant**, thin it with water or simple syrup and carefully warm to 100°F (38°C). Watch the temperature; when overheated, the fondant will lose its opacity and will dry with an uneven appearance. Commercially prepared fondant will keep for several months at room temperature in an airtight container. The surface of the fondant should be coated with simple syrup, however, to prevent a crust from forming.

Rolled fondant is a very stiff doughlike type of fondant that is used for covering cakes and for making flowers and other decorations. As the name implies, it is rolled out to the desired thickness, then draped over a cake or torte to create a very smooth, flat

Cocoa fudge frosting

glucose a thick, sweet syrup made from cornstarch, composed primarily of dextrose; light corn syrup can usually be substituted for it in baked goods or candy making

Celebration cake covered with rolled fondant

TABLE 33.6	TROUBLESHOOTING CHART FOR FROSTINGS	
PROBLEM	**CAUSE**	**SOLUTION**
Frosting breaks or curdles	Fat added too slowly or eggs too hot when fat was added	Add shortening or sifted powdered sugar
	Butter too cold when added	Soften butter before adding
Frosting is lumpy	Powdered sugar not sifted	Sift dry ingredients
	Ingredients not blended	Use softened fats
	Sugar syrup lumps in frosting	Add sugar syrups carefully
Frosting is too stiff	Not enough liquid	Adjust formula; add small amount of water or milk to thin the frosting
	Too cold	Bring frosting to room temperature; heat gently over simmering water
Frosting will not adhere to cake	Cake too hot	Cool cake completely
	Frosting too thin	Adjust frosting formula
	Frosting too stiff	Adjust frosting formula
	Frosting too cold	Soften frosting at room temperature before using

coating. Rolled fondant is available in a ready-to-use form. It can be flavored or colored if desired. Be sure to keep the rolled fondant tightly wrapped in plastic and stored in an airtight container to prevent it from drying out and cracking.

Glaze

A glaze is a thin coating meant to be poured or drizzled onto a cake or pastry. A glaze is usually too thin to apply with a knife or spatula. It is used to add moisture and flavor to cakes on which a heavy frosting would be undesirable—for example, a chiffon or angel food cake—and is often tinted with food coloring.

Flat frosting or water frosting is a specific type of glaze used on Danish pastries and coffeecakes. It is pure white and dries to a firm gloss. A glaze made from fondant is also used for this purpose. The glucose in fondant prevents it from crystallizing.

PROCEDURE FOR **PREPARING SUGAR GLAZES**

❶ Blend sifted powdered sugar with a small amount of liquid and flavorings.
❷ Use immediately.

BASIC SUGAR GLAZE

MISE EN PLACE
▶ Sift powdered sugar.
▶ Melt butter.

Yield: Approximately 12 oz. (360 g)

Powdered sugar, sifted	9½ oz.	285 g
Light cream or milk	2 fl. oz.	60 ml
Unsalted butter, melted	1 oz.	30 g
Vanilla, lemon or almond extract	2 tsp.	10 ml

❶ Stir the ingredients together in a small bowl until smooth.
❷ Adjust the consistency by adding more cream or milk to thin the glaze if necessary.
❸ Adjust the flavor as necessary.
❹ Use immediately, before the glaze begins to dry.

VARIATION:

Flavored Sugar Glaze—Stir ¼ teaspoon (1 milliliter) lemon or orange oil into the glaze. Fruit juice and other flavorings may be substituted for the vanilla extract.

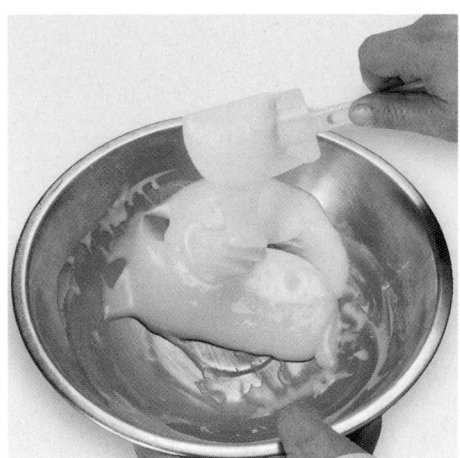

Approximate values per 1-oz. (30-g) serving: **Calories** 110, **Total fat** 2 g, **Saturated fat** 1.5 g, **Cholesterol** 5 mg, **Sodium** 0 mg, **Total carbohydrates** 23 g, **Protein** 0 g, **Claims**—low fat; low cholesterol; no sodium

Royal Icing

Royal icing, also known as **decorator's icing**, is similar to flat frosting except it is much stiffer and becomes hard and brittle when dry. It is an uncooked mixture of powdered sugar and pasteurized egg whites and can be dyed with food coloring pastes.

Royal icing is used for making decorations, particularly intricate flowers or lace patterns. Prepare royal icing in small quantities, and always keep any unused portion well covered with a damp towel and plastic wrap to prevent hardening.

PROCEDURE FOR **PREPARING ROYAL ICING**

1. Combine pasteurized egg white and lemon juice, if using.
2. Beat in sifted powdered sugar until the correct consistency is reached.
3. Beat until very smooth and firm enough to hold a stiff peak.
4. Color as desired with paste food colorings.
5. Store covered with a damp cloth and plastic wrap.

ROYAL ICING

Yield: Approximately 7 oz. (210 g)

Powdered sugar	6 oz.	180 g
Egg white, pasteurized, room temperature	1	1
Lemon juice	¼ tsp.	1 ml

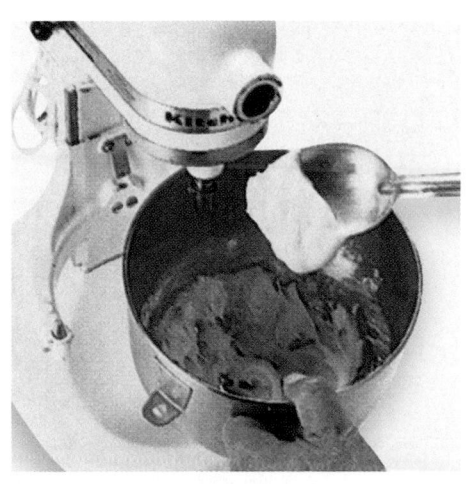

1. Sift the sugar and set aside.
2. Place the egg white and lemon juice in a stainless steel bowl.
3. Add 4 ounces (120 grams) sugar and beat with an electric mixer or metal spoon until blended. The mixture should fall from a spoon in heavy globs. If it pours, it is too thin and will need the remaining 2 ounces (60 grams) sugar.
4. Once the consistency is correct, continue beating for 3 to 4 minutes. The icing should be white, smooth and thick enough to hold a stiff peak. Food coloring paste can be added at this time if desired.
5. Cover the icing with a damp towel and plastic wrap to prevent it from hardening. Royal icing will keep refrigerated for 1 to 2 days.

Approximate values per 1-oz. (30-g) serving: **Calories** 120, **Total fat** 0 g, **Saturated fat** 0 g, **Cholesterol** 0 mg, **Sodium** 10 mg, **Total carbohydrates** 28 g, **Protein** 1 g, **Claims**—fat free; no saturated fat; no cholesterol; very low sodium

Ganache

Ganache is a sublime blending of pure chocolate and cream. It can also include butter, liqueur or other flavorings. Any bittersweet, semisweet or dark chocolate may be used; the choice depends on personal preference and cost considerations.

Depending on its consistency, ganache may be used as a candy or as a filling, frosting or glaze-type coating on cakes or pastries. The ratio of chocolate to cream determines how thick the cooled ganache will be. Equal parts by weight of chocolate and cream generally are best for frostings and fillings. Increasing the percentage of chocolate produces a thicker ganache. Warm ganache can be poured over a cake or pastry and allowed to harden as a thin glaze, or it can be cooled and whipped to create a rich, smooth frosting. If it becomes too firm, ganache can be remelted over a bain marie.

PROCEDURE FOR **PREPARING GANACHE**

❶ Melt finely chopped chocolate with cream in a double boiler. Alternatively, bring cream just to a boil; then pour it over finely chopped chocolate and allow the cream's heat to gently melt the chocolate. Do not attempt to melt chocolate and then add cool cream. This will cause the chocolate to resolidify and lump.

❷ Stir the ganache with a rubber spatula to emulsify the cream and chocolate. (Whisking the ganache using a whip may be quicker, but the ganache will be grainy and less creamy.)

❸ Whichever method is used, cool the cream and chocolate mixture over an ice bath.

❶ Pouring the hot cream over the chopped chocolate.

❷ Cool, firm ganache.

CHOCOLATE GANACHE

Yield: 2 lb. (960 g)

Bittersweet chocolate	1 lb.	480 g
Heavy cream	1 pt.	480 ml
Almond or coffee liqueur	1 fl. oz.	30 ml

❶ Chop the chocolate into small pieces and place in a large metal bowl.
❷ Bring the cream just to a boil, then immediately pour it over the chocolate, stirring with a rubber spatula to blend. Stir gently until all the chocolate has melted.
❸ Stir in the liqueur.
❹ Allow to cool, stirring frequently with a rubber spatula until the desired consistency is achieved.

Approximate values per 1-oz. (30-g) serving: **Calories** 130, **Total fat** 10 g, **Saturated fat** 6 g, **Cholesterol** 20 mg, **Sodium** 5 mg, **Total carbohydrates** 8 g, **Protein** 1 g, **Vitamin A** 6%

CHOCOLATE TRUFFLES

Ganache is also the foundation of one of the world's most sophisticated candies, the chocolate truffle. Truffles take their name from the rough, black, highly prized fungus they resemble, but there the similarity ends. Chocolate truffles should have a rich, creamy ganache center with a well-balanced, refined flavor.

To prepare chocolate truffles, a firm ganache is flavored as desired, then piped or allowed to harden. Once firm, the ganache is rolled in cocoa powder, confectioner's sugar or melted chocolate. The classic French truffle is a small, irregularly shaped ball of bittersweet chocolate dusted with cocoa powder. Americans, however, seem to prefer larger candies, coated with melted chocolate and decorated with nuts or additional chocolate, toasted sliced almonds, chocolate shavings, or candied citrus peel. The following recipe can be prepared in either style.

DARK CHOCOLATE TRUFFLES

Yield: 150 Medium-Sized Truffles; 4 lb. 4 oz. (2 kg)

Dark chocolate	2 lb.	1 kg
Unsalted butter	1 lb.	480 g
Heavy cream	1 pt.	480 ml
Brandy, bourbon or liqueur	4 fl. oz.	120 ml

1. Chop the chocolate and butter into small pieces and place in a large metal bowl.
2. Bring the cream to a boil. Immediately pour the hot cream over the chocolate and butter. Stir until the chocolate and butter are completely melted.
3. Stir in the brandy. Pour the ganache into a flat, shallow, ungreased pan and chill until firm.
4. Shape the ganache into rough balls using a melon ball cutter. Immediately drop each ball into a pan of sifted cocoa powder or confectioner's sugar, rolling it around to coat completely.
5. Truffles can be stored in the refrigerator for 7 to 10 days. Allow them to soften slightly at room temperature before serving.

Approximate values per truffle: **Calories** 70, **Total fat** 6 g, **Saturated fat** 3.5 g, **Cholesterol** 10 mg, **Sodium** 0 mg, **Total carbohydrates** 4 g, **Protein** 0 g

1. Shaping chocolate truffles with a melon ball scoop and coating with cocoa powder.

2. Alternately, chocolate truffles may be dipped into tempered chocolate using a dipping spoon.

3. After dipping in tempered chocolate, truffles may also be coated with chopped toasted nuts.

ASSEMBLING AND DECORATING CAKES

Much of a cake's initial appeal lies in its appearance. This is true whether the finished cake is a simple sheet cake topped with swirls of buttercream or an elaborate wedding cake with intricate garlands and bouquets of marzipan roses. Any cake assembled and decorated with care and attention to detail is preferable to a carelessly assembled or garishly overdecorated one.

Thousands of decorating styles or designs are possible, of course. This section describes a few simple options that beginning pastry cooks can prepare using a minimum of specialized tools. In planning a cake's design, consider the flavor, texture and color of the components used as well as the number of guests or portions that must be served. Consider who will be cutting and eating the cake and how long the dessert must stand before service.

ADVANCED PÂTISSERIE

Sugar can be used to create a number of doughs, pastes and syrups used for artistic and decorative work. Mastering even some of these products takes years of experience and practice. Although formulas and preparation methods are beyond the scope of this book, it is important that all pastry cooks be able to recognize and identify certain decorative sugar products.

Blown sugar—a boiled mixture of sucrose, glucose and tartaric acid that is colored and shaped (in a manner very similar to glass blowing) using an air pump. It is used for making pieces of fruit and containers such as bowls and vases.

Gum paste—a smooth dough made of sugar and gelatin; it dries relatively slowly, becoming very firm and hard. The paste can be colored and rolled out, cut and shaped, or molded. It is used for making flowers, leaves and small figures.

Marzipan—a mixture of almond paste and sugar that may be colored and used like modeling clay for sculpting small fruits, flowers or other objects. Marzipan can also be rolled out and cut into various shapes or used to cover cakes or pastries.

Nougat—a candy made of caramelized sugar and almonds that can be molded into shapes or containers. Unlike other sugar decorations, nougat remains deliciously edible.

Pastillage—a paste made with sugar, cornstarch and gelatin. It can be rolled into sheets, then cut into shapes. It dries in a very firm and sturdy form, like plaster. Naturally pure white, it can be painted with cocoa or food colorings. Pastillage is used for showpieces and large decorative items.

Pulled sugar—a doughlike mixture of sucrose, glucose and tartaric acid that is colored, then shaped by hand. Pulled sugar is used for making birds, flowers, leaves, bows and other items.

Spun sugar—long, fine, hairlike threads of sugar made by flicking caramelized sugar rapidly across dowels. Mounds or wreaths of these threads are used to decorate ice cream desserts, croquembouche and gâteaux.

Assembling Cakes

Before a cake can be decorated, it must be assembled and coated with frosting. Most cakes can be assembled in a variety of shapes and sizes; sheet cakes, round layer cakes and rectangular layer cakes are the most common. When assembling any cake, the goal is to fill and stack the cake layers evenly and to apply an even coating of frosting that is smooth and free of crumbs. (A thin underlayer of frosting called a **crumb coat** may be spread on an assembled cake to seal loose surface crumbs before a final decorative layer of frosting is applied.)

Most of the photographs used in this section show the assembly and decoration of a celebration cake shown in the photograph to the left.

❶ Split the cake horizontally into thin layers if desired. Use cake boards to support each layer as it is removed. Brush away any loose crumbs with a dry pastry brush or your hand.

❷ Position the bottom layer on a cake board. Place the layer on a revolving cake stand, if available. Pipe a border of buttercream around the cake, then top the layer with a mound of filling. Use a cake spatula to spread it evenly.

❸ Position the next cake layer over the filling and continue layering and filling the cake as desired.

④ Place a mound of frosting in the center of the cake top. Push it to the edge of the cake with a cake spatula. Do not drag the frosting back and forth or lift the spatula off the frosting, as these actions tend to pick up crumbs.

⑤ Smooth a thin layer of frosting (the crumb coat) over the top of the cake. Cover the sides with excess frosting from the top. Chill the cake.

⑥ Place another mound of frosting in the center of the cake top. Frost the cake with a second layer of icing. Hold the spatula upright against the side of the cake and, pressing gently, turn the cake stand slowly. This smooths and evens the sides. When the sides and top are smooth, the cake is ready to be decorated as desired.

Simple Decorating Techniques

An extremely simple yet effective way to decorate an iced cake is with a garnish of chopped nuts, fruit, toasted coconut, shaved chocolate or other foods arranged in patterns or sprinkled over the cake. Be sure to use a garnish that complements the cake and frosting flavors or reflects one of the cake's ingredients. For example, finely chopped pecans would be an appropriate garnish for a carrot cake that contains pecans; shaved chocolate would not.

Side masking is the technique of coating only the sides of a cake with garnish. Be sure to apply the garnish while the frosting is still moist enough for it to adhere. The top may be left plain or decorated with frosting designs or a message.

Stencils can be used to apply patterns of finely chopped garnishes, powdered sugar or cocoa powder to the top of a cake. A design can be cut from cardboard, or thin plastic forms can be purchased. Even simple strips of parchment paper can be used to create an attractive pattern. If using a stencil on an iced cake, allow the frosting to set somewhat before laying the stencil on top of it. After the garnishes have been sprinkled over the stencil, carefully lift the stencil to avoid spilling the excess garnish and messing up the pattern.

A **cake** or **baker's comb** or a serrated knife can be used to create patterns on a cake iced with buttercream, fudge or ganache. Hold the comb against the side of an iced cake and rotate the cake turntable slowly and steadily to create horizontal lines in the frosting.

Side masking—coating the sides of a carrot cake with chopped pistachios.

Stencils—creating a design with confectioner's sugar and strips of parchment paper.

Cake comb—creating a pattern on a frosted cake.

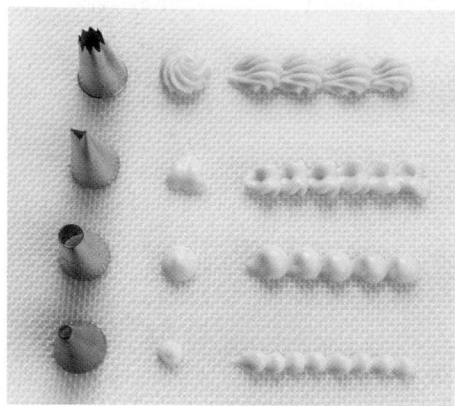

Tip patterns

Piping Techniques

More elaborate and difficult decorations can be produced with the aid of a piping bag and an assortment of pastry tips. With these tools, buttercream or royal icing can be used to create borders, flowers and messages. Before applying any decorations, however, plan a design or pattern that is appropriate for the size and shape of the item being decorated.

When used properly, colored frostings can bring cake decorations to life. Buttercream, royal icing and fondant are easily tinted using paste food coloring. Liquid food colorings are not recommended as they may thin the frosting too much. Always add coloring gradually with a toothpick. Frosting colors tend to darken as they sit. It is easy to add more later to darken the color if necessary, but it is difficult to lighten the color if too much is added.

Piping bags made from plastic, nylon or plastic-coated canvas are available in a range of sizes. A disposable piping cone can also be made from parchment paper.

Most decorations and designs are made by using a piping bag fitted with a pastry tip. Pastry tips are available with dozens of different openings and are referred to by standardized numbers. Some commonly used tips are shown in the photo above. A variety of borders and designs can be produced by changing the pressure, the angle of the bag and the distance between the tip and the cake surface.

PROCEDURE FOR **MAKING A PARCHMENT-PAPER CONE**

1 Begin with an equilateral triangle of uncreased paper. Shape it into a cone as shown.

2 Fold the top edges together to hold the shape.

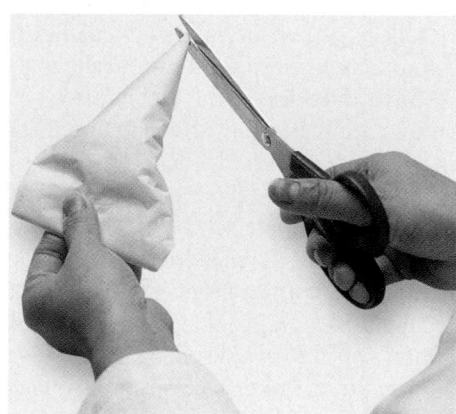

3 Cut the tip of the filled parchment cone.

PROCEDURE FOR **FILLING A PIPING BAG**

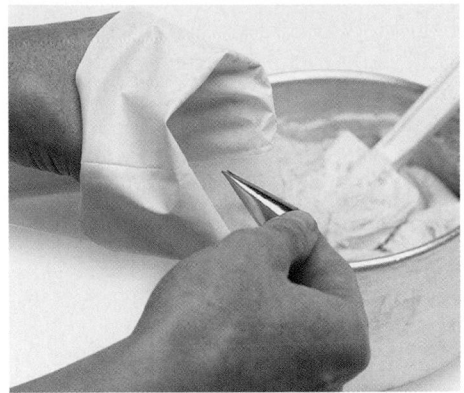

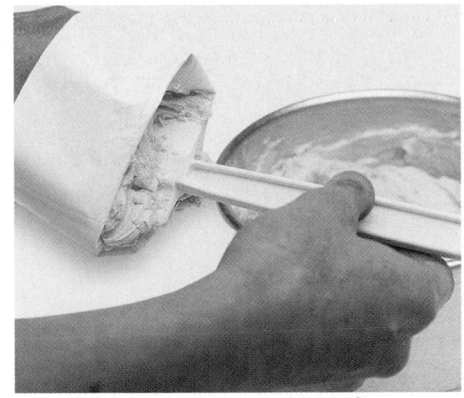

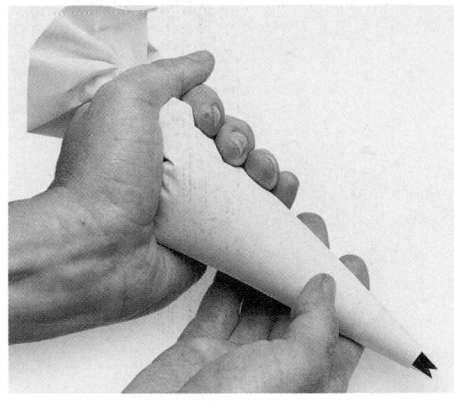

❶ Select the proper size piping bag for your task. Insert the desired tip.

❷ Fold down the top of the bag, then fill approximately half full with frosting. Do not overfill the bag.

❸ Be sure to close the open end tightly before you start piping. Hold the bag firmly in your palm and squeeze from the top. Do not squeeze from the bottom or you may force the contents out the wrong end. Use the fingers of your other hand to guide the bag as you work.

PIPED-ON DECORATING TECHNIQUES

Instead of leaving the sides of a frosted cake smooth or coating them with chopped nuts or crumbs, many designs can be piped on in artful patterns. Some simple but elegant designs are the vine border and basket weave shown here. Normally, a border pattern will be piped around the base of the cake and along the top edge. Borders should be piped on after nuts or any other garnishes are applied.

Applying a vine and leaf border onto a celebration cake.

Applying a bead border onto a celebration cake.

Applying a basket weave pattern to the sides of a celebration cake.

Applying a shell border to a celebration cake.

Each slice or serving of cake can be marked with its own decoration. For example, a rosette of frosting or a whole nut or piece of fruit could be used as shown. This makes it easier to portion the cake evenly.

Delicate flowers such as roses can be piped, allowed to harden, then placed on the cake in attractive arrangements. Royal icing is particularly useful for making decorations in advance because it dries very hard and lasts indefinitely.

The key to success with a piping bag is practice, practice, practice. Use plain all-purpose shortening piped onto parchment paper to practice and experiment with piping techniques. Once comfortable using a piping bag, try applying these newfound skills directly to cakes and pastries.

Placing royal icing flowers onto cake portions.

PROCEDURE FOR **PIPING BUTTERCREAM ROSES**

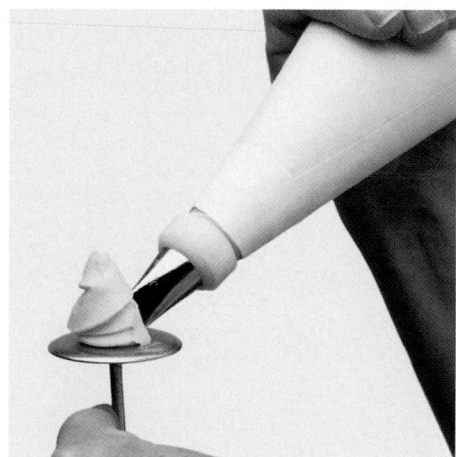

❶ Using a #104 tip, pipe a mound of frosting onto a rose nail.

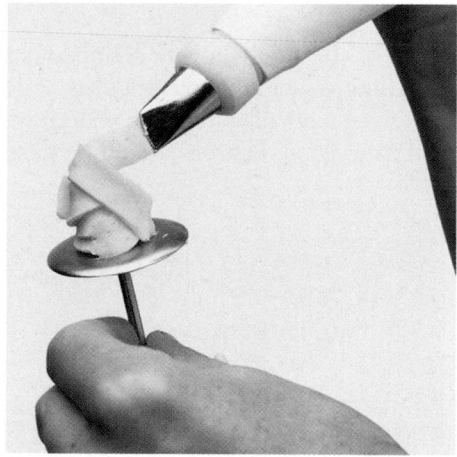

❷ Pipe a curve of frosting around the mound to create the center of the rose.

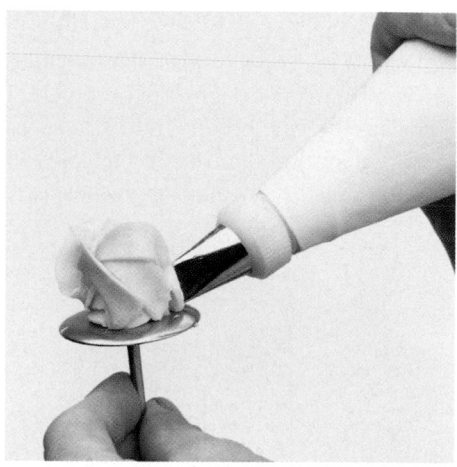

❸ Pipe three overlapping petals around the center.

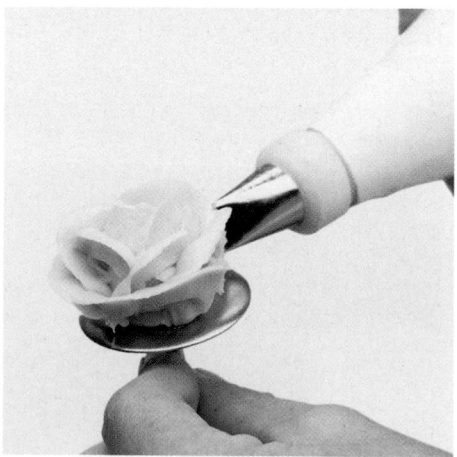

❹ Pipe five more overlapping petals around the first three petals.

❺ Use a small palette knife or spatula to place a finished rose on the cake.

CONVENIENCE PRODUCTS

Packaged cake mixes are a tremendous time-saver for commercial food service operations. Almost any operation can serve a variety of cakes made by relatively unskilled employees using prepared mixes. The results are consistent and the texture and flavor are acceptable to most consumers. Indeed, a well-prepared packaged mix cake is preferable to a poorly prepared cake made from scratch. Most packaged cake mixes can be adapted to include flavorings, nuts, spices or fruits, which can improve the product's overall quality. The convenience of mixes is not without cost, however. Packaged cake mixes are often more expensive than the ingredients needed for an equal number of cakes made from scratch. Cakes made from mixes are also softer and more cottony than scratch cakes, and their flavor tends to be more artificial.

Cake mixes are blends of flour, shortening, emulsifiers, chemical leavening and flavorings that are moistened with water or other liquid. Some mixes require the addition of eggs, fats and flavorings. Mixing techniques vary, so follow package directions carefully. Most cake mixes are not creamed but simply blended with the paddle attachment. To aerate the batter in an angel food cake mix, a whip may be specified. Some mixes require the addition of liquids in two stages. As with any cake batter, scraping down the bowl frequently in the early stages of mixing ensures that the dry mix is properly moistened. Once mixed, panning, baking and assembly techniques are the same as for scratch preparations.

Storing Cakes

Plain cake layers or sheets can be stored at room temperature for 2 or 3 days if well covered, although they may be easier to handle when chilled. Iced or filled cakes are usually refrigerated to prevent spoilage. Simple buttercreams or sugar glazes made without eggs or dairy products, however, can be left at room temperature for 1 or 2 days. Any cake containing custard filling, mousse or whipped cream must be refrigerated. Cakes made with foam-type frosting should be eaten the day they are prepared.

Cakes can usually be frozen with great success; this makes them ideal for baking in advance. Unfrosted layers or sheets should be well covered with plastic wrap and frozen at 0°F (−18°C) or lower. High-fat cakes will keep for up to 6 months; egg-foam cakes begin to deteriorate after 2 or 3 months.

Frostings and fillings do not freeze particularly well, often losing flavor or changing texture when frozen. Buttercreams made with egg whites or sugar syrups tend to develop crystals and graininess. Foam frostings weep, expelling beads of sugar and becoming sticky. If a filled or a frosted cake must be frozen, it is best to freeze it unwrapped first, until the frosting is firm. The cake can then be covered with plastic wrap without damaging the frosting design. Leave the cake wrapped until completely thawed. It is best to thaw cakes in the refrigerator; do not refreeze a thawed cake.

----

1 Cake ingredients can be classified into six categories according to the function they perform. List them and give an example of each.

2 What is the primary leavening agent in cakes made with the foaming method? How is this similar to or different from cakes made with the creaming method?

3 What is the difference between a spongecake and a classic genoise?

4 Discuss for which types of cakes would a glaze be suitable. Why would buttercream be unsuitable for such a cake?

5 List the steps employed in assembling and frosting a three-layer cake.

6 Wedding cakes vary greatly from one region or culture to another. Investigate the various types or styles of cakes traditionally served at weddings in three or four different cultures. Discuss which recipes in this book would be appropriate for a wedding cake. **WWW**

QUESTIONS FOR DISCUSSION

Terms to Know

creamed fat (creaming method)	foam frosting
	fondant
	flat frosting
whipped eggs	royal icing
butter cake	decorator's icing
genoise	ganache
high-ratio cake	mousseline
angel food cake	boiled frosting
chiffon	crumb coat
icing	side masking
buttercream	

ADDITIONAL CAKE AND FROSTING FORMULAS

CARROT CAKE WITH CREAM CHEESE FROSTING

Yield: 5 Half-Sheet Cakes or 6 Rounds, 10 in. (25 cm) each   **Method:** Creaming

Vegetable oil	1 lb. 12 oz.	840 g
Granulated sugar	1 lb. 14 oz.	900 g
Eggs	9	9
Carrots, shredded	2 lb. 4 oz.	1080 g
Crushed pineapple, with juice	1 lb. 9 oz.	750 g
Baking soda	¾ oz.	21 g
Cinnamon, ground	1 oz.	30 g
Pumpkin pie spice	¾ oz.	21 g
Salt	¾ oz.	21 g
Baking powder	1½ Tbsp.	45 ml
Cake flour	2 lb. 5 oz.	1100 g
Coconut, shredded	8 oz.	240 g
Walnut pieces	10 oz.	300 g
Cream Cheese Frosting (recipe follows)	as needed	as needed

1. Blend the oil and sugar in the large bowl of a mixer fitted with the paddle attachment. Add the eggs, beating to incorporate.
2. Blend in the carrots and pineapple.
3. Sift the baking soda, cinnamon, pumpkin pie spice, salt, baking powder and flour together, and then add them to the batter. Stir in the coconut and walnuts.
4. Divide the batter into greased and floured pans.
5. Bake at 340°F (170°C) until springy to the touch and a cake tester comes out almost clean, approximately 30 to 40 minutes.
6. Allow the cakes to cool, then fill and frost as desired with Cream Cheese Frosting.

Approximate values per 5-oz. (150-g) serving: **Calories** 390, **Total fat** 22 g, **Saturated fat** 4 g, **Cholesterol** 40 mg, **Sodium** 490 mg, **Total carbohydrates** 44 g, **Protein** 5 g, **Vitamin A** 100%

CREAM CHEESE FROSTING

Yield: 5 lb. 4 oz. (2.5 kg)

Unsalted butter, softened	6 oz.	180 g
Cream cheese, softened	1 lb. 8 oz.	720 g
Margarine	6 oz.	180 g
Vanilla extract	1 Tbsp.	15 ml
Powdered sugar, sifted	3 lb.	1440 g

1. Cream the butter and cream cheese until smooth. Add the margarine and beat well.
2. Beat in the vanilla. Slowly add the sugar, scraping down the bowl frequently. Beat until smooth.

Approximate values per serving: **Calories** 130, **Total fat** 6 g, **Saturated fat** 3 g, **Cholesterol** 15 mg, **Sodium** 45 mg, **Total carbohydrates** 17 g, **Protein** 1 g, **Vitamin A** 6%

MARBLE CAKE

Yield: 1 Sheet Cake, 18 in. × 24 in. (45 cm × 60 cm)   **Method:** Creaming

Cake flour, sifted	1 lb. 11 oz.	810 g
Baking powder	2½ Tbsp.	45 ml
Salt	1½ tsp.	7 ml
Unsalted butter	12 oz.	360 g
Granulated sugar	1 lb. 11 oz.	810 g
Milk	24 fl. oz.	720 ml
Vanilla extract	1 tsp.	5 ml
Dark chocolate, melted	4½ oz.	130 g
Baking soda	¼ tsp.	1 ml
Coffee extract	2 tsp.	10 ml
Egg whites	12 oz.	360 g
Basic Fudge Frosting (page 1027), Cocoa Fudge Frosting variation	as needed	as needed

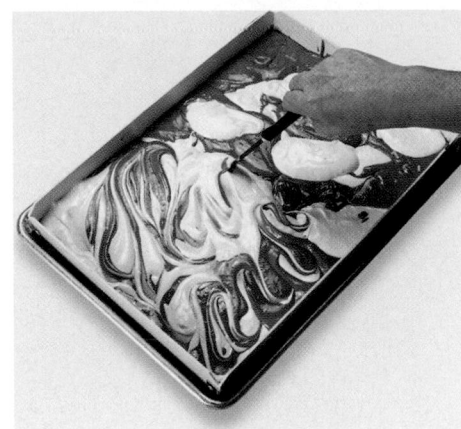

1. Sift the flour, baking powder and salt together. Set aside.
2. Cream the butter and sugar until light and fluffy.
3. Combine the milk and vanilla.
4. Add the dry ingredients to the creamed butter alternately with the milk. Stir the batter only until smooth.
5. Separate the batter into two equal portions. Add the melted chocolate, baking soda and coffee extract to one portion.
6. Whip the egg whites until stiff but not dry. Fold half of the whites into the vanilla batter and half into the chocolate batter.
7. Spoon the batters onto a greased sheet pan, lined with a pan extender, alternating the two colors. Pull a paring knife through the batter to swirl the colors together.
8. Bake at 350°F (180°C) until a tester comes out clean, approximately 25 minutes.
9. Allow the cake to cool, and then cover the top with Cocoa Fudge Frosting.

Approximate values per 5-oz. (150-g) serving: **Calories** 480, **Total fat** 17 g, **Saturated fat** 11 g, **Cholesterol** 40 mg, **Sodium** 250 mg, **Total carbohydrates** 75 g, **Protein** 7 g, **Vitamin A** 15%, **Calcium** 15%

GERMAN CHOCOLATE CAKE

Yield: 1 Layer Cake, 9 in. (22 cm) **Method:** Creaming

Sweet baking chocolate	8 oz.	240 g
Water, boiling	4 fl. oz.	120 ml
Unsalted butter	8 oz.	240 g
Granulated sugar	1 lb.	480 g
Egg yolks	4	4
Vanilla extract	1 tsp.	5 ml
Cake flour	10 oz.	300 g
Baking soda	1 tsp.	5 ml
Salt	½ tsp.	2 ml
Buttermilk	8 fl. oz.	240 ml
Egg whites	4	4
Coconut Pecan Frosting (recipe follows)	1 lb. 13 oz.	870 g

1. Chop the chocolate and melt it with the boiling water over a bain marie.
2. In the bowl of a mixer fitted with the paddle attachment, cream together the butter and sugar until light and fluffy.
3. Add the egg yolks, one at a time, to the butter, then stir in the vanilla and the melted chocolate.
4. Sift the dry ingredients together and add them alternately with the buttermilk, beating well after each addition.
5. Whip the egg whites to stiff peaks and fold into the batter.
6. Divide the batter into three 9-inch (22-centimeter) layer pans that have been greased and lined with parchment paper.
7. Bake at 350°F (180°C) until set and just beginning to pull away from the sides, approximately 30 to 40 minutes. When the cake has cooled completely, spread the Coconut Pecan Frosting between each layer and on top. The sides of this cake are traditionally left plain.

Approximate values per ½-cake serving: **Calories** 840, **Total fat** 47 g, **Saturated fat** 24 g, **Cholesterol** 210 mg, **Sodium** 240 mg, **Total carbohydrates** 101 g, **Protein** 10 g, **Vitamin A** 25%, **Calcium** 15%, **Iron** 20%

COCONUT PECAN FROSTING

Yield: 1 lb. 13 oz. (870 g), enough for 1 three-layer cake

Evaporated milk	8 fl. oz.	240 ml
Granulated sugar	8 oz.	240 g
Egg yolks	3	3
Unsalted butter	4 oz.	120 g
Vanilla extract	1 tsp.	5 ml
Coconut, flaked	4 oz.	120 g
Pecans, chopped	4 oz.	120 g

1. Combine the milk, sugar, egg yolks and butter in a saucepan over medium heat. Cook, stirring constantly, until the mixture thickens, approximately 12 minutes.
2. Remove from the heat and add the vanilla, coconut and pecans. Beat until cool and spreadable.

Approximate values per 1-oz. (30-g) serving: **Calories** 140, **Total fat** 11 g, **Saturated fat** 7 g, **Cholesterol** 25 mg, **Sodium** 10 mg, **Total carbohydrates** 10 g, **Protein** 1 g, **Vitamin A** 8%

SACHER TORTE

Yield: 2 Cakes, 9 in. (22 cm) each   **Method:** Creaming

Cake:

All-purpose flour	10 oz.	300 g
Cocoa powder, alkalized	3 oz.	90 g
Unsalted butter	12½ oz.	375 g
Granulated sugar	18 oz.	540 g
Egg yolks	14	14
Hazelnuts, toasted and ground	3 oz.	90 g
Egg whites	14	14
Apricot jam	18 oz.	540 g
Apricot glaze	as needed	as needed
Dark Chocolate Glaze (recipe follows)	as needed	as needed

1. Grease two 9-inch (22-centimeter) springform pans lightly with butter and line with parchment paper.
2. Sift the flour and cocoa powder together twice. Set aside.
3. Cream the butter and 7 ounces (210 grams) sugar together until light and fluffy. Gradually add the egg yolks and beat well.
4. Fold in the sifted flour and cocoa and the hazelnuts by hand.
5. Whip the egg whites to soft peaks, then gradually add the remaining sugar and continue whipping until stiff, glossy peaks form.
6. Lighten the batter with approximately one-fourth of the egg whites, then fold in the remaining whites.
7. Pour the batter into the prepared pans and bake at 350°F (180°C) until the cakes are set, approximately 35 to 45 minutes.
8. Cool the cakes for 5 minutes before removing from the pans.
9. Cool completely, then cut each cake horizontally into two layers. Spread apricot jam on each layer and restack them, creating two two-layer cakes.
10. Heat the apricot glaze until spreadable. Pour it over the top and sides of each cake.
11. Allow the apricot glaze to cool completely, and then pour the Chocolate Glaze over the top and sides of each cake to create a smooth, glossy coating.

Approximate values per ⅒-cake serving: **Calories** 450, **Total fat** 21 g, **Saturated fat** 10 g, **Cholesterol** 185 mg, **Sodium** 60 mg, **Total carbohydrates** 56 g, **Protein** 7 g, **Vitamin A** 20%

DARK CHOCOLATE GLAZE

Yield: 4 lb. (1.9 kg)

Evaporated milk	14 oz.	420 g
Corn syrup	3 oz.	90 g
Simple syrup	14 oz.	420 g
Dark chocolate coating	17 oz.	510 g
Extra-bittersweet couverture, chopped fine	17 oz.	510 g

1. Bring the milk, corn syrup and simple syrup to a boil, stirring carefully. Do not whisk vigorously or you will incorporate too much air.
2. In a bowl, combine the dark chocolate coating and the extra-bittersweet chocolate.
3. Slowly pour the cream mixture onto the chocolate. Let it sit for approximately a minute. Using a whisk, stir the mixture slowly to incorporate the chocolate and cream.
4. Keep the mixture refrigerated. When ready to use, warm it over a water bath to 100°F (38°C). If the temperature gets any hotter, the glaze will not be as shiny.

Approximate values per 1-oz. (30-g) serving: **Calories** 90, **Total fat** 6 g, **Saturated fat** 3 g, **Cholesterol** 0 mg, **Sodium** 10 mg, **Total carbohydrates** 12 g, **Protein** 1 g

SWEDISH APPLE CAKE

UNIVERSITY OF WISCONSIN-STOUT, MENOMINEE, WI

Associate Professor Philip McGuirk

Cake crumbs have many uses. When trimming plain buttercakes, genoise or sponge cake layers, reserve the crumbs and scraps. Dry them out in a low oven and then grind the scraps in a food processor. Use these crumbs to side-mask cakes, garnish fruit pies or for making cakes such as this apple cake.

Yield: 12 Servings

Tart green apples, peeled and cored	3 lb.	1.3 kg
Lemon juice	1 Tbsp.	15 ml
Whole butter	4 oz.	120 g
Dry crumbs made from genoise, zwieback or biscotti	5 oz.	150 g
Granulated sugar	6 oz.	180 g
Cinnamon, ground	2 tsp.	10 ml
Lemon zest, grated	1 tsp.	5 ml
Whipped cream, unsweetened	1 pt.	480 ml
Sliced almonds, toasted	4 oz.	120 g

1. Slice the apples into wedges approximately ½ inch (1.2 centimeters) thick. Toss with the lemon juice and set aside.

2. Melt 3 ounces (90 grams) butter in a heavy sauté pan. Add the bread crumbs, sugar and cinnamon. Cook, stirring constantly, until the crumbs begin to toast and become fragrant, approximately 2 minutes. Set aside.

3. Melt the remaining 1 ounce (30 grams) butter in a large sauté pan over medium heat. Add the apples and lemon zest, then cover the pan. Cook, turning the apples frequently, until the apples soften and most of their juices have been absorbed, approximately 10 minutes.

4. Sprinkle one-third of the crumb mixture evenly over the bottom of a 9-inch (22-centimeter) springform pan. Spread half of the apple mixture evenly over the crumbs. Repeat, then cover the top of the apples with the remaining crumb mixture.

5. Cover and chill at least 12 hours.

6. Unmold, cut into wedges and serve with the whipped cream and toasted sliced almonds.

Approximate values per serving: **Calories** 420, **Total fat** 28 g, **Saturated fat** 15 g, **Cholesterol** 75 mg, **Sodium** 45 mg, **Total carbohydrates** 40 g, **Protein** 4 g, **Vitamin A** 15%, **Vitamin C** 15%

CHOCOLATE FLOURLESS CAKE

VINCENT ON CAMELBACK, PHOENIX, AZ

Chef Vincent Guerithault

Yield: 21 Servings   **Method:** Egg foam

Unsalted butter	1 lb.	480 g
Dark chocolate	27 oz.	810 g
Eggs, separated	20	20
Granulated sugar	7 oz.	210 g
Powdered sugar	as needed	as needed

1. Melt the butter and chocolate over a bain marie.

2. Whisk the egg yolks into the melted chocolate.

3. Whip the egg whites until shiny. Add the granulated sugar and whip until very stiff. Fold into the chocolate. Pour the batter into a full-size hotel pan lined with buttered parchment.

4. Bake at 400°F (200°C) for 10 minutes. Lower the oven temperature to 350°F (180°C) and continue baking until done, approximately 40 minutes. A cake tester will not come out clean, even though the cake will be done.

5. Invert the cake onto the back of a sheet pan. Cool completely, then dust with powdered sugar.

Approximate values per 4-oz. (120-g) serving: **Calories** 470, **Total fat** 35 g, **Saturated fat** 20 g, **Cholesterol** 250 mg, **Sodium** 65 mg, **Total carbohydrates** 32 g, **Protein** 8 g, **Vitamin A** 25%

LADYFINGERS

Ladyfingers are made from a spongecake batter that is piped into finger-length strips. After baking, these soft cakes may be eaten plain as a cookie or petit four. They are equally good when dried out in the oven, like biscotti. These versatile cakes are used to line the mold for a Charlotte dessert. For convenience, the batter may be piped close together to form a strip after baking and used to line a mold or torte ring.

Yield: Approximately 95 Cookies, 4 in. (10 cm) each   **Method:** Spongecake

Bread flour	5 oz.	150 g
Cornstarch	4 oz.	120 g
Egg yolks	7 oz.	210 g
Vanilla extract	1 tsp.	5 ml
Egg whites	12 oz.	360 g
Granulated sugar	7.5 oz.	235 g
Powdered sugar	as needed	as needed

1. Sift the flour and cornstarch together. Set aside.
2. Whip the egg yolks and vanilla together in the bowl of a mixer fitted with the whip attachment until the mixture is thick and creamy.
3. Simultaneously, in a second mixer fitted with the whip attachment, whip the egg whites and granulated sugar until the mixture holds stiff peaks.
4. Using a balloon whisk, gently stir the egg whites to restore a smooth appearance. Add the whipped yolks all at once into the egg whites. Gently fold the two together using a rubber spatula or a balloon whisk until the mixture is streaked in appearance and is not completely combined. Gently fold in the flour, taking care not to deflate the batter.
5. Place the batter into a pastry bag fitted with a medium plain tip. Pipe 4-inch- (10-centimeter-) long cookies onto paper-lined sheet pans.
6. Sprinkle the surface of the piped batter with powdered sugar. Let it sit for a few minutes until the powdered sugar dissolves. Sprinkle a second time with more powdered sugar.
7. Bake immediately at 400°F (200°C) until the cookies bounce back when lightly pressed, approximately 9 to 11 minutes.

Approximate values per cookie: **Calories** 20, **Total fat** 0 g, **Saturated fat** 0 g, **Cholesterol** 15 mg, **Sodium** 0 mg, **Total carbohydrates** 4 g, **Protein** 1 g, **Claims**—fat free; no saturated fat; low cholesterol; no sodium; low calorie

FUDGE BROWNIES

Yield: 4 Dozen Squares, 2 in. (5 cm) each, or 1 Half-Sheet Pan

Method: Egg foam

Unsweetened chocolate	1 lb.	480 g
Unsalted butter	18 oz.	540 g
Eggs	10	10
Granulated sugar	2 lb. 8 oz.	1.2 kg
Salt	1 tsp.	5 ml
Vanilla extract	1 fl. oz.	30 ml
All-purpose flour	1 lb.	480 g
Pecan pieces	8 oz.	240 g
Powdered sugar (optional)	as needed for garnish	

1. Melt the chocolate with the butter over a double boiler.
2. While the chocolate is melting, whip the eggs, granulated sugar and salt in the large bowl of a mixer fitted with the paddle attachment for 10 minutes.
3. Scrape down the bowl and add the melted chocolate and vanilla to the eggs. Stir to blend completely. Stir in the flour and nuts.
4. Spread the batter evenly onto a parchment-lined and buttered half-sheet pan. The pan will be very full. Bake at 325°F (160°C) until the center is set, approximately 40 minutes.
5. Allow to cool completely before cutting. Dust the brownies with powdered sugar (if using).

Approximate values per 2-in. (5-cm) square: **Calories** 343, **Total fat** 18 g, **Saturated fat** 9 g, **Cholesterol** 70 mg, **Sodium** 16 mg, **Total carbohydrates** 41 g, **Protein** 4 g

CHOCOLATE PEANUT BUTTER BROWNIES

Yield: 4 Dozen Brownies, 2 in. (5 cm) each

Method: Egg foam

Pastry flour	1 lb.	480 g
Baking powder	2 tsp.	10 ml
Eggs	5	5
Granulated sugar	12 oz.	360 g
Brown sugar	12 oz.	360 g
Peanut butter	12 oz.	360 g
Vanilla extract	1 Tbsp.	15 ml
Unsalted butter, melted	3 oz.	90 g
Peanuts, toasted	6 oz.	180 g
Semisweet chocolate chunks	6 oz.	180 g
Ganache (page 993)	1 lb. 8 oz.	720 g
Chocolate decorations (optional)	as needed	as needed
Peanut halves	as needed	as needed

1. Sift together the flour and baking powder. Set aside.
2. In the bowl of a mixer fitted with the paddle attachment, blend the eggs and sugars. Add the peanut butter and vanilla. Mix until well combined, then beat in the butter. Stir in the flour, peanuts and chocolate chunks.
3. Spread the batter on a paper-lined half sheet pan. Bake at 350°F (175°C) until set, approximately 35 to 38 minutes.
4. Let cool completely, turn over onto the back of a clean sheet pan and frost the surface with ganache heated to 110°F (43°C).
5. Cut into 2-inch (5-centimeter) squares and decorate with chocolate decorations (if using) and peanut halves.

Approximate values per 2-in. (5-cm) square: **Calories** 250, **Total fat** 13 g, **Saturated fat** 6 g, **Cholesterol** 35 mg, **Sodium** 65 mg, **Total carbohydrates** 31 g, **Protein** 5 g, **Claims**—low fat; low cholesterol; no sodium

GERMAN CHOCOLATE LAYERED BROWNIES

Yield: 8 Dozen Squares, 2-in. (5-cm) each, or 1 Full Sheet Pan

Method: Egg Foam

Semi-sweet chocolate	1 lb.	480 g
Unsalted butter	1 lb. 4 oz.	600 g
Vanilla extract	1 Tbsp.	15 ml
Eggs	12 eggs	600 g
Salt	½ tsp.	2 ml
Granulated sugar	2 lb.	960 g
Cocoa powder	2 oz.	60 g
All purpose flour	14 oz.	420 g
Pecans, chopped	1 lb.	480 g
Topping:		
Unsalted butter	12 oz.	360 g
Shredded coconut	12 oz.	360 g
Coconut flavoring	4 tsp.	20 ml
Vanilla extract	4 tsp.	20 ml
Powdered sugar	1 lb. 4 oz	600 g
Cream cheese, softened	1 lb. 8 oz.	720 g

❶ Placing coconut topping on brownie batter spread in the sheet pan.

1. Melt chocolate and butter together and set aside. Stir in the vanilla extract.

2. Beat eggs, salt and sugar together in another bowl.

3. In a large bowl, stir together the cocoa powder, flour and pecans. Add the egg mixture to the flour, then stir in the melted chocolate.

4. Pour into a greased and floured sheet pan, spreading evenly.

5. To make the topping, melt the butter in a large saucepan and then stir in the remaining ingredients except for the cream cheese. Cook over low heat until the sugar has dissolved and the mixture is creamy.

6. Cream the cream cheese in a mixer or food processor. Add the hot butter/sugar mixture and blend until no lumps of cheese remain.

7. Immediately spoon the topping over the unbaked chocolate brownie batter. Spread the topping into a thin layer using an offset spatula.

8. Bake at 300°F (149°C) until the center has set and the surface is golden brown, approximately 1 hour. Cool, then wrap and chill completely overnight before cutting into 2-x-2-inch (5-x-5-centimeter) squares.

❷ Spreading topping on layered brownie before baking.

Approximate values per bar cookie: **Calories** 220, **Total fat** 15 g, **Saturated fat** 8 g, **Cholesterol** 50 mg, **Sodium** 45 mg, **Total carbohydrates** 22 g, **Protein** 2 g

<blockquote>
" Like a host at a good party, vanilla encourages all the elements present to rise to the occasion and make their own contributions to the whole, without calling undue attention to itself. "

—RICHARD SAX, AMERICAN FOOD WRITER,
COOKBOOK AUTHOR AND TEACHER (1954–1995)
</blockquote>

CHAPTER THIRTY-FOUR

CUSTARDS, CREAMS, FROZEN DESSERTS AND DESSERT SAUCES

After studying this chapter, you will be able to:

- prepare a variety of custards and creams

- prepare a variety of ice creams, sorbets and frozen dessert items

- prepare a variety of dessert sauces

- use these products in preparing and serving other pastry and dessert items

THE BAKESHOP IS RESPONSIBLE FOR MORE than just quick breads, yeast breads, pies, pastries, cookies and cakes. It also produces many delightfully sweet concoctions that are not baked and often not even cooked. These include sweet custards, creams, frozen desserts and dessert sauces. Sweet custards are cooked mixtures of eggs, sugar and milk; flour or cornstarch may be added. Sweet custards can be flavored in a variety of ways and eaten hot or cold. Some are served alone as a dessert or used as a filling, topping or accompaniment for pies, pastries or cakes. Creams include whipped cream and mixtures lightened with whipped cream such as Bavarians, chiffons and mousses. Frozen desserts include ice cream and sorbet as well as the still-frozen mousses called semifreddi.

Sauces for these desserts, including fruit purées, caramel sauces and chocolate syrup, are also made in the bakeshop and are discussed in this chapter. Indeed, many of the items presented in this chapter are components, meant to be combined with pastries (Chapter 32) or cakes (Chapter 33) to form complete desserts. Guidelines for assembling desserts are given at this chapter's end.

CUSTARDS

A **custard** is any liquid thickened by the coagulation of egg proteins. A custard's consistency depends on the ratio of eggs to liquid, whether whole eggs or just yolks are used, and the type of liquid used. The more eggs used, the thicker and richer the final product will be. The richer the liquid (cream versus milk, for example), the thicker the final product. Most custards, with the notable exception of pastry creams, are not thickened by starch.

A custard can be stirred or baked. A **stirred custard** tends to be soft, rich and creamy. A **baked custard**, typically prepared in a bain marie, is usually firm enough to unmold and slice.

Stirred Custards

A stirred custard is cooked on the stove top either directly in a saucepan or over a double boiler. It must be stirred throughout the cooking process to prevent curdling (overcooking).

A stirred custard can be used as a dessert sauce, incorporated into a complex dessert or eaten alone. The stirred custards most commonly used in food service operations are **vanilla custard sauce** and **pastry cream**. Other popular stirred custards are lemon curd and **sabayon**.

VANILLA CUSTARD SAUCE

Vanilla custard sauce (Fr. *crème anglaise*) is made with egg yolks, sugar and milk or half-and-half. Usually flavored with vanilla bean or pure vanilla extract, a custard sauce can also be flavored with liqueur, chocolate, ground nuts or extracts.

Custard sauce is prepared on the stovetop over direct heat in a nonreactive saucepan. (If a nonreactive pan is unavailable, cook the custard in a stainless steel bowl set over a bain marie of simmering water.) When making a custard sauce, be extremely careful to stir the mixture continually and do not allow it to boil, or it will curdle. Do not allow the temperature to exceed 190°F (88°C) or the custard will break. Use a thermometer to monitor the custard as it cooks, removing it from the heat when it reaches 185°F (85°C). A properly made custard sauce should be smooth and thick enough to coat the back of a spoon. It should not contain any noticeable bits of cooked egg.

A custard sauce can be served with cakes, pastries, fruits and soufflés and is often used for decorating dessert plates. It may be served hot or cold. It is also used as the base for many ice creams.

A very thick version of custard sauce can be made using heavy cream and additional egg yolks. Its consistency is more like a **pudding** than a sauce. This custard is often served over fruit in a small ramekin or other container and then topped with caramelized sugar for a dessert known as **crème brûlée** ("burnt cream"). See the recipe on page 1069.

PASTRY CREAM

Pastry cream (Fr. *crème pâtissière*) is a stirred custard made with egg yolks, sugar and milk and thickened with starch (flour, cornstarch or a combination of the two). Because the starch protects the egg yolks from curdling, pastry cream can be boiled. In fact, it must be boiled to fully gelatinize the starch and eliminate the taste of raw starch.

Pastry cream can be flavored with chocolate, liquors, extracts or fruits. (Pudding is nothing more than a flavored pastry cream.) It is used for filling éclairs, cream puffs, napoleons, fruit tarts and other pastries. Pastry cream thickened with cornstarch is also the filling for cream pies (see Chapter 32, Pies, Pastries and Cookies). Pastry cream is thick enough to hold its shape without making pastry doughs soggy.

Pastry cream can be rather heavy. It can be lightened by folding in whipped cream to produce a **mousseline**, or Italian meringue can be folded in to produce a **crème Chiboust**.

PROCEDURE FOR PREPARING VANILLA CUSTARD SAUCE AND PASTRY CREAM

❶ Place milk and/or cream in a heavy, nonreactive saucepan; add vanilla bean to **steep** in the cream if desired.

❷ In a mixing bowl, whisk together the egg yolks, sugar and starch (if using). Do not use an electric mixer, as it incorporates too much air.

❸ Bring the liquid just to a boil. **Temper** the egg mixture with approximately one-third of the hot liquid.

❹ Pour the tempered eggs into the remaining hot liquid and return the mixture to the heat. The stove's temperature can be as hot as you dare: The lower the temperature, the longer the custard will take to thicken; the higher the temperature, the greater the risk of curdling.

❺ Cook, stirring constantly, until thickened. Custard sauce should reach a temperature of 185°F (85°C). Pastry cream should be allowed to boil for a few moments.

❻ Immediately remove the cooked custard from the hot saucepan to avoid overcooking. Butter or other flavorings can be added at this time.

❼ Cool in an ice bath. Store in a clean, shallow container. Cover to prevent pastry cream from developing a thick skin and refrigerate.

pudding a thick, spoonable dessert custard, usually made with eggs, milk, sugar and flavorings and thickened with flour or another starch

crème brûlée (krehm broo-lay) French for "burnt cream"; used to describe a rich dessert custard topped with a crust of caramelized sugar

mousseline (moos-uh-leen) a cream or sauce lightened by folding in whipped cream

crème Chiboust (krehm chee-boos) a vanilla pastry cream lightened by folding in Italian meringue; traditionally used in a gâteau St. Honoré

steep to soak food in a hot liquid in order to either extract its flavor or soften its texture

temper to heat gently and gradually; refers to the process of slowly adding a hot liquid to eggs or other foods to raise their temperature without causing them to curdle

SAFETY ALERT
Eggs

Eggs are high-protein foods that are easily contaminated by bacteria such as salmonella that cause food-borne illnesses. Because custards cannot be heated to temperatures high enough to destroy these bacteria without first curdling the eggs, it is especially important that sanitary guidelines be followed in preparing the egg products discussed in this chapter.

❶ Cleanliness is important: Wash your hands thoroughly before beginning; be sure to use clean, sanitized bowls, utensils and storage containers.

❷ When breaking or separating eggs, do not allow the exterior of the eggshell to come into contact with the raw egg.

❸ Heat the milk to just below a boil before combining it with the eggs. This reduces the final cooking time.

❹ Chill the finished product quickly over an ice bath and refrigerate immediately below 40°F (4°C).

❺ Do not store any custard mixture, cooked or uncooked, at room temperature.

PROCEDURE FOR **SALVAGING CURDLED VANILLA CUSTARD SAUCE**

1. Strain the sauce into a bowl. Place the bowl over an ice bath and whisk vigorously.
2. If this does not smooth out the overcooked sauce, place the sauce in a blender and process for a few moments.

Although these steps may reincorporate the curdled eggs, the resulting sauce will be thin and less creamy than a properly prepared vanilla custard sauce.

MISE EN PLACE

▶ Split vanilla bean in half.
▶ Set up an ice bath.

1. Mise en place for vanilla sauce.

2. Tempering the eggs.

VANILLA CUSTARD SAUCE (CRÈME ANGLAISE)

Yield: 36 fl. oz. (1.2 lt)   **Method:** Stirred custard

Half-and-half	1 qt.	960 ml
Vanilla bean, split	1	1
Egg yolks	12	12
Granulated sugar	10 oz.	300 g

1. Using a heavy nonreactive saucepan, bring the half-and-half and vanilla bean just to a boil.
2. Whisk the egg yolks and sugar together in a mixing bowl. Temper the egg mixture with approximately one-third of the hot half-and-half, then return the entire mixture to the saucepan with the remaining half-and-half.
3. Cook the sauce over medium heat, stirring constantly, until it is thick enough to coat the back of a spoon. Do not allow the sauce to exceed 185°F (85°C) or the mixture will curdle.
4. As soon as the sauce thickens, remove it from the heat and pour it through a fine mesh strainer into a clean bowl. Chill the sauce in an ice bath, then cover and keep refrigerated. The sauce should last 3 to 4 days.

VARIATIONS:

Chocolate Custard Sauce—Stir 6 ounces (180 grams) finely chopped dark chocolate into the strained custard while it is still warm. The heat of the custard will melt the chocolate.

Coffee Custard Sauce—Add 1–1½ fluid ounces (30–45 milliliters) coffee (café) extract or compound to the warm custard.

Frangelico Custard Sauce—Omit the vanilla bean. Stir in ½ teaspoon (2 milliliters) vanilla extract and 2–3 tablespoons (30–45 milliliters) Frangelico, to taste.

Ginger Custard Sauce—Omit the vanilla bean. Steep 3 ounces (90 grams) chopped fresh ginger for 10 minutes in the half-and-half. Reheat and continue preparing the sauce as directed. The chopped ginger will be strained out in Step 4.

Pistachio Custard Sauce—Omit the vanilla bean. Place 4 ounces (120 grams) finely chopped pistachio nuts in the saucepan with the barely boiling half-and-half. Remove from the heat, cover and steep for up to 1 hour. Uncover the mixture, reheat and continue preparing the sauce as directed. The ground nuts will be strained out in Step 4.

Approximate values per 1-fl.-oz. (30-ml) serving: **Calories** 80, **Total fat** 4.5 g, **Saturated fat** 2.5 g, **Cholesterol** 75 mg, **Sodium** 15 mg, **Total carbohydrates** 8 g, **Protein** 2 g, **Vitamin A** 6%

❸ The properly cooked sauce.

❹ Straining the sauce into a bowl.

PASTRY CREAM (CRÈME PÂTISSIÈRE)

Yield: Approximately 3 lb. (1.4 kg) **Method:** Stirred custard

Ingredient	US	Metric
Milk	1 qt.	960 ml
Granulated sugar	7½ oz.	225 g
Egg yolks	10	10
Cornstarch	2.5 oz.	75 g
Unsalted butter	2 oz.	60 g

❶ Boil the milk and 3 ounces (120 grams) sugar in a large nonreactive saucepan.

❷ Whisk the egg yolks in a mixing bowl and gradually add the remaining sugar. Whisk in the cornstarch to combine.

❸ Temper the egg yolk mixture with one-quarter of the boiling milk. Return the egg mixture to the pan and cook, whisking vigorously until the cream boils and is well thickened. Allow the pastry cream to boil approximately 1 minute, stirring constantly.

❹ Remove the pastry cream from the heat and immediately pour it into a clean mixing bowl.

❺ Fold in the butter until melted. Do not overmix, as this will thin the custard.

❻ Cover by placing plastic wrap on the surface of the custard. Chill over an ice bath. Remove the vanilla bean just before using the pastry cream.

VARIATIONS:

Chocolate Pastry Cream—Stir 4 ounces (120 grams) finely chopped dark chocolate into the strained custard while it is still warm. The heat of the custard will melt the chocolate.

Coffee Pastry Cream—Add 1 fluid ounce (30 milliliters) coffee extract or compound to the warm custard.

Mousseline Pastry Cream—Whip 12 fluid ounces (360 milliliters) heavy cream to stiff peaks. Fold into the chilled Pastry Cream Filling.

Approximate values per 1-fl.-oz. (30-ml) serving: **Calories** 50, **Total fat** 2.5 g, **Saturated fat** 1.5 g, **Cholesterol** 55 mg, **Sodium** 10 mg, **Total carbohydrates** 6 g, **Protein** 1 g

MISE EN PLACE
◀ Split vanilla bean in half.
◀ Set up an ice bath.

❶ Stirring the pastry cream as it comes to a boil.

❷ Folding butter into the cooked pastry cream.

SABAYON

Sabayon (sah-bay-own; It. *zabaglione*) is a foamy, stirred custard sauce made by whisking eggs, sugar and wine over low heat. The egg proteins coagulate, thickening the mixture, while the whisking incorporates air to make it light and fluffy. Usually a sweet wine is used; marsala and champagne are the most popular choices. The flavor of the sabayon depends on the quality of the wine from which it is made; use the best quality available.

The mixture can be served warm, or it can be chilled and lightened with whipped cream or whipped egg whites. Sabayon may be served alone or as a sauce or topping with fruit or pastries such as spongecake or ladyfingers.

PROCEDURE FOR **PREPARING SABAYON**

1. Combine egg yolks, sugar and wine in the top of a double boiler.
2. Place the double boiler over low heat and whisk constantly until the sauce is foamy and thick enough to form a ribbon when the whisk is lifted.
3. Remove from the heat and serve immediately, or whisk over an ice bath until cool. If allowed to sit, the hot mixture may separate.
4. Whipped egg whites or whipped cream may be folded into the cooled sabayon.

CHAMPAGNE SABAYON

Yield: Approximately 1 qt. (1 lt)		**Method:** Stirred custard
Egg yolks	8	8
Granulated sugar	4 oz.	120 g
Salt	¼ tsp.	1 ml
Marsala wine	2 fl. oz.	60 ml
Dry champagne	6 fl. oz.	180 ml
Heavy cream (optional)	8 fl. oz.	240 ml

1. Combine the egg yolks, sugar and salt in a stainless steel bowl.
2. Add the marsala and champagne to the egg mixture.
3. Place the bowl over a pan of barely simmering water. Whisk vigorously until the sauce is thick and pale yellow, approximately 10 minutes. Serve immediately.
4. To prepare a sabayon mousseline, place the bowl of sabayon in an ice bath and continue whisking until completely cold. Whip the cream to soft peaks and fold it into the cold sabayon. Serve the sabayon over fresh berries and ladyfingers or as a sauce for another dessert preparation.

Approximate values per 1-fl.-oz. (30-ml) serving: **Calories** 50, **Total fat** 4 g, **Saturated fat** 2 g, **Cholesterol** 60 mg, **Sodium** 25 mg, **Total carbohydrates** 4 g, **Protein** 1 g, **Vitamin A** 6%

Baked Custards

A baked custard is based on the same principle as a stirred custard: A liquid thickens by the coagulation of egg proteins. However, with a baked custard, the thickening occurs in an oven. The container of custard is usually placed in a water bath (bain marie) to protect the eggs from curdling. Even though the water bath's temperature will not exceed 212°F (100°C), care must be taken not to bake the custards for too long or at too high a temperature. An overbaked custard will be watery or curdled; a properly baked custard should be smooth-textured and firm enough to slice.

Baked custards include simple mixtures of whole eggs or yolks, sugar and milk such as crème caramel, called **flan** in Spain and Mexico. Baked custards also include mixtures in which other ingredients are suspended—for example, cheesecake, rice pudding, bread pudding and quiche.

CRÈME CARAMEL

Crème caramel, crème renversée and flan all refer to an egg custard baked over a layer of caramelized sugar and inverted for service. The caramelized sugar produces a golden-brown surface on the inverted custard and a thin caramel sauce.

✗ 8 TOFFEE CARAMEL FLAN

Yield: 10 Ramekins, 6 oz. (180 ml) each   **Method:** Baked custard

Granulated sugar	1 lb. 4 oz.	600 g
Water	8 fl. oz.	240 ml
Milk	24 fl. oz.	720 ml
Heavy cream	24 fl. oz.	720 ml
Cinnamon sticks	2	2
Vanilla bean, split	1	1
Eggs	8	8
Egg yolks	4	4
Brown sugar	6 oz.	180 g
Molasses	1 Tbsp.	15 ml
Amaretto liqueur	2 Tbsp.	30 ml

1. Combine the granulated sugar with the water in a small heavy saucepan; bring to a boil. Cook until the sugar reaches a deep golden brown. Immediately pour about 2 tablespoons (30 milliliters) caramelized sugar into each ramekin. Tilt each ramekin to spread the caramel evenly along the bottom. Arrange the ramekins in a 2-inch- (5-centimeter-) deep hotel pan and set aside.
2. Combine the milk, cream, cinnamon sticks and vanilla bean in a large saucepan. Bring just to a boil, cover and remove from the heat. Allow this mixture to steep for about 30 minutes.
3. Whisk the eggs, egg yolks, brown sugar, molasses and amaretto together in a large bowl.
4. Uncover the milk mixture and return it to the stove top. Bring just to a boil. Temper the egg-and-sugar mixture with approximately one-third of the hot milk. Whisk in the remaining hot milk.
5. Strain the custard through a fine mesh strainer. Pour into the caramel-lined ramekins, filling to just below the rim.
6. Pour enough warm water into the hotel pan to reach halfway up the sides of the ramekins. Bake at 325°F (160°C) for approximately 30 to 40 minutes. The custards should be almost set, but still slightly soft in the center.
7. Completely chill the baked custards before serving. To unmold, run a small knife around the edge of the custard, invert onto the serving plate and give the ramekin a firm sideways shake. Garnish with fresh fruit or caramelized almonds.

Approximate values per serving: **Calories** 670, **Total fat** 33 g, **Saturated fat** 19 g, **Cholesterol** 355 mg, **Sodium** 120 mg, **Total carbohydrates** 82 g, **Protein** 10 g, **Vitamin A** 40%, **Calcium** 20%

MISE EN PLACE

◀ Gather the ramekins and hotel pan.
◀ Preheat the oven to 325°F (160°C).
◀ Split vanilla bean in half.

SAFETY ALERT

Be extremely careful when working with hot sugar syrups. Because sugar can be heated to very high temperatures, these syrups can cause severe burns. Do not touch the liquefied or caremelized sugar with your bare hand until it has cooled completely.

CRÈME BRÛLÉE

Crème brûlée (krehm broo-LAY) can be made as either a stirred or a baked custard. Neither version should be considered superior, however; they are simply different. The stirred or stove top method is quicker, but requires constant attention and a practiced feel for the custard's consistency. The finished custard will be heavier, creamier and softer than its baked counterpart. The baked version is served in the ramekin or bowl in which it was baked. Unlike crème caramel or flan, baked crème brûlée is not inverted or removed from its baking dish for service. A formula for the baked version follows; a stirred version appears on page 1069.

Gentle heat is important for both methods. Overcooked stirred custard will curdle, turning into scrambled eggs. Overcooked baked custard will become watery, its texture marred with small bubbles.

Additional flavors and textures can be added to the custard in several ways:

▶ Placing a layer of fresh berries or fruit compote under the custard
▶ Incorporating fruit, nuts or liqueurs directly into the custard
▶ Adding flavoring compounds and extracts to the custard
▶ Infusing the heavy cream with nuts, herbs, spices, tea or other flavorings before making the custard

If fruit purées or other liquids are used, the quantity of cream will have to be adjusted or else the custard may be too watery or unable to set properly.

MISE EN PLACE

▶ Split vanilla bean in half.
▶ Preheat the oven to 325°F (160°C).

SAFETY ALERT

Training on how to operate a propane torch is recommended before using it to brown sugar or other dessert preparations. Use extreme caution and follow appropriate safety procedures. Keep the gas bottle away from sources of heat. Do not leave the torch unattended. Rest the bottle on a stable surface away from any flammable materials.

BAKED CRÈME BRÛLÉE

Yield: 10 Servings, 4 oz. (120 g) each   **Method:** Baked custard

Heavy cream	1 qt.	1 lt
Vanilla bean, split	½	½
Granulated sugar	4 oz.	120 g
Egg yolks	10	10
Granulated sugar	as needed	as needed

1. Heat the cream and the vanilla bean in a medium saucepan over medium-high heat until bubbles appear along the sides of the pan.
2. Quickly whisk the sugar into the egg yolks.
3. When the cream is hot, slowly pour it into the yolk mixture. Whisk until well combined.
4. Strain the mixture through a fine sieve into a pitcher or large measuring cup. Scrape the vanilla bean with the tip of a paring knife to remove the remaining seeds; stir the seeds into the custard.
5. Preheat the oven to 325°F (160°C). Arrange the ramekins in a 2-inch- (5-centimeter-) deep hotel pan or baking dish. Pour the custard into the ramekins. Set the pan of ramekins inside the preheated oven, then carefully pour enough water into the pan to come two-thirds of the way up the sides of the ramekins. Bake until just set, approximately 45 to 50 minutes. Start checking the custards early; baking time will depend on the thickness and depth of your ramekins. The custard should be set, not soupy, with only a small area of jiggle in the center.
6. When the custards are done, carefully remove the baking dish from the oven and allow the ramekins to cool in the water bath. When the ramekins are cool enough to handle, remove them from the water, cover with plastic wrap, and refrigerate for at least 4 hours or up to 2 days before service.
7. At service, sprinkle the top of each custard with granulated sugar, then immediately caramelize the sugar with a propane torch or under a broiler.

Approximate values per serving: **Calories** 430, **Total fat** 40 g, **Saturated fat** 24 g, **Cholesterol** 345 mg, **Sodium** 45 mg, **Total carbohydrates** 14 g, **Protein** 5 g, **Vitamin A** 35%

CHEESECAKE

Cheesecakes, which are almost as old as western civilization, have undergone many changes and variations since the ancient Greeks devised the first known recipe. Americans revolutionized the dessert with the development of cream cheese in 1872.

Cheesecake is a baked custard that contains a smooth cheese, usually a soft, fresh cheese such as cream, ricotta, cottage or farmer cheese. A cheesecake may be prepared without a crust, or it may have a base or sides of short dough, cookie crumbs, ground nuts or spongecake. The filling can be dense and rich (New York style) or light and fluffy (Italian style). Fruit, nuts and flavorings may also be included in the filling. Cheesecakes are often topped with fruit or sour cream glaze. Recipes for both dense and light cheesecakes are at the end of this chapter.

Some cheesecakes are unbaked and rely on gelatin for thickening; others are frozen. These are not really custards, however, but are more similar to the chiffons or mousses discussed later.

BREAD PUDDING

Bread pudding is a home-style dessert in which chunks of bread, flavorings and raisins or other fruit are mixed with an egg custard and baked. The result is somewhat of a cross between a cake and a pudding. It is often served with custard sauce, ice cream, whipped cream or a whiskey-flavored butter sauce. Bread pudding is a delicious way to use stale or leftover bread or overripe fruit. A recipe for bread pudding with bourbon sauce appears at the end of this chapter.

Soufflés

A soufflé is made with a custard base that is lightened with whipped egg whites and then baked. The air in the egg whites expands to create a light, fluffy texture and tall rise. A soufflé is not as stable as a cake or other pastry item, however, and will collapse very quickly when removed from the oven.

Soufflés can be prepared in a wide variety of sweet and savory flavors. The flavorings can be incorporated into the custard, as in the following recipe. Alternatively, an unflavored pastry cream can be used as the base; the liqueur, fruit or chocolate is then added to each portion separately.

When making a soufflé, the custard base and egg whites should be at room temperature. First, the egg whites will whip to a better volume; second, if the base is approximately the same temperature as the egg whites, the two mixtures can be more easily incorporated. The egg whites are whipped to stiff peaks with a portion of the sugar for stability. The whipped egg whites are then gently folded into the base immediately before baking.

A soufflé is baked in a straight-sided mold or individual ramekin. The finished soufflé should be puffy with a lightly browned top. It should rise well above the rim of the baking dish. A soufflé must be served immediately, before it collapses. A warm custard sauce (crème anglaise) is often served as an accompaniment to a sweet soufflé.

A frozen soufflé is not a true soufflé. Rather, it is a creamy custard mixture thickened with gelatin, lightened with whipped egg whites or whipped cream and placed in a soufflé dish wrapped with a paper or acetate collar. When the collar is removed, the mixture looks as if it has risen above the mold like a hot soufflé.

BURNT CREAM

James Beard called crème brûlée "one of the greatest desserts in the realm of cooking." The secret to crème brûlée's success probably lies in its comfort-food familiarity. It is a rich, creamy concoction of egg yolks, sugar and cream served very cold and topped with a crisp, crunchy layer of deeply caramelized sugar. The contrast of textures and flavors satisfies multiple taste desires.

Despite its French name, crème brûlée (literally, "burnt cream") is most likely a product of Great Britain. Perhaps the earliest recipe for burnt cream appears in a 17th-century cookbook from Dorset, England. Numerous sources credit a member of the faculty at Trinity College in Cambridge, England, with successfully introducing this caramelized custard to his peers in the mid-1800s.

Burnt cream was also popular in America, with recognizable versions appearing in Thomas Jefferson's personal recipe collection and in several cookbooks from the 1800s.

Considered a trendy dessert for upscale American restaurants in the 1980s, crème brûlée now appears on all types of menus and is equally at home in neighborhood diners and four-star, white-tablecloth eateries.

PROCEDURE FOR **PREPARING BAKED SOUFFLÉS**

❶ Butter the mold or ramekins and dust with granulated sugar. Preheat the oven to approximately 425°F (220°C).

❷ Prepare the custard base. Add flavorings as desired.

❸ Whip the egg whites and sugar to stiff peaks. Fold the whipped egg whites into the base.

❹ Pour the mixture into the prepared mold or ramekins and bake immediately.

CHOCOLATE SOUFFLÉS

MISE EN PLACE

▶ Separate eggs.
▶ Chop chocolate finely.
▶ Melt butter.

Yield: 8 Servings

Orange juice	1 pt.	480 ml
Eggs, separated	8	8
Granulated sugar	4 oz.	120 g
All-purpose flour	3 oz.	90 g
Bittersweet chocolate, chopped fine	8 oz.	240 g
Orange liqueur	2 fl. oz.	60 ml
Butter, melted	as needed	as needed
Granulated sugar	as needed	as needed

① Folding the whipped egg whites into the chocolate base.

① To prepare the base, heat the orange juice to lukewarm in a heavy saucepan.

② Whisk the egg yolks with 3 ounces (90 grams) sugar in a large mixing bowl. Whisk in the flour and warm orange juice, then return the mixture to the saucepan.

③ Cook over medium-low heat, stirring constantly, until the custard is thick. Do not allow it to boil. Remove from the heat.

④ Stir in the chocolate until completely melted. Stir in the liqueur. Cover this base mixture with plastic wrap to prevent a skin from forming. Hold for use at room temperature. (Unused base can be kept overnight in the refrigerator; it should be brought to room temperature before mixing with the egg whites.)

⑤ To prepare the soufflés, brush 4-fluid-ounce (120-milliliter) ramekins with melted butter and dust with granulated sugar.

⑥ Preheat the oven to 425°F (220°C). Place a sheet pan in the oven, onto which you will place the soufflés for baking. (This makes it easier to remove the hot soufflé cups from the oven.)

⑦ Whip the egg whites to stiff peaks with the remaining 1 ounce (30 grams) sugar. Fold the whites into the chocolate base and spoon the mixture into the prepared ramekins. The ramekins should be filled to within ¼ inch (6 millimeters) of the rim. Smooth the top of each soufflé with a spatula and bake immediately.

⑧ The soufflés are done when well risen, brown on top and the edges appear dry, approximately 12 minutes. Do not touch a soufflé to test doneness.

⑨ Sprinkle the soufflés with powdered sugar if desired and serve immediately.

Approximate values per serving: **Calories** 350, **Total fat** 15 g, **Saturated fat** 8 g, **Cholesterol** 210 mg, **Sodium** 65 mg, **Total carbohydrates** 48 g, **Protein** 10 g, **Vitamin A** 10%, **Vitamin C** 50%

② Filling the ramekins.

③ The finished soufflé, ready for service.

TABLE 34.1	CREM (CRÈME) COMPONENTS		
FOR A	**BEGIN WITH A BASE OF**	**THICKEN WITH**	**THEN FOLD IN**
Bavarian	Custard	Gelatin	Whipped cream
Chiffon	Custard or starch-thickened fruit	Gelatin	Whipped egg whites
Mousse	Melted chocolate, puréed fruit or custard	Nothing or gelatin	Whipped cream, whipped egg whites or both

CREAMS

Creams (Fr. *crèmes*) include light, fluffy or creamy-textured dessert items made with whipped egg whites or whipped cream. Some, such as **Bavarian creams** and **chiffons**, are thickened with gelatin. Others, such as **mousses** and **crèmes Chantilly**, are softer and lighter. (See Table 34.1.) The success of all, however, depends on properly whipping and incorporating egg whites or heavy cream.

Review the material on whipping cream found in Chapter 7, Dairy Products. Note that whipping cream has a butterfat content of 30 to 36 percent. When preparing any whipped cream, be sure that the cream, the mixing bowl and all utensils are well chilled and clean. A warm bowl can melt the butterfat, destroying the texture of the cream. Properly whipped cream should increase two to three times in volume.

Overwhipped cream loses volume, curdles and separates.

Crème Chantilly

Crème Chantilly is simply heavy cream whipped to soft peaks and flavored with sugar and vanilla. It can be used for garnishing pastry or dessert items, or it can be folded into cooled custard or pastry cream and used as a component in a pastry.

When making crème Chantilly, the vanilla extract and sugar should be added after the cream begins to thicken. Either granulated or powdered sugar may be used; there are advantages and disadvantages to both. Granulated sugar assists in forming a better foam than powdered sugar, but it may cause the cream to feel gritty. Powdered sugar dissolves more quickly and completely than granulated sugar, but does nothing to assist with foaming. Whichever sugar is used, it should be added just before the whipping is complete to avoid interfering with the cream's volume and stability. When properly whipped, heavy cream expands two to two and a half times in volume.

CRÈME CHANTILLY (CHANTILLY CREAM)

Yield: 2–2½ qt. (2–2.5 lt)

Heavy cream, chilled	1 qt.	1 lt
Powdered sugar	3 oz.	90 g
Vanilla extract	2 tsp.	10 ml

MISE EN PLACE
◄ Chill cream, mixing bowl and whisk.

① Place the cream in a chilled mixing bowl. Using a balloon whisk, whisk the cream until slightly thickened.

② Add the sugar and vanilla and continue whisking to the desired consistency. The cream should be smooth and light, not grainy. Do not overwhip.

③ Crème Chantilly may be stored in the refrigerator for several hours. If the cream begins to soften, gently rewhip as necessary.

VARIATION:

Chocolate Chantilly—Melt 1 pound 2 ounces (540 grams) bittersweet chocolate to 120°F (49°C) and remove from heat. Whip the cream to medium peaks. Whisk one-fourth of the whipped cream into the chocolate vigorously. Gently fold in the remaining cream. This mixture will have the texture of velvety ganache.

Properly whipped Crème Chantilly.

Approximate values per 1-fl.-oz. (30-ml) serving: **Calories** 60, **Total fat** 6 g, **Saturated fat** 3.5 g, **Cholesterol** 20 mg, **Sodium** 5 mg, **Total carbohydrates** 2 g, **Protein** 0 g

Bavarian Cream

A Bavarian cream (Fr. *bavarois*) is prepared by first thickening custard sauce with gelatin, then folding in whipped cream. The final product is poured into a mold and chilled until firm enough to unmold and slice. Although a Bavarian cream can be molded into individual servings, it is often poured into a round mold lined with spongecake or ladyfingers to create the classic dessert known as a **charlotte**.

Bavarians can be flavored by adding chocolate, puréed fruit, chopped nuts, extracts or liquors to the custard sauce base. Layers of fruit or liquor-soaked spongecake can also be added for flavor and texture.

When thickening a dessert cream with gelatin, it is important to use the correct amount of gelatin. If not enough gelatin is used or it is not incorporated completely, the cream will not become firm enough to unmold. If too much gelatin is used, the cream will be tough and rubbery. The recipe given here uses sheet gelatin, although an equal amount by weight of granulated gelatin can be substituted. Refer to Chapter 29, Principles of the Bakeshop, for information on using gelatin.

PROCEDURE FOR **PREPARING BAVARIAN CREAMS**

❶ Prepare a custard sauce of the desired flavor.

❷ While the custard sauce is still quite warm, stir in softened gelatin. Make sure the gelatin is completely incorporated.

❸ Chill the custard until almost thickened, then fold in the whipped cream.

❹ Pour the Bavarian into a mold or charlotte form. Chill until set.

BAVARIAN CREAM

MISE EN PLACE

▶ Split vanilla bean in half.
▶ Soften gelatin.

Charlotte Bavarian.

Yield: Approximately 2 qt. (2 lt)

Milk	14 fl. oz.	420 ml
Heavy cream	14 fl. oz.	420 ml
Granulated sugar	6 oz.	180 g
Vanilla bean, split in half	1	1
Egg yolks	8	8
Sheet gelatin, softened	¾ oz.	21 g
Heavy cream, whipped to soft peaks	1 qt.	960 ml

❶ To prepare the custard sauce, combine the milk, cream, 2 ounces (60 grams) sugar and the vanilla bean in a heavy saucepan. Bring to a boil.

❷ Whisk the egg yolks and remaining 4 ounces (120 grams) sugar together to the ribbon stage. Temper the yolk mixture with one-quarter of the heated milk, whisking constantly.

❸ Pour the egg mixture into the saucepan with the rest of the milk. Stir constantly with a rubber spatula until the custard reaches 185°F (85°C).

❹ Remove the custard from the heat and pour it through a fine mesh strainer into a clean bowl.

❺ Add the softened gelatin to the hot custard. Chill until thick in an ice bath, until the custard reaches 75°F (24°C) or slightly cooler. Fold in the whipped cream.

❻ Pour the Bavarian cream immediately into serving dishes or a ladyfinger-lined mold. Chill completely before serving.

Note: Gelatin may separate in the freezer, so quick chilling is not recommended. Products made with gelatin keep well for 1 to 2 days but stiffen with age.

① Adding gelatin to the custard base.

② Folding in the whipped cream.

VARIATION:

Charlotte Bavarian—Line a 2–2½-quart (2–2.5-liter) charlotte mold with ladyfingers (page 1043), then fill with alternating layers of fruit and Bavarian cream. Chill completely, then invert onto a serving platter when firm and garnish with whipped cream.

Approximate values per 3.5-oz. (105-g) serving: **Calories** 230, **Total fat** 15 g, **Saturated fat** 9 g, **Cholesterol** 135 mg, **Sodium** 30 mg, **Total carbohydrates** 19 g, **Protein** 3 g, **Vitamin A** 20%

Chiffon

A chiffon is similar to a Bavarian except that whipped egg whites instead of whipped cream are folded into the thickened base. The base may be a custard or a fruit mixture thickened with cornstarch. Although a chiffon may be molded like a Bavarian, it is most often used as a pie or tart filling.

PROCEDURE FOR **PREPARING CHIFFONS**

① Prepare the base, which is usually a custard or a fruit mixture thickened with cornstarch.
② Add gelatin to the warm base.
③ Fold in whipped egg whites.
④ Pour into a mold or pie shell and chill.

CHARLOTTE, SWEET CHARLOTTE

The original charlotte was created during the 18th century and named for the wife of King George III of England. It consisted of an apple compote baked in a round mold lined with toast slices. A few decades later, the great French chef Carême adopted the name but altered the concept in response to a kitchen disaster. When preparing a grand banquet for King Louis XVIII, he found that his gelatin supply was insuffi-

cient for the Bavarian creams he was making, so Carême steadied the sides of his sagging desserts with ladyfingers. The result became known as charlotte russe, probably due to the reigning fad for anything Russian. A fancier version, known as charlotte royale, is made with pinwheels or layers of spongecake and jam instead of ladyfingers. The filling for either should be a classic Bavarian cream.

LIME CHIFFON

Yield: 8 servings

Granulated gelatin	¼ oz.	7 g
Water	5 fl. oz.	150 ml
Granulated sugar	7 oz.	210 g
Fresh lime juice	3 fl. oz.	90 ml
Lime zest, grated fine	1 Tbsp.	15 ml
Egg yolks, pasteurized	4	4
Egg whites, pasteurized	4	4
Crumb or other pie crust, baked (optional)	1	1

1. Soften the gelatin in 1 fluid ounce (30 milliliters) water.
2. Combine 4 ounces (120 grams) sugar with the remaining water, lime juice, lime zest and egg yolks in a bowl over a pan of simmering water.
3. Whisk the egg-and-lime mixture together vigorously until it begins to thicken. Add the softened gelatin and continue whipping until very thick and foamy.
4. Remove from the heat, cover and refrigerate until cool and as thick as whipping cream.
5. Meanwhile, whip the egg whites to soft peaks. Whip in the remaining sugar and continue whipping until stiff but not dry.
6. Fold the whipped egg whites into the egg-and-lime mixture. Pour into serving dishes or a prepared pie crust and chill for several hours, until firm.

VARIATIONS:

Lemon Chiffon—Substitute lemon juice and lemon zest for the lime juice and zest.

Orange Chiffon—Substitute orange juice for the lime juice and for 4 fluid ounces (120 milliliters) water. Substitute orange zest for the lime zest. Reduce the amount of sugar in the egg yolk mixture to 1 ounce (30 grams).

Approximate values per serving: **Calories** 140, **Total fat** 2.5 g, **Saturated fat** 1 g, **Cholesterol** 105 mg, **Sodium** 35 mg, **Total carbohydrates** 26 g, **Protein** 4 g, **Claims**—low fat; low saturated fat; low sodium

Mousse

The term *mousse* applies to an assortment of dessert creams not easily classified elsewhere. A mousse is similar to a Bavarian or chiffon in that it is lightened with whipped cream, whipped egg whites or both. A mousse is generally softer than these other products, however, and only occasionally contains a small amount of gelatin. A mousse is generally too soft to mold.

A mousse may be served alone as a dessert or used as a filling in cakes or pastry items. Sweet mousses can be based on a custard sauce, melted chocolate or puréed fruit. Savory mousses are discussed in Chapter 27, Charcuterie.

SAFETY ALERT
Egg Products in Uncooked Mousses

Pasteurized egg products are recommended for most mousse formulas, because mousses require no further cooking. One exception is Italian meringue; the hot sugar syrup cooks the egg whites to a temperature that makes them safe for consumption.

PROCEDURE FOR **PREPARING MOUSSES**

1. Prepare the base, which is usually a custard sauce, melted chocolate or puréed fruit.
2. If gelatin is used, it is softened first, then dissolved in the warm base.
3. Fold in whipped pasteurized egg whites, if using. If the base is slightly warm when the egg whites are added, their proteins will coagulate, making the mousse firmer and more stable.
4. Allow the mixture to cool completely, then fold in whipped cream, if using. Note that the egg whites are folded in before any whipped cream. Although the egg whites may deflate somewhat during folding, if the cream is added first it may become overwhipped when the egg whites are added, creating a grainy or coarse product.

CLASSIC CHOCOLATE MOUSSE

Yield: 1½–2 qt. (1.5–2 lt)

Bittersweet chocolate	15 oz.	450 g
Unsalted butter	9 oz.	270 g
Egg yolks, pasteurized	7	7
Egg whites, pasteurized	11	11
Granulated sugar	2½ oz.	75 g
Heavy cream	8 fl. oz.	240 ml

1 Melt the chocolate and butter in a double boiler over low heat. Stir until no lumps remain.

2 Allow the mixture to cool slightly, then whisk in the egg yolks one at a time.

3 Beat the egg whites until soft peaks form. Slowly beat in the sugar and continue beating until stiff peaks form. Whisk one-fourth of the whipped egg whites into the chocolate mixture to lighten, then fold in the remaining whites.

4 Whip the cream to soft peaks. Allow the mousse to cool to 90°F–95°F (32°C–35°C), then fold in the whipped cream. Make sure no streaks of egg white or cream remain.

5 Spoon the mousse into serving bowls and garnish with whipped cream, fresh berries, shaved chocolate or mint. Or chill the mousse completely, then pipe it into bowls or baked tartlet shells. The mousse may also be used as a cake or pastry filling.

Approximate values per 3-fl.-oz. (90-ml) serving: **Calories** 370, **Total fat** 31 g, **Saturated fat** 18 g, **Cholesterol** 215 mg, **Sodium** 50 mg, **Total carbohydrates** 16 g, **Protein** 7 g, **Vitamin A** 25%

1 Folding in the whipped egg whites.

2 Folding in the whipped cream.

FROZEN DESSERTS

Frozen desserts include **ice cream** and **gelato** and desserts assembled with ice cream such as baked Alaska, bombes and parfaits. Frozen fruit purées, known as **sorbets** and **sherbets**, are also included in this category. Still-frozen desserts, known as **semifreddi**, are made from custards or mousses that are frozen without churning.

When making any frozen mixture, remember that cold dulls flavors. Although perfect at room temperature, flavors seem weaker when the mixture is cold. Thus, it may be necessary to oversweeten or overflavor creams or custards that will be frozen for service. Although liquors and liqueurs are common flavoring ingredients, alcohol drastically lowers a liquid mixture's freezing point. Too much alcohol will prevent the mixture from freezing; thus any liqueurs or liquors must be used in moderation.

ICE CREAM: FROM ANCIENT CHINA TO DOUBLE-FUDGE-BROWNIE-CHOCOLATE-CHIP WITH COOKIE DOUGH AND TOASTED ALMOND SLIVERS

Despite claims to the contrary, it is impossible to identify any one country as having invented ice cream. More likely, it was invented in several places around the world at various times.

Early ancestors of today's ice creams were flavored water ices, which have been popular in China since prehistoric times. They have also been popular in the Mediterranean and Middle East since the Golden Age of Greece. In fact, Alexander the Great had a penchant for wine-flavored ices, made with ice brought down from the mountains by runners. The Roman emperor Nero served his guests mixtures of fruit crushed with snow and honey. The Saracens brought their knowledge of making flavored ices with them when they migrated to Sicily in the ninth century. And 12th-century crusaders returned to Western Europe with memories of Middle Eastern sherbets.

The Italians are said to have developed gelato from a recipe brought back from China by Marco Polo in the 13th century. Somehow the dish spread to England by the 15th century, where it was recorded that King Henry V served it at his coronation banquet. Catherine de Medici brought the recipe with her when she married the future king of France in 1533. A different flavor was served during each of the 34 days of their marriage festivities.

Ice cream was first sold to the public in Paris during the late 17th century. It was available at fashionable cafés serving another new treat: coffee. French chefs quickly developed many elaborate desserts using ice creams, including bombes, coupes and parfaits.

Many of this country's founders—Thomas Jefferson, Alexander Hamilton and James and Dolley Madison—were confirmed ice cream addicts. George Washington spent more than $200, a very princely sum, for ice cream during the summer of 1790.

The mechanized ice cream freezer was invented in 1846, setting the stage for mass production and wide availability. By the late 19th century, ice cream parlors were popular gathering places. (Some of today's ice cream parlors still take their décor from "Gay Nineties" motifs.)

Despite the disappearance of most ice cream wagons, soda fountains and lunch counters, all of which were popular ice cream purveyors for much of the 20th century, ice cream sales have never waned. Today, more than 80 percent of all ice cream is sold in supermarkets or convenience stores. The public's demand for high-fat, homemade-style "super-premium" ice creams with rich and often-elaborate flavor combinations shows no sign of declining.

SAFETY ALERT
Ice Cream

It is important to exercise extra care when preparing ice cream products because ice cream contains several potentially hazardous foods, such as cream, milk and eggs. Properly cooking ice cream bases that use pasteurized egg products helps ensure a safe product. Ice cream freezers have many grooves and crevices where bacteria can hide and grow. Always break down and clean an ice cream maker after each use, and sanitize all pieces according to the manufacturer's directions. Never store frozen ice cream products in a container that held raw or unprocessed custard without first cleaning and sanitizing the container. And, of course, wash your hands thoroughly and wear gloves when working with ice cream products.

Ice Cream and Gelato

Ice cream and gelato are custards that are churned during freezing. They can be flavored with a seemingly endless variety of fruits, nuts, extracts, liqueurs and the like. The USDA has established standards for the labeling of frozen products. They require that products labeled "ice cream" contain at least 10 percent milkfat and 20 percent milk solids and have no more than 50 percent **overrun**. French-style ice creams (frozen custards) contain a higher percentage of egg yolks and cream than standard ice cream. Gelato is an Italian-style ice cream made primarily with milk. Although it has a low milkfat content—from 4 to 9 percent—it is denser than American-style products because less air is incorporated during churning. "Ice milk" refers to products that do not meet the standards for ice cream. Low-fat products made without cream or egg yolks are also available for the calorie-conscious. Frozen yogurt uses yogurt as its base. Although touted as a nutritious substitute for ice cream, frozen yogurt may have whole milk or cream added for richness and smoothness.

One hallmark of good ice cream and gelato is smoothness. The ice crystals that would normally form during freezing can be avoided by incorporating air through constant stirring or churning. The air causes the mixture to expand. Gelato is denser because it has little incorporated air. Good-quality ice creams have enough air to make them light; inferior products often contain excessive overrun. The difference becomes obvious when equal volumes are weighed.

Many food service operations use ice cream makers that have internal freezing units to chill the mixture while churning it. Most commercial machines are suitable for churning either ice cream or sorbet. Follow the manufacturer's directions for using and cleaning any ice cream maker.

PROCEDURE FOR **PREPARING ICE CREAMS**

❶ Place the milk and/or cream in a heavy saucepan. If a vanilla bean is being used, it may be added at this time.

❷ Whisk the egg yolks and sugar together in a mixing bowl.

❸ Bring the liquid just to a boil. Temper the egg mixture with approximately one-third of the hot liquid.

❹ Pour the tempered eggs into the remaining hot liquid and return the mixture to the heat.

❺ Cook, stirring constantly, until the custard reaches 180°F to 185°F (82°C to 85°C).

❻ Remove the cooked custard sauce from the hot saucepan immediately. If left in the hot saucepan, it will overcook. Flavorings may be added at this time.

❼ Cool the cooked custard sauce over an ice bath. Store covered and refrigerated at 36°F (2°C) 24 hours to mature the ice cream base.

❽ Process according to the machine manufacturer's directions.

overrun a measure of the air churned into an ice cream; expressed as a percentage, which reflects the increase in volume of the ice cream greater than the amount of the base used to produce the product

---

ICE CREAM BASE

Yield: 2½ qt. (2.5 lt)

Whole milk	1½ qt.	1.5 lt
Heavy cream	1 pt.	480 ml
Vanilla bean, split (optional)	1	1
Egg yolks	16	16
Granulated sugar	20 oz.	600 g

❶ Combine the milk and cream in a heavy saucepan and bring to a boil. Add the vanilla bean (if using).

❷ Whisk the egg yolks and sugar together in a mixing bowl.

❸ Temper the eggs with one-third of the hot milk. Return the egg mixture to the saucepan.

❹ Cook over medium heat, stirring constantly, until the custard reaches 180°F to 185°F (82°C to 85°C). Pour through a fine mesh strainer into a clean bowl.

❺ Chill the cooked ice cream base in an ice bath, then refrigerate overnight before processing.

MISE EN PLACE
◀ Set up an ice bath.

VARIATIONS:

Chocolate Ice Cream—Add approximately 9 ounces (270 grams) finely chopped bitter-sweet chocolate per quart (liter) of ice cream base. Add the chocolate to the hot mixture after it has been strained. Stir until completely melted.

Cappuccino Ice Cream—Steep the hot milk and cream with the vanilla bean and 2 or 3 cinnamon sticks. After the ice cream base is made, stir in 1–1½ fluid ounces (30–45 milliliters) coffee extract.

Brandied Cherry Ice Cream—Drain the liquid from one 16-ounce (500-gram) can tart, pitted cherries. Soak the cherries in 1½ fluid ounces (45 milliliters) brandy. Reduce the sugar to 16 ounces (480 grams) and prepare the ice cream base as directed, omitting the vanilla bean. Add the brandy-soaked cherries to the cooled custard before processing.

Approximate values per 6-fl.-oz. (180-ml) serving: **Calories** 370, **Total fat** 20 g, **Saturated fat** 11 g, **Cholesterol** 270 mg, **Sodium** 65 mg, **Total carbohydrates** 41 g, **Protein** 7 g, **Vitamin A** 25%

Scraping Mango Sorbet from a batch ice cream machine.

Sorbet and Sherbet

Sorbet is a churned mixture of sugar, water and fruit juice, wine, liqueurs or other flavorings. (Even some herb and vegetable flavorings are suitable for sorbet.) It is served as a first course, a palate refresher between courses or a dessert.

Sorbet may be made with fresh, frozen or canned fruit. A wide variety of quality, all-natural frozen purées are available for sorbet making. Granulated sugar or sugar syrup is added for flavor and body. Pasteurized egg whites may also be added during churning for improved texture; the protein in the whites coats the water crystals as the sorbet freezes. Often an invert sugar such as corn syrup or glucose replaces some of the granulated sugar to prevent graininess. *Sherbet* is an Americanization of the French word *sorbet*, which has taken on a slightly different meaning on this side of the Atlantic. When it contains fruit juice and sugar, sherbet is identical to sorbet. But milk is often added to the mixture before churning, making it somewhat richer than sorbet and better served at the end of a meal.

The ratio of sugar to fruit purée or juice depends to some extent on the natural sweetness of the specific fruit as well as personal preference. If too much sugar is used, however, the mixture will be soft and syrupy. If too little sugar is used, the sorbet will be very hard and grainy. Following the formula carefully helps avoid this problem.

GRAPEFRUIT SORBET

Yield: 1½ qt. (1.5 lt)

Fresh grapefruit juice	1 qt.	1 lt
Granulated sugar	8 oz.	250 g

1. Combine the juice and sugar.
2. Process in an ice cream maker according to the manufacturer's directions.
3. Pack into a clean container and freeze until firm.

VARIATIONS:

Mango Sorbet—Combine 2.2 pounds (1 kilogram) mango purée with 8 fluid ounces (240 milliliters) medium sugar syrup.

Raspberry Sorbet—Combine 2.2 pounds (1 kilogram) puréed, strained raspberries with 1 pound (500 grams) granulated sugar and 1 fluid ounce (30 milliliters) lemon juice.

Approximate values per 3-fl.-oz. (90-ml) serving: **Calories** 94, **Total fat** 0 g, **Saturated fat** 0 g, **Cholesterol** 0 mg, **Sodium** 1 mg, **Total carbohydrates** 23 g, **Protein** 0.5 g, **Vitamin C** 36%, **Claims**—no fat; no cholesterol; very low sodium; low calorie

SERVING SUGGESTIONS FOR ICE CREAMS AND SORBETS

Ice creams and sorbets are usually served by the scoop, often in cookie cones. Or they can be served as sundaes. More formal presentations include baked Alaska, bombes, coupes and parfaits.

Still-Frozen Desserts

Still-frozen desserts (It. *semifreddi*) are made with frozen mousse, custard or cream. Layers of spongecake and/or fruit may be added for flavor and texture. Because these mixtures are frozen without churning, air must be incorporated by folding in relatively large amounts of whipped cream or meringue. The air helps keep the mixture smooth and prevents it from becoming too hard.

Still-frozen products include frozen soufflés, **marquise**, mousses and neapolitans. The Chocolate Hazelnut Marquise Recipe at the end of this chapter (page 1076) is an example of a still-frozen dessert.

baked Alaska ice cream set on a layer of spongecake and encased in meringue, then baked until the meringue is warm and golden

bombe two or more flavors of ice cream, or ice cream and sherbet, shaped in a spherical mold; each flavor is a separate layer that forms the shell for the next flavor

parfait ice cream served in a long, slender glass with alternating layers of topping or sauce; also the name of the mousselike preparation that forms the basis for some still-frozen desserts

marquise a frozen mousselike dessert, usually chocolate

DESSERT SAUCES

Pastries and desserts are often accompanied by sweet sauces. Dessert sauces provide moisture, flavor and texture and enhance plate presentation. Sauces may be based on milk and cream, such as Vanilla Custard Sauce (page 1050), the principal dessert sauce. Like any master sauce, it can be flavored and colored with chocolate, coffee extract, liquor or fruit compound as desired. Other dessert sauces include fruit purées, caramel sauce and chocolate syrup. Sauces should be selected to contrast or complement the dessert or pastry with which they are served. For example, a raspberry soufflé can be complemented by an intense raspberry purée or contrasted with a rich chocolate sauce. Plan on 1 to 2 ounces (30 to 60 milliliters) sauce per plated dessert.

Fruit Purées

Many types of fruit can be puréed for dessert sauces; strawberries, raspberries, blackberries, apricots, mangoes and papayas are popular choices. They produce thick sauces with strong flavors and colors. Ripe, fresh or individually quick-frozen (IQF) fruits are recommended. Several commercial brands of prepared fruit purées are available. The best use only natural fruits and are excellent for making sauces and sorbets. They provide consistent flavor and color, reduce preparation time, and make out-of-season or hard-to-obtain tropical fruits available at a reasonable price.

Puréed fruit sauces, also known as **coulis**, can be cooked or uncooked. Cooking thickens the sauces by reduction and allows any starch thickener to gelatinize. They can also be sweetened with granulated sugar or a sugar syrup. The amount of sweetener will vary depending on the fruit's natural sweetness and personal preference.

Sundae or coupe with raspberry coulis, Chantilly cream and nuts.

coulis (coo-lee) a sauce made from a purée of fruits or vegetables

PROCEDURE FOR **PREPARING A FRUIT COULIS**

❶ Wash, peel and chop the fruit if necessary.

❷ Purée the fruit in a food mill, blender or food processor. Strain to remove seeds.

❸ Combine the purée with flavorings and sweeteners (if using).

RASPBERRY SAUCE

Yield: 1 qt. (1 lt)

Raspberries, fresh or IQF	2 lb.	1 kg
Granulated sugar	1 lb.	500 g
Lemon juice	1 fl. oz.	30 ml

❶ Purée the berries and strain through a fine chinois.

❷ Stir in the sugar and lemon juice. Adjust the flavor with additional sugar if necessary.

Approximate values per 1-fl.-oz. (30-ml) serving: **Calories** 70, **Total fat** 0 g, **Saturated fat** 0 g, **Cholesterol** 0 mg, **Sodium** 0 mg, **Total carbohydrates** 17 g, **Protein** 0 g, **Claims**—fat free; no saturated fat; no cholesterol; no sodium

Caramel Sauce

Caramel sauce is a mixture of caramelized sugar and heavy cream. A liqueur or citrus juice may be used for added flavor. Review the material on caramelizing sugar in Chapter 29, Principles of the Bakeshop, before making caramel sauce.

MISE EN PLACE

◀ Thaw raspberries if necessary.

CARAMEL SAUCE

MISE EN PLACE

▶ Bring cream to room temperature.
▶ Cut butter into pieces.

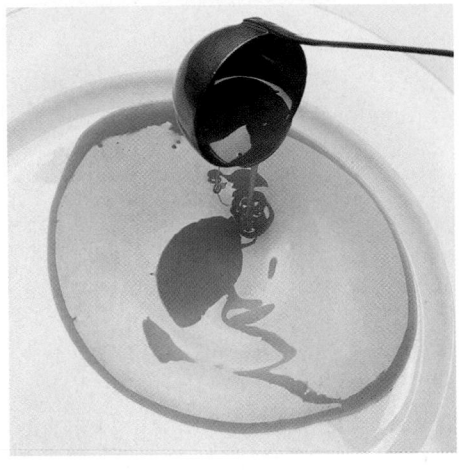

Yield: 4 qt. (4 lt)

Granulated sugar	4 lb. 8 oz.	2.1 kg
Water	1 pt.	480 ml
Lemon juice	2 fl. oz.	60 ml
Heavy cream, room temperature	1 qt	960 ml
Unsalted butter, cut into pieces	5 oz.	150 g

1. Combine the sugar and water in a large heavy saucepan. Stir to moisten the sugar completely. Place the saucepan on the stove top over high heat and bring to a boil. Brush down the sides of the pan with water to remove any sugar granules.

2. When the sugar comes to a boil, add the lemon juice. Do not stir the sugar, as this may cause lumping. Continue boiling until the sugar caramelizes, approximately 338°F (170°C), turning a dark golden brown and producing a rich aroma.

3. Remove the saucepan from the heat. Gradually add the cream. Be extremely careful, as the hot caramel may splatter. Whisk in the cream to blend.

4. Add the pieces of butter. Stir until the butter melts completely. If necessary, return the sauce to the stove to reheat enough to melt the butter.

5. Strain the sauce and cool completely at room temperature. The sauce may be stored for several weeks under refrigeration. Stir before using.

Approximate values per 1-fl.-oz. (30-ml) serving: **Calories** 130, **Total fat** 7 g, **Saturated fat** 4 g, **Cholesterol** 25 mg, **Sodium** 5 mg, **Total carbohydrates** 16 g, **Protein** 0 g, **Vitamin A** 8%

Chocolate Syrup

Chocolate syrup or sauce can be prepared by adding finely chopped chocolate to warm vanilla custard sauce. A darker syrup can also be made with unsweetened chocolate or cocoa powder. Fudge-type sauces, like the one at the end of this chapter (page 1077), are really just variations on ganache, discussed in Chapter 33, Cakes and Frostings.

DARK CHOCOLATE SYRUP

Yield: 1 pt. (480 ml)

Cocoa powder	2 oz.	60 g
Water	12 fl. oz.	360 ml
Granulated sugar	8 oz.	240 g
Unsalted butter	3 oz.	90 g
Heavy cream	2 Tbsp.	30 ml

1. Mix the cocoa powder with just enough of the water to make a smooth paste.

2. Bring the sugar and remaining water to a boil in a small, heavy saucepan. Immediately add the cocoa paste, whisking until smooth.

3. Simmer for 15 minutes, stirring constantly, then remove from the heat.

4. Stir the butter and cream into the warm cocoa mixture. Serve warm or at room temperature.

Approximate values per 1-fl.-oz. (30-ml) serving: **Calories** 120, **Total fat** 6 g, **Saturated fat** 3 g, **Cholesterol** 15 mg, **Sodium** 0 mg, **Total carbohydrates** 16 g, **Protein** 1 g, **Vitamin A** 6%

ASSEMBLING DESSERTS

As noted previously, many pastries and other desserts are assembled from the baked doughs discussed in Chapter 32, Pies, Pastries and Cookies; the cakes, icings and glazes discussed in Chapter 33, Cakes and Frostings; and the creams, custards and other products discussed in this chapter. Many of these desserts are classic presentations requiring the precise arrangement of specific components. With a basic mastery of the skills discussed in this book, student chefs can use creativity, taste and judgment to combine these components into a wide selection of new, unique and tempting desserts.

Assembled pastries and other desserts generally consist of three principal components: the base, the filling and the garnish. The **base** is the dough, crust or cake product that provides structure and forms the foundation for the final product. The **filling** refers to whatever is used to add flavor, texture and body to the final product. The **garnish** is any glaze, fruit, sauce or accompaniment used to complete the dish.

GUIDELINES FOR **ASSEMBLING DESSERTS**

❶ There should be a proper blend of complementary and contrasting flavors. For example, pears, red wine and blue cheese go well together, as do chocolate and raspberries. Do not combine flavors simply for the sake of originality, however.

❷ There should be a proper blend of complementary and contrasting textures. For example, crisp puff pastry, soft pastry cream and tender strawberries are combined for a strawberry napoleon.

❸ There should be a proper blend of complementary and contrasting colors. For example, a garnish of red raspberries and green mint adds life to a brown-on-brown chocolate torte.

❹ Garnishes should not be overly fussy or garish.

❺ The base should be strong enough to hold the filling and garnish without collapsing, yet thin or tender enough to cut easily with a fork.

❻ The filling or garnish may cause the base to become soft or even soggy. This may or may not be desirable. If you want a crisp base, assemble the product very close to service. If you want this softening to occur, assemble the product in advance of service.

❼ Consider the various storage and keeping qualities of the individual components. It may be best to assemble or finish some products at service time.

❽ The final construction should not be so elaborate or fragile that it cannot be portioned or served easily or attractively.

❾ Consider whether the product would be better prepared as individual portions or as one large item. This may depend on the desired plate presentation and the ease and speed with which a large product can be cut and portioned for service.

Cheesecake baked in individual molds, pineapple kebab and mango sorbet garnished with fresh fruit and chopped nuts.

Desserts and the pastry chefs who create them are getting top billing along with the heretofore more prominent chefs de cuisine. Plated desserts may include several sweets on one visually stunning plate: a main item served hot accompanied by a contrasting cold garnish and something acidic or crunchy as a contrast. Today's restaurant desserts are a far cry from a humble slice of apple pie and scoop of ice cream, although a well-crafted pie using ripe fruit in season cannot be beat. With the popularity of plated desserts, pastry chefs have more opportunity to develop their style. Many concepts for presenting desserts are covered in more detail in Chapter 35, Plate Presentation. Striking a balance among contrasting tastes, textures and temperatures on a dessert plate makes desserts that appeal to all the senses.

Terms to Know

pastry cream	gelato
sabayon	sorbet
Bavarian cream	semifreddi
chiffon	churned
mousse	custard
charlotte	

1. Eggs and dairy products are susceptible to bacterial contamination. What precautions should be taken to avoid food-borne illnesses when preparing custards?

2. Explain why pastry cream should be boiled and why custard sauce should not be boiled.

3. Identify three desserts that are based on a baked custard.

4. Compare a classically prepared Bavarian, chiffon, mousse and soufflé. How are they similar? How are they different?

5. Describe the procedure for making a typical still-frozen dessert. What is the purpose of including whipped cream or whipped egg whites?

6. Explain three ways in which sweet sauces can be used in preparing or presenting a dessert.

7. Locate the Web sites of three manufacturers or distributors of prepared dessert sauces. How do you think these products compare with sauces that you could make from scratch? What additional information—not available on the Internet—would you need in order to make a decision about using these sauces? **WWW**

CRÈME BRÛLÉE

VINCENT ON CAMELBACK, PHOENIX, AZ
Chef Vincent Guerithault

Yield: 3½ qt. (3.5 lt) **Method:** Stirred custard

Heavy cream	2 qt.	2 lt
Vanilla beans, split	2	2
Egg yolks	50	50
Granulated sugar	20 oz.	600 g
Fresh berries	as needed	as needed
Tulipe Cookie cups (page 1005)	as needed	as needed
Granulated sugar	as needed	as needed

1. Place the cream and the vanilla beans in a large, heavy saucepan. Heat just to a boil.
2. Whisk the egg yolks and sugar together until smooth and well blended.
3. Temper the egg mixture with one-third of the hot cream. Return the egg mixture to the saucepan and cook, stirring constantly, until very thick. Do not allow the custard to boil.
4. Remove from the heat and strain into a clean bowl. Cool over an ice bath, stirring occasionally.
5. To serve, place fresh berries in the bottom of each Tulipe Cookie cup. Top with several spoonsful of custard.
6. Sprinkle granulated sugar over the top of the custard and caramelize with a propane torch. Serve immediately.

VARIATION:

Passion Fruit Crème Brûlée—Replace ½ quart (500 milliliters) cream with ½ quart (500 milliliters) frozen, thawed passion fruit purée.

Approximate values per 5-fl.-oz. (150-ml) serving: **Calories** 460, **Total fat** 36 g, **Saturated fat** 20 g, **Cholesterol** 480 mg, **Sodium** 135 mg, **Total carbohydrates** 26 g, **Protein** 7 g, **Vitamin A** 50%

CHOCOLATE POTS DE CRÈME

Yield: 8 Servings, 4 oz. (120 ml) each **Method:** Baked custard

Milk	1 pt.	480 ml
Bittersweet chocolate	8 oz.	240 g
Granulated sugar	7 oz.	210 g
Vanilla extract	1 tsp.	5 ml
Coffee liqueur	1 fl. oz.	30 ml
Egg yolks	7	7

1. Heat the milk just to a simmer. Add the chocolate and sugar. Stir constantly until the chocolate melts; do not allow the mixture to boil. Remove from the heat and add the vanilla and liqueur.
2. Whisk the egg yolks together, then slowly whisk them into the chocolate mixture.
3. Pour the custard into ramekins. Place the ramekins in a hotel pan and add enough hot water to reach halfway up the sides of the ramekins.
4. Bake at 325°F (160°C) until the custards are almost set in the center, approximately 30 minutes. Remove from the water bath and refrigerate until thoroughly chilled. Serve garnished with whipped cream and chocolate shavings.

Approximate values per serving: **Calories** 360, **Total fat** 16 g, **Saturated fat** 9 g, **Cholesterol** 195 mg, **Sodium** 40 mg, **Total carbohydrates** 46 g, **Protein** 6 g, **Vitamin A** 10%, **Calcium** 10%

NEW YORK CHEESECAKE

Yield: 2 Cakes, 8 in. (20 cm) each   **Method:** Baked custard

Graham crackers, crushed	1 lb.	480 g
Butter, melted	6 oz.	180 g
Cream cheese, room temperature	3 lb. 6 oz.	1620 g
Granulated sugar	14 oz.	420 g
Eggs	8	8
Cake flour or cornstarch	2 oz.	60 g
Vanilla extract	1 Tbsp.	15 ml
Lemon zest, grated fine	1½ tsp.	7 ml
Heavy cream	14 fl. oz.	420 ml

1. Combine the graham cracker crumbs with the melted butter. Press the mixture into the bottom of two 8-inch (20-centimeter) round springform pans. Bake for 12 to 15 minutes at 375°F (180°C) until the crust is dry to the touch. Set aside.
2. Blend the cream cheese and sugar on low speed in the bowl of a mixer fitted with the paddle attachment until no lumps remain. Scrape down the bowl often.
3. Add the eggs one at a time, waiting for each egg to be fully incorporated before adding more. Scrape down the bowl and paddle between each addition.
4. Add the flour and mix until combined. Add the remaining ingredients and mix to blend.
5. Divide the cheesecake batter evenly between the two pans. Wrap the bottom and sides of each pan in several layers of aluminum foil.
6. Preheat the oven to 300°F (150°C). Place the batter-filled pans in a hotel pan and set the hotel pan in the preheated oven. Pour in enough water to come halfway up the sides of the pans. Bake until the batter is set and no longer trembles, approximately 75 to 90 minutes.
7. Cool the cakes on a wire rack in their pans, then refrigerate them overnight. Remove the cakes from the pan.

Approximate values per ⅛-cake serving: **Calories** 770, **Total fat** 57 g, **Saturated fat** 34 g, **Cholesterol** 265 mg, **Sodium** 500 mg, **Total carbohydrates** 53 g, **Protein** 13 g, **Vitamin A** 40%, **Iron** 15%

TURTLE CHEESECAKE

Yield: 2 Cakes, 8 in. (20 cm) each   **Method:** Baked custard

Granulated sugar	6 oz.	180 g
Corn syrup	1½ oz.	45 g
Water	3 fl. oz.	90 ml
Honey	2 oz.	60 g
Heavy cream, heated	6 fl. oz.	180 ml
Walnuts	5 oz.	150 g
Pecans	4 oz.	120 g
Vanilla extract	½ fl. oz.	15 ml
New York Cheesecake (page 1070), baked	2	2
Crème Chantilly (page 1057; optional)	as needed	as needed

1. In a deep saucepan, bring the sugar, corn syrup and water to a boil.
2. Wash down any crystals that cling to the sides of the pan with a brush dipped in water. Cook the mixture without stirring until it turns a golden caramel color, approximately 350°F (175°C).
3. Add the honey and heated cream; be aware that the caramel mixture will rise when these ingredients are added. Reboil the mixture until it darkens to a medium amber color, approximately 3 to 4 minutes.

④ Remove from heat and add walnuts and pecans. Let cool to room temperature, then stir in the vanilla.

⑤ Spread the warmed icing over the cheesecakes. Once the caramel topping has cooled, decorate with Crème Chantilly (if using). Let the caramel filling set before cutting.

Approximate values per ½-cake serving: **Calories** 660, **Total fat** 114 g, **Saturated fat** 63 g, **Cholesterol** 442 mg, **Sodium** 615 mg, **Total carbohydrates** 103 g, **Protein** 22 g, **Vitamin A** 45%, **Iron** 15%

BREAD PUDDING WITH BOURBON SAUCE

Yield: 20 Servings

Method: Baked custard

Raisins	8 oz.	240 g
Brandy	4 fl. oz.	120 ml
Unsalted butter, melted	2 oz.	60 g
White bread, day-old	24 oz.	720 g
Heavy cream	2 qt.	1.9 lt
Eggs	6	6
Granulated sugar	1 lb. 10 oz.	780 g
Vanilla extract	1 fl. oz.	30 ml
Bourbon Sauce (recipe follows)	as needed	as needed

① Combine the raisins and brandy in a small saucepan. Heat just to a simmer, cover and set aside.

② Use a portion of the butter to thoroughly coat a 2-inch- (5-centimeter-) deep hotel pan. Reserve the remaining butter.

③ Tear the bread into chunks and place in a large bowl. Pour the cream over the bread and set aside until soft.

④ Beat the eggs and sugar until smooth and thick. Add the vanilla, the remaining melted butter and the raisins and brandy.

⑤ Toss the egg mixture with the bread gently to blend. Pour into the hotel pan and bake at 350°F (180°C) until browned and almost set, approximately 45 minutes.

⑥ Serve warm with 1–1½ fluid ounces (30–45 milliliters) Bourbon Sauce.

VARIATION:

Chocolate Bread Pudding—Omit the brandy, raisins and butter. Melt 6 ounces (180 grams) unsalted butter and 12 ounces (360 grams) bittersweet chocolate together. Add the chocolate and butter to the egg mixture in Step 4. Serve with Vanilla Custard Sauce (page 1050).

Approximate values per serving: **Calories** 700, **Total fat** 44 g, **Saturated fat** 26 g, **Cholesterol** 270 mg, **Sodium** 260 mg, **Total carbohydrates** 67 g, **Protein** 9 g, **Vitamin A** 50%, **Calcium** 10%, **Iron** 10%

BOURBON SAUCE

Yield: 1 qt. (960 ml)

Unsalted butter	8 oz.	240 g
Granulated sugar	1 lb.	480 g
Eggs	2	2
Bourbon	8 fl. oz.	240 ml

① Melt the butter; stir in the sugar and eggs and simmer to thicken.

② Add the bourbon and hold in a warm place for service.

Approximate values per 1-fl.-oz. (30-ml) serving: **Calories** 150, **Total fat** 8 g, **Saturated fat** 5 g, **Cholesterol** 40 mg, **Sodium** 50 mg, **Total carbohydrates** 19 g, **Protein** 1 g, **Vitamin A** 8%

CHERRY CLAFOUTI

Yield: 1 Cake, 10 in. (25 cm)	**Method:** Baked custard	
Dark cherries, fresh or canned, pitted	1 lb.	480 g
Eggs	4	4
Milk	12 fl. oz.	360 ml
Granulated sugar	2 oz.	60 g
Vanilla extract	1 tsp.	5 ml
All-purpose flour	2 oz.	60 g
Powdered sugar	as needed	as needed

1. Drain the cherries and pat them completely dry with paper towels. Arrange them evenly on the bottom of a buttered 10-inch (25-centimeter) pan. Do not use a springform pan or removable-bottom tartlet pan.
2. Make the custard by whisking the eggs and milk together. Add the granulated sugar, vanilla and flour and continue whisking until all the lumps are removed.
3. Pour the custard over the cherries and bake at 325°F (160°C) for 1 to 1½ hours. The custard should be lightly browned and firm to the touch when done.
4. Dust with powdered sugar and serve the clafouti while still warm.

Approximate values per ⅒-cake serving: **Calories** 170, **Total fat** 3.5 g, **Saturated fat** 1.5 g, **Cholesterol** 90 mg, **Sodium** 4.5 mg, **Total carbohydrates** 30 g, **Protein** 5 g, **Vitamin A** 6%

Clafouti is a country-style dessert from the Loire region of France and is similar to a quiche. Stone fruits such as cherries, peaches or plums are baked in an egg custard, then served piping hot or at room temperature.

LEMON CURD

Yield: 1½ qt. (1.4 lt)	**Method:** Stirred custard	
Eggs	12	12
Egg yolks	4	4
Granulated sugar	2 lb.	960 g
Unsalted butter, cubed	1 lb.	480 g
Lemon zest	1 oz.	30 g
Fresh lemon juice	12 fl. oz.	360 ml

1. Whisk everything together in a large metal bowl.
2. Place the bowl over a pan of simmering water and cook, stirring frequently, until very thick, approximately 20 to 25 minutes.
3. Strain, cover and chill completely. Serve with scones or use as a filling for tartlets or layer cakes.

VARIATION:

Lime Curd—Substitute lime juice and zest for the lemon juice.

Approximate values per 1-fl.-oz. (30-ml) serving: **Calories** 170, **Total fat** 9 g, **Saturated fat** 5 g, **Cholesterol** 90 mg, **Sodium** 20 mg, **Total carbohydrates** 20 g, **Protein** 2 g, **Vitamin A** 10%

WHITE CHOCOLATE FRANGELICO BAVARIAN

Yield: 4 qt. (3.8 lt)

Heavy cream	2 qt.	1.9 lt
White chocolate, chopped	2 lb.	960 g
Frangelico (hazelnut liqueur)	10 fl. oz.	300 ml
Sheet gelatin, softened	¾ oz.	21 g
Vanilla extract	2 tsp.	10 ml

1. Bring 1 quart (1 liter) cream just to a boil. Immediately pour over the chopped chocolate. Stir until the chocolate melts.
2. Gently heat the Frangelico just to a simmer. Remove from the heat and stir in the gelatin, one softened sheet at a time.
3. Add the gelatin mixture to the chocolate. Stir to blend well. Cool over an ice bath, stirring frequently.
4. Whip the remaining cream with the vanilla to stiff peaks.
5. Fold the whipped cream into the chocolate mixture. Chill several hours until set.

Approximate values per 4-fl.-oz. (120-ml) serving: **Calories** 400, **Total fat** 32 g, **Saturated fat** 21 g, **Cholesterol** 90 mg, **Sodium** 50 mg, **Total carbohydrates** 22 g, **Protein** 5 g, **Vitamin A** 25%

CHEESE SOUFFLÉ

Yield: 6 Servings

Butter	2 oz.	60 g
All-purpose flour	3 oz.	90 g
Milk	12 fl. oz.	360 ml
Salt	½ tsp.	2 ml
Cayenne pepper	¼ tsp.	1 ml
Eggs, separated	6	6
Gruyère cheese, grated	8 oz.	240 g
Cream of tartar	⅛ tsp.	0.5 g
Parmesan, grated	4 Tbsp.	60 ml

1. Make a blond roux with the butter and flour. Cook 1 minute, then whisk in the milk. Cook, stirring constantly, until thickened, approximately 2 minutes. Whisk in the salt, cayenne and egg yolks. Let cool slightly.
2. Stir in the Gruyère. Scrape the soufflé base into a large bowl.
3. Whip the egg whites until foamy, then add the cream of tartar. Whip the mixture until stiff but not dry. Fold the whites into the soufflé base in three additions.
4. To bake the soufflés, brush 6 individual-serving-sized ramekins lightly with melted butter and sprinkle with 2 tablespoons (30 milliliters) Parmesan. Pipe the mixture into the prepared ramekins to within ¼ inch (6 millimeters) of the rim. Sprinkle with the remaining Parmesan.
5. Bake immediately at 400°F (200°C) until well puffed and lightly browned, approximately 20 to 25 minutes. Do not touch the soufflés to test doneness.

Approximate values per serving: **Calories** 400, **Total fat** 28 g, **Saturated fat** 6 g, **Cholesterol** 280 mg, **Sodium** 470 mg, **Total carbohydrates** 14 g, **Protein** 22 g, **Vitamin A** 20%, **Calcium** 50%

RASPBERRY MOUSSE

Yield: 1 qt. (1 lt)

Raspberries, puréed	12 oz.	360 g
Granulated sugar	3 oz.	90 g
Raspberry brandy	1 fl. oz.	30 ml
Sheet gelatin, softened	¼ oz.	7 g
Heavy cream	8 fl. oz.	240 ml

1 Place the raspberry purée, sugar and brandy in a nonreactive saucepan and warm just to dissolve the sugar. Remove from the heat and strain through a fine chinois.

2 Add the softened gelatin, stirring until it is dissolved. Chill the mixture until thick but not set.

3 Whip the cream to soft peaks and fold it into the raspberry mixture.

Approximate values per 3-fl.-oz. (90-ml) serving: **Calories** 180, **Total fat** 11 g, **Saturated fat** 7 g, **Cholesterol** 40 mg, **Sodium** 15 mg, **Total carbohydrates** 16 g, **Protein** 5 g, **Vitamin A** 10%

1 Adding the softened gelatin sheets to the warm raspberry purée.

2 Folding the softly whipped cream into the chilled raspberry purée.

LEMON SORBET

VINCENT ON CAMELBACK, PHOENIX, AZ

Chef Vincent Guerithault

Yield: 1½ qt. (1.5 lt)

Lemon juice	1 pt.	500 ml
Water	1 pt.	500 ml
Granulated sugar	1 lb.	500 g

1 Combine all the ingredients in a large bowl. Stir until the sugar dissolves completely.

2 Pour the mixture into an ice cream/sorbet machine and process according to the manufacturer's directions.

3 The finished sorbet will be rather soft. Pack it into a storage container and freeze at a temperature of 0°F (−18°C) or lower until firm.

Approximate values per 1½-fl.-oz. (45-ml) serving: **Calories** 25, **Total fat** 0 g, **Saturated fat** 0 g, **Cholesterol** 0 mg, **Sodium** 0 mg, **Total carbohydrates** 6 g, **Protein** 0 g, **Claims**—fat free; no sodium; low calorie

COFFEE GRANITA

Granita (Fr. granité), which is very similar to an Italian ice, is made with fruit or other flavorings but with less sugar than sorbet. This produces a mixture that will freeze harder than sorbet. Instead of being churned, the granita mixture is still-frozen in a shallow stainless steel container, then scraped with a fork or spoon to obtain grainy flakes. Or, as the mixture freezes and ice crystals form, the mixture is periodically stirred until granulation is complete.

Yield: 1½ pt. (720 ml)

Water	20 fl. oz.	600 ml
Granulated sugar	5 oz.	150 g
Coffee, ground	¾ oz.	21 g

1 Bring 4 fluid ounces (120 milliliters) water and the sugar to a boil. Stir to dissolve the sugar. Remove the syrup from the heat and let cool.

2 Bring the remaining 16 fluid ounces (480 milliliters) water to a boil. Add the coffee and steep for 5 minutes. Strain the mixture and set aside to cool.

3 Combine the sugar syrup with the coffee liquid.

4 Pour into a shallow stainless steel pan and freeze until the granita begins to harden, approximately 3 hours.

5 Scrape the surface of the granita with a metal fork or spoon to break up the ice crystals. Return the granita to the freezer until firm.

6 Scrape the surface of the frozen granita to loosen the ice crystals. Scoop into serving dishes and serve immediately.

Approximate values per 4-fl.-oz. (120-ml) serving: **Calories** 100, **Total fat** 0 g, **Saturated fat** 0 g, **Cholesterol** 0 mg, **Sodium** 0 mg, **Total carbohydrates** 26 g, **Protein** 0 g, **Vitamin C** 15%. **Claims**—no fat; no cholesterol; very low sodium

1 When the mixture has begun to freeze, scrape the ice crystals as they form in the granita.

2 Spoon the finished granita into a serving dish and serve immediately.

CHOCOLATE HAZELNUT MARQUISE
WITH FRANGELICO SAUCE

Yield: 12 Servings

Melted butter	as needed	as needed
Dark chocolate	1 lb.	480 g
Unsalted butter	4 oz.	120 g
Hazelnuts, roasted, skinned and chopped coarse	4 oz.	120 g
Egg yolks, pasteurized	6	6
Frangelico (hazelnut liqueur)	2 fl. oz.	60 ml
Egg whites, pasteurized	6	6
Salt	1 pinch	1 pinch
Frangelico Custard Sauce (page 1050)	as needed	as needed
Hazelnuts, roasted and chopped coarse	as needed for garnish	
Raspberries	as needed for garnish	
Fresh mint	as needed for garnish	

1. Line a terrine mold with melted butter and parchment paper.
2. Melt the chocolate and unsalted butter over a bain marie. Remove from the heat and stir in the nuts, egg yolks and Frangelico. Set aside to cool to room temperature. Do not use an ice bath, as the chocolate will solidify.
3. Whip the egg whites with the salt until stiff but not dry. Fold the whipped whites into the chocolate mixture.
4. Pour the mixture into the terrine mold and freeze overnight.
5. Remove the marquise from the mold and peel off the paper. (Work quickly because this melts quickly.) While the loaf is still frozen, use a hot knife to slice it into ⅓-inch- (8-millimeter-) thick slices. Return the marquise to the freezer until just before service.
6. Serve two slices on a pool of Frangelico Custard Sauce. Garnish with coarsely chopped hazelnuts, fresh raspberries and fresh mint.

Approximate values per serving: **Calories** 380, **Total fat** 28 g, **Saturated fat** 14 g, **Cholesterol** 125 mg, **Sodium** 35 mg, **Total carbohydrates** 25 g, **Protein** 6 g, **Vitamin A** 10%

FRUIT COULIS

Yield: 1 lb. 4 oz. (600 g)

Fruit purée, strained	16 oz.	480 g
Granulated sugar	2½ oz.	75 g
Glucose or corn syrup	1 oz.	30 g
Lemon juice	½ fl. oz.	15 ml

1. Combine the strained fruit purée with the sugar and glucose or corn syrup. Add as much lemon juice as needed to balance the flavor of the sauce.
2. Serve warm or cold.

Approximate values per 1-oz. (30-g) serving: **Calories** 35, **Total fat** 0 g, **Saturated fat** 0 g, **Cholesterol** 0 mg, **Sodium** 5 mg, **Total carbohydrates** 8 g, **Protein** 0 g, **Claims** low fat; no cholesterol; low sodium

BUTTERSCOTCH SAUCE

Yield: Approximately 2 qt. (2 lt)

Granulated sugar	1 lb. 8 oz.	720 g
Light corn syrup	2 lb. 4 oz.	1 kg
Unsalted butter	4 oz.	120 g
Heavy cream	10 fl. oz.	300 ml
Scotch whisky	4 fl. oz.	120 ml

1 Cook the sugar to a dark brown caramel. Add the corn syrup.

2 Remove the sugar from the heat and slowly add the butter and cream, stirring until the butter is completely melted.

3 Stir in the Scotch and cool.

Approximate values per 1-fl.-oz. (30-ml) serving: **Calories** 120, **Total fat** 3 g, **Saturated fat** 2 g, **Cholesterol** 23 mg, **Sodium** 20 mg, **Total carbohydrates** 23 g, **Protein** 0 g, **Vitamin A** 4%, **Claims**—low fat; low cholesterol; very low sodium

CHOCOLATE FUDGE SAUCE

Yield: Approximately 1 gal. (4 lt)

Heavy cream	2 qt.	1.9 lt
Light corn syrup	6 fl. oz.	180 ml
Granulated sugar	8 oz.	240 g
Bittersweet chocolate	4 lb.	1.9 kg

1 Combine the cream, corn syrup and sugar in a saucepan and bring just to a boil, stirring frequently.

2 Chop the chocolate and place in a large bowl.

3 Pour the hot cream over the chocolate and stir until completely melted.

4 Store well covered and refrigerated. Gently rewarm over a bain marie if desired.

Approximate values per 1-fl.-oz. (30-ml) serving: **Calories** 130, **Total fat** 9 g, **Saturated fat** 6 g, **Cholesterol** 20 mg, **Sodium** 10 mg, **Total carbohydrates** 10 g, **Protein** 1 g, **Vitamin A** 6%

ESPRESSO SAUCE

CHRISTOPHER'S RESTAURANT AND CRUSH LOUNGE, PHOENIX, AZ
Chef-Owner Christopher Gross

Yield: Approximately 1½ pt. (720 ml)

Egg yolks	8	8
Granulated sugar	3½ oz.	100 g
Half-and-half	1 pt.	480 ml
Espresso beans, whole	3 oz.	90 g
Vanilla bean	½	½

1 Whisk the egg yolks and sugar together in a medium bowl.

2 Bring the half-and-half, espresso beans and vanilla bean to a simmer in a heavy saucepan.

3 Temper the egg yolks with a portion of the hot half-and-half, then return the mixture to the saucepan. Cook over low heat, stirring constantly, until the sauce is thick enough to coat the back of a spoon. Strain and cool over an ice bath.

Approximate values per 1-fl.-oz. (30-ml) serving: **Calories** 60, **Total fat** 4 g, **Saturated fat** 2 g, **Cholesterol** 75 mg, **Sodium** 10 mg, **Total carbohydrates** 5 g, **Protein** 2 g, **Vitamin A** 6%

CHAPTER THIRTY-FIVE

PLATE PRESENTATION

FINALLY, THE REAL TEST HAS COME. It is time to put down the spatula and set the whisk aside. The food must be served. But it is important that the creativity and skill that went into cooking, baking or otherwise preparing the foods are not wasted because of a sloppy presentation or an unattractive setting.

Although food preparation is very much a science, food presentation is an art. Good plate presentation results from careful attention to the colors, shapes, textures and arrangements of the foods. Great plate presentation requires experience and style.

This chapter describes several methods of presenting foods. For every guideline suggested, there are exceptions. Nor are these examples meant to take the place of more traditional techniques. They are intended only to spark the imagination. With experience, a chef's personal style will evolve. The final step in food preparation is to justify the hours of hard work spent cooking the food by serving and presenting it properly.

Service is the process of delivering the selected foods to diners in the proper fashion. Hot foods should be served very hot and on heated plates; cold foods should be served very cold and on chilled plates. Foods should be cooked to the proper degree of doneness: A roast rack of lamb ordered medium rare should be medium rare—not medium, not rare. Pasta should be served al dente—slightly chewy, not mushy. Bread should be fresh, not stale. Portion sizes should be appropriate. First courses and appetizers should be small enough so that the diner can still appreciate the courses that follow.

Presentation is the process of offering the selected foods to diners in a fashion that is visually pleasing. When presenting foods, always bear in mind that diners consume first with their eyes and then with their mouths. The foods must be pleasantly and appropriately colored, cut or molded. The colors, textures, shapes and arrangements of all foods must work together to form a pleasing composition on the plate. Any decorative touches such as the manipulation of sauces or the addition of garnishes should be done thoughtfully and well. Most important, plates should be neat and clean. Inspect all plates before they leave the kitchen; wipe fingerprints, drops of sauce or specks of food from their rims with a clean towel.

Presentation techniques are divided here into two broad categories: those applied to specific foods and those applied to the plate as a whole. Most of the techniques and concepts described here are illustrated with foods or recipes that appear elsewhere in the text. A brief discussion on small plates concludes the chapter.

THE FOOD

The most attractive foods will always be the ones that are properly prepared, but they can be made even more attractive by cutting or molding them into various shapes. Both of these techniques preserve the integrity of the food; that is, neither changes the food itself, but only changes the way the food is presented.

Preparing Foods Properly

Foods look best when prepared properly. A sirloin steak grilled medium rare should be pink inside; its surface should glisten and be branded with well-defined and neatly executed crosshatch marks. When serving asparagus with hollandaise, the stalks should be bright green and crisp looking; the hollandaise sauce should be smooth and shiny, not grainy and dingy. A lemon meringue pie should be attractively browned on top; the filling should be a true lemony yellow and the crust golden brown and without cracks.

Whether a recipe calls for browning foods under a salamander before service, poaching a galantine of chicken wrapped in cheesecloth to maintain its shape or adding vinegar when braising red cabbage, proper cooking procedures can enhance the texture, shape and color of many cooked foods. Throughout this text, we have discussed the proper cooking procedures for many, many foods. Use them.

Fried Julienned Carrots

Cutting Foods

The careful cutting of foods often increases their visual appeal and reflects the chef's attention to detail. Here we distinguish between cutting foods to decorate the plate and cutting the foods to be consumed. Decorative garnishes such as tomato and radish roses, scallion brushes, watermelon boats and the like, fall within the former category. Cutting foods into beautiful garnishes is an art unto itself, requiring skill and practice. Although beyond the scope of this text, books on creating food garnishes are listed in the Bibliography.

The latter category includes the meats, poultry, fish, shellfish, vegetables and starches that are the meal. Each should be carefully cut. Vegetables can be cut into uniform shapes and sizes such as julienne, bâtonnet or tournée. Firm vegetables such as beets, carrots, leeks, lotus root, parsnips, potatoes, scallions and turnips can be sliced or julienned and deep-fried to add color, flavor and texture to a plated dish.

Fried Julienned Leeks

If serving sliced meats or poultry, the slices should be of an even thickness; fish can be cut into tranches. Individual stew ingredients and soup or salad garnishes should be of uniform sizes. All these techniques are simple, fundamental and effective.

Some foods take the shape of the pan in which they are cooked. Polenta and gratin or escalloped potatoes, for example, can be presented attractively when baked in and removed from individual casseroles, or they can be baked in a hotel pan and then cut into various shapes.

Fried Sliced Lotus Root

PROCEDURE FOR **CUTTING POLENTA**

Cutting polenta into various shapes.

1 Cook the polenta according to the recipe. When it is done, pour it onto a well-oiled half-sheet pan. Then chill it until firm.

2 Once the polenta is firm, flip the pan over onto a worktable. Lift off the pan; the polenta will come out easily. Using a chef's knife or circular cutters, cut the polenta into the desired shape. The polenta can be sautéed or grilled for service.

PROCEDURE FOR **CUTTING GRATIN OR ESCALLOPED POTATOES**

Cutting potatoes with a circular cutter.

1 Select a recipe that produces a firm finished product so that the finished dish will hold its shape after cutting.

2 Bake the potatoes in a well-greased pan and refrigerate until cold and firm. Then cut the potatoes into various shapes with a chef's knife or circular cutters and remove them to a clean pan with a spatula.

3 For service, reheat the potatoes in a 325°F (160°C) oven until hot.

Molding Foods

Some foods, particularly grains or vegetables bound by sauces, can be molded into attractive shapes by using metal rings, circular cutters or other forms. These molded forms create height and keep the plate neat and clean.

PROCEDURE FOR **MOLDING GRAINS**

Unmolding a timbale of rice.

1 Fill a timbale, soup cup or other mold of the appropriate size and shape with the hot grains, firmly pressing them together.

2 For à la carte service, immediately unmold the grains onto the serving plate by placing the mold upside down on the plate and tapping its rim.

3 For banquet service, place the filled molds in a hotel pan and refrigerate until needed. Shortly before service, fill the hotel pan with hot water to a point about two-thirds up the side of the molds. Be careful not to splash any water onto the grains. Cover the pan with foil and place in the oven. Heat until the grains are hot, then plate as desired.

PROCEDURE FOR **MOLDING VEGETABLES**

1 Position a ring mold on the plate and fill it with the vegetables. Press the foods into the ring to help them hold the shape. Level the top.

2 Carefully lift off the ring.

Many soft and creamy foods can be molded into small ovals such as for the dumpling-shaped quenelle discussed in Chapter 27, Charcuterie. Purées and mousses such as mashed potatoes, risotto and salmon mousseline as well as ice creams, custards and sorbets can be attractively shaped using two large spoons.

THE PLATE

Properly cooked, carefully cut and appropriately molded foods should not be haphazardly slapped onto a plate. Rather, choose and position the foods carefully to achieve a plate presentation with a balanced, harmonious **composition**.

The composition can be further enhanced by decorating the plate with garnishes, crumbs or sauces. Some of these techniques (for example, decorating the plate with powdered sugar) do not substantially affect the flavors of the foods; they only make the completed presentation more attractive. Other techniques (for example, garnishing a dessert with finely chopped nuts or painting a plate with two sauces) add flavor and texture to the finished dish.

Choosing Plates

Restaurant china designed to withstand the rigors of repeated use is available in many different shapes, sizes, colors and styles. It is often the chef's responsibility to choose the china appropriate for the food being served. Frequently, specific plates will be used for specific dishes, such as a tulip sundae glass for an ice cream dish.

SIZES AND SHAPES

Most plates are round, but oval plates (also referred to as platters) and rectangular, square and triangular plates are becoming more common. Plates are available in a variety of sizes from a small 4-inch (10-centimeter) bread plate to a huge 14-inch (35-centimeter) charger or base plate. Plates are typically concave; their depths vary within a limited range of about 1 inch (2.5 centimeters). Most plates have rims; rim widths also vary. Soup bowls can be rimmed or rimless. Soup plates are usually larger and shallower than soup bowls and have wide rims. Soup cups are also available. There are also dozens of plate designs intended

Forming grapefruit sorbet into a quenelle shape using two spoons.

composition a completed plate's structure of colors, shapes and arrangements

Salmon mousse with smoked salmon garnish.

Grilled prawn brochette with butternut squash risotto.

for a specific purpose, such as plates with small indentations for holding escargots, or long, rectangular plates with grooves for holding asparagus.

Choose plates large enough to hold the food comfortably without overcrowding or spilling. Oversized, rimmed soup plates are popular for serving any food with a sauce. Be careful when using oversized plates, however, as the food may look sparse, creating poor value perception.

Whether a round, oval or less conventionally shaped plate is used, be sure to choose one with a size and shape that best highlights the food and supports the composition. For example, in the photograph to the left, the pentagon-shaped bowl with graceful curved edges and raised rim accentuates the geometrically simple yet effective composition of the oval salmon timbale draped with a slice of smoked salmon.

COLORS AND PATTERNS

White and cream are by far the most common colors for restaurant china. Almost any food looks good on these neutral colors.

Colored and patterned plates can be used quite effectively to accent food, however. The obvious choice is to contrast dark plates with bright- or light-colored foods and light plates with dark-colored foods. The food should always be the focal point of any plate. The colors and shapes in the pattern should blend well and harmonize with the foods served. The crisp pattern of blue dots along the plate rim shown at left, for example, harmonizes well with the beige sauce and symmetrically placed shrimp skewers.

Arranging Foods on Plates

Plates should be composed to make the food appetizing to the customer. Strive for a well-balanced plate composition that can be achieved with careful consideration of the shapes, colors, textures and arrangement of foods on the plate.

SHAPES

For visual interest and pure drama, combine a variety of shapes on the plate. The plate shown below is an excellent example of simple shapes artfully combined: round venison medallions with oval fingerling potatoes and long spears of carrots and baby zucchini. The three complementary shapes lend harmony and character to the dish.

COLORS

Foods come in a rainbow of colors and to the extent appropriate, foods of different colors should be presented together. Generally, the colors should provide balance and contrast. But no matter how well prepared or planned, some dishes simply have dull, boring or similar colors. If so, try adding another ingredient or garnish for a splash of color. The flecks of crisp green chives shown here add striking color notes to a lobster dish that would otherwise be monochromatic. The artful placement of the lobster claws adds to the visual interest.

Venison medallions with black currant sauce.

Lobster à l'Americaine.

TEXTURES

Texture refers to the sensation perceived when eating a food as well as the appearance of the surface of the food. It may be crisp, crumbly, grainy, flaky, smooth or creamy. Mashed potatoes and carrot purée both look smooth and soft. Salmon mousseline and spinach soufflé both have slightly grainy surfaces. Rösti potatoes and meatloaf both appear coarse. The flavors of each food in these pairs differ; their visual textures do not.

Typically, foods with similar textures look boring together; foods with different textures look more exciting. Serve carrots cut into julienne with the mashed potatoes to achieve a balance of hard and soft textures; steamed leaf spinach with the salmon mousseline for a combination of smooth and grainy textures; and a baked potato with the meatloaf for pairing fluffy and coarse textures. These pairs generally maintain the same range of flavors as the first set of pairs while providing different visual textures.

Achieving a balance of texture on a plate can be as simple as adding a crisp garnish such as the fried julienned vegetables shown here served with a rack of lamb. The rack of lamb shown to the right harmoniously combines several textures in one dish: the pebbly rice, the slices of smooth lamb and coarse fried vegetables.

Rack of lamb garnished with fried julienned vegetables.

ARRANGEMENTS

Having decided on the colors, textures and shapes of the foods that will go on the plate, the next choice is where to place each individual item to achieve a balanced and unified composition. Mostly this takes judgment and style, but there are a few general guidelines.

GUIDELINES FOR **ARRANGING FOODS ON A PLATE**

1. Strike a balance between overcrowding the plate and leaving large gaps of space. Foods should not touch the plate rim nor necessarily be confined to the very center.

2. Choose a focal point for the plate—that is, the point to which the eye is drawn. This is usually the highest point on the plate. Design the plate with the highest point to the rear or center. Avoid placing foods of equal heights around the edge of the plate, leaving a hole in the center—the eye will naturally be drawn to that gap.

3. The plate's composition should flow naturally. For example, make the highest point the back of the plate and have the rest of the food become gradually shorter toward the front of the plate. Slicing and fanning foods can attract the eye and help establish flow.

Grilled duck with roasted vegetables.

The grilled duck with roasted vegetables shown here elegantly illustrates these principles. Height is established by a structure composed of the duck leg and thigh, sliced turnips and baby carrots. The structure sits toward the back of the plate. Its height, placement and striking appearance make it the focal point. The neatly sliced duck breast is then fanned across the plate in front of this focal point, drawing the viewer into the plate.

Decorating Plates

The colors, textures, shapes and arrangements of foods on a plate can be improved or highlighted by decorating a plate with herbs, greens, spices and other garnishes and sauces. If any of these are to be applied after the principal food is placed on the plate, be prepared to do so quickly so that the food is served at its proper temperature.

GARNISHING PLATES WITH HERBS AND GREENS

Using fresh herbs and greens is one of the easiest ways to add color, texture and flow to a plate. Whether the herbs or greens are an ingredient in the dish or merely a decoration, they should always complement the foods and be consistent with their seasonings. A sprig of fresh rosemary garnishing a beautifully roasted rack of lamb or tiny leaves of chervil garnishing delicately poached fillets of sole are natural combinations. Microgreens add a delicate-tasting, light and lacy garnish to many dishes. Sprigs of fresh green mint

Using herbs to garnish a plate of roast chicken.

Garnishing a plate with chopped fresh rosemary.

Garnishing an appetizer with microgreens.

Pistachio-crusted salmon with gingered dal and cilantro chutney.

Adding a foamed sauce to a risotto appetizer plate.

(often with a fresh berry or two or a strawberry cut in a fan) can be the perfect decoration for a dessert plate.

Provided they complement the food, very finely chopped nuts can also be used to decorate plates for sweet or savory foods. Plates for savory foods can also be decorated by sprinkling them with finely chopped herbs such as thyme or minced vegetables such as a combination of brightly colored peppers.

DECORATING PLATES WITH SAUCES

The sauce is an integral part of most any dish: It adds flavor and moisture; it also adds color, texture and flow to the plate. A rich, glossy bordelaise or Madeira sauce pooled beneath sautéed tournedos of beef is a classic example. A chunky cilantro chutney dabbed around a spicy nut-crusted salmon shown above is a more contemporary approach.

Sauces are also used in other, less traditional ways to add visual appeal. For example, cream sauces and light mousses can be foamed and applied as a complementary garnish using a whipped cream charger, such as that shown in this plate of risotto garnished with shrimp and corm mousse. Or, if a dish calls for a generous amount of sauce, allow the service staff to pour the sauce tableside after the dish is presented, as shown here. Tableside service adds drama to the presentation while keeping the sauce warm for service.

One or more colored sauces can also be used to paint plates. One technique is simply to drizzle or spoon the sauce onto the plate. In the photograph shown here, a rich

Pouring sauce over a fish and vegetable plate tableside.

Marinated loin of venison roasted with mustard.

Seared diver scallops with tomatillo sauce, avocado relish and tomato syrup.

game fond is boldly spooned onto the plate in an abstract swirl echoed in the curved shape of the venison chop. Such technique requires a deft hand.

Alternatively, one or more colored sauces can be applied to a plate using squirt bottles. On the preceding page, a tomato syrup is added to a plate of seared scallops with tomatillo sauce. Squirt bottles can also be used to create abstract patterns or representational designs. Salad dressings or reduced balsamic vinegar can be artfully squirted over some or all of a plate to create interest and eye appeal as shown here.

Painting plates with different-colored sauces also facilitates flow and adds color. Although this technique can be used with hot sauces, it is more often used with cold sauces (such as vanilla, caramel, chocolate and fruit-flavored ones) for dessert presentations. The sauces must be thick enough to hold the pattern and they should all be the same viscosity.

Macadamia nut-crusted halibut.

PROCEDURE FOR **PAINTING A SPIDER WEB DESIGN**

1 Pool one sauce evenly across the entire base of the plate, then apply a contrasting sauce onto the base sauce in a spiral.

2 Draw a thin-bladed knife or a toothpick through the sauces from the center point toward the edge. Then draw a knife blade or toothpick from the edge to the center.

Ring molds, skewers, spoons, spatulas and other simple kitchen tools help when applying sauces, as shown in the following examples.

Pulling a skewer through chocolate and raspberry-sauce dots to create a border of hearts.

Painting balsamic reduction on a plate with a pastry brush.

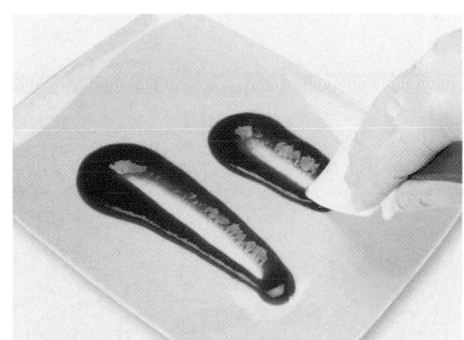

Running a spatula through a line of fruit coulis to create a shadow effect.

SMALL PLATES

Diminutive dishes once reserved for the start of a meal have taken hold as an eating style all its own, referred to as *small-plate dining*. For consumers seeking variety, eating three or more small plates can replace ordering a traditional appetizer and entrée. Each dish on a small-plate menu is usually reduced in size and price, often reducing the cost of dining out. Exposure to chef tasting menus where numerous dishes are served in dainty portions may be one reason why many are comfortable with this style of dining. Or perhaps ethnic dining styles such as Spanish tapas, Chinese dim sum and Middle Eastern mezze are giving consumers a taste for eclectic eating. Studies suggest that consumers view eating a variety of small plates as a less formal, more relaxed way of dining. Small plates allow customers to experiment and try new dishes while offering an alternative to larger portions of protein-dominated entrées at a lower cost.

Whatever the reason for the popularity of such menu offerings, the principles for composing a small plate are the same as for preparing and presenting any dish. Shapes, colors and textures of food should be chosen to enhance each item on the plate. Foods should be arranged with eye appeal, an essential component in ensuring guests' satisfaction. Although composition on each plate is important, balance in the selections of dishes offered on a small-plate menu is of prime consideration because guests often order three or more dishes to create a meal.

GUIDELINES FOR **CREATING SMALL PLATES**

▶ **Reduce the portion size of a conventional entrée.** From stews to sautés, any entrée can be adapted by reducing the portion size. In the photograph shown here, a 2- to 3-ounce portion of seared salmon accompanied by braised cabbage and sauce makes an appealing yet satisfying miniature dish.

Small portion of grilled salmon on a bed of braised cabbage and sauce.

▶ **Reduce the number of units served.** A single crab cake, grilled sausage or soft-shell crab, as shown here, would make an appealing small plate. Or serve an unconventionally large diver scallop accompanied by mushrooms and a few crisp potatoes. This dish satisfies the palate without satiating the diner.

Grilled soft-shell crab with citrus aïoli.

Seared diver scallop with chanterelles, potato gaufrettes and blood orange cream.

▶ **Use an unexpected garnish with a traditional protein.** Pairing a dish with a salad or vegetable instead of a heavier starch garnish lightens a conventional entrée. In the photograph below, baby greens dressed with hazelnut vinaigrette accompany a grilled duck breast more commonly served with scalloped potatoes or wild rice.

Warm duck breast salad with Asian spices and hazelnut vinaigrette.

▶ **Present entrée items in a new format.** Grilled brochettes or skewers of fish, game, meat or poultry served without garnishes are candidates for small-plate menus. A solitary jumbo shrimp wrapped in potato perched on a mold of spinach and two sauces is an elegant dish that provides visual appeal as well as a palate-pleasing textural contrast between the crisp potato crust and creamy spinach.

Veal kebabs.

Freshwater shrimp wrapped in potato.

▶ **Offer an assortment of starch dishes.** Small potato or grain dishes complement a variety of dishes. Perfectly crisp French fries or a more unexpected plate of grilled sweet potato dish make excellent accompaniments to any number of foods. Do not overlook pasta or risotto served in small portions. Guests are free to compose their own menu by combining a few small plates with a suitable starch.

Grilled sweet potatoes with poblano chiles.

▶ **Highlight vegetables as center of the plate items.** Vegetable dishes, especially in season, shine on small-plate menus. Early vegetables such as the grilled baby squash shown here make compelling small plates. Salads presented in a novel manner such as a mold of beet and corn salad or in a trio that can be shared among guests at the table satisfy the need for variety on small-plate menus.

Grilled baby squash with honey cardamom butter.

Beet and corn salad.

Trio of salads.

▶ **Look to the breakfast, lunch and appetizer menu for inspiration.** Crêpes, quiche and egg dishes make compelling small plates. Scotch eggs, hard-boiled eggs with assorted fillings, individual cheese soufflés, crêpes stuffed with mushrooms or mini quiches are often overlooked as components on small-plate menus. Also bear in mind the diminutive size of many appetizers, which naturally work well in the lineup of smaller dishes.

Spinach and mushroom crêpe.

▶ **Simplify the plating to compensate for the increased number of dishes needed.** When portions are small, customers will order more dishes, which means more plates to send out from the kitchen. Consider the time and labor needed to compose each plate when designing small-plate menus. Streamline the presentation accordingly.

❶ Explain why proper service and presentation are important in food service operations.

❷ Distinguish between cutting and molding foods for visual appeal and creating garnishes out of foods.

❸ How can the selection of serviceware such as bowls and platters affect the visual appeal of the foods served?

❹ List and describe four techniques for garnishing plates.

❺ Describe how color, texture, shape and arrangement can be used to create a well-balanced plate composition.

❻ Restaurant menus composed entirely of small dishes are popular across the country in both ethnic and traditional American-style restaurants. Use the Internet to research small-plate menus. Analyze two or three menus and discuss how many items are offered and how customers can create an evening's meal from the list of offerings. WWW

QUESTIONS FOR DISCUSSION

Terms to Know

service	painting sauces
presentation	eye appeal
garnishing	small-plate dining

CHAPTER THIRTY-SIX

BUFFET PRESENTATION

After studying this chapter, you will be able to:

- understand the basic principles of buffet presentation

- use a variety of techniques to create and maintain appealing buffets

A BUFFET OFFERS DINERS ALL THE DISHES from a selected menu, usually at one time, in a single, attractive setting. A buffet offers food service professionals the opportunity to exercise their creativity by identifying themes and then creating menus, displays and decorations with these themes in mind.

In this chapter, we use the word *buffet* to describe both the event at which all the dishes from a menu are served at once as well as the table on which these foods are displayed and from which diners serve themselves or are served by wait staff. Buffet foods can be virtually any of those found in this book.

PLANNING THE BUFFET

Buffets must be carefully designed to provide foods from a planned menu in an attractive fashion to a given number of people within a specified time. Doing this well requires a collaborative effort among the chef, the catering sales staff and the dining room manager, banquet manager or other senior front-of-the-house staff. Together, they identify the theme for the event and choose the menu. If the event is designed for a specific client, then the client should be invited to join in the planning.

The **theme** sets the tone of the event. It defines a motif: an elegant Sunday brunch, a black-and-white formal, a Mexican fiesta, a New England clambake. Regardless of the purpose for the event—a wedding, bar mitzvah, business luncheon, charity ball or the

Mozart-themed dessert buffet, Hotel Adlon Kempinski, Berlin, Germany.

like—the theme defines the menu, decorations, props, linens and dinnerware; it can even define the music, lighting and wait staff uniforms. In Figures 36.1 through 36.4, we present examples of menus, decorations and buffet plans for various themed events.

Once the theme is identified, a **menu** is designed. Essentially, a lunch or dinner buffet offers an à la carte menu; the only differences are that at a buffet, the foods are presented all at once and the diners generally serve themselves or are served by wait staff stationed at the buffet table. Like an à la carte menu, the buffet menu should contain selections of first courses (soups and/or salads), entrées (hot and/or cold meat, poultry, fish and/or shellfish dishes), accompaniments (vegetables, starches and breads), desserts and beverages. Depending on the event, the menu may need to reflect particular dietary or religious concerns, such as the need for vegetarian entrées or kosher-style selections. Although costs are a consideration, the principal factors limiting a menu are the client's desires and the chef's imagination.

When planning the menu, it is important to offer dishes consistent with the theme. If the theme is a Greek wedding feast, do not offer tortilla chips and salsa. It may be necessary, however, to occasionally bend this rule in order to include one of the client's favorite foods or to offer an item not traditionally associated with the theme, such as beef at a Hawaiian luau.

It is also important to consider visual appeal and avoid repetition. Therefore:

White asparagus festival centerpiece, Hotel Adlon Kempinski, Berlin, Germany.

▶ **Offer dishes featuring different principal ingredients**—This avoids repetition and offers diners a wider array of choices. Even fussy diners should be able to find something they want to eat. Therefore, if the buffet features two entrées, make one beef and the other poultry; if there is a third, use fish or shellfish. If there are two starch dishes, make one a pasta and the other a potato dish. Also, avoid repeating ingredients in different dishes; for example, if the entrée is a stir-fry of beef and broccoli, do not offer steamed broccoli as a vegetable side dish.

▶ **Offer foods cooked by different methods**—For example, serve beef bourguignonne (a hot braised meat dish), roast turkey (a hot or cold roasted poultry dish) and salmon with dill sauce (a cold poached fish dish). Again, this avoids repetition.

▶ **Offer foods with different colors**—Fettuccine Alfredo and poached fish in a béarnaise sauce may both taste good, but they look boring next to each other. Offer a salsa verde or pesto instead of the béarnaise sauce, or a penne with asparagus and tomatoes in place of the Alfredo. This will increase the buffet's visual appeal.

▶ **Offer foods with different textures**—If two or more soups are served, make one a clear soup and the other a cream or purée soup; use a variety of tossed and bound salads, each with different principal ingredients.

▶ **Offer seasonally appropriate foods**—A rich lamb stew may be easy to prepare and may hold well in a chafing dish, but it is not appropriate to offer at a summer luncheon. Offer sliced grilled leg of lamb as a lighter option.

▶ **Offer foods appropriate to the time of year**—Buffet menus may be planned months in advance. Consider the availability of the produce needed in the menu being offered. A fresh tomato, basil and mozzarella salad is ideal for a summer buffet but a poor choice in the winter months when hothouse tomatoes may be all that is available.

When defining the theme and creating the menu, costs must be considered. Often a client will place a limit on what he or she wants to spend for the buffet. It is then the responsibility of the chef, sales staff and/or dining room manager to create an attractive and satisfying buffet that meets this budget, while providing a reasonable profit to the food service operation. One typical method of meeting these sometimes-conflicting needs is to plan a menu that balances both high-end and less expensive items.

DESIGNING THE BUFFET

After the theme is set, members of the planning group should study the room, garden, patio or other space where the event will be held. They need to allocate space for the buffet table(s), the dining tables and, depending on the function, one or more bars, a dance floor, a stage for musicians, a podium for speakers, audiovisual equipment for presentations and so on. When doing so, common sense should be used: The buffet should be in an area with easy access to both the kitchen and the dining tables—neither the wait staff nor the diners should have to cross a dance floor or walk in front of a podium to get to the food. Similarly, a stage or podium should be within good sightlines of the dining tables.

Once the room's layout is determined, the chef and/or banquet or dining room manager decides on the shape of the buffet table. A buffet table is usually composed of one or more standard-sized tables grouped together in a functional and attractive shape. Standard table shapes and sizes are found in Table 36.1; arrangements of the various sizes and shapes are shown in Figures 36.1 through 36.4. The buffet table can then be draped with a floor-length linen tablecloth, or a tablecloth with a detachable skirt can be used. An alternative to standard-sized tables shrouded in linen is to use unique pieces of furniture such as cabinets, sideboards, consoles, armoires, desks or other furniture, draped with linens or not.

The number of diners is a critical consideration when determining the size, arrangement and placement of the buffet table. As a general rule, a single-sided buffet can comfortably serve 50–75 people. See Figure 36.1. If more than 100 guests are expected, the buffet should be designed with at least two service lines. See Figure 36.2. Even so, many guests will still have to wait in line, although their wait should not be excessive.

Several techniques can be used to serve large groups efficiently. One option is to use a double-sided buffet line. On a double-sided buffet, the same foods are served on both sides of the table. See Figure 36.2. All diners approach the table from the same direction and at the start of the buffet, the line is split, with half of the diners diverted to either side. Or a single-sided buffet can be divided into two, three or more zones, each of which offers the identical foods. See Figure 36.3. Either option requires that the buffet provide the diners with appropriate visual cues to recognize that the two sides of the table or two ends of the table are offering identical fare.

TABLE 36.1 STANDARD BUFFET TABLES

SHAPE	SIZES	SIZES FOR TABLECLOTHS OR SKIRTING
Rectangle	6 feet × 30 inches	90 × 128 inches (floor length)
	8 feet × 30 inches	60 × 125 inches (lap length) or 90 × 153 inches (floor length)
Round	24-inch diameter	80-inch diameter (floor length)
	36-inch diameter	96-inch diameter (floor length)
	48-inch diameter	80-inch diameter (lap) or 108-inch diameter (floor)
	60-inch diameter	96-inch diameter (lap) or 120-inch diameter (floor)
	72-inch diameter	108-inch diameter (lap) or 132-inch diameter (floor)
Half-round	30-inch radius at 180° angle (i.e., half of a 60-inch diameter round)	160 inches of skirting
Quarter-round (wedge)	30-inch radius at 90° angle (i.e., one-quarter of a 60-inch-diameter round)	110 inches of skirting
Serpentine	Outside curve measures 8 feet, inside curve measures 4 feet, ends measure 30 inches (i.e., one-quarter of a circle's circumference)	Specialty cloths needed

DÉCOR

Linens: buffet and dining tables draped with floor-length colored linens, buffet table with a contrasting overlay; linen napkins in the same colors as the table-cloths and overlay.

Centerpieces: fresh flowers (tulips, mums, lilies and greenery).

Serviceware: polished stainless steel or brass trays and chafing dishes; ceramic bowls.

Dinnerware: white or ivory china, stainless flatware and plain stemware.

Music: none

Wait staff uniforms: bistro attire (white button-down shirts, long tie, black pants and long aprons).

KEY FOR THE BUFFET TABLE

   a. Rectangular table, 8 feet x 30 inches
1. Basket of flatware rolled in linen napkins
2. Dinner plates
3. Sunset Salad
4. Raspberry Vinaigrette
5. Caesar Salad
6. Chafing dish of Vegetable Medley
7. Centerpiece
8. Chafing dish of Dauphine Potatoes
9. Sweet and Flavored Butters
10. Baskets of Rolls
11. Chafing dish of Chicken with Wild Mushroom Sauce
12. Chafing dish of Salmon Fillets
13. Dessert plates
14. Cheesecake
15. Fruit Platter
16. Sacher Torte
17. Caramel Sauce for the Cheesecake
18. Raspberry Sauce for the Sacher Torte

Note: Beverages will be in pitchers on the table and replenished by the wait staff; coffee will be offered by circulating wait staff.

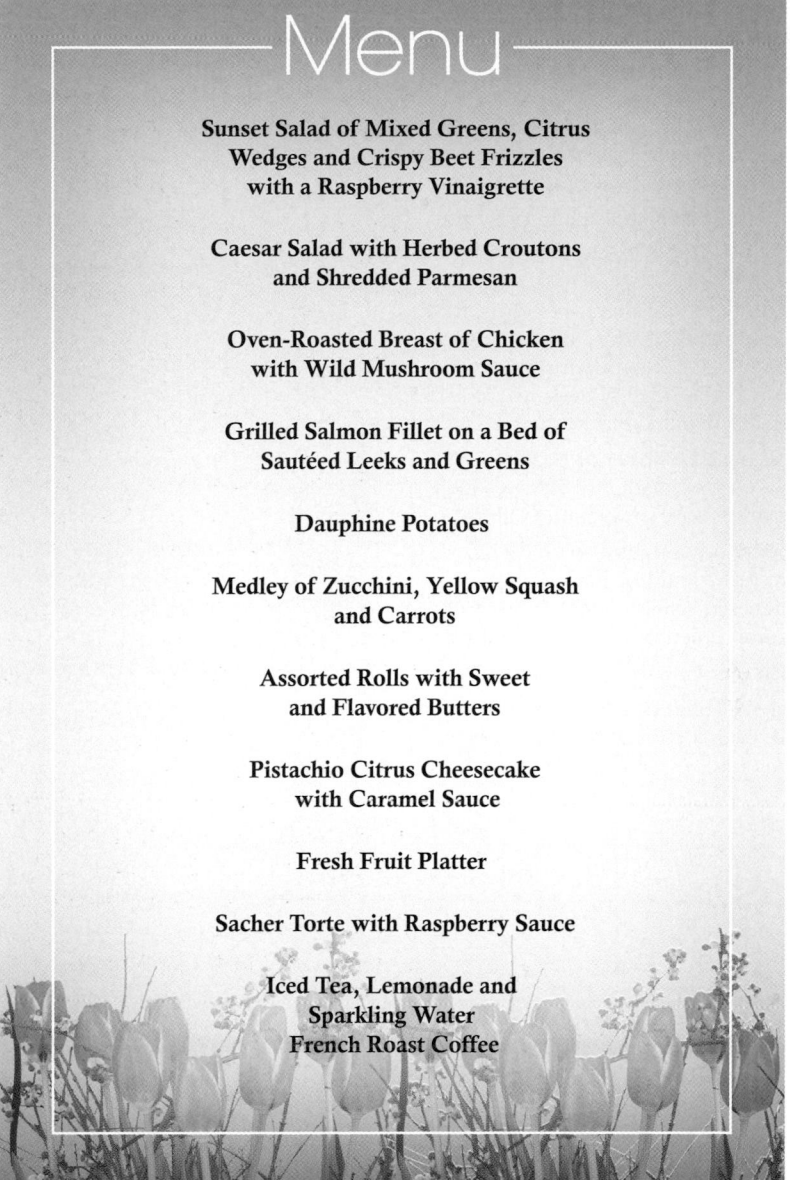

Sunset Salad of Mixed Greens, Citrus Wedges and Crispy Beet Frizzles with a Raspberry Vinaigrette

Caesar Salad with Herbed Croutons and Shredded Parmesan

Oven-Roasted Breast of Chicken with Wild Mushroom Sauce

Grilled Salmon Fillet on a Bed of Sautéed Leeks and Greens

Dauphine Potatoes

Medley of Zucchini, Yellow Squash and Carrots

Assorted Rolls with Sweet and Flavored Butters

Pistachio Citrus Cheesecake with Caramel Sauce

Fresh Fruit Platter

Sacher Torte with Raspberry Sauce

Iced Tea, Lemonade and Sparkling Water French Roast Coffee

A SINGLE-SIDED BUFFET TO FEED 50 PEOPLE

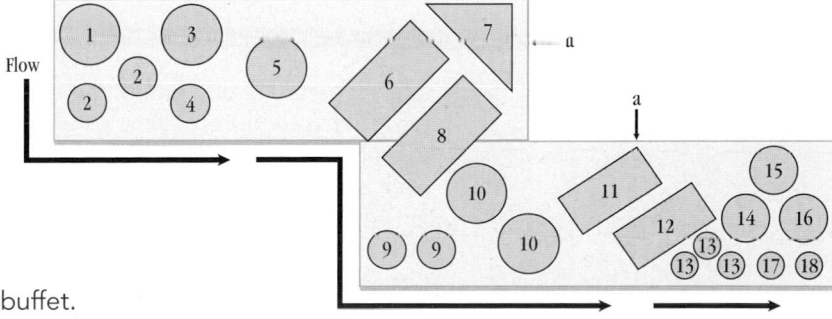

FIGURE 36.1 ▶ Business luncheon buffet.

DÉCOR

Linens: buffet and dining tables draped in bright colors (yellow, orange, red, fuschia and/or turquoise) with overlays of brightly colored Mexican serapes; brightly colored linen napkins tied with raffia.

Centerpieces: large cacti in pots with raffia ties, surrounded with river rocks and sand.

Decorations: piñatas, sombreros, fresh chiles, brightly colored paper flowers, brightly colored papier maché vegetables, raffia, small potted cacti in turquoise-painted terra-cotta pots.

Serviceware: copper or beaten tin trays, copper chafing dishes, wooden or earthenware bowls and platters.

Dinnerware: brightly colored china (red, yellow and/or turquoise), hammered stainless steel flatware and Mexican green or blue glass stemware.

Music: strolling mariachi band.

Wait staff uniforms: jeans and white shirts with a colored serape over the shoulders.

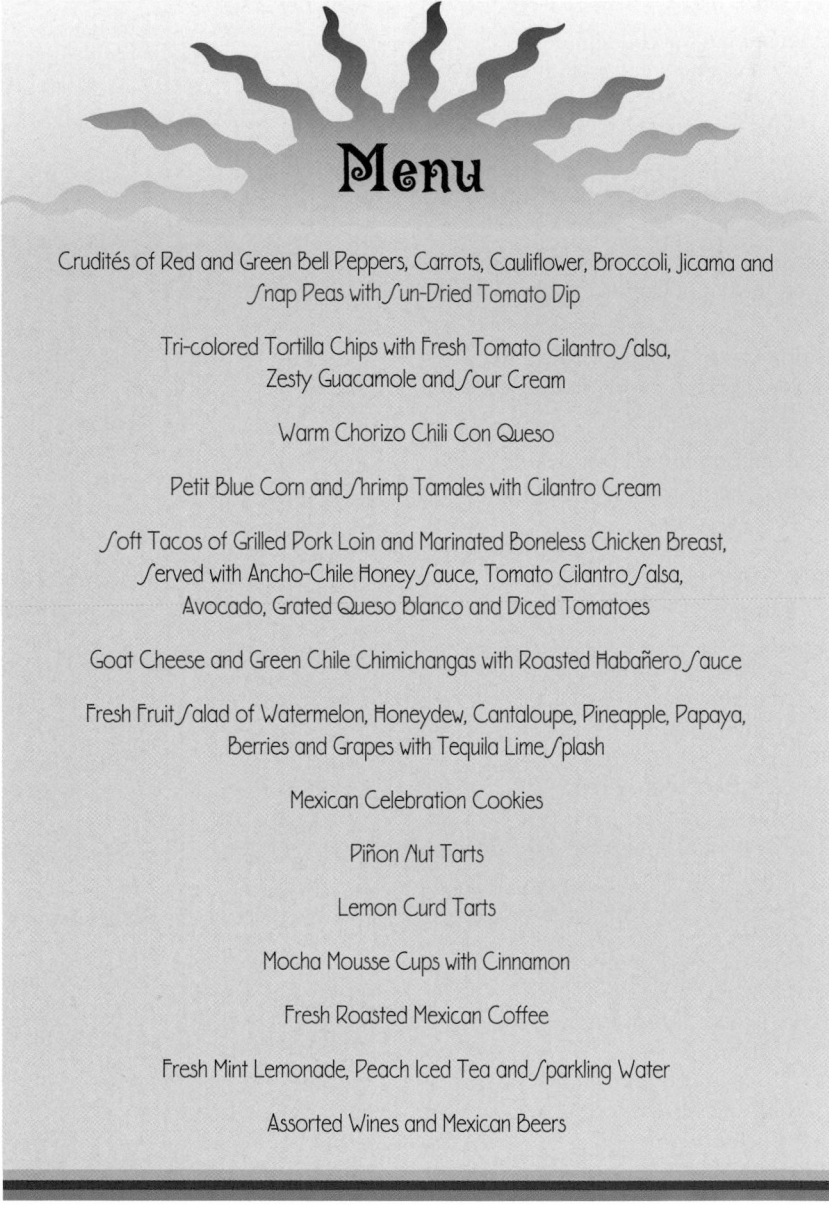

Menu

Crudités of Red and Green Bell Peppers, Carrots, Cauliflower, Broccoli, Jicama and Snap Peas with Sun-Dried Tomato Dip

Tri-colored Tortilla Chips with Fresh Tomato Cilantro Salsa, Zesty Guacamole and Sour Cream

Warm Chorizo Chili Con Queso

Petit Blue Corn and Shrimp Tamales with Cilantro Cream

Soft Tacos of Grilled Pork Loin and Marinated Boneless Chicken Breast, Served with Ancho-Chile Honey Sauce, Tomato Cilantro Salsa, Avocado, Grated Queso Blanco and Diced Tomatoes

Goat Cheese and Green Chile Chimichangas with Roasted Habañero Sauce

Fresh Fruit Salad of Watermelon, Honeydew, Cantaloupe, Pineapple, Papaya, Berries and Grapes with Tequila Lime Splash

Mexican Celebration Cookies

Piñon Nut Tarts

Lemon Curd Tarts

Mocha Mousse Cups with Cinnamon

Fresh Roasted Mexican Coffee

Fresh Mint Lemonade, Peach Iced Tea and Sparkling Water

Assorted Wines and Mexican Beers

FIGURE 36.2 ▶ Mexican fiesta.

Another option for serving larger crowds is to divide the menu among various stations that are scattered throughout the room or series of rooms. See Figure 36.4. One station can be devoted to cold salads or to an elaborate display of cold fish and shellfish surrounding an ice sculpture. Another can be devoted to pasta prepared to order by a line cook assigned to the station; equipped with a portable gas or electric burner, the chef can finish precooked pasta in the diner's choice of sauce. Other stations can offer roasted meats and poultry kept warm by an infrared heat lamp and carved to order by the station chef. See Figure 36.4.

The excitement and beauty of a well-designed buffet table depends principally on two factors: (1) the arrangement of the foods on their individual serving pieces, and (2) the arrangement of the foods and decorations on the buffet table.

A DOUBLE-SIDED BUFFET TO FEED 125 PEOPLE

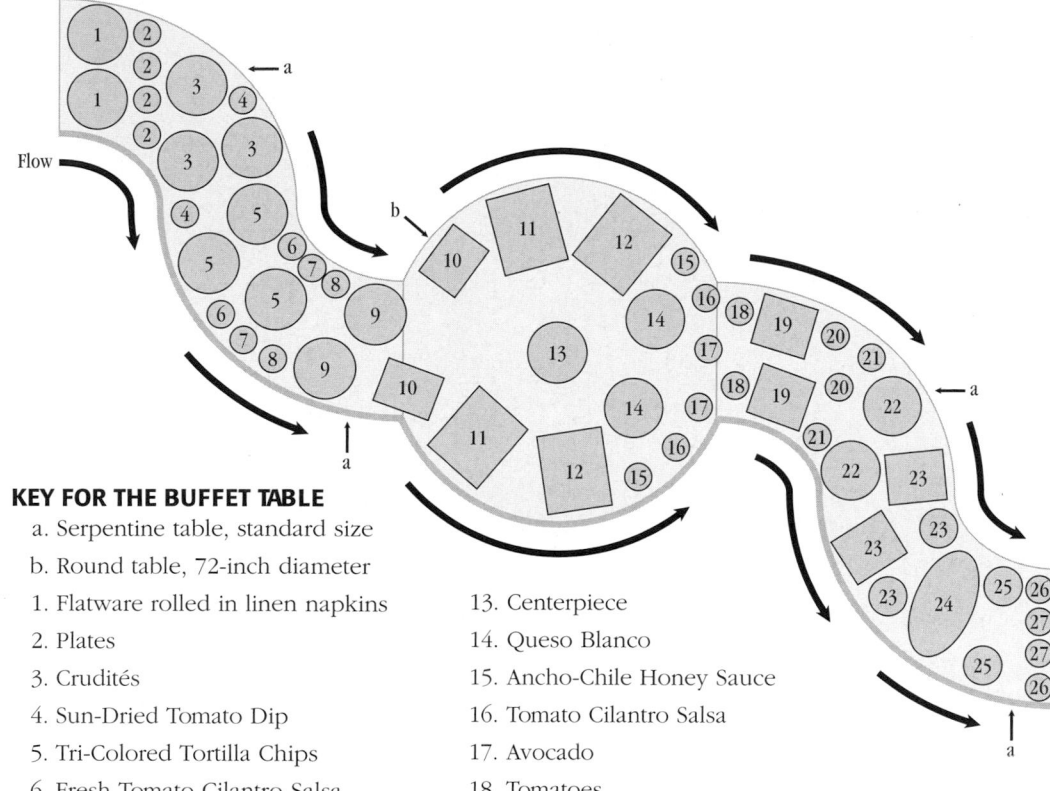

Flow

KEY FOR THE BUFFET TABLE

a. Serpentine table, standard size

b. Round table, 72-inch diameter

1. Flatware rolled in linen napkins
2. Plates
3. Crudités
4. Sun-Dried Tomato Dip
5. Tri-Colored Tortilla Chips
6. Fresh Tomato Cilantro Salsa
7. Zesty Guacamole
8. Sour Cream
9. Chorizo Chili Con Queso
10. Chafing dish of Blue Corn and Shrimp Tamales with Cilantro Cream
11. Chafing dish of Soft Pork Tacos
12. Chafing dish of Soft Chicken Tacos

13. Centerpiece
14. Queso Blanco
15. Ancho-Chile Honey Sauce
16. Tomato Cilantro Salsa
17. Avocado
18. Tomatoes
19. Chafing dish of Goat Cheese and Green Chile Chimichangas
20. Habañero Sauce
21. Dessert plates
22. Fruit Salad
23. Platters of Cookies and Tarts
24. Coffee cups and spoons
25. Coffee

26. Cream
27. Sweeteners

Note: Beers and wines will be available at a separate bar; soft drinks will be in pitchers on the tables and replenished by wait staff.

FIGURE 36.2 ▶ *(continued)*

Arranging Foods on Serving Pieces

The chef is responsible for determining how the foods will be arranged on their serving pieces. Most hot foods will be presented in chafing dishes, whereas cold or room-temperature foods are usually served on trays, platters, bowls or mirrors.

Chafing dishes are metal dishes, usually rectangular or round, with a heat source (flame or electric) located beneath, which is used to keep the foods warm; the foods are usually placed in a hotel pan or other receptacle that sits inside the chafing dish above a pan of hot water. Chafing dishes are usually covered in copper, silver or stainless steel.

Trays, platters and mirrors for presenting foods are available in four basic shapes: square, rectangle, round and oval. They come in a wide variety of materials, including metal (silver, copper, tin and steel), ceramics (china and earthenware), glass, mirrors (glass and acrylic), plastic, wood and stone (especially marble). The choice depends on the theme. Silver and mirror trays create a more formal feel at an event; ceramic and wood lend a more casual look.

Chafing dishes set up on a curved buffet.

DÉCOR

Linens: buffet and dining tables draped with blue denim tablecloths and red bandanna overlays; cobalt and red linen napkins with silver cow head napkin rings.

Centerpieces: fresh flowers (daisies, red mums and yellow lilies), decorated with barbed wire (dulled) and raffia.

Decorations: lanterns, horseshoes, cowbells, miniature hay bales, leather saddles, saddle blankets and western rope.

Serviceware: tin and copper trays and copper chafing dishes, earthenware bowls.

Dinnerware: cobalt china on tin chargers, hammered stainless steel flatware and cobalt-rimmed stemware.

Music: Country and Western band.

Wait staff uniforms: cowboy and cowgirl outfits.

KEY FOR THE BUFFET TABLE

a. Rectangular table, 8 feet × 30 inches

b. Quarter-round table, 30-inch radius

c. Half-round table, 30-inch radius

1. Centerpiece

2. Prop or decoration

3. Plates

4. Fruit Salad

5. Corn, Tomato and Confetti Pepper Salad

6. Grilled Vegetable Platter

7. Chafing dish of Corn on the Cob

8. Chafing dish of Grilled Potatoes

9. Red Chile Sour Cream

10. Butter

11. Prop or decoration

12. Chafing dish of Barbecued Chicken

13. Flour Tortillas

14. Chafing dish of New York Strip Steak

15. Chipotle Lime Sauce

16. Southwestern Béarnaise

17. Prop or decoration

18. Dessert plates

19. Strawberry Rhubarb Tarts

20. Brownies

21. Blackberry Cobbler

22. Vanilla Bean Ice Cream

Note: Beers and wines will be available at a separate bar; soft drinks will be in pitchers on the table and replenished by the wait staff; coffee will be offered by circulating wait staff.

MENU

Fresh Fruit Salad of Watermelon, Honeydew, Cantaloupe, Pineapple, Papaya, Mango, Berries and Grapes

Platter of Chilled Carrots, Cauliflower, Broccoli, Asparagus, Snap Peas, Bell Peppers, Eggplant, Bermuda Onions, Summer Squash and Zucchini Marinated in Flavored Oils, Seasoned with Fresh Herbs and Grilled

Chilled Corn, Tomato and Confetti Pepper Salad with Creamy Basil Dressing

Corn on the Cob Grilled in the Husk Grilled Yukon Gold Potatoes with Red Chile Sour Cream and Butter

Barbecued Chicken and Chile-Rubbed Black Angus New York Strip Steak Served with Chipotle Lime Sauce, Southwestern Béarnaise and Flour Tortillas

Warm Blackberry Cobbler with Vanilla Bean Ice Cream Strawberry Rhubarb Tarts with Fresh Whipped Cream Fudgy Homemade Brownies

Fresh Mint Lemonade and Sparkling Water Kettle Coffee with Cream and Sweeteners Assorted Wines and Beers

BUFFET DIVIDED INTO TWO ZONES TO FEED 150 PEOPLE

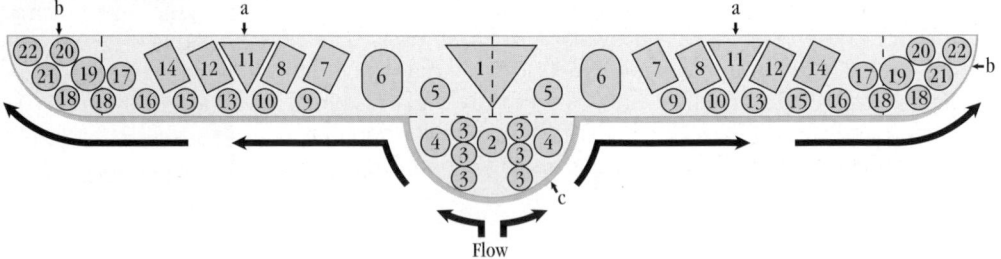

FIGURE 36.3 ▶ Western barbecue buffet.

Once the tray, platter, bowl or mirror is chosen, the chef must artfully arrange the food on it. When designing the presentation, the chef should consider the following:

❶ **Height**—The eye is naturally drawn toward the highest point on a tray; typically, this will be the centerpiece. It can be a garnish or a **grosse piece**. Although it is sometimes in the center of the tray, it is more often located toward the rear, either in the middle or off to one side. Foods placed at a level higher than the centerpiece usually distract from the overall appearance.

❷ **Pattern**—Whenever possible, foods should be arranged in an interesting pattern. Three different types of canapés, each chosen for contrasting shapes, colors and textures, can march across a mirrored surface in alternating lines. Crudités can flow from baskets, hollowed squashes or bell peppers. Spirals of different pâtés can swirl around one another. Foods should generally flow toward the diner. Stack foods higher in the center or rear of the tray so that they cascade toward the front or edges. (Trays that are higher around all the edges than in the center tend to draw the eye into the hole in the center.)

❸ **Color**—The colors of the principal foods should complement or contrast with each other. If they cannot (for example, a tray of pâtés or cheeses), they should be garnished with attractively contrasting colored foods such as fruits, vegetables and herbs.

❹ **Texture and shape**—Try to use a variety of shapes and textures. Avoid building trays with circular slices of galantine garnished with circular liver mousse molds and round tartlets of a vegetable purée; all have the same shape and very similar textures. Instead, try molding the mousse or tartlets into different shapes or preparing a vegetable salad rather than a purée for the tartlets.

❺ **Negative space**—This refers to the areas left unused. It is important because the space enhances the appeal of the object it surrounds and prevents overcrowding. Try leaving a border of space around the tray and some space within clusters of food on the platter.

grosse piece a centerpiece consisting of a large piece of the principal food offered; for example, a large wheel of cheese with slices of the cheese cascading around it

Display of seafood and meats for brunch buffet, Hotel Adlon Kempinski, Berlin, Germany.

THE HOTEL ADLON KEMPINSKI

The Hotel Adlon Kempinski is a storied hotel in the heart of Berlin overlooking the Brandenberg Gate. From its opening in 1907, the Hotel Adlon catered to a "who's who" of Europe; Kaiser Wilhelm II officiated at its opening and Auguste Escoffier was its legendary chef. The hotel's founder, Lorenz Adlon, also managed the largest wine store in the world with an assortment of more than one million bottles of wine. Consumed by a fire in 1945, the hotel was rebuilt on the same spot in 1997. Today, with more than 350 rooms and suites, five restaurants, three of which hold coveted Michelin stars, and the Palace ballroom capable of serving 500 guests, the Hotel Adlon Kempinski is ranked consistently among the finest hotels in the world. Its catered events and sumptuous breakfast buffets at Restaurant Quarré are pictured throughout this chapter.

Menu

— *Butlered Hors d'Oeuvre* —

Red Potatoes with Gorgonzola, Bacon and Walnuts   Popovers with Shrimp and Chive Filling

Mushroom Phyllo Triangles   Asparagus Spears Tied with Red Pepper

— *Buffet* —

Station One
Tropical Fruit Display
Caesar Salad with Herbed Croutons and Shredded Parmesan
Salad of Bibb Lettuce and Blue Cheese
with Citrus Vinaigrette
Platter of Assorted Pâtés, Galantines and Ballotines
Assorted Rolls with Sweet and Flavored Butters
Tiered Display of Imported Cheeses, including Stilton, Saint
André, Port Salut, Gouda, Black Diamond Cheddar and
Brie Baked in Phyllo with Apricots and Fresh Basil,
Garnished with Apple Slices and Grape Clusters
Lavosh and Cracker Bread

Station Two
Antipasto of Assorted Salami, Prosciutto, Sliced Cheeses,
Marinated Mushrooms and Artichokes, Olives, Roasted
Peppers and Wedges of Melon Wrapped with Prosciutto
Penne with Fresh Tomatoes and Basil Tossed with
Extra Virgin Olive Oil
Cheese-Filled Tortellini with Wild Mushroom Alfredo Sauce
Pastas Prepared to Order by the Chef
Wheel of Parmesan
Focaccia, Garlic Twists, Breadsticks and Assorted Rolls
Sweet and Flavored Butters

Station Three
Herb-Rubbed, Grilled Tenderloin of Beef Carved by the
Chef with Béarnaise Sauce and Sage-Merlot Sauce
Assorted Rolls with Sweet and Flavored Butters
Chicken Satay with Chile Peanut Sauce
Grilled Swordfish with Tomatillo Sauce

Station Four
Three-Tiered Wedding Cake
bottom layer – Black Forest
middle layer – White Cake with White Chocolate Mousse,
Strawberries and Chocolate Ganache
top layer – Carrot Cake
Petits Fours
Fruit Tartlets
Chocolate-Dipped Strawberries
French Roast Coffee and Hot Tea with Deluxe Condiments

Assorted Beers, Alcoholic Beverages, Still and Sparkling Wines,
Sparkling Water and Soft Drinks

DÉCOR

Linens: buffet and dining tables draped with floor-length ivory linens with overlays of tulle and lace, accented with gold ribbons and tassels, linen napkins tied with ribbons and tassels and decorated with flowers.

Centerpieces: fresh flowers (calla lilies, white orchids, roses, tulips, ivy and greenery) and candles (votives, pillars or hurricanes) wrapped in ivy.

Serviceware: fancy silver and mirror trays, silver chafing dishes, china or glass bowls.

Dinnerware: ivory gold-rimmed china on gold chargers, silver flatware and gold-rimmed stemware.

Music: harpist, violinist or quartet.

Wait staff uniforms: tuxedos.

FIGURE 36.4 ▶ Formal wedding buffet.

A FOUR-STATION BUFFET (INCLUDING TWO STAFFED BY CHEFS) TO FEED 200 PEOPLE

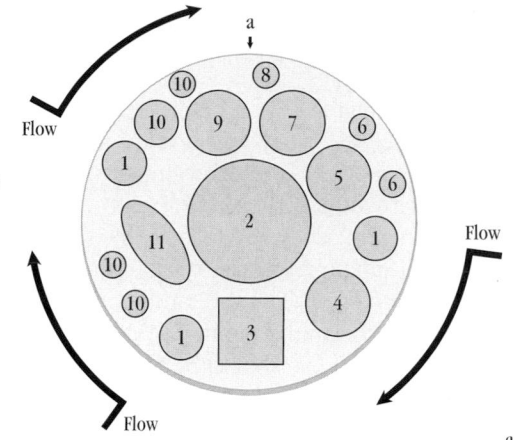

KEY FOR STATION ONE:

a. Round table, 72-inch diameter
1. Salad plates
2. Centerpiece
3. Tropical Fruit Display
4. Caesar Salad
5. Basket of Rolls overflowing onto the table
6. Sweet and Flavored Butters
7. Bibb Lettuce Salad
8. Citrus Vinaigrette
9. Platter of Pâtés, Galantines and Ballotines
10. Baskets of Lavosh and Cracker Breads
11. Tiered Cheese Display

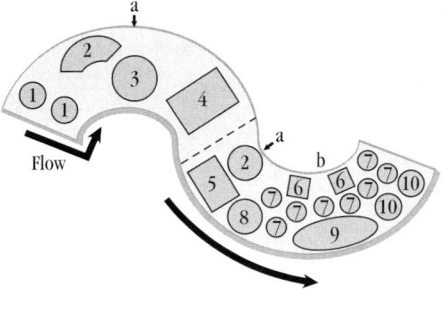

KEY FOR STATION TWO:

a. Serpentine table, standard size
b. Chef's station
1. Plates
2. Centerpiece
3. Antipasto
4. Chafing dish of Penne Pasta
5. Chafing dish of Cheese Tortellini
6. Induction burners for chef
7. Garnishes for the pastas made to order, including
mushrooms, grilled chicken, walnuts, peas, roasted bell peppers and shrimp, and sauces for the pasta, including Alfredo and tomato basil
8. Large hollowed wheel of Parmesan
9. Basket of Focaccia, Garlic Twists, Breadsticks and Assorted Rolls
10. Sweet and Flavored Butters

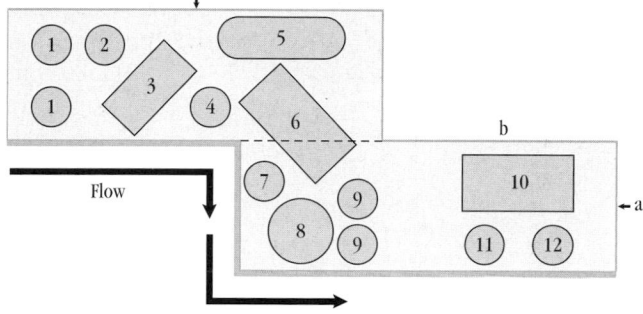

KEY FOR STATION THREE:

a. Rectangular table, 6 feet x 30 inches
b. Chef's station
1. Plates
2. Decoration or prop
3. Chafing dish of Swordfish
4. Tomatillo Sauce
5. Centerpiece
6. Chafing dish of Chicken Satay
7. Chile Peanut Sauce
8. Basket of Assorted Rolls
9. Sweet and Flavored Butters
10. Carving station with heat lamp for the Tenderloin of Beef
11. Sage-Merlot Sauce
12. Béarnaise Sauce

KEY FOR STATION FOUR:

a. Round table, 48-inch diameter
b. Serpentine table, standard size
1. Three-Tiered Wedding Cake
2. Cake and dessert plates
3. Petits Fours
4. Fruit Tartlets
5. Chocolate-Dipped Strawberries
6. Tray of coffee mugs
7. Carafe of hot water with assorted tea bags
8. Urn of regular coffee
9. Garnishes for coffee including raw sugar cubes, artificial sweeteners, cream, whipped cream, candied citrus peel, mint swizzle sticks, cinnamon sticks, rock sugar sticks and chocolate shavings
10. Urn of decaffeinated coffee
Note: Soft drinks as well as assorted wines, beers and other alcoholic beverages will be available at a separate bar; sparkling water, assorted wines and champagne will be served by the wait staff.

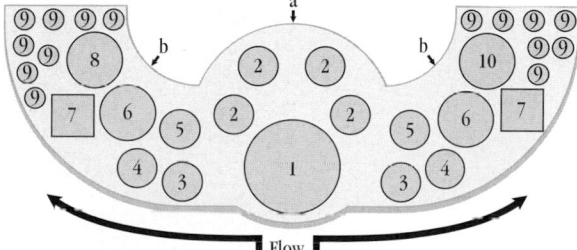

FIGURE 36.4 ▶ *(continued)*

Plates positioned at the beginning of a long double-sided buffet.

Arranging Foods and Other Items on the Buffet Table

When designing the shape of the buffet table, the chef and/or banquet or dining room manager must also consider how the various foods, centerpieces and props will be laid out on the table. Besides color, height, shape and texture, they should consider the following:

❶ **Flow**—Regardless of whether a single buffet table, a main buffet table with one or more stations or only stations are used, the foods should be placed in a logical order that affords the diner the chance to construct a meal in the same order as one that would be served to him or her. The start of the buffet line should be obvious and accessible; usually, it is near the entrance to the room.

Typically, on a single- or double-sided buffet table, the first items offered the diner are plates. (Flatware and napkins can be located at the start or the end of the buffet or on the dining tables.) The first foods to be offered should be soups and salads. These should be followed by appetizers such as cold sliced meats, pâtés and shellfish. Entrées should be next, along with their vegetable and starch accompaniments. Desserts should be the last items on the buffet. (Beverages can be available on the buffet table, at a bar, or on the dining tables or offered by circulating wait staff.)

Stations offer the designer greater flexibility. They also help minimize the line that usually forms at a single buffet table, allowing diners to go in various directions, although this can sometimes cause traffic problems. Like a single buffet table, each station can be designed so that it offers diners sufficient selections to create a complete meal. The stations can also be arranged around a room in a sequence mirroring a meal: soups and salads on the first station diners would approach, appetizers on the next, and so on. A third option is to arrange the stations so that the one with the most spectacular display of centerpiece, foods and decorations or the one featuring a chef making foods to order will be the center of attention, with the other stations scattered around the room. Regardless of how they are arranged, each should be self-contained with plates and accompaniments for the main items.

❷ **Spacing**—Allow approximately 1 linear foot for each item on the buffet. Thus, if 16 items are to be placed on the table, including plates, a centerpiece and large props, then the buffet table must be approximately 16 feet long. If extremely large

Display of cheeses for a private event, Hotel Adlon Kempinski, Berlin, Germany.

centerpieces are used or if food is presented on oversized platters, this will, of course, affect the total table space needed.

❸ **Reach**—Try to place all foods within easy reach of the diners. Try to avoid stacking one item behind another. But if items must be placed farther back on the table, try setting them on **risers** or on pedestals in order to add height to the platter. This extra height not only adds visual interest, it allows the diner to reach over the dish in front without disturbing its arrangement. Also, if possible, place foods that will not drip or splatter behind ones that will; that way, sauce from the back dish will not drip into the front dish on its way to the diner's plate. Trays with foods that will not shift can be propped at a slight angle to make the contents more accessible and attractive.

❹ **Accompaniments**—Place the appropriate garnishes, sauces or other accompaniments near their principal foods. Also, place a small plate or napkin near a platter for any serving utensils.

❺ **Centerpieces**—A centerpiece brings focus to the buffet, and its height or dominance increases the visual appeal of the overall table design. A centerpiece can be a floral arrangement or a sculpture made of ice, tallow, pastillage, chocolate, blown or pulled sugar or other material. The centerpiece can also be a grosse piece such as a whole roast turkey or whole poached salmon decorated with sauce chaud-froid. See Chapter 27, Charcuterie.

❻ **Decorations**—In addition to the centerpiece, other nonedible objects or props may grace the buffet table. Sometimes these are nothing more than smaller or modified versions of the centerpiece, such as flowers or leaves from a floral

risers boxes (including the plastic crates used to store glassware) covered with linens, paper or other decorative items and used on a buffet table as a base for platters, trays or displays

Display of fresh fruit and pastries for Sunday brunch buffet, The Phoenician, Scottsdale, AZ.

THE PHOENICIAN RESORT

The Phoenician Resort in Scottsdale, Arizona, is one of America's premier resorts. It offers several dining options, including the award-winning fine-dining room Mary Elaine's. Sunday brunch is a popular event at The Phoenician, especially in the Terrace Dining Room, where chefs create a lavish multistationed buffet using interior spaces and exterior patios. The Terrace's Sunday brunch buffet, which is pictured throughout this chapter, typically serves 450 guests and is prepared and maintained by 20 cooks. It takes the staff 12 hours to set up some 13 stations for each week's 4-hour-long brunch. In addition to a wide selection of hot and cold entrées, meat and poultry carving stations, fresh fruits and vegetables, pasta, salads, pâtés, freshly baked breads and pastries, guests enjoy four varieties of imported caviar and consume an average of 120 pounds of boiled shrimp.

centerpiece. Of course, anything from a saddle to a silver candelabra can be used, depending on the buffet's theme. Whatever items are chosen, they should be well cleaned and arranged artfully but not in a manner that interferes with a diner's ability to see and reach the food. Props can also be used to mark divisions in the meal; for example, grouping all salads between one set of props divides them from the entrées. Sometimes, unusable or dead space will result because of constrictions of room or food. If it cannot be avoided, try filling the space with props or other decorations.

❼ **Labels**—Unlike a restaurant with a printed menu and an attentive wait staff, an unattended buffet may not give the diner an opportunity to inquire about particular dishes. This can be remedied by placing attractively printed cards bearing the name of the dish in front of any items that the chef feels need identification.

PRESENTING AND MAINTAINING THE BUFFET

Portioning Foods

A common problem when planning a buffet is overproduction. Many novice chefs want to make enough of each menu item to serve the entire group. But this is unnecessary. Most people tend to sample a little from many dishes and try not to gorge themselves. Some chefs use a simple, although far from foolproof, formula of 1 pound (450 grams) of food per person as a starting point and then adjust this number depending on factors such as the general composition of the group (a luncheon for female executives may require less food than one for male football players), the number of items offered (the more dishes to choose from, the smaller the portions most people will take), the structure of the event (that is, whether it will be convenient for people to return to the buffet for second helpings) and whether diners serve themselves or are served by wait staff or chefs at the buffet.

Generally, portions should be small, especially if more than one item is served in each food category. For example, if a grilled salmon fillet with lyonnaise potatoes and a medley of sautéed vegetables is served as an entrée from an à la carte menu, a typical serving would be 6 ounces (180 grams) fish, 4 ounces (120 grams) potato and 4 ounces (120 grams) vegetables. If the same salmon fillet with its accompaniments is served as one of three entrées on a dinner buffet for 100 people, the total of available fish should be 2 to 3 ounces (60 to 90 grams) fish per portion multiplied by 100 portions, 1 to 1.5 ounces (30 to 45 grams) potatoes per portion multiplied by 100 portions and 1 ounce (30 grams) vegetables per portion (diners tend to take smaller portions of vegetables than of starches) multiplied by 100 portions. Similarly, if a dessert tart from an à la carte menu has a 4-inch (10-centimeter) diameter, the version offered on a dessert buffet should have a 2-inch (5-centimeter) diameter.

Experience suggests that most diners tend to serve themselves larger portions of foods found at the start of the buffet than at its middle. Thus, if caviar is being served, it may make economic sense to place it somewhere farther down the line than at the start of the buffet.

Presenting Hot Foods

Keeping hot foods hot on a buffet is a particular challenge, and an important one, for both food safety and presentation concerns. If possible, hot foods should be served in relatively small quantities on warm platters that are exchanged frequently. This is not always possible, however. More often, hot foods are maintained in chafing dishes or under heat lamps.

To maintain the quality of foods kept in a chafing dish, use the following guidelines:

▶ Choose foods that hold well. Rare meats and delicate pastas do not hold well in a chafing dish; they become overcooked and unattractive quickly. Instead, try braised meats (which may actually benefit from the extended cooking) or hearty pastas such as tortellini or penne. This guideline also applies to garnishes: Bunches of delicate

Braised veal sloppy joe sliders served from a hot buffet.

Pasta station, The Phoenician, Scottsdale, AZ.

herbs such as basil do not do well in a chafing dish; instead, try sprigs of rosemary or thyme.

▶ Cook small amounts of delicate foods at a time and change the insert pan in a chafing dish often. This prevents foods from sitting too long.

▶ Ladle a small amount of sauce in the bottom of the pan before placing sliced meats in the pan, or serve sliced meats, poultry or fish on a bed of vegetables. The sauce or the vegetable bed helps to absorb the heat from the chafing dish, insulating the more delicate items and providing a bit of steam to help keep the foods moist.

▶ Keep the chafing dish closed whenever possible. This holds in the steam, which helps keep the food moist. But a closed chafing dish distracts from a buffet's appeal and slows down the flow of diners through the buffet line.

Heat lamps are generally used for keeping large cuts of meats or poultry warm during carving. These foods, however, become dry rapidly and should be replaced periodically. Of course, time and temperature principles of food safety must also be followed.

Presenting Cold Foods

Keeping cold foods cold on a buffet table is a little less of a challenge. As with hot foods, it is best if cold foods are served in relatively small quantities on cold platters that are exchanged frequently. Alternatively, the items can be set on a bed of ice—usually a large bowl filled with ice into which a smaller bowl containing the food is placed.

Replenishing Foods

Dishes from the buffet table should be removed when they are approximately two-thirds empty or have deteriorated in some fashion (for example, when the aspic on pâtés has softened, cut fruits have browned or a hot food has crusted over). Once the old dish has been removed, its fresh replacement should be placed on the buffet immediately, and it should be as carefully arranged and garnished as the original. If items from the old dish are to be combined with a replacement dish, this should be done in the kitchen and not at the buffet table. Batches of temperature-sensitive or potentially hazardous foods should not be combined, however.

A BLOCK OF ICE, A CHAIN SAW, A CHISEL AND A LITTLE CAUTION AND CREATIVITY

Ice carvings have long been popular buffet centerpieces; they add elegance and sophistication to the setting and occasion. As with other arts, it may take years to master ice carving. Nevertheless, with some practice and care, chefs can usually create acceptable ice sculptures after only a few tries.

Blocks of carving ice are specially prepared to remove air bubbles. These large blocks (20 × 10 × 46 inches [50 × 25 × 115 centimeters]) weigh approximately 300 pounds (135 kilograms), and special ice tongs and caution are required when handling them.

At 0°F (−18°C), ice is very brittle and difficult to carve without breaking. Therefore, carving ice must be tempered before carving. To temper the ice, remove it from the freezer and allow it to rest at room temperature for approximately 1 hour. When the surface is clear of frost, carving can begin.

A single carving can take from one to several hours to complete. Although chisels and specially designed saws for ice carving work quite well, chain saws are commonly used to speed up the process. Because most carving is done indoors, electric saws are used; unlike gas saws, they do not leave a greasy residue on the ice's surface. Be very careful when using any chain saw, particularly an electric one, around melting ice and pools of water.

To begin, trace the outline of the figure you want to carve on the surface of all four sides of the block of ice. There are several excellent ice carving books, some of which provide stencils for this purpose. Then start removing the ice using a large saw or a chainsaw. As the figure begins to take shape, use smaller chisels and specialized tools to create the desired effect. Some carvers use chain saws for the entire process, however. After some practice, you will develop your own style and preferences.

When the carving is complete, carefully return the ice to the freezer until needed. When setting it on a buffet, use a pan designed to hold an ice carving and provide drainage. Avoid placing ice sculptures under hot air vents. At room temperature and average humidity, ice melts at the rate of approximately ½ inch (1.2 centimeters) per hour from all sides. Keep this in mind when carving thin pieces or small details into the surface.

An ice carving dominates a seafood buffet at a New Year's Gala, Hotel Adlon Kempinski, Berlin, Germany.

Serving Foods

Once the banquet or restaurant manager has completed the planning for a buffet, it usually falls to a captain to supervise the actual event. The captain directs the crew setting up the room as well as the stewards who bring the food, flatware, china and glassware from the kitchen to the buffet.

The captain also supervises the wait staff. One of the front waiters' principal responsibilities is to maintain the appearance of the buffet and to replenish items as needed. Depending on the function, front waiters can be stationed behind the buffet table to serve diners, circulate in the crowd with trays of hors d'oeuvre or drinks (passing foods in this fashion is called **butler service**) or serve beverages to diners seated at the dining tables. Back waiters generally police the room and clear tables. They should be particularly vigilant in removing used plates from a dining table after a diner has gone to the buffet for more food and before he or she returns to the dining table with a new plate.

Typically, servers or chefs are placed only at stations where foods are prepared or carved to order. This helps control portioning. It also provides a greater opportunity for staff to police the buffet and therefore ensure that the table and the individual items remain neat, attractive and fresh. Finally, placing wait staff or kitchen staff at the buffet allows diners to ask questions about the foods presented.

THE BUFFET: AN ANCIENT EXTRAVAGANZA

The origin of the buffet is obscure, but it is possible that the idea evolved from Italian banquets of the early Renaissance. Gathering together to eat and drink on festive occasions was not new; one only has to think of banqueting scenes on ancient Egyptian or Roman frescoes. But the word *banchetto* was new, and referred not only to the event but to the long table or bench at which the many guests were seated.

As the influence of Italian art and manners spread throughout Europe, the French adopted the *banquet*. Not only was it an occasion for eating and drinking prodigious amounts, but the resplendent display of food was often accompanied by an equally resplendent display of silver on dining room buffets or sideboards. And it was the chefs who were responsible for these imaginative displays. Paintings from the period of Louis XIV depict the unbridled creativity that went into these tableaux.

From France to England to America, the idea of the buffet migrated across time. There is *rijstaffel* in the Netherlands and *smorgasbord* in Scandinavia. In America, the Chinese restaurant buffet began around the time of the 1849 gold rush, perhaps the first instance of the "all you can eat" experience. It cost $1.00. The "midnight chuck wagon" buffet at the El Rancho in 1940s Las Vegas popularized the "all you can eat" buffet. It cost $1.50.

Whatever the case, the buffet has come a long way from the 16th-century Medici banquet that featured a ram poached in water, reinserted into its skin (horns and all) and set lifelike into a gold basin.

QUESTIONS FOR DISCUSSION

1. What is a grosse piece? How is it different from a centerpiece?

2. What food safety and sanitation factors must be considered when planning a buffet? Explain your answer.

3. Describe three things that can be done to keep hot foods attractive and fresh when using a chafing dish.

4. Describe two things that can be done to keep cold foods cold on a buffet.

5. List five different stations serving hot foods at a buffet and the equipment necessary for each.

6. Redesign the Western-themed buffet in Figure 36.3 to include three stations.

7. Where can you go for current information on new trends and styles of buffet arrangements? What resources are available to assist caterers in business management? **www**

Terms to Know

buffet
theme
layout
single-sided
    buffet
double-sided
    buffet
stations
chafing dish
butler service

APPENDIX I
PROFESSIONAL ORGANIZATIONS

American Cheese Society

455 South Fourth Street, Suite 650
Louisville, KY 40202
(502) 574-9950
www.cheesesociety.org

American Culinary Federation (ACF)

180 Center Place Way
St. Augustine, FL 32095
(800) 624-9458
www.acfchefs.org

American Dietetic Association (ADA)

120 South Riverside Plaza, Suite 2000
Chicago, Illinois 60606-6995
(800) 877-1600
www.eatright.org

American Institute of Baking (AIB)

P.O. Box 3999
Manhattan, KS 66505-3999
(800) 633-5137
www.aibonline.org

American Institute of Wine & Food (AIWF)

26364 Carmel Rancho Lane, Suite 201
Carmel, CA 93923
(800) 274-2493
www.aiwf.org

Chefs Collaborative

89 South Street, Lower Level
Boston, MA 02111
(617) 236-5200
www.chefscollaborative.org

Club Managers Association of America (CMAA)

1733 King Street
Alexandria, VA 22314
(703) 739-9500
www.cmaa.org

International Association of Culinary Professionals (IACP)

1100 Johnson Ferry Road, Suite 300
Atlanta, GA 30342
(800) 928-4227
www.iacp.com

International Food Service Executives Association

Synergy Communications
500 Ryland Street, Suite 200
Reno, NV 89502
(800) 893-5499
www.ifsea.com

The James Beard Foundation

167 West 12th Street
New York, NY 10011
(800) 36-BEARD
www.jamesbeard.org

Les Dames d'Escoffier International

P.O. Box 4961
Louisville, KY 40204
(502) 456-1851
www.ldei.org

National Ice Carving Association

P.O. Box 3593
Oak Brook, IL 60522-3593
(630) 871-8431
www.nica.org

National Restaurant Association

1200 17th Street NW
Washington, DC 20036
(202) 331-5900
www.restaurant.org

Oldways Preservation Trust

266 Beacon Street
Boston, MA 02116
(617) 421-5500
www.oldwayspt.org

Research Chefs Association

1100 Johnson Ferry Road, Suite 300
Atlanta, GA 30342
(404) 252-3663
www.culinology.org

Share Our Strength (SOS)

1730 M Street NW, Suite 700
Washington, DC 20036
(800) 969-4767
www.strength.org

Slow Food USA

20 Jay Street, M04
Brooklyn, NY 11201
(718) 260-8000
www.slowfoodusa.org

Southern Foodways Alliance

Center for the Study of Southern Culture
Barnard Observatory
P.O. Box 1848
University, MS 38677
(662) 915-5993
www.southernfoodways.com

U.S. Personal Chef Association

610 Quantum
Rio Rancho, NM 87124
(800) 995-2138
www.uspca.com

Women Chefs and Restaurateurs (WCR)

P.O. Box 1875
Madison, AL 35758
(877) 927-7787
www.womenchefs.org

APPENDIX II
Measurement and Conversion Charts

FORMULAS FOR EXACT MEASURES

	WHEN YOU KNOW:	MULTIPLY BY:	TO FIND:
Mass (weight)	ounces	28.35	grams
	pounds	0.45	kilograms
	grams	0.035	ounces
	kilograms	2.2	pounds
Volume (capacity)	teaspoons	5.0	milliliters
	tablespoons	15.0	milliliters
	fluid ounces	29.57	milliliters
	cups	0.24	liters
	pints	0.47	liters
	quarts	0.95	liters
	gallons	3.785	liters
	milliliters	0.034	fluid ounces
Temperature	Fahrenheit	⅝ (after subtracting 32)	Celsius
	Celsius	⅝ (then add 32)	Fahrenheit

ROUNDED MEASURES FOR QUICK REFERENCE

1 oz.		= 30 g
4 oz.		= 120 g
8 oz.		= 240 g
16 oz.	= 1 lb.	= 480 g
32 oz.	= 2 lb.	= 960 g
36 oz.	= 2¼ lb.	= 1000 g (1 kg)
¼ tsp.	= ¹⁄₂₄ fl. oz.	= 1 ml
½ tsp.	= ¹⁄₁₂ fl. oz.	= 2 ml
1 tsp.	= ⅙ fl. oz.	= 5 ml
1 Tbsp.	= ½ fl. oz.	= 15 ml
1 c.	= 8 fl. oz.	= 240 ml
2 c. (1 pt.)	= 16 fl. oz.	= 480 ml
4 c. (1 qt.)	= 32 fl. oz.	= 960 ml
4 qt. (1 gal.)	= 128 fl. oz.	= 3.75 lt
32°F		= 0°C
122°F		= 50°C
212°F		= 100°C

CONVERSION GUIDELINES

1 gallon	=	4 quarts
		8 pints
		16 cups (8 fluid ounces)
		128 fluid ounces
1 fifth bottle	=	approximately 1½ pints or exactly 26.5 fluid ounces
1 measuring cup	=	8 fluid ounces (a coffee cup generally holds 6 fluid ounces)
1 large egg white	=	1 ounce (average)
1 lemon	=	1 to 1¼ fluid ounces juice
1 orange	=	3 to 3½ fluid ounces juice

SCOOP SIZES

SCOOP NUMBER	LEVEL MEASURE
6	⅔ cup
8	½ cup
10	⅖ cup
12	⅓ cup
16	¼ cup
20	3⅕ tablespoons
24	2⅔ tablespoons
30	2⅕ tablespoons
40	1⅗ tablespoons

The number of the scoop determines the number of servings in each quart of a mixture: for example, with a No. 16 scoop, one quart of mixture will yield 16 servings.

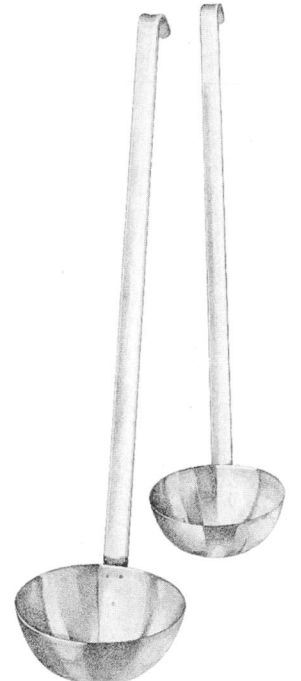

LADLE SIZES

SIZE	PORTION OF A CUP	NUMBER PER QUART	NUMBER PER LITER
1 fl. oz.	⅛	32	34
2 fl. oz.	¼	16	17
2⅔ fl. oz.	⅓	12	13
4 fl. oz.	½	8	8.6
6 fl. oz.	¾	5⅓	5.7

Various standard cans—(left to right, front row) No. ½ flat, No. ¼; (middle row) No. 300, No. 1 tall, No. ½; (back row) No. 10, No. 3 cylinder, No. 5

CANNED GOOD SIZES

SIZE	NO. OF CANS PER CASE	AVERAGE WEIGHT	AVERAGE NO. CUPS PER CAN
No. ¼	1 & 2 doz.	4 oz.	½
No. ½	8	8 oz.	1
No. 300	1 & 2 doz.	14 oz.	1¾
No. 1 tall (also known as 303)	2 & 4 doz.	16 oz.	2
No. 2	2 doz.	20 oz.	2½
No. 2½	2 doz.	28 oz.	3½
No. 3	2 doz.	33 oz.	4
No. 3 cylinder	1 doz.	46 oz.	5⅔
No. 5	1 doz.	3 lb. 8 oz.	5½
No. 10	6	6 lb. 10 oz.	13

APPENDIX III
FRESH PRODUCE AVAILABILITY CHART

The availability of fresh, locally grown produce depends on local climate and growing conditions. Gardeners in central Arizona may be enjoying vine-ripened tomatoes in March, while gardeners in Michigan or New England may still be buried under snow. Just by looking at what's available in the produce department of your local supermarket, you may not be able to tell whether it is July or January. That's because consumers have become accustomed to having the same foods available all year. Modern transportation and storage methods allow us to have out-of-season foods anytime, anywhere. But though we depend on and enjoy this convenience, it contributes to hidden costs that are not usually considered. These include loss of farmlands and natural resources involved in the marketing and movement of these foods.

Chefs across the country are now shopping for fruits and vegetables at local farmer's markets and working with local farmers who grow products especially for their kitchens. Although good produce wholesalers or even supermarkets will carry out-of-season, imported produce, the taste will be inferior and the cost will be much higher.

Locally grown, in-season products appeal to restaurant patrons and demonstrate your concern for both food quality and the viability of local farmers and foragers. Chefs can also work with local farmers before planting begins to determine what specialty items grow well in the area and to encourage farmers to grow products that the restaurant agrees to purchase at harvest. Many states now have programs to assist and encourage chefs and farmers to work together. It's a shift from demand-driven (chef) to supply-driven (farm) choices.

With only 2 percent of the U.S. population farming the land, few Americans give a second thought to the sources of their food. Many of us may have lost our connection to agriculture, but none of us has lost our dependence on that connection. By creating markets for local agriculture, we can ensure that farmland remains active and viable. What happens to farmers remains crucial to our nation's well-being. Even if we never set foot on a farm, our connection to the farmer and the land is there every time we buy a loaf of bread, munch an apple, plan a daily special or design a restaurant's menu.

The following chart is intended as only a general guide to the best availability of freshly harvested produce items grown in the continental United States. State departments of agriculture can provide charts of local produce availability and information on local farmer's markets and sustainable agriculture programs. The Web sites of environmental groups such as the Natural Resources Defense Council and other public and private organizations also provide lists of seasonally available produce organized by state.

PRODUCT	JAN	FEB	MAR	APR	MAY	JUN	JUL	AUG	SEP	OCT	NOV	DEC
	WINTER DEC 21–MAR 19		SPRING MAR 20–JUN 20			SUMMER JUN 21–SEP 21			AUTUMN SEP 22–DEC 20			
Apples								X	X	X	X	
Apricots						X	X					
Artichokes			X	X	X							
Asparagus				X	X	X						
Avocados, Hass				X	X	X	X	X	X	X		
Beans, green					X	X	X	X	X			
Beets								X	X	X		
Blueberries					X	X	X	X				
Broccoli	X	X	X						X	X	X	X
Brussels sprouts	X	X							X	X	X	X
Cabbage	X	X	X	X	X				X	X	X	X
Cantaloupe						X	X	X	X			
Cauliflower	X	X	X	X	X				X	X	X	X
Celery root	X	X	X	X					X	X	X	X
Cherries					X	X	X	X				
Chestnuts									X	X	X	X
Citrus	X	X	X	X	X	X			X	X	X	X
Collards	X										X	X
Corn						X	X	X				
Cranberries									X	X	X	X
Cucumbers					X	X	X	X				
Dates										X	X	X
Eggplants						X	X	X	X			
Figs						X	X	X	X	X		
Grapes						X	X	X	X	X	X	
Greens			X	X	X	X						
Kohlrabi						X	X					
Leeks	X	X	X							X	X	X
Lettuce			X	X	X	X	X	X	X			
Lychees						X	X					
Mangos					X	X	X	X				
Mushrooms, morels			X	X	X							

PRODUCT	JAN	FEB	MAR	APR	MAY	JUN	JUL	AUG	SEP	OCT	NOV	DEC
	WINTER DEC 21–MAR 19		SPRING MAR 20–JUN 20			SUMMER JUN 21–SEP 21			AUTUMN SEP 22–DEC 20			
Mushrooms, truffles	X	X									X	X
Okra					X	X	X	X	X			
Onions						X	X	X	X			
Onions, sweet				X	X	X						
Papayas			X	X	X	X						
Peaches					X	X	X	X				
Pears	X	X	X	X						X	X	X
Peas, English				X	X							
Peas, field							X	X				
Pecans											X	X
Peppers, bell						X	X	X	X			
Peppers, chile									X	X	X	X
Persimmons										X	X	X
Pineapples			X	X	X	X	X	X				
Plums						X	X	X	X			
Pome-granates									X	X	X	X
Potatoes								X	X	X		
Prickly pears									X	X	X	X
Pumpkins									X	X	X	
Raspberries						X	X	X	X			
Rhubarb		X	X	X	X							
Spinach	X	X	X	X	X					X	X	X
Squash, summer				X	X	X	X	X	X			
Squash, winter	X	X	X							X	X	X
Strawberries		X	X	X	X	X						
Tomatoes						X	X	X	X			
Turnips				X	X					X	X	
Water-melons						X	X	X				

VITAMIN AND MINERAL FUNCTIONS AND SOURCES

VITAMINS: THEIR FUNCTIONS, SOURCES AND TECHNIQUES FOR RETAINING MAXIMUM NUTRIENT CONTENT

VITAMIN	KNOWN FUNCTIONS IN THE HUMAN BODY	SOURCES	TECHNIQUES FOR NUTRIENT RETENTION
Vitamin A	Keeps skin healthy; protects eyes; protects mouth and nose linings; supports immune functioning	Deep yellow and orange vegetables, leafy green vegetables, deep orange fruits, egg yolks, liver, fortified milk	Serve fruits and vegetables raw or lightly cooked; store vegetables covered and refrigerated; steam vegetables; roast or broil meats
Vitamin D	Helps body absorb calcium; regulates calcium and phosphorus in the bones; assists bone mineralization	Fortified milk, butter, some fish oils, egg yolks (exposure to sunlight produces vitamin D in the body)	Stable under heat and insoluble in water; therefore unaffected by cooking
Vitamin E	Antioxidant; protects membranes and cell walls	Vegetable oils, whole grains, dark leafy vegetables, wheat germ, nuts, seeds, whole grains	Use whole-grain flours, store foods in airtight containers; avoid exposing food to light and air
Vitamin K	Assists blood-clotting proteins	Liver, dark green leafy vegetables (bacteria in the intestinal tract also produce some vitamin K)	Steam or microwave vegetables; do not overcook meats
Vitamin C (ascorbic acid)	Supports immune system functioning; repairs connective tissues; promotes healing; assists amino acid metabolism	Citrus fruits, green vegetables, strawberries, cantaloupes, tomatoes, broccoli, potatoes	Serve fruits and vegetables raw; steam or microwave vegetables
Thiamin (vitamin B_1)	Assists energy metabolism; supports nervous system functioning	Meats (especially pork), legumes, whole grains	Use enriched or whole-grain pasta or rice; do not wash whole grains before cooking or rinse afterward; steam or microwave vegetables; roast meats at moderate temperatures; cook meats only until done
Riboflavin (vitamin B_2)	Assists energy metabolism	Milk, cheese, yogurt, fish, enriched grain breads and cereals, dark green leafy vegetables	Store foods in opaque containers; roast or broil meats or poultry
Niacin (vitamin B_3)	Promotes normal digestion; supports nervous system functioning; assists energy metabolism	Meats, poultry, fish, dark green leafy vegetables, whole-grain or enriched breads and cereals, nuts	Steam or microwave vegetables; roast or broil beef, veal, lamb and poultry (pork retains about the same amount of niacin regardless of cooking method)
Vitamin B_6	Necessary for protein metabolism and red blood cell formation	Meats, fish, poultry, shellfish, whole grains, dark green vegetables, potatoes, liver	Serve vegetables raw; cook foods in a minimum amount of water and for the shortest possible time; roast or broil meats and fish
Vitamin B_{12}	Helps produce red blood cells; assists metabolism	Animal foods only, particularly milk, eggs, poultry and fish	Roast or broil meats, poultry and fish
Folate	Necessary for protein metabolism and red blood cell formation	Orange juice, dark green leafy vegetables, organ meats, legumes, seeds	Serve vegetables raw; steam or microwave vegetables; store vegetables covered and refrigerated
Biotin	Coenzyme in energy metabolism, glycogen synthesis and fat metabolism	Widespread in foods	
Pantothenic acid	Coenzyme in energy metabolism	Widespread in foods	

MINERALS: THEIR FUNCTIONS AND SOURCES

MINERAL	KNOWN FUNCTIONS IN THE HUMAN BODY	SOURCES
Major Minerals		
Calcium	Helps build bones and teeth; helps blood clot; promotes muscle and nerve functions	Dairy products, canned salmon and sardines, broccoli, kale, tofu, turnips
Magnesium	Muscle contraction; assists energy metabolism, bone formation	Green leafy vegetables, whole grains, legumes, fish, shellfish, cocoa
Phosphorus	Helps build bones and teeth; assists energy metabolism; formation of DNA	All animal tissues, milk, legumes, nuts
Potassium	Maintains electrolyte and fluid balance; promotes normal body functions; assists protein metabolism	Meats, poultry, fish, fruits (especially bananas, oranges, and cantaloupes), legumes, vegetables
Sodium	Maintains normal fluid balance; necessary for nerve impulse transmission	Salt, soy sauce, processed foods, MSG
Chloride	With sodium, involved in fluid balance; a component of stomach acid	Salt, soy sauce, meats, milk, processed foods
Sulfur	A component of some proteins, insulin, and the vitamins biotin and thiamin	All protein-containing foods
Trace Minerals		
Iron	Part of hemoglobin (the red substance in blood that carries oxygen); prevents anemia	Liver, meats, shellfish, enriched breads and cereals, legumes
Zinc	A component of insulin; enhances healing; a component of many enzymes; involved in taste perception; bone formation	Protein foods, whole-grain breads and cereals, fish, shellfish, poultry, vegetables
Selenium	Antioxidant	Fish, shellfish, meats, eggs, grains (depends on soil conditions)
Iodine	A component of thyroid hormone	Iodized salt, fish, shellfish, bread, plants grown in iodide-rich soil
Copper	Facilitates iron absorption; part of enzymes	Meats, fish, shellfish, nuts, seeds
Fluoride	Necessary for bone and teeth formation; helps teeth resist tooth decay	Fluoridated drinking water, fish, shellfish
Chromium	Insulin cofactor	Liver, whole grains, brewer's yeast, nuts, oils
Molybdenum	Cofactor in metabolism	Legumes, cereals
Manganese	Cofactor in metabolism	Whole grains, nuts, organ meats
Cobalt	Component of vitamin B_{12} (cobalamin)	Liver, shellfish, lean beef, seafood, eggs, dairy, poultry, fermented soybeans (miso)

GLOSSARY

à la—(ah lah) French for "in the manner or style of"; used in relation to a food, it designates a style of preparation or presentation

à la carte—(ah lah kart) (1) a menu on which each food and beverage is listed and priced separately; (2) foods cooked to order as opposed to foods cooked in advance and held for later service

à la grecque—(ah lah grehk) a preparation style in which vegetables are marinated in olive oil, lemon juice and herbs, then served cold

à point—(ah PWAN) (1) French term for cooking to the ideal degree of doneness; (2) when applied to meat, refers to cooking it medium rare

absorption—the ability of flour to absorb moisture when mixed into dough, which varies according to protein content, growing, and storage conditions

acid—a substance that neutralizes a base (alkaline) in a liquid solution; foods such as citrus juice, vinegar and wine that have a sour or sharp flavor (most foods are slightly acidic); acids have a pH of less than 7

acidulation—the browning of cut fruit caused by the reaction of an enzyme (polyphenoloxidase) with the phenolic compounds present in these fruits; this browning is often mistakenly attributed to exposure to oxygen

additives—substances added to many foods to prevent spoilage or improve appearance, texture, flavor or nutritional value; they may be synthetic materials copied from nature (for example, sugar substitutes) or naturally occurring substances (for example, lecithin). Some food additives may cause allergic reactions in sensitive people.

adobo seasoning—a commercial spice blend; although several brands are available, most include dried chiles,

Mexican oregano, cumin, black pepper, garlic powder and onion powder

aerate—to incorporate air into a mixture through sifting and mixing

aerobic bacteria—those that thrive on oxygen

aging—(1) the period during which freshly killed meat is allowed to rest so that the effects of rigor mortis dissipate; (2) the period during which freshly milled flour is allowed to rest so that it will whiten and produce less sticky doughs; the aging of flour can be chemically accelerated

agneau pre-salé—distinctively flavored lamb that grazes on salt marshes in France

airline breast—a boneless chicken breast with the first wing bone attached

albumen—the principal protein found in egg whites

al dente—(al DEN-tay) Italian for "to the tooth"; used to describe a food, usually pasta, that is cooked only until it gives a slight resistance when one bites into it

alkali—also known as a base, any substance with a pH higher than 7; baking soda is one of the few alkaline foods

allemande—(ah-leh-MAHND) an intermediary sauce made by adding lemon juice and a liaison to chicken or veal velouté

allergens—substances that may cause allergic reactions in some people

allumette—(al-yoo-MEHT) (1) a matchstick cut of ⅛ inch × ⅛ inch × 2 inches (3 millimeters × 3 millimeters × 5 centimeters) usually used for potatoes; (2) a strip of puff pastry with a sweet or savory filling

amino acid—the basic molecular component of proteins; each of the approximately two dozen amino acids contains oxygen, hydrogen, carbon and nitrogen atoms

anadromous—describes a fish that migrates from a saltwater habitat to spawn in fresh water

anaerobic bacteria—those that are able to live and grow without the presence of oxygen

andouille—(an-DOO-ee) a very spicy smoked pork sausage, popular in Cajun cuisine

angus beef, certified—a brand created in 1978 to distinguish the highest-quality beef produced from descendants of the black, hornless Angus cattle of Scotland

anterior—at or toward the front of an object or place; opposite of posterior

appetizers—also known as first courses, usually small portions of hot or cold foods intended to whet the appetite in anticipation of the more substantial courses to follow

aquafarming—also known as aquaculture, the business, science and practice of raising large quantities of fish and shellfish in tanks, ponds or ocean pens

aroma—the sensations, as interpreted by the brain, of what we detect when a substance comes in contact with sense receptors in the nose

aromatic—a food added to enhance the natural aromas of another food; aromatics include most flavorings, such as herbs and spices, as well as some vegetables

artisan—a person who works in a skilled craft or trade; one who works with his or her hands; applied to bread bakers, cheese makers, confectioners, charcutiers and other craftspeople who prepare foods using traditional methods

aspic; aspic jelly—a clear jelly usually made from a clarified stock thickened with gelatin; used to coat foods, especially charcuterie items, and for garnish

as purchased (A.P.)—the condition or cost of an item as it is purchased or received from the supplier

au gratin—(oh GRAH-tan) foods with a browned or crusted top; often made by browning a food with a bread-crumb, cheese and/or sauce topping under a broiler or salamander

au jus—(oh zhew) roasted meats, poultry or game served with their natural, unthickened juices

au sec—(oh sek) cooked until nearly dry

bacteria—single-celled microorganisms, some of which can cause diseases, including food-borne diseases

bagel—a dense, donut-shaped yeast roll; it is cooked in boiling water, then baked, which gives it a shiny glaze and chewy texture

bain marie—(bane mah-ree) (1) a hot-water bath used to gently cook food or keep cooked food hot; (2) a container for holding food in a hot-water bath

baked Alaska—ice cream set on a layer of spongecake and encased in meringue, then baked until the meringue is warm and golden

baked blind—describes a pie shell or tart shell that is baked unfilled, using baking weights or beans to support the crust as it bakes

baking—a dry-heat cooking method in which foods are surrounded by hot, dry air in a closed environment; similar to roasting, the term *baking* is usually applied to breads, pastries, vegetables and fish

baking powder—a mixture of sodium bicarbonate and one or more acids, generally cream of tartar and/or sodium aluminum sulfate, used to leaven baked goods; it releases carbon dioxide gas if moisture is present in a formula. Single-acting baking powder releases carbon dioxide gas in the presence of moisture only; double-acting baking powder releases some carbon dioxide gas upon contact with moisture, and more gas is released when heat is applied.

baking soda—sodium bicarbonate, an alkaline compound that releases carbon dioxide gas when combined with an acid and moisture; used to leaven baked goods

ballotine—(bahl-lo-teen) similar to a galantine; usually made by stuffing a deboned poultry leg with forcemeat; it is then poached or braised and normally served hot

barbecue—(1) to cook foods over dry heat created by the burning of hardwood or hardwood charcoals; (2) a tangy tomato- or vinegar-based sauce used for grilled foods; (3) foods cooked by this method and/or with this sauce

barding—tying thin slices of fat, such as bacon or pork fatback, over meats or poultry that have little to no natural fat covering in order to protect and moisten them during roasting

barista—Italian for "bartender"; now used to describe someone who has been professionally trained in the art of preparing espresso and espresso-based beverages

base—a substance that neutralizes an acid in a liquid solution; ingredients such as sodium bicarbonate (baking soda) that have an alkaline or bitter flavor; bases have a pH of more than 7

baste—to moisten foods during cooking (usually grilling, broiling or roasting) with melted fat, pan drippings, a sauce or other liquids to prevent drying and to add flavor

bâtonnet—(bah-toh-nah) foods cut into matchstick shapes of ¼ inch × ¼ inch × 2 inches (6 millimeters × 6 millimeters × 5 centimeters)

batter—(1) a semiliquid mixture containing flour or other starch used to make cakes and breads. The gluten development is minimized and the liquid forms the continuous medium in which other ingredients are disbursed; generally contains more fat, sugar and liquids than a dough; (2) a semiliquid mixture of liquid and starch used to coat foods for deep-frying.

Baumé scale—(boh-may) *see* hydrometer

bavarian cream—a sweet dessert mixture made by thickening custard sauce with gelatin and then folding in whipped cream; the final product is poured into a mold and chilled until firm

bean flour—cooked beans including chickpeas, soybeans and white beans that are dried, then ground into a fine powder. Many bean flours, especially soy flour with a 50% protein content, are added to wheat flour mixtures to boost protein content.

beard—a clump of dark threads found on a mussel

béarnaise—(bare-NAYZ) a sauce made of butter and egg yolks and flavored with a reduction of vinegar, shallots, tarragon and peppercorns

beating—a mixing method in which foods are vigorously agitated to incorporate air or develop gluten; a spoon or electric mixer with its paddle attachment is used

béchamel—(bay-shah-mell) a leading sauce made by thickening milk with a white roux and adding seasonings

beefalo—the product of crossbreeding a bison (American buffalo) and a domestic beef animal.

beer—an alcoholic beverage made from water, hops and malted barley, fermented by yeast

beignets—squares or strips of éclair paste deep-fried and dusted with powdered sugar

Berkshire pork—a breed of black pig named for the region of Great Britain where they were discovered, also known as Kurobuta in Japan; considered a rare and endangered breed, hogs produce pork that is well-marbled, moist and tender.

berry—(1) the kernel of certain grains such as wheat; (2) small, juicy fruits that grow on vines and bushes

beurre blanc—(burr BLANHK) French for "white butter"; an emulsified butter sauce made from shallots, white wine and butter

beurre composé—(burr kom-poh-ZAY) *see* compound butter

beurre fondu—(burr fon-DOO) French for "melted butter"; it is often served over steamed vegetables such as asparagus or poached white fish

beurre manié—(burr man-YAY) a combination of equal amounts by weight of flour and soft, whole butter; it is whisked into a simmering sauce at the end of the cooking process for quick thickening and added sheen and flavor

beurre noir—(burr NWAR) French for "black butter"; used to describe whole butter cooked until dark brown (not black); sometimes flavored with vinegar or lemon juice, capers and parsley and served over fish, eggs and vegetables

beurre noisette—(burr nwah-ZEHT) French for "brown butter"; used to describe butter cooked until it is a light brown color; it is flavored and used in much the same manner as beurre noir

beurre rouge—(burr ROOGE) French for "red butter"; an emulsified butter sauce made from shallots, red wine and butter

biological hazard—a danger to the safety of food caused by disease-causing microorganisms such as bacteria, molds, yeasts, viruses or fungi

biscotti—twice-baked cookies with a long-lasting, firm, crisp texture; Italian in origin, they are usually served with coffee, wine or other beverages

biscuit method—a mixing method used to make biscuits, scones and flaky doughs; it involves cutting cold fat into the flour and other dry ingredients before any liquid is added

bisque—(bisk) a soup made from shellfish; classic versions are thickened with rice

bivalves—mollusks such as clams, oysters and mussels that have two bilateral shells attached at a central hinge

blanching—very briefly and partially cooking a food in boiling water or hot fat; used to assist preparation (for example, to loosen peels from vegetables), as part of a combination cooking method or to remove undesirable flavors

blanquette—(blahn-KEHT) a white stew made of a white sauce and meat or poultry that is simmered without first browning

blending—a mixing method in which two or more ingredients are combined just until they are evenly distributed

bloom—(1) a white, powdery layer that sometimes appears on chocolate if the cocoa butter separates; (2) a measure of gelatin's strength; (3) to soften granulated gelatin in a cold liquid before dissolving and using

blue cheese—(1) a generic term for any cheese containing visible blue-green molds that contribute a characteristic tart, sharp flavor and aroma; also known as a blue-veined cheese or bleu; (2) a group of Roquefort-style cheeses made in the United States and Canada from cow's or goat's milk rather than ewe's milk and injected with molds that form blue-green veins; also known as blue mold cheese or blue-veined cheese

boiling—a moist-heat cooking method that uses convection to transfer heat from a hot (approximately 212°F/100°C) liquid to the food submerged in it; the turbulent waters and higher temperatures cook foods more quickly than do poaching or simmering

bombe—two or more flavors of ice cream, or ice cream and sherbet, shaped in a spherical mold; each flavor is a separate layer that forms the shell for the next flavor

bouchées—(boo-SHAY) small puff pastry shells that can be filled and served as bite-size hors d'oeuvre or petit fours

bound salad—a salad composed of cooked meats, poultry, fish, shellfish, pasta or potatoes combined with a dressing

bouquet garni—(boo-KAY gar-NEE) fresh herbs and vegetables tied into a bundle with twine and used to flavor stocks, sauces, soups and stews

boxed beef—industry terminology for primal and subprimal cuts of beef that are vacuum sealed and packed into cardboard boxes for shipping from the packing plant to retailers and food service operations

braising—a combination cooking method in which foods are first browned in hot fat, then covered and slowly cooked in a small amount of liquid over low heat; braising uses a combination of simmering and steaming to transfer heat from the liquid (conduction) and the air (convection) to the foods

bran—the tough outer layer of a cereal grain and the part highest in fiber

brandy—an alcoholic beverage made by distilling wine or the fermented mash of grapes or other fruits.

brawn—also called an aspic terrine, made from simmered meats packed into a terrine and covered with aspic

brazier; brasier—a pan designed for braising; usually round with two handles and a tight-fitting lid

breading—(1) a coating of bread or cracker crumbs, cornmeal or other dry meal applied to foods that will typically be deep-fried or pan-fried; (2) the process of applying this coating

brigade—a system of staffing a kitchen so that each worker is assigned a set of specific tasks; these tasks are often related by cooking method, equipment or the types of foods being produced

brine—a mixture of salt, water and seasonings used to preserve foods

brioche—(bree-OHSH) a rich yeast bread containing large amounts of eggs and butter

brochettes—(bro-SHETTS) skewers, either small hors d'oeuvre or large entrée size, threaded with meat, poultry, fish, shellfish and/or vegetables and grilled, broiled or baked; sometimes served with a dipping sauce

broiling—a dry-heat cooking method in which foods are cooked by heat radiating from an overhead source

broth—a flavorful liquid obtained from the long simmering of meats and/or vegetables

brown sauce—*see* espagnole

brown stew—a stew in which the meat is first browned in hot fat

brown stock—a richly colored stock made of chicken, veal, beef or game bones and vegetables, all of which are caramelized before they are simmered in water with seasonings

brunoise—(BROO-nwaz) (1) foods cut into cubes of ⅛ inch × ⅛ inch × ⅛ inch (3 millimeters × 3 millimeters × 3 millimeters); a 1/16-inch (1.5-millimeter) cube is referred to as a fine brunoise; (2) foods garnished with vegetables cut in this manner

buckwheat flour—a dark, nutty-tasting flour milled from the seeds of the buckwheat plant; used for centuries in Middle Eastern and Asian countries to make bread, cereals and baked goods

buffet service—restaurant service in which diners generally serve themselves foods arranged on a counter or table or are served by workers assigned to specific areas of the buffet. Usually buffet-service-style restaurants charge by the meal; restaurants offering buffet service that charge by the dish are known as cafeterias.

bun—any of a variety of small, round yeast rolls; can be sweet or savory

butcher—to slaughter and/or dress or fabricate animals for consumption

butler service—restaurant service in which servers pass foods (typically hors d'oeuvre) or drinks arranged on trays

buttercream—a light, smooth, fluffy frosting of sugar, fat and flavorings; egg yolks or whipped egg whites are sometimes added. There are three principal kinds: simple, Italian and French.

butterfly—to slice boneless meat, poultry or fish nearly in half lengthwise so that it spreads open like a book

caffeine—an alkaloid found in coffee beans, tea leaves and cocoa beans that acts as a stimulant

cake—in American usage, refers to a broad range of pastries, including layer cakes, coffeecakes and gâteaux; can refer to almost anything that is baked, tender, sweet and sometimes frosted

calf—(1) a young cow or bull; (2) the meat of calves slaughtered when they are older than five months

calorie—the unit of energy measured by the amount of heat required to raise 1000 grams of water one degree Celsius; it is also written as kilocalorie or kcal

canapé—(KAN-ah-pay) a tiny open-faced sandwich served as an hors d'oeuvre; usually composed of a small piece of bread or toast topped with a savory spread and garnish

capicola—Italian dry-cured salami made from pork shoulder that is seasoned with garlic, hot pepper, spices and wine, then smoked and cured

capon—(kay-pahn) the class of surgically castrated male chickens; they have well-flavored meat and soft, smooth skin

capsaicin—(kap-SAY-ee-zin) an alkaloid found in a chile pepper's placental ribs that provides the pepper's heat

caramelization—the process of cooking sugars; the browning of sugar enhances the flavor and appearance of foods

carbohydrates—a group of compounds composed of oxygen, hydrogen and carbon that supply the body with energy (4 calories per gram); carbohydrates are classified as simple (including certain sugars) and complex (including starches and fiber)

carotenoid—a naturally occurring pigment that predominates in red and yellow vegetables such as carrots and red peppers

carryover cooking—the cooking that occurs after a food is removed from a heat source; it is accomplished by the residual heat remaining in the food

cartilage—also known as gristle; a tough, elastic, whitish connective tissue that helps give structure to an animal's body

carve—to cut cooked meat or poultry into portions

casings—membranes used to hold forcemeat for sausages; they can be natural animal intestines or manufactured from collagen extracted from cattle hides

casserole—(1) a heavy dish, usually ceramic, for baking foods; (2) foods baked in a casserole dish

caul fat—a fatty membrane from pig or sheep intestines; it resembles fine netting and is used to bard roasts and pâtés and to encase forcemeat for sausages

caviar—traditionally, the salted roe (eggs) of sturgeon fish; imported sturgeon caviar is classified by species, size and color as beluga, osetra, or sevruga

cellulose—a complex carbohydrate found in the cell wall of plants; it is edible but indigestible by humans

cephalopods—mollusks with a single, thin internal shell called a pen or cuttlebone, well-developed eyes, a number of arms that attach to the head and a saclike fin-bearing mantle; include squid and octopus

Certified Angus Beef—a brand created in 1978 to distinguish the highest-quality beef produced from descendants of the black, hornless Angus cattle of Scotland. The meat must meet American Angus Association standards for yield, marbling and age, and be graded as high choice or prime.

chafing dish—a metal dish with a heating unit (flame or electric) used to keep foods warm at tableside or during buffet service

chalazae cords—thick, twisted strands of egg white that anchor the yolk in place

challah—(HAH-la) a yeast bread enriched with eggs and flavored with honey; loaves are traditionally braided and topped with sesame or poppy seeds

charcuterie—(shahr-COO-tuhr-ree) the production of pâtés, terrines, galantines, sausages and similar foods

chaud-froid—(shoh-FRAWH) French for "hot-cold"; refers to a white sauce made with either mayonnaise or cream and stock thickened with gelatin; used to coat foods such as whole fish or poultry for decorative purposes

cheesecloth—a light, fine mesh gauze used to strain liquids and make sachets

chef de cuisine—(chef duh qui-zine) also known simply as chef; the person responsible for all kitchen operations, developing menu items and setting the kitchen's tone and tempo

chef's knife—an all-purpose knife used for chopping, slicing and mincing; its tapering blade is 8–14 inches (20–35 centimeters) long

chemical hazard—a danger to the safety of food caused by chemical substances, especially cleaning agents, pesticides and toxic metals

chèvre—(SHEHV-ruh) French for "goat"; generally refers to a cheese made from goat's milk

chiffon—(1) a cake leavened with whipped egg whites and enriched with egg yolks and oil, usually flavored with citrus and baked in a tube pan; (2) a pie filling or dessert preparation lightened with whipped egg whites and thickened with gelatin

chiffonade—(chef-fon-nahd) to finely slice or shred leafy vegetables or herbs

chile—a member of the *Capsicum* family; may be used fresh or dried or dried and ground into a powder

chili—a stewlike dish containing chiles

chilli—a commercial spice powder containing a blend of seasonings

china cap—a cone-shaped strainer made of perforated metal

chine—the backbone or spine of an animal; a subprimal cut of beef, veal, lamb, pork or game carcass containing a portion of the backbone with some adjoining flesh

chinois—(sheen-WAH) a conical strainer made of fine mesh, used for straining and puréeing foods

chlorophyll—a naturally occurring pigment that predominates in green vegetables such as cabbage

cholesterol—a fatty substance found in foods derived from animal products and in the human body; it has been linked to heart disease

chop—(1) a cut of meat, including part of the rib; (2) to cut into pieces when uniformity of size and shape is not important

chorizo—(chor-EE-zoh) a coarse, spicy pork sausage flavored with ground chiles and removed from its casing before cooking; used in Mexican and Spanish cuisines

choux pastry—(shoo paste-re) *see* éclair paste

chowder—a hearty soup made from fish, shellfish and/or vegetables, usually containing milk and potatoes and often thickened with roux

churros—a Spanish and Mexican pastry in which sticks of éclair paste flavored with cinnamon are deep-fried and rolled in sugar while still hot

chutney—a sweet-and-sour condiment made of fruits and/or vegetables cooked in vinegar with sugar and spices; some chutneys are reduced to a purée, while others retain recognizable pieces of their ingredients

cider—mildly fermented apple juice; nonalcoholic apple juice may also be labeled cider

citrus—fruits characterized by a thick rind, most of which is a bitter white pith (albedo) with a thin exterior layer of colored skin (zest); their flesh is segmented and juicy and varies from bitter to tart to sweet

clarification—(1) the process of transforming a broth into a clear consommé by trapping impurities with a clearmeat consisting of the egg white protein albumen, ground meat, an acidic product, mirepoix and other ingredients; (2) the clearmeat used to clarify a broth

clarified butter—purified butterfat; the butter is melted and the water and milk solids are removed

classic cuisine—a late 19th- and early 20th-century refinement and simplification of French grande cuisine. Classic (or classical) cuisine relies on the thorough exploration of culinary principles and techniques, and emphasizes the refined preparation and presentation of superb ingredients.

clean—to remove visible dirt and soil

clear soups—unthickened soups, including broths, consommés and broth-based soups

clearmeat—*see* clarification

club roll—a small oval-shaped roll made of crusty French bread

coagulation—the irreversible transformation of proteins from a liquid or semiliquid state to a solid state

cocoa butter—the fat found in cocoa beans and used in fine chocolates; it is white, solid at room temperature and tasteless

coconut cream—(1) a coconut-flavored liquid made like coconut milk but with less water; it is creamier and thicker than coconut milk; (2) the thick fatty portion that separates and rises to the top of canned or frozen coconut milk; do not substitute cream of coconut for true coconut cream

coconut milk—a coconut-flavored liquid made by pouring boiling water over shredded coconut; may be sweetened or unsweetened; do not substitute cream of coconut for coconut milk

coconut water—the thin, slightly opaque liquid contained within a fresh coconut

colander—a perforated bowl, with or without a base or legs, used to strain foods

collagen—a protein found in connective tissue; it is converted into gelatin when cooked with moisture

combination cooking methods—cooking methods, principally braising and stewing, that employ both dry-heat and moist-heat procedures

composed salad—a salad prepared by arranging each of the ingredients (the base, body, garnish and dressing) on individual plates in an artistic fashion

composition—a completed plate's structure of colors, shapes and arrangements

compound butter—also known as a beurre composé, a mixture of softened whole butter and flavorings used as a sauce or to flavor and color other sauces

compound sauces—*see* small sauces

concassée—peeled, seeded and diced tomato

concentrate—also known as a fruit paste or compound; a reduced fruit purée, without a gel structure, used as a flavoring

conching—stirring melted chocolate with large stone or metal rollers to create a smooth texture in the finished chocolate

condiment—traditionally, any item added to a dish for flavor, including herbs, spices and vinegars; now also refers to cooked or prepared flavorings such as prepared mustards, relishes, bottled sauces and pickles

conduction—the transfer of heat from one item to another through direct contact

confit—(kohn-FEE) meat or poultry (often lightly salt-cured) slowly cooked and preserved in its own fat and served hot

connective tissue—tissue found throughout an animal's body that binds together and supports other tissues such as muscles

consommé—(kwang-soh-MAY) a rich stock or broth that has been clarified with clearmeat to remove impurities

contaminants—biological, chemical or physical substances that can be harmful when consumed in sufficient quantities

contamination—the presence, generally unintentional, of harmful organisms or substances

convection—the transfer of heat caused by the natural movement of molecules in a fluid (whether air, water or fat) from a warmer area to a cooler one; mechanical convection is the movement of molecules caused by stirring

conversion factor (C.F.)—the number used to increase or decrease ingredient quantities and recipe yields

cookery—the art, practice or work of cooking

cookie press—also known as a cookie gun, a hollow tube fitted with a plunger and an interchangeable decorative tip or plate; soft cookie dough is pressed through the tip to create shapes or patterns

cookies—small, sweet, flat pastries; usually classified by preparation or makeup techniques as drop, icebox, bar, sheet, cutout, pressed, rolled or molded and wafer

cooking—(1) the transfer of energy from a heat source to a food; this energy alters the food's molecular structure, changing its texture, flavor, aroma and appearance; (2) the preparation of food for consumption

cooking medium—the air, fat, water or steam in which a food is cooked

coring—the process of removing the seeds or pit from a fruit or fruit-vegetable

cost of goods sold—the total cost of food items sold during a given period; calculated as beginning inventory plus purchases minus ending inventory

cost per portion—the amount of the total recipe cost divided by the number of portions produced from that recipe; the cost of one serving

coulibiac—a creamy mixture of salmon fillet, rice, hard-cooked eggs, mushrooms, shallots and dill enclosed in a pastry envelope usually made of brioche dough

coulis—(koo-LEE) a sauce made from a purée of vegetables and/or fruit; may be served hot or cold

count—the number of individual items in a given measure of weight or volume

coupe—another name for an ice cream sundae, especially one served with a fruit topping

court bouillon—(kort boo-yon) water simmered with vegetables, seasonings and an acidic product such as vinegar or wine; used for simmering or poaching fish, shellfish or vegetables

couverture—(coo-vehr-TYOOR) high quality chocolate containing at least 32% cocoa butter

cracking—a milling process in which grains are broken open

cream filling—a pie filling made of flavored pastry cream thickened with cornstarch

creaming—a mixing method in which softened fat and sugar are vigorously combined to incorporate air

cream of coconut—a canned commercial product consisting of thick, sweetened coconut-flavored liquid; used for baking and in beverages

cream puffs—baked rounds of éclair paste cut in half and filled with pastry cream, whipped cream, fruit or other filling

creams—also known as crèmes; include light, fluffy or creamy-textured dessert foods made with whipped cream or whipped egg whites, such as Bavarian creams, chiffons, mousses and crème Chantilly

cream sauce—a sauce made by adding cream to a béchamel sauce

cream soup—a soup made from vegetables cooked in a liquid that is thickened with a starch and puréed; cream is then incorporated to add richness and flavor

crème anglaise—(khrem ahn-GLEHZ) also known as crème à l'anglaise; *see* vanilla custard sauce

crème brûlée—(krehm broo-lay) French for "burnt cream"; used to describe a rich dessert custard topped with a crust of caramelized sugar

crème caramel—(khrem kair-ah-MEHL) like crème renversée (rehn-vehr-SAY) and flan, a custard baked over a layer of caramelized sugar and inverted for service

crème Chantilly—(khrem shan-TEE) heavy cream whipped to soft peaks and flavored with sugar and vanilla; used to garnish pastries or desserts or folded into cooled custard or pastry cream for fillings

crème Chiboust—(krehm chee-boos) a vanilla pastry cream lightened by folding in Italian meringue; traditionally used in a gâteau St. Honoré

crème pâtissière—(khrem pah-tees-SYEHR) *see* pastry cream

crêpe—(krayp) a thin, delicate unleavened griddlecake made with a very thin egg batter cooked in a very hot sauté pan; used in sweet and savory preparations

critical control point—a step during the processing of food when a mistake can result in the transmission, growth or survival of pathogenic bacteria

croissant—(krwah-SAHN) a crescent-shaped roll made from a rich, rolled-in yeast dough

croquembouche—(krow-kem-BOOSH) a pyramid of small puffs, each filled with pastry cream; a French tradition for Christmas and weddings, it is held together with caramelized sugar and decorated with spun sugar or marzipan flowers

croquette—(crow-keht) a food that has been puréed or bound with a thick sauce (usually béchamel or velouté), made into small shapes and then breaded and deep-fried

cross-contamination—the transfer of bacteria or other contaminants from one food, work surface or piece of equipment to another

croûte, en—(awn KROOT) describes a food encased in a bread or pastry crust

crouton—(KROO-tawn) a bread or pastry garnish, usually toasted or sautéed until crisp

crudités—(croo-dee-TAYS) generally refers to raw or blanched vegetables served as an hors d'oeuvre and often accompanied by a dip

crullers—a Dutch pastry in which a loop or strip of twisted éclair paste is deep-fried

crumb—the interior of bread or cake; may be elastic, aerated, fine grained or coarse grained

crustaceans—shellfish characterized by a hard outer skeleton or shell and jointed appendages; include lobsters, crabs and shrimp

cuisine—the ingredients, seasonings, cooking procedures and styles attributable to a particular group of people; the group can be defined by geography, history, ethnicity, politics, culture or religion

cuisson—(kwee-sohn) the liquid used for shallow poaching

cupping—testing coffee or tea for taste and quality, often performed by a professional taster trained to identify key coffee or tea characteristics

curd—(1) the solid portion of milk when it separates; what becomes cheese; (2) a stirred custard made from eggs, sugar, butter and fruit juice, usually citrus

curdling—the separation of milk or egg mixtures into solid and liquid components; caused by overcooking, high heat or the presence of acids

curing salt—a mixture of salt and sodium nitrite that inhibits bacterial growth; used as a preservative, often for charcuterie items

custard—any liquid thickened by the coagulation of egg proteins; its consistency depends on the ratio of eggs to liquid and the type of liquid used; custards can be baked in the oven or cooked in a bain marie or on the stove top

cutlet—a relatively thick, boneless slice of meat

cutting—(1) reducing a food to smaller pieces; (2) a mixing method in which solid fat is incorporated into dry ingredients until only lumps of the desired size remain

cutting loss—the unavoidable and unrecoverable loss of food during fabrication; the loss is usually the result of food particles sticking to the cutting board or the evaporation of liquids

cuttlebone—also known as the pen, the single, thin internal shell of cephalopods

dairy products—include cow's milk and foods produced from cow's milk such as butter, yogurt, sour cream and cheese; sometimes other milks and products made from them are included (e.g., goat's milk cheese)

decant—to separate liquid from solids without disturbing the sediment by pouring off the liquid; vintage wines are often decanted to remove sediment

decoction—(1) boiling a food until its flavor is removed; (2) a procedure used for brewing coffee

deep-frying—a dry-heat cooking method that uses convection to transfer heat to a food submerged in hot fat; foods to be deep-fried are usually first coated in batter or breading

deglaze—to swirl or stir a liquid (usually wine or stock) in a pan to dissolve cooked food particles remaining on the bottom; the resulting mixture often becomes the base for a sauce

degrease—to remove fat from the surface of a liquid such as a stock or sauce by skimming, scraping or lifting congealed fat

demi-glace—(deh-me glass) French for "half-glaze"; a mixture of half brown stock and half brown sauce reduced by half

density—the relationship between the mass and volume of a substance ($D = m/v$). For example, as more and more sugar is dissolved in a liquid, the heavier or denser the liquid will become. Sugar density is measured on the Baumé scale using a hydrometer or saccharometer.

dessert wines—sweet wines made from grapes left on the vine until they are overly ripe, such as Sauternes or wines labeled "Late Harvest"; during fermentation, some of the sugar is not converted to alcohol, but remains in the wine, giving it its characteristic intense sweet taste

détrempe—a paste made with flour and water during the first stage of preparing a pastry dough, especially rolled-in doughs

deveining—the process of removing a shrimp's digestive tract

deviled—describes meat, poultry or other food seasoned with mustard, vinegar and other spicy seasonings

diagonals—oval-shaped slices

dice—to cut into cubes with six equal-sized sides

dip—a thick, creamy sauce, served hot or cold, to accompany crudités, crackers, chips or other foods, especially as an hors d'oeuvre; dips are often based on sour cream, mayonnaise or cream cheese

direct contamination—the contamination of raw foods in their natural setting or habitat

distillation—the separation of alcohol from a liquid (or, during the production of alcoholic beverages, from a fermented mash); it is accomplished by heating the liquid or mash to a gas that contains alcohol vapors; this steam is then condensed into the desired alcoholic liquid (beverage)

diver scallops—scallops that are harvested from the ocean by divers who hand-pick each one; diver scallops tend to be less gritty than those harvested by dragging, and hand-harvesting is more ecologically friendly

dock—to prick small holes in an unbaked dough or crust to allow steam to escape and to prevent the dough from rising when baked

dough—a mixture of flour and other ingredients used in baking; has a low moisture content, and gluten forms the continuous medium into which other ingredients are embedded; it is often stiff enough to cut into shapes

drawn—a market form for fish in which the viscera is removed

dredging—coating a food with flour or finely ground crumbs; usually done prior to sautéing or frying or as the first step of the standard breading procedure

dress—to trim or otherwise prepare an animal carcass for consumption

dressed—a market form for fish in which the viscera, gills, fins and scales are removed

dressing—another name for a bread stuffing used with poultry

drupes—*see* stone fruits

dry-heat cooking methods—cooking methods, principally broiling, grilling, roasting and baking, sautéing, pan-frying and deep-frying, that use air or fat to transfer heat through conduction and convection; dry-heat cooking methods allow surface sugars to caramelize

drying—a preservation method in which the food's moisture content is dramatically reduced; drying changes the food's texture, flavor and appearance

duchesse potatoes—(duh-shees) a purée of cooked potatoes, butter and egg yolks, seasoned with salt, pepper and nutmeg; can be eaten as is or used to prepare several classic potato dishes

duckling—a duck slaughtered before it is eight weeks old

dumpling—any of a variety of small starchy products made from doughs or batters that are simmered or steamed; can be plain or filled

durum wheat—a species of very hard wheat with a particularly high amount of protein; it is used to make couscous or milled into semolina, which is used for making pasta

duxelles—a coarse paste made of finely chopped mushrooms sautéed with shallots in butter used in sauces and stuffing

éclair paste—(ay-clahr) also known as pâte à choux; a soft dough that produces hollow baked products with crisp exteriors; used for making éclairs, cream puffs and savory products

éclairs—baked fingers of éclair paste filled with pastry cream; the top is then coated with chocolate glaze or fondant

edible portion (E.P.)—the amount of a food item available for consumption or use after trimming or fabrication; a smaller, more convenient portion of a larger or bulk unit

egg wash—a mixture of beaten eggs (whole eggs, yolks or whites) and a liquid, usually milk or water, used to coat doughs before baking to add sheen

elastin—a protein found in connective tissues, particularly ligaments and tendons; it often appears as the white or silver covering on meats known as silverskin

émincé—a small, thin, boneless piece of meat

emulsification—the process by which generally unmixable liquids, such as oil and water, are forced into a uniform distribution

emulsion—a uniform mixture of two unmixable liquids; it is often temporary (for example, oil in water)

endosperm—the largest part of a cereal grain and a source of protein and carbohydrates (starch); the part used primarily in milled products

en papillote—(awn pa-pee-yote) a cooking method in which food is wrapped in paper or foil and then heated so that the food steams in its own moisture

entrée—the main dish of an American meal, usually meat, poultry, fish or shellfish accompanied by a vegetable and starch; in France, the first course, served before the fish and meat courses

escalope—(eh-SKAL-ohp) *see* scallop

escargot—(ays-SKAHR-go) French for "snail"; those used for culinary purposes are land snails (genus *Helix*); the most popular are the large Burgundy snails and the smaller but more flavorful common or garden snail known as *petit gris*

espagnole—(ess-spah-nyol) also known as brown sauce, a leading sauce made of brown stock, mirepoix and tomatoes thickened with brown roux; often used to produce demi-glace

espresso—a unique method for brewing coffee in which hot water is forced through finely ground and packed coffee under high pressure, the coffee beans used are traditionally roasted very dark before grinding. Espresso coffee is the base for many drinks, such as cappuccino and caffé latte, to which steamed and/or foamed milk is added.

essence—a sauce made from a concentrated vegetable juice

essential nutrients—nutrients that must be provided by food because the body cannot or does not produce them in sufficient quantities

essential oils—pure oils extracted from the skins, peels and other parts of plants used to give their aroma and taste to flavoring agents in foods, cosmetics and other products

ethnic cuisine—the cuisine of a group of people having a common cultural heritage, as opposed to the cuisine of a group of people bound together by geography or political factors

ethylene gas—a colorless, odorless hydrocarbon gas naturally emitted from fruits and fruit-vegetables that encourages ripening

evaporation—the process by which heated water molecules move faster and faster until the water turns to a gas (steam) and vaporizes; evaporation is responsible for the drying of foods during cooking

ewe's milk—milk produced by a female sheep; it has approximately 7.9% milkfat, 11.4% milk solids and 80.7% water

extracts—concentrated mixtures of ethyl alcohol and flavoring oils such as vanilla, almond and lemon

extrusion—the process of forcing pasta dough through perforated plates to create various shapes; pasta dough that is not extruded must be rolled and cut

fabricate—to cut a larger portion of raw meat (for example, a primal or subprimal), poultry or fish into smaller portions

fabricated cuts—individual portions cut from a subprimal

facultative bacteria—those that can adapt and will survive with or without oxygen

fancy—(1) fish that has been previously frozen; (2) a quality grade for fruits, especially canned or frozen

farm-to-table movement—an awareness of the source of ingredients with an emphasis on serving locally grown and minimally processed foods in season

fatback—fresh pork fat from the back of the pig, used primarily for barding

fats—(1) a group of compounds composed of oxygen, hydrogen and carbon atoms that supply the body with energy (9 calories per gram); fats are classified as saturated, monounsaturated or polyunsaturated; (2) the general term for butter, lard, shortening, oil and margarine used as cooking media or ingredients

fermentation—the process by which yeast converts sugar into alcohol and carbon dioxide; it also refers to the time that yeast dough is left to rise—that is, the time it takes for carbon dioxide gas cells to form and become trapped in the gluten network

feuilletées—(fuh-yuh-TAY) square, rectangular or diamond-shaped puff pastry boxes; may be filled with a sweet or savory mixture

fiber—also known as dietary fiber; indigestible carbohydrates found in grains, fruits and vegetables; fiber aids digestion

FIFO (first in, first out)—a system of rotating inventory, particularly perishable and semiperishable goods, in which items are used in the order in which they are received

filé—(fee-lay) a seasoning and thickening agent made from dried, ground sassafras leaves

filet, fillet—(fee-lay) (1) filet: a boneless tenderloin of meat; (2) fillet: the side of a fish removed intact, boneless or semiboneless, with or without skin; (3) to cut such a piece

fish velouté—a velouté sauce made from fish stock

flambé—(flahm-BAY) food served flaming; produced by igniting brandy, rum or other liquor

flan—a firm savory or sweet egg custard; dessert variety is baked over a layer of caramelized sugar and inverted for service

flash-frozen—describes food that has been frozen very rapidly using metal plates, extremely low temperatures or chemical solutions

flash point—the temperature at which a fat ignites and small flames appear on the surface of the fat

flatfish—fish with asymmetrical, compressed bodies that swim in a horizontal position and have both eyes on the top of the head; include sole, flounder and halibut

flavonoids—plant pigments that dissolve readily in water, found in red, purple and white vegetables such as blueberries, red cabbage, onions and tea

flavor—an identifiable or distinctive quality of a food, drink or other substance perceived with the combined senses of taste, touch and smell

flavored tea—tea to which flavorings such as oils, dried fruit, spices, flowers and herbs have been added

flavoring—an item that adds a new taste to a food and alters its natural flavors; flavorings include herbs, spices, vinegars

and condiments; the terms *seasoning* and *flavoring* are often used interchangeably

flax—a grain plant also known as linseed; rich in omega-3 fatty acids, a compound in oily fish found to be beneficial for promoting heart and arterial health. Flax hulls and seeds are crushed into a meal or flour to release beneficial compounds.

fleuron—(fluh-rawng) a crescent-shaped piece of puff pastry used as a garnish

flour—a powdery substance of varying degrees of fineness made by milling grains such as wheat, corn or rye

foamed milk—milk that is heated and frothed with air and steam generated by an espresso machine; it will be slightly cooler than steamed milk

foie gras—(fwah grah) liver of specially fattened geese

fold—(1) a mixing method; (2) a measurement of the strength of vanilla extract

folding—a mixing method in which light, airy ingredients are incorporated into heavier ingredients by gently moving them from the bottom of the bowl up over the top in a circular motion, usually with a rubber spatula

fond—(1) French for "stock" or "base"; (2) the concentrated juices, drippings and bits of food left in pans after foods are roasted or sautéed; it is used to flavor sauces made directly in the pans in which foods were cooked

fondant—(FAHN-dant) a sweet, thick opaque sugar paste commonly used for glazing pastries such as napoleons or making candies

fond lié—(fahn lee-ay) *see* jus lié

fondue—a Swiss specialty made with melted cheese, wine and flavorings; eaten by dipping pieces of bread into the hot mixture with long forks

food cost—the cost of the materials that go directly into the production of menu items

food cost percentage—the ratio of the cost of foods used to the total food sales during a set period, calculated by dividing the cost of food used by the total sales in a restaurant

forcemeat—a preparation made from uncooked ground meats, poultry, fish or shellfish, seasoned, and emulsified with fat; commonly prepared as country-style, basic and mousseline and used for charcuterie items

fork tender—describes braised meat that is so tender it shows little resistance when pierced with a fork

formula—the standard term used throughout the industry for a bakeshop recipe; formulas rely on weighing to ensure accurate measuring of ingredients

frangipane—(fran-juh-pahn) a sweet almond and egg filling cooked inside pastry

free-range chickens—chickens allowed to move freely and forage for food; as opposed to chickens raised in coops

free-range veal—the meat of calves that are allowed to roam freely and eat grasses and other natural foods; this meat is pinker and more strongly flavored than that of milk-fed calves

freezer burn—the surface dehydration and discoloration of food that results from moisture loss at below-freezing temperatures

French dressing—classically, a vinaigrette dressing made from oil, vinegar, salt and pepper; in the United States, the term also refers to a commercially prepared dressing that is creamy, tartly sweet and red-orange in color

frenching—a method of trimming racks or individual chops of meat, especially lamb, in which the excess fat is cut away, leaving the eye muscle intact; all meat and connective tissue are removed from the rib bone

fresh-frozen—describes a food that has been frozen while still fresh

fricassee—(FRIHK-uh-see) a white stew in which the meat is cooked in fat without browning before the liquid is added

frittata—(free-TAH-ta) an open-faced omelet of Spanish-Italian origin

fritters—deep-fried sweet or savory cakes or spheres often made with chopped fruits or vegetables coated in batter

frosting—also known as icing, a sweet decorative coating used as a filling between the layers or as a coating over the top and sides of a cake

fruit—the edible organ that develops from the ovary of a flowering plant and contains one or more seeds (pips or pits)

frying—a dry-heat cooking method in which foods are cooked in hot fat; includes sautéing and stir-frying, pan-frying and deep-frying

fumet—(foo-may) a stock made from fish bones or shellfish shells and vegetables simmered in a liquid with flavorings

fungi—a large group of plants ranging from single-celled organisms to giant mushrooms; the most common are molds and yeasts

fusion cuisine—the blending or use of ingredients and/or preparation methods from various ethnic, regional or national cuisines in the same dish; also known as transnational cuisine

galantine—(GAL-uhn-teen) similar to a ballotine; a charcuterie item made from a forcemeat of poultry, game or suckling pig usually wrapped in the skin of the bird or animal and poached in an appropriate stock; often served cold, usually in aspic

game—birds and animals hunted for sport or food; many game birds and animals are now ranch-raised and commercially available

game hen—the class of young or immature progeny of Cornish chickens or of a Cornish chicken and White Rock chicken; they are small and very flavorful

ganache—(ga-NOSH) a rich blend of chocolate and heavy cream and, optionally, flavorings, used as a pastry or candy filling or frosting

garde-manger—(gar mawn-zhay) (1) also known as the pantry chef, the cook in charge of cold food production, including salads and salad dressings,

charcuterie items, cold appetizers and buffet items; (2) the work area where these foods are prepared

garnish—(1) food used as an attractive decoration; (2) a subsidiary food used to add flavor or character to the main ingredient in a dish (for example, noodles in chicken noodle soup)

gastrique—(gas-streek) caramelized sugar deglazed with vinegar; used to flavor tomato or savory fruit sauces

gastronomy—the art and science of eating well

gâteau—(gah-toe) (1) in American usage, refers to any cake-type dessert; (2) in French usage, refers to various pastry items made with puff pastry, éclair paste, short dough or sweet dough

gaufrette—(goh-FREHT) a thin lattice or waffle-textured slice of vegetable, especially potatoes, cut on a mandoline

gelatin—a tasteless and odorless mixture of proteins (especially collagen) extracted from boiling bones, connective tissue and other animal parts; when dissolved in a hot liquid and then cooled, it forms a jellylike substance used as a thickener and stabilizer

gelatinization—the process by which starch granules are cooked; they absorb moisture when placed in a liquid and heated; as the moisture is absorbed, the product swells, softens and clarifies slightly

gelato—(jah-laht-to) an Italian-style ice cream that is denser, softer and often more intensely flavored than American-style ice cream

genoise—(zhen-waahz) (1) a form of whipped-egg cake that uses whole eggs whipped with sugar; (2) a French spongecake

germ—the smallest portion of a cereal grain and the only part that contains fat

ghee—a form of clarified butter in which the milk solids remain with the fat and are allowed to brown; originating in India and now used worldwide as an ingredient and cooking medium, it has a long shelf life, a high smoke point and a nutty, caramel-like flavor

gianduja—(zhahn-DOO-yah) chocolate blended with hazelnut paste

giblets—the collective term for edible poultry viscera, including gizzards, hearts, livers and necks.

gizzard—a bird's second stomach

glaçage—(glah-sahge) browning or glazing a food, usually under a salamander or broiler

glace de poisson—(glahss duh pwah-sawng) a syrupy glaze made by reducing a fish stock

glace de viande—(glahss duh vee-awnd) a dark, syrupy meat glaze made by reducing a brown stock

glace de volaille—(glahss duh vo-lahy) a light brown, syrupy glaze made by reducing a chicken stock

glaze—(1) any shiny coating applied to food or created by browning; (2) the dramatic reduction and concentration of a stock; (3) a thin, flavored coating poured or dripped onto a cake or pastry

global cuisine—foods (often commercially produced items) or preparation methods that have become ubiquitous throughout the world; for example, curries and French fried potatoes

glucose—(1) energy source for the body, also known as blood sugar; (2) a thick, sweet syrup made from cornstarch, composed primarily of dextrose; light corn syrup can usually be substituted for it in baked goods or candy making

gluten—an elastic network of proteins created when wheat flour is moistened and manipulated

goat—meat of the species *Capra hircus,* closely related to lamb; this ruminant thrives in rocky mountainous terrains, preferring scrub and bark to grass. Tender young goat is called kid. Most goats are bred for milk and cheese production. In Mediterranean countries as well as in the West Indies, goat or kid is served whole and spit-roasted or in stews and curries.

goat's milk—milk produced by a female goat; it has approximately 4.1% milkfat, 8.9% milk solids and 87% water

gougère—éclair pastry flavored with cheese or herbs, baked and served as a savory hors d'oeuvre

gourmand—a connoisseur of fine food and drink, often to excess

gourmet—a connoisseur of fine food and drink

gourmet foods—foods of the highest quality, perfectly prepared and beautifully presented

grading—a series of voluntary programs offered by the U.S. Department of Agriculture to designate a food's overall quality

grains—(1) grasses that bear edible seeds, including corn, rice and wheat; (2) the fruit (that is, the seed or kernel) of such grasses

gram—the basic unit of weight in the metric system; equal to approximately 1/30 of an ounce

grande cuisine—the rich, intricate and elaborate cuisine of the 18th- and 19th-century French aristocracy and upper classes. It is based on the rational identification, development and adoption of strict culinary principles. By emphasizing the how and why of cooking, grande cuisine was the first to distinguish itself from regional cuisines, which tend to emphasize the tradition of cooking.

grate—to cut a food into small, thin shreds by rubbing it against a serrated metal plate known as a grater

gravy—a sauce made from meat or poultry juices combined with a liquid and thickening agent; usually made in the pan in which the meat or poultry was cooked

gremolata—(greh-moa-LAH-tah) an aromatic garnish of chopped parsley, garlic and lemon zest used for osso buco

grilling—a dry-heat cooking method in which foods are cooked by heat radiating from a source located below the cooking surface; the heat can be generated by electricity or by burning gas, hardwood or hardwood charcoals

grind—to pulverize or reduce food to small particles using a mechanical grinder or food processor

grinding—a milling process in which grains are reduced to a powder; the powder can be of differing degrees of fineness or coarseness

gristle—*see* cartilage

grosse piece—a centerpiece consisting of a large piece of the principal food offered; for example, a large wheel of cheese with slices of the cheese cascading around it

gum paste—a smooth dough of sugar and gelatin that can be colored and used to make decorations, especially for pastries

HACCP—*see* Hazard Analysis Critical Control Points

halal—describes food prepared in accordance with Muslim dietary laws

hanging—the practice of allowing eviscerated (drawn or gutted) game to age in a dry, well-ventilated place; hanging helps tenderize the flesh and strengthen its flavor

Hazard Analysis Critical Control Points (HACCP)—a rigorous system of self-inspection used to manage and maintain sanitary conditions in all types of food service operations; it focuses on the flow of food through the food service facility to identify any point or step in preparation (known as a critical control point) where some action must be taken to prevent or minimize a risk or hazard

herb—any of a large group of aromatic plants whose leaves, stems or flowers are used as a flavoring; used either dried or fresh

heritage or heirloom breed—a loosely defined term that refers to older breeds of pork, meat or poultry less commonly raised in modern agricultural systems or food production; many believe that protecting a genetically diverse population of livestock by raising and consuming such animals is important culturally and scientifically and will help ensure human survival

high-ratio cake—a form of creamed-fat cake that uses emulsified shortening and a two-stage mixing method

hollandaise—(ohll-uhn-daze) an emulsified sauce made of butter, egg yolks and flavorings (especially lemon juice)

homogenization—the process by which milk fat is prevented from separating out of milk products

hors d'oeuvre—(ohr durv) very small portions of hot or cold foods served before the meal to stimulate the appetite

hotel pan—a rectangular, stainless steel pan with a lip allowing it to rest in a storage shelf or steam table; available in several standard sizes

hull—also known as the husk, the outer covering of a fruit, seed or grain

hulling—a milling process in which the hull or husk is removed from grains

hybrid—the result of crossbreeding different species that are genetically unalike; often a unique product

hydrogenated fat—unsaturated, liquid fats that are chemically altered to remain solid at room temperature, such as solid shortening or margarine

hydrogenation—the process used to harden oils; hydrogen atoms are added to unsaturated fat molecules, making them partially or completely saturated and thus solid at room temperature

hydrometer—a device used to measure specific gravity; it shows degrees of concentration on the Baumé scale

hygroscopic—describes a food that readily absorbs moisture from the air

icing—*see* frosting

IMPS/NAMP—*see* NAMP/IMPS

induction cooking—a cooking method that uses a special coil placed below the stove top's surface in combination with specially designed cookware to generate heat rapidly with an alternating magnetic field

infection—in the food safety context, a disease caused by the ingestion of live pathogenic bacteria that continue their life processes in the consumer's intestinal tract

infrared cooking—a heating method that uses an electric or ceramic element heated to such a high temperature that it gives off waves of radiant heat that cook the food

infuse—to flavor a liquid by steeping it with ingredients such as tea, coffee, herbs or spices

infusion—(1) the extraction of flavors from a food at a temperature below boiling; (2) a group of coffee brewing techniques, including steeping, filtering and dripping; (3) the liquid resulting from this process

instant-read thermometer—a thermometer used to measure the internal temperature of foods; the stem is inserted in the food, producing an instant temperature readout

intoxication—in the food safety context, a disease caused by the toxins that bacteria produce during their life processes

inventory—the listing and counting of all foods in the kitchen, storerooms and refrigerators

IQF (individually quick-frozen)—describes the technique of rapidly freezing each individual item of food such as slices of fruit, berries or pieces of fish before packaging; IQF foods are not packaged with syrup or sauce

irradiation—a preservation method used for certain fruits, vegetables, grains, spices, meat and poultry in which ionizing radiation sterilizes the food, slows ripening and prevents sprouting

jam—a fruit gel made from fruit pulp and sugar

jelly—a fruit gel made from fruit juice and sugar

juice—the liquid extracted from any fruit or vegetable

julienne—(ju-lee-en) (1) to cut foods into stick-shaped pieces, approximately ⅛ inch × ⅛ inch × 2 inches (3 millimeters × 3 millimeters × 5 centimeters); a fine julienne has dimensions of ¹⁄₁₆ inch × ¹⁄₁₆ inch × 2 inches (1.5 millimeters × 1.5 millimeters × 5 centimeters); (2) the stick-shaped pieces of cut food

jus lié—(zhoo lee-ay) also known as fond lié; a sauce made by thickening brown stock with cornstarch or similar starch; often used like a demi-glace, especially to produce small sauces

Kaiser roll—a large round yeast roll with a crisp crust and a curved pattern stamped on the top; used primarily for sandwiches

kneading—working a dough to develop gluten

Kobe beef—an exclusive type of beef traditionally produced in Kobe, Japan. Wagyu cattle are fed a special diet, which includes beer to stimulate the animal's appetite during summer months. The animals are massaged with sake to relieve stress and muscle stiffness in the belief that calm, contented cattle produce better-quality meat. This special treatment produces meat that is extraordinarily tender and full-flavored, and extraordinarily expensive. Kobe Beef America introduced Wagyu cattle to the United States in 1976. KBA's cattle are raised without hormones and the meat is dry-aged for 21 days prior to sale.

kosher—describes food prepared in accordance with Jewish dietary laws

lactose—a disaccharide that occurs naturally in mammalian milk; milk sugar

ladyfingers—small cakes or cookies made from spongecake batter piped into finger-length strips; used to line molds for desserts or layered with fillings

lamb—the meat of sheep slaughtered under the age of one year

lard—the rendered fat of hogs

larding—inserting thin slices of fat, such as pork fatback, into low-fat meats in order to add moisture

lardons—diced, blanched, fried bacon

leading sauces—also known as mother sauces, the foundation for the entire classic repertoire of hot sauces; the five leading sauces (béchamel, velouté, espagnole [also known as brown], tomato and hollandaise) are distinguished by the liquids and thickeners used to make them; they can be seasoned and garnished to create a wide variety of small or compound sauces

leavener—an ingredient or process that produces or incorporates gases in a baked product in order to increase volume, provide structure and give texture

lecithin—a natural emulsifier found in egg yolks

legumes—(lay-gyooms) (1) French for "vegetables"; (2) a large group of vegetables with double-seamed seed pods; depending upon the variety, the seeds, pod and seeds together, or the dried seeds are eaten

liaison—(lee-yeh-zon) a mixture of egg yolks and heavy cream used to thicken and enrich sauces

liqueur—a strong, sweet, syrupy alcoholic beverage made by mixing or redistilling neutral spirits with fruits, flowers, herbs, spices or other flavorings; also known as a cordial

liquor—an alcoholic beverage made by distilling grains, fruits, vegetables or other foods; includes rum, whiskey and vodka

liter—the basic unit of volume in the metric system, equal to slightly more than a quart

lozenges—diamond-shaped pieces, usually of firm vegetables

macaroni—any dried pasta made with wheat flour and water; only in the United States does the term refer to elbow-shaped tubes

macerate—to soak foods in a liquid, usually alcoholic, to soften them

macronutrients—the nutrients needed in large quantities: carbohydrates, proteins, fats and water

Madeira—(muh-DEH-rah) a Portuguese fortified wine heated during aging to give it a distinctive flavor and brown color

magret—(may-gray) a duck breast, traditionally taken from the ducks that produce foie gras; it is usually served boneless but with the skin intact

maître d'hotel (maître d')—(may-tr doh tel) (1) the leader of the dining room brigade, also known as the dining room manager; oversees the dining room or "front of the house" staff; (2) a compound butter flavored with chopped parsley and lemon juice

Maillard reaction—the process whereby sugar breaks down in the presence of protein

make-up—the cutting, shaping and forming of dough products before baking

marbling—whitish streaks of inter- and intramuscular fat

marinade—the liquid used to marinate foods; it generally contains herbs, spices and other flavoring ingredients as well as an acidic product such as wine, vinegar or lemon juice

marinate—to soak a food in a seasoned liquid in order to tenderize the food and add flavor to it

marmalade—a citrus jelly that also contains unpeeled slices of citrus fruit

marquise—a frozen mousselike dessert, usually chocolate

marrow—soft tissue in the center of animal bones, especially leg bones

Marsala—(mar-SAH-lah) a flavorful fortified sweet-to-semidry Sicilian wine

marzipan—(MAHR-sih-pan) a paste of ground almonds, sugar and egg whites used to fill and decorate pastries

masa harina—Spanish for "dough flour;" finely ground flour made from dried hominy, it is used to make tamales and tortillas

mass—*see* weight

matignon—a standard mirepoix plus diced smoked bacon or smoked ham and, depending on the dish, mushrooms and herbs; sometimes called an edible mirepoix, it is usually cut more uniformly than a standard mirepoix and left in the finished dish as a garnish

matzo—thin, crisp unleavened bread made only with flour and water; can be ground into meal that is used for matzo balls and pancakes

mayonnaise—a thick, creamy sauce consisting of oil and vinegar emulsified with egg yolks, usually used as a salad dressing

meal—(1) the coarsely ground seeds of any edible grain such as corn or oats; (2) any dried, ground substance (such as bonemeal); (3) food eaten at one time

mealy potatoes—also known as starchy potatoes; those with a high starch content and thick skin; they are best for baking

medallion—a small, round, relatively thick slice of meat

melting—the process by which certain foods, especially those high in fat,

gradually soften and then liquefy when heated

menu—a list of foods and beverages available for purchase

meringue—(muh-reng) a foam made of beaten egg whites and sugar

metabolism—all the chemical reactions and physical processes that occur continuously in living cells and organisms

meter—the basic unit of length in the metric system, equal to slightly more than 1 yard

micronutrients—the nutrients needed only in small amounts; vitamins and minerals

microorganisms—single-celled organisms as well as tiny plants and animals that can be seen only through a microscope

microwave cooking—a heating method that uses radiation generated by a special oven to penetrate the food; it agitates water molecules, creating friction and heat; this energy then spreads throughout the food by conduction (and by convection in liquids)

mignonette—(1) a medallion; (2) a vinegar sauce with shallots

milk-fed veal—also known as formula-fed veal; the meat of calves fed only a nutrient-rich liquid and kept tethered in pens; this meat is whiter and more mildly flavored than that of free-range calves

millet—a high-protein cereal grain cooked and eaten like rice; used in combination with wheat flour in conventional baking when it is ground

milling—the process by which grain is ground into flour or meal

mince—to cut into very small pieces when uniformity of shape is not important

minerals—inorganic micronutrients necessary for regulating body functions and proper bone and tooth structures

mirepoix—(meer-pwa) a mixture of coarsely chopped onions, carrots and celery used to flavor stocks, stews and other foods; generally, a mixture of

50 percent onions, 25 percent carrots and 25 percent celery, by weight, is used

mise en place—(meez on plahs) French for "putting in place"; refers to the preparation and assembly of all necessary ingredients and equipment

mix—to combine ingredients in such a way that they are evenly dispersed throughout the mixture

moist-heat cooking methods—cooking methods, principally simmering, poaching, boiling and steaming, that use water or steam to transfer heat through convection; moist-heat cooking methods are used to emphasize the natural flavors of foods

mojo criollo—a citrus and herb marinade used in Latino cuisines; bottled brands are available in Hispanic markets

molding—the process of shaping foods, particularly grains and vegetables bound by sauces, into attractive, hard-edged shapes by using metal rings, circular cutters or other forms

molds—(1) algaelike fungi that form long filaments or strands; for the most part, molds affect only food appearance and flavor; (2) containers used for shaping foods

molecular gastronomy—a contemporary scientific movement that investigates the chemistry and physics behind the preparation of foods and dishes

mollusks—shellfish characterized by a soft, unsegmented body, no internal skeleton and a hard outer shell

monounsaturated fats—*see* unsaturated fats

monter au beurre—(mohn-tay ah burr) to finish a sauce by swirling or whisking in butter (raw or compound) until it is melted; used to give sauces shine, flavor and richness

mortadella—(mohr-tah-DEH-lah) an Italian smoked sausage made with ground beef, pork and pork fat, flavored with coriander and white wine; it is air-dried and has a delicate flavor; also a large American bologna-type pork sausage studded with pork fat and garlic

mortar and pestle—a hard bowl (the mortar) in which foods such as spices are ground or pounded into a powder with a club-shaped tool (the pestle)

mother sauces—(Fr. *sauces mères*), *see* leading sauces

mousse—(moose) a soft, creamy food, either sweet or savory, lightened by adding whipped cream, beaten egg whites or both

mousseline—(moos-uh-leen) a cream or sauce lightened by folding in whipped cream

mouthfeel—the sensation created in the mouth by a combination of a food's taste, smell, texture and temperature

muesli—(MYOOS-lee) a breakfast cereal made from raw or toasted cereal grains, dried fruits, nuts and dried milk solids and usually eaten with milk or yogurt; sometimes known as granola

muffin method—a mixing method used to make quick-bread batters; it involves combining liquid fat with other liquid ingredients before adding them to the dry ingredients

muscles—animal tissues consisting of bundles of cells or fibers that can contract and expand; they are the portions of a carcass usually consumed

mushrooms—members of a broad category of plants known as fungi; they are often used and served like vegetables

mutton—the meat of sheep slaughtered after they reach the age of one year

NAMP/IMPS—the Institutional Meat Purchasing Specifications (IMPS) published by the U.S. Department of Agriculture; the IMPS are illustrated and described in The Meat Buyer's Guide published by the National Association of Meat Purveyors (NAMP)

nappé—(nap-ay) the consistency of a liquid, usually a sauce, that will coat the back of a spoon; from the verb *naper* in French or *nap* in English, meaning to coat a food with sauce

national cuisine—the characteristic cuisine of a nation

navarin—(nah-veh-rahng) a brown ragoût generally made with turnips, other root vegetables, onions, peas and lamb

neapolitan—a three-layered loaf or cake of ice cream; each layer is a different flavor and a different color, a typical combination being chocolate, vanilla and strawberry

nectar—the diluted, sweetened juice of peaches, apricots, guavas, black currants or other fruits, the juice of which would be too thick or too tart to drink straight

neutral spirits or grain spirits—pure alcohol (ethanol or ethyl alcohol); they are odorless, tasteless and a very potent 190 proof (95% alcohol)

New American cuisine—a late-20th-century movement that began in California but has spread across the United States; it stresses the use of fresh, locally grown, seasonal produce and high-quality ingredients simply prepared in a fashion that preserves and emphasizes natural flavors

niche pork—industry term for alternative or specialty pork products; meat from a specific breed such as Duroc or Tamworth hogs, or meat raised using a particular feeding method such as free-range or without antibiotics and hormones is considered a niche product

noisette—a small, usually round, portion of meat cut from the rib

noodles—flat strips of pasta-type dough made with eggs; may be fresh or dried

nouvelle cuisine—French for "new cooking"; a mid-20th-century movement away from many classic cuisine principles and toward a lighter cuisine based on natural flavors, shortened cooking times and innovative combinations

nut—(1) the edible single-seed kernel of a fruit surrounded by a hard shell; (2) generally, any seed or fruit with an edible kernel in a hard shell

nutrients—the chemical substances found in food that nourish the body by promoting growth, facilitating body functions and providing energy; there are six categories of nutrients: proteins, carbohydrates, fats, water, minerals and vitamins

nutrition—the science that studies nutrients

oblique cuts—(oh-BLEEK) small pieces with two angle-cut sides

offal—(OFF-uhl) also called variety meats; edible entrails (for example, the heart, kidneys, liver, sweetbreads and tongue) and extremities (for example, oxtail and pig's feet) of an animal

oignon brûlé—(ohn-neang brew-LAY) French for "burnt onion"; made by charring onion halves; used to flavor and color stocks and sauces

oignon piqué—(ohn-neang pee-KAY) French for "pricked onion"; a bay leaf tacked with a clove to a peeled onion; used to flavor sauces and soups

oil—a type of fat that remains liquid at room temperature

organic farming—a method of farming that does not rely on synthetic pesticides, fungicides, herbicides or fertilizers

orzo—a rice-shaped pasta

oven spring—the rapid rise of yeast goods in a hot oven, resulting from the production and expansion of trapped gases

overhead costs—expenses related to operating a business, including but not limited to costs for advertising, equipment leasing, insurance, property rent, supplies and utilities

overrun—a measure of the air churned into an ice cream; expressed as a percentage, which reflects the increase in volume of the ice cream greater than the amount of the base used to produce the product

paillard—a scallop of meat pounded until thin, usually grilled

palate—(1) the complex of smell, taste and touch receptors that contribute to a person's ability to recognize and appreciate flavors; (2) the range of an individual's recognition and appreciation of flavors

panada; panade—(pah-nahd) (1) something other than fat added to a forcemeat to enhance smoothness, aid emulsification or both; it is often

béchamel, rice or crustless white bread soaked in milk; (2) a mixture for binding stuffings and dumplings, notably quenelles, often choux pastry, bread crumbs, frangipane, puréed potatoes or rice

pan-broiling—a dry-heat cooking method that uses conduction to transfer heat to a food resting directly on a cooking surface; no fat is used and the food remains uncovered

pan-dressed—a market form for fish in which the viscera, gills and scales are removed and the fins and tail are trimmed

panettone—(pan-eh-TONE-nay) sweet Italian yeast bread filled with raisins, candied fruits, anise seeds and nuts; traditionally baked in a rounded cylindrical mold and served as a breakfast bread or dessert during the Christmas holidays

pan-frying—a dry-heat cooking method in which food is placed in a moderate amount of hot fat

pan gravy—a sauce made by deglazing pan drippings from roast meat or poultry and combining them with a roux or other starch and stock

papain—an enzyme found in papayas that breaks down proteins; used as the primary ingredient in many commercial meat tenderizers

papillote, en—(awn pa-pee-yote) a cooking method in which food is wrapped in paper or foil and then heated so that the food steams in its own moisture

pappadam—(PAH-pah-dahm) thin waferlike flatbread made from chickpea, lentil or rice flour flavored with spices and served in India and other south Asian countries; pappadam are usually deep-fried before serving with chutney, raita and Indian curries

parboiling—partially cooking a food in boiling or simmering liquid; similar to blanching but the cooking time is longer

parchment (paper)—heat-resistant paper used throughout the kitchen for tasks such as lining baking pans, wrapping foods to be cooked en

papillote and covering foods during shallow poaching

parcooking—partially cooking a food by any cooking method

parfait—ice cream served in a long, slender glass with alternating layers of topping or sauce; also the name of the mousselike preparation that forms the basis for some still-frozen desserts

paring knife—a short knife used for detail work, especially cutting fruits and vegetables; it has a rigid blade approximately 2–4 inches (5–10 centimeters) long

Paris-Brest—rings of baked éclair paste cut in half horizontally and filled with light pastry cream and/or whipped cream; the top is dusted with powdered sugar or drizzled with chocolate glaze

parisienne—(pah-REE-zee-en) spheres of fruits or vegetables cut with a small melon ball cutter

parstock (par)—the amount of stock necessary to cover operating needs between deliveries

pasta—(1) an unleavened paste or dough made from wheat flour (often semolina), water and eggs; the dough can be colored and flavored with a wide variety of herbs, spices or other ingredients and cut or extruded into a wide variety of shapes and sizes; it can be fresh or dried and is boiled for service; (2) general term for any macaroni product or egg noodle

pasteurization—the process of heating something to a certain temperature for a specific period in order to destroy pathogenic bacteria

pastillage—(pahst-tee-azh) a paste made of sugar, cornstarch and gelatin; it may be cut or molded into decorative shapes

pastry cream—also known as crème pâtissière, a stirred custard made with egg yolks, sugar and milk and thickened with starch; used for pastry and pie fillings

pâte—(paht) French for *dough*

pâté—(pah-TAY) traditionally, a fine savory meat filling wrapped in pastry, baked and served hot or cold; as opposed to a terrine, which was a coarsely ground and highly seasoned meat mixture baked in an earthenware mold and served cold; today, the words pâté and terrine are generally used interchangeably

pâte à choux—(paht ah shoo) *see* éclair paste

pâte au pâté—(paht oh pah-TAY) a specially formulated pastry dough used for wrapping pâté when making pâté en croûte

pâte brisée—(paht bree-zay) a dough that produces a very flaky baked product containing little or no sugar; flaky dough is used for prebaked pie shells or crusts; mealy dough is a less flaky product used for custard, cream or fruit pie crusts

pâte en croûte—(pah-tay awn croot) a pâté baked in pastry dough such as pâte au pâté

pâte feuilletée—(paht fuh-yuh-tay) also known as puff pastry; a rolled-in dough used for pastries, cookies and savory products; it produces a rich and buttery but not sweet baked product with hundreds of light, flaky layers

pâte sucrée—(paht soo-kray) a dough containing sugar that produces a very rich, crisp (not flaky) baked product; also known as sweet dough, it is used for tart shells

pathogen—any organism that causes disease; usually refers to bacteria; undetectable by smell, sight or taste, pathogens are responsible for as many as 95 percent of all food-borne illnesses

pâtissier—(pah-tees-see-yay) a pastry chef; the person responsible for all baked items, including breads, pastries and desserts

paupiette—(poe-pee-yet) a thin slice of meat or fish that is rolled around a filling of finely ground meat or vegetables, then fried, baked or braised in wine or stock

paysanne—(pahy-sahn) foods cut into flat square, round or triangular items with dimensions of ½ inch × ½ inch × ⅛ inch (1.2 centimeters × 1.2 centimeters × 3 millimeters)

pearling—a milling process in which all or part of the hull, bran and germ are removed from grains

pectin—a gelatin-like carbohydrate obtained from certain fruits; used to thicken jams and jellies

pepperoni—(peh-peh-ROH-nee) a hard, thin, air-dried Italian sausage seasoned with red and black pepper

persillade—(payr-see-yad) (1) a food served with or containing parsley; (2) a mixture of bread crumbs, parsley and garlic used to coat meats, especially lamb

pH—a measurement of the acid or alkali content of a solution, expressed on a scale of 0 to 14.0. A pH of 7.0 is considered neutral or balanced. The lower the pH value, the more acidic the substance. The higher the pH value, the more alkaline the substance.

PHF/TCS foods—*see* potentially hazardous foods

physical hazard—a danger to the safety of food caused by particles such as glass chips, metal shavings, bits of wood or other foreign matter

pickle—(1) to preserve food in a brine or vinegar solution; (2) food that has been preserved in a seasoned brine or vinegar, especially cucumbers. Pickled cucumbers are available whole, sliced, in wedges, or chopped as a relish, and may be sweet, sour, dill-flavored or hot and spicy.

pie—food item composed of a sweet or savory filling in a baked crust, generally prepared in a round, slope-sided pan

pigment—any substance that gives color to an item

pilaf—a cooking method for grains in which the grains are lightly sautéed in hot fat and then a hot liquid is added; the mixture is simmered without stirring until the liquid is absorbed

pimentón—Spanish paprika produced from one of several varieties of *Capsicum annuum* peppers; in Extremadura, these peppers are dried over an oak fire, giving the region's *Pimentón de la Vera* a subtle smoky flavor

poaching—a moist-heat cooking method that uses convection to transfer heat from a hot (approximately 160°F–180°F [71°C–82°C]) liquid to the food submerged in it

poêléing—(pwah-lay) moist heat cooking method used for tender cuts of meat or poultry; the food is cooked in an oven in a covered pot and is often browned in hot fat first

polyunsaturated fats—*see* unsaturated fats

pomes—members of the *Rosaceae* family; tree fruits with a thin skin and firm flesh surrounding a central core containing many small seeds (called pips or carpels); include apples, pears and quince

ponzu—(pon zoo) Japanese dipping sauce traditionally made with lemon juice or rice wine vinegar, soy sauce, mirin or sake, seaweed and dried bonito flakes

popovers—crisp hollow muffin-shaped breads made from a rich egg batter and leavened with steam

pork—the meat of hogs, usually slaughtered under the age of one year

posole—also known as hominy or samp; dried corn that has been soaked in hydrated lime or lye; posole (Sp. *pozole*) also refers to a stewlike soup made with pork and hominy served in Mexico and Central America

posterior—at or toward the rear of an object or place; opposite of anterior

potentially hazardous foods (PHF)—foods on which bacteria can thrive, they are generally high in protein and include animal-based products, cooked grains and some raw and cooked vegetables; also known as time/temperature controlled for safety (TCS) foods

poultry—the collective term for domesticated birds bred for eating; they include chickens, ducks, geese, guineas, pigeons and turkeys

poussin—a French term for a small, immature chicken; in the United States, *poussin* is another name for a small chicken such as a Rock Cornish game hen

preserve—a fruit gel that contains large pieces or whole fruits

primal cuts—the primary divisions of muscle, bone and connective tissue produced by the initial butchering of the carcass

prix fixe—(pree feeks) French for "fixed price"; refers to a menu offering a complete meal for a set price; also known as table d'hôte

professional cooking—a system of cooking based on a knowledge of and appreciation for ingredients and procedures

profiteroles—small baked rounds of éclair paste filled with ice cream and topped with chocolate sauce

proofing—the rise given shaped yeast products just prior to baking

proteins—a group of compounds composed of oxygen, hydrogen, carbon and nitrogen atoms necessary for manufacturing, maintaining and repairing body tissues and as an alternative source of energy (4 calories per gram); protein chains are constructed of various combinations of amino acids

pudding—a thick, spoonable dessert custard, usually made with eggs, milk, sugar and flavorings and thickened with flour or another starch

puff pastry—*see* pâte feuilletée

pulled sugar—a doughlike mixture of sucrose, glucose and tartaric acid that can be colored and shaped by hand into decorative items

pulses—dried seeds from a variety of legumes

pumpernickel—(1) coarsely ground rye flour; (2) bread made with this flour

purée—(pur-ray) (1) to process food to achieve a smooth pulp; (2) food that is processed by mashing, straining or fine chopping to achieve a smooth pulp

purée soup—a soup usually made from starchy vegetables or legumes; after the main ingredient is simmered in a liquid, the mixture, or a portion of it, is puréed

putrefactives—bacteria that spoil food without rendering it unfit for human consumption

quality grades—a guide to the eating qualities of meat—its tenderness, juiciness and flavor—based on an animal's age and the meat's color, texture and degree of marbling

quenelle—(kuh-nehl) a small, dumpling-shaped portion of a mousseline forcemeat poached in an appropriately flavored stock; it is shaped by using two spoons

quiche—a savory tart or pie consisting of a custard baked in a pastry shell with a variety of flavorings and garnishes

quick bread—a bread, including loaves and muffins, leavened by chemical leaveners or steam rather than yeast

quinoa—tiny, spherical seeds of a plant native to South America; cooked like grain or ground and used like flour

radiation cooking—a heating process that does not require physical contact between the heat source and the food being cooked; instead, energy is transferred by waves of heat or light striking the food. Two kinds of radiant heat used in the kitchen are infrared and microwave.

raft—a crust formed during the process of clarifying consommé; it is composed of the clearmeat and impurities from the stock, which rise to the top of the simmering stock and release additional flavors

ragoût—(rah-goo) (1) traditionally, a well-seasoned, rich stew containing meat, vegetables and wine; (2) any stewed mixture

ramekin—a small, ovenproof dish, usually ceramic

rancidity—the decomposition of fats by exposure to oxygen, resulting in off-flavors and destruction of nutritive components

ratites—a family of flightless birds with small wings and flat breastbones; they include the ostrich, emu and rhea

recipe—a set of written instructions for producing a specific food or beverage; also known as a formula

recovery time—the length of time it takes a cooking medium such as fat or water to return to the desired cooking temperature after food is submerged in it

red rice—an unmilled short- or long-grain rice from the Himalayas; it has a russet-colored bran and an earthy, nutty flavor

reduction—cooking a liquid such as a sauce until its quantity decreases through evaporation. To reduce by one-half means that one-half of the original amount remains. To reduce by three-fourths means that only one-fourth of the original amount remains. To reduce au sec means that the liquid is cooked until nearly dry.

refreshing—submerging a food in cold water to quickly cool it and prevent further cooking, also known as shocking; usually used for vegetables

regional cuisine—a set of recipes based on local ingredients, traditions and practices; within a larger geographical, political, cultural or social unit, regional cuisines are often variations of one another that blend together to create a national cuisine

relish—a cooked or pickled sauce usually made with vegetables or fruits and often used as a condiment; can be smooth or chunky, sweet or savory and hot or mild

remouillage—(rhur-moo-yahj) French for "rewetting"; a stock produced by reusing the bones left from making another stock. After draining the original stock from the stockpot, add fresh mirepoix, a new sachet and enough water to cover the bones and mirepoix, and a second stock can be made. A remouillage is treated like the original stock; allow it to simmer for 4 to 5 hours before straining. A remouillage will not be as clear or as flavorful as the original stock, however. It is often used to make glazes or in place of water when making stocks.

render—(1) to melt and clarify fat; (2) to cook meat in order to remove the fat

respiration rate—the speed with which the cells of a fruit use oxygen and produce carbon dioxide during ripening

restaurateur—a person who owns or operates an establishment serving food, such as a restaurant

ribbon stage—a term used to describe the consistency of a batter or mixture, especially a mixture of beaten egg and sugar; when the beater or whisk is lifted, the mixture will fall back slowly onto its surface in a ribbonlike pattern

ricer—a sievelike utensil with small holes through which soft food is forced; it produces particles about the size of a grain of rice

rillette—(ree-yeh) meat or poultry slowly cooked, mashed and preserved in its own fat; served cold and usually spread on toast

ripe—fully grown and developed; a ripe fruit's flavor, texture and appearance are at their peak, and the fruit is ready to eat

risers—boxes (including the plastic crates used to store glassware) covered with linens, paper or other decorative items and used on a buffet table as a base for platters, trays or displays

risotto—(re-zot-toe) (1) a cooking method for grains in which the grains are lightly sautéed in butter and then a liquid is gradually added; the mixture is simmered with near-constant stirring until the still-firm grains merge with the cooking liquid; (2) a Northern Italian rice dish prepared this way

roasting—a dry-heat cooking method that heats food by surrounding it with hot, dry air in a closed environment or on a spit over an open fire; similar to baking, the term *roasting* is usually applied to meats, poultry, game and vegetables

roe—(roh) fish eggs; *see* caviar

roll cuts—*see* oblique cuts

rolled fondant—a cooked mixture of sugar, glucose and water formulated to drape over cakes

rolled-in dough—a dough in which a fat is incorporated in many layers by using a rolling and folding procedure; it is used for flaky baked goods such as croissants, puff pastry and Danish pastry

rondeau—(ron-doe) a shallow, wide, straight-sided pot with two loop handles

rondelles—(ron-dellz) disk-shaped slices

rotate stock—to use products in the order in which they were received; all perishable and semiperishable goods, whether fresh, frozen, canned or dry, should be used according to the first in, first out (FIFO) principle

rotisserie—cooking equipment that slowly rotates meat or other foods in front of a heating element

roulade—(roo-lahd) (1) a slice of meat, poultry or fish rolled around a stuffing; (2) a filled and rolled spongecake

round fish—fish with round, oval or compressed bodies that swim in a vertical position and have eyes on both sides of their heads; include salmon, swordfish and cod

rounding—the process of shaping dough into smooth, round balls; used to stretch the outside layer of gluten into a smooth coating

roux—(roo) a cooked mixture of equal parts flour and fat, by weight, used as a thickener for sauces and other dishes; cooking the flour in fat coats the starch granules with the fat and prevents them from lumping together or forming lumps when introduced into a liquid

rub—a mixture of fresh or dried herbs and spices ground together; it can be used dried, or it can be mixed with a little oil, lemon juice, prepared mustard or ground fresh garlic or ginger to make a wet rub

sabayon—(sa-by-on) also known as zabaglione; a foamy, stirred custard sauce made by whisking eggs, sugar and wine over low heat

sachet d'épices; sachet—(sah-shay day-peace) French for "bag of spices"; aromatic ingredients tied in a cheesecloth bag and used to flavor stocks and other foods; a standard sachet contains parsley stems, cracked peppercorns, dried thyme, bay leaf, cloves and, optionally, garlic

salad—a single food or a mix of different foods accompanied or bound by a dressing

salad dressing—a sauce for a salad; most are based on a vinaigrette, mayonnaise or other emulsified product

salad greens—a variety of leafy vegetables that are usually eaten raw

salamander—a small broiler used primarily for browning or glazing the tops of foods

salsa—(sahl-sah) Spanish for "sauce"; (1) generally, a cold chunky mixture of fresh herbs, spices, fruits and/or vegetables used as a sauce for meat, poultry, fish or shellfish; (2) in Italian usage, a general term for pasta sauces

salt-curing—the process of surrounding a food with salt or a mixture of salt, sugar, nitrite-based curing salt, herbs and spices; salt-curing dehydrates the food, inhibits bacterial growth and adds flavor

sanding sugar—granulated sugar with a large, coarse crystal structure that prevents it from dissolving easily; used for decorating cookies and pastries

sanitation—the creation and maintenance of conditions that will prevent food contamination or food-borne illness

sanitize—to reduce pathogenic organisms to safe levels

sansho—dried berries of the prickly ash tree, ground into a powder that is also known as Szechuan pepper, fagara and Chinese pepper; generally used in Japanese cooking to season fatty foods

sashimi—(sah-shee-mee) raw fish eaten without rice; usually served as the first course of a Japanese meal

saturated fats—fats found mainly in animal products such as milk, butter, cheese, eggs and meat as well as in tropical oils such as coconut and palm; usually solid at room temperature. Research suggests that high fat diets, especially those high in saturated fat, may be linked to heart disease, obesity and certain forms of cancer.

sauce—generally, a thickened liquid used to flavor and enhance other foods

saucisson sec—(soh-see-SOHN seck) a hard, air-dried French sausage seasoned with garlic and black pepper

sausage—a seasoned forcemeat usually stuffed into a casing; a sausage can be fresh, smoked and cooked, dried or hard

sautéing—(saw-tay-ing) a dry-heat cooking method that uses conduction to transfer heat from a hot pan to food with the aid of a small amount of hot fat; cooking is usually done quickly over high temperatures

sauteuse—(saw-toose) the basic sauté pan with sloping sides and a single long handle

sautoir—(saw-twahr) a sauté pan with straight sides and a single long handle

savory—describes spiced or seasoned, as opposed to sweet, foods

scald—to heat a liquid, usually milk, to just below the boiling point

scallop—(1) (Fr. *escalope*, It. *scaloppa*, *scaloppine* pl) a thin, boneless slice of meat; (2) (Fr. *coquilles Saint Jacques*) a bivalve shellfish with an edible white muscle and fan-shaped shells

scorch—to burn the surface of a food, changing its color and/or flavor

score—to cut shallow gashes across the surface of a food before cooking

Scoville Heat Units—a subjective rating for measuring a chile's heat; the sweet bell pepper usually rates 0 units, the tabasco pepper rates from 30,000 to 50,000 units and the habanero pepper rates from 100,000 to 300,000 units

seafood—an inconsistently used term encompassing some or all of the following: saltwater fish, freshwater fish, saltwater shellfish, freshwater shellfish and other edible marine life

sear—to brown food quickly over high heat; usually done as a preparatory step for combination cooking methods

season—(1) traditionally, to enhance flavor by adding salt; (2) more commonly, to enhance flavor by adding salt and/or pepper as well as herbs and spices; (3) to mature and bring a food (usually beef or game) to a proper condition by aging or special preparation; (4) to prepare a pot, pan or other cooking surface to prevent sticking

seasoning—an item added to enhance the natural flavors of a food without dramatically changing its taste; salt is the most common seasoning

seitan—(SAY-tan) a form of wheat gluten; it has a firm, chewy texture and a bland flavor; traditionally simmered in a broth of soy sauce or tamari with ginger, garlic and kombu (seaweed)

semifreddi—(seh-mee-frayd-dee) also known as still-frozen desserts; items made with frozen mousse, custard or cream into which large amounts of whipped cream or meringue are folded in order to incorporate air; layers of spongecake and/or fruits may be added for flavor and texture; include frozen soufflés, marquise, mousses and neapolitans

sfoglia—(sfo-glee-ah) a thin, flat sheet of pasta dough that can be cut into ribbons, circles, squares or other shapes

shallow poaching—a moist-heat cooking method that combines poaching and steaming; the food (usually fish) is placed on a vegetable bed and partially covered with a liquid (cuisson) and simmered

shank—the leg of beef, veal, pork or lamb (foreshanks are the front legs, hindshanks are the rear legs); although flavorful, the meat is filled with connective tissue and should be cooked with moist heat

shellfish—aquatic invertebrates with shells or carapaces

sherbet—a frozen mixture of fruit juice or fruit purée that contains milk and/or eggs for creaminess

shocking—also called refreshing; the technique of quickly chilling blanched or parcooked foods in ice water; prevents further cooking and sets colors

shortening—(1) a white, flavorless, solid fat formulated for baking or deep-frying; (2) any fat used in baking to tenderize the product by shortening gluten strands

shred—to cut into thin but irregular strips

shrinkage—the loss of weight in a food due to evaporation of liquid or melting of fat during cooking

shuck—(1) a shell, pod or husk; (2) to remove the edible portion of a food (for example, clam meat, peas or an ear of corn) from its shell, pod or husk

sifting—shaking one or more dry substances through a sieve or sifter to remove lumps, incorporate air and mix

silverskin—the tough connective tissue that surrounds certain muscles; *see* elastin

simmering—(1) a moist-heat cooking method that uses convection to transfer heat from a hot (approximately 185°F–205°F [85°C–96°C]) liquid to the food submerged in it; (2) maintaining the temperature of a liquid just below the boiling point

skim—to remove fat and impurities from the surface of a liquid during cooking

slice—to cut an item into relatively broad, thin pieces

slurry—a mixture of raw starch and cold liquid used for thickening

small sauces—also known as compound sauces; made by adding one or more ingredients to a leading sauce; they are grouped together into families based on their leading sauce; some small sauces have a variety of uses, while others are traditional accompaniments for specific foods

smoke point—the temperature at which a fat begins to break down and smoke

smoking—any of several methods for preserving and flavoring foods by exposing them to smoke; includes cold smoking (in which the foods are not fully cooked) and hot smoking (in which the foods are cooked)

smørbrød—(SMURR-brur) Norwegian cold open-faced sandwiches; similarly, the Swedish term *smörgåsbord* (SMORE-guhs-bohrd) refers to a buffet table of bread and butter, salads, open-faced sandwiches, pickled or marinated fish, sliced meats and cheeses

solid pack—canned fruits or vegetables with little or no water added

soppressata—(soh-preh-SAH-tah) a hard, aged Italian salami, sometimes coated with cracked peppercorns or herbs

sorbet—(sore-bay) a frozen mixture of fruit juice or fruit purée; similar to sherbet but without milk products

sorghum—grain harvested from a plant that resembles corn, used primarily for animal feed and food processing applications; also called *milo*. When ground, sorghum may be blended with other flours to make gluten-free preparations.

soufflé—(soo-flay) either a sweet or savory fluffy dish made with a custard base lightened with whipped egg whites and then baked; the whipped egg whites cause the dish to puff when baked

sourdough—a fermented mixture of flour and water added to dough for leavening and flavor

sous-chef—(soo-shef) a cook who supervises food production and who reports to the executive chef; he or she is second in command of a kitchen

sous-vide—(soo-veed) French for "under vacuum"; a type of low-temperature cooking in which foods are vacuum-sealed in pouches, then cooked for an extended period in a water bath

specifications; specs—standard requirements to be followed in procuring items from suppliers

spice—any of a large group of aromatic plants whose bark, roots, seeds, buds or berries are used as a flavoring; usually used in dried form, either whole or ground

sponge—a thick flour and water batter, which may or may not contain yeast, used to improve the flavor and texture of breads

springform pan—a circular baking pan with a separate bottom and a side wall held together with a clamp that is released to free the baked product

spring lamb—young lamb born in the early spring and slaughtered when 3 to 5 months old; spring lamb is often served roasted whole

spun sugar—a decoration made by flicking dark caramelized sugar rapidly over a dowel to create long, fine, hairlike threads

squab—the class of young pigeon used in food service operations

staling—also known as starch retrogradation; a change in the distribution and location of water molecules within baked products; stale products are firmer, drier and more crumbly than fresh baked goods

standard breading procedure—the procedure for coating foods with crumbs or meal by passing the food through flour, then an egg wash and then the crumbs; it

gives foods a relatively thick, crisp coating when deep-fried or pan-fried

standardized recipe—a recipe producing a known quality and quantity of food for a specific operation

staples—(1) certain foods regularly used throughout the kitchen; (2) certain foods, usually starches, that help form the basis for a regional or national cuisine and are principal components in the diet

starch—(1) complex carbohydrates from plants that are edible and either digestible or indigestible (fiber); (2) a rice, grain, pasta or potato accompaniment to a meal

starch retrogradation—the process whereby starch molecules in a batter or dough lose moisture after baking; the result is baked goods that are dry or stale

starchy potatoes—*see* mealy potatoes

station chef—the cook in charge of a particular department in a kitchen

steak—(1) a cross-section slice of a round fish with a small section of the bone attached; (2) a cut of meat, either with or without the bone

steamed milk—milk that is heated with steam generated by an espresso machine; it should be approximately 150°F to 170°F (66°C to 77°C)

steamer—(1) a set of stacked pots with perforations in the bottom of each pot; they fit over a larger pot filled with boiling or simmering water and are used to steam foods; (2) a perforated insert made of metal or bamboo placed in a pot and used to steam foods; (3) a type of soft-shell clam from the East Coast; (4) a piece of gas or electric equipment in which foods are steamed in a sealed chamber

steaming—a moist-heat cooking method in which heat is transferred from steam to the food being cooked by direct contact; the food to be steamed is placed in a basket or rack above a boiling liquid in a covered pan

steel—a tool, usually made of steel, used to hone or straighten knife blades

steep—to soak food in a hot liquid in order to either extract its flavor or soften its texture

steers—male cattle castrated prior to maturity and principally raised for beef

sterilize—to destroy all living microorganisms

stewing—a combination cooking method similar to braising but generally involving smaller pieces of meat that are first blanched or browned, then cooked in a small amount of liquid that is served as a sauce

stir-frying—a dry-heat cooking method similar to sautéing in which foods are cooked over very high heat using little fat and are stirred constantly and briskly; often done in a wok

stirring—a mixing method in which ingredients are gently mixed by hand until blended, usually with a spoon, whisk or rubber spatula

stock—(Fr. *fond*) a clear, unthickened liquid flavored by soluble substances extracted from meat, poultry or fish and their bones as well as from a mirepoix, other vegetables and seasonings

stone fruits—members of the genus *Prunus*, also known as drupes; tree or shrub fruits with a thin skin, soft flesh and one woody stone or pit; include apricots, cherries, nectarines, peaches and plums

straight dough method—a mixing method for yeast breads in which all ingredients are simply combined and mixed

strain—to pour foods through a sieve, mesh strainer or cheesecloth to separate or remove the liquid component

streusel—a crumbly mixture of fat, flour, sugar and sometimes nuts and spices, used to top baked goods

strudel—a sweet or savory pastry made with a filling, such as sautéed apples or creamed mushrooms, that is rolled in many layers of a very thin dough, then baked until crisp and brown

subcutaneous fat—also known as exterior fat; the fat layer between the hide and muscles

submersion poaching—a poaching method in which the food is completely covered with the poaching liquid

subprimal cuts—the basic cuts produced from each primal

suckling lamb—young lamb that has never been fed any grass or grains

suckling pig—(Fr. *cochon de lait*) very young, very small whole pigs used for roasting or barbecuing whole

sucrose—the chemical name for common refined sugar; it is a disaccharide, composed of one molecule each of glucose and fructose

sugar—a carbohydrate that provides the body with energy and gives a sweet taste to foods

sugar syrups—either simple syrups (thin mixtures of sugar and water) or cooked syrups (melted sugar cooked until it reaches a specific temperature)

sundae—a dessert concoction of ice cream, sauces (hot fudge, marshmallow and caramel, for example), toppings (nuts, candies and fresh fruit to name a few) and whipped cream

suprême—(soo-prem) an intermediary sauce made by adding cream to chicken velouté

supreme—(soo-pream) an intact segment of citrus fruit with all membrane removed

sushi—(szu-she) cooked or raw fish or shellfish rolled in or served on seasoned rice

sweat—to cook a food in a pan (usually covered), without browning, over low heat until the item softens and releases moisture; sweating allows the food to release its flavor more quickly when cooked with other foods

syrup—sugar that is dissolved in liquid, usually water, and often flavored with spices or citrus zest

syrup pack—canned fruits with a light, medium or heavy syrup added

tahini—(tah-HEE-nee) a thick, oily paste made from crushed sesame seeds

tamale—a Mexican steamed dish consisting of seasoned meats, poultry and/or vegetables wrapped in a corn husk spread with masa dough

tang—the portion of a knife's blade that extends inside the handle

tapioca—starch produced from the root of the cassava (manioc) plant, sometimes used for thickening sauces or fruit mixtures

tart—a sweet or savory filling in a baked crust made in a shallow, straight-sided pan without a top crust

tartlet—a small, single-serving tart

taste—the sensations, as interpreted by the brain, of what we detect when food, drink or other substances come in contact with our taste buds

TCS foods—*see* potentially hazardous foods

tempeh—(TEHM-pay) fermented whole soybeans mixed with a grain such as rice or millet; it has a chewy consistency and a yeasty, nutty flavor

temper—to heat gently and gradually; refers to the process of slowly adding a hot liquid to eggs or other foods to raise their temperature without causing them to curdle

temperature danger zone—the broad range of temperatures between 41°F and 135°F (5°C and 57°C) at which bacteria multiply rapidly

tempering—(1) a process for melting chocolate during which the temperature of the cocoa butter is carefully stabilized; this keeps the chocolate smooth and glossy; (2) gradually raising the temperature of a cold liquid

terrine—(teh-reen) (1) traditionally, a loaf of coarse forcemeat cooked in a covered earthenware mold without a crust; today, the word is used interchangeably with pâté; (2) the mold used to cook such items, usually a ceramic rectangle or oval shape

thickening agents—ingredients used to thicken sauces; include starches (flour, cornstarch and arrowroot), gelatin and liaisons

timbale—(tim-bahl) (1) a small pail-shaped mold used to shape foods; (2) a preparation made in such a mold

tisanes—(tee-ZAHNS) beverages made from herbal infusions that do not contain any tea

tofu—also known as bean curd; it is created from soymilk using a method similar to the way animal milk is separated into curds and whey in the production of cheese

tomato sauce—a leading sauce made from tomatoes, vegetables, seasonings and white stock; it may or may not be thickened with roux

toque—(toke) the tall white hat worn by chefs

torchon—(TOR-shahn) French for a cloth or towel, such as a dishcloth. The term is sometimes used to refer to dishes in which the item has been shaped into a cylinder by being wrapped in a cloth or towel.

torte—in Central and Eastern European usage, refers to a rich cake in which all or part of the flour is replaced with finely chopped nuts or bread crumbs

tossed salad—a salad prepared by placing the greens, garnishes and salad dressing in a large bowl and tossing to combine

total recipe cost—the total cost of ingredients for a particular recipe; it does not reflect overhead, labor, fixed expenses or profit

tourner—(toor-NAY) to cut into football-shaped pieces with seven equal sides and blunt ends

toxins—by-products of living bacteria that can cause illness if consumed in sufficient quantities

tranche—(tranch) an angled slice cut from fish fillets

trans fats—a type of fat created when vegetable oils are solidified through hydrogenation

tripe—the edible lining of a cow's stomach

truffles—(1) flavorful tubers that grow near the roots of oak or beech trees; (2) rich chocolate candies made with ganache

truss—to tie poultry with butcher's twine into a compact shape for cooking

tube pan—a deep round baking pan with a hollow tube in the center

tuber—the fleshy root, stem or rhizome of a plant from which a new plant will grow; some, such as potatoes, are eaten as vegetables

tunneling—large tubular holes in muffins and cakes, a defect caused by improper mixing

umami—from the Japanese term for "delicious," often called the fifth taste; refers to the savory or rich, full taste perceived from the natural amino acid glutamate and its commercially produced counterpart, monosodium glutamate (MSG); cheeses, meats, rich stocks, soy sauce, shellfish, fatty fish, tomatoes, mushrooms and wine are all high in glutamate

unit cost—the price paid to acquire one of the specified units

univalves—single-shelled mollusks with a single muscular foot, such as abalone

unsaturated fats—fats that are normally liquid (oils) at room temperature; they may be monounsaturated (from plants such as olives and avocados) or polyunsaturated (from grains and seeds such as corn, soybeans and safflower as well as from fish)

vacuum packaging—a food preservation method in which fresh or cooked food is placed in an airtight container (usually plastic). Virtually all air is removed from the container through a vacuum process, and the container is then sealed.

vanilla custard sauce—also known as crème anglaise; a stirred custard made with egg yolks, sugar and milk or half-and-half and flavored with vanilla; served with or used in dessert preparations

variety—the result of breeding plants of the same species that have different qualities or characteristics; the new plant often combines features from both parents

variety meats—*see* offal

veal—the meat of calves under the age of nine months

vegan—(VEE-gun) a vegetarian who does not eat dairy products, eggs, honey or any other animal product; vegans usually also avoid wearing and using animal products such as fur, leather or wool

vegetable—any herbaceous plant (one with little or no woody tissue) that can be partially or wholly eaten; vegetables can be classified as cabbages, fruit-vegetables, gourds and squashes, greens, mushrooms and truffles, onions, pods and seeds, roots and tubers and stalks

vegetarian—a person who does not eat any meat, poultry, game, fish, shellfish or animal by-products such as gelatin or animal fats; may also exclude dairy products or eggs from the diet

velouté—(veh-loo-tay) a leading sauce made by thickening a white stock (fish, veal, or chicken) with roux

venison—flesh from any member of the deer family, including antelope, elk, moose, reindeer, red-tailed deer, white-tailed deer, mule deer and axis deer

vent—(1) to allow the circulation or escape of a liquid or gas; (2) to cool a pot of hot liquid by setting the pot on blocks in a cold water bath and allowing cold water to circulate around it

vinaigrette—a temporary emulsion of oil and vinegar seasoned with salt and pepper

vinegar—a thin, sour liquid used as a preservative, cooking ingredient and cleaning solution

viniculture—the art and science of making wine from grapes

vintner—a winemaker

viruses—the smallest known form of life; they invade the living cells of a host and take over those cells' genetic material, causing the cells to produce more viruses; some viruses can enter a host through the ingestion of food contaminated with those viruses

viscera—internal organs

vitamins—compounds present in foods in very small quantities; they do not provide energy but are essential for regulating body functions

viticulture—the art and science of growing grapes used to make wines; factors considered include soil, topography (particularly, sunlight and drainage) and microclimate (temperature and rainfall)

vol-au-vents—deep, individual portion–sized puff pastry shells, often shaped as a heart, fish or fluted circle; they are filled with a savory mixture and served as an appetizer or main course

volume—the space occupied by a substance; volume measurements are commonly expressed as liters, teaspoons, tablespoons, cups, pints and gallons

wash—a glaze applied to dough before baking; a commonly used wash is made with whole egg and water

water bath—*see* bain marie

water buffalo's milk—milk produced by a female water buffalo; it has approximately 7.5% milkfat, 10.3% milk solids and 82.2% water

water pack—canned fruits with water or fruit juice added

waxy potatoes—those with a low starch content and thin skin; they are best for boiling

weight—the mass or heaviness of a substance; weight measurements are commonly expressed as grams, ounces and pounds

whetstone—a dense, grained stone used to sharpen or hone a knife blade

whipping—a mixing method in which foods are vigorously beaten in order to incorporate air; a whisk or an electric mixer with its whip attachment is used

white stew—*see* fricassee *and* blanquette

white stock—a light-colored stock made from chicken, veal, beef or fish bones simmered in water with vegetables and seasonings

whitewash—a thin mixture or slurry of flour and cold water used like cornstarch for thickening

whole butter—butter that is not clarified, whipped or reduced-fat

wine—an alcoholic beverage made from the fermented juice of grapes; may be sparkling (effervescent) or still (non-effervescent) or fortified with additional alcohol

work section—*see* work station

work station—a work area in the kitchen dedicated to a particular task, such as broiling or salad making; work stations using the same or similar equipment for related tasks are grouped together into work sections

yeasts—microscopic fungi whose metabolic processes are responsible for fermentation; they are used for leavening bread and in cheese, beer and wine making

yield—the total amount of a product made from a specific recipe; also, the amount of a food item remaining after cleaning or processing

yield grades—a grading program for meat that measures the amount of usable meat on a carcass

yield percentage—the ratio of the usable weight of an ingredient after cleaning and trimming to the quantity purchased, calculated by dividing the trimmed weight by the as-purchased weight of the ingredient

yield test—measuring and weighing an ingredient before and after trimming to determine the usable portion; used to determine the quantity of an ingredient to purchase as well as actual ingredient cost

zabaglione—*see* sabayon

zest—the colored outer portion of the rind of citrus fruit; contains the oil that provides flavor and aroma

zushi—(zhoo-she) the seasoned rice used for sushi

BIBLIOGRAPHY
AND RECOMMENDED READING

GENERAL INTEREST

Bennion, Marion, and Barbara Scheule. *Introductory Foods.* 13th ed. Upper Saddle River, N.J.: Prentice Hall, 2009.

Davidson, Alan. *The Oxford Companion to Food.* 2nd ed. Oxford, England: Oxford University Press, 2006.

Dornenburg, Andrew, and Karen Page. *Becoming a Chef.* New York: Wiley, 2003.

———. *Culinary Artistry.* New York: Wiley, 1996.

Escoffier, Auguste. *The Escoffier Cook Book and Guide to the Fine Art of Cookery for Connoisseurs, Chefs, Epicures.* (Trans. of *Le Guide culinaire.*) New York: Crown, 1969.

Herbst, Sharon Tyler, and Ron Herbst. *The New Food Lover's Companion.* 4th ed. Hauppauge, N.Y.: Barron's Educational Series, 2007.

Labensky, Steven, Gaye G. Ingram, and Sarah R. Labensky. *Webster's New World Dictionary of Culinary Arts.* 2nd ed. Upper Saddle River, N.J.: Prentice Hall, 2000.

Larousse Gastronomique. English ed. New York: Clarkson Potter, 2001.

Molt, Mary. *Food for Fifty.* 12th ed. Upper Saddle River, N.J.: Prentice Hall, 2005.

Pépin, Jacques. *The Art of Cooking.* New York: Knopf, 1987.

———. *La Technique.* New York: Pocket Books, 1987.

Peterson, James. *Essentials of Cooking.* New York: Artisan, 2000.

Point, Fernand. *Fernand Point: Ma Gastronomie.* English ed. Wilton, Conn.: Lyceum Books, 1974.

Rhulman, Michael. *Ratio: The Simple Codes behind the Craft of Everyday Cooking.* New York: Scribner, 2009.

Saulnier, Louis. *Le Répertoire de la Cuisine.* Revised ed. New York: Barron's Educational Series, 1977.

FOOD HISTORY

Anderson, Jean. *The American Century Cookbook: The Most Popular Recipes of the 20th Century.* New York: Clarkson Potter, 1997.

Cooper, Ann. *A Woman's Place Is in the Kitchen: The Evolution of Women Chefs.* Stamford, Conn.: Thomson, 1997.

Freedman, Paul. *Food: The History of Taste.* Davis: University of California Press, 2008.

Fussell, Betty. *The Story of Corn.* New York: Knopf, 1992.

Kurlansky, Mark. *Cod: A Biography of the Fish That Changed the World.* New York: Walker, 1997.

Lovegren, Sylvia. *Fashionable Food: Seven Decades of Food Fads.* New York: Macmillan General Reference, 1995.

Mintz, Sidney W. *Sweetness and Power: The Place of Sugar in Modern History.* New York: Viking Press, 1995.

Revel, Jean-François. *Culture and Cuisine.* (Trans. of *Un Festin en paroles.*) New York: Da Capo Press, 1982.

Rupp, Rebecca. *Blue Corn and Square Tomatoes.* Pownal, Vt.: Garden Way, 1987.

Schlossberg, Eli W. *The World of Orthodox Judaism.* Northvale, N.J.: Aronson, 1996.

Schwartz, Arthur. *Arthur Schwartz's New York City Food: An Opinionated History and More Than 100 Legendary Recipes.* New York: Abrams, 2004.

Shapiro, Laura. *Perfection Salad: Women and Cooking at the Turn of the Century.* New York: Farrar, Straus & Giroux, 1986.

Tannahill, Reay. *Food in History.* Revised ed. New York: Crown, 1995.

Toussaint-Samat, Maguelonne. *A History of Food*, trans. Anthea Bell. Cambridge, Mass.: Blackwell, 1992.

Wheaton, Barbara Ketcham. *Savoring the Past: The French Kitchen and Table from 1300 to 1789.* Reprint ed. New York: Touchstone Books, 1996.

Willan, Anne. *Great Cooks and Their Recipes: From Taillevent to Escoffier.* Boston: Little, Brown, 1992.

SANITATION AND SAFETY

International Life Sciences Institute. *A Simple Guide to Understanding and Applying the Hazard Analysis Critical Control Point Concept.* Washington, D.C.: ILSI Press, 1993.

Loken, Joan K. *The HACCP Food Safety Manual.* New York: Wiley, 1995.

McSwane, David, Nancy Rue, and Richard Linton. *Essentials of Food Safety and Sanitation.* 4th ed. Upper Saddle River, N.J.: Prentice Hall, 2004.

National Assessment Institute. *Handbook for Safe Food Service Management.* 2nd ed. Upper Saddle River, N.J.: Prentice Hall, 1998.

National Restaurant Association Educational Foundation. *ServSafe Essentials.* 5th ed. Upper Saddle River, N.J.: Prentice Hall, 2008.

FOOD COSTING AND BUSINESS SKILLS

Cullen, Noel. *Life Beyond the Line: A Front-of-the-House Companion for Culinarians.* Upper Saddle River, N.J.: Prentice Hall, 2001.

Drysdale, John, and Jennifer A. Galipee. *Profitable Menu Planning.* 4th ed. Upper Saddle River, N.J.: Prentice Hall, 2008.

Labensky, Sarah R. *Applied Math for Food Service.* Upper Saddle River, N.J.: Prentice Hall, 1998.

Schmidt, Arno. *Chef's Book of Formulas, Yields, and Sizes.* 2nd ed. New York: Van Nostrand Reinhold, 1996.

TOOLS

Hiromitsu, Nozaki, Kate Klippensteen, and Yasuo Konishi. *Japanese Kitchen Knives: Essential Techniques and Recipes.* Tokyo: Kodansha International, 2009.

Weinstein, Norman. *Mastering Knife Skills: The Essential Guide to the Most Important Tools in Your Kitchen.* New York: Stewart, Tabori & Chang, 2008.

Williams, Chuck, ed. *Williams-Sonoma Kitchen Companion.* New York: Time-Life Books, 2000.

Wolf, Burton, ed. *The New Cooks' Catalogue.* New York: Knopf, 2000.

GENERAL INGREDIENTS

Anderson, Burton. *Treasures of the Italian Table: Italy's Celebrated Foods and the Artisans Who Make Them.* New York: Morrow, 1994.

Cost, Bruce. *Asian Ingredients: A Guide to Foodstuffs of China, Japan, Korea, Thailand and Vietnam.* New York: Quill HarperCollins, 2000.

Dowell, Philip, and Adrian Bailey. *Cook's Ingredients.* New York: Morrow, 1980.

Kummer, Corby. *The Joy of Coffee: The Essential Guide to Buying, Brewing, and Enjoying.* New York: Houghton Mifflin Harcourt, 2003.

Jordan, Michele Anna. *The Good Cook's Book of Oil and Vinegar.* Reading, Mass.: Addison-Wesley, 1992.

Morris, Sallie, and Lesley Mackley. *The Spice Ingredients Cookbook.* New York: Lorenz Books, 1997.

Norman, Jill. *The Complete Book of Spices.* American ed. New York: Viking Studio Books, 1991.

Ortiz, Elisabeth Lambert. *The Encyclopedia of Herbs, Spices and Flavorings.* 1st American ed. New York: Dorling Kindersley, 1992.

Ward, Susie, et al. *The Gourmet Atlas.* New York: Macmillan, 1997.

FLAVORS AND FOOD SCIENCE

Coates, Clive. *An Encyclopedia of the Wines and Domaines of France.* Davis: University of California Press, 2001.

Delwiche, Jeannine. "Are There 'Basic' Tastes?" *Trends in Food Science & Technology* 7, Special Issue on Flavor Perception (December 1996): 411–415.

MacNeil, Karen. *The Wine Bible.* New York: Workman, 2001.

McGee, Harold. *On Food and Cooking.* Revised ed. New York: Scribner, 2004.

McWilliams, Margaret. *Foods: Experimental Perspectives.* 4th ed. Upper Saddle River, N.J.: Prentice Hall, 2001.

Page, Karen, and Andrew Dornenburg. *The Flavor Bible: The Essential Guide to Culinary Creativity, Based on the Wisdom of America's Most Imaginative Chefs.* New York: Little, Brown, 2008.

Parsons, Russ. *How to Read a French Fry.* Boston: Houghton Mifflin, 2001.

Robinson, Jancis. *The Oxford Companion to Wine.* 2nd ed. Oxford, England: Oxford University Press, 1999.

Schmid, Albert. *Hospitality Managers Guide to Wines, Beers and Spirits.* Upper Saddle River, NJ: Prentice Hall, 2004.

This, Hervé. *Building a Meal: From Molecular Gastronomy to Culinary Constructivism.* New York: Columbia University Press, 2008.

———. *Molecular Gastronomy: Exploring the Science of Flavor.* New York: Columbia University Press, 2008.

DAIRY AND CHEESE

Fletcher, Janet. *The Cheese Course.* San Francisco: Chronicle Books, 2002.

Jenkins, Steven. *Steven Jenkins' Cheese Primer.* New York: Workman, 1996.

Lambert, Paula. *The Cheese Lover's Cookbook & Guide.* New York: Simon & Schuster, 2000.

Masui, Kazuko, and Tomoko Yamada. *French Cheeses.* New York: Dorling Kindersley, 1996.

McCalman, Max, and David Gibbons. *Cheese: A Connoisseur's Guide to the World's Best.* New York: Clarkson Potter, 2005.

Mendelson, Anne. *Milk. The Surprising Story of Milk through the Ages.* New York: Random House, 2008.

Werlin, Laura. *Laura Werlin's Cheese Essentials: An Insider's Guide to Buying and Serving Cheese.* New York: Stewart, Tabori & Chang, 2007.

STOCKS, SAUCES AND SOUPS

Clayton, Bernard. *The Complete Book of Soups and Stews.* New York: Simon & Schuster, 1987.

Davis, Deidre. *A Fresh Look at Saucing Foods.* Reading, Mass.: Addison-Wesley, 1993.

Kafka, Barbara. *Soup: A Way of Life.* New York: Artisan, 1998.

Larousse, David Paul. *The Sauce Bible: Guide to the Saucier's Craft.* New York: Wiley, 1993.

Peterson, James. *Sauces: Classical and Contemporary Sauce Making.* 3rd ed. New York: Wiley, 2008.

Sokolov, Raymond A. *The Saucier's Apprentice.* New York: Knopf, 1976.

MEAT

Aidells, Bruce, and Denis Kelly. *The Complete Meat Cookbook.* New York: Houghton Mifflin, 1998.

Fearnley-Whittingstall, Hugh. *The Hugh River Cottage Meat Book.* Berkeley, Calif.: Ten Speed Press, 2007.

Henderson, Fergus. *The Whole Beast: Nose to Tail Eating.* New York: Ecco Press, 2004.

Keller, Thomas. *Under Pressure: Cooking Sous Vide.* New York: Artisan, 2008.

Knox, Luc, and Keith Richmond. *The World Encyclopedia of Meat, Game and Poultry.* New York: Lorenz Books, 2000.

North American Meat Processors Association. *The Meat Buyer's Guide.* New York: Wiley, 2006.

GAME

Cameron, Angus, and Judith Jones. *The L. L. Bean Game and Fish Cookbook.* New York: Random House, 1983.

Hibler, Jane. *Wild about Game: 150 Recipes for Cooking Farm-Raised and Wild Game from Alligator and Antelope to Venison and Wild Turkey.* New York: Broadway Books, 1998.

Little, Carolyn. *The Game Cookbook*. Wiltshire, England: Crowood Press, 1988.

Marrone, Teresa. *Dressing and Cooking Wild Game*. New York: Prentice Hall, 1987.

Webster, Harold W., Jr. *The Complete Venison Cookbook*. Brandon, Miss.: Quail Ridge Press, 1996.

FISH AND SHELLFISH

The Commercial Guide to Fish and Shellfish. Toms River, N.J.: Urner Barry, 2006.

King, Shirley. *Fish, the Basics*. Revised and updated ed. New York: Chapters, 1996.

———. *Saucing the Fish*. New York: Simon & Schuster, 1986.

Kurlansky, Mark. *The Last Fish Tale*. New York: Riverhead Books, 2009.

Loomis, Susan Herrmann. *The Great American Seafood Cookbook*. New York: Workman, 1988.

McClane, A. J. *The Encyclopedia of Fish Cookery*. New York: Holt, Rinehart & Winston, 1989.

Moonen, Rich, and Roy Finamore. *Fish without a Doubt: The Cook's Essential Companion*. New York: Houghton Mifflin Harcourt, 2008.

Peterson, James. *Fish and Shellfish*. New York: Morrow, 1998.

The Seafood Handbook: Seafood Standards. Rockland, Maine: Seafood Business Magazine, 2009.

The Seafood List: FDA Guide to Acceptable Market Names for Food Fish Sold in Interstate Commerce. Washington, D.C.: Center for Food Safety and Applied Nutrition, 2009.

EGGS AND BREAKFAST COOKERY

Bristow, Linda Kay. *Bread and Breakfast*. San Ramon, Calif.: 101 Productions, 1985.

Davids, Kenneth. *Coffee: A Guide to Buying, Brewing, and Enjoying*. 5th ed. New York: St. Martin's Griffin, 2001.

Eggcyclopedia. 2nd ed. Park Ridge, Ill.: American Egg Board, 1989.

Fox, Margaret S., and John Bear. *Morning Food from Café Beaujolais*. Berkeley, Calif.: Ten Speed Press, 1994.

Gand, Gale, and Christie Matheson. *Gale Gand's Brunch! 100 Fantastic Recipes for the Weekend's Best Meal*. New York: Clarkson Potter, 2009.

Jamison, Cheryl A., and Bill Jamison. *A Real American Breakfast: The Best Meal of the Day, Any Time of the Day*. New York: Morrow, 2002.

Pettigrew, Jane. *The Tea Companion*. Jackson, Tenn.: Running Press, 2004.

VEGETABLES AND FRUITS

Andrews, Jean. *Peppers: The Domesticated Capsicums*. Austin: University of Texas Press, 1984.

Brown, Marlene. *International Produce Cookbook and Guide*. Los Angeles: HP Books, 1989.

Davidson, Alan. *Fruit: A Connoisseur's Guide and Cookbook*. New York: Simon & Schuster, 1991.

DeWitt, Dave, and Nancy Gerlach. *The Whole Chile Pepper Book*. Boston: Little, Brown, 1990.

Goldstein, Joyce. *Italian Slow and Savory*. San Francisco: Chronicle Books, 2004.

Greenburg, Patricia. *The Whole Soy Cookbook*. New York: Random House, 1998.

Ingram, Christine. *The New Guide to Vegetables*. New York: Hermes House, 1997.

Kafka, Barbara. *Vegetable Love*. New York: Artisan, 2005.

Madison, Deborah. *Local Flavors: Cooking and Eating from America's Farmer's Markets*. New York: Broadway Books, 2002.

Masumoto, David Mas. *Epitaph for a Peach: Four Seasons on My Family Farm*. New York: HarperOne, 1996.

———. *Wisdom of the Last Farmer: Harvesting Legacies from the Land*. New York: Free Press, 2009.

Miller, Mark, with John Harrisson. *The Great Chile Book*. Berkeley, Calif.: Ten Speed Press, 1991.

Murdich, Jack. *Buying Produce*. New York: Morrow, 1986.

Payne, Rolce Redard, and Dorrit Speyer Senior. *Cooking with Fruit*. New York: Crescent Books, 1995.

Peterson, James, and Justin Schwartz. *Vegetables*. New York: Morrow, 1998.

Schneider, Elizabeth. *Vegetables from Amaranth to Zucchini: The Essential Reference*. New York: Morrow, 2001.

GRAINS AND PASTA

Bugialli, Giuliano. *On Pasta*. New York: Simon & Schuster, 1988.

Della Croce, Julia. *Pasta Classica*. Reprint ed. San Francisco: Chronicle Books, 1996.

Kummer, Corby. "Pasta." *The Atlantic* 258, no. 1 (July 1986): 35–47.

Leblang, Bonnie Tandy, and Joanne Lamb Hayes. *Rice*. New York: Harmony Books, 1991.

Sass, Lorna. *Whole Grains Every Day, Every Way*. New York: Clarkson Potter, 2006.

NUTRITION

Baskette, Michael, and Eleanor Mainella. *The Art of Nutritional Cooking*. 3rd ed. Upper Saddle River, N.J.: Prentice Hall, 2008.

Drummond, Nina, and Lisa M. Brefore. *Nutrition for Foodservice and Culinary Professionals*. New York: Wiley, 2003.

Freyberg, Nicholas, and Willis A. Gortner. *The Food Additives Book*. New York: Bantam Books, 1982.

VEGETARIAN COOKING

Bergeron, Ken. *Professional Vegetarian Cooking*. New York: Wiley, 1999.

Harris, William. *The Scientific Basis of Vegetarianism*. Honolulu, Hawaii: Health, 1995.

Holthaus, Fusako. *Tofu Cookery*. Tokyo: Kodansha International, 1992.

Madison, Deborah. *Vegetarian Cooking for Everyone*. New York: Broadway Books, 1997.

Melino, Vesanto, and Brenda Davis. *The New Becoming Vegetarian: The Essential Guide to a Healthy Vegetarian Diet*. Summertown, Tenn.: Healthy Living, 2003.

Messina, Mark, and Virginia Messina. *The Vegetarian Way*. New York: Three Rivers Press, 1996.

CHARCUTERIE

Bertoli, Paul. *Cooking by Hand*. New York: Clarkson Potter, 2003.

Ehlert, Friedrich W., et al. *Pâtés and Terrines*. Reprint ed. London: Hearst Books, 1990.

Grigson, Jane. *The Art of Charcuterie*. Reprint ed. New York: Echo Press, 1991.

Rhulman, Michael, and Brian Polcyn. *Charcuterie*. New York: Norton, 2009.

HORS D'OEUVRE AND BUFFETS

Aloni, Nicole. *Secrets from a Caterer's Kitchen*. Tucson, Ariz.: HP Books, 2001.

Barber, Kimiko, and Hiroki Takemura. *Sushi: Taste and Techniques*. Upper Saddle River, N.J.: Prentice Hall, 2008.

Duffy, Gillian. *Hors d'Oeuvres*. New York: Morrow, 1998.

Janericco, Terence. *The Book of Great Hors d'Oeuvre*. New York: Wiley, 1990.

Jasa, Michael A., and Carlos R. Brenda. *Ice Carving 101*. Upper Saddle River, N.J.: Prentice Hall, 2008.

Larousse, David Paul. *The Professional Garde Manger*. New York: Wiley, 1996.

Sanders, Ed, et al. *Catering Solutions*. Upper Saddle River, N.J.: Prentice Hall, 2000.

Schmidt, Arno, and Inja Nam. *The Book of Hors d'Oeuvres and Canapes*. New York: Van Nostrand Reinhold, 1996.

Simmons, Bob, and Coleen Simmons. *Tapas Fantasticas: Appetizers with a Spanish Flair*. San Leandro, Calif.: Bristol Books, 1999.

BREADS

Albright, Barbara, and Leslie Weiner. *Mostly Muffins*. New York: St. Martin's Press, 1984.

Alston, Elizabeth. *Biscuits and Scones*. New York: Clarkson Potter, 1988.

Clayton, Bernard. *Bernard Clayton's New Complete Book of Breads*. Revised ed. New York: Fireside Books, 1995.

Colicchio, Tom, and Sisha Ortuzar. '*Wichcraft: Craft a Sandwich into a Meal—and a Meal into a Sandwich*. New York: Crown, 2009.

David, Elizabeth. *English Bread and Yeast Cookery*. Notes by Karen Hess. American ed. New York: Viking Press, 1980.

Glezer, Maggie. *Artisan Baking across America*. New York: Artisan, 2000.

Leader, Daniel, and Lauren Chattman. *Local Breads: Sourdough and Whole-Grain Recipes from Europe's Best Artisan Bakers*. New York: Norton, 2008.

Reinhart, Peter. *The Bread Baker's Apprentice*. Berkeley, Calif.: Ten Speed Press, 2001.

PASTRIES AND DESSERTS

Braker, Flo. *The Simple Art of Perfect Baking*. Shelburne, Vt.: Chapters, 1992.

Daley, Regan. *In the Sweet Kitchen: The Definitive Baker's Companion*. New York: Artisan, 2001.

Friberg, Bo. *The Professional Pastry Chef*. 4th ed. New York: Wiley, 2002.

Healy, Bruce, and Paul Bugat. *Mastering the Art of French Pastry*. Woodbury, N.Y.: Barron's Educational Series, 1984.

Heatter, Maida. *Maida Heatter's Book of Great Desserts*. Kansas City, Mo.: Andrews McMeel, 1999.

Hyman, Philip, and Mary Hyman, trans. *The Best of Gaston Lenotre's Desserts*. Woodbury, N.Y.: Barron's Educational Series, 1983.

Iuzzini, Johnny, and Roy Finamore. *Dessert Fourplay*. New York: Clarkson Potter, 2008.

Labensky, Sarah, Priscilla Martel, and Eddy Van Damme. *On Baking: A Textbook of Baking and Pastry Fundamentals*. 2nd ed. Upper Saddle River, N.J.: Prentice Hall, 2009.

London, Sheryl, and Mel London. *Fresh Fruit Desserts: Classic and Contemporary*. New York: Prentice Hall, 1990.

Luchetti, Emily. *A Passion for Ice Cream*. San Francisco: Chronicle Books, 2007.

Purdy, Susan G. *A Piece of Cake*. Reprint ed. New York: Macmillan, 1993.

Schreiber, Cory, and Julie Richardson. *Rustic Fruit Desserts: Crumbles, Buckles, Cobblers, Pandowdies, and More*. Berkeley, Calif.: Ten Speed Press, 2009.

Silverton, Nancy. *Desserts by Nancy Silverton*. New York: Harper & Row, 1986.

Teubner, Christian, ed. *The Chocolate Bible*. New York: Penguin Studio, 1997.

GARNISHING

Budgen, June. *The Book of Garnishes*. Los Angeles: HP Books, 1986.

De Costa, Narahenapitage Sumith Premalal. *Edible Art: Tricks and Tools for Master Centerpieces*. Atglen, Pa.: Schiffer, 2006.

Hongwiwat, Nidda, ed. *Complete Step by Step Vegetable and Fruit Carving*. 3rd ed. Bangkok: Sangdad, 2005.

Huang, Su-Huei. *Great Garnishes*. Monterey Park, Calif.: Wei-Chuan, 1990.

Jasa, Michael A., and Carlos R. Brenda. *Ice Carving 101*. Upper Saddle River, N.J.: Prentice Hall, 2008.

Lynch, Francis Talyn. *Garnishing: A Feast for Your Eyes*. Los Angeles: HP Books, 1987.

Rosen, Harvey. *How to Garnish*. Lakewood, N.J.: International Culinary Consultants, 1998.

INTERNATIONAL CUISINES

Adrià, Ferran, Julie Soler, and Albert Adrià. *A Day at el Bulli*. London: Phaidon Press, 2008.

Alford, Jeffrey. *Hot Sour Salty Sweet: A Culinary Journey through Southeast Asia*. New York: Artisan, 2000.

Andoh, Elizabeth. *Washoku: Recipes from the Japanese Home Kitchen*. San Francisco: Ten Speed Press, 2005.

Bayless, Rick, with Deann Groen Bayless. *Authentic Mexican: Regional Cooking from the Heart of Mexico*. New York: Morrow, 1987.

Bugialli, Giuliano. *The Fine Art of Italian Cooking*. New York: Random House, 1990.

Casas, Penelope. *The Foods and Wines of Spain*. New York: Knopf, 1991.

Garces, Jose. *Latin Evolution*. New York: Lake Isle Press, 2008.

Gin, Maggie. *Regional Cooking of China*. San Francisco: 101 Productions, 1984.

Harris, Jessica. *The Africa Cookbook: Tastes of a Continent*. New York: Simon & Schuster, 1998.

Hazan, Marcella. *Essentials of Classic Italian Cooking*. New York: Knopf, 1993.

Jaffrey, Madhur. *An Invitation to Indian Cooking*. New York: Ecco Press, 1999.

Kasper, Lynn Rossetto. *The Splendid Table: Recipes from Emilia-Romagna, the Heartland of Northern Italian Food*. New York: Morrow, 1992.

Kennedy, Diana. *The Cuisines of Mexico*. Revised ed. New York: Harper & Row, 1986.

Lo, Kenneth. *The Encyclopedia of Chinese Cooking*. New York: Bristol Books, 1997.

McDermott, Nancie. *Real Thai: The Best of Thailand's Regional Cooking*. San Francisco: Chronicle Books, 1992.

Morimoto, Masaharu. *Morimoto: The New Art of Japanese Cooking*. New York: Dorling Kindersley, 2008.

Pham, Mai. *Pleasures of the Vietnamese Table*. New York: HarperCollins, 2001.

Roden, Claudia. *The New Book of Middle Eastern Food*. New York: Knopf, 2000.

Rojas-Lombardi, Felipe. *The Art of South American Cooking*. New York: HarperCollins, 1991.

Rose, Evelyn. *The New Complete International Jewish Cookbook*. New York: Carroll & Graf, 1992.

Routhier, Nicole. *Foods of Vietnam*. New York: Stewart, Tabori & Chang, 1989.

Rozin, Elisabeth. *Ethnic Cuisine: How to Create the Authentic Flavors of 30 International Cuisines*. Reprint ed. New York: Penguin, 1992.

Solomon, Charmaine. *The Complete Asian Cookbook*. Revised ed. Boston: Tuttle, 2002.

———. *Encyclopedia of Asian Food*. Boston: Periplus Editions, 1998.

Toomre, Joyce. *Classic Russian Cooking: Elena Molokhovets' A Gift to Young Housewives*, trans., introduced and annotated by Joyce Toomre. Bloomington: Indiana University Press, 1992.

Von Bremzen, Anya, and John Welchman. *Please to the Table: The Russian Cookbook*. New York: Workman, 1990.

Young, Grace, and Alan Richardson. *The Breath of a Wok: Unlocking the Spirit of Chinese Wok Cooking through Recipes and Lore*. New York: Simon & Schuster, 2004.

BOOKS BY CONTRIBUTING CHEFS

Ash, John. *From the Earth to the Table: John Ash's Wine Country Cuisine*. San Francisco: Chronicle Books, 2007.

Atkinson, Leland. *Cocina! A Hands-On Guide to the Techniques of Southwestern Cooking*. Berkeley, Calif.: Ten Speed Press, 1996.

Beranbaum, Rose Levy. *The Cake Bible*. New York: Morrow, 1988.

———. *Rose's Heavenly Cakes*. New York: Wiley, 2009.

Bishop, John. *Bishop's: The Cookbook*. Vancouver, Canada: Douglas & McIntyre, 1997.

Brennan, Pip, Jimmy Brennan, and Ted Brennan. *Breakfast at Brennan's and Dinner, Too*. New Orleans, La.: Brennan's, 1994.

Carpenter, Hugh, and Teri Sandison. *Chopstix: Quick Cooking with Pacific Flavors*. New York: Stewart, Tabori & Chang, 1990.

Danhi, Robert. *Southeast Asian Flavors*. El Segundo, Calif.: Mortar & Press, 2008.

Golden, Harris. *Golden's Kitchen: The Artistry of Cooking and Dining on the Light Side*. Revised 2nd ed. Phoenix, Ariz.: Quail Run Books, 1989.

Goldstein, Joyce. *Back to Square One: Old-World Food in a New-World Kitchen*. New York: Morrow, 1992.

———. *Sephardic Flavors: Jewish Cooking of the Mediterranean*. San Francisco: Chronicle Books, 2000.

———. *Tapas: Sensational Small Plates From Spain*. San Francisco: Chronicle Books, 2009.

Guerithault, Vincent. *Vincent's Cookbook*. Berkeley, Calif.: Ten Speed Press, 1994.

Harris, Jessica. *Beyond Gumbo: Creole Fusion Food from the Atlantic Rim*. New York: Simon & Schuster, 2003.

———. *Tasting Brazil: Brazilian Recipes and Reminiscences*. New York: Macmillan, 1992.

Lukins, Sheila. *Sheila Lukins USA Cookbook*. New York: Workman, 1997.

Medrich, Alice. *BitterSweet: Recipes and Tales from a Life in Chocolate*. New York: Artisan, 2003.

———. *Chocolat*. New York: Warner Books, 1990.

Miller, Mark. *Coyote Cafe*. Berkeley, Calif.: Ten Speed Press, 1989.

Milliken, Mary Sue, and Susan Feniger. *City Cuisine*. New York: Morrow, 1989.

Pépin, Jacques. *The Apprentice: My Life in the Kitchen*. Boston: Houghton Mifflin, 2003.

———. *Jacques Pépin Celebrates*. New York: Knopf, 2001.

Puck, Wolfgang. *Wolfgang Puck Adventures in the Kitchen*. New York: Gramercy, 2004.

———. *The Wolfgang Puck Cookbook: Recipes from Spago, Chinois and Points East and West*. New York: Random House, 1996.

Richard, Michel. *Happy in the Kitchen: The Craft of Cooking, the Art of Eating*. New York: Artisan, 2006.

Roberts, Michael. *Secret Ingredients*. New York: Bantam Books, 1988.

Smith, Andrew F. *The Oxford Companion to American Food and Drink*. Oxford, England: Oxford University Press, 2009.

———. *The Tomato in America: Early History, Culture and Cookery*. Reprint ed. Champaign: University of Illinois Press, 2001.

Somerville, Annie. *Fields of Greens: New Vegetarian Recipes from the Celebrated Greens Restaurant*. New York: Bantam Books, 1993.

Susser, Allen. *Allen Susser's New World Cuisine and Cookery*. New York: Doubleday, 1995.

———. *The Great Mango Book: A Guide with Recipes*. Berkeley, Calif.: Ten Speed Press, 2004.

Tausend, Marilyn. *Cocina de la Familia: More Than 200 Authentic Recipes from Mexican-American Home Kitchens*. New York: Fireside Books, 1999.

Tropp, Barbara. *China Moon Cookbook*. New York: Workman, 1992.

INDEX

545

PHOTO CREDITS

CHAPTER OPENER PHOTOS

p. 3: Paul Poplis\Jupiter Images – FoodPix – Creatas

p. 17: Eric Futran\Jupiter Images – FoodPix – Creatas

p. 37: Carlos Sanchez Pereyra\Jupiter Images

p. 53: Thinkstock Royalty Free

p. 77: Michael Piazza\Jupiter Images – FoodPix – Creatas

p. 91: Lew Robertson\Jupiter Images – FoodPix – Creatas

p. 131: Jennifer Harrington\Jupiter Images – FoodPix – Creatas

p. 149: © Stockphoto

p. 161: Jupiter Images – Comstock Images

pp. 183, 271: Richard Embery\Pearson Education/PH College

p. 233: Valerie Janssen\Jupiter Images – FoodPix – Creatas

p. 301: E. Jane Armstrong\Jupiter Images – FoodPix – Creatas

p. 327: Ben Fink\Jupiter Images – FoodPix – Creatas

p. 349, 533: Ann Stratton\Jupiter Images – FoodPix - Creatas

p. 371: Jupiterimages\Jupiter Images – FoodPix – Creatas

p. 393: Maura McEvoy\Jupiter Images – FoodPix - Creatas

p. 449: Alexandra Grablewski\Jupiter Images – FoodPix – Creatas

p. 463: FabFoodPix\StockFood America – Royalty Free

p. 565: © Miki Duisterhof/FoodPix/Getty Images, Inc.

p. 625: © Chang/Stockphoto

p. 679: Leigh Beisch\Jupiter Images – FoodPix – Creatas

p. 711: © Richard Embery/Pearson PH College

p. 749: © Reggie Casagrande/Stockbyte RF/Getty Images, Inc.

p. 787: Sabine Scheckel/Photodisk/Getty Images

p. 809: © Tracey Kusiewicz/Foodie Photography/Getty Images, Inc.

p. 847: © Stockfood America

p. 881: © Food Collection/Stock Food America

p. 905: © Stockphoto

p. 923: © Tracey Kusiewicz/Food Collection RF/Stockfood America

p. 959: © Eric Futari/Stockfood America

p. 1007: © Carrie Bottomley/Stockphoto

p. 1047: © Paolo Scarlata/iStockphoto

p. 1079: © Darryl Jacobson/Blend Images/SuperStock

p. 1093: © Steven Miric/Stockphoto

INTERIOR PHOTOS

p. 5: Pearson Education/PH College

pp. 5, 75: Courtesy of Barbara Wheaton

p. 6: Musée Escoffier de l'Art Culinaire, Villeneuve-Lubet (06), France

p. 8: © Sophie Bassouls/CORBIS SYGMA

p. 9: © Albert Gea / Reuters / Corbis

p. 14: © Sophie Bassouls/CORBIS SYGMA

p. 41: Courtesy of The Schlesinger Library, Radcliffe Institute, Harvard University

p. 62: Courtesy of Demarle Inc.

p. 116: Andy Crawford © Dorling Kindersley

p. 116, bottom: Dave King © Dorling Kindersley

p. 120: Steve Gorton © Dorling Kindersley

pp. 126 (bottom left), 128: Francesca Yorke © Dorling Kindersley

pp. 126 (middle and bottom right), 567: Priscilla Martel

p. 127: Sarah R Labensky

p. 129: Getty Images / De Agostini Editore Picture Library

p. 199, left: Kip Peticolas\Fundamental Photographs, NYC; right: Charles D. Winters\Photo Researchers, Inc.

p. 372: Mapes Livestock Photos, Steven R. Mapes, Milford Center, OH

p. 399: Peter Dean / Getty Images, Inc. – Stone Allstock

p. 455: William Harnett, "After the Hunt," 1885. Fine Arts Museum of San Francisco

p. 472, box: Phillip Dowell © Dorling Kindersley

p. 473 (fresh oysters): Clive Streeter © Dorling Kindersley

p. 555: David Murray © Dorling Kindersley

p. 756: SGM/Stock Connection

p. 764: Pacific Organic Foods

p. 827, top: Neil Mersh © Dorling Kindersley

p. 831: Clive Streeter © Dorling Kindersley

p. 872: Neil Mersh © Dorling Kindersley

p. 996: David Murray & Jules Selmes © Dorling Kindersley

All uncredited photos: Pearson Education/PH College